W9-CUK-788

Service Book

and

Hymnal

THE PUBLISHERS

Augsburg Publishing House
Minneapolis, Minnesota

Board of Publication
Lutheran Church in America
Philadelphia, Pennsylvania

Service Book
and
Hymnal

Authorized by the Lutheran Churches

cooperating in

The Commission on the Liturgy and Hymnal

MUSIC EDITION

Printed in the United States of America

First printing, March, 1958
Second printing, May, 1958
Third printing, December, 1958
Fourth printing, April, 1960
Fifth printing, September, 1961
Sixth printing, October, 1962
Seventh printing, September, 1963
Eighth printing, August, 1964
Ninth printing, September, 1965
Tenth printing, January, 1967
Eleventh printing, January, 1968
Twelfth printing, July, 1969
Thirteenth printing, August, 1971
Fourteenth printing, November, 1972
Fifteenth printing, January, 1974
Sixteenth printing, January, 1975

Contents

Preface to the Liturgy

IN worship, as in doctrine, the Lutheran Church is part of the "one, holy, catholic and apostolic Church." It claims as its rightful inheritance all that is truly ecumenical in the Church of every age and every land. Not the least part of its legacy is the liturgy, which has moved from beginnings in Asia Minor to the western end of the Mediterranean, to northern Europe and to the Western Hemisphere. In this transition it has crossed the barriers of language from Greek to Latin to German to English. The Lutheran churches which have prepared the Common Liturgy are located in the New World and worship in the English language.

In the transmission of the liturgy from beginnings remote in space and time to this our day and place, the Church has been conscious of the continuing guidance of the Holy Spirit, without whose presence the historical process would have been beset with insuperable difficulties. Not the least of these occurred in the sixteenth century when the mass, after more than a millennium of use in the Western Church in the Latin language, was put into the language of the people. At the same time it was restored to the people as an act of the whole congregation, purified of accretions of unscriptural and late medieval provenance, and enriched with new devotional and liturgical material.

Under the hand of God, this task fell first to the Lutheran reformers. Beginning in 1524 there appeared many service books in areas which are now parts of Germany, Scandinavia, France, Austria, Czecho-Slovakia, Poland, Russia and the Baltic countries, purifying the medieval mass and translating it into the vernacular. Following the lead of the Lutheran reformers on the continent, th English reformers brought out in 154 the First Prayer Book of Edward VI, i which they performed the same task fo English-speaking peoples. Not only wa there a striking similarity between th North European and English missal from which the two groups of reformer worked, but the English reformers wer aware of and were influenced by Luther an Orders which had appeared durin the twenty-five years.

Omitting only such elements as we inconsistent with the scriptural basis c the mass, the reformers devoutly re tained what had been evangelical in liturgy as old as the Church itself. The preserved the structure both of th Church year and the communion servic the principle of historic propers and per copes, vestments and altar appoin ments. By their emphasis on the partic pation of the congregation through re sponses and canticles, and the singing hymns, as well as on the essential plac of sacrament and sermon, they restore biblical balance to the liturgical servic Of unique importance to the Wester Church was the rendition of the text the liturgy in the language of the peopl

Thus when, a century later, Europear began to establish permanent settlemen in the New World, they brought wi them their vernacular liturgies. Luthe ans among them brought a variety mother-tongues. Their liturgies exhi ited a fundamental unity among them selves and with the service of the Wes ern Church, but also certain variatio resulting from their own peculiar cu toms and uses. As long as immigratic continued in appreciable numbers, t languages of the motherlands continu to be used in the New World, and, i

Preface to the Liturgy

1748, Henry Melchior Muhlenberg laid a foundation for an American liturgy on historical principles in the German Liturgy adopted at that time by the Ministerium of Pennsylvania.

As the number of native born Americans increased there developed an increasing demand for an English liturgy. Stimulated by this need, as well as by a deepening interest in the European churches in liturgical recoveries, typified by the work of Wilhelm Loehe in his *Agende*, the Ministerium of Pennsylvania prepared an English liturgy for America in 1860. This was followed by a new hymnbook, and the excellent English liturgy of the General Council in 1868 which restored forms and usages which had been obscured by Pietism and Rationalism as well as by the exigencies of frontier life in America. In the preparation of much of this material the Lutheran Church acknowledged its indebtedness to the high standards of expression of the English prayer-books.

In an effort to unite the Church in a common liturgy, the General Synod and the United Synod of the South joined with the General Council to establish a form on the principle of the common consent of the pure Lutheran liturgies of the sixteenth century. The result was the *Common Service* of 1888, the finest liturgical achievement of American Lutheranism up to that time. Further endeavors by the Joint Committee of the three bodies made possible a complete service book, including occasional services and musical settings for the liturgy, as well as hymns. This became the *Common Service Book* of 1917. Its appearance coincided with the formation of the United Lutheran Church in America, which thus had a common liturgy and a common hymnal. Many other Lutheran bodies in America adopted the *Common Service*, incorporating it into their own service books and hymnals.

Following a fundamental tenet of the confessions, expressed in the Formula of Concord, we "believe, teach and confess that the Church of God in every place and every time has the power, according to circumstances, to change ceremonies (instituted by man) in such manner as may be most useful and edifying." As Lutherans of different backgrounds and from various sections of America have come to understand each other, they have in increasing measure found it "useful and edifying" to worship together in one tongue with one mind and one spirit. In 1945, the greater part of the Church found it possible to embark on the venture of a Common Hymnal, and this led naturally to a desire for a Common Liturgy grounded upon both the *Common Service* and upon other forms significant to American Lutherans, especially those of Scandinavian origin.

At the same time that our Churches in America have come more fully to appreciate each other, they have also discovered through deepened scholarship and broader fellowship, the rich treasury of ecumenical liturgy, especially in the ancient Greek tradition antedating the Roman Rite from which European usage has been derived. A vision clearer than was sometimes possible in the turmoil of the Reformation controversy has revealed the enduring value of some elements which were lost temporarily in the sixteenth century reconstruction of the liturgy, as, for instance, the proper use of the Prayer of Thanksgiving and the essential meaning of the term 'catholic' in the creeds. At the same time the study of the liturgy has demonstrated more fully the profound inner identity of the liturgical endeavors of the reformers with the evangelical nature of the original eucharistic service. And witnessing also to a contemporary growth in congregational devotion is the increased number of collects and prayers and the richer variety in the musical settings of the liturgy.

The Common Liturgy is rooted in the developed worship of the ancient and medieval Christian Church, both East and West, and grounded on the historic German, Scandinavian and American uses of the post-reformation centuries. Prepared especially for the use of Lutherans in the Western Hemisphere, the Common Liturgy presents the full Service of the Church with all its provisions for all who wish to use it. Essential material is preceded by a *shall* rubric; optional material by a *may* rubric. Freedom and flexibility in matters liturgical are our birthright, and there is room for ample variety in ceremonial, music, and architectural appointments. Some parishes may desire and have the resources to provide full and ornate services. However, the most ornate structure should not incorporate extraneous or unauthorized texts. Other parishes may desire or be able to provide only services of a much simpler character. Likewise, the simplest service should not omit essential or important parts, or change their order. Every service, whether elaborat or simple, sung or said, should be withi the framework of the common rite au thorized by the Church, and its integrit should be respected and maintained un der all circumstances and conditions.

In a real sense the Common Liturg testifies to the unity of the whole Lu theran Church in America, and to it participation in the heritage of the hol treasures of the Church of Christ whic Luther defined as "a holy assembly an congregation upon earth of pure saint under one head, even Christ, called to gether by the Holy Ghost in one faith one mind and understanding, with mani fold gifts, yet one in love, without sect or schisms."

The American Evangelical Lutheran Church
The American Lutheran Church
The Augustana Evangelical Lutheran Church
The Evangelical Lutheran Church
The Finnish Evangelical Lutheran Churc of America—Suomi Synod
The Lutheran Free Church
The United Evangelical Lutheran Church
The United Lutheran Church in America

The Music of the Liturgy

JUST as the text of the liturgy and the order of its parts come down to us from the earliest Christian sources, so the liturgical music used at the time of the Reformation was the most ancient music of the Christian Church, plainchant. And in the same way that many of the texts of the sixteenth century hymns were set to adaptations of plainsong melodies already familiar to the people, so the text of the liturgy, translated into the vernacular, was set to th traditional music.

The transition, however, was n without difficulties, since the translate texts sometimes failed to fit the accus tomed musical phrases. In some case versifications of the texts replaced th original words, and these were set t chorale-type melodies. Some of thes paraphrases, as those of the *Gloria i excelsis* and the *Credo*, have continue in European Lutheran use to the present time.

In the New World, the Lutheran Church had to undergo another transition in language. Following consistently the Reformation principle of making the liturgy available in the language of the people, the church accepted along with the English text, the chant form characteristic of liturgical music in the English use. The *Common Service*, set in chant form, was more widely adopted than any other service among English-speaking Lutherans. The pointing used was the so-called 'cathedral' pointing, which was standard in all English language churches in the nineteenth century.

Thus the Lutheran Church in the English-speaking world reflects three distinct musical traditions in its liturgical music: plainsong, the chorale, and the English chant. While it may appear that the cause of unity would have been served better with only one musical setting of the liturgy, all three traditions survive in the Church and find recognition in the provision of three musical settings.

THE FIRST SETTING

The first musical setting of The Service, and the music for Matins and Vespers, are in chant form. The 'cathedral' pointing, however, has been replaced by contemporary pointing which brings the normal accents of the text upon the natural accents of the chant. This is a return to the ancient manner of performing psalms, canticles and responses. While the music is divided into measures and the text is set beneath certain notes, these divisions have no bearing on the time required to chant the words. The notes have no time value. The time that any note receives will be determined solely by the time the spoken words require. All other time values, especially those of the notes, must be forgotten. The notes indicate changes of pitch alone.

The chants should be read first, then sung on a single note, and finally, the inflections of pitch of the chant should be introduced. In all cases the right sense of the text will govern the time and phrasing of the music. The accompaniment must never dominate, but should simply support the proper rendition of the text.

Bar lines are devices to aid the eye in grouping certain words and syllables of the text to certain notes of the music. They have nothing to do with measuring time. In the printing of the text, a vertical line (ˈ) at the top of the text sets off the division of the text into measures of music. It is the counterpart of the bar line in the music. A dot (.) indicates the division of the text between notes within a single measure. Where three syllables of text occur to two notes of musical inflection the first two syllables are sung to the first note, and the third syllable to the second note. Keys are not binding, but the music may be transposed freely to suit the circumstances.

Intonations have been provided for the minister, but their use is permissive and not mandatory, and in every case the rubric states that he may sing or say. The ancient usage in the Church was to intone if the response was chanted; to read if the response was said. Where intonations are not provided, as for the collects, lessons and extended prayers, intonation on a single note with simple inflections similar to those of the opening versicles is proper.

THE SECOND SETTING

The second setting, based on the melodic form of the chorale, requires little in the way of special directions. Some of the music, notably the brief responses, is common to the first setting and should be chanted in the same manner. A few of the intonations are more extended and complex, and this music reflects more of the spirit of continental Lutheran use, though all paraphrases of the extended chants have been eliminated in favor of the straight liturgical English text. The notes of the music have a general time value, but should be sung freely, devotionally and in flowing style.

THE THIRD SETTING

It is much to be regretted that limitations of space have not permitted the printing in this book of the third setting of The Service. However, a complete setting, an adaptation of the *Missa orbis factor*, is available as a separate publication. This is the most ancient and historic form of liturgical music, and while it is used by fewer churches at the present time than the type of music represented in settings one and two, the contemporary free style of both the chant and the chorale indicates a return by both to the plainsong sources from whict they developed.

CONCLUSION

It is recognized that the introductio of new musical settings to the liturgica services of the church is attended by a period of unfamiliarity and strangenes until the music has been fully mastered Worship in our churches has been char acterized by the hearty participation o the people in the liturgical song, as i the beloved hymns. In sending forth thi book, with settings which are at least i some degree new and unfamiliar t many people, it is hoped that the prope study, rehearsal, and patience on th part of choirs and congregations, wil lead to an acquaintance with the musi that will issue in a fresh chorus of prais and thanksgiving to our Lord and Re deemer.

NOTE

It is to be observed that the Music Edition of the Service Book and Hymnal contains only a part of the Common Liturgy adopted by the Churches. Limitations of space have made necessary the omission of certain of the Occasional Services and other material. The Text Edition includes the whole body of the liturgical services.

The Calendar

THE SEASON OF ADVENT—Four Weeks.

The First Sunday in Advent	(The Sunday nearest St. Andrew's Day)
St. Andrew, Apostle	November 30
St. Thomas, Apostle	December 21

THE CHRISTMAS SEASON—Twelve Days.

CHRISTMAS DAY. The Nativity of Our Lord	December 25
St. Stephen, Martyr	December 26
St. John, Apostle, Evangelist	December 27
The Holy Innocents	December 28
The Circumcision of Our Lord	January 1

THE SEASON OF THE EPIPHANY—One to Six Weeks.

THE EPIPHANY OF OUR LORD	January 6
Septuagesima Sunday	
Sexagesima Sunday	
Quinquagesima Sunday	
The Conversion of St. Paul	January 25
The Presentation of Our Lord	February 2
St. Matthias, Apostle	February 24

THE SEASON OF LENT—Forty Days.

Ash Wednesday. The First Day of Lent

The Sundays in Lent

I. Invocabit
II. Reminiscere
III. Oculi
IV. Laetare
V. Judica, Passion Sunday
VI. Palmarum, Palm Sunday

The Days in Holy Week

Monday
Tuesday
Wednesday

Maundy Thursday		
Good Friday		
Saturday, Easter Eve		
THE EASTER (*or* Paschal) SEASON.		
EASTER DAY. The Resurrection of Our Lord		
The Annunciation	March	2
The Sundays after Easter		
I. Quasi Modo Geniti		
II. Misericordia		
III. Jubilate		
IV. Cantate		
V. Rogate		
The Ascension of Our Lord		
(VI.) Exaudi, The Sunday after the Ascension		
St. Mark, Evangelist	April	2
St. Philip and St. James, Apostles	May	
THE SEASON AFTER PENTECOST (The Trinity Season).		
THE DAY OF PENTECOST. Whitsunday		
Trinity Sunday		
The Nativity of St. John, the Baptist	June	2
St. Peter and St. Paul, Apostles	June	2
The Visitation	July	
St. James the Elder, Apostle	July	2
The Transfiguration of Our Lord	August	
St. Bartholomew, Apostle	August	2
St. Matthew, Apostle, Evangelist	September	2
St. Michael and All Angels	September	2
St. Luke, Evangelist	October	1
St. Simon and St. Jude, Apostles	October	2
Reformation Day	October	3
All Saints' Day	November	

The Service

¶ *The General Rubrics contain directions additional to those which* ***appear in the Services.***

¶ *The Congregation shall rise. The Minister shall sing or say:*

N the Name of the Father, and of the Son, and of the Holy Ghost.

¶ *The Congregation shall sing or say:*

Amen.

THE CONFESSION OF SINS

¶ *The Minister shall say:*

BELOVED in the Lord! Let us draw near with a true heart, and confess our sins unto God our Father, beseeching him, in the Name of our Lord sus Christ, to grant us forgiveness.

¶ *The Minister and Congregation may kneel.*

¶ *They shall sing or say:*

Our help is in the Name of the Lord.
Response. Who made heaven and earth.
I said, I will confess my transgressions unto the Lord.
℟. And thou forgavest the iniquity of my sin.

¶ *Then shall the Minister say:*

ALMIGHTY God, our Maker and Redeemer, we poor sinners confess unto thee, that we are by nature sinful and unclean, and that we have ned against thee by thought, word, and deed. Wherefore we flee for refuge thine infinite mercy, seeking and imploring thy grace, for the sake of our rd Jesus Christ.

¶ *The Congregation shall say with the Minister:*

O MOST merciful God, who hast given thine only-begotten Son to die for us, have mercy upon us, and for his sake grant us remission of all our s; and by thy Holy Spirit increase in us true knowledge of thee and of thy ll, and true obedience to thy Word, that by thy grace we may come to erlasting life; through Jesus Christ our Lord. Amen.

¶ *Then the Minister, standing, and facing the Congregation, shall say:*

ALMIGHTY God, our heavenly Father, hath had mercy upon us, and hath given his only Son to die for us, and for his sake forgiveth us all our sins. them that believe on his Name, he giveth power to become the sons of God, d bestoweth upon them his Holy Spirit. He that believeth, and is baptized, all be saved. Grant this, O Lord, unto us all.

¶ *Or, he may say:*

THE Almighty and merciful God grant unto you, being penitent, pardo and remission of all your sins, time for amendment of life, and the gra and comfort of his Holy Spirit.

¶ *The Congregation shall sing or say:*

Amen.

¶ *A brief Silence may be kept before the Introit for the Day.*

¶ *The Congregation shall stand until the close of the Collect.*

INTROIT

¶ *The Introit for the Day with the Gloria Patri shall be sung or said.*

GLORIA PATRI

GLORY be to the Father, and to the Son, and to the Holy Ghost: as it wa in the beginning, is now, and ever shall be, world without end. Amen.

¶ *Then shall be sung or said the Kyrie.*

KYRIE

IN peace let us pray to the Lord.
℟. Lord, have mercy.
For the peace that is from above, and for the salvation of our souls, let pray to the Lord.
℟. Lord, have mercy.
For the peace of the whole world, for the well-being of the churches of Go and for the unity of all, let us pray to the Lord.
℟. Lord, have mercy.
For this holy house, and for them that in faith, piety and fear of God off here their worship and praise, let us pray to the Lord.
℟. Lord, have mercy.
Help, save, pity, and defend us, O God, by thy grace.
℟. Amen.

¶ *In place of the foregoing, the following Kyrie may be sung or said:*

KYRIE

LORD, have mercy upon us.
℟. Lord, have mercy upon us.
Christ, have mercy upon us.
℟. Christ, have mercy upon us.
Lord, have mercy upon us.
℟. Lord, have mercy upon us.

¶ *Then shall be sung or said the Gloria in Excelsis.*

GLORIA IN EXCELSIS

¶ *The Minister shall sing or say:*

Glory be to God on high!

¶ *The Congregation shall sing or say:*

AND on earth peace, good will toward men. We praise thee, we bless thee, we worship thee, we glorify thee, we give thanks to thee for thy great lory, O Lord God, heavenly King, God the Father Almighty.

O Lord, the only-begotten Son, Jesus Christ; O Lord God, Lamb of God, on of the Father, that takest away the sin of the world, have mercy upon us. hou that takest away the sin of the world, receive our prayer. Thou that ttest at the right hand of God the Father, have mercy upon us.

For thou only art holy; thou only art the Lord; thou only, O Christ, with e Holy Ghost, art most high in the glory of God the Father. Amen.

¶ *Then shall the Minister sing or say:*

The Lord be with you.

℟. And with thy spirit.

¶ *The Minister shall say:*

Let us pray.

¶ *Then shall the Minister say the Collect for the Day.*

THE COLLECT

¶ *The Collect ended, the Congregation shall sing or say:*

Amen.

¶ *Here the Minister may read the appointed Lesson from the Old Testament, saying:* The Lesson is written in the ________ Chapter of ____________, beginning at the ________ Verse. *The Lesson ended, he shall say,* Here endeth the Lesson.

¶ *Then may be sung a Psalm or a hymn version of a Psalm.*

¶ *Then shall the Minister announce the Epistle for the Day, saying:* The Epistle for *ere he shall name the Festival or Day*) is written in the ________ Chapter of ____________, eginning at the ________ Verse.

THE EPISTLE

¶ *The Epistle ended, the Minister shall say:* Here endeth the Epistle for the Day.

¶ *Then may the Gradual for the Day be sung.*

THE GRADUAL

¶ *When the Gradual for the Day is omitted, the Alleluia or the Gradual for the Season may be sung.*

THE ALLELUIA

Alleluia.

¶ *In Lent this Sentence shall be sung instead of the Alleluia:*

Christ hath humbled himself, and become obedient unto death: even th death of the Cross.

¶ *Then shall the Minister announce the Gospel for the Day, saying:* The Holy Gosp is written in the ________ Chapter of St. ________________, beginning at the ______ Verse.

¶ *The Congregation shall rise and sing or say:*

Glory be to thee, O Lord.

¶ *Then shall the Minister read the Gospel for the Day.*

THE GOSPEL

¶ *The Gospel ended, the Minister shall say:* Here endeth the Gospel for the Day.

¶ *The Congregation shall sing or say:*

Praise be to thee, O Christ.

¶ *Then shall be said or sung the Creed.*

THE CREED

¶ *The Nicene Creed shall be said or sung on all Festivals and whenever there is a Com munion.*

THE NICENE CREED

I BELIEVE in one God, the Father Almighty, Maker of heaven and eart And of all things visible and invisible.

And in one Lord Jesus Christ, the only-begotten Son of God, Begotten his Father before all worlds, God of God, Light of Light, Very God of ve God, Begotten, not made, Being of one substance with the Father, By who all things were made: Who for us men, and for our salvation, came dow from heaven, And was incarnate by the Holy Ghost of the Virgin Mary, An was made man; And was crucified also for us under Pontius Pilate. He su fered and was buried; And the third day he rose again according to the Scri tures, And ascended into heaven, And sitteth on the right hand of the Fathe And he shall come again with glory to judge both the quick and the dea Whose kingdom shall have no end.

And I believe in the Holy Ghost, The Lord and Giver of Life, Who pr ceedeth from the Father and the Son, Who with the Father and the Son t gether is worshipped and glorified, Who spake by the Prophets. And I belie one Holy Christian* and Apostolic Church. I acknowledge one Baptism f

* *Or,* "And I believe one Holy catholic and Apostolic Church," *the original and ge erally accepted text.*

ıe remission of sins. And I look for the Resurrection of the dead, And the ife of the world to come. Amen.

THE APOSTLES' CREED

BELIEVE in God the Father Almighty, Maker of heaven and earth:
And in Jesus Christ his only Son our Lord, Who was conceived by the Holy host, Born of the Virgin Mary, Suffered under Pontius Pilate, Was crucified, ead, and buried: He descended into hell; The third day he rose again from ıe dead; He ascended into heaven, And sitteth on the right hand of God the ather Almighty; From thence he shall come to judge the quick and the dead.
I believe in the Holy Ghost; The Holy Christian* Church, the Communion f Saints; The Forgiveness of sins; The Resurrection of the body, And the ife everlasting. Amen.

¶ *Then shall be sung the Hymn.*

THE HYMN

¶ *Then shall follow the Sermon.*

THE SERMON

The Sermon being ended, the Congregation shall rise and the Minister shall then say:

THE Peace of God, which passeth all understanding, keep your hearts and minds through Christ Jesus.

¶ *The Congregation shall sing or say:*

Amen.

¶ *Then shall the Offering be received and presented at the Altar.*

THE OFFERING

Then shall follow the Offertory, the Congregation standing meanwhile. One of the Offertories here following, or any other suitable Offertory, may be sung or said.
When there is a Communion, the Minister, after Silent Prayer, and during the singing of the Offertory, shall uncover the Vessels and reverently prepare for the Administration of the Holy Sacrament.

THE OFFERTORY

I

THE sacrifices of God are a broken spirit: a broken and a contrite heart, O God, thou wilt not despise.
Do good in thy good pleasure unto Zion: build thou the walls of Jerusalem.
Then shalt thou be pleased with the sacrifices of righteousness: with burnt-fering and whole burnt-offering.

* *Or,* "The Holy catholic Church," *the original and generally accepted text.*

II

WHAT shall I render unto the Lord: for all his benefits toward me?
I will offer to thee the sacrifice of thanksgiving: and will call upc the Name of the Lord.
I will take the cup of salvation: and call upon the Name of the Lord.
I will pay my vows unto the Lord now in the presence of all his people: the courts of the Lord's house, in the midst of thee, O Jerusalem.

III

CREATE in me a clean heart, O God: and renew a right spirit within m
Cast me not away from thy presence: and take not thy Holy Spir from me.
Restore unto me the joy of thy salvation: and uphold me with thy fr Spirit.

¶ *Then shall follow the Prayer of the Church.*

THE PRAYER OF THE CHURCH

¶ *The indented paragraphs in the Prayer of the Church may be omitted, at the discretion the Minister.*

¶ *If special prayers are desired by or for members of the Church, the Minister may make me tion of them before beginning the Prayer of the Church, as occasion may require, or follows:*

Intercessions: The prayers of the Church are asked for the following brethren wl are sick (*or*, in adversity, *or*, in suffering, *or*, in need): *N. N.*
Thanksgivings: N. N. desires to return thanks to God, for special blessings (*or*, for rest ration from illness, *or*, for gifts of grace), and asks the prayers of the Church.
Commemorations: Let us remember with thanksgiving before God our brethren wl have departed this life with the sign of faith: *N. N.* (*or*, our *brother N. N.*, who h departed this life).

Let us pray.

ALMIGHTY God, the Father of our Lord Jesus Christ: We give th praise and hearty thanks for all thy goodness and tender mercies. V bless thee for the love which hath created and doth sustain us from day to da We praise thee for the gift of thy Son, our Saviour, through whom thou ha made known thy will and grace. We thank thee for the Holy Ghost, tl Comforter; for thy holy Church, for the Means of Grace, for the lives of faithful and godly men, and for the hope of the life to come. Help us to trea ure in our hearts all that our Lord hath done for us; and enable us to sho our thankfulness by lives that are given wholly to thy service;

℟. We beseech thee to hear us, good Lord.

SAVE and defend thy Church Universal, purchased with the precious Blo of Christ. Give it pastors and ministers according to thy Spirit, a strengthen it through the Word and the holy Sacraments. Make it perfect love and in all good works, and establish it in the faith delivered to the sain anctify and unite thy people in all the world, that one holy Church may bear 'itness to thee, the God and Father of all;

R. We beseech thee to hear us, good Lord.

UPON all in any holy office in thy Church bestow thy wisdom and heavenly grace, and enable them to fulfill their duties in thy fear and in purity of heart. Let thy gracious benediction rest upon our clergy and people, and upon all who are set over us in the Lord; that faith may abound, and thy kingdom increase;

R. We beseech thee to hear us, good Lord.

SEND forth thy light and thy truth into all the earth, O Lord. Raise up, we pray thee, faithful servants of Christ to labor in the Gospel at home and in istant lands;

R. We beseech thee to hear us, good Lord.

ACCORDING to thy merciful goodness, O God, extend thy saving health and strength to the younger Churches. Grant that they may rejoice in a rich harvest of souls for thy kingdom. Support them in times of trial and weakness, and make them steadfast, abounding in the work of the Lord;

R. We beseech thee to hear us, good Lord.

PRESERVE our Nation in righteousness and honor, and continue thy blessings to us as a people, that we may lead a quiet and peaceable life, all godliness and honesty. Grant health and favor to all who bear office in ur land (especially to the President and the Congress, the Governor and egislature of this State)*, and help them to acknowledge and obey thy oly will;

R. We beseech thee to hear us, good Lord.

GIVE to all men the mind of Christ, and dispose our days in thy peace, O God. Take from us all hatred and prejudice, and whatever may hinder unity of spirit and concord. Prosper the labors of those who take counsel for the nations of the world, that mutual understanding and common endeavor may be increased among all peoples;

R. We beseech thee to hear us, good Lord.

BLESS, we pray thee, the schools of the Church, universities and centers of research, all institutions of learning, and those who exercise the care of souls therein. Withhold not, we pray thee, thy Word and Wisdom, but bestow it in such measure that men may serve thee in Church and State, and our common life be brought under the rule of thy truth and righteousness;

R. We beseech thee to hear us, good Lord.

* *In Canadian Churches, the following may be said:* especially to Her Gracious Majesty he Queen, the Prime Minister and the Parliament, and all Provincial Authorities.

WE pray thee especially, heavenly Father, to sanctify our homes wi thy light and joy. Keep our children in the covenant of their bap tism, and enable their parents to rear them in a life of faith and godlines By the spirit of affection and service unite the members of all Christia families, that they may show forth thy praise in our land and in all th world;

℟. We beseech thee to hear us, good Lord.

GOD of mercies, we pray thee to comfort with the grace of thy Holy Spir all who are in sorrow or need, sickness or adversity. Remember thos who suffer persecution for the faith. Have mercy upon those to whom deat draws near. Bring consolation to those in sorrow or mourning. And to a grant a measure of thy love, taking them into thy tender care;

℟. We beseech thee to hear us, good Lord.

LET thy blessing rest upon the seed-time and harvest, the commerce an industry, the leisure and rest, and the arts and culture of our peopl Take under thy special protection those whose toil is difficult or dange ous, and be with all who lay their hands to any useful task. Give them ju rewards for their labor, and the knowledge that their work is good in th sight, who art the Maker and Sustainer of all things;

℟. We beseech thee to hear us, good Lord.

WE remember with thanksgiving those who have loved and served th in thy Church on earth, who now rest from their labors (especially tho most dear to us, whom we name in our hearts before thee). Keep us in fellov ship with all thy saints, and bring us at length to the joy of thy heavenly kin dom;

℟. We beseech thee to hear us, good Lord.

¶ *Here special Supplications, Intercessions, and Thanksgivings may be made.*

ALL these things, and whatever else thou seest that we need, grant us, Father, for his sake who died and rose again, and now liveth and reigne with thee in the unity of the Holy Ghost, one God, world without end.

℟. Amen.

¶ *If there be no Communion the Minister and Congregation shall say the Lord's Prayer.*

OUR Father, who art in heaven, Hallowed be thy Name, Thy kingdo come, Thy will be done, on earth as it is in heaven. Give us this d our daily bread; And forgive us our trespasses, as we forgive those wh trespass against us; And lead us not into temptation, But deliver us fro evil. For thine is the kingdom, and the power, and the glory, for ev and ever. Amen.

¶ *A Hymn may then be sung.*

¶ *Then the Minister, standing at the Altar, shall sing or say the Benediction.*

THE LORD bless thee, and keep thee.
The LORD make his face shine upon thee, and be gracious unto thee.
The LORD lift up his countenance upon thee, and give thee peace:
IN the Name of the Father, and of the Son, and of the Holy Ghost.

¶ *The Congregation shall sing or say:*

Amen.

THE THANKSGIVING

¶ *A Hymn shall be sung.*

¶ *The Congregation shall rise at the beginning of the Preface.*

THE PREFACE

¶ *The Minister and Congregation shall sing or say:*

THE Lord be with you.
℟. And with thy spirit.

Lift up your hearts.
℟. We lift them up unto the Lord.

Let us give thanks unto the Lord our God.
℟. It is meet and right so to do.

¶ *Then shall the Minister turn to the Altar and sing or say:*

IT is truly meet, right, and salutary, that we should at all times, and in all places, give thanks unto thee, O Lord, Holy Father, Almighty, Everlasting God:

Here shall follow the Proper Preface for the Day or Season. If there be none especially appointed, then shall follow immediately, Therefore with Angels, *etc.*

PROPER PREFACES

For Advent

WHO didst comfort thy people with the promise of the Redeemer, through whom thou wilt also make all things new in the day when he shall come again to judge the world in righteousness. Therefore with Angels, *&c.*

For Christmas

FOR in the mystery of the Word made flesh, thou hast given us a new revelation of thy glory; that seeing thee in the person of thy Son, we may be drawn to the love of those things which are not seen. Therefore with Angels, *&c.*

For Epiphany

AND now do we praise thee, that thou didst send unto us thine onl begotten Son, and that in him, being found in fashion as a man, tho didst reveal the fullness of thy glory. Therefore with Angels, *etc.*

For Lent

WHO on the Tree of the Cross didst give salvation unto mankind; th whence death arose, thence life also might rise again; and that he wh by a tree once overcame, might likewise by a Tree be overcome, throug Christ our Lord; through whom with Angels, *etc.*

For Easter

BUT chiefly are we bound to praise thee for the glorious Resurrection thy Son, Jesus Christ our Lord: for he is the very Paschal Lamb, whi was offered for us, and hath taken away the sin of the world; who by his dea hath destroyed death, and by his rising to life again hath restored to us eve lasting life. Therefore with Angels, *etc.*

For the Ascension of our Lord

THROUGH Jesus Christ our Lord, who, after his Resurrection, appear openly to all his disciples, and in their sight was taken up into heave that he might make us partakers of his divine Nature. Therefore with Ange *etc.*

For the Day of Pentecost

THROUGH Jesus Christ our Lord, who, ascending above the heave and sitting at thy right hand, poured out on this day the Holy Spirit, as had promised, upon the chosen disciples; whereat the whole earth rejoic with exceeding joy. Therefore with Angels, *etc.*

For Trinity Sunday

WHO with thine only-begotten Son, and the Holy Ghost, art one Go one Lord. And in the confession of the only true God, we worship t Trinity in Person, and the Unity in Substance, of Majesty co-equal. Therefo with Angels, *etc.*

For All Saints' Day (or at any time when the faithful departed are remembere

THROUGH Jesus Christ our Lord, who in the blessedness of thy sai hath given us a glorious pledge of the hope of our calling; that, followi their example and being strengthened by their fellowship, we may exult thee for thy mercy, even as they rejoice with thee in glory. Therefore wi Angels, *etc.*

¶ *After the Preface shall follow immediately:*

THEREFORE with Angels and Archangels, and with all the company of heaven, we laud and magnify thy glorious Name; evermore praising thee, nd saying:

¶ *Then shall be sung or said the Sanctus.*

THE SANCTUS

HOLY, holy, holy, Lord God of Sabaoth; Heaven and earth are full of thy glory; Hosanna in the highest.
Blessed is he that cometh in the Name of the Lord; Hosanna in the highest.

¶ *Then may the Congregation kneel.*

The Minister standing before the Altar, and facing it, shall say the Prayer of Thanksgiving.

THE PRAYER OF THANKSGIVING

HOLY art thou, Almighty and Merciful God. Holy art thou, and great is the Majesty of thy glory.

Thou didst so love the world as to give thine only-begotten Son, that whoever believeth in him might not perish, but have everlasting life; Who, ving come into the world to fulfill for us thy holy will and to accomplish all ings for our salvation, IN THE NIGHT IN WHICH HE AS BETRAYED, [a]TOOK BREAD; AND, WHEN HE HAD VEN THANKS, HE BRAKE IT AND GAVE IT TO HIS DISPLES, SAYING, TAKE, EAT; THIS IS MY BODY, WHICH IS GIVEN FOR YOU; THIS) IN REMEMBRANCE OF ME.

(a) Here he shall take the BREAD *in his hand.*

AFTER THE SAME MANNER ALSO, HE [b]TOOK THE CUP, HEN HE HAD SUPPED, AND, WHEN HE HAD GIVEN IANKS, HE GAVE IT TO THEM, SAYING, DRINK YE ALL IT; THIS CUP IS THE NEW TESTAMENT in MY BLOOD, WHICH IS SHED FOR YOU, ND FOR MANY, FOR THE REMISSION OF SINS; THIS DO, AS OFT AS YE DRINK IT, IN MEMBRANCE OF ME.

(b) Here he shall take the CUP *in his hand.*

Remembering, therefore, his salutary precept, his life-giving Passion and eath, his glorious Resurrection and Ascension and the promise of his ming again, we give thanks to thee, O Lord God Almighty, not as we ought, it as we are able; and we beseech thee mercifully to accept our praise and anksgiving, and with thy Word and Holy Spirit to bless us, thy servants, d these thine own gifts of bread and wine, so that we and all who partake ereof may be filled with heavenly benediction and grace, and, receiving the mission of sins, be sanctified in soul and body, and have our portion with thy saints.

And unto thee, O God, Father, Son, and Holy Spirit, be all honor and glory thy holy Church, world without end. Amen.

¶ *Then shall the Minister sing or say:*

OUR Father, who art in heaven, Hallowed be thy Name, Thy kingdo come, Thy will be done, on earth as it is in heaven. Give us this day o daily bread; And forgive us our trespasses, as we forgive those who trespa against us; And lead us not into temptation, But deliver us from evil.

¶ *The Congregation shall sing or say:*

FOR thine is the kingdom, and the power, and the glory, for ever and eve Amen.

¶ *Or, instead of the above Prayer of Thanksgiving,* "Holy art thou, Almighty and Merci God," *the Minister may say the Words of Institution, followed by the Lord's Prayer.*

THE WORDS OF INSTITUTION

OUR LORD JESUS CHRIST, IN THE NIGHT IN WHICH HE WAS BETRAYED, [a]TOOK BREAD; AND, WHEN HE HAD GIVEN THANKS, HE BRAKE IT AND GAVE IT TO HIS DISCIPLES, SAYING, TAKE, EAT; THIS IS MY BODY, WHICH IS GIVEN FOR YOU; TI DO IN REMEMBRANCE OF ME.

(a) Here he shall ta the BREAD *in his hand.*

AFTER THE SAME MANNER ALSO, HE [b]TOOK THE CUP, WHEN HE HAD SUPPED, AND, WHEN HE HAD GIVEN THANKS, HE GAVE IT TO THEM, SAYING, DRINK YE ALL OF IT; THIS CUP IS THE NEW TESTAMENT IN MY BLOOD, WHICH IS SHED FOR YO AND FOR MANY, FOR THE REMISSION OF SINS; THIS DO, AS OFT AS YE DRINK IT, REMEMBRANCE OF ME.

(b) Here he shall ta the CUP *in his hand.*

THE LORD'S PRAYER

OUR Father, who art in heaven, . . .

¶ *Then shall the Minister turn to the Congregation and sing or say:*

The peace of the Lord be with you alway.

¶ *The Congregation shall sing or say:*

And with thy spirit.

¶ *Then, the Congregation standing, shall be sung or said the Agnus Dei.*

AGNUS DEI

O CHRIST, thou Lamb of God, that takest away the sin of the worl have mercy upon us.

O Christ, thou Lamb of God, that takest away the sin of the world, ha mercy upon us.

O Christ, thou Lamb of God, that takest away the sin of the world, gra us thy peace. Amen.

¶ *Then shall the Communicants present themselves before the Altar and receive the Holy Sacrament.*

THE COMMUNION

¶ *When the Minister giveth the* Bread *he shall say:*

The Body of Christ, given for thee.

¶ *When he giveth the* Cup *he shall say:*

The Blood of Christ, shed for thee.

¶ *The Communicant may say* Amen *after each Element has been received.*

¶ *After he hath given the* Bread *and the* Cup, *or after all have been communicated, the Minister shall say:*

The Body of our Lord Jesus Christ and his precious Blood strengthen and eserve you unto eternal life.

THE POST-COMMUNION

¶ *Then shall the Congregation rise, and the Nunc Dimittis may be sung or said.*

NUNC DIMITTIS

ORD, now lettest thou thy servant depart in peace: according to thy word;
For mine eyes have seen thy salvation: which thou hast prepared before e face of all people;
A light to lighten the Gentiles: and the glory of thy people Israel.
Glory be to the Father, and to the Son, and to the Holy Ghost;
As it was in the beginning, is now, and ever shall be, world without end. nen.

¶ *Then shall be said The Prayer.*

THE PRAYER

¶ *The Minister shall say one of the following Prayers; or he may say the Collect for Thursday in Holy Week.*

O give thanks unto the Lord, for he is good.
℟. And his mercy endureth for ever.

WE give thanks to thee, Almighty God, that thou hast refreshed us with this thy salutary gift; and we beseech thee, of thy mercy, to strengthen through the same gift, in faith toward thee and in fervent love toward one other; through Jesus Christ, thy dear Son, our Lord, who liveth and reign- with thee and the Holy Ghost, one God, world without end.

Or,

POUR forth upon us, O Lord, the spirit of thy love, that by thy mercy thou mayest make of one will those whom thou hast fed with one heavenly od; through thy Son, Jesus Christ our Lord, who liveth and reigneth with ee and the Holy Ghost, one God, world without end.

Or,

ALMIGHTY God, who givest the true Bread which cometh down fro heaven, even thy Son, Jesus Christ our Lord: Grant, we beseech thee, th we who have received the Sacrament of his Body and Blood may abide him, and he in us, that we may be filled with the power of his endless lif who liveth and reigneth with thee and the Holy Ghost, one God, world witho end.

Or,

ALMIGHTY God, who hast given thine only Son to be unto us both a sa rifice for sin and also an ensample of godly life: Give us grace that we m always most thankfully receive that his inestimable benefit, and also daily e deavor ourselves to follow the blessed steps of his most holy life; through t same Jesus Christ our Lord, who liveth and reigneth with thee and the Ho Ghost, one God, world without end.

¶ *The Congregation shall sing or say:*

Amen.

¶ *Then may be sung or said the Salutation and the Benedicamus.*

The Lord be with you.
℟. And with thy spirit.

Bless we the Lord.
℟. Thanks be to God.

¶ *Then the Minister, standing at the Altar, shall sing or say the Benediction.*

THE BENEDICTION

THE LORD bless thee, and keep thee.
The LORD make his face shine upon thee, and be gracious unto thee.
The LORD lift up his countenance upon thee, and give thee peace:
IN the Name of the Father, and of the Son, and of the Holy Ghost.

¶ *The Congregation shall sing or say:*

Amen.

The Service

FIRST SETTING

¶ The General Rubrics contain directions additional to those which appear in the Services. Intonations provided for the Minister's parts of the Services represent a permissive use. They are not to be considered directive.

¶ The preparatory office up to the Introit may be said. If it be sung, the following musical setting may be used.

¶ The Congregation shall rise. The Minister shall sing or say:

IN the Name of the Father, and of the Son, and of the Holy Ghost.

¶ The Congregation shall sing or say:

A - men.

THE CONFESSION OF SINS

¶ The Minister shall say:

BELOVED in the Lord! Let us draw near with a true heart, and confess our sins unto God our Father, beseeching him, in the Name of our Lord Jesus Christ, to grant us forgiveness.

¶ The Minister and Congregation may kneel.

¶ They shall sing or say:

Minister
Congregation
Our help is in the Name of the Lord.
℟. Who made heaven and earth.
Minister
Congregation
I said, I will confess my transgressions unto the Lord.
℟. And thou forgavest the iniquity of my sin.

For notes on the chant, see p. ix.

¶ *Then shall the Minister say:*

ALMIGHTY God, our Maker and Redeemer, we poor sinners conf unto thee, that we are by nature sinful and unclean, and that we ha sinned against thee by thought, word, and deed. Wherefore we flee for refu to thine infinite mercy, seeking and imploring thy grace, for the sake of o Lord Jesus Christ.

¶ *The Congregation shall say with the Minister:*

O MOST merciful God, who hast given thine only-begotten Son to die us, have mercy upon us, and for his sake grant us remission of all o sins; and by thy Holy Spirit increase in us true knowledge of thee and of t will, and true obedience to thy Word, that by thy grace we may come to ev lasting life; through Jesus Christ our Lord. Amen.

¶ *Then the Minister, standing, and facing the Congregation, shall say:*

ALMIGHTY God, our heavenly Father, hath had mercy upon us, and ha given his only Son to die for us, and for his sake forgiveth us all our si To them that believe on his Name, he giveth power to become the sons God, and bestoweth upon them his Holy Spirit. He that believeth, and is ba tized, shall be saved. Grant this, O Lord, unto us all.

¶ *Or, he may say:*

THE Almighty and merciful God grant unto you, being penitent, pard and remission of all your sins, time for amendment of life, and the gra and comfort of his Holy Spirit.

¶ *The Congregation shall sing or say:*

A - men.

¶ ***A brief Silence may be kept before the Introit for the Day.***

The Communion

¶ *The Congregation shall stand until the close of the Collect.*

INTROIT

The Introit for the Day with the Gloria Patri shall be sung or said. The Introit should be sung by the choir, or it may be said by the Minister.

GLORIA PATRI

Congregation
HENRY SMART
Glory be to the Father, and to the Son, and to the Ho - ly Ghost:
as it was in the beginning, is now and ev - er shall be, world with-out end. A-men.
Or,
Congregation
HAROLD W. GILBERT
Glory be to the Father, and to the Son, and to the Ho - ly Ghost:
as it was in the be - ginning, is now, and ever shall be, world with-out end. A - men.

¶ *Then shall be sung or said the Kyrie.*

KYRIE

Minister

IN peace let us pray to the Lord. ℟.

For the peace that is from above, and for the salvation of our souls, let pray to the Lord. ℟.

For the peace of the whole world, for the well-being of the churches of Gc and for the unity of all, let us pray to the Lord. ℟.

For this holy house, and for them that in faith, piety and fear of God of here their worship and praise, let us pray to the Lord. ℟.

Help, save, pity and defend us, O God, by thy grace. ℟.

ARNOLD RICHARDSON
ARR. HAROLD W. GILBERT

Congregation. After the first four petitions
℟. Lord, have mer - - cy.
Congregation. After the final petition
℟. A - - - - - - - men.

Or,

HAROLD W. GILBERT

Congregation. After the first four petitions *After the final petition*

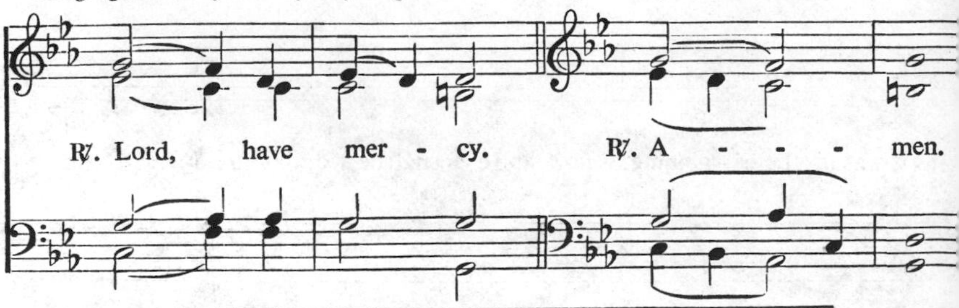
℟. Lord, have mer - cy.
℟. A - - - men.

¶ *In place of the foregoing, the following Kyrie may be sung or said:*

KYRIE

Minister

1. Lord, have mercy upon us. 2. Christ, have mercy upon us. 3. Lord, have mercy upon us.

Congregation
1. ℟. Lord, have mer - cy up - on us.
2. ℟. Christ, have mer - cy up - on us.
3. ℟. Lord, have mer - cy up - on us.

¶ *Then shall be sung or said the Gloria in Excelsis.*

GLORIA IN EXCELSIS

¶ *The Minister shall sing or say:*

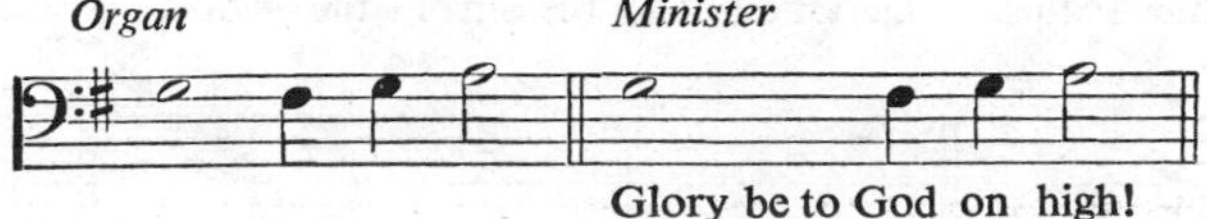
Organ
Minister

Glory be to God on high!

The Service

Congregation
Old Scottish Chant
And on earth peace, good - will toward men. We praise thee, we bless thee,
we worship thee, we glorify thee, we give thanks to thee for thy great glory,
O Lord God, heaven - ly King, God the Father Al - mighty.
O Lord, the only-begotten Son, Je - sus Christ; O Lord God, Lamb of God,
Son of the Father, that takest away the sin of the world, have mercy

up-on us. Thou that takest away the sin of the world, re-ceive our prayer.
Thou that sittest at the right hand of God the Father, have mercy up-on us. For thou
on-ly art holy; thou on-ly art the Lord; thou only, O Christ, with the
Ho-ly Ghost, art most high in the glory of God the Father. A-men.
Or,
Leo Sowerby
Adapted by Harold W. Gilbert
Organ
Minister
Congregation
Glo-ry be to God on high! And on earth peace, goodwill toward men.

We praise thee, we bless thee, we worship thee, we glorify thee, we give thanks to thee
(♯) (♮)
for thy great glory, O Lord God, heaven-ly King, God the Father Al-mighty.
O Lord, the only-begotten Son, Je - sus Christ; O Lord God, Lamb of God, Son of
the Father, that takest away the sin of the world, have mercy up - on us.
Thou that takest away the sin of the world, re - ceive our prayer.

Thou that sittest at the right hand of God the Father, have mercy up - on us.
For thou only art holy; thou on - ly art the Lord; thou only, O Christ, with the
Ho - ly Ghost, art most high in the glory of God the Father. A - men.
¶ Then shall the Minister sing or say:
Organ
Congregation
The Lord be with you. ℟. And with thy spirit.
¶ The Minister shall say:
Let us pray.
¶ Then shall the Minister say the Collect for the Day.
THE COLLECT
¶ The Collect ended, the Congregation shall sing or say:
A - men.

¶ *Here the Minister may read the appointed Lesson from the Old Testament, saying:* The Lesson is written in the ______ Chapter of ____________, beginning at the __________ Verse. *The Lesson ended, he shall say:* Here endeth the Lesson.

¶ *Then may be sung a Psalm or a hymn version of a Psalm.*

¶ *Then shall the Minister announce the Epistle for the Day, saying:* The Epistle fo (*here he shall name the Festival or Day*) is written in the ________ Chapter of ________ beginning at the ______ Verse.

THE EPISTLE

¶ *The Epistle ended, the Minister shall say:* Here endeth the Epistle for the Day.

¶ *Then may the Gradual for the Day be sung.*

THE GRADUAL

¶ *When the Gradual for the Day is omitted, the Alleluia or the Gradual for the Season (pp. 117–128) may be sung.*

THE ALLELUIA

W. H. MONK

Al - le - lu - ia, Al - le - lu - ia, Al - le - lu - ia.
Org.

¶ *In Lent this Sentence shall be sung instead of the Alleluia:*

JOHN MERBECKE
Arr. HAROLD W. GILBERT

Unison

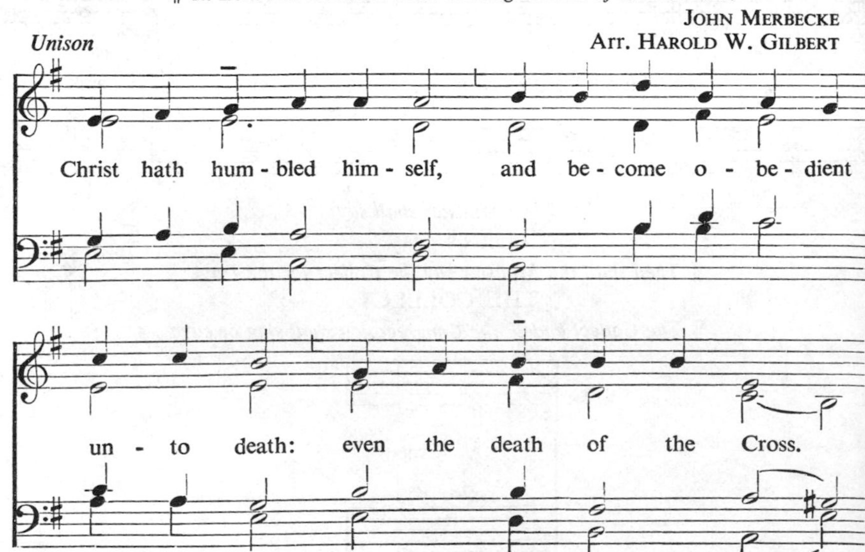
Christ hath hum - bled him - self, and be - come o - be - dient
un - to death: even the death of the Cross.

¶ *Then shall the Minister announce the Gospel for the Day, saying:* The Holy Gospel written in the ________ Chapter of St. ________________, beginning at the ________ Verse.

¶ *The Congregation shall rise and sing or say:*

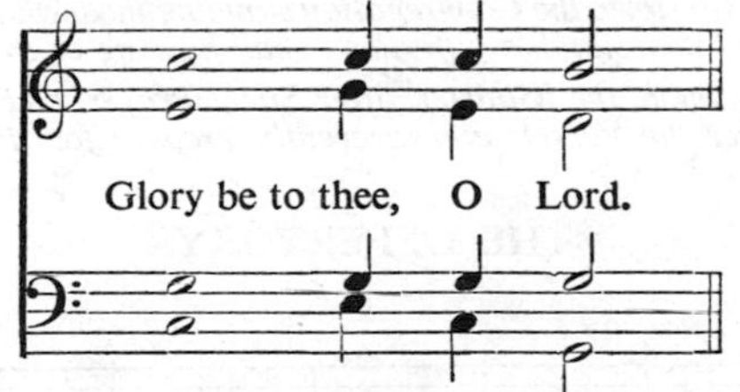
Glory be to thee, O Lord.

¶ *Then shall the Minister read the Gospel for the Day.*

THE GOSPEL

¶ *The Gospel ended, the Minister shall say:* Here endeth the Gospel for the Day.

¶ *The Congregation shall sing or say:*

Praise be to thee, O Christ.

¶ *Then shall be said or sung the Creed.*

THE CREED

The Nicene Creed shall be said or sung on all Festivals and whenever there is a Communion.

THE NICENE CREED

I BELIEVE in one God, . . . (*page 4*)

THE APOSTLES' CREED

I BELIEVE in God the Father Almighty, . . . (*page 5*)

¶ *Then shall be sung the Hymn.*

THE HYMN

¶ *Then shall follow the Sermon.*

THE SERMON

The Sermon being ended, the Congregation shall rise and the Minister shall then say:

THE Peace of God, which passeth all understanding, keep your hearts and minds through Christ Jesus.

Congregation

A - men.

¶ *Then shall the Offering be received and presented at the Altar.*

THE OFFERING

¶ *Then shall follow the Offertory, the Congregation standing meanwhile. One of the Offertori here following, or any other suitable Offertory, shall be sung or said.*

¶ *When there is a Communion, the Minister, after Silent Prayer, and during the singing of tl Offertory, shall uncover the Vessels and reverently prepare for the Administration of tl Holy Sacrament.*

THE OFFERTORY

I

W. Crotch

II

J. Alcock

I

THE sacrifices of God are a ˈ broken ˈ spirit:
 * a broken and a contrite heart O God ˈ thou wilt ˈ not de ˈ spise.
Do good in thy good ˈ pleasure · unto ˈ Zion:
 * build ˈ thou the ˈ walls · of Je ˈ rusalem.
Then shalt thou be pleased with the ˈ sacrifices of ˈ righteousness:
 * with burnt ˈ offering and ˈ whole burnt ˈ offering.

II

WHAT shall I ˈ render · unto the ˈ Lord:
 * for ˈ all his ˈ benefits ˈ toward me?
I will offer to thee the ˈ sacrifice of ˈ thanksgiving:
 * and will ˈ call up · on the ˈ Name of the ˈ Lord.
I will take the ˈ cup of sal ˈ vation:
 * and ˈ call up · on the ˈ Name of the ˈ Lord.
I will pay my vows unto the Lord now in the presence of ˈ all his ˈ peopl
 * in the courts of the Lord's house, in the ˈ midst of thee ˈ O Je ˈ rusale

The Communion

III

CREATE in me a clean ' heart O ' God:
  * and re ' new a right ' spirit with ' in me.
Cast me not a ' way from thy ' presence:
  * and take not thy ' Holy ' Spirit ' from me.
Restore unto me the joy of ' thy sal ' vation:
  * and up ' hold me with ' thy free ' Spirit.

Or,

From a Melody by J. A. FREYLINGHAUSEN
Adapted, HAROLD W. GILBERT

Cre - ate in me a clean heart, O God: and re -
new a right spir - it with - in me. Cast me not a -
way from thy pres - ence: and take not thy Ho - ly
Spir - it from me. Re - store un - to me the joy of

thy sal - va - tion: and up - hold me with thy free Spir - it.

¶ *Then shall follow the Prayer of the Church.* (*p.* 6.)

THE PRAYER OF THE CHURCH

Let us pray.

ALMIGHTY God, the Father of our Lord Jesus Christ, . . .

¶ *If there be no Communion the Minister and Congregation shall say the Lord's Prayer.*

OUR Father, who art in heaven, . . .

¶ *A Hymn may then be sung. Then the Minister, standing at the Altar, shall sing or say th Benediction.*

THE BENEDICTION

The LORD bless thee, and keep thee.

The LORD make his face shine upon thee, and be gracious unto thee.

The LORD lift up his countenance upon thee, and give thee peace:

In the Name of the Father, and of the Son, and of the Holy Ghost.

¶ *The Congregation shall sing or say:*

Amen.

¶ *For music, see p.* 40.

THE THANKSGIVING

¶ *A Hymn shall be sung.*

¶ *The Congregation shall rise at the beginning of the Preface.*

THE PREFACE

¶ *The Minister and Congregation shall sing or say:*

Ancient Church melodies
Harm. after J. H. Arnold

Organ
Minister
Congregation. Unison
The Lord be with you. ℟. And with thy spir - it.
Minister
Lift up your hearts.
Congregation
℟. We lift them up un - to the Lord.
Minister
Let us give thanks un - to the Lord our God.
Congregation
℟. It is meet and right so to do.

¶ *Then shall the Minister turn to the Altar and sing or say:*

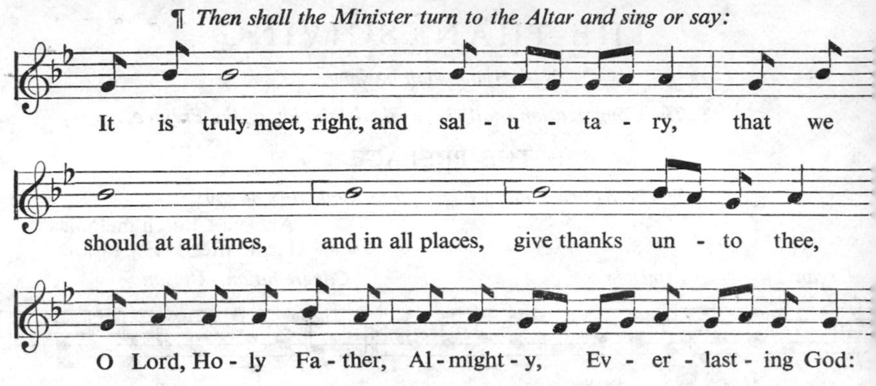
It is truly meet, right, and sal - u - ta - ry, that we
should at all times, and in all places, give thanks un - to thee,
O Lord, Ho - ly Fa - ther, Al - might - y, Ev - er - last - ing God:

¶ *Here shall follow the Proper Preface for the Day or Season. If there be none especiall appointed, then shall follow immediately,* Therefore with Angels, *etc.*

PROPER PREFACES

For Advent

WHO didst comfort thy people with the promise of the Redeeme through whom thou wilt also make all things new in the day when h shall come again to judge the world in righteousness. Therefore with Angel *etc.*

For Christmas

FOR in the mystery of the Word made flesh, thou hast given us a ne revelation of thy glory; that seeing thee in the person of thy Son, we ma be drawn to the love of those things which are not seen. Therefore wit Angels, *etc.*

For Epiphany

AND now do we praise thee, that thou didst send unto us thine onl begotten Son, and that in him, being found in fashion as a man, thou did reveal the fullness of thy glory. Therefore with Angels, *etc.*

For Lent

WHO on the Tree of the Cross didst give salvation unto mankind; th whence death arose, thence life also might rise again; and that he wh by a tree once overcame, might likewise by a Tree be overcome, throug Christ our Lord; through whom with Angels, *etc.*

For Easter

BUT chiefly are we bound to praise thee for the glorious Resurrection thy Son, Jesus Christ our Lord: for he is the very Paschal Lamb, whic was offered for us, and hath taken away the sin of the world; who by his deat hath destroyed death, and by his rising to life again hath restored to us eve lasting life. Therefore with Angels, *etc.*

¶ *For music of the Proper Prefaces, see pp. 71–74.*

For the Ascension of our Lord

THROUGH Jesus Christ our Lord, who, after his Resurrection, appeared openly to all his disciples, and in their sight was taken up into heaven, hat he might make us partakers of his divine Nature. Therefore with Angels, *tc.*

For the Day of Pentecost

THROUGH Jesus Christ our Lord, who, ascending above the heavens and sitting at thy right hand, poured out on this day the Holy Spirit, as he ad promised, upon the chosen disciples; whereat the whole earth rejoices vith exceeding joy. Therefore with Angels, *etc.*

For Trinity Sunday

WHO with thine only-begotten Son, and the Holy Ghost, art one God, one Lord. And in the confession of the only true God, we worship the rinity in Person, and the Unity in Substance, of Majesty co-equal. Therefore vith Angels, *etc.*

or All Saints' Day (or at any time when the faithful departed are remembered)

THROUGH Jesus Christ our Lord, who in the blessedness of thy saints hath given us a glorious pledge of the hope of our calling; that, following eir example and being strengthened by their fellowship, we may exult in ee for thy mercy, even as they rejoice with thee in glory. Therefore with ngels, *etc.*

¶ *After the Preface shall follow immediately:*

There-fore with An - gels and Arch - an - gels, and with all

the com - pa - ny of heav - en, we laud and magnify thy

glo - rious Name; ev - er - more prais - ing thee, and say - ing:

¶ *Then shall be sung or said the Sanctus.*

THE SANCTUS

XI cent. Plainsong, adapted, J. S. BACH
STEINAU, 1726
Adapted, REGINA H. FRYXELL

Unison
Ho - ly, ho - ly, ho - ly, Lord God of Sa - ba - oth;
Heaven and earth are full of thy glo - ry; Ho - san - na
in the high - est. Bless - ed is he that com - eth in the
Name of the Lord; Ho - san - na in the high - est.

The Communion

Or,
HEALEY WILLAN
Arranged, HAROLD W. GILBERT
Unison
Ho - ly, ho - ly, ho - - - - ly,
Lord God of Sa - ba - oth; Heaven and earth are full of thy
glo - ry; Ho - san - na in the high - - est.
Bless - ed is he that com - eth in the
Name of the Lord; Ho - san - na in the high - est.

¶ *Then may the Congregation kneel.*

¶ *The Minister standing before the Altar, and facing it, shall say the Prayer of Thanksgivin*

THE PRAYER OF THANKSGIVING

HOLY art thou, Almighty and Merciful God. Holy art thou, and great the Majesty of thy glory.

Thou didst so love the world as to give thine only-begotten Son, that who soever believeth in him might not perish, but have everlasting life; Wh having come into the world to fulfill for us thy holy will and to accomplis all things for our salvation, IN THE NIGHT IN WHICH HE WAS BETRAYED, [a]TOOK BREAD; AND, WHEN HE HAD GIVEN THANKS, HE BRAKE IT AND GAVE IT TO HIS DISCIPLES, SAYING, TAKE, EAT; THIS IS MY BODY, WHICH IS GIVEN FOR YOU; THIS D IN REMEMBRANCE OF ME.

(*a*) *Here he shall take the* BREAD *in his hand.*

AFTER THE SAME MANNER ALSO, HE [b]TOOK THE CUP, WHEN HE HAD SUPPED, AND, WHEN HE HAD GIVEN THANKS, HE GAVE IT TO THEM, SAYING, DRINK YE ALL OF IT; THIS CUP IS THE NEW TESTAMENT IN MY BLOOD, WHICH IS SHED FOR YO AND FOR MANY, FOR THE REMISSION OF SINS; THIS DO, AS OFT AS YE DRINK IT, REMEMBRANCE OF ME.

(*b*) *Here he shall take the* CUP *in his hand.*

Remembering, therefore, his salutary precept, his life-giving Passion an Death, his glorious Resurrection and Ascension and the promise of h coming again, we give thanks to thee, O Lord God Almighty, not as we ough but as we are able; and we beseech thee mercifully to accept our praise ar thanksgiving, and with thy Word and Holy Spirit to bless us, thy servants, ar these thine own gifts of bread and wine, so that we and all who partake there may be filled with heavenly benediction and grace, and, receiving the remissic of sins, be sanctified in soul and body, and have our portion with all thy saint

And unto thee, O God, Father, Son, and Holy Spirit, be all honor ar glory in thy holy Church, world without end. Amen.

¶ *Then shall the Minister sing or say:*

OUR Father, who art in heaven, Hallowed be thy Name, Thy kingdo come, Thy will be done, on earth as it is in heaven. Give us this d our daily bread; And forgive us our trespasses, as we forgive those w trespass against us; And lead us not into temptation, But deliver us from ev

¶ *The Congregation shall sing or say:*

Ancient Church melody
Harm. by WINFRED DOUGLAS

Unison

For thine is the king - dom, and the power, and the

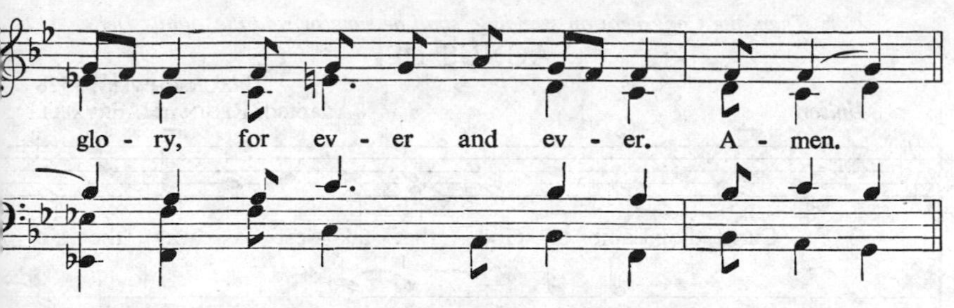
glo - ry, for ev - er and ev - er. A - men.

Or, instead of the above Prayer of Thanksgiving, "Holy art thou, Almighty and Merciful God," *the Minister may say the Words of Institution, followed by the Lord's Prayer.*

THE WORDS OF INSTITUTION

OUR LORD JESUS CHRIST, IN THE NIGHT IN WHICH HE WAS BETRAYED, [a]TOOK BREAD; AND, WHEN HE HAD GIVEN THANKS, HE BRAKE IT AND GAVE IT TO HIS DISCIPLES, SAYING, TAKE, EAT; THIS IS MY BODY, WHICH IS GIVEN FOR YOU; THIS DO IN REMEMBRANCE OF ME.

(a) Here he shall take the BREAD *in his hand.*

AFTER THE SAME MANNER ALSO, HE [b]TOOK THE CUP, WHEN HE HAD SUPPED, AND, WHEN HE HAD GIVEN THANKS, HE GAVE IT TO THEM, SAYING, DRINK YE ALL OF IT; THIS CUP IS THE NEW TESTAMENT IN MY BLOOD, WHICH IS SHED FOR YOU, AND FOR MANY, FOR THE REMISSION OF SINS; THIS DO, AS OFT AS YE DRINK IT, IN REMEMBRANCE OF ME.

(b) Here he shall take the CUP *in his hand.*

THE LORD'S PRAYER

OUR Father, who art in heaven, . . .

¶ *Then shall the Minister turn to the Congregation and sing or say:*

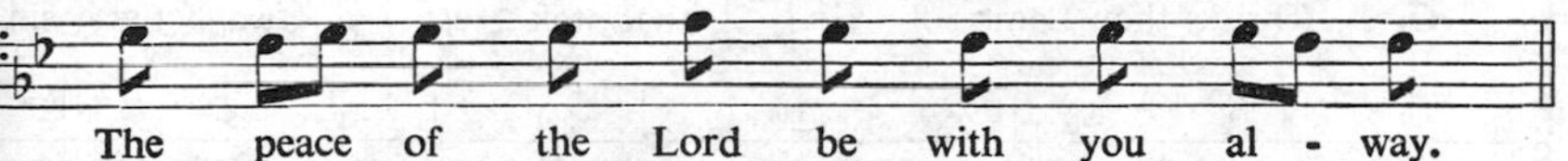
The peace of the Lord be with you al - way.

¶ *The Congregation shall sing or say:*

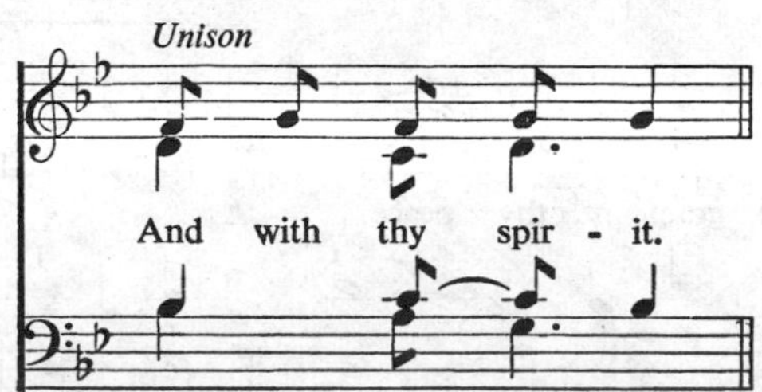
Unison
And with thy spir - it.

¶ *Then, the Congregation standing, shall be sung or said the Agnus Dei.*

AGNUS DEI

BRAUNSCHWEIG, 1528
Unison Adapted, REGINA H. FRYXELL

O Christ, thou Lamb of God, that tak - est a - way the sin
of the world, have mer - cy up - on us. O Christ, thou Lamb of God,
that tak - est a - way the sin of the world, have mer - cy up - on us.
O Christ, thou Lamb of God, that tak - est a - way the sin
of the world, grant us thy peace. A - - - - men.

Or,
XIII cent. Plainsong
Swedish Mässbok, 1942
Adapted, REGINA H. FRYXELL
Unison
O Christ, thou Lamb of God, that tak - est a - way the sin
of the world, have mer-cy up - on us. O Christ, thou Lamb of God,
that tak - est a - way the sin of the world, have mer -
cy up - on us. O Christ, thou Lamb of God, that tak - est
a - way the sin of the world, grant us thy peace. A - men.

¶ *Then shall the Communicants present themselves before the Altar and receive the Holy Sacrament.*

THE COMMUNION

¶ *When the Minister giveth the* Bread *he shall say:*

The Body of Christ, given for thee.

¶ *When he giveth the* Cup *he shall say:*

The Blood of Christ, shed for thee.

¶ *The Communicant may say* Amen *after each Element has been received.*

¶ *After he hath given the* Bread *and the* Cup, *or after all have been communicated, the Minis shall say:*

The Body of our Lord Jesus Christ and his precious Blood strengthen ar preserve you unto eternal life.

THE POST-COMMUNION

¶ *Then shall the Congregation rise, and the Nunc Dimittis may be sung or said.*

NUNC DIMITTIS

John Blow

Lord, now lettest thou thy servant de ' part in ' peace:
  * ac ' cording to ' thy ' word;
For mine eyes have ' seen thy sal ' vation:
  * which thou hast prepared before the ' face of ' all ' people;
A light to ' lighten the ' Gentiles:
  * and the ' glory · of thy ' people ' Israel.
Glory ' be to the ' Father,
  * and to the ' Son · and to the ' Holy ' Ghost;
As it ' was in · the be ' ginning,
  * is now, and ever shall be, ' world without ' end. A ' men.

¶ *Then shall be said The Prayer.*

THE PRAYER

¶ *The Minister shall say one of the following Prayers; or he may say the Collect for Thursday in Holy Week.*

Minister *Congregation*

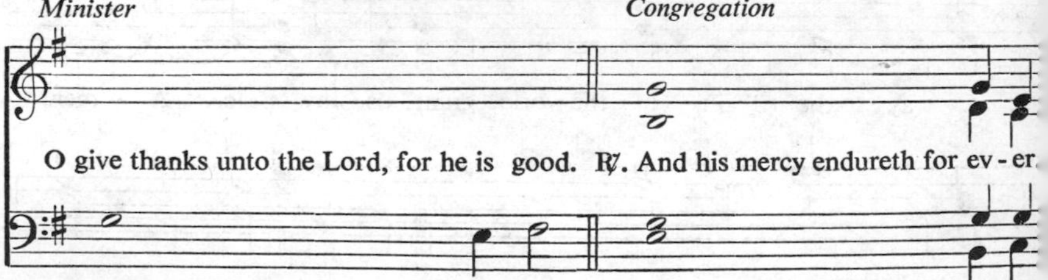
O give thanks unto the Lord, for he is good. R/. And his mercy endureth for ev - er.

WE give thanks to thee, Almighty God, that thou hast refreshed us with this thy salutary gift; and we beseech thee, of thy mercy, to strengthen ; through the same gift, in faith toward thee and in fervent love toward one ıother; through Jesus Christ, thy dear Son, our Lord, who liveth and reign- h with thee and the Holy Ghost, one God, world without end.

Or,

POUR forth upon us, O Lord, the spirit of thy love, that by thy mercy thou mayest make of one will those whom thou hast fed with one heav- ıly food; through thy Son, Jesus Christ our Lord, who liveth and reigneth ıth thee and the Holy Ghost, one God, world without end.

Or,

ALMIGHTY God, who givest the true Bread which cometh down from heaven, even thy Son, Jesus Christ our Lord: Grant, we beseech thee, at we who have received the Sacrament of his Body and Blood may abide him, and he in us, that we may be filled with the power of his endless life; ıo liveth and reigneth with thee and the Holy Ghost, one God, world thout end.

Or,

ALMIGHTY God, who hast given thine only Son to be unto us both a sacrifice for sin and also an ensample of godly life: Give us grace that we ay always most thankfully receive that his inestimable benefit, and also ily endeavor ourselves to follow the blessed steps of his most holy life; rough the same Jesus Christ our Lord, who liveth and reigneth with thee d the Holy Ghost, one God, world without end.

¶ *The Congregation shall sing or say:*

A - men.

¶ *Then may be sung or said the Salutation and the Benedicamus.*

Minister *Congregation*

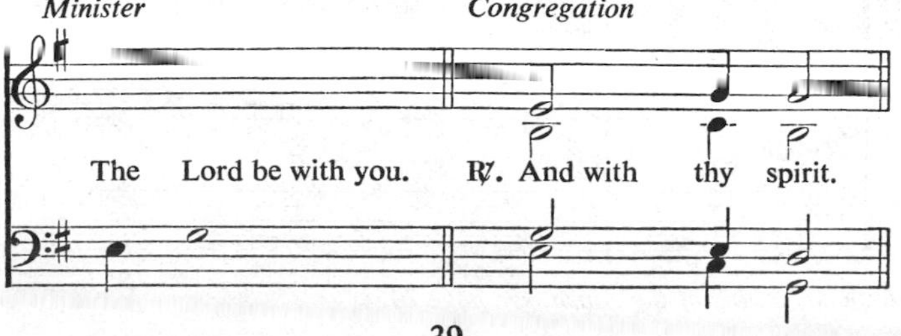
The Lord be with you.
℟. And with thy spirit.

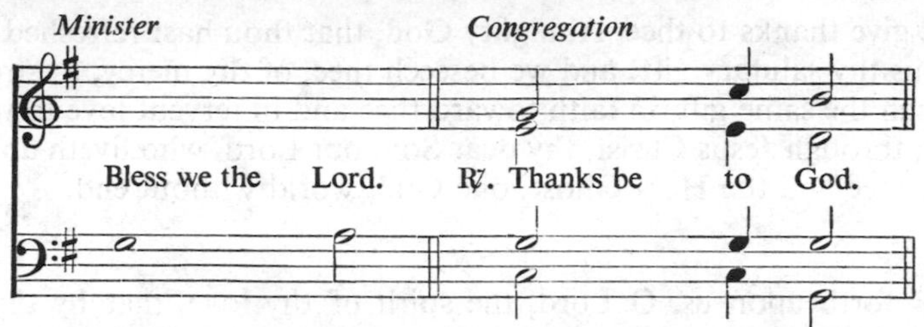
Minister
Congregation
Bless we the Lord.
℟. Thanks be to God.

¶ *Then the Minister, standing at the Altar, shall sing or say the Benediction.*

THE BENEDICTION

THE LORD bless thee, and keep thee.

The LORD make his face shine upon thee, and be gracious unto thee.

The LORD lift up his countenance upon thee, and give thee peace:

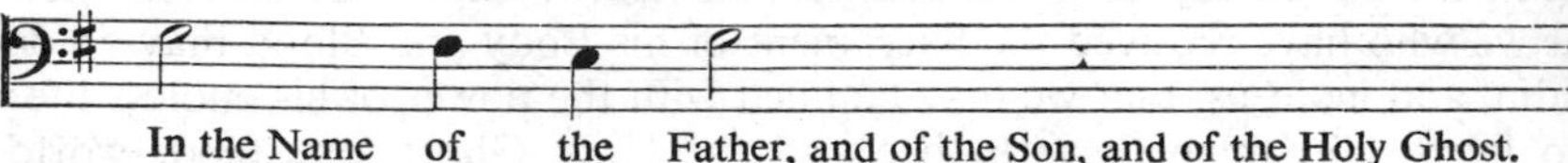
In the Name of the Father, and of the Son, and of the Holy Ghost.

¶ *The Congregation shall sing or say:*

I.

A - men.

II.

A - men.

III.

Based on T. TERTIUS NOBLE

A - men. A - men. A - - - men.

p *f*

Organ

For additional setting of the Amen, see page 70.

The Service

SECOND SETTING

The General Rubrics contain directions additional to those which appear in the Services.

Intonations provided for the Minister's parts of the Services represent a permissive use. They are not to be considered directive.

The preparatory office up to the Introit may be said. If it be sung, the following musical setting may be used.

¶ *The Congregation shall rise. The Minister shall sing or say:*

IN the Name of the Father, and of the Son, and of the Holy Ghost.

¶ *The Congregation shall sing or say:*

A - men.

THE CONFESSION OF SINS

¶ *The Minister shall say:*

BELOVED in the Lord! Let us draw near with a true heart, and confess our sins unto God our Father, beseeching him, in the Name of our Lord sus Christ, to grant us forgiveness.

¶ *The Minister and Congregation may kneel.*

¶ *They shall sing or say:*

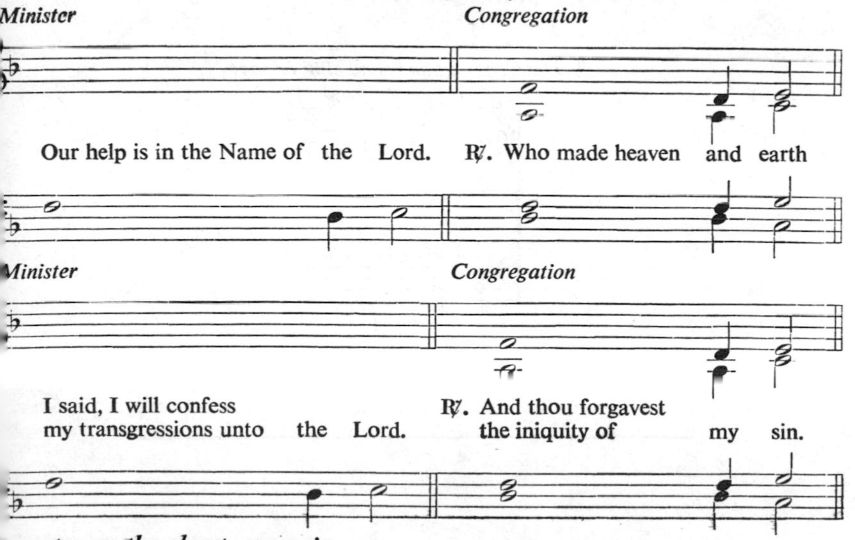
Minister
Congregation
Our help is in the Name of the Lord.
℟. Who made heaven and earth
Minister
Congregation
I said, I will confess my transgressions unto the Lord.
℟. And thou forgavest the iniquity of my sin.

r notes on the chant, see p. ix.

¶ *Then shall the Minister say:*

ALMIGHTY God, our Maker and Redeemer, we poor sinners confe unto thee, that we are by nature sinful and unclean, and that we ha sinned against thee by thought, word, and deed. Wherefore we flee for refug to thine infinite mercy, seeking and imploring thy grace, for the sake of o Lord Jesus Christ.

¶ *The Congregation shall say with the Minister:*

O MOST merciful God, who hast given thine only-begotten Son to die f us, have mercy upon us, and for his sake grant us remission of all o sins; and by thy Holy Spirit increase in us true knowledge of thee and of t will, and true obedience to thy Word, that by thy grace we may come to eve lasting life; through Jesus Christ our Lord. Amen.

¶ *Then the Minister, standing, and facing the Congregation, shall say:*

ALMIGHTY God, our heavenly Father, hath had mercy upon us, a hath given his only Son to die for us, and for his sake forgiveth us all o sins. To them that believe on his Name, he giveth power to become the so of God, and bestoweth upon them his Holy Spirit. He that believeth, and baptized, shall be saved. Grant this, O Lord, unto us all.

¶ *Or, he may say:*

THE Almighty and merciful God grant unto you, being penitent, pard and remission of all your sins, time for amendment of life, and the gra and comfort of his Holy Spirit.

¶ *The Congregation shall sing or say:*

A - men.

The Communion

¶ *A brief Silence may be kept before the Introit for the Day.*

¶ *The Congregation shall stand until the close of the Collect.*

INTROIT

The Introit for the Day with the Gloria Patri shall be sung or said. The Introit should be sung by the choir, or it may be said by the Minister.

GLORIA PATRI

Plainsong, Tone V
PFALZ, 1557
Adapted, REGINA H. FRYXELL

Congregation. Unison
Glo - ry be to the Fa - ther, and to the Son,
and to the Ho - ly Ghost: as it was in the be - gin - ning,
is now, and ev - er shall be, world with-out end. A - men.

¶ *Then shall be sung or said the Kyrie.*

KYRIE

X cent. Plainsong (*Orbis factor*)
Swedish *Mässbok*, 1942
Adapted, REGINA H. FRYXELL

Minister

In peace let us pray to the Lord.

Congregation. Unison

℟. Lord, - - - - - - have mer - cy.

Minister

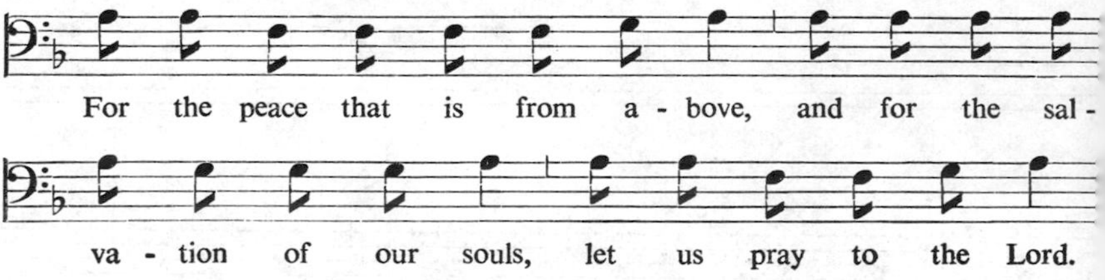

For the peace that is from a - bove, and for the sal -
va - tion of our souls, let us pray to the Lord.

Congregation

℟. Lord, - - - - - - have mer - cy.

Minister

For the peace of the whole world, for the well - be - ing of the church -

of God, and for the u - ni - ty of all, let us pray to the Lor

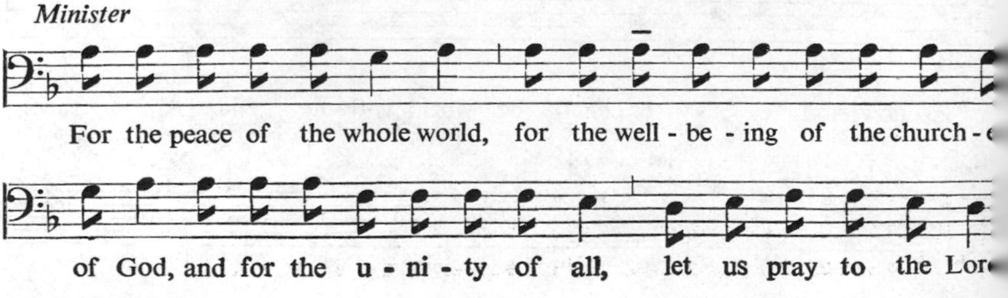

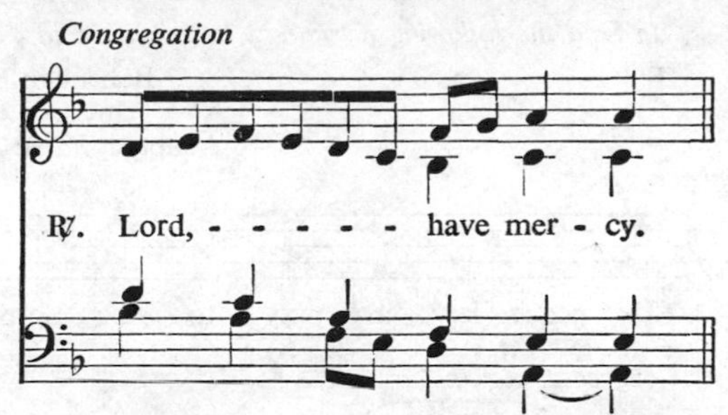
Congregation
℟. Lord, - - - - - have mer - cy.

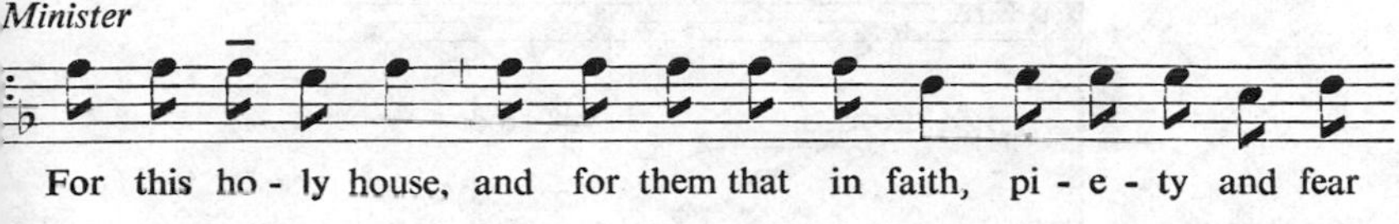
Minister
For this ho - ly house, and for them that in faith, pi - e - ty and fear

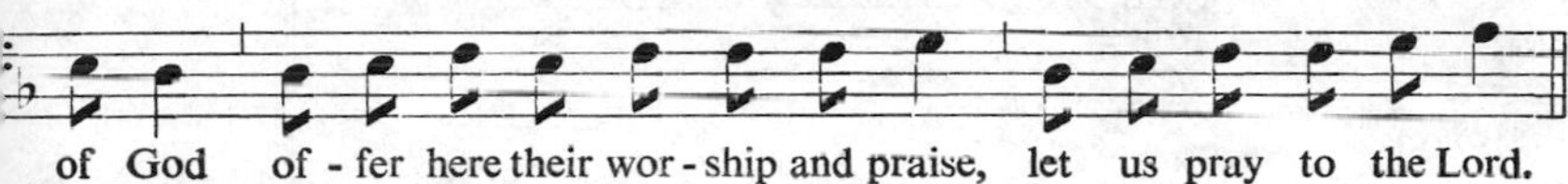
of God of - fer here their wor - ship and praise, let us pray to the Lord.

Congregation
℟. Lord, - - - - - have mer - cy.

Minister
Help, save, pi - ty and de - fend us, O God, by thy grace.

Congregation
℟. A - - - men.

¶ *In Lent the following Kyrie may be sung or said:*

Bohemian Brethren, 1544
Swedish *Mässbok*, 1942
Adapted, REGINA H. FRYXELL

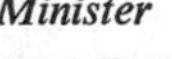
Minister

In peace let us pray to the Lord.

Congregation. Unison

℟. Lord, - - - have mer - cy.

Minister

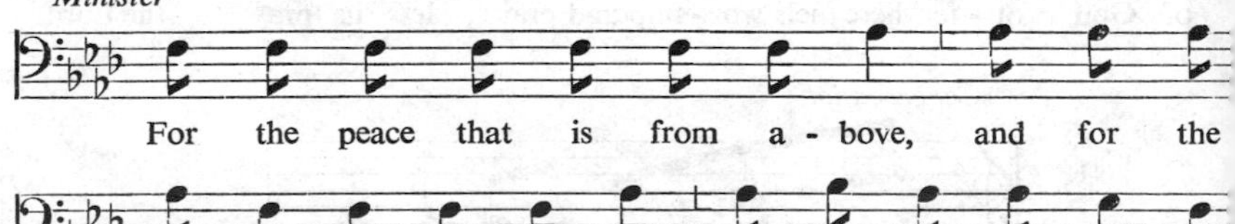
For the peace that is from a - bove, and for the

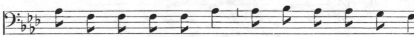

sal - va - tion of our souls, let us pray to the Lord

Congregation

℟. Lord, - - - have mer - cy.

Minister

For the peace of the whole world, for the well - be - ing of the church-

of God, and for the u - ni - ty of all, let us pray to the Lord

Congregation

℟. Lord, - - - have mer - cy.

Minister

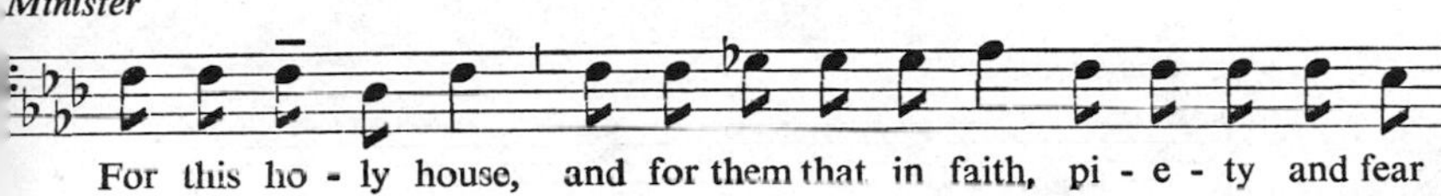
For this ho - ly house, and for them that in faith, pi - e - ty and fear

of God of - fer here their wor-ship and praise, let us pray to the Lord.

Congregation

℟. Lord, - - - have mer - cy.

Minister

Help, save, pi - ty and de - fend us, O God, by thy grace.

Congregation

℟. A - - men.

¶ *In place of the foregoing, the following Kyrie may be sung or said:*

KYRIE

Minister

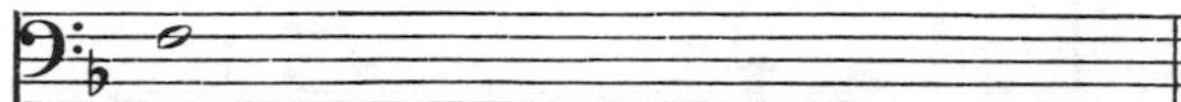

1. Lord, have mercy upon us.
2. Christ, have mercy upon us.
3. Lord, have mercy upon us.

Congregation

1. ℟. Lord, have mer - cy up - on us.

2. ℟. Christ, have mer - cy up - on us.

3. ℟. Lord, have mer - cy up - on us.

¶ *Then shall be sung or said the Gloria in Excelsis.*

GLORIA IN EXCELSIS

X cent. Plainsong (*Lux et origo*)
N. DECIUS, *Allein Gott in der Höh' sei Ehr*
Adapted, REGINA H. FRYXELL

Minister
Glo - - ry be to God on high!
Congregation. Unison
And on earth peace, good will toward men.
We praise thee, we bless thee, we wor - ship thee, we glo - ri - fy thee,
we give thanks to thee for thy great glo - ry, O Lord God,
heaven - ly King, God the Fa - ther Al - might - y.

O Lord, the on - ly be - got - ten Son, Je - sus Christ; O Lord God
Lamb of God, Son of the Fa - ther, that tak - est a - way th
sin of the world, have mer - cy up - on us. Thou that tak - est
way the sin of the world, re - ceive our prayer. Thou that sit - test at t
right hand of God the Fa - ther, have mer - cy up - on us

Or,

XI cent. Plainsong (*De angelis*)
Adapted, REGINA H. FRYXELL

Unison

Al - le - lu - ia, Al - le - lu - ia, Al - - - - le - lu - ia.

¶ *In Lent this Sentence shall be sung instead of the Alleluia:*

JOHN MERBECKE
ARR. HAROLD W. GILBERT

Unison

Christ hath hum - bled him - self, and be - come o - be - dient un - to death: even the death of the Cross.

¶ *Then shall the Minister announce the Gospel for the Day, saying:* The Holy Gospel is written in the ——— Chapter of St. ———, beginning at the ——— Verse.

¶ *The Congregation shall rise and sing or say:*

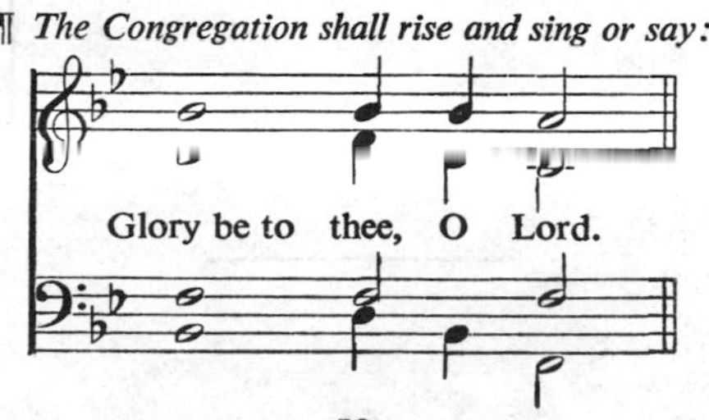
Glory be to thee, O Lord.

¶ *Then shall the Minister read the Gospel for the Day.*

THE GOSPEL

¶ *The Gospel ended, the Minister shall say:* Here endeth the Gospel for the Day.

¶ *The Congregation shall sing or say:*

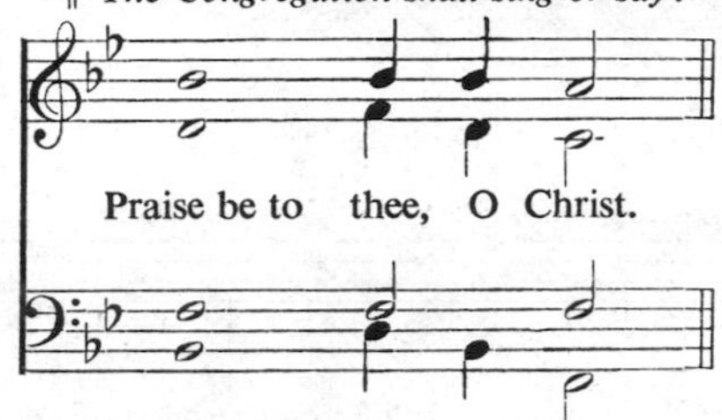
Praise be to thee, O Christ.

¶ *Then shall be said or sung the Creed.*

THE CREED

¶ *The Nicene Creed shall be said or sung on all Festivals and whenever there is a Communion*

THE NICENE CREED

I BELIEVE in one God, . . . (*page 4*)

THE APOSTLES' CREED

I BELIEVE in God the Father Almighty, . . . (*page 5*)

¶ *Then shall be sung the Hymn.*

THE HYMN

¶ *Then shall follow the Sermon.*

THE SERMON

¶ *The Sermon being ended, the Congregation shall rise and the Minister shall then say:*

THE peace of God, which passeth all understanding, keep your hearts and minds through Christ Jesus.

Congregation

A - men.

The Communion

¶ *Then shall the Offering be received and presented at the Altar.*

THE OFFERING

¶ *Then shall follow the Offertory, the Congregation standing meanwhile. One of the Offertories here following, or any other suitable Offertory, shall be sung or said.*

¶ *When there is a Communion, the Minister, after Silent Prayer, and during the singing of the Offertory, shall uncover the Vessels and reverently prepare for the Administration of the Holy Sacrament.*

THE OFFERTORY

I

Litany in Phrygian Mode
Swedish *Mässbok*, 1942
Adapted, REGINA H. FRYXELL

Unison

The sac - ri - fic - es of God are a bro - ken spir - it:
a bro ken and a con-trite heart, O God, thou wilt not de-spise.
Do good in thy good pleas-ure un - to Zi - on: build thou the
walls of Je - ru - sa - lem. Then shalt thou be pleased with the sac - ri -

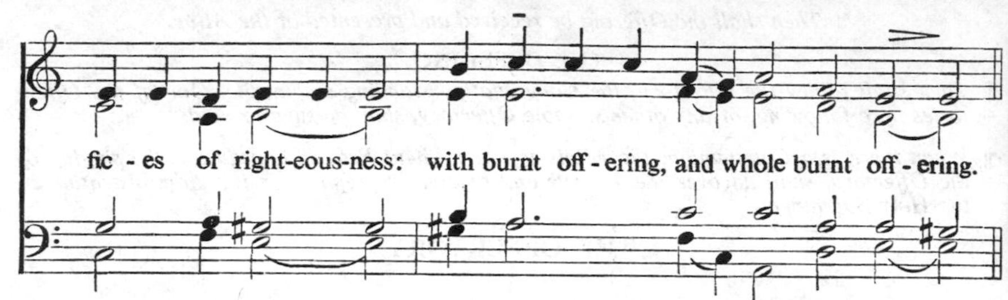
fic - es of right-eous-ness: with burnt off - ering, and whole burnt off - ering.

II

For music of the second Offertory text, What shall I render unto the Lord . . . , see First Setting, page 26.

III

Melody by J. G. WINER
Adapted, REGINA H. FRYXELL

Cre - ate in me a clean heart, O God: and re- new a

right spir - it with - in me. Cast me not a - way

from thy pres - ence: and take not thy Ho - ly Spir - it

from me. Re - store un - to me the joy of thy sal -
va - tion: and up - hold me with thy free Spir - it.

For another setting of this Offertory text, see page 27.

¶ *Then shall follow the Prayer of the Church. (p. 6.)*

THE PRAYER OF THE CHURCH

Let us pray.

ALMIGHTY God, the Father of our Lord Jesus Christ . . .

¶ *If there be no Communion the Minister and Congregation shall say the Lord's Prayer.*

OUR Father, who art in heaven, . . .

¶ *A Hymn may then be sung. Then the Minister, standing at the Altar, shall sing or say the Benediction.*

THE BENEDICTION

THE LORD bless thee, and keep thee.
The LORD make his face shine upon thee, and be gracious unto thee.
The LORD lift up his countenance upon thee, and give thee peace:
In the Name of the Father, and of the Son, and of the Holy Ghost.

¶ *The Congregation shall sing or say:*

Amen.

For music, see p. 70.

THE THANKSGIVING

¶ *A Hymn shall be sung.*

¶ *The Congregation shall rise at the beginning of the Preface.*

THE PREFACE

¶ *The Minister and Congregation shall sing or say:*

Ancient Church melodies
Harm. after J. H. ARNOLD

Organ *Minister*

The LORD be with you.

Congregation. Unison

℟. And with thy spir - it.

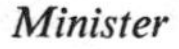
Minister

Lift up your hearts.

Congregation

℟. We lift them up un - to the Lord.

Minister

Let us give thanks un - to the Lord our God.

Congregation

℟. It is meet and right so to do.

¶ *Then shall the Minister turn to the Altar and sing or say:*

It is truly meet, right, and sal - u - ta - ry, that we
should at all times, and in all places, give thanks un - to thee,
O Lord, Ho - ly Fa - ther, Al - might - y, Ev - er - last - ing God:

¶ *Here shall follow the Proper Preface for the Day or Season. If there be none especially appointed, then shall follow immediately,* Therefore with Angels, *etc.*

¶ *For music of the Proper Prefaces, see pp. 71–74.*

PROPER PREFACES

For Advent

WHO didst comfort thy people with the promise of the Redeemer, through whom thou wilt also make all things new in the day when he shall come again to judge the world in righteousness. Therefore with Angels, *etc.*

For Christmas

FOR in the mystery of the Word made flesh, thou hast given us a new revelation of thy glory; that seeing thee in the person of thy Son, we may be drawn to the love of those things which are not seen. Therefore with Angels, *etc.*

For Epiphany

AND now do we praise thee, that thou didst send unto us thine only-begotten Son, and that in him, being found in fashion as a man, thou didst reveal the fullness of thy glory. Therefore with Angels, *etc.*

For Lent

WHO on the Tree of the Cross didst give salvation unto mankind; that whence death arose, thence life also might rise again; and that he who by a tree once overcame, might likewise by a Tree be overcome, through Christ our Lord: through whom with Angels, *etc.*

For Easter

BUT chiefly are we bound to praise thee for the glorious Resurrection of thy Son, Jesus Christ our Lord: for he is the very Paschal Lamb, which was offered for us, and hath taken away the sin of the world; who by his death hath destroyed death, and by his rising to life again hath restored to us everlasting life. Therefore with Angels, *etc.*

For the Ascension of our Lord

THROUGH Jesus Christ our Lord, who, after his Resurrection, appeared openly to all his disciples, and in their sight was taken up into heaven that he might make us partakers of his divine Nature. Therefore with Angels *etc.*

For the Day of Pentecost

THROUGH Jesus Christ our Lord, who, ascending above the heaven and sitting at thy right hand, poured out on this day the Holy Spirit, a he had promised, upon the chosen disciples; whereat the whole earth rejoice with exceeding joy. Therefore with Angels, *etc.*

For Trinity Sunday

WHO with thine only-begotten Son, and the Holy Ghost, art one God one Lord. And in the confession of the only true God, we worship th Trinity in Person, and the Unity in Substance, of Majesty co-equal. Therefor with Angels, *etc.*

For All Saints' Day (or at any time when the faithful departed are remembered

THROUGH Jesus Christ our Lord, who in the blessedness of thy saint hath given us a glorious pledge of the hope of our calling; that, followin their example and being strengthened by their fellowship, we may exult in the for thy mercy, even as they rejoice with thee in glory. Therefore with Angels *etc.*

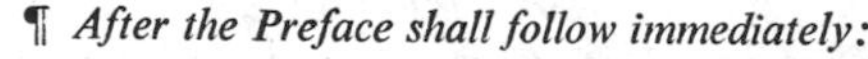

¶ *After the Preface shall follow immediately:*

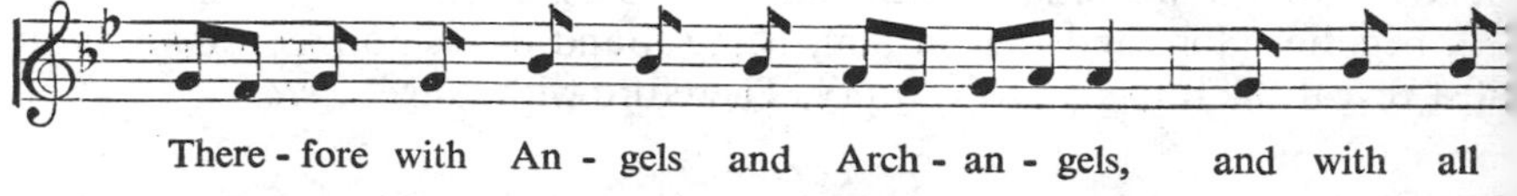
There - fore with An - gels and Arch - an - gels, and with all

the com - pa - ny of heav - en, we laud and magnify thy

glo - rious Name; ev - er - more prais - ing thee, and say - ing:

The Communion

¶ *Then shall be sung or said the Sanctus.*

THE SANCTUS

X cent. Plainsong
Swedish *Mässbok*, 1942
Adapted, REGINA H. FRYXELL

Slowly, in unison
Ho - ly, ho - - - ly, ho - - ly, Lord God of Sa - ba - oth;
Heav - en and earth are full of thy glo - ry; Ho -
san - na in the high - est. Bless - ed is he that com - eth
in the Name of the Lord; Ho - san - na in the high - est.

For another setting of the Sanctus, see p. 32.

¶ *Then may the Congregation kneel.*

¶ *The Minister standing before the Altar, and facing it, shall say the Prayer of Thanksgiving.*

THE PRAYER OF THANKSGIVING

HOLY art thou, Almighty and Merciful God. Holy art thou, and great is the Majesty of thy glory.

Thou didst so love the world as to give thine only-begotten Son, that whosoever believeth in him might not perish, but have everlasting life; Who, having come into the world to fulfill for us thy holy will and to accomplish all things for our salvation, IN THE NIGHT IN WHICH HE WAS BETRAYED, [a]TOOK BREAD; AND, WHEN HE HAD GIVEN THANKS, HE BRAKE IT AND GAVE IT TO HIS DISCIPLES, SAYING, TAKE, EAT; THIS IS MY BODY, WHICH IS GIVEN FOR YOU; THIS DO IN REMEMBRANCE OF ME.

(a) *Here he shall take the* BREAD *in his hand.*

AFTER THE SAME MANNER ALSO, HE [b]TOOK THE CUP, WHEN HE HAD SUPPED, AND, WHEN HE HAD GIVEN THANKS, HE GAVE IT TO THEM, SAYING, DRINK YE ALL OF IT; THIS CUP IS THE NEW TESTAMENT IN MY BLOOD, WHICH IS SHED FOR YOU, AND FOR MANY, FOR THE REMISSION OF SINS; THIS DO, AS OFT AS YE DRINK IT, IN REMEMBRANCE OF ME.

(b) *Here he shall take the* CUP *in his hand.*

Remembering, therefore, his salutary precept, his life-giving Passion and Death, his glorious Resurrection and Ascension and the promise of his coming again, we give thanks to thee, O Lord God Almighty, not as we ought, but as we are able; and we beseech thee mercifully to accept our praise and thanksgiving, and with thy Word and Holy Spirit to bless us, thy servants, and these thine own gifts of bread and wine, so that we and all who partake thereof may be filled with heavenly benediction and grace, and, receiving the remission of sins, be sanctified in soul and body, and have our portion with all thy saints.

And unto thee, O God, Father, Son, and Holy Spirit, be all honor and glory in thy holy Church, world without end. Amen.

¶ *Then shall the Minister sing or say:*

OUR Father, who art in heaven, Hallowed be thy Name, Thy kingdom come, Thy will be done, on earth as it is in heaven. Give us this day our daily bread; And forgive us our trespasses, as we forgive those who trespass against us; And lead us not into temptation, But deliver us from evil.

¶ *The Congregation shall sing or say:*

Ancient Church Melody
Harm. by WINFRED DOUGLAS

For thine is the king - dom, and the power, and the

glo - ry, for - ev - er and ev - er. A - men.

Or, instead of the above Prayer of Thanksgiving, "Holy art thou, Almighty and Merciful God," *the Minister may say the Words of Institution, followed by the Lord's Prayer.*

THE WORDS OF INSTITUTION

OUR LORD JESUS CHRIST, IN THE NIGHT IN WHICH HE WAS BETRAYED, [a]TOOK BREAD; AND, WHEN HE AD GIVEN THANKS, HE BRAKE IT AND GAVE IT TO HIS ISCIPLES, SAYING, TAKE, EAT; THIS IS MY BODY, WHICH IS GIVEN FOR YOU; THIS O IN REMEMBRANCE OF ME.

(a) Here he shall take the BREAD *in his hand.*

AFTER THE SAME MANNER ALSO, HE [b]TOOK THE CUP, HEN HE HAD SUPPED, AND, WHEN HE HAD GIVEN HANKS, HE GAVE IT TO THEM, SAYING, DRINK YE ALL F IT; THIS CUP IS THE NEW TESTAMENT IN MY BLOOD, WHICH IS SHED FOR YOU, ND FOR MANY, FOR THE REMISSION OF SINS; THIS DO, AS OFT AS YE DRINK IT, IN EMEMBRANCE OF ME.

(b) Here he shall take the CUP *in his hand.*

THE LORD'S PRAYER

OUR Father, who art in heaven, . . .

¶ *Then shall the Minister turn to the Congregation and sing or say:*

The peace of the Lord be with you al - way.

¶ *The Congregation shall sing or say:*

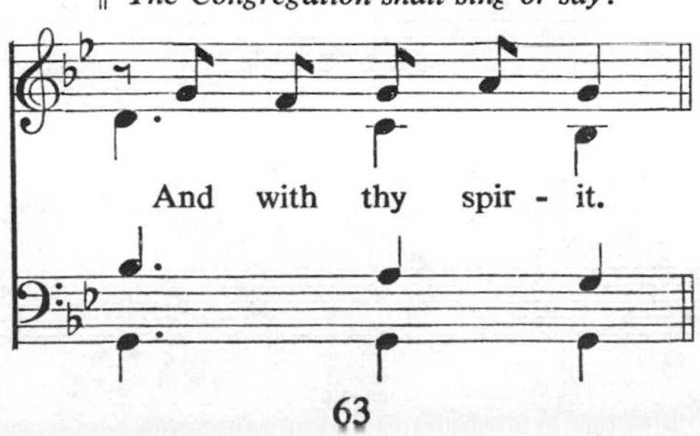
And with thy spir - it.

¶ *Then, the Congregation standing, shall be sung or said the Agnus Dei.*

AGNUS DEI

BRAUNSCHWEIG, 1528
Adapted, REGINA H. FRYXELL

Unison
O Christ, thou Lamb of God, that tak - est a - way the sin
of the world, have mer - cy up - on us. O Christ, thou Lamb of God,
that tak - est a - way the sin of the world, have mer - cy up - on us.
O Christ, thou Lamb of God, that tak - est a - way the sin

of the world, grant us thy peace. A - - - - - - - men.
Or,
XIII cent. Plainsong
Swedish Mässbok, 1942
Adapted, REGINA H. FRYXELL
Unison
O Christ, thou Lamb of God, that tak - est a - way the sin
of the world, have mer - cy up - on us. O Christ, thou Lamb of God,
that tak - est a - way the sin of the world, have mer -

cy up - on us. O Christ, thou Lamb of God, that tak - est
a - way the sin of the world, grant us thy peace. A - men.

¶ *Then shall the Communicants present themselves before the Altar and receive the Holy Sacrament.*

THE COMMUNION

¶ *When the Minister giveth the* BREAD *he shall say:*

The Body of Christ, given for thee.

¶ *When he giveth the* CUP *he shall say:*

The Blood of Christ, shed for thee.

¶ *The Communicant may say* Amen *after each Element has been received.*

¶ *After he hath given the* BREAD *and the* CUP, *or after all have been communicated, th Minister shall say:*

The Body of our Lord Jesus Christ and his precious Blood strengthen a preserve you unto eternal life.

THE POST-COMMUNION

¶ *Then shall the Congregation rise, and the Nunc Dimittis may be sung or said:*

NUNC DIMITTIS

Plainsong, Tone V
SOEST, 1532; PFALZ, 1557
Adapted, REGINA H. FRYXELL

Lord, now let - test thou thy ser - vant de - part in peac

ac - cord - ing to thy word; For mine eyes have
seen thy sal - va - tion: which thou hast pre - pared be - fore the
face of all peo - ple, A light to light - en the
Gen - tiles: and the glo - ry of thy peo - ple Is - - ra - el.
Glo - ry be to the Fa - ther, and to the Son, and to the

Ho - ly Ghost: As it was in the be - gin - ning, is now, and

ev - - - - er shall be, world with - out end. A - men.

¶ *Then shall be said The Prayer.*

THE PRAYER

¶ *The Minister shall say one of the following Prayers; or he may say the Collect for Thursday in Holy Week.*

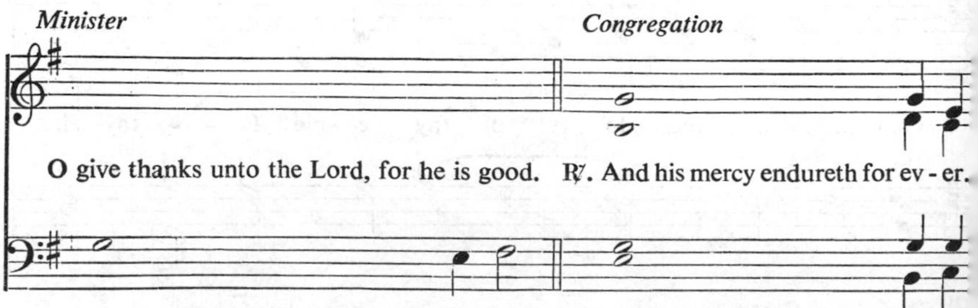
Minister
Congregation
O give thanks unto the Lord, for he is good.
℟. And his mercy endureth for ev - er.

WE give thanks to thee, Almighty God, that thou hast refreshed us wi this thy salutary gift; and we beseech thee, of thy mercy, to strength us through the same gift, in faith toward thee and in fervent love toward o another; through Jesus Christ, thy dear Son, our Lord, who liveth and reig eth with thee and the Holy Ghost, one God, world without end.

Or,

POUR forth upon us, O Lord, the spirit of thy love, that by thy mercy thou mayest make of one will those whom thou hast fed with one heaven- food; through thy Son, Jesus Christ our Lord, who liveth and reigneth with ee and the Holy Ghost, one God, world without end.

Or,

ALMIGHTY God, who givest the true Bread which cometh down from heaven, even thy Son, Jesus Christ our Lord: Grant, we beseech thee, at we who have received the Sacrament of his Body and Blood may abide him, and he in us, that we may be filled with the power of his endless life; 10 liveth and reigneth with thee and the Holy Ghost, one God, world without d.

Or,

ALMIGHTY God, who hast given thine only Son to be unto us both a sacrifice for sin and also an ensample of godly life: Give us grace that may always most thankfully receive that his inestimable benefit, and also ily endeavor ourselves to follow the blessed steps of his most holy life; ough the same Jesus Christ our Lord, who liveth and reigneth with thee d the Holy Ghost, one God, world without end.

¶ *The Congregation shall sing or say:*

A - men.

¶ *Then may be sung or said the Salutation and the Benedicamus.*

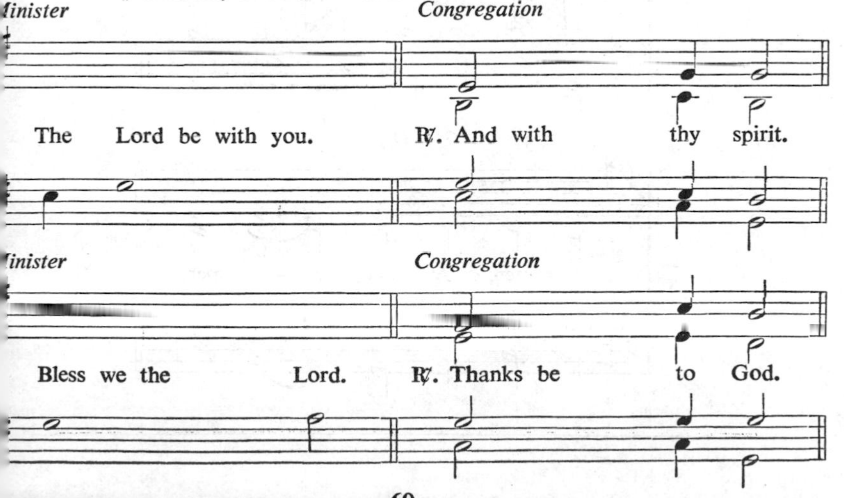
inister
Congregation
The Lord be with you.
℟. And with thy spirit.
inister
Congregation
Bless we the Lord.
℟. Thanks be to God.

¶ *Then the Minister, standing at the Altar, shall sing or say the Benediction.*

THE BENEDICTION

Minister

THE LORD bless thee, and keep thee.
The LORD make his face shine upon thee, and be gracious unto thee.
The LORD lift up his countenance up thee, and give thee peace:

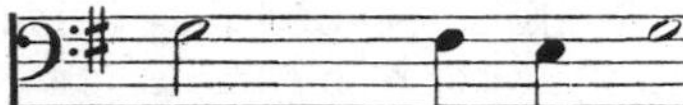

In the Name of the Father, and of the Son, and of the Holy Ghost.

¶ *The Congregation shall sing or say:*

A - men. *Or,* A - - men.

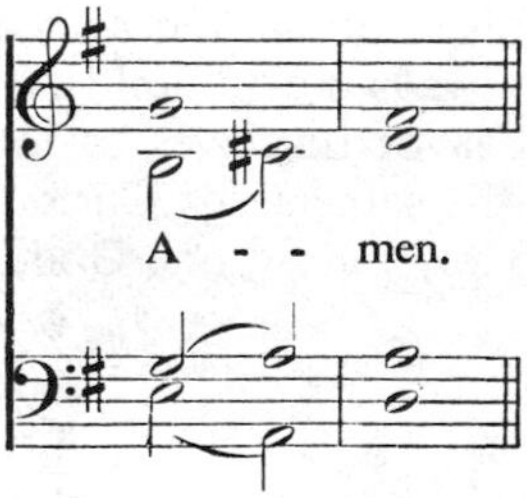

Or,

A - men, A - men, A - - - men.

Or,

A - men, A - men, A - - men.

Proper Prefaces

FOR THE DAY OR SEASON

For Advent

Who didst comfort thy people with the promise of the Re - deem - er,
through whom thou wilt also make all things new in the day when he shall
come a - gain to judge the world in right-eous-ness. Therefore, *etc.*
For Christmas
For in the mystery of the Word made flesh, thou hast given us a new
rev - e - la - tion of thy glo - ry; that seeing thee in the person of thy Son,
we may be drawn to the love of those things which are not seen. Therefore, *etc.*
For Epiphany
And now do we praise thee, that thou didst send unto us thine
on - ly - be - got - ten Son, and that in him, being found in fashion
as a man, thou didst re-veal the full - ness of thy glo - ry. Therefore, *etc.*

Proper Prefaces

For Lent

Who on the Tree of the Cross didst give salvation unto man - kind;
that whence death a - rose, thence life al - so might rise a - gain;
and that he who by a tree once o - ver-came, might like-wise by a Tree
be o - ver - come, through Christ our Lord; through whom wit
For Easter
But chief-ly are we bound to praise thee for the glo - ri - ous Res-ur - rec-tion
of thy Son, Je - sus Christ our Lord: for he is the very Pas-chal Lamb,
which was of - fer-ed for us, and hath ta - ken a - way the sin of the worl
who by his death hath de - stroy-ed death, and by his ris - ing to life agai
hath restored to us ev - er - last - ing life. There-fore, et

Proper Prefaces

For the Ascension of Our Lord

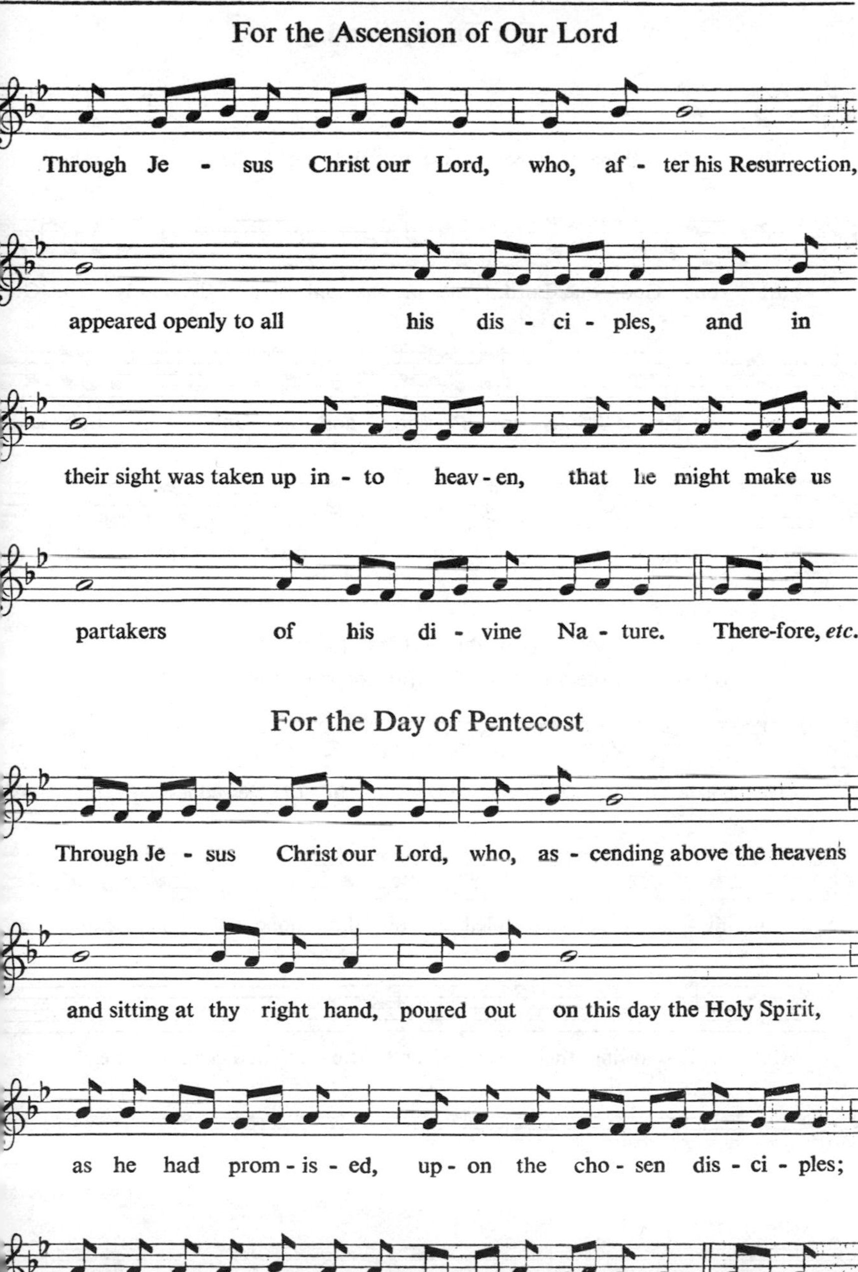

Through Je - sus Christ our Lord, who, af - ter his Resurrection,
appeared openly to all his dis - ci - ples, and in
their sight was taken up in - to heav - en, that he might make us
partakers of his di - vine Na - ture. There-fore, *etc.*

For the Day of Pentecost

Through Je - sus Christ our Lord, who, as - cending above the heavens
and sitting at thy right hand, poured out on this day the Holy Spirit,
as he had prom - is - ed, up - on the cho - sen dis - ci - ples;
where - at the whole earth re - joic - es with ex - ceed-ing joy. There-fore, *etc.*

Proper Prefaces

For Trinity Sunday

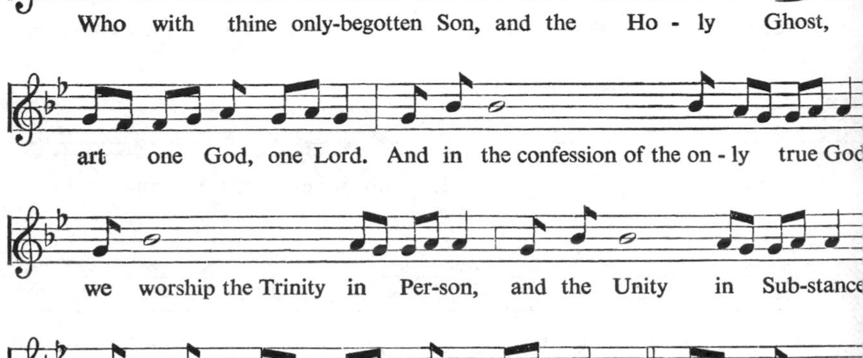
Who with thine only-begotten Son, and the Ho - ly Ghost,
art one God, one Lord. And in the confession of the on - ly true God
we worship the Trinity in Per-son, and the Unity in Sub-stance
of Maj - es - ty co - e - qual. There - fore. . . , etc

For All Saints' Day

(or at any time when the faithful departed are remembered)

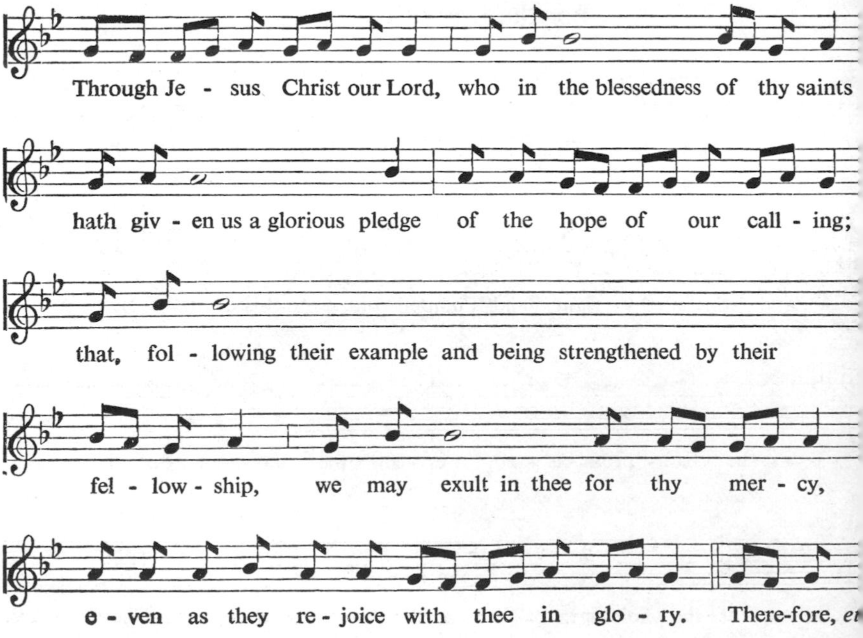

Through Je - sus Christ our Lord, who in the blessedness of thy saints

hath giv - en us a glorious pledge of the hope of our call - ing;

that, fol - lowing their example and being strengthened by their

fel - low - ship, we may exult in thee for thy mer - cy,

e - ven as they re - joice with thee in glo - ry. There-fore, *etc*

The Proper of the Service

INTROITS, COLLECTS, LESSONS, EPISTLES, GRADUALS AND GOSPELS

The First Sunday in Advent

INTROIT

JNTO thee, O Lord, do I lift up my soul : O my God, I trust in thee; me not be ashamed : let not mine ene-es triumph over me; yea, let none that it on thee : be ashamed. *Psalm.* Show thy ways, O Lord : teach me thy ths. Glory be to the Father . . .

COLLECT

TIR up, we beseech thee, thy power, O Lord, and come; that by thy pro-tion we may be rescued from the eatening perils of our sins, and saved thy mighty deliverance; who livest d reignest with the Father and the Holy Ghost, one God, world without end. *Amen.*

LESSON. Jeremiah 31:31–34

EPISTLE. Romans 13:11–14
(*Begin:* "Brethren, ye know the time . . .")

GRADUAL

LET none that wait on thee : be ashamed. *Verse.* Show me thy ways, O Lord : teach me thy paths.

Alleluia, alleluia. *V.* Show us thy mercy, O Lord : and grant us thy salva-tion. Alleluia.

GOSPEL. Matthew 21:1–9,
or Luke 3:1–6

The Second Sunday in Advent

INTROIT

)AUGHTER of Zion : behold thy salvation cometh. The Lord shall ise his glorious voice to be heard : and shall have gladness of heart. *Ps.* Give , O Shepherd of Israel : thou that dest Joseph like a flock. Glory be to Father . . .

COLLECT

TIR up our hearts, O Lord, to make ready the way of thine only-begotten n, so that by his coming we may be ibled to serve thee with pure minds; ough the same thy Son, Jesus Christ r Lord, who liveth and reigneth with e and the Holy Ghost, one God, world without end. *Amen.*

LESSON. Malachi 4:1–6

EPISTLE. Romans 15:4–13

GRADUAL

OUT of Zion, the perfection of beau-ty, God hath shined : our God shall come. *V.* Gather my saints together with me : those that have made a cove-nant with me by sacrifice.

Alleluia, alleluia. *V.* I was glad when they said unto me : Let us go into the house of the Lord. *V.* Our feet shall stand within thy gates : O Jerusalem. Alleluia.

GOSPEL. Luke 21:25–33

The Third Sunday in Advent

INTROIT

REJOICE in the Lord alway : and again I say, Rejoice. Let your moderation be known unto all men : the Lord is at hand. Be careful for nothing : but in everything by prayer and supplication with thanksgiving let your requests be made known unto God. *Ps.* Lord, thou hast been favorable unto thy land : thou hast brought back the captivity of Jacob. Glory be to the Father . . .

COLLECT

LORD, we beseech thee, give ear to our prayers, and lighten the darkness of our hearts by thy gracious visitation; who livest and reignest with the Fath and the Holy Ghost, one God, wo without end. *Amen.*

LESSON. Isaiah 40:1–8

EPISTLE. 1 Corinthians 4:1–5

GRADUAL

THOU that dwellest between t Cherubim, shine forth : stir up t strength and come. *V.* Give ear, O She herd of Israel : thou that leadest Jose like a flock.

Alleluia, alleluia. *V.* Stir up t strength : and come and save us. Al luia.

GOSPEL. Matthew 11:2–10

The Fourth Sunday in Advent

INTROIT

DROP down, ye heavens, from above : and let the skies pour down righteousness. Let the earth open : and let them bring forth salvation. *Ps.* The heavens declare the glory of God : and the firmament showeth his handiwork. Glory be to the Father . . .

COLLECT

STIR up, O Lord, we beseech thee, thy power, and come, and with great might succor us, that by the help of thy grace whatsoever is hindered by our sins may be speedily accomplished through thy mercy and satisfaction; who livest and reignest with the Father and the Holy Ghost, one God, world witho end. *Amen.*

LESSON. Deuteronomy 18:15–19, *or* Isaiah 40:9–11

EPISTLE. Philippians 4:4–7

GRADUAL

THE Lord is nigh unto all them th call upon him : to all that call up him in truth. *V.* My mouth shall spe the praise of the Lord : and let all fle bless his holy Name.

Allelulia, alleluia. *V.* Thou art help and my deliverer : make no tar ing, O my God. Alleluia.

GOSPEL. John 1:19–28

OTHER COLLECTS FOR ADVENT

O LORD, mercifully hear the prayers of thy people, that as they rejoice in the advent of thine only-begotten Son according to the flesh, so when he cometh a second time in his Majesty, they may receive the reward of eternal life; through the same thy Son, Jesus Christ our Lord *Amen.*

MOST merciful God, who hast given thine eternal Word to be made incarnate of the pure Virgin : Grant unto thy people grace to put away fles lusts, so that they may be ready for t visitation; through the same thy So Jesus Christ our Lord. *Amen.*

O LORD, we beseech thee, mer fully to hear the prayers of t people, that we, who for our sins a justly afflicted, may be consoled by t visitation; who livest and reignest w the Father and the Holy Ghost, o God, world without end. *Amen.*

Christmas Day. The Nativity of Our Lord

I. For the Early Service

INTROIT

THE Lord hath said unto me : Thou art my Son, this day have I begotten ee. *Ps.* The Lord reigneth, he is clothed ith majesty : the Lord is clothed with rength, wherewith he hath girded himlf. Glory be to the Father . . .

COLLECT

O GOD, who hast made this most holy night to shine with the brightss of the true Light : Grant, we beech thee, that, as we have known on rth the mysteries of that Light, we may o come to the fulness of his joys in aven; who liveth and reigneth with thee and the Holy Ghost, one God, world without end. *Amen.*

LESSON. Isaiah 9:2–7

EPISTLE. Titus 2:11–14,
or 1 John 4:7–16

GRADUAL

THY people shall be willing in the day of thy power : in the beauties of holiness from the womb of the morning. *V.* The Lord said unto my Lord . Sit thou at my right hand, until I make thine enemies thy footstool.

Alleluia, alleluia. *V.* The Lord hath said unto me : Thou art my Son, this day have I begotten thee. Alleluia.

GOSPEL. Luke 2:1–14

II. For the Later Service

INTROIT

UNTO us a Child is born, unto us a Son is given : and the government all be upon his shoulder. And his ame shall be called Wonderful, Counlor, The mighty God : The everlasting ther, The Prince of Peace. *Ps.* O sing to the Lord a new song : for he hath ne marvellous things. Glory be to the ther . . .

COLLECT

GRANT, we beseech thee, Almighty God, that the new birth of thine ly-begotten Son in the flesh may set us e who are held in the old bondage der the yoke of sin; through the same sus Christ, thy Son, our Lord, who liveth and reigneth with thee and the Holy Ghost, one God, world without end. *Amen.*

LESSON. Isaiah 45:1–8

EPISTLE. Hebrews 1:1–12

GRADUAL

ALL the ends of the earth have seen the salvation of our God : make a joyful noise unto the Lord, all the earth. *V.* The Lord hath made known his salvation : his righteousness hath he openly showed in the sight of the heathen.

Alleluia, alleluia. *V.* O come, let us sing unto the Lord : let us worship and bow down. Alleluia.

GOSPEL. John 1:1–14

III. At Vespers: LESSON. Luke 2:15–20

St. Stephen, Martyr

December 26

INTROIT

PRINCES also did sit and speak against me : the wicked have waited for me to stroy me. Help me, O Lord God : for ave kept thy testimonies. *Ps.* Blessed the undefiled in the way : who walk the law of the Lord. Glory be to the ther . . .

COLLECT

GRANT us grace, O Lord, that like St. Stephen we may learn to love even our enemies, and seek forgiveness for those who desire our hurt; through thy Son, Jesus Christ our Lord, who liveth and reigneth with thee and the Holy Ghost, one God, world without end. *Amen.*

LESSON. 2 Chronicles 24:17–22

EPISTLE. Acts 7:54–60, *or* 6:8–7:60

GRADUAL

BLESSED are they who are persecuted for righteousness' sake : for theirs is the kingdom of heaven. *V.* Be thou faithful unto death : and I will give th a crown of life.

Alleluia, alleluia. *V.* I see the heave opened : and Jesus standing at the rig hand of God. Alleluia.

GOSPEL. Matthew 23:34–39

St. John, Apostle, Evangelist

December 27

¶ *For Introit and Gradual see Apostles' Days, p. 106.*

COLLECT

MERCIFUL Lord, we beseech thee to cast the bright beams of thy light upon thy Church; that it, being instructed by the doctrine of thy blessed Apostle and Evangelist St. John, may so walk in the light of thy truth, that it may at length attain to the light of everlasting life; through thy Son, Jesus Christ o Lord, who liveth and reigneth with th and the Holy Ghost, one God, wor without end. *Amen.*

LESSON. Hosea 14:1–9, *or* 11:1–4

EPISTLE. 1 John 1:1–10

GOSPEL. John 21:19b–24

The Holy Innocents, Martyrs

December 28

INTROIT

OUT of the mouth of babes and sucklings hast thou ordained strength : because of thine enemies. *Ps.* O Lord, our Lord : how excellent is thy Name in all the earth. Glory be to the Father . . .

COLLECT

O GOD our Father, who by the birth and infancy of thy Son didst sanctify and bless childhood : We commend to thy love all children, and beseech thee to protect them from every hurt and harm, and to lead them to the knowledge of thyself and the obedience of thy will; through the same Jesus Christ our Lord, who liveth and reigneth with thee a the Holy Ghost, one God, world witho end. *Amen.*

LESSON. Jeremiah 31:15–17

EPISTLE. Revelation 14:1–5

GRADUAL

OUR soul is escaped as a bird out the snare of the fowlers : the sna is broken, and we are escaped. *V.* O help is in the Name of the Lord : w made heaven and earth.

Alleluia, alleluia. *V.* Praise, O ye se ants of the Lord : praise the Name of t Lord. Alleluia.

GOSPEL. Matthew 2:13–18

The First Sunday after Christmas

INTROIT

THY testimonies are very sure : holiness becometh thine house, O Lord, forever. Thy throne is established of old : thou art from everlasting. *Ps.* The Lord reigneth, he is clothed with majesty : the Lord is clothed with strength, wherewith he hath girded himself. Glory be to the Father . . .

COLLECT

ALMIGHTY and everlasting God, rect our actions according to t good pleasure, that in the Name of t beloved Son, we may be made to abou in good works; through the same t Son, Jesus Christ our Lord, who live and reigneth with thee and the Holy Gho one God, world without end. *Amen.*

LESSON. Isaiah 63:7–16

EPISTLE. Galatians 4:1–7

GRADUAL

⁊HOU art fairer than the children of men : grace is poured into thy lips. My heart is inditing a good matter, I ·ak of the things which I have made touching the king : my tongue is the pen of a ready writer.

Alleluia, alleluia. *V.* The Lord reigneth, he is clothed with majesty : the Lord is clothed with strength, wherewith he hath girded himself. Alleluia.

GOSPEL. Luke 2:33–40

The Circumcision and The Name of Jesus

[New Year's Day]

INTROIT

) LORD our Lord, how excellent is thy Name in all the earth : who ·t set thy glory above the heavens. ·at is man that thou art mindful of ı : and the son of man that thou visit- him? *Ps.* Thou, O Lord, art our Fa- r, our Redeemer : thy Name is from ·rlasting. Glory be to the Father . . .

COLLECT

) LORD God, who, for our sakes, hast made thy blessed Son our ·iour subject to the Law, and caused ı to endure the circumcision of the h : Grant us the true circumcision of spirit, that our hearts may be pure ·n all sinful desires and lusts; through same thy Son, Jesus Christ our Lord, o liveth and reigneth with thee and Holy Ghost, one God, world without ·. *Amen.*

LESSON. Joshua 24:14–24

EPISTLE. Galatians 3:23–29

GRADUAL

LL the ends of the earth have seen the salvation of our God : make a joyful noise unto the Lord, all the earth. *V.* The Lord hath made known his salvation : his righteousness hath he openly showed in the sight of the heathen.

Alleluia, alleluia. *V.* God, who of old time spake in divers ways unto the fathers by the prophets : hath in these last days spoken unto us by his Son. Alleluia.

GOSPEL. Luke 2:21

COLLECT FOR NEW YEAR

ALMIGHTY and everlasting God, from whom cometh down every good and perfect gift : We give thee thanks for all thy benefits, temporal and spiritual, bestowed upon us in the year past, and we beseech thee of thy goodness, grant us a favorable and joyful year, defend us from all dangers and adversities, and send upon us the fulness of thy blessing; through thy Son, Jesus Christ our Lord, who liveth and reigneth with thee and the Holy Ghost, one God, world without end. *Amen.*

The Second Sunday after Christmas

¶ *Introit, Collect and Gradual the same as for The First Sunday after Christmas.*

LESSON. 1 Samuel 2:1–10 EPISTLE. Titus 3:4–7

GOSPEL. John 1:14–18

The Epiphany of Our Lord

INTROIT

BEHOLD the Lord, the Ruler, hath come : and the kingdom, and the power, and the glory are in his hand. *Ps.* Give the King thy judgments, O God : and thy righteousness unto the King's Son. Glory be to the Father . . .

COLLECT

O GOD, who on this day by the leading of a star didst reveal thine only-begotten Son to the Gentiles : Mercifully grant that we, who know thee now by faith, may be brought to contemplate the beauty of thy Majesty; through the same thy Son, Jesus Christ our Lord, who liveth and reigneth with thee and the Holy Ghost, one G world without end. *Amen.*

LESSON. Isaiah 60:1–6

EPISTLE. Colossians 1:23–27, *or* Ephesians 3:1–12

GRADUAL

ALL they from Sheba shall come, t shall bring gold and incense : they shall show forth the praises of Lord. *V.* Arise, shine, for thy ligh come : and the glory of the Lord is ri upon thee.

Alleluia, alleluia. *V.* We have seen star in the east : and are come to wors him. Alleluia.

GOSPEL. Matthew 2:1–12

¶ *When only the Epistle and the Gospel are read, the Epistle shall be Isaiah 60:1–*

The First Sunday after the Epiphany

INTROIT

I SAW also the Lord, sitting upon a throne : high and lifted up. And I heard the voice of a great multitude, saying : Alleluia, for the Lord God omnipotent reigneth. *Ps.* Make a joyful noise unto the Lord, all ye lands : serve the Lord with gladness. Glory be to the Father . . .

COLLECT

O LORD, we beseech thee mercifully to receive the prayers of thy people who call upon thee; and grant that they may both perceive and know what things they ought to do, and also may have grace and power faithfully to fulfill the same; through thy Son, Jesus Christ our Lord, who liveth and reigneth w thee and the Holy Ghost, one G world without end. *Amen.*

LESSON. Ecclesiastes 12:1–7

EPISTLE. Romans 12:1–5

GRADUAL

BLESSED be the Lord God, the C of Israel, who only doeth wondr things : and blessed be his glorious Na forever. *V.* The mountains shall b peace to the people: and the little h by righteousness.

Alleluia, alleluia. *V.* Make a jo noise unto the Lord, all ye lands : se the Lord with gladness. Alleluia.

GOSPEL. Luke 2:41–52

The Second Sunday after the Epiphany

INTROIT

ALL the earth shall worship thee, and shall sing unto thee : they shall sing to thy Name, O thou most High. *Ps.* Make a joyful noise unto God, all ye lands : sing forth the honor of his Name, make his praise glorious. Glory be to Father . . .

COLLECT

ALMIGHTY and everlasting G who dost govern all things in hea

d earth : Mercifully hear the supplica-
ns of thy people, and grant us thy
ace all the days of our life; through thy
n, Jesus Christ our Lord, who liveth
d reigneth with thee and the Holy
host, one God, world without end.
nen.

LESSON. Isaiah 61:1–6

EPISTLE. Romans 12:6–16a

GRADUAL

HE sent his Word and healed them : and delivered them from their destructions. *V.* O that men would praise the Lord for his goodness : and for his wonderful works to the children of men.

Alleluia, alleluia. *V.* Praise ye him, all his angels : praise ye him, all his hosts. Alleluia.

GOSPEL. John 2:1–11

The Third Sunday after the Epiphany

INTROIT

VORSHIP him, all ye his angels : Zion heard and was glad. The
ughters of Judah rejoiced : because of
/ judgments, O Lord. *Ps.* The Lord
gneth, let the earth rejoice : let the
ltitude of isles be glad thereof. Glory
to the Father . . .

COLLECT

LMIGHTY and everlasting God,
mercifully look upon our infirmities,
d in all our dangers and necessities
etch forth the right hand of thy Maj-
y to help and defend us; through thy
n, Jesus Christ our Lord, who liveth
d reigneth with thee and the Holy
Ghost, one God, world without end. *Amen.*

LESSON. 2 Kings 5:1–15a
(*End:* ". . . but in Israel.")

EPISTLE. Romans 12:16b–21

GRADUAL

SO the heathen shall fear the Name of the Lord : and all the kings of the earth thy glory. *V.* When the Lord shall build up Zion : he shall appear in his glory.

Alleluia, alleluia. *V.* The Lord reigneth, let the earth rejoice : let the multitude of isles be glad thereof. Alleluia.

GOSPEL. Matthew 8:1–13,
or John 1:29–34

The Fourth Sunday after the Epiphany

¶ *Introit and Gradual the same as for The Third Sunday after the Epiphany.*

COLLECT

LMIGHTY God, who knowest us to
be set in the midst of so many and
at dangers, that by reason of the frail-
of our nature we cannot always stand
ight : Grant to us such strength and
tection as may support us in all dan-
s, and carry us through all tempta-
tions; through thy Son, Jesus Christ our Lord, who liveth and reigneth with thee and the Holy Ghost, one God, world without end. *Amen.*

LESSON. Exodus 14:21–31

EPISTLE. Romans 13:8–10

GOSPEL. Matthew 8:23–27

The Fifth Sunday after the Epiphany

¶ *Introit and Gradual the same as for The Third Sunday after the Epiphany.*

COLLECT

) LORD, we beseech thee to keep
thy Church and household con-
ually in thy true religion; that they
o do lean only upon the hope of thy
heavenly grace may evermore be defended by thy mighty power; through thy Son, Jesus Christ our Lord, who liveth and reigneth with thee and the Holy Ghost, one God, world without

end. *Amen.*

LESSON. Ezekiel 33:10–16

EPISTLE. Colossians 3:12–17

GOSPEL. Matthew 13:24–30

The Sixth Sunday after the Epiphany

¶ *For the Propers, see The Transfiguration of Our Lord, p. 111.*
¶ *The Propers for this Sunday may be used on The Last Sunday after the Epipha except when there is only one Sunday after the Epiphany.*

Septuagesima Sunday

INTROIT

THE sorrows of death compassed me : the sorrows of hell compassed me about. In my distress I called upon the Lord : and he heard my voice out of his temple. *Ps.* I will love thee, O Lord my strength : the Lord is my rock and my fortress. Glory be to the Father . . .

COLLECT

O LORD, we beseech thee favorably to hear the prayers of thy people : that we, who are justly punished for our offences, may be mercifully delivered by thy goodness, for the glory of thy Name; through thy Son, Jesus Christ our Lord, who liveth and reigneth with thee and the Holy Ghost, one God, world without end. *Amen.*

LESSON. Jeremiah 9:23–24

EPISTLE. 1 Corinthians 9:24–10:5

GRADUAL

THE Lord also will be a refuge for t oppressed, a refuge in times of tro ble : and they that know thy Name w put their trust in thee; for thou, Lo hast not forsaken them that seek th *V.* For the needy shall not alway be f gotten : the expectation of the poor sh not perish forever. Arise, O Lord; let n man prevail.

Tract. Out of the depths have I cr unto thee, O Lord : Lord, hear my voi

GOSPEL. Matthew 20:1–16

Sexagesima Sunday

INTROIT

AWAKE, why sleepest thou, O Lord : arise, cast us not off for ever. Wherefore hidest thou thy face : and forgettest our affliction? Our soul is bowed down to the dust : arise for our help and redeem us. *Ps.* We have heard with our ears, O God : our fathers have told us what work thou didst in their days. Glory be to the Father . . .

COLLECT

O LORD God, who seest that we put not our trust in anything that we do : Mercifully grant that by thy power we may be defended against all adversity; through thy Son, Jesus Christ our Lord, who liveth and reigneth with th and the Holy Ghost, one God, wo without end. *Amen.*

LESSON. Amos 8:11–12

EPISTLE. 2 Corinthians 11:19–12:

GRADUAL

LET men know that thou, wh Name alone is Jehovah : art the m High over all the earth. *V.* O my G make them like a wheel : as the stub before the wind.

Tract. Thou hast given a banner them that fear thee : that it may be d played because of the truth.

GOSPEL. Luke 8:4–15

Quinquagesima Sunday

INTROIT

BE thou my strong rock : for an house of defence to save me. Thou art my ock and my fortress : therefore for thy ame's sake lead me and guide me. *Ps.* thee, O Lord, do I put my trust; let me ever be ashamed : deliver me in thy ghteousness. Glory be to the Father . . .

COLLECT

O LORD, we beseech thee mercifully hear our prayers, and, having set free from the bonds of sin, defend us om all evil; through thy Son, Jesus hrist our Lord, who liveth and reigneth with thee and the Holy Ghost, one God, world without end. *Amen.*

LESSON. Jeremiah 8:4b–9

EPISTLE. 1 Corinthians 13:1–13

GRADUAL

THOU art the God that doest wonders : thou hast declared thy strength among the people. *V.* Thou hast with thine arm redeemed thy people : the sons of Jacob and Joseph.

Tract. Make a joyful noise unto the Lord, all ye lands : serve the Lord with gladness.

GOSPEL. Luke 18:31–43

Ash Wednesday. The First Day of Lent

INTROIT

WILL cry unto God most High : unto God that performeth all things for e. Yea, in the shadow of thy wings will nake my refuge : until these calamities overpast. *Ps.* Be merciful unto me, God, be merciful unto me : for my ul trusteth in thee. Glory be to the ther . . .

COLLECT

ALMIGHTY and everlasting God, who hatest nothing that thou hast ade, and dost forgive the sins of all ose who are penitent : Create and ake in us new and contrite hearts, that , worthily lamenting our sins, and knowledging our wretchedness, may tain of thee, the God of all mercy, per-t remission and forgiveness; through Son, Jesus Christ our Lord, who liveth and reigneth with thee and the Holy Ghost, one God, world without end. *Amen.*

This Collect may also be used on weekdays during Lent.

LESSON. Joel 2:12–19

EPISTLE. 1 John 1:5–9,
or Philippians 3:7–12

GRADUAL

BE merciful unto me, O God, be merciful unto me : for my soul trusteth in thee. *V.* He shall send from heaven : and save me from the reproach of him that would swallow me up.

Tract. He hath not dealt with us after our sins : nor rewarded us according to our inquities. Help us, O God of our salvation : for the glory of thy Name.

GOSPEL. Matthew 6:16–2

¶ *When only the Epistle and the Gospel are read, the Epistle shall be Joel 2:12–19.*

Invocabit. The First Sunday in Lent

INTROIT

HE shall call upon me, and I will answer him : I will deliver him and nor him. With long life will I satisfy n : and show him my salvation. *Ps.* He that dwelleth in the secret place of the most High : shall abide under the shadow of the Almighty. Glory be to the Father . . .

COLLECT

O LORD, mercifully hear our prayer, and stretch forth the right hand of thy Majesty to defend us from them that rise up against us; through thy Son, Jesus Christ our Lord, who liveth and reigneth with thee and the Holy Ghost, one God, world without end. *Amen.*

LESSON. Genesis 22:1–14

EPISTLE. 2 Corinthians 6:1–10

GRADUAL

FOR he shall give his angels charg over thee : to keep thee in all th ways. *V.* They shall bear thee up in the hands : lest thou dash thy foot against stone.

Tract. He that dwelleth in the secr place of the most High : shall abide u der the shadow of the Almighty.

GOSPEL. Matthew 4:1–11

Reminiscere. The Second Sunday in Lent

INTROIT

REMEMBER, O Lord, thy tender mercies and thy lovingkindnesses : for they have been ever of old. Let not mine enemies triumph over me : redeem Israel, O God, out of all his troubles. *Ps.* Unto thee, O Lord, do I lift up my soul : O my God, I trust in thee; let me not be ashamed. Glory be to the Father . . .

COLLECT

O GOD, who seest that of ourselves we have no strength : Keep us both outwardly and inwardly; that we may be defended from all adversities which may happen to the body, and from all evil thoughts which may assault and hurt the soul; through thy Son, Jes Christ our Lord, who liveth and reigne with thee and the Holy Ghost, one Go world without end. *Amen.*

LESSON. Exodus 33:12–23

EPISTLE. 1 Thessalonians 4:1–7

GRADUAL

THE troubles of my heart are e larged : O bring thou me out of n distresses. *V.* Look upon mine afflicti and my pain : and forgive all my sins.

Tract. O give thanks unto the Lo for he is good : for his mercy endure forever.

GOSPEL. Matthew 15:21–28

Oculi. The Third Sunday in Lent

INTROIT

MINE eyes are ever toward the Lord : for he shall pluck my feet out of the net. Turn thee unto me, and have mercy upon me : for I am desolate and afflicted. *Ps.* Unto thee, O Lord, do I lift up my soul : O my God, I trust in thee; let me not be ashamed. Glory be to the Father . . .

COLLECT

WE beseech thee, Almighty God, look upon the hearty desires of thy humble servants, and stretch forth the right hand of thy Majesty to be our defence against all our enemies; through thy Son, Jesus Christ our Lord, who liveth and reigneth with thee and the Ho Ghost, one God, world without en *Amen.*

LESSON. Jeremiah 26:1–15

EPISTLE. Ephesians 5:1–9

GRADUAL

ARISE, O Lord; let not man prevai let the heathen be judged in t sight. *V.* When mine enemies are turn back : they shall fall and perish at t presence.

Tract. Unto thee lift I up mine ey O thou that dwellest in the heaven have mercy upon us, O Lord, have me upon us.

GOSPEL. Luke 11:14–28

Laetare. The Fourth Sunday in Lent

INTROIT

REJOICE ye with Jerusalem, and be glad with her : all ye that love her. Rejoice for joy with her : all ye that mourn for her. *Ps.* I was glad when they said unto me : Let us go into the house of the Lord. Glory be to the Father . . .

COLLECT

GRANT, we beseech thee, Almighty God, that we, who for our evil deeds do worthily deserve to be punished, by the comfort of thy grace may mercifully be relieved; through thy Son, Jesus Christ our Lord, who liveth and reigneth with thee and the Holy Ghost, one God, world without end. *Amen.*

LESSON. Isaiah 55:1–7

EPISTLE. Galatians 4:21–5:1a

GRADUAL

I WAS glad when they said unto me : Let us go into the house of the Lord. *V.* Peace be within thy walls : and prosperity within thy palaces.

Tract. They that trust in the Lord shall be as Mount Zion : which cannot be removed, but abideth forever.

GOSPEL. John 6:1–15

Judica. Passion Sunday

INTROIT

JUDGE me, O God : and plead my cause against an ungodly nation. O deliver me from the deceitful and unjust man : for thou art the God of my strength. *Ps.* O send out thy light and thy truth : let them lead me; let them bring me unto thy holy hill. Glory be to the Father . . .

COLLECT

WE beseech thee, Almighty God, mercifully to look upon thy people, that by thy great goodness they may be governed and preserved evermore, both in body and soul; through thy Son, Jesus Christ our Lord, who liveth and reigneth with thee and the Holy Ghost, one God, world without end. *Amen.*

LESSON. Numbers 21:4–9

EPISTLE. Hebrews 9:11–15

GRADUAL

DELIVER me, O Lord, from mine enemies : teach me to do thy will. *V.* He delivereth me from mine enemies; yea, thou liftest me up above those that rise up against me : thou hast delivered me from the violent man.

Tract. Many a time have they afflicted me from my youth. *V.* May Israel now say : Many a time have they afflicted me from my youth. *V.* Yet they have not prevailed against me.

GOSPEL. John 8:46–59

Palmarum. The Sixth Sunday in Lent

INTROIT

BE not thou far from me, O Lord : O my Strength, haste thee to help me. Save me from the lion's mouth : and deliver me from the horns of the unicorns. *Ps.* My God, my God, why hast thou forsaken me : why art thou so far from helping me? Glory be to the Father . . .

COLLECT

ALMIGHTY and everlasting God, who hast sent thy Son, our Saviour Jesus Christ, to take upon him our flesh, and to suffer death upon the Cross, that all mankind should follow the example of his great humility : Mercifully grant that we may both follow the example of his patience, and also be made partakers of his Resurrection; through the same thy Son, Jesus Christ our Lord, who liveth and reigneth with thee and the Holy Ghost, one God, world without end. *Amen.*

LESSON. Zechariah 9:9–12
EPISTLE. Philippians 2:5–11

GRADUAL

THOU hast holden me by my right hand : thou shalt guide me with thy counsel, and afterward receive me to glory. *V.* Truly God is good to Israel : even to such as are of a clean heart.

Tract. My God, my God, why hast thou forsaken me : why art thou so far from helping me? *V.* Our fathers trusted in thee : they cried unto thee and were delivered.

GOSPEL. Matthew 21:1–9,
or Matthew 26:1–27:66

Monday in Holy Week

INTROIT

PLEAD my cause, O Lord, with them that strive with me : fight against them that fight against me. Take hold of shield and buckler : and stand up for mine help. *Ps.* Draw out also the spear, and stop the way against them that persecute me : say unto my soul, I am thy salvation. Glory be to the Father . . .

COLLECT

GRANT, we beseech thee, Almighty God, that we, who amid so many adversities do fail through our own infirmities, may be restored through the Passion and Intercession of thine only-begotten Son, who liveth and reigneth with thee and the Holy Ghost, one God, world without end. *Amen.*

LESSON. Isaiah 50:5–10

EPISTLE. 1 Peter 2:21–24

GRADUAL

STIR up thyself, and awake to my judgment : even unto my cause, my God and my Lord. *V.* Draw out also the spear : and stop the way against them that persecute me.

Tract. Help us, O God of our salvation, for the glory of thy Name : and deliver us and purge away our sins for thy Name's sake.

GOSPEL. John 12:1–36

Tuesday in Holy Week

INTROIT

GOD forbid that I should glory : save in the Cross of our Lord Jesus Christ. In him is salvation, life, and resurrection from the dead : by him we are redeemed and set at liberty. *Ps.* God be merciful unto us, and bless us : and cause his face to shine upon us. Glory be to the Father . . .

COLLECT

ALMIGHTY and everlasting God, grant us grace so to contemplate the Passion of our Lord, that we may find therein forgiveness for our sins; through the same thy Son, Jesus Christ our Lord, who liveth and reigneth with thee and the Holy Ghost, one God, world without end. *Amen.*

LESSON. Jeremiah 11:18–20

EPISTLE. 1 Timothy 6:12–14

GRADUAL

AS for me my clothing was sackcloth : I humbled my soul with fasting; and my prayer returned into mine own bosom. *V.* Plead my cause, O Lord, with them that strive with me : take hold of shield and buckler, and stand up for mine help.

GOSPEL John 12:37–50, *or* Mark 14:1–15:46

Wednesday in Holy Week

INTROIT

AT the Name of Jesus every knee shall bow : of things in heaven, and things in earth, and things under the earth. For he became obedient unto death, even the death of the Cross : wherefore he is Lord, to the glory of God the Father. *Ps.* Hear my prayer, O Lord : and let my cry come unto thee. Glory be to the Father . . .

COLLECT

GRANT, we beseech thee, Almighty God, that we, who for our evil deeds are continually afflicted, may mercifully be relieved by the Passion of thine only-begotten Son, who liveth and reigneth with thee and the Holy Ghost, one God, world without end. *Amen.*

LESSON. Isaiah 62:11–63:7, *or* 52:13–53:3

EPISTLE. Revelation 1:5b–7

GRADUAL

HIDE not thy face from thy servant, for I am in trouble : hear me speedily. *V.* Save me, O God, for the waters are come in unto my soul : I sink in deep mire, where there is no standing.

Tract. Hear my prayer, O Lord : and let my cry come unto thee. *V.* Thou shalt arise and have mercy upon Zion : for the time to favor her, yea, the set time, is come.

GOSPEL. Luke 22:1–23:53

Thursday in Holy Week

¶ *Introit the same as for Tuesday in Holy Week.*

COLLECT

O LORD God, who hast left unto us in a wonderful Sacrament a memorial of thy Passion : Grant, we beseech thee, that we may so partake of this Sacrament of thy Body and Blood, that the fruits of thy redemption may continually be manifest in us; who livest and reignest with the Father and the Holy Ghost ever, one God, world without end. *Amen.*

LESSON. Exodus 12:1–14

EPISTLE. 1 Corinthians 11:20–32

GRADUAL

CHRIST hath humbled himself, and become obedient unto death : even the death of the Cross. *V.* Wherefore God also hath highly exalted him: and given him a Name which is above every name.

GOSPEL. John 13:1–15, *or* John 6:28–37

Good Friday

¶ *Introit the same as for Tuesday in Holy Week; or this:*

INTROIT

SURELY he hath borne our griefs and carried our sorrows : he was wounded for our transgressions, he was bruised for our iniquities. All we like sheep have gone astray : and the Lord hath laid on him the iniquity of us all. *Ps.* Hear my prayer, O Lord : and let my cry come unto thee. Glory be to the Father . . .

COLLECT

ALMIGHTY God, we beseech thee graciously to behold this thy family, for which our Lord Jesus Christ was contented to be betrayed and given up into the hands of wicked men, and to suffer death upon the Cross; through the same thy Son, Jesus Christ our Lord, who liveth and reigneth with thee and the Holy Ghost, one God, world without end. *Amen.*

LESSON. Isaiah 53:4–12, *or* Hosea 6:1–6

EPISTLE. Revelation 5:1–14

GRADUAL

HE was wounded for our transgressions, he was bruised for our iniquities : the chastisement of our peace was upon him; and with his stripes we are healed. *V.* He shall see of the travail of his soul : and shall be satisfied.

GOSPEL. John 18:1–19:42

OTHER COLLECTS FOR GOOD FRIDAY

MERCIFUL and everlasting God, who hast not spared thine only Son, but delivered him up for us all, that he might bear our sins upon the Cross : Grant that our hearts may be so fixed with steadfast faith in him that we may not fear the power of any adversaries; through the same thy Son, Jesus Christ our Lord. *Amen.*

ALMIGHTY and everlasting God, who hast willed that thy Son should bear for us the pains of the Cross, that thou mightest remove from us the power of the adversary : Help us so to remember and give thanks for our Lord's Passion that we may obtain remission of sin and redemption from everlasting death; through the same Jesus Christ, our Lord. *Amen.*

Saturday in Holy Week—Easter Eve

INTROIT

MY soul waiteth for the Lord : more than they that watch for the morning. I wait for the Lord, my soul doth wait : and in his word do I hope. *Ps.* Out of the depths have I cried unto thee, O Lord : Lord, hear my voice. Glory be to the Father . . .

COLLECT

O GOD, who didst enlighten this most holy night with the glory of the Lord's Resurrection : Preserve in all thy people the spirit of adoption which thou hast given, so that renewed in body and soul they may perform unto thee a pure service; through thy Son, Jesus Christ our Lord, who liveth and reigneth with thee and the Holy Ghost, one God, world without end. *Amen.*

LESSON. Exodus 13:17–22

EPISTLE. 1 Peter 3:17–22

GRADUAL

MY flesh also shall rest in hope : for thou wilt not leave my soul in hell. *V.* Into thy hand I commit my spirit : thou hast redeemed me, O Lord God of truth. *V.* In thee, O Lord, do I put my trust : let me never be ashamed.

GOSPEL. Matthew 27:57–66

Easter Day. The Resurrection of Our Lord

I. For an early Service

INTROIT

HE is risen, alleluia : why seek ye the living among the dead? Alleluia. Remember how he spake unto you, alleluia : The Son of Man must be crucified, and the third day rise again. Alleluia, alleluia. *Ps.* Thou hast crowned him with glory and honor : thou madest him to have dominion over the works of thy hands. Glory be to the Father . . .

COLLECT

O GOD, who for our redemption didst give thine only-begotten Son, Jesus Christ, to suffer death upon the Cross, and by his glorious Resurrection hast delivered us from the power of the enemy : Grant us so to die daily unto sin, that we may evermore live with him who died and rose again for us; through the same Jesus Christ our Lord, who liveth and reigneth with thee and the Holy Ghost, one God, world without end. *Amen.*

LESSON. Isaiah 25:6–9
(*Begin:* "In this mountain . . ."),
or Daniel 3:8–25

EPISTLE. 1 Peter 1:3–9

GRADUAL

THIS is the day which the Lord hath made : we will rejoice and be glad in it. *V.* O give thanks unto the Lord for he is good : for his mercy endureth forever.

Alleluia, alleluia. *V.* Christ our Passover : is sacrificed for us. *V.* Let us keep the feast : with the unleavened bread of sincerity and truth. Alleluia.

GOSPEL. John 20:1–18

II. For The Service

INTROIT

WHEN I awake, I am still with thee. Alleluia : thou hast laid thine hand upon me. Alleluia. Such knowledge is too wonderful for me : it is high, I cannot attain unto it. Alleluia, alleluia. *Ps.* O Lord, thou hast searched me, and known me : thou knowest my downsitting and mine uprising. Glory be to the Father . . .

COLLECT

ALMIGHTY God, who through thine only-begotten Son Jesus Christ hast overcome death, and opened unto us the gate of everlasting life : We humbly beseech thee, that as thou dost put into our minds good desires, so by thy continual help we may bring the same to good effect; through the same, Jesus Christ our Lord, who liveth and reigneth with thee and the Holy Ghost, one God, world without end. *Amen.*

LESSON. Daniel 3:8–25,
or Isaiah 25:6–9
(*Begin:* "In this mountain . . .")

EPISTLE. 1 Corinthians 5:7–8,
or 1 Corinthians 15:20–26

GRADUAL

THIS is the day which the Lord hath made : we will rejoice and be glad in it. *V.* O give thanks unto the Lord for he is good : for his mercy endureth forever.

Alleluia, alleluia. *V.* Christ our Passover : is sacrificed for us. *V.* Let us keep the feast : with the unleavened bread of sincerity and truth. Alleluia.

GOSPEL. Mark 16:1–7

III. At Vespers: LESSON. Luke 24:13–35

OTHER EASTER COLLECTS

GRANT, we beseech thee, Almighty God, that we who celebrate thy Paschal Feast, kindled with heavenly desires, may ever thirst for the fountain of life, Jesus Christ our Lord, who liveth and reigneth with thee and the Holy Ghost, one God, world without end. *Amen.*

GRANT, we beseech thee, Almighty God, that we who celebrate the solemnities of the Lord's Resurrection, may by the renewal of thy Holy Spirit rise again from the death of the soul; through the same Jesus Christ our Lord. *Amen.*

Monday after Easter

¶ *Introit, Collect and Gradual the same as for The Service on Easter Day.*

LESSON. Exodus 15:1–18 EPISTLE. Acts 10:34–43

GOSPEL. Luke 24:13–35

Quasi Modo Geniti. The First Sunday after Easter

INTROIT

AS newborn babes, alleluia : desire the sincere milk of the Word, alleluia. Hear, O my people, and I will testify unto thee : O Israel, if thou wilt hearken unto me. Alleluia, alleluia, alleluia. *Ps.* Sing aloud unto God our strength : make a joyful noise unto the God of Jacob. Glory be to the Father . . .

COLLECT

GRANT, we beseech thee, Almighty God, that we who have celebrated the solemnities of the Lord's Resurrection may, by the help of thy grace, bring forth the fruits thereof in our life and conversation; through the same thy Son, Jesus Christ our Lord, who liveth and reigneth with thee and the Holy Ghost, one God, world without end. *Amen.*

LESSON. Genesis 32:22–30

EPISTLE. 1 John 5:4–12

(*Verse 7, which does not appear in ancient manuscripts, may be omitted when the Authorized Version is read.*)

GRADUAL

ALLELUIA, alleluia. *V.* The angel of the Lord descended from heaven and came and rolled back the stone from the door, and sat upon it.

Alleluia. *V.* After eight days came Jesus, the doors being shut, and stood in the midst of his disciples : and saith unto them, Peace be unto you. Alleluia.

GOSPEL. John 20:19–31

Misericordia Domini. The Second Sunday after Easter

INTROIT

THE earth is full of the goodness of the Lord, alleluia : by the word of the Lord were the heavens made. Alleluia, alleluia. *Ps.* Rejoice in the Lord, O ye righteous : for praise is comely for the upright. Glory be to the Father . . .

COLLECT

GOD, who, by the humiliation of thy Son, didst raise up the fallen world: Grant unto thy faithful ones perpetual gladness, and those whom thou hast delivered from the danger of everlasting death, do thou make partakers of eternal joys; through the same thy Son, Jesus Christ our Lord, who liveth and reigneth with thee and the Holy Ghost, one God, world without end. *Amen.*

LESSON. Ezekiel 34:11–16

EPISTLE. 1 Peter 2:21b–25

GRADUAL

ALLELUIA, alleluia. *V.* Then was the Lord Jesus known of the disciples : in the breaking of bread.

Alleluia. *V.* I am the Good Shepherd : and know my sheep, and am known of mine. Alleluia.

GOSPEL. John 10:11–16

Jubilate. The Third Sunday after Easter

INTROIT

MAKE a joyful noise unto God, all ye lands, alleluia : sing forth the honor of his Name, alleluia; make his praise glorious. Alleluia, alleluia, alleluia. *Ps.* Say unto God, How terrible art thou in thy works : through the greatness of thy power shall thine enemies submit themselves unto thee. Glory be to the Father . . .

COLLECT

ALMIGHTY God, who showest to them that be in error the light of thy truth, to the intent that they may return into the way of righteousness : Grant unto all them that are admitted into the fellowship of Christ's religion that they may eschew those things that are contrary to their profession, and follow all such things as are agreeable to the same; through thy Son, Jesus Christ our Lord, who liveth and reigneth with thee and the Holy Ghost, one God, world without end. *Amen.*

LESSON. Isaiah 40:25–31

EPISTLE. 1 Peter 2:11–20

GRADUAL

ALLELUIA, alleluia. *V.* The Lord hath sent redemption : unto his people.

Alleluia. *V.* It behooved Christ to suffer, and to rise from the dead : and thus to enter into his glory. Alleluia.

GOSPEL. John 16:16–22

Cantate. The Fourth Sunday after Easter

INTROIT

O SING unto the Lord a new song, alleluia : for he hath done marvellous things, alleluia. The Lord hath made known his salvation : his righteousness hath he openly showed in the sight of the heathen. Alleluia, alleluia, alleluia. *Ps.* His right hand, and his holy arm : hath gotten him the victory. Glory be to the Father . . .

COLLECT

O GOD, who makest the minds of the faithful to be of one will : Grant unto thy people that they may love what thou commandest, and desire what thou dost promise; that, among the manifold changes of this world, our hearts may there be fixed where true joys are to be found; through thy Son, Jesus Christ our Lord, who liveth and reigneth with thee and the Holy Ghost, one God, world without end. *Amen.*

LESSON. Isaiah 29:9–14

EPISTLE. James 1:17–21

GRADUAL

ALLELUIA, alleluia. *V.* The right hand of the Lord is exalted : the right hand of the Lord doeth valiantly.

Alleluia. *V.* Christ, being raised from the dead, dieth no more : death hath no more dominion over him. Alleluia.

GOSPEL. John 16:4b–15

Rogate. The Fifth Sunday after Easter

INTROIT

WITH a voice of singing declare ye, and tell this, alleluia; utter it even to the end of the earth : The Lord hath redeemed his servant Jacob. Alleluia, alleluia. *Ps.* Make a joyful noise unto God, all ye lands : sing forth the honor of his Name; make his praise glorious. Glory be to the Father . . .

COLLECT

O GOD, from whom all good things do come : Grant to us thy humble servants, that by thy holy inspiration we may think those things that be right, and by thy merciful guiding may perform the same; through thy Son, Jesus Christ our Lord, who liveth and reigneth with thee and the Holy Ghost, one God, world without end. *Amen.*

LESSON. Isaiah 55:6–11

EPISTLE. James 1:22–27

GRADUAL

ALLELUIA, alleluia. *V.* It behooved Christ to suffer, and to rise from the dead : and thus to enter into his glory.

Alleluia. *V.* I came forth from the Father, and am come into the world : again I leave the world, and go to the Father. Alleluia.

GOSPEL. John 16:23b–30

The Ascension of Our Lord

INTROIT

YE men of Galilee : why stand ye gazing up into heaven? Alleluia. This same Jesus which is taken up from you into heaven : shall so come in like manner as ye have seen him go into heaven. Alleluia, alleluia, alleluia. *Ps.* O clap your hands, all ye people : shout unto God with the voice of triumph. Glory be to the Father . . .

COLLECT

GRANT, we beseech thee, Almighty God, that like as we do believe thy only-begotten Son, our Lord Jesus Christ, to have ascended into the heavens; so may we also in heart and mind thither ascend, and with him continually dwell; who liveth and reigneth with thee and the Holy Ghost, one God, world without end. *Amen.*

Or,

O KING of Glory, Lord of Hosts, who didst this day ascend in triumph far above all heavens : We beseech thee leave us not comfortless, but send to us the Spirit of Truth, promised of the Father; who livest and reignest with the Father and the same Spirit, one God, world without end. *Amen.*

LESSON. 2 Kings 2:9–15,
or Genesis 5:21–24

EPISTLE. Acts 1:1–11

GRADUAL

ALLELUIA, alleluia. *V.* God is gone up with a shout : the Lord with the sound of a trumpet.

Alleluia. *V.* Thou hast ascended on high : thou hast led captivity captive. Alleluia.

GOSPEL. Mark 16:14–20

Exaudi. The Sunday after The Ascension

INTROIT

HEAR, O Lord, when I cry with my voice, alleluia : when thou saidst, Seek ye my face; my heart said unto thee, Thy face, Lord, will I seek. Hide not thy face from me : alleluia, alleluia.

s. The Lord is my light and my salva-on : whom shall I fear? Glory be to the ather . . .

COLLECT

ALMIGHTY, everlasting God, make us to have always a devout will owards thee, and to serve thy Majesty ith a pure heart; through thy Son, esus Christ our Lord, who liveth and eigneth with thee and the Holy Ghost, ne God, world without end. *Amen.*

LESSON. Isaiah 32:14–20

EPISTLE. 1 Peter 4:7b–11

(*Begin:* "Be ye sober and watch . . .")

GRADUAL

ALLELUIA, alleluia. *V.* God reigneth over the heathen : God sitteth upon the throne of his holiness.

Alleluia. *V.* I will not leave you comfortless : I go, and I will come again to you, and your heart shall rejoice. Alleluia.

GOSPEL. John 15:26–16:4a

The Day of Pentecost. Whitsunday

INTROIT

THE Spirit of the Lord filleth the world, alleluia : let the righteous be lad, let them rejoice before God; yea, t them exceedingly rejoice. Alleluia, lleluia, alleluia. *Ps.* Let God arise, let is enemies be scattered : let them also at hate him flee before him. Glory be the Father . . .

COLLECT

O GOD, who didst teach the hearts of thy faithful people, by sending them the light of thy Holy Spirit : rant us by the same Spirit to have a ght judgment in all things, and evermore to rejoice in his holy comfort; through thy Son, Jesus Christ our Lord, who liveth and reigneth with thee and the Holy Ghost, one God, world without end. *Amen.*

LESSON. Joel 2:28–32

EPISTLE. Acts 2:1–11

GRADUAL

ALLELUIA, alleluia. *V.* Thou sendest forth thy Spirit, they are created : and thou renewest the face of the earth.

Alleluia. *V.* Come, Holy Spirit, fill the hearts of the faithful : and kindle in them the fire of thy love. Alleluia.

GOSPEL. John 14:23–31a

At Vespers: LESSON. Acts 2:14–21

Monday after Pentecost

¶ *Introit and Gradual the same as for Pentecost.*

COLLECT

O GOD, who didst give thy Holy Spirit to thine Apostles : Grant nto thy people the performance of their etitions, so that on us to whom thou ast given faith, thou mayest also beow peace; through thy Son, Jesus Christ our Lord, who liveth and reigneth with thee and the Holy Ghost, one God, world without end. *Amen.*

LESSON. Isaiah 57:15–21

EPISTLE. Acts 10:42–48a

GOSPEL. John 3:16–21

Trinity Sunday

[The Octave of Pentecost]

INTROIT

BLESSED be the Holy Trinity, and the undivided Unity : let us give glory to him because he hath shown his mercy to us. *Ps.* O Lord our Lord : how excellent is thy Name in all the earth. Glory be to the Father . . .

Or,

HOLY, holy, holy is the Lord of Hosts : of him, and through him, and to him, are all things. *Ps.* O Lord our Lord : how excellent is thy Name in all the earth. Glory be to the Father . . .

COLLECT

ALMIGHTY and everlasting God, who hast given unto us thy servants grace, by the confession of a true faith, to acknowledge the glory of the eternal Trinity, and in the power of the Divine Majesty to worship the Unity : We beseech thee, that thou wouldest keep u steadfast in this faith, and evermore d fend us from all adversities; who live and reignest, one God, world witho end. *Amen.*

LESSON. Isaiah 6:1–8

EPISTLE. Romans 11:33–36

GRADUAL

BLESSED art thou, O Lord, who b holdest the deep : and who dwelle between the Cherubim. *V.* Blessed a thou, O Lord, in the firmament of hea en : and greatly to be praised, and glor fied, and highly exalted forever.

Alleluia, alleluia. *V.* Blessed art tho O Lord God of our fathers : and great to be praised and glorified forever. All luia.

GOSPEL. Matthew 28:18–20, *or* John 3:1–15

The First Sunday after Trinity

[The Second Sunday after Pentecost]

INTROIT

O LORD, I have trusted in thy mercy : my heart shall rejoice in thy salvation. I will sing unto the Lord : because he hath dealt bountifully with me. *Ps.* How long wilt thou forget me, O Lord : how long wilt thou hide thy face from me? Glory be to the Father . . .

COLLECT

O GOD, the strength of all them that put their trust in thee : Mercifully accept our prayers; and because through the weakness of our mortal nature we can do no good thing without thee, grant us the help of thy grace, that in keeping thy commandments we may please thee, both in will and deed; through thy Son, Jesus Christ our Lord, who liveth an reigneth with thee and the Holy Ghos one God, world without end. *Amen.*

LESSON. Deuteronomy 6:4–13

EPISTLE. 1 John 4:16b–21

GRADUAL

I SAID, Lord, be merciful unto me heal my soul, for I have sinne against thee. *V.* Blessed is he that co sidereth the poor : the Lord will deliv him in time of trouble.

Alleluia, alleluia. *V.* O Lord my Go in thee do I put my trust : save me fro all them that persecute me, and deliv me. Alleluia.

GOSPEL. Luke 16:19–31

The Second Sunday after Trinity

[The Third Sunday after Pentecost]

INTROIT

THE Lord was my stay : he brought me forth also into a large place. He elivered me : because he delighted in ne. *Ps.* I will love thee, O Lord, my trength : the Lord is my rock, and my ortress. Glory be to the Father . . .

COLLECT

O LORD, who never failest to help and govern those whom thou dost ring up in thy steadfast fear and love : Make us to have a perpetual fear and ove of thy holy Name; through thy Son, esus Christ our Lord, who liveth and reigneth with thee and the Holy Ghost, one God, world without end. *Amen.*

LESSON. Proverbs 9:1–10

EPISTLE. 1 John 3:13–18

GRADUAL

IN my distress I cried unto the Lord : and he heard me. *V.* Deliver my soul, O Lord, from lying lips : and from a deceitful tongue.

Alleluia, alleluia. *V.* I will praise the Lord according to his righteousness : and will sing praise to the Name of the Lord most High. Alleluia.

GOSPEL. Luke 14:15–24

The Third Sunday after Trinity

[The Fourth Sunday after Pentecost]

INTROIT

TURN thee unto me, and have mercy upon me : for I am desolate and fflicted. Look upon mine affliction and ny pain : and forgive all my sins. *Ps.* Unto thee, O Lord, do I lift up my soul: my God, I trust in thee, let me not be shamed. Glory be to the Father . . .

COLLECT

O GOD, the protector of all that trust in thee, without whom nothing is strong, nothing is holy : Increase nd multiply upon us thy mercy; that, nou being our ruler and guide, we may pass through things temporal, that we nally lose not the things eternal; through thy Son, Jesus Christ our Lord, who liveth and reigneth with thee and the Holy Ghost, one God, world without end. *Amen.*

LESSON. Isaiah 12:1–6

EPISTLE. 1 Peter 5:6–11

GRADUAL

CAST thy burden upon the Lord : and he shall sustain thee. *V.* I will call upon God; and the Lord shall save me : he hath delivered my soul in peace.

Alleluia, alleluia. *V.* I will love thee, O Lord, my strength : the Lord is my rock, and my fortress, and my deliverer. Alleluia.

GOSPEL. Luke 15:1–10

The Fourth Sunday after Trinity

[The Fifth Sunday after Pentecost]

INTROIT

THE Lord is my light and my salvation, whom shall I fear : the Lord is ne strength of my life, of whom shall I be afraid? When the wicked, even mine enemies and my foes, came upon me : they stumbled and fell. *Ps.* Though an host should encamp against me : my heart shall not fear. Glory be to the Father . . .

COLLECT

GRANT, O Lord, we beseech thee, that the course of this world may be so peaceably ordered by thy governance, that thy Church may joyfully serve thee in all godly quietness; through thy Son, Jesus Christ our Lord, who liveth and reigneth with thee and the Holy Ghost, one God, world without end. *Amen.*

LESSON. Numbers 6:22–27

EPISTLE. Romans 8:18–23

GRADUAL

FORGIVE our sins, O Lord : lest th heathen say, Where is their God? *V* Help us, O God of our salvation, for th glory of thy Name : and deliver us.

Alleluia, alleluia. *V.* The king shall jo in thy strength, O Lord : and in thy sal vation how greatly shall he rejoice. Alle luia.

GOSPEL. Luke 6:36–42

The Fifth Sunday after Trinity

[The Sixth Sunday after Pentecost]

INTROIT

HEAR, O Lord, when I cry with my voice : thou hast been my help. Leave me not, neither forsake me : O God of my salvation. *Ps.* The Lord is my light and my salvation : whom shall I fear? Glory be to the Father . . .

COLLECT

O GOD, who hast prepared for them that love thee such good things as pass man's understanding : Pour into our hearts such love toward thee, that we, loving thee above all things, may obtain thy promises, which exceed all that we can desire; through thy Son, Jesus Christ our Lord, who liveth an reigneth with thee and the Holy Ghos one God, world without end. *Amen.*

LESSON. Lamentations 3:22–33

EPISTLE. 1 Peter 3:8–15a

GRADUAL

BEHOLD, O God our shield : an look upon the face of thine anointe *V.* O Lord God of hosts : hear m prayer.

Alleluia, alleluia. *V.* In thee, O Lor do I put my trust; let me never b ashamed : deliver me in thy righteou ness. Alleluia.

GOSPEL. Luke 5:1–11

The Sixth Sunday after Trinity

[The Seventh Sunday after Pentecost]

INTROIT

THE Lord is the strength of his people : he is the saving strength of his anointed. Save thy people, and bless thine inheritance : feed them also, and lift them up forever. *Ps.* Unto thee will I cry, O Lord, my rock; be not silent to me : lest if thou be silent to me, I become like them that go down into the pit. Glory be to the Father . . .

COLLECT

LORD of all power and might, who a the author and giver of all goo things : Graft in our hearts the love o thy Name, increase in us true religio nourish us with all goodness, and of th great mercy keep us in the same; throug thy Son, Jesus Christ our Lord, who li eth and reigneth with thee and the Ho Ghost, one God, world without en *Amen.*

LESSON. Ruth 1:1–18

EPISTLE. Romans 6:3–11

GRADUAL

RETURN, O Lord, how long : and let it repent thee concerning thy servants. *V.* Lord, thou hast been our dwelling place : in all generations.

Alleluia, alleluia. *V.* O clap your hands, all ye people : shout unto God with the voice of triumph. Alleluia.

GOSPEL. Matthew 5:20–26

The Seventh Sunday after Trinity

[The Eighth Sunday after Pentecost]

INTROIT

O CLAP your hands, all ye people : shout unto God with the voice of iumph. *Ps.* He shall subdue the people ıder us : and the nations under our et. Glory be to the Father . . .

COLLECT

O GOD, whose never-failing providence ordereth all things both in aven and earth : We humbly beseech ee to put away from us all hurtful ings, and to give us those things which profitable for us; through thy Son, sus Christ our Lord, who liveth and reigneth with thee and the Holy Ghost, one God, world without end. *Amen.*

LESSON. Isaiah 62:6–12

EPISTLE. Romans 6:19–23

GRADUAL

COME, ye children, hearken unto me : I will teach you the fear of the Lord. *V.* They looked unto him and were lightened : and their faces were not ashamed.

Alleluia, alleluia. *V.* Deliver me from mine enemies, O my God : defend me from them that rise up against me. Alleluia.

GOSPEL. Mark 8:1–9

The Eighth Sunday after Trinity

[The Ninth Sunday after Pentecost]

INTROIT

WE have thought of thy lovingkindness, O God : in the midst of thy nple. According to thy Name, O God, is thy praise unto the ends of the rth : thy right hand is full of rightusness. *Ps.* Great is the Lord, and eatly to be praised : in the city of our od, in the mountain of his holiness. lory be to the Father . . .

COLLECT

GRANT to us, Lord, we beseech thee, the spirit to think and do always ch things as are right; that we, who nnot do anything that is good without ee, may by thee be enabled to live according to thy will; through thy Son, Jesus Christ our Lord, who liveth and reigneth with thee and the Holy Ghost, one God, world without end. *Amen.*

LESSON. Jeremiah 23:16–29

EPISTLE. Romans 8:12–17

GRADUAL

BE thou my strong rock : for an house of defence to save me. *V.* In thee, O Lord, do I put my trust : let me never be ashamed.

Alleluia, alleluia. *V.* The Lord knoweth the way of the righteous : but the way of the ungodly shall perish. Alleluia.

GOSPEL. Matthew 7:15–21

The Ninth Sunday after Trinity

[The Tenth Sunday after Pentecost]

INTROIT

BEHOLD, God is mine helper : the Lord is with them that uphold my soul. He shall reward evil unto mine enemies : cut them off in thy truth. *Ps.* Save me, O God, by thy Name : and judge me by thy strength. Glory be to the Father . . .

COLLECT

LET thy merciful ears, O Lord, be open to the prayers of thy humble servants; and, that they may obtain their petitions, make them to ask such things as shall please thee; through thy Son, Jesus Christ our Lord, who liveth and reigneth with thee and the Holy Ghost, one Go world without end. *Amen.*

LESSON. Proverbs 16:1–9

EPISTLE. 1 Corinthians 10:1–13

GRADUAL

O LORD our Lord, how excellent thy Name in all the earth : wl hast set thy glory above the heavens.

Alleluia, alleluia. *V.* Give ear, O n people, to my law : incline your ears the words of my mouth. Alleluia.

GOSPEL. Luke 16:1–9, *or* Luke 15:11–32

The Tenth Sunday after Trinity

[The Eleventh Sunday after Pentecost]

INTROIT

AS for me, I will call upon God, and he shall hear my voice : he hath delivered my soul in peace from the battle that was against me. God shall hear and afflict them, even he that abideth of old : cast thy burden upon the Lord, and he shall sustain thee. *Ps.* Give ear to my prayer, O God : and hide not thyself from my supplication. Glory be to the Father . . .

COLLECT

O GOD, who declarest thine almighty power chiefly in showing mercy and pity : Mercifully grant unto us such a measure of thy grace, that we, running the way of thy commandments, may obtain thy gracious promises, and be made partakers of thy heavenly treasure; through thy Son, Jesus Christ our Lo who liveth and reigneth with thee a the Holy Ghost, one God, world witho end. *Amen.*

LESSON. Jeremiah 7:1–11

EPISTLE. 1 Corinthians 12:1–11

GRADUAL

KEEP me, O Lord, as the apple of t eye : hide me under the shadow thy wings. *V.* Let my sentence come fo from thy presence : let thine eyes beh the things that are equal.

Alleluia, alleluia. *V.* Deliver me fr mine enemies, O my God : defend from them that rise up against me. Al luia.

GOSPEL. Luke 19:41–47a

The Eleventh Sunday after Trinity

[The Twelfth Sunday after Pentecost]

INTROIT

GOD is in his holy habitation; God setteth the solitary in families : the od of Israel is he that giveth strength d power unto his people. *Ps.* Let God ise, let his enemies be scattered : let em also that hate him flee before him. lory be to the Father . . .

COLLECT

ALMIGHTY and everlasting God, who art always more ready to hear an we to pray, and art wont to give ore than either we desire or deserve : our down upon us the abundance of y mercy, forgiving us those things hereof our conscience is afraid, and ving us those good things which we are ot worthy to ask, but through the merits and mediation of Jesus Christ, thy Son, our Lord, who liveth and reigneth with thee and the Holy Ghost, one God, world without end. *Amen.*

LESSON. Daniel 9:15–19

EPISTLE. 1 Corinthians 15:1–10

GRADUAL

MY heart trusteth in God, and I am helped : therefore my heart greatly rejoiceth; and with my song will I praise him. *V.* Unto thee will I cry, O Lord my rock : be not silent to me. Hear the voice of my supplications.

Alleluia, alleluia. *V.* Praise waiteth for thee, O God, in Sion : and unto thee shall the vow be performed. Alleluia.

GOSPEL. Luke 18:9–14

The Twelfth Sunday after Trinity

[The Thirteenth Sunday after Pentecost]

INTROIT

MAKE haste, O God, to deliver me : make haste to help me, O Lord. t them be ashamed and confounded : at seek after my soul. *Ps.* Let them be rned backward, and put to confusion : at desire my hurt. Glory be to the ather . . .

COLLECT

ALMIGHTY and merciful God, of whose only gift it cometh that thy ithful people do unto thee true and laudle service : Grant, we beseech thee, that e may so faithfully serve thee in this life, at we fail not finally to attain thy heavly promises; through thy Son, Jesus Christ our Lord, who liveth and reigneth with thee and the Holy Ghost, one God, world without end. *Amen.*

LESSON. Isaiah 29:17–21

EPISTLE. 2 Corinthians 3:4–9

GRADUAL

I WILL bless the Lord at all times : his praise shall continually be in my mouth. *V.* My soul shall make her boast in the Lord : the humble shall hear thereof and be glad.

Alleluia, alleluia. *V.* Sing aloud unto God our strength : make a joyful noise unto the God of Jacob. Alleluia.

GOSPEL. Mark 7:31–37

The Thirteenth Sunday after Trinity

[The Fourteenth Sunday after Pentecost]

INTROIT

HAVE respect to the covenant : O let not the oppressed return ashamed. Arise, O God, plead thine own cause : forget not the voice of thine enemies. *Ps.* O God, why hast thou cast us off forever : why doth thine anger smoke against the sheep of thy pasture? Glory be to the Father . . .

COLLECT

ALMIGHTY and everlasting God, give unto us the increase of faith, hope, and charity; and that we may obtain that which thou dost promise, make us to love that which thou dost command; through thy Son, Jesus Christ our Lord, who liveth and reigneth with thee and the Holy Ghost, one God, world without end. *Amen.*

LESSON. Zechariah 7:4–10

EPISTLE. Galatians 3:16–22

GRADUAL

HAVE respect to the covenant : O le[t] not the oppressed return ashamed *V.* Arise, O God, plead thine own cause forget not the voice of thine enemies.

Alleluia, alleluia. *V.* O Lord God o[f] my salvation : I have cried day and nigh[t] before thee. Alleluia.

GOSPEL. Luke 10:23–37

The Fourteenth Sunday after Trinity

[The Fifteenth Sunday after Pentecost]

INTROIT

BEHOLD, O God our shield, and look upon the face of thine anointed : for a day in thy courts is better than a thousand. *Ps.* How amiable are thy tabernacles, O Lord of Hosts : my soul longeth, yea, even fainteth for the courts of the Lord. Glory be to the Father . . .

COLLECT

KEEP, we beseech thee, O Lord, thy Church with thy perpetual mercy; and, because the frailty of man without thee cannot but fall, keep us ever by thy help from all things hurtful, and lead us to all things profitable to our salvation; through thy Son, Jesus Christ our Lor[d] who liveth and reigneth with thee an[d] the Holy Ghost, one God, world withou[t] end. *Amen.*

LESSON. Proverbs 4:10–23

EPISTLE. Galatians 5:16–24

GRADUAL

IT is better to trust in the Lord : than t[o] put confidence in man. *V.* It is bette[r] to trust in the Lord : than to put conf[i]dence in princes.

Alleluia, alleluia. *V.* Lord, thou ha[st] been our dwelling place : in all genera[]tions. Alleluia.

GOSPEL. Luke 17:11–19

The Fifteenth Sunday after Trinity

[The Sixteenth Sunday after Pentecost]

INTROIT

BOW down thine ear, O Lord, hear me : O thou, my God, save thy servant that trusteth in thee. Be merciful unto me, O Lord : for I cry unto thee daily. *Ps.* Rejoice the soul of thy servant : for unto thee, O Lord, do I lift up my soul. Glory be to the Father . . .

COLLECT

O LORD, we beseech thee, let th[y] continual pity cleanse and defen[d] thy Church; and because it cannot co[n]tinue in safety without thy succor, pr[e]serve it evermore by thy help and goo[d]ness; through thy Son, Jesus Christ ou[r] Lord, who liveth and reigneth with th[ee] and the Holy Ghost, one God, wor[ld] without end. *Amen.*

LESSON. 1 Kings 17:8–16

EPISTLE. Galatians 5:25–6:10

GRADUAL

T is a good thing to give thanks unto the Lord : and to sing praises unto thy Name, O most High. *V.* To show forth thy lovingkindness in the morning : and thy faithfulness every night.

Alleluia, alleluia. *V.* O God, my heart is fixed : I will sing and give praise, even with my glory. Alleluia.

GOSPEL. Matthew 6:24–34

The Sixteenth Sunday after Trinity

[The Seventeenth Sunday after Pentecost]

INTROIT

E merciful unto me, O Lord : for I cry unto thee daily. For thou, Lord, 't good, and ready to forgive : and enteous in mercy unto all them that ll upon thee. *Ps.* Bow down thine ear, Lord, hear me : for I am poor and eedy. Glory be to the Father . . .

COLLECT

ORD, we pray thee, that thy grace may always go before and follow ter us, and make us continually to be ven to all good works; through thy on, Jesus Christ our Lord, who liveth d reigneth with thee and the Holy Ghost, one God, world without end. *Amen.*

LESSON. Job 5:17–26

EPISTLE. Ephesians 3:13–21

GRADUAL

THE heathen shall fear the Name of the Lord : and all the kings of the earth thy glory. *V.* When the Lord shall build up Zion : he shall appear in his glory.

Alleluia, alleluia. *V.* O sing unto the Lord a new song : for he hath done marvellous things. Alleluia.

GOSPEL. Luke 7:11–16

The Seventeenth Sunday after Trinity

[The Eighteenth Sunday after Pentecost]

INTROIT

IGHTEOUS art thou, O Lord : and upright are thy judgments. Deal th thy servant : according unto thy ercy. *Ps.* Blessed are the undefiled in e way : who walk in the law of the ord. Glory be to the Father . . .

COLLECT

ORD, we beseech thee, grant thy people grace to withstand the temptans of the devil, and with pure hearts d minds to follow thee, the only God, rough thy Son, Jesus Christ our Lord, ho liveth and reigneth with thee and e Holy Ghost, one God, world without d. *Amen.*

LESSON. Proverbs 25:6–14

EPISTLE. Ephesians 4:1–6

GRADUAL

BLESSED is the nation whose God is the Lord : and the people whom he hath chosen for his own inheritance. *V.* By the word of the Lord were the heavens made : and all the host of them by the breath of his mouth.

Alleluia, alleluia. *V.* I love the Lord : because he hath heard my voice and my supplications. Alleluia.

GOSPEL. Luke 14:1–11

The Eighteenth Sunday after Trinity

[The Nineteenth Sunday after Pentecost]

INTROIT

REWARD them that wait for thee, O Lord : and let thy prophets be found faithful. Hear the prayer of thy servants : and of thy people Israel. *Ps.* I was glad when they said unto me : Let us go into the house of the Lord. Glory be to the Father . . .

COLLECT

O GOD, forasmuch as without thee we are not able to please thee : Mercifully grant, that thy Holy Spirit may in all things direct and rule our hearts; through thy Son, Jesus Christ our Lord, who liveth and reigneth with the and the Holy Ghost, one God, worl without end. *Amen.*

LESSON. 2 Chronicles 1:7–12

EPISTLE. 1 Corinthians 1:4–9

GRADUAL

I WAS glad when they said unto me Let us go into the house of the Lor *V.* Peace be within thy walls : and pro perity within thy palaces.

Alleluia, alleluia. *V.* O praise the Lor all ye nations : praise him, all ye peopl Alleluia.

GOSPEL. Matthew 22:34-46

The Nineteenth Sunday after Trinity

[The Twentieth Sunday after Pentecost]

INTROIT

SAY unto my soul : I am thy salvation. The righteous cry, and the Lord heareth, and delivereth them out of all their troubles : for this God is our God for ever and ever. *Ps.* Give ear, O my people, to my law : incline your ears to the words of my mouth. Glory be to the Father . . .

COLLECT

O ALMIGHTY and most merciful God, of thy bountiful goodness keep us, we beseech thee, from all things that may hurt us; that we, being ready, both in body and soul, may cheerfully accomplish those things that thou woul est have done; through thy Son, Jes Christ our Lord, who liveth and reignet with thee and the Holy Ghost, one Go world without end. *Amen.*

LESSON. Genesis 28:10–17

EPISTLE. Ephesians 4:17–28

GRADUAL

LET my prayer be set forth before the as incense : and the lifting up of m hands as the evening sacrifice.

Alleluia, alleluia. *V.* The right hand the Lord is exalted : the right hand of t Lord doeth valiantly. Alleluia.

GOSPEL. Matthew 9:1–8

The Twentieth Sunday after Trinity

[The Twenty-first Sunday after Pentecost]

INTROIT

THE Lord our God is righteous in all his works which he doeth : for we obeyed not his voice. Give glory to thy Name, O Lord : and deal with us accor ing to the multitude of thy mercies. *P* Great is the Lord, and greatly to praised : in the city of our God, in t ıountain of his holiness. Glory be to ıe Father . . .

COLLECT

GRANT, we beseech thee, merciful Lord, to thy faithful people pardon nd peace, that they may be cleansed om all their sins, and serve thee with a uiet mind; through thy Son, Jesus hrist our Lord, who liveth and reigneth ith thee and the Holy Ghost, one God, orld without end. *Amen.*

LESSON. Proverbs 2:1–9

EPISTLE. Ephesians 5:15–21

GRADUAL

THE eyes of all wait upon thee, O Lord : and thou givest them their meat in due season. *V.* Thou openest thine hand : and satisfiest the desire of every living thing.

Alleluia, alleluia. *V.* O give thanks unto the Lord, call upon his Name : make known his deeds among the people. Alleluia.

GOSPEL. Matthew 22:1–14

The Twenty-first Sunday after Trinity

[The Twenty-second Sunday after Pentecost]

INTROIT

THE whole world is in thy power, O Lord, King Almighty : there is no ıan that can gainsay thee. For thou hast ıade heaven and earth, and all the wonrous things under the heaven : thou art ord of all. *Ps.* Blessed are the undefiled ı the way : who walk in the law of the ord. Glory be to the Father . . .

COLLECT

ORD, we beseech thee to keep thy household, the Church, in continual odliness; that through thy protection it ıay be free from all adversities, and deoutly given to serve thee in good works, the glory of thy Name; through thy on, Jesus Christ our Lord, who liveth ıd reigneth with thee and the Holy Ghost, one God, world without end. *Amen.*

LESSON. 2 Samuel 7:18–29

EPISTLE. Ephesians 6:10–17

GRADUAL

LORD, thou hast been our dwelling place : in all generations. *V.* Before the mountains were brought forth or ever thou hadst formed the earth and the world : even from everlasting to everlasting, thou art God.

Alleluia, alleluia. *V.* They that trust in the Lord shall be as Mount Zion : which cannot be removed, but abideth forever. Alleluia.

GOSPEL. John 4:46b–53

(*Begin:* "There was a certain nobleman . . .")

The Twenty-second Sunday after Trinity

[The Twenty-third Sunday after Pentecost]

INTROIT

F thou, Lord, shouldest mark iniquities : O Lord, who shall stand? But ere is forgiveness with thee : that thou ayest be feared. *Ps.* Out of the depths ve I cried unto thee, O Lord : Lord, ar my voice. Glory be to the Father . . .

COLLECT

O GOD, our refuge and strength, who art the author of all godliness : Be ready, we beseech thee, to hear the devout prayers of thy Church; and grant that those things which we ask faithfully, we may obtain effectually;

through thy Son, Jesus Christ our Lord, who liveth and reigneth with thee and the Holy Ghost, one God, world without end. *Amen.*

LESSON. Proverbs 3:11–20

EPISTLE. Philippians 1:3–11

GRADUAL

BEHOLD, how good and how pleasa it is : for brethren to dwell togeth in unity. *V.* The Lord commanded t blessing : even life for evermore.

Alleluia, alleluia. *V.* Praise the Lor O my soul; while I live will I praise t Lord : I will sing praises unto my Go Alleluia.

GOSPEL. Matthew 18:21–35

The Twenty-third Sunday after Trinity

[The Twenty-fourth Sunday after Pentecost]

INTROIT

I KNOW the thoughts that I think toward you, saith the Lord : thoughts of peace, and not of evil. Then shall ye call upon me, and pray unto me, and I will hearken unto you : and I will turn your captivity, and gather you from all nations and from all places. *Ps.* Lord, thou hast been favorable unto thy land : thou hast brought back the captivity of Jacob. Glory be to the Father . . .

COLLECT

ABSOLVE, we beseech thee, O Lord, thy people from their offences; that from the bonds of our sins which, by reason of our frailty, we have brought upon us, we may be delivered by thy bountiful goodness; through thy So Jesus Christ our Lord, who liveth a reigneth with thee and the Holy Gho one God, world without end. *Amen.*

LESSON. Proverbs 8:11–22

EPISTLE. Philippians 3:17–21

GRADUAL

THOU hast saved us from our en mies : and hast put them to shan that hated us. *V.* In God we boast all t day long : and praise thy Name foreve

Alleluia, alleluia. *V.* Ye that fear t Lord, trust in the Lord : he is their he and their shield. Alleluia.

GOSPEL. Matthew 22:15–22

The Twenty-fourth Sunday after Trinity

[The Twenty-fifth Sunday after Pentecost]

INTROIT

O COME, let us worship and bow down : let us kneel before the Lord our maker. For he is our God : and we are the people of his pasture, and the sheep of his hand. *Ps.* O come, let us sing unto the Lord : let us make a joyful noise to the rock of our salvation. Glory be to the Father . . .

COLLECT

STIR up, we beseech thee, O Lord, t wills of thy faithful people; th they, plenteously bringing forth the fr of good works, may of thee be plenteou ly rewarded; through thy Son, Jes Christ our Lord, who liveth and reigne with thee and the Holy Ghost, one Go world without end. *Amen.*

LESSON. 1 Kings 17:17–24

EPISTLE. Colossians 1:9–14

GRADUAL

BLESSED is the man : that walketh not in the counsel of the ungodly. . His delight is in the law of the Lord : and in his law doth he meditate day and night.

Alleluia, alleluia. *V.* He shall call upon me, and I will answer him: with long life will I satisfy him, and show him my salvation. Alleluia.

GOSPEL. Matthew 9:18–26

¶ *The Propers for the following three Sundays may be used on the last three Sundays after Trinity.*

The Twenty-fifth Sunday after Trinity

[The Twenty-sixth Sunday after Pentecost]

INTROIT

HAVE mercy upon me, O Lord, for I am in trouble : deliver me from the and of mine enemies, and from them at persecute me. Let me not be ashamed, Lord : for I have called upon thee. *Ps.* thee, O Lord, do I put my trust : let e never be ashamed. Glory be to the ather . . .

COLLECT

ALMIGHTY God, we beseech thee, show thy mercy unto thy humble rvants; that we, who put no trust in ır own merits, may not be dealt with ter the severity of thy judgment, but cording to thy mercy; through thy Son, Jesus Christ our Lord, who liveth and reigneth with thee and the Holy Ghost, one God, world without end. *Amen.*

LESSON. Job 14:1–6

EPISTLE. 1 Thessalonians 4:13–18

GRADUAL

I WILL say of the Lord, He is my refuge and my fortress : my God, in him will I trust. *V.* His truth : shall be thy shield and buckler.

Alleluia, alleluia. *V.* He that dwelleth in the secret place of the most High : shall abide under the shadow of the Almighty. Alleluia.

GOSPEL. Matthew 24:15–28

The Twenty-sixth Sunday after Trinity

[The Twenty-seventh Sunday after Pentecost]

INTROIT

SAVE me, O God, by thy Name : and judge me by thy strength. Hear my ayer, O God : give ear to the words of y mouth. *Ps.* He shall reward evil unto ine enemies : cut them off in thy truth. lory be to the Father . . .

COLLECT

O GOD, so rule and govern our hearts and minds by thy Holy Spirit, that, being ever mindful of the end of all things and the day of thy just judgment, we may be stirred up to holiness of living here, and dwell with thee forever hereafter; through thy Son, Jesus Christ our Lord, who liveth and reigneth with thee and the Holy Ghost, one God, world without end. *Amen.*

LESSON. Daniel 7:9–14

EPISTLE. 1 Thessalonians 5:1–11

GRADUAL

WHO shall ascend into the hill of the Lord : or who shall stand in his holy place? *V.* He that hath clean hand and a pure heart : he shall receive th blessing from the Lord.

Alleluia, alleluia. *V.* Fear not, for have redeemed thee : I have called the by thy Name; thou art mine. Alleluia.

GOSPEL. Matthew 25:31–46

The Last Sunday after Trinity

[The Last Sunday after Pentecost]

¶ *The Introit, Collect, Lesson, Epistle, Gradual and Gospel here following shall be us on the Last Sunday after Trinity of each year.*

INTROIT

I AM Alpha and Omega, the beginning and the ending : which is, and which was, and which is to come, the Almighty. Behold, the tabernacle of God is with men, and he will dwell with them : and they shall be his people, and God himself shall be with them, and be their God. *Ps.* Lift up your heads, O ye gates; and be ye lift up, ye everlasting doors : and the King of Glory shall come in. Glory be to the Father . . .

COLLECT

ABSOLVE, we beseech thee, O Lord, thy people from their offences; that from the bonds of our sins which, by reason of our frailty, we have brought upon us, we may be delivered by thy bountiful goodness; through thy So Jesus Christ our Lord, who liveth an reigneth with thee and the Holy Ghos one God, world without end. *Amen.*

LESSON. Isaiah 35:3–10

EPISTLE. 2 Peter 3:8–14

GRADUAL

I AM the light of the world : he th followeth me shall not walk in dar ness, but shall have the light of life. The Spirit and the bride say, Come; ar let him that heareth say, Come : and l him that is athirst come.

Alleluia, alleluia. *V.* Even so : com Lord Jesus. Alleluia.

GOSPEL. Matthew 25:1–13

Apostles' Days

INTROIT

I KNOW whom I have believed : and am persuaded that he is able to keep that which I have committed unto him against that day. There is laid up for me a crown of righteousness : which the Lord, the righteous Judge, shall give me. *Ps.* O Lord, thou hast searched me and known me : thou knowest my downsitting and mine uprising. Glory be to the Father . . .

GRADUAL

THEIR sound went forth through the earth : and their words to the e of the world. *V.* The heavens declare t glory of God : and the firmament sho eth his handiwork.

Alleluia, alleluia. *V.* I have chos you, and ordained you : that ye should and bring forth fruit, and that your fr should remain. Alleluia.

Evangelists' Days

INTROIT

GO ye into all the world : and preach the gospel to every creature. Their ound went forth through all the earth : nd their words to the end of the world. *'s.* Thy word is a lamp unto my feet : nd a light unto my path. Glory be to ne Father . . .

GRADUAL

THEIR sound went forth through all the earth : and their words to the end of the world. *V.* The heavens declare the glory of God : and the firmament showeth his handiwork.

Alleluia, alleluia. *V.* I have chosen you, and ordained you : that ye should go and bring forth fruit, and that your fruit should remain. Alleluia.

St. Andrew, Apostle

November 30

¶ *For Introit and Gradual see Apostles' Days, p. 106.*

COLLECT

ALMIGHTY God, who didst give such grace unto thy holy Apostle Saint ndrew, that he readily obeyed the callıg of thy Son Jesus Christ, and followed im without delay : Grant unto us all, ıat we, being called by thy holy Word, ıay forthwith give up ourselves obediently to fulfil thy holy commandments; through the same, thy Son, Jesus Christ our Lord, who liveth and reigneth with thee and the Holy Ghost, one God, world without end. *Amen.*

LESSON. Ezekiel 3:16–21

EPISTLE. Romans 10:10–18

GOSPEL. Matthew 4:18–22

St. Thomas, Apostle

December 21

¶ *For Introit and Gradual see Apostles' Days, p. 106.*

COLLECT

ALMIGHTY and everliving God, who hast given to them that believe xceeding great and precious promises : rant us so perfectly, and without all oubt, to believe in thy Son Jesus Christ, ıat our faith in thy sight may never be proved; through the same, thy Son, Jesus Christ our Lord, who liveth and reigneth with thee and the Holy Ghost, one God, world without end. *Amen.*

LESSON. Judges 6:36–40

EPISTLE. Ephesians 1:3–6

GOSPEL. John 20:24–29

The Conversion of St. Paul

January 25

¶ *For Introit and Gradual see Apostles' Days, p. 106.*

COLLECT

O GOD, who didst teach the multitude of the Gentiles by the preachg of blessed Paul the Apostle : Grant us grace, that we, who this day recall his conversion, may by his example be led to thee; through thy Son, Jesus Christ our Lord, who liveth and reigneth with thee and the Holy Ghost, one God, world without end. *Amen.*

LESSON. Jeremiah 1:4–10
EPISTLE. Acts 9:1–22
GOSPEL. Matthew 19:27–29

The Presentation of Our Lord

February 2

INTROIT

WE have thought of thy lovingkindness, O God : in the midst of thy temple. According to thy Name, O God, so is thy praise unto the ends of the earth : thy right hand is full of righteousness. *Ps.* Great is the Lord, and greatly to be praised : in the city of our God, in the mountain of his holiness. Glory be to the Father . . .

COLLECT

ALMIGHTY and everliving God, we humbly beseech thy Majesty, that as thine only-begotten Son was this day presented in the temple in substance of our flesh, so we may be presented unto thee with pure and clean hearts; through the same thy Son, Jesus Christ our Lord, who liveth and reigneth with thee and the Holy Ghost, one God, world without end. *Amen.*

LESSON. Haggai 2:6–9

EPISTLE. 1 Corinthians 1:26–31

GRADUAL

WE have thought of thy lovingkindness, O God : in the midst of thy temple. *V.* According to thy Name, O God: so is thy praise unto the ends of the earth.

Alleluia, alleluia. He shall set up an ensign for the nations : and gather together the dispersed of Judah from the four corners of the earth. Alleluia.

GOSPEL. Luke 2:22–32

St. Matthias, Apostle

February 24

¶ *For Introit and Gradual see Apostles' Days, p. 106.*

COLLECT

ALMIGHTY God, who didst number thy servant Matthias among the twelve Apostles : Grant that thy Church may ever be instructed and guided by faithful and true pastors; through thy Son, Jesus Christ our Lord, who liveth and reigneth with thee and the Holy Ghost, one God, world without end. *Amen.*

LESSON. Isaiah 66:1–2

EPISTLE. Acts 1:15–26

GOSPEL. Matthew 11:25–30

The Annunciation

March 25

INTROIT

ALL the rich among the people shall entreat thy favor : she shall be brought unto the king in raiment of needlework. Her companions shall be brought unto thee : with gladness and rejoicing. *Ps.* My heart is inditing a good matter : I speak of the things which ve made touching the king. Glory be the Father . . .

COLLECT

VE beseech thee, O Lord, pour thy grace into our hearts; that as we ve known the Incarnation of thy Son sus Christ by the message of an angel, by his Cross and Passion we may be ought unto the glory of his Resurrec-n; through the same thy Son, Jesus rist our Lord, who liveth and reigneth th thee and the Holy Ghost, one God, orld without end. *Amen.*

LESSON. Micah 5:2–4

EPISTLE. Philippians 4:4–9

GRADUAL

GRACE is poured into thy lips : therefore God hath blessed thee forever. *V.* Thou lovest righteousness and hatest wickedness : therefore God hath anointed thee.

V. Behold a Virgin shall conceive and bear a Son : and shall call his Name Emmanuel.

GOSPEL. Luke 1:26–38

St. Mark, Evangelist

April 25

¶ *For Introit and Gradual see Evangelists' Days, p. 107.*

COLLECT

) ALMIGHTY God, who hast instructed thy holy Church with the avenly doctrine of thy Evangelists : ve us grace, that, being not like chilen carried away with every blast of ln doctrine, we may be established in : truth of thy holy Gospel; through thy Son, Jesus Christ our Lord, who liveth and reigneth with thee and the Holy Ghost, one God, world without end. *Amen.*

LESSON. Isaiah 55:1–5

EPISTLE. Ephesians 4:7–16

GOSPEL. John 15:1–11

St. Philip and St. James, Apostles

May 1

¶ *For Introit and Gradual see Apostles' Days, p. 106.*

COLLECT

) ALMIGHTY God, whom to know is everlasting life : Grant us per-tly to know thy Son Jesus Christ to the way, the truth, and the life; that lowing his steps we may steadfastly lk in the way that leadeth to eternal life; through the same thy Son, Jesus Christ our Lord, who liveth and reigneth with thee and the Holy Ghost, one God, world without end. *Amen.*

LESSON. Malachi 3:16–18

EPISTLE. Ephesians 2:19–22

GOSPEL. John 14:1–13a

The Nativity of St. John, the Baptist

June 24

INTROIT

THE voice of him that crieth in the wilderness : Prepare ye the way of : Lord, make straight in the desert a ghway for our God. And the glory of the Lord : shall be revealed. *Ps.* It is a good thing to give thanks unto the Lord : and to sing praises unto thy Name, O most High. Glory be to the Father . . .

COLLECT

O LORD God, heavenly Father, who, through thy servant John the Baptist, didst bear witness that Jesus Christ is the Lamb of God which taketh away the sin of the world, and that all who believe in him shall inherit eternal life : We humbly pray thee to enlighten us by thy Holy Spirit that we may at all times find comfort and joy in this witness, continue steadfast in the true faith, and at last with all believers attain unto eternal life; through the same thy Son, Jesus Christ our Lord, who liveth and reigneth with thee and the Holy Ghost, one God, world without end. *Amen.*

LESSON. Malachi 4:4–6

EPISTLE. 1 John 1:1–4

GRADUAL

AND thou, child, shalt be called t prophet of the Highest : for th shalt go before the face of the Lord prepare his ways. *V.* John bare witness him, and cried saying, This was he whom I spake, He that cometh after is preferred before me : for he was b fore me.

Alleluia, alleluia. *V.* Behold the La of God : which taketh away the sin the world. Alleluia.

GOSPEL. Luke 1:57–80

St. Peter and St. Paul, Apostles

June 29

¶ *For Introit and Gradual see Apostles' Days, p. 106.*

COLLECT

O ALMIGHTY God, who by thy Son Jesus Christ didst give to thy holy Apostles many excellent gifts, and commandedst them earnestly to feed thy flock : Make, we beseech thee, all pastors diligently to preach thy holy word, and the people obediently to follow the same, that they may receive the crown of everlasting glory; through thy Son, Jesus Christ our Lord, who liveth and reign with thee and the Holy Ghost, one G world without end. *Amen.*

LESSON. Jeremiah 26:12–16, *or* Isaiah 22:20–23

EPISTLE. Acts 12:1–11, *or* Galatians 1:11–20

GOSPEL. Matthew 16:13–19

The Visitation

July 2

¶ *For Introit and Gradual see The Annunciation, p. 108.*

COLLECT

ALMIGHTY God, who hast dealt wonderfully with thy handmaiden the Virgin Mary, and hast chosen her to be the mother of thy Son, and hast graciously made known that thou regardest the poor and the lowly and the despised : Grant us grace in all humility and meekness to receive thy word with hearty faith, and so to be made one with dear Son, who liveth and reigneth w thee and the Holy Ghost, one G world without end. *Amen.*

LESSON. Judges 13:2–7, *or* Song of Solomon 2:8–14

EPISTLE. 1 Peter 3:1–5a

GOSPEL. Luke 1:39–47

St. James the Elder, Apostle

July 25

¶ *For Introit and Gradual see Apostles' Days, p. 106.*

COLLECT

) ALMIGHTY God, who hast built thy Church upon the foundation the Apostles and Prophets, Jesus ırist himself being the head cornerɔne : Grant us so to be joined together unity of spirit by their doctrine, that may be made a holy temple acceptaunto thee; through the same thy Son, Jesus Christ our Lord, who liveth and reigneth with thee and the Holy Ghost, one God, world without end. *Amen.*

LESSON. 1 Kings 19:9–18

(*Begin:* "And Elijah came thither . . .")

EPISTLE. 1 Corinthians 4:9–15

GOSPEL. Matthew 20:20–28

The Transfiguration of Our Lord

August 6

¶ *The Propers for this Day shall be used on the Sixth Sunday after the Epiphany; and may used on the last Sunday after the Epiphany, except when there is only one Sunday after the iphany.*

INTROIT

⁻HE lightnings lightened the world : the earth trembled and shook. *Ps.* ɔw amiable are thy tabernacles, O Lord hosts : my soul longeth, yea, even nteth for the courts of the Lord. ory be to the Father . . .

COLLECT

) GOD, who, in the glorious Transfiguration of thy only-begotten n, hast confirmed the mysteries of the th by the testimony of the Fathers, d who, in the voice that came from the ght cloud, didst in a wonderful manforeshow the adoption of sons : ercifully vouchsafe to make us coirs with the King of his glory, and ng us to the enjoyment of the same; through the same thy Son, Jesus Christ our Lord, who liveth and reigneth with thee and the Holy Ghost, one God, world without end. *Amen.*

LESSON. Exodus 34:29–35

EPISTLE. 2 Peter 1:16–21

GRADUAL

THOU art fairer than the children of men : grace is poured into thy lips. *V.* The Lord said unto my Lord, Sit thou at my right hand : until I make thine enemies thy footstool.

Alleluia, alleluia. *V.* Sing unto the Lord, bless his Name; show forth his salvation from day to day: declare his glory among the heathen, his wonders among all people. Alleluia.

GOSPEL. Matthew 17:1–9

St. Bartholomew, Apostle

August 24

¶ *For Introit and Gradual see Apostles' Days, p. 106.*

COLLECT

LMIGHTY God, who hast made the remembrance of thine apostles days of gladness and joy to thy Church : Grant that we may ever love thee whom they loved, and set forth the doctrine which they taught; through thy Son, Jesus Christ our Lord, who liveth and reigneth with thee and the Holy Ghost, one God, world without end. *Amen.*

LESSON. Proverbs 3:1–7

EPISTLE. 1 Corinthians 12:27–31a

GOSPEL. Luke 22:24–30

St. Matthew, Apostle, Evangelist

September 21

¶ *For Introit and Gradual see Apostles' Days,* *p. 106.*

COLLECT

O ALMIGHTY God, who by thy blessed Son didst call Matthew from the receipt of custom to be an Apostle and Evangelist : Grant us grace to forsake all covetous desires and inordinate love of riches, and to follow the same thy Son Jesus Christ, who liveth and reigneth with thee and the Holy Gho[st,] one God, world without end. *Amen.*

LESSON. Ezekiel 1:4–14, *or* Proverbs 30:7–9

EPISTLE. Ephesians 4:7–16

GOSPEL. Matthew 9:9–13

St. Michael and All Angels

September 29

INTROIT

BLESS the Lord, ye his angels, that excel in strength : that do his commandments, hearkening unto the voice of his word. Bless ye the Lord, all ye his hosts : ye ministers of his that do his pleasure. *Ps.* Bless the Lord, O my soul : and all that is within me, bless his holy Name. Glory be to the Father . . .

COLLECT

O EVERLASTING God, who hast ordained and constituted the services of angels and men in a wonderful order : Mercifully grant, that as thy holy angels always do thee service in heaven, so by thy appointment they may succor and defend us on earth; through thy Son, Jesus Christ our Lord, who liveth a[nd] reigneth with thee and the Holy Gho[st,] one God, world without end. *Amen.*

LESSON. 2 Kings 6:8–17

EPISTLE. Revelation 12:7–12

GRADUAL

BLESS the Lord, ye his angels, th[at] excel in strength : that do his co[m]mandments, hearkening unto the vo[ice] of his word. *V.* Bless the Lord, O [my] soul : and all that is within me, bless [his] holy Name.

Alleluia, alleluia. God hath given [his] angels charge over thee : to keep thee [in] all thy ways. Alleluia.

GOSPEL. Matthew 18:1–10

St. Luke, Evangelist

October 18

¶ *For Introit and Gradual see Evangelists' Days,* *p. 107.*

COLLECT

ALMIGHTY God, who didst call Saint Luke the Physician, whose praise is in the Gospel, to be an evangelist a[nd] physician of the soul : Strengthen t[hy] Church, we beseech thee, in a like vo[...]

on, that men may learn the message of thy love, and receive healing for their souls and bodies; through the merits of thy Son, Jesus Christ our Lord, who liveth and reigneth with thee and the Holy Ghost, one God, world without end. *Amen.*

LESSON. Isaiah 35:5–8

EPISTLE. 2 Timothy 4:5–11

GOSPEL. Luke 10:1–9

St. Simon and St. Jude, Apostles

October 28

¶ *For Introit and Gradual see Apostles' Days, p. 106.*

COLLECT

O ALMIGHTY God, who hast built thy Church upon the foundation of the Apostles and Prophets, Jesus Christ himself being the head cornerstone : Grant us so to be joined together in unity of spirit by their doctrine, that we may be made a holy temple acceptable unto thee; through the same thy Son, Jesus Christ our Lord, who liveth and reigneth with thee and the Holy Ghost, one God, world without end. *Amen.*

LESSON. Jeremiah 26:16–19

EPISTLE. 1 Peter 1:3–9

GOSPEL. John 15:17–25

Reformation Day

October 31

¶ *The Sunday preceding October 31 may be observed as Reformation Sunday.*

INTROIT

THE Lord of hosts is with us : the God of Jacob is our refuge. Therefore will not we fear, though the earth be removed : and though the mountains be carried into the midst of the sea. *Ps.* God is our refuge and strength : a very present help in trouble. Glory be to the Father . . .

COLLECT

O LORD God, heavenly Father, pour out, we beseech thee, thy Holy Spirit upon thy faithful people, keep them steadfast in thy grace and truth, protect and comfort them in all temptation, defend them against all enemies of thy Word, and bestow upon Christ's Church militant thy saving grace; through the same thy Son, Jesus Christ our Lord, who liveth and reigneth with thee and the Holy Ghost, one God, world without end. *Amen.*

Or,

ALMIGHTY God, who through the preaching of thy servants, the blessed Reformers, hast caused the light of the Gospel to shine forth : Grant, we beseech thee, that, knowing its saving power, we may faithfully guard and defend it against all enemies, and joyfully proclaim it, to the salvation of souls and the glory of thy holy Name; through thy Son, Jesus Christ our Lord, who liveth and reigneth with thee and the Holy Ghost, one God, world without end. *Amen.*

LESSON. 1 Samuel 3:19–4:1a

EPISTLE. Romans 3:21–28

GRADUAL

GREAT is the Lord, and greatly to be praised : in the city of our God, in the mountain of his holiness. *V.* Walk about Zion : tell the towers thereof. Mark ye well her bulwarks, consider her palaces : that ye may tell it to the generation following.

Alleluia, alleluia. *V.* For this God our God for ever and ever : he will b our guide even unto death. Alleluia.

GOSPEL. John 8:31–36

All Saints' Day

November 1

¶ *The Sunday after November 1 may be observed as All Saints' Sunday.*

INTROIT

THESE are they which came out of great tribulation : and have washed their robes and made them white in the blood of the Lamb. Therefore are they before the throne of God : and serve him day and night in his temple. *Ps.* Rejoice in the Lord, O ye righteous : for praise is comely for the upright. Glory be to the Father . . .

COLLECT

O ALMIGHTY God, who hast knit together thine elect in one communion and fellowship in the mystical body of thy Son, Christ our Lord : Grant us grace so to follow thy blessed Saints in all virtuous and godly living, that we may come to those unspeakable joys which thou hast prepared for those who unfeignedly love thee; through th same Jesus Christ our Lord, who live and reigneth with thee and the Ho Ghost, one God, world without en *Amen.*

LESSON. Deuteronomy 33:1–3

EPISTLE. Revelation 7:2–17

GRADUAL

O FEAR the Lord, ye his saints : f there is no want to them that fe him. *V.* They that seek the Lord : sh not want any good thing.

Alleluia, alleluia. *V.* Come unto m all ye that labor and are heavy lader and I will give you rest. Alleluia.

GOSPEL. Matthew 5:1–12

The Festival of Harvest

INTROIT

O LORD, thou crownest the year with thy goodness : and thy paths drop fatness. Thou visitest the earth and waterest it : thou blessest the springing thereof. *Ps.* Praise waiteth for thee, O God, in Sion : and unto thee shall the vow be performed. Glory be to the Father . . .

COLLECT

ALMIGHTY God, most merciful Father, who openest thine hand, and satisfiest the desire of every living thing : We give thee most humble and hearty thanks that thou hast crowned the fiel with thy blessing, and hast permitted once more to gather in the fruits of t earth; and we beseech thee to bless a protect the living seed of thy word so in our hearts, that in the plenteous fru of righteousness we may always pres to thee an acceptable thank-offeri through thy Son, Jesus Christ our Lo who liveth and reigneth with thee a the Holy Ghost, one God, world with end. *Amen.*

LESSON. Deuteronomy 11:8–21

EPISTLE. Acts 14:11–18

GRADUAL

THE eyes of all wait upon thee : and thou givest them their meat in due ason. *V.* Thou openest thine hand : nd satisfiest the desire of every living ing.

Alleluia, alleluia. *V.* Bless the Lord, O my soul, and all that is within me, bless his holy Name : bless the Lord, O my soul, and forget not all his benefits. Alleluia.

GOSPEL. Luke 12:15–34

A Day of Humiliation and Prayer

INTROIT

HEAR, O heavens, and give ear, O earth, for the Lord hath spoken : I ave nourished and brought up children, d they have rebelled against me. They ave forsaken the Lord, they have pro-ked the Holy One of Israel unto anger : ey are gone away backward. *Ps.* If ou, Lord, shouldest mark iniquities : Lord, who shall stand? Glory be to e Father . . .

COLLECT

ALMIGHTY and most merciful God, our heavenly Father, of whose com-ssion there is no end; who art long-ffering, gracious, and plenteous in odness and truth; forgiving iniquity, nsgression and sin : We have sinned d done perversely, we have sinned and evously offended thee; against thee, e only, have we sinned and done evil thy sight; but, we beseech thee, O Lord, remember not against us former iniquities; let thy tender mercies speedily prevent us, for we are brought very low; help us, O God of our salvation, and purge away our sins, for the glory of thy holy Name, and for the sake of thy dear Son, Jesus Christ our Saviour, who liveth and reigneth with thee and the Holy Ghost, one God, world without end. *Amen.*

LESSON. 1 Samuel 7:3–12

EPISTLE. Acts 3:12–19a

GRADUAL

SEEK ye the Lord while he may be found : call ye upon him while he is near. *V.* Let the wicked forsake his way : and the unrighteous man his thoughts;

V. And let him return unto the Lord, and he will have mercy upon him : and to our God, for he will abundantly pardon.

GOSPEL. Matthew 7:6–12

A Day of General or Special Thanksgiving

INTROIT

ET every thing that hath breath praise the Lord : praise ye the Lord. Praise n for his mighty acts : praise him ac-ding to his excellent greatness. *Ps.* ise ye the Lord. Praise God in his ctuary : praise him in the firmament his power. Glory be to the Father . . .

COLLECT

ALMIGHTY God, our heavenly Father, whose mercies are new unto us every morning, and who, though we have in no wise deserved thy goodness, dost abundantly provide for all our wants of body and soul : Give us, we pray thee, thy Holy Spirit, that we may heartily acknowledge thy merciful goodness toward us, give thanks for all thy benefits, and serve thee in willing obedience; through thy Son, Jesus Christ our Lord, who liveth and reigneth with thee and the Holy Ghost, one God, world without end. *Amen.*

LESSON. Deuteronomy 8:1–20, *or* Isaiah 61:10–11

EPISTLE. 1 Timothy 2:1–8, *or* Acts 14:8–18

GRADUAL

THE eyes of all wait upon thee : an thou givest them their meat in du season. *V.* Thou openest thine hand and satisfiest the desire of every livin thing.

Alleluia, alleluia. *V.* Bless the Lord, my soul, and all that is within me, ble his holy Name : bless the Lord, O m soul, and forget not all his benefit Alleluia.

GOSPEL. Matthew 6:25–33

Graduals for the Seasons

ADVENT

HAROLD W. GILBERT

Let none that wait on thee : be a - shamed.
℣. Show me thy ways, O Lord: teach me thy paths. Al - le -
lu - ia, al - le - lu - ia. ℣. Show us thy mer - cy, O
3
3

Lord: and grant us thy sal - va - tion. Al - le - lu - ia.

CHRISTMAS

HAROLD W. GILBERT

Unison

All the ends of the earth have seen the sal - va - tion of our God:

Harmony

make a joy - ful noise un - to the Lord, all the earth. *V.* The

V. The Lord

Lord hath made known his sal - va - tion: his right-eous-ness hath he

hath made known his sal - va - tion: his

o - pen - ly showed in the sight of the hea - then.
Unison
Harmony
Al - - - - - - - le - lu - ia, al - - - le - lu - ia.
Unison
Harmony
V. O come, let us sing un - to the Lord: let us
wor - ship and bow down. Al - - - le - lu - ia.
Al - - - le - lu - ia.

EPIPHANY

HAROLD W. GILBERT

Bless-ed be the Lord God, the God of Is-ra-el, who on-ly
do-eth won-drous things: and bless-ed be his glo-rious Name for-
ev-er. V. The moun-tains shall bring peace to the peo-ple: and the
lit-tle hills, by right-eous-ness. Al-le-lu-ia, al-le-

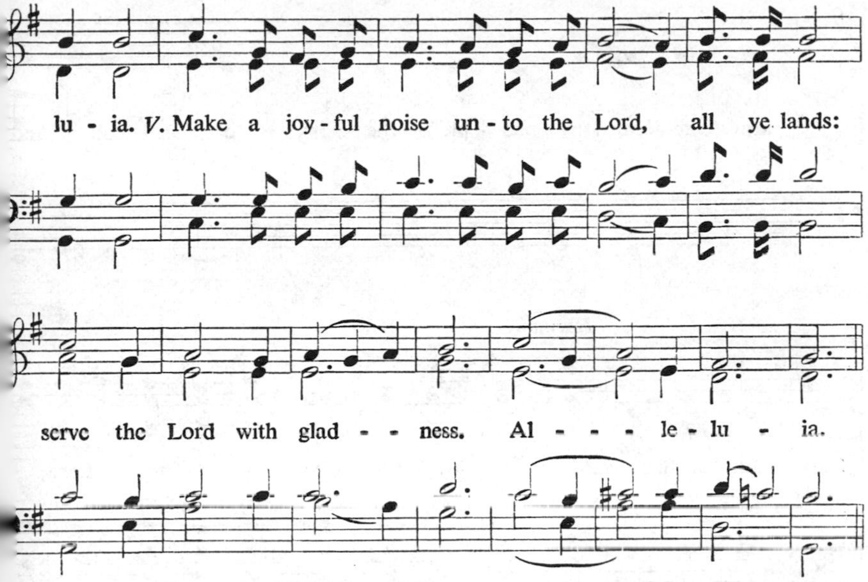

lu - ia. *V.* Make a joy - ful noise un - to the Lord, all ye lands:

serve the Lord with glad - - ness. Al - - - le - lu - ia.

SEPTUAGESIMA TO LENT

HAROLD W. GILBERT

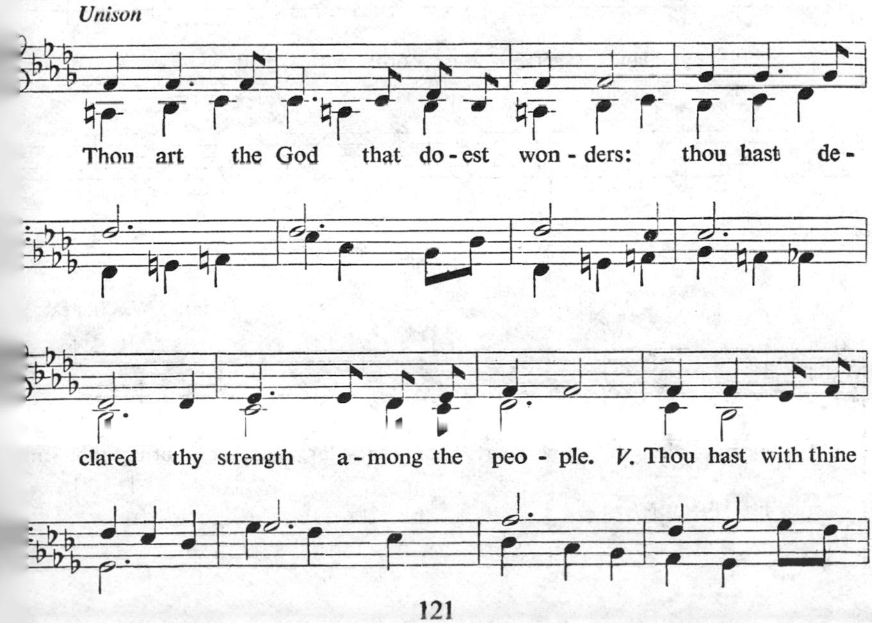

Unison

Thou art the God that do - est won - ders: thou hast de -

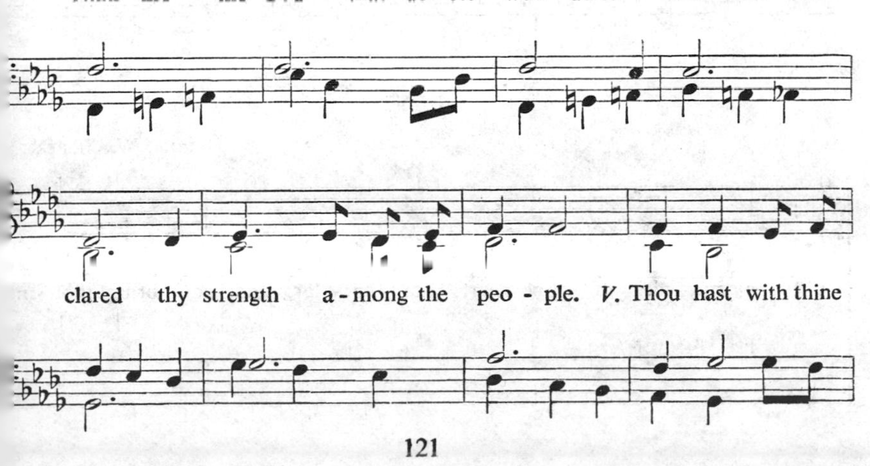
clared thy strength a - mong the peo - ple. V. Thou hast with thine

arm re-deemed thy peo - ple: the sons of Ja - cob and

Harmony

Jo - seph. *Tract.* Make a joy - ful noise un - to the Lord,

all ye lands: serve the Lord with glad - - - ness.

LENT

HAROLD W. GILBERT

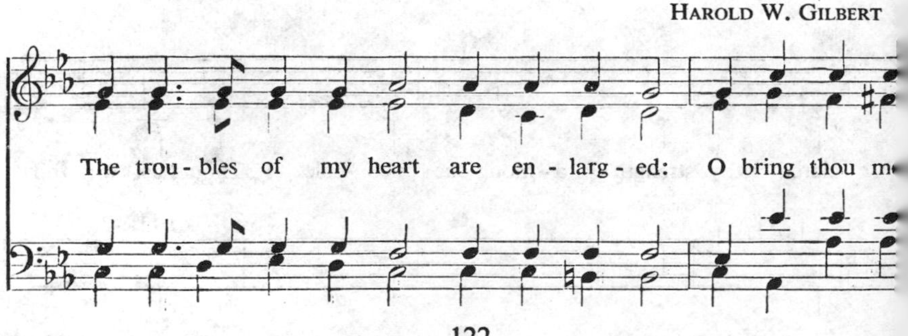
The trou - bles of my heart are en - larg - ed: O bring thou me

out of my dis - tress - es. V. Look up - on mine af -
flic - tion and my pain: and for - give all my sins.
Tract. O give thanks un - to the Lord, for he is good:
for his mer - cy - - en - dur - - eth for - ev - er.
for his mer - cy en - dur - eth for - ev - - - - - - er.

EASTER

HAROLD W. GILBERT

Al - le - lu - ia, al - le - lu - ia. V. The Lord hath sent re-
demp-tion: un - to his peo - ple. Al - le - lu - ia. V. It be-
hoov - ed Christ to suf - fer, and to rise from the dead: and
thus to en - ter in - to his glo - ry. Al - - - - - - le - lu - ia.
3
3
3
3

PENTECOST
HAROLD W. GILBERT
Al - - le - lu - ia, al - - le - lu - ia. V. Thou send - est forth
thy Spir - it, they are cre - a - ted: and thou re - new - est the
face of the earth. Al - le - lu - ia. V. Come, Ho - ly Spir - it,
fill the hearts of the faith - ful: and kin - dle in
3
3

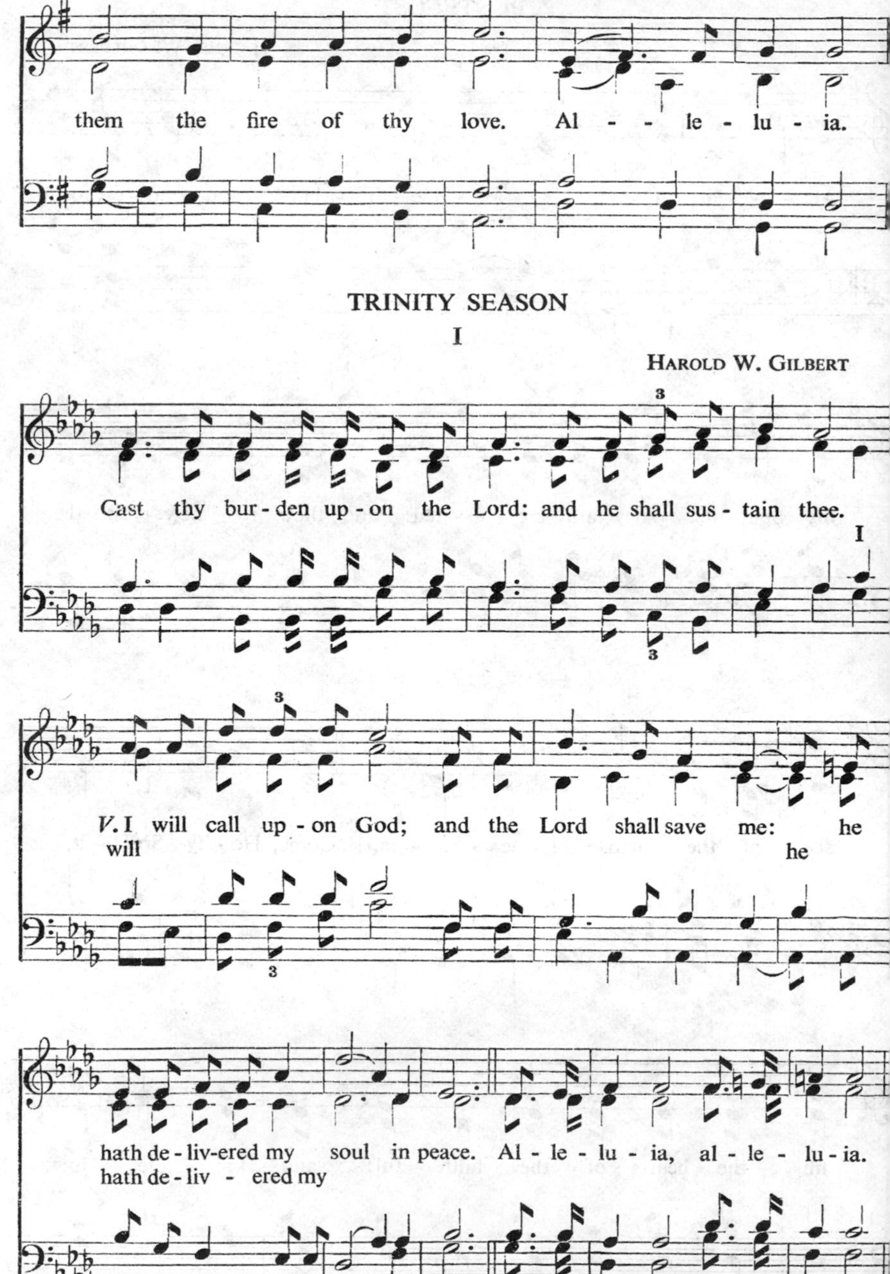
them the fire of thy love. Al - - le - lu - ia.
TRINITY SEASON
I
HAROLD W. GILBERT
Cast thy bur-den up-on the Lord: and he shall sus- tain thee.
V. I will call up-on God; and the Lord shall save me: he will
he
hath de-liv-ered my soul in peace. Al - le - lu - ia, al - le - lu - ia.
hath de-liv - ered my

V. I will love thee, O Lord, my strength: the Lord is my rock, and my
fort-ress, and my de-liv-er-er. Al-le-lu-ia.
TRINITY SEASON
II
HAROLD W. GILBERT
Unison
For-give our sins, O Lord: lest the hea-then say, Where is their God?
Harmony
V. Help us, O God of our sal-va-tion, for the glo-ry

of thy Name: and de - liv - er us. Al - - - le - lu - ia, al - le -
lu - ia. V. The king shall joy in thy strength, O Lord: and in thy sal -
va - tion how great - ly shall he re - joice. Al - - - - le - lu - ia.

Matins

¶ *Intonations provided for the Minister's parts of the Services represent a permissive use. They are not to be considered directive.*

¶ *The Versicles with the Gloria Patri shall be sung or said, the Congregation standing until the end of the Venite.*

¶ *The Alleluia shall be omitted in Lent.*

THE VERSICLES

Organ *Minister* TALLIS

O Lord, open thou my lips.

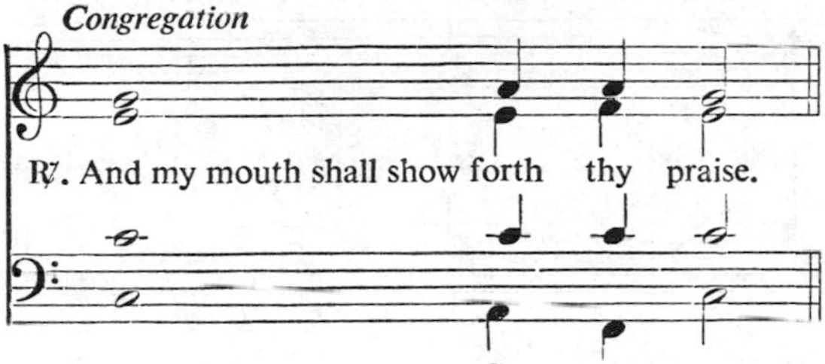

Congregation

℟. And my mouth shall show forth thy praise.

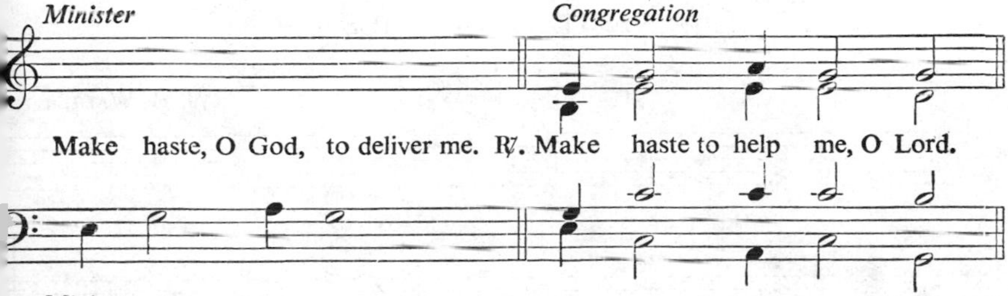

Minister Make haste, O God, to deliver me. *Congregation* ℟. Make haste to help me, O Lord.

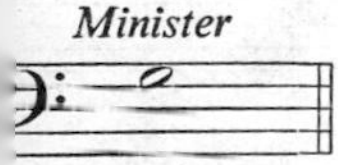

Minister Glory be to the Father, and to the Son, and to the Holy Ghost:

Congregation

℟. As it was in the beginning, is now, and ever shall be, world with-out end. A-men.

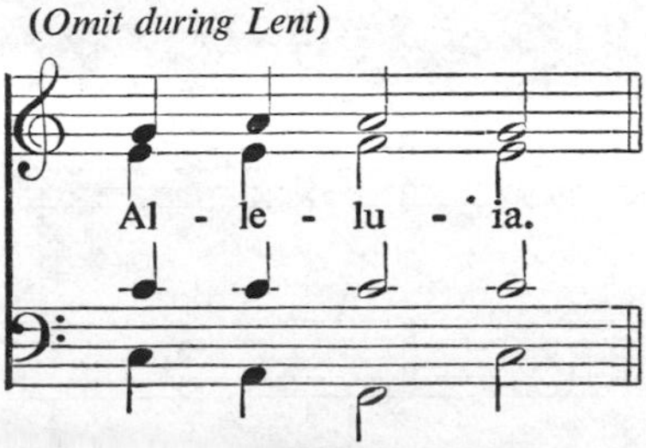

(*Omit during Lent*)

Al - le - lu - ia.

¶ *Then may follow the Invitatory with the Venite.*

THE INVITATORY

Minister

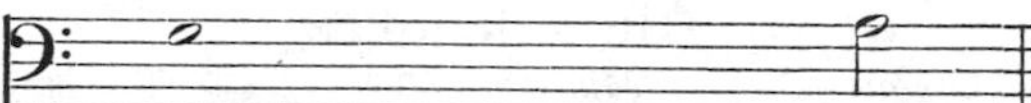
O come, let us worship the Lord.

Congregation

℟. For he is our Ma - ker.

VENITE EXULTEMUS

I

W. H. WALTER

II

W. SAVAGE

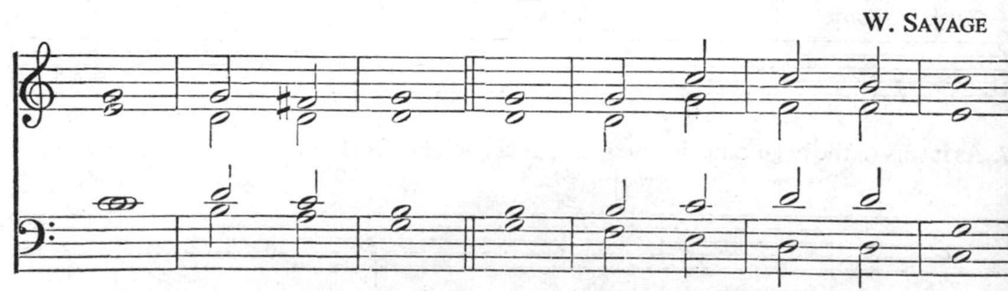

III

W. RUSSELL

O COME, let us ' sing · unto the ' LORD:
* let us make a joyful noise to the ' Rock of ' our sal ' vation.
Let us come before his ' presence with ' thanksgiving:
* and make a joyful ' noise · unto ' him with ' psalms.
For the LORD is a ' great ' God:
* and a great ' King above ' all ' gods.
In his hand are the ' deep places · of the ' earth:
* the strength of the ' hills is ' his ' also.
The sea is ' his and he ' made it:
* and his hands ' formed the ' dry ' land.
O come let us worship, and ' bow ' down:
* let us ' kneel be · fore the ' LORD our ' Maker.
For ' he is our ' God:
* and we are the people of his ' pasture · and the ' sheep of his ' hand.
GLORY ' be to the ' Father:
* and to the ' Son · and to the ' Holy ' Ghost;
As it ' was in · the be ' ginning,
* is now, and ever shall be, ' world without ' end. A ' men.

¶ *Then shall be sung the Hymn.*

THE HYMN

¶ *Then, all standing, shall be sung or said one or more Psalms.*

THE PSALM

¶ *At the end of each Psalm, the Congregation shall sing or say the Gloria Patri.*

GLORIA PATRI

I

HENRY SMART

GLORY ' be to the ' Father:
* and to the ' Son · and to the ' Holy ' Ghost;
As it ' was in · the be ' ginning,
* is now, and ever shall be, ' world without ' end. A ' men.

II

G. A. MacFarren

III

In Lent H. W. Gilbert

Glory ' be to the ' Father:
* and to the ' Son · and to the ' Holy ' Ghost;
As it ' was in · the be ' ginning:
* is now, and ever shall be, ' world without ' end. A ' men.

THE LESSON

¶ *The Lessons shall then be read. After each Lesson shall be sung or said the Response.*

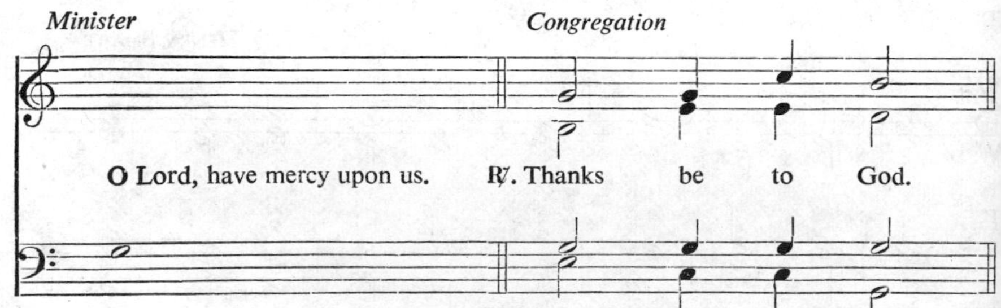
Minister
Congregation
O Lord, have mercy upon us.
℟. Thanks be to God.

¶ *After the Lesson a Responsory or a Hymn may be sung.*

¶ *A brief Sermon or Address may then follow.*

THE CANTICLE

¶ *The Congregation shall rise and sing or say the Canticle.*

TE DEUM LAUDAMUS

I

SYDNEY H. NICHOLSON
Arr. by H. W. G.

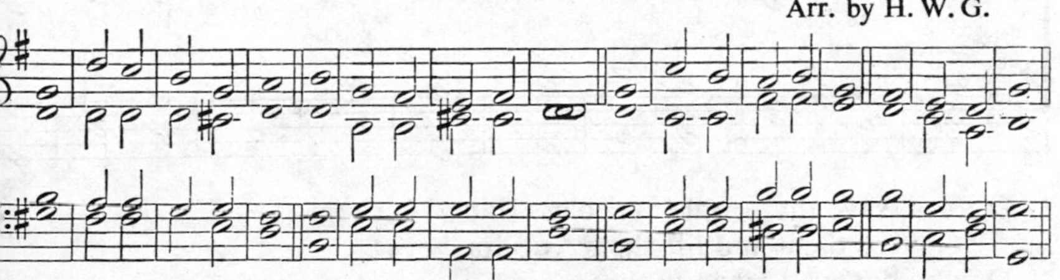

WE ' praise ' thee O ' God: *We acknowledge ' thee to ' be the ' Lord.
All the ' earth doth ' worship ' thee: *The ' Father · ever ' lasting.
To thee all ' angels ' cry a ' loud: *The heavens and ' all the ' powers there ' in.
To thee ' Cheru ' bim and ' Seraphim: *Con ' tinual · ly do ' cry:
Holy, ' holy ' ho - ' ly: *Lord ' God of ' Saba ' oth;
Heaven and ' earth are ' full of the ' Majesty: *Of ' thy ' glory.
The glorious company of the A ' postles ' praise ' thee:
  *The goodly fellowship of the ' Prophets ' praise ' thee:
The ' noble ' army of ' Martyrs: *Praise ' - - ' thee.
The holy Church throughout all the ' world · doth ac ' knowledge ' thee:
  *The ' Father · of an ' infinite ' Majesty:
Thine adorable ' true and ' only ' Son,
  *Also the Holy ' Ghost the ' Comforter.

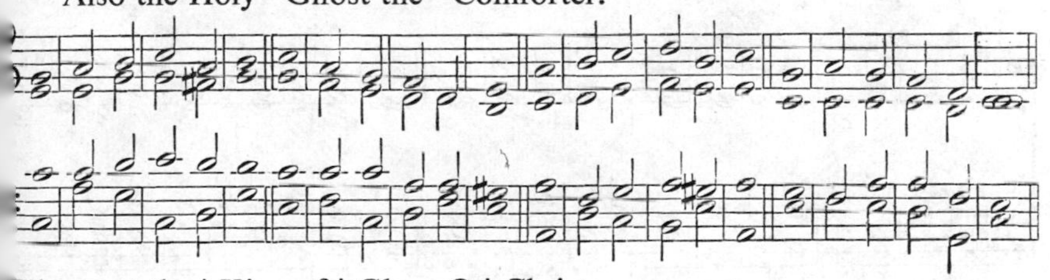

Thou art the ' King of ' Glory O ' Christ;
  *Thou art the ever ' lasting ' Son of the ' Father.
When thou tookest upon thee ' to de ' liver ' man:
  *Thou didst humble thy ' self · to be ' born · of a ' Virgin.
When thou hadst over ' come the ' sharpness of ' death:
  *Thou didst open the kingdom of ' heaven to ' all be ' lievers.
Thou sittest at the ' right ' hand of ' God:
  *In the ' glory ' of the ' Father.
  **We believe that thou shalt ' come to ' be our ' Judge.
We therefore ' pray thee ' help thy ' servants
  *Whom thou hast re ' deemed · with thy ' precious ' Blood.
Make them to be ' numbered ' with thy ' saints
  *In ' glory ' ever ' lasting.

Note: The text of the Te deum laudamus is to be sung continuously to the four parts of chant, with one exception (**)*: here, the text is sung to the fourth part, repeated.*

O Lord, save thy people and bless thine ' heritage.
  *Govern them and lift them ' up for ' ever.
Day by day we ' magnify thee;
  *And we worship thy Name ever ' world without ' end.
Vouchsafe, O ' Lord:
  *To keep us this ' day without ' sin.
O Lord, have mercy up ' on us:
  *Have ' mercy up ' on us.
O Lord, let thy mercy be up ' on us:
  *As our ' trust is in ' thee.
O Lord, in thee have I ' trusted:
  *Let me never ' be con ' founded.

SYDNEY H. NICHOLSON
Arr. by H. W. G.

II

WE ' praise ' thee O ' God: *We acknowledge ' thee to ' be the ' Lord
All the ' earth doth ' worship ' thee: *The ' Father · ever ' lasting.
To thee all ' angels ' cry a ' loud: *The heavens and ' all the ' powers there '
To thee ' Cheru ' bim and ' Seraphim: *Con ' tinual · ly do ' cry:
Holy ' holy ' ho - ' ly: *Lord ' God of ' Saba ' oth;
Heaven and ' earth are ' full of the ' Majesty: *Of ' thy ' glory.
The glorious company of the A ' postles ' praise ' thee:
  *The goodly fellowship of the ' Prophets ' praise ' thee:
The ' noble ' army of ' Martyrs: *Praise ' — ' thee.
The holy Church throughout all the ' world · doth ac ' knowledge ' the
  *The ' Father · of an ' infinite ' Majesty:
Thine adorable ' true and ' only ' Son,
  *Also the Holy ' Ghost the ' Comforter.

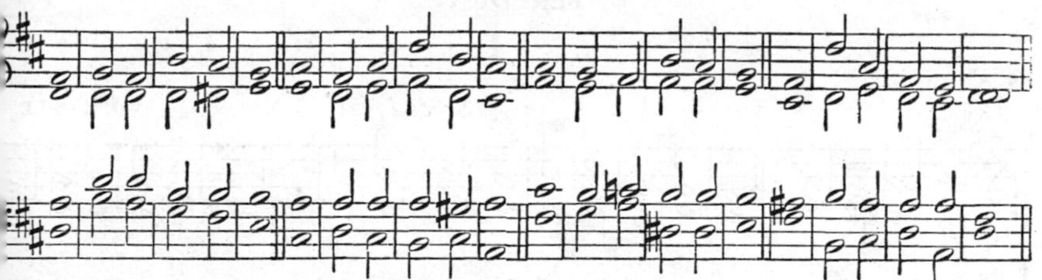

Thou art the ' King of ' Glory O ' Christ;
*Thou art the ever ' lasting ' Son of the ' Father.
When thou tookest upon thee ' to de ' liver ' man:
*Thou didst humble thy ' self · to be ' born · of a ' Virgin.
When thou hadst over ' come the ' sharpness of ' death:
*Thou didst open the kingdom of ' heaven to ' all be ' lievers.
Thou sittest at the ' right ' hand of ' God:
*In the ' glory ' of the ' Father.
**We believe that thou shalt ' come to ' be our ' Judge.
We therefore ' pray thee ' help thy ' servants
*Whom thou hast re ' deemed · with thy ' precious ' Blood.
Make them to be ' numbered ' with thy ' saints
*In ' glory ' ever ' lasting.

(** *repeat last phrase of chant to this verse*)

O Lord, save thy people and bless thine ' heritage.
*Govern them and lift them ' up for ' ever.
Day by day we ' magnify thee;
*And we worship thy Name ever ' world without ' end.
Vouchsafe, O ' Lord:
*To keep us this ' day without ' sin.
O Lord, have mercy up ' on us.
*Have ' mercy up ' on us.
O Lord, let thy mercy be up ' on us:
*As our ' trust is in ' thee.
O Lord, in thee have I ' trusted:
*Let me never ' be con ' founded.

BENEDICTUS

I

Second part
J. TURLE

BLESSED be the Lord ' God of ' Israel:
* for he hath ' visited · and re ' deemed his ' people;
And hath raised up an horn of sal ' vation ' for us:
* in the ' house of his ' servant ' David;
As he spake by the mouth of his ' holy ' prophets:
* which have been ' since the ' world be ' gan;
That we should be ' saved · from our ' enemies:
* and from the ' hand of ' all that ' hate us;
To perform the mercy ' promised · to our ' fathers:
* and to re ' member his ' holy ' covenant;
The oath ' which he ' sware:
* to ' our ' father ' Abraham,
That he would grant unto us, that we, being delivered out of the ' hand of our ' enemies:
* might ' serve him with ' out ' fear,
In holiness and ' righteousness · be ' fore him:
* all the ' days of ' our ' life.
And thou, child, shalt be called the ' prophet · of the ' Highest:
* for thou shalt go before the face of the ' Lord · to pre ' pare his ' w
To give knowledge of salvation unto his people by the re ' mission of · their ' sins:
* through the ' tender ' mercy · of our ' God;

Second Part

Whereby the Dayspring from on ' high hath ' visited us:
* to give light to them that sit in darkness and in the shadow of death, to guide our ' feet · into the ' way of ' peace.
GLORY ' be to the ' Father:
* and to the ' Son · and to the ' Holy ' Ghost;
As it ' was in · the be ' ginning,
* is now and ever shall be ' world without ' end. A ' men.

II

Second part
H. Skeats

ESSED be the Lord ' God of ' Israel:
* for he hath ' visited · and re ' deemed his ' people;
d hath raised up an horn of sal ' vation ' for us:
* in the ' house of his ' servant ' David;
he spake by the mouth of his ' holy ' prophets:
* which have been ' since the ' world be ' gan;
at we should be ' saved · from our ' enemies:
* and from the ' hand of ' all that ' hate us;
perform the mercy ' promised · to our ' fathers:
* and to re ' member his ' holy ' covenant;
e oath ' which he ' sware:
* to ' our ' father ' Abraham,
at he would grant unto us, that we, being delivered out
of the ' hand of our ' enemies:
might ' serve him with ' out ' fear,
holiness and ' righteousness · be ' fore him:
all the ' days of ' our ' life.
d thou, child, shalt be called the ' prophet · of the ' Highest:
for thou shalt go before the face of the ' Lord · to pre ' pare his ' ways;
give knowledge of salvation unto his people by the re ' mission of ·
their ' sins:
through the ' tender ' mercy · of our ' God;

ond Part

ereby the Dayspring from on ' high hath ' visited us:
to give light to them that sit in darkness and in
the shadow of death, to guide our ' feet · into the ' way of ' peace.
ORY ' be to the ' Father:
and to the ' Son · and to the ' Holy ' Ghost;
it ' was in · the be ' ginning,
is now and ever shall be ' world without '
end. A ' men.

THE PRAYER

¶ *Then shall be said the Prayers.*

¶ *The Minister shall sing or say:*

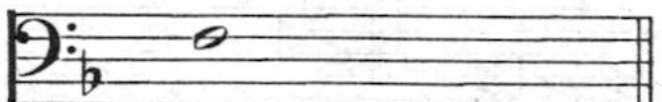

Lord, have mercy upon us.

I

THOMAS TALLIS
Arr. by BARNBY

Congregation

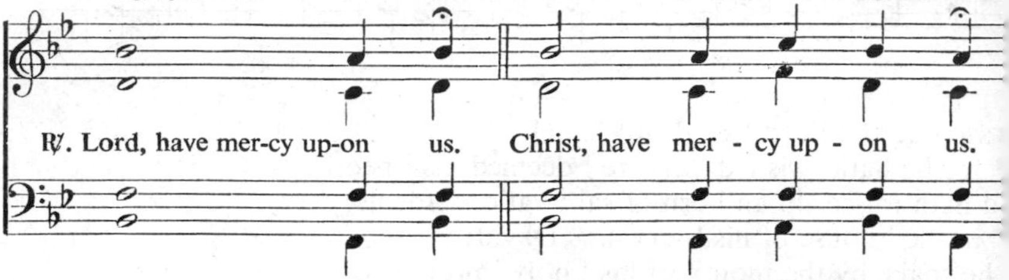

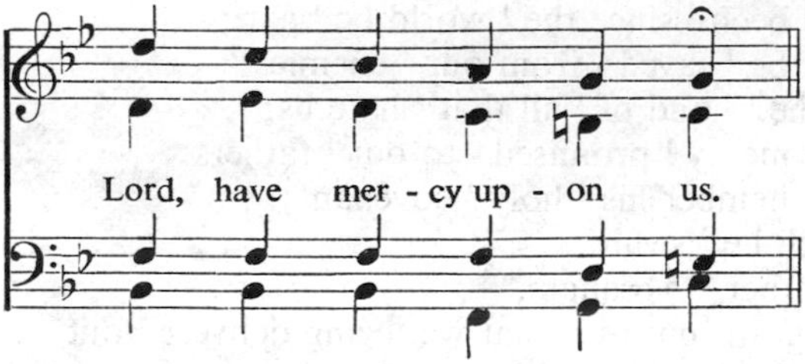

℟. Lord, have mer-cy up-on us. Christ, have mer - cy up - on us.

Lord, have mer - cy up - on us.

II

Congregation. Unison

J. MERBECKE

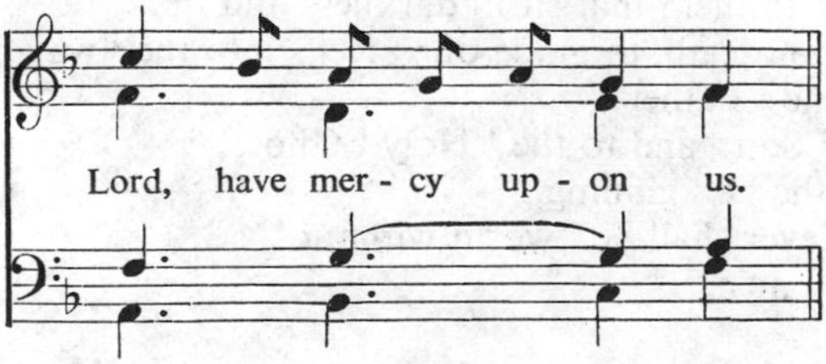

℟. Lord, have mer - cy up - on us. Christ, have mer - cy up - on us.

Lord, have mer - cy up - on us.

¶ *Then shall all say the Lord's Prayer.*

OUR Father, who art in heaven , . . .

¶ *Then may be sung or said:*

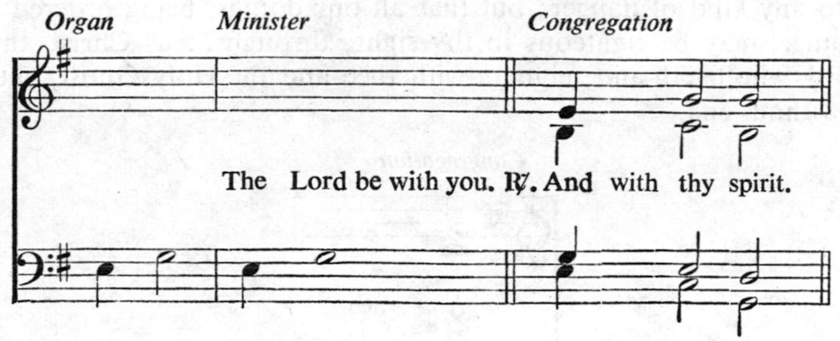
Organ
Minister
Congregation
The Lord be with you. ℟. And with thy spirit.

Minister
Let us pray.

¶ *Then shall be said the Collect for the Day.*

THE COLLECT FOR THE DAY

Congregation
A - men.

¶ *Other Collects may then be said, and after them this Collect for Grace, with which a Versicle may be used.*

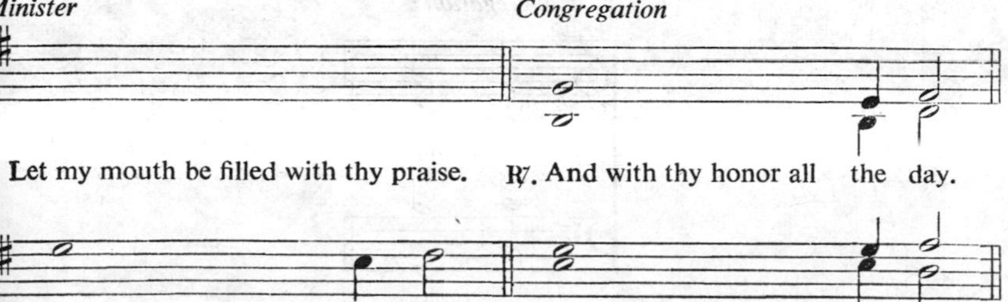
Minister
Congregation
Let my mouth be filled with thy praise. ℟. And with thy honor all the day.

THE COLLECT FOR GRACE

O LORD, our heavenly Father, Almighty and everlasting God, who ha safely brought us to the beginning of this day: Defend us in the sar with thy mighty power; and grant that this day we fall into no sin, neith run into any kind of danger; but that all our doings, being ordered by t governance, may be righteous in thy sight; through Jesus Christ, thy So our Lord, who liveth and reigneth with thee and the Holy Ghost, one Go world without end.

Congregation
A - men.

¶ *Then may be sung or said the Benedicamus.*

Minister
Congregation
Bless we the Lord. ℟. Thanks be to God.

¶ *Then shall the Minister sing or say the Benediction.*

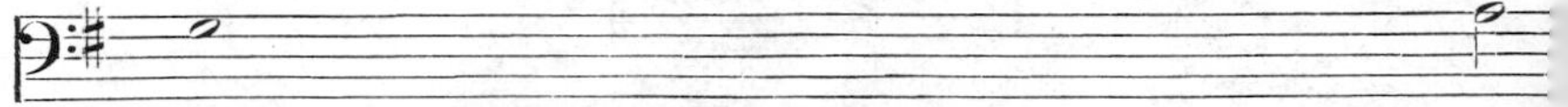

The Grace of our Lord Jesus Christ, and the Love of God, and the Communion of the Holy Ghost, be with you all.

Congregation
A - men.

Vespers

Intonations provided for the Minister's parts of the Services represent a permissive use. They are not to be considered directive.

¶ *The Versicles with the Gloria Patri shall be sung or said, the Congregation standing until the end of the Psalm.*

¶ *The Alleluia shall be omitted in Lent.*

THE VERSICLES

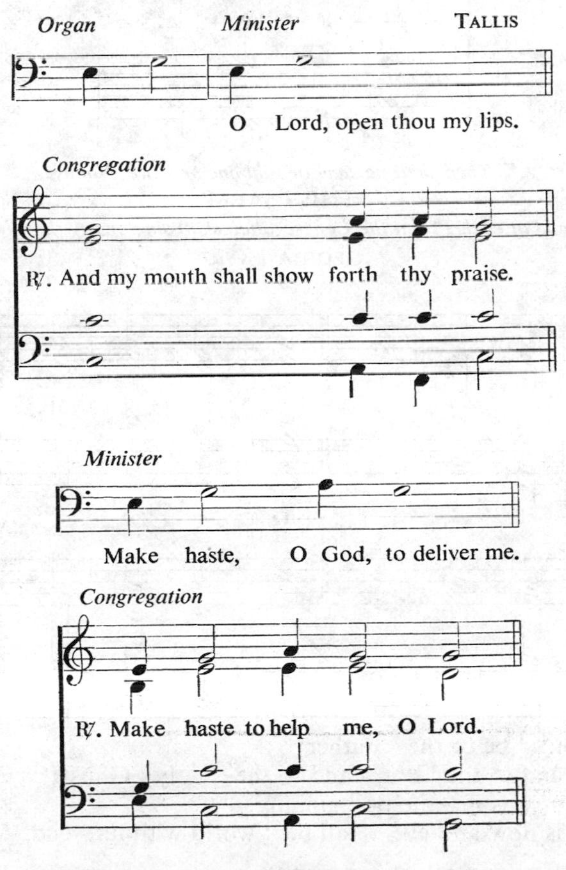

Organ
Minister
TALLIS
O Lord, open thou my lips.
Congregation
℟. And my mouth shall show forth thy praise.
Minister
Make haste, O God, to deliver me.
Congregation
℟. Make haste to help me, O Lord.

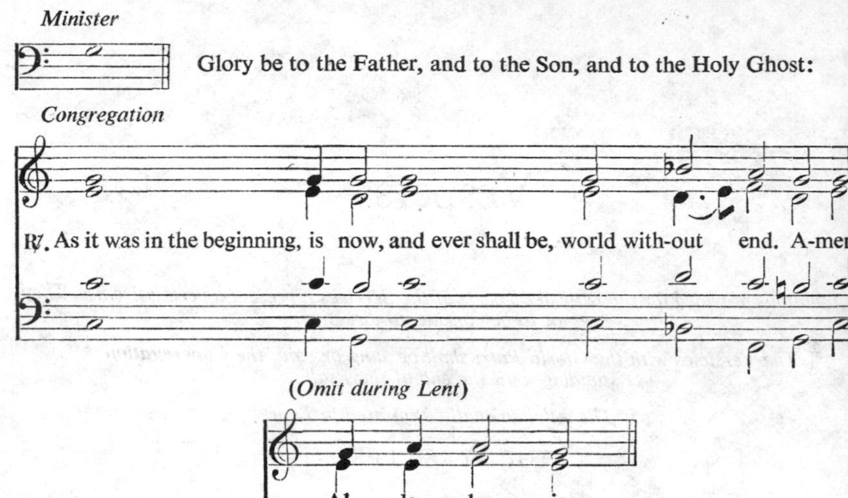
Minister
Glory be to the Father, and to the Son, and to the Holy Ghost:
Congregation
℟. As it was in the beginning, is now, and ever shall be, world with-out end. A-men

(Omit during Lent)

Al - le - lu - ia.

¶ *Then shall be sung or said one or more Psalms.*

THE PSALM

¶ *At the end of each Psalm the Congregation shall sing or say the Gloria Patri.*

GLORIA PATRI

I
S. Arnold
II
V. Novello

Glory ˈ be to the ˈ Father:
    * and to the ˈ Son · and to the ˈ Holy ˈ Ghost;
As it ˈ was in · the be ˈ ginning:
    * is now and ever shall be, ˈ world without ˈ end. A ˈ men.

III

(*In Lent*) H. W. GILBERT

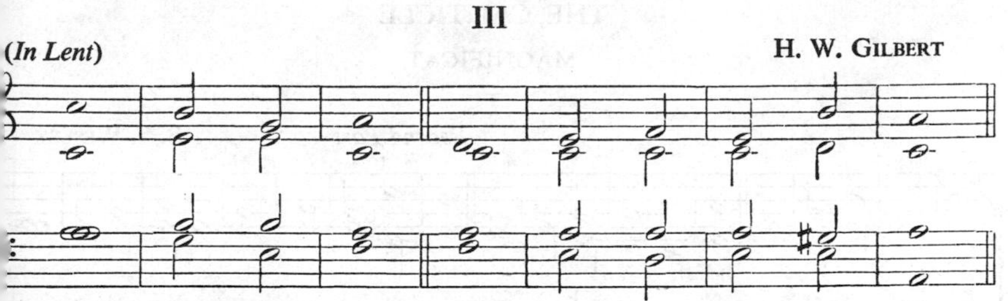

GLORY ' be to the ' Father:
 * and to the ' Son · and to the ' Holy ' Ghost;
As it ' was in · the be ' ginning:
 * is now and ever shall be, ' world without ' end. A ' men.

THE LESSON

¶ *The Lessons shall then be read. After each Lesson shall be sung or said the Response.*

Minister *Congregation*

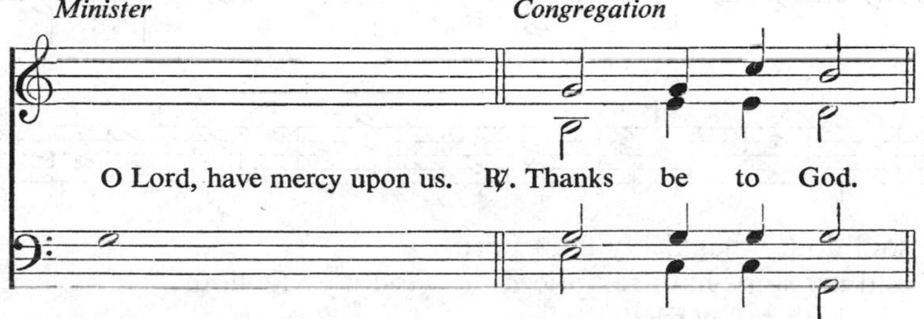
O Lord, have mercy upon us. ℟. Thanks be to God.

¶ *After the Lesson a Responsory or a Hymn may be sung.*
¶ *A Sermon or a brief Address may then follow.*
¶ *The Offering may then be received and placed upon the Altar.*
¶ *Then shall be sung the Hymn.*

THE HYMN

¶ *The Congregation shall rise and sing or say the Canticle.*
¶ *A Versicle shall be used with the Canticle.*

Minister

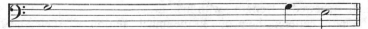

Let my prayer be set forth before thee as in - cense.

Congregation

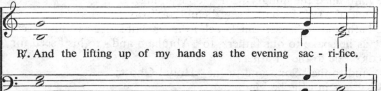

℟. And the lifting up of my hands as the evening sac - ri-fice.

THE CANTICLE

MAGNIFICAT

I

Second Part S. S. WESLEY

II

Second Part S. ELVEY

MY soul doth ' magni · fy the ' Lord,
* and my spirit hath re ' joiced in ' God my ' Saviour.
For ' he hath re ' garded
* the ' low es ' tate of his ' handmaiden.
For be ' hold from ' henceforth
* all gener ' ations shall ' call me ' blessed.
For he that is mighty hath done to me ' great ' things;
* and ' holy ' is his ' Name.

Repeat second part of Chant for following verse only:

And his mercy is on ' them that ' fear him
* from gener ' ation to ' gener ' ation.
He hath shewed ' strength · with his ' arm;
* he hath scattered the proud in the imagi ' nation of ' their ' hearts.
He hath put down the ' mighty · from their ' seats,
* and exalted ' them of ' low de ' gree.
He hath filled the hungry with ' good ' things;
* and the rich he hath ' sent ' empty a ' way.
He hath holpen his servant Israel, in re ' membrance · of his ' mercy;
* as he spake to our fathers, to ' Abraham and · to his ' seed for ' e
GLORY ' be to the ' Father:
* and to the ' Son · and to the ' Holy ' Ghost;
As it ' was in · the be ' ginning,
* is now and ever shall be ' world without ' end. A ' men.

NUNC DIMITTIS

I

J. Goss

II

C. H. Stewart

Lord, now lettest thou thy servant de ' part in ' peace:
 * ac ' cording to ' thy ' word;
For mine eyes have ' seen thy sal ' vation:
 * which thou hast prepared before the ' face of ' all ' people;
A light to ' lighten the ' Gentiles:
 * and the ' glory · of thy ' people ' Israel.
Glory ' be to the ' Father,
 * and to the ' Son · and to the ' Holy ' Ghost;
As it ' was in · the be ' ginning,
 * is now, and ever shall be, ' world without ' end. A ' men.

THE PRAYER

¶ *Then shall be said the Prayers.*

¶ *The Minister shall sing or say:*

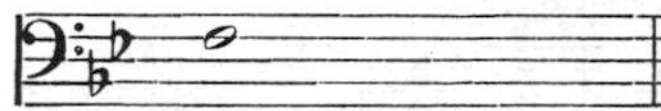

Lord, have mercy upon us.

THOMAS TALLIS
Arr. by BARNBY

Congregation

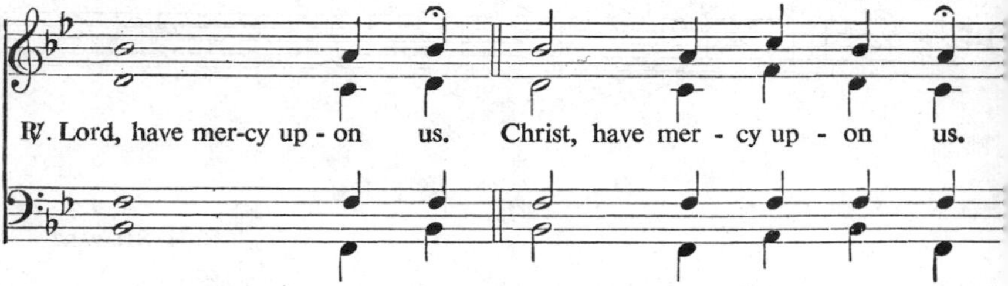

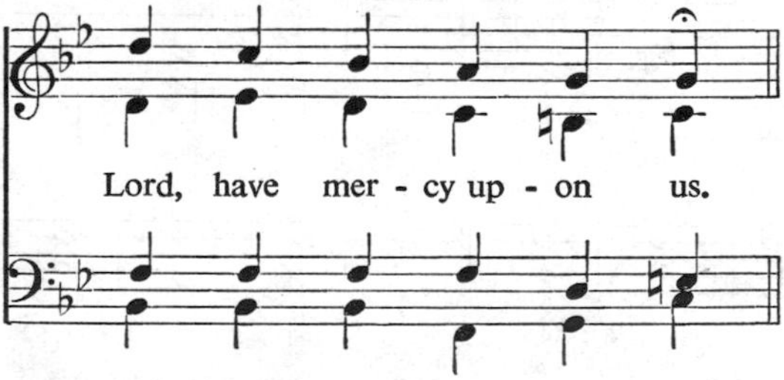

℟. Lord, have mer-cy up - on us. Christ, have mer - cy up - on us.

Lord, have mer - cy up - on us.

Or,

Congregation. Unison

J. MERBECKE

℟. Lord, have mer - cy up - on us. Christ, have mer - cy up - on us.

Lord, have mer - cy up - on us.

¶ *Then shall all say the Lord's Prayer.*

OUR Father, who art in heaven, . . .

¶ *Then may be sung or said:*

Organ *Minister* *Congregation*

The Lord be with you. ℟. And with thy spirit.

(*When the Collect is intoned.*)

Minister

Let us pray.

¶ *Then shall be said the Collect for the Day.*

THE COLLECT FOR THE DAY

Congregation

A - men.

¶ *Other Collects may then be said, and after them this Collect for Peace, with which a Versicle may be used.*

Minister

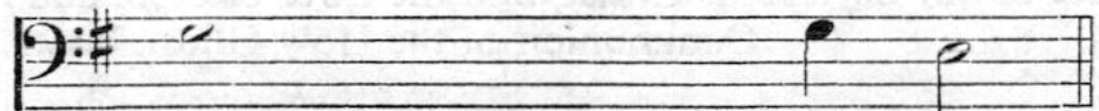

The Lord will give strength unto his peo - ple.

Congregation

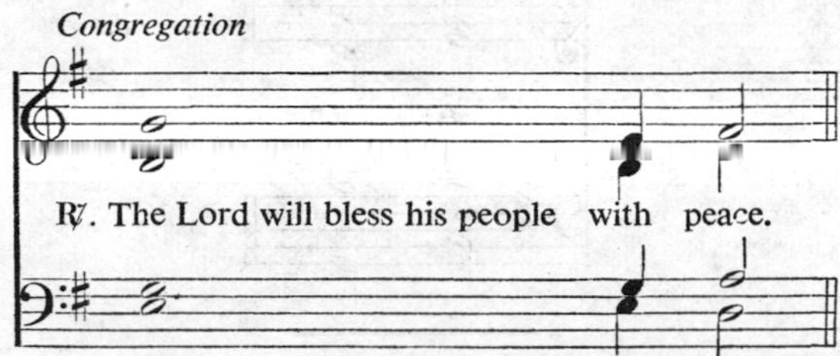
℟. The Lord will bless his people with peace.

COLLECT FOR PEACE

O GOD, from whom all holy desires, all good counsels, and all just work do proceed: Give unto thy servants that peace which the world cann give; that our hearts may be set to obey thy commandments, and also th by thee, we, being defended from the fear of our enemies, may pass our tim in rest and quietness; through the merits of Jesus Christ our Saviour, wh liveth and reigneth with thee and the Holy Ghost, one God, world witho end.

A - men.

¶ *Then may be sung or said the Benedicamus.*

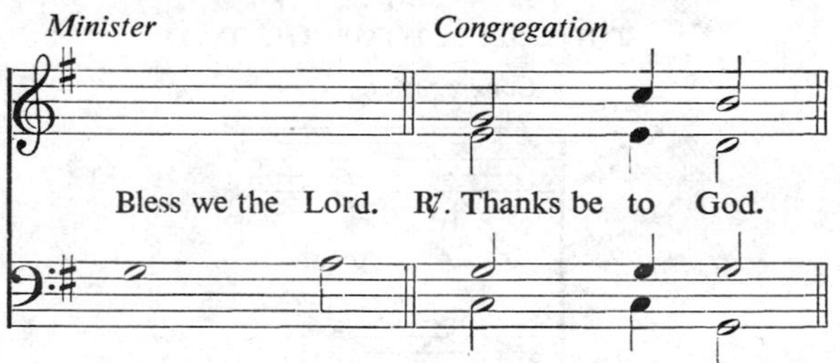
Minister
Congregation
Bless we the Lord. R̸. Thanks be to God.

¶ *Then shall the Minister sing or say the Benediction.*

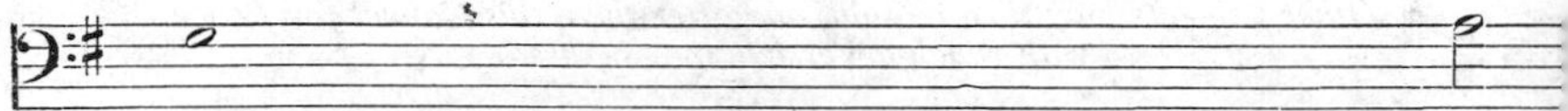

The Grace of our Lord Jesus Christ, and the Love of God, and the Communion of the Holy Ghost, be with you all.

A - men.

Invitatories, Antiphons and Responsories

Advent

INVITATORY

BEHOLD, the King cometh : O come, let us worship him.

ANTIPHONS

Behold, the Name of the Lord cometh rom far : and let the whole earth be filled with his glory.

Come, O Lord, and make no tarrying : oosen the bonds of thy people Israel.

Rejoice greatly, O Jerusalem : behold, hy King cometh.

Behold, the Lord shall come, and all is saints with him : and in that day the ight shall be great. Alleluia.

RESPONSORY

BEHOLD, the days come, saith the Lord, that I will raise unto David a righteous Branch, and a King shall reign and prosper, and shall execute judgment and justice in the earth. And this is his Name whereby he shall be called, The Lord our Righteousness.

V. In his days shall Judah be saved, and Israel shall dwell safely.

And this is his Name whereby he shall be called, The Lord our Righteousness.

Glory be to the Father, and to the Son, and to the Holy Ghost.

And this is his Name whereby he shall be called, The Lord our Righteousness.

Christmas

INVITATORY

UNTO us the Christ is born : O come, let us worship him.

ANTIPHONS

The Lord hath said unto me : Thou rt my Son, this day have I begotten hee.

The Lord hath sent redemption unto is people : he hath commanded his ovenant forever.

Of the fruit of thy body : will I set pon thy throne.

Christ the Lord, our Saviour, ever-asting God and Mary's Son : we praise hee evermore.

RESPONSORY

THE Word was made flesh and dwelt among us. And we beheld his glory, the glory as of the only-begotten of the Father, full of grace and truth.

V. In the beginning was the Word, and the Word was with God, and the Word was God.

And we beheld his glory, the glory as of the only-begotten of the Father, full of grace and truth.

Glory be to the Father, and to the Son, and to the Holy Ghost.

And we beheld his glory, the glory as of the only-begotten of the Father, full of grace and truth.

Epiphany

INVITATORY

CHRIST hath appeared unto us : O come, let us worship him.

ANTIPHONS

Give unto the Lord glory and strength : worship the Lord in the beauty of holiness.

The Lord hath made known his Word, alleluia : the Word of his salvation. Alleluia, alleluia.

A light to lighten the Gentiles : and the glory of thy people Israel.

We have seen his star in the east : and are come to worship him.

RESPONSORY

ARISE, shine, for thy light is come, and the glory of the Lord is risen upon thee.

V. And the Gentiles shall come to thy light, and kings to the brightness of thy rising.

And the glory of the Lord is risen upon thee.

Glory be to the Father, and to the Son and to the Holy Ghost.

And the glory of the Lord is risen upon thee.

Lent

ANTIPHONS

Man shall not live by bread alone : but by every word that proceedeth out of the mouth of God.

Behold, now is the accepted time : behold, now is the day of salvation.

The kings of the earth set themselves, and the rulers take counsel together : against the Lord and against his Anointed.

He was oppressed, and he was afflicted, yet he opened not his mouth : and the Lord hath laid on him the iniquity of us all.

RESPONSORY

HE was brought as a lamb to the slaughter, he was oppressed and he was afflicted, yet he opened not his mouth; he was delivered up to death that he might quicken his people.

V. In Salem also is his tabernacle, and his dwelling place in Zion.

He was delivered up to death, that he might quicken his people.

Easter

INVITATORY

THE Lord is risen indeed : Alleluia.

ANTIPHONS

Alleluia, alleluia, alleluia.

I laid me down and slept; I awaked : for the Lord sustained me. Alleluia, alleluia.

Alleluia. The Lord is risen. Alleluia : as he said unto you. Alleluia, alleluia.

Alleluia. Abide with us, for it is toward evening : and the day is far spent. Alleluia, alleluia.

RESPONSORY

CHRIST being raised from the dead dieth no more; death hath no more dominion over him. In that he liveth, he liveth unto God. Alleluia, alleluia.

V. Christ was delivered for our offences and raised again for our justification.

In that he liveth, he liveth unto God. Alleluia, alleluia.

Glory be to the Father, and to the Son and to the Holy Ghost.

In that he liveth, he liveth unto God. Alleluia, alleluia.

Propers for Matins and Vespers

Ascension Day

INVITATORY

ALLELUIA. The King ascendeth into heaven : O come, let us worship him. Alleluia.

ANTIPHONS

If I go not away, the Comforter will not come unto you : but if I depart, I will send him unto you. Alleluia.

Alleluia. Christ hath ascended up on high, alleluia : and hath led captivity captive. Alleluia, alleluia.

I ascend unto my Father and your Father: and to my God and your God. Alleluia.

RESPONSORY

GO ye into all the world, and preach the Gospel. Alleluia. He that believeth and is baptized shall be saved. Alleluia, alleluia.

V. In the Name of the Father, and of the Son, and of the Holy Ghost.

He that believeth and is baptized, shall be saved. Alleluia, alleluia.

Glory be to the Father, and to the Son, and to the Holy Ghost.

He that believeth and is baptized, shall be saved. Alleluia, alleluia.

Pentecost

INVITATORY

ALLELUIA. The Spirit of the Lord filleth the world : O come, let us worship him. Alleluia.

ANTIPHONS

Come, Holy Ghost, and fill the hearts of thy faithful people, and kindle in them the fire of thy love : thou, who through divers tongues gatherest together the nations in the unity of the faith. Alleluia, alleluia.

Thou sendest forth thy Spirit, they are created : and thou renewest the face of the earth. Alleluia, alleluia.

I will not leave you comfortless. Alleluia : I will come to you, and your heart shall rejoice. Alleluia.

RESPONSORY

AND there appeared unto the Apostles cloven tongues, like as of fire. Alleluia. And the Holy Ghost sat upon each of them. Alleluia, alleluia.

V. And they began to speak with other tongues the wonderful works of God.

And the Holy Ghost sat upon each of them. Alleluia, alleluia.

Glory be to the Father, and to the Son, and to the Holy Ghost.

And the Holy Ghost sat upon each of them. Alleluia, alleluia.

Trinity Sunday

INVITATORY

THE true God, One in Three and Three in One : O come, let us worship him.

ANTIPHONS

Unto thee do we call, thee do we praise, thee do we worship : O Blessed Trinity.

Glory be to thee, co-equal Trinity : one God before all worlds began, and now, and for evermore.

Holy, holy, holy, Lord God Almighty: which was, and is, and is to come.

RESPONSORY

WE bless the Father, and the Son, and the Holy Ghost. Praise him and magnify him forever.

V. Blessed art thou, O Lord, in the firmament of heaven, and above all to be praised and glorified forever.

Praise him and magnify him forever.

Glory be to the Father, and to the Son, and to the Holy Ghost.

Praise him and magnify him forever.

Apostles' and Evangelists' Days

RESPONSORY

TAKE my yoke upon you, saith the Lord, and learn of me, for I am meek and lowly of heart; and ye shall find rest unto your souls.

V. For my yoke is easy and my burden is light. And ye shall find rest unto your souls.

Glory be to the Father, and to the Son, and to the Holy Ghost.

And ye shall find rest unto your souls.

The Presentation of Our Lord

¶ *The proper Responsory for this Day is:* The Word was made flesh. . ., *p. 149.*

The Annunciation

RESPONSORY

THEN said Mary unto the angel : Behold the handmaid of the Lord : be it unto me according to thy word.

V. The Holy Ghost shall come upon thee. And when the angel thus made answer, Mary said:

Be it unto me according to thy word

Glory be to the Father, and to the Son and to the Holy Ghost.

Be it unto me according to thy word

The Visitation

¶ *The proper Responsory for this Day is:* The Word was made flesh. . ., *p. 149.*

Reformation Day

ANTIPHON

I will speak of thy testimonies also before kings : and will not be ashamed.

RESPONSORY

FOREVER, O Lord, thy word is settled in heaven. Lord, I have loved the habitation of thy house, and the place where thine honor dwelleth.

V. Thy word is a lamp unto my feet and a light unto my path.

Lord, I have loved the habitation of thy house, and the place where thine honor dwelleth.

Glory be to the Father, and to the Son and to the Holy Ghost.

Lord, I have loved the habitation of thy house, and the place where thine honor dwelleth.

The Suffrages

The General Suffrages

¶ *The General Suffrages may be said at Matins or Vespers immediately following the Canticle.*

LORD, have mercy upon us.
℟. Lord, have mercy upon us.
Christ, have mercy upon us.
℟. Christ, have mercy upon us.
Lord, have mercy upon us.
℟. Lord, have mercy upon us.

¶ *Then shall the Minister say:*

OUR Father, who art in heaven, Hallowed be thy Name, Thy kingdom come, Thy will be done, on earth as it is in heaven. Give us this day our daily bread; And forgive us our trespasses, as we forgive those who trespass against us; And lead us not into temptation:
℟. But deliver us from evil.

I SAID, O Lord, be merciful unto me:
℟. Heal my soul; for I have sinned against thee.
Return, O Lord, how long?
℟. And let it repent thee concerning thy servants.
Let thy mercy, O Lord, be upon us:
℟. According as we hope in thee.
Let thy priests be clothed with righteousness:
℟. And let thy saints shout for joy.
O Lord, save our rulers:
℟. Let the King hear us when we call.
Save thy people, and bless thine inheritance:
℟. Feed them also, and lift them up for ever.
Remember thy congregation:
℟. Which thou hast purchased of old.
Peace be within thy walls:
℟. And prosperity within thy palaces.
Let us pray for our absent brethren:
℟. O thou our God, save thy servants that trust in thee.
Let us pray for the broken-hearted and the captives:
℟. Redeem Israel, O God, out of all his troubles.
Send them help from the sanctuary:
℟. And strengthen them out of Zion.
Hear my prayer, O LORD:
℟. And let my cry come unto thee.

¶ *At Matins may then be said responsively the Psalm (130), De profundis; and at Vespers may be said the Psalm (51), Miserere mei, Deus, secundum.*
¶ *Then shall be said:*

TURN us again, O God of hosts:
℟. Cause thy face to shine, and we shall be saved.
Arise, O Christ, for our help:
℟. And redeem us, for thy mercy's sake.
Hear my prayer, O LORD:
℟. And let my cry come unto thee.
The Lord be with you.
℟. And with thy spirit.
Let us pray.

¶ *Then shall the Minister say the Collect for the Day, after which he may say any other suitable Collects, ending with this Collect for Peace.*

O LORD, let there be peace in thy strength:
℟. And abundance in thy towers.

O GOD, from whom all holy desires, all good counsels, and all just works do proceed: Give unto thy servants that peace, which the world cannot give; that our hearts may be set to obey thy commandments, and also that by thee, we, being defended from the fear of our enemies, may pass our time in rest and quietness; through the merits of Jesus Christ our Saviour, who liveth and reigneth with thee and the Holy Ghost, one God, world without end. *Amen.*

¶ *Then may be said the Benedicamus.*

Bless we the Lord.
℟. Thanks be to God.

¶ *Then shall be said the Benediction.*

THE Grace of our Lord Jesus Chris and the Love of God, and the Com munion of the Holy Ghost, be with yo all. *Amen.*

The Morning Suffrages

¶ *The Morning Suffrages may be said at Matins, or in the Morning Prayer of the Househol or alone as a brief Office.*

¶ *When said at Matins, the Morning Suffrages shall immediately follow the Canticle.*

¶ *When used as a special Office, the Morning Suffrages shall begin:* In the Name o the Father, and of the Son, and of the Holy Ghost. ℟. Amen.

LORD, have mercy upon us.
℟. Lord, have mercy upon us.
Christ, have mercy upon us.
℟. Christ, have mercy upon us.
Lord, have mercy upon us.
℟. Lord, have mercy upon us.

¶ *Then shall all say the Lord's Prayer and the Apostles' Creed.*

OUR Father, who art in heaven, . . .

I BELIEVE . . .

¶ *When the Morning Suffrages are used as a special Office, here shall follow the Psalm, the Lesson, and the Hymn.*

¶ *Then shall the Minister say:*

UNTO thee have I cried, O LORD:
℟. And in the morning shall my prayer come before thee.
Let my mouth be filled with thy praise:
℟. And with thy honor all the day.
O Lord, hide thy face from my sins:
℟. And blot out all mine iniquities.
Create in me a clean heart, O God:
℟. And renew a right spirit within me.
Cast me not away from thy presence:
℟. And take not thy Holy Spirit from me.
Restore unto me the joy of thy salva tion:
℟. And uphold me with thy fre Spirit.
Vouchsafe, O Lord, this day:
℟. To keep us without sin.
Have mercy upon us, O Lord:
℟. Have mercy upon us.
O Lord, let thy mercy be upon us:
℟. As our trust is in thee.
Hear my prayer, O LORD:
℟. And let my cry come unto the

The Lord be with you.
℟. And with thy spirit.
Let us pray.

¶ *Then shall be said the Collect for the Da and any other suitable Collects; after whic may be said the Prayer here following.*

WE give thanks to thee, heaven Father, through Jesus Christ, th dear Son, that thou hast protected u through the night from all danger an harm; and we beseech thee to preserv and keep us, this day also, from all si and evil; that in all our thoughts, wor and deeds, we may serve and please the Into thy hands we commend our bodi and souls, and all that is ours. Let th holy angel have charge concerning u that the wicked one have no power ov us. *Amen.*

Then may be said the Benedicamus.

Bless we the Lord.
℟. Thanks be to God.

When the Morning Suffrages are said as a pecial Office, the following Blessing may be aid.

MAY the Lord Almighty dispose our days and our deeds in his peace. *men.*

¶ *At Matins shall be said this Benediction.*

THE Grace of our Lord Jesus Christ, and the Love of God, and the Communion of the Holy Ghost, be with you all. *Amen.*

The Evening Suffrages

The Evening Suffrages may be said at Vespers, or in the Evening Prayer of the Household, or alone as a brief Office.
When said at Vespers, the Evening Suffrages shall immediately follow the Canticle.
When used as a special Office, the Evening Suffrages shall begin: In the Name of the Father, and of the Son, and of the Holy Ghost. ℟. Amen.

ORD, have mercy upon us.
℟. Lord, have mercy upon us.
Christ, have mercy upon us.
℟. Christ, have mercy upon us.
Lord, have mercy upon us.
℟. Lord, have mercy upon us.

Then shall all say the Lord's Prayer and e Apostles' Creed.

OUR Father, who art in heaven, . . .

BELIEVE . . .

When the Evening Suffrages are used as special Office, here shall follow the Psalm, e Lesson, and the Hymn.

Then shall the Minister say:

BLESSED art thou, O Lord God of our fathers:
℟. And greatly to be praised and orified forever.
Bless we the Father, and the Son, and e Holy Ghost:
℟. We praise and magnify him forer.
Blessed art thou, O Lord, in the firmaent of heaven:
℟. And greatly to be praised, and orified, and highly exalted forever.

The Almighty and merciful Lord, bless and preserve us.
℟. Amen.
Vouchsafe, O Lord, this night:
℟. To keep us without sin.
O Lord, have mercy upon us:
℟. Have mercy upon us.
O Lord, let thy mercy be upon us:
℟. As our trust is in thee.
Hear my prayer, O LORD:
℟. And let my cry come unto thee.

The Lord be with you.
℟. And with thy spirit.
Let us pray.

¶ *Then shall be said the Collect for the Day, and any other suitable Collects; after which may be said the Prayer here following.*

WE give thanks unto thee, heavenly Father, through Jesus Christ, thy dear Son, that thou hast this day so graciously protected us; and we beseech thee to forgive us all our sins, and the wrong which we have done, and by thy great mercy defend us from all the perils and dangers of this night. Into thy hands we commend our bodies and souls, and all that is ours. Let thy holy angel have charge concerning us, that the wicked one have no power over us. *Amen.*

¶ *Then may be said the Benedicamus.*

Bless we the Lord.
℟. Thanks be to God.

¶ *When the Evening Suffrages are said as a special Office, the following Blessing may be said.*

MAY the Almighty and Merciful Lord, the Father, the Son, and the Holy Ghost, bless and preserve us. *Amen.*

¶ *At Vespers shall be said this Benediction.*

THE Grace of our Lord Jesus Christ and the Love of God, and the Communion of the Holy Ghost, be with you all. *Amen.*

The Litany

¶ *The Litany may be used at The Service on Sundays in place of the Prayer of the Church except on Festivals or when there is a Communion.*

¶ *It may be used at Matins and Vespers, except on Festivals.*

¶ *When used at Matins or Vespers, it shall immediately follow the Canticle, and after it shall be said the Benedicamus and the Benediction.*

¶ *It may be used alone on Days of Humiliation and Prayer, or as a Penitential Office or at specially appointed times; the ancient litany days being Wednesday and Friday.*

¶ *When used as a special Office, the Order shall be: The Minister shall say:* In the Name of the Father, and of the Son, and of the Holy Ghost. ℟. Amen. *Then shall be said one or more of the Psalms with the Gloria Patri. A brief Lesson with the Response and a Hymn may follow. Then shall the Litany follow, and after the last Collect shall follow this Benediction:* The Blessing of Almighty God, the Father, the Son, and the Holy Ghost, be with you all. ℟. Amen.

¶ *The Responses shall be sung or said by the Congregation.*

Traditional Melody
adapted by
HAROLD W. GILBERT

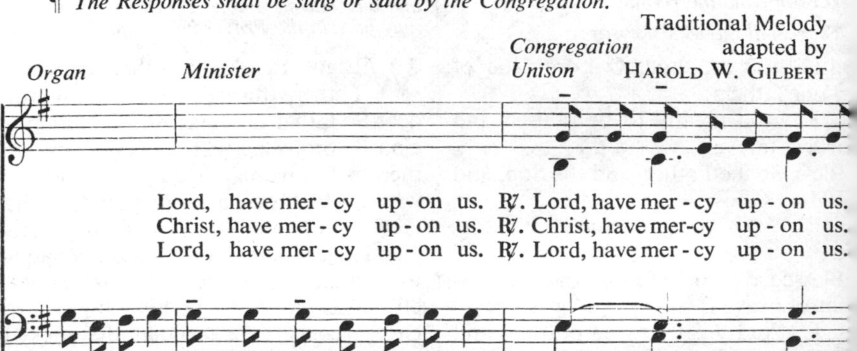
Organ
Minister
Congregation Unison
Lord, have mer - cy up - on us. ℟. Lord, have mer - cy up - on us.
Christ, have mer - cy up - on us. ℟. Christ, have mer-cy up - on us.
Lord, have mer - cy up - on us. ℟. Lord, have mer - cy up - on us.

The Litany

Minister
Minister
O Christ, hear us. ℟. O Christ, hear us. O God, the Father in heav-en:
Minister
℟. Have mer - cy up - on us. O God the Son, Redeemer of the world:
O God the Holy - - - - - Ghost:
Minister
℟. Have mer - cy up - on us. O Holy Trinity, One God:
℟. Have mer - cy up - on us.
Minister
℟. Have mer-cy up-on us. Be gra-cious un-to us. ℟. Spare us, good Lord.
Be gra-cious un-to us. ℟. Help us, good Lord.
Minister
From all sin; from all error; from all e - vil: ℟. Good Lord, de-liv-er us.

The Litany

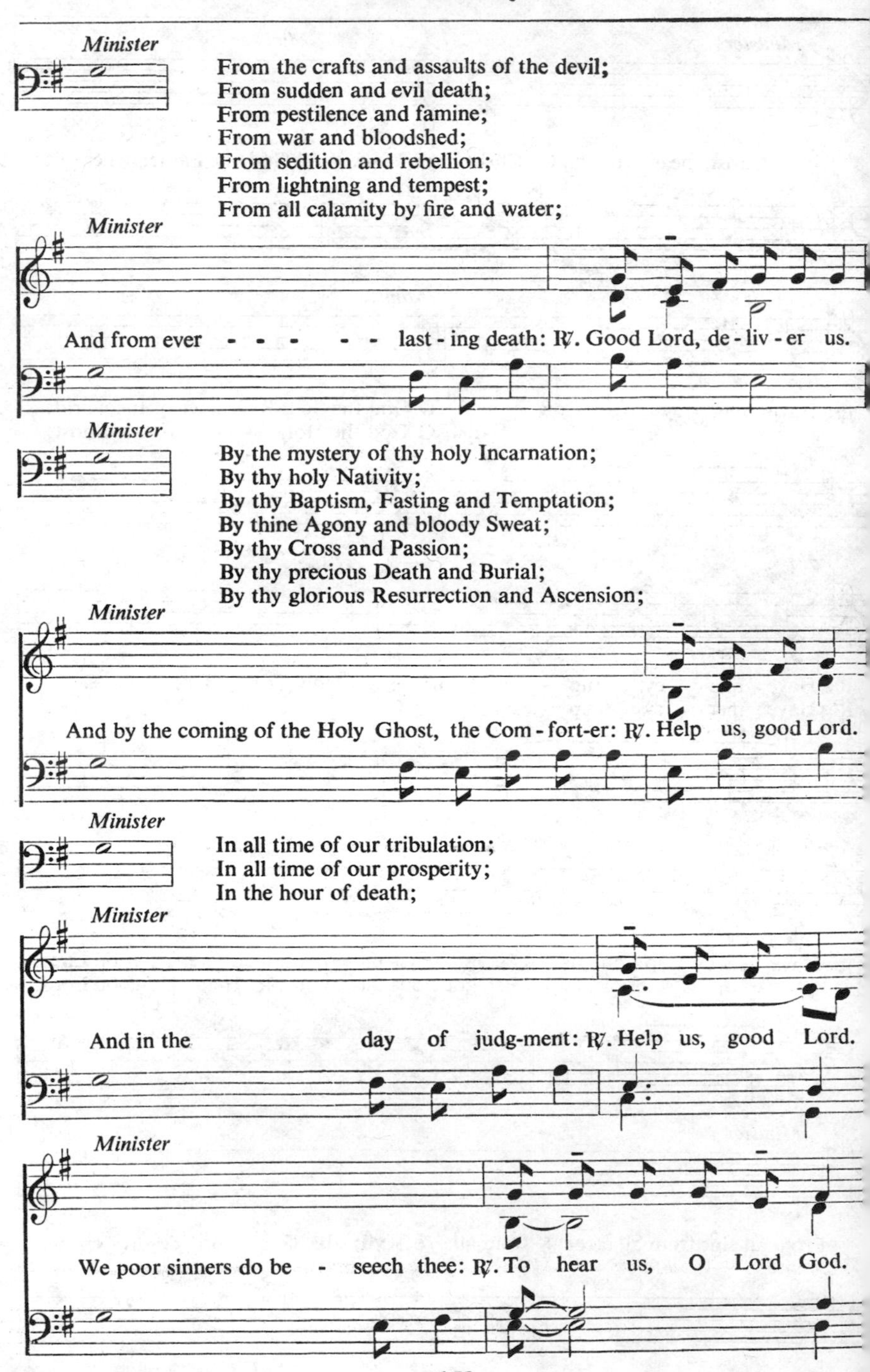
Minister
From the crafts and assaults of the devil;
From sudden and evil death;
From pestilence and famine;
From war and bloodshed;
From sedition and rebellion;
From lightning and tempest;
From all calamity by fire and water;
Minister
And from ever - - - - - - last - ing death: ℟. Good Lord, de - liv - er us.
Minister
By the mystery of thy holy Incarnation;
By thy holy Nativity;
By thy Baptism, Fasting and Temptation;
By thine Agony and bloody Sweat;
By thy Cross and Passion;
By thy precious Death and Burial;
By thy glorious Resurrection and Ascension;
Minister
And by the coming of the Holy Ghost, the Com - fort-er: ℟. Help us, good Lord.
Minister
In all time of our tribulation;
In all time of our prosperity;
In the hour of death;
Minister
And in the day of judg-ment: ℟. Help us, good Lord.
Minister
We poor sinners do be - seech thee: ℟. To hear us, O Lord God.

Minister
And to rule and govern thy holy Christian Church;
To preserve all pastors and ministers of thy Church in the true knowledge and understanding of thy Word, and in holiness of life;
To put an end to all schisms and causes of offence;
To bring into the way of truth all such as have erred, and are deceived;
To beat down Satan under our feet;
To send faithful laborers into thy harvest;
To accompany thy Word with thy Spirit and grace;
To raise up them that fall, and to strengthen such as do stand;
Minister
And to comfort and help the weak-hearted and the dis-tress-ed: R. We be-seech thee to hear us, good Lord.
Minister
To give to all nations peace and concord;
To preserve our country from discord and contention;
To direct and defend our President (or, our gracious Sovereign), and all in authority;
Minister
And to bless and keep our magistrates, and all our peo-ple: R. We be-seech thee to hear us, good Lord.
Minister
To behold and succor all who are in danger, necessity and tribulation;
To protect all who travel by land, air or water;
To preserve all women in the perils of childbirth;
To strengthen and keep all sick persons and young children;
To set free all who are innocently imprisoned;
To defend and provide for all fatherless children and widows;
Minister
And to have mercy up-on all men: R. We be-seech thee to hear us, good Lord.

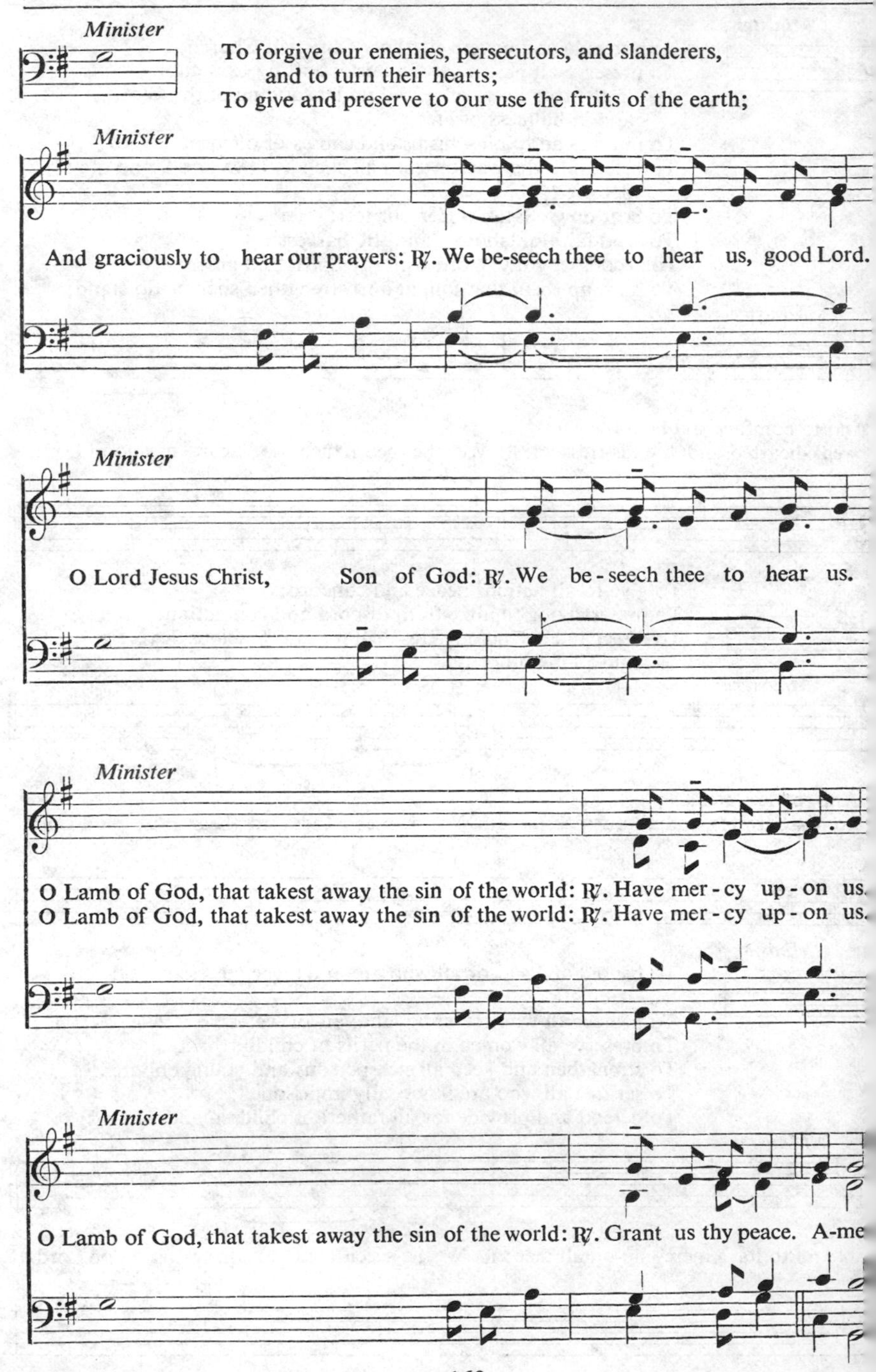
Minister
To forgive our enemies, persecutors, and slanderers,
and to turn their hearts;
To give and preserve to our use the fruits of the earth;
Minister
And graciously to hear our prayers: ℟. We be-seech thee to hear us, good Lord.
Minister
O Lord Jesus Christ, Son of God: ℟. We be-seech thee to hear us.
Minister
O Lamb of God, that takest away the sin of the world: ℟. Have mer-cy up-on us.
O Lamb of God, that takest away the sin of the world: ℟. Have mer-cy up-on us.
Minister
O Lamb of God, that takest away the sin of the world: ℟. Grant us thy peace. A-me

¶ *Then shall the Minister, and the Congre-
ıtion with him, say the Lord's Prayer.*

)UR Father, who art in heaven, . . .

¶ *Then shall the Minister say the Collect
r the Day, except when The Litany is used
The Service. Then may be said one or more
the Litany Collects here following.*

℣. O Lord, deal not with us after our
ıs.
℟. Neither reward us according to
ır iniquities.

LMIGHTY God, our heavenly Father, who desirest not the death of sinner, but rather that he should turn ɔm his evil way and live: We beseech ee graciously to turn from us those ınishments which we by our sins have served, and to grant us grace ever reafter to serve thee in holiness and reness of living; through Jesus Christ, y Son, our Lord. *Amen.*

℣. Help us, O God of our salvation,
the glory of thy Name.
℟. Deliver us, and purge away our
s, for thy Name's sake.

LMIGHTY and everlasting God, who by thy Holy Spirit dost govern d sanctify the whole Christian Church: ar our prayers for all members of the ne, and mercifully grant, that by thy ce they may serve thee in true faith; ough Jesus Christ, thy Son, our Lord. *ıen.*

℣. O Lord, deal not with us after our
s.
℟. Neither reward us according to
iniquities.

) GOD, merciful Father, who despisest not the sighing of a contrite ırt, nor the desire of such as are sorrowful: Mercifully assist our prayers which we make before thee in all our troubles and adversities, whensoever they oppress us; and graciously hear us, that those evils which the craft and subtilty of the devil or man worketh against us, may, by thy good providence, be brought to naught; that we thy servants, being hurt by no persecutions, may evermore give thanks unto thee in thy holy Church; through Jesus Christ, thy Son, our Lord. *Amen.*

℣. O Lord, enter not into judgment with thy servant.
℟. For in thy sight shall no man living be justified.

ALMIGHTY God, who knowest us to be set in the midst of so many and great dangers, that by reason of the frailty of our nature we cannot always stand upright: Grant us such strength and protection, as may support us in all dangers, and carry us through all temptations; through Jesus Christ, thy Son, our Lord. *Amen.*

℣. Call upon me in the day of trouble.
℟. I will deliver thee, and thou shalt glorify me.

SPARE us, O Lord, and mercifully forgive us our sins, and though by our continual transgressions we have merited thy punishments, be gracious unto us, and grant that all those evils which we have deserved may be turned from us, and overruled to our everlasting good; through Jesus Christ, thy Son, our Lord. *Amen.*

¶ *In the Morning the final Collect shall be the Collect for Grace with its Versicle (p. 139).*

¶ *In the Evening the final Collect shall be the Collect for Peace with its Versicle (p. 147).*

The Psalms

PSALM 1. *Beatus vir.*

BLESSED is the man that walketh not in the counsel of the ungodly : nor standeth in the way of sinners, nor sitteth in the seat of the scornful.

But his delight is in the law of the LORD : and in his law doth he meditate day and night.

And he shall be like a tree planted by the rivers of water : that bringeth forth his fruit in his season;

His leaf also shall not wither : a whatsoever he doeth shall prosper.

The ungodly are not so : but are li the chaff which the wind driveth awa

Therefore the ungodly shall not sta in the judgment : nor sinners in the co gregation of the righteous.

For the LORD knoweth the way of righteous : but the way of the ungo shall perish.

PSALM 2. *Quare fremuerunt gentes?*

WHY do the heathen rage : and the people imagine a vain thing?

The kings of the earth set themselves, and the rulers take counsel together : against the LORD, and against his anointed, saying,

Let us break their bands asunder : and cast away their cords from us.

He that sitteth in the heavens shall laugh : the Lord shall have them in derision.

Then shall he speak unto them in his wrath : and vex them in his sore displeasure.

Yet have I set my king : upon my holy hill of Zion.

I will declare the decree : the LORD hath said unto me, Thou art my S this day have I begotten thee.

Ask of me, and I shall give thee heathen for thine inheritance : and uttermost parts of the earth for thy p session.

Thou shalt break them with a rod iron : thou shalt dash them in pieces l a potter's vessel.

Be wise now therefore, O ye kings : instructed, ye judges of the earth.

Serve the LORD with fear : and rejo with trembling.

Kiss the Son, lest he be angry, and perish from the way, when his wrath kindled but a little : blessed are all th that put their trust in him.

PSALM 3. *Domine, quid multiplicati?*

LORD, how are they increased that trouble me : many are they that rise up against me.

Many there be which say of my soul : There is no help for him in God.

But thou, O LORD, art a shield for me : my glory, and the lifter up of mine head.

I cried unto the LORD with my voice : and he heard me out of his holy hill.

I laid me down and slept : I awaked; for the LORD sustained me.

I will not be afraid of ten thousands people : that have set themselves agai me round about.

Arise, O LORD : save me, O my G

For thou hast smitten all mine e mies upon the cheekbone : thou h broken the teeth of the ungodly.

Salvation belongeth unto the Lor thy blessing is upon thy people.

PSALM 4. *Cum invocarem, exaudivit.*

HEAR me when I call, O God of my righteousness : thou hast enlarged me when I was in distress.

Have mercy upon me : and hear my prayer.

O ye sons of men, how long will ye turn my glory into shame : how long will ye love vanity, and seek after falsehood?

But know that the LORD hath set apart him that is godly for himself : the LORD will hear when I call unto him.

Stand in awe, and sin not : commune with your own heart upon your bed, and be still.

Offer the sacrifices of righteousness : and put your trust in the LORD.

There be many that say, Who will show us any good : LORD, lift thou up the light of thy countenance upon us.

Thou hast put gladness in my heart : more than in the time that their corn and their wine increased.

I will both lay me down in peace, and sleep : for thou, LORD, only makest me dwell in safety.

PSALM 6. *Domine, ne in furore.*

[A PENITENTIAL PSALM]

O LORD, rebuke me not in thine anger : neither chasten me in thy hot displeasure.

Have mercy upon me, O LORD, for I am weak : O LORD, heal me, for my bones are vexed.

My soul is also sore vexed : but thou, O LORD, how long?

Return, O LORD, deliver my soul : O save me for thy mercies' sake.

For in death there is no remembrance of thee : in the grave who shall give thee thanks?

I am weary with my groaning, all the night make I my bed to swim : I water my couch with my tears.

Mine eye is consumed because of grief : it waxeth old because of all mine enemies.

Depart from me, all ye workers of iniquity : for the LORD hath heard the voice of my weeping.

The LORD hath heard my supplication : the LORD will receive my prayer.

Let all mine enemies be ashamed and sore vexed : let them return and be ashamed suddenly.

PSALM 8. *Domine, Dominus noster.*

O LORD, our Lord, how excellent is thy Name in all the earth : who hast set thy glory above the heavens.

Out of the mouth of babes and sucklings hast thou ordained strength because of thine enemies : that thou mightest still the enemy and the avenger.

When I consider thy heavens, the work of thy fingers : the moon and the stars, which thou hast ordained;

What is man, that thou art mindful of him : and the son of man, that thou visitest him?

For thou hast made him a little lower than the angels : and hast crowned him with glory and honor.

Thou madest him to have dominion over the works of thy hands : thou hast put all things under his feet;

All sheep and oxen : yea, and the beasts of the field;

The fowl of the air, and the fish of the sea : and whatsoever passeth through the paths of the seas.

O LORD our Lord : how excellent is thy Name in all the earth!

PSALM 9. *Confitebor tibi.*

I WILL praise thee, O LORD, with my whole heart : I will show forth all thy marvelous works.

I will be glad and rejoice in thee : I will sing praise to thy Name, O thou most High.

When mine enemies are turned back : they shall fall and perish at thy presence.

For thou hast maintained my right and my cause : thou satest in the throne judging right.

Thou hast rebuked the heathen, thou hast destroyed the wicked : thou hast put out their name for ever and ever.

O thou enemy, destructions are come to a perpetual end : and thou hast destroyed cities, their memorial is perished with them.

But the LORD shall endure for ever : he hath prepared his throne for judgment.

And he shall judge the world in righteousness : he shall minister judgment to the people in uprightness.

The LORD also will be a refuge for the oppressed : a refuge in times of trouble.

And they that know thy Name will put their trust in thee : for thou, LORD, hast not forsaken them that seek thee.

Sing praises to the LORD, which dwell- eth in Zion : declare among the peopl his doings.

When he maketh inquisition fo blood, he remembereth them : he for- getteth not the cry of the humble.

Have mercy upon me, O LORD; con- sider my trouble which I suffer of then that hate me : thou that liftest me u from the gates of death:

That I may show forth all thy prais in the gates of the daughter of Zion : will rejoice in thy salvation.

The heathen are sunk down in the pi that they made : in the net which the hid is their own foot taken.

The LORD is known by the judgmen which he executeth : the wicked i snared in the work of his own hands.

The wicked shall be turned into hell and all the nations that forget God.

For the needy shall not always be for gotten : the expectation of the poor sha not perish for ever.

Arise, O LORD, let not man prevail let the heathen be judged in thy sight.

Put them in fear, O LORD : that th nations may know themselves to be bu men.

PSALM 11. *In Domino confido.*

IN the LORD put I my trust : how say ye to my soul, Flee as a bird to your mountain?

For lo, the wicked bend their bow, they make ready their arrow upon the string : that they may privily shoot at the upright in heart.

If the foundations be destroyed : what can the righteous do?

The LORD is in his holy temple, the LORD's throne is in heaven : his eyes behold, his eyelids try, the children o men.

The LORD trieth the righteous : bu the wicked and him that loveth violenc his soul hateth.

Upon the wicked he shall rain snare fire and brimstone, and a horrible tem pest : this shall be the portion of their cu

For the righteous LORD loveth righ eousness : his countenance doth behol the upright.

PSALM 13. *Usquequo, Domine, oblivisceris?*

HOW long wilt thou forget me, O LORD, for ever : how long wilt thou ide thy face from me?

How long shall I take counsel in my oul, having sorrow in my heart daily : ow long shall mine enemy be exalted ver me?

Consider and hear me, O LORD my od : lighten mine eyes, lest I sleep the sleep of death;

Lest mine enemy say, I have prevailed against him : and those that trouble me rejoice when I am moved.

But I have trusted in thy mercy : my heart shall rejoice in thy salvation.

I will sing unto the LORD : because he hath dealt bountifully with me.

PSALM 14. *Dixit insipiens in corde suo.*

THE fool hath said in his heart : There is no God.

They are corrupt, they have done bominable works : there is none that oeth good.

The LORD looked down from heaven pon the children of men : to see if there ere any that did understand, and seek od.

They are all gone aside, they are all gether become filthy : there is none at doeth good, no, not one.

Have all the workers of iniquity no knowledge? who eat up my people as they eat bread : and call not upon the LORD.

There were they in great fear : for God is in the generation of the righteous.

Ye have shamed the counsel of the poor : because the LORD is his refuge.

O that the salvation of Israel were come out of Zion : when the LORD bringeth back the captivity of his people, Jacob shall rejoice, and Israel shall be glad.

PSALM 15. *Domine, quis habitabit?*

ORD, who shall abide in thy tabernacle : who shall dwell in thy holy ill?

He that walketh uprightly : and workh righteousness, and speaketh the uth in his heart.

He that backbiteth not with his tongue, or doeth evil to his neighbor : nor takh up a reproach against his neighbor.

In whose eyes a vile person is contemned, but he honoreth them that fear the LORD : he that sweareth to his own hurt, and changeth not.

He that putteth not out his money to usury : nor taketh reward against the innocent.

He that doeth these things : shall never be moved.

PSALM 16. *Conserva me, Domine.*

PRESERVE me, O God : for in thee do I put my trust.

O my soul, thou hast said unto the ORD : Thou art my LORD, my goodness xtendeth not to thee;

But to the saints that are in the earth, nd to the excellent : in whom is all my elight.

Their sorrows shall be multiplied : that hasten after another god.

Their drink offerings of blood will I not offer : nor take up their names into my lips.

The LORD is the portion of mine inheritance and of my cup : thou maintainest my lot.

The lines are fallen unto me in pleasant places : yea, I have a goodly heritage.

I will bless the LORD, who hath given me counsel : my heart also instructs me in the night seasons.

I have set the LORD always before me : because he is at my right hand, I shall not be moved.

Therefore my heart is glad, and n glory rejoiceth : my flesh also shall re in hope.

For thou wilt not leave my soul hell : neither wilt thou suffer thine Ho One to see corruption.

Thou wilt show me the path of life : thy presence is fulness of joy, at thy rig hand there are pleasures for evermore.

PSALM 17. *Exaudi, Domine, justitiam.*

HEAR the right, O LORD, attend unto my cry : give ear unto my prayer, that goeth not out of feigned lips.

Let my sentence come forth from thy presence : let thine eyes behold the things that are equal.

Thou hast proved mine heart, thou hast visited me in the night, thou hast tried me, and shalt find nothing : I am purposed that my mouth shall not transgress.

Concerning the works of men : by the word of thy lips I have kept me from the paths of the destroyer.

Hold up my goings in thy paths : that my footsteps slip not.

I have called upon thee, for thou wilt hear me, O God : incline thine ear unto me, and hear my speech.

Show thy marvellous lovingkindness, O thou that savest by thy right har them which put their trust in thee : fro those that rise up against them.

Keep me as the apple of the eye : hi me under the shadow of thy wings.

From the wicked that oppress me from my deadly enemies, who compa me about.

Arise, O LORD, disappoint him, ca him down : deliver my soul from t wicked, which is thy sword;

From men which are thy hand, LORD, from men of the world : whi have their portion in this life, and who belly thou fillest with thy hid treasure

They are full of children : and lea the rest of their substance to their babe

As for me, I will behold thy face righteousness : I shall be satisfied, wh I awake, with thy likeness.

PSALM 18. *Diligam te, Domine.*

I WILL love thee : O LORD, my strength.

The LORD is my rock, and my fortress, and my deliverer : my God, my strength, in whom I will trust; my shield, and the horn of my salvation, and my high tower.

I will call upon the LORD, who is worthy to be praised : so shall I be saved from mine enemies.

The sorrows of death compassed me : and the floods of ungodly men made me afraid.

The sorrows of hell compassed n about : the snares of death came upo me.

In my distress I called upon the LORI and cried unto my God;

He heard my voice out of his temple and my cry came before him, even in his ears.

Then the earth shook and trembled the foundations also of the hills move and were shaken, because he wa wroth.

There went up a smoke out of his no

ils, and fire out of his mouth devoured : oals were kindled by it.

He bowed the heavens also, and came own : and darkness was under his feet.

And he rode upon a cherub, and did y : yea, he did fly upon the wings of the ind.

He made darkness his secret place : is pavilion round about him were dark aters and thick clouds of the skies.

At the brightness that was before him is thick clouds passed : hailstones and oals of fire.

The LORD also thundered in the heavns, and the Highest gave his voice : ailstones and coals of fire.

Yea, he sent out his arrows, and scattered them : and he shot out lightnings, and discomfited them.

Then the channels of waters were seen, and the foundations of the world were discovered : at thy rebuke, O LORD, at the blast of the breath of thy nostrils.

He sent from above, he took me : he drew me out of many waters.

He delivered me from my strong enemy, and from them which hated me : for they were too strong for me.

They came upon me in the day of my calamity : but the LORD was my stay.

He brought me forth also into a large place : he delivered me, because he delighted in me.

PSALM 19. *Caeli enarrant.*

THE heavens declare the glory of God : and the firmament showeth is handywork.

Day unto day uttereth speech : and ight unto night showeth knowledge.

There is no speech nor language : here their voice is not heard.

Their line is gone out through all the arth : and their words to the end of the orld.

In them hath he set a tabernacle for e sun : which is as a bridegroom comg out of his chamber, and rejoiceth as strong man to run a race.

His going forth is from the end of the eaven, and his circuit unto the ends of : and there is nothing hid from the eat thereof.

The law of the LORD is perfect, conerting the soul : the testimony of the ORD is sure, making wise the simple.

The statutes of the LORD are right, rejoicing the heart : the commandment of the LORD is pure, enlightening the eyes.

The fear of the LORD is clean, enduring forever : the judgments of the LORD are true and righteous altogether.

More to be desired are they than gold, yea, than much fine gold : sweeter also than honey and the honeycomb.

Moreover by them is thy servant warned : and in keeping of them there is great reward.

Who can understand his errors : cleanse thou me from secret faults.

Keep back thy servant also from presumptuous sins, let them not have dominion over me : then shall I be upright, and I shall be innocent from the great transgression.

Let the words of my mouth, and the meditation of my heart, be acceptable in thy sight : O LORD, my strength, and my redeemer.

PSALM 20. *Exaudiat te Dominus.*

THE LORD hear thee in the day of trouble : the Name of the God of acob defend thee;

Send thee help from the sanctuary : nd strengthen thee out of Zion;

Remember all thy offerings : and accept thy burnt sacrifice;

Grant thee according to thine own heart : and fulfil all thy counsel.

We will rejoice in thy salvation, and in

the Name of our God we will set up our banners : the LORD fulfil all thy petitions.

Now know I that the LORD saveth his anointed : he will hear him from his holy heaven, with the saving strength of his right hand.

Some trust in chariots, and some i horses : but we will remember the Nam of the LORD our God.

They are brought down and fallen but we are risen, and stand upright.

Save, Lord : let the king hear us whe we call.

PSALM 21. *Domine, in virtute tua.*

THE king shall joy in thy strength, O LORD : and in thy salvation how greatly shall he rejoice!

Thou hast given him his heart's desire : and hast not withholden the request of his lips.

For thou meetest him with the blessings of goodness : thou settest a crown of pure gold on his head.

He asked life of thee, and thou gavest it him : even length of days for ever and ever.

His glory is great in thy salvation : honor and majesty hast thou laid upon him.

For thou hast made him most blessed for ever : thou hast made him exceeding glad with thy countenance.

For the king trusteth in the LORD : and through the mercy of the most High he shall not be moved.

Thine hand shall find out all thine en mies : thy right hand shall find out thos that hate thee.

Thou shalt make them as a fiery ove in the time of thine anger : the LOR shall swallow them up in his wrath, an the fire shall devour them.

Their fruit shalt thou destroy from th earth : and their seed from among th children of men.

For they intended evil against thee they imagined a mischievous devic which they are not able to perform.

Therefore shalt thou make them tur their back : when thou shalt make read thine arrows upon thy strings against th face of them.

Be thou exalted, LORD, in thine ow strength : so will we sing and praise th power.

PSALM 22. *Deus, Deus meus.*

[A PSALM OF THE PASSION]

MY GOD, my God, why hast thou forsaken me : why art thou so far from helping me, and from the words of my roaring?

O my God, I cry in the daytime, but thou hearest not : and in the night season, and am not silent.

But thou art holy : O thou that inhabitest the praises of Israel.

Our fathers trusted in thee : they trusted, and thou didst deliver them.

They cried unto thee, and were delivered : they trusted in thee, and were not confounded.

But I am a worm, and no man : a re proach of men, and despised of the peopl

All they that see me laugh me to scorn they shoot out the lip, they shake th head, saying,

He trusted on the LORD that he woul deliver him : let him deliver him, seein he delighted in him.

But thou art he that took me out of th womb : thou didst make me hope whe I was upon my mother's breasts.

I was cast upon thee from the womb thou art my God since my mother bo me.

Be not far from me, for trouble is ear : for there is none to help.

Many bulls have compassed me : trong bulls of Bashan have beset me ound.

They gaped upon me with their nouths : as a ravening and a roaring ion.

I am poured out like water, and all my ones are out of joint : my heart is like ax, it is melted in the midst of my bowls.

My strength is dried up like a potherd, and my tongue cleaveth to my aws : and thou hast brought me into he dust of death.

For dogs have compassed me : the ssembly of the wicked have inclosed ne, they pierced my hands and my feet.

I may tell all my bones : they look and tare upon me.

They part my garments among them : nd cast lots upon my vesture.

But be not thou far from me, O LORD : my strength, haste thee to help me.

Deliver my soul from the sword : my arling from the power of the dog.

Save me from the lion's mouth : for hou hast heard me from the horns of he unicorns.

I will declare thy Name unto my brethren : in the midst of the congregation will I praise thee.

Ye that fear the LORD, praise him, all ye the seed of Jacob, glorify him : and fear him, all ye the seed of Israel.

For he hath not despised nor abhorred the affliction of the afflicted : neither hath he hid his face from him, but when he cried unto him, he heard.

My praise shall be of thee in the great congregation : I will pay my vows before them that fear him.

The meek shall eat and be satisfied : they shall praise the LORD that seek him, your heart shall live for ever.

All the ends of the world shall remember and turn unto the LORD : and all the kindreds of the nations shall worship before thee.

For the kingdom is the LORD's : and he is the governor among the nations.

All they that be fat upon earth : shall eat and worship;

All they that go down to the dust shall bow before him : and none can keep alive his own soul.

A seed shall serve him : it shall be accounted to the Lord for a generation.

They shall come, and shall declare his righteousness unto a people that shall be born : that he hath done this.

PSALM 23. *Dominus regit me.*

THE LORD is my shepherd : I shall not want.

He maketh me to lie down in green astures : he leadeth me beside the still aters.

He restoreth my soul : he leadeth me n the paths of righteousness for his Name's sake.

Yea, though I walk through the valley f the shadow of death, I will fear no evil : for thou art with me, thy rod and thy staff they comfort me.

Thou preparest a table before me in the presence of mine enemies : thou anointest my head with oil, my cup runneth over.

Surely goodness and mercy shall follow me all the days of my life : and I will dwell in the house of the LORD for ever.

PSALM 24. *Domini est terra.*

THE earth is the LORD's, and the fulness thereof : the world, and they hat dwell therein.

For he hath founded it upon the seas : and established it upon the floods.

Who shall ascend into the hill of the LORD : or who shall stand in his holy place?

He that hath clean hands, and a pure heart : who hath not lifted up his soul unto vanity, nor sworn deceitfully.

He shall receive the blessing from the Lord : and righteousness from the God of his salvation.

This is the generation of them that seek him : that seek thy face, O God of Jacob.

Lift up your heads, O ye gates, and be ye lift up, ye everlasting doors : and th
King of glory shall come in.

Who is this King of glory : the Lor
strong and mighty, the Lord mighty i
battle.

Lift up your heads, O ye gates, eve
lift them up, ye everlasting doors : an
the King of glory shall come in.

Who is this King of glory : the Lor
of hosts, he is the King of glory.

PSALM 25. *Ad te, Domine, levavi.*

UNTO thee, O Lord : do I lift up my soul.

O my God, I trust in thee : let me not be ashamed, let not mine enemies triumph over me.

Yea, let none that wait on thee be ashamed : let them be ashamed which transgress without cause.

Show me thy ways, O Lord : teach me thy paths.

Lead me in thy truth, and teach me : for thou art the God of my salvation, on thee do I wait all the day.

Remember, O Lord, thy tender mercies and thy lovingkindnesses : for they have been ever of old.

Remember not the sins of my youth, nor my transgressions : according to thy mercy remember thou me for thy goodness' sake, O Lord.

Good and upright is the Lord : therefore will he teach sinners in the way.

The meek will he guide in judgment : and the meek will he teach his way.

All the paths of the Lord are mercy and truth : unto such as keep his covenant and his testimonies.

For thy Name's sake, O Lord, pardo
mine iniquity : for it is great.

What man is he that feareth th
Lord : him shall he teach in the way tha
he shall choose.

His soul shall dwell at ease : and hi
seed shall inherit the earth.

The secret of the Lord is with the
that fear him : and he will show them hi
covenant.

Mine eyes are ever toward the Lord
for he shall pluck my feet out of the ne

Turn thee unto me, and have merc
upon me : for I am desolate and afflicte

The troubles of my heart are enlarged
O bring thou me out of my distresses.

Look upon mine affliction and m
pain : and forgive all my sins.

Consider mine enemies, for they ar
many : and they hate me with crue
hatred.

O keep my soul, and deliver me : le
me not be ashamed, for I put my trus
in thee.

Let integrity and uprightness preserv
me : for I wait on thee.

Redeem Israel, O God : out of all hi
troubles.

PSALM 26. *Judica me, Domine.*

JUDGE me, O Lord, for I have walked in mine integrity : I have trusted also in the Lord, therefore I shall not slide.

Examine me, O Lord, and prove me : try my heart and my mind.

For thy lovingkindness is before min
eyes : and I have walked in thy truth.

I have not sat with vain persons
neither will I go in with dissemblers.

I have hated the congregation of evi

ers : and will not sit with the wicked.
I will wash mine hands in innocency : will I compass thine altar, O LORD;
That I may publish with the voice of anksgiving : and tell of all thy wonous works.
LORD, I have loved the habitation of y house : and the place where thine nor dwelleth.

Gather not my soul with sinners : nor my life with bloody men;
In whose hands is mischief : and their right hand is full of bribes.
But as for me, I will walk in mine integrity : redeem me, and be merciful unto me.
My foot standeth in an even place : in the congregations will I bless the LORD.

PSALM 27. *Dominus illuminatio.*

THE LORD is my light and my salvation, whom shall I fear : the LORD is e strength of my life, of whom shall I afraid?
When the wicked, even mine enemies d my foes, came upon me to eat up y flesh : they stumbled and fell.
Though an host should encamp against e, my heart shall not fear : though war ould rise against me, in this will I be nfident.
One thing have I desired of the LORD, at will I seek after : that I may dwell the house of the LORD all the days of y life, to behold the beauty of the ORD, and to enquire in his temple.
For in the time of trouble he shall hide e in his pavilion : in the secret of his bernacle shall he hide me, he shall set e up upon a rock.
And now shall mine head be lifted up : ove mine enemies round about me;
Therefore will I offer in his tabernacle crifices of joy : I will sing, yea, I will ng praises unto the LORD.

Hear, O LORD, when I cry with my voice : have mercy also upon me, and answer me.
When thou saidst, Seek ye my face : my heart said unto thee, Thy face, LORD, will I seek.
Hide not thy face far from me : put not thy servant away in anger;
Thou hast been my help : leave me not, neither forsake me, O God of my salvation.
When my father and my mother forsake me : then the LORD will take me up.
Teach me thy way, O LORD : and lead me in a plain path, because of mine enemies.
Deliver me not over unto the will of mine enemies : for false witnesses are risen up against me, and such as breathe out cruelty.
I had fainted : unless I had believed to see the goodness of the LORD in the land of the living.
Wait on the LORD : be of good courage, and he shall strengthen thine heart; wait, I say, on the LORD.

PSALM 28. *Ad te, Domine, clamabo.*

UNTO thee will I cry, O LORD my rock, be not silent to me : lest, if ou be silent to me, I become like them at go down into the pit.
Hear the voice of my supplications, hen I cry unto thee : when I lift up my nds toward thy holy oracle.
Draw me not away with the wicked, d with the workers of iniquity : which speak peace to their neighbors, but mischief is in their hearts.
Give them according to their deeds : and according to the wickedness of their endeavors.
Give them after the work of their hands : render to them their desert.
Because they regard not the works of the LORD, nor the operation of his

hands : he shall destroy them, and not build them up.

Blessed be the LORD : because he hath heard the voice of my supplications.

The LORD is my strength and my shield, my heart trusted in him, and I am helped : therefore my heart greatly rejoiceth, and with my song will I prai him.

The LORD is their strength : and he the saving strength of his anointed.

Save thy people, and bless thine i heritance : feed them also, and lift the up for ever.

PSALM 29. *Afferte Domino.*

GIVE unto the LORD, O ye mighty : give unto the LORD glory and strength.

Give unto the LORD the glory due unto his Name : worship the LORD in the beauty of holiness.

The voice of the LORD is upon the waters : the God of glory thundereth, the LORD is upon many waters.

The voice of the LORD is powerful : the voice of the LORD is full of majesty.

The voice of the LORD breaketh the cedars : yea, the LORD breaketh the cedars of Lebanon.

He maketh them also to skip like a calf : Lebanon and Sirion like a you unicorn.

The voice of the LORD : divideth t flames of fire.

The voice of the LORD shaketh t wilderness : the LORD shaketh the w derness of Kadesh.

The voice of the LORD maketh t hinds to calve, and discovereth the fc ests : and in his temple doth every o speak of his glory.

The LORD sitteth upon the flood : ye the LORD sitteth King for ever.

The LORD will give strength unto h people : the LORD will bless his peop with peace.

PSALM 30. *Exaltabo te, Domine.*

I WILL extol thee, O LORD, for thou hast lifted me up : and hast not made my foes to rejoice over me.

O LORD my God, I cried unto thee : and thou hast healed me.

O LORD, thou hast brought up my soul from the grave : thou hast kept me alive, that I should not go down to the pit.

Sing unto the LORD, O ye saints of his : and give thanks at the remembrance of his holiness.

For his anger endureth but a moment, in his favor is life : weeping may endure for a night, but joy cometh in the morning.

And in my prosperity I said : I shall never be moved.

LORD, by thy favor thou hast ma my mountain to stand strong : th didst hide thy face, and I was trouble

I cried to thee, O LORD : and unto t LORD I made supplication.

What profit is there in my blood, wh I go down to the pit : shall the du praise thee? shall it declare thy truth?

Hear, O LORD, and have mercy up me : LORD, be thou my helper.

Thou hast turned for me my mourni into dancing : thou hast put off my sac cloth, and girded me with gladness;

To the end that my glory may si praise to thee, and not be silent : LORD my God, I will give thanks un thee for ever.

PSALM 31. *In te, Domine, speravi.*

N thee, O LORD, do I put my trust, let me never be ashamed : deliver me in ıy righteousness.

Bow down thine ear to me, deliver me ›eedily : be thou my strong rock, for an ɔuse of defence to save me.

For thou art my rock and my fortress : ıerefore for thy Name's sake lead me, ıd guide me.

Pull me out of the net that they have id privily for me : for thou art my rength.

Into thine hand I commit my spirit : ıou hast redeemed me, O LORD God of uth.

I have hated them that regard lying ınities : but I trust in the LORD.

I will be glad and rejoice in thy mercy, ›r thou hast considered my trouble : ıou hast known my soul in adversities;

And hast not shut me up into the hand ' the enemy : thou hast set my feet in a rge room.

Have mercy upon me, O LORD, for I n in trouble : mine eye is consumed ith grief, yea, my soul and my belly.

For my life is spent with grief, and my ·ars with sighing : my strength faileth ɛcause of mine iniquity, and my bones ·e consumed.

I was a reproach among all mine ene- ıies, but especially among my neigh- ɔrs, and a fear to mine acquaintance : ıey that did see me without fled from ıe.

I am forgotten as a dead man out of ıind : I am like a broken vessel.

For I have heard the slander of many, fear was on every side : while they took counsel together against me, they de- vised to take away my life.

But I trusted in thee, O LORD : I said, Thou art my God.

My times are in thy hand : deliver me from the hand of mine enemies, and from them that persecute me.

Make thy face to shine upon thy serv- ant : save me for thy mercies' sake.

Let me not be ashamed, O LORD, for I have called upon thee : let the wicked be ashamed, and let them be silent in the grave.

Let the lying lips be put to silence : which speak grievous things proudly and contemptuously against the righteous.

O how great is thy goodness, which thou hast laid up for them that fear thee : which thou hast wrought for them that trust in thee before the sons of men!

Thou shalt hide them in the secret of thy presence from the pride of man : thou shalt keep them secretly in a pavil- ion from the strife of tongues.

Blessed be the LORD : for he hath showed me his marvellous kindness in a strong city.

For I said in my haste, I am cut off from before thine eyes : nevertheless thou heardest the voice of my supplica- tions when I cried unto thee.

O love the LORD, all ye his saints : for the LORD preserveth the faithful, and plentifully rewardeth the proud doer.

Be of good courage : and he shall strengthen your heart, all ye that hope in the LORD.

PSALM 32. *Beati quorum.*

[A PENITENTIAL PSALM]

ƁLESSED is he whose transgression is forgiven : whose sin is covered.

Blessed is the man unto whom the ORD imputeth not iniquity : and in hose spirit there is no guile.

When I kept silence : my bones waxed old through my roaring all the day long.

For day and night thy hand was heavy upon me : my moisture is turned into the drought of summer.

I acknowledged my sin unto thee : and mine iniquity have I not hid.

I said, I will confess my transgressions unto the LORD : and thou forgavest the iniquity of my sin.

For this shall every one that is godly pray unto thee in a time when thou mayest be found : surely in the floods of great waters they shall not come nigh unto him.

Thou art my hiding place, thou shalt preserve me from trouble : thou shalt compass me about with songs of deliverance.

I will instruct thee and teach thee the way which thou shalt go : I will guic thee with mine eye.

Be ye not as the horse, or as the mul which have no understanding : who mouth must be held in with bit ar bridle, lest they come near unto thee.

Many sorrows shall be to the wicked but he that trusteth in the LORD, merc shall compass him about.

Be glad in the LORD, and rejoice, y righteous : and shout for joy, all ye th are upright in heart.

PSALM 33. *Exultate, justi, in Domino.*

REJOICE in the LORD, O ye righteous : for praise is comely for the upright.

Praise the LORD with harp : sing unto him with the psaltery and an instrument of ten strings.

Sing unto him a new song : play skillfully with a loud noise.

For the word of the LORD is right : and all his works are done in truth.

He loveth righteousness and judgment : the earth is full of the goodness of the LORD.

By the word of the LORD were the heavens made : and all the host of them by the breath of his mouth.

He gathereth the waters of the sea together as an heap : he layeth up the depth in storehouses.

Let all the earth fear the LORD : let all the inhabitants of the world stand in awe of him.

For he spake, and it was done : he commanded, and it stood fast.

The LORD bringeth the counsel of the heathen to nought : he maketh the devices of the people of none effect.

The counsel of the LORD standeth for ever : the thoughts of his heart to a generations.

Blessed is the nation whose God is th LORD : and the people whom he ha chosen for his own inheritance.

The LORD looketh from heaven : h beholdeth all the sons of men.

From the place of his habitation h looketh : upon all the inhabitants of th earth.

He fashioneth their hearts alike : h considereth all their works.

There is no king saved by the mult tude of an host : a mighty man is n delivered by much strength.

A horse is a vain thing for safety neither shall he deliver any by his gre strength.

Behold, the eye of the LORD is upc them that fear him : upon them th hope in his mercy;

To deliver their soul from death : ar to keep them alive in famine.

Our soul waiteth for the LORD : he our help and our shield.

For our heart shall rejoice in him : b cause we have trusted in his holy Nam

Let thy mercy, O LORD, be upon us according as we hope in thee.

PSALM 34. *Benedicam Dominum.*

WILL bless the LORD at all times : his praise shall continually be in my outh.

My soul shall make her boast in the ORD : the humble shall hear thereof, d be glad.

O magnify the LORD with me : and let exalt his Name together.

I sought the LORD, and he heard me : d delivered me from all my fears.

They looked unto him, and were lighted : and their faces were not ashamed.

This poor man cried, and the LORD ard him : and saved him out of all his oubles.

The angel of the LORD encampeth und about them that fear him : and livereth them.

O taste and see that the LORD is good : essed is the man that trusteth in m.

O fear the LORD, ye his saints : for ere is no want to them that fear him.

The young lions do lack, and suffer nger : but they that seek the LORD all not want any good thing.

Come, ye children, hearken unto me : vill teach you the fear of the LORD.

What man is he that desireth life : and loveth many days, that he may see good?

Keep thy tongue from evil : and thy lips from speaking guile.

Depart from evil, and do good : seek peace, and pursue it.

The eyes of the LORD are upon the righteous : and his ears are open unto their cry.

The face of the LORD is against them that do evil : to cut off the remembrance of them from the earth.

The righteous cry, and the LORD heareth : and delivereth them out of all their troubles.

The LORD is nigh unto them that are of a broken heart : and saveth such as be of a contrite spirit.

Many are the afflictions of the righteous : but the LORD delivereth him out of them all.

He keepeth all his bones : not one of them is broken.

Evil shall slay the wicked : and they that hate the righteous shall be desolate.

The LORD redeemeth the soul of his servants : and none of them that trust in him shall be desolate.

PSALM 36. *Dixit injustus.*

THE transgression of the wicked saith within my heart : that there is fear of God before his eyes.

For he flattereth himself in his own es : until his iniquity be found to be teful.

The words of his mouth are iniquity d deceit : he hath left off to be wise, d to do good.

He deviseth mischief upon his bed, he teth himself in a way that is not good : abhorreth not evil.

Thy mercy, O LORD, is in the heavens : d thy faithfulness reacheth unto the ouds.

Thy righteousness is like the great ountains, thy judgments are a great ep : O LORD, thou preservest man and ast.

How excellent is thy lovingkindness, O God : therefore the children of men put their trust under the shadow of thy wings.

They shall be abundantly satisfied with the fatness of thy house : and thou shalt make them drink of the river of thy pleasures.

For with thee is the fountain of life : in thy light shall we see light.

O continue thy lovingkindness unto them that know thee: and thy righteousness to the upright in heart.

Let not the foot of pride come against me : and let not the hand of the wicked remove me.

There are the workers of iniquity fallen : they are cast down, and shall not be able to rise.

PSALM 38. *Domine, ne in furore.*

[A PENITENTIAL PSALM]

O LORD, rebuke me not in thy wrath : neither chasten me in thy hot displeasure.

For thine arrows stick fast in me : and thy hand presseth me sore.

There is no soundness in my flesh because of thine anger : neither is there any rest in my bones because of my sin.

For mine iniquities are gone over mine head : as an heavy burden they are too heavy for me.

Lord, all my desire is before thee : and my groaning is not hid from thee.

My heart panteth, my strength faileth me : as for the light of mine eyes, it also is gone from me.

My lovers and my friends stand aloof from my sore : and my kinsmen stand afar off.

They also that seek after my life lay snares for me : and they that seek my hurt speak mischievous things, and imagine deceits all the day long.

But I, as a deaf man, heard not : and I was as a dumb man that openeth not [illegible] mouth.

Thus I was as a man that heareth no[illegible] and in whose mouth are no reproofs.

For in thee, O LORD, do I hope : th[illegible] wilt hear, O Lord my God.

For I said, Hear me, lest otherw[illegible] they should rejoice over me : when [illegible] foot slippeth, they magnify themsel[illegible] against me.

For I am ready to halt : and my so[illegible]row is continually before me.

For I will declare mine iniquity [illegible] will be sorry for my sin.

But mine enemies are lively, and th[illegible] are strong : and they that hate me wron[illegible]fully are multiplied.

They also that render evil for good a[illegible] mine adversaries : because I follow t[illegible] thing that good is.

Forsake me not, O LORD : O my Go[illegible] be not far from me.

Make haste to help me : O Lord [illegible] salvation.

PSALM 40. *Expectans, expectavi Dominum.*

I WAITED patiently for the LORD : and he inclined unto me, and heard my cry.

He brought me up also out of a horrible pit, out of the miry clay : and set my feet upon a rock, and established my goings.

And he hath put a new song in my mouth, even praise unto our God : many shall see it, and fear, and shall trust in the LORD.

Blessed is that man that maketh the LORD his trust : and respecteth not the proud, nor such as turn aside to lies.

Many, O LORD my God, are thy wonderful works which thou hast done, and thy thoughts which are to us-ward : they cannot be reckoned up in order unto thee;

If I would declare and speak of them : they are more than can be numbered.

Sacrifice and offering thou didst n[illegible] desire, mine ears hast thou opened[illegible] burnt offering and sin offering hast th[illegible] not required.

Then said I, Lo, I come : in the vo[illegible]ume of the book it is written of me,

I delight to do thy will, O my God[illegible] yea, thy law is within my heart.

I have preached righteousness in t[illegible] great congregation : lo, I have not r[illegible]frained my lips, O LORD, thou knowe[illegible]

I have not hid thy righteousness with[illegible] my heart : I have declared thy faithfu[illegible]ness and thy salvation.

I have not concealed thy lovingkin[illegible]ness and thy truth : from the great co[illegible]gregation.

Withhold not thou thy tender merci[illegible] from me, O LORD : let thy lovingkin[illegible]ness and thy truth continually preser[illegible] me.

For innumerable evils have compassed
e about : mine iniquities have taken
ɔld upon me, so that I am not able to
ok up;
They are more than the hairs of mine
ead : therefore my heart faileth me.
Be pleased, O LORD, to deliver me : O
ɔRD, make haste to help me.
Let them be ashamed and confounded
gether that seek after my soul to de-
roy it : let them be driven backward
ıd put to shame that wish me evil.

Let them be desolate for a reward of their shame : that say unto me, Aha, aha.

Let all those that seek thee rejoice and be glad in thee : let such as love thy salvation say continually, The LORD be magnified.

But I am poor and needy : yet the Lord thinketh upon me;

Thou art my help and my deliverer : make no tarrying, O my God.

PSALM 42. *Quemadmodum desiderat cervus.*

S the hart panteth after the water
brooks : so panteth my soul after
ee, O God.
My soul thirsteth for God, for the liv-
g God : when shall I come and appear
fore God?
My tears have been my meat day and
ght : while they continually say unto
e, Where is thy God?
When I remember these things, I pour
t my soul in me : for I had gone with
e multitude,
I went with them to the house of God,
th the voice of joy and praise : with a
ıltitude that kept holyday.
Why art thou cast down, O my soul :
d why art thou disquieted in me?
Hope thou in God : for I shall yet
aise him for the help of his counte-
nce.
O my God, my soul is cast down with-
me : therefore will I remember thee
from the land of Jordan, and of the Hermonites, from the hill Mizar.

Deep calleth unto deep at the noise of thy waterspouts : all thy waves and thy billows are gone over me.

Yet the LORD will command his lovingkindness in the daytime : and in the night his song shall be with me, and my prayer unto the God of my life.

I will say unto God my rock, Why hast thou forgotten me : why go I mourning because of the oppression of the enemy?

As with a sword in my bones, mine enemies reproach me : while they say daily unto me, Where is thy God?

Why art thou cast down, O my soul : and why art thou disquieted within me?

Hope thou in God : for I shall yet praise him, who is the health of my countenance, and my God.

PSALM 43. *Judica me, Deus.*

JDGE me, O God, and plead my
cause against an ungodly nation : O
liver me from the deceitful and unjust
ın.
For thou art the God of my strength,
ıy dost thou cast me off : why go I
ɔurning because of the oppression of
e enemy?
O send out thy light and thy truth, let
em lead me : let them bring me unto
thy holy hill, and to thy tabernacles.

Then will I go unto the altar of God, unto God my exceeding joy : yea, upon the harp will I praise thee, O God my God.

Why art thou cast down, O my soul? and why art thou disquieted within me? hope thou in God : for I shall yet praise him, who is the health of my countenance, and my God.

PSALM 44. *Deus, auribus.*

WE have heard with our ears, O God, our fathers have told us : what work thou didst in their days, in the times of old.

How thou didst drive out the heathen with thy hand, and plantedst them : how thou didst afflict the people, and cast them out.

For they got not the land in possession by their own sword : neither did their own arm save them;

But thy right hand, and thine arm, and the light of thy countenance : because thou hadst a favor unto them.

Thou art my King, O God : command deliverances for Jacob.

Through thee will we push down our enemies : through thy Name will we tread them under that rise up against us.

For I will not trust in my bow : neither shall my sword save me.

But thou hast saved us from our enemies : and hast put them to shame that hated us.

In God we boast all the day long : and praise thy Name for ever.

But thou hast cast off, and put us to shame : and goest not forth with our armies.

Thou makest us to turn back from the enemy : and they which hate us spoil for themselves.

Thou hast given us like sheep appointed for meat : and hast scattered us among the heathen.

Thou sellest thy people for nought : and dost not increase thy wealth by their price.

Thou makest us a reproach to ou neighbors : a scorn and a derision t them that are round about us.

Thou makest us a byword among th heathen : a shaking of the head amon the people.

My confusion is continually before m and the shame of my face hath covere me,

For the voice of him that reproache and blasphemeth : by reason of the en my and avenger.

All this is come upon us, yet have w not forgotten thee : neither have w dealt falsely in thy covenant.

Our heart is not turned back : neith have our steps declined from thy way;

Though thou hast sore broken us the place of dragons : and covered with the shadow of death.

If we have forgotten the Name of o God : or stretched out our hands to strange god;

Shall not God search this out : for knoweth the secrets of the heart.

Yea, for thy sake are we killed all t day long : we are counted as sheep f the slaughter.

Awake, why sleepest thou, O Lord arise, cast us not off for ever.

Wherefore hidest thou thy face : a forgettest our affliction and our oppre sion?

For our soul is bowed down to t dust : our belly cleaveth unto the eart

Arise for our help : and redeem us f thy mercies' sake.

PSALM 45. *Eructavit cor meum.*

MY heart is inditing a good matter, I speak of the things which I have made touching the king : my tongue is the pen of a ready writer.

Thou art fairer than the children of men : grace is poured into thy lips, therefore God hath blessed thee forever.

Gird thy sword upon thy thigh, most mighty : with thy glory and t majesty.

And in thy majesty ride prosperous because of truth and meekness and righ eousness : and thy right hand shall teac thee terrible things.

Thine arrows are sharp in the heart of he king's enemies : whereby the people all under thee.

Thy throne, O God, is for ever and ver : the sceptre of thy kingdom is a ight sceptre.

Thou lovest righteousness, and hatest vickedness : therefore God, thy God, ath anointed thee with the oil of gladess above thy fellows.

All thy garments smell of myrrh, and loes, and cassia : out of the ivory palces, whereby they have made thee glad.

Kings' daughters were among thy onorable women : upon thy right hand id stand the queen in gold of Ophir.

Hearken, O daughter, and consider, nd incline thine ear : forget also thine wn people, and thy father's house;

So shall the king greatly desire thy beauty : for he is thy Lord, and worship thou him.

And the daughter of Tyre shall be there with a gift : even the rich among the people shall intreat thy favor.

The king's daughter is all glorious within: her clothing is of wrought gold.

She shall be brought unto the king in raiment of needlework : the virgins her companions that follow her shall be brought unto thee.

With gladness and rejoicing shall they be brought : they shall enter into the king's palace.

Instead of thy fathers shall be thy children : whom thou mayest make princes in all the earth.

I will make thy Name to be remembered in all generations : therefore shall the people praise thee for ever and ever.

PSALM 46. *Deus noster refugium.*

GOD is our refuge and strength : a very present help in trouble.

Therefore will not we fear, though the arth be removed : and though the ountains be carried into the midst of e sea;

Though the waters thereof roar and be oubled : though the mountains shake ith the swelling thereof.

There is a river, the streams whereof hall make glad the city of God : the oly place of the tabernacles of the most ligh.

God is in the midst of her, she shall ot be moved : God shall help her, and at right early.

The heathen raged, the kingdoms were moved : he uttered his voice, the earth melted.

The LORD of hosts is with us : the God of Jacob is our refuge.

Come, behold the works of the LORD : what desolations he hath made in the earth.

He maketh wars to cease unto the end of the earth : he breaketh the bow, and cutteth the spear in sunder, he burneth the chariot in the fire.

Be still, and know that I am God : I will be exalted among the heathen, I will be exalted in the earth.

The LORD of hosts is with us : the God of Jacob is our refuge.

PSALM 47. *Omnes gentes, plaudite.*

O CLAP your hands, all ye people : shout unto God with the voice of iumph.

For the LORD most high is terrible : he a great King over all the earth.

He shall subdue the people under us : ıd the nations under our feet.

He shall choose our inheritance for us : the excellency of Jacob whom he loved.

God is gone up with a shout : the LORD with the sound of a trumpet.

Sing praises to God, sing praises : sing praises unto our King, sing praises.

For God is the King of all the earth : sing ye praises with understanding.

God reigneth over the heathen : God sitteth upon the throne of his holiness.
The princes of the people are gathered together, even the people of the God o[f] Abraham : for the shields of the eart[h] belong unto God, he is greatly exalte[d]

PSALM 48. *Magnus Dominus.*

GREAT is the LORD, and greatly to be praised : in the city of our God, in the mountain of his holiness.
Beautiful for situation, the joy of the whole earth, is mount Zion : on the sides of the north, the city of the great King.
God is known in her palaces : for a refuge.
For, lo, the kings were assembled : they passed by together.
They saw it, and so they marvelled : they were troubled, and hasted away.
Fear took hold upon them there, and pain : as of a woman in travail.
Thou breakest the ships of Tarshish : with an east wind.
As we have heard, so have we seen in the city of the LORD of hosts, in the city of our God : God will establish it fo[r] ever.
We have thought of thy lovingkin[d]ness, O God : in the midst of thy templ[e]
According to thy Name, O God, so thy praise unto the ends of the earth thy right hand is full of righteousness.
Let mount Zion rejoice, let the daugh[t]ers of Judah be glad : because of th[y] judgments.
Walk about Zion, and go round abou[t] her : tell the towers thereof.
Mark ye well her bulwarks, conside[r] her palaces : that ye may tell it to th[e] generation following.
For this God is our God for ever an[d] ever : he will be our guide even unt[o] death.

PSALM 50. *Deus deorum.*

THE mighty God, even the LORD, hath spoken : and called the earth from the rising of the sun unto the going down thereof.
Out of Zion, the perfection of beauty : God hath shined.
Our God shall come, and shall not keep silence : a fire shall devour before him, and it shall be very tempestuous round about him.
He shall call to the heavens from above : and to the earth, that he may judge his people.
Gather my saints together unto me : those that have made a covenant with me by sacrifice.
And the heavens shall declare his righteousness : for God is judge himself.
Hear, O my people, and I will speak : O Israel, and I will testify against thee; I am God, even thy God.
I will not reprove thee for thy sacrifices or thy burnt offerings : to have been continually before me.
I will take no bullock out of thy house : nor he goats out of thy folds;
For every beast of the forest is mine and the cattle upon a thousand hills.
I know all the fowls of the mountains and the wild beasts of the field are min[e]
If I were hungry, I would not tell thee for the world is mine, and the fulne[ss] thereof.
Will I eat the flesh of bulls : or drin[k] the blood of goats?
Offer unto God thanksgiving : an[d] pay thy vows unto the most High;
And call upon me in the day of trou[]ble : I will deliver thee, and thou sha[lt] glorify me.
But unto the wicked God saith, Wh[at] hast thou to do to declare my statutes or that thou shouldest take my covena[nt] in thy mouth?
Seeing thou hatest instruction : an[d] castest my words behind thee.
When thou sawest a thief, then tho[u] consentedst with him : and hast bee[n] partaker with adulterers.
Thou givest thy mouth to evil : an[d]

[m]y tongue frameth deceit.

Thou sittest and speakest against thy [b]rother : thou slanderest thine own [m]other's son.

These things hast thou done, and I [k]ept silence, thou thoughtest that I was [a]ltogether such a one as thyself : but I [w]ill reprove thee, and set them in order before thine eyes.

Now consider this, ye that forget God : lest I tear you in pieces, and there be none to deliver.

Whoso offereth praise glorifieth me : and to him that ordereth his conversation aright will I show the salvation of God.

PSALM 51. *Miserere mei, Deus, secundum.*

[A PENITENTIAL PSALM]

HAVE mercy upon me, O God, according to thy lovingkindness : [a]ccording unto the multitude of thy ten[d]er mercies, blot out my transgressions.

Wash me thoroughly from mine in[i]quity : and cleanse me from my sin.

For I acknowledge my transgressions : [a]nd my sin is ever before me.

Against thee, thee only, have I sinned, [a]nd done this evil in thy sight : that thou [m]ightest be justified when thou speakest, [a]nd be clear when thou judgest.

Behold, I was shapen in iniquity : and [in] sin did my mother conceive me.

Behold, thou desirest truth in the in[w]ard parts : and in the hidden part thou [sh]alt make me to know wisdom.

Purge me with hyssop, and I shall be [cl]ean : wash me, and I shall be whiter [th]an snow.

Make me to hear joy and gladness : [th]at the bones which thou hast broken [m]ay rejoice.

Hide thy face from my sins : and blot [o]ut all mine iniquities.

Create in me a clean heart, O God : [a]nd renew a right spirit within me.

Cast me not away from thy presence : and take not thy holy spirit from me.

Restore unto me the joy of thy salvation : and uphold me with thy free spirit.

Then will I teach transgressors thy ways : and sinners shall be converted unto thee.

Deliver me from bloodguiltiness, O God, thou God of my salvation : and my tongue shall sing aloud of thy righteousness.

O Lord, open thou my lips : and my mouth shall show forth thy praise.

For thou desirest not sacrifice, else would I give it : thou delightest not in burnt offering.

The sacrifices of God are a broken spirit : a broken and a contrite heart, O God, thou wilt not despise.

Do good in thy good pleasure unto Zion : build thou the walls of Jerusalem.

Then shalt thou be pleased with the sacrifices of righteousness, with burnt offering and whole burnt offering : then shall they offer bullocks upon thine altar.

PSALM 54. *Deus, in nomine tuo.*

SAVE me, O God, by thy Name : and judge me by thy strength.

Hear my prayer, O God : give ear to [th]e words of my mouth.

For strangers are risen up against me : [a]nd oppressors seek after my soul, they [h]ave not set God before them.

Behold, God is mine helper : the Lord is with them that uphold my soul.

He shall reward evil unto mine enemies : cut them off in thy truth.

I will freely sacrifice unto thee : I will praise thy Name, O LORD, for it is good.

For he hath delivered me out of all trouble : and mine eye hath seen his desire upon mine enemies.

PSALM 56. *Miserere mei, Deus, quoniam.*

BE merciful unto me, O God, for man would swallow me up : he fighting daily oppresseth me.

Mine enemies would daily swallow me up : for they be many that fight against me, O thou most High.

What time I am afraid : I will trust in thee.

In God I will praise his word, in God I have put my trust : I will not fear what flesh can do unto me.

Every day they wrest my words : all their thoughts are against me for evil.

They gather themselves together, they hide themselves : they mark my steps, when they wait for my soul.

Shall they escape by iniquity : in thine anger cast down the people, O Go

Thou tellest my wanderings, put tho my tears into thy bottle : are they not i thy book?

When I cry unto thee, then shall mi enemies turn back : this I know, for Go is for me.

In God will I praise his word : in th LORD will I praise his word.

In God have I put my trust : I will n be afraid what man can do unto me.

Thy vows are upon me, O God : I w render praises unto thee.

For thou hast delivered my soul fro death, wilt not thou deliver my feet fro falling : that I may walk before God i the light of the living?

PSALM 57. *Miserere mei, Deus, miserere.*

BE merciful unto me, O God, be merciful unto me, for my soul trusteth in thee : yea, in the shadow of thy wings will I make my refuge, until these calamities be overpast.

I will cry unto God most high : unto God that performeth all things for me.

He shall send from heaven, and save me from the reproach of him that would swallow me up : God shall send forth his mercy and his truth.

My soul is among lions : and I lie even among them that are set on fire,

Even the sons of men, whose teeth are spears and arrows : and their tongue a sharp sword.

Be thou exalted, O God, above the heavens : let thy glory be above all th earth.

They have prepared a net for my step my soul is bowed down : they hav digged a pit before me, into the mid whereof they are fallen themselves.

My heart is fixed, O God, my heart fixed : I will sing and give praise.

Awake up, my glory; awake, psalte and harp : I myself will awake early.

I will praise thee, O Lord, among th people : I will sing unto thee among th nations.

For thy mercy is great unto the hea ens : and thy truth unto the clouds.

Be thou exalted, O God, above th heavens : let thy glory be above all th earth.

PSALM 60. *Deus, repulisti nos.*

O GOD, thou hast cast us off, thou hast scattered us : thou hast been displeased, O turn thyself to us again.

Thou hast made the earth to tremble, thou hast broken it : heal the breaches thereof, for it shaketh.

Thou hast showed thy people hard things : thou hast made us to drink the wine of astonishment.

Thou hast given a banner to them th fear thee : that it may be displayed b cause of the truth.

That thy beloved may be delivered save with thy right hand, and he me.

God hath spoken in his holiness, I w rejoice : I will divide Shechem, and me out the valley of Succoth.

Gilead is mine, and Manasseh is mine : Ephraim also is the strength of mine head, Judah is my lawgiver;

Moab is my washpot, over Edom will I cast out my shoe : Philistia, triumph thou because of me.

Who will bring me into the strong city : who will lead me into Edom?

Wilt not thou, O God, which hadst cast us off : and thou, O God, which didst not go out with our armies?

Give us help from trouble : for vain is the help of man.

Through God we shall do valiantly : for he it is that shall tread down our enemies.

PSALM 61. *Exaudi, Deus, deprecationem.*

HEAR my cry, O God : attend unto my prayer.

From the end of the earth will I cry unto thee, when my heart is overwhelmed : lead me to the rock that is higher than I.

For thou hast been a shelter for me : and a strong tower from the enemy.

I will abide in thy tabernacle for ever : I will trust in the covert of thy wings.

For thou, O God, hast heard my vows : thou hast given me the heritage of those that fear thy Name.

Thou wilt prolong the king's life : and his years as many generations.

He shall abide before God for ever : O prepare mercy and truth, which may preserve him.

So will I sing praise unto thy Name for ever : that I may daily perform my vows.

PSALM 62. *Nonne Deo subjecta?*

TRULY my soul waiteth upon God : from him cometh my salvation.

He only is my rock and my salvation : he is my defence, I shall not be greatly moved.

How long will ye imagine mischief against a man : ye shall be slain all of you; as a bowing wall shall ye be, and as a tottering fence.

They only consult to cast him down from his excellency : they delight in lies; they bless with their mouth, but they curse inwardly.

My soul, wait thou only upon God : for my expectation is from him.

He only is my rock and my salvation : he is my defence, I shall not be moved.

In God is my salvation and my glory : the rock of my strength, and my refuge, is in God.

Trust in him at all times, ye people, pour out your heart before him : God is a refuge for us.

Surely men of low degree are vanity, and men of high degree are a lie : to be laid in the balance, they are altogether lighter than vanity.

Trust not in oppression, and become not vain in robbery : if riches increase, set not your heart upon them.

God hath spoken once, twice have I heard this : that power belongeth unto God.

Also unto thee, O Lord, belongeth mercy : for thou renderest to every man according to his work.

PSALM 63. *Deus, Deus meus, ad te.*

O GOD, thou art my God : early will I seek thee;

My soul thirsteth for thee : my flesh longeth for thee in a dry and thirsty land, where no water is;

To see thy power and thy glory : so as I have seen thee in the sanctuary.

Because thy lovingkindness is better than life : my lips shall praise thee.

Thus will I bless thee while I live : I will lift up my hands in thy Name.

My soul shall be satisfied as with mar-row and fatness : and my mouth shall praise thee with joyful lips;

When I remember thee upon my bed : and meditate on thee in the night watches.

Because thou hast been my help therefore in the shadow of thy wing will I rejoice.

My soul followeth hard after thee thy right hand upholdeth me.

PSALM 65. *Te decet hymnus, Deus.*

PRAISE waiteth for thee, O God, in Sion : and unto thee shall the vow be performed.

O thou that hearest prayer : unto thee shall all flesh come.

Iniquities prevail against me : as for our trangressions, thou shalt purge them away.

Blessed is the man whom thou choosest, and causest to approach unto thee : that he may dwell in thy courts;

We shall be satisfied with the goodness of thy house : even of thy holy temple.

By terrible things in righteousness wilt thou answer us : O God of our salvation;

Who art the confidence of all the ends of the earth : and of them that are afar off upon the sea;

Which by his strength setteth fast the mountains : being girded with power;

Which stilleth the noise of the seas : the noise of their waves, and the tumul of the people.

They also that dwell in the uttermos parts are afraid at thy tokens : thou makest the outgoings of the morning and evening to rejoice.

Thou visitest the earth, and wateres it : thou greatly enrichest it with the river of God, which is full of water.

Thou preparest them corn : whe thou hast so provided for it.

Thou waterest the ridges thereof abundantly : thou settlest the furrows thereof

Thou makest it soft with showers thou blessest the springing thereof.

Thou crownest the year with thy goodness : and thy paths drop fatness.

They drop upon the pastures of the wilderness : and the little hills rejoice on every side.

The pastures are clothed with flocks the valleys also are covered over with corn : they shout for joy, they also sing

PSALM 66. *Jubilate Deo, omnis terra.*

MAKE a joyful noise unto God, all ye lands : sing forth the honor of his Name, make his praise glorious.

Say unto God, How terrible art thou in thy works : through the greatness of thy power shall thine enemies submit themselves unto thee.

All the earth shall worship thee, and shall sing unto thee : they shall sing to thy Name.

Come and see the works of God : he is terrible in his doing toward the children of men.

He turned the sea into dry land : they went through the flood on foot, there did we rejoice in him.

He ruleth by his power for ever, hi eyes behold the nations : let not the rebellious exalt themselves.

O bless our God, ye people : and make the voice of his praise to be heard;

Which holdeth our soul in life : and suffereth not our feet to be moved.

For thou, O God, hast proved us thou hast tried us, as silver is tried.

Thou broughtest us into the net : thou laidst affliction upon our loins.

Thou hast caused men to ride over ou

heads : we went through fire and through water, but thou broughtest us out into a wealthy place.

I will go into thy house with burnt offerings : I will pay thee my vows, which my lips have uttered, and my mouth hath spoken, when I was in trouble.

I will offer unto thee burnt sacrifices of fatlings, with the incense of rams : I will offer bullocks with goats.

Come and hear, all ye that fear God : and I will declare what he hath done for my soul.

I cried unto him with my mouth : and he was extolled with my tongue.

If I regard iniquity in my heart : the Lord will not hear me;

But verily God hath heard me : he hath attended to the voice of my prayer.

Blessed be God, which hath not turned away my prayer : nor his mercy from me.

PSALM 67. *Deus misereatur nostri.*

GOD be merciful unto us, and bless us: and cause his face to shine upon us;

That thy way may be known upon earth : thy saving health among all nations.

Let the people praise thee, O God : let all the people praise thee.

O let the nations be glad and sing for joy : for thou shalt judge the people righteously, and govern the nations upon earth.

Let the people praise thee, O God : let all the people praise thee.

Then shall the earth yield her increase ; and God, even our own God, shall bless us.

God shall bless us : and all the ends of the earth shall fear him.

PSALM 68. *Exsurgat Deus.*

I. EXSURGAT DEUS.

LET God arise, let his enemies be scattered : let them also that hate him flee before him.

As smoke is driven away, so drive them away : as wax melteth before the fire, so let the wicked perish at the presence of God.

But let the righteous be glad, let them rejoice before God : yea, let them exceedingly rejoice.

Sing unto God, sing praises to his Name : extol him that rideth upon the heavens by his Name JAH, and rejoice before him.

A father of the fatherless, and a judge of the widows : is God in his holy habitation.

God setteth the solitary in families, he bringeth out those which are bound with chains : but the rebellious dwell in a dry land.

O God, when thou wentest forth before thy people : when thou didst march through the wilderness,

The earth shook, the heavens also dropped at the presence of God : even Sinai itself was moved at the presence of God, the God of Israel.

Thou, O God, didst send a plentiful rain : whereby thou didst confirm thine inheritance, when it was weary.

Thy congregation hath dwelt therein : thou, O God, hast prepared of thy goodness for the poor.

The Lord gave the word : great was the company of those that published it.

Kings of armies did flee apace : and she that tarried at home divided the spoil.

Though ye have lain among the pots, yet shall ye be as the wings of a dove : covered with silver, and her feathers with yellow gold.

When the Almighty scattered kings in it : it was white as snow in Salmon.

The hill of God is as the hill of Bashan : an high hill as the hill of Bashan.

Why leap ye, ye high hills ? this is the hill which God desireth to dwell in : yea, the LORD will dwell in it for ever.

The chariots of God are twenty thousand, even thousands of angels : the Lord is among them, as in Sinai, in th holy place.

Thou hast ascended on high, thou has led captivity captive, thou hast receive gifts for men : yea, for the rebelliou also, that the LORD God might dwel among them.

II. BENEDICTUS DOMINUS DIE.

Blessed be the Lord, who daily loadeth us with benefits : even the God of our salvation.

He that is our God is the God of salvation : and unto GOD the Lord belong the issues from death.

But God shall wound the head of his enemies : and the hairy scalp of such a one as goeth on still in his trespasses.

The Lord said, I will bring again from Bashan : I will bring my people again from the depths of the sea;

That thy foot may be dipped in the blood of thine enemies : and the tongue of thy dogs in the same.

They have seen thy goings, O God : even the goings of my God, my King, in the sanctuary.

The singers went before, the players on instruments followed after : among them were the damsels playing with timbrels.

Bless ye God in the congregations : even the Lord, from the fountain of Israel.

There is little Benjamin with their ruler, the princes of Judah and their council : the princes of Zebulun, an the princes of Naphtali.

Thy God hath commanded th strength : strengthen, O God, that whic thou hast wrought for us.

Because of thy temple at Jerusalem shall kings bring presents unto thee.

Rebuke the company of spearmen, th multitude of the bulls, with the calves o the people, till every one submit himse with pieces of silver : scatter thou th people that delight in war.

Princes shall come out of Egypt : Ethiopia shall soon stretch out her hand unto God.

Sing unto God, ye kingdoms of th earth : O sing praises unto the Lord;

To him that rideth upon the heavens c heavens, which were of old : lo, he dot send out his voice, and that a might voice.

Ascribe ye strength unto God, his ex cellency is over Israel : and his strengt is in the clouds.

O God, thou art terrible out of th holy places : the God of Israel is he tha giveth strength and power unto his peo ple. Blessed be God.

PSALM 69. *Salvum me fac, Deus.*

SAVE me, O God : for the waters are come in unto my soul.

I sink in deep mire, where there is no standing : I am come into deep waters, where the floods overflow me.

I am weary of my crying, my throat is dried : mine eyes fail while I wait for my God.

They that hate me without a cause ar more than the hairs of mine head : the that would destroy me, being mine ene mies wrongfully, are mighty; then I re stored that which I took not away.

O God, thou knowest my foolishness and my sins are not hid from thee.

Let not them that wait on thee, C

ord God of hosts, be ashamed for my ıke : let not those that seek thee be con-ounded for my sake, O God of Israel.

Because for thy sake I have borne eproach : shame hath covered my face.

I am become a stranger unto my rethren : and an alien unto my moth-r's children.

For the zeal of thine house hath eaten e up : and the reproaches of them that eproached thee are fallen upon me.

When I wept, and chastened my soul ith fasting : that was to my reproach.

I made sackcloth also my garment : nd I became a proverb to them.

They that sit in the gate speak against e : and I was the song of the drunk-rds.

But as for me, my prayer is unto thee,) Lord, in an acceptable time : O God, ı the multitude of thy mercy hear me, ı the truth of thy salvation.

Deliver me out of the mire, and let me ot sink : let me be delivered from them hat hate me, and out of the deep waters.

Let not the waterflood overflow me, either let the deep swallow me up : and et not the pit shut her mouth upon me.

Hear me, O Lord, for thy lovingkind-ess is good : turn unto me according to he multitude of thy tender mercies.

And hide not thy face from thy serv-nt, for I am in trouble : hear me speed-y.

Draw nigh unto my soul, and redeem it : deliver me because of mine enemies.

Thou hast known my reproach, and my shame, and my dishonor : mine ad-versaries are all before thee.

Reproach hath broken my heart : and I am full of heaviness.

And I looked for some to take pity, but there was none : and for comforters, but I found none.

They gave me also gall for my meat : and in my thirst they gave me vinegar to drink.

I am poor and sorrowful : let thy sal-vation, O God, set me up on high.

I will praise the Name of God with a song : and will magnify him with thanks-giving.

This also shall please the Lord : better than an ox or bullock that hath horns and hoofs.

The humble shall see this, and be glad : and your heart shall live that seek God.

For the Lord heareth the poor : and despiseth not his prisoners.

Let the heaven and earth praise him : the seas, and every thing that moveth therein.

For God will save Zion, and will build the cities of Judah : that they may dwell there, and have it in possession.

The seed also of his servants shall in-herit it : and they that love his Name shall dwell therein.

PSALM 71. *In te, Domine, speravi.*

IN thee, O Lord, do I put my trust : let me never be put to confusion.

Deliver me in thy righteousness, and ause me to escape : incline thine ear ınto me, and save me.

Be thou my strong habitation, where-ınto I may continually resort : thou hast iven commandment to save me, for hou art my rock and my fortress.

Deliver me, O my God, out of the and of the wicked : out of the hand of he unrighteous and cruel man.

For thou art my hope, O Lord God : thou art my trust from my youth.

Through thee have I been holden up ever since I was born : thou art he that took me out of my mother's womb, my praise shall be always of thee.

I am as a wonder unto many : but thou art my strong refuge.

Let my mouth be filled with thy praise : and with thy honor all the day.

Cast me not off in the time of old age : forsake me not when my strength faileth.

For mine enemies speak against me : and they that lay wait for my soul take counsel together,

Saying, God hath forsaken him : persecute and take him for there is none to deliver him.

O God, be not far from me : O my God, make haste for my help.

Let them be confounded and consumed that are adversaries to my soul : let them be covered with reproach and dishonor that seek my hurt.

But I will hope continually : and will yet praise thee more and more.

My mouth shall show forth thy righteousness and thy salvation all the day : for I know not the numbers thereof.

I will go in the strength of the Lord GOD : I will make mention of thy righteousness, even of thine only.

O God, thou hast taught me from my youth : and hitherto have I declared thy wondrous works.

Now also when I am old and greyheaded, O God, forsake me not : unti have showed thy strength unto this ge eration, and thy power to every one th is to come.

Thy righteousness also, O God, very high, who hast done great things O God, who is like unto thee!

Thou, which hast showed me gre and sore troubles, shalt quicken r again : and shalt bring me up again fro the depths of the earth.

Thou shalt increase my greatness : a comfort me on every side.

I will also praise thee with the psalte even thy truth, O my God : unto th will I sing with the harp, O thou Ho One of Israel.

My lips shall greatly rejoice when I si unto thee : and my soul, which thou ha redeemed.

My tongue also shall talk of thy righ eousness all the day long : for they a confounded, for they are brought un shame, that seek my hurt.

PSALM 72. *Deus, judicium.*

GIVE the king thy judgments, O God : and thy righteousness unto the king's son.

He shall judge thy people with righteousness : and thy poor with judgment.

The mountains shall bring peace to the people : and the little hills, by righteousness.

He shall judge the poor of the people, he shall save the children of the needy : and shall break in pieces the oppressor.

They shall fear thee as long as the sun and moon endure : throughout all generations.

He shall come down like rain upon the mown grass : as showers that water the earth.

In his days shall the righteous flourish : and abundance of peace so long as the moon endureth.

He shall have dominion also from s to sea : and from the river unto the en of the earth.

They that dwell in the wilderness sh bow before him : and his enemies sh lick the dust.

The kings of Tarshish and of the is shall bring presents : the kings of She and Seba shall offer gifts.

Yea, all kings shall fall down befo him : all nations shall serve him.

For he shall deliver the needy when crieth : the poor also, and him that ha no helper.

He shall spare the poor and needy and shall save the souls of the needy.

He shall redeem their soul from dec and violence : and precious shall the blood be in his sight.

And he shall live, and to him shall be given of the gold of Sheba : prayer also shall be made for him continually, and daily shall he be praised.

There shall be an handful of corn in the earth upon the top of the mountains : the fruit thereof shall shake like Lebanon, and they of the city shall flourish like grass of the earth.

His Name shall endure for ever, his Name shall be continued as long as the sun : and men shall be blessed in him; all nations shall call him blessed.

Blessed be the LORD God, the God of Israel : who only doeth wondrous things.

And blessed be his glorious Name for ever : and let the whole earth be filled with his glory. Amen, and Amen.

PSALM 73. *Quam bonus Israel!*

TRULY God is good to Israel : even to such as are of a clean heart.

But as for me, my feet were almost gone : my steps had well nigh slipped.

For I was envious at the foolish : when I saw the prosperity of the wicked.

For there are no bands in their death : but their strength is firm.

They are not in trouble as other men : neither are they plagued like other men.

Therefore pride compasseth them about as a chain : violence covereth them as a garment.

Their eyes stand out with fatness : they have more than heart could wish.

They are corrupt, and speak wickedly concerning oppression: they speak loftily.

They set their mouth against the heavens : and their tongue walketh through the earth.

Therefore his people return hither : and waters of a full cup are wrung out to them.

And they say, How doth God know : and is there knowledge in the most High?

Behold, these are the ungodly who prosper in the world: they increase in riches.

Verily I have cleansed my heart in vain : and washed my hands in innocency.

For all the day long have I been plagued : and chastened every morning.

If I say, I will speak thus : behold, I should offend against the generation of thy children.

When I thought to know this : it was too painful for me;

Until I went into the sanctuary of God : then understood I their end.

Surely thou didst set them in slippery places : thou castedst them down into destruction.

How are they brought into desolation, as in a moment : they are utterly consumed with terrors.

As a dream when one awaketh : so, O Lord, when thou awakest, thou shalt despise their image.

Thus my soul was grieved : and I was pricked in my heart.

So foolish was I, and ignorant : I was as a beast before thee.

Nevertheless I am continually with thee : thou hast holden me by my right hand.

Thou shalt guide me with thy counsel : and afterward receive me to glory.

Whom have I in heaven but thee : and there is none upon earth that I desire beside thee.

My flesh and my heart faileth : but God is the strength of my heart, and my portion for ever.

PSALM 74. *Ut quid, Deus?*

O GOD, why hast thou cast us off for ever : why doth thine anger smoke against the sheep of thy pasture?

Remember thy congregation : which thou hast purchased of old;

The rod of thine inheritance, which thou hast redeemed : this mount Zion, wherein thou hast dwelt.

Lift up thy feet unto the perpetual desolations : even all that the enemy hath done wickedly in the sanctuary.

Thine enemies roar in the midst of thy congregations : they set up their ensigns for signs.

A man was famous : according as he had lifted up axes upon the thick trees.

But now they break down the carved work thereof : at once with axes and hammers.

They have cast fire into thy sanctuary : they have defiled by casting down the dwelling place of thy Name to the ground.

They said in their hearts, Let us destroy them together : they have burned up all the synagogues of God in the land.

We see not our signs, there is no more any prophet : neither is there among us any that knoweth how long.

O God, how long shall the adversary reproach : shall the enemy blaspheme thy Name for ever?

Why withdrawest thou thy hand, even thy right hand : pluck it out of thy bosom.

For God is my King of old : working salvation in the midst of the earth.

Thou didst divide the sea by thy strength : thou brakest the heads of the dragons in the waters.

Thou breakest the heads of leviathan in pieces : and gavest him to be meat to the people inhabiting the wilderness.

Thou didst cleave the fountain and the flood : thou driedst up mighty rivers.

The day is thine, the night also is thine : thou hast prepared the light and the sun.

Thou hast set all the borders of the earth : thou hast made summer and winter.

Remember this, that the enemy hath reproached, O LORD : and that the foolish people have blasphemed thy Name.

O deliver not the soul of thy turtle-dove unto the multitude of the wicked : forget not the congregation of thy poor for ever.

Have respect unto the covenant : for the dark places of the earth are full of the habitations of cruelty.

O let not the oppressed return ashamed : let the poor and needy praise thy Name.

Arise, O God, plead thine own cause : remember how the foolish man reproacheth thee daily.

Forget not the voice of thine enemies : the tumult of those that rise up against thee increaseth continually.

PSALM 77. *Voce mea ad Dominum clamavi.*

I CRIED unto God with my voice : even unto God with my voice, and he gave ear unto me.

In the day of my trouble I sought the Lord : I stretched forth my hands unto him, and ceased not in the night season, my soul refused comfort.

I remembered God, and was troubled : I complained, and my spirit was overwhelmed.

Thou holdest mine eyes waking : I am so troubled that I cannot speak.

I have considered the days of old : the years of ancient times.

I call to remembrance my song in the night : I commune with mine own heart, and my spirit made diligent search.

Will the Lord cast off for ever : and will he be favorable no more?

Is his mercy clean gone for ever : doth ɪis promise fail for evermore?

Hath God forgotten to be gracious : ɪath he in anger shut up his tender mer-:ies?

And I said, This is my infirmity : but I vill remember the years of the right hand ɔf the most High.

I will remember the works of the ˌORD : surely I will remember thy won-lers of old.

I will meditate also of all thy work : ɪnd talk of thy doings.

Thy way, O God, is in the sanctuary : vho is so great a God as our God?

Thou art the God that doest wonders : hou hast declared thy strength among he people.

Thou hast with thine arm redeemed thy people : the sons of Jacob and Joseph.

The waters saw thee, O God, the waters saw thee, they were afraid : the depths also were troubled.

The clouds poured out water, the skies sent out a sound : thine arrows also went abroad.

The voice of thy thunder was in the heaven : the lightnings lightened the world, the earth trembled and shook.

Thy way is in the sea, and thy path in the great waters : and thy footsteps are not known.

Thou leddest thy people like a flock : by the hand of Moses and Aaron.

PSALM 80. *Qui regis Israel.*

GIVE ear, O Shepherd of Israel, thou that leadest Joseph like a flock : hou that dwellest between the cherub-ms, shine forth.

Before Ephraim and Benjamin and Ianasseh stir up thy strength : and ome and save us.

Turn us again, O God : and cause thy ace to shine, and we shall be saved.

O LORD God of hosts : how long wilt hou be angry against the prayer of thy eople?

Thou feedest them with the bread of ears : and givest them tears to drink in reat measure.

Thou makest us a strife unto our eighbors : and our enemies laugh mong themselves.

Turn us again, O God of hosts : and ause thy face to shine, and we shall be aved.

Thou hast brought a vine out of Egypt : thou hast cast out the heathen, nd planted it.

Thou preparedst room before it : and lidst cause it to take deep root, and it illed the land.

The hills were covered with the shadow of it : and the boughs thereof were like the goodly cedars.

She sent out her boughs unto the sea : and her branches unto the river.

Why hast thou then broken down her hedges : so that all they which pass by the way do pluck her?

The boar out of the wood doth waste it : and the wild beast of the field doth devour it.

Return, we beseech thee, O God of hosts : look down from heaven, and behold, and visit this vine;

And the vineyard which thy right hand hath planted : and the branch that thou madest strong for thyself.

It is burned with fire, it is cut down : they perish at the rebuke of thy countenance.

Let thy hand be upon the man of thy right hand : upon the son of man whom thou madest strong for thyself.

So will not we go back from thee : quicken us, and we will call upon thy Name.

Turn us again, O LORD God of hosts : cause thy face to shine, and we shall be saved.

PSALM 81. *Exultate Deo.*

SING aloud unto God our strength : make a joyful noise unto the God of Jacob.

Take a psalm, and bring hither the timbrel : the pleasant harp with the psaltery.

Blow up the trumpet in the new moon : in the time appointed, on our solemn feast day.

For this was a statute for Israel : and a law of the God of Jacob.

This he ordained in Joseph for a testimony, when he went out through the land of Egypt : where I heard a language that I understood not.

I removed his shoulder from the burden : his hands were delivered from the pots.

Thou calledst in trouble, and I delivered thee : I answered thee in the secret place of thunder.

I proved thee : at the waters of Meribah.

Hear, O my people, and I will testify unto thee : O Israel, if thou wilt hearken unto me;

There shall no strange god be in thee neither shalt thou worship any strang god.

I am the LORD thy God, which brough thee out of the land of Egypt : open th mouth wide, and I will fill it.

But my people would not hearken t my voice : and Israel would none of me

So I gave them up unto their ow hearts' lust : and they walked in thei own counsels.

O that my people had hearkened unt me : and Israel had walked in my ways

I should soon have subdued their ene mies : and turned my hand against thei adversaries.

The haters of the LORD should hav submitted themselves unto him : bu their time should have endured for eve

He should have fed them also with th finest of the wheat : and with honey ou of the rock should I have satisfied thee

PSALM 84. *Quam dilecta tabernacula.*

HOW amiable are thy tabernacles, O LORD of hosts! My soul longeth, yea, even fainteth for the courts of the LORD : my heart and my flesh crieth out for the living God.

Yea, the sparrow hath found an house, and the swallow a nest for herself, where she may lay her young : even thine altars, O LORD of hosts, my King and my God.

Blessed are they that dwell in thy house : they will be still praising thee.

Blessed is the man whose strength is in thee : in whose heart are thy ways.

Who passing through the valley of Baca make it a well : the rain also filleth the pools.

They go from strength to strength every one of them in Zion appearet before God.

O LORD God of hosts, hear my prayer give ear, O God of Jacob.

Behold, O God our shield : and loo upon the face of thine anointed.

For a day in thy courts is better than thousand : I had rather be a doorkeepe in the house of my God, than to dwell i the tents of wickedness.

For the LORD God is a sun and shield the LORD will give grace and glory;

No good thing will he withhold fro them that walk uprightly : O LORD c hosts, blessed is the man that trusteth i thee.

PSALM 85. *Benedixisti, Domine.*

ORD, thou hast been favorable unto thy land : thou hast brought back ie captivity of Jacob.

Thou hast forgiven the iniquity of iy people : thou hast covered all ieir sin.

Thou hast taken away all thy wrath : iou hast turned thyself from the fierce-ess of thine anger.

Turn us, O God of our salvation : and iuse thine anger toward us to cease.

Wilt thou be angry with us for ever : ilt thou draw out thine anger to all enerations?

Wilt thou not revive us again : that iy people may rejoice in thee?

Show us thy mercy, O LORD : and rant us thy salvation.

I will hear what God the LORD will speak : for he will speak peace unto his people, and to his saints, but let them not turn again to folly.

Surely his salvation is nigh them that fear him : that glory may dwell in our land.

Mercy and truth are met together : righteousness and peace have kissed each other.

Truth shall spring out of the earth : and righteousness shall look down from heaven.

Yea, the LORD shall give that which is good : and our land shall yield her increase.

Righteousness shall go before him : and shall set us in the way of his steps.

PSALM 86. *Inclina, Domine.*

BOW down thine ear, O LORD, hear me : for I am poor and needy.

Preserve my soul, for I am holy : O iou my God, save thy servant that usteth in thee.

Be merciful unto me, O Lord : for I y unto thee daily.

Rejoice the soul of thy servant : for nto thee, O Lord, do I lift up my soul.

For thou, Lord, art good, and ready forgive : and plenteous in mercy unto l them that call upon thee.

Give ear, O LORD, unto my prayer : nd attend to the voice of my supplica-ons.

In the day of my trouble I will call pon thee : for thou wilt answer me.

Among the gods there is none like nto thee, O Lord : neither are there any orks like unto thy works.

All nations whom thou hast made iall come and worship before thee, O ord : and shall glorify thy Name.

For thou art great, and doest wondrous things : thou art God alone.

Teach me thy way, O LORD, I will walk in thy truth : unite my heart to fear thy Name.

I will praise thee, O Lord my God, with all my heart : and I will glorify thy Name for evermore.

For great is thy mercy toward me : and thou hast delivered my soul from the lowest hell.

O God, the proud are risen against me : and the assemblies of violent men have sought after my soul, and have not set thee before them.

But thou, O Lord, art a God full of compassion, and gracious : longsuffering and plenteous in mercy and truth.

O turn unto me, and have mercy upon me : give thy strength unto thy servant, and save the son of thine handmaid.

Show me a token for good, that they which hate me may see it, and be ashamed : because thou, LORD, hast holpen me, and comforted me.

PSALM 87. *Fundamenta ejus.*

HIS foundation is in the holy mountains : the LORD loveth the gates of Zion more than all the dwellings of Jacob.

Glorious things are spoken of thee : O city of God.

I will make mention of Rahab and Babylon : to them that know me;

Behold Philistia, and Tyre, with Ethiopia : this man was born there.

And of Zion it shall be said, This an that man was born in her : and th Highest himself shall establish her.

The LORD shall count, when he writet up the people : that this man was bor there.

As well the singers as the players o instruments shall be there : all m springs are in thee.

PSALM 89. *Misericordias Domini.*

I WILL sing of the mercies of the LORD for ever : with my mouth will I make known thy faithfulness to all generations.

For I have said, Mercy shall be built up for ever : thy faithfulness shalt thou establish in the very heavens.

I have made a covenant with my chosen : I have sworn unto David my servant.

Thy seed will I establish for ever : and build up thy throne to all generations.

And the heavens shall praise thy wonders, O LORD : thy faithfulness also in the congregation of the saints.

For who in the heaven can be compared unto the LORD : who among the sons of the mighty can be likened unto the LORD?

God is greatly to be feared in the assembly of the saints : and to be had in reverence of all them that are about him.

O LORD God of hosts, who is a strong LORD like unto thee : or to thy faithfulness round about thee?

Thou rulest the raging of the sea : when the waves thereof arise, thou stillest them.

Thou hast broken Rahab in pieces, as one that is slain : thou hast scattered thine enemies with thy strong arm.

The heavens are thine, the earth also is thine : as for the world and the fulness thereof, thou hast founded them.

The north and the south thou ha created them : Tabor and Hermon sha rejoice in thy Name.

Thou hast a mighty arm : strong is th hand, and high is thy right hand.

Justice and judgment are the habita tion of thy throne : mercy and trut shall go before thy face.

Blessed is the people that know th joyful sound : they shall walk, O LORI in the light of thy countenance.

In thy Name shall they rejoice all th day : and in thy righteousness shall the be exalted.

For thou art the glory of their strength and in thy favor our horn shall be e alted.

For the LORD is our defence : and th Holy One of Israel is our king.

Then thou spakest in vision to th holy one, and saidst : I have laid hel upon one that is mighty, I have exalte one chosen out of the people.

I have found David my servant : wi my holy oil have I anointed him;

With whom my hand shall be esta lished : mine arm also shall strengthe him.

The enemy shall not exact upon him nor the son of wickedness afflict him.

And I will beat down his foes befo his face : and plague them that hate hir

But my faithfulness and my mer shall be with him : and in my name sha his horn be exalted.

I will set his hand also in the sea : and his right hand in the rivers.

He shall cry unto me, Thou art my father : my God, and the rock of my salvation.

Also I will make him my firstborn : higher than the kings of the earth.

My mercy will I keep for him for evermore : and my covenant shall stand fast with him.

His seed also will I make to endure for ever : and his throne as the days of heaven.

If his children forsake my law : and walk not in my judgments;

If they break my statutes : and keep not my commandments;

Then will I visit their transgression with the rod : and their iniquity with stripes.

Nevertheless my lovingkindness will I not utterly take from him : nor suffer my faithfulness to fail.

Lord, where are thy former lovingkindnesses : which thou swarest unto David in thy truth?

Remember, Lord, the reproach of thy servants : how I do bear in my bosom the reproach of all the mighty people;

Wherewith thine enemies have reproached, O LORD : wherewith they have reproached the footsteps of thine anointed.

BLESSED be the LORD for evermore: Amen, and Amen.

PSALM 90. *Domine, refugium.*

LORD, thou hast been our dwelling place : in all generations.

Before the mountains were brought forth, or ever thou hadst formed the earth and the world : even from everlasting to everlasting, thou art God.

Thou turnest man to destruction : and sayest, Return, ye children of men.

For a thousand years in thy sight are but as yesterday when it is past : and as a watch in the night.

Thou carriest them away as with a flood, they are as a sleep : in the morning they are like grass which groweth up.

In the morning it flourisheth and groweth up : in the evening it is cut down, and withereth.

For we are consumed by thine anger : and by thy wrath are we troubled.

Thou hast set our iniquities before thee : our secret sins in the light of thy countenance.

For all our days are passed away in thy wrath : we spend our years as a tale that is told.

The days of our years are threescore years and ten, and if by reason of strength they be fourscore years : yet is their strength labor and sorrow, for it is soon cut off, and we fly away.

Who knoweth the power of thine anger : even according to thy fear, so is thy wrath.

So teach us to number our days : that we may apply our hearts unto wisdom.

Return, O LORD, how long : and let it repent thee concerning thy servants.

O satisfy us early with thy mercy : that we may rejoice and be glad all our days.

Make us glad according to the days wherein thou hast afflicted us : and the years wherein we have seen evil.

Let thy work appear unto thy servants : and thy glory unto their children.

And let the beauty of the LORD our God be upon us : and establish thou the work of our hands upon us; yea, the work of our hands establish thou it.

PSALM 91. *Qui habitat.*

HE that dwelleth in the secret place of the most High : shall abide under the shadow of the Almighty.

I will say of the LORD, He is my refuge and my fortress : my God, in him will I trust.

Surely he shall deliver thee from the snare of the fowler : and from the deadly pestilence.

He shall cover thee with his feathers, and under his wings shalt thou trust : his truth shall be thy shield and buckler.

Thou shalt not be afraid for the terror by night : nor for the arrow that flieth by day;

Nor for the pestilence that walketh in darkness : nor for the destruction that wasteth at noonday.

A thousand shall fall at thy side, and ten thousand at thy right hand : but it shall not come nigh thee.

Only with thine eyes shalt thou behold : and see the reward of the wicked.

Because thou hast made the LORD, which is my refuge : even the most High, thy habitation;

There shall no evil befall thee : neither shall any plague come nigh thy dwelling.

For he shall give his angels charge over thee : to keep thee in all thy ways.

They shall bear thee up in their hands : lest thou dash thy foot against a stone.

Thou shalt tread upon the lion and adder : the young lion and the dragon shalt thou trample under feet.

Because he hath set his love upon me, therefore will I deliver him : I will set him on high, because he hath known my Name.

He shall call upon me, and I will answer him : I will be with him in trouble; I will deliver him, and honor him.

With long life will I satisfy him : and show him my salvation.

PSALM 92. *Bonum est confiteri.*

IT is a good thing to give thanks unto the LORD : and to sing praises unto thy Name, O most High;

To show forth thy lovingkindness in the morning : and thy faithfulness every night,

Upon an instrument of ten strings, and upon the psaltery : upon the harp with a solemn sound.

For thou, LORD, hast made me glad through thy work : I will triumph in the works of thy hands.

O LORD, how great are thy works : and thy thoughts are very deep.

A brutish man knoweth not : neither doth a fool understand this.

When the wicked spring as the grass, and when all the workers of iniquity do flourish : it is that they shall be destroyed for ever, but thou, LORD, art most high for evermore.

For, lo, thine enemies, O LORD, for lo, thine enemies shall perish : all the workers of iniquity shall be scattered.

But my horn shalt thou exalt like the horn of an unicorn : I shall be anointed with fresh oil.

Mine eye also shall see my desire on mine enemies : and mine ears shall hear my desire of the wicked that rise up against me.

The righteous shall flourish like the palm tree : he shall grow like a cedar in Lebanon.

Those that be planted in the house of the LORD : shall flourish in the courts of our God.

They shall still bring forth fruit in old age : they shall be fat and flourishing;

To show that the LORD is upright, he is my rock : and there is no unrighteousness in him.

The Psalms

PSALM 93. *Dominus regnavit.*

THE LORD reigneth, he is clothed with majesty : the LORD is clothed with ·ength, wherewith he hath girded him-lf.

The world also is stablished : that it nnot be moved.

Thy throne is established of old : thou t from everlasting.

The floods have lifted up, O LORD, the floods have lifted up their voice : the floods lift up their waves.

The LORD on high is mightier than the noise of many waters : yea, than the mighty waves of the sea.

Thy testimonies are very sure : holiness becometh thine house, O LORD, for ever.

PSALM 95. *Venite, exultemus.*

O COME, let us sing unto the LORD : let us make a joyful noise to the ck of our salvation.

Let us come before his presence with anksgiving : and make a joyful noise to him with psalms.

For the LORD is a great God : and a eat King above all gods.

In his hand are the deep places of the rth : the strength of the hills is his also.

The sea is his, and he made it : and his nds formed the dry land.

O come, let us worship and bow wn : let us kneel before the LORD our aker.

For he is our God : and we are the people of his pasture, and the sheep of his hand.

Today if ye will hear his voice, harden not your heart : as in the provocation, and as in the day of temptation in the wilderness;

When your fathers tempted me : proved me, and saw my work.

Forty years long was I grieved with this generation, and said : It is a people that do err in their heart, and they have not known my ways;

Unto whom I sware in my wrath : that they should not enter into my rest.

PSALM 96. *Cantate Domino.*

O SING unto the LORD a new song : sing unto the LORD, all the earth.

Sing unto the LORD, bless his Name : ow forth his salvation from day to y.

Declare his glory among the heathen : s wonders among all people.

For the LORD is great, and greatly to praised : he is to be feared above all ds.

For all the gods of the nations are ols : but the LORD made the heavens.

Honor and majesty are before him : rength and beauty are in his sanctuary.

Give unto the LORD, O ye kindreds of e people : give unto the LORD glory d strength.

Give unto the LORD the glory due unto his Name : bring an offering, and come into his courts.

O worship the LORD in the beauty of holiness : fear before him, all the earth.

Say among the heathen that the LORD reigneth, the world also shall be established that it shall not be moved : he shall judge the people righteously.

Let the heavens rejoice, and let the earth be glad : let the sea roar, and the fulness thereof.

Let the field be joyful, and all that is therein : then shall all the trees of the wood rejoice before the LORD;

For he cometh, for he cometh to judge the earth : he shall judge the world with righteousness, and the people with his truth.

PSALM 97. *Dominus regnavit, exultet.*

THE LORD reigneth, let the earth rejoice : let the multitude of isles be glad thereof.

Clouds and darkness are round about him : righteousness and judgment are the habitation of his throne.

A fire goeth before him : and burneth up his enemies round about.

His lightnings enlightened the world : the earth saw and trembled.

The hills melted like wax at the presence of the LORD : at the presence of the Lord of the whole earth.

The heavens declare his righteousness : and all the people see his glory.

Confounded be all they that serve graven images, that boast themselves idols : worship him, all ye gods.

Zion heard, and was glad : and t daughters of Judah rejoiced because thy judgments, O LORD.

For thou, LORD, art high above all t earth : thou art exalted far above all go

Ye that love the LORD, hate evil : preserveth the souls of his saints, he d livereth them out of the hand of t wicked.

Light is sown for the righteous : a gladness for the upright in heart.

Rejoice in the LORD, ye righteous and give thanks at the remembrance his holiness.

PSALM 98. *Cantate Domino.*

O SING unto the LORD a new song : for he hath done marvellous things;

His right hand, and his holy arm : hath gotten him the victory.

The LORD hath made known his salvation : his righteousness hath he openly showed in the sight of the heathen.

He hath remembered his mercy and his truth toward the house of Israel : all the ends of the earth have seen the salvation of our God.

Make a joyful noise unto the LORD, all the earth : make a loud noise, and rejoice, and sing praise.

Sing unto the LORD with the harp with the harp, and the voice of a psal

With trumpets and sound of corne make a joyful noise before the LORD, t King.

Let the sea roar, and the fulness the of : the world, and they that dwell the in.

Let the floods clap their hands, let t hills be joyful together before the LOR for he cometh to judge the earth;

With righteousness shall he judge t world : and the people with equity.

PSALM 99. *Dominus regnavit, irascantur.*

THE LORD reigneth, let the people tremble : he sitteth between the cherubims, let the earth be moved.

The LORD is great in Zion : and he is high above all the people.

Let them praise thy great and terrible Name : for it is holy.

The king's strength also loveth judgment, thou dost establish equity : thou executest judgment and righteousness in Jacob.

Exalt ye the LORD our God, and worship at his footstool : for he is holy.

Moses and Aaron among his pries and Samuel among them that call up his Name : they called upon the LO and he answered them.

He spake unto them in the clou pillar : they kept his testimonies, and t ordinance that he gave them.

Thou answeredst them, O LORD c God : thou wast a God that forgav them, though thou tookest vengeance their inventions.

Exalt the LORD our God, and wors at his holy hill : for the LORD our G is holy.

PSALM 100. *Jubilate Deo.*

MAKE a joyful noise unto the LORD, all ye lands : serve the LORD with 'adness, come before his presence with nging.

Know ye that the LORD he is God : it he that hath made us, and not we our- lves; we are his people, and the sheep f his pasture.

Enter into his gates with thanksgiving, and into his courts with praise : be thankful unto him, and bless his Name.

For the LORD is good, his mercy is everlasting : and his truth endureth to all generations.

PSALM 102. *Domine, exaudi orationem meam.*

[A PENITENTIAL PSALM]

I. DOMINE, EXAUDI ORATIONEM MEAM.

HEAR my prayer, O LORD : and let my cry come unto thee.

Hide not thy face from me in the ay when I am in trouble : incline thine ır unto me; in the day when I call an- wer me speedily.

For my days are consumed like smoke : nd my bones are burned as an hearth.

My heart is smitten, and withered like rass : so that I forget to eat my bread.

By reason of the voice of my groan- ıg : my bones cleave to my skin.

I am like a pelican of the wilderness : I m like an owl of the desert.

I watch, and am as a sparrow : alone pon the house top.

Mine enemies reproach me all the ay : and they that are mad against me re sworn against me.

For I have eaten ashes like bread : and mingled my drink with weeping,

Because of thine indignation and thy wrath : for thou hast lifted me up, and cast me down.

My days are like a shadow that declineth : and I am withered like grass.

But thou, O LORD, shalt endure for ever : and thy remembrance unto all generations.

Thou shalt arise, and have mercy upon Zion : for the time to favor her, yea, the set time, is come.

For thy servants take pleasure in her stones : and favor the dust thereof.

So the heathen shall fear the Name of the LORD : and all the kings of the earth thy glory.

II. QUIA AEDIFICAVIT DOMINUS SION.

WHEN the LORD shall build up Zion : e shall appear in his glory.

He will regard the prayer of the destiıte : and not despise their prayer.

This shall be written for the generation ı come : and the people which shall be 'eated shall praise the LORD.

For he hath looked down from the eight of his sanctuary : from heaven id the LORD behold the earth;

To hear the groaning of the prisoner : ı loose those that are appointed to eath;

To declare the Name of the LORD in Zion : and his praise in Jerusalem;

When the people are gathered together : and the kingdoms, to serve the LORD.

He weakened my strength in the way : he shortened my days.

I said, O my God, take me not away in the midst of my days : thy years are throughout all generations.

Of old hast thou laid the foundation of the earth : and the heavens are the work of thy hands.

They shall perish, but thou shalt endure : yea, all of them shall wax old like a garment;

As a vesture shalt thou change them : and they shall be changed;

But thou art the same : and thy yea shall have no end.

The children of thy servants shall co tinue : and their seed shall be esta lished before thee.

PSALM 103. *Benedic, anima mea, Domino, et omnia.*

BLESS the LORD, O my soul : and all that is within me, bless his holy Name.

Bless the LORD, O my soul : and forget not all his benefits;

Who forgiveth all thine iniquities : who healeth all thy diseases;

Who redeemeth thy life from destruction : who crowneth thee with loving-kindness and tender mercies;

Who satisfieth thy mouth with good things : so that thy youth is renewed like the eagle's.

The LORD executeth righteousness and judgment : for all that are oppressed.

He made known his ways unto Moses : his acts unto the children of Israel.

The LORD is merciful and gracious : slow to anger, and plenteous in mercy.

He will not always chide : neither will he keep his anger forever.

He hath not dealt with us after our sins : nor rewarded us according to our iniquities.

For as the heaven is high above the earth : so great is his mercy toward them that fear him.

As far as the east is from the west : so far hath he removed our transgressions from us.

Like as a father pitieth his children so the LORD pitieth them that fear hi

For he knoweth our frame : he r membereth that we are dust.

As for man, his days are as grass : as flower of the field, so he flourisheth.

For the wind passeth over it, and it gone : and the place thereof shall kno it no more.

But the mercy of the LORD is fro everlasting to everlasting upon the that fear him : and his righteousne unto children's children;

To such as keep his covenant : and those that remember his commandmen to do them.

The LORD hath prepared his throne the heavens : and his kingdom rule over all.

Bless the LORD, ye his angels, th excel in strength : that do his comman ments, hearkening unto the voice of h word.

Bless ye the LORD, all ye his hosts : ministers of his, that do his pleasure.

Bless the LORD, all his works in places of his dominion : bless the LOR O my soul.

PSALM 104. *Benedic, anima mea, Domine Deus meus.*

BLESS the LORD, O my soul : O LORD my God, thou art very great, thou art clothed with honor and majesty.

Who coverest thyself with light as with a garment : who stretchest out the heavens like a curtain;

Who layeth the beams of his chambers in the waters : who maketh the clouds his chariot, who walketh upon the wings of the wind;

Who maketh his angels spirits : his ministers a flaming fire;

Who laid the foundations of the earth that it should not be removed for eve

Thou coveredst it with the deep with a garment : the waters stood abo the mountains.

At thy rebuke they fled : at the voi of thy thunder they hasted away.

They go up by the mountains, they g down by the valleys : unto the pla which thou hast founded for them.

Thou hast set a bound that they ma

not pass over : that they turn not again to cover the earth.

He sendeth the springs into the valleys : which run among the hills.

They give drink to every beast of the field : the wild asses quench their thirst.

By them shall the fowls of the heaven have their habitation : which sing among the branches.

He watereth the hills from his chambers : the earth is satisfied with the fruit of thy works.

He causeth the grass to grow for the cattle : and herb for the service of man;

That he may bring forth food out of the earth, and wine that maketh glad the heart of man : and oil to make his face to shine, and bread which strengtheneth man's heart.

The trees of the LORD are full of sap : the cedars of Lebanon, which he hath planted;

Where the birds make their nests : as for the stork, the fir trees are her house.

The high hills are a refuge for the wild goats : and the rocks for the conies.

He appointed the moon for seasons : the sun knoweth his going down.

Thou makest darkness, and it is night : wherein all the beasts of the forest do creep forth.

The young lions roar after their prey : and seek their meat from God.

The sun ariseth, they gather themselves together : and lay them down in their dens.

Man goeth forth unto his work and to his labor : until the evening.

O LORD, how manifold are thy works : in wisdom hast thou made them all, the earth is full of thy riches.

So is this great and wide sea : wherein are things creeping innumerable, both small and great beasts.

There go the ships, there is that leviathan : whom thou hast made to play therein.

These wait all upon thee : that thou mayest give them their meat in due season.

That thou givest them they gather : thou openest thine hand, they are filled with good.

Thou hidest thy face, they are troubled : thou takest away their breath, they die, and return to their dust.

Thou sendest forth thy spirit, they are created : and thou renewest the face of the earth.

The glory of the LORD shall endure for ever : the LORD shall rejoice in his works.

He looketh on the earth, and it trembleth : he toucheth the hills, and they smoke.

I will sing unto the LORD as long as I live : I will sing praise to my God while I have my being.

My meditation of him shall be sweet : I will be glad in the LORD.

Let the sinners be consumed out of the earth, and let the wicked be no more : bless thou the LORD, O my soul. Praise ye the LORD.

PSALM 110. *Dixit Dominus.*

THE LORD said unto my Lord : Sit thou at my right hand, until I make thine enemies thy footstool.

The LORD shall send the rod of thy strength out of Zion : rule thou in the midst of thine enemies.

Thy people shall be willing in the day of thy power, in the beauties of holiness from the womb of the morning : thou hast the dew of thy youth.

The LORD hath sworn, and will not repent : Thou art a priest for ever after the order of Melchizedek.

The Lord at thy right hand : shall strike through kings in the day of his wrath.

He shall judge among the heathen, he shall fill the places with the dead bodies : he shall wound the heads over many countries.

He shall drink of the brook in the way: therefore shall he lift up the head.

PSALM 111. *Confitebor tibi.*

PRAISE ye the LORD. I will praise the LORD with my whole heart : in the assembly of the upright, and in the congregation.

The works of the LORD are great : sought out of all them that have pleasure therein.

His work is honorable and glorious : and his righteousness endureth for ever.

He hath made his wonderful works to be remembered : the LORD is gracious and full of compassion.

He hath given meat unto them that fear him : he will ever be mindful of his covenant.

He hath showed his people the powe of his works : that he may give them th heritage of the heathen.

The works of his hands are verity an judgment : all his commandments a sure.

They stand fast for ever and ever : an are done in truth and uprightness.

He sent redemption unto his people he hath commanded his covenant fc ever, holy and reverend is his Name.

The fear of the LORD is the beginnin of wisdom : a good understanding hav all they that do his commandments, h praise endureth for ever.

PSALM 112. *Beatus vir qui timet.*

PRAISE ye the LORD. Blessed is the man that feareth the LORD : that delighteth greatly in his commandments.

His seed shall be mighty upon earth : the generation of the upright shall be blessed.

Wealth and riches shall be in his house : and his righteousness endureth for ever.

Unto the upright there ariseth light in the darkness : he is gracious, and full of compassion, and righteous.

A good man showeth favor, and lendeth : he will guide his affairs with discretion.

Surely he shall not be moved for ever the righteous shall be in everlasting remembrance.

He shall not be afraid of evil tidings his heart is fixed, trusting in the LORD.

His heart is established, he shall not b afraid : until he see his desire upon h enemies.

He hath dispersed, he hath given t the poor : his righteousness endureth fc ever; his horn shall be exalted with hono

The wicked shall see it, and be grieved he shall gnash with his teeth, and me away; the desire of the wicked sha perish.

PSALM 113. *Laudate, pueri.*

PRAISE ye the LORD. Praise, O ye servants of the LORD : praise the Name of the LORD.

Blessed be the Name of the LORD : from this time forth and for evermore.

From the rising of the sun unto the going down of the same : the LORD's Name is to be praised.

The LORD is high above all nations : and his glory above the heavens.

Who is like unto the LORD our God, who dwelleth on high : who humblet himself to behold the things that are i heaven, and in the earth!

He raiseth up the poor out of th dust : and lifteth the needy out of th dunghill;

That he may set him with princes even with the princes of his people.

He maketh the barren woman to kee house : and to be a joyful mother of chi dren. Praise ye the LORD.

PSALM 114. *In exitu Israel.*

WHEN Israel went out of Egypt : the house of Jacob from a people strange language;

Judah was his sanctuary : and Israel s dominion.

The sea saw it, and fled : Jordan was iven back.

The mountains skipped like rams : d the little hills like lambs.

What ailed thee, O thou sea, that thou fleddest : thou Jordan, that thou wast driven back?

Ye mountains, that ye skipped like rams : and ye little hills, like lambs?

Tremble, thou earth, at the presence of the Lord : at the presence of the God of Jacob;

Which turned the rock into a standing water : the flint into a fountain of waters.

PSALM 115. *Non nobis, Domine.*

NOT unto us, O LORD, not unto us, but unto thy Name give glory : for y mercy, and for thy truth's sake.

Wherefore should the heathen say : here is now their God?

But our God is in the heavens : he th done whatsoever he hath pleased.

Their idols are silver and gold : the ork of men's hands.

They have mouths, but they speak t : eyes have they, but they see not;

They have ears, but they hear not : ses have they, but they smell not;

They have hands, but they handle not, et have they, but they walk not : neier speak they through their throat.

They that make them are like unto em : so is every one that trusteth in em.

O Israel, trust thou in the LORD : he their help and their shield.

O house of Aaron, trust in the LORD : he is their help and their shield.

Ye that fear the LORD, trust in the LORD : he is their help and their shield.

The LORD hath been mindful of us, he will bless us : he will bless the house of Israel, he will bless the house of Aaron.

He will bless them that fear the LORD : both small and great.

The LORD shall increase you more and more : you and your children.

Ye are blessed of the LORD : which made heaven and earth.

The heaven, even the heavens, are the LORD's : but the earth hath he given to the children of men.

The dead praise not the LORD : neither any that go down into silence.

But we will bless the LORD : from this time forth and for evermore. Praise the LORD.

PSALM 116. *Dilexi, quoniam.*

LOVE the LORD : because he hath heard my voice and my supplications.

Because he hath inclined his ear unto e : therefore will I call upon him as ng as I live.

The sorrows of death compassed me, d the pains of hell gat hold upon me : found trouble and sorrow

Then called I upon the Name of the ORD : O LORD, I beseech thee, deliver y soul.

Gracious is the LORD, and righteous : a, our God is merciful.

The LORD preserveth the simple : I was brought low, and he helped me.

Return unto thy rest, O my soul : for the LORD hath dealt bountifully with thee.

For thou hast delivered my soul from death : mine eyes from tears, and my feet from falling.

I will walk before the LORD : in the land of the living.

I believed, therefore have I spoken, I was greatly afflicted : I said in my haste, All men are liars.

What shall I render unto the LORD : for all his benefits toward me?

I will take the cup of salvation : and call upon the Name of the LORD.

I will pay my vows unto the LORD now : in the presence of all his people.

Precious in the sight of the LORD : is the death of his saints.

O LORD, truly I am thy servant : I am thy servant, and the son of thine handmaid; thou hast loosed my bonds.

I will offer to thee the sacrifice thanksgiving : and will call upon t Name of the LORD.

I will pay my vows unto the LORD nc in the presence of all his people : in t courts of the LORD's house, in the mic of thee, O Jerusalem. Praise ye the LOR

PSALM 117. *Laudate Dominum.*

O PRAISE the LORD, all ye nations : praise him, all ye people.

For his merciful kindness is great toward us : and the truth of t LORD endureth for ever. Praise ye t LORD.

PSALM 118. *Confitemini Domino.*

O GIVE thanks unto the LORD, for he is good : because his mercy endureth for ever.

Let Israel now say : that his mercy endureth for ever.

Let the house of Aaron now say : that his mercy endureth for ever.

Let them now that fear the LORD say : that his mercy endureth for ever.

I called upon the LORD in distress : the LORD answered me, and set me in a large place.

The LORD is on my side, I will not fear : what can man do unto me?

The LORD taketh my part with them that help me : therefore shall I see my desire upon them that hate me.

It is better to trust in the LORD : than to put confidence in man.

It is better to trust in the LORD : than to put confidence in princes.

All nations compassed me about : but in the Name of the LORD will I destroy them.

They compassed me about, yea, they compassed me about : but in the Name of the LORD I will destroy them.

They compassed me about like bees, they are quenched as the fire of thorns : for in the Name of the LORD I will destroy them.

Thou hast thrust sore at me that I might fall : but the LORD helped me.

The LORD is my strength and song : and is become my salvation.

The voice of rejoicing and salvation in the tabernacles of the righteous : t right hand of the LORD doeth valiant

The right hand of the LORD is exalte the right hand of the LORD doeth va antly.

I shall not die, but live : and decla the works of the LORD.

The LORD hath chastened me sore but he hath not given me over un death.

Open to me the gates of righteo ness : I will go into them, and I w praise the LORD:

This gate of the LORD : into which t righteous shall enter.

I will praise thee, for thou hast hea me : and art become my salvation.

The stone which the builders refuse is become the head-stone of the corn

This is the LORD's doing : it is marv lous in our eyes.

This is the day which the LORD ha made : we will rejoice and be glad in

Save now, I beseech thee, O LORD : LORD, I beseech thee, send now prosp ity.

Blessed be he that cometh in the Nar of the LORD : we have blessed you out the house of the LORD.

God is the LORD, which hath show us light : bind the sacrifice with cor even unto the horns of the altar.

Thou art my God, and I will prai

hee : thou art my God, I will exalt thee.
O give thanks unto the LORD, for he is good : for his mercy endureth for ever.

PSALM 119. *Beati immaculati.*

I. BEATI IMMACULATI.

BLESSED are the undefiled in the way : who walk in the law of the LORD.

Blessed are they that keep his testimonies : and that seek him with the whole heart.

They also do no iniquity : they walk n his ways.

Thou hast commanded us : to keep hy precepts diligently.

O that my ways were directed : to keep thy statutes!

Then shall I not be ashamed : when I have respect unto all thy commandments.

I will praise thee with uprightness of heart : when I shall have learned thy righteous judgments.

I will keep thy statutes : O forsake me not utterly.

II. IN QUO CORRIGIT.

WHEREWITHAL shall a young nan cleanse his way : by taking heed hereto according to thy word.

With my whole heart have I sought hee : O let me not wander from thy ommandments.

Thy word have I hid in mine heart : hat I might not sin against thee.

Blessed art thou, O LORD : teach me hy statutes.

With my lips have I declared : all the judgments of thy mouth.

I have rejoiced in the way of thy testimonies : as much as in all riches.

I will meditate in thy precepts : and have respect unto thy ways.

I will delight myself in thy statutes : I will not forget thy word.

III. RETRIBUE SERVO TUO.

DEAL bountifully with thy servant : hat I may live, and keep thy word.

Open thou mine eyes : that I may behold wondrous things out of thy law.

I am a stranger in the earth : hide not hy commandments from me.

My soul breaketh for the longing : hat it hath unto thy judgments at all imes.

Thou hast rebuked the proud that are cursed : which do err from thy commandments.

Remove from me reproach and contempt : for I have kept thy testimonies.

Princes also did sit and speak against me : but thy servant did meditate in thy statutes.

Thy testimonies also are my delight : and my counsellors.

PSALM 121. *Levavi oculos.*

I WILL lift up mine eyes unto the hills : from whence cometh my help.

My help cometh from the LORD : which made heaven and earth.

He will not suffer thy foot to be moved: he that keepeth thee will not slumber.

Behold, he that keepeth Israel : shall neither slumber nor sleep.

The LORD is thy keeper : the LORD is thy shade upon thy right hand.

The sun shall not smite thee by day : nor the moon by night.

The LORD shall preserve thee from all evil : he shall preserve thy soul.

The LORD shall preserve thy going out and thy coming in : from this time forth, and even for evermore.

PSALM 122. *Laetatus sum.*

I WAS glad when they said unto me : Let us go into the house of the LORD.

Our feet shall stand within thy gates : O Jerusalem.

Jerusalem is builded as a city : that is compact together;

Whither the tribes go up, the tribes of the LORD : unto the testimony of Israel, to give thanks unto the Name of the LORD.

For there are set thrones of judgment : the thrones of the house of David.

Pray for the peace of Jerusalem : the shall prosper that love thee.

Peace be within thy walls : and pros perity within thy palaces.

For my brethren and companion: sakes : I will now say, Peace be withi thee.

Because of the house of the LORD ou God : I will seek thy good.

PSALM 124. *Nisi quia Dominus.*

IF it had not been the LORD who was on our side : now may Israel say;

If it had not been the LORD who was on our side : when men rose up against us;

Then they had swallowed us up quick : when their wrath was kindled against us;

Then the waters had overwhelmed us : the stream had gone over our soul;

Then the proud waters : had gone ove our soul.

Blessed be the LORD : who hath no given us as a prey to their teeth.

Our soul is escaped as a bird out of th snare of the fowlers : the snare is broke and we are escaped.

Our help is in the Name of the LORD who made heaven and earth.

PSALM 125. *Qui confidunt in Domino.*

THEY that trust in the LORD shall be as mount Zion : which cannot be removed, but abideth for ever.

As the mountains are round about Jerusalem : so the LORD is round about his people from henceforth even for ever.

For the rod of the wicked shall not rest upon the lot of the righteous : lest the righteous put forth their hands unt iniquity.

Do good, O LORD, unto those that b good : and to them that are upright i their hearts.

As for such as turn aside unto the crooked ways : the LORD shall lead the forth with the workers of iniquity; b peace shall be upon Israel.

PSALM 126. *In convertendo.*

WHEN the LORD turned again the captivity of Zion : we were like them that dream.

Then was our mouth filled with laughter : and our tongue with singing;

Then said they among the heathen : The LORD hath done great things for them.

The LORD hath done great things for us : whereof we are glad.

Turn again our captivity, O LORD : a the streams in the south.

They that sow in tears : shall reap i joy.

He that goeth forth and weepet bearing precious seed : shall doubtle come again with rejoicing, bringing h sheaves with him.

PSALM 127. *Nisi Dominus ædificaverit.*

EXCEPT the LORD build the house : they labor in vain that build it;

Except the LORD keep the city : the atchman waketh but in vain.

It is vain for you to rise up early, to t up late, to eat the bread of sorrows : r so he giveth his beloved sleep.

Lo, children are an heritage of the LORD : and the fruit of the womb is his reward.

As arrows are in the hand of a mighty man : so are children of the youth.

Happy is the man that hath his quiver full of them : they shall not be ashamed, but they shall speak with the enemies in the gate.

PSALM 128. *Beati omnes.*

BLESSED is every one that feareth the LORD : that walketh in his ways.

For thou shalt eat the labor of thine ınds : happy shalt thou be, and it shall : well with thee.

Thy wife shall be as a fruitful vine by ıe sides of thine house : thy children ce olive plants round about thy table.

Behold, that thus shall the man be blessed : that feareth the LORD.

The LORD shall bless thee out of Zion : and thou shalt see the good of Jerusalem all the days of thy life.

Yea, thou shalt see thy children's children : and peace upon Israel.

PSALM 130. *De profundis.*

[A PENITENTIAL PSALM]

OUT of the depths : have I cried unto thee, O LORD.

Lord, hear my voice : let thine ears be tentive to the voice of my supplicaons.

If thou, LORD, shouldest mark iniquies : O Lord, who shall stand?

But there is forgiveness with thee : at thou mayest be feared.

I wait for the LORD, my soul doth wait : and in his word do I hope.

My soul waiteth for the Lord more than they that watch for the morning : I say, more than they that watch for the morning.

Let Israel hope in the LORD, for with the LORD there is mercy : and with him is plenteous redemption.

And he shall redeem Israel : from all his iniquities.

PSALM 132. *Memento, Domine.*

LORD, remember David : and all his afflictions;

How he sware unto the LORD : and owed unto the mighty God of Jacob;

Surely I will not come into the tabercle of my house : nor go up into my d,

I will not give sleep to mine eyes : or umber to mine eyelids,

Until I find out a place for the LORD : ı habitation for the mighty God of cob.

Lo, we heard of it at Ephratah : we found it in the fields of the wood.

We will go into his tabernacles : we will worship at his footstool.

Arise, O LORD, into thy rest : thou, and the ark of thy strength.

Let thy priests be clothed with righteousness : and let thy saints shout for joy.

For thy servant David's sake : turn not away the face of thine anointed.

The LORD hath sworn in truth unto David : he will not turn from it;

Of the fruit of thy body : will I set upon thy throne.

If thy children will keep my covenant and my testimony that I shall teach them : their children shall also sit upon thy throne for evermore.

For the LORD hath chosen Zion : he hath desired it for his habitation.

This is my rest for ever : here will I dwell, for I have desired it.

I will abundantly bless her provisior
I will satisfy her poor with bread.

I will also clothe her priests with sa
vation : and her saints shall shout alo
for joy.

There will I make the horn of David
bud : I have ordained a lamp for mi
anointed.

His enemies will I clothe with sham
but upon himself shall his crown flouris

PSALM 133. *Ecce, quam bonum.*

BEHOLD, how good and how pleasant it is : for brethren to dwell together in unity!

It is like the precious ointment upon the head, that ran down upon the beard : even Aaron's beard, that went down to the skirts of his garments;

As the dew of Hermon : and as t
dew that descended upon the mountai
of Zion.

For there the LORD commanded t
blessing : even life for evermore.

PSALM 134. *Ecce nunc.*

BEHOLD, bless ye the LORD, all ye servants of the LORD : which by night stand in the house of the LORD.

Lift up your hands in the sanctuar
and bless the LORD.

The LORD that made heaven a
earth : bless thee out of Zion.

PSALM 135. *Laudate nomen Domini.*

PRAISE ye the LORD. Praise ye the Name of the LORD : praise him, O ye servants of the LORD.

Ye that stand in the house of the LORD : in the courts of the house of our God,

Praise the LORD, for the LORD is good : sing praises unto his Name, for it is pleasant.

For the LORD hath chosen Jacob unto himself : and Israel for his peculiar treasure.

For I know that the LORD is great : and that our Lord is above all gods.

Whatsoever the LORD pleased, that did he in heaven, and in earth : in the seas, and all deep places.

He causeth the vapors to ascend from the ends of the earth : he maketh lig
nings for the rain, he bringeth the wi
out of his treasuries.

Who smote the firstborn of Egyp
both of man and beast.

Who sent tokens and wonders into t
midst of thee, O Egypt : upon Pharac
and upon all his servants.

Who smote great nations : and sl
mighty kings;

Sihon king of the Amorites, and
king of Bashan : and all the kingdoms
Canaan;

And gave their land for an heritag
an heritage unto Israel his people.

Thy Name, O LORD, endureth
ever : and thy memorial, O LO
throughout all generations.

For the LORD will judge his people : nd he will repent himself concerning his ervants.

The idols of the heathen are silver and old : the work of men's hands.

They have mouths, but they speak ot : eyes have they, but they see not;

They have ears, but they hear not : either is there any breath in their ouths.

They that make them are like unto them : so is every one that trusteth in them.

Bless the LORD, O house of Israel : bless the LORD, O house of Aaron;

Bless the LORD, O house of Levi : ye that fear the LORD, bless the LORD.

Blessed be the LORD out of Zion : which dwelleth at Jerusalem. Praise ye the LORD.

PSALM 136. *Confitemini Domino.*

O GIVE thanks unto the LORD, for he is good : for his mercy endureth r ever.

O give thanks unto the God of gods : r his mercy endureth for ever.

O give thanks to the Lord of lords : r his mercy endureth for ever.

To him who alone doeth great woners : for his mercy endureth for ever.

To him that by wisdom made the eavens : for his mercy endureth for ver.

To him that stretched out the earth bove the waters : for his mercy endureth r ever.

To him that made great lights : for his ercy endureth for ever;

The sun to rule by day : for his mercy ndureth for ever;

The moon and stars to rule by night : r his mercy endureth for ever.

To him that smote Egypt in their firstorn : for his mercy endureth for ever;

And brought out Israel from among em : for his mercy endureth for ever;

With a strong hand, and with a retched out arm : for his mercy enureth for ever.

To him which divided the Red Sea to parts : for his mercy endureth for ver;

And made Israel to pass through the midst of it : for his mercy endureth for ever;

But overthrew Pharaoh and his host in the Red Sea : for his mercy endureth for ever.

To him which led his people through the wilderness : for his mercy endureth for ever.

To him which smote great kings : for his mercy endureth for ever;

And slew famous kings : for his mercy endureth for ever;

Sihon king of the Amorites : for his mercy endureth for ever;

And Og the king of Bashan : for his mercy endureth for ever;

And gave their land for an heritage : for his mercy endureth for ever;

Even an heritage unto Israel his servant: for his mercy endureth for ever.

Who remembered us in our low estate : for his mercy endureth for ever;

And hath redeemed us from our enemies : for his mercy endureth for ever.

Who giveth food to all flesh : for his mercy endureth for ever.

O give thanks unto the God of heaven: for his mercy endureth for ever.

PSALM 137. *Super flumina.*

BY the rivers of Babylon, there we sat down, yea, we wept : when we reembered Zion.

We hanged our harps upon the willows : in the midst thereof.

For there they that carried us away

captive required of us a song : and they that wasted us required of us mirth, saying, Sing us one of the songs of Zion.

How shall we sing the LORD's song : in a strange land?

If I forget thee, O Jerusalem : let m right hand forget her cunning.

If I do not remember thee, let m tongue cleave to the roof of my mouth if I prefer not Jerusalem above my chi joy.

PSALM 138. *Confitebor tibi.*

I WILL praise thee with my whole heart : before the gods will I sing praise unto thee.

I will worship toward thy holy temple, and praise thy Name for thy lovingkindness and for thy truth : for thou hast magnified thy word above all thy Name.

In the day when I cried thou answeredst me : and strengthenedst me with strength in my soul.

All the kings of the earth shall praise thee, O LORD : when they hear the words of thy mouth.

Yea, they shall sing in the ways of the LORD : for great is the glory of th LORD.

Though the LORD be high, yet hath h respect unto the lowly : but the proud h knoweth afar off.

Though I walk in the midst of troubl thou wilt revive me : thou shalt stretc forth thine hand against the wrath c mine enemies, and thy right hand sha save me.

The LORD will perfect that which con cerneth me : thy mercy, O LORD, en dureth for ever; forsake not the work of thine own hands.

PSALM 139. *Domine, probasti me.*

O LORD, thou hast searched me, and known me : thou knowest my downsitting and mine uprising; thou understandest my thought afar off.

Thou compassest my path and my lying down : and art acquainted with all my ways.

For there is not a word in my tongue : but, lo, O LORD, thou knowest it altogether.

Thou hast beset me behind and before : and laid thine hand upon me.

Such knowledge is too wonderful for me : it is high, I cannot attain unto it.

Whither shall I go from thy spirit : or whither shall I flee from thy presence?

If I ascend up into heaven, thou art there : if I make my bed in hell, behold, thou art there.

If I take the wings of the morning : and dwell in the uttermost parts of the sea;

Even there shall thy hand lead me: and thy right hand shall hold me.

If I say, Surely the darkness shall cove me : even the night shall be light abou me.

Yea, the darkness hideth not fron thee, but the night shineth as the day the darkness and the light are both alik to thee.

For thou hast possessed my reins thou hast covered me in my mother womb.

I will praise thee, for I am fearfull and wonderfully made : marvellous a thy works, and that my soul knowet right well.

My substance was not hid from the when I was made in secret : and cur ously wrought in the lowest parts of th earth.

Thine eyes did see my substance, y being unperfect : and in thy book all m members were written,

Which in continuance were fashioned when as yet there was none of them.

How precious also are thy thoughts unto me, O God : how great is the sum of them!

If I should count them, they are more in number than the sand : when I awake, I am still with thee.

Surely thou wilt slay the wicked, O God : depart from me therefore, ye bloody men.

For they speak against thee wickedly : and thine enemies take thy Name in vain.

Do not I hate them, O LORD, that hate thee : and am not I grieved with those that rise up against thee?

I hate them with perfect hatred : I count them mine enemies.

Search me, O God, and know my heart : try me, and know my thoughts;

And see if there be any wicked way in me : and lead me in the way everlasting.

PSALM 142. *Voce mea ad Dominum.*

I CRIED unto the LORD with my voice : with my voice unto the LORD did I make my supplication.

I poured out my complaint before him : I showed before him my trouble.

When my spirit was overwhelmed within me, then thou knewest my path : in the way wherein I walked have they privily laid a snare for me.

I looked on my right hand, and beheld, but there was no man that would know me : refuge failed me; no man cared for my soul.

I cried unto thee, O LORD : I said, Thou art my refuge and my portion in the land of the living.

Attend unto my cry, for I am brought very low : deliver me from my persecutors, for they are stronger than I.

Bring my soul out of prison, that I may praise thy Name : the righteous shall compass me about; for thou shalt deal bountifully with me.

PSALM 143. *Domine, exaudi.*

[A PENITENTIAL PSALM]

HEAR my prayer, O LORD, give ear to my supplications : in thy faithfulness answer me, and in thy righteousness.

And enter not into judgment with thy servant : for in thy sight shall no man living be justified.

For the enemy hath persecuted my soul, he hath smitten my life down to the ground : he hath made me to dwell in darkness, as those that have been long dead.

Therefore is my spirit overwhelmed within me : my heart within me is desolate.

I remember the days of old, I meditate on all thy works : I muse on the work of thy hands.

I stretch forth my hands unto thee : my soul thirsteth after thee, as a thirsty land.

Hear me speedily, O LORD, my spirit faileth : hide not thy face from me, lest I be like unto them that go down into the pit.

Cause me to hear thy lovingkindness in the morning, for in thee do I trust : cause me to know the way wherein I should walk, for I lift up my soul unto thee.

Deliver me, O LORD, from mine enemies : I flee unto thee to hide me.

Teach me to do thy will, for thou art my God : thy spirit is good; lead me into the land of uprightness.

Quicken me, O LORD, for thy Name's sake : for thy righteousness' sake bring my soul out of trouble.

And of thy mercy cut off mine enemies : and destroy all them that afflict my soul, for I am thy servant.

PSALM 144. *Benedictus Dominus.*

BLESSED be the LORD my strength : which teacheth my hands to war, and my fingers to fight;

My goodness and my fortress, my high tower, and my deliverer : my shield, and he in whom I trust; who subdueth my people under me.

LORD, what is man, that thou takest knowledge of him : or the son of man, that thou makest account of him!

Man is like to vanity : his days are as a shadow that passeth away.

Bow thy heavens, O LORD, and come down : touch the mountains, and they shall smoke.

Cast forth lightning, and scatter them : shoot out thine arrows, and destroy them.

Send thine hand from above : rid me, and deliver me out of great waters, from the hand of strange children;

Whose mouth speaketh vanity : and their right hand is a right hand of falsehood.

I will sing a new song unto thee, O God : upon a psaltery and an instrument of ten strings will I sing praises unto thee.

It is he that giveth salvation unto kings : who delivereth David his servant from the hurtful sword.

Rid me, and deliver me from the hand of strangers : whose mouth speaketh vanity, and their right hand is a right hand of falsehood;

That our sons may be as plants grown up in their youth : that our daughters may be as corner stones, polished after the similitude of a palace;

That our garners may be full, affording all manner of store : that our sheep may bring forth thousands and ten thousands in our streets;

That our oxen may be strong to labor : that there be no breaking in, nor going out; that there be no complaining in our streets.

Happy is that people, that is in such a case : yea, happy is that people, whose God is the LORD.

PSALM 145. *Exaltabo te, Deus.*

I WILL extol thee, my God, O King : and I will bless thy Name for ever and ever.

Every day will I bless thee : and I will praise thy Name for ever and ever.

Great is the LORD, and greatly to be praised : and his greatness is unsearchable.

One generation shall praise thy works to another : and shall declare thy mighty acts.

I will speak of the glorious honor of thy majesty : and of thy wondrous works.

And men shall speak of the might of thy terrible acts : and I will declare thy greatness.

They shall abundantly utter the memory of thy great goodness : and shall sing of thy righteousness.

The LORD is gracious, and full of compassion : slow to anger, and of great mercy.

The LORD is good to all : and his tender mercies are over all his works.

All thy works shall praise thee, O LORD : and thy saints shall bless thee.

They shall speak of the glory of thy kingdom : and talk of thy power;

To make known to the sons of men his mighty acts : and the glorious majesty of his kingdom.

Thy kingdom is an everlasting kingdom : and thy dominion endureth throughout all generations.

The LORD upholdeth all that fall : and raiseth up all those that be bowed down.

The eyes of all wait upon thee : and thou givest them their meat in due season.

Thou openest thine hand : and satisfiest the desire of every living thing.

The LORD is righteous in all his ways : and holy in all his works.

The LORD is nigh unto all them that call upon him : to all that call upon him in truth.

He will fulfill the desire of them that fear him : he also will hear their cry, and will save them.

The LORD preserveth all them that love him : but all the wicked will he destroy.

My mouth shall speak the praise of the LORD : and let all flesh bless his holy Name for ever and ever.

PSALM 146. *Lauda, anima mea.*

PRAISE ye the LORD : praise the LORD, O my soul.

While I live will I praise the LORD : I will sing praises unto my God while I have any being.

Put not your trust in princes, nor in the son of man : in whom there is no help.

His breath goeth forth, he returneth to his earth : in that very day his thoughts perish.

Happy is he that hath the God of Jacob for his help : whose hope is in the LORD his God;

Which made heaven and earth, the sea, and all that therein is : which keepeth truth for ever;

Which executeth judgment for the oppressed : which giveth food to the hungry.

The LORD looseth the prisoners : the LORD openeth the eyes of the blind;

The LORD raiseth them that are bowed down : the LORD loveth the righteous;

The LORD preserveth the strangers, he relieveth the fatherless and widow : but the way of the wicked he turneth upside down.

The LORD shall reign for ever, even thy God, O Zion : unto all generations. Praise ye the LORD.

PSALM 147. *Laudate Dominum.*

PRAISE ye the LORD, for it is good to sing praises unto our God : for it is pleasant, and praise is comely.

The LORD doth build up Jerusalem : he gathereth together the outcasts of Israel.

He healeth the broken in heart : and bindeth up their wounds.

He telleth the number of the stars : he calleth them all by their names.

Great is our Lord, and of great power : his understanding is infinite.

The LORD lifteth up the meek : he casteth the wicked down to the ground.

Sing unto the LORD with thanksgiving : sing praise upon the harp unto our God;

Who covereth the heaven with clouds, who prepareth rain for the earth : who maketh grass to grow upon the mountains.

He giveth to the beast his food : and to the young ravens which cry.

He delighteth not in the strength of the horse : he taketh not pleasure in the legs of a man.

The LORD taketh pleasure in them that fear him : in those that hope in his mercy.

Praise the LORD, O Jerusalem : praise thy God, O Zion.

For he hath strengthened the bars of thy gates : he hath blessed thy children within thee.

He maketh peace in thy borders : and filleth thee with the finest of the wheat.

He sendeth forth his commandment upon earth : his word runneth very swiftly.

He giveth snow like wool : he scattereth the hoarfrost like ashes.

He casteth forth his ice like morsels : who can stand before his cold?

He sendeth out his word, and melteth them : he causeth his wind to blow, and the waters flow.

He showeth his word unto Jacob : his statutes and his judgments unto Israel.

He hath not dealt so with any nation : and as for his judgments, they have not known them. Praise ye the LORD.

PSALM 148. *Laudate Dominum, de cœlis.*

PRAISE ye the LORD. Praise ye the LORD from the heavens : praise him in the heights.

Praise ye him, all his angels : praise ye him, all his hosts.

Praise ye him, sun and moon : praise him, all ye stars of light.

Praise him, ye heavens of heavens : and ye waters that be above the heavens.

Let them praise the Name of the LORD : for he commanded, and they were created.

He hath also stablished them for ever and ever : he hath made a decree which shall not pass.

Praise the LORD from the earth : ye dragons, and all deeps;

Fire, and hail, snow, and vapors : stormy wind fulfilling his word;

Mountains, and all hills : fruitful trees, and all cedars;

Beasts, and all cattle : creeping things, and flying fowl;

Kings of the earth, and all people : princes, and all judges of the earth;

Both young men, and maidens : old men, and children;

Let them praise the Name of the LORD : for his Name alone is excellent, his glory is above the earth and heaven.

He also exalteth the horn of his people, the praise of all his saints : even of the children of Israel, a people near unto him. Praise ye the LORD.

PSALM 149. *Cantate Domino.*

PRAISE ye the LORD. Sing unto the LORD a new song : and his praise in the congregation of saints.

Let Israel rejoice in him that made him : let the children of Zion be joyful in their King.

Let them praise his Name in the dance : let them sing praises unto him with the timbrel and harp.

For the LORD taketh pleasure in his people : he will beautify the meek with salvation.

Let the saints be joyful in glory : let them sing aloud upon their beds.

Let the high praises of God be in their mouth : and a two-edged sword in their hand;

To execute vengeance upon the heathen : and punishments upon the people;

To bind their kings with chains : and their nobles with fetters of iron;

To execute upon them the judgment written : this honor have all his saints. Praise ye the LORD.

PSALM 150. *Laudate Dominum in sanctis ejus.*

PRAISE ye the LORD. Praise God in his sanctuary : praise him in the firmament of his power.

Praise him for his mighty acts : praise him according to his excellent greatness.

Praise him with the sound of the trumpet : praise him with the psaltery and harp.

Praise him with the timbrel and dance : praise him with stringed instruments and organs.

Praise him upon the loud cymbals : praise him upon the high sounding cymbals.

Let every thing that hath breath : praise the LORD. Praise ye the LORD.

GLORY BE TO THE FATHER, AND TO THE SON, AND TO THE HOLY GHOST: AS IT WAS IN THE BEGINNING, IS NOW, AND EVER SHALL BE, WORLD WITHOUT END. AMEN.

The Canticles

1. *Magnificat*. St. Luke 1:46–55.
2. *Nunc Dimittis*. St. Luke 2:29–32.
3. *Te Deum laudamus*.
4. *Benedictus*. St. Luke 1:68–79.

Note that the texts of Canticles Numbers 1 to 4 are not given here. The Magnificat and the Nunc Dimittis will be found in Vespers; and the Te Deum laudamus and the Benedictus will be found in Matins.

5. *Benedicite, omnia opera.*

O ALL ye Works of the Lord, bless ye the Lord : praise him and magnify him for ever.

O ye Angels of the Lord, bless ye the Lord : O ye Heavens, bless ye the Lord.

O ye Waters that be above the firmament, bless ye the Lord : O ye Powers of the Lord, bless ye the Lord.

O ye Sun and Moon, bless ye the Lord : O ye Stars of heaven, bless ye the Lord.

O ye Showers and Dew, bless ye the Lord : O ye Winds of God, bless ye the Lord.

O ye Fire and Heat, bless ye the Lord : O ye Winter and Summer, bless ye the Lord.

O ye Dews and Frost, bless ye the Lord : O ye Frost and Cold, bless ye the Lord.

O ye Ice and Snow, bless ye the Lord : O ye Nights and Days, bless ye the Lord.

O ye Light and Darkness, bless ye the Lord : O ye Lightnings and Clouds, bless ye the Lord.

O let the Earth bless the Lord : yea, let it praise him, and magnify him for ever.

O ye Mountains and Hills, bless ye the Lord : O all ye Green Things upon the earth, bless ye the Lord.

O ye Wells, bless ye the Lord : O ye Seas and Floods, bless ye the Lord.

O ye Whales and all that move in the waters, bless ye the Lord : O all ye Fowls of the air, bless ye the Lord.

O all ye Beasts and Cattle, bless ye the Lord : O ye Children of Men, bless ye the Lord.

O let Israel bless the Lord : praise him and magnify him for ever.

O ye Priests of the Lord, bless ye the Lord : O ye Servants of the Lord, bless ye the Lord.

O ye Spirits and Souls of the Righteous, bless ye the Lord : O ye holy and humble Men of heart, bless ye the Lord.

Bless we the Father, and the Son, and the Holy Ghost : let us praise him and magnify him for ever.

Blessed art thou, O Lord, in the firmament of heaven : and greatly to be praised, and glorified, and highly exalted for ever.

6. *Confitebor tibi*. Isaiah 12:1–6.

O LORD, I will praise thee, though thou wast angry with me, thine anger is turned away : and thou comfortedst me.

Behold, God is my salvation : I will trust, and not be afraid;

For the LORD JEHOVAH is my strength and my song : he also is become my salvation.

Therefore with joy shall ye draw water : out of the wells of salvation.

And in that day shall ye say, Praise the LORD, call upon his Name : declare his doings among the people, make mention that his Name is exalted.

Sing unto the LORD, for he hath done excellent things : this is known in all the earth.

Cry out and shout, thou inhabitant of Zion : for great is the Holy One of Israel in the midst of thee.

Glory be to the Father, . . .

7. *Exultavit cor meum.* 1 Samuel 2:1–10.

MY heart rejoiceth in the LORD : mine horn is exalted in the LORD;

My mouth is enlarged over mine enemies : because I rejoice in thy salvation.

There is none holy as the LORD, for there is none beside thee : neither is there any rock like our God.

Talk no more so exceeding proudly : let not arrogancy come out of your mouth;

For the LORD is a God of knowledge : and by him actions are weighed.

The bows of the mighty men are broken : and they that stumbled are girded with strength.

The LORD killeth, and maketh alive : he bringeth down to the grave, and bringeth up.

The LORD maketh poor, and maketh rich : he bringeth low, and lifteth up.

He raiseth up the poor out of the dust : and lifteth up the beggar from the dunghill,

To set them among princes : and to make them inherit the throne of glory;

For the pillars of the earth are the LORD's : and he hath set the world upon them.

He will keep the feet of his saints, and the wicked shall be silent in darkness : for by strength shall no man prevail.

The adversaries of the LORD shall be broken to pieces : out of heaven shall he thunder upon them;

The LORD shall judge the ends of the earth : and he shall give strength unto his king, and exalt the horn of his anointed.

Glory be to the Father, . . .

8. *Cantemus Domino.* Exodus 15.

I WILL sing unto the LORD, for he hath triumphed gloriously : the horse and his rider hath he thrown into the sea.

The LORD is my strength and song : and he is become my salvation;

He is my God, and I will prepare him an habitation : my father's God, and I will exalt him.

Thy right hand, O LORD, is become glorious in power : thy right hand, O LORD, hath dashed in pieces the enemy.

Who is like unto thee, O LORD : among the gods?

Who is like thee : glorious in holiness, fearful in praises, doing wonders?

Thou in thy mercy hast led forth the people : which thou hast redeemed;

Thou hast guided them in thy strength : unto thy holy habitation.

Thou shalt bring them in, and plant them : in the mountain of thine inheritance.

In the place, O LORD, which thou hast made for thee to dwell in : in the Sanctuary, O Lord, which thy hands have established.

The LORD shall reign : for ever and ever.

Glory be to the Father, . . .

9. *Domine, audivi.* Habakkuk 3.

O LORD, I have heard thy speech, and was afraid : O LORD, revive thy work in the midst of the years;

In the midst of the years make known : in wrath remember mercy.

God came from Teman : and the Holy One from mount Paran.

His glory covered the heavens : and the earth was full of his praise.

His brightness was as the light, he had horns coming out of his hand : and there was the hiding of his power.

Before him went the pestilence : and burning coals went forth at his feet.

He stood, and measured the earth : he beheld, and drove asunder the nations;

And the everlasting mountains were

scattered, the perpetual hills did bow : his ways are everlasting.

Thou wentest forth for the salvation of thy people : even for salvation with thine anointed.

I will rejoice in the LORD : I will joy in the God of my salvation.

The LORD God is my strength : and he will make me to walk upon mine high places.

Glory be to the Father, . . .

10. *Audite cœli.* Deuteronomy 32.

GIVE ear, O ye heavens, and I will speak : and hear, O earth, the words of my mouth.

My doctrine shall drop as the rain, my speech shall distil as the dew : as the small rain upon the tender herb, and as the showers upon the grass;

Because I will publish the Name of the LORD : ascribe ye greatness unto our God.

He is the Rock, his work is perfect : for all his ways are judgment;

A God of truth and without iniquity : just and right is he.

The LORD's portion is his people : Jacob is the lot of his inheritance.

For the LORD shall judge his people : and repent himself for his servants;

When he seeth that their power is gone : and there is none shut up, or left.

And he shall say, I lift up my hand to heaven : and say, I live for ever.

Rejoice, O ye nations, with his people : for he will avenge the blood of his servants,

And will render vengeance to his adversaries : and will be merciful unto his land, and to his people.

Glory be to the Father, . . .

11. *Song of Hezekiah.* Isaiah 38:10–20.

I SAID in the cutting off of my days, I shall go to the gates of the grave : I am deprived of the residue of my years.

I said, I shall not see the LORD, even the LORD, in the land of the living : I shall behold man no more with the inhabitants of the world.

Mine age is departed : and is removed from me as a shepherd's tent.

I have cut off like a weaver my life : he will cut me off with pining sickness, from day even to night wilt thou make an end of me.

I reckoned till morning, that, as a lion, so will he break all my bones : from day even to night wilt thou make an end of me.

Like a crane or a swallow, so did I chatter, I did mourn as a dove : mine eyes fail with looking upward.

O LORD, I am oppressed : undertake for me.

What shall I say? he hath both spoken unto me : and himself hath done it.

I shall go softly all my years : in the bitterness of my soul.

O LORD, by these things men live : and in all these things is the life of my spirit.

So wilt thou recover me : and make me to live.

Behold, for peace, I had great bitterness, but thou hast in love to my soul delivered it from the pit of corruption : for thou hast cast all my sins behind thy back.

For the grave cannot praise thee : death can not celebrate thee.

They that go down into the pit : cannot hope for thy truth.

The living, the living, he shall praise thee : as I do this day.

The father to the children : shall make known thy truth.

The LORD was ready to save me : therefore we will sing my songs to the stringed instruments all the days of our life in the house of the LORD.

Glory be to the Father, . . .

12. *Song of David.* I Chronicles 29:10–18.

BLESSED be thou, LORD God of Israel : our father, for ever and ever.

Thine, O LORD, is the greatness, and the power, and the glory, and the victory, and the majesty : for all that is in the heaven and in the earth is thine.

Thine is the kingdom, O LORD : and thou art exalted as head above all.

Both riches and honor come of thee : and thou reignest over all;

And in thine hand is power and might : and in thine hand it is to make great, and to give strength unto all.

Now therefore, our God, we thank thee : and praise thy glorious Name.

But who am I, and what is my people : that we should be able to offer so willingly after this sort?

For all things come of thee : and of thine own have we given thee.

For we are strangers before thee, and sojourners : as were all our fathers.

Our days on the earth are as a shadow : and there is none abiding.

O LORD our God, all this store that we have prepared to build thee an house for thine holy Name cometh of thine hand : and is all thine own.

I know also, my God, that thou triest the heart : and hast pleasure in uprightness.

As for me, in the uprightness of mine heart I have willingly offered all these things : and now have I seen with joy thy people, which are present here, to offer willingly unto thee.

O LORD God of Abraham, Isaac, and of Israel, our fathers, keep this for ever in the imagination of the thoughts of the heart of thy people : and prepare their heart unto thee.

Glory be to the Father, . . .

Collects and Prayers

THE CHURCH

1. *For the Church*

O GOD of unchangeable power and eternal light, look favorably on thy whole Church, that wonderful and sacred mystery; and, by the tranquil operation of thy perpetual Providence, carry out the work of man's salvation; and let the whole world feel and see that things which were cast down are being raised up, that things which had grown old are being made new, and that all things are returning to perfection through him from whom they took their origin, even thy Son, Jesus Christ our Lord. *Amen.*

2. *For the Church*

GRANT, we beseech thee, Almighty God, unto thy Church, thy Holy Spirit, and the wisdom which cometh down from above; that thy word, as becometh it, may not be bound, but have free course and be preached to the joy and edifying of Christ's holy people; that in steadfast faith we may serve thee, and in the confession of thy Name abide unto the end; through Jesus Christ, thy Son, our Lord. *Amen.*

3. *For the Church*

O LORD, favorably receive the prayers of thy Church; that, being delivered from all adversity and error, it may serve thee in safety and freedom; and grant us thy peace in our time; through Jesus Christ, thy Son, our Lord. *Amen.*

4. *For the Church*

MOST gracious Father, we humbly beseech thee for thy holy catholic Church. Fill it with all truth, in all peace. Where it is corrupt, purify it; where it is in error, direct it; where anything is amiss, reform it; where it is right, strengthen and confirm it; where it is in want, provide for it; where it is divided and rent asunder, heal the breaches thereof, O thou Holy One of Israel; through Jesus Christ our Lord. *Amen.*

5. *For the Church*

O MOST Holy Spirit of God, from whom alone floweth the fulness of wisdom and life: Come in thine everlasting power and glory, we beseech thee, upon thy Church and into the hearts of men; to bring to the world a new birth of holiness, new interpretations of truth, and new unity in love; through Jesus Christ our Lord, who with the Father and thee liveth and reigneth, one God, world without end. *Amen.*

6. *For the Church Militant*

HEAVENLY Father, the author of all wisdom, understanding, and true strength: We beseech thee to look mercifully upon thy servants and send thy Holy Spirit into their hearts; that when they must join to fight in the field for the glory of thy holy Name, then they, being strengthened with the defense of thy right hand, may manfully stand in the confession of thy faith and of thy truth, and continue in the same unto the end of their lives; through Jesus Christ our Lord. *Amen.*

7. *For Church Unity*

O GOD our Father, good beyond all that is good, fair beyond all that is fair, in whom is calmness and peace: Do thou make up the dissensions which divide us from each other, and bring us back into a unity of love, which may bear some likeness to thy sublime Nature; grant that we may be spiritually one, as well in ourselves as in each other; through that peace of thine which maketh all things peaceful, and through the grace, mercy and compassion of thy Son, Jesus Christ, our Lord. *Amen.*

8. *For Church Unity*

O GOD, the physician of men and nations, the restorer of the years that have been destroyed: Look upon the distractions of the world, and be pleased to complete the work of thy healing hand; draw all men unto thee and one to another by the bands of thy love; make thy Church one, and fill it with thy Spirit, that by thy power it may unite the world in a sacred brotherhood of nations, wherein justice, mercy and faith, truth and freedom may flourish, and thou mayest be ever glorified; through Jesus Christ our Lord. *Amen.*

9. *For the Parish*

ALMIGHTY and everlasting God, who dost govern all things in heaven and earth: Mercifully hear our supplications, and grant unto this parish all things that are needful for its spiritual welfare. Strengthen and increase the faithful; visit and relieve the sick; rouse the careless; restore the fallen and penitent; remove all hindrances to the advancement of thy truth; and bring all to be of one heart and mind within the fold of thy holy Church, to the honor and glory of thy holy Name; through Jesus Christ our Lord. *Amen.*

10. *For the Spread of the Gospel*
(*Evangelistic Work*)

INCREASE, O God, the faith and the zeal of all thy people, that they may more earnestly desire, and more diligently seek, the salvation of their fellowmen, through the message of thy love in Jesus Christ our Lord. Send forth a mighty call unto all thy servants, granting unto them hearts of love, sincerity of speech, and the power of the Holy Spirit, that they may be able to persuade men to forsake sin and return unto thee. And so bless and favor the work of thine evangelists, that multitudes may be brought from the bondage of evil into the kingdom of thy dear Son; through the same Jesus Christ our Lord. *Amen.*

11. *For the Anniversary of a Church Building*

O GOD, who hast promised to be present with thy Church even unto the end of the world: We thank thee for this House builded to thine honor and glory. For the faith and life and worship for which it has witnessed, for the love which thou hast manifested to thy people here (from age to age), for the blessing which thou hast vouchsafed to them in worship and in work, and for all who in this place have testified to things unseen and eternal, and handed on the light of truth from generation to generation: Glory be to thee, O Lord, most High.

Guide and bless thy people still, we beseech thee; increase in them the spirit of faith and love, make them worthy of the heritage they have received, knit them together in the communion of thy saints, and grant that this place may be unto all who worship here none other than the House of God and the Gate of Heaven; through Jesus Christ, thy Son, our Lord. *Amen.*

12. *A Church Anniversary*

O GOD, who year after year dost return to us the day of the founding of this congregation, and ever dost bring us again into the presence of thy holy mysteries: Hear the prayers of thy people, and grant that whosoever shall enter this temple to seek blessings may rejoice in his desires wholly fulfilled; through Jesus Christ our Lord. *Amen.*

13. *For Synods of the Church*

¶ *The following prayer may be said in churches on the Sunday, or during the week, before the meeting of a Synod or other ecclesiastical body, or during its sessions.*

O LORD, the only Source of true wisdom: We invoke thy blessing upon the ———————— about to assemble (*or*, now assembled) in thy Name to deliberate upon those things which make for the well-being and extension of thy holy Church among us and throughout the world; and as thou hast promised to send thy Holy Spirit to lead thy people into all truth, so guide the representatives of thy Church that they may seek only thy glory and the welfare of those whom thou hast redeemed by the death of thy Son; through the same thy Son, Jesus Christ our Lord. *Amen*

14. *For the Church in Time of War or Distress*

O GOD, who dost will that thy Church bear witness to thee among all nations: Grant unto thy faithful people, amid the labors and distresses of this present time, boldness to confess thy Name; enable them, by thy Holy Spirit, to be among their fellow men as those who serve, turning the hearts of men to thee, uplifting the weak, comforting the sorrowing, and speaking peace to the desolate and afflicted; through Jesus Christ our Lord, who liveth and reigneth with thee and the Holy Ghost, one God, world without end. *Amen.*

15. *For the Protection and Peace of the Church*

ALMIGHTY God, who wilt have all men to be saved and come to the knowledge of the truth: Impart, we beseech thee, the grace of thy Holy Spirit to thy ministers, so that they may teach thy truth to the saving of men. Bring to naught the counsels of the enemies of thy word, who by corrupt teaching or with violent hands would destroy it; and enlighten them with its saving power. Increase and enrich our faith, and lead us in the way of quietness and peace; through Jesus Christ, thy Son, our Lord. *Amen.*

16. *For Catechumens*

ALMIGHTY and everlasting God, who dost always multiply thy Church, and with thy light and grace dost strengthen the hearts of those whom thou hast regenerated, confirming unto them thy covenant and faithfulness: Grant unto our Catechumens increase both of faith and knowledge, that they may rejoice in their Baptism and really and heartily renew their covenant with thee; through Jesus Christ, thy Son, our Lord. *Amen.*

17. *For the Children of the Church*

ALMIGHTY and everlasting God, who hast sent thine only Son to eek and to save that which was lost, nd through him hast said, Suffer the ttle children to come unto me, and forid them not, for of such is the kingdom f God: Most heartily we beseech thee to bless and govern the children of ny Church, by thy Holy Spirit, that they ay grow in grace and in the knowledge f thy word; protect and defend them gainst all danger and harm, and give y holy angels charge over them; rough the same Jesus Christ, thy Son, ur Lord. *Amen.*

18. *For a Conference of Christian People*

O GOD, whose beloved Son ministered to men in the market place d in the country, by the hearth and in y holy House: We beseech thee to bless who are gathered in thy Name. Help to learn and to do thy will. Guide us thy Spirit; comfort us with the sense thy presence; and let our life and felwship be to the praise of thy Name and e advancement of thy kingdom; rough the same Jesus Christ, our Lord. *men.*

THE MINISTRY

19. *For the Ministry*

ALMIGHTY and everlasting God, who alone doest great wonders: nd down upon thy Ministers and upon e Congregations committed to their arge, the healthful Spirit of thy grace; d, that they may truly please thee, ur upon them the continual dew of y blessing; through Jesus Christ, thy n, our Lord. *Amen.*

20. *For the Ministry*

O LORD, we beseech thee to raise up for the work of the Ministry faith- and able men, who shall count it all to spend and be spent for the sake of dear Son, and for the souls for whom shed his most precious Blood upon the Cross; and fit them, we pray thee, for their holy office by thy bountiful grace and heavenly benediction; through the same Jesus Christ our Lord. *Amen.*

21. *For the Increase of the Ministry*

O ALMIGHTY God, look mercifully upon the world, which thou hast redeemed by the Blood of thy dear Son, and incline the hearts of many to offer themselves for the sacred Ministry of thy Church; so that by their labors thy light may shine in the darkness, and the coming of thy kingdom may be hastened by the perfecting of thine elect; through the same thy Son, Jesus Christ our Lord. *Amen.*

22. *For Theological Seminaries*

O GOD, who through thy Holy Spirit dost illuminate the minds and sanctify the lives of those whom thou dost call to the work of pastors and teachers: Look with thy favor upon all seminaries for the instruction and discipline of those who are to serve in the sacred Ministry of thy Church; bless those who teach and those who learn, that they may apply themselves with such diligence to the knowledge which is able to make men wise unto salvation, and submit themselves with such ready obedience to the law of thy Son our Saviour, that they may fulfill their ministry with joy; through the same Jesus Christ, our Lord. *Amen.*

MISSIONS

23. *For Missions*

O GOD our Protector, behold, and look upon the face of thine Anointed, who hath given himself for the redemption of all, and grant that, from the rising of the sun to the going down thereof, thy Name may be great among the Gentiles; and that in every place, sacrifice and a pure offering may be made unto thy Name; through the same Jesus Christ, thy Son, our Lord. *Amen.*

24. *For Missions*

ALMIGHTY God, who hast called the Church out of the world that she might bring the world to thee: Make her faithful, we beseech thee, in the work thou hast entrusted to her hands. Stir up the hearts of thy people here and everywhere, that by their prayers, gifts, and labors, they may have due part in the spreading of thy Gospel over all the earth; and hasten the time when all the ends of the world shall remember and turn unto the Lord, and all the kindreds of the nations shall worship before thee; through Jesus Christ our Lord. *Amen.*

25. *For Missionary Work*

ALMIGHTY and everlasting God, who hast wrought the redemption of man after a miraculous manner, in sending thine only Son to fulfill the promises made unto our fathers: Open up more and more the knowledge of that salvation, that in all places of the earth thy truth and power may be made known, to the intent that all nations may praise, honor, and glorify thee; through the same thy Son, Jesus Christ our Lord. *Amen.*

26. *For Missions*

O GOD, who didst so love the world as to give thine only-begotten Son, that whosoever believeth in him should not perish, but have everlasting life: Look with compassion upon the heathen who know thee not, and on the multitudes that are scattered as sheep having no shepherd; and so bestow upon us thy grace, that we, with all thy believing people, may be the messengers of thy Gospel, seek them that are lost, and restore them unto thee; that they, being gathered out of all places whither they have wandered, may be strengthened, nurtured, protected and guided by the true Shepherd and Bishop of souls, Jesus Christ our Lord; to whom, with thee and the Holy Ghost, be honor and power, dominion and glory, world without end. *Amen.*

27. *For the Maintenance of the Gospel*

ALMIGHTY God, our heavenly Fa- ther, who givest us our daily brea in answer to our prayers: Withhold n from us, nor from our children's ch dren, nor from our land, nor from t people of any nation of the earth, t Bread of Life; but grant that the livi seed of thy word may everywhere sown plenteously, and that the frui thereof may abound by thy grace un life everlasting; through the same Jes Christ, thy Son, our Lord. *Amen.*

28. *For the Coming of the Kingdom*

O GOD, who didst send thy bless Son Jesus Christ to preach pea to them that are afar off, and to the that are nigh: Grant that all the peopl of the world may feel after thee and fi thee; and hasten, O God, the fulfillme of thy promise to pour out thy Spi upon all flesh; through Jesus Christ o Lord. *Amen.*

29. *For Missionary Work*

ALMIGHTY God, heavenly Fathe who through thy Son Jesus Chri hast given commandment unto thy pe ple to go into all the world and prea the Gospel to every creature: Grant a ready will to obey thy word; and as have entered into the labors of oth men, help us to serve thee, that othe may enter into our labors; and that with them, and they with us, may atta unto everlasting life; through the sar Jesus Christ, thy Son, our Lord. *Ame*

30. *For the Heathen*

O GOD of all the nations of the eart remember the multitudes of t heathen, who, though created in thi image, are ignorant of thy love; and a cording to the propitiation of thy S Jesus Christ grant that by the praye and labors of thy holy Church, they m be delivered from all superstition a unbelief, and brought to worship the through him whom thou hast sent to our salvation, the Resurrection and t ife of all the faithful, the same thy Son, ›sus Christ our Lord. *Amen.*

31. *For the Jews*

) GOD, the God of Abraham, look upon thine everlasting covenant, ıd cause the captivity of Judah and Is-el to return. They are thy people; O be ou their Saviour, that all who love Je-salem and mourn for her may rejoice ith her, for Jesus Christ's sake, their viour and ours. *Amen.*

32. *For Islam*

LMIGHTY God, our heavenly Fa- ther, who in thy goodness hast used the light of the Gospel to shine our land: Extend thy mercy, we be-ech thee, to the nations of the world at still walk in darkness. Enlighten the oslems with the knowledge of thy ıth; and grant that the Gospel of sal-tion may be made known in every nd, that the hearts of all people may be rned unto thee; through Jesus Christ r Lord. *Amen.*

33. *For the Consummation*

) LORD Jesus Christ, who wilt come again in glory and bring in thine ernal reign: Establish us in the Faith, ıd by thy might defend us amid the mptations and cares of this life; that steadfast devotion we may look for e consummation of thy glorious king-m; who livest and reignest with the ther and the Holy Ghost, one God, orld without end. *Amen.*

INTERCESSIONS

34. *For Those in Affliction and Sorrow*

OD of all comfort, we commend to thy mercy all those upon whom any oss or tribulation is laid : the nations ich are afflicted with famine, pesti-ce, or war; those of our brethren who ffer persecution for the sake of the ospel; all such as are in danger by sea land or in the air; and all persons op-essed with poverty, sickness, or any infirmity of body or sorrow of mind. We pray particularly for the sick and afflicted members of this church, and for those who desire to be remembered in our prayers (and for any such known to ourselves, whom we name in our hearts before thee). May it please thee to show them thy fatherly kindness, chastening them for their good, that their hearts may turn unto thee, and receive perfect consolation, and deliverance from all their troubles; for the sake of Christ our Lord. *Amen.*

35. *For Those in Affliction*

ALMIGHTY and everlasting God, the comfort of the sad, the strength of them that suffer: Let the prayers of thy children who cry out of any tribulation come unto thee; and unto every soul that is distressed grant thou mercy, grant relief, grant refreshment; through Jesus Christ, our Lord. *Amen.*

See also the Order for the Burial of the Dead, p. 266.

36. *For Those in Affliction*

O LORD, look down from heaven, behold, visit and relieve thy servants, for whom we offer our supplications; look upon them with the eyes of thy mercy; give them comfort and sure confidence in thee; defend them from the danger of the enemy, and keep them in perpetual peace and safety; through Jesus Christ, thy Son, our Lord. *Amen.*

37. *For the Sick*

ALMIGHTY, everlasting God, the eternal Salvation of them that believe: Hear our prayers in behalf of thy servants who are sick, for whom we implore the aid of thy mercy; that being restored to health, they may render thanks to thee in thy Church; through Jesus Christ, thy Son, our Lord. *Amen.*

38. *For Friends*

O GOD, who, through the grace of the Holy Spirit, dost pour the gifts of thy love into the hearts of the faithful: Grant unto all our friends, for whom we entreat thy clemency, health of mind and body; so that they may love thee with all their strength, and in gladness accomplish all things pleasing unto thee; through Jesus Christ, thy Son, our Lord. *Amen.*

39. *For Home and Kindred*

O GOD, our heavenly Father, look in favor, we beseech thee, upon the homes of thy people; defend them against all evil, and supply all their needs according to the riches of thy grace; make them sanctuaries of purity and peace, love and joy. Bless all dear to us wheresoever they are, and grant that they and we may follow thee at every step of our daily life; that, though our paths may lead us far from one another, we may all abide within the safe shelter of thy love; through Jesus Christ, thy Son, our Lord. *Amen.*

40. *For Children*

O HEAVENLY Father, who long ago didst watch thy Son on earth grow as in stature so in wisdom and in perfect love of thee: Teach, by the wondrous tale of Jesus and his Church, the children whom thou watchest now; that they may grow into his likeness, loving thee, obedient to thy will, and happy in thy House; through the same Jesus Christ our Lord. *Amen.*

41. *For Our Children*

HEAVENLY Father, from whom all fatherhood in heaven and earth is named: Bless, we beseech thee, all children, and give to their fathers and mothers the spirit of wisdom and love; so that the homes in which they grow up may be to them an image of thy kingdom, and the care of their parents a likeness of thy love; through our Lord Jesus Christ. *Amen.*

42. *For the Sanctity of Marriage*

O LORD God, who didst institute matrimony in Eden: Preserve in our land the sanctity of the marriage bond; that those who enter therein ma in honor and fidelity to each other b enriched with thy blessing; throug Jesus Christ, thy Son, our Lord. *Ame.*

43. *Thanksgiving for the Faithful Depart*

WITH reverence and affection we r member before thee, O everlastir God, all our friends and kindred wh have passed within the veil. Keep us i union with them here, through faith ar love towards thee, that hereafter we ma enter into thy blessed presence, and b numbered with those who serve thee ar behold thy face, in glory everlastin through Jesus Christ our Lord, un whom with thee and the Holy Spirit, b glory and praise, now and for evermo *Amen.*

44. *For the Fellowship of Saints*

O GOD, who hast brought us near an innumerable company of a gels, and to the spirits of just men ma perfect: Grant us during our earthly p grimage to abide in their fellowsh and in our heavenly country to becor partakers of their joy; through Jes Christ our Lord. *Amen.*

NATION AND WORLD

45. *For the Nation*

O GOD, who in this land hast ma the people the ministers of thy j rule: So turn their hearts unto thee th holding their citizenship as a sacr trust, they may guard, defend and use according to thy will; and that, servi thee with willing, joyful and obedie hearts, they may cherish their freedom a blessing of thy Gospel, and strive bring it unto all peoples; through Jes Christ, thy Son, our Lord. *Amen.*

46. *For Our Nation*

O GOD, who by thy Providence di lead our forefathers to this la wherein they found refuge from oppr sion and freedom to worship thee: V beseech thee ever to guide our Nation e way of thy truth and peace, so that may never fail in the blessing which ou hast promised to that people whose od is the Lord; through Jesus Christ r Lord. *Amen.*

47. *For Our Country*

LMIGHTY God, who hast given us a land wherein we are free to read d hear thy word, to confess thy Name, d to labor together for the extension thy kingdom: Grant, we beseech thee, at the liberty vouchsafed unto us may continued to our children, and our ildren's children; and that the power the Gospel may here abound to the essing of all the nations of the earth, d to thine eternal glory; through Jesus rist our Lord. *Amen.*

48. *For the President and Those in Authority*

LMIGHTY and everlasting God, we humbly implore thee graciously to gard the President of the United States, counselors, and all others in authority over us; that, guided by thy Holy irit, they may be high in purpose, wise counsel, and unwavering in duty; and the administration of their solemn arge may wholly serve thy will, uphold e honor of our Nation, secure the protion of our people, and set forward ery righteous cause; through Jesus rist, thy Son, our Lord. *Amen.*

. *For Those in Our Country's Service in Time of War*

LMIGHTY God, our heavenly Father, let thy protection be upon all ose who are in the service of our Coun-; guard them from all harm and dan- of body and soul; sustain and com-t those at home, especially in their urs of loneliness, anxiety, and sor-v; prepare the dying for death and the ing for thy service; give success to our ns on land and sea and in the air; and nt unto us and all nations a speedy, t and lasting peace, to the glory of thy Name and the coming of thy kingdom; through Jesus Christ our Lord. *Amen.*

50. *For the Armed Forces of the Nation (For Those in the Services)*

ALMIGHTY and everlasting God, whose Providence hath given us as a people this great land stored with treasure and around it hath cast like a mantle the sea: Bless, we pray thee, the officers and men of our armed forces as they perform the duties of their calling; give them not only true love of Country, but also love of thee, and understanding of thy love for all mankind; so that, relying upon thine almighty aid, they may promote righteousness, honor, and unity among our people in time of peace, and be a means of fostering mutual respect and understanding among the peoples of the world; through Jesus Christ our Lord. *Amen.*

51. *For Seafarers*

O ETERNAL Lord God, who alone spreadest out the heavens and rulest the raging of the sea: Be pleased to receive into thy protection all those who go down to the sea in ships and do business in great waters. Make thou their voyages safe to their persons and their goods (especially in this present storm); and be thyself their way and light till journeying shall end; through Jesus Christ our Lord. *Amen.*

52. *For Chaplains and Those Who Minister to the Sick and Wounded*

O MOST merciful Father, who dost commit to our love and care our fellow men in their necessities: Graciously be with and prosper all those who are seeking and ministering to the sick and wounded; let their ministry be abundantly blessed in bringing ease to the suffering, comfort to the sorrowing, and peace to the dying; and let them know that inasmuch as they do it unto the least of these, Christ's brethren, they do it unto him, who liveth and reigneth with thee and the Holy Ghost, one God, world without end. *Amen.*

53. *For the Bereaved*

HAVE compassion, O Lord, upon all who mourn and upon all who are lonely and desolate; be thou their Comforter and Friend; give them such earthly solace as thou seest to be best for them; bring them to fuller knowledge of thy love, and wipe away all their tears; for the sake of Jesus Christ our Lord. *Amen.*

54. *For Victory*

O GOD, our refuge and strength, our very present help in trouble: Protect and prosper, we beseech thee, our beloved Country in this time of war; make of us, by thy grace, a people worthy to be entrusted with victory; and so use, direct and bless our armed forces that they may be thy servants in overcoming wrong and establishing liberty, truth and righteousness in the earth; through Jesus Christ, thy Son, our Lord. *Amen.*

55. *Against Evildoers*

O LORD God Almighty, who alone riddest away tyrants and stillest the noise and tumult of the people: Scatter, we beseech thee, the counsels of them that secretly devise mischief, and bring the dealings of the violent to naught; cast down the unjust from high places and cause the unruly to cease from troubling; put down all envious and malicious passions and subdue the haters and evil-doers, that the whole world may have rest before thee, and that all nations may serve thee; through Jesus Christ our Lord. *Amen.*

56. *National Thanksgiving*

ALMIGHTY God, our heavenly Father, whose mercies are new unto us every morning, and who, though we have in no wise deserved thy goodness, dost abundantly provide for all our wants of body and soul: Give us, we pray thee, thy Holy Spirit, that we may heartily acknowledge thy merciful goodness toward us, give thanks for all thy benef and serve thee in willing obedien through Jesus Christ, thy Son, our Lo *Amen.*

57. *For Peace*

O GOD, who wouldst fold both hea en and earth in a single peace: l the design of thy great love lighten up the waste of our wraths and sorrov and give peace to thy Church, pea among nations, peace in our dwellin and peace in our hearts; through t Son, our Saviour, Jesus Christ. *Amen*

58. *For Peace*

O GOD, the Father in heaven: Gra thy mighty aid to the efforts of m to establish peace among the nations the world. Give strength of purpose those who lead; enlighten those who in council; and so transform the hea of men everywhere by thy gracious G pel, that they may exalt peace above w service above gain, and righteousn above glory; through Jesus Christ o Lord. *Amen.*

59. *For Peace*

ETERNAL Father, who in the send of thy Son didst speak peace to world, and in the Blood of his Cross h opened to all mankind the way to pe with thee: Turn all men to the Cr that, following his holy example a burning with his zeal of service, they m become one brotherhood in him, and peace possess every heart and rule in the nations of the world; through same Jesus Christ, thy Son, our Lo *Amen.*

60. *For Brotherhood*

O GOD, who hast made man in th own likeness, and who dost love whom thou hast made: Teach us unity of thy family and the breadth thy love. By the example of thy S Jesus Christ our Saviour, enable while loving and serving our own, enter into the fellowship of the wh ıman family; and forbid that, from ide of race or hardness of heart, we ould despise any for whom he died, or jure any in whom he lives; through the me Jesus Christ our Lord. *Amen.*

61. *For the Church and the World*

LMIGHTY Father, who hast so formed man for thyself that his art is restless till it find rest in thee: By e ministry of thy Church and the lives those who humbly love and follow ee, convince the world that thou art e sure refuge of all who are weary and stressed in mind and body, the safe rbor for all who seek certainty and ace of heart, and the eternal salvation every burdened soul; through Jesus rist our Lord. *Amen.*

SOCIETY AND COMMUNITY

62. *For All People*

) GOD our Father, who hast promised that the kingdoms of this orld shall become the kingdom of thy n: Purge the nations of error and corption; overthrow the power of sin, and ablish the kingdom of grace in every d; incline the hearts of all rulers and oples to the Lord of lords and King of ory, that he may enter into their cities, urches and homes, to dwell there and vern all things by his word and Holy irit; through Jesus Christ our Lord. *nen.*

63. *For Those Who Seek Peace*

) HEAVENLY Father, we thank thee for all those who, even at this ne of strife and loss, are seeking a more cellent way for the nations of the orld, whereby justice and order may be ablished and the differences of peoples resolved in equity. We pray thee to their purpose on sure foundations d to prosper their labors, that thy will y be done; for the sake of Jesus Christ r Lord. *Amen.*

64. *For the Kingdom*

O LORD, who hast set before us a great hope that thy kingdom shall come on earth, and hast taught us to pray for its coming: Make us ever ready to thank thee for the signs of its dawning, and to pray and work for the perfect day when thy will shall be done, on earth as it is in heaven; who livest and reignest with the Father and the Holy Ghost, one God, world without end. *Amen.*

65. *For World Peace*

WE beseech thee, O Lord our God, to set the peace of heaven within the hearts of men, that it may bind the nations also in a covenant which cannot be broken; through Jesus Christ our Lord. *Amen.*

66. *For the New World*

O GOD, at whose word chaos became an ordered creation: Brood over this troubled world as once thy Spirit moved upon the face of the waters, and create in the nations such love for thee and for each other, that this world may be a new creation in righteousness, peace and brotherhood: through thy Son, Jesus Christ our Lord. *Amen.*

67. *The Church and the Community*

O GOD, who through the gift of thy Holy Spirit hast established the Church in this place: Grant unto all who have been converted unto thee such a knowledge of thy will and trust in thy grace that they may truly exemplify the life they profess, and by their good works enable men to glorify thee, the only true God; through Jesus Christ our Lord. *Amen.*

68. *Christian Service* (*Social Missions*)

O LORD, our heavenly Father, whose blessed Son came not to be ministered unto, but to minister: We beseech thee to bless all who, following in his steps, give themselves to the service of

For Christian Service, see also Nos. 24–29.

their fellow men. Endue them with wisdom, patience, and courage to strengthen the weak and raise up those who fall; that, being inspired by thy love, they may worthily minister in thy Name to the suffering, the friendless, and the needy; for the sake of him who laid down his life for us, thy Son our Saviour, Jesus Christ. *Amen.*

69. *For Deaconesses*

O GOD, the Father of Jesus Christ our Lord, who in olden time didst call holy women to the service of thy Church: Let thy blessing rest upon all who are set apart for the work of serving love; grant them knowledge of thy Gospel, sincerity of purpose, true diligence in service, and beauty of life in Christ; that many souls may rise up to bless them, and that thy holy Name may be glorified; through the same thy Son, Jesus Christ our Lord. *Amen.*

70. *For Compassion (For a Social Conscience)*

O GOD our King, who hast called us through Jesus Christ to be kings and priests unto thee: Teach us to bear one another's burdens and the burdens of the commonwealth. Open our eyes to see the woes of our land, the despair in the lives of many, and the deep and shameful wrongs that cry to be put right. Give to us also a vision of our land as thou wouldst have it be, and as thou alone canst fashion it. Make us thy servants, giving us no rest or discharge until thou hast wrought this work of compassion, that generations yet unborn may praise thy Name. We ask this for Jesus Christ's sake. *Amen.*

71. *For the Relations of Men to One Another*

O GOD, the King of righteousness, lead us, we pray thee, in the ways of justice and of peace; inspire us to break down all oppression and wrong, to gain for every man his due reward, and from every man his due service; th each may live for all, and all may ca for each; in the Name of Jesus Christ o Lord. *Amen.*

72. *For Industrial Peace*

O GOD, who in thy providence do appoint to every man his wor We humbly beseech thee to still all str and contention amongst those who a engaged in industry (*especially the who are now at variance*); defend the from all greed and covetousness, a grant that they, seeking only that whi is just, may live and work together brotherly unity and concord, to th own well-being, and the prosperity this land; through Jesus Christ our Lo *Amen.*

73. *For the Labors of Men*

PROSPER our industries, we pr thee, God most high, that our la may be full with all manner of store, a there be no complaining in our stree and, as thy Son our Lord plied tools earth, so give to all that labor pride their work, a just reward, and joy bo in supplying need and serving th through the same Jesus Christ our Lo *Amen.*

74. *The Perils of Abundance*

O GOD, who in thy love hast b stowed upon us gifts such as o fathers neither knew nor dreamed Mercifully grant that we be not so occ pied with material things that we for the things which are spiritual; lest, ha ing gained the whole world, we lose o own soul; for thy mercy's sake. *Amen*

75. *For the Right Use of Wealth*

O GOD, who in thine infinite lo hast entrusted to us both the know edge of thy truth and the gifts of t bounty: Help us to use them as go stewards, giving liberally, praying stantly, and working diligently, that may share in bringing all men to t truth and in hastening the coming of t kingdom; through Jesus Christ o Lord. *Amen.*

76. *For the Unemployed*

O LORD, our heavenly Father, we commend to thy protecting care and compassion the men and women of our land now suffering distress and anxiety through lack of work. Support and strengthen them, we beseech thee; and so prosper the counsels of those who order our common life, that thy people may be set free from want and fear, and be enabled to work in security and peace, for the relief of their necessities, and for the well-being of our land; through Jesus Christ our Lord. *Amen.*

77. *For the Fruits of the Earth*

ALMIGHTY God, who hast blessed the earth that it should be fruitful and bring forth abundantly whatsoever is needful for the life of man: Prosper, we beseech thee, the labors of the husbandman, and grant such seasonable weather that we may gather in the fruits of the earth, and ever rejoice in thy goodness, to the praise of thy holy Name; through Jesus Christ our Lord. *Amen.*

78. *For the Fruits of the Earth*

O ALMIGHTY God, who hast created the earth for man, and man for thy glory: Mercifully hear the supplications of thy people, and be mindful of thy covenant; that the earth may yield her increase, and the good seed bring forth abundantly, to the glory of thy holy Name; through Jesus Christ our Lord. *Amen.*

MORNING AND EVENING

79. *For the Right Use of the Lord's Day*

LORD, who dost ask of thy people love for love, and worship in return for life: Assist us to keep holy, week by week, the day of thy Son's mighty rising from the dead, and bless us in the breaking of the bread and the prayers; that other thy children who behold our joy may seek thy lovingkindness in the midst of thy temple; through the same Jesus Christ our Lord. *Amen.*

80. *Morning*

GRANT us, O Lord, to pass this day in gladness and peace, without stumbling and without stain, that reaching the eventide victorious over all temptation through thy ever present aid, we may praise thee, the eternal God, who dost govern all things and art blessed for evermore; through Jesus Christ, thy Son, our Lord. *Amen.*

81. *Morning*

O LORD, King of heaven and earth, may it please thee this day to order and hallow, to rule and govern our hearts and bodies, our thoughts, words and works, according to thy commandments; through Jesus Christ, thy Son, our Lord. *Amen.*

See also the Collect for Grace in Matins, and the Prayer in the Morning Suffrages.

82. *Morning*

O GOD, Lord of all power and might, preserver of all thy creatures: Keep us this day in health of body and soundness of mind, in purity of heart and cheerfulness of spirit, in contentment with our lot and charity with our neighbor; and further all our lawful undertakings with thy blessing. In our labor strengthen us; in our pleasure purify us; in our difficulties direct us; in our perils defend us; in our troubles comfort us; and supply all our needs, according to the riches of thy grace in Christ Jesus our Lord. *Amen.*

83. *Evening*

O GOD, with whom there is no darkness, but the night shineth as the day: Keep and defend us and all thy children, in soul and body, during the coming night. Make us to rest in the peace of a good conscience, in the hope of a better life, in the faith of thy providence, and in the comfort of thy love; through Jesus Christ our Lord. *Amen.*

84. *Evening*

O GOD, who hast drawn over weary day the restful veil of night, enfold us in thy heavenly peace. Lift from our hands our tasks, and bear in thy bosom the weight of our burdens and sorrows; that in untroubled slumber we may press our weariness close to thy strength, and win from thee new power for the morrow's labors; through Jesus Christ our Lord. *Amen.*

85. *Evening*

WATCH thou, dear Lord, with those who wake, or watch, or weep tonight, and give thine angels charge over those who sleep. Tend thy sick ones, O Lord. Rest thy weary ones. Bless thy dying ones. Soothe thy suffering ones. Pity thine afflicted ones. Shield thy joyous ones. And grant all, for thy love's sake, in Jesus Christ our Lord. *Amen.*

86. *Evening*

LIGHTEN our darkness, we beseech thee, O Lord; and by thy great mercy defend us from all perils and dangers of this night; for the love of thy only Son, our Saviour, Jesus Christ, who liveth and reigneth with thee and the Holy Ghost, one God, world without end. *Amen.*

87. *For Divine Protection*

O LORD, support us all the day long of this troublous life, until the shadows lengthen, and the evening comes, and the busy world is hushed, and the fever of life is over, and our work is done. Then in thy mercy, grant us a safe lodging and a holy rest, and peace at the last; through Jesus Christ our Lord. *Amen.*

SPIRITUAL GIFTS

88. *For Spiritual Renewal*

O LORD God, heavenly Father, who hast given thine only Son to die for our sins, and to rise again for our justification: Quicken us, we beseech thee, by thy Holy Spirit, unto newness of life, that, through the power of his Resurrection, we may dwell with Christ forever; who liveth and reigneth with thee and the Holy Ghost, one God, world without end. *Amen.*

89. *For Spiritual Renewal*

ALMIGHTY God, who hast given us thine only-begotten Son to take our nature upon him: Grant that we, being regenerate and made thy children by adoption and grace, may daily be renewed by thy Holy Spirit; through the same Jesus Christ, thy Son, our Lord. *Amen.*

90. *For the Holy Spirit*

ALMIGHTY and everlasting God, who of thy great mercy in Jesus Christ thy Son dost grant us forgiveness of sin, and all things pertaining to life and godliness: Grant us, we beseech thee, thy Holy Spirit, that we may strive to mortify the flesh and overcome the world; and, serving thee in holiness and pureness of living, may give thee continual thanks for all thy goodness; through the same Jesus Christ, thy Son, our Lord. *Amen.*

91. *For the Holy Spirit*

SEND, we beseech thee, Almighty God, thy Holy Spirit into our hearts, that he may rule and direct us according to thy will, comfort us in all our temptations and afflictions, defend us from all error, and lead us into all truth; that we, being steadfast in the faith, may increase in love and in all good works, and in the end obtain everlasting life; through Jesus Christ, thy Son, our Lord. *Amen.*

92. *For Guidance into Truth*

ENLIGHTEN our minds, we beseech thee, O God, by the Spirit who proceedeth from thee; that, as thy Son hath promised, we may be led into all truth; through the same Jesus Christ our Lord. *Amen.*

93. *For Grace to Receive the Word*

BLESSED Lord, who hast caused all Holy Scriptures to be written for our learning: Grant that we may in such wise hear them, read, mark, learn, and inwardly digest them, that by patience and comfort of thy holy word, we may embrace, and ever hold fast the blessed hope of everlasting life, which thou hast given us in our Saviour Jesus Christ, who liveth and reigneth with thee and the Holy Ghost, one God, world without end. *Amen.*

94. *For Guidance*

ALMIGHTY and everlasting God, who makest us both to will and to do those things which are good, and acceptable unto thy Divine Majesty: Let thy fatherly hand, we beseech thee, ever be over us; let thy Holy Spirit ever be with us; and so lead us in the knowledge and obedience of thy word, that in the end we may obtain everlasting life; through Jesus Christ, thy Son, our Lord. *Amen.*

95. *For Guidance*

O GOD, by whom the meek are guided in judgment, and light riseth up for the godly: Grant us in all our doubts and uncertainties the grace to ask what thou wouldst have us do; that the spirit of wisdom may save us from false choices, and that in thy light we may see light and in thy straight path may not stumble; through our Lord and Saviour Jesus Christ. *Amen.*

96. *For Guidance*

O LORD God, who hast called us thy servants to ventures of which we cannot see the ending, by paths as yet untrodden and through perils unknown: Give us faith to go out with good courage, not knowing whither we go, but only that thy hand is leading us and thy love supporting us; through Jesus Christ our Lord. *Amen.*

97. *For Faith, Hope and Love*

GRANT us, we beseech thee, Almighty God, a steadfast faith in Jesus Christ, a cheerful hope in thy mercy, and a sincere love to thee and to all our fellow men; through the same Jesus Christ, thy Son, our Lord. *Amen.*

98. *For Love to God*

O GOD, who through the grace of thy Holy Spirit dost pour the gifts of charity into the hearts of thy faithful people: Grant unto thy servants health both of mind and body, that they may love thee with their whole strength, and with their whole heart perform those things which are pleasing unto thee; through Jesus Christ, thy Son, our Lord. *Amen.*

99. *For Love to God*

O GOD, who hast prepared for them that love thee such good things as pass man's understanding: Pour into our hearts such love toward thee, that we, loving thee above all things, may obtain thy promises, which exceed all that we can desire; through Jesus Christ, thy Son, our Lord. *Amen.*

100. *For Charity*

O LORD, who hast taught us that all our doings without charity are nothing worth: Send thy Holy Ghost, and pour into our hearts that most excellent gift of charity, the very bond of peace and of all virtues, without which whosoever liveth is counted dead before thee; grant this for thine only Son Jesus Christ's sake. *Amen.*

101. *For Grace to Do God's Will*

ALMIGHTY God, give us grace that we may cast away the works of darkness, and put upon us the armor of light, now in the time of this mortal life, in which thy Son Jesus Christ came to visit us in great humility; that in the last day, when he shall come again in his glorious Majesty to judge both the quick and the dead, we may rise to the life immortal; through the same Jesus Christ, thy Son, our Lord. *Amen.*

102. *For Faith*

O MOST loving Father, who willest us to give thanks for all things, and to dread nothing but the loss of thee, and to cast all our care upon thee who carest for us: Preserve us from faithless fears and worldly anxieties; and grant that no clouds of this mortal life may hide from us the light of that love which is immortal, and which thou hast manifested unto us in thy Son, Jesus Christ our Lord. *Amen.*

103. *For Faith*

ALMIGHTY and everliving God, who hast given to them that believe exceeding great and precious promises: Grant us so perfectly, and without all doubt, to believe in thy Son Jesus Christ, that our faith in thy sight may never be reproved. Hear us, O Lord, through the same, our Saviour Jesus Christ. *Amen.*

104. *For Zeal*

O GOD, the sovereign good of the soul, who requirest the hearts of all thy children: Deliver us from all sloth in thy work and all coldness in thy cause; and grant us by looking unto thee to rekindle our love, and by waiting upon thee to renew our strength; through Jesus Christ our Lord. *Amen.*

105. *Consecration*

O ALMIGHTY and everlasting God, vouchsafe, we beseech thee, to direct, sanctify and govern both our hearts and bodies in the ways of thy laws, and in the works of thy commandments; that, through thy most mighty protection, both here and ever, we may be preserved in body and soul; through Jesus Christ, thy Son, our Lord. *Amen.*

106. *For Grace to Use Our Gifts*

O LORD God Almighty, who dost endue thy servants with singular gifts of the Holy Ghost: Leave us not, we beseech thee, destitute of thy manifold gifts, nor yet of grace to use them alway to thy honor and glory; through Jesus Christ, thy Son, our Lord. *Amen.*

107. *For Grace to Follow Christ*

ALMIGHTY God, who hast given thine only Son to be unto us both a sacrifice for sin and also an ensample of godly life: Give us grace that we may always most thankfully receive that his inestimable benefit, and also daily endeavor ourselves to follow the blessed steps of his most holy life; through the same Jesus Christ, thy Son, our Lord. *Amen.*

108. *For Patience*

O GOD, who by the meek endurance of thine only-begotten Son didst beat down the pride of the old enemy: Help us, we beseech thee, rightly to treasure in our hearts what our Lord hath of his goodness borne for our sakes; that after his example we may bear with patience whatsoever things are adverse to us; through the same Jesus Christ, thy Son, our Lord. *Amen.*

109. *For Meekness and Gentleness of Heart*

O GOD our Father, whose chastenings are for our purification and strengthening: Teach us, by the things we suffer, both meekness of heart and gentleness of spirit; that we may endure all things manfully, and enduring, conquer for thy Name's sake; through Jesus Christ, thy Son, our Lord. *Amen.*

110. *For Contentment*

ALMIGHTY God, our heavenly Father, who dost feed the birds and clothe the flowers, and who carest for us as a father for his children: Guard us against distrust and anxiety; and help us, through thy Holy Spirit, to live to the hallowing of thy Name, the coming of thy kingdom, and the doing of thy will; so that in unwavering faith we may cast all our care upon thee; through Jesus Christ our Lord. *Amen.*

111. *For Steadfastness in Affliction*

ALMIGHTY and most merciful God, who hast appointed us to endure sufferings and death with our Lord Jesus Christ before we enter with him into eternal glory: Grant us grace at all times to subject ourselves to thy holy will, and to continue steadfast in the true faith unto the end of our lives, and at all times to find peace and joy in the blessed hope of the resurrection of the dead, and of the glory of the world to come; through Jesus Christ, thy Son, our Lord. *Amen.*

112. *For Purity*

ALMIGHTY God, unto whom all hearts are open, all desires known, and from whom no secrets are hid : Cleanse the thoughts of our hearts by the inspiration of thy Holy Spirit, that we may perfectly love thee, and worthily magnify thy holy Name; through Jesus Christ, thy Son, our Lord. *Amen.*

113. *For Divine Assistance*

DIRECT us, O Lord, in all our doings, with thy most gracious favor, and further us with thy continual help; that in all our works begun, continued, and ended in thee, we may glorify thy holy Name; and finally, by thy mercy, obtain everlasting life; through Jesus Christ, thy Son, our Lord. *Amen.*

114. *For the Blessings of Redemption*

O LORD God, heavenly Father, we give thee thanks, that of thy great goodness and mercy, thou didst suffer thine only-begotten Son to become incarnate, and to redeem us from sin and everlasting death; and we beseech thee, enlighten our hearts by thy Holy Spirit, that we may evermore yield thee unfeigned thanks for this thy grace, and therein find comfort in time of tribulation and distress; through the same Jesus Christ, thy Son, our Lord. *Amen.*

115. *For the Blessings of Redemption*

O LORD, who art God from eternity, yet man for our sakes: Grant us, thine unworthy servants, what thou hast promised to all alike; that thy Passion may be our deliverance, thy wounds our healing, thy Cross our redemption, thy death our life; and that, as thou wast raised upon the Cross, so by thy Cross we may be lifted up to thy Father, with whom thou livest and reignest in the unity of the Spirit, one God. *Amen.*

116. *For Increase in the Knowledge of God*

O GOD, who didst send thy Son to live with men that, through him, they might know thee truly, love thee purely, and worship thee aright: Remove far from us all the wrong desires that cloud our vision when we look on him; and bestow upon us the aid of thy Holy Spirit, that, knowing Christ, we may come to an ever truer knowledge of thyself; through the same, thy Son, Jesus Christ our Lord. *Amen.*

117. *Vocation*

REMEMBER, O God, what thou hast wrought in us, and not what we deserve; and, as thou hast called us to thy service, make us worthy of our calling; through Jesus Christ our Lord. *Amen.*

118. *For the Blessedness of Heaven*

ALMIGHTY, everlasting God, who didst give thine only Son to be a High Priest of good things to come: Hereafter grant unto us, thine unworthy servants, to have our share in the company of the blessed; through the same Jesus Christ, thy Son, our Lord. *Amen.*

119. *For Inner Peace*

O GOD, who art the author of peace and lover of concord, in knowledge of whom standeth our eternal life, whose service is perfect freedom: Defend us, thy humble servants, in all assaults of our enemies; that we, surely trusting in thy defence, may not fear the power of any adversaries; through Jesus Christ, thy Son, our Lord. *Amen.*

120. *For the Spirit of Prayer*

O ALMIGHTY God, from whom every good prayer cometh, and who pourest out on all who desire it the spirit of grace and supplication: Deliver us, when we draw nigh to thee, from coldness of heart and wanderings of mind; that with steadfast thoughts and kindled affections we may worship thee in spirit and in truth; through Jesus Christ our Lord. *Amen.*

121. *For Answer to Prayer*

ALMIGHTY God, who hast given us grace at this time with one accord to make our common supplications unto thee; and dost promise that when two or three are gathered together in thy Name, thou wilt grant their requests: Fulfill now, O Lord, the desires and petitions of thy servants as may be most expedient for them; granting us in this world knowledge of thy truth, and in the world to come life everlasting. *Amen.*

122. *For Answer to Prayer*

ALMIGHTY God, the fountain of all wisdom, who knowest our necessities before we ask and our ignorance in asking: We beseech thee to have compassion upon our infirmities, and those things which for our unworthiness we dare not, and for our blindness we cannot ask, vouchsafe to give us, for the worthiness of Jesus Christ, thy Son, our Lord. *Amen.*

123. *For Answer to Prayer*

ALMIGHTY God, who hast promised to hear the petitions of those who ask in thy Son's Name: We beseech thee mercifully to incline thine ear to us who have now made our prayers and supplications unto thee; and grant that those things which we have faithfully asked according to thy will, may effectually be obtained, to the relief of our necessity and to the setting forth of thy glory; through Jesus Christ our Lord. *Amen.*

PRIVATE DEVOTION

1. *Before Service*

BLESS me, O God, with a reverent sense of thy Presence, that I may be still and adore thee; through Jesus Christ our Lord. *Amen.*

2. *Before Service*

DISPEL for this hour, O Lord, the manifold distractions of the world; that we may be able with quiet minds to receive the promptings of thy still small voice; through Jesus Christ our Lord. *Amen.*

3. *Before Service*

SEND forth, O God, thy good grace, and sanctify our souls, bodies, and spirits; turn our thoughts to holiness, so that with pure conscience we may offer to thee the sacrifice of praise; through the mercy and compassion of thine only-begotten Son, with whom thou art blessed, together with thy Holy, and Good, and Quickening Spirit, now and always. *Amen.*

4. *Penitence, Confession (Before Worship)*

O GOD, whose goodness is great, and the multitudes of thy mercies without number; we have sinned against thee, and done evil in thy sight; yet, since thou art the God of mercy and the Fountain of eternal purity, we present unto thee the sacrifice of a troubled spirit, beseeching thee to let the fire of thy love consume our sins and purify our souls. Make clean our hearts, O God; though our sins be as scarlet, yet make them like wool, though they be as crimson, yet make them white as snow. Restore to us the voice of joy and gladness; give us the comforts of thy Presence again, and let thy free Spirit establish us in the liberty of the sons of God; so shall we sing of thy righteousness, and our lips shall give thee praise in the congregation of thy redeemed, now, henceforth, and forever. *Amen.*

5. *Before Holy Communion*

O LORD our God, who from the Name of thine only-begotten Son hast called us to be Christians, and hast given us the Baptism of the new birth for the remission of sins: Make us, we beseech thee, worthy now to receive this Communion for the forgiveness of all our sins, and to give thanks with grateful hearts, as to thee so to the Son and to the Holy Ghost, now and forever. *Amen.*

6. *Before Holy Communion*

DIRECT and control us, O Lord, always and everywhere with heavenly light; that we may both discern with clear vision and share with worthy effect that mystery of which thou hast willed us to partake; through Jesus Christ our Lord. *Amen.*

7. *Before Holy Communion*

WE do not presume to come to this thy Table, O merciful Lord, trusting in our own righteousness, but in thy manifold and great mercies: We are not worthy so much as to gather up the crumbs under thy Table; but thou art the same Lord whose property is always to have mercy. Grant us therefore, gracious Lord, so to eat the Flesh of thy dear Son, and to drink his Blood in these holy mysteries, that we may continually dwell in him and he in us, that our sinful bodies may be made clean by his Body, and our souls washed through his most precious Blood. *Amen.*

8. *After Holy Communion*

PRESERVE in us, O Lord, the gift of thy grace, that, by the power and virtue of the Eucharist which we have received, we may be fortified against all evils now and evermore; through Jesus Christ our Lord. *Amen.*

9. *After Holy Communion*

O MERCIFUL Father, we render thee thanks and praise that thou hast vouchsafed to feed us, thine unworthy servants, with the precious Body and Blood of thy dear Son; and we pray that by thy grace we may walk worthy of our holy calling, and learn to adorn the doctrine of God our Saviour in all things; through the same Jesus Christ, thy Son, our Lord. *Amen.*

10. *After Holy Communion*

ALMIGHTY God, who givest the true Bread which cometh down from heaven, even thy Son, Jesus Christ our Lord: Grant, we beseech thee, that we who have received the Sacrament of his Body and Blood may abide in him, and he in us, that we may be filled with the power of his endless life; who liveth and reigneth with thee and the Holy Ghost, one God, world without end. *Amen.*

11. *After Holy Communion*

WE give thanks to thee, Almighty God, that thou hast refreshed us with this Sacrament of thy love, and hast granted to us the presence of thy Son, even Jesus Christ our Lord; and we beseech thee to strengthen our faith in thee and to increase our love toward one another; through the same thy Son, Jesus Christ our Lord. *Amen.*

12. *For Aid in Temptation*

O GOD, who by thy Son, our Saviour, hast promised us forgiveness of sins and everlasting life: Lead us by thy Spirit to seek help from Christ in our daily need, especially in times of temptation; that by faith we may obtain thy promises, and live as thy children; through the same Jesus Christ our Lord. *Amen.*

13. *For Repentance*

MERCIFUL Father, give us grace that we may never presume to sin; but if at any time we offend thy Divine Majesty, may we truly repent and lament our offence, and by a lively faith obtain remission of all our sins; solely through the merits of Jesus Christ, thy Son, our Lord. *Amen.*

14. *In Time of Affliction*

LORD, who knowest the deep places through which our lives must go: Help us, when we enter them, to lift our hearts to thee, to be patient when we are afflicted, to be humble when we are in distress; and grant that the hope of thy mercy may never fail us, and the consciousness of thy lovingkindness may never be clouded nor hidden from our eyes; through Jesus Christ, thy Son, our Lord. *Amen.*

15. *Evening: Personal Prayer*

WATCH over us, O Lord, our heavenly Father. Preserve us from all evil, and grant that we may this night rest secure beneath thy care. Bless thy Church and our government. Remember the sick and those who are in need or in peril. Have mercy upon all men. And when our last evening shall come, grant us to fall asleep in thy peace and to awake in thy glory; through Jesus Christ, thy Son, our Lord. *Amen.*

See also the Prayer in the Evening Suffrages.

Prayers in the preceding collection which are also suited for private devotion are these: Numbers 32–39, 42, 43, 56, 57, 81–84, 87–123.

The Bidding Prayer

¶ *By ancient usage this Prayer was specially appointed for Good Friday. It may also be used on Wednesdays and Fridays in Lent and at other times.*

¶ *When this Prayer is said, a quiet moment should be kept after each bid, during which the people may make their silent petitions. The Collect, said by the Minister, is followed by the response,* Amen, *said by the people.*

LET us pray, dearly beloved, for the *holy Church of God*, that our Lord God would grant it peace and unity, and preserve it throughout the world, keeping it perpetually upon the true foundation, Jesus Christ.

ALMIGHTY and everlasting God, who hast revealed thy glory to all nations in Jesus Christ and the word of his truth: Keep in safety, we beseech thee, the works of thy mercy, that thy Church, spread throughout all nations, may serve thee in true faith, and persevere in the confession of thy Name; through Jesus Christ, thy Son, our Lord. *Amen.*

Let us pray for *the chief pastor of the Church*, that the Lord God who called him to his office, may keep him in health and safety, for the good of the holy Church and the leadership of the people of God.

ALMIGHTY and everlasting God, by whose will all things are established: Mercifully hear our prayer, and of thy goodness preserve him whom thou hast called as our chief pastor, that under his guidance the Christian people, subject to thy rule, may grow in faith and in all good works; through Jesus Christ, thy Son, our Lord. *Amen.*

Let us pray for *all estates of men in the holy Church*, for pastors and ministers, for missionaries and deaconesses, for all faithful laymen, and for all the people of God.

ALMIGHTY and everlasting God, by whose Spirit the whole body of the Church is governed and sanctified: Receive our supplications and prayers for all estates of men in thy holy Church, that every member of the same, in his vocation and ministry, may faithfully serve thee; through Jesus Christ, thy Son, our Lord. *Amen.*

Let us pray for our *Catechumens*, that our Lord God would open their hearts and the door of his mercy, that having received the remission of all their sins by the washing of regeneration, they may be mindful of their baptismal covenant, and evermore be found in Christ Jesus our Lord.

O ALMIGHTY and eternal God, who dost always provide new children for thy Church: Increase the faith and understanding of our catechumens, that, being born again in the waters of baptism, they may be numbered among thine adopted children and daily renew their covenant with thee; through Jesus Christ, thy Son, our Lord. *Amen.*

Let us pray for *all in authority*, and especially for the Government (*of the United States*, or, *of the Dominion of Canada*), that we may lead a quiet and peaceable life in all godliness and honesty.

) MERCIFUL Father in heaven, of whom is all earthly rule and au- ›rity: Graciously regard thy serv- ts, the President of the United States, ,Her Majesty the Queen), and those .o serve in public office, that under ›ir direction this people may walk in › ways of thy commandments and be ssed with thy continued favor; 'ough Jesus Christ, thy Son, our Lord. *ıen.*

Let us pray our Lord God Almighty ıt he would deliver the world from all *'or*, take away *disease*, ward off *famine*, free *those in bondage*, grant health to › *sick*, and a safe passage to *all vellers.*

LMIGHTY and everlasting God, the consolation of the sorrowful and › strength of the weak: May the pray- of them that in any tribulation or dis- ss cry unto thee graciously come be- e thee, so that in all their necessities ›y may mark and receive thy manifold 'p and comfort; through Jesus Christ, ' Son, our Lord. *Amen.*

Let us pray for *all who are without the 'urch*, that our Lord God would be ›ased to deliver them from all their 'ors, call them to faith in the true and ing God and his only Son, Jesus ›rist our Lord, and gather them into › holy family, the Church.

LMIGHTY and everlasting God, who seekest not the death but the › of all mankind: Hear our prayers for those who have no right knowledge thee; free them from their errors, and › the glory of thy Name bring them o the fellowship of thy holy Church; 'ough Jesus Christ, thy Son, our Lord. *ıen.*

¶ *Here may also be said Collects 30, 31, and 32.*

Let us pray for *peace throughout the 'rld*, and for the guidance of God's irit in the councils of men.

ALMIGHTY and everlasting God, King of Glory, and Lord of heaven and earth, by whose Spirit all things are governed: Bestow thy heavenly peace and concord upon the nations of the earth, that all men may serve thee in true fear, to the praise and glory of thy holy Name; through Jesus Christ, thy Son, our Lord. *Amen.*

Let us pray for our *enemies*, that God would remember them in mercy, and graciously vouchsafe unto them such things as are both needful for them and profitable unto their salvation.

O ALMIGHTY, everlasting God, who, through thine only Son, our blessed Lord, has commanded us to love our enemies, to do good to them that hate us, and to pray for them that persecute us: We earnestly beseech thee, that by thy gracious visitation all our enemies may have the same love, and be of one accord and of one mind and heart, with us and with thy whole Christian Church; through the same Jesus Christ, thy Son, our Lord. *Amen.*

Let us pray for the *fruits of the earth*, that God would send down his blessing upon them, and graciously dispose our hearts to enjoy them in obedience to his holy will.

O LORD, Father Almighty, who by thy Word hast created and dost bless and uphold all things: We pray thee so to reveal unto us thy Word, our Lord Jesus Christ, that, he dwelling in our hearts, we may by thy grace be made meet to receive thy blessing on all the fruits of the earth, and whatsoever pertains to our bodily need; through the same Jesus Christ, thy Son, our Lord. *Amen*

Finally, let us pray for all those things which our Lord would have us ask, saying:

OUR Father, who art in heaven, . . .

General Prayers

I

O LORD our God, who hast bidden the light to shine out of darkness, who hast again brought us to thy house of prayer, to praise thy goodness and ask for thy grace: Accept now, in thy endless mercy, the sacrifice of our worship and thanksgiving, and grant unto us all such requests as may be wholesome for us. Make us to be children of the light and of the day, and heirs of thy everlasting inheritance. Remember, O Lord, according to the multitude of thy mercies, thy whole Church, all who join with us in prayer, all our brethr by land and sea, or wherever they m be in thy vast kingdom, who stand need of thy grace and succour. Po out upon them the riches of thy mer so that we, redeemed in soul and bo and steadfast in faith, may ever pra thy wonderful and holy Name; throu Jesus Christ our Lord, who liveth a reigneth with thee in the unity of Holy Ghost, one God, world with end. *Amen.*

II

ALMIGHTY God, our heavenly Father, we, thine unworthy servants, do give thee most humble and hearty thanks for all thy goodness and lovingkindness to us, and to all men. We bless thee for our creation, preservation, and all the blessings of this life; but above all, for thine inestimable love in the redemption of the world by our Lord Jesus Christ, for the means of grace, and for the hope of glory. And, we beseech thee, give us that due sense of all thy mercies, that our hearts may be unfeignedly thankful, and that we may show forth thy praise, not only with our lips, but in our lives; that walking before thee in holiness and righteousness all our days, we may enjoy the testimony of a good conscience and the hope of thy favor, be sustained and comforted under the troubles of this life, and finally be received into thine everlasting kingdom; through thine infinite mercy in Jesus Christ, our Lord.

We offer unto thee our common supplications for the good estate of thy Church throughout the world: that it may be so guided and governed by thy good Spirit, that all who prof themselves Christians may be led in the way of truth, and hold the faith unity of spirit, in the bond of pea and in righteousness of life. Send do upon all pastors and ministers, and up the congregations committed to th charge, the healthful spirit of thy gra and that they may truly please th pour upon them the continual dew thy blessing.

Most heartily we beseech thee, w thy favor to behold (the President a the Congress of the United States, a all others in authority;)* and so plenish them with thy grace, that t may always incline to thy will, and w in thy way. Prosper all good coun and all just works, that peace and hap ness, truth and righteousness, relig and piety, may be established am us throughout all generations.

We humbly entreat thee also for

* *In Canadian Churches, the follo may be said:* especially Her Graci Majesty the Queen, the Prime Mini and the Parliament, and all Provin Authorities.

:ts and conditions of men; that thou ·uldest be pleased to make thy ways ·own unto them, thy saving health to all nations.

May it please thee to preserve all ıt travel by land, air, or water; to ccour all that are in peril or need; d to satisfy the wants of all thy atures.

We also commend to thy fatherly odness all those who are in any way licted or distressed, in mind, body, estate; that it may please thee to comfort and relieve them according to their several necessities, giving them patience under their sufferings, and a happy issue out of all their afflictions.

¶ *Here special Supplications, Intercessions, and Prayers may be made.*

Hear us, merciful Lord, in these our humble prayers, which we offer unto thee in the Name of Jesus Christ our Lord, who liveth and reigneth with thee and the Holy Ghost, one God, world without end. *Amen.*

III

LMIGHTY and everlasting God, who art worthy to be had in erence by all the children of men, we e thee most humble and hearty nks for the innumerable blessings, th temporal and spiritual, which, thout any merit or worthiness on our rt, thou hast bestowed upon us.

We praise thee, especially, that thou st preserved unto us, in their purity, saving Word, and the sacred dinances of thy house. And we be-ech thee, O Lord, to grant and pre-ve unto thy holy Church, through-t the world, purity of doctrine, and thful pastors who shall preach thy ord with power; and help all who ar, rightly to understand, and truly believe the same. Be thou the pro-tor and defender of thy people in time of tribulation and danger; and ıy we, in communion with thy urch, and in brotherly unity with our fellow-Christians, fight the good ht of faith, and in the end receive salvation of our souls.

Bestow thy grace upon all the nations the earth. Especially do we entreat e to bless our land, and all its in-bitants, and all who are in authority. use thy glory to dwell among us, and mercy and truth, righteousness and peace, everywhere prevail. To this end, we commend to thy care all our schools, and pray thee to make them nurseries of useful knowledge and of Christian virtues, that they may bring forth the wholesome fruits of life.

Graciously defend us from all calamities by fire and water, from war and pestilence, from scarcity and famine. Protect and prosper every one in his appropriate calling, and cause all useful arts to flourish among us. Be thou the God and Father of the widow and the fatherless children, the helper of the sick and needy, and the comforter of the forsaken and distressed.

¶ *Here special Supplications, Intercessions, and Prayers may be made.*

And as we are strangers and pilgrims on earth, help us by true faith and a godly life to prepare for the world to come; doing the work which thou hast given us to do while it is day, before the night cometh when no man can work. And when our last hour shall come, support us by thy power, and receive us into thine everlasting kingdom; through Jesus Christ, thy Son, our Lord, who liveth and reigneth with thee and the Holy Ghost, one God, world without end. *Amen.*

IV

¶ *When the following Prayer is said, a quiet moment should be kept after each bid, dur which the Congregation may make their silent petitions. The Collect, said by Minister, is followed by the response,* Amen, *by the people.*

Let us pray.

ALMIGHTY and most merciful Father, from whom cometh every good and perfect gift: We give thee praise and hearty thanks for all thy mercies. For thy goodness that hath created us, thy bounty that hath sustained us, thy fatherly discipline that hath chastened and corrected us, thy patience that hath borne with us, and thy love that hath redeemed us, we praise thee, O Lord. For thy Son our Saviour, for thy Spirit our Comforter, for thy Church our home, for the lives of all good and godly men, and for the hope of the life to come: we praise thee, O God.

Grant unto us, with all thy gifts, a heart to love and praise thee; and enable us to show our thankfulness for all thy benefits by giving up ourselves to thy service, and cheerfully conforming in all things to thy blessed will; through Jesus Christ our Lord. *Amen.*

Let us pray for the whole Church of God.

MOST gracious Father, we humbly beseech thee for thy holy catholic Church. Fill it with all truth, and in all truth with all peace. Where it is in error, reform it; where it is in want, furnish it; where it is right, strengthen and confirm it; and where it is rent asunder, heal thou the divisions thereof; through Jesus Christ our Lord. *Amen.*

Let us pray for all who serve the Lord in his Church.

O GOD, who hast bestowed upon thy Church the holy ministry of the Word and the Sacraments, and dost continue it from age to age: Endue thy ministers with thy Spirit; enable all who are called to serve thee in thy Church to fulfil their office with fidelity and zeal; and grant unto all thy peo that they may worship thee in truth, a alway labor and pray for the com of thy kingdom; through our L and Saviour, Jesus Christ. *Amen.*

Let us pray for the peace of the whole world.

O GOD, who hast revealed thy p pose for mankind in him who King of Righteousness and Prince Peace: Inspire the hearts of all men follow after justice; and hasten the ti when nation shall not lift up sw against nation, neither shall they le war any more; through the same Je Christ, thy Son, our Lord. *Amen.*

Let us pray for the President (*or*, H Gracious Majesty the Queen), and for those in authority.

O GOD, the King of kings and L of lords: Bestow thy blessing up thy servant, the President of the Uni States (*or*, Her Gracious Majesty Queen), and upon all in authority o us, and grant them thy grace and gu ance; that they may ever labor for welfare of the people, the honor of land, and the glory of thy Nan through Jesus Christ our Lord. *Am*

Let us pray for all who are in suffer and distress.

GOD of all comfort, we comme unto thee all who are in any w afflicted, all persons oppressed w poverty, sickness, or other trouble body or sorrow of mind, and all su as we name in our hearts before th .... Grant them the consolations which they have need, and overr their present sufferings to their eter good; through Jesus Christ our Lo *Amen.*

[Le]t us remember with thanksgiving those who have gone before.

[O] LORD most High, we give thee thanks for all thy saints, martyrs, [an]d confessors; for thy faithful servants [wh]o in their lives have witnessed a good [co]nfession; and for all dear to us whom [th]ou hast taken to thy nearer presence ..... Grant us grace to follow them as they followed Christ; and bring us, with them, to those things which eye hath not seen, nor ear heard, which thou hast prepared for them that love thee; through Jesus Christ our Lord. *Amen.*

Let us pray in the words which our Saviour hath taught us.

OUR Father, . . .

Occasional Services

ORDER FOR THE BAPTISM OF INFANTS

¶ *Baptism shall ordinarily be administered in the Church at any of the stated services, or a specially appointed service. At Matins or Vespers, the Order here given may follow Lessons or the Sermon; at The Service it may follow the Sermon.*

¶ *When circumstances demand, Baptism may be administered privately, and public announ ment thereof shall afterward be made. Infants should be brought to the Church for H Baptism as soon as possible after birth.*

¶ *The names of the Parents, of the Sponsors, of the Child, and of the Minister, with the d and place of birth and of baptism, shall be entered in the Record of the Congregation, a proper certificate issued.*

¶ *Only members of the Church shall be accepted as Sponsors, and they shall be instruc as to their spiritual responsibility to the Child.*

¶ *This Order may be preceded and followed by a Hymn.*

¶ *The Sponsors (and the Assistant), together with the Congregation, shall say,* Amen, *at end of each prayer.*

¶ *The Minister shall say:*

IN the Name of the Father, and of the Son, and of the Holy Ghc *Amen.*

DEARLY Beloved: Forasmuch as all men are born in sin, and our Savi Jesus Christ hath said, Except a man be born of Water and of the Spi he cannot enter into the kingdom of God: Let us call upon God the Fath through our Lord Jesus Christ, that of his goodness and mercy he will rece *this Child* by baptism, and make *him* a living member of his holy Chur

¶ *Then may the Minister make the sign of the Cross on the Child's forehead, saying:* Rec the sign of the holy Cross, in token that henceforth thou shalt know the Lord, and power of his Resurrection, and the fellowship of his sufferings.

¶ *The Congregation shall stand until the end of the Lord's Prayer.*

¶ *The Minister shall say:*

Let us pray.

ALMIGHTY and everlasting God, the Father of our Lord Jesus Chr We call upon thee for *this Child*, and beseech thee to bestow upon *h* the gift of thy baptism and thine everlasting grace by the washing of regene tion. Receive *him*, O Lord, as thou hast promised by thy well-beloved S saying: Ask, and it shall be given unto you; seek, and ye shall find; kno and it shall be opened unto you; through the same Jesus Christ, thy S our Lord. *Amen.*

¶ *Then shall the Minister say:*

HEAR the Holy Gospel, which saith: They brought young children to him that he should touch them; and his disciples rebuked those that ought them. But when Jesus saw it, he was much displeased, and said unto em, Suffer the little children to come unto me, and forbid them not, for of ch is the kingdom of God. Verily I say unto you, whosoever shall not receive e kingdom of God as a little child, he shall not enter therein. And he took em up in his arms, put his hands upon them, and blessed them.

¶ *Then shall all say the Lord's Prayer.*

¶ *During the Prayer the Minister may lay his hand upon the head of the Child.*

OUR Father, who art in heaven, Hallowed be thy Name, Thy kingdom come, Thy will be done, on earth as it is in heaven. Give us this day r daily bread; And forgive us our trespasses, as we forgive those who tres- ss against us; And lead us not into temptation, But deliver us from evil. r thine is the kingdom, and the power, and the glory, for ever and ever. nen.

¶ *Then shall the Minister say to those who present the Child:*

SINCE in Christian love you present *this Child* for Holy Baptism, I charge you that you diligently and faithfully teach *him* the Ten Commandments, e Creed, and the Lord's Prayer; and that, as *he* grows in years, you place *his* hands the Holy Scriptures, bring *him* to the services of God's House, d provide for *his* instruction in the Christian Faith; that, abiding in the venant of *his* Baptism and in communion with the Church, *he* may be ought up to lead a godly life until the day of Jesus Christ. I therefore call on you to answer in *his* stead:

¶ *Then may the Minister say:*

Do you renounce the devil, and all his works, and all his ways?
Answer: I renounce them.

¶ *Then shall the Minister say:*

Do you believe in God the Father Almighty, Maker of heaven and earth?
Answer: I believe.

Do you believe in Jesus Christ, his only Son our Lord, Who was conceived the Holy Ghost, Born of the Virgin Mary, Suffered under Pontius Pilate, as crucified, dead, and buried: Descended into hell, The third day rose ain from the dead; Ascended into heaven, And sitteth on the right hand of od the Father Almighty; Whence he shall come to judge the quick and the ad?
Answer: I believe.

Do you believe in the Holy Ghost; The Holy Christian (*or*, catholic) Churc the Communion of Saints; The Forgiveness of sins; The Resurrection of tl body, And the Life everlasting?

Answer: I believe.

¶ *Then shall the Minister say to those who present the Child:*

Do you present *this Child* to be baptized into this Christian Faith?

Answer: I do.

¶ *The Congregation shall rise, and the Minister shall say:*

Let us pray.

ALMIGHTY, everlasting God, whose dearly beloved Son, Jesus Chri hath said to his disciples: All power is given unto me in heaven and earth, and hath commanded them to go and teach all nations, baptizing the in the Name of the Father, and of the Son, and of the Holy Ghost; and ha promised to be with them alway, even unto the end of the world: Regard t prayers of thy people, and grant unto *this Child* now to be baptized, t fulness of thy grace, that *he* may ever remain in the number of thy faithf and elect children; through the same Jesus Christ our Lord. *Amen.*

¶ *The Minister may now ask,* How shall this Child be named? *and shall then baptize h by applying water three times as he saith:*

N., I BAPTIZE thee: In the Name of the Father, and of the Son, and the Holy Ghost. Amen.

¶ *Then the Minister, laying his hand on the head of the Child, shall say:*

ALMIGHTY God, the Father of our Lord Jesus Christ, who hath begott thee again of Water and the Holy Ghost, and hath forgiven thee all t sin, strengthen thee with his grace unto life everlasting. Amen.

Peace be with thee.

¶ *Then shall the Minister say:*

Let us pray.

ALMIGHTY and most merciful God and Father: We thank thee that th dost graciously preserve and extend thy Church, and that thou ha granted to *this Child* the new birth in Holy Baptism, and received *him* as t *Child* and *heir* to thy kingdom; and we humbly beseech thee to defend a keep *him* in this grace, that *he* may never depart from thee but may alwa live according to thy will, and finally receive the fulness of thy promise thine eternal kingdom; through Jesus Christ, thy Son, our Lord, who live and reigneth with thee and the Holy Ghost, one God, world without en *Amen.*

¶ *Then shall the Minister say:*

THE Blessing of Almighty God, the Father, the Son, and the Holy Gho be with you alway. *Amen.*

ORDER FOR CONFIRMATION

Candidates for Confirmation shall be instructed in the Christian Faith as it is set forth in the Small Catechism, and be approved in such manner as may be deemed satisfactory by the Pastor and the Church Council.

Confirmation shall be administered at a public service of the Congregation. In case of serious illness or pressing necessity, it may be administered privately in the presence of members of the Church. In such case the Confirmation shall be publicly announced to the Congregation.

When Confirmation is administered at The Service, and there be no Communion, this Order shall follow the Prayer of the Church.

If the Holy Communion be administered, this Order shall follow the Sermon; and at the conclusion of this Order, The Service shall be continued with the Offering, the Offertory, and the Prayer of the Church.

Before the Epistle and the Gospel for the Day, one or more of the following Lessons may be read: Acts 8:14–17; Romans 10:8–11 (Begin: The word is nigh thee); *Ephesians 2:13–22; Ecclesiastes 12:1–7; John 15:1–16.*

The Hymn, Come, Holy Ghost, our souls inspire, *(No. 117), or another Hymn of Invocation of the Holy Ghost, shall be sung.*

¶ *The Minister shall say:*

THE following persons, having been instructed in the Christian Faith and approved by the Church, are now presented for the Rite of Confirmation.

Then shall the Minister announce the names of the persons to be confirmed, after which they shall come to the Altar.

¶ *Then shall the Minister say:*

DEARLY Beloved: In Holy Baptism you were received by our Lord Jesus Christ and made members of his holy Church. In accordance with our ord's command, you have been instructed in the Word of God and led to ıe knowledge of his will and of his gracious Gospel, and you now desire to ıake public profession of your faith, and to be confirmed. I therefore ask ıch of you:

¶ *The Minister may then say:*

DO you renounce the devil, and all his works, and all his ways?
Answer: I renounce them.

¶ *Then shall the Minister say:*

Do you believe in God the Father Almighty?
Answer: I believe in God the Father Almighty, Maker of heaven and arth.

Do you believe in Jesus Christ?
Answer: I believe in Jesus Christ his only Son our Lord, Who was conęived by the Holy Ghost, Born of the Virgin Mary, Suffered under Pontius ilate, Was crucified, dead, and buried: He descended into hell; The third ay he rose again from the dead; He ascended into heaven, And sitteth on ıe right hand of God the Father Almighty; From thence he shall come to ıdge the quick and the dead.

Do you believe in the Holy Ghost?

Answer: I believe in the Holy Ghost; The Holy Christian (*or*, catholic Church, the Communion of Saints; The Forgiveness of sins; The Resurrec tion of the body, and the Life everlasting.

Do you promise to abide in this Faith and in the covenant of your baptism and as a member of the Church to be diligent in the use of the Means of Grac and in prayer?

¶ *Then shall each candidate answer in turn:*

I do, by the help of God.

¶ *Then shall the Minister say:*

Let us pray.

ALMIGHTY and everlasting God, who hast vouchsafed to regenerate thes thy servants by Water and the Spirit, and hast forgiven them all the sins: Strengthen them, we beseech thee, with the Holy Ghost, the Comforte and daily increase in them thy manifold gifts of grace: the spirit of wisdo and understanding; the spirit of counsel and might; the spirit of knowledg and of the fear of the Lord, now and forever; through Jesus Christ, thy So our Lord. *Amen.*

¶ *Then shall the candidates kneel, and the Minister shall lay his hand, or hands, on the he of each and say the Prayer of Blessing.*

THE Father in Heaven, for Jesus' sake, renew and increase in thee the gi of the Holy Ghost, to thy strengthening in faith, to thy growth in grac to thy patience in suffering, and to the blessed hope of everlasting life.

¶ *Each one confirmed shall say:*

Amen.

¶ *Then shall they rise, and the Minister shall say:*

FORASMUCH as you have made confession of your faith and hav received Holy Baptism, I do now, in the Name of the Lord Jesus Chris the great King and Head of the Church, admit you to the fellowship of th Lord's Table, and to participation in all the spiritual privileges of the Churc

God the Father, God the Son, and God the Holy Ghost, bless, preserv and keep you, now and forevermore. *Amen.*

¶ *Then shall the Congregation rise, and the Minister shall say:*

The Lord be with you.

℟. And with thy spirit.

Let us pray.

ALMIGHTY and merciful God, heavenly Father, who only workest in to will and to do the things that please thee: Confirm, we beseech the the work which thou hast begun in these thy servants; that, abiding in th ommunion of thy Church and in the faith of thy Gospel, no false doctrine, o lusts of the flesh, nor love of the world may lead them away from thee, or from the truth which they have confessed; but that in joyful obedience thy Word, they may ever know thee more perfectly, love thee more fer-ently, and serve thee in every good word and deed, to the blessing of their llow men, the edification of thy people and the glory of thy Name; through sus Christ, thy Son, our Lord, who liveth and reigneth with thee, and the oly Ghost, one God, world without end. *Amen.*

¶ *Then shall all say:*

OUR Father, who art in heaven, . . .

¶ *Then shall the Minister dismiss them, saying:*

THE Blessing of Almighty God, the Father, the Son, and the Holy Ghost, be with you alway. *Amen.*

A BRIEF ORDER FOR PUBLIC CONFESSION

WHEN THE CONFESSION OCCURS IMMEDIATELY BEFORE THE SERVICE OF THE DAY

¶ *A Hymn may be sung.*
¶ *The Minister shall say:*

IN the Name of the Father, and of the Son, and of the Holy Ghost. *Amen.*

Let us pray.

ALMIGHTY God, unto whom all hearts are open, all desires known, and from whom no secrets are hid: Cleanse the thoughts of our hearts by the inspiration of thy Holy Spirit, that we may perfectly love thee, and worthily magnify thy holy Name; through Jesus Christ, thy Son, our Lord. *Amen.*

¶ *Here may follow Psalm 51, Miserere mei, Deus, secundum and the Gloria Patri.*
¶ *A brief Address or the Exhortation (p. 250) may follow.*

¶ *Then shall the Minister say:*

Let us humbly kneel, and make confession unto God, imploring his forgiveness, through Jesus Christ our Lord.

¶ *Then shall all kneel.*

¶ *Silence shall be kept for a space for self-examination.*

¶ *Then shall all say:*

O GOD, our heavenly Father, I confess unto thee that I have grievous sinned against thee in many ways; not only by outward transgression but also by secret thoughts and desires which I cannot fully understand, b which are all known unto thee. I do earnestly repent, and am heartily sor for these my offences, and I beseech thee of thy great goodness to have mer upon me, and for the sake of thy dear Son, Jesus Christ our Lord, to forgi my sins, and graciously to help my infirmities. Amen.

¶ *The Minister shall rise. The Congregation shall remain kneeling until after the Benedictic*

¶ *Then shall the Minister say the Absolution according to one of the following forms.*

ALMIGHTY GOD, our heavenly Father, hath had mercy upon us, and f the sake of the sufferings, death, and resurrection of his dear Son, Jes Christ our Lord, forgiveth us all our sins. As a Minister of the Church Christ, and by his authority, I therefore declare unto you who do truly repe and believe in him, the entire forgiveness of all your sins: In the Name the Father, and of the Son, and of the Holy Ghost. *Amen.*

Or:

THE Almighty and merciful God grant unto you, being penitent, pardc and remission of all your sins, time for amendment of life, and the gra and comfort of his Holy Spirit. *Amen.*

¶ *Or, where customary, the Minister may lay his hand on the heads of the penitents and sa*

BY the authority of God and of this our office and ministry, I declare un thee the gracious forgiveness of all thy sins: In the Name of the Fathe and of the Son, and of the Holy Ghost. *Amen.*

¶ *Then shall the Minister say:*

THE Grace of our Lord Jesus Christ, and the Love of God, and the Cor munion of the Holy Ghost, be with you all. *Amen.*

¶ *Then shall The Service begin with the Introit for the Day.*

THE ORDER FOR PUBLIC CONFESSION

FOR A SPECIALLY APPOINTED PREPARATORY SERVICE

This Order is provided for use when a Service of Preparation for Holy Communion is held on a day before the administration of the Sacrament. It is specially appropriate as the Vesper Office on Wednesday and Friday in Holy Week.

A Hymn of Invocation of the Holy Ghost, or another suitable Hymn may be sung. The Versicles with the Gloria Patri shall be sung or said, the Congregation standing until the end of the Psalm.

MAKE haste, O God, to deliver me.
℟. Make haste to help me, O Lord.
I said, I will confess my transgressions unto the Lord.
℟. And thou forgavest the iniquity of my sin.
GLORY be to the Father, and to the Son, and to the Holy Ghost:
℟. As it was in the beginning, is now, and ever shall be, world without nd. Amen.

¶ *Then shall be sung or said this Psalm:*

PSALM 51. *Miserere mei, Deus, secundum.*

HAVE mercy upon me, O God, according to thy lovingkindness: according unto the multitude of thy tender mercies, blot out my transgressions.
Wash me thoroughly from mine iniquity: and cleanse me from my sin.
For I acknowledge my transgressions: and my sin is ever before me.
Against thee, thee only, have I sinned, and done this evil in thy sight: at thou mightest be justified when thou speakest, and be clear when thou dgest.
Behold, I was shapen in iniquity: and in sin did my mother conceive me.
Behold, thou desirest truth in the inward parts: and in the hidden part ou shalt make me to know wisdom.
Purge me with hyssop, and I shall be clean: wash me, and I shall be whiter an snow.
Make me to hear joy and gladness: that the bones which thou hast broken ay rejoice.
Hide thy face from my sins: and blot out all mine iniquities.
Create in me a clean heart, O God: and renew a right spirit within me.
Cast me not away from thy presence: and take not thy holy spirit from e.
Restore unto me the joy of thy salvation: and uphold me with thy free irit.
Then will I teach transgressors thy ways: and sinners shall be converted to thee.

Deliver me from bloodguiltiness, O God, thou God of my salvation: a my tongue shall sing aloud of thy righteousness.

O Lord, open thou my lips: and my mouth shall show forth thy prai

For thou desirest not sacrifice, else would I give it: thou delightest not burnt offering.

The sacrifices of God are a broken spirit: a broken and a contrite hea O God, thou wilt not despise.

Do good in thy good pleasure unto Zion: build thou the walls of Jer salem.

Then shalt thou be pleased with the sacrifices of righteousness, with bur offering and whole burnt offering: then shall they offer bullocks upon thi altar.

GLORY be to the Father, and to the Son, and to the Holy Ghost:

As it was in the beginning, is now, and ever shall be, world without en Amen.

¶ *Then shall be read one or more of the following Lessons:*

Exodus 20:1–17	Matthew 11:25–30
Daniel 9:4–9, 17–19	Mark 12:28–31
Isaiah 57:14–21	Luke 13:1–9
Isaiah 1:11–18	Luke 15:1, 2, 11–31
1 John 1:5–9	John 13:1–17
1 Corinthians 11:23–29	John 20:19–23

¶ *A Hymn may be sung after the Lesson.*
¶ *Then may follow an Address or Sermon, after which may be sung a Hymn.*

THE EXHORTATION

¶ *Then shall the Congregation rise, and the Minister shall read the following Exhortatic*

DEARLY Beloved: The Holy Supper of our Lord Jesus Christ ha been instituted for the special comfort and strengthening of those wl humbly confess their sins, and who hunger and thirst after righteousne Forasmuch as we intend to come to the Lord's Table, it becometh us diligen to examine ourselves as St. Paul exhorteth us.

We find, when we do this, that we are under the dominion of sin a death. To save us from death, make us children of God and exalt us to eve lasting life, our Lord Jesus Christ had mercy on us, took our nature up him, and himself became obedient unto death.

In order that we should believe this with greater confidence and be strengt ened in cheerful obedience to his will, he hath instituted the Sacrament of t Altar in which he giveth us his Body and his Blood to eat and to drink. Wh ever eateth this Bread and drinketh this Cup, firmly believing the words Christ, liveth in Christ and Christ in him, and hath eternal life.

We should also do this in remembrance of him, showing his death, that he 'as delivered for our offences and raised again for our justification. For all ıat he hath done we are bound to give him most hearty thanks, to take up ur cross and follow him, and as he gave commandment, to love one another s he hath loved us. For as we are all partakers of this one Bread and drink of ıis one Cup, so are we all one body in him.

¶ *Then shall the Minister say:*

Let us pray.

ALMIGHTY God, unto whom all hearts are open, all desires known, and from whom no secrets are hid: Cleanse the thoughts of our hearts by the ıspiration of thy Holy Spirit, that we may perfectly love thee, and worthily ıagnify thy holy Name; through Jesus Christ, thy Son, our Lord. *Amen.*

¶ *Then may the Minister conduct the Examination of Conscience, saying as follows:*

I ASK you, in the presence of God, who searcheth the heart:

DO you confess that you are by nature a most unworthy sinner, and that you have grievously offended against him, in thought, word, and deed, nd have merited only his wrath and condemnation?

Answer: I do so confess.

DO you trust entirely in the mercy of God in Jesus Christ?

Answer: I do so trust.

DO you promise heartily to forgive others, as you believe that God forgives you, and to serve him henceforth in newness of life, to the glory of his ıoly Name?

Answer: I do so promise.

¶ *Then shall the Minister begin the Confession, saying:*

Let us humbly kneel, and make confession unto God, imploring his for-iveness through Jesus Christ our Lord.

¶ *Then shall all kneel and say:*

O God, our heavenly Father, I confess unto thee that I have grievously sinned against thee in many ways; not only by outward transgressions, ut also by secret thoughts and desires which I cannot fully understand, but which are all known unto thee. I do earnestly repent, and am heartily sorry or these my offences, and I beseech thee of thy great goodness to have mercy ıpon me, and for the sake of thy dear Son, Jesus Christ our Lord, to forgive ny sins, and graciously to help my infirmities. Amen.

¶ *Then shall the Minister rise and say the Absolution. The Congregation shall remain kneelir until after the Benediction. Where customary, the Minister may lay his hand on the hea of the penitents as he says the Absolution.*

ALMIGHTY God, our heavenly Father, hath had mercy upon us, and fc the sake of the sufferings, death, and resurrection of his dear Son, Jesu Christ our Lord, forgiveth us all our sins. As a Minister of the Church c Christ, and by his authority, I therefore declare unto you who do truly reper and believe in him, the entire forgiveness of all your sins: In the Name c the Father, and of the Son, and of the Holy Ghost. *Amen.*

¶ *Here the Minister may also say:*

ON the other hand, by the same authority, I declare unto the impeniter and unbelieving, that so long as they continue in their impenitenc God hath not forgiven their sins, and will assuredly visit their iniquities upo them, if they turn not from their evil ways, and come to true repentance an faith in Christ, ere the day of grace be ended.

¶ *Then shall the Minister kneel, and all shall say the Lord's Prayer.*

OUR Father, who art in heaven, . . .

¶ *Then shall the Minister say the Collect for the Day. Other suitable collects may then l said, and after them the Collect for Peace.*

℣. The Lord will give strength unto his people.
℟. The Lord will bless his people with peace.

O GOD, from whom all holy desires, all good counsels, and all just work do proceed: Give unto thy servants that peace which the world cannc give; that our hearts may be set to obey thy commandments, and also th: by thee, we, being defended from the fear of our enemies, may pass our tim in rest and quietness; through the merits of Jesus Christ our Saviour, wh liveth and reigneth with thee and the Holy Ghost, one God, world withou end. *Amen.*

¶ *The Minister shall rise and say the Benediction.*

THE Grace of our Lord Jesus Christ, and the Love of God, and the Con munion of the Holy Ghost, be with you all. *Amen.*

ORDER FOR THE BURIAL OF THE DEAD

¶ *The Order for the Burial of the Dead is provided for the burial of those who depart this life in the Christian Faith.*

¶ *The death of a member of the Church should be reported immediately to the Pastor, and no arrangements for the burial should be made without consultation with him.*

¶ *This Order may be used in the Church, or at the house, before the burial. The service should be held in the Church whenever possible.*

¶ *The Minister, in his customary vestments, shall go before the body as it is brought into the Church. The Congregation shall stand. The coffin shall be placed before the Chancel in a lengthwise position. During the service the coffin shall remain closed. The Congregation may provide a funeral pall.*

¶ *When a brief service is held at the house before going to the Church, it may include a Hymn or Psalm, a Lesson, a Collect or Prayer, and a Benediction.*

¶ *Before the service, the altar-candles shall be lighted. Only flowers of the immediate family should be permitted in the Chancel.*

¶ *This Order may be used as a Memorial Service after the Burial.*

¶ *The Order of the Church herein provided shall in no case be interrupted by the exercises of secular organizations, and shall close with the Benediction immediately following the final Collect.*

¶ *The service may begin with a Hymn, after which the Minister shall sing or say:*

Organ *Minister*

In the Name of the Father, and of the Son, and of the Holy Ghost. ℟. A-men.
¶ Then shall be sung or said the Kyrie.
Minister
Congregation. Unison
Lord, have mer - cy up - on us. ℟. Lord, have mer - cy up - on us.

Minister *Congregation*

Christ, have mer - cy up - on us. ℟. Christ, have mer - cy up - on us.

Minister *Congregation*

Lord, have mer - cy up - on us. ℟. Lord, have mer - cy up - on us.

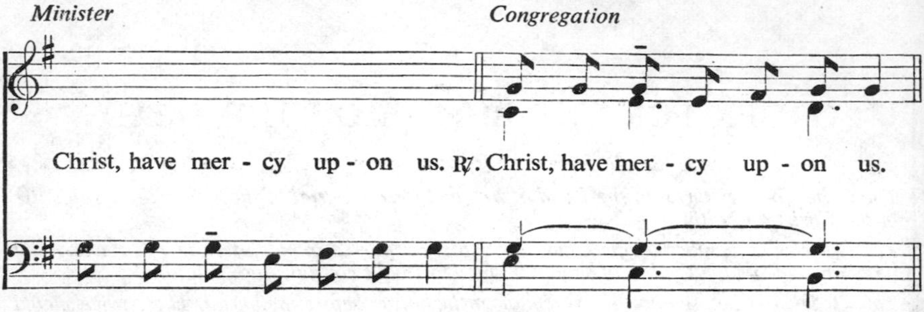

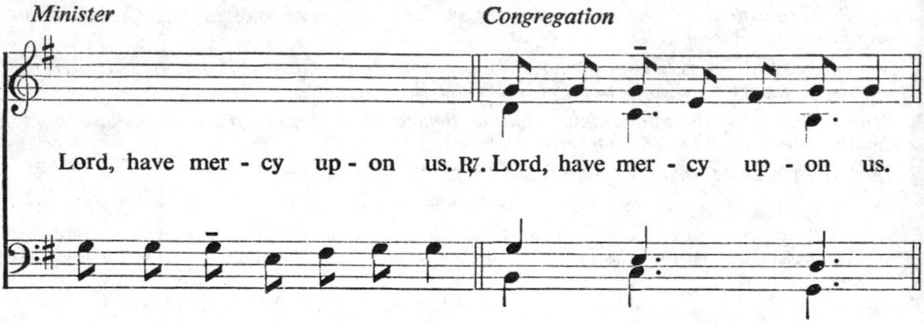

¶ *Then shall be sung or said one or more of the Psalms here following. The Psalm may be preceded and followed by an Antiphon.*

PSALM 130. *De profundis.*

Antiphon. Unison

If thou, Lord, should-est mark in - iq - ui - ties: O Lord, who shall stand?

J. TURLE, from H. PURCELL

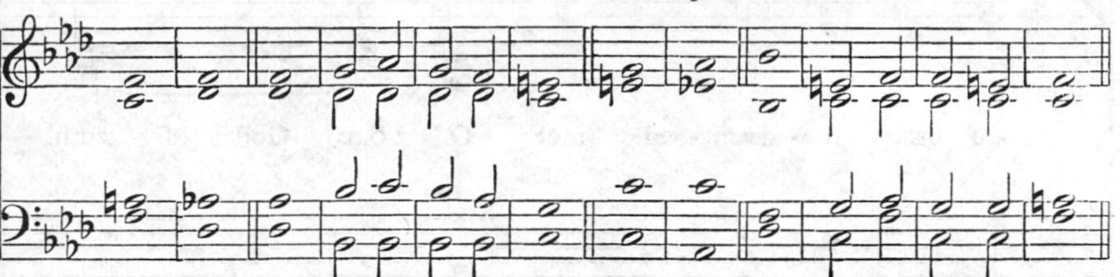
Second part

OUT of the ' depths:
* have I ' cried · unto ' thee, O ' LORD.
Lord, hear my ' voice:
* let thine ears be attentive to the ' voice of my ' suppli- ' cations.
If thou, LORD, shouldest mark in ' iquities:
* O ' Lord, ' who shall ' stand?
But there is forgiveness with ' thee:
* that ' thou ' mayest be ' fear-ed.
I wait for the LORD, my soul doth ' wait:
* and in ' his ' Word do I ' hope.
My soul waiteth for the Lord more than they that watch for the ' morning:
* I say, more than ' they that ' watch · for the ' morning.
Let Israel hope in the ' LORD:
* for with the ' Lord ' there is ' mercy;
And with ' him:
* is ' plen- ' teous re- ' demption.

Second part

And he shall redeem ' Israel:
* from ' all ' his in ' iquities.
GLORY be to the ' Father:
* and to the ' Son, · and to the ' Holy ' Ghost;
As it was in the be- ' ginning:
* is now and ever shall be ' world without ' end. A ' men.

Antiphon repeated.

PSALM 23. *Dominus regit me.*

Antiphon. Unison

In - to thy hands, O LORD: I com - mit my spir - it.

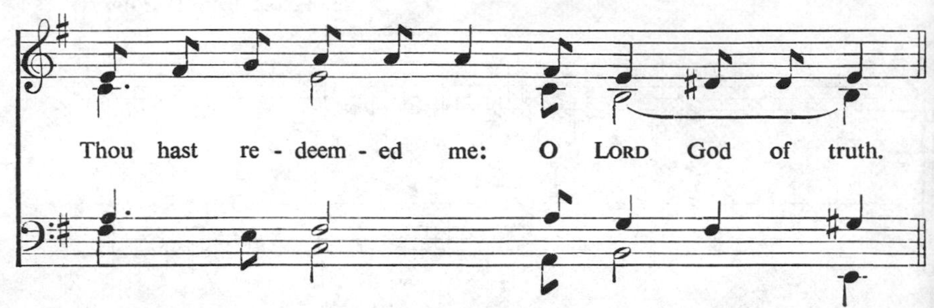
Thou hast re - deem - ed me: O LORD God of truth.

After J. Goss

THE ' LORD is my ' Shepherd:
* I ' shall not ' want.
He maketh me to lie down in ' green ' pastures:
* he leadeth me beside the ' still ' waters.
He re- ' storeth my ' soul:
* he leadeth me in the paths of ' righteousness · for his ' Name's sake.
Yea, though I walk through the valley of the shadow of death,
I will ' fear no ' evil:
* for thou art with me; thy rod and
thy ' staff they ' comfort me.
Thou preparest a table before me in the ' presence of mine ' enemies:
* thou anointest my head with oil; my ' cup · runneth ' over.
Surely goodness and mercy shall follow me all the ' days of my ' life:
* and I will dwell in the house of the ' LORD for ' ever.
GLORY ' be to the ' Father:
* and to the Son, and to the ' Holy ' Ghost;
As it ' was in · the be- ' ginning:
* is now, and ever shall be, world without ' end. A ' men.

Antiphon repeated.

¶ *Instead of these, Psalms 27, 34, 42, 73, 84, 90, 103, 116, 121, 126, 139, or 146 may be used.*

¶ *Then shall be read one or more of the following Lessons:*

WHAT shall we then say to these things? If God be for us, who can be against us? He that spared not his own Son, but delivered him up for us all, how shall he not with him also freely give us all things? Who shall lay anything to the charge of God's elect? It is God that justifieth. Who is he that condemneth? It is Christ that died, yea rather, that is risen again, who is even at the right hand of God, who also maketh intercession for us.

Who shall separate us from the love of Christ? shall tribulation, or distress, or persecution, or famine, or nakedness, or peril, or sword? As it is written, For thy sake we are killed all the day long; we are accounted as sheep for the slaughter.

Nay, in all these things we are more than conquerors through him that loved us. For I am persuaded, that neither death, nor life, nor angels, nor principalities, nor powers, nor things present, nor things to come, nor height, nor depth, nor any other creature, shall be able to separate us from the love of God, which is in Christ Jesus our Lord. *Rom.* 8:31–39.

NOW if Christ be preached that he rose from the dead, how say some among you that there is no resurrection of the dead? But if there be no resurrection of the dead, then is Christ not risen: and if Christ be not risen, then is our preaching vain, and your faith is also vain. Yea, and we are found false witnesses of God; because we have testified of God that he raised up Christ: whom he raised not up, if so be that the dead rise not. For if the dead rise not, then is not Christ raised: and if Christ be not raised, your faith is vain; ye are yet in your sins. Then they also which are fallen asleep in Christ are perished.

If in this life only we have hope in Christ, we are of all men most miserable.

But now is Christ risen from the dead, and become the firstfruits of them that slept. For since by man came death, by man came also the resurrection of the dead. For as in Adam all die, even so in Christ shall all be made alive.

But every man in his own order: Christ the firstfruits; afterward they that are Christ's at his coming. Then cometh the end, when he shall have delivered up the kingdom to God, even the Father; when he shall have put down all rule and all authority and power. For he must reign, till he hath put all enemies under his feet. The last enemy that shall be destroyed is death. *1 Cor.* 15:12–26.

BLESSED be the God and Father of our Lord Jesus Christ, which according to his abundant mercy hath begotten us again unto a lively hope by the resurrection of Jesus Christ from the dead, to an inheritance incorruptible, and undefiled, and that fadeth not away, reserved in heaven for you, who are kept by the power of God through faith unto salvation ready to be revealed in the last time. Wherein ye greatly rejoice, though now for a season, if need be, ye are in heaviness through manifold temptations: that the trial of your faith, being much more precious than of gold that perisheth, though it be tried with fire, might be found unto praise and honor and glory at the appearing of Jesus Christ: whom having not seen, ye love; in whom, though now ye see him not, yet believing, ye rejoice with joy unspeakable and full of glory: receiving the end of your faith, even the salvation of your souls. *1 Pet.* 1:3–9.

AFTER this I beheld, and lo, a great multitude which no man could number, of all nations, and kindreds, and people, and tongues, stood before the throne, and before the Lamb, clothed with white robes, and palms in their hands; and cried with a loud voice, saying, Salvation to our God which sitteth upon the throne, and unto the Lamb.

And all the angels stood round about the throne, and about the elders and the four beasts, and fell before the throne on their faces, and worshipped God, saying, Amen: Blessing, and glory, and wisdom, and thanksgiving, and honor, and power, and might, be unto our God for ever and ever. Amen.

And one of the elders answered, saying unto me, What are these which are arrayed in white robes? and whence came they? And I said unto him, Sir, thou knowest. And he said unto me, These are they which came out of great tribulation, and have washed their robes, and made them white in the blood of the Lamb. Therefore are they before the throne of God, and serve him day and night in his temple: and he that sitteth on the throne shall dwell among them. They shall hunger no more, neither thirst any more; neither shall the sun light on them, nor any heat. For the Lamb which is in the midst of the throne shall feed them, and shall lead them unto living fountains of waters: and God shall wipe away all tears from their eyes. *Rev.* 7:9–17.

AND I heard a great voice out of heaven saying, Behold, the tabernacle of God is with men, and he will dwell with them, and they shall be his people, and God himself shall be with them, and be their God. And God shall wipe away all tears from their eyes; and there shall be no more death, neither sorrow, nor crying, neither shall there be any more pain: for the former things are passed away. And he that sat upon the throne said, Behold, I make all things new. And he said unto me, Write: for these words are true and faithful. And he said unto me, It is done. I am Alpha and Omega, the beginning and the end. I will give unto him that is athirst of the fountain of the water of life freely. He that overcometh shall inherit all things; and I will be his God, and he shall be my son. *Rev.* 21:3–7.

VERILY, verily, I say unto you, He that heareth my word, and believeth on him that sent me, hath everlasting life, and shall not come into condemnation; but is passed from death unto life. Verily, verily, I say unto you, The hour is coming, and now is, when the dead shall hear the voice of the Son of God: and they that hear shall live. For as the Father hath life in himself; so hath he given to the Son to have life in himself; and hath given him authority to execute judgment also, because he is the Son of man. Marvel not at this: for the hour is coming, in the which all that are in the graves shall hear his voice, and shall come forth; they that have done good, unto the resurrection of life; and they that have done evil, unto the the resurrection of damnation. *John* 5:24–29.

THEN said Martha unto Jesus, Lord, if thou hadst been here, my brother had not died. But I know, that even now, whatsoever thou wilt ask of God, God will give it thee. Jesus saith unto her, Thy brother shall rise again. Martha saith unto him, I know that he shall rise again in the resurrection at the last day.

Jesus said unto her, I am the resurrection, and the life: he that believeth in me, though he were dead, yet shall he live: and whosoever liveth and believeth in me shall never die. Believest thou this?

She saith unto him, Yea, Lord: I believe that thou art the Christ, the Son of God, which should come into the world. *John* 11:21–27.

LET not your heart be troubled: ye believe in God, believe also in me. In my Father's house are many mansions: if it were not so, I would have told you. I go to prepare a place for you.

And if I go and prepare a place for you, I will come again, and receive you unto myself; that where I am, there ye may be also. And whither I go ye know, and the way ye know.

Thomas saith unto him, Lord, we know not whither thou goest; and how can we know the way? Jesus saith unto him, I am the way, the truth, and the life: no man cometh unto the Father, but by me. *John* 14:1–6.

At the Burial of a Child

AND they brought young children to him, that he should touch them: and his disciples rebuked those that brought them.

But when Jesus saw it, he was much displeased, and said unto them, Suffer the little children to come unto me, and forbid them not; for of such is the kingdom of God. Verily I say unto you, Whosoever shall not receive the kingdom of God as a little child, he shall not enter therein.

And he took them up in his arms, put his hands upon them, and blessed them. *Mark* 10:13–16.

Burial of the Dead

¶ *One or more of the following Lessons may also be read:* I *Cor.* 15:50–58;
I Thess. 4:13–18 (*Epistle for the Twenty-fifth Sunday after Trinity*);
Matt. 9:18, 19, 23–26 (*Gospel for the Twenty-fourth Sunday after Trinity*);
Luke 7:11–16 (*Gospel for the Sixteenth Sunday after Trinity*).

¶ *Then may be sung a Responsory, or a Hymn, or a suitable Anthem.*

THE RESPONSORIES

I. *Si bona suscepimus.*

Adapted by HAROLD W. GILBERT
From BARTHOLOMÄUS GESIUS, 1605

Shall we re - ceive - - good at the hand of the LORD, and
shall we not re - ceive e - - - vil? The LORD - - gave, and the
ceive - - e - vil?
LORD hath ta - - - ken a - way. V. Bless - ed be the Name of the
LORD hath ta - - ken a - way.
LORD hath ta - ken a - - way.
LORD. The LORD gave, and the LORD hath ta - - - ken a - way.
LORD hath ta - - ken a - way.
LORD hath ta - ken a - - way.

Burial of the Dead

II. *Credo, quod Redemptor meus.*

JEREMIAH FRANKLIN OHL, 1916

I know that my re - deem - er liv - - eth, and that he shall
stand at the lat - ter day up - on the earth; and in my
flesh shall I see God. V. Whom I shall see for my - self, and mine eyes
shall be-hold, and not an - oth - er. And in my flesh shall I see God.

Burial of the Dead

III. *Ecce, quomodo moritur justus.*

Adapted by Harold W. Gilbert
From Jacob Handl (c. 1590–1591)

Be - hold, how the right - eous di - - eth, and no man lay - eth
it to heart, and the just are tak - en - a - way, and
none - con - sid - er - eth. From - the e - vil to come is he
ta-ken a - way; and his mem - o - ry shall - - be in peace. V.
peace - - he rests in the earth, and in Zi - on is his hab - i
He rests

ta - - tion. His mem - o - ry shall be in peace.

¶ *Then may follow a Sermon.*

¶ *Then may a Hymn be sung.*

¶ *Then may the following Canticle be sung, and with it an Antiphon.*

NUNC DIMITTIS

Antiphon Based on LUCAS LOSSIUS

O how glo - ri - ous is that king - dom where - in all the

saints do re - joice with Christ. They are cloth - ed with white robes,

and fol - low the Lamb whith - er - so - ev - er he go - eth.

JOHN BLOW

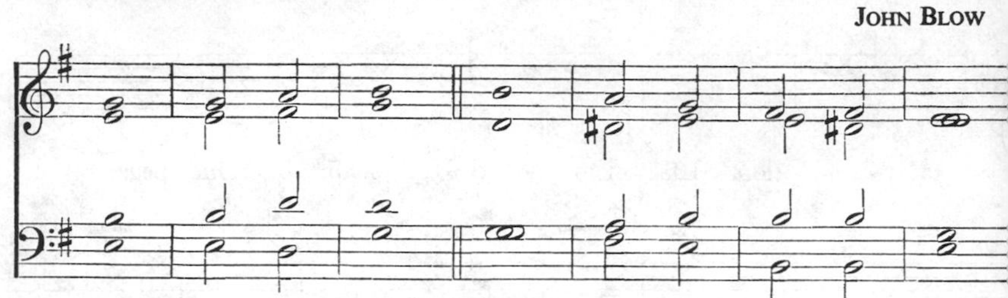

LORD, now lettest thou thy servant de- ' part in ' peace:
* ac- ' cording to ' thy ' word;
For mine eyes have ' seen thy sal ' vation:
* which thou hast prepared before the ' face of ' all ' people;
A light to ' lighten the ' Gentiles:
* and the ' glory · of thy ' people ' Israel.
GLORY ' be to the ' Father:
* and to the ' Son · and to the ' Holy ' Ghost;
As it ' was in · the be- ' ginning:
* is now, and ever shall be ' world without ' end. A ' men.

Antiphon repeated.

¶ *In place of the Nunc Dimittis, the Benedictus may be sung as the Canticle (Matins, p. 13*

¶ *Then shall the Congregation rise and the following Prayers, or other Prayers, shall be sa*

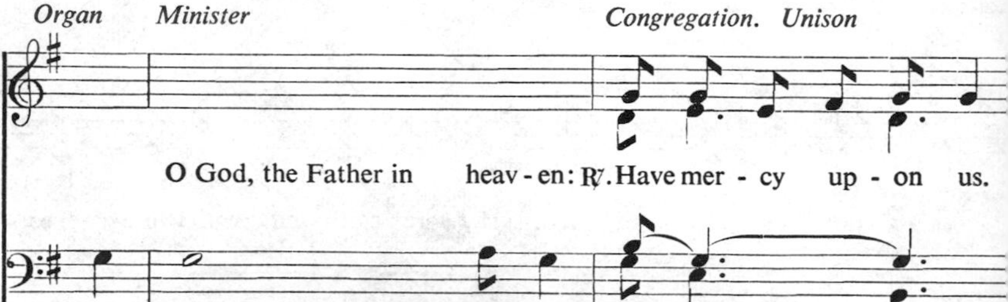
Organ
Minister
Congregation. Unison
O God, the Father in heav - en: ℟. Have mer - cy up - on us.

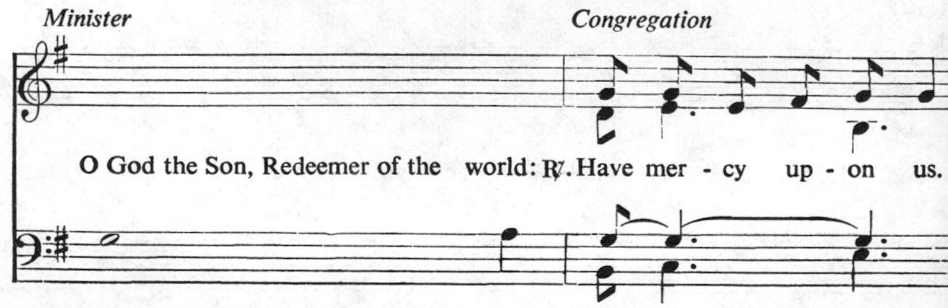
Minister
Congregation
O God the Son, Redeemer of the world: ℟. Have mer - cy up - on us.

Minister
Congregation
O God the Holy Ghost, the Com - forter: R̸. Grant us thy peace.

¶ *Then shall all say:*

OUR Father, who art in heaven, . . .

¶ *Then may the Minister say one or more of the following Collects:*

O GOD, our heavenly Father, who has taught us by thy holy Apostle not to sorrow overmuch for them that sleep in Jesus: Mercifully grant, at after this life, we, with all thy saints, may be received into everlasting y; through Jesus Christ, thy Son, our Lord. *Amen.*

(*After the Collects*)

A - - men.

ALMIGHTY God, with whom do live the spirits of those who depart hence in the Lord, and with whom the souls of the faithful, after they are livered from the burden of the flesh, are in joy and felicity: We give thee arty thanks for thy grace bestowed upon thy servants, who, having finished eir course in faith, do now rest from their labors; and we beseech thee, at we, with all who have departed in the true faith of thy holy Name, may ve our perfect consummation and bliss, both in body and soul, in thy ernal glory; through Jesus Christ, thy Son, our Lord. *Amen.*

ALMIGHTY and most merciful God, who hast appointed us to endu sufferings and death with our Lord Jesus Christ before we enter wi him into eternal glory: Grant us grace at all times to subject ourselves thy holy will, and to continue steadfast in the true faith unto the end of o lives; and at all times to find peace and joy in the blessed hope of the resu rection of the dead, and of the glory of the world to come; through the san Jesus Christ our Lord. *Amen.*

ALMIGHTY and everlasting God, the consolation of the sorrowful, a the strength of the weak: May the prayers of them that in any tribulati or distress cry unto thee, graciously come before thee, so that in all the necessities they may mark and receive thy manifold help and comfo through Jesus Christ, thy Son, our Lord. *Amen.*

O GOD, before whose face the generations rise and pass away, the streng of those who labor, and the repose of the blessed dead: We rejoice the communion of thy saints; we remember all who have faithfully live all who have peacefully died; and especially those most dear to us who re in thee. Give us at length our portion with those who have trusted in th and striven in all things to do thy holy will; and unto thy Name, with t Church on earth and the Church in heaven, we ascribe all honor and glo world without end. *Amen.*

O GOD, whose days are without end, and whose mercies cannot numbered: Make us deeply sensible of the shortness and uncertain of human life; and let thy Holy Spirit lead us through this present world holiness and righteousness all the days of our life; that, when we have serv thee in our day and generation, we may be gathered to our fathers, havi the testimony of a good conscience, in the communion of thy Church, the confidence of a certain faith, in the comfort of a holy hope, in fav with thee our God, and in perfect charity with all mankind; through Jes Christ our Lord. *Amen.*

O GOD, who healest the broken in heart, and bindest up their wound Look in tender pity and compassion upon thy servants whose joy h been turned into mourning. Leave them not comfortless, but grant that th may be drawn closer to thee and to one another by their common sorro Fill their souls with the light and comfort of thy presence. Grant unto the such a vision of that life wherein all mysteries shall be revealed, and all te be wiped away, that they may be able to endure as seeing thee who invisible. So dwell with them and be their God, until the day break and t shadows flee away; through Jesus Christ our Lord. *Amen.*

ALMIGHTY, everlasting God, who by reason of sin causest man to die and return to the dust: So teach us to number our days, that we may pply our hearts unto wisdom. Grant us a true faith in thine only-begotten on, Jesus Christ, who was delivered for our offences, was raised again for ur justification, and reigneth to all eternity. Help us by thy grace that we ay die daily unto sin and live according to thy holy will, so that, when our st hour shall come, we may be prepared for a peaceful departure. Receive ur souls unto thyself, and grant that at the last day our bodies may rise gain from the grave unto everlasting life; through Jesus Christ our Lord. *men.*

At the Burial of a Child

O GOD, whose most dear Son took little children into his arms and blessed them: Give us grace, we beseech thee, to entrust the soul of this child thy never-failing care and love, and bring us all to thy heavenly kingdom; rough the same thy Son, Jesus Christ our Lord. *Amen.*

O GOD our Father, we pray that thou wilt keep in tender love the life which we shall hold in blessed memory. Help us who continue here to rve thee with constancy, trusting in thy promise of eternal life, that hereafter e may be united with thy blessed children in glory everlasting; through sus Christ our Lord. *Amen.*

Special Prayers and Supplications may here be said. The following are suitable: Numbers 43, 53, 87, 101, and 110; No. 14 in Prayers for Private Devotion; and the Collect for All Saints' Day.

¶ Then shall be said the Prayer:

GOD of all Grace, who didst send thy Son, our Saviour Jesus Christ, to bring life and immortality to light: Most humbly and heartily we give ee thanks, that by his death he hath destroyed the power of death, and by s glorious resurrection hath opened the kingdom of heaven to all believers. rant us assuredly to know that because he lives we shall live also, and that ither death nor life, nor things present nor things to come, shall be able separate us from thy love, which is in Christ Jesus our Lord, who liveth d reigneth with thee and the Holy Ghost ever, one God, world without end. *men.*

¶ *Then shall the Minister say:*

THE Grace of our Lord Jesus Christ, and the Love of God, and the Com-munion of the Holy Ghost, be with you all.

Congregation
A - - - men.

¶ *If the foregoing Order be not used, then the Service may include the following parts, in th order: Invocation; one or more Psalms, with the Gloria Patri; one or more Lessons fro Holy Scripture; a Canticle; Prayers; and the Benediction. A brief Address may follo the Lesson. A Hymn may be sung after the Lessons, or after the Address.*

THE SERVICE AT THE GRAVE

¶ *When the body has been committed to the grave, the Minister may say:*

BLESSED are the dead which die in the Lord from henceforth; Yea, sai the Spirit, that they may rest from their labors. I am the Resurrectic and the Life, saith the Lord; he that believeth in me, though he were dea yet shall he live; and whosoever liveth and believeth in me shall never di

¶ *Or, he may say:*

IN the midst of life we are in death. Of whom may we seek for succor, b of thee, O Lord, who for our sins art justly displeased? Yet, O Lord Gc most holy, O Lord most mighty, O holy and most merciful Saviour: Suff us not, at our last hour, for any pains of death, to fall from thee.

¶ *Then, as earth is cast upon the coffin, the Minister shall say:*

FORASMUCH as it hath pleased Almighty God of his great mercy, take unto himself the soul of our *brother:* we therefore commit *his* bo to the ground;* earth to earth, ashes to ashes, dust to dust; in sure and certa hope of the resurrection to eternal life through our Lord Jesus Christ; wl shall change the body of our low estate, that it may be fashioned like un his glorious body, according to the working whereby he is able even to subd all things unto himself.

¶ *Or, he may say:*

FORASMUCH as it hath pleased Almighty God in his wise providen to call out of this world the soul of our *brother*, we therefore comn *his* body to the ground. Dust thou art, to dust thou shalt return. Jesus Chri our Saviour, shall at the latter day raise thee from the dead.

---

* *At the Burial of the Dead at sea, the words* to the deep, *shall be substituted for the wor* to the ground; *and the words* earth to earth, ashes to ashes, dust to dust, *shall be omitt*

¶ *Then may the Benedictus or a Hymn be sung.*

¶ *Then may the Minister say one or more of the following Prayers:*

ALMIGHTY God, who by the death of thy Son, Jesus Christ, hast destroyed death, and by his rest in the tomb hast sanctified the graves of thy saints, and by his glorious resurrection hast brought life and immortality to light, so that all who die in him abide in peace and hope: Receive, we beseech thee, our unfeigned thanks for the victory over death and the grave which he hath obtained for us, and for all who sleep in him; and keep us, who are still in the body, in everlasting fellowship with all that wait for thee on earth, and with all around thee in heaven, in union with him who is the Resurrection and the Life, even Jesus Christ our Lord. *Amen.*

O LORD Jesus Christ, who by thy death didst take away the sting of death: Grant unto us thy servants so to follow in faith where thou hast led the way, that we may at length fall peacefully asleep in thee, and awake after thy likeness; through thy mercy, O our Lord, who livest and reignest with the Father and the Holy Ghost, one God, world without end. *Amen.*

¶ *Then shall the Minister say:*

NOW the God of peace, that brought again from the dead our Lord Jesus, the great Shepherd of the sheep, through the blood of the everlasting covenant: Make you perfect in every good work to do his will; working in you that which is well pleasing in his sight; through Jesus Christ, to whom be glory for ever and ever. *Amen.*

Or,

THE LORD bless thee and keep thee. The LORD make his face shine upon thee, and be gracious unto thee. The LORD lift up his countenance upon thee, and give thee peace. *Amen.*

ORDER FOR MARRIAGE

¶ *Before solemnizing a Marriage, the Minister shall counsel with the persons about to be married, and shall diligently inquire: first, as to whether the union contemplated be in accordance with the Word of God; second, whether it be in accordance with the laws of the State. No Marriage shall be solemnized unless the Minister be convinced that God's blessing may properly be asked upon it.*

¶ *The Minister may publish the Banns in the Church, one or more Sundays before the day appointed for the Marriage, saying:* N.N. and N.N. purpose to enter into the holy estate of Matrimony, according to God's ordinance. They desire that prayer be made for them, that they may enter into this union in the Name of the Lord, and be prospered in it. If any one can show just cause why they may not be joined together, I exhort him to make known such objection before the day of the marriage.

¶ *All arrangements for the Marriage service shall be made in consultation with the Pastor. Due reverence shall be maintained in the preparation for, and the celebration of, the marriage. The use of secular music shall not be permitted in the Church.*

¶ *When a Marriage is solemnized in the Church, a Hymn may be sung, and Psalm 67 or Psalm 128 may be sung or said, ending with the Gloria Patri. If there be an Address it may then follow.*

¶ *The Congregation shall stand for the Invocation.*

¶ *The persons to be married having presented themselves at the entrance to the Chancel, or before the Altar, the Man to the right of the Woman, the Minister shall say:*

IN the Name of the Father, and of the Son, and of the Holy Ghost *Amen.*

DEARLY Beloved: Forasmuch as Marriage is a holy estate, ordained of God, and to be held in honor by all, it becometh those who enter therein to weigh, with reverent minds, what the Word of God teacheth concerning it

THE Lord God said:

It is not good that the man should be alone; I will make him an help meet for him.

Our Lord Jesus Christ said:

HAVE ye not read that he which made them at the beginning made them male and female, and said, For this cause shall a man leave father and mother, and shall cleave to his wife, and they twain shall be one flesh? Wherefore, they are no more twain, but one flesh. What therefore God hath joined together, let not man put asunder.

¶ *Then shall be read one or both of the following Lections:*

The Apostle Paul, speaking by the Holy Spirit, saith:

HUSBANDS, love your wives, even as Christ also loved the Church and gave himself for it. He that loveth his wife, loveth himself; for no man ever yet hated his own flesh, but nourisheth it, even as the Lord the Church. Wives, submit yourselves unto your own husbands, as unto the Lord; for the husband is the head of the wife, even as Christ is the Head of the Church.

The Apostle Peter, speaking by the Holy Spirit, saith:

YE wives, let your adorning be the ornament of a meek and quiet spirit, which is, in the sight of God, of great price. Likewise, ye husbands, dwell with them according to knowledge, giving honor unto the wife as unto the weaker vessel and as being heirs together of the grace of life.

¶ *Then shall the Minister say:*

AND although, by reason of sin, many a cross hath been laid thereon, nevertheless our gracious Father in heaven doth not forsake his children in an estate so holy and acceptable to him, but is ever present with his abundant blessing.

¶ *If the Banns have not been published, then the Minister may say:*

INTO this holy estate this Man and this Woman come now to be united. If any one, therefore, can show just cause why they may not be lawfully joined together, let him now speak, or else forever hold his peace.

¶ *Then shall the Minister say to the Man:*

N., WILT thou have this Woman to thy wedded wife, to live together after God's ordinance in the holy estate of Matrimony? Wilt thou love her, comfort her, honor and keep her in sickness and in health, and, forsaking all others, keep thee only unto her, so long as ye both shall live?

¶ *The Man shall say:*

I will.

¶ *Then shall the Minister say to the Woman:*

N., WILT thou have this Man to thy wedded husband, to live together after God's ordinance in the holy estate of Matrimony? Wilt thou love him, comfort him, honor and keep him in sickness and in health, and, forsaking all others, keep thee only unto him, so long as ye both shall live?

¶ *The Woman shall say:*

I will.

¶ *If the Woman be given in Marriage, the Minister shall say:*

Who giveth this Woman to be married to this Man?

¶ *The Minister shall then receive her at the hands of her father (or guardian or any friend), the Woman placing her right hand in the hand of the Minister. Then shall the Minister place the right hand of the Woman in the right hand of the Man. Then shall they loose their hands.*

¶ *If the first part of the service has been conducted at the entrance to the Chancel, the Minister shall now precede the Man and Woman to the Altar.*

¶ *The Man shall take the right hand of the Woman and say after the Minister:*

I, N., take thee, N., to my wedded wife, to have and to hold from this day forward, for better for worse, for richer for poorer, in sickness and in health, to love and to cherish, till death us do part, according to God's holy ordinance; and thereto I plight thee my troth.

¶ *Then shall the Woman, in like manner, say after the Minister:*

I, N., take thee, N., to my wedded husband, to have and to hold from this day forward, for better for worse, for richer for poorer, in sickness and in health, to love and to cherish, till death us do part, according to God's holy ordinance; and thereto I plight thee my troth.

¶ *Should a shorter form be desired, the following may be said:*

I, N., take thee, N., to my wedded (wife, *or*, husband), and plight thee my troth, till death us do part.

¶ *If the wedding Ring be used, the Minister shall now receive it and give it to the Man to put on the fourth finger of the Woman's left hand.*
¶ *Then shall the Man say, or if two rings be used, the Man and the Woman, in turn, shall say, after the Minister:*

Receive this Ring as a token of wedded love and troth.

¶ *Then shall the Minister say:*

Join your right hands.

¶ *Then shall the Minister lay his right hand upon their hands and say:*

FORASMUCH as N. and N. have consented together in holy wedlock, and have declared the same before God and in the presence of this company, I pronounce them Man and Wife: In the Name of the Father and of the Son and of the Holy Ghost. Amen.

What God hath joined together, let not man put asunder.

¶ *Then may they kneel, and the Minister shall bless them, saying:*

THE Lord God, who created our first parents and sanctified their union in Marriage: Sanctify and bless you, that ye may please him both in body and soul, and live together in holy love until life's end. Amen.

¶ *Then shall the Minister say:*

Let us pray.

ALMIGHTY and most merciful God, who hast now united this Man and this Woman in the holy estate of Matrimony: Grant them grace to live therein according to thy holy Word; strengthen them in constant fidelity and true affection toward each other; sustain and defend them amidst all trials and temptations; and help them so to pass through this world in faith toward thee, in communion with thy holy Church, and in loving service one of the other, that they may enjoy forever thy heavenly benediction; through Jesus Christ, thy Son, our Lord, who liveth and reigneth with thee and the Holy Ghost, one God, world without end. *Amen.*

¶ *The Minister may add one or both of the following prayers:*

O ALMIGHTY God, Creator of mankind, who only art the well-spring of life: Bestow upon these thy servants, if it be thy will, the gift and heritage of children; and grant that they may see their children brought up in thy faith and fear, to the honor and glory of thy Name; through Jesus Christ our Lord. *Amen.*

O GOD, who art our dwelling-place in all generations: Look with favor upon the homes of our land; enfold husbands and wives, parents and children, in the bonds of thy pure love; and so bless our homes, that they may be a shelter for the defenceless, a bulwark for the tempted, a resting-place for the weary, and a foretaste of our eternal home in thee; through Jesus Christ our Lord. *Amen.*

¶ *Then shall all say:*

OUR Father, who art in heaven, . . .

¶ *Then shall the Minister say the Benediction:*

THE Lord bless thee and keep thee. The Lord make his face shine upon thee, and be gracious unto thee. The Lord lift up his countenance upon thee, and give thee peace. *Amen.*

Or,

GOD Almighty send you his light and truth to keep you all the days of your life. The hand of God protect you; his holy Angels accompany you. God the Father, God the Son, and God the Holy Ghost, cause his grace to be mighty upon you. *Amen.*

General Rubrics

These General Rubrics, together with the Rubrics appointed in the services, are a directory for the conduct of Divine Worship.

Rubrics are of two kinds: directive, expressed by 'shall'; and permissive, expressed by 'may'.

I. FOR THE SERVICE, MATINS, AND VESPERS

Worshippers should offer Silent Prayer upon entering and before leaving the Church.

The Congregation shall rise at the beginning of every service.

A Hymn of Invocation of the Holy Ghost, or another suitable Hymn, may be sung at the beginning of any service.

The Minister may face the Altar except in such parts of the services as are a direct address to the Congregation.

A Hymn may be sung after the Benediction at any service.

Intonations provided for the Minister's parts of the Services represent a permissive use. They are not to be considered directive.

THE PROPERS. *The Propers for the Day, the Introit, Collect, Lesson, Epistle, Gradual, and Gospel, shall be used throughout the week following, except on those Days for which other appointments are made.*

When a Greater Festival falls within the week, the Propers for the Festival shall be used until the following Sunday.

THE COLLECTS. *The Collect for the Sunday is said at Matins throughout the week. It is also said at Vespers daily except on Saturday, when the Collect for the following Sunday is said.*

Should a Festival fall within the week, the Collect for the Festival shall be said first on that Day, and if it be a Greater Festival, throughout the remainder of the week.

Whenever the Collect for the Day is said, the full termination as appointed shall be used. If other Collects are said after it, as at Matins and Vespers, the full termination shall be used with the Collect for the Day and with the last Collect only.

The short termination of the Collects used after the Collect for the Day, will usually be: through Jesus Christ, thy Son, our Lord, or, through the same Jesus Christ, thy Son, our Lord Exceptions to this rule will be found printed in full in the Collects and Prayers.

II. THE SERVICE

For the Invocation, the Confession, and the Declaration of Grace, the Minister may stand in the Chancel before the Altar. At the Introit, he shall stand at the Altar.

When The Service begins with the Introit, the Minister shall go immediately to the Altar.

THE INTROIT. *The Introit for the Day with the Gloria Patri should be sung by the Choir; but the Introit may be sung by the Choir, the Congregation uniting in the Gloria Patri; or the Introit may be said by the Minister, the Choir and the Congregation singing the Gloria Patri.*

The Introits have their proper music, but they may be sung to the Psalm Tones. When sung, the Antiphon of the Introit may be repeated after the Gloria Patri.

THE KYRIE. *The Kyrie is the invariable responsive prayer which begins the Liturgy proper. It consists of invitations to prayer, sung or said by the Minister, with responses by the Choir and Congregation. The alternate form may be used instead of that which is first provided.*

THE GLORIA IN EXCELSIS. *The Gloria in Excelsis shall be used on all Festival Days or when there is a Communion. At other times another Canticle or Hymn of Praise may be sung.*

THE LESSONS. *Before the Epistle for the Day a Lesson from the Old Testament, as provided in the Lectionary, or other Lessons of Holy Scripture, may be read; but the Epistle and the Gospel for the Day shall always be read.*

THE GRADUAL FOR THE DAY AND THE ALLELUIA. *The Gradual for the Day should be sung by the choir; or, instead thereof, the Season Gradual or the Alleluia may be sung by the Choir and the Congregation.*

THE CREED. *The Nicene Creed shall be used on all Festivals and whenever there is a Communion; at other times the Apostles' Creed may be used in its stead. After the Creed the Minister may make any needful announcements.*

THE PRAYER OF THE CHURCH. *Before the Prayer of the Church the Minister shall make mention of any special Petitions, Intercessions, or Thanksgivings, which may have been requested. He may also make mention of the death of any members of the Congregation.*

The Prayer of the Church, or one of the General Prayers (p. 238), shall be used on Festivals and whenever there is a Communion. At other times the Litany or a selection from the Collects and Prayers (p. 218), or any other suitable Prayer, may be said.

THE LORD'S PRAYER. *The Lord's Prayer shall be omitted after the Prayer of the Church when there is a Communion, or when one of the Occasional Services is used in connection with The Service.*

THE HOLY COMMUNION. *The Proper Preface for a Festival shall be used on the Festival and during the week following. The Proper Prefaces for Advent, Lent, and Easter shall be used throughout those seasons.*

In making ready the Elements for the Holy Communion so much of the Bread and Wine shall be placed in the proper Vessels as, in the judgment of the Minister, will be required for the administration.

The Minister himself may first receive the Bread and Wine and shall then administer the same to the people.

When all have received the Holy Sacrament, the Minister shall cover that which remaineth of the Bread and Wine with the Veil.

III. MATINS

THE INVITATORY. *The Invitatory is always used with the Venite. It may vary with the season.*

The first part: O Come, let us worship the Lord, *may be sung or said before the Venite by the Minister, or by a single voice; the Choir and Congregation reponding:* For he is our Maker. *After the Venite and Gloria Patri, the whole Invitatory should be repeated, in the same manner.*

THE PSALM. *In the reading or singing of the Psalter at Matins, Psalm 95 (Venite) shall not be used.*

An Antiphon may be sung with each Psalm.

When an Antiphon is used with the Psalm, it should be sung by a single voice before the Psalm, and repeated after the Psalm and Gloria Patri by the entire Choir.

THE LESSON. *One or more Lessons shall be read. On Sundays or Festivals the Lessons shall be read according to the Table (Chapter VIII, below).*

In announcing the Lesson the Minister shall say: The First *(or* Second, *or* Third*)* Lesson is written in the —— Chapter of —— beginning at the —— Verse. *The Lesson ended, he shall say:* Here endeth the First *(or* Second, *or* Third*)* Lesson. *After that he shall say:* O Lord, have mercy upon us.

THE RESPONSORY. *The Responsory varies with the Season and may be sung by the Choir after the last Lesson.*

THE SERMON. *The Sermon or Address may follow the Lesson and Responsory as appointed. Or it may follow the Benedicamus; the Sermon shall then be followed by a Hymn, a Collect, and the Benediction.*

THE CANTICLES. *The Te Deum. Proper on all Sundays except in Advent and from Septuagesima to Easter Eve.*

The Benedictus. Proper at Matins in Advent, and from Septuagesima to Easter Eve.

The Benedicite is proper on Festivals and during Eastertide.

Any of the other Canticles, except the Magnificat and the Nunc Dimittis, which are appointed for use at Vespers, may be used at Matins on any day except a Sunday or a Festival.

An Antiphon may be sung with any of the Canticles except the Te Deum. It should be sung by a single voice before the Canticle and repeated after the Canticle by the entire Choir.

THE PRAYER. *Instead of the Prayer appointed, the General Suffrages, the Morning Suffrages, the Litany or other Prayers may be said. The Congregation may kneel for the Prayer.*

IV. VESPERS

THE PSALM. *An Antiphon may be sung with each Psalm.*

When an Antiphon is used with a Psalm it should be sung by a single voice before the Psalm and repeated after the Psalm and Gloria Patri by the entire Choir.

THE LESSON. *One or more Lessons shall be read.*

In announcing the Lesson the Minister shall say: The First (or Second, or Third) Lesson is written in the —— Chapter of —— beginning at the —— Verse. The Lesson ended, he shall say: Here endeth the First (or Second, or Third) Lesson. After that he shall say: O Lord, have mercy upon us.

THE RESPONSORY. *The Responsory varies with the Season and may be sung by the Choir after the last Lesson.*

THE SERMON. *The Sermon or Address may follow the Lesson and Responsory as appointed. Or it may follow the Benedicamus; the Sermon shall then be followed by a Collect and the Benediction.*

VESPER CANTICLES. *The Magnificat. Proper at any time.*

The Nunc Dimittis may be used at any time except the Greater Festivals.

On Festivals a special Versicle may be used with the Canticle.

An Antiphon may be sung with the Canticle.

THE PRAYER. *Instead of the Prayer appointed, the General Suffrages, the Evening Suffrages, the Litany or other Prayers may be said. The Congregation may kneel for the Prayer.*

THE COLLECT. *The Collect for the Sunday is said at Vespers through Friday; but on Saturday the Collect for the following Sunday is said. The Collect proper for any Sunday or other Festival may be used at Vespers of the day before.*

Additional rubrics governing the use of Collects are given on p. 274.

V. LITURGICAL COLORS

The Liturgical Colors are: White, Red, Green, Violet, Black. The proper use of the Liturgical Colors is as follows: the Color of all Paraments: Altar Hangings, Pulpit and Lectern Falls Stoles, etc., shall be of the Proper Color of the Day or Season. The Celebration of the Holy Communion, or the use of any of the Occasional Services, including the Order for Marriage and the Order for the Burial of the Dead, shall not affect the Proper Color for the Day or the Season.

WHITE. *From and with the Vespers of the Eve of the Nativity, through the Epiphany Season (except the Days of St. Stephen, Martyr, The Holy Innocents, Martyrs, and the Conversion of St. Paul, on which Days the color is Red).*

From the Vespers of Easter Eve to, but not including, the Vespers of the Eve of Pentecost

On the Festival of the Presentation.

On Trinity Sunday and through its Octave.

On the Days of the Annunciation and of the Visitation.

On the Transfiguration of our Lord.

On the Day of St. Michael and All Angels.

RED. *From the Vespers of the Eve of Pentecost to, but not including, the Vespers of the Eve of Trinity Sunday.*

On Reformation Day, or on the Sunday of its observance.

On the Apostles' Days and on Evangelists' Days (excepting St. John, Apostle, Evangelist, on which Day the color is White).

On Martyrs' Days.

On All Saints' Day and the Sunday following.

For the Dedication of a Church and its Anniversaries.

For the Festival of Harvest.

For the Day of Thanksgiving.

GREEN. *From and with Vespers of the Saturday before Septuagesima to, but not including, Vespers of the day before Ash Wednesday. Beginning with Monday after the First Sunday after Trinity Sunday and throughout the Trinity Season to, but not including, Vespers of the Saturday before the first Sunday in Advent, except on such Festivals and Days for which there is a special appointment.*

VIOLET. *From and with Vespers of the Saturday before the First Sunday in Advent to, but not including, Vespers of Christmas Eve.*

From and with Vespers of the day before Ash Wednesday and throughout Lent (excepting Good Friday) to, but not including, Vespers of Easter Eve.

BLACK. *For Good Friday, and for a Day of Humiliation.*

THE ALTAR LINENS. *The Fair Linen, a cloth covering the Altar, extending one-third or two-thirds to the floor at the narrow ends, shall always be upon the Altar.*

SACRAMENTAL LINENS. *The Corporal, a square of very fine linen, is laid on the center of the Fair Linen cloth. Upon it the Sacramental Vessels are placed.*

The Pall, a small square of heavy cardboard covered with linen, is used to cover the Chalice. It should be removed at the Offertory.

The Purificators, squares of heavy linen, are used to cleanse the rim of the Chalice during the Administration.

The Veil, made of silk or of the finest linen, is used to cover the Sacramental Vessels upon the Altar. It is removed at the Offertory and should be folded carefully and laid upon the Altar and again placed over the Sacramental Vessels after the Administration at the Nunc Dimittis.

The Sacramental Linens when not in use should be properly folded and kept in the Burse, a square envelope made of strong cardboard covered with silk or heavy linen.

VI. THE CHURCH YEAR

Note: For the Festivals and Days of the Church Year, see the Calendar, page xi.

CALENDAR RUBRICS

The Moveable Festivals and Days all depend upon Easter except Advent Sunday.

Advent Sunday is always the Sunday nearest to St. Andrew's Day, the thirtieth day of November, whether before or after.

Easter is always the first Sunday after the Full Moon which happens upon, or next after the twenty-first day of March; and if the Full Moon happens upon a Sunday, Easter is the Sunday after.

The time of Easter being found, the other Festivals occur as follows:

Septuagesima Sunday is nine weeks before Easter.

Ash Wednesday, the First Day of Lent, is forty-six days before Easter.

Palm Sunday, or the beginning of Holy Week, is the Sunday next before Easter.
Holy, or Maundy, Thursday is the Thursday before Easter.
Good Friday is the Friday before Easter.
Ascension Day is forty days after Easter.
Pentecost or Whitsunday is seven weeks after Easter.
Trinity Sunday is the Sunday next after Pentecost.

PRECEDENCE OF FESTIVALS AND DAYS

I. The following days shall be observed invariably as appointed in the Calendar. A Day or Festival concurring with any of these here noted may be observed the first open day thereafter.

GREATER FESTIVALS AND DAYS

The Sundays of Advent
The Nativity
The Circumcision
The Epiphany
Septuagesima
Sexagesima
Quinquagesima
Ash Wednesday
The Sundays in Lent
The Days of Holy Week
Easter Day and the Day following
The Sundays after Easter
The Ascension and the Sunday following
Pentecost and the Day following
Trinity Sunday
Reformation Day
All Saints' Day

II. When a Lesser Festival falls on a Sunday not noted in Rubric I, the Introit, Collect, Epistle, Gradual, and Gospel, for the Festival shall be used, and the Collect for the Sunday shall be said after the Collect for the Day.

The Propers for a Lesser Festival may be used on the Sunday following the Festival, provided that the Sunday be not noted in Rubric I.

LESSER FESTIVALS:

All Apostles', Evangelists', and Martyrs' Days
The Presentation, the Visitation, and the Annunciation
The Transfiguration
St. Michael and All Angels

THE EASTER TABLE

A Table of Days on Which Easter Will Fall from 1955–2002

1955	April	10	1967	March	26	1979	April	15	1991	March	31
1956	"	1	1968	April	14	1980	"	6	1992	April	19
1957	"	21	1969	"	6	1981	"	19	1993	"	11
1958	"	6	1970	March	29	1982	"	11	1994	"	3
1959	March	29	1971	April	11	1983	"	3	1995	"	16
1960	April	17	1972	"	2	1984	"	22	1996	"	7
1961	"	2	1973	"	22	1985	"	7	1997	March	30
1962	"	22	1974	"	14	1986	March	30	1998	April	12
1963	"	14	1975	March	30	1987	April	19	1999	"	4
1964	March	29	1976	April	18	1988	"	3	2000	"	23
1965	April	18	1977	"	10	1989	March	26	2001	"	15
1966	"	10	1978	March	26	1990	April	15	2002	March	31

TABLE OF THE MOVEABLE FESTIVALS

According to the Several Days upon Which Easter May Fall

Easter	*	*Septuagesima*	*Ash Wednesday*	*Ascension*	*Pentecost*	§	*Advent*
March 22	1	January 18	February 4	April 30	May 10	27	November 29
23	1	19	5	May 1	11	27	30
24	1	20	6	2	12	27	December 1
25	2	21	7	3	13	27	2
26	2	22	8	4	14	27	3
27	2	23	9	5	15	26	November 27
28	2	24	10	6	16	26	28
29	2	25	11	7	17	26	29
30	2	26	12	8	18	26	30
31	2	27	13	9	19	26	December 1
April 1	3	28	14	10	20	26	2
2	3	29	15	11	21	26	3
3	3	30	16	12	22	25	November 27
4	3	31	17	13	23	25	28
5	3	February 1	18	14	24	25	29
6	3	2	19	15	25	25	30
7	3	3	20	16	26	25	December 1
8	4	4	21	17	27	25	2
9	4	5	22	18	28	25	3
10	4	6	23	19	29	24	November 27
11	4	7	24	20	30	24	28
12	4	8	25	21	31	24	29
13	4	9	26	22	June 1	24	30
14	4	10	27	23	2	24	December 1
15	5	11	28	24	3	24	2
16	5	12	March 1	25	4	24	3
17	5	13	2	26	5	23	November 27
18	5	14	3	27	6	23	28
19	5	15	4	28	7	23	29
20	5	16	5	29	8	23	30
21	5	17	6	30	9	23	December 1
22	6	18	7	31	10	23	2
23	6	19	8	June 1	11	23	3
24	6	20	9	2	12	22	November 27
25	6	21	10	3	13	22	28

* *Sundays after Epiphany. In a Leap Year, the number of Sundays after Epiphany is the same as if Easter had fallen one day later than it really does; and Septuagesima Sunday and Ash Wednesday fall one day later than that given in the Table, unless the Table gives some day in March for Ash Wednesday; for in that case the day in the table is right.*

§ *Sundays after Trinity.*

Note: Section VII of the General Rubrics, "Lessons, Epistles, and Gospels" (for The Service), is omitted from this edition.

VIII. LESSONS FOR MATINS AND VESPERS

SUNDAY or HOLYDAY	MATINS I Lesson	MATINS II Lesson	VESPERS I Lesson	VESPERS II Lesson
1 Advent	Is 28:14–22	Lk 1:1–25	Is 62:1–12	Col 1:9–23
2 "	Is 52:1–10	Lk 1:26–38	Amos 3:1–8	Rom 2:1–16
3 "	Jer 1:4–10, 17–19	Lk 1:39–56	Nah 1:3–8, 15	Rom 1:16–25
4 "	Jer 33:7–16	Lk 1:67–80	Is 40:12–26	Heb 12:11–29
Christmas	Is 9:2–7	Jn 1:1–14	Mic 4:1–5 and 5:2–4	Lk 2:15–20
1 after "	Is 49:8–13	Lk 2:22–32	Job 28:12–28	Heb 2:9–16
Circumcision	Dt 30:1–10	Lk 4:16–21	Dt 30:11–20	Jas 4:13–17
2 a. Christmas	Is 44:1–8, 21–23	Mt 3:1–12	Hag 2:1–9	Rom 3:23–31
Epiphany	Is 2:2–5	Mt 3:13–17	Is 61:1–11	Rom 3:23–31
1 a. "	Prov 8:22–35	Mk 10:13–16	Is 49:1–7	Eph 6:1–4
2 " "	Is 41:8–10, 17–20	Lk 19:1–10	Num 20:1–11	Eph 5:22–33
3 " "	Dt 4:5–13, 32–40	Lk 17:5–10	Dan 10:10–19	Heb 11:1–16
4 " "	Jos 3:14–17	Mt 14:22–33	Job 38:1–11	Rom 4:16–25
5 " "	Joel 3:9–17	Mt 13:44–52	Amos 5:14–24	1 Cor 3:3–23
6 " "	Ex 3:1–6	Mt 11:25–30	Ex 24:12–18	2 Cor 4:5–6
Septuagesima	Jos 1:1–9	Mt 25:14–30	Is 5:1–7	Acts 17:22–34
Sexagesima	Is 50:4–10	Mk 4:26–32	Eccl 11:1–6	2 Tim 3:10–4:5
Quinquagesima	Dt 10:12–11:1	Jn 12:23–36	Lev 19:1–2, 9–18	1 Pet 3:18–22
Ash Wednesday	Is 59:12–21	Lk 6:20–36	Jon 3:1–4:11	1 Jn 1:5–10
1 in Lent	Is 58:1–12	Lk 22:24–32	Jer 17:5–14	Jas 1:2–15
2 " "	1 K 8:37–43	Mk 9:17–29	2 Sam 12:1–10, 13–14	Jas 5:13–20
3 " "	Zech 1:1–6, 12–17	Jn 8:42–51	Amos 4:4–13	Rev 2:1–7
4 " "	Ex 16:4–15	Jn 6:35–51	Is 52:7–10	2 Pet 1:2–11
5 " "	Is 1:10–20	Mt 10:32–42	Hos 6:1–6	1 Cor 1:21–31
6 Palmarum	Is 59:1–3, 9–16	Mk 14:3–9	Jer 8:9–15, 18–22	Heb 12:1–11
M in Holy Wk	Ex 19:1–9	Lk 21:34–38	Ex 15:27–16:7*a*	Rom 5:1–5
T in Holy Wk	Is 41:26–42:4	Mk 10:35–45	Is 1:16–19	2 Cor 1:3–5
W in Holy Wk	Lam 3:1–21	Jn 11:45–54	Is 42:5–12	Acts 4:8–12
Thurs in HW	Jer 31:31–34	Lk 22:14–20	Lam 3:40–58	1 Cor 10:16–17
Good Friday	Gen 22:1–18	Mt 27:33–54	Is 52:13–53:12	Rev 5:6–10
Sat in HW	Zech 12:10–11a	Mt 16:24–27	Lev 23:26–32	Heb 10:32–39
Easter Day	Is 25:1–9	Mt 28:1–8	Is 51:9–16	Lk 24:13–35
Easter Mon	Jer 17:13–18	Lk 24:36–47	Is 51:4–8	Rom 8:3–11
1 after Easter	Is 43:1–12	Jn 21:15–19	Zeph 3:14–20	1 Pet 1:17–2:3
2 " "	Is 40:1–11	Jn 10:22–30	Ez 34:22–31	Heb 13:20–21
3 " "	2 Sam 12:15b–23	Jn 14:1–14	Prov 4:7–18	Heb 4:14–16
4 " "	Ez 37:1–14	Jn 8:21–36	Dan 12:1–4, 13	2 Cor 5:14–21
5 " "	Ez 34:22–31	Jn 17:1–19	Is 48:12–21	Rom 8:24–28
Ascension Day	Dan 7:9–10, 13–14	Lk 24:45–53	Is 33:5–6, 17, 20–22	Eph 1:3–14
Exaudi	Is 4:2–6	Jn 17:20–26	Is 32:13–20	Rom 8:29–39
Pentecost	Ez 36:22–28	Jn 14:15–21	Is 11:1–9	Acts 2:14–21
Whitmonday	1 K 3:5–14	Lk 9:1–6	Ez 37:21–27	Eph 4:7–16
Trinity Sunday	Gen 1:1–2:3	Mt 28:19–20	Job 38:1–11, 16–18	2 Cor 13:11–14
1 after Trin.	Job 29:11–16	Lk 12:13–21	Is 42:5–12	1 Tim 6:6–19
2 " "	Dt 20:1–9	Lk 14:25–33	Jer 7:25–28	Rev 3:14–22
3 " "	Jer 31:1–14	Lk 15:11–32	Jer 23:1–8	Acts 9:1–18
4 " "	Dt 32:1–4, 20–39	Mt 5:43–48	Gen 18:20–33	Rom 14:7–17
5 " "	Eccl 2:1–11, 18–23	Mt 16:13–25	Prov 3:1–7, 11–12	1 Pet 2:1–10
6 " "	2 Sam 19:16–23	Mt 19:16–30	Gen 4:1–16	Eph 2:4–10
7 " "	Hos 14:1–9	Mt 10:24–31	Dan 5:1–9, 13–20	Acts 14:8–23
8 " "	Zech 4:1–10	Mt 7:21–29	1 Sam 26:1–7, 12–17, 21–25	Acts 20:17–38
9 " "	Ex 32:1–6	Lk 12:32–48	Is 38:1–8	2 Tim 1:3–14
10 " "	Jer 26:1–19	Mt 11:16–24	Lam 1:1–12	Heb 3:7–15

VIII. LESSONS FOR MATINS AND VESPERS

SUNDAY or HOLYDAY	MATINS I Lesson	MATINS II Lesson	VESPERS I Lesson	VESPERS II Lesson
1 after Trin.	Is 26:12–16, 19	Lk 7:36–50	Eccl 5:1–7	Rom 10:4–18
2 " "	Gen 41:1a, 8, 14–40	Mt 12:31–42	2 Sam 15:1–23	Jas 3:1–12
3 " "	Hab 1:12–2:4	Mt 20:20–28	Dt 15:7–15	1 Tim 1:5–17
4 " "	Mic 6:1–8	Jn 5:1–15	Dt 8:1–14, 17–20	Acts 3:1–10
5 " "	Dt 7:6–12	Lk 10:38–42	Joel 2:21–27	Acts 8:26–39
6 " "	Jer 32:36–42	Jn 11:19–45	1 K 17:17–24	1 Cor 15:21–28
7 " "	Jer 13:15–25	Mk 2:18–28	Mal 2:1–10	Jude 20–25
8 " "	Amos 8:4–12	Jn 15:1–17	Jer 17:5–10	1 Jn 3:1–8
9 " "	Job 24:1–17	Jn 1:35–51	Jer 5:7–19	1 Cor 12:12–27
0 " "	Eccl 9:4–10	Mt 21:28–44	Jer 2:1–9, 13	Rom 11:25–32
1 " "	Ex 33:1, 12–23	Jn 4:31–42	Gen 15:1–6	Rev 3:7–13
2 " "	Num 20:14–21	Mt 18:1–20	1 K 8:46–53	Eph 4:30–32
3 " "	Jer 29:1, 4–14	Mk 12:41–44	2 K 23:1–4, 11–14, 21–23	Rom 13:1–7
4 " "	Jos 23:1–3, 11–16	Jn 5:17–29	2 K 4:18–37	2 Cor 5:1–10
5 " "	Dan 12:1–4	Lk 17:20–33	Dan 9:24–27	2 Pet 3:3–15
6 " "	Jer 3:14–18	Mt 11:25–30	Eccl 11:9–12:7	Heb 4:9–13
ast " "	Is 2:6–19	Mt 5:13–16	Gen 19:1–3, 10–17, 24–28	Rev 21:1–7
Andrew	Is 55:1–5	Jn 1:29–42	Zech 8:20–23	1 Cor 4:1–16
Thomas	Job 42:1–6	Jn 11:1–16	Is 43:8–13	Jn 14:1–14
Stephen	2 Chr 24:17–22	Acts 6:1–15	Jer 26:8–15	Acts 7:59–8:8
John	Ex 33:12–19	Jn 13:20–35	Jer 1:7–10	Rev 4:1–11
Ioly Innocents	Jer 31:15–17	Mt 2:19–23	Ez 18:1–4	Rom 1:1–7
Conv S Paul	Is 45:15–19	Acts 26:1–23	Jer 4:1–10	2 Tim 3:10–4:8
resentation	1 Sam 1:21–28	1 Jn 3:1–8	Hag 2:1–9	Gal 3:15–4:7
Matthias	1 Sam 2:27–35	Lk 12:22–40	1 Sam 12:1–5	1 Jn 2:15–17
nnunciation	Is 52:7–10	Jn 1:1–18	1 Sam 2:1–10	Lk 1:39–56
Mark	Is 62:6–12	Acts 12:24–13:13	Zech 4:6–9	1 Pet 5:1–14
s Philip & Jas	Job 23:3–12	Jn 6:1–14	Is 30:18–21	Acts 15:1–31
John Baptist	Mal 3:1–6	Mt 3:1–17	Mal 4:1–6	Mk 6:14–29
s Peter & Paul	Ez 2:1–7	Jn 21:1–22	Ez 34:11–16	1 Pet 4:12–5:11
isitation	1 Sam 9:11–21	Lk 1:39–56	Jer 33:14–16	Jn 1:1–18
James	Jer 45:1–5	Mk 1:14–22	Jer 26:8–15	Lk 9:46–48
ransfiguration	Is 61:10, 11	Mk 9:2–13	Ex 24:12–18	Rev 1:1–20
Bartholomew	Gen 28:10–12, 16–17	Lk 6:12–23	Is 66:1–2, 18–23	1 Pet 1:22–2:10
Matthew	1 K 19:15–16, 19–21	Lk 5:27–32	Job 28:12–23	Rom 10:1–15
Michael	Job 38:1–7	Acts 12:1–17	2 K 6:8–17	Heb 1:13–2:10
Luke	Is 52:7–10	Lk 1:1–4	Is 45:20–25	Acts 15:36–16:15
s Simon & Jude	Is 28:9–16	Mk 6:1–13	Deut 32:1–4	Eph 2:1–22
Reformation Day	2 K 23:1–25	Jn 2:13–17	1 K 19:13–18	Gal 2:16–21
All Saints'	2 K 6:14–17	Heb 11:32–12:2	Dan 12:1–3	Rev 19:1–16
Iarvest	Gen 8:20–22	Lk 12:13–21	Deut 16:9–17	Jas 1:17–18
Iumiliation	Dan 9:3–19	Mt 3:1–12	Joel 2:12–17	Heb 10:19–25
hanksgiving	Deut 26:1–11	Lk 17:11–19	Neh 8:9–12	Gal 6:7–10

IX. TABLE OF PSALMS

For the Sundays and Festivals of the Church Year

DAY	MATINS	VESPERS
1 S. in Advent	25, 85	6, 8, 19
2 " "	50, 80, 122	21, 24, 25
3 " "	80, 85	42, 93, 96
4 " "	19, 145	98, 110, 111
CHRISTMAS	2, 98, 110	19, 132
1 S. after Christmas	45, 93	147, 148
Circumcision	98	8, 40, 65, 90
2 S. after Christmas	98, 110	45, 93, 110
EPIPHANY	72	47, 48, 66
1 S. after Epiphany	72, 100	67, 84, 86
2 S. " "	66, 148	87, 96, 97
3 S. " "	97, 102	100, 135
4 S. " "	24	19, 72, 93
5 S. " "	65	46, 48, 104
6 S. " "	19	19, 67, 150
Septuagesima	18, 99, 130	27, 31, 116
Sexagesima	44, 60	18, 67, 119, 143
Quinquagesima	31, 77, 100	116, 145
Ash Wednesday	57, 103	32, 51, 130
1 in Lent	91	25, 34, 38
2 " "	25, 136	43, 86, 90
3 " "	9, 25	91, 121, 122
4 " "	122, 125	130, 139, 143
5 " "	18, 43, 143	6, 32, 38
Palm Sunday	22, 73	24, 61, 97, 110
Monday	42	27, 32
Tuesday	67	43, 51, 57
Wednesday	69, 102	63, 67, 71
Thursday	67, 118	116, 142
Friday	102	22, 40, 51, 139
Saturday		91, 4, 16, 31
EASTER DAY	8, 118, 136	23, 30, 33
1 S. after Easter	81	66, 98, 100
2 S. " "	33	23, 111, 118, 124
3 S. " "	66, 111	33, 65, 66
4 S. " "	98, 118	100, 111, 124
5 S. " "	100	146, 148, 150
Ascension Day	47, 68	8, 21, 24, 47, 97
S. after Ascension	27, 47	110, 111, 150
PENTECOST	68, 104	19, 48, 113, 145
Trinity Sunday	8	29, 33, 93, 96, 148, 150
1 S. after Trinity	13	1, 2, 3
2 S. " "	18	4, 6
3 S. " "	18, 25	8, 9, 11
4 S. " "	21, 27, 29	13, 14, 15
5 S. " "	27, 31, 84	16, 17

IX. TABLE OF PSALMS

For the Sundays and Festivals of the Church Year

DAY	MATINS	VESPERS
6 S. after Trinity	28, 47, 90	18
7 S. " "	34, 47	19, 20, 21
8 S. " "	1, 31, 48	23, 24, 25
9 S. " "	8, 54	26, 27, 28
10 S. " "	17	29, 30
11 S. " "	28, 65, 68	31
12 S. " "	34, 81	32, 33
13 S. " "	74	34
14 S. " "	84, 90, 118	36
15 S. " "	92	38, 40
16 S. " "	86, 98, 102	42, 43, 44
17 S. " "	33, 116, 119	45
18 S. " "	117, 122	46, 47, 48
19 S. " "	118	50
20 S. " "	48, 145	56, 57
21 S. " "	90, 119, 125	61, 62, 63
22 S. " "	130, 133, 146	65, 66
23 S. " "	44, 85, 115	67, 68
24 S. " "	1, 91	69
25 S. " "	31, 91	73
26 S. " "	24, 54	77
27 S. " "	24	84, 85, 86
Apostles', Evangelists', Martyrs' Days	1, 15, 19, 34	112, 121, 139, 146, 148
S. Stephen	119	27, 89
Presentation	48	92
Annunciation	45	96
S. John Baptist	92	99
Visitation	45	89
Transfiguration	45, 84, 96, 110	8, 27, 47, 61, 93
S. Michael	34, 91	103, 148
Reformation	46, 48, 87	116, 125
All Saints'	33, 48	103, 148, 150
Harvest	65, 67	104, 118
Humiliation and Prayer	6, 20, 51, 56	80, 90, 130, 143
Thanksgiving	65, 67, 92, 100, 103	145, 147, 148, 150
National	46, 47, 48, 65, 66, 67, 68	100, 124, 144, 145, 146, 148
Missions	2, 24, 47, 67, 72, 96, 97	115, 126
Education	1, 25, 91, 119	143
Death, Burial	23, 27, 42, 90, 91	116, 121, 126, 130, 139, 146
Christian Comfort	13, 23, 25, 27, 30, 34	40, 62, 91, 121, 130, 139, 143

The Penitential Psalms are: 6, 32, 38, 51, 102, 130, 143.

PSALM PARAPHRASES

ACKNOWLEDGMENTS

THANKS are due to the following authors, copyright owners, and publishers for permission to use their prayers; to the Oxford University Press for the use of the following prayers from the *Book of Common Order of the Church of Scotland* (1940): Collects and Prayers, Nos. 11, 24, 39, 40, 43, 73, 76, 82, also several collects on pp. 240 and 241, two prayers used in the Order for the Burial of the Dead, and the Proper Preface for All Saints' Day; to the Oxford University Press and Eric Milner-White for several prayers from *Daily Prayer;* to the Oxford University Press for selections from *Prayers for the Christian Year* (1952); to the Methodist Publishing House for the use of prayers from *The Book of Worship for Church and Home;* to the United Church Publishing House for several prayers from *The Book of Common Order of the United Church of Canada* (1932); to the British Broadcasting Corporation for several prayers from *Each Returning Day* and *New Every Morning;* to Longmans, Green and Company for a prayer from *A Cambridge Bede Book.*

If the Commissions have unwittingly transgressed any copyright, they make sincere apologies and will acknowledge any such oversight in future printings.

The Hymnal

Introduction to the Common Hymnal

THE birth of Jesus was announced in song, and the last act of worship of our Lord and his Disciples was the singing of a hymn. Sacred song, rooted in the Hebrew tradition, occupied from the first a preeminent position in Christian worship. The earliest hymns were psalms and canticles. Initially the people sang them, though by the fourth century in the East, and by the seventh in the West, they had become part of the liturgy and a matter for the clergy and the choirs. Not again until the time of the Reformation was the hymn restored to the people as their rightful heritage in worship.

In 1524, Luther published the *Achtliederbuch* which led the way for an outburst of evangelical hymnody in the countries of Northern and Central Europe. Next there came a new type of music, the chorale, based sometimes on plainsong, sometimes on secular melodies. The hymn was incorporated into the services of the Church and once more was congregational. In sharp contrast, the Reformed churches employed only the Psalter, often crudely paraphrased, and it was not until the eighteenth century that the hymn made its way in the English-speaking world.

When Lutherans came to the New World, they brought with them the hymnals of their homelands, but as their descendants grew up in an English-speaking environment, English Lutheran hymnals began to appear. Attempts were made to translate hymns of the Lutheran heritage and to incorporate the finest English hymns. Each Lutheran body used its own hymnal, but there was a growing feeling that there was a body of common hymnody sufficient to permit the preparation of a common hymnal. In 1944, the United Lutheran Church directed its Common Service Book Committee (which had been engaged for four years in studies envisaging the revision of its own hymnal) "to seek the fullest possible cooperation with other Lutheran bodies, in the hope of producing a Common Lutheran Hymnal in America." Upon the subsequent invitation, representatives of the American Lutheran Church, the Augustana Lutheran Church, the Evangelical Lutheran Church, and the United Lutheran Church, met in Pittsburgh, Pa., June, 1945, to inaugurate this work.

The Commission on a Common Hymnal followed these basic principles:

the Common Hymnal must be a new work, not simply a conflation of the existing hymnals; it must contain only good hymns providing, as a companion to the liturgy, for the full round of the Christian Year and the Christian Life; the hymns should be devotional rather than didactic or homiletical, and their direction Godward, not manward; the hymnal must be ecumenical in character, expressing the continuity and catholicity of the life of the Church; the final criterion is not Lutheran authorship, but agreement with the teachings of the Word of God; the hymnal must have the highest standards of literary excellence, and each hymn, being an act of worship, should be exalted in language, noble in thought and reverent in feeling.

One of the most difficult problems was the application of this final principle, especially to hymns of our own heritage where pressure was great for their inclusion. Inferior translations have been accepted in the past because of the affection felt for the original, or because of a majestic chorale tune with which the original text was associated. What is often forgotten, or perhaps charitably overlooked, is the fact that a translation seldom succeeds in recreating either the poetic beauty or depth of message of the original. The Commission has found it necessary to edit and, in some cases, retranslate, some of these hymns. It hopes that it has thus enriched the hymnal by many hymns from sources largely unknown in the New World, and that some of these may eventually become part of the ecumenical treasury of Christian hymnody.

In addition to hymns of Lutheran provenance, and the best of the ancient Greek and Latin hymns, nearly two-thirds of the hymns are of English and American authorship. Many of them have been in our hymnals for years, and the nearly eighty of American authorship will correct a weakness common to our hymnals. A few original hymns appear here for the first time. In general, the Commission has respected the original texts of the authors, though in some cases, generally-accepted alterations have been adopted. Where this has been done, *a.* (altered) follows the author's name.

As far as possible, hymns have been placed where they will be of the greatest general use, and only a minimum appear under the more restrictive rubrics of the Church Year. Extensive cross-references at the end of each section of the hymnal and indexes at the end of the book, afford an increased selection of hymns for particular occasions.

The music, like the texts, is ecumenical. The characteristic Lutheran form, the chorale, is well-represented in rhythmic, isometric and Bach arrangements. An increased number of plainsong melodies on the one hand, and some Gospel hymns on the other, will provide for a wide variety of taste among our people. About two hundred fifty hymns have tunes of English origin, including both the standard tunes of the nineteenth century and some by contemporary composers. Psalm tunes from English, Scottish, Swiss and French sources appear as well as eight Welsh tunes and a number of French tunes based on plainsong. Carols and more than thirty folksongs, largely from North European sources, add much new and interesting music. American composers are well represented, some by tunes which appear here for the first time.

The Commission has tried not to disturb the association of certain hymns with certain tunes, except in instances where the traditional tune has become worn by usage. In such cases a second tune has been provided in the hope of lending new freshness to the text, and often, where a new tune appears, a cross-reference indicates where the older tune may be located. The pitch of many of the hymns has been lowered to encourage congregational singing by men as well as women. Solid notes have usually been employed in notation, except in the case of psalm tunes, some chorales and modern compositions of grave character. Eighth notes have been used in plainsong. For every hymn, a direction indicates the mood and tempo of the tune, and organists and choirmasters should note these suggestions carefully. *Amen* has not been provided for hymns which are didactic, hortatory, narrative or contemplative, but it appears, properly, at the conclusion of hymns which end in prayer or praise. Double bars are employed at the end of musical rather than textual phrases.

The Commission expresses its appreciation to all who have granted permission for the use of copyrighted material, and hopes that all such material has been properly credited. It also records, with a deep sense of sorrow and loss, the death of five of its members since the inception of its work: the Rev. Paul Zeller Strodach, D.D., of the United Lutheran Church; the Rev. C. A. Wendell, D.D., Litt.D., and the Rev. Carl J. Sodergren, D.D., both of the Augustana Lutheran Church; and the Rev. Albert Jagnow, Ph.D., and the Rev. Leonard O. Burry, both of the American Lutheran Church. All of them made important contributions and it is to be regretted that they did not live to see the completion of this work.

Since 1945, four additional bodies of Lutherans have become associated in this project: the Lutheran Free Church, The United Evangelical Lutheran Church, the Finnish Evangelical Lutheran Church, and the American Evangelical Lutheran Church. This assures the use of the Common Hymnal by more than two-thirds of the Lutherans in the United States and Canada. After the appearance of the Common Liturgy and Hymnal, a permanent Commission on the Liturgy and Hymnal, will come into being and will have full jurisdiction over this book, other and subsequent editions and companion volumes.

The Lutheran Churches in America are in process of becoming the Lutheran Church in America. We share the rich endowments of a common faith, a common history, a common heritage of liturgy and hymnody, and the recognition of a common mission and destiny in the New World. This book will contribute to the unity of our Church and to the advent of the day when Henry Melchior Muhlenberg's vision of "one Church and one book" will become a reality. May God accept the worship this volume brings. To his glory we dedicate the *Service Book and Hymnal* with the prayer that he may bless it and use it as an instrument of his grace and power for the advancement of his kingdom.

Contents

The Church Year

1 **ADVENT**

MERTON. 8 7, 8 7. WILLIAM HENRY MONK, 1823–89

In moderate time

1. Hark! a thrill - ing voice is sound - ing; 'Christ is
2. Wak - ened by the sol - emn warn - ing, Let the
nigh,' it seems to say, 'Cast a - way the
earth - bound soul a - rise; Christ, her sun, all
works of dark-ness, O ye chil - dren of the day.'
ill dis - pel - ling, Shines up - on the morn - ing skies. A - men.

3 Lo, the Lamb, so long expected,
Comes with pardon down from heaven;
Let us haste, with tears of sorrow,
One and all to be forgiven;

4 So when next he comes in glory,
And the world is wrapped in fear,
With his mercy may he shield us,
And with words of love draw near.

5 Honor, glory, might, and blessing
Be to God: the Father, Son,
And the everlasting Spirit,
While eternal ages run. Amen.

Latin hymn, V cent.
Tr. Edward Caswall, 1814–78 a.

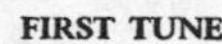

FIRST TUNE

VENI, EMMANUEL. 8 8, 8 8, 8 8. Plainsong Melody, Mode I
Arr. by ERNEST WHITE, 1899-

In unison

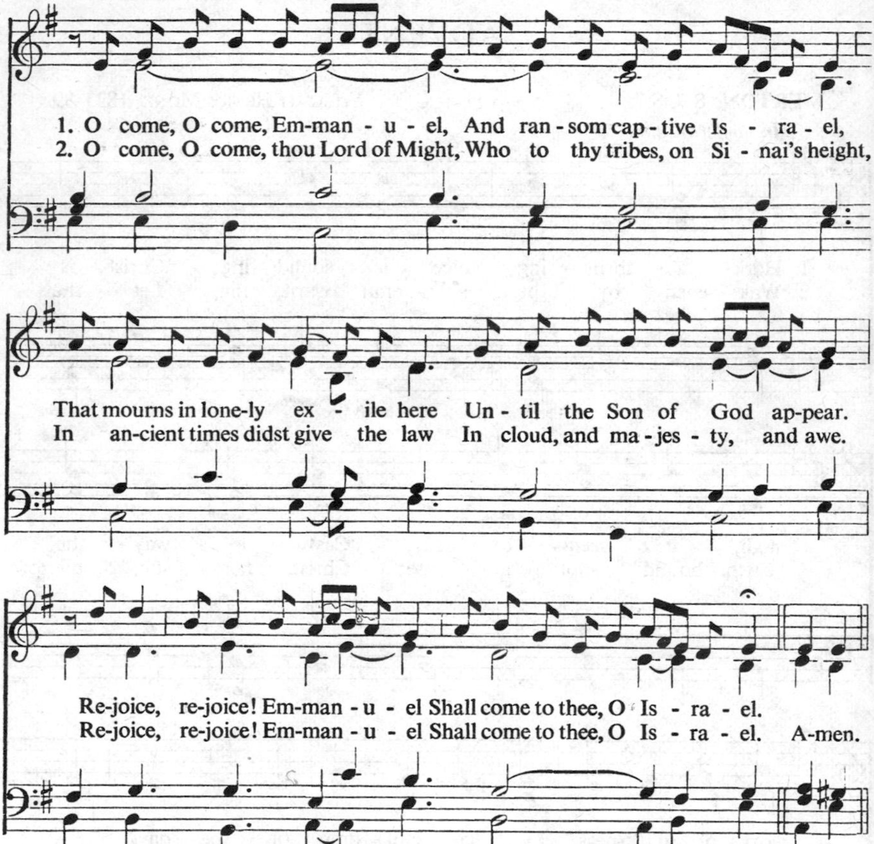

1. O come, O come, Em-man - u - el, And ran - som cap - tive Is - ra - el,
2. O come, O come, thou Lord of Might, Who to thy tribes, on Si - nai's height,

That mourns in lone-ly ex - ile here Un - til the Son of God ap-pear.
In an-cient times didst give the law In cloud, and ma - jes - ty, and awe.

Re-joice, re-joice! Em-man - u - el Shall come to thee, O Is - ra - el.
Re-joice, re-joice! Em-man - u - el Shall come to thee, O Is - ra - el. A-men.

3 O come, thou Rod of Jesse, free
Thine own from Satan's tyranny;
From depths of hell thy people save,
And give them victory o'er the grave.
Rejoice, rejoice! Emmanuel
Shall come to thee, O Israel.

4 O come, thou Dayspring, come and cheer
Our spirits by thine advent here;
Disperse the gloomy clouds of night,
And death's dark shadows put to flight.
Rejoice, rejoice! Emmanuel
Shall come to thee, O Israel.

5 O come, thou Key of David, come,
And open wide our heavenly home;
Make safe the way that leads on high,
And close the path to misery.
Rejoice, rejoice! Emmanuel
Shall come to thee, O Israel. Amen.

Medieval Antiphons
Latin Hymn, 1710
Tr. John Mason Neale, 1818–66

2

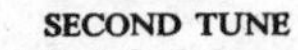

SECOND TUNE

VENI, VENI, EMMANUEL. 8 8, 8 8, 8 8. **Plainsong Melody, Mode I**

Unison, in free rhythm

1. O come, O come, Em - man - u - el, And ran-som cap-tive Is - ra - el,
2. O come, O come, thou Lord of Might, Who to thy tribes, on Si - nai's height,

That mourns in lone - ly ex - ile here Un - til the Son of God ap - pear.
In an-cient times didst give the law In cloud, and ma - jes - ty, and awe.

Harmony

Re-joice, re-joice! Em-man - u - el Shall come to thee, O Is - ra - el.
Re-joice, re-joice! Em-man - u - el Shall come to thee, O Is - ra - el. A-men.

3 O come, thou Rod of Jesse, free
Thine own from Satan's tyranny;
From depths of hell thy people save
And give them victory o'er the grave.
Rejoice, rejoice! Emmanuel
Shall come to thee, O Israel.

4 O come, thou Dayspring, come and cheer
Our spirits by thine advent here;
Disperse the gloomy clouds of night,
And death's dark shadows put to flight.
Rejoice, rejoice! Emmanuel
Shall come to thee, O Israel.

5 O come, thou Key of David, come,
And open wide our heavenly home;
Make safe the way that leads on high,
And close the path to misery.
Rejoice, rejoice! Emmanuel
Shall come to thee, O Israel. Amen.

Medieval Antiphons
Latin Hymn, 1710
Tr. John Mason Neale, 1818–66

DONCASTER. S. M. SAMUEL WESLEY, 1766–1837

With dignity

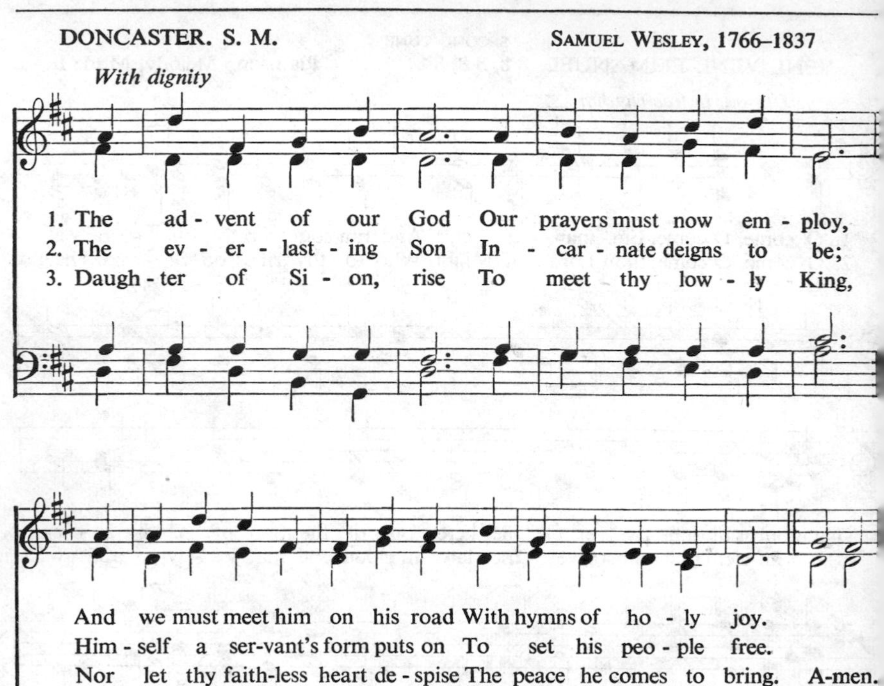
1. The ad - vent of our God Our prayers must now em - ploy,
2. The ev - er - last - ing Son In - car - nate deigns to be;
3. Daugh - ter of Si - on, rise To meet thy low - ly King,
And we must meet him on his road With hymns of ho - ly joy.
Him - self a ser-vant's form puts on To set his peo - ple free.
Nor let thy faith-less heart de - spise The peace he comes to bring. A-men.

4 As Judge, on clouds of light,
He soon will come again,
And all his scattered saints unite
With him in heaven to reign.

5 Before the dawning day
Let sin's dark deeds be gone;
The old man all be put away,
The new man all put on.

6 All glory to the Son,
Who comes to set us free,
With Father, Spirit, ever One,
Through all eternity. Amen.

Charles Coffin, 1676–174
Tr. John Chandler, 1806–7

Advent

ALSTONE. L. M. CHRISTOPHER EDWIN WILLING, 1830–1904

In moderate time

1. On Jor-dan's banks the Bap-tist's cry An-nounc-es that the Lord is nigh;
2. Then cleansed be ev-ery breast from sin, Make straight the way for God with-in;

A-wake and heark-en, for he brings Glad ti-dings of the King of kings.
And let us all our hearts pre-pare For Christ to come and en-ter there. A-men.

3 For thou art our salvation, Lord,
Our refuge and our great reward;
Without thy grace we waste away
Like flowers that wither and decay.

4 Stretch forth thy hand, to health restore,
And make us rise to fall no more;
Once more upon thy people shine,
And fill the world with love divine.

5 All praise, eternal Son, to thee
Whose advent sets thy people free,
Whom with the Father we adore,
And Holy Ghost, for evermore. Amen.

Charles Coffin, 1676–1749
Tr. John Chandler, 1806–76 a.

5

ST. HILARY. 8 7, 8 7. D.
Origin uncertain
With dignity
1. Come, thou long - ex - pect - ed Je - sus, Born to set thy
2. Born thy peo - ple to de - liv - er, Born a child, and
peo - ple free; From our fears and sins re - lease us, Let us
yet a king; Born to reign in us for - ev - er, Now thy
find our rest in thee. Is - rael's strength and con - so - la - tion,
gra - cious king - dom bring. By thine own e - ter - nal Spir - it
Hope of all the earth thou art; Dear de - sire of ev - ery
Rule in all our hearts a - lone; By thine all - suf - fi - cient

na - tion, Joy of ev - ery long - ing heart.
mer - it Raise us to thy glo - rious throne. A - men.

Charles Wesley, 1707–88

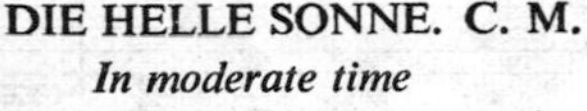

DIE HELLE SONNE. C. M. SIGMUND GOTTLIEB STADEN, 1605–55

In moderate time

1. Hark, the glad sound! the Sav - iour comes, The Sav - iour prom-ised long;
2. He comes, the pris-oners to re - lease In Sa - tan's bond-age held;

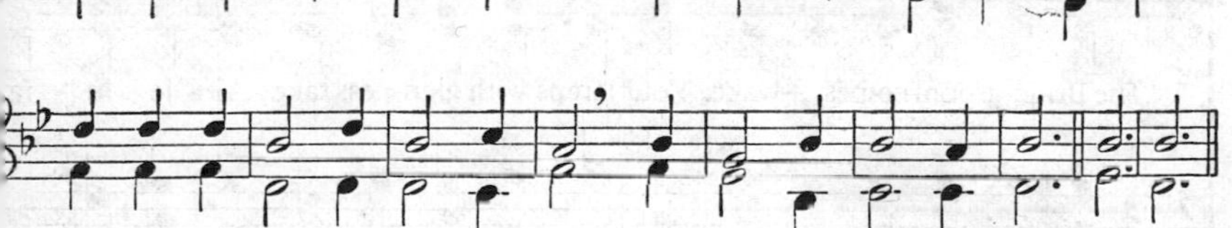

Let ev - ery heart pre-pare a throne, And ev - ery voice a song.
The gates of brass be-fore him burst, The i - ron fet - ters yield. A-men.

3 He comes, the broken heart to bind,
The bleeding soul to cure,
And with the treasures of his grace
To enrich the humble poor

4 Our glad hosannas, Prince of Peace,
Thy welcome shall proclaim;
And heaven's eternal arches ring
With thy belovèd Name. Amen.

Philip Doddridge, 1702–51

FIRST TUNE
WACHET AUF. Irregular.
PHILIPP NICOLAI, 1556–1608
Jubilantly
1. Wake, a - wake, for night is fly - ing, The watch-men on the heights are cry - ing, A - wake, Je - ru - sa - lem, at last!
Mid - night hears the wel-come voic - es And at the thril-ing cry re - joic - es: Come forth, ye vir - gins, night is past!
The Bride-groom comes, a-wake, Your lamps with glad-ness take; Al - le - lu - ia
And for his mar - riage feast pre-pare, For ye must go to meet him there. A-men

2 Zion hears the watchmen singing,
And all her heart with joy is springing,
She wakes, she rises from her gloom;
For her Lord comes down all-glorious,
The strong in grace, in truth victorious,
Her Star is risen, her Light is come.
Ah come, thou blessèd One,
God's own belovèd Son,
Alleluia!
We follow till the halls we see
Where thou hast bid us sup with thee.

Now let all the heavens adore thee,
And men and angels sing before thee,
With harp and cymbal's clearest tone;
Of one pearl each shining portal,
Where we are with the choir immortal
Of angels round thy dazzling throne;
Nor eye hath seen, nor ear
Hath yet attained to hear
What there is ours;
But we rejoice, and sing to thee
Our hymn of joy eternally. Amen.

Philipp Nicolai, 1556–1608
Tr. Catherine Winkworth, 1829–78

SECOND TUNE

WACHET AUF. Irregular.

PHILIPP NICOLAI, 1556–1608
Adapted and harm. by J. S. BACH, 1685–1750

Jubilantly

1. Wake, a - wake, for night is fly - ing, The watch-men on the
Mid - night hears the wel-come voic - es And at the thrill-ing
Wake, a-wake, for
heights are cry - ing, A - wake, Je - ru - sa - lem, at last!
cry re - joic - es: Come forth, ye vir - gins, night is past!
The Bride-groom comes, a - wake, Your lamps with glad-ness take; Al - le - lu - ia!
And for his mar - riage feast pre-pare, For ye must go to meet him there. A-men.

For stanzas 2 and 3, see above.

For another version of this tune, see the hymn, Glorious Majesty (No. 189).

FIRST VERSION

TRURO. L. M. — THOMAS WILLIAMS

With spirit — *Psalmodia Evangelica*, 1789

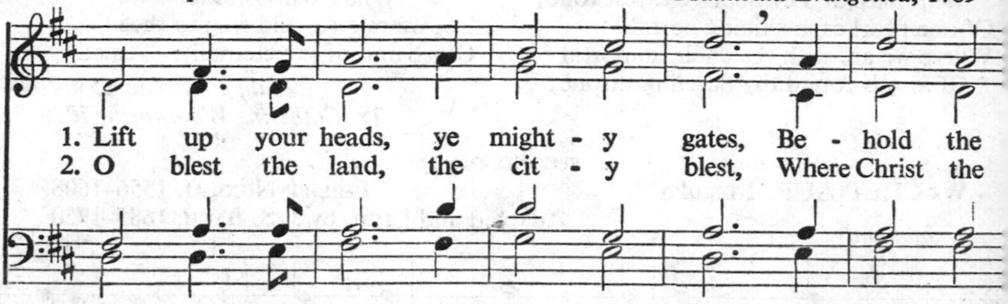

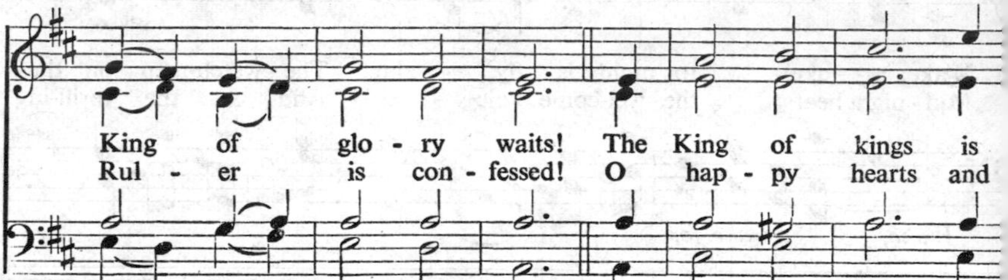

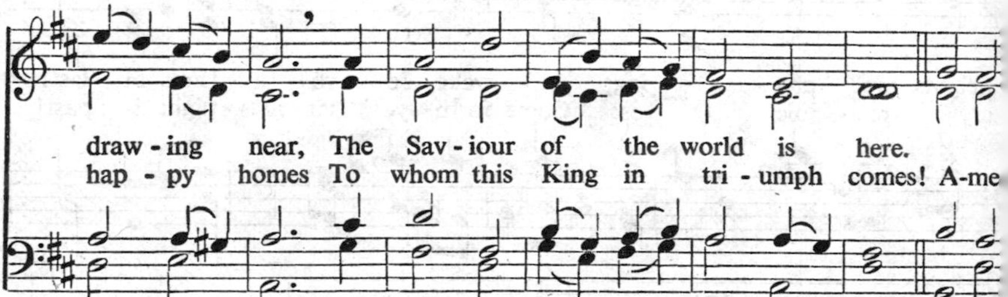

1. Lift up your heads, ye might - y gates, Be - hold the King of glo - ry waits! The King of kings is draw - ing near, The Sav - iour of the world is here.
2. O blest the land, the cit - y blest, Where Christ the Rul - er is con - fessed! O hap - py hearts and hap - py homes To whom this King in tri - umph comes! A-men

3 Fling wide the portals of your heart,
Make it a temple set apart
From earthly use for heaven's employ,
Adorned with prayer and love and joy.

4 Redeemer, come! with us abide;
Our hearts to thee we open wide,
Let us thy inner presence feel,
Thy grace and love in us reveal. Amen

Georg Weissel, 1590–16
Tr. Catherine Winkworth, 1829–

8

SECOND VERSION

MACHT HOCH DIE TÜR. 8 8, 8 8, 8 8, 6 6. — FREYLINGHAUSEN'S

Joyfully — *Gesangbuch*, 1704

1. Lift up your heads, ye might - y gates; Be - hold the King of
2. The Lord is just, a help - er tried, With mer - cy ev - er

Advent

Glo - ry waits! The King of kings is draw - ing near;
at his side; His king - ly crown is ho - li - ness,
The Sav - iour of the world is here; Life and sal - va - tion
His scep - tre, pit - y in dis - tress, The end of all our
he doth bring, Where - fore re - joice and glad - ly sing:
woe he brings; Where - fore the earth is glad and sings:
We praise thee, Fa - ther, now, Cre - a - tor, wise art thou.
We praise thee, Sav - iour, now, Might-y in deed art thou. A-men.

3 O blest the land, the city blest,
Where Christ the Ruler is confest!
O happy hearts and happy homes
To whom this King of triumph comes!
The cloudless Sun of joy he is,
Who bringeth pure delight and bliss:
O Comforter divine,
What boundless grace is thine.

4 Redeemer, come! I open wide
My heart to thee: here, Lord, abide!
Let me thy inner presence feel,
Thy grace and love in me reveal.
Thy Holy Spirit guide us on,
Until our glorious goal is won:
Eternal praise and fame
We offer to thy Name. Amen.

Georg Weissel, 1590–1635
Tr. Catherine Winkworth, 1829–78 a.

MESSIAH. 7 6, 7 6, 7 7, 6 6.
Swedish Melody, XVII cent.
In stately manner
1. Pre-pare the way, O Zi-on! Ye aw-ful deeps, rise high;
Sink low, ye loft-y moun-tains, The Lord is draw-ing nigh;
2. O Zi-on, he ap-proach-es, Your Lord and King for aye;
Strew palms where he ad-vanc-es, Spread gar-ments in his way;
The right-eous King of glo-ry, Fore-told in sa-cred sto-ry.
God's prom-ise fail-eth nev-er, Ho-san-na sound for-ev-er.
Refrain
O blest is he that came In God the Fa-ther's Name!

3 Fling wide your portals, Zion,
And hail your glorious King;
His tidings of salvation
To every people bring,
Who, waiting still in sadness,
Would sing his praise with gladness.

The throne which he ascended
Is fixed in heaven above;
His everlasting kingdom
Is light and joy and love;
Let us his praise be sounding
For grace and peace abounding.

Frans Mikael Franzén, 1772–184
Tr. Augustus Nelson, 1863–194

FARRANT. C. M. RICHARD FARRANT, *cir.* 1530–80

In moderate time

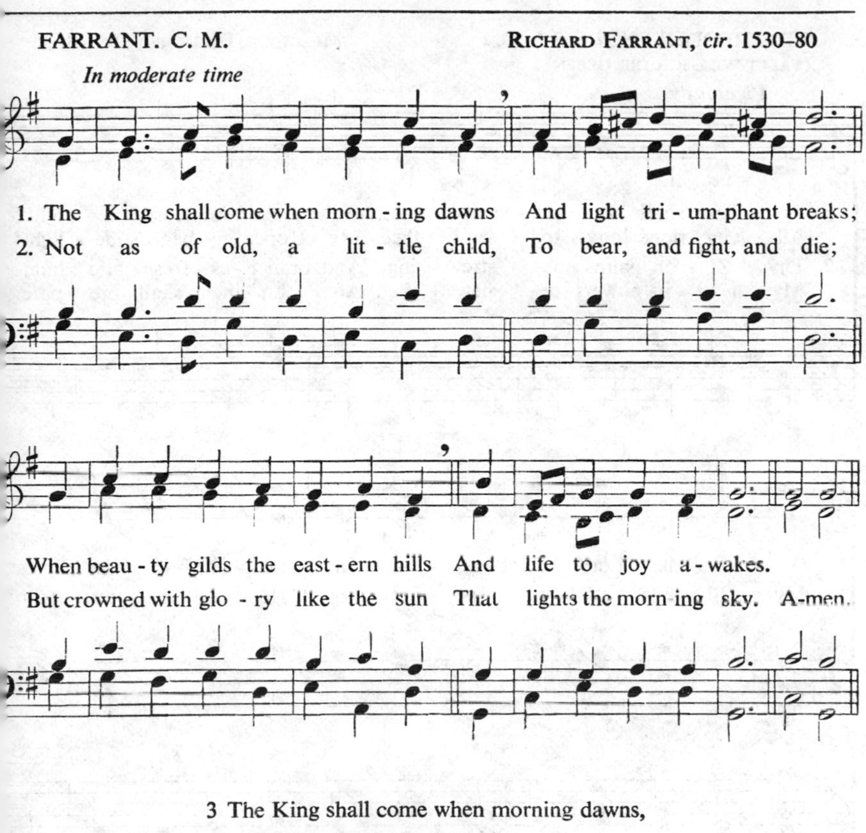
1. The King shall come when morn - ing dawns And light tri - um-phant breaks;
2. Not as of old, a lit - tle child, To bear, and fight, and die;
When beau - ty gilds the east - ern hills And life to joy a - wakes.
But crowned with glo - ry like the sun That lights the morn-ing sky. A-men.

3 The King shall come when morning dawns,
And earth's dark night is past;
O haste the rising of that morn,
The day that aye shall last;

4 And let the endless bliss begin,
By weary saints foretold,
When right shall triumph over wrong,
And truth shall be extolled.

5 The King shall come when morning dawns,
And light and beauty brings:
Hail, Christ the Lord! Thy people pray,
Come quickly, King of kings. Amen.

John Brownlie, 1859–1925
Based on the Greek

From HYMNS OF THE RUSSIAN CHURCH *by permission of the Oxford University Press*

ST. THEODULPH. 7 6, 7 6. D. (VALET WILL ICH DIR GEBEN)

MELCHIOR TESCHNER, 1584–1635

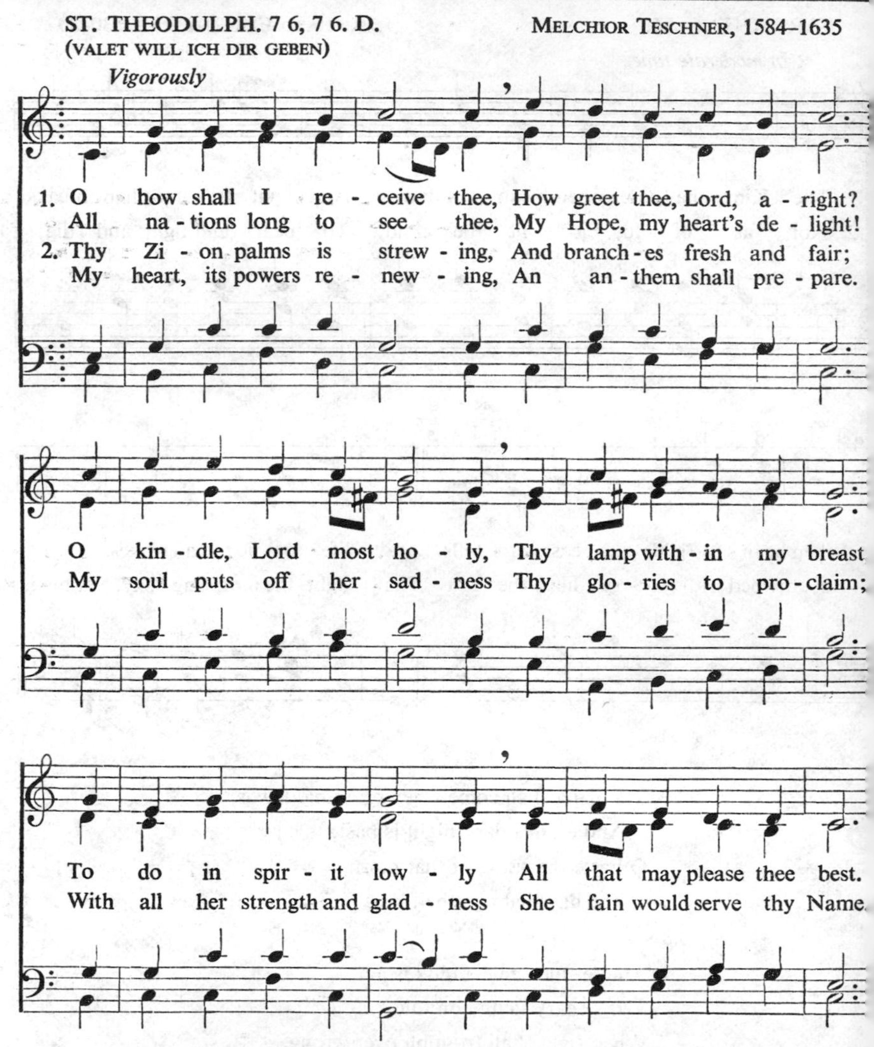
Vigorously
1. O how shall I re - ceive thee, How greet thee, Lord, a - right?
All na - tions long to see thee, My Hope, my heart's de - light!
2. Thy Zi - on palms is strew - ing, And branch - es fresh and fair;
My heart, its powers re - new - ing, An an - them shall pre - pare.
O kin - dle, Lord most ho - ly, Thy lamp with - in my breast
My soul puts off her sad - ness Thy glo - ries to pro - claim;
To do in spir - it low - ly All that may please thee best.
With all her strength and glad - ness She fain would serve thy Name.

3 Love caused thine incarnation,
Love brought thee down to me;
Thy thirst for my salvation
Procured my liberty.
O love beyond all telling
That led thee to embrace,
In love all love excelling,
Our lost and fallen race.

4 Rejoice then, ye sad-hearted,
Who sit in deepest gloom,
Who mourn o'er joys departed
And tremble at your doom,
He who alone can cheer you
Is standing at the door;
He brings his pity near you,
And bids you weep no more.

Paul Gerhardt, 1607–
Tr. Compos

PSALM 42 (**FREU DICH SEHR**). **8 7, 8 7, 7 7, 8 8.** *Genevan Psalter*, **1551**

Brightly
1. Com-fort, com-fort ye, my peo - ple, Speak ye peace, thus saith our God;
Com-fort those who sit in dark - ness, Bowed be-neath their sor - row's load;
Of the peace that waits for them Speak ye to Je - ru - sa - lem;
Tell her that her sins I cov - er, And her war - fare now is o - ver.

2 For the herald's voice is crying
In the desert far and near,
Bidding all men to repentance,
Since the kingdom now is here.
O, that warning cry obey!
Now prepare for God a way;
Let the valleys rise to meet him,
And the hills bow down to greet him.

3 Make ye straight what long was crooked,
Make the rougher places plain;
Let your hearts be true and humble,
As befits his holy reign;
For the glory of the Lord
Now o'er earth is shed abroad,
And all flesh shall see the token
That his word is never broken.

Johannes Olearius, 1611–84
Tr. Catherine Winkworth, 1829–78 a.

13

STÖRL. 8 7, 8 7, 4 7. JOHANN G. C. STÖRL, 1675–1719

Majestically

1. Lo! he comes with clouds de - scend-ing, Once for fa - vored sin - ners slain;
2. Ev - ery eye shall now be - hold him Robed in glo - rious maj - es - ty;
Thou-sand thou-sand saints at - tend - ing Swell the tri - umph of his train:
Those who set at nought and sold him, Pierced and nailed him to the Tree,
Al - le - lu - ia! God ap - pears, on earth to reign.
Deep - ly wail - ing, Shall their true Mes - si - ah see. A - men.

3 Those dear tokens of his passion
Still his dazzling body bears;
Cause of wondering exultation
To his ransomed worshippers;
With what rapture
Praise we him for all his scars.

4 Yea, amen, let all adore thee,
High on thine eternal throne;
Saviour, take the power and glory,
Claim the kingdom for thine own:
Alleluia!
Thou shalt reign, and thou alone! Amen.

Charles Wesley, 1707–88

This hymn may also be sung to ST. THOMAS (HOLYWOOD) (No. 61).

14 Advent

VIGIL. 7 6, 7 6. D.
Swedish Folk Melody
Brightly
1. Re - joice, all ye be - liev - ers, And let your lights ap - pear;
2. The watch - ers on the moun - tain Pro - claim the Bride-groom near;
The eve - ning is ad - vanc - ing And dark - er night is near;
Go meet him as he com - eth With hal - le - lu - jahs clear;
The Bride-groom is a - ris - ing, And soon he draw - eth nigh;
The mar - riage-feast is wait - ing, The gates wide o - pen stand;
Up, pray, and watch, and wres - tle, At mid-night comes the cry!
Up, up, ye heirs of glo - ry, The Bride-groom is at hand! A - men.

3 Ye saints, who here in patience
Your cross and sufferings bore,
Shall live and reign for ever
When sorrow is no more.
Around the throne of glory
The Lamb ye shall behold,
In triumph cast before him
Your diadems of gold!

4 Our hope and expectation,
O Jesus, now appear;
Arise, thou Sun so longed for,
O'er this benighted sphere!
With hearts and hands uplifted,
We plead, O Lord, to see
The day of earth's redemption
That brings us unto thee! Amen.

Laurentius Laurenti, 1660–1722
Tr. Sarah Borthwick Findlater, 1823–1907

This hymn may also be sung to LANCASHIRE (No. 550).

ANTIOCH, C. M. Melody arr. by LOWELL MASON, 1792–1872

In moderate time

1. Joy to the world! the Lord is come; Let earth re - ceive her King;
2. Joy to the world! the Sav - iour reigns; Let men their songs em - ploy,
Let ev - ery heart pre - pare him room, And heaven and na - ture
While fields and floods, rocks, hills and plains Re - peat the sound-ing
And
sing, And heaven and nature sing, And heaven, and heaven and na - ture sing.
joy, Re-peat the sound-ing joy, Re - peat, re - peat the sound-ing joy.
heaven and na - ture sing, and heaven and na-ture sing,

3 No more let sins and sorrows grow,
Nor thorns infest the ground;
He comes to make his blessings flow
Far as the curse is found.

4 He rules the world with truth and grace,
And makes the nations prove
The glories of his righteousness,
And wonders of his love.

Isaac Watts, 1674–1748

See also:

74 All glory, laud and honor
208 Christ, whose glory fills
328 Hail to the Lord's Anointed
321 Hills of the North
424 Hosanna to the living Lord
356 Mine eyes have seen the glory
541 Rise up, O men of God
327 The Lord will come
586 The world is very evil
329 Thy kingdom come, O God
331 Thy kingdom come, on bended
348 Turn back, O man
525 Watchman, tell us of the night
309 Thou, whose almighty word

16 CHRISTMAS

STILLE NACHT. Irregular. FRANZ XAVER GRUBER, 1787–1863

Tenderly
1. Si - lent night, ho - ly night, All is calm, all is bright
Round yon Vir - gin Moth - er and Child. Ho - ly In - fant, so ten-der and mild,
Sleep in heav - en - ly peace, Sleep in heav - en - ly peace.

2 Silent night, holy night,
Shepherds quake at the sight;
Glories stream from heaven afar,
Heavenly hosts sing, Alleluia,
Christ, the Saviour, is born!

3 Silent night, holy night,
Son of God, love's pure light
Radiant beams from thy holy face,
With the dawn of redeeming grace,
Jesus, Lord, at thy birth.

Joseph Mohr, 1792–1849
Tr. Unknown

DIVINUM MYSTERIUM. 8 7, 8 7, 8 7 7. XIII cent. Plainsong, Mode V,
(CORDE NATUS EX PARENTIS) Arr. by WINFRED DOUGLAS, 1867–1944

Unison, in moderate time FIRST TUNE

1. Of the Fa-ther's love be - got - ten Ere the worlds be - gan to be,
2. O that birth for ev - er bless - ed, When the Vir - gin, full of grace,
He is Al - pha and O - me - ga, He the source, the end - ing he,
By the Ho - ly Ghost con - ceiv - ing, Bare the Sav - iour of our race;
Of the things that are, that have been, And that
And the Babe, the world's Re - deem - - - er, First re -

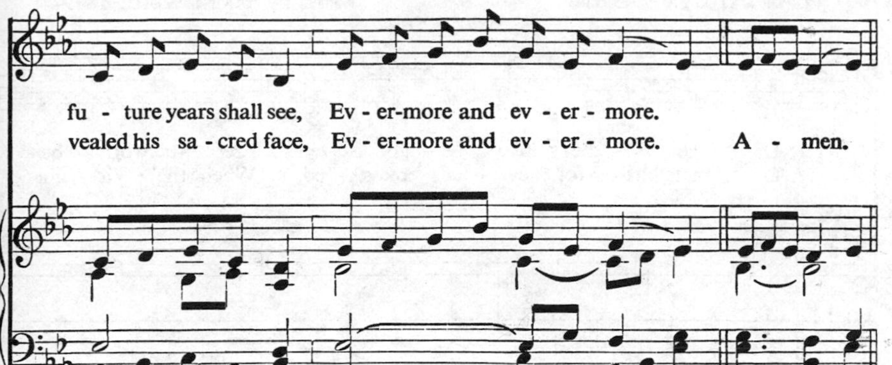
fu - ture years shall see, Ev - er-more and ev - er - more.
vealed his sa - cred face, Ev - er-more and ev - er - more. A - men.

3 This is he whom seers in old time
Chanted of with one accord;
Whom the voices of the prophets
Promised in their faithful word;
Now he shines, the long-expected;
Let creation praise its Lord,
Evermore and evermore.

4 O ye heights of heaven, adore him;
Angel hosts, his praises sing;
Powers, dominions, bow before him,
And extol our God and King;
Let no tongue on earth be silent,
Every voice in concert ring,
Evermore and evermore.

5 Christ, to thee, with God the Father,
And, O Holy Ghost, to thee,
Hymn and chant and high thanksgiving,
And unwearied praises be:
Honor, glory, and dominion,
And eternal victory,
Evermore and evermore. Amen.

Aurelius Clemens Prudentius, 348–413
Tr. St. 1–4, John Mason Neale, 1818–66
Tr. St. 5, Henry Williams Baker, 1821–77

DIVINUM MYSTERIUM. 8 7, 8 7, 8 7 7. (CORDE NATUS EX PARENTIS)

XIII cent. Plainsong, Mode V, Arr. by ERNEST WHITE, 1899–

Unison SECOND TUNE

1. Of the Fa - ther's love be - got - ten Ere the worlds be - gan to be, He is Al - pha and O - me - ga, He the source, the end - ing he, Of the things that are, that have been, And that fu - ture years shall see, Ev - er-more and ev - er - more.
2. O that birth for ev - er bless - ed, When the Vir - gin, full of grace, By the Ho - ly Ghost con - ceiv - ing, Bare the Sav - iour of our race, And the Babe, the world's Re-deem - er, First re-vealed his sa - cred face, Ev - er-more and ev - er - more. A-men.

3 This is he whom seers in old time
Chanted of with one accord,
Whom the voices of the prophets
Promised in their faithful word;
Now he shines, the long-expected;
Let creation praise its Lord,
Evermore and evermore.

4 O ye heights of heaven, adore him;
Angel hosts, his praises sing;
Powers, dominions, bow before him,
And extol our God and King;
Let no tongue on earth be silent,
Every voice in concert ring,
Evermore and evermore.

5 Christ, to thee, with God the Father,
And, O Holy Ghost, to thee,
Hymn and chant and high thanksgiving
And unwearied praises be:
Honor, glory, and dominion,
And eternal victory,
Evermore and evermore. Amen.

Aurelius Clemens Prudentius, 348–413
Tr. St. 1–4, John Mason Neale, 1818–66
Tr. St. 5, Henry Williams Baker, 1821–77

18

ST. ALPHEGE. 7 6, 7 6. HENRY J. GAUNTLETT, 1805–76

In moderate time

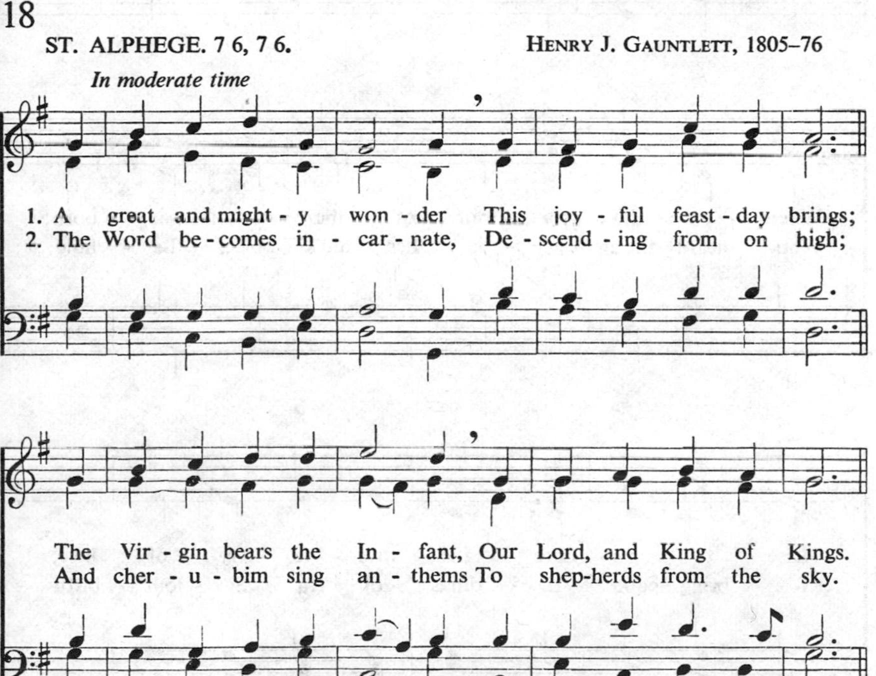
1. A great and might - y won - der This joy - ful feast - day brings;
2. The Word be - comes in - car - nate, De - scend - ing from on high;
The Vir - gin bears the In - fant, Our Lord, and King of Kings.
And cher - u - bim sing an - thems To shep-herds from the sky.

3 And we with them triumphant
Repeat the hymn again,
'To God on high be glory,
And peace on earth to men!'

4 While thus they sing your Monarch
Those bright angelic bands,
Rejoice, ye vales and mountains!
Ye oceans, clap your hands!

5 Since all he comes to ransom,
By all be he adored,
The Infant born in Bethlehem,
The Saviour and the Lord!

6 All idol forms shall perish,
And error shall decay,
And Christ shall wield His sceptre,
Our Lord and God for aye.

St. Germanus, cir. 634–734
Tr. John Mason Neale, 1818–66, a.

YORKSHIRE. 10 10, 10 10, 10 10. JOHN WAINWRIGHT, *cir.* 1723–68

Broadly, with vigor
1. Chris - tians, a - wake! sa - lute the hap - py morn
2. Then to the watch - ful shep - herds it was told,
Where - on the Sav - iour of the world was born;
Who heard the an - gel - ic her - ald's voice, 'Be - hold,
Rise to a - dore the mys - te - ry of love,
I bring good ti - dings of a Sav - iour's birth
Which hosts of an - gels chant - ed from a - bove;
To you and all the na - tions up - on earth;

Christmas

With them the joy - ful ti - dings first be - gun
This day hath God ful- filled his prom - ised word,
Of God In - car - nate and the Vir - gin's Son.
This day is born a Sav - iour, Christ the Lord.'

3 He spake; and straightway the celestial choir
In hymns of joy, unknown before, conspire;
The praises of redeeming love they sang,
And heaven's whole orb with alleluias rang;
God's highest glory was their anthem still,
Peace upon earth, and unto men good will.

4 To Bethlehem straight the enlightened shepherds ran,
To see the wonder God had wrought for man,
And found, with Joseph and the blessèd Maid,
Her Son, the Saviour, in a manger laid;
Amazed, the wondrous story they proclaim,
The first apostles of his infant fame.

5 Like Mary, let us ponder in our mind
God's wondrous love in saving lost mankind;
Trace we the Babe, who has retrieved our loss,
From his poor manger to his bitter Cross;
Treading his steps, assisted by his grace,
Till man's first heavenly state again takes place.

6 Then may we hope, the angelic thrones among,
To sing, redeemed, a glad triumphal song;
He that was born upon this joyful day
Around us all his glory shall display;
Saved by his love, incessant we shall sing
Eternal praise to heaven's Almighty King.

John Byrom, 1692–1763

A SOLIS ORTUS CARDINE Plainsong, Mode III

Arr. by E. T. Cook in the *BBC Hymn Book*

FIRST TUNE

Unison
1. From east to west, from shore to shore, Let ev - ery heart a - wake and sing The ho - ly Child whom Ma - ry bore, The Christ, the ev - er - last - ing King.
2. Be - hold, the world's Cre - a - tor wears The form and fash - ion of a slave; Our ver - y flesh our Mak - er shares, His fall - en crea - ture, man, to save. A - men.

3 For this how wondrously he wrought!
A maiden, in her lowly place,
Became, in ways beyond all thought,
The chosen vessel of his grace.

4 And while the angels in the sky
Sang praise above the silent field,
To shepherds poor the Lord most high,
The one great Shepherd, was revealed.

5 All glory for this blessèd morn
To God the Father ever be;
All praise to thee, O Virgin-born,
All praise, O Holy Ghost, to thee. Amen.

Coelius Sedulius,† cir. 450
Tr. John Ellerton, 1826–93

CHRISTUM WIR SOLLEN LOBEN SCHON. L. M. *Geistliche Lieder,* Wittenberg, 1535

SECOND TUNE

With dignity
1. From east to west, from shore to shore, Let ev - ery heart a - wake and sing The ho - ly Child whom Ma - ry bore, The Christ, the ev - er - last - ing King.
2. Be - hold, the world's Cre - a - tor wears The form and fash - ion of a slave; Our ver - y flesh our Mak - er shares, His fall - en crea - ture, man, to save. A - men.

3 For this how wondrously he wrought!
A maiden, in her lowly place,
Became, in ways beyond all thought,
The chosen vessel of his grace.

4 And while the angels in the sky
Sang praise above the silent field,
To shepherds poor the Lord most high,
The one great Shepherd, was revealed.

5 All glory for this blessèd morn
To God the Father ever be,
All praise to thee, O Virgin-born,
All praise, O Holy Ghost, to thee. Amen.

Coelius Sedulius,† cir. 450
Tr. John Ellerton, 1826–93

This hymn may also be sung to O JESU CHRIST, MEIN LEBENS LICHT (No. 376).

TALLIS' CANON. L. M.
THOMAS TALLIS, *cir.* 1505–85
With dignity
1. All praise to thee, E - ter - nal Lord, Clothed in a garb of flesh and blood; Choos - ing a man - ger for thy throne, While worlds on worlds are thine a - lone.
2. Once did the skies be - fore thee bow, A Vir - gin's arms con - tain thee now; An - gels, who did in thee re - joice, Now lis - ten for thine in - fant voice.

3 A little child, thou art our guest,
That weary ones in thee may rest;
Forlorn and lowly is thy birth,
That we may rise to heaven from earth.

4 Thou comest in the darksome night,
To make us children of the light,
To make us in the realms divine,
Like thine own angels, 'round thee shine.

5 All this for us thy love hath done,
By this to thee our love is won,
For this we tune our cheerful lays,
And shout our thanks in ceaseless praise.

Latin Hymn of XI cent.
German Hymn of XIV cent.
Martin Luther, 1483–1546
Tr. anonymous, 1858

This hymn may also be sung to CANONBURY (No. 538).

VOM HIMMEL HOCH. L. M. MARTIN LUTHER, 1483–1546

In flowing style
1. From heaven a - bove to earth I come To bear good news to ev - ery home; Glad ti - dings of great joy I bring, Where - of I now will say and sing.
2. To you this night is born a child Of Ma - ry, cho - sen moth - er mild; This lit - tle child, of low - ly birth, Shall be the joy of all the earth.

3 Were earth a thousand times as fair,
Beset with gold and jewels rare,
She yet were far too poor to be
A narrow cradle, Lord, to thee.

4 Ah, dearest Jesus, Holy Child,
Make thee a bed, soft undefiled,
Within my heart, that it may be
A quiet chamber kept for thee.

5 'Glory to God in highest heaven,
Who unto man his Son hath given,'
While angels sing with pious mirth
A glad new year to all the earth.

Martin Luther, 1483–1546
Tr. Catherine Winkworth, 1829–78

For harmonization of this tune by J. S. Bach, see No. 34.

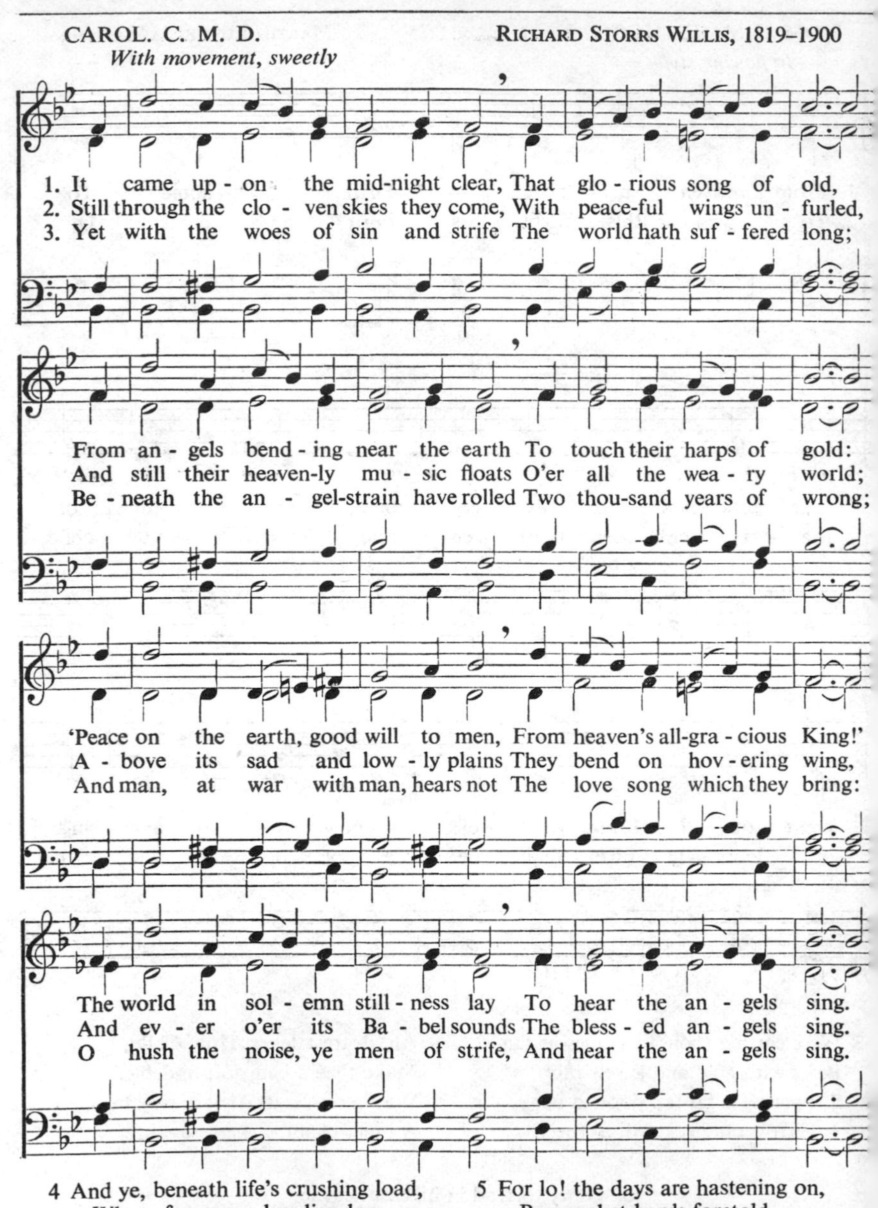
CAROL. C. M. D.
RICHARD STORRS WILLIS, 1819–1900
With movement, sweetly
1. It came up - on the mid-night clear, That glo - rious song of old,
2. Still through the clo - ven skies they come, With peace-ful wings un - furled,
3. Yet with the woes of sin and strife The world hath suf - fered long;
From an - gels bend - ing near the earth To touch their harps of gold:
And still their heaven-ly mu - sic floats O'er all the wea - ry world;
Be - neath the an - gel-strain have rolled Two thou-sand years of wrong;
'Peace on the earth, good will to men, From heaven's all-gra - cious King!'
A - bove its sad and low - ly plains They bend on hov - ering wing,
And man, at war with man, hears not The love song which they bring:
The world in sol - emn still - ness lay To hear the an - gels sing.
And ev - er o'er its Ba - bel sounds The bless - ed an - gels sing.
O hush the noise, ye men of strife, And hear the an - gels sing.

4 And ye, beneath life's crushing load,
Whose forms are bending low,
Who toil along the climbing way
With painful steps and slow:
Look now! for glad and golden hours
Come swiftly on the wing;
O rest beside the weary road,
And hear the angels sing.

5 For lo! the days are hastening on,
By prophet-bards foretold,
When, with the ever-circling years,
Shall come the Age of Gold;
When peace shall over all the earth
Its heavenly splendors fling,
And all the world give back the song
Which now the angels sing.

Edmund Hamilton Sears, 1810–

BETHLEHEM. C. M. D. GOTTFRIED WILHELM FINK, 1783–1846

Joyfully
1. While shep-herds watched their flocks by night, All, seat-ed on the ground,
The an-gel of the Lord came down, And glo-ry shone a-round.
'Fear not,' said he, for might-y dread Had seized their trou-bled mind;
'Glad ti-dings of great joy I bring To you and all man-kind.'

2 'To you, in David's town this day
Is born of David's line
A Saviour, who is Christ the Lord;
And this shall be the sign:
The heavenly Babe you there shall find
To human view displayed,
All meanly wrapped in swathing bands,
And in a manger laid.'

3 Thus spake the seraph, and forthwith
Appeared a shining throng
Of angels praising God, who thus
Addressed their joyful song:
'All glory be to God on high,
And to the earth be peace;
Good will henceforth from heaven to men
Begin and never cease!'

Nahum Tate, 1652–1715

MENDELSSOHN. 77, 77. D. With Refrain. FELIX MENDELSSOHN-BARTHOLDY, 1809–47
In moderate time
1. Hark! the her - ald an - gels sing, 'Glo - ry to the new - born King;
Peace on earth, and mer - cy mild, God and sin - ners rec - on - ciled!'
Joy - ful, all ye na - tions, rise, Join the tri - umph of the skies,
With the an - gel - ic host pro-claim, 'Christ is born in Beth - le - hem.'
Unison
Hark, the her - ald an - gels sing, 'Glo - ry to the new-born King!'
Org.

2 Christ, by highest heaven adored,
Christ, the everlasting Lord,
Late in time behold him come,
Offspring of a Virgin's womb.
Veiled in flesh the Godhead see;
Hail, the incarnate Deity,
Pleased as Man with man to dwell,
Jesus, our Immanuel!

3 Hail, the heaven-born Prince of Peace!
Hail, the Sun of Righteousness!
Light and life to all he brings,
Risen with healing in his wings.
Mild he lays his glory by,
Born that man no more may die,
Born to raise the sons of earth,
Born to give them second birth.

Charles Wesley, 1707–88, a.

6

WARUM SOLLT ICH. 8, 3 3, 6. D. JOHANN GEORG EBELING, 1637–76

Briskly
1. All my heart this night re - joic - es As I hear, far and
near, Sweet - est an - gel voic - es; 'Christ is born,' their choirs are
sing - ing, Till the air ev - ery-where Now with joy is ring - ing.

2 Hark! a voice from yonder manger,
Soft and sweet, doth entreat,
'Flee from woe and danger;
Brethren, come; from all that grieves you
You are freed; all you need
I will surely give you.'

3 Come then, let us hasten yonder;
Here let all, great and small,
Kneel in awe and wonder,
Love him who with love is yearning;
Hail the star that from far
Bright with hope is burning.

Paul Gerhardt, 1607–76
Tr. Catherine Winkworth, 1829–78

ST. LOUIS (REDNER). 8 6, 8 6, 7 6, 8 6. LEWIS HENRY REDNER, 1831–1908

Quietly FIRST TUNE

1. O lit - tle town of Beth - le - hem, How still we see thee lie!
2. For Christ is born of Ma - - ry, And gath - ered all a - bove,
A - bove thy deep and dream-less sleep The si - lent stars go by;
While mor - tals sleep, the an - gels keep Their watch of won-dering love.
Yet in thy dark streets shin - eth The ev - er - last - ing Light;
O morn - ing stars, to - geth - er Pro - claim the ho - ly birth,
The hopes and fears of all the years Are met in thee to-night.
And prais - es sing to God the King, And peace to men on earth! A-me

3 How silently, how silently,
The wondrous Gift is given!
So God imparts to human hearts
The blessings of his heaven.
No ear may hear his coming,
But in this world of sin,
Where meek souls will receive him, still
The dear Christ enters in.

4 O holy Child of Bethlehem,
Descend to us, we pray;
Cast out our sin, and enter in,
Be born in us today.
We hear the Christmas angels
The great glad tidings tell;
O come to us, abide with us,
Our Lord Immanuel! Amen.

Phillips Brooks, 1835-

CHRISTMAS CAROL. 8 6, 8 6, 7 6, 8 6. HENRY WALFORD DAVIES, 1869–1941

SECOND TUNE

In moderate time
1. O little town of Bethlehem, How still we see thee lie!
2. For Christ is born of Mary, And gathered all above,
Above thy deep and dreamless sleep The silent stars go by;
While mortals sleep, the angels keep Their watch of wondering love.
Yet in thy dark streets shineth The everlasting Light;
O morning stars, together Proclaim the holy birth,
The hopes and fears of all the years Are met in thee to-night.
And praises sing to God the King, And peace to men on earth! A-men.

3 How silently, how silently,
The wondrous Gift is given!
So God imparts to human hearts
The blessings of his heaven.
No ear may hear his coming,
But in this world of sin,
Where meek souls will receive him, still
The dear Christ enters in.

4 O holy Child of Bethlehem,
Descend to us, we pray;
Cast out our sin, and enter in,
Be born in us today.
We hear the Christmas angels
The great glad tidings tell;
O come to us, abide with us,
Our Lord Immanuel! Amen.

Phillips Brooks, 1835–93

EMMANUEL. L. M.
CARL C. N. BALLE, 1806–55
Joyfully
1. The hap - py Christ-mas comes once more, The heaven - ly guest is
2. The low - ly Sav - iour meek - ly lies, Laid off the splen - do
at the door, The bless - ed words the shep - herds thrill,
of the skies; No crown be - decks his fore - head fair,
The joy - ous ti - dings, 'Peace, good - will.'
No pearl, nor gem, nor silk is there. A - men.

3 O wake, our hearts, in gladness sing,
And keep our Christmas with our King,
Till living song, from loving souls,
Like sound of mighty water rolls.

4 O holy Child, thy manger gleams
Till earth and heaven glow with its beams,
Till midnight noon's broad light hath won,
And Jacob's star outshines the sun.

5 Thou patriarchs' joy, thou prophets' son
Thou heavenly Dayspring, looked for lon
Thou Son of Man, incarnate Word,
Great David's Son, great David's Lord

6 Come, Jesus, glorious heavenly guest,
Keep thine own Christmas in our brea
Then David's harpstrings, hushed so lon
Shall swell our jubilee of song. Amen

Nikolai F. S. Grundtvig, 1783–18
Tr. Charles Porterfield Krauth, 1823–

SCHOP. 8 7, 8 7, 8 8, 7 7.
JOHANN SCHOP, *cir.* 1600–65
Harm. J. S. BACH, 1685–1750
Joyously
1. Break forth, O beau-teous heaven-ly light, And ush - er in the
Ye shep-herds, shrink not with af-fright, But hear the an-gel's
morn - ing; This Child, now born in in - fan - cy, Our
warn - ing.
con - fi - dence and joy shall be, The power of Sa - tan
break - ing, Our peace e - ter - nal mak - ing. A-men.

2 All blessing, thanks and praise to thee,
  Lord Jesus Christ, be given:
Thou hast our brother deigned to be,
  Our foes in sunder riven.
O grant us through our day of grace
  With constant praise to seek thy face;
Grant us ere long in glory
  With praises to adore thee. Amen.

Johann Rist, 1607–67
Tr. St. 1, composite
Tr. St. 2, Arthur Tozer Russell, 1806–74

GLORIA (IRIS). 7 7, 7 7. With Refrain. French Carol
Arr. by EDWARD SHIPPEN BARNES, 1887–

Brightly
1. An - gels we have heard on high, Sing - ing sweet - ly through the night,
2. Shep-herds, why this ju - bi - lee? Why these songs of hap - py cheer?
And the moun-tains in re - ply Ech - o - ing their brave de - light.
What great bright-ness did you see? What glad ti - dings did you hear?
Glo - - - - - - - - - - - ri - a
in ex - cel - sis De - o,
Glo - - - - - - - - - - - - ri - a in ex - cel - sis De - o.

3 Come to Bethlehem and see
Him whose birth the angels sing;
Come, adore on bended knee
Christ, the Lord, the new-born King.

4 See him in a manger laid
Whom the angels praise above;
Mary, Joseph, lend your aid,
While we raise our hearts in love.

Traditional French carol
Alt., Earl Marlatt, 1892–

31

REGENT SQUARE. 8 7, 8 7, 8 7. HENRY SMART, 1813–79

Moderately slow, with dignity

1. An - gels, from the realms of glo - ry, Wing your flight o'er all the earth;
2. Shep-herds, in the fields a - bid - ing, Watch-ing o'er your flocks by night,
Ye, who sang cre - a - tion's sto - ry, Now pro-claim Mes - si - ah's birth:
God with man is now re - sid - ing, Yon - der shines the in - fant light:
Come and wor - ship, come and wor - ship, Wor-ship Christ, the new-born King.

3 Sages, leave your contemplations,
Brighter visions beam afar;
Seek the great Desire of nations,
Ye have seen his natal star:

4 All creation, join in praising
God, the Father, Spirit, Son,
Evermore your voices raising
To the eternal Three in One:

James Montgomery, 1771–1854, a.

WIE SCHÖN LEUCHTET. Irregular. PHILIPP NICOLAI, 1556–1608

With movement

Re - joice, re - joice this hap - py morn, A Sav - iour
His low - ly birth in Beth - le - hem The an - gels
un - to us is born, The Christ, the Lord of glo - ry;
from on high pro - claim, And sing re - demp - tion's sto - ry;
My soul, ex - tol God's great fa - vor, bless him ev - er,
For sal - va - tion Give him praise and ad - o - ra - tion.

Birgitte Cathrine Boye, 1742–1824
Tr. Carl Doving, 1867–1937

WIE SCHÖN LEUCHTET. Irregular. PHILIPP NICOLAI, 1556–1608

With movement

1. All hail to thee, O bless - ed morn, To ti - dings
O sa - cred and im - mor - tal day, When un - to
long by proph - ets borne Hast thou ful - fill - ment giv - en;
earth, in glo - rious ray, De - scends the grace of heav - en!
Young and old their voic - es blend-ing, Praise are send - ing
Un - to heav - en For the Sav - iour to us giv - en.

2 Like other men, he tears will shed,
Our sorrows share, and be our aid,
Through his eternal power,
The love of God on us bestow,
And mingle in our cup of woe
The drops of mercy's shower;
Dearly buying through his passion
Our salvation,
And to mortals
Opening wide the heavenly portals.

3 He comes, for our redemption sent,
And by his glory heaven is rent
To close upon us never;
Our blessèd Shepherd he would be,
Whom we may follow faithfully
To live with him forever,
Unto realms of glory winging,
Praises singing
To the Father
And the Son, and Spirit, ever.

Johann Olof Wallin, 1779–1839
Based on German Hymn of 1621
Tr. Ernst William Olson, 1870–1958

VOM HIMMEL HOCH. L. M. *Geistliche Lieder*, Leipzig, 1539
Harm. J. S. BACH, 1685–1750

Slowly, with dignity
1. The ho - ly Son of God most high, For love of A - dam's laps - ed race, Quit the sweet pleas-ures of the sky To bring us to that hap - py place.
2. His robes of light he laid a - side, Which did his maj - es - ty a - dorn, And the frail state of mor - tals tried, In hu - man flesh and fig - ure born.

3 Whole choirs of angels loudly sing
The mystery of his sacred birth,
And the blest news to shepherds bring,
Filling their watchful souls with mirth.

4 The Son of God thus man became,
That men the sons of God might be,
And by their second birth regain
A likeness to his deity.

Henry More, 1614–87

This hymn may also be sung in the rhythmic form of the Chorale at No. 22.

CHRISTMAS DAWN. 7 6, 7 6. German Folksong, 1823

Simply
1. When Christ-mas morn is dawn - ing In faith I would re - pair
Un - to the low - ly man - ger; My Sav - iour li - eth there,
Un - to the low - ly man - ger; My Sav - iour li - eth there. A-men.

2 How kind, O loving Saviour,
To come from heaven above;
From sin and evil save us,
And keep us in thy love.

3 We need thee, blessèd Jesus,
Our dearest friend thou art;
Forbid that we by sinning
Should grieve thy loving heart. Amen.

Arr. by Elisabeth Ehrenborg-Posse, 1818–80
Tr. Claude William Foss, 1855–1935

CRANHAM. Irregular. GUSTAV THEODORE HOLST, 1874–1934

In moderate time

1. In the bleak mid - win - ter, Frost - y wind made moan,
2. Heav - en can - not hold him, Nor . . earth sus - tain;
Earth stood hard as i - ron, Wa - ter like a stone;
Heaven and earth shall flee a - way When he comes to reign;
Snow had fall - en, snow on snow, Snow . . on . . snow,
In the bleak mid - win - ter A sta - ble place suf - ficed The
In the bleak mid - win - ter, Long a - go.
Lord . . God Al - might - y, Je - sus Christ.

3 Angels and archangels
May have gathered there,
Cherubim and seraphim
Throngèd the air;
But his mother only,
In her maiden bliss,
Worshipped the Belovèd
With a kiss.

4 What can I give him,
Poor as I am?
If I were a shepherd
I would bring a lamb;
If I were a wise man
I would do my part;
Yet what I can I give him—
Give my heart.

Christina Georgina Rossetti, 1830–94

7

GARTAN. 6 7, 6 7.
Traditional Irish Air
Brightly
1. Love came down at Christ-mas, Love all love - ly, Love di - vine;
Love was born at Christ-mas, Star and an - gels gave the sign.

2 Worship we the Godhead,
Love incarnate, Love divine;
Worship we our Jesus:
But wherewith for sacred sign?

3 Love shall be our token,
Love be yours and love be mine,
Love to God and all men,
Love for plea and gift and sign.

Christina Georgina Rossetti, 1830–94

ES IST EIN' ROS' ENTSPRUNGEN. 7 6, 7 6, 6 7 6.

Geistliche Kirchengesäng, Cologne, 1599

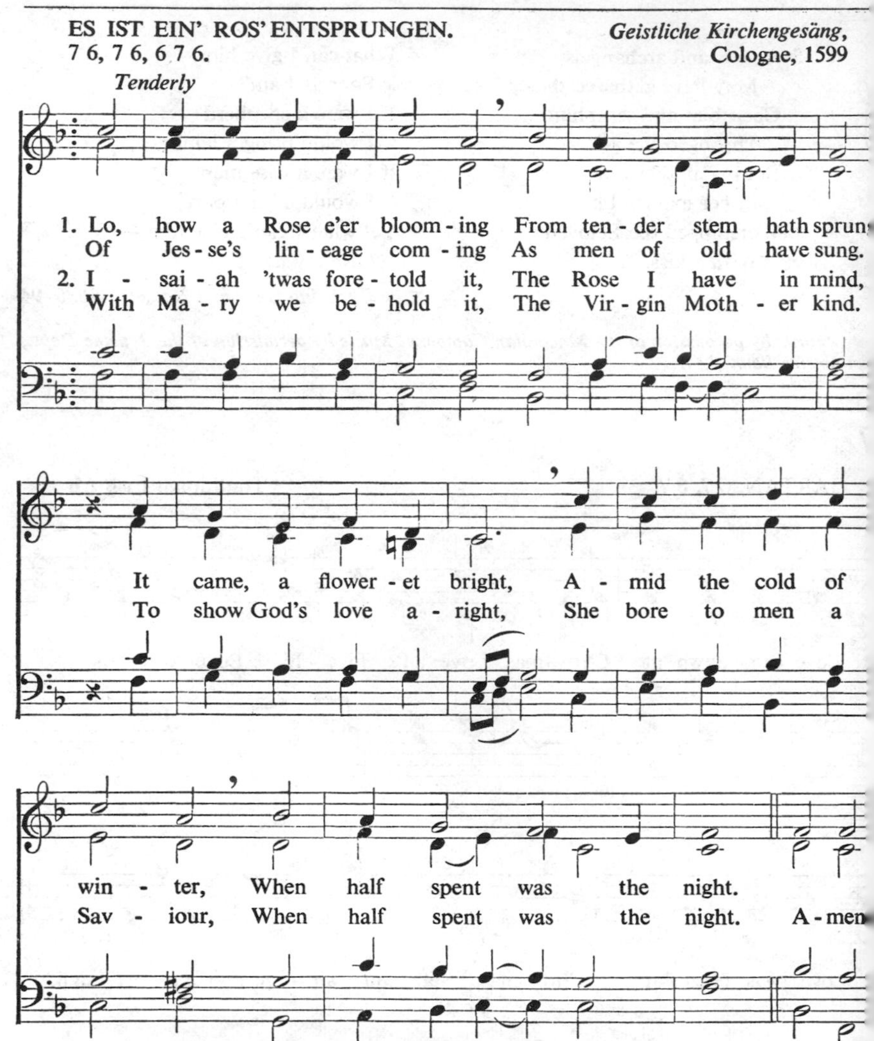
Tenderly
1. Lo, how a Rose e'er bloom-ing From ten-der stem hath sprung!
Of Jes-se's lin-eage com-ing As men of old have sung.
2. I-sai-ah 'twas fore-told it, The Rose I have in mind,
With Ma-ry we be-hold it, The Vir-gin Moth-er kind.
It came, a flower-et bright, A-mid the cold of win-ter, When half spent was the night.
To show God's love a-right, She bore to men a Sav-iour, When half spent was the night. A-men

3 This Flower, whose fragrance tender
With sweetness fills the air,
Dispels with glorious splendor
The darkness everywhere.
True Man, yet very God,
From sin and death he saves us
And lightens every load.

4 O Saviour, Child of Mary,
Who felt our human woe;
O Saviour, King of glory,
Who dost our weakness know,
Bring us at length we pray
To the bright courts of heaven,
And to the endless day. Amen.

XVI ce
Tr. St. 1, 2, Theodore Baker, 1851–19
St. 3, Harriet R. Krauth, 1845–19
St. 4, John Caspar Mattes, 1876–19

IN DULCI JUBILO. Irregular.
XIV cent. German Melody
Smoothly, in quiet time
1. Good Chris-tian men, re - joice, With heart, and soul, and voice;
Give ye heed to what we say: Je - sus Christ is born to - day;
Ox and ass be - fore him bow, And he is in the
man - ger now. Christ is born to - day! Christ is born to - day!

2 Good Christian men, rejoice,
With heart, and soul, and voice;
Now ye hear of endless bliss:
Jesus Christ was born for this!
He hath ope'd the heavenly door,
And man is blessèd evermore.
Christ was born for this!

3 Good Christian men, rejoice,
With heart, and soul, and voice;
Now ye need not fear the grave:
Jesus Christ was born to save!
Calls you one and calls you all
To gain his everlasting hall.
Christ was born to save!

Medieval Latin Carol
Tr. John Mason Neale, 1818–66

THE FIRST NOWELL. Irregular. With Refrain. Traditional English Carol

With spirit
1. The first No - el the an - gel did say Was to cer - tain poor shep-herds in fields as they lay; In fields where they lay, keep - ing their sheep, On a cold win - ter's night that was so deep.
2. They look - ed up and saw a star Shin - ing in the east be - yond them far, And to the earth it gave great light, And so it con - tin - ued both day and night.
No - el, No - el, No - el, No - el,
Born is the King of Is - ra - el.

And by the light of that same star
Three wise men came from country far;
To seek for a king was their intent,
And to follow the star wherever it went.

This star drew nigh to the northwest,
O'er Bethlehem it took its rest,
And there it did both stop and stay
Right over the place where Jesus lay.

5 Then entered in those wise men three
Full reverently upon their knee,
And offered there in his presence
Their gold, and myrrh, and frankincense.

6 Then let us all with one accord
Sing praises to our heavenly Lord,
That hath made heaven and earth of naught,
And with his Blood mankind hath bought.

Traditional English Carol

41

IRBY. 8 7, 8 7, 7 7. HENRY J. GAUNTLETT, 1805–76

Slowly. May be sung in unison

1. Once in roy - al Da - vid's cit - y Stood a low - ly cat - tle - shed,
Where a Moth - er laid her ba - by In a man - ger for his bed;
2. He came down to earth from heav - en Who is God and Lord of all,
And his shel - ter was a sta - ble, And his cra - dle was a stall;

Ma - ry was that Moth - er mild, Je - sus Christ her lit - tle Child.
With the poor and mean and low-ly, Lived on earth our Sav - iour ho - ly.

3 And through all his wondrous childhood
He would honor and obey,
Love and watch the lowly maiden
In whose gentle arms he lay;
Christian children all must be
Mild, obedient, good as he.

4 For he is our childhood's pattern:
Day by day like us he grew;
He was little, weak, and helpless;
Tears and smiles like us he knew;
And he feeleth for our sadness,
And he shareth in our gladness.

5 And our eyes at last shall see him
Through his own redeeming love,
For that Child so dear and gentle
Is our Lord in heaven above;
And he leads his children on
To the place where he is gone.

6 Not in that poor lowly stable,
With the oxen standing by,
We shall see him; but in heaven,
Set at God's right hand on high,
When like stars his children crowned
All in white shall wait around.

Cecil Frances Alexander, 1823–95

ADESTE FIDELES. Irregular. JOHN F. WADE'S *Cantus diversi*, 1751

In moderate time

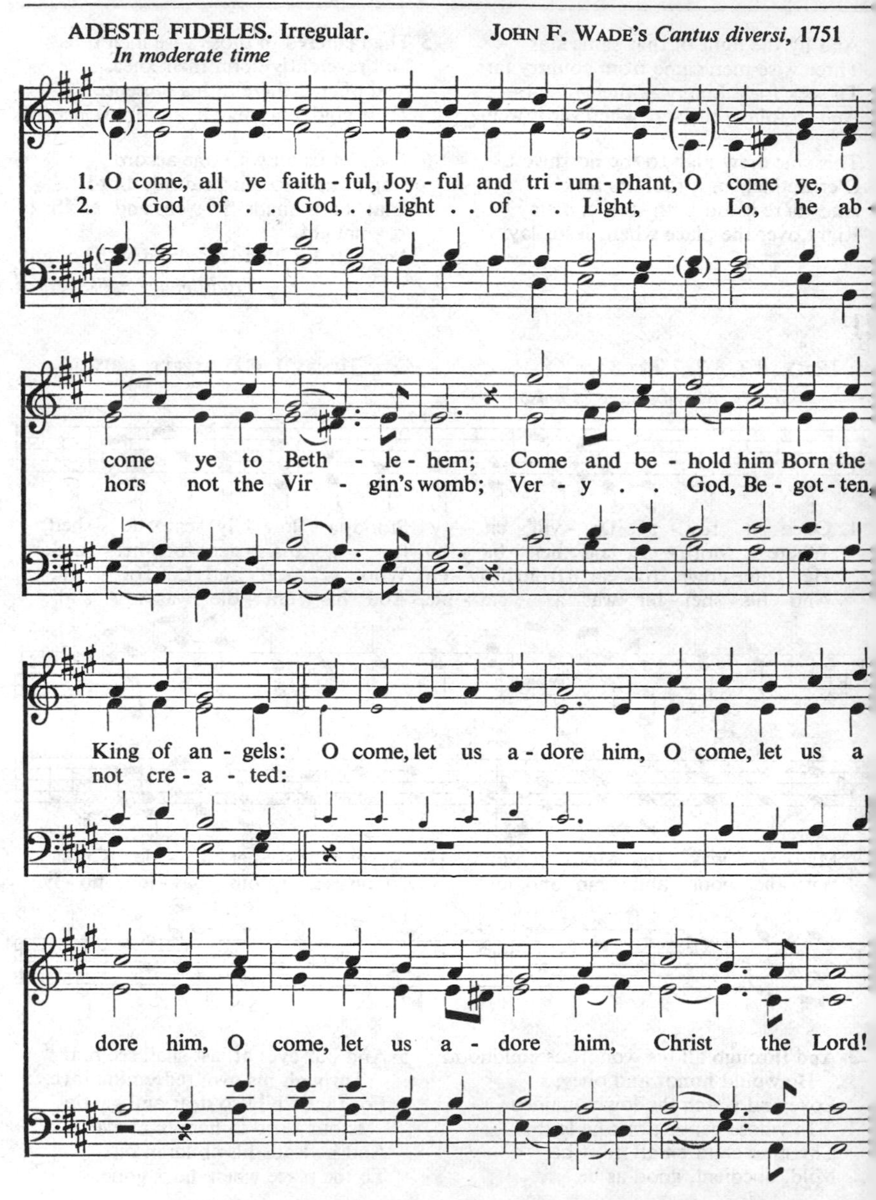
1. O come, all ye faith - ful, Joy - ful and tri - um - phant, O come ye, O
2. God of . . God, . . Light . . of . . Light, Lo, he ab -
come ye to Beth - le - hem; Come and be - hold him Born the
hors not the Vir - gin's womb; Ver - y . . God, Be - got - ten,
King of an - gels: O come, let us a - dore him, O come, let us a
not cre - a - ted:
dore him, O come, let us a - dore him, Christ the Lord!

3
Sing, choirs of angels,
Sing in exultation,
Sing, all ye citizens of heaven above!
Glory to God
In the highest:

4
Yea, Lord, we greet thee,
Born this happy morning,
Jesus, to thee be glory given;
Word of the Father,
Now in flesh appearing:

Latin Hymn, XVIII ce
Tr. Frederick Oakeley, 1802–80, and oth

HOLY MANGER. 8 8, 9 9, 8 8. **Arnold F. Keller, 1890–**

Tenderly, in unison

1. Un - der the fee - ble sta - ble light Come and be - hold the
won-drous sight! Lies here a babe so heav - en - ly sweet,
Moth - er and an - gels the In - fant keep. An - gels on wing,
What do they sing? 'Glo - ry to God, the Sav - iour, King!'
Refrain

2 Brighter the radiant heavens shine,
Shepherds afield hear voices divine,
'For unto you a child is born!'
Go and behold him, this blessed morn.

3 Far away too, in eastern lands,
Wise Men obey the star's commands;
Follow the gleam to where the child lay,
Offer their royal gifts this day.

Arnold Frederick Keller, 1890–

RESONET IN LAUDIBUS. German Carol Melody, 14th cent.
Irregular. With Refrain. Harm. by R. VAUGHAN WILLIAMS, 1872–1958

Brightly in unison
1. Long a - go and far a - way Heav - en rang with joy to - day,
2. Shep-herds heard and won-dered why An - gels sang up in the sky
3. Said the an - gel, 'For a sign Ye shall find the Babe di - vine
Je - sus in the man - ger lay In Beth - le - hem Up -
'Glo - ry be to God most high,' In Beth - le - hem Up -
Cra - dled with the low - ing kine, In Beth - le - hem Up -
on a Christ-mas morn-ing.
on a Christ-mas morn-ing. He came a - mong us at Christ-mas-tide, At
on a Christ-mas morn-ing.
Christ-mas-tide, in Beth - le - hem; Men shall bring him from far and wide Love
di - a - dem: Je - sus, Je - sus, Lo, he comes, and loves, and saves, and frees us.

4 Hard upon the angel's word
Came they all with one accord,
In the manger found the Lord,
In Bethlehem
Upon a Christmas morning.

5 Glory, honor, laud and praise
Be to God for endless days
For the Babe his love displays
In Bethlehem
Upon a Christmas morning.

Edward Traill Horn, III, 1909–
Written for this book and copyrighted
Refrain XV cent., German, Tr. Oxford Book of Carols, 1928

Harmony from THE REVISED CHURCH HYMNARY *by permission of the Oxford University Press*

45

CHRISTMAS EVE. C. M. PEDER KNUDSEN, 1819–63

With movement

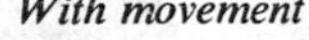

1. I am so glad each Christ-mas Eve, The night of Je - sus' birth!
2. The lit - tle Child in Beth - le - hem, He was a King in - deed!
3. He dwells a - gain in heav-en's realm, The Son of God to - day;

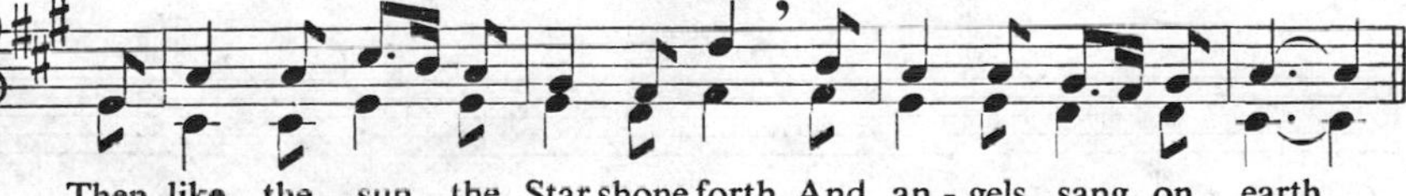

Then like the sun the Star shone forth, And an - gels sang on earth.
For he came down from heaven a-bove To help a world in need.
And still he loves his lit - tle ones And hears them when they pray.

4 I am so glad on Christmas Eve!
His praises then I sing;
He opens then for every child
The palace of the King.

5 When mother trims the Christmas tree
Which fills the room with light,
She tells me of the wondrous Star
That made the dark world bright.

6 She says the Star is shining still,
And never will grow dim;
And if it shines upon my way,
It leads me up to him,

7 And so I love each Christmas Eve
And I love Jesus, too;
And that he loves me every day
I know so well is true.

Marie Wexelsen, 1832–1911
Tr. Peter Andrew Sveeggen, 1881–

St. 5–7, for use in the home

CHRISTMAS BRINGS JOY. 8 7, 9 7, 8 7, 8 7. C. E. F. WEYSE, 1774–1842

With flowing melody

1. Christ-mas brings joy to ev - ery heart, Sets old and young re -

joic - ing, What an - gels sang once to all on earth, Oh,

hear the chil - dren voic - ing. Bright is the tree with

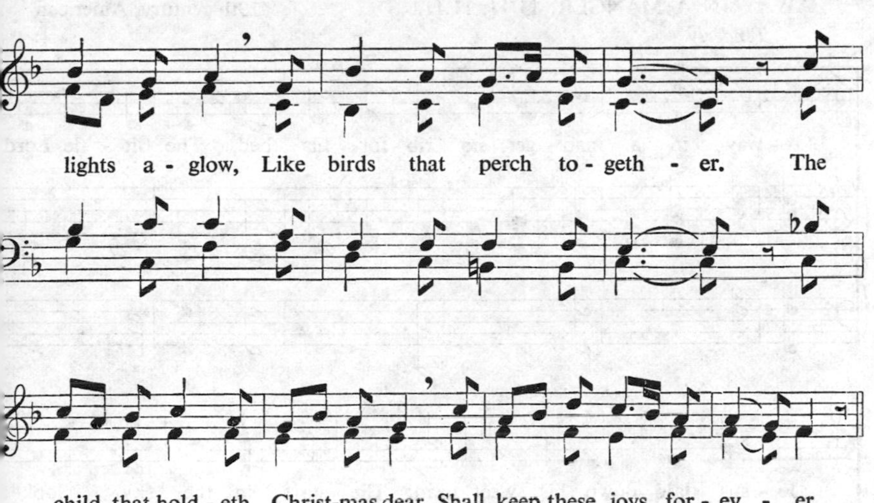
lights a - glow, Like birds that perch to - geth - er. The
child that hold - eth Christ-mas dear Shall keep these joys for - ev - er.

2 Joy comes to all the world today,
To halls and cottage hasting.
Come, sparrow and dove, from roof tree tall,
And share our Christmas feasting.
Dance, little child, on mother's knee,
The lovely day is dawning;
The road to Paradise is found
This blessèd Christmas morning.

3 Once to this earth our Saviour came,
An infant poor and lowly,
To open for us those gardens fair
Where dwell his angels holy.
Christmas joy he bringeth us,
The Christ-child King of heaven,
'To every little child,' he saith,
'Shall angel wings be given.'

Bernhardt Severin Ingemann, 1789–1862
Tr. Cecil Cowdrey

AWAY IN A MANGER. 11 11, 11 11. 19th century, American

Tenderly

1. A - way in a man - ger, no crib for his bed, The lit - tle Lord
Je - sus laid down his sweet head; The stars in the sky looke
down where he lay, The lit - tle Lord Je - sus, a - sleep on the hay. A-men.

2 The cattle are lowing, the poor baby wakes,
But little Lord Jesus no crying he makes.
I love thee, Lord Jesus, look down from the sky,
And stay by my cradle to watch lullaby.

3 Be near me, Lord Jesus; I ask thee to stay
Close by me for ever, and love me, I pray.
Bless all the dear children in thy tender care,
And fit us for heaven, to live with thee there. Amen.

St. 1, 2, Anonymo
St. 3, John Thomas McFarland, 1851–19

GREENSLEEVES. 8 7, 8 7. With Refrain.
English, before 1642
In moderate time
1. What child is this, who, laid to rest, On Ma-ry's lap is sleep-ing?
Whom an-gels greet with an-thems sweet, While shep-herds watch are keep-ing?
Refrain
This, this is Christ the King, Whom shep-herds guard and an-gels sing;
Haste, haste to bring him laud, The Babe, the son of Ma-ry.

2 Why lies he in such mean estate
Where ox and ass are feeding?
Good Christian, fear; for sinners here
The silent Word is pleading.

3 So bring him incense, gold, and myrrh,
Come, peasant, king, to own him;
The King of kings salvation brings,
Let loving hearts enthrone him.

William Chatterton Dix, 1837–98

(CHRISTMAS)

PAEDIA. L. M. J. A. P. SCHULZ, 1747–1800

Simply

1. Thy lit - tle ones, dear Lord, are we, And come thy low - ly bed to see; En - light - en ev - ery soul and mind, That we the way to thee may find.
2. With songs we has - ten thee to greet, And kiss the dust be - fore thy feet; O bless - ed hour, O sweet - est night, That gave thee birth, our soul's de - light. A-men.

3 O draw us wholly to thee, Lord.
Do thou to us thy grace accord,
True faith and love to us impart,
That we may hold thee in our heart.

4 Until at last we too proclaim
With all thy saints, thy glorious Name;
In paradise our songs renew,
And praise thee as the angels do. Amen.

Hans Adolph Brorson, 1694–17
Tr. Harriet Reynolds Krauth Spaeth, 1845–19

See also:

424 Hosanna to the living Lord
15 Joy to the world
428 O for a thousand tongues
419 O Saviour, precious Saviour
432 Songs of praise the angels sang
433 Thou didst leave thy throne
437 Ye watchers and ye holy ones

UNIVERSITY COLLEGE. 7 7, 7 7. HENRY JOHN GAUNTLETT, 1805–76

Slowly, with dignity

1. Je - sus, Name of won-drous love, Name all oth - er names a - bove!
2. Je - sus, Name of price - less worth To the fall - en sons of earth,
3. Je - sus, Name of mer - cy mild, Giv - en to the ho - ly Child

Un - to which must ev - ery knee Bow in deep hu - mil - i - ty.
For the prom - ise that it gave, 'Je - sus shall his peo - ple save.'
When the cup of hu - man woe First he tast - ed here be - low. A-men.

4 Jesus, only Name that's given
Under all the mighty heaven,
Whereby man, to sin enslaved,
Bursts his fetters and is saved.

5 Jesus, Name of wondrous love!
Human Name of God above;
Pleading only this we flee,
Helpless, O our God, to thee. Amen.

William Walsham How, 1823–97

See also:

426 All hail the power
430 At the Name of Jesus
434 Beautiful Saviour
509 Conquering kings
[illegible] the Name
481 Jesus, the very thought
412 Join all the glorious names
428 O for a thousand tongues
468 O Jesus, King most wonderful
419 O Saviour, precious Saviour

The Church Year

51 EPIPHANY

STUTTGART. 8 7, 8 7. CHRISTIAN FRIEDRICH WITT, 1660–1716

With dignity

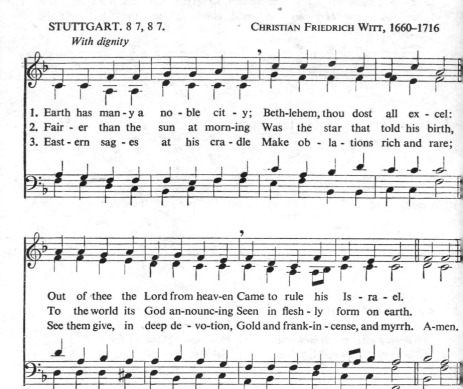

1. Earth has man - y a no - ble cit - y; Beth-lehem, thou dost all ex - cel:
2. Fair - er than the sun at morn-ing Was the star that told his birth,
3. East - ern sag - es at his cra - dle Make ob - la - tions rich and rare;

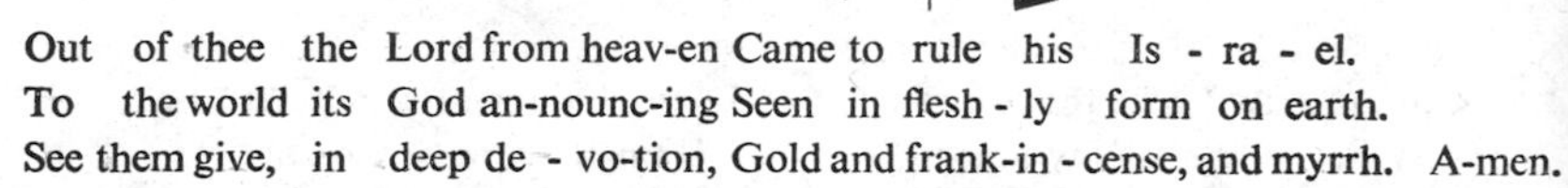

Out of thee the Lord from heav-en Came to rule his Is - ra - el.
To the world its God an-nounc-ing Seen in flesh - ly form on earth.
See them give, in deep de - vo-tion, Gold and frank-in - cense, and myrrh. A-men.

4 Sacred gifts of mystic meaning:
   Incense doth their God disclose,
Gold the King of kings proclaimeth,
   Myrrh his sepulchre foreshows.

5 Jesu, whom the Gentiles worshipped
   At thy glad Epiphany,
Unto thee, with God the Father
   And the Spirit, glory be. Amen.

Aurelius Clemens Prudentius, 348–413
Tr. Edward Caswall, 1814–78

DIX (TREUER HEILAND). 7 7, 7 7, 7 7.
CONRAD KOCHER, 1786–1872
In moderate time
1. As with glad - ness men of old Did the guid - ing star be - hold;
2. As with joy - ful steps they sped To that low - ly man - ger - bed,
3. As they of - fered gifts most rare At that man - ger rude and bare;
As with joy they hailed its light, Lead - ing on - ward, beam - ing bright;
There to bend the knee be - fore Him whom heaven and earth a - dore;
So may we with ho - ly joy, Pure and free from sin's al - loy,
So, most gra - cious God, may we Ev - er - more be led to thee.
So may we with will - ing feet Ev - er seek thy mer - cy - seat.
All our cost - liest treas - ures bring, Christ, to thee, our heaven - ly King. A - men.

4 Holy Jesus, every day
Keep us in the narrow way;
And, when earthly things are past,
Bring our ransomed souls at last
Where they need no star to guide,
Where no clouds thy glory hide.

5 In the heavenly country bright
Need they no created light;
Thou its light, its joy, its crown,
Thou its sun which goes not down;
There for ever may we sing
Alleluias to our King. Amen.

William Chatterton Dix, 1837–98

FIRST TUNE

MORNING STAR. 11 10, 11 10. JAMES P. HARDING, *cir.* 1860–1911

With devotion

1. Bright - est and best of the sons of the morn - ing, Dawn on our dark-ness and lend us thine aid; Star of the east, the hor - i - zon a - dorn - ing, Guide where our in - fant Re - deem - er is laid.
2. Cold on his cra - dle the dew - drops are shin - ing, Low lies his head with the beasts of the stall; An - gels a - dore him in slum-ber re - clin - ing, Mak - er, and Mon - arch, and Sav - iour of all.
3. Say, shall we yield him, in cost - ly de - vo - tion, O - dors of E - dom and of - ferings di - vine; Gems of the moun-tain and pearls of the o - cean, Myrrh from the for - est, or gold from the mine?

4 Vainly we offer each ample oblation,
Vainly with gifts would his favor secure;
Richer by far is the heart's adoration,
Dearer to God are the prayers of the poor.

5 Brightest and best of the sons of the morning,
Dawn on our darkness and lend us thine aid;
Star of the east, the horizon adorning,
Guide where our infant Redeemer is laid.

Reginald Heber, 1783–18

SECOND TUNE

LIEBSTER IMMANUEL. 11 10, 11 10.

Himmels-Lust, Leipzig, 1675
Harm. J. S. BACH, 1685–1750

Slowly, with dignity

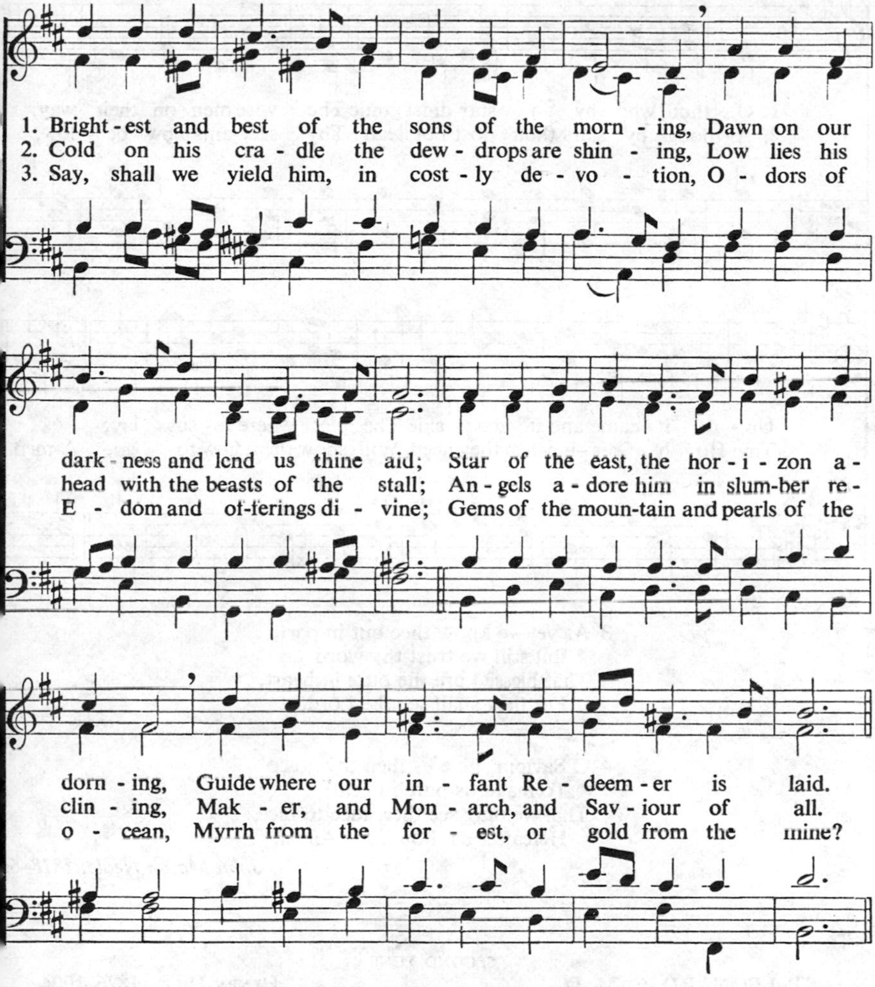

1. Bright - est and best of the sons of the morn - ing, Dawn on our
2. Cold on his cra - dle the dew - drops are shin - ing, Low lies his
3. Say, shall we yield him, in cost - ly de - vo - tion, O - dors of

dark - ness and lend us thine aid; Star of the east, the hor - i - zon a -
head with the beasts of the stall; An - gels a - dore him in slum - ber re -
E - dom and of - ferings di - vine; Gems of the moun - tain and pearls of the

dorn - ing, Guide where our in - fant Re - deem - er is laid.
clin - ing, Mak - er, and Mon - arch, and Sav - iour of all.
o - cean, Myrrh from the for - est, or gold from the mine?

4 Vainly we offer each ample oblation,
Vainly with gifts would his favor secure;
Richer by far is the heart's adoration,
Dearer to God are the prayers of the poor.

5 Brightest and best of the sons of the morning,
Dawn on our darkness and lend us thine aid;
Star of the east, the horizon adorning,
Guide where our infant Redeemer is laid.

Reginald Heber, 1783–1826

FIRST TUNE

CREDITON. C. M. THOMAS CLARK, 1775–1859

In moderate time

1. O thou, who by a star didst guide The wise men on their way,
2. Al-though by stars thou dost not lead Thy serv-ants now be - low,

Un - til it came and stood be - side The place where Je - sus lay;
Thy Ho - ly Spir - it, when they need, Will show them how to go. A-men.

3 As yet we know thee but in part,
But still we trust thy word
That blessèd are the pure in heart,
For they shall see the Lord.

4 O Saviour, give us then thy grace
To make us pure in heart,
That we may see thee, face to face,
Hereafter as thou art. Amen.

John Mason Neale, 1818–66

54

SECOND TUNE

ST. LEONARD. C. M. D. HENRY HILES, 1826–1904

In moderate time

1. O thou, who by a star didst guide The wise men on their way,

Un - til it came and stood be - side The place where Je - sus lay;

2. Al-though by stars thou dost not lead Thy serv - ants now be - low,

Thy Ho - ly Spir - it, when they need, Will show them how to go. A-men.

3 As yet we know thee but in part,
But still we trust thy word
That blessèd are the pure in heart,
For they shall see the Lord.

4 O Saviour, give us then thy grace
To make us pure in heart,
That we may see thee, face to face,
Hereafter as thou art. Amen.

John Mason Neale, 1818–66

TICHFIELD. 7 7, 7 7. D. JOHN RICHARDSON, 1816–79

In moderate time

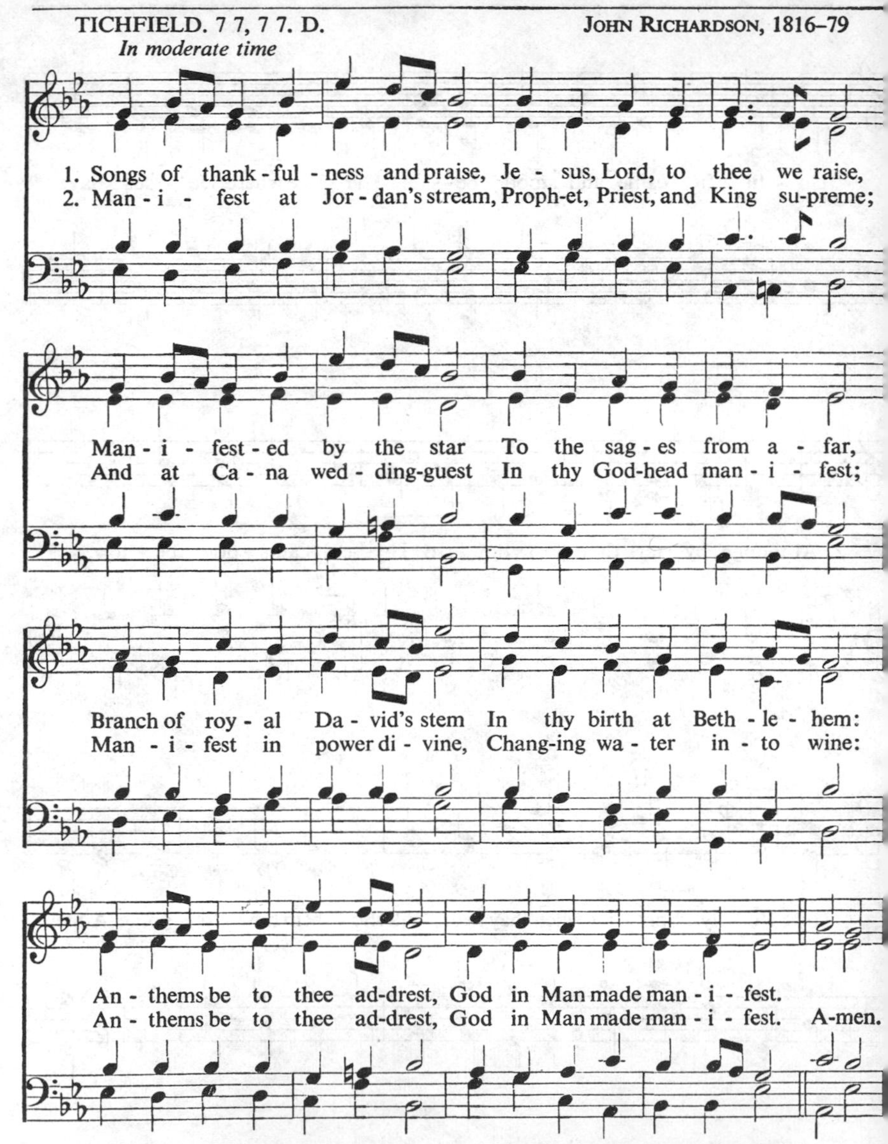
1. Songs of thank - ful - ness and praise, Je - sus, Lord, to thee we raise,
2. Man - i - fest at Jor - dan's stream, Proph-et, Priest, and King su-preme;
Man - i - fest - ed by the star To the sag - es from a - far,
And at Ca - na wed - ding-guest In thy God-head man - i - fest;
Branch of roy - al Da - vid's stem In thy birth at Beth - le - hem:
Man - i - fest in power di - vine, Chang-ing wa - ter in - to wine:
An - thems be to thee ad-drest, God in Man made man - i - fest.
An - thems be to thee ad-drest, God in Man made man - i - fest. A-men.

3 Manifest in making whole
Palsied limbs and fainting soul;
Manifest in valiant fight,
Quelling all the devil's might;
Manifest in gracious will,
Ever bringing good from ill:
Anthems be to thee addrest,
God in Man made manifest.

4 Grant us grace to see thee, Lord,
Mirrored in thy holy word;
May we imitate thee now,
And be pure, as pure art thou;
That we like to thee may be
At thy great Epiphany:
And may praise thee, ever blest,
God in Man made manifest. Amen.

Christopher Wordsworth, 1807–85

This hymn may also be sung to SALZBURG (No. 95).

ROTTERDAM. 7 6, 7 6, D. BERTHOLD TOURS, 1838–97

With movement

1. O one with God the Fa - ther In maj - es - ty and might,
2. Yet, Lord, we see but dark - ly; O heaven - ly Light, a - rise,
The bright-ness of his glo - ry, E - ter - nal Light of Light,
Dis - pel these mists that shroud us, And hide thee from our eyes.
O'er this our home of dark - ness Thy rays are stream-ing now;
We long to track the foot - prints That thou thy - self hast trod;
The shad - ows flee be - fore thee, The world's true Light art thou.
We long to see the path - way That leads to thee, our God.

3 O Jesus, shine around us
With radiance of thy grace;
O Jesus, turn upon us
The brightness of thy face.
We need no star to guide us
As on our way we press,
If thou thy light vouchsafest,
O Sun of Righteousness.

William Walsham How, 1823–97

CELESTIA. 7 7, 8 8, 7 7. **Danish Melody**

Brightly

1. Bright and glo - rious is the sky, Ra - diant are the heav-ens high
2. On that ho - ly Christ-mas night Through the dark-ness beamed a light;
Where the gold - en stars were shin - ing And their rays to earth in - clin - ing,
All the stars a - bove were pal - ing, All their lus - ter slow - ly fail - ing,
Beck-oning us to heaven a - bove, Beck-oning us to heaven a - bove.
As the Christ-mas star drew nigh, As the Christ-mas star drew nigh.

3 Sages from the East afar,
When they saw this wondrous star,
Went to find the King of nations
And to offer their oblations
Unto him as Lord and King.

4 Him they found in Bethlehem,
Yet he wore no diadem;
They but saw a maiden lowly
With an infant pure and holy,
Resting in her loving arms.

5 Guided by the star they found
Him whose praise the ages sound.
We too have a star to guide us
Which forever will provide us
With the light to find our Lord.

6 As a star God's holy word
Leads us to our King and Lord;
Brightly from its sacred pages
Shall this light throughout the ages
Shine upon our path of life.

Nikolai F. S. Grundtvig, 1783–187
Hymnal Version, 19

See also:

434 Beautiful Saviour
208 Christ, whose glory fills
509 Conquering kings their titles take
315 Fling out the banner
333 Full many shall come
319 Hail to the brightness
328 Hail to the Lord's
321 Hills of the North
404 How brightly beams
326 I love to tell the story
342 In Christ there is no East or West
307 Jesus shall reign
481 Jesus, the very thought
483 Jesus, thou joy of loving hearts
412 Join all the glorious names
343 Judge eternal, throned in splendor
418 Let all the world in every corner
475 Light of the anxious heart
428 O for a thousand tongues
468 O Jesus, King most wonderful
163 O worship the King
542 Son of God, eternal Saviour
323 Spread, O spread, thou mighty word
545 The wise may bring their learning
329 Thy kingdom come, O God
525 Watchman, tell us

TANTUM ERGO (DULCE CARMEN). 8 7, 8 7, 8 7.

Essay on The Church Plain Chant, 1782

With dignity
1. Al - le - lu - ia, song of sweet-ness, Voice of joy that can - not die;
2. Al - le - lu - ia thou re-sound - est, True Je - ru - sa - lem and free;
Al - le - lu - ia is the an - them Ev - er dear to choirs on high;
Al - le - lu - ia, joy - ful moth - er, All thy chil - dren sing with thee;
In the house of God a - bid - ing Thus they sing e - ter - nal - ly.
But by Ba - by - lon's sad wa - ters Mourn-ing ex - iles now are we. A-men.

3 Alleluia cannot always
Be our song while here below;
Alleluia our transgressions
Make us for a while forego;
For the solemn time is coming
When our tears for sin must flow.

4 Therefore in our hymns we pray thee
Grant us, blessèd Trinity,
At the last to keep thine Easter
In our home beyond the sky,
There to thee forever singing
Alleluia joyfully. Amen.

Medieval Latin Hymn
Tr. John Mason Neale, 1818–66 a.

This hymn may also be sung to REGENT SQUARE (No. 31).

JESU. 8 7, 8 7. D. GUSTAF DÜBEN, 1671–1730

In moderate time

1. Hark! the voice of Je - sus cry - ing, 'Who will go and work to - day?
Fields are white and har - vests wait - ing, Who will bear the sheaves a - way?'
Loud and long the Mas - ter call - eth, Rich re - ward he of - fers free;
Who will an - swer, glad - ly say - ing, 'Here am I; send me, send me?'

2 If you cannot speak like angels,
  If you cannot preach like Paul,
You can tell the love of Jesus,
  You can say he died for all.
If you cannot rouse the wicked
  With the judgment's dread alarms,
You can lead the little children
  To the Saviour's waiting arms.

3 Let none hear you idly saying,
  'There is nothing I can do,'
While the souls of men are dying,
  And the Master calls for you:
Take the task he gives you gladly,
  Let his work your pleasure be;
Answer quickly when he calleth,
  'Here am I; send me, send me.'

Daniel March, 1816–1909

This hymn may also be sung to RIPLEY (No. 403).

RELEASE. C. M. D. Danish Melody

Broadly

1. How bless-ed from the bonds of sin And earth-ly fet-ters free,
2. With will-ing heart and long-ing eyes To watch be-fore thy gate,
In sin-gle-ness of heart and aim Thy serv-ant, Lord, to be!
Read-y to run the wea-ry race, To bear the heav-y weight;
The hard-est toil to un-der-take With joy at thy com-mand,
No voice of thun-der to ex-pect, But fol-low, calm and still,
The mean-est of-fice to re-ceive With meek-ness at thy hand!
For love can eas-i-ly di-vine The One Be-lov-ed's will.

3 Thus may we serve thee, gracious Lord!
Thus ever thine alone,
Our souls and bodies given to thee,
The purchase thou hast won;
Through evil or through good report
Still keeping by thy side.
By life or death, in this poor flesh
Let Christ be magnified!

4 How happily the working days
In this dear service fly!
How rapidly the closing hour,
The time of rest, draws nigh!
When all the faithful gather home,
A joyful company,
And ever where the Master is,
Shall his blest servants be.

Karl Johann Philipp Spitta, 1801–59
Tr. Jane Borthwick, 1813–97

This hymn may also be sung to ST. LEONARD (No. 54).

Septuagesima to Lent, see also:

---

61 LENT

PANGE LINGUA. 8 7, 8 7, 8 7. — FIRST TUNE — Plainsong Melody, Mode III, Arr. ERNEST WHITE

In unison

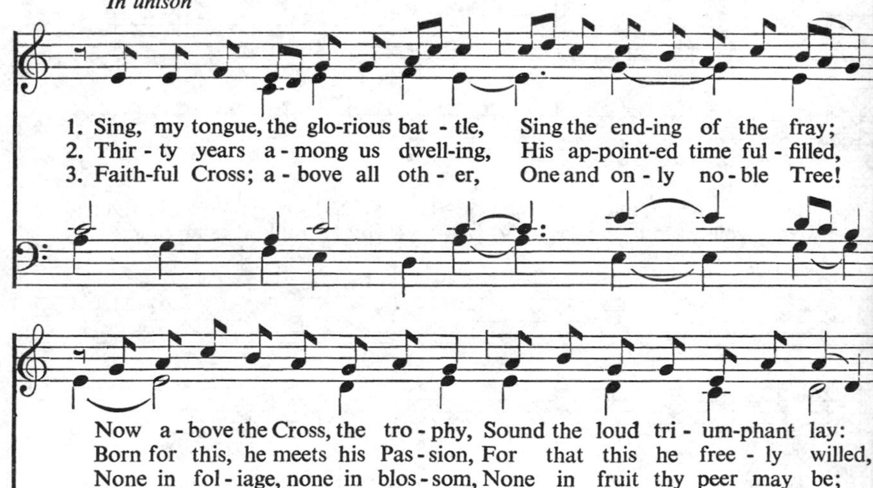
1. Sing, my tongue, the glo-rious bat - tle, Sing the end-ing of the fray;
2. Thir - ty years a - mong us dwell-ing, His ap-point-ed time ful - filled,
3. Faith-ful Cross; a - bove all oth - er, One and on - ly no - ble Tree!
Now a - bove the Cross, the tro - phy, Sound the loud tri - um-phant lay:
Born for this, he meets his Pas - sion, For that this he free - ly willed,
None in fol - iage, none in blos - som, None in fruit thy peer may be;

Tell how Christ, the world's Re-deem-er, As a Vic - tim won the day.
On the Cross the Lamb is lift - ed Where his life-blood shall be spilled.
Sweet - est wood and sweet-est i - ron; Sweet-est weight is hung on thee. A - men.

4 Bend thy boughs, O Tree of Glory,
Thy relaxing sinews bend;
For awhile the ancient rigor
That thy birth bestowed, suspend;
And the King of heavenly beauty
On thy bosom gently tend.

5 To the Trinity be glory
Everlasting, as is meet;
Equal to the Father, equal
To the Son, and Paraclete:
God the Three in One, whose praises
All created things repeat. Amen.

Venantius Fortunatus, 530–609
Tr. John Mason Neale, 1818–66 a.

61

ST. THOMAS (HOLYWOOD). 8 7, 8 7, 8 7. Traditional Melody, 18th cent.

Slowly and majestically SECOND TUNE

1. Sing, my tongue, the glo - rious bat - tle, Sing the end-ing of the fray;
2. Thir - ty years a - mong us dwell-ing, His ap - point-ed time ful - filled,
3. Faith - ful Cross; a - bove all oth - er, One and on - ly no - ble Tree!

Now a - bove the Cross, the tro - phy, Sound the loud tri - um-phant lay:
Born for this, he meets his Pas - sion, For that this he free - ly willed,
None in fol - iage, none in blos - som, None in fruit thy peer may be;

Tell how Christ, the world's Re-deem-er, As a Vic - tim won the day.
On the Cross the Lamb is lift - ed Where his life - blood shall be spilled.
Sweet-est wood and sweet-est i - ron; Sweet-est weight is hung on thee. A-men.

4 Bend thy boughs, O Tree of Glory,
Thy relaxing sinews bend;
For awhile the ancient rigor
That thy birth bestowed, suspend;
And the King of heavenly beauty
On thy bosom gently tend.

5 To the Trinity be glory
Everlasting, as is meet;
Equal to the Father, equal
To the Son, and Paraclete:
God the Three in One, whose praises
All created things repeat. Amen.

Venantius Fortunatus, 530–609
Tr. John Mason Neale, 1818–66 a.

CROMER. L. M. JOHN AMBROSE LLOYD, 1815–74

FIRST TUNE

With breadth, slowly
1. O Christ, our King, Cre - a - tor, Lord, Sav - iour of all who trust thy word, To them who seek thee ev - er near, Now to our prais - es bend thine ear.
2. In thy dear Cross a grace is found, It flows from ev - ery stream-ing wound, Whose power our in - bred sin con - trols, Breaks the firm bond, and frees our souls.
3. Thou didst cre - ate the stars of night, Yet thou hast veiled in flesh thy light, Hast deigned a mor - tal form to wear, A mor - tal's pain - ful lot to bear. A-men.

4 When thou didst hang upon the Tree
The quaking earth acknowledged thee,
When thou didst there yield up thy breath
The world grew dark as shades of death.

5 Now in the Father's glory high,
Great Conqueror, never more to die,
Us by thy mighty power defend,
And reign through ages without end. Amen.

St. Gregory, 540–604
Tr. Ray Palmer, 1808–87

GRACE CHURCH. L. M. IGNAZ JOSEPH PLEYEL, 1757–1831

SECOND TUNE

1. O Christ, our King, Cre - a - tor, Lord, Sav - iour of all who trust thy word, To them who seek thee ev - er near, Now to our prais - es bend thine ear.
2. In thy dear Cross a grace is found, It flows from ev - ery stream - ing wound, Whose power our in - bred sin con - trols, Breaks the firm bond, and frees our souls.
3. Thou didst cre - ate the stars of night, Yet thou hast veiled in flesh thy light, Hast deigned a mor - tal form to wear, A mor - tal's pain - ful lot to bear. A - men.

4 When thou didst hang upon the Tree
The quaking earth acknowledged thee,
When thou didst there yield up thy breath
The world grew dark as shades of death.

5 Now in the Father's glory high,
Great Conqueror, never more to die,
Us by thy mighty power defend,
And reign through ages without end. Amen.

St. Gregory, 540–604
Tr. Ray Palmer, 1808–87

FREIBURG (ES LIEGT EIN SCHLOSS). 8 7, 8 7. German Folksong, XVI cent.

Slowly FIRST TUNE

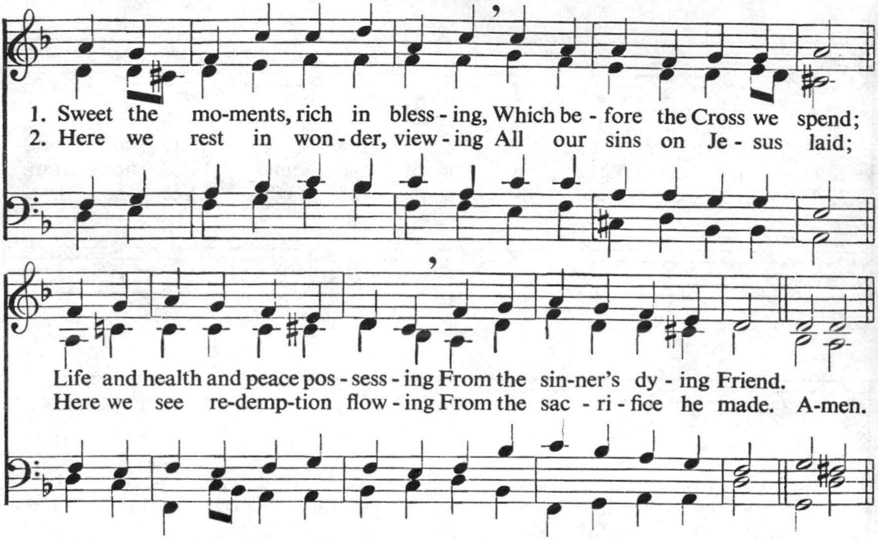

1. Sweet the moments, rich in blessing, Which before the Cross we spend;
Life and health and peace possessing From the sinner's dying Friend.

2. Here we rest in wonder, viewing All our sins on Jesus laid;
Here we see redemption flowing From the sacrifice he made. Amen.

3 Here we find the dawn of heaven,
While upon the Cross we gaze;
See our trespasses forgiven,
And our songs of triumph raise.

4 Lord, in ceaseless contemplation
Fix our hearts and eyes on thee,
Till we taste thy full salvation,
And unveiled thy glories see. Amen.

James Allen, 1734–1804
Walter Shirley, 1725–86
St. 4, Cooke and Denton's Church Hymnal, 1853

63

BATTY (RINGE RECHT). 8 7, 8 7. THOMMEN'S *Christen-Schatz*, 1745

Quietly SECOND TUNE

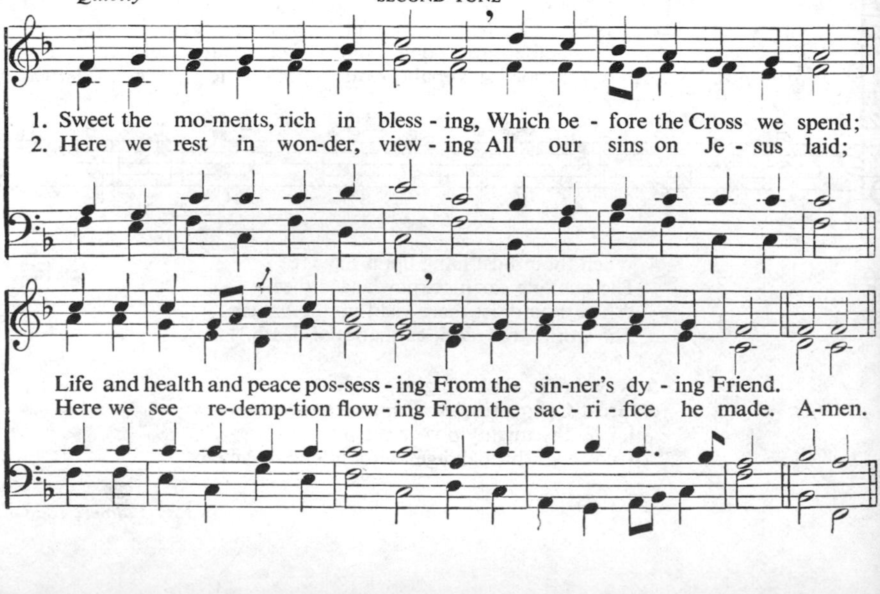

1. Sweet the moments, rich in blessing, Which before the Cross we spend;
Life and health and peace possessing From the sinner's dying Friend.

2. Here we rest in wonder, viewing All our sins on Jesus laid;
Here we see redemption flowing From the sacrifice he made. Amen.

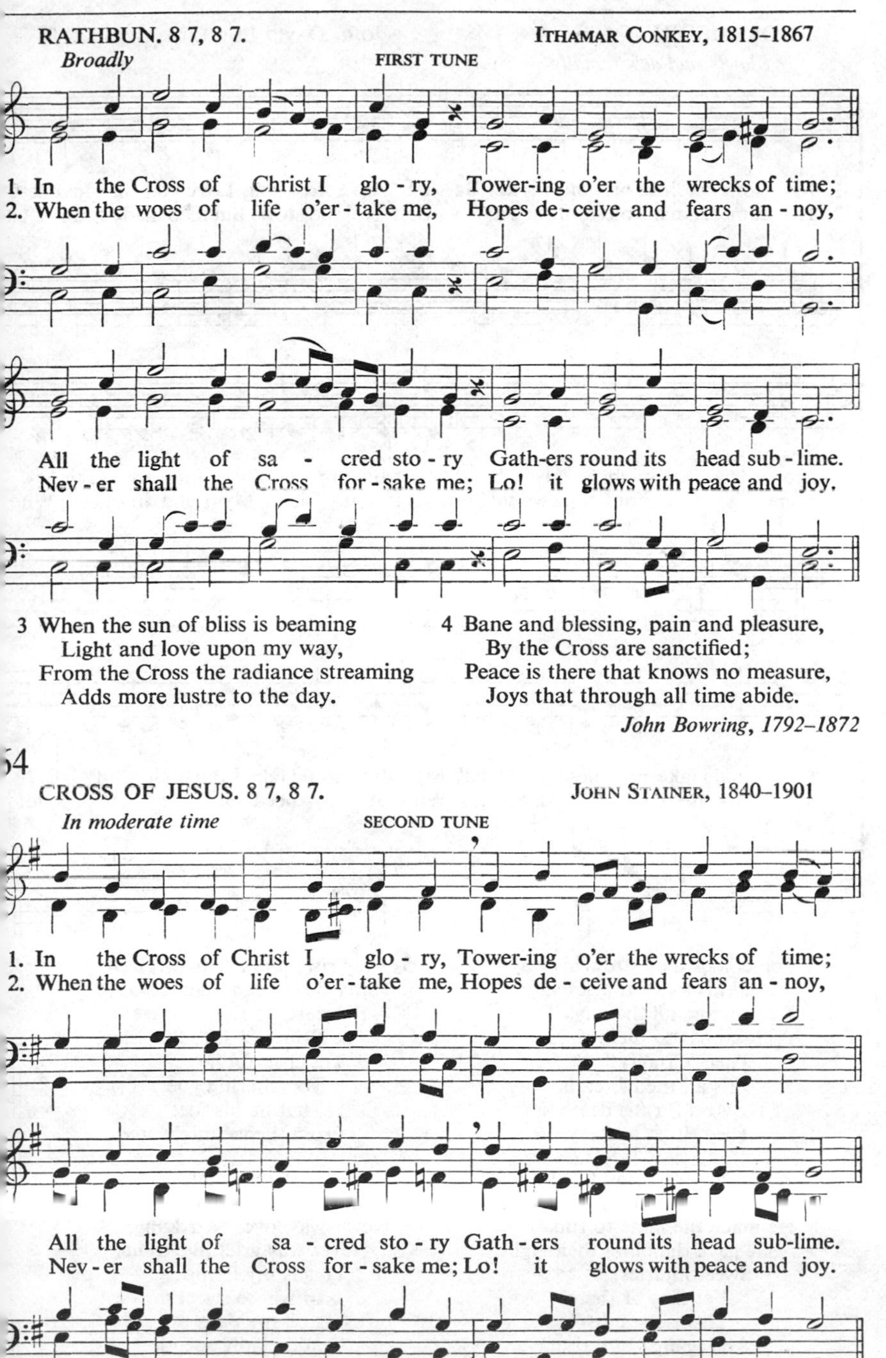
RATHBUN. 8 7, 8 7.
ITHAMAR CONKEY, 1815–1867
Broadly
FIRST TUNE
1. In the Cross of Christ I glo - ry, Tower-ing o'er the wrecks of time;
2. When the woes of life o'er - take me, Hopes de - ceive and fears an - noy,
All the light of sa - cred sto - ry Gath-ers round its head sub - lime.
Nev - er shall the Cross for - sake me; Lo! it glows with peace and joy.
3 When the sun of bliss is beaming
Light and love upon my way,
From the Cross the radiance streaming
Adds more lustre to the day.
4 Bane and blessing, pain and pleasure,
By the Cross are sanctified;
Peace is there that knows no measure,
Joys that through all time abide.
John Bowring, 1792–1872
54
CROSS OF JESUS. 8 7, 8 7.
JOHN STAINER, 1840–1901
In moderate time
SECOND TUNE
1. In the Cross of Christ I glo - ry, Tower-ing o'er the wrecks of time;
2. When the woes of life o'er - take me, Hopes de - ceive and fears an - noy,
All the light of sa - cred sto - ry Gath - ers round its head sub-lime.
Nev - er shall the Cross for - sake me; Lo! it glows with peace and joy.

RHOSYMEDRE. 6 6, 6 6, 4 4, 4 4. JOHN DAVID EDWARDS, *cir.* 1805–85

Slowly and devotionally

1. My song is love un-known, My Sav-iour's love to me; Love to the love-less
2. He came from his blest throne Sal - va-tion to be-stow; But men made strange, an
shown That they might love-ly be. O who am I, That for my sake My
none The longed-for Christ would know. But O, my friend, My friend in - deed, Who
Lord should take Frail flesh, and die? My Lord should take Frail flesh, and die?
at my need His life did spend! Who at my need His life did spend!

3 Sometimes they strew his way
And his sweet praises sing;
Resounding all the day
Hosannas to their king.
Then 'Crucify!'
Is all their breath,
And for his death
They thirst and cry.

4 Why, what hath my Lord done?
What makes this rage and spite?
He made the lame to run,
He gave the blind their sight.
Sweet injuries!
Yet they at these
Themselves displease,
And 'gainst him rise.

5 They rise, and needs will have
My dear Lord made away;
A murderer they save,
The Prince of Life they slay.
Yet cheerful he
To suffering goes,
That he his foes
From thence might free.

6 Here might I stay and sing,
No story so divine;
Never was love, dear King,
Never was grief like thine.
This is my friend,
In whose sweet praise
I all my days
Could gladly spend.

Samuel Crossman, 1624–8

LEOMINSTER. S. M. D.
GEORGE WILLIAM MARTIN, 1828–1881
Arr. by ARTHUR S. SULLIVAN, 1842–1900
In moderate time
1. Wide o - pen are thy hands, Pay - ing with more than gold
The aw - ful debt of guilt - y men, For - ev - er and of old.
Ah, let me grasp those hands, That we may nev - er part,
And let the pow - er of their blood Sus - tain my faint - ing heart.

2 Wide open are thine arms,
A fallen world to embrace;
To take to love and endless rest
Our whole forsaken race.
Lord, I am sad and poor,
But boundless is thy grace;
Give me the soul-transforming joy
For which I seek thy face.

3 Draw all my mind and heart
Up to thy throne on high,
And let thy sacred Cross exalt
My spirit to the sky.
To these, thy mighty hands,
My spirit I resign;
Living, I live alone to thee,
Dying, alone am thine.

Ascribed to St. Bernard of Clairvaux, 1091–1153
Tr. Charles Porterfield Krauth, 1823–83

Music by permission of Novello and Company, Ltd.

NAME OF JESUS. 7 6, 7 6, 8 8, 7 7. RALPH ALVIN STROM, 1901–

FIRST TUNE

1. Je - sus, Name all names a - bove; Je - sus, best and dear - est;
2. Je - sus, crowned with bit - ter thorn, By man - kind for - sak - en,
3. Je - sus, o - pen me the gate That of old he en - tered
Je - sus, fount of per - fect love, Ho - liest, ten - derest, near - est;
Je - sus, who through scourge and scorn Held thy faith un - shak - en,
Who, in that most lost es - tate, Whol - ly on thee ven - tured;
Thou the source of grace com-plet - est, Thou the pur - est, thou the sweet-est,
Je - sus, clad in pur - ple rai-ment, For man's e - vils mak-ing pay-ment:
Je - sus, leave me not to lan-guish: Help - less, hope-less, full of an-guish!
Thou the well of power di - vine, Make me, keep me, seal me thine!
Let not all thy woe and pain, Let not Cal-vary be in vain!
Je - sus, let me hear thee say, 'Thou shalt be with me to - day!' A-men.

Theoctistus of the Studium, cir. 890
Tr. John Mason Neale, 1818–66 a.

Music composed for this book and copyrighted

WERDE MUNTER (ALTERED). 7 6, 7 6, 8 8, 7 7. JOHANN SCHOP, *cir.* 1600–65
Harm. J. S. BACH, 1685–1750

SECOND TUNE

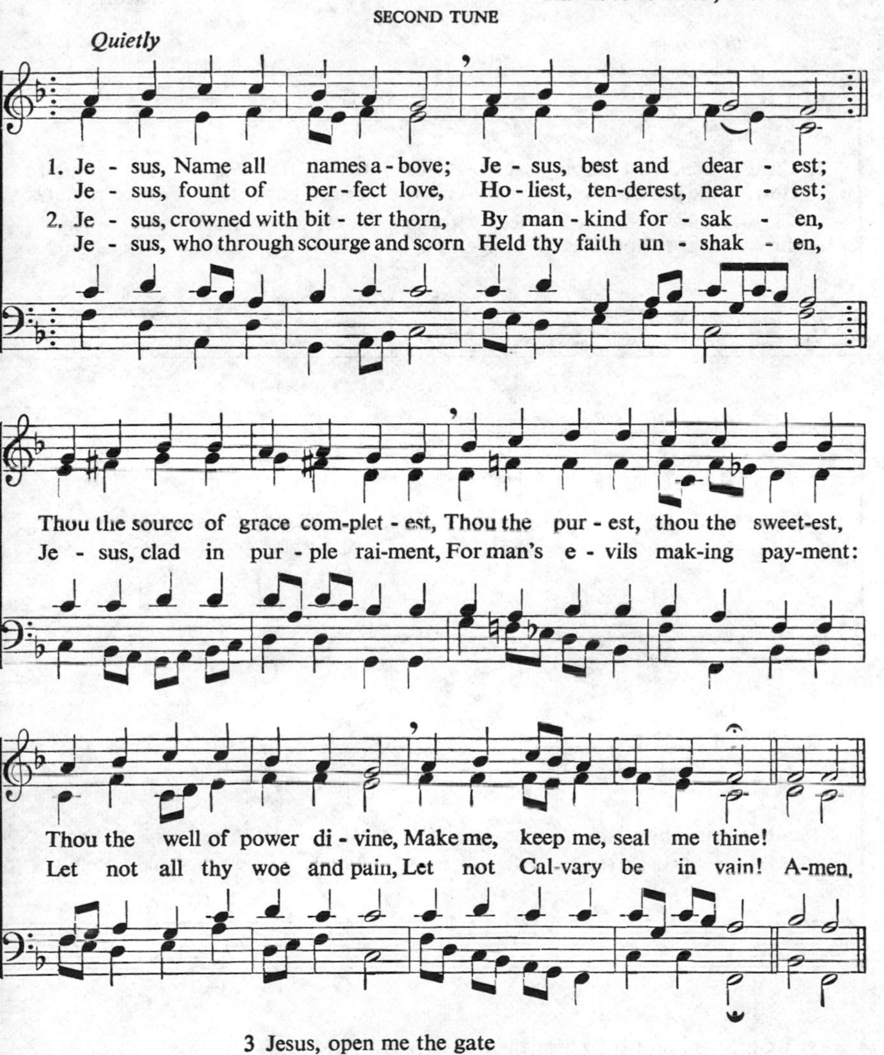
Quietly
1. Je - sus, Name all names a - bove; Je - sus, best and dear - est;
Je - sus, fount of per - fect love, Ho - liest, ten-derest, near - est;
2. Je - sus, crowned with bit - ter thorn, By man - kind for - sak - en,
Je - sus, who through scourge and scorn Held thy faith un - shak - en,
Thou the source of grace com-plet - est, Thou the pur - est, thou the sweet-est,
Je - sus, clad in pur - ple rai-ment, For man's e - vils mak-ing pay-ment:
Thou the well of power di - vine, Make me, keep me, seal me thine!
Let not all thy woe and pain, Let not Cal-vary be in vain! A-men.

3 Jesus, open me the gate
That of old he entered
Who, in that most lost estate,
Wholly on thee ventured;
Jesus, leave me not to languish:
Helpless, hopeless, full of anguish!
Jesus, let me hear thee say,
'Thou shalt be with me today!' Amen.

Theoctistus of the Studium, cir. 890
Tr. John Mason Neale, 1818–66 a.

GUTE BÄUME BRINGEN. 6 5, 6 5. D. *Praxis Pietatis Melica,* Frankfurt, 1668

FIRST TUNE

With energy

1. Chris - tian, dost thou see them On the ho - ly ground,
How the powers of dark - ness Com - pass thee a - round?
2. Chris - tian, dost thou feel them, How they work with - in,
Striv - ing, tempt - ing, lur - ing, Goad - ing in - to sin?
Chris - tian, up and smite them, Count - ing gain but loss;
Chris - tian, nev - er trem - ble, Nev - er be down - cast;
Smite them by the mer - it Of the ho - ly Cross.
Gird thee for the bat - tle, Watch and pray and fast.

3 Christian, dost thou hear them,
How they speak thee fair:
Always fast and vigil,
Always watch and prayer?
Christian, answer boldly,
'While I breathe, I pray.'
Peace shall follow battle,
Night shall end in day.

4 Well I know thy trouble,
O my servant true,
Thou art very weary,
I was weary too;
But that toil shall make thee
Some day all mine own,
And the end of sorrow
Shall be near my throne.

Andrew of Crete, cir. 660–732
Tr. John Mason Neale, 1818–66

ST. ANDREW OF CRETE. 6 5, 6 5. D.
JOHN BACCHUS DYKES, 1823–76
Thoughtfully
SECOND TUNE
1. Chris - tian, dost thou see them On the ho - ly ground,
2. Chris - tian, dost thou feel them, How they work with - in,
How the powers of dark - ness Com-pass thee a - round?
Striv - ing, tempt-ing, lur - ing, Goad-ing in - to sin?
Chris - tian, up and smite them, Count - ing gain but loss;
Chris - tian, nev - er trem - ble, Nev - er be down - cast;
Smite them by the mer - it Of the ho - ly Cross.
Gird thee for the bat - tle, Watch and pray and fast.
3 Christian, dost thou hear them,
How they speak thee fair:
Always fast and vigil,
Always watch and prayer?
Christian, answer boldly,
'While I breathe, I pray.'
Peace shall follow battle,
Night shall end in day.
4 Well I know thy trouble,
O my servant true,
Thou art very weary,
I was weary too;
But that toil shall make thee
Some day all mine own,
And the end of sorrow
Shall be near my throne.
Andrew of Crete, cir. 660–732
Tr. John Mason Neale, 1818–66

O DU LIEBE MEINER LIEBE. 8 7, 8 7. D. — JOHANN THOMMEN'S *Christenschatz*, 1745

With movement

1. Je - sus, ref - uge of the wea - ry, Ob - ject of the spir - it's love,
Foun-tain in life's des - ert drear - y, Sav - iour from the world a - bove;
O how oft thine eyes, of - fend - ed, Gaze up - on the sin-ner's fall;
Yet up - on the Cross ex - tend-ed, Thou didst bear the pain of all. A-men.

2 Do we pass that Cross unheeding,
Breathing no repentant vow,
Though we see thee wounded, bleeding,
See thy thorn-encircled brow?
Yet thy sinless death hath brought us
Life eternal, peace, and rest;
Only what thy grace hath taught us
Calms the sinner's stormy breast.

3 Jesus, may our hearts be burning
With more fervent love for thee;
May our eyes be ever turning
To thy Cross of agony;
Till in glory, parted never
From the blessèd Saviour's side,
Graven in our hearts forever,
Dwell the Cross, the Crucified. Amen

Girolamo Savonarola, 1452–9
Tr. Jane Francesca Wilde, 1826–9

O LAMM GOTTES. 7 7, 7 7, 7 7 7. NIKOLAUS DECIUS, †1541

Slowly
St. 1, 2, 3.
O Lamb of God most ho - ly! Who on the Cross didst
suf - fer, And pa - tient still and low - ly, Thy - self to scorn didst
of - fer; Our sins by thee were tak - en, Or hope had us for -
sak - en:
St. 1, 2.
Have mer - cy on us, Je - sus!
St. 3.
Thy peace be with us, Je - sus! A - men.

Nikolaus Decius, †1541
Tr. Arthur Tozer Russell, 1806–74 a.

PSALM 42. 8 7, 8 7, 7 7, 8 8.
(FREU DICH SEHR)

Genevan Psalter, 1551
Adapted and harm. by J. S. BACH, 1685–1750

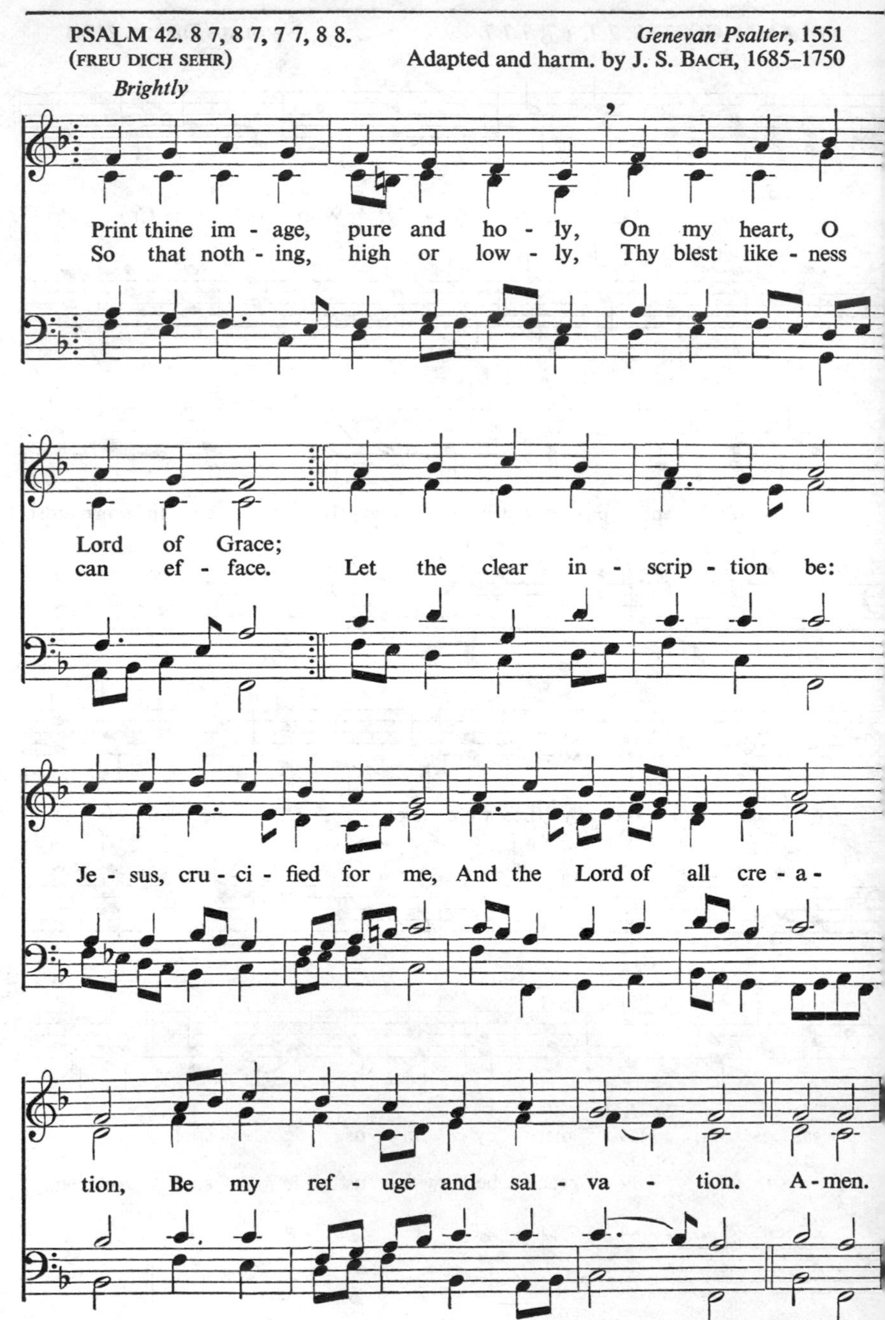
Brightly
Print thine im - age, pure and ho - ly, On my heart, O
So that noth - ing, high or low - ly, Thy blest like - ness
Lord of Grace;
can ef - face. Let the clear in - scrip - tion be:
Je - sus, cru - ci - fied for me, And the Lord of all cre - a -
tion, Be my ref - uge and sal - va - tion. A - men.

Thomas Hansen Kingo, 1634–170.
Tr. Jens Christian Aaberg, 1877-

72

SPANISH HYMN. 7 7, 7 7. D.
Arranged by BENJAMIN CARR, 1768–1831
In moderate time
1. Sav - iour, when in dust to thee Low we bend the a - dor - ing knee;
2. By thy help - less in - fant years, By thy life of want and tears,
When, re - pent - ant, to the skies, Scarce we lift our weep - ing eyes;
By thy days of sore dis - tress In the sav - age wil - der-ness,
O by all thy pains and woe Suf - fered once for man be - low,
By the dread mys - ter - ious hour Of the in-sult - ing tempt-er's power;
Bend - ing from thy throne on high, Hear our sol-emn lit - a - ny!
Turn, O turn a fa-voring eye, Hear our sol-emn lit - a - ny! A-men.

3 By thine hour of dire despair,
By thine agony of prayer;
By the cross, the nail, the thorn,
Piercing spear, the torturing scorn;
By the gloom that veiled the skies
O'er the dreadful sacrifice;
Listen to our humble cry,
Hear our solemn litany!

4 By thy deep expiring groan,
By the sad sepulchral stone;
By the vault whose dark abode
Held in vain the rising God;
O from earth to heaven restored,
Mighty, re-ascended Lord,
Listen, listen to the cry
Of our solemn litany! Amen.

Robert Grant, 1779–1838

Lent, see also:

517 Art thou weary
388 As pants the hart
527 Brief life
79 Christ, the Life of all the living
569 Come, ye disconsolate
467 Dear Lord and Father
435 Hail, thou once despisèd Jesus
499 I heard the voice of Jesus
479 I need thee every hour
561 In the hour of trial
514 Jesus, and shall it ever be
393 Jesus, Lover of my soul
504 Jesus, my Lord, my God
481 Jesus, the very thought
370 Just as I am
368 Lord, it belongs not to my care
365 Lord Jesus, think on me
403 Lord, with glowing heart
375 My faith looks up to thee
466 O for a closer walk
389 O for a heart to praise my God
489 O God, I love thee
386 O Jesus, thou art standing
402 O Love that wilt not let me go
480 O thou in all thy might so far
384 One who is all unfit to count
411 Praise to the Holiest
379 Rock of Ages, cleft for me
463 Saviour, thy dying love
75 The royal banners
586 The world is very evil
391 Thou hidden Love of God
348 Turn back, O man
494 We sing the praise
503 When I survey the wondrous Cross
367 With broken heart

PALM SUNDAY

73

ST. DROSTANE. L. M. JOHN BACCHUS DYKES, 1823–76

Broadly, with dignity FIRST TUNE

1. Ride on, ride on in ma - jes - ty! Hark! all the tribes Ho - san - na cry;
2. Ride on, ride on in ma - jes - ty! In low - ly pomp ride on to die!
3. Ride on, ride on in ma - jes - ty! The wing - ed squad-rons of the sky

O Sav-iour meek, pur - sue thy road With palms and scat-tered gar-ments strowed
O Christ, thy tri-umphs now be - gin O'er cap - tive death and con-quered sin.
Look down with sad and wondering eyes To see the ap-proach-ing sac-ri - fice.

4 Ride on, ride on in majesty!
Thy last and fiercest strife is nigh:
The Father on his sapphire throne
Expects his own anointed Son.

5 Ride on, ride on in majesty!
In lowly pomp ride on to die!
Bow thy meek head to mortal pain,
Then take, O God, thy power and reign

Henry Hart Milman, 1791–1868 a

73

THE KING'S MAJESTY. L. M.
GRAHAM GEORGE, 1912–
In unison, with dignity
SECOND TUNE
1. Ride on, ride on in ma - jes - ty! Hark! all the tribes Ho - san - na cry, O Sav - iour meek, pur - sue thy road With palms and scat - tered gar - ments strowed.
2. Ride on, ride on in ma - jes - ty! In low - ly pomp ride on to die! O Christ, thy tri - umphs now be - gin O'er cap - tive death and con - quered sin.
3. Ride on, ride on in ma - jes - ty! The wing - ed squad - rons of the sky Look down with sad and won-dering eyes To see the ap - proach - ing sac - ri - fice.

4 Ride on, ride on in majesty!
Thy last and fiercest strife is nigh:
The Father on his sapphire throne
Expects his own anointed Son.

5 Ride on, ride on in majesty!
In lowly pomp ride on to die!
Bow thy meek head to mortal pain,
Then take, O God, thy power and reign.

Henry Hart Milman, 1791–1868 a.

ST. THEODULPH (VALET WILL ICH DIR GEBEN). 7 6, 7 6. D.

Vigorously MELCHIOR TESCHNER, 1585–1635

Refrain
1. All glo - ry, laud, and hon - or To thee, Re - deem - er, King;
To whom the lips of chil - dren Made sweet ho - san - nas ring.
Stanzas 2, 3, 4, 5, and 6.
2. Thou art the King of Is - rael, Thou Da - vid's roy - al Son,
Repeat refrai
Who in the Lord's Name com - est, The King and Bless - ed One!

3 The company of angels
Are praising thee on high,
And mortal men and all things
Created make reply. *Refrain.*

4 The people of the Hebrews
With palms before thee went;
Our praise and prayer and anthems
Before thee we present. *Refrain.*

5 To thee before thy Passion
They sang their hymns of praise;
To thee, now high exalted,
Our melody we raise. *Refrain.*

6 Thou didst accept their praises;
Accept the prayers we bring,
Who in all good delightest,
Thou good and gracious King. *Refrai*

Theodulph of Orleans, cir. 760–82
Tr. John Mason Neale, 1818–6

Another form of this Chorale is provided at No. 11.

See also:

430 At the Name of Jesus
76 Glory be to Jesus
424 Hosanna to the living Lord
62 O Christ, our King, Creator
419 O Saviour, precious Saviour
61 Sing, my tongue
75 The royal banners
562 The Son of God goes forth
77 There is a green hill

VEXILLA REGIS PRODEUNT.
FIRST TUNE
Plainsong Melody, Mode I
Arr. Ernest White, 1899–
Unison
1. The royal banners forward go, The Cross shines forth in mystic glow Where he, as man, who gave man breath, Now bows beneath the yoke of death.
2. Fulfilled is all that David told In true prophetic song of old; How God the nations' King should be, For God is reigning from the Tree. Amen.

3 O Tree of beauty, Tree most fair,
Ordained those holy limbs to bear;
Gone is thy shame, each crimsoned bough
Proclaims the King of glory now.

4 Blest Tree, whose chosen branches bore
The wealth that did the world restore,
The price of humankind to pay,
And spoil the spoiler of his prey.

5 O Cross, our one reliance, hail!
Still may thy power with us avail
More good for righteous souls to win,
And save the sinner from his sin.

6 To thee, eternal Three in One
Let homage meet by all be done:
As by the Cross thou dost restore,
So rule and guide us evermore. Amen.

Sts. 1–4, Venantius Fortunatus, 530–609
Sts. 5, 6, Anonymous
Tr. Episcopal Hymnal, 1940

PARKER. L. M.
HORATIO PARKER, 1863–1919
SECOND TUNE
In unison, majestically
1. The roy - al ban - ners for - ward go, The Cross shines forth in mys - tic glow Where he, as man, who gave man breath, Now bows be - neath the yoke of death.
2. Ful - filled is all that Da - vid told In true pro - phet - ic song of old; How God the na - tions' King should be, For God is reign - ing from the Tree. A-men.

3 O Tree of beauty, Tree most fair,
Ordained those holy limbs to bear;
Gone is thy shame, each crimsoned bough
Proclaims the King of glory now.

4 Blest Tree, whose chosen branches bore
The wealth that did the world restore,
The price of humankind to pay,
And spoil the spoiler of his prey.

5 O Cross, our one reliance, hail!
Still may thy power with us avail
More good for righteous souls to win,
And save the sinner from his sin.

6 To thee, eternal Three in One,
Let homage meet by all be done:
As by the Cross thou dost restore,
So rule and guide us evermore. Amen.

Sts. 1–4, Venantius Fortunatus, 530–60
Sts. 5, 6, Anonymou
Tr. Episcopal Hymnal, 194

CASWALL. 6 5, 6 5. FRIEDRICH FILITZ, 1804–76

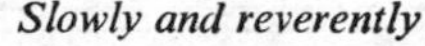
Slowly and reverently

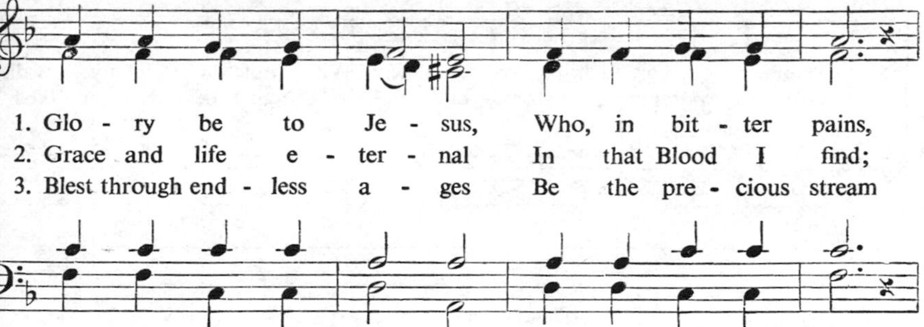
1. Glo - ry be to Je - sus, Who, in bit - ter pains,
2. Grace and life e - ter - nal In that Blood I find;
3. Blest through end - less a - ges Be the pre - cious stream

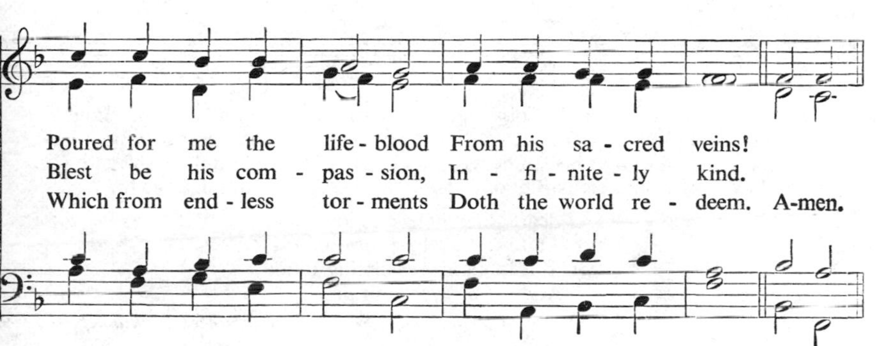
Poured for me the life - blood From his sa - cred veins!
Blest be his com - pas - sion, In - fi - nite - ly kind.
Which from end - less tor - ments Doth the world re - deem. A-men.

4 Abel's blood for vengeance
Pleaded to the skies;
But the Blood of Jesus
For our pardon cries.

5 Oft as earth exulting
Wafts its praise on high,
Angel-hosts, rejoicing,
Make their glad reply.

6 Lift we then our voices,
Swell the mighty flood;
Louder still and louder
Praise the precious Blood! Amen.

Italian, XVIII cent.
Tr. Edward Caswall, 1814–78

MEDITATION (GOWER). C. M. FIRST TUNE JOHN HENRY GOWER, 1855–1922

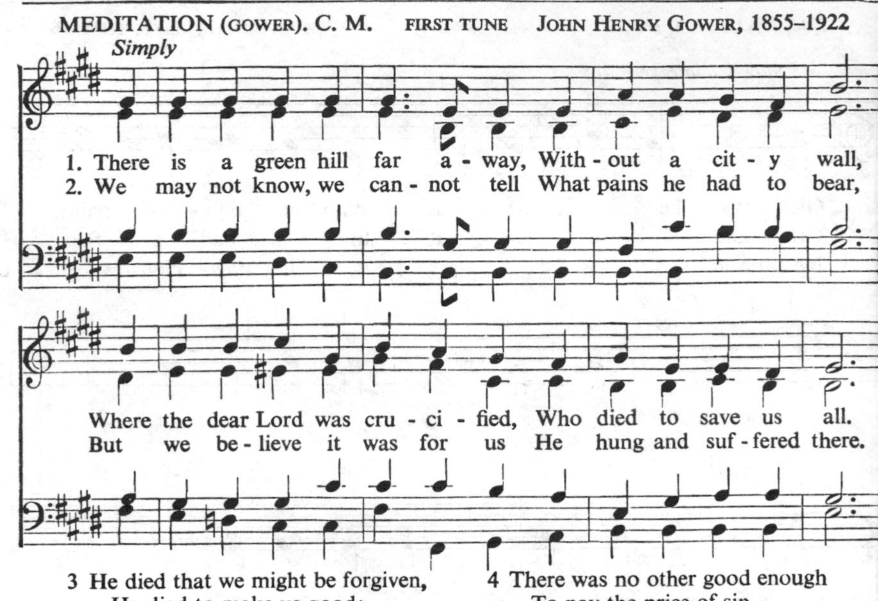
Simply
1. There is a green hill far a - way, With - out a cit - y wall,
2. We may not know, we can - not tell What pains he had to bear,
Where the dear Lord was cru - ci - fied, Who died to save us all.
But we be - lieve it was for us He hung and suf - fered there.

3 He died that we might be forgiven,
He died to make us good;
That we might go at last to heaven,
Saved by his precious Blood.

4 There was no other good enough
To pay the price of sin,
He only could unlock the gate
Of heaven, and let us in.

5 O dearly, dearly has he loved,
And we must love him too,
And trust in his redeeming Blood,
And try his works to do.

Cecil Frances Alexander, 1823–9

77

HORSLEY. C. M. SECOND TUNE WILLIAM HORSLEY, 1774–1858

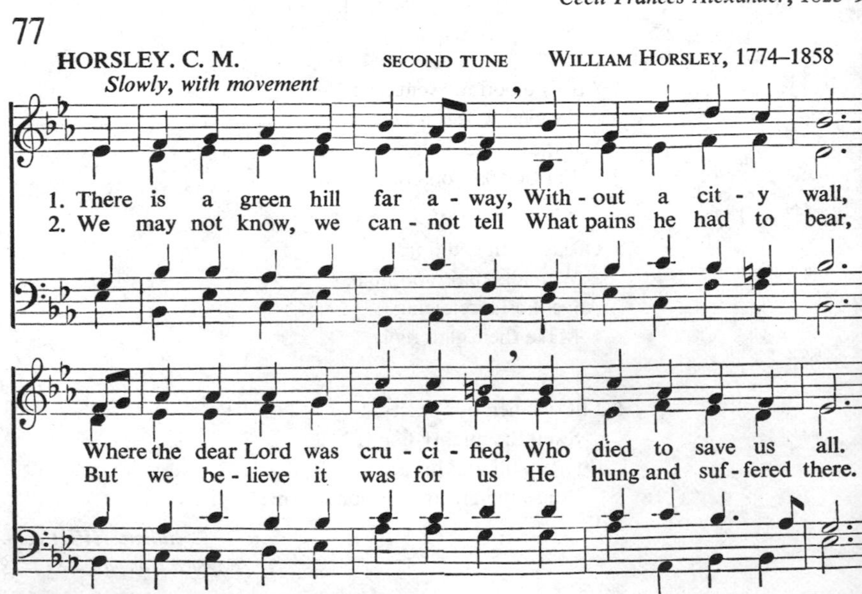
Slowly, with movement
1. There is a green hill far a - way, With - out a cit - y wall,
2. We may not know, we can - not tell What pains he had to bear,
Where the dear Lord was cru - ci - fied, Who died to save us all.
But we be - lieve it was for us He hung and suf - fered there.

PETRA (REDHEAD NO. 76). 7 7, 7 7, 7 7. RICHARD REDHEAD, 1820–1901

Moderately slow

1. Go to dark Geth-sem-a-ne, Ye that feel the tempt-er's power;
Your Re-deem-er's con-flict see, Watch with him one bit-ter hour;
Turn not from his griefs a-way, Learn of Je-sus Christ to pray.

2. Fol-low to the judg-ment-hall, View the Lord of life ar-raigned;
O the worm-wood and the gall! O the pangs his soul sus-tained!
Shun not suf-fering, shame, or loss; Learn of him to bear the cross. A-men.

3 Calvary's mournful mountain climb;
There, adoring at his feet,
Mark that miracle of time,
God's own Sacrifice complete;
'It is finished,' hear him cry;
Learn of Jesus Christ to die.

4 Early hasten to the tomb,
Where they laid his breathless clay;
All is solitude and gloom;
Who hath taken him away?
Christ is risen!—He meets our eyes;
Saviour, teach us so to rise. Amen.

James Montgomery, 1771–1854

JESU, MEINES LEBENS LEBEN. 8 7, 8 7, 7 7, 7 7.

With dignity and movement Darmstadt *Gesangbuch*, 1687

1. Christ, the Life of all the liv - ing, Christ the Death of death, our foe,
Who thy - self for us once giv - ing To the dark - est depths of woe,
Pa - tient - ly didst yield thy breath But to save my soul from death;
Praise and glo - ry ev - er be, Bless - ed Je - sus, un - to thee. A-men.

2 Thou, O Christ, hast taken on thee
Bitter strokes, a cruel rod;
Pain and scorn were heaped upon thee,
O thou sinless Son of God,
Only thus for me to win
Rescue from the bonds of sin;
Praise and glory ever be,
Blessèd Jesus, unto thee.

3 Thou didst bear the smiting only
That it might not fall on me;
Stoodest falsely charged and lonely
That I might be safe and free;
Comfortless that I might know
Comfort from thy boundless woe.
Praise and glory ever be,
Blessèd Jesus, unto thee.

4 Then for all that wrought our pardon,
For thy sorrows deep and sore,
For thine anguish in the garden,
I will thank thee evermore;
Thank thee with my latest breath
For thy sad and cruel death,
For that last and bitter cry
Praise thee evermore on high. Amen.

Ernst Christoph Homburg, 1605–81
Tr. Catherine Winkworth, 1829–78 a.

MARLEE. 6 6, 6 6, 8 8. LELAND B. SATEREN, 1913–

Unison. Devotionally with movement

1. Deep were his wounds, and red, On cru - el Cal - va - ry,
As on the Cross he bled In bit - ter ag - o - ny; But they, whom
sin has wound - ed sore, Find heal - ing in the wounds he bore.

2 He suffered shame and scorn,
And wretched, dire disgrace;
Forsaken and forlorn,
He hung there in our place.
But such as would from sin be free
Look to his Cross for victory.

3 His life, his all, he gave
When he was crucified;
Our burdened souls to save,
What fearful death he died!
But each of us, though dead in sin,
Through him eternal life may win.

William Johnson, 1906–

THE WORDS ON THE CROSS

PART I

'Father, forgive them; for they know not what they do'—Luke xxiii:34

SWEDISH LITANY. 7 7, 7 6. Swedish Melody, 1697

Solemnly

1. Je - sus, in thy dy - ing woes, E - ven while thy life-blood flows,
Crav - ing par - don for thy foes: Hear us, ho - ly Je - sus. A-men.

2 Saviour, for our pardon sue,
When our sins thy pangs renew,
For we know not what we do:
Hear us, holy Jesus.

3 O may we, who mercy need,
Be like thee in heart and deed,
When with wrong our spirits bleed:
Hear us, holy Jesus. Amen.

PART II

'Today shalt thou be with me in paradise'—Luke xxiii:43

1 Jesus, pitying the sighs
Of the thief, who near thee dies,
Promising him paradise:
Hear us, holy Jesus.

2 May we in our guilt and shame
Still thy love and mercy claim,
Calling humbly on thy Name:
Hear us, holy Jesus.

3 May our hearts to thee incline,
Looking from our cross to thine;
Cheer our souls with hope divine:
Hear us, holy Jesus. Amen.

PART III

'Woman, behold thy son!' 'Behold thy mother!'—John xix:26, 27

1 Jesus, loving to the end
Her whose heart thy sorrows rend,
And thy dearest human friend:
Hear us, holy Jesus.

2 May we in thy sorrows share,
For thy sake all peril dare,
And enjoy thy tender care:
Hear us, holy Jesus.

THE WORDS ON THE CROSS—Continued

3 May we all thy loved ones be,
All one holy family,
Loving for the love of thee:
Hear us, holy Jesus. Amen.

PART IV

'My God, my God, why hast thou forsaken me?'—Matt. xxvii:46

1 Jesus, whelmed in fears unknown,
With our evil left alone,
While no light from heaven is shown:
Hear us, holy Jesus.

2 When we seem in vain to pray,
And our hope seems far away,
In the darkness be our stay:
Hear us, holy Jesus.

3 Though no Father seem to hear,
Though no light our spirits cheer,
May we know that God is near:
Hear us, holy Jesus. Amen.

PART V

'I thirst'—John xix:28

1 Jesus, in thy thirst and pain,
While thy wounds thy life-blood drain,
Thirsting more our love to gain:
Hear us, holy Jesus.

2 Thirst for us in mercy still,
All thy holy work fulfill,
Satisfy thy loving will:
Hear us, holy Jesus.

3 May we thirst thy love to know;
Lead us in our sin and woe
Where the healing waters flow:
Hear us, holy Jesus. Amen.

PART VI

'It is finished'—John xix:30

1 Jesus, all our ransom paid,
All thy Father's will obeyed;
By thy sufferings perfect made:
Hear us, holy Jesus.

2 Save us in our soul's distress;
Be our help to cheer and bless,
While we grow in holiness:
Hear us, holy Jesus.

3 Brighten all our heavenward way
With an ever holier ray
Till we pass to perfect day:
Hear us, holy Jesus. Amen.

PART VII

'Father, into thy hands I commend my spirit'—Luke xxiii:46

1 Jesus, all thy labor vast,
All thy woe and conflict past;
Yielding up thy soul at last:
Hear us, holy Jesus.

2 When the death shades round us lower,
Guard us from the tempter's power,
Keep us in that trial hour:
Hear us, holy Jesus.

3 May thy life and death supply
Grace to live and grace to die,
Grace to reach the home on high:
Hear us, holy Jesus. Amen.

Thomas Benson Pollock, 1836–96

HOLY MOUNTAIN. 8 7, 8 7, 7 7. LUDVIG M. LINDEMAN, 1812–87

In flowing style

1. Come to Cal-vary's ho - ly moun-tain, Sin - ners, ru - ined by the fall;
2. Come in pov - er - ty and mean-ness, Come de - filed, with - out, with - in;
Here a pure and heal - ing foun-tain Flows to you, to me, to all;
From in - fec - tion and un-clean-ness, From the lep - ro - sy of sin,
In a full per - pet - ual tide, O-pened when our Sav - iour died.
Wash your robes and make them white; Ye shall walk with God in light.

3 Come in sorrow and contrition,
Wounded, impotent, and blind;
Here the guilty, free remission,
Here the troubled, peace may find:
Health this fountain will restore;
He that drinks shall thirst no more.

4 He that drinks shall live forever;
'Tis a soul-renewing flood:
God is faithful; God will never
Break his covenant of blood,
Signed when our Redeemer died,
Sealed when he was glorified.

James Montgomery, 1771–1854

This hymn may also be sung to DANA (No. 456).

See also:

WIGAN. 6 6 6 4, 8 8 4. SAMUEL SEBASTIAN WESLEY, 1810–76

Devotionally

1. Be - hold the Lamb of God! O thou for sin - ners slain,
2. Be - hold the Lamb of God! In - to the sa - cred flood
Let it not be in vain That thou hast died.
Of thy most pre - cious Blood My soul I cast;
Thee for my Sav - iour let me take, My on - ly ref - uge
Wash me and make me clean with - in, And keep me pure from
let me make Thy pierc - ed side!
ev - ery sin, Till life be past. A-men.

3 Behold the Lamb of God!
All hail, incarnate Word!
Thou everlasting Lord,
Saviour most blest!
Fill us with love that never faints,
Grant us, with all thy blessèd saints,
Eternal rest.

4 Behold the Lamb of God!
Worthy is he alone
To sit upon the throne
Of God above,
One with the Ancient of all days,
One with the Comforter in praise,
All Light, all Love! Amen.

Matthew Bridges, 1800–94 ***a.***

STABAT MATER (MAINZ). 8 8 7. D. Mainz *Gesangbuch*, 1661

Slowly, with dignity
1. At the Cross, her sta - tion keep - ing, Stood the mourn - ful
For her soul, of joy be - reav - ed, Bowed with an - guish,
2. O, how sad and sore dis - tress - ed Now was she, that
Deep the woe of her af - flic - tion, When she saw the
moth - er weep - ing, Where he hung, the dy - ing Lord;
deep - ly griev - ed, Felt the sharp and pierc - ing sword.
moth - er bless - ed Of the sole - be - got - ten One.
cru - ci - fix - ion Of her ev - er - glo - rious Son. A-men.

3 Who, on Christ's dear mother gazing,
Pierced by anguish so amazing,
Born of woman, would not weep?
Who, on Christ's dear mother thinking,
Such a cup of sorrow drinking,
Would not share her sorrows deep?

4 For his people's sins chastisèd,
She beheld her Son despisèd,
Scourged, and crowned with thorns entwined;
Saw him then from judgment taken,
And in death by all forsaken,
Till his spirit he resigned.

5 Jesus, may her deep devotion
Stir in me the same emotion,
Fount of love, Redeemer kind,
That my heart, fresh ardor gaining
And a purer love attaining,
May with thee acceptance find. Amen.

XIII cen
Tr. Edward Caswall, 1814–78, and other

HERZLIEBSTER JESU. 11 11 11, 5.
JOHANN CRÜGER, 1598–1662
Slowly and solemnly
1. Ah, holy Jesus, how hast thou offended, That man to judge thee hath in hate pretended? By foes derided, by thine own rejected, O most afflicted.
2. Who was the guilty? Who brought this upon thee? Alas, my treason, Jesus, hath undone thee. 'Twas I, Lord Jesus, I it was denied thee: I crucified thee. Amen.

3 Lo, the good Shepherd for the sheep is offered;
The slave hath sinnèd, and the Son hath suffered;
For man's atonement, while he nothing heedeth,
God intercedeth.

4 For me, kind Jesus, was thine Incarnation,
Thy mortal sorrow, and thy life's oblation;
Thy death of anguish and thy bitter Passion,
For my salvation.

5 Therefore, kind Jesus, since I cannot pay thee,
I do adore thee, and will ever pray thee,
Think on thy pity and thy love unswerving,
Not my deserving. Amen.

Johann Heermann, 1585–1647
Tr. Robert Bridges, 1844–1930

ST. CROSS. L. M. JOHN BACCHUS DYKES, 1823–76

Slowly
1. O come and mourn with me a - while; O come ye to the Sav - iour's side; O come, to - geth - er let us mourn: Je - sus, our Lord, is cru - ci - fied.
2. Have we no tears to shed for him, While sol - diers scoff and foes de - ride? Ah! look how pa - tient - ly he hangs: Je - sus, our Lord, is cru - ci - fied.

3 Seven times he spake, seven words of love;
And all three hours his silence cried
For mercy on the souls of men:
Jesus, our Lord, is crucified.

4 O love of God, O sin of man!
In this dread act your strength is tried,
And victory remains with love:
For he, our Love, is crucified!

Frederick William Faber, 1814–63

87 Good Friday

O TRAURIGKEIT. 4 4, 7 7 6.
Mainz, 1628
Tenderly
1. O dark - est woe! Ye tears, forth flow! Has earth so sad a won - der? God the Fa - ther's on - ly Son Now lies bur - ied yon - der.
2. O sin - ful man, It was the ban Of death on thee that brought him Down to suf - fer for thy sins, And such woe hath wrought him. A - men.

3 Behold thy Lord,
The Lamb of God
Blood-sprinkled lies before thee,
Pouring out his life that he
May to life restore thee.

4 O Jesus blest,
My help and rest!
With tears I pray, Lord hear me,
Make me love thee to the last,
And in death be near me. Amen.

St. 1, Anonymous
St. 2–4, Johann Rist, 1607–67
Tr. Catherine Winkworth, 1829–78

PASSION CHORALE. 7 6, 7 6. D. HANS LEO HASSLER, 1564–1612

FIRST TUNE

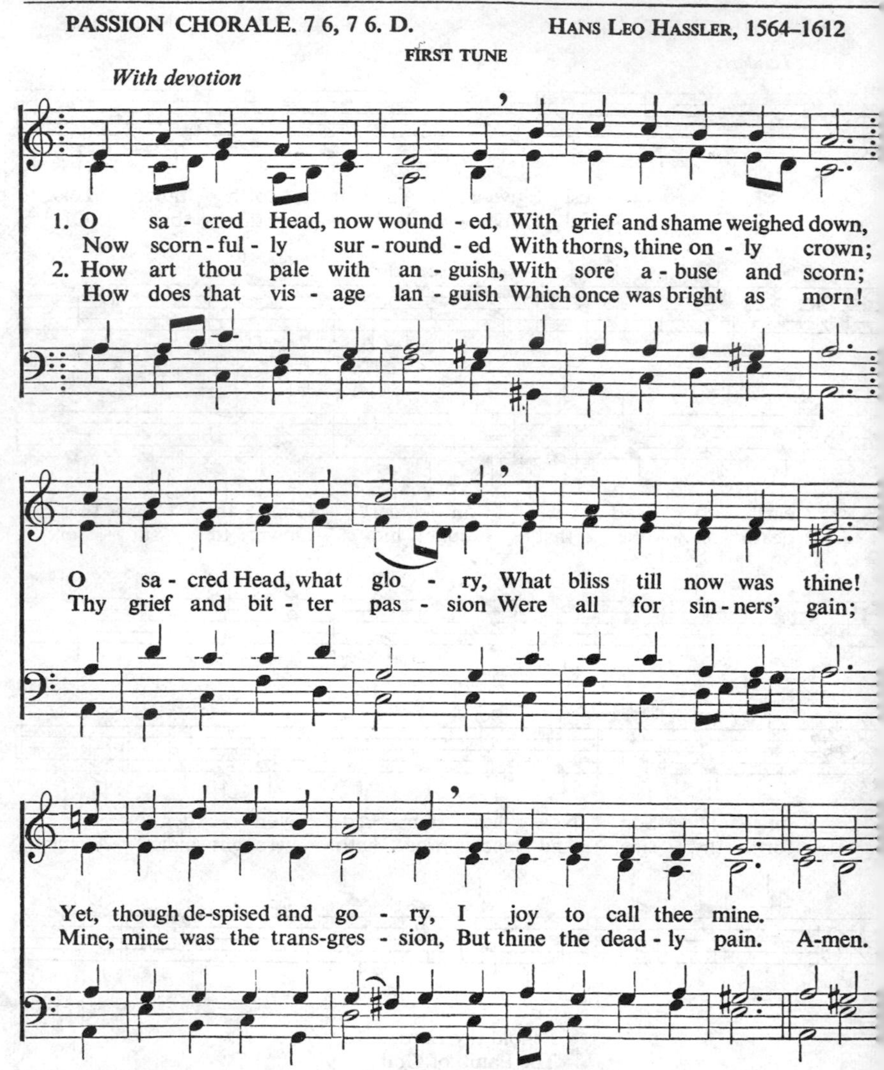
With devotion
1. O sa - cred Head, now wound - ed, With grief and shame weighed down,
Now scorn - ful - ly sur - round - ed With thorns, thine on - ly crown;
2. How art thou pale with an - guish, With sore a - buse and scorn;
How does that vis - age lan - guish Which once was bright as morn!
O sa - cred Head, what glo - ry, What bliss till now was thine!
Thy grief and bit - ter pas - sion Were all for sin - ners' gain;
Yet, though de-spised and go - ry, I joy to call thee mine.
Mine, mine was the trans-gres - sion, But thine the dead - ly pain. A-men.

3 What language shall I borrow
To thank thee, dearest friend,
For this thy dying sorrow,
Thy pity without end?
O make me thine for ever,
And should I fainting be,
Lord, let me never, never
Outlive my love to thee.

4 Be near when I am dying,
O show thy Cross to me!
And, for my succor flying,
Come, Lord, to set me free.
These eyes, new faith receiving,
From thee shall never move;
For he who dies believing
Dies safely in thy love. Amen.

Ascribed to St. Bernard of Clairvaux, 1091–115
Paul Gerhardt, 1607–7
Tr. James Waddell Alexander, 1804–59

PASSION CHORALE. 7 6, 7 6. D.

HANS LEO HASSLER, 1564–1612
Adapted and harm. by J. S. BACH, 1685–1750

SECOND TUNE

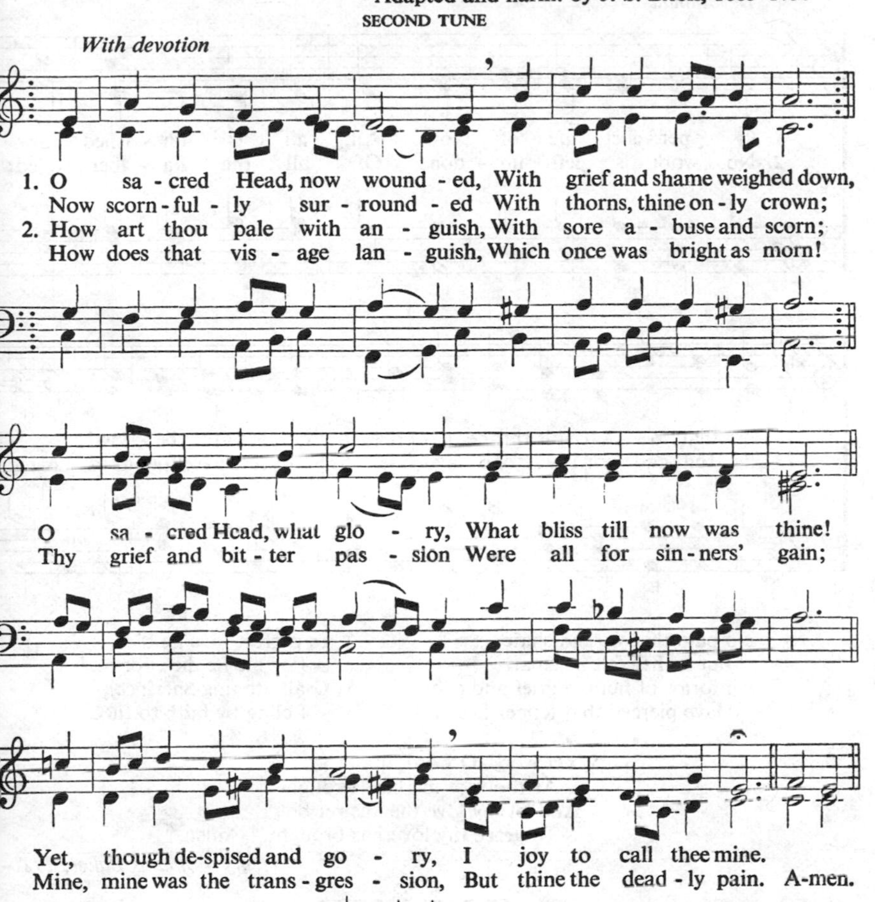
With devotion
1. O sa - cred Head, now wound - ed, With grief and shame weighed down,
Now scorn - ful - ly sur - round - ed With thorns, thine on - ly crown;
2. How art thou pale with an - guish, With sore a - buse and scorn;
How does that vis - age lan - guish, Which once was bright as morn!
O sa - cred Head, what glo - ry, What bliss till now was thine!
Thy grief and bit - ter pas - sion Were all for sin - ners' gain;
Yet, though de-spised and go - ry, I joy to call thee mine.
Mine, mine was the trans - gres - sion, But thine the dead - ly pain. A-men.

3 What language shall I borrow
  To thank thee, dearest friend,
For this thy dying sorrow,
  Thy pity without end?
O make me thine for ever
  And should I fainting be,
Lord, let me never, never
  Outlive my love to thee.

4 Be near when I am dying
  O show thy Cross to me!
And, for my succor flying,
  Come, Lord, to set me free.
These eyes, new faith receiving,
  From thee shall never move;
For he who dies believing
  Dies safely in thy love. Amen.

Ascribed to St. Bernard of Clairvaux, 1091–1153
Paul Gerhardt, 1607–76
Tr. James Waddell Alexander, 1804–59 a.

89

GORTON. S. M. Arr. LUDVIG VON BEETHOVEN, 1770–1827

Devotionally

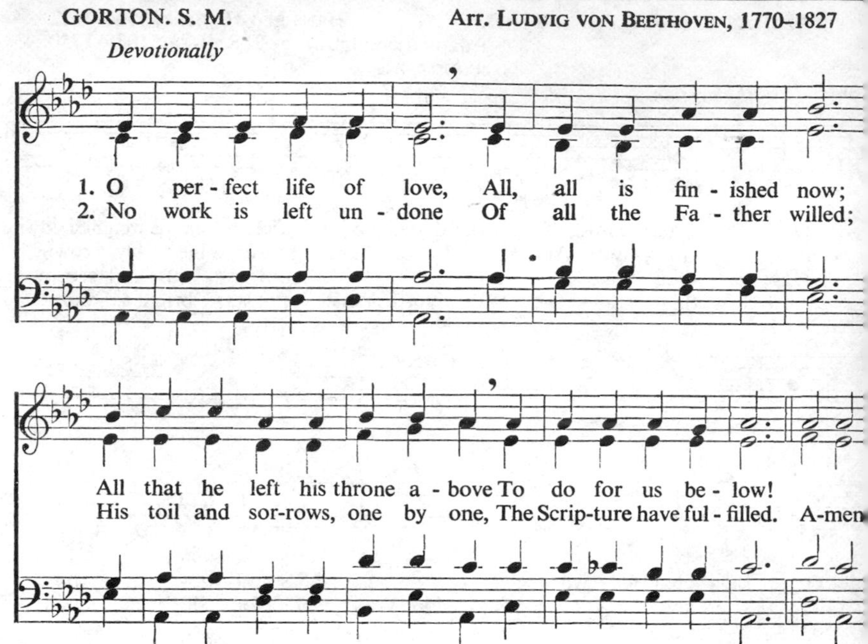
1. O per - fect life of love, All, all is fin - ished now;
2. No work is left un - done Of all the Fa - ther willed;
All that he left his throne a - bove To do for us be - low!
His toil and sor-rows, one by one, The Scrip-ture have ful - filled. A-men

3 No pain that we can share
But he has felt its smart;
All forms of human grief and care
Have pierced that tender heart.

4 In perfect love he dies;
For me he dies, for me!
O all-atoning Sacrifice,
I cling by faith to thee.

5 Yet work, O Lord, in me,
As thou for me hast wrought;
And let my love the answer be
To grace thy love has brought. Amen.

Henry Williams Baker, 1821–

See also:

486 Alas! and did my Saviour
482 Beneath the Cross of Jesus
80 Deep were his wounds
568 If thou but suffer God
64 In the Cross of Christ
512 Jesus, I my cross have taken
81 Jesus, in thy dying woes
370 Just as I am
580 My Jesus, as thou wilt
577 Nearer, my God, to thee
541 Rise up, O men of God
373 There is a fountain filled
77 There is a green hill
494 We sing the praise of him
503 When I survey

For Easter Eve, see:

482 Beneath the Cross of Jesus
413 Come, let us join our cheerful songs
435 Hail, thou once despisèd Jesus
87 O darkest woe

EASTER

90

VICTORY. 8 8 8. With Alleluias. GIOVANNI PIERLUIGI DA PALESTRINA, 1525–94
Adapted by WILLIAM HENRY MONK, 1823–89
Alleliuas by WILLIAM HENRY MONK, 1823–89

Broadly, with dignity

Al - le - lu - ia! Al - le - lu - ia! Al - le - lu - ia!
Org.
1. The strife is o'er, the bat - tle done; Now is the Vic - tor's
2. The powers of death have done their worst, But Christ their le - gions
3. The three sad days have quick - ly sped, He ris - es glo - rious
tri - umph won; Now be the song of praise be - gun, Al - le - lu - ia!
hath dis-persed; Let shouts of ho - ly joy out-burst, Al - le - lu - ia!
from the dead; All glo - ry to our ris - en Head! Al - le - lu - ia!

4 He brake the age-bound chains of hell,
The bars from heaven's high portals fell;
Let hymns of praise his triumph tell.
Alleluia!

5 Lord, by the stripes which wounded thee,
From death's dread sting thy servants free,
That we may live and sing to thee,
Alleluia!
Alleluia! Alleluia! Alleluia!

Latin, XVII cent.
Tr. Francis Pott, 1832–1909

ST. GEORGE'S, WINDSOR. 7 7, 7 7. D. GEORGE JOB ELVEY, 1816–93

With spirit
1. Christ the Lord is risen to-day, Sons of men and an-gels say;
Raise your joys and tri-umphs high, Sing, ye heavens, and earth, re-ply.
Love's re-deem-ing work is done, Fought the fight, the bat-tle won;
Lo! the Sun's e-clipse is o'er, Lo! he sets in blood no more. A-men

2 Vain the stone, the watch, the seal,
Christ hath burst the gates of hell;
Death in vain forbids his rise,
Christ hath opened Paradise.
Lives again our glorious King,
Where, O death, is now thy sting?
Once he died our souls to save,
Where thy victory, O grave?

3 Soar we now where Christ hath led,
Following our exalted Head:
Made like him, like him we rise;
Ours the cross, the grave, the skies.
Hail the Lord of earth and heaven,
Praise to thee by both be given;
Thee we greet triumphant now,
Hail, the Resurrection Thou! Amen.

Charles Wesley, 1707–

EASTER HYMN (WORGAN). 7 7, 7 7. With Alleluias. *Lyra Davidica*, 1708

With dignity

1. Je - sus Christ is risen to - day, Al - - le - lu - ia!
2. Hymns of praise then let us sing, Al - - le - lu - ia!
Our tri - um-phant ho - ly day, Al - - le - lu - ia!
Un - to Christ, our heaven-ly King, Al - - le - lu - ia!
Who did once, up - on the Cross, Al - - le - lu - ia!
Who en - dured the Cross and grave, Al - - le - lu - ia!
Suf - fer to re - deem our loss. Al - le - lu - ia!
Sin - ners to re - deem and save. Al - le - lu - ia! A-men.

3 But the pains which he endured, Alleluia!
Our salvation have procured, Alleluia!
Now above the sky he's King, Alleluia!
Where the angels ever sing. Alleluia!

4 Sing we to our God above, Alleluia!
Praise eternal as his love; Alleluia!
Praise him, all ye heavenly host, Alleluia!
Father, Son, and Holy Ghost. Alleluia!
Amen.

Latin, XIV cent.
Tr. Lyra Davidica, 1708
St. 4, Charles Wesley, 1707–88

FORTUNATUS. 11 11, 11 11. With Refrain. ARTHUR S. SULLIVAN, 1842–1900

Brightly
1. 'Wel - come, hap - py morn - ing!' age to age shall say,
2. Earth with joy con - fess - es, cloth - ing her for spring,
'Hell to - day is van-quished, heaven is won to - day!'
All good gifts re - turn with her re - turn - ing King;
Lo! the dead is liv - ing, God for ev - er - more!
Bloom in ev - ery mea - dow, leaves on ev - ery bough,
Him, their true Cre - a - tor, all his works a - dore.
Speak his sor - rows end - ed, hail his tri - umph now.

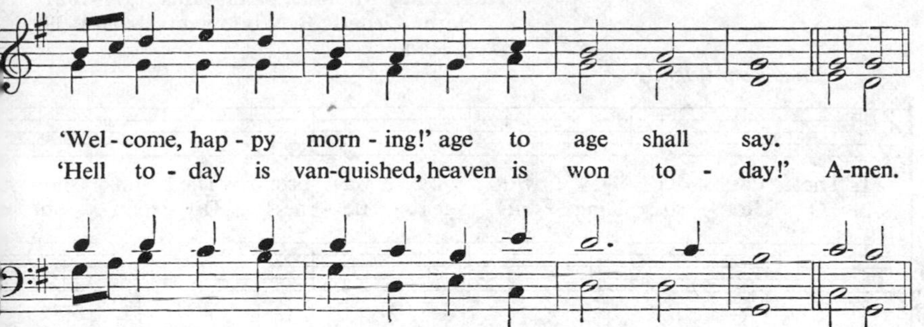
'Wel - come, hap - py morn - ing!' age to age shall say.
'Hell to - day is van-quished, heaven is won to - day!' A-men.

3 Months in due succession, days of lengthening light,
Hours and passing moments praise thee in their flight;
Brightness of the morning, sky and fields and sea,
Vanquisher of darkness, bring their praise to thee:
'Welcome, happy morning!' age to age shall say.

4 Maker and Redeemer, life and health of all,
Thou from heaven beholding man's abasing fall,
Of the Eternal Father true and only Son,
Manhood to deliver, manhood didst put on:
'Hell today is vanquished, heaven is won today!'

5 Thou, of life the author, death didst undergo,
Tread the path of darkness, saving strength to show;
Come then, true and faithful, now fulfil thy word;
'Tis thine own third morning; rise, O buried Lord!
'Welcome, happy morning!' age to age shall say.

6 Loose the souls long prisoned, bound with Satan's chain;
All that now is fallen raise to life again;
Show thy face in brightness, bid the nations see;
Bring again our daylight; day returns with thee;
'Hell today is vanquished, heaven is won today!' Amen.

Venantius Fortunatus, 530–609
Tr. John Ellerton, 1826–93

PUER NOBIS. L. M.

Plainsong Melody
Adapted by MICHAEL PRAETORIUS, 1571–1621
Harm. GEORGE R. WOODWARD, 1848–1939

FIRST TUNE

In unison. Brightly

1. That Eas - ter Day with joy was bright, The sun shone out with fair - er light, When, to their long - ing eyes re - stored, The A - pos - tles saw their ris - en Lord.
2. O Je - sus, King of gen - tle - ness, Do thou our in - most hearts pos - sess; And we to thee will ev - er raise The trib - ute of our grate - ful praise. A - men.

3 Jesus, who art the Lord of all,
In this our Easter festival,
From every weapon death can wield,
Thine own redeemed, thy people, shield!

4 All praise, O risen Lord, we give
To thee, who, dead, again dost live;
To God the Father equal praise,
And God the Holy Ghost, we raise.
Amen

Latin hymn, IV or V cen.
Tr. John Mason Neale, 1818–66

Tune from THE COWLEY CAROL BOOK (*Mowbrays*).

94

CLARO PASCHALI GAUDIO.
Plainsong, Mode VIII
SECOND TUNE
1. That Eas - ter Day with joy was bright, The sun shone out with fair - er light, . . When, to their long - ing eyes re - stored, The A - pos - tles saw their ris - en Lord.
2. O Je - sus, King of gen - tle - ness, Do thou our in - most hearts pos - sess; . . And we to thee will ev - er raise The trib - ute of our grate - ful praise. A - men.

3 Jesus, who art the Lord of all,
In this our Easter festival,
From every weapon death can wield,
Thine own redeemed, thy people, shield!

4 All praise, O risen Lord, we give
To thee, who, dead, again dost live;
To God the Father equal praise,
And God the Holy Ghost, we raise.
Amen.

Latin hymn, IV or V cent.
Tr. John Mason Neale, 1818–66 a.

SALZBURG (ALLE MENSCHEN). 7 7, 7 7. D.
JAKOB HINTZE, 1622–1702
With vigor
FIRST TUNE
Harm. by J. S. BACH, 1685–1750
1. At the Lamb's high feast we sing Praise to our vic - to - rious King,
2. Where the Pas - chal Blood is poured, Death's dark an - gel sheathes his sword;
Who hath washed us in the tide Flow - ing from his pierc - ed side;
Is - rael's hosts tri - umph - ant go Through the wave that drowns the foe.
Praise we him, whose love di - vine Gives his sa - cred Blood for wine,
Praise we Christ, whose Blood was shed, Pas - chal vic - tim, Pas - chal bread;
Gives his Bod - y for the feast, Christ the vic - tim, Christ the priest.
With sin - cer - i - ty and love Eat we man - na from a - bove. A-men.

3 Mighty victim from the sky,
Hell's fierce powers beneath thee lie;
Thou hast conquered in the fight,
Thou hast brought us life and light;
Now no more can death appall,
Now no more the grave enthrall;
Thou hast opened paradise,
And in thee thy saints shall rise.

4 Paschal triumph, Paschal joy,
Sin alone can this destroy;
From sin's power do thou set free
Souls new-born, O Lord, in thee.
Hymns of glory, songs of praise,
Father, unto thee we raise:
Risen Lord, all praise to thee
With the Spirit ever be. Amen.

Based on the Lati
Tr. Robert Campbell, 1814–68 a

TICHFIELD. 7 7, 7 7. D. SECOND TUNE JOHN RICHARDSON, 1816–79

In moderate time

1. At the Lamb's high feast we sing Praise to our vic - to - rious King,
2. Where the Pas - chal Blood is poured, Death's dark an - gel sheathes his sword;
Who hath washed us in the tide Flow - ing from his pierc - ed side;
Is - rael's hosts tri - um - phant go Through the wave that drowns the foe.
Praise we him, whose love di - vine Gives his sa - cred Blood for wine,
Praise we Christ, whose Blood was shed, Pas - chal vic - tim, Pas - chal bread;
Gives his Bod - y for the feast, Christ the vic - tim, Christ the priest.
With sin - cer - i - ty and love Eat we man - na from a - bove. A-men.

3 Mighty victim from the sky,
Hell's fierce powers beneath thee lie;
Thou hast conquered in the fight,
Thou hast brought us life and light;
Now no more can death appall,
Now no more the grave enthrall;
Thou hast opened paradise,
And in thee thy saints shall rise.

4 Paschal triumph, Paschal joy,
Sin alone can this destroy;
From sin's power do thou set free
Souls new-born, O Lord, in thee.
Hymns of glory, songs of praise,
Father, unto thee we raise:
Risen Lord, all praise to thee
With the Spirit ever be. Amen.

Based on the Latin
Tr. Robert Campbell, 1814–68 a.

O FILII ET FILIAE. 8 8 8. With Alleluias. XV cent. French Melody, Mode II

In unison
Al - le - lu - ia! Al - le - lu - ia! Al - - le - lu - ia!
1. O sons and daugh-ters, let us sing! The King of heaven, the glo - rious King, O'er death to - day rose tri - umph - ing. Al - - - - le - lu - ia!
2. That Eas - ter morn, at break of day, The faith - ful wo - men went their way To seek the tomb where Je - sus lay. Al - - - - le - lu - ia!
3. An an - gel clad in white they see, Who sat, and spake un - to the three, 'Your Lord doth go to Gal - i - lee.' Al - - - - le - lu - ia!

4 That night the apostles met in fear;
Amidst them came their Lord most dear,
And said, 'My peace be on all here.'
Alleluia!

5 When Thomas first the tidings heard,
How they had seen the risen Lord,
He doubted the disciples' word.
Alleluia!

6 'My piercèd side, O Thomas, see;
My hands, my feet, I show to thee;
Not faithless, but believing be.'
Alleluia!

7 No longer Thomas then denied;
He saw the feet, the hands, the side;
'Thou art my Lord and God,' he cried.
Alleluia!

8 How blest are they who have not seen,
And yet whose faith has constant been,
For they eternal life shall win.
Alleluia!

9 On this most holy day of days,
To God your hearts and voices raise
In laud and jubilee and praise.
Alleluia!
Alleluia! Alleluia! Alleluia!

Jean Tisserand, †1494
Tr. John Mason Neale, 1818–66

97

HAWARDEN. 6 6, 6 5. D. — SAMUEL SEBASTIAN WESLEY, 1810–76

In moderate time

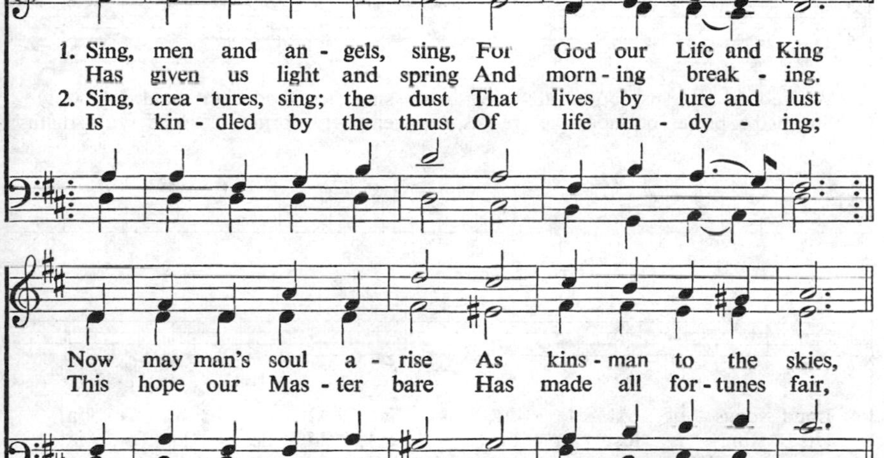

1. Sing, men and an - gels, sing, For God our Life and King
Has given us light and spring And morn - ing break - ing.
2. Sing, crea - tures, sing; the dust That lives by lure and lust
Is kin - dled by the thrust Of life un - dy - ing;
Now may man's soul a - rise As kins - man to the skies,
This hope our Mas - ter bare Has made all for - tunes fair,
And God un - seals his eyes To an a - wak - ing.
And man can on and dare, His death de - fy - ing.

3 After the winter snows
A wind of healing blows,
And thorns put forth a rose
And lilies cheer us;
Life's everlasting spring
Hath robbed death of his sting,
Henceforth a cry can bring
Our Master near us.

John Masefield, 1878–

CHRIST LAG IN TODESBANDEN. 8 7, 8 7, 7 8, 7 4.

Geistliches Gesangbüchlein, Wittenberg 1524

FIRST TUNE

Majestically

1. Christ Je - sus lay in death's strong bands For our of - fenc - es giv - en;
But now at God's right hand he stands, And brings us life from heav - en;
2. It was a strange and dread-ful strife When Life and death con - tend - ed;
The vic - to - ry re-mained with Life, The reign of death was end - ed;
Where-fore let us joy - ful be, And sing to God right thank-ful - ly
Stripped of power, no more he reigns, An emp - ty form a - lone re - mains;
Loud songs of Al - le - lu - ia! Al - le - lu - ia!
His sting is lost for ev - er! Al - le - lu - ia!

3 So let us keep the festival
Whereto the Lord invites us;
Christ is himself the joy of all,
The Sun that warms and lights us;
By his grace he doth impart
Eternal sunshine to the heart;
The night of sin is ended!
Alleluia!

4 Then let us feast this Easter Day
On the true Bread of heaven;
The Word of grace hath purged away
The old and wicked leaven;
Christ alone our souls will feed,
He is our meat and drink indeed,
Faith lives upon no other!
Alleluia!

Martin Luther, 1483–1546
Based on the Sequence Victimae Paschali
Tr. Richard Massie, 1800–87

CHRIST LAG IN TODESBANDEN. 8 7, 8 7, 7 8, 7 4.

Geistliches Gesangbüchlein, Wittenberg 1524
Harm. J. S. Bach, 1685–1750

SECOND TUNE

Majestically

1. Christ Je-sus lay in death's strong bands For our of - fenc - es giv - en;
But now at God's right hand he stands, And brings us life from heav - en;
2. It was a strange and dread-ful strife When Life and death con - tend - ed;
The vic - to - ry re-mained with Life, The reign of death was end - ed;

Where-fore let us joy - ful be, And sing to God right thank-ful - ly
Stripped of power, no more he reigns, An emp - ty form a - lone re-mains;

Loud songs of Al - le - lu - ia! Al - le - lu - ia!
His sting is lost for ev - er! Al - le - lu - ia!

3 So let us keep the festival
Whereto the Lord invites us;
Christ is himself the joy of all,
The Sun that warms and lights us;
By his grace he doth impart
Eternal sunshine to the heart;
The night of sin is ended!
Alleluia!

4 Then let us feast this Easter Day
On the true Bread of heaven;
The Word of grace hath purged away
The old and wicked leaven;
Christ alone our souls will feed,
He is our meat and drink indeed,
Faith lives upon no other!
Alleluia!

Martin Luther, 1483–1546
Based on the Sequence Victimae Paschali
Tr. Richard Massie, 1800–87

LLANFAIR. 7 7, 7 7. With Alleluias.
ROBERT WILLIAMS, cir. 1781–1821
Broadly, with dignity
1. Christ, the Lord, is risen to - day; Al - le - lu - ia!
2. For the sheep the Lamb hath bled, Al - le - lu - ia!
3. Christ, the Vic - tim un - de - filed, Al - le - lu - ia!
Chris - tians, haste your vows to pay; Al - le - lu - ia!
Sin - less in the sin - ner's stead; Al - le - lu - ia!
God and man hath rec - on - ciled; Al - le - lu - ia!
Of - fer ye your prais - es meet, Al - le - lu - ia!
Christ is risen, to - day we cry; Al - le - lu - ia!
Whilst in strange and aw - ful strife, Al - le - lu - ia!
Voices in unison
At the Pas-chal Vic-tim's feet. Al - le - lu - ia!
Now he lives no more to die. Al - le - lu - ia!
Met to - geth - er death and Life. Al - le - lu - ia! A - men.

Christians, on this happy day, Alleluia!
Haste with joy your vows to pay; Alleluia!
Christ is risen, today we cry; Alleluia!
Now he lives no more to die. Alleluia!

5 Christ who once for sinners bled, Alleluia!
Now the first-born from the dead, Alleluia!
Throned in endless might and power, Alleluia!
Lives and reigns for evermore. Alleluia!

6 Hail, Eternal Hope on high! Alleluia!
Hail, thou King of Victory! Alleluia!
Hail, thou Prince of Life adored! Alleluia!
Help and save us, gracious Lord. Alleluia! Amen.

Latin Sequence, Victimae Paschali
Tr. Jane Eliza Leeson, 1807–82

00

EASTER GLORY (FRED TIL BOD). 7 7, 7 7, 7 7.
Triumphantly
LUDVIG MATTHIAS LINDEMAN, 1812–87

1. Al - le - lu - ia! Je - sus lives! Won the bat - tle glo - ri - ous!
From the gloom-y vault of death He hath come vic - to - ri - ous,
Lead-ing to their heaven-ly home Count-less mul - ti - tudes to come. A-men.

2 Alleluia! O my soul,
Life eternal waits for thee;
Saved by him, the Living One,
Where he is, thou too shalt be,
Safe within the promised land,
With the Lord at God's right hand.

3 Alleluia! heavenly choirs
Joyfully their voices raise!
Let us mortals here below
Blend with theirs our songs of praise.
Glory to the eternal Son!
Glory to the Risen One! Amen.

Carl B. Garve, 1763–1841
Tr. Laurence N. Field, 1896–

WIE SCHÖN LEUCHTET. Irregular. PHILIPP NICOLAI, 1556–1608

With movement

Our Lord is ris - en from the dead, And rays of glo - ry crown his head, New hope has come to mor - tals.
He rose in power to smite his foes, He lives to free us from our woes And o - pen heav - en's por - tals.
O sing, our King now is ris - en! Come and lis - ten To the sto - ry, Christ the Lord is risen in glo - ry!

Birgitte Cathrine Boye, 1742–18
Tr. Fred C. M. Hansen, 188

LOB SEI DEM ALLMÄCHTIGEN GOTT. L. M.

With dignity JOHANN CRÜGER, 1598–1662

1. O Pas - chal Feast, what joy is thine! We praise, dear Lord,
2. The Tree where thou wast of - fered up Now bears the fruit
thy Name di - vine, For thou hast tri - umphed o'er the tomb;
of life and hope; Thy pre - cious Blood for us was shed
No more we need to dread its gloom.
That we might eat of heaven - ly bread. A - men.

3 We thank thee, Jesus, that thy hand
Hath freed us from sin's galling band;
No more its bondage need we fear,
The year of liberty is here.

4 O Paschal Lamb, God's holy Son,
Through whom redemption now is won,
Thou givest saving strength indeed
In all our conflicts, all our need.

5 As thou didst rise on Easter Day,
Help us to rise from sin, we pray;
And at the end of earthly strife
Raise us, O Lord, to endless life. Amen.

Early Latin Hymn
Tr. Olavus Petri, 1493–1552
Tr. George Henry Trabert, 1843–1931 a.

This hymn may also be sung to SPLENDOR PATERNAE (No. 206).

LASST UNS ERFREUEN. 8 8, 4 4, 8 8, 4 4. With Alleluias.

Geistliche Kirchengesänge, Cologne 1623

In unison; boldly

1. Now let the vault of heaven re - sound In praise of Love that
2. E - ter - nal is the gift he brings, Where - fore our heart with
doth a - bound, 'Christ hath tri - umphed, al - le - lu - ia;'
rap - ture sings, 'Christ hath tri - umphed, Je - sus liv - eth!'
Sing, choirs of an - gels, loud and clear, Re - peat their song
Now doth he come and give us life, Now doth his pres -

of glo - ry here, 'Christ hath tri-umphed, Christ hath tri-umphed!'
ence still all strife Through his tri - umph; Je - sus reign - eth!
Al - le - lu - ia, al - le - lu - ia, al - le - lu - ia.
Al - le - lu - ia, al - le - lu - ia, al - le - lu - ia. A-men.

3 O fill us, Lord, with dauntless love;
Set heart and will on things above
That we conquer through thy triumph,
Grant grace sufficient for life's day
That by our life we ever say,
'Christ hath triumphed, and he liveth!'
Alleluia, alleluia, alleluia.

4 Adoring praises now we bring
And with the heavenly blessèd sing,
'Christ hath triumphed, Alleluia!'
Be to the Father, and our Lord,
To Spirit blest, most holy God,
Thine the glory never ending!
Alleluia, alleluia, alleluia! Amen.

Paul Zeller Strodach, 1876–1947

RIDDARHOLM (UPP, MIN TUNGA). 8 7, 8 7, 8 7.
Swedish *Koralbok*, 1697
Triumphantly
1. Praise the Sav - iour, now and ev - er, Praise him, all be -
2. Day of glad - ness, gone is sad - ness; Christ hath bruised the
neath the skies; Come be - fore him, and a - dore him,
ser - pent's head; Death no long - er is the strong - er,
God's own per - fect Sac - ri - fice; Vic - tory gain - ing,
Hell it - self is cap - tive led. Christ our Sav - iour
life ob - tain - ing, Now in glo - ry he doth rise.
lives for - ev - er, O'er the tomb his light is shed. A-men.

3 Anthems glorious, hymns victorious,
Raise we to our Paschal King;
Bonds are broken, heaven is open,
Sing, ye ransomed mortals, sing!
Christ is risen from death's prison
Healing in his wings to bring.

4 Earth rejoices, all its voices
Glory to the Father sing;
Praise the Saviour, laud him ever,
Son of God, our Lord and King;
Praise the Spirit, through Christ's merit
Life eternal he doth bring. Amen.

Swedish hymn based on Venantius Fortunatus, 530-6(
Tr. Hymnal Version, 19.

105 Easter

ROTTERDAM. 7 6, 7 6. D. — BERTHOLD TOURS, 1838–97

With movement

1. The Day of Res - ur - rec - tion, Earth, tell it out a - broad;
The Pass - o - ver of glad - ness, The Pass - o - ver of God!
From death to life e - ter - nal, From earth un - to the sky,
Our Christ hath brought us o - ver With hymns of vic - to - ry.

2 Our hearts be pure from evil,
   That we may see aright
The Lord in rays eternal
   Of resurrection light;
And, listening to his accents,
   May hear so calm and plain
His own 'All hail,' and, hearing,
   May raise the victor strain.

3 Now let the heavens be joyful,
   Let earth her song begin,
The round world keep high triumph,
   And all that is therein;
In grateful exultation
   Their notes let all things blend,
For Christ the Lord hath risen,
   Our joy that hath no end!

St. John of Damascus, VIII cent.
Tr. John Mason Neale, 1818–66 a.

This hymn may also be sung to LANCASHIRE (No. 550).

ST. KEVIN. 7 6, 7 6. D. Trochaic. ARTHUR S. SULLIVAN, 1842–1900

With movement
FIRST TUNE
1. Come, ye faith-ful, raise the strain Of tri-um-phant glad-ness;
2. Now the queen of sea-sons, bright With the day of splen-dor,
God hath brought his Is-ra-el In-to joy from sad-ness;
With the roy-al feast of feasts, Comes its joy to ren-der;
'Tis the spring of souls to-day: Christ hath burst his pris-on,
Comes to glad-den Chris-tian men, Who with true af-fec-tion
And from three days' sleep in death, As a sun hath ris-en.
Wel-come in un-wea-ried strains Je-sus' res-ur-rec-tion.

3 All the winter of our sins,
  Long and dark, is flying
From his light, to whom we give
  Laud and praise undying.
Neither might the gates of death,
  Nor the tomb's dark portal,
Nor the watchers, nor the seal,
  Hold thee as a mortal;

4 But today amidst the Twelve
  Thou didst stand, bestowing
That thy peace, which evermore
  Passeth human knowing.
Come, ye faithful, raise the strain
  Of triumphant gladness;
God hath brought his Israel
  Into joy from sadness.

St. John of Damascus, VIII cen
Tr. John Mason Neale, 1818–66

SPRING OF SOULS. 7 6, 7 6. D. Trochaic. LUDVIG M. LINDEMAN, 1812–87

SECOND TUNE

Triumphantly
1. Come, ye faith-ful, raise the strain Of tri-um-phant glad-ness;
2. Now the queen of sea-sons, bright With the day of splen-dor,
God hath brought his Is-ra-el In-to joy from sad-ness;
With the roy-al feast of feasts, Comes its joy to ren-der;
'Tis the spring of souls to-day: Christ hath burst his pris-on,
Comes to glad-den Chris-tian men, Who with true af-fec-tion
And from three days' sleep in death, As a sun hath ris-en.
Wel-come in un-wea-ried strains Je-sus' res-ur-rec-tion.

3 All the winter of our sins,
Long and dark, is flying
From his light, to whom we give
Laud and praise undying.
Neither might the gates of death,
Nor the tomb's dark portal,
Nor the watchers, nor the seal,
Hold thee as a mortal;

4 But today amidst the Twelve
Thou didst stand, bestowing
That thy peace, which evermore
Passeth human knowing.
Come, ye faithful, raise the strain
Of triumphant gladness;
God hath brought his Israel
Into joy from sadness.

St. John of Damascus, VIII cent.
Tr. John Mason Neale, 1818–66 a.

CHRIST IST ERSTANDEN. 7 7, 7 7. With Alleluia.

German Carol, XII cent.

Joyfully
In unison

1. Christ, the Lord, is risen a - gain, Christ hath bro - ken ev - ery chain!
2. He who gave for us his life, Who for us en - dured the strife,

Hark, an - gel - ic voic - es cry, Sing - ing ev - er - more on high,
Is our Pas - chal Lamb to - day; We too sing for joy, and say:

Refrain, after stanzas 2, 4, 6.

Al - le - lu - ia! Al - le - lu - ia, Al - le - lu - ia,

Al - le - lu - ia. Hark, an - gel - ic voic - es cry,
Sing - ing ev - er - more on high, Al - le - lu - ia.

3 He who bore all pain and loss
Comfortless upon the Cross,
Lives in glory now on high,
Pleads for us, and hears our cry:
Alleluia!

4 He who slumbered in the grave,
Is exalted now to save;
Now through Christendom it rings
That the Lamb is King of kings,
Alleluia!

5 Now he bids us tell abroad
How the lost may be restored,
How the penitent forgiven,
How we too may enter heaven,
Alleluia!

6 Thou, our Paschal Lamb indeed,
Christ, thy ransomed people feed,
Take our sins and guilt away,
Let thy people sing for aye:
Alleluia!

Michael Weisse, cir. 1480–1534
Tr. Catherine Winkworth, 1829–78 a.

LUX EOI. 8 7, 8 7. D. ARTHUR S. SULLIVAN, 1842–1900

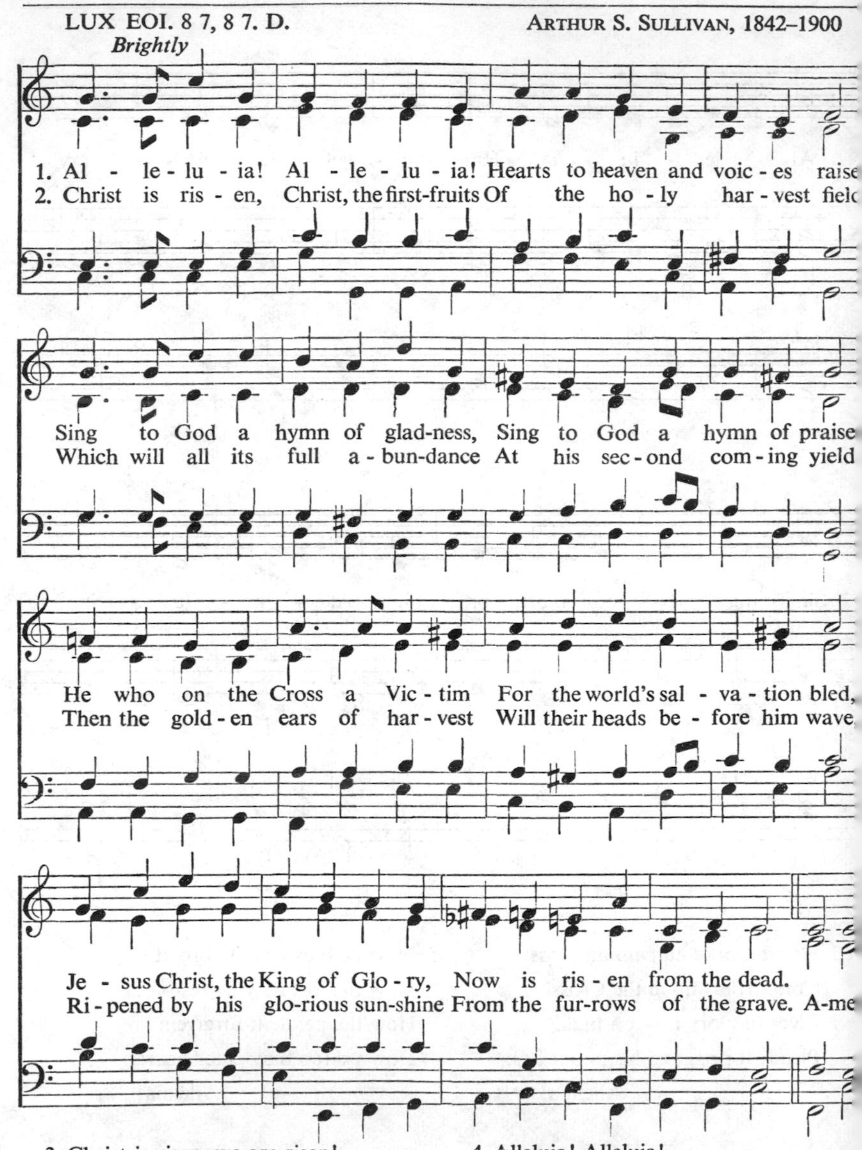
Brightly
1. Al - le - lu - ia! Al - le - lu - ia! Hearts to heaven and voic - es raise
2. Christ is ris - en, Christ, the first-fruits Of the ho - ly har - vest field
Sing to God a hymn of glad-ness, Sing to God a hymn of praise
Which will all its full a - bun-dance At his sec - ond com - ing yield
He who on the Cross a Vic - tim For the world's sal - va - tion bled,
Then the gold - en ears of har - vest Will their heads be - fore him wave,
Je - sus Christ, the King of Glo - ry, Now is ris - en from the dead.
Ri - pened by his glo-rious sun-shine From the fur-rows of the grave. A-men

3 Christ is risen, we are risen!
Shed upon us heavenly grace,
Rain and dew and gleams of glory
From the brightness of thy face;
That we, Lord, with hearts in heaven,
Here on earth may fruitful be,
And by angel hands be gathered
And be ever safe with thee.

4 Alleluia! Alleluia!
Glory be to God on high;
Alleluia! to the Saviour
Who has gained the victory;
Alleluia! to the Spirit,
Font of love and sanctity;
Alleluia! Alleluia!
To the Triune Majesty. Amen.

Christopher Wordsworth, 1807

This hymn may also be sung to DEERHURST (No. 143).

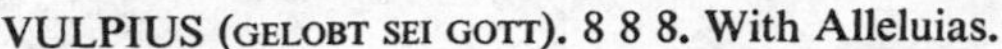

VULPIUS (GELOBT SEI GOTT). 8 8 8. With Alleluias.

MELCHIOR VULPIUS, cir. 1560
Harm. by ERNEST MACMILLAN, 1893–

With exultation

1. Good Chris - tian men, re - joice and sing! Now is the
2. The Lord of Life is risen for aye; Bring flowers of

tri - umph of our King! To all the world glad news we bring:
song to strew his way; Let all man - kind re - joice and say:

Al - le - lu - ia! Al - le - lu - ia! Al - le - lu - ia!
Al - le - lu - ia! Al - le - lu - ia! Al - le - lu - ia!

3 Praise we in songs of victory
That love, that life which cannot die,
And sing with hearts uplifted high:
Alleluia!

4 Thy Name we bless, O risen Lord,
And sing today with one accord
The life laid down, the life restored:
Alleluia!

Cyril A. Alington, 1872–1955

By permission of the author

See also:

417 Alleluia! sing to Jesus
180 Arise, my soul, arise
430 At the Name of Jesus
166 Blessing and honor
311 Christ for the world we sing
413 Come, let us join
441 Give to our God immortal praise
387 I know that my Redeemer lives
326 I love to tell the story
307 Jesus shall reign
412 Join all the glorious names
418 Let all the world in every corner
414 Let the whole creation cry
182 O day of rest and gladness
428 O for a thousand tongues
427 Praise the Lord of heaven
407 Praise the Lord! Ye heavens
408 Praise to the Lord, the Almighty
436 Rejoice, the Lord is King
390 Thou art the Way; to thee alone
437 Ye watchers and ye holy ones

The Church Year

ASCENSION

110

PARK STREET. L. M. FREDERICK M. A. VENUA, 1788–1872

Slowly, with movement

1. A hymn of glo - ry let us sing, New hymns through-out the
2. May our af - fec - tions thith - er tend, And thith - er con - stant -
world shall ring; By a new way none ev - er trod Christ mount-eth
ly as - cend, Where, seat - ed on the Fa-ther's throne, Thee, reign-ing
to the throne of God, Christ mount-eth to the throne of God.
in the heavens, we own! Thee, reign-ing in the heavens, we own! A - men.

3 Be thou our present joy, O Lord,
Who wilt be ever our reward;
So shall the light that springs from thee
Be ours through all eternity.

4 O risen Christ, ascended Lord,
All praise to thee let earth accord,
Who art, while endless ages run,
With Father and with Spirit, One. Ame

The Venerable Bede, 673–7.
Tr. St. 1–3, Elizabeth Rundle Charles, 1820–
Tr. St. 4, Benjamin Webb, 1820–

ASCENSION. 7 7, 7 7. With Alleluias.
WILLIAM HENRY MONK, 1823–89
Triumphantly
1. Hail the day that sees him rise, Al - le - lu - ia!
2. There the glo - rious tri - umph waits; Al - le - lu - ia!
Glo - rious to his na - tive skies, Al - le - lu - ia!
Lift your heads, e - ter - nal gates, Al - le - lu - ia!
Christ, a - while to mor - tals given, Al - le - lu - ia!
Wide un - fold the ra - diant scene, Al - le - lu - ia!
En - ters now the high - est heaven. Al - le - lu - ia!
Take the King of glo - ry in. Al - le - lu - ia! A-men.

3 See, he lifts his hands above, Alleluia!
See, he shows the prints of love: Alleluia!
Hark! his gracious lips bestow, Alleluia!
Blessings on his church below. Alleluia!

4 Lord beyond our mortal sight, Alleluia!
Raise our hearts to reach thy height,
Alleluia!
There thy face unclouded see, Alleluia!
Find our heaven of heavens in thee.
Alleluia! Amen.

Charles Wesley, 1707–88 a.

This hymn may also be sung to LLANFAIR (No. 99).

REX GLORIAE. 8 7, 8 7. D. HENRY SMART, 1813–79

Broadly, with dignity
1. See the Con-queror mounts in tri - umph, See the King in roy - al state,
2. Who is this that comes in glo - ry With the trump of ju - bi - lee?
Rid - ing on the clouds his char - iot To his heaven-ly pal - ace gate!
Lord of bat - tles, God of ar - mies, He has gained the vic - to - ry!
Hark! the choir of an - gel voic - es Joy - ful al - le - lu - ias sing,
He who on the Cross did suf - fer, He who from the grave a - rose,
And the por - tals high are lift - ed To re-ceive their heaven-ly King.
He has van-quished sin and Sa - tan, He by death has spoiled his foes. A-men.

3 Thou hast raised our human nature
On the clouds to God's right hand;
There we sit in heavenly places,
There with thee in glory stand;
Jesus reigns, adored by angels;
Man with God is on the throne;
Mighty Lord, in thine Ascension
We by faith behold our own.

4 Glory be to God the Father;
Glory be to God the Son,
Dying, risen, ascending for us,
Who the heavenly realm has won;
Glory to the Holy Spirit;
To One God, in Persons Three;
Glory both in earth and heaven,
Glory, endless glory, be. Amen.

Christopher Wordsworth, 1807–8.

NUN FREUT EUCH. 8 7, 8 7, 8 8 7. *Geistliche Lieder*, Wittenberg, 1535

With dignity

1. Let all the mul-ti-tudes of light, Their songs in con-cert rais - ing,
With earth's tri - um-phant hymns u-nite, The ris - en Sav-iour prais - ing.
Ye heavens, his fes - ti - val pro-claim! Our King re-turn-eth
whence he came, With vic - to - ry a - maz - ing. A-men.

2 For us he bore the bitter Tree,
To death's dark realm descending;
Our foe he slew, and set us free,
Man's ancient bondage ending.
No more the tyrant's chains oppress;
O conquering Love, thy Name we bless,
With thee to heaven ascending.

3 Jesus, to thee be endless praise
For this thy great salvation!
O holy Father, thine always
Be thanks and adoration!
Spirit of life and light, to thee
Eternal praise and glory be:
One God of all creation! Amen.

Frederick Brodie Macnutt, 1873–1949

TRIUMPH. 8 7, 8 7, 4 4 7. HENRY JOHN GAUNTLETT, 1805–76

FIRST TUNE

Majestically

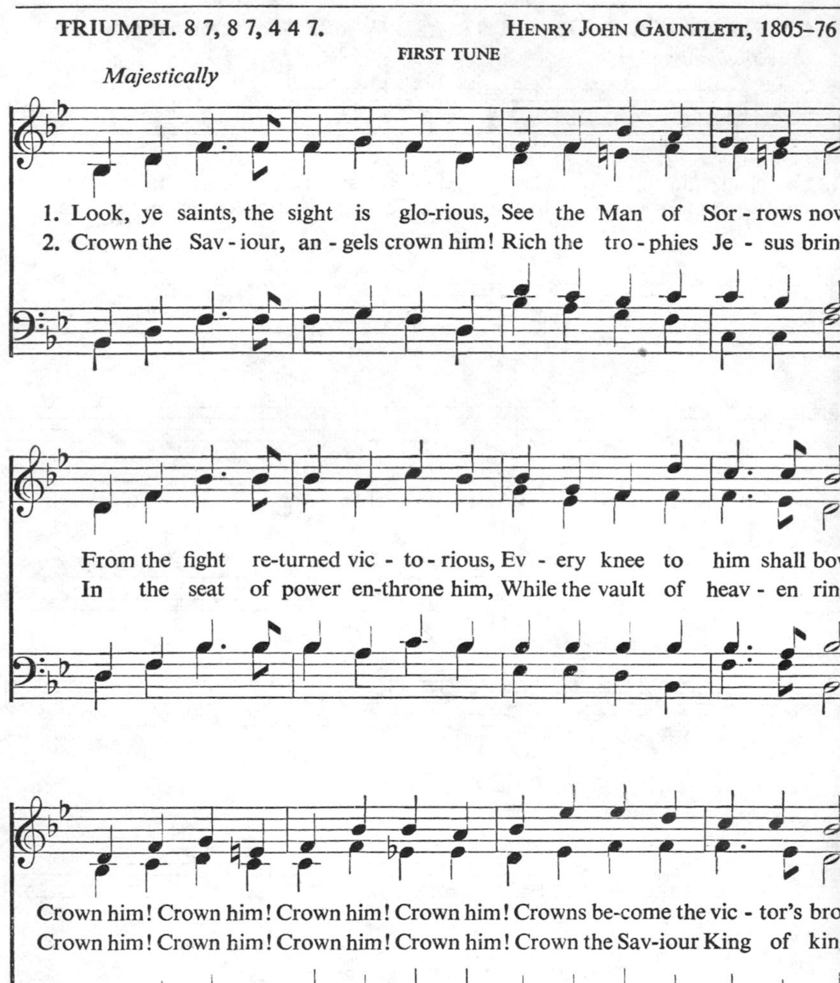
1. Look, ye saints, the sight is glo-rious, See the Man of Sor - rows now
2. Crown the Sav - iour, an - gels crown him! Rich the tro - phies Je - sus bring
From the fight re-turned vic - to - rious, Ev - ery knee to him shall bow
In the seat of power en-throne him, While the vault of heav - en ring
Crown him! Crown him! Crown him! Crown him! Crowns be-come the vic - tor's brov
Crown him! Crown him! Crown him! Crown him! Crown the Sav-iour King of king

3 Sinners in derision crowned him,
Mocking thus the Saviour's claim;
Saints and angels crowd around him,
Own his title, praise his Name;
Crown him! Crown him!
Crown him! Crown him!
Spread abroad the victor's fame.

4 Hark, those bursts of acclamation,
Hark, those loud triumphant chord
Jesus takes the highest station;
O what joy the sight affords!
Crown him! Crown him!
Crown him! Crown him!
King of kings, and Lord of lords.

Thomas Kelly, 1769–1

114

BRYN CALFARIA. 8 7, 8 7, 4 7. WILLIAM OWEN, 1814–93

SECOND TUNE

Broadly

1. Look, ye saints, the sight is glo - rious, See the Man of Sor-rows now;
From the fight re - turned vic - to - rious, Ev - ery knee to him shall bow;
2. Crown the Sav-iour, an - gels crown him! Rich the tro - phies Je - sus brings;
In the seat of power en-throne him, While the vault of heav - en rings;

Crown him! Crown him! Crown him! Crown him! Crown him! Crown him!
Crown him! Crown him! Crown him! Crown him! Crown him! Crown him!

Crowns be - come the vic - tor's brow; Crowns be-come the vic - tor's brow.
Crown the Sav-iour King of kings; Crown the Sav - iour King of kings.

3 Sinners in derision crowned him,
Mocking thus the Saviour's claim;
Saints and angels crowd around him,
Own his title, praise his Name;
Crown him! Crown him!
Crown him! Crown him!
Spread abroad the victor's fame.

4 Hark, those bursts of acclamation,
Hark, those loud triumphant chords!
Jesus takes the highest station,
O what joy the sight affords!
Crown him! Crown him!
Crown him! Crown him!
King of kings, and Lord of lords.

Thomas Kelly, 1769–1854

HERMAS. 6 5, 6 5. D. With Refrain. FRANCES RIDLEY HAVERGAL, 1836–79

Brightly
1. Gold - en harps are sound - ing, An - gel voic - es ring, Pearl - y
gates are o - pened, O - pened for the King. Christ, the King of
Glo - ry, Je - sus, King of Love, Is gone up in tri - umph
Refrain
To his throne a - bove. 'All his work is end - ed,' Joy - ful -
ly we sing, 'Je - sus hath as - cend - ed, Glo - ry to our King.'

2 He who came to save us,
He who bled and died,
Now is crowned with glory
At his Father's side.
Never more to suffer,
Never more to die,
Jesus, King of Glory,
Has gone up on high.

3 Praying for his children
In that blessèd place,
Calling them to glory,
Sending them his grace;
His bright home preparing,
Faithful ones, for you,
Jesus ever liveth,
Ever loveth, too.

Frances Ridley Havergal, 1836–79

16

MACH'S MIT MIR, GOTT (EISENACH). 8 7, 8 7, 8 8.

Joyfully JOHANN HERMANN SCHEIN, 1586–1630

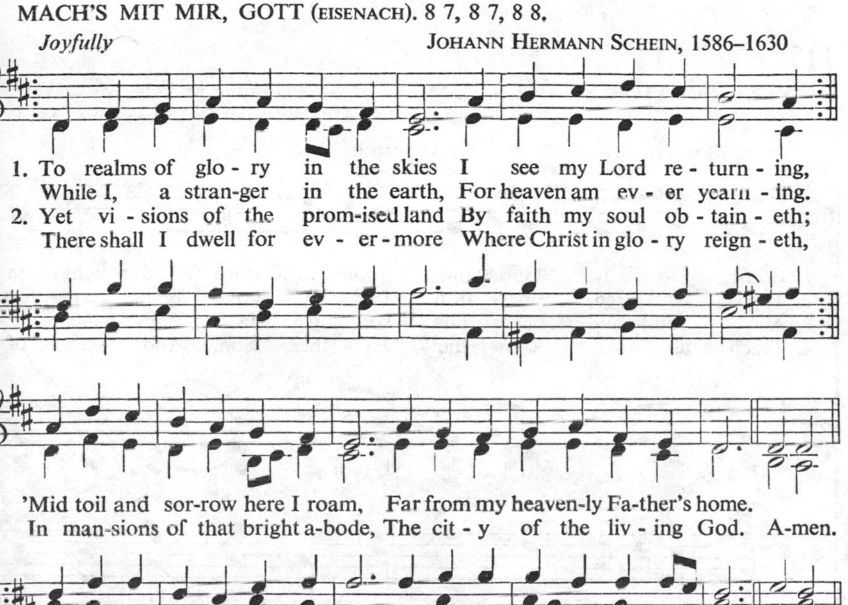

1. To realms of glo - ry in the skies I see my Lord re - turn - ing,
While I, a stran-ger in the earth, For heaven am ev - er yearn - ing.
2. Yet vi - sions of the prom-ised land By faith my soul ob - tain - eth;
There shall I dwell for ev - er - more Where Christ in glo - ry reign - eth,
'Mid toil and sor-row here I roam, Far from my heaven-ly Fa-ther's home.
In man-sions of that bright a-bode, The cit - y of the liv - ing God. A-men.

3 In that blest city is no night,
Nor any pain or weeping;
There is my treasure, there my heart,
Safe in the Saviour's keeping;
In heaven, my risen Lord, with thee
May all my thought and living be.

4 How blessèd shall those servants be,
O Lord, at thy returning,
Whose hearts are waiting still for thee,
Whose lamps are trimmed and burning;
Them wilt thou take to dwell with thee
In joy and peace eternally. Amen.

Johan Olof Wallin, 1779–1839
Tr. Claude William Foss, 1855–1935

See also:

426 All hail the power
417 Alleluia, sing to Jesus
430 At the Name of Jesus
413 Come, let us join
431 Crown him with many crowns
441 Give to our God immortal
435 Hail, thou once despisèd Jesus
307 Jesus shall reign
170 Lord of all being
570 Majestic sweetness
400 O Christ, our hope
419 O Saviour, precious Saviour
436 Rejoice, the Lord is King
177 Round the Lord in glory
97 Sing, men and angels, sing
439 The head that once was crowned

The Church Year

PENTECOST

117

VENI, CREATOR SPIRITUS. L. M. — Plainsong Melody, Mode VIII
Arr. WINFRED DOUGLAS, 1867–1944

Unison, broadly — FIRST TUNE

1. Come, Ho - ly Ghost, our souls in - spire And light - en
2. Thy bless - ed unc - tion from a - bove Is com - fort,
3. A - noint and cheer our soil - ed face With the a -
4. Teach us to know the Fa - ther, Son, And thee, of
with ce - les - tial fire; Thou the a - noint - ing
life, and fire of love. En - a - ble with per
bun - dance of thy grace. Keep far our foes; give
both, to be but One; That through the a - ges

Pentecost—The Holy Ghost

Spir - it art Who dost thy seven - fold gifts im - part.
pet - ual light The dull - ness of our blind - ed sight.
peace at home; Where thou art guide, no ill can come.
all a - long This .... may be our end - less song!
After the last stanza only
Praise to thy e - ter - nal mer - it,
Fa - ther, Son, and Ho - ly Spir - it. A - men.

Based on Veni, Creator Spiritus
Tr. John Cosin, 1594–1672

THANKSGIVING. L. M. JOHN BACCHUS DYKES, 1823–76

Slowly SECOND TUNE

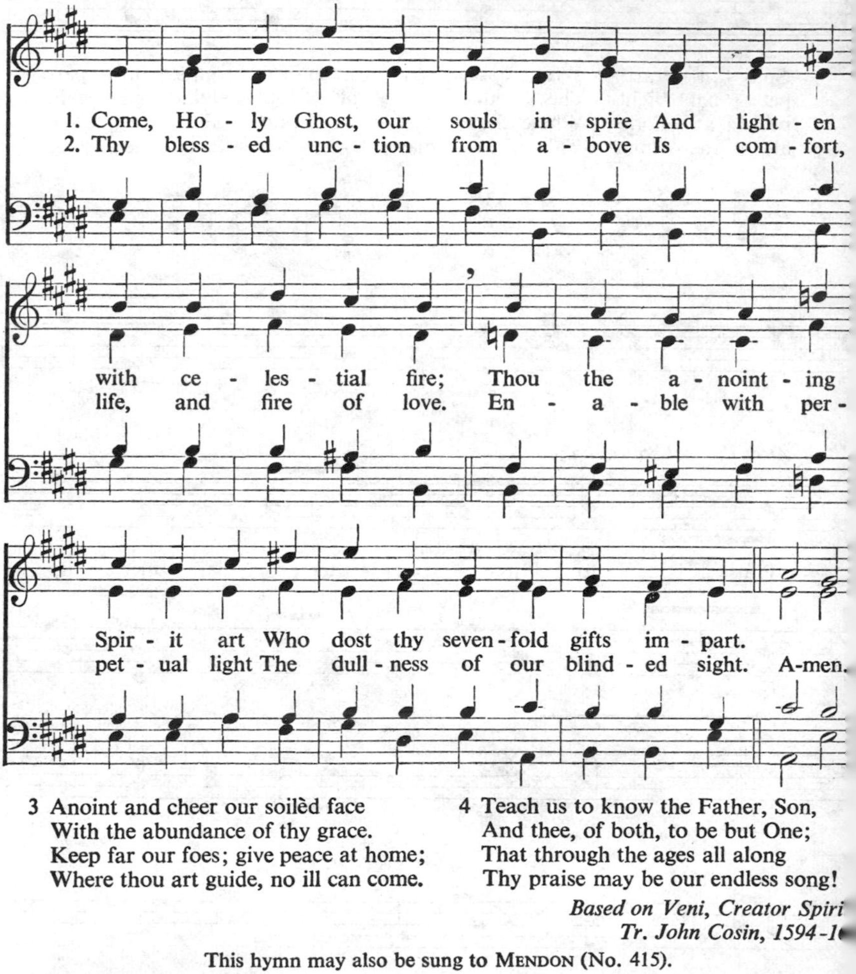

1. Come, Ho - ly Ghost, our souls in - spire And light - en
2. Thy bless - ed unc - tion from a - bove Is com - fort,

with ce - les - tial fire; Thou the a - noint - ing
life, and fire of love. En - a - ble with per -

Spir - it art Who dost thy seven - fold gifts im - part.
pet - ual light The dull - ness of our blind - ed sight. A-men.

3 Anoint and cheer our soilèd face
With the abundance of thy grace.
Keep far our foes; give peace at home;
Where thou art guide, no ill can come.

4 Teach us to know the Father, Son,
And thee, of both, to be but One;
That through the ages all along
Thy praise may be our endless song!

Based on Veni, Creator Spiri
Tr. John Cosin, 1594-1

This hymn may also be sung to MENDON (No. 415).

118

OMBERSLEY. L. M. WILLIAM HENRY GLADSTONE, 1840–91

With devotion

1. Spir - it of mer - cy, truth, and love, O shed thine

in - fluence from a - bove, And still from age to age con -
vey The won - ders of this sa - cred day. A-men.

2 In every clime, by every tongue,
Be God's amazing glory sung;
Let all the listening earth be taught
The wonders by our Saviour wrought.

3 Unfailing Comfort, heavenly Guide,
Still o'er thy holy Church preside;
Still let mankind thy blessings prove,
Spirit of mercy, truth, and love. Amen.

London Foundling Hospital Collection, 1774

Music by permission of Novello and Company, Ltd.

This hymn may also be sung to FEDERAL STREET (No. 514).

119

CAPETOWN. 7 7, 7 5. FRIEDRICH FILITZ, 1804–76

Moderately slow

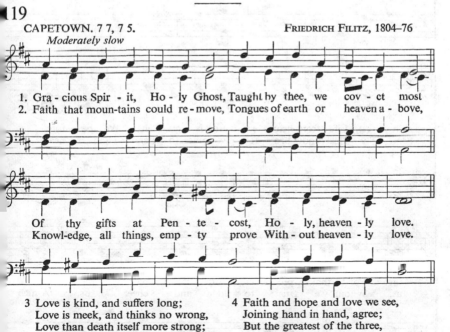

1. Gra - cious Spir - it, Ho - ly Ghost, Taught by thee, we cov - et most
Of thy gifts at Pen - te - cost, Ho - ly, heaven - ly love.

2. Faith that moun-tains could re - move, Tongues of earth or heaven a - bove,
Knowl-edge, all things, emp - ty prove With - out heaven - ly love.

3 Love is kind, and suffers long;
Love is meek, and thinks no wrong,
Love than death itself more strong;
Therefore give us love.

4 Faith and hope and love we see,
Joining hand in hand, agree;
But the greatest of the three,
And the best, is love.

Christopher Wordsworth, 1807–85

WIE SCHÖN LEUCHTET. Irregular.
PHILIPP NICOLAI, 1556–1608
Adapted and harm. by J. S. BACH, 1685–1750
With movement
1. O Ho - ly Spir - it, en - ter in, A - mong these hearts thy
Sun of the soul, thou light di - vine, A - round and in us
2. Left to our - selves we shall but stray, O lead us on the
And give us stead - fast - ness, that we May hence-forth tru - ly
work be - gin, Thy tem - ple deign to make us;
bright-ly shine, To strength and glad-ness wake us. Where thou
nar - row way, With wis - est coun-sel guide us;
fol - low thee, What - ev - er woes be - tide us; Heal thou
shin - est, Life from heav - en there is giv - en; We be - fore
gent - ly Hearts now bro - ken, give some to - ken Thou art near
thee. For that pre - cious gift im - plore thee.
us, Whom we trust to light and cheer us. A-men.

O mighty Rock, O Source of life!
Let thy dear word, 'mid doubt and strife,
Be so within us burning,
That we be faithful unto death
In thy pure love and holy faith,
From thee true wisdom learning.
Lord, thy graces
On us shower; by thy power
Christ confessing,
Let us win his grace and blessing.

4 Grant that our days, while life shall last,
In purest holiness be passed;
Our minds so rule and strengthen
That they may rise o'er things of earth,
The hopes and joys that here have birth;
And if our course thou lengthen,
Keep thou pure, Lord,
From offences, heart and senses;
Blessèd Spirit,
Bid us thus true life inherit. Amen.

Michael Schirmer, 1606–73
Tr. Catherine Winkworth, 1829–78

21

MALVERN. 6 6 4, 6 6 6 4. The Hallelujah, 1849
In moderate time Arr. by JOHN ROBERTS, 1822–77

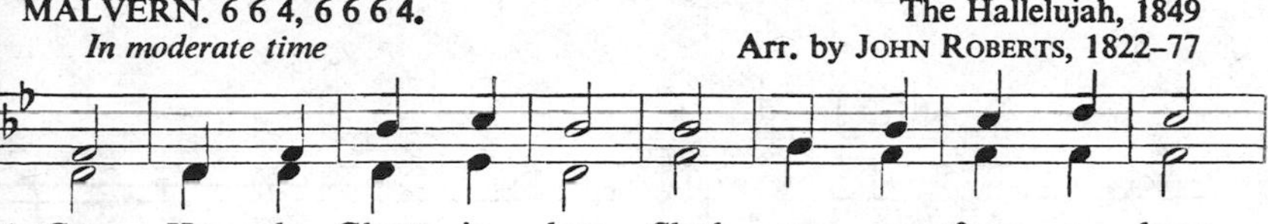

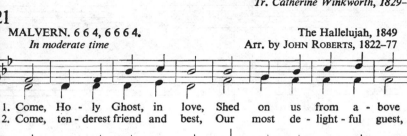

1. Come, Ho - ly Ghost, in love, Shed on us from a - bove
2. Come, ten - derest friend and best, Our most de - light - ful guest,

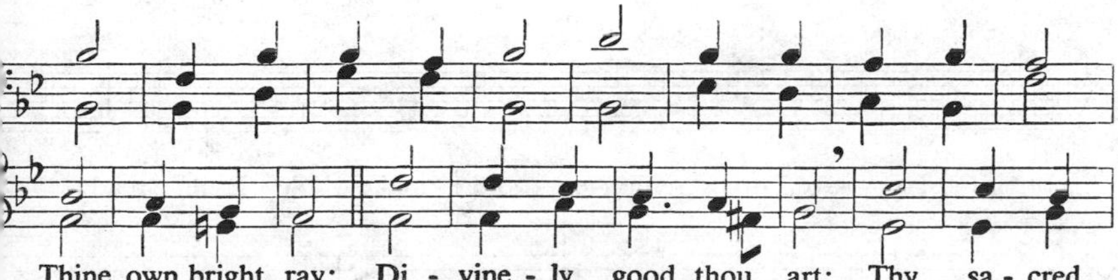

Thine own bright ray; Di - vine - ly good thou art; Thy sa - cred
With sooth - ing power; Rest, which the wea - ry know, Shade, 'mid the

gifts im - part To glad-den each sad heart; O come to - day.
noon - tide glow, Peace, when deep griefs o'er-flow; Cheer us, this hour. A-men.

3 Come, Light serene, and still
Our inmost bosoms fill;
Dwell in each breast;
We know no dawn but thine;
Send forth thy beams divine,
On our dark souls to shine,
And make us blest.

4 Come, all the faithful bless;
Let all, who Christ confess,
His praise employ;
Give virtue's rich reward;
Victorious death accord,
And, with our glorious Lord,
Eternal joy! Amen.

Based on Veni, Sancte Spiritus
Tr. Ray Palmer, 1808–87

KOMM HEILIGER GEIST, HERRE GOTT. L. M. D. With Alleluias.

Pre-Reformation Melody
Erfurt Gesangbuch, 1524

With dignity
In unison
FIRST TUNE
1. Come, Ho - ly Spir - it, God and Lord; Be all thy gifts in plen - ty
poured To save, to strength- en and make whole Each read - y
mind, each wait - ing soul. O, by the bright-ness of thy light In

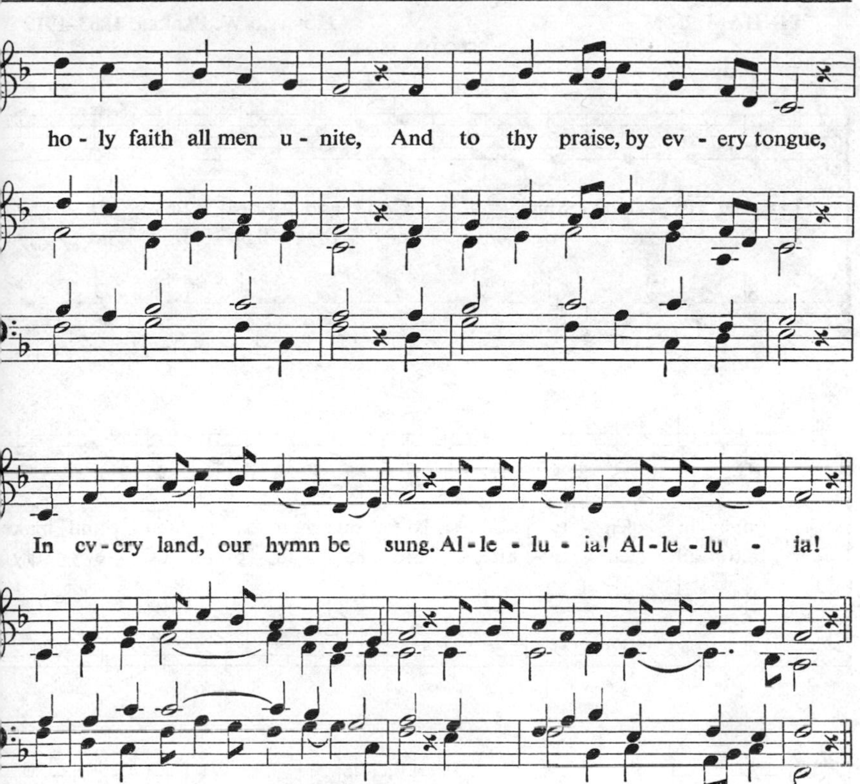
ho - ly faith all men u - nite, And to thy praise, by ev - ery tongue,
In ev - ery land, our hymn be sung. Al - le - lu - ia! Al - le - lu - ia!

2 O strong Defence, O holy Light!
That we may know our God aright,
And call him Father from the heart,
The word of life and truth impart.
Make us to trust in God alone,
And Jesus for our Master own,
His yoke and teaching ne'er to change
For other doctrines new and strange.
Alleluia! Alleluia!

3 O sacred Ardor, Comfort sweet!
Make willing hearts and ready feet
That, come what may, in storm and test
We answer only thy behest.
O quicken us with all thy powers,
Make strong our faith in weaker hours,
That, as good Christians in the strife,
We turn to thee in death and life.
Alleluia! Alleluia!

Martin Luther, 1483–1546
Tr. Edward Traill Horn III, 1909–

PIXHAM. L. M.

HORATIO W. PARKER, 1863–1919

SECOND TUNE

Prayerfully
1. Come, Ho - ly Spir - it, God and Lord; Be all thy gifts in plen - ty poured To save, to strength-en and make whole Each read - y mind, each wait - ing soul.
2. O, by the bright - ness of thy light In ho - ly faith all men u - nite, And to thy praise, by ev - ery tongue, In ev - ery land, our hymn be sung. A - men.

3 O strong Defence, O holy Light!
That we may know our God aright,
And call him Father from the heart,
The word of life and truth impart.

4 Make us to trust in God alone,
And Jesus for our Master own,
His yoke and teaching ne'er to change
For other doctrines new and strange.

5 O sacred Ardor, Comfort sweet!
Make willing hearts and ready feet
That, come what may, in storm and tes
We answer only thy behest.

6 O quicken us with all thy powers,
Make strong our faith in weaker hours,
That, as good Christians in the strife,
We turn to thee in death and life. Ame

Martin Luther, 1483–15
Tr. Edward Traill Horn III, 190

DOWN AMPNEY. 6 6, 11. D. R. VAUGHAN WILLIAMS, 1872–1958

Moderately slow; may be sung in unison

1. Come down, O Love di - vine, Seek thou this soul of mine,
2. O let it free - ly burn, Till earth - ly pas - sions turn
And vis - it it with thine own ar - dor glow - ing;
To dust and ash - es in its heat con - sum - ing;
O Com-fort - er, draw near, With - in my heart ap - pear,
And let thy glo - rious light Shine ev - er on my sight,
And kin - dle it, thy ho - ly flame be - stow - ing.
And clothe me round, the while my path il - lum - ing.

3 Let holy charity
Mine outward vesture be,
And lowliness become mine
inner clothing;
True lowliness of heart
Which takes the humbler part,
And o'er its own shortcomings
weeps with loathing.

4 And so the yearning strong,
With which the soul will long,
Shall far outpass the power
of human telling;
For none can guess its grace,
Till he become the place
Wherein the Holy Spirit makes
his dwelling.

Bianco da Siena, †1434
Tr. Richard Frederick Littledale, 1833–90

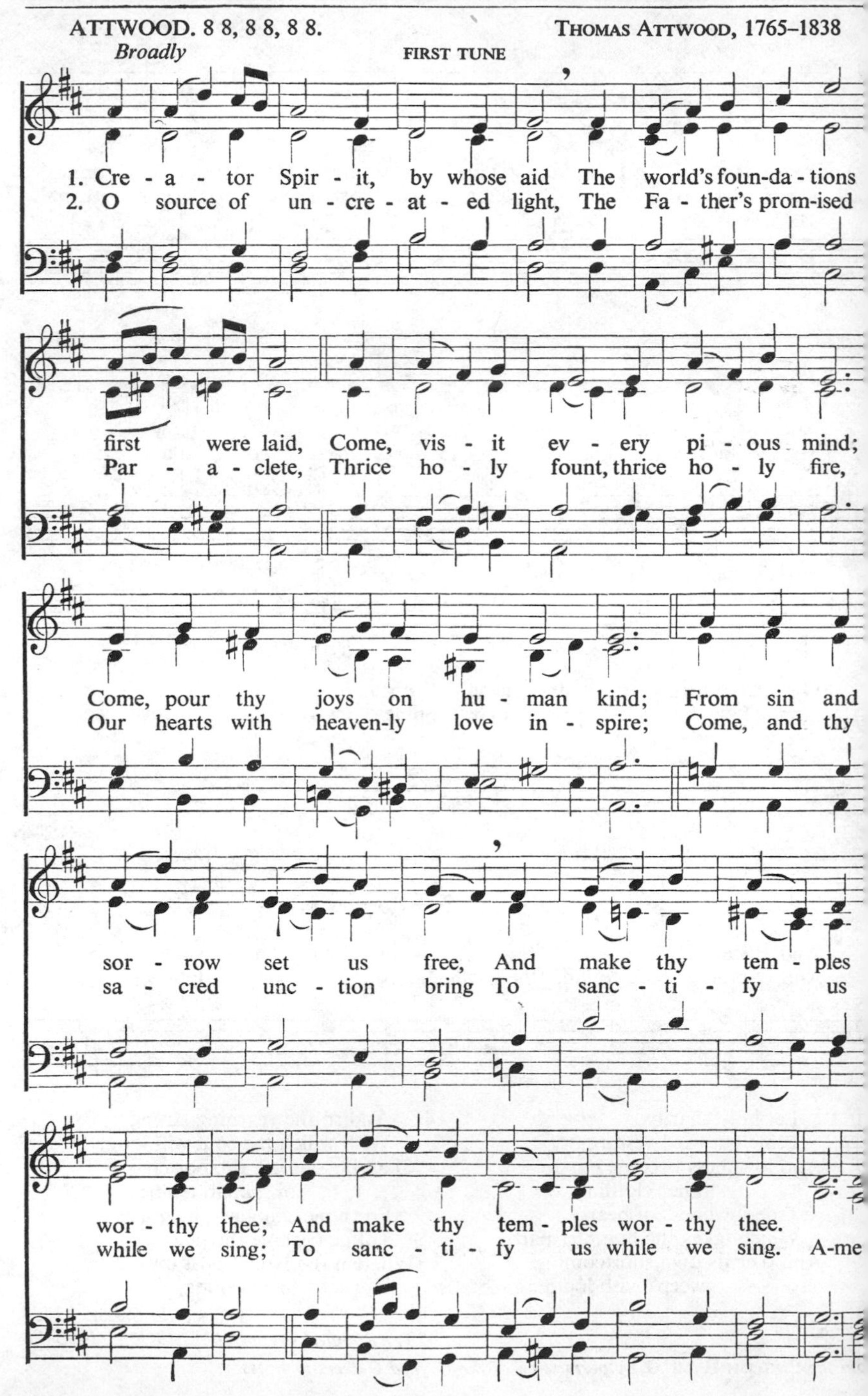
ATTWOOD. 8 8, 8 8, 8 8.
THOMAS ATTWOOD, 1765–1838
Broadly
FIRST TUNE
1. Cre - a - tor Spir - it, by whose aid The world's foun-da - tions first were laid, Come, vis - it ev - ery pi - ous mind; Come, pour thy joys on hu - man kind; From sin and sor - row set us free, And make thy tem - ples wor - thy thee; And make thy tem - ples wor - thy thee.
2. O source of un - cre - at - ed light, The Fa - ther's prom-ised Par - a - clete, Thrice ho - ly fount, thrice ho - ly fire, Our hearts with heaven-ly love in - spire; Come, and thy sa - cred unc - tion bring To sanc - ti - fy us while we sing; To sanc - ti - fy us while we sing. A-me

3 Plenteous of grace, descend from high
Rich in thy sevenfold energy;
Make us eternal truths receive,
And practise all that we believe;
Give us thyself, that we may see
The Father and the Son by thee.

4 Immortal honor, endless fame,
Attend the almighty Father's Name;
The Saviour Son be glorified,
Who for lost man's redemption died;
And equal adoration be,
Eternal Paraclete, to thee. Amen.

John Dryden, 1631–1700
Based on Veni, Creator Spiritus

124

MELITA. 8 8, 8 8, 8 8. JOHN BACCHUS DYKES, 1823–76

SECOND TUNE

With dignity

1. Cre - a - tor Spir - it, by whose aid The world's foun-da - tions first were laid,
2. O source of un - cre - at - ed light, The Fa-ther's prom-ised Par - a - clete,

Come, vis - it ev - ery pi - ous mind; Come, pour thy joys on hu-man kind;
Thrice ho - ly fount, thrice ho - ly fire, Our hearts with heaven-ly love in - spire;

From sin and sor-row set us free, And make thy tem-ples wor - thy thee.
Come, and thy sa-cred unc-tion bring To sanc - ti - fy us while we sing. A-men.

SONG 22. 10 10, 10 10. ORLANDO GIBBONS, 1583–1625

With movement
1. Love of the Fa - ther, Love of God the Son,
From whom all came, in whom was all be - gun;
Who form - est heaven-ly beau - ty out of strife,
Cre - a - tion's whole de - sire and breath of life: A-men.

2 Thou the all-holy, thou supreme in might,
Thou dost give peace, thy presence maketh right;
Thou with thy favor all things dost enfold,
With thine all-kindness free from harm wilt hold.

3 Eternal glory, all men thee adore,
Who art and shalt be worshipped evermore:
Us whom thou madest, comfort with thy might,
And lead us to enjoy thy heavenly light. Amen.

Latin hymn, XII ce
Paraphrase, Robert Bridges, 1844–19

This hymn may also be sung to LANGRAN (No. 366).

From THE YATTENDON HYMNAL, *edited by Robert Bridges*
By permission of the Clarendon Press, Oxford

126

KOMM, O KOMM, DU GEIST DES LEBENS. 8 7, 8 7, 7 7.

Meiningen Gesangbuch, 1693

With movement

1. Come, O come, thou quick-ening Spir - it, God be - fore the dawn of time!
2. On - ly that which thou de - sir - est Be our ob - ject; with thy hand

Fire our hearts with ho - ly ar - dor, Bless - ed Com-fort - er sub - lime!
Lead our ev - ery thought and ac - tion That they be but thy com-mand.

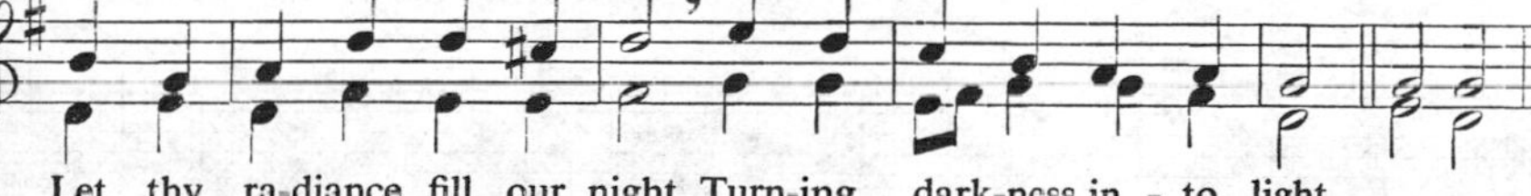

Let thy ra-diance fill our night, Turn-ing dark-ness in - to light.
All our sin - ful - ness e - rase With the in-crease of thy grace. A-men.

3 Blessèd Spirit, who renewest
All that dwell upon the earth,
When the evil one assails us
Help us prove our heavenly birth;
Arm us with thy mighty sword
In the legions of the Lord.

4 Help us keep the faith forever;
Let not Satan, death or shame
Draw us from thee, or deprive us
Of the honor of thy Name.
When the foe would lure us hence,
Be thou, God, our sure defence. Amen.

Heinrich Held, †cir. 1659
Tr. Edward Traill Horn III, 1909–

WAREHAM. L. M. WILLIAM KNAPP, 1698–1768

In moderate time

1. Come, gra - cious Spir - it, heaven-ly Dove, With light and
2. The light of truth to us dis - play, And make us
com - fort from a - bove; Be thou our guard-ian, thou our
know and choose thy way; Plant ho - ly fear in ev - ery
guide, O'er ev - ery thought and step pre - side.
heart, That we from God may ne'er de - part. A - men.

3 Lead us to Christ, the living way,
Nor let us from his pastures stray;
Lead us to holiness, the road
That we must take to dwell with God.

4 Lead us to heaven, that we may share
Fulness of joy for ever there;
Lead us to God our final rest,
To be with him for ever blest. Amen.

Simon Browne, 1680–173

BERGGREN (ALT.). 12 10, 11 10. ANDREAS PETER BERGGREN, 1801–80

Serenely
1. Lord, let thy Spir - it, from earth - ly pas - sion wean - ing,
Lead me a - long thy will's all - ho - ly way,
To find by faith, on Je - sus' bos - om lean - ing,
'Mid tri - al, doubt and need, in him my stay. A-men.

2 Lord, let thy Spirit, new love and life bestowing,
Create a holy heart my breast within;
That I, into my Saviour's likeness growing,
May bear his image through a world of sin.

3 Lord, let thy Spirit, thy word's deep wealth unsealing,
Lighten mine eyes with truth's celestial fire;
In life, in death, the narrow path revealing
Unto the Promised Land of our desire. Amen.

Valdimar Briem, 1848–1930

MORECAMBE. 10 10, 10 10. Ascribed to FREDERICK COOK ATKINSON, 1841–97

With reverence

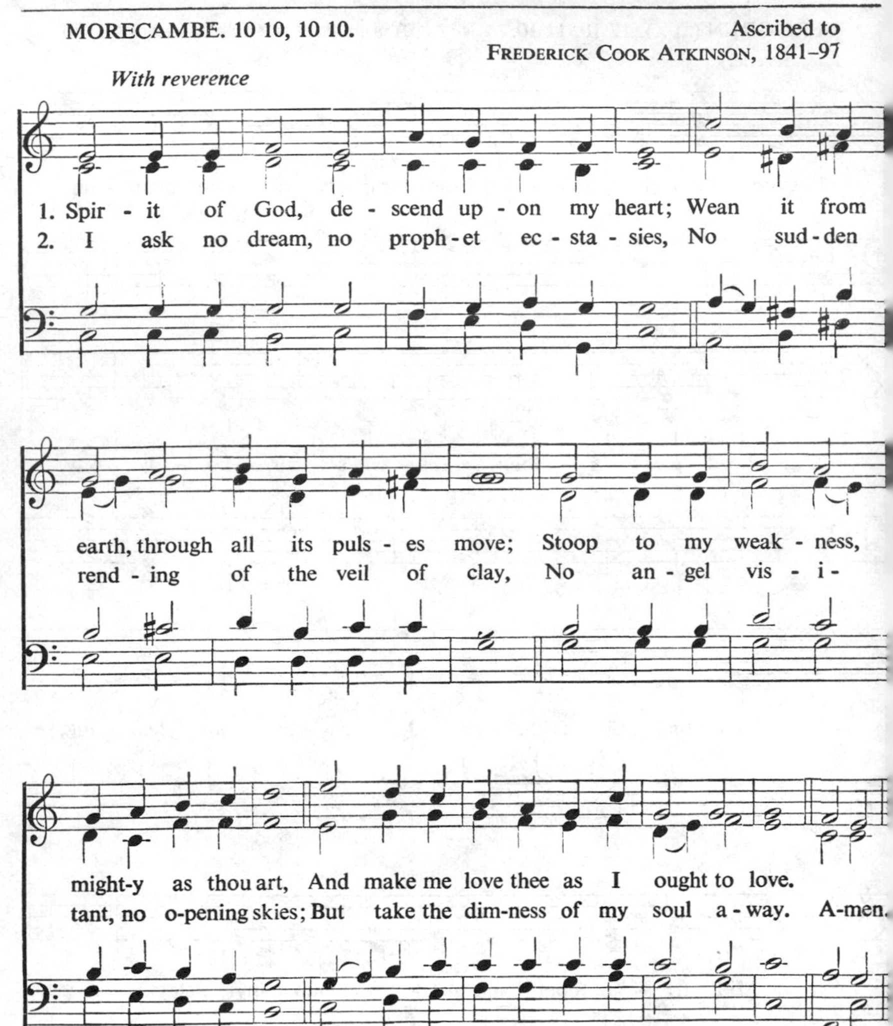
1. Spir - it of God, de - scend up - on my heart; Wean it from
2. I ask no dream, no proph - et ec - sta - sies, No sud - den
earth, through all its puls - es move; Stoop to my weak - ness,
rend - ing of the veil of clay, No an - gel vis - i -
might-y as thou art, And make me love thee as I ought to love.
tant, no o-pening skies; But take the dim-ness of my soul a - way. A-men.

3 Hast thou not bid me love thee, God and King;
All, all thine own, soul, heart and strength and mind?
I see thy Cross; there teach my heart to cling;
O let me seek thee, and O let me find!

4 Teach me to love thee as thine angels love,
One holy passion filling all my frame:
The baptism of the heaven-descended Dove,
My heart an altar, and thy love the flame. Amen.

George Croly, 1780–1860

SONG 13. 7 7, 7 7. **Orlando Gibbons, 1583–1625**

Quietly

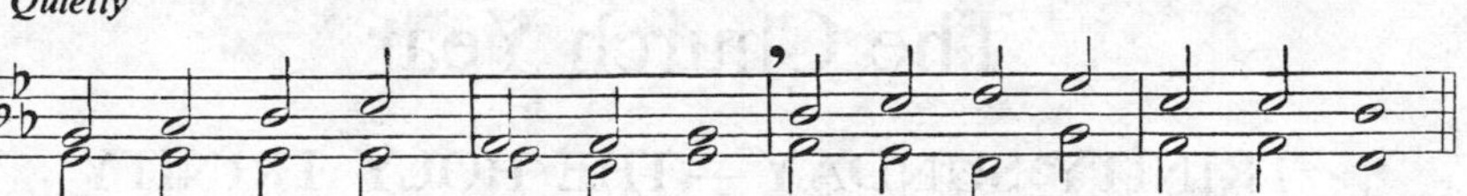

1. Ho - ly Spir - it, truth di - vine, Dawn up - on this soul of mine;
2. Ho - ly Spir - it, love di - vine, Glow with - in this heart of mine;

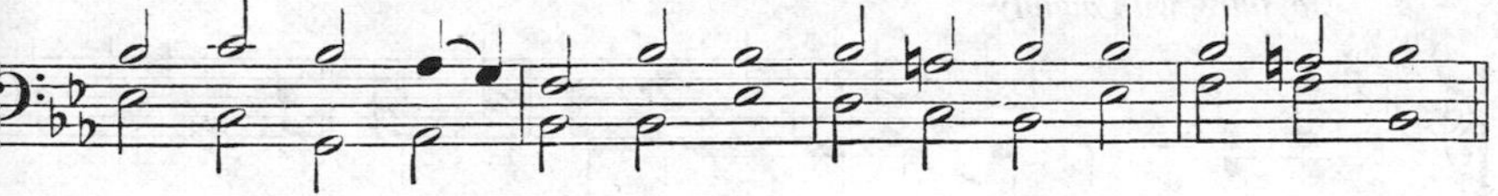

Word of God, and in - ward light, Wake my spir - it, clear my sight.
Kin - dle ev - ery high de - sire; Per - ish self in thy pure fire. A-men.

3 Holy Spirit, power divine,
Fill and nerve this will of mine;
By thee may I strongly live,
Bravely bear, and nobly strive.

4 Holy Spirit, peace divine,
Still this restless heart of mine;
Speak to calm this tossing sea,
Stayed in thy tranquillity.

5 Holy Spirit, right divine,
King within my conscience reign;
Be my law, and I shall be
Firmly bound, for ever free. Amen.

Samuel Longfellow, 1819–92

See also:

470 Breathe on me, Breath of God
476 Immortal Love, forever full
186 Light of light, enlighten me
306 O Spirit of the living God
405 Sometimes a light surprises
474 Walk in the light

The Church Year

TRINITY SUNDAY — THE HOLY TRINITY

131

NICAEA. Irregular. JOHN BACCHUS DYKES, 1823–76

Joyfully, with dignity

1. Ho - ly, ho - ly, ho - ly, Lord God Al-might - y! Ear - ly in the
2. Ho - ly, ho - ly, ho - ly! all the saints a-dore thee, Cast-ing down their
morn- ing our song shall rise to thee; Ho - ly, ho - ly, ho - ly,
golden crowns a - round the glass - y sea, Cher - u - bim and ser - a-phim
mer - ci - ful and might-y, God in three Per-sons, bless-ed Trin - i - ty!
fall - ing down be-fore thee, Which wert, and art, and ev-er-more shalt be. A-men

3 Holy, holy, holy! though the darkness hide thee,
  Though the eye of sinful man thy glory may not see,
Only thou art holy; there is none beside thee,
  Perfect in power, in love, and purity.

4 Holy, holy, holy, Lord God Almighty!
  All thy works shall praise thy Name, in earth and sky and sea;
Holy, holy, holy, merciful and mighty,
  God in three Persons, blessèd Trinity! Amen.

Reginald Heber, 1783–182

32 Trinity Sunday—The Holy Trinity

ALLEIN GOTT IN DER HÖH. 8 7, 8 7, 8 8 7.
NIKOLAUS DECIUS, †1541
Joyfully; with breadth
1. All glo - ry be to God on high, Who hath our race be - friend - ed;
To us no harm shall now come nigh, The strife at last is end - ed;
God show - eth his good will to men, And peace shall reign on
earth a - gain; O thank him for his good - ness. A-men.

2 We praise, we worship thee, we trust,
And give thee thanks for ever,
O Father, that thy rule is just
And wise, and changes never;
Thy boundless power o'er all things reigns,
Thou dost whate'er thy will ordains:
'Tis well thou art our Ruler!

3 O Jesus Christ, our God and Lord,
Begotten of the Father,
Who hast our fallen race restored
And straying sheep dost gather,
Thou Lamb of God, enthroned on high,
Behold our need, and hear our cry:
Have mercy on us, Jesus!

4 O Holy Spirit, precious Gift,
Thou Comforter unfailing,
Do thou our troubled souls uplift,
Against the foe prevailing;
Since Christ for us his Blood hath shed,
Avert our woes and calm our dread;
We trust in thee to help us! Amen.

Ascribed to Nikolaus Decius, †1541
Tr. Catherine Winkworth, 1829–78 a.

O LUX BEATA TRINITAS. FIRST TUNE

Plainsong Melody, Mode VIII
Arr. by ERNEST WHITE, 1899–

1. O Trin - i - ty of bless-ed light, O U - ni - ty of prince - ly might, The fier - y sun now goes his way; Shed thou with - in our hearts thy ray. A - men.

2 To thee our morning song of praise,
To thee our evening prayer we raise;
Thy glory suppliant we adore
For ever and for evermore.

3 All laud to God the Father be,
All praise, eternal Son, to thee,
All glory, as is ever meet,
To God the holy Paraclete. Amen.

Ascribed to St. Ambrose, 340–9
Tr. John Mason Neale, 1818–6

Music arranged for this book and copyrighted

133

AETERNA CHRISTI MUNERA. L. M. SECOND TUNE

Rouen Church Melody

With movement

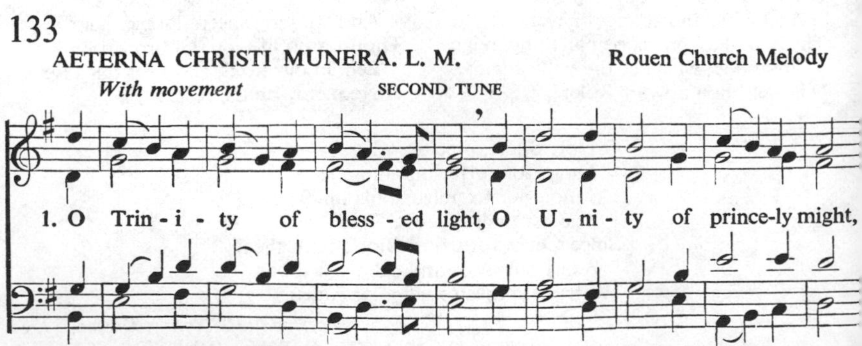
1. O Trin - i - ty of bless - ed light, O U - ni - ty of prince-ly might,

The fier - y sun now goes his way; Shed thou with-in our hearts thy ray. A-men.

2 To thee our morning song of praise,
To thee our evening prayer we raise;
Thy glory suppliant we adore
For ever and for evermore.

3 All laud to God the Father be,
All praise, eternal Son, to thee,
All glory, as is ever meet,
To God the holy Paraclete. Amen.

Ascribed to St. Ambrose, 340–397
Tr. John Mason Neale, 1818–66

33

ILLSLEY. L. M. JOHN BISHOP, 1665–1737

Slowly

THIRD TUNE

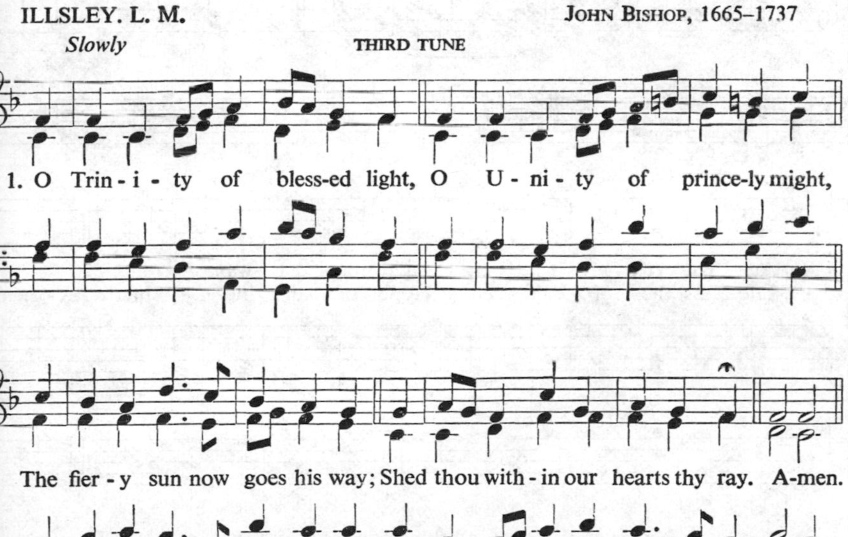
1. O Trin - i - ty of bless-ed light, O U - ni - ty of prince-ly might,
The fier - y sun now goes his way; Shed thou with - in our hearts thy ray. A-men.

2 To thee our morning song of praise,
To thee our evening prayer we raise;
Thy glory suppliant we adore
For ever and for evermore.

3 All laud to God the Father be,
All praise, eternal Son, to thee,
All glory, as is ever meet,
To God the holy Paraclete. Amen.

Ascribed to St. Ambrose, 340–397
Tr. John Mason Neale, 1818–66

CHRISTE SANCTORUM. 11 11, 11 5. XVIII cent. French Church Melody

Unison, in moderate time Harm. by R. VAUGHAN WILLIAMS, 1872–1958

1. Fa - ther most ho - ly, mer - ci - ful and ten - der; Je - sus our
2. Trin - i - ty sa - cred, U - ni - ty un - shak - en; De - i - ty
Sav - iour, with the Fa - ther reign - ing; Spir - it all - kind - ly,
per - fect, giv - ing and for - giv - ing, Light of the an - gels,
Ad - vo - cate, De - fend - er, Light nev - er wan - ing;
Life of the for - sak - en, Hope of all liv - ing. A - men.

3 Maker of all things, all thy creatures praise thee;
  Lo, all things serve thee through thy whole creation:
Hear us, Almighty, hear us, as we raise thee
  Heart's adoration.

4 To the all-ruling triune God be glory:
  Highest and greatest, help thou our endeavor,
We too would praise thee, giving honor worthy,
  Now and for ever. Amen.

Latin Hymn, cir. X cen
Tr. Percy Dearmer, 1867–19.

Trinity Sunday — The Holy Trinity

ST. ATHANASIUS. 7 7, 7 7, 7 7. EDWARD JOHN HOPKINS, 1818–1901

With dignity, in moderate time

1. Ho - ly, ho - ly, ho - ly Lord God of Hosts, e - ter - nal King,
2. Since by thee were all things made, And in thee do all things live,

By the heavens and earth a - dored; An - gels and arch - an - gels sing,
Be in thee all hon - or paid; Praise to thee may all things give,

Chant - ing ev - er - last - ing - ly To the bless - ed Trin - i - ty.
Sing - ing ev - er - last - ing - ly To the bless - ed Trin - i - ty. A-men.

3 Thousands, tens of thousands stand,
Spirits blest, before thy throne,
Speeding thence at thy command;
And when thy behests are done,
Singing everlastingly
To the blessèd Trinity.

4 Alleluia! Lord, to thee,
Father, Son, and Holy Ghost,
Godhead One, and Persons Three;
Join we with the heavenly host,
Singing everlastingly
To the blessèd Trinity. Amen.

Christopher Wordsworth, 1807–85

MOSCOW (ITALIAN HYMN). 6 6 4, 6 6 6 4. FELICE DE GIARDINI, 1716–96

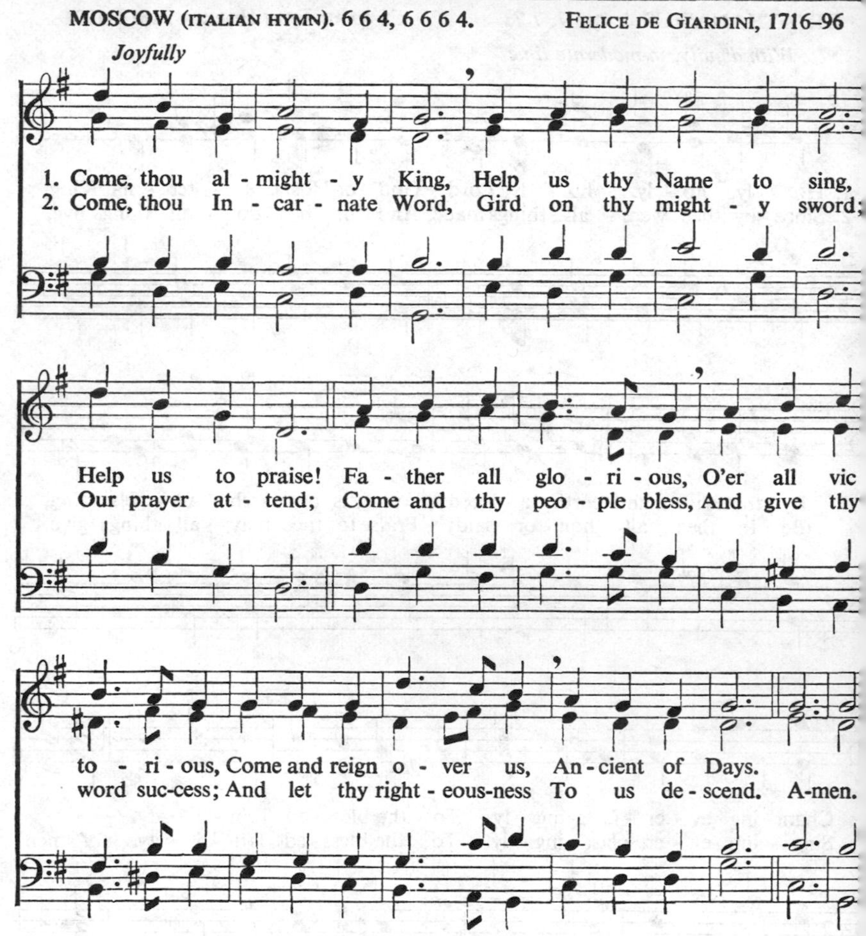
Joyfully
1. Come, thou al - might - y King, Help us thy Name to sing,
2. Come, thou In - car - nate Word, Gird on thy might - y sword;
Help us to praise! Fa - ther all glo - ri - ous, O'er all vic
Our prayer at - tend; Come and thy peo - ple bless, And give thy
to - ri - ous, Come and reign o - ver us, An - cient of Days.
word suc-cess; And let thy right - eous-ness To us de - scend. A-men.

3 Come, Holy Comforter,
Thy sacred witness bear
In this glad hour:
Thou who almighty art,
Now rule in every heart,
And ne'er from us depart,
Spirit of power.

4 To thee, great One in Three,
Eternal praises be,
Hence, evermore!
Thy sovereign majesty
May we in glory see,
And to eternity
Love and adore. Amen.

Authorship uncert
Whitefield's Collection, 1757

ANCIENT OF DAYS. (ALBANY) 11 10, 11 10.
In unison, with dignity
JOHN ALBERT JEFFERY, 1855–1929
1. An - cient of Days, who sit - test throned in glo - ry, To thee all
2. O Ho - ly Fa - ther, who hast led thy chil - dren In all the
knees are bent, all voic - es pray; Thy love has blessed the wide world's
a - ges with the fire and cloud Through seas dry-shod, through wea - ry
won-drous sto - ry With light and life since E-den's dawn - ing day.
wastes be - wil-dering: To thee, in rev-erent love, our hearts are bowed. A - men.

3 O holy Jesus, Prince of Peace and Saviour,
To thee we owe the peace that still prevails;
Stilling the rude wills of men's wild behavior
And calming passion's fierce and stormy gales.

4 O Holy Ghost, the Lord and the Life-giver,
Thine is the quickening power that gives increase;
From thee have flowed, as from a pleasant river,
Our plenty, wealth, prosperity and peace.

5 O Triune God, with heart and voice adoring,
Praise we the goodness that doth crown our days;
Pray we that thou wilt hear us, still imploring
Thy love and favor, kept to us always. Amen.

William Croswell Doane, 1832–1913

ST. FLAVIAN. C. M. JOHN DAY'S PSALTER, 1562

In moderate time

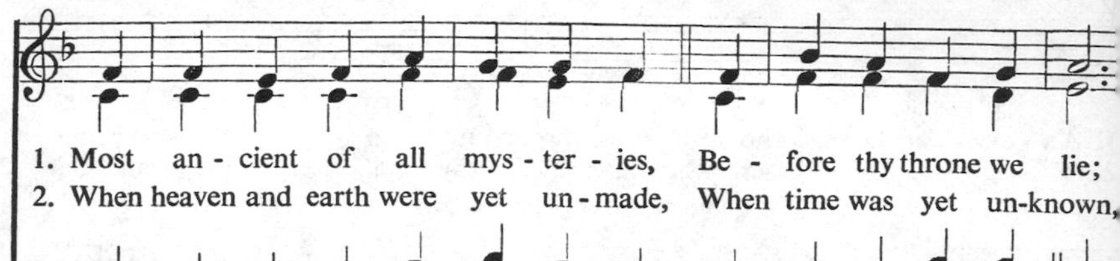
1. Most an - cient of all mys - ter - ies, Be - fore thy throne we lie;
2. When heaven and earth were yet un - made, When time was yet un-known,

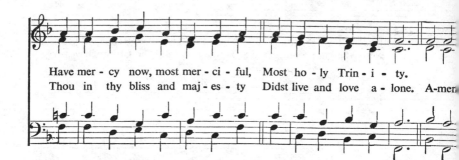

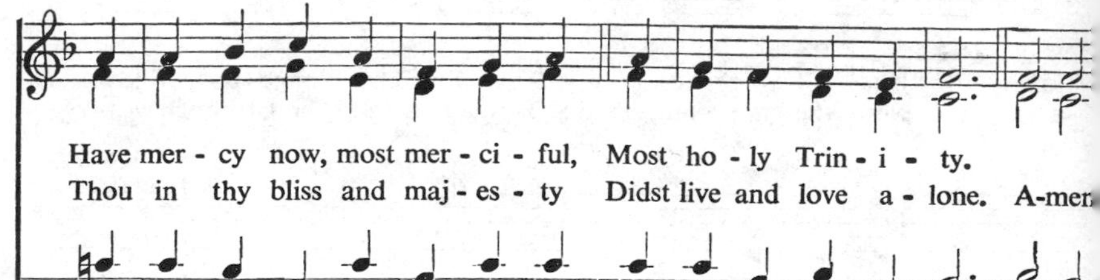
Have mer - cy now, most mer - ci - ful, Most ho - ly Trin - i - ty.
Thou in thy bliss and maj - es - ty Didst live and love a - lone. A-men

3 Thou wert not born; there was no fount
From which thy Being flowed;
There is no end which thou canst reach;
But thou art simply God.

4 How wonderful creation is,
The work which thou didst bless,
And O, what then must thou be like,
Eternal loveliness!

5 O listen then, most pitiful,
To thy poor creature's heart:
It blesses thee that thou art God,
That thou art what thou art.

6 Most ancient of all mysteries,
Still at thy throne we lie;
Have mercy now, most merciful,
Most holy Trinity. Amen.

Frederick William Faber, 1814-6.

Trinity Sunday—The Holy Trinity

ST. NICHOLAS. 8 7, 8 7. JOHANN CRÜGER, 1598–1662

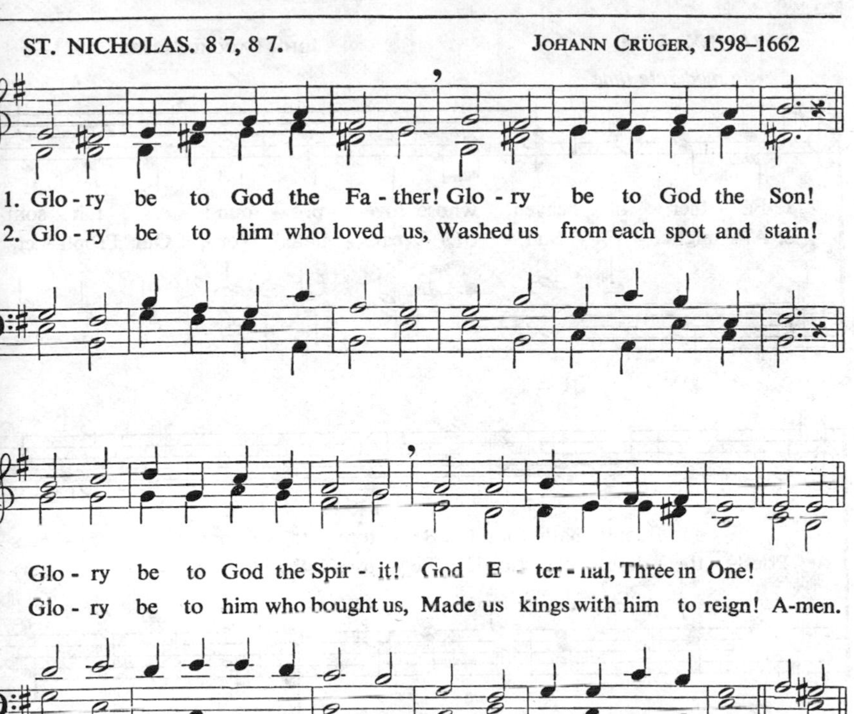
1. Glo-ry be to God the Fa-ther! Glo-ry be to God the Son!
2. Glo-ry be to him who loved us, Washed us from each spot and stain!
Glo-ry be to God the Spir-it! God E-ter-nal, Three in One!
Glo-ry be to him who bought us, Made us kings with him to reign! A-men.

3 Glory to the King of angels!
Glory to the Church's King!
Glory to the King of nations!
Heaven and earth, your praises bring!

4 Glory, blessing, praise eternal!
Thus the choir of angels sings,
Honor, riches, power, dominion!
Thus its praise creation brings.

5 Glory be to God the Father!
Glory be to God the Son!
Glory be to God the Spirit!
God Eternal, Three in One! Amen.

***Horatius Bonar*, 1808–89**

This hymn may also be sung to ARUNDEL (No. 407).

RIVAULX. L. M. JOHN BACCHUS DYKES, 1823–76

In moderate time

1. Fa - ther of heaven, whose love pro - found A ran - som for our souls hath found, Be - fore thy throne we sin - ners bend: To us thy par - doning love ex - tend.
2. Al - might - y Son, In - car - nate Word, Our Proph - et, Priest, Re - deem- er, Lord! Be - fore thy throne we sin - ners bend: To us thy sav - ing grace ex - tend. A - men.

3 Eternal Spirit! By whose breath
The soul is raised from sin and death,
Before thy throne we sinners bend:
To us thy quickening power extend.

4 Thrice Holy! Father, Spirit, Son,
Mysterious Godhead, Three in One!
Before thy throne we sinners bend:
Grace, pardon, life, to us extend. Amen.

Edward Cooper, 1770–1833

See also:

178 Eternal God, before thy throne
167 Holy God, we praise thy Name
172 Immortal, invisible, God
170 Lord of all being, throned afar
181 My God, how wonderful thou art
353 O God of wondrous grace
163 O worship the King
421 Praise ye the Father
410 The God of Abraham praise

ST. MICHAEL (OLD 134TH). S. M. *Genevan Psalter*, **1551**

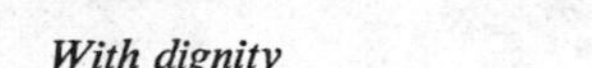
With dignity

1. For all thy saints, O Lord, Who strove in thee to live,

Who fol-lowed thee, o-beyed, a-dored, Our grate-ful hymn re-ceive. A-men.

2 For all thy saints, O Lord,
Accept our thankful cry;
Who counted thee their great reward,
And strove in thee to die.

3 They all, in life or death,
With thee, their Lord, in view,
Learned from thy Holy Spirit's breath
To suffer and to do.

4 For this, thy Name we bless,
And humbly pray that we
May follow them in holiness,
And live and die in thee. Amen.

Richard Mant, 1776–1848

MANNHEIM. 8 7, 8 7, 8 7. FRIEDRICH FILITZ, 1804–76

In stately rhythm

The Presentation

1. In his tem - ple now be - hold him, See the long - ex - pect - ed Lord; An - cient proph - ets had fore - told him, God has now ful - filled his word. Now to praise him, his re - deem-ed Shall break forth with one ac - cord.
2. In the arms of her who bore him, Vir - gin pure, be - hold him lie, While his a - ged saints a - dore him, Ere in per - fect faith they die. Al - le - lu - ia! Al - le - lu - ia! Lo, the in - car - nate God Most High! A-men.

3 Jesus, by thy Presentation,
  Thou who didst for us endure,
Make us see thy great salvation,
  Seal us with thy promise sure;
And present us, in thy glory,
  To thy Father, cleansed and pure. Amen.

Henry John Pye, 1825–190

DEERHURST. 8 7, 8 7. D. JAMES LANGRAN, 1835–1909

In moderate time

1. Hark! the sound of holy voices Chanting at the crystal sea,
2. They have come from tribulation, And have washed their robes in blood,
Alleluia, Alleluia, Alleluia, Lord, to thee!
Washed them in the Blood of Jesus; Tried they were, and firm they stood;
Multitude, which none can number, Like the stars in glory stands
Mocked, imprisoned, stoned, tormented, Sawn asunder, slain with sword,
Clothed in white apparel, holding Palms of victory in their hands.
They have conquered death and Satan By the might of Christ the Lord. Amen.

3 God of God, the One-begotten,
Light of Light, Emmanuel,
In whose body joined together
All the saints for ever dwell;
Pour upon us of thy fullness
That we may for evermore
God the Father, God the Son, and
God the Holy Ghost adore. Amen.

Christopher Wordsworth, 1807–85 a.

This hymn may also be sung to SANCTUARY (No. 403).

SINE NOMINE. 10 10 10. With Alleluias.
R. VAUGHAN WILLIAMS, 1872–1958
FIRST TUNE
Unison, in moderate time
1. For all the saints who from their la - bors rest, Who thee . . . by faith be - fore the world con - fessed, Thy Name, O Je - sus, be for ev - er blest.
2. Thou wast their rock, their for - tress and their might; Thou, Lord, their Cap - tain in their well - fought fight; Thou, in the dark - ness drear, their one true light.
3. O may thy sol - diers, faith - ful, true and bold, Fight as the saints who no - bly fought of old, And win, with them, the vic - tor's crown of gold.
7. But lo! there breaks a yet more glo - rious day: The saints . . tri - umph - ant rise in bright ar - ray; The King of Glo - ry pass - es on his way.
8. From earth's wide bounds, from o - cean's far - thest coast, Through gates . . of pearl streams in the count - less host, Sing - ing to Fa - ther, Son, and Ho - ly Ghost:

Al - le - lu - ia! Al - le - lu - ia!
Harmony
A-men.
Harmony
4. O blest com-mun - ion, fel - low - ship di - vine! We fee - bly strug - gle,
5. And when the strife is fierce, the war-fare long, Steals on the ear the
6. The gold - en eve - ning bright-ens in the west; Soon, soon to faith - ful
(small notes st. 6)
they in glo - ry shine; Yet all are one in thee, for all are
dis - tant tri-umph-song, And hearts are brave a - gain, and arms are
war-riors com-eth rest; Sweet is the calm of par - a - dise the
thine.
strong. Al - le - lu - ia! Al - le - lu - ia!
blest.

William Walsham How, 1823–97

PRO OMNIBUS SANCTIS (SARUM). 10 10 10, 4. JOSEPH BARNBY, 1838–86

Broadly, with spirit SECOND TUNE

1. For all the saints who from their la - bors rest, Who thee by faith be - fore the world con - fessed, Thy Name, O Je - sus, be for ev - er blest. Al - le - lu - ia! Al - le - lu - ia!
2. Thou wast their rock, their for - tress and their might; Thou, Lord, their Cap - tain in their well - fought fight; Thou, in the dark - ness drear, their one true light. Al - le - lu - ia! Al - le - lu - ia!
3. O may thy sol - diers, faith - ful, true and bold, Fight as the saints who no - bly fought of old, And win, with them, the vic - tor's crown of gold. Al - le - lu - ia! Al - le - lu - ia!

4 O blest communion, fellowship divine!
We feebly struggle, they in glory shine;
Yet all are one in thee, for all are thine. Alleluia!

5 And when the strife is fierce, the warfare long,
Steals on the ear the distant triumph-song,
And hearts are brave again, and arms are strong. Alleluia!

6 The golden evening brightens in the west;
Soon, soon to faithful warriors cometh rest;
Sweet is the calm of paradise the blest. Alleluia!

7 But lo! there breaks a yet more glorious day:
The saints triumphant rise in bright array;
The King of Glory passes on his way. Alleluia!

8 From earth's wide bounds, from ocean's farthest coast,
Through gates of pearl streams in the countless host,
Singing to Father, Son, and Holy Ghost: Alleluia!

William Walsham How, 1823–9

NYBERG. 8 8, 8 8, 88. BERNDT MIKAEL NYBERG, 1871–1940

Smoothly
1. The saints of God! their con - flict past, And life's long bat - tle won at last, No more they need the shield or sword, They cast them down be - fore the Lord: O hap - py saints, for ev - er blest, At Je - sus' feet how safe your rest!
2. The saints of God! their wan-derings done, No more their wea - ry course they run, No more they faint, no more they fall, No foes op - press, no fears ap - pall: O hap - py saints, for ev - er blest, In that dear home how sweet your rest!
3. The saints of God! life's voy - age o'er, Safe land - ed on that bliss - ful shore, No storm - y tem - pests now they dread, No roar - ing bil - lows lift their head: O hap - py saints, for ev - er blest, In that calm ha - ven of your rest!
A - men.

4 The saints of God their vigil keep,
While yet their mortal bodies sleep,
Till from the dust they too shall rise
And soar triumphant to the skies:
O happy saints, rejoice and sing;
He quickly comes, your Lord and King!

5 O God of saints! to thee we cry;
O Saviour! plead for us on high;
O Holy Ghost! our guide and friend,
Grant us thy grace till life shall end;
That with all saints our rest may be
In that bright Paradise with thee! Amen.

William Dalrymple Maclagan, 1826–1910

This hymn may also be sung to ST. MATTHIAS (No. 199).

LAURINUS. 8 6, 8 6, 8 8 6. Swedish *Koralbok*, 1697

Majestically FIRST TUNE

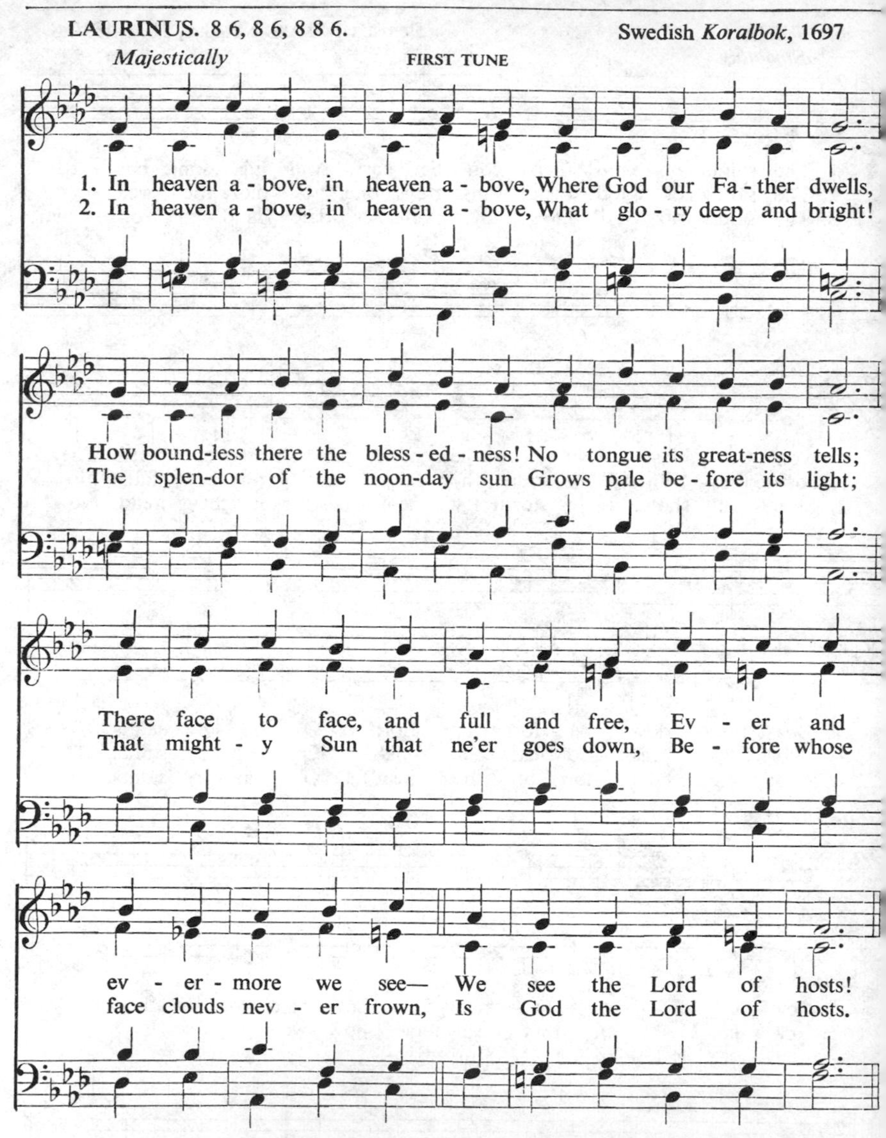
1. In heaven a - bove, in heaven a - bove, Where God our Fa - ther dwells,
2. In heaven a - bove, in heaven a - bove, What glo - ry deep and bright!
How bound-less there the bless - ed - ness! No tongue its great-ness tells;
The splen-dor of the noon-day sun Grows pale be - fore its light;
There face to face, and full and free, Ev - er and
That might - y Sun that ne'er goes down, Be - fore whose
ev - er - more we see— We see the Lord of hosts!
face clouds nev - er frown, Is God the Lord of hosts.

3 In heaven above, in heaven above,
No tears of pain are shed;
There nothing e'er shall fade or die;
Life's fullness round is spread,
And, like an ocean, joy o'erflows,
And with immortal mercy glows
Our God the Lord of hosts.

4 In heaven above, in heaven above,
God hath a joy prepared,
Which mortal ear hath never heard,
Nor mortal vision shared,
Which never entered mortal breast,
By mortal lips was ne'er expressed,
'Tis God, the Lord of Hosts!

Laurentius Laurentii Laurinus, 1573–1655
Revised Johan Åstrom, 1767–1844
Tr. William Maccall, 1812–88

HAUGE. 8 6, 8 6, 8 8 6. Norwegian Folk Melody

With movement SECOND TUNE

1. In heaven a - bove, in heaven a - bove, Where God our Fa - ther dwells,
2. In heaven a - bove, in heaven a - bove, What glo - ry deep and bright!
How bound-less there the bless - ed - ness! No tongue its great-ness tells;
The splen - dor of the noon - day sun Grows pale be - fore its light;
There face to face, and full and free, Ev - er and
That might - y Sun that ne'er goes down, Be - fore whose
ev - er - more we see— We see the Lord of hosts!
face clouds nev - er frown, Is God the Lord of hosts.

3 In heaven above, in heaven above,
No tears of pain are shed;
There nothing e'er shall fade or die,
Life's fullness round is spread,
And, like an ocean, joy o'erflows,
And with immortal mercy glows
Our God the Lord of hosts.

4 In heaven above, in heaven above,
God hath a joy prepared,
Which mortal ear hath never heard,
Nor mortal vision shared,
Which never entered mortal breast,
By mortal lips was ne'er expressed,
'Tis God, the Lord of hosts!

Laurentius Laurentii Laurinus, 1573–1655
Revised Johan Åstrom, 1767–1844
Tr. William Maccall, 1812–88

CONDITOR ALME SIDERUM.
Mode IV
Arr. by ERNEST WHITE, 1899–
Unison
FIRST TUNE
The Transfiguration
1. O won-drous type, O vi - sion fair Of glo - ry that the
2. With shin - ing face and bright ar - ray, Christ deigns to man - i -
Church shall share, Which Christ up - on the moun - tain shows,
fest to - day What glo - ry shall be theirs a - bove,
Where bright - er than the sun he glows!
Who joy in God with per - fect love. A - men.

3 And faithful hearts are raisèd on high
By this great vision's mystery,
For which in joyful strains we raise
The voice of prayer, the hymn of praise.

4 O Father, with the eternal Son
And Holy Spirit ever One,
Vouchsafe to bring us by thy grace
To see thy glory face to face. Amen.

Latin hymn, XV ce
Tr. John Mason Neale, 1818–6

CAMERONIAN MIDNIGHT HYMN. L. M.
Scottish Hymn Melody
In moderate time
SECOND TUNE
The Transfiguration
1. O won - drous type, O vi - sion fair Of glo - ry that the
2. With shin - ing face and bright ar - ray, Christ deigns to man - i -
Church shall share, Which Christ up - on the moun - tain shows,
fest to - day What glo - ry shall be theirs a - bove,
Where bright - er than the sun he glows!
Who joy in God with per - fect love. A - men.

3 And faithful hearts are raised on high
By this great vision's mystery,
For which in joyful strains we raise
The voice of prayer, the hymn of praise.

4 O Father, with the eternal Son
And Holy Spirit ever One,
Vouchsafe to bring us by thy grace
To see thy glory face to face. Amen.

Latin hymn, XV cent.
Tr. John Mason Neale, 1818–66 a.

This hymn may also be sung to WAREHAM (No. 127).

TRISAGION. 10 10, 10 10. HENRY SMART, 1813–79

In moderate time

St. Michael and All Angels

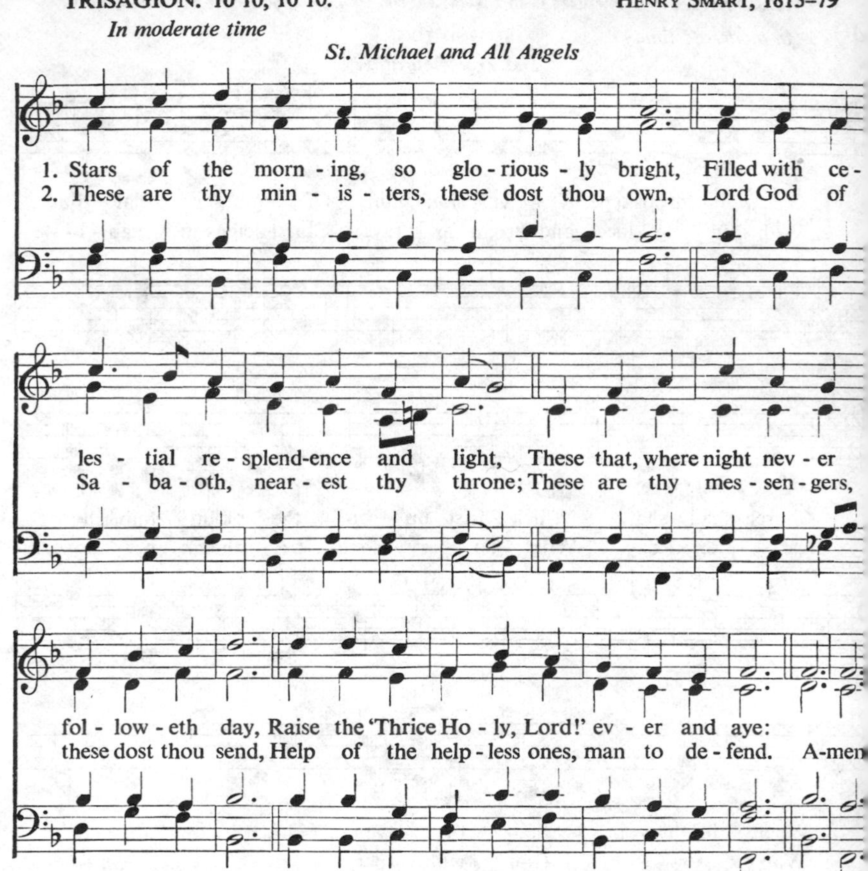
1. Stars of the morn - ing, so glo - rious - ly bright, Filled with ce - les - tial re - splend-ence and light, These that, where night nev - er fol - low - eth day, Raise the 'Thrice Ho - ly, Lord!' ev - er and aye:
2. These are thy min - is - ters, these dost thou own, Lord God of Sa - ba - oth, near - est thy throne; These are thy mes - sen - gers, these dost thou send, Help of the help - less ones, man to de - fend. A-men

3 Still let them succor us; still let them fight,
Lord of angelic hosts, battling for right,
Till, where their anthems they ceaselessly pour,
We with the angels may bow and adore. Amen.

St. Joseph the Hymnographer, †88
Tr. John Mason Neale, 1818–

This hymn may also be sung to QUEDLINBURG (No. 596).

See also:

554	Am I a soldier of the Cross	560	Onward, Christian soldiers
245	Blessèd city, heavenly Salem	555	Rejoice, ye pure in heart
527	Brief life is here our portion	564	Soldiers of Christ, arise
594	Give me the wings of faith	595	Ten thousand times ten thousand
587	Jerusalem, my happy home	562	The Son of God goes forth
584	Jerusalem, the golden	415	Thee we adore, eternal Lord
553	Jesus calls us	585	Thy word, O God, declareth
591	Light's abode, celestial Salem	409	Ye holy angels bright
247	O Light, from age to age	437	Ye watchers and ye holy ones

The Church

49

AURELIA. 7 6, 7 6. D. SAMUEL SEBASTIAN WESLEY, 1810–76

With breadth and dignity

1. The Church's one foun - da - tion Is Je - sus Christ her Lord;
2. E - lect from ev - ery na - tion, Yet one o'er all the earth,
She is his new cre - a - tion By wa - ter and the word:
Her char - ter of sal - va - tion One Lord, one faith, one birth;
From heaven he came and sought her To be his ho - ly bride,
One ho - ly Name she bless - es, Par - takes one ho - ly food,
With his own Blood he bought her, And for her life he died.
And to one hope she press - es, With ev - ery grace en - dued. A-men.

3 'Mid toil and tribulation,
And tumult of her war,
She waits the consummation
Of peace for evermore;
Till with the vision glorious
Her longing eyes are blest,
And the great Church victorious
Shall be the Church at rest.

4 Yet she on earth hath union
With God, the Three in One,
And mystic sweet communion
With those whose rest is won.
O happy ones and holy!
Lord, give us grace that we
Like them, the meek and lowly,
On high may dwell with thee. Amen.

Samuel John Stone, 1839–1900

150

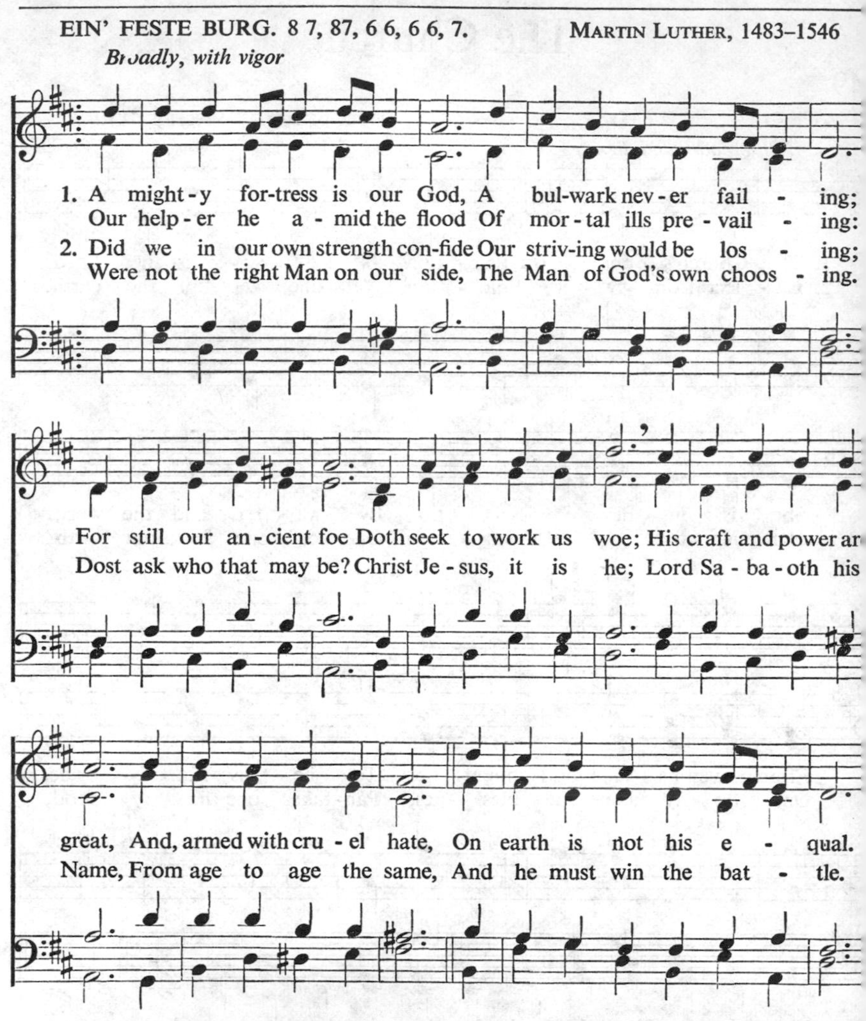
EIN' FESTE BURG. 8 7, 87, 6 6, 6 6, 7.
MARTIN LUTHER, 1483–1546
Broadly, with vigor
1. A might - y for-tress is our God, A bul-wark nev - er fail - ing;
Our help - er he a - mid the flood Of mor - tal ills pre - vail - ing:
2. Did we in our own strength con-fide Our striv-ing would be los - ing;
Were not the right Man on our side, The Man of God's own choos - ing.
For still our an - cient foe Doth seek to work us woe; His craft and power ar
Dost ask who that may be? Christ Je - sus, it is he; Lord Sa - ba - oth his
great, And, armed with cru - el hate, On earth is not his e - qual.
Name, From age to age the same, And he must win the bat - tle.

3 And though this world, with devils filled,
Should threaten to undo us;
We will not fear, for God hath willed
His truth to triumph through us:
The prince of darkness grim,
We tremble not for him;
His rage we can endure,
For lo! his doom is sure,
One little word shall fell him.

4 That word above all earthly powers,
No thanks to them, abideth;
The Spirit and the gifts are ours
Through him who with us sideth:
Let goods and kindred go,
This mortal life also;
The body they may kill:
God's truth abideth still,
His kingdom is forever.

Martin Luther, 1483–15
Tr. Frederick H. Hedge, 1805–
Based on Psalm

KIRKEN. 8 8, 8 8, 8 8, 8. LUDVIG M. LINDEMAN, 1812–87

With vigor

1. Built on a rock the church doth stand, E - ven when stee - ples are fall - ing; Crum-bled have spires in ev - ery land, Bells still are chim - ing and call - ing; Call - ing the young and old to rest, Call - ing the souls of men dis-tressed, Long-ing for life ev - er - last - ing.
2. Not in our tem - ples made with hands God, the al - might - y, is dwell - ing; High in the heavens his tem - ple stands, All earth - ly tem - ples ex - cell - ing; Yet he who dwells in heaven a - bove Deigns to a - bide with us in love, Mak-ing our bod - ies his tem - ple.
3. We are God's house of liv - ing stones, Built for his own hab - i - ta - tion; He fills our hearts, his hum - ble thrones, Grant-ing us life and sal - va - tion; Were two or three to seek his face, He in their midst would show his grace, Bless-ings up - on them be - stow - ing.

4 Yet in this house, an earthly frame,
Jesus the children is blessing;
Hither we come to praise his Name,
Faith in our Saviour confessing;
Jesus to us his Spirit sent,
Making with us his covenant,
Granting his children the kingdom.

5 Through all the passing years, O Lord,
Grant that, when church bells are ringing,
Many may come to hear God's word
Where he this promise is bringing:
I know mine own, mine own know me,
Ye, not the world, my face shall see;
My peace I leave with you, amen.

Nikolai F. S. Grundtvig, 1783–1872; Tr. Carl Doving, 1867–1937
Revised, Fred C. M. Hansen, 1888–

HARWELL. 8 7, 8 7. D. FIRST TUNE LOWELL MASON, 1792–1872

Slowly
1. Glo - rious things of thee are spo - ken, Zi - on, cit - y of our God;
2. See the streams of liv - ing wa - ters Spring-ing from e - ter - nal love,
He, whose word can-not be bro - ken, Formed thee for his own a - bode.
Well sup - ply thy sons and daugh-ters And all fear of want re - move.
On the Rock of A - ges found - ed, What can shake thy sure re - pose?
Who can faint while such a riv - er Ev - er flows their thirst to assuag
With sal - va - tion's walls sur-round - ed, Thou may'st smile at all thy foes.
Grace which, like the Lord, the giv - er, Nev - er fails from age to age?

3 Round each habitation hovering,
See the cloud and fire appear
For a glory and a covering,
Showing that the Lord is near;
Thus deriving from their banner
Light by night and shade by day,
Safe they feed upon the manna
Which he gives them when they pray.

4 Saviour, if of Zion's city
I, through grace, a member am,
Let the world deride or pity,
I will glory in thy Name.
Fading is the worldling's pleasure,
All his boasted pomp and show;
Solid joys and lasting treasure
None but Zion's children know.

John Newton, 1725–18

This hymn may also be sung to REX GLORIAE (No. 112).

AUSTRIAN HYMN. 8 7, 8 7. D. FRANZ JOSEPH HAYDN, 1732–1809

SECOND TUNE

With dignity
1. Glo-rious things of thee are spo-ken, Zi - on, cit - y of our God;
2. See the streams of liv - ing wa - ters Spring-ing from e - ter - nal love,
He, whose word can - not be bro-ken, Formed thee for his own a - bode.
Well sup - ply thy sons and daugh-ters, And all fear of want re - move.
On the Rock of A - ges found-ed, What can shake thy sure re - pose?
Who can faint while such a riv - er Ev - er flows their thirst to assuage,
With sal - va - tion's walls sur-round-ed, Thou may'st smile at all thy foes.
Grace which, like the Lord, the giv - er, Nev - er fails from age to age?

3 Round each habitation hovering,
See the cloud and fire appear
For a glory and a covering,
Showing that the Lord is near;
Thus deriving from their banner
Light by night and shade by day,
Safe they feed upon the manna
Which he gives them when they pray.

4 Saviour, if of Zion's city
I, through grace, a member am,
Let the world deride or pity,
I will glory in thy Name.
Fading is the worldling's pleasure,
All his boasted pomp and show;
Solid joys and lasting treasure
None but Zion's children know.

John Newton, 1725–1807

This hymn may also be sung to REX GLORIAE (No. 112).

SCHEFFLER. 7 7 7, 6. JOHANN SCHEFFLER'S *Heilige Seelenlust*, 1657

FIRST TUNE

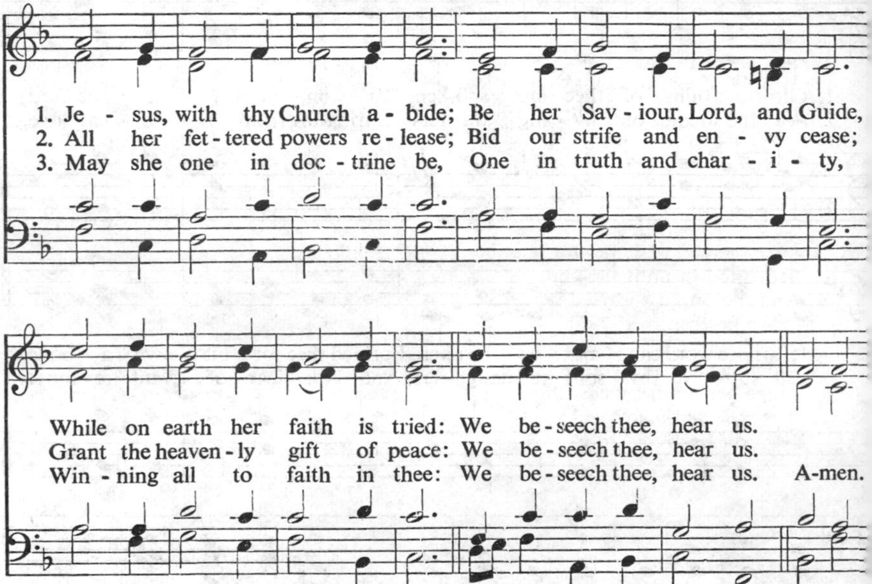

1. Je - sus, with thy Church a - bide; Be her Sav - iour, Lord, and Guide,
While on earth her faith is tried: We be - seech thee, hear us.

2. All her fet - tered powers re - lease; Bid our strife and en - vy cease;
Grant the heaven - ly gift of peace: We be - seech thee, hear us.

3. May she one in doc - trine be, One in truth and char - i - ty,
Win - ning all to faith in thee: We be - seech thee, hear us. A-men.

4 May she guide the poor and blind,
Seek the lost until she find,
And the broken-hearted bind:
We beseech thee, hear us.

5 Judge her not for work undone,
Judge her not for fields unwon,
Bless her works in thee begun:
We beseech thee, hear us.

6 May her lamp of truth be bright;
Bid her bear aloft its light
Through the realms of heathen night:
We beseech thee, hear us.

7 May she holy triumphs win,
Overthrow the hosts of sin,
Gather all the nations in:
We beseech thee, hear us. Amen.

Thomas Benson Pollock, 1836–9

153

LITANY. 7 7 7, 6. WILLIAM HENRY MONK, 1823–89

SECOND TUNE

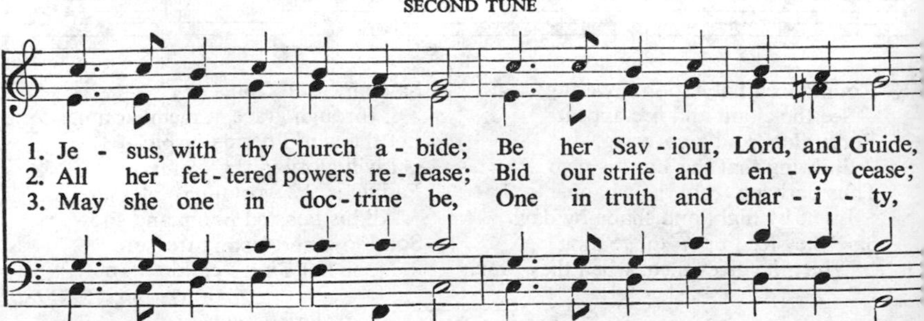
1. Je - sus, with thy Church a - bide; Be her Sav - iour, Lord, and Guide,
2. All her fet - tered powers re - lease; Bid our strife and en - vy cease;
3. May she one in doc - trine be, One in truth and char - i - ty,

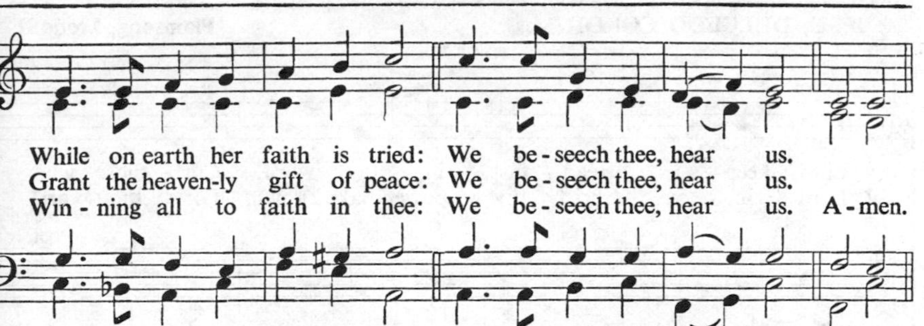
While on earth her faith is tried: We be - seech thee, hear us.
Grant the heaven-ly gift of peace: We be - seech thee, hear us.
Win - ning all to faith in thee: We be - seech thee, hear us. A - men.

4 May she guide the poor and blind,
Seek the lost until she find,
And the broken-hearted bind:
We beseech thee, hear us.

5 Judge her not for work undone,
Judge her not for fields unwon,
Bless her works in thee begun:
We beseech thee, hear us.

6 May her lamp of truth be bright;
Bid her bear aloft its light
Through the realms of heathen night:
We beseech thee, hear us.

7 May she holy triumphs win,
Overthrow the hosts of sin,
Gather all the nations in:
We beseech thee, hear us. Amen.

Thomas Benson Pollock, 1836–96

154

TALLIS' ORDINAL. C. M. THOMAS TALLIS, *cir.* 1505–85

In moderate time

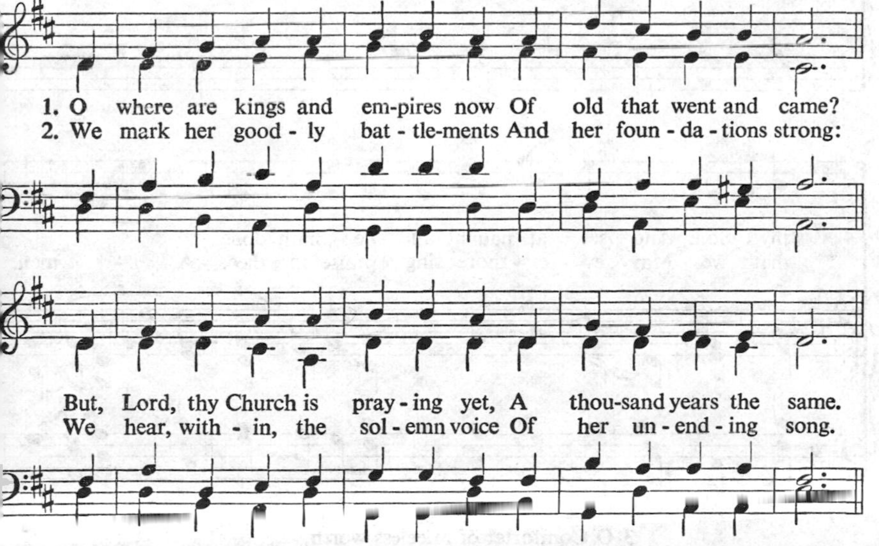
1. O where are kings and em-pires now Of old that went and came?
2. We mark her good - ly bat - tle-ments And her foun - da - tions strong:
But, Lord, thy Church is pray - ing yet, A thou-sand years the same.
We hear, with - in, the sol - emn voice Of her un - end - ing song.

3 For not like kingdoms of the world
Thy holy Church, O God,
Though earthquake shocks are threatening her,
And tempests are abroad;

4 Unshaken as eternal hills,
Immovable she stands,
A mountain that shall fill the earth,
A house not made with hands.

Arthur Cleveland Coxe, 1818–96

JESU, DULCEDO CORDIUM. Plainsong, Mode II

FIRST TUNE

1. Lord, keep us stead - fast in thy word, Curb those who fain by craft or sword Would wrest the king - dom from thy Son, And set at naught all he hath done.
2. Lord Je - sus Christ, thy power make known, For thou art Lord of lords a - lone; De - fend thy Chris - ten - dom, that we May ev - er - more sing praise to thee. A - men.

3 O Comforter of priceless worth,
Send peace and unity on earth;
Support us in our final strife,
And lead us out of death to life. Amen.

Martin Luther, 1483–1546
Tr. Catherine Winkworth, 1829–78

ERHALT UNS, HERR. L. M.

MARTIN LUTHER, 1483–1546
Based on Plainsong Melody, Mode II,
Jesu, dulcedo cordium

SECOND TUNE

Devotionally
1. Lord, keep us stead - fast in thy word, Curb
2. Lord Je - sus Christ, thy power make known, For
those who fain by craft or sword Would wrest the king-dom from thy
thou art Lord of lords a - lone; De - fend thy Chris-ten - dom, that
Son, And set at naught all he hath done.
we May ev - er - more sing praise to thee. A - men.

3 O Comforter of priceless worth,
Send peace and unity on earth;
Support us in our final strife,
And lead us out of death to life. Amen.

Martin Luther, 1483–1546
Tr. Catherine Winkworth, 1829–78

ASCENDIT DEUS. 8 8 7, 8 8 7.
JOHANN GOTTFRIED SCHICHT, 1753–1823
FIRST TUNE
In moderate time, with dignity
1. Fear not, thou faith - ful Chris - tian flock; God is thy shel - ter
and thy rock: Fear not for thy sal - va - tion. Though
fierce the foe and dark the night, The Lord of hosts shall
be thy might, Christ thine il - lu - mi - na - tion.

2 Arise, arise, the foe defy!
Call on the Name of God most high,
That he with might endue you.
And Christ, your everlasting Priest,
In all your conflicts shall assist,
From strength to strength renew you.

Johann Michael Altenburg(?), 1584–1630
Tr. Robert Bridges, 1844–1930

From the YATTENDON HYMNAL, *Edited by Robert Bridges*
By permission of the Clarendon Press, Oxford

KOMMT HER ZU MIR. 8 8 7, 8 8 7. German Folksong, XV cent.

SECOND TUNE

With confidence
1. Fear not, thou faith - ful Chris - tian flock; God is thy
shel - ter and thy rock: Fear not for thy sal - va - tion.
Though fierce the foe and dark the night, The Lord of
hosts shall be thy might, Christ thine il - lu - mi - na - tion.

2 Arise, arise, the foe defy!
Call on the Name of God most high,
That he with might endue you.
And Christ, your everlasting Priest,
In all your conflicts shall assist,
From strength to strength renew you.

Johann Michael Altenburg(?), 1584–1630
Tr. Robert Bridges, 1844–1930

CLOISTERS. 11 11 11, 5. JOSEPH BARNBY, 1838–96

Moderately fast, in strict time

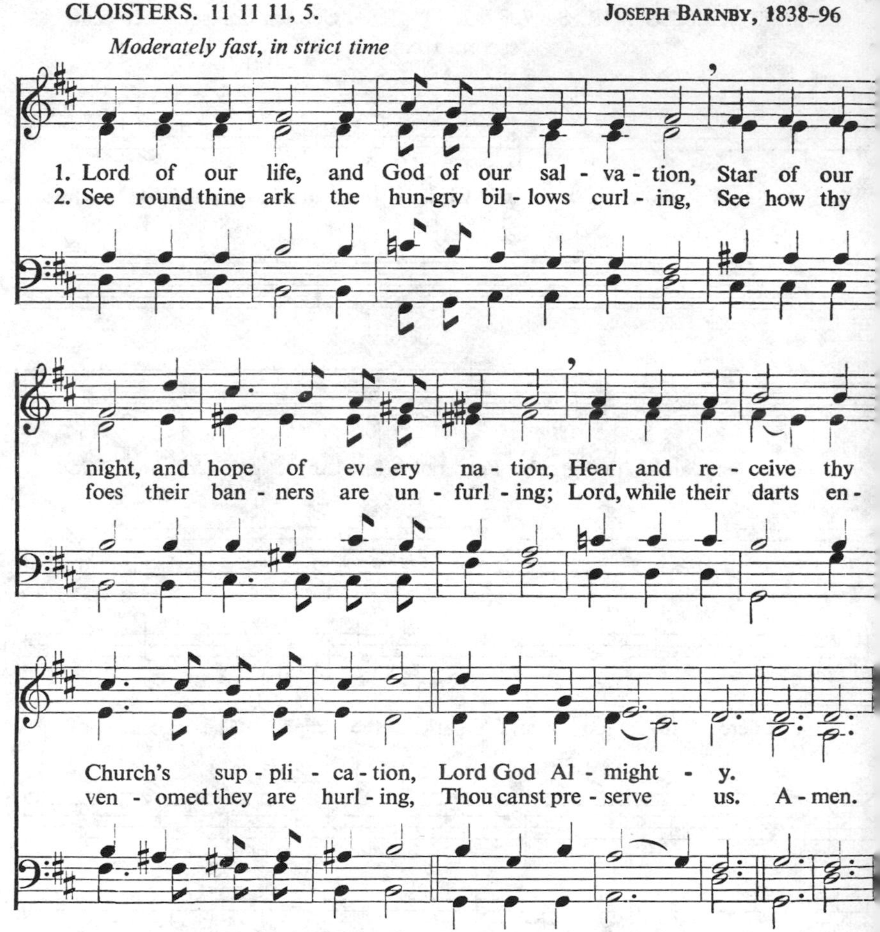
1. Lord of our life, and God of our sal - va - tion, Star of our
2. See round thine ark the hun-gry bil - lows curl - ing, See how thy
night, and hope of ev - ery na - tion, Hear and re - ceive thy
foes their ban - ners are un - furl - ing; Lord, while their darts en -
Church's sup - pli - ca - tion, Lord God Al - might - y.
ven - omed they are hurl - ing, Thou canst pre - serve us. A - men.

3 Lord, thou canst help when earthly armor faileth,
Lord, thou canst save when deadly sin assaileth,
Lord, o'er thy rock nor death nor hell prevaileth;
Grant us thy peace, Lord.

4 Peace in our hearts, our evil thoughts assuaging,
Peace in thy Church, where brothers are engaging,
Peace when the world its busy war is waging;
Calm thy foes' raging.

5 Grant us thy help till backward they are driven;
Grant them thy truth, that they may be forgiven;
Grant peace on earth, and, after we have striven,
Peace in thy heaven. Amen.

Matthäus Apelles von Löwenstern, 1594–164
Paraphrase, Philip Pusey, 1799–185

ST. THOMAS. S. M. AARON WILLIAMS, 1731–76

Slowly

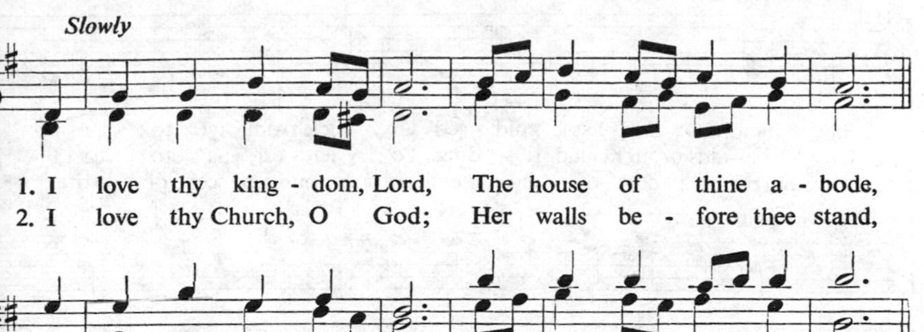
1. I love thy king - dom, Lord, The house of thine a - bode,
2. I love thy Church, O God; Her walls be - fore thee stand,

The Church our blest Re - deem - er saved With his own pre-cious Blood.
Dear as the ap - ple of thine eye, And grav - en on thy hand. A-men.

3 For her my tears shall fall,
For her my prayers ascend;
To her my cares and toils be given,
Till toils and cares shall end.

4 Beyond my highest joy
I prize her heavenly ways,
Her sweet communion, solemn vows,
Her hymns of love and praise.

5 Jesus, thou Friend divine,
Our Saviour and our King,
Thy hand from every snare and foe
Shall great deliverance bring.

6 Sure as thy truth shall last,
To Sion shall be given
The brightest glories earth can yield,
And brighter bliss of heaven. Amen.

Timothy Dwight, 1752–1817

THORNBURY. 7 6, 7 6. D. BASIL HARWOOD, 1859–1949

Slowly; in unison
1. Thy hand, O God, has guid - ed Thy flock from age to age;
2. Thy her-alds brought glad ti - dings To great - est, as to least;
3. Through man-y a day of dark - ness, Through man-y a scene of strife,
The won-drous tale is writ - ten, Full clear, on ev - ery page;
They bade men rise, and has - ten To share the great King's feast;
The faith - ful few fought brave - ly To guard the na - tion's life.
Our fa - thers owned thy good - ness, And we their deeds re -
And this was all their teach - ing, In ev - ery deed and
Their Gos - pel of re - demp - tion, Sin par-doned, man re -
cord; And both of this bear wit - ness, One Church,
word, To all a - like pro - claim - ing, One Church,
stored, Was all in this en - fold - ed, One Church,
Org.

one Faith, one Lord. . . . .
one Faith, one Lord, one Faith, one Lord.
org.)

4 And we, shall we be faithless?
Shall hearts fail, hands hang down?
Shall we evade the conflict,
And cast away our crown?
Not so; in God's deep counsels
Some better thing is stored;
We will maintain, unflinching,
One Church, one Faith, one Lord.

5 Thy mercy will not fail us,
Nor leave thy work undone;
With thy right hand to help us,
The victory shall be won;
And then by men and angels
Thy Name shall be adored,
And this shall be their anthem,
One Church, one Faith, one Lord.

Edward Hayes Plumptre, 1821–91

See also:

242 Christ is made the sure foundation
330 City of God, how broad and far
557 Fight the good fight
565 Forward! be our watchword
342 In Christ there is no east or west
584 Jerusalem the golden
550 Lead on, O King eternal
356 Mine eyes have seen the glory
168 O God, our help in ages past
560 Onward, Christian soldiers
541 Rise up, O men of God
556 Rise, ye children of salvation
564 Soldiers of Christ, arise
562 The Son of God goes forth to war
566 Thine is the glory
529 Through the night of doubt and sorrow

160

PRAISE, MY SOUL. 8 7, 8 7, 8 7. — JOHN GOSS, 1800–80

FIRST TUNE

Slowly, with joy

1. Praise, my soul, the King of heav - en; To his feet thy trib-ute bring;
2. Praise him for his grace and fa - vor To our fa-thers in dis - tress;

Ran-somed, healed, re - stored, for - giv - en, Who like me his praise should sing
Praise him, still the same for ev - er, Slow to chide, and swift to bless:

Al - le - lu - ia! Al - le - lu - ia! Praise the ev - er - last - ing King.
Al - le - lu - ia! Al - le - lu - ia! Glo - rious in his faith - ful - ness.

3 Father-like he tends and spares us,
Well our feeble frame he knows;
In his hands he gently bears us,
Rescues us from all our foes:
Alleluia! Alleluia!
Widely as his mercy flows.

4 Angels, help us to adore him,
Ye behold him face to face;
Sun and moon, bow down before him;
Dwellers all in time and space:
Alleluia! Alleluia!
Praise with us the God of grace.

Henry Francis Lyte, 1793–18
Based on Psalm 1

OUR LADY, TRONDHJEM. 8 7, 8 7, 8 7.

LUDVIG MATTHIAS LINDEMAN, 1812–87

SECOND TUNE

With dignity

1. Praise, my soul, the King of heav - en; To his feet thy trib - ute bring;
2. Praise him for his grace and fa - vor To our fa - thers in dis - tress;

Ran-somed, healed, re-stored, for - giv - en, Who like me his praise should sing?
Praise him, still the same for ev - er, Slow to chide, and swift to bless:

Al - le - lu - ia! Al - le - lu - ia! Praise the ev - er - last - ing King.
Al - le - lu - ia! Al - le - lu - ia! Glo - rious in his faith - ful - ness.

3 Father-like he tends and spares us,
Well our feeble frame he knows;
In his hands he gently bears us,
Rescues us from all our foes:
Alleluia! Alleluia!
Widely as his mercy flows.

4 Angels, help us to adore him,
Ye behold him face to face;
Sun and moon, bow down before him;
Dwellers all in time and space:
Alleluia! Alleluia!
Praise with us the God of grace.

Henry Francis Lyte, 1793–1847
Based on Psalm 103

OLD HUNDREDTH. L. M.

LOUIS BOURGEOIS, *cir.* 1510–61
Genevan Psalter, 1551

With great dignity

1. Be - fore Je - ho - vah's awe - ful throne, Ye na - tions bow with sa - cred joy: Know that the Lord is God a - lone, He can cre - ate, and he de - stroy.
2. His sov - ereign power, with - out our aid, Made us of clay, and formed us men; And when like wan-dering sheep we strayed, He brought us to his fold a - gain.

3 We are his people, we his care,
  Our souls and all our mortal frame:
What lasting honors shall we rear,
  Almighty Maker, to thy Name?

4 We'll crowd thy gates with thankful songs,
  High as the heavens our voices raise,
And earth, with her ten thousand tongues,
  Shall fill thy courts with sounding praise.

5 Wide as the world is thy command,
  Vast as eternity thy love;
Firm as a rock thy truth shall stand,
  When rolling years shall cease to move.

Isaac Watts, 1674–174
Revised by John Wesley, 1703–9
Psalm 10

WINCHESTER NEW. 8 8, 8 8, 8 8.

GEORG WITTWE'S *Musikalisch Handbuch*, 1690

With dignity
1. Lo, God is here! let us a - dore, And own how
Let all with - in us feel his power, And si - lent
dread - ful is this place!
bow be - fore his face; Who know his power, his grace who
prove, Serve him with awe, with rev - erence love. A - men.

2 Lo, God is here! him day and night
United choirs of angels sing;
To him, enthroned above all height,
The hosts of heaven their praises bring;
Disdain not, Lord, our meaner song,
Who praise thee with a faltering tongue.

3 Being of beings, may our praise
Thy courts with grateful fragrance fill!
Still may we stand before thy face
Still hear and do thy sovereign will;
To thee may all our thoughts arise
A true and ceaseless sacrifice. Amen.

Gerhard Tersteegen, 1697–1769
Tr. John Wesley, 1703–91

This hymn may also be sung to VATER UNSER (No. 380).

HANOVER. 10 10, 11 11. WILLIAM CROFT, 1678–1727

With dignity

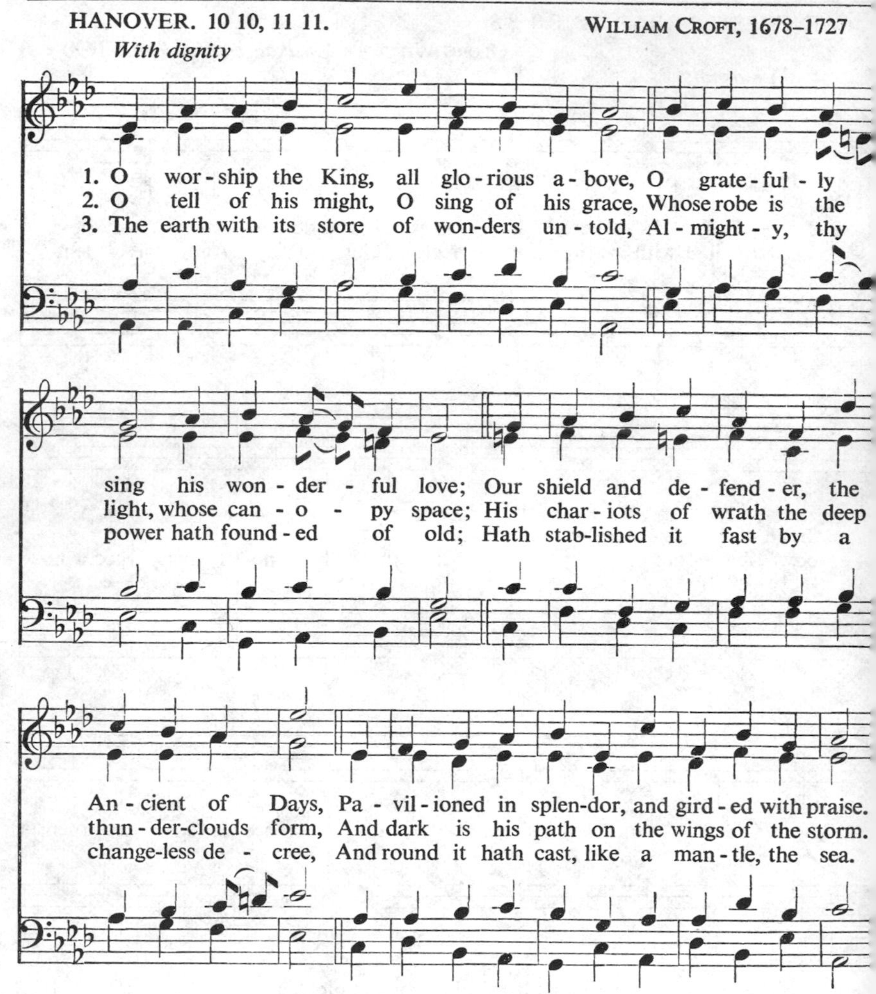
1. O wor-ship the King, all glo-rious a-bove, O grate-ful-ly sing his won-der-ful love; Our shield and de-fend-er, the An-cient of Days, Pa-vil-ioned in splen-dor, and gird-ed with praise.
2. O tell of his might, O sing of his grace, Whose robe is the light, whose can-o-py space; His char-iots of wrath the deep thun-der-clouds form, And dark is his path on the wings of the storm.
3. The earth with its store of won-ders un-told, Al-might-y, thy power hath found-ed of old; Hath stab-lished it fast by a change-less de-cree, And round it hath cast, like a man-tle, the sea.

4 Thy bountiful care what tongue can recite?
It breathes in the air, it shines in the light;
It streams from the hills, it descends to the plain,
And sweetly distils in the dew and the rain.

5 Frail children of dust, and feeble as frail,
In thee do we trust, nor find thee to fail;
Thy mercies how tender, how firm to the end,
Our Maker, Defender, Redeemer, and Friend.

6 O measureless Might, ineffable Love,
While angels delight to hymn thee above,
The humbler creation, though feeble their lays,
With true adoration shall sing to thy praise.

Robert Grant, 1779–18
Psalm 1

164

ARNSBERG (WUNDERBARER KÖNIG). 6 6 8, 6 6 8, 3 3, 6 6.

JOACHIM NEANDER, 1650–80

Reverently

1. God him-self is pres-ent, Let us now a-dore him,
And with awe ap-pear be-fore him!
God is in his tem-ple, All with-in keep si-lence,
Pros-trate lie with deep-est rev-erence. Him a-lone God we own,
Him, our God and Sav-iour; Praise his Name for-ev-er! A-men.

2 God himself is present,
Hear the harps resounding;
See the crowds the throne surrounding!
'Holy, Holy, Holy,'
Hear the hymn ascending,
Angels, saints, their voices blending!
Bow thine ear
To us here!
Hear, O Christ, the praises
That thy Church now raises.

3 O thou Fount of blessing,
Purify my spirit,
Trusting only in thy merit;
Like the holy angels
Who behold thy glory,
May I ceaselessly adore thee.
Let thy will
Ever still
Rule thy Church terrestrial,
As the hosts celestial. Amen.

Gerhard Tersteegen, 1697–1769
Tr. Frederick William Foster, 1760–1835
John Miller, 1756–1790

KANE. S. M. D. LOWELL MASON, 1792–1872

With spirit
1. Come, we that love the Lord, And let our joys be known;
Join in a song with sweet ac - cord, And thus sur-round the throne.
Let those re - fuse to sing That nev - er knew our God;
But chil - dren of the heaven-ly King Must speak their joys a - broad.

2 The men of grace have found
Glory begun below;
Celestial fruits on earthly ground
From faith and hope may grow.
The hill of Zion yields
A thousand sacred sweets,
Before we reach the heavenly fields
Or walk the golden streets.

3 There shall we see his face,
And never, never sin;
There from the rivers of his grace
Drink endless pleasures in.
Then let our songs abound,
And every tear be dry;
We're marching through Immanuel's
To fairer worlds on high. [groun

Isaac Watts, 1674–174

AMERICAN HYMN. 10 10, 10 10. MATTHIAS KELLER, 1813–90

With dignity
1. Bless - ing and hon - or, and glo - ry and power, Wis - dom, and
2. Dwell - eth the light of the glo - ry with him, Light of a
rich - es, and strength ev - er - more, Give ye to him who our
glo - ry that can - not grow dim, Light in its si - lence and
bat - tle hath won, Whose are the king-dom, the crown and the throne,
beau - ty and calm, Light in its glad-ness and bright-ness and balm,
Whose are the king - dom, the crown and the throne.
Light in its glad - ness and bright - ness and balm.

3 Ever ascendeth the song and the joy,
Ever descendeth the love from on high,
Blessing, and honor, and glory, and praise,
This is the theme of the hymns that we raise.

4 Give we the glory and praise to the Lamb;
Take we the robe and the harp and the palm;
Sing we the song of the Lamb that was slain,
Dying in weakness, but rising to reign.

Horatius Bonar, 1808–89

This hymn may also be sung to TRISAGION (No. 148).

TE DEUM (GROSSER GOTT). 7 8, 7 8, 77.

Allgemeines Katholisches Gesangbuch, Vienna 1774

Boldly, with movement
1. Ho - ly God, we praise thy Name; Lord of all, we bow be - fore thee!
All on earth thy scep - tre claim, All in heaven a - bove a - dore thee;
In - fi - nite thy vast do - main, Ev - er - last - ing is thy reign. A - men.

2 Hark! the loud celestial hymn
Angel choirs above are raising,
Cherubim and seraphim,
In unceasing chorus praising;
Fill the heavens with sweet accord:
Holy, holy, holy, Lord.

3 Lo! the Apostolic train
Join the sacred Name to hallow;
Prophets swell the loud refrain,
And the white-robed martyrs follow;
And from morn to set of sun,
Through the Church the song goes on.

4 Holy Father, Holy Son,
Holy Spirit, Three we name thee;
While in essence only One,
Undivided God we claim thee;
And adoring bend the knee,
While we own the mystery. Amen.

German, XVIII cen
Tr. Clarence A. Walworth, 1820–190

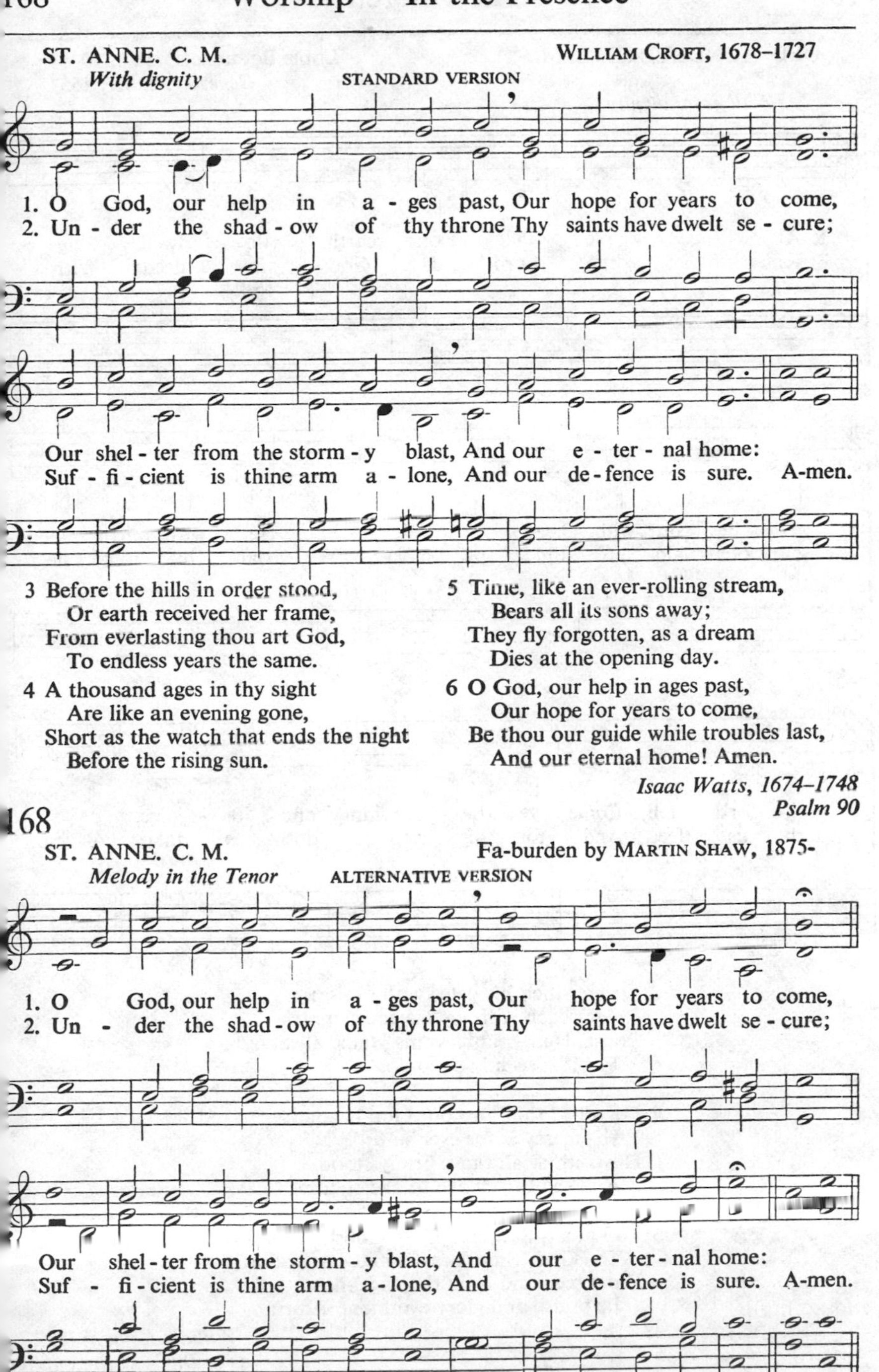
ST. ANNE. C. M.
WILLIAM CROFT, 1678–1727
With dignity
STANDARD VERSION
1. O God, our help in a - ges past, Our hope for years to come,
2. Un - der the shad - ow of thy throne Thy saints have dwelt se - cure;
Our shel - ter from the storm - y blast, And our e - ter - nal home:
Suf - fi - cient is thine arm a - lone, And our de - fence is sure. A-men.
3 Before the hills in order stood,
Or earth received her frame,
From everlasting thou art God,
To endless years the same.
4 A thousand ages in thy sight
Are like an evening gone,
Short as the watch that ends the night
Before the rising sun.
5 Time, like an ever-rolling stream,
Bears all its sons away;
They fly forgotten, as a dream
Dies at the opening day.
6 O God, our help in ages past,
Our hope for years to come,
Be thou our guide while troubles last,
And our eternal home! Amen.
Isaac Watts, 1674–1748
Psalm 90
168
ST. ANNE. C. M.
Fa-burden by MARTIN SHAW, 1875-
Melody in the Tenor
ALTERNATIVE VERSION
1. O God, our help in a - ges past, Our hope for years to come,
2. Un - der the shad - ow of thy throne Thy saints have dwelt se - cure;
Our shel - ter from the storm - y blast, And our e - ter - nal home:
Suf - fi - cient is thine arm a - lone, And our de - fence is sure. A-men.

OLD HUNDREDTH. L. M.
LOUIS BOURGEOIS, cir. 1510–61
Genevan Psalter, 1551
With great dignity
1. All peo - ple that on earth do dwell, Sing
2. Know that the Lord is God in - deed; With -
to the Lord with cheer - ful voice; Him serve with mirth, his
out our aid he did us make; We are his folk, he
praise forth tell, Come ye be - fore him, and re - joice.
doth us feed, And for his sheep he doth us take. A-men.

3 O enter then his gates with praise;
Approach with joy his courts unto;
Praise, laud, and bless his Name always,
For it is seemly so to do.

4 For why? the Lord our God is good:
His mercy is for ever sure;
His truth at all times firmly stood,
And shall from age to age endure.

5 To Father, Son, and Holy Ghost,
The God whom heaven and earth adore,
From men and from the angel-host
Be praise and glory evermore. Amen.

William Kethe, †1608 ?
As in Day's Psalter, 1561
Psalm 100

LOUVAN. L. M. VIRGIL CORYDON TAYLOR, 1817–91

In moderate time

1. Lord of all be - ing, throned a - far, Thy glo - ry flames from sun and star; Cen - ter and soul of ev - ery sphere, Yet to each lov - ing heart how near!
2. Sun of our life, thy quick - ening ray Sheds on our path the glow of day; Star of our hope, thy sof - tened light Cheers the long watch - es of the night. A - men.

3 Our midnight is thy smile withdrawn,
Our noontide is thy gracious dawn,
Our rainbow arch thy mercy's sign;
All, save the clouds of sin, are thine.

4 Lord of all life, below, above,
Whose light is truth, whose warmth is love,
Before thy ever-blazing throne
We ask no lustre of our own.

5 Grant us thy truth to make us free,
And kindling hearts that burn for thee,
Till all thy living altars claim
One holy light, one heavenly flame. Amen.

Oliver Wendell Holmes, 1809–94

This hymn may also be sung to OMBERSLEY (No. 118).

DARMSTADT. 6 7, 6 7, 6 6, 6 6.

AHASUERUS FRITSCH, 1629–1701
Adapted and harm. by J. S. BACH, 1685–1750

Moderately

1. Our God, to whom we turn When wea - ry with il - lu - sion,
Whose stars se - rene - ly burn A - bove this earth's con - fu - sion,
Thine is the might-y plan, The stead - fast or - der sure,
In which the world be - gan, En - dures, and shall en - dure.

2. Thou art thy - self the truth; Though we, who fain would find thee,
Have tried, with thoughts un - couth, In fee - ble words to bind thee,
It is be - cause thou art We're driv - en to the quest;
Till truth from false - hood part Our souls can find no rest.

3. All beau - ty speaks of thee: The moun-tains and the riv - ers,
The line of lift - ed sea, Where spread-ing moon-light quiv - ers,
The deep-toned or - gan blast That rolls through arch - es dim,
Hints of the mu - sic vast Of thy e - ter - nal hymn. A-men.

4 Wherever goodness lurks
We catch thy tones appealing;
Where man for justice works
Thou art thyself revealing;
The blood of man, for man
On friendship's altar spilt,
Betrays the mystic plan
On which thy house is built.

5 Thou hidden fount of love,
Of peace, and truth, and beauty,
Inspire us from above
With joy and strength for duty.
May thy fresh light arise
Within each clouded heart,
And give us open eyes
To see thee as thou art. Amen.

Edward Grubb, 1854–1939

72

ST. DENIO. 11 11, 11 11. Welsh Hymn Melody

Majestically

1. Im - mor - tal, in - vis - i - ble, God on - ly wise,
In light in - ac - ces - si - ble hid from our eyes,
Most bless - ed, most glo - rious, the An - cient of Days,
Al - might - y, vic - to - rious, thy great Name we praise. A - men.

2 Unresting, unhasting, and silent as light,
Nor wanting, nor wasting, thou rulest in might;
Thy justice like mountains high soaring above,
Thy clouds which are fountains of goodness and love.

3 To all life thou givest, to both great and small;
In all life thou livest, the true life of all;
We blossom and flourish like leaves on the tree,
And wither and perish; but naught changeth thee.

4 Great Father of glory, pure Father of light,
Thine angels adore thee, all veiling their sight;
All laud we would render: O help us to see
'Tis only the splendor of light hideth thee. Amen.

Walter Chalmers Smith, 1824–1908

173 The Church

LASST UNS ERFREUEN. 8 8, 4 4, 8 8. With Refrain.

Geistliche Kirchengesänge, Cologne, 1623

In unison, boldly
1. All crea-tures of our God and King, Lift up your voice and
2. Thou rush-ing wind that art so strong, Ye clouds that sail in
with us sing Al - le - lu - ia, al - le - lu - ia!
heaven a - long, O . . . praise him, al - le - lu - ia!
Thou burn-ing sun with gold - en beam, Thou sil - ver moo
Thou ris - ing morn, in praise re - joice, Ye . lights of eve

Refrain
with soft - er gleam: O praise him, O praise him,
ning, find a voice:
Al - le - lu - ia, al - le - lu - ia, al - le - lu - ia!

Thou flowing water, pure and clear,
Make music for thy Lord to hear,
Alleluia, alleluia!
Thou fire so masterful and bright,
That givest man both warmth and light:

Dear mother earth, who day by day
Unfoldest blessings on our way,
O praise him, alleluia!
The flowers and fruits that in thee grow,
Let them his glory also show:

5 And all ye men of tender heart,
Forgiving others, take your part,
O sing ye, alleluia!
Ye who long pain and sorrow bear,
Praise God and on him cast your care:

6 And thou, most kind and gentle death,
Waiting to hush our latest breath,
O praise him, alleluia!
Thou leadest home the child of God,
And Christ our Lord the way hath trod:

7 Let all things their Creator bless,
And worship him in humbleness;
O praise him, alleluia!
Praise, praise the Father, praise the Son,
And praise the Spirit, Three in One:

St. Francis of Assisi, 1182–1226
Tr. William H. Draper, 1855–1933

TER SANCTUS. 8 8, 10 10. *Rostockerhandboken,* 1529

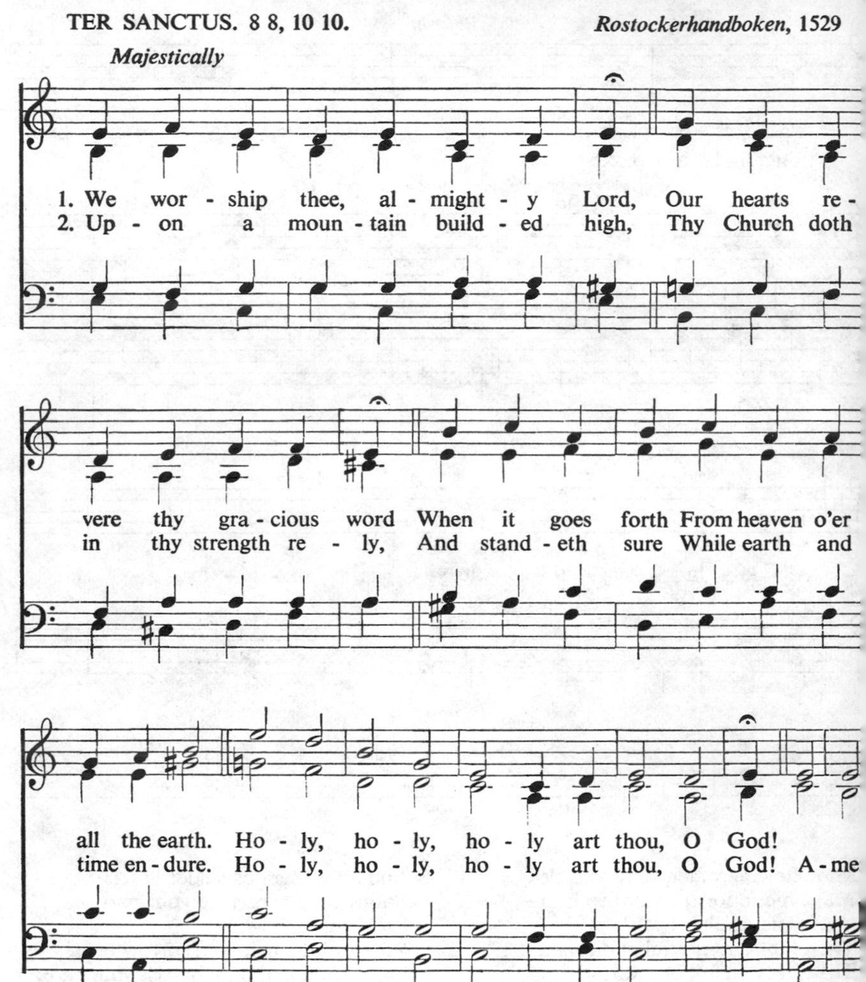
Majestically
1. We wor - ship thee, al - might - y Lord, Our hearts re - vere thy gra - cious word When it goes forth From heaven o'er all the earth. Ho - ly, ho - ly, ho - ly art thou, O God!
2. Up - on a moun - tain build - ed high, Thy Church doth in thy strength re - ly, And stand - eth sure While earth and time en - dure. Ho - ly, ho - ly, ho - ly art thou, O God! A - me

3 Through her shall every land proclaim
The sacred might of Jesus' Name,
And all rejoice
With Christian heart and voice.
Holy, holy, holy art thou, O God!

4 All nations to thy throne shall throng
And raise on high the victory song,
While cherubim
Reply to seraphim,
'Holy, holy, holy art thou, O God!' Amen.

Johan Olof Wallin, 1779–1
Tr. Charles Wharton Stork, 18

LEICESTER. 8 8, 8 8, 8 8. JOHN BISHOP, *cir.* 1665–1737

With movement

1. O King of kings, be - fore whose throne The an - gels bow, no gift can we Pre - sent that is in - deed our own, Since heaven and earth be - long to thee; Yet this our souls through grace im - part, The of - fering of a thank - ful heart. A-men.

2 O Jesu, set at God's right hand,
With thine eternal Father plead
For all thy loyal-hearted band,
Who still on earth thy succor need:
For them in weakness strength provide,
And through the world their footsteps [guide.

3 O Holy Spirit, fount of breath,
Whose comforts never fail nor fade,
Vouchsafe the life that knows no death,
Vouchsafe the light that knows no shade;
And grant that we through all our days
May share thy gifts, and sing thy praise.
Amen.

John Quarles, 1624–65
Alt. Thomas Darling, 1816–93

This hymn may also be sung to ST. CHRYSOSTOM (No. 504).

MIRIAM. 7 6, 7 6. D. JOSEPH PARRY HOLBROOK, 1822–88

FIRST TUNE

With dignity

1. O God, the Rock of A - ges, Who ev - er - more hast been,
What time the tem - pest rag - es, Our dwell - ing - place se - rene;
Be - fore thy first cre - a - tions, O Lord, the same as now,
To end - less gen - er - a - tions The ev - er - last - ing Thou. A-me

2 Our years are like the shadows
On sunny hills that lie,
Or grasses in the meadows
That blossom but to die;
A sleep, a dream, a story
By strangers quickly told,
An unremaining glory
Of things that soon are old.

3 O thou who canst not slumber,
Whose light grows never pale,
Teach us aright to number
Our years before they fail;
On us thy mercy lighten,
On us thy goodness rest,
And let thy Spirit brighten
The hearts thyself hast blessed. Am

Edward Henry Bickersteth, 1825–19

DU MEINE SEELE SINGE. 7 6, 7 6. D. JOHANN GEORG EBELING, 1637–76

SECOND TUNE

In flowing style

1. O God, the Rock of A - ges, Who ev - er-more hast been,
What time the tem - pest rag - es, Our dwell - ing-place se - rene;
Be - fore thy first cre - a - tions, O Lord, the same as now,
To end - less gen - er - a - tions The ev - er - last - ing Thou. A-men.

2 Our years are like the shadows
  On sunny hills that lie,
Or grasses in the meadows
  That blossom but to die;
A sleep, a dream, a story
  By strangers quickly told,
An unremaining glory
  Of things that soon are old.

3 O thou who canst not slumber,
  Whose light grows never pale,
Teach us aright to number
  Our years before they fail;
On us thy mercy lighten,
  On us thy goodness rest,
And let thy Spirit brighten
  The hearts thyself hast blessed. Amen.

Edward Henry Bickersteth, 1825–1906

ADORATION. 8 7, 8 7. D. GEORGE JOB ELVEY, 1816–93

FIRST TUNE

Brightly
1. Round the Lord in glo - ry seat - ed, Cher - u - bim and ser - a - phim
Filled his tem - ple, and re - peat - ed Each to each the al-ter - nate hym
Refrain
'Lord, thy glo - ry fills the heav - en, Earth is with its ful - ness store
Un - to thee be glo - ry giv - en, Ho - ly, ho - ly, ho - ly Lord!' A-me

2 Heaven is still with glory ringing,
Earth takes up the angels' cry,
'Holy, holy, holy,' singing,
'Lord of Hosts, the Lord most high!'

3 With his seraph-train before him,
With his holy Church below,
Thus unite we to adore him,
Bid we thus our anthem flow:

Richard Mant, 1776–

MOULTRIE. 8 7, 8 7. D. GERARD FRANCIS COBB, 1838–1904

SECOND TUNE

In moderate time

1. Round the Lord in glo - ry seat - ed, Cher - u - bim and ser - a - phim
Filled his tem - ple, and re - peat - ed Each to each the al - ter - nate hymn:

Refrain

'Lord, thy glo - ry fills the heav - en, Earth is with its ful - ness stored;
Un - to thee be glo - ry giv - en, Ho - ly, ho - ly, ho - ly Lord!' A-men.

2 Heaven is still with glory ringing,
Earth takes up the angels' cry,
'Holy, holy, holy,' singing,
'Lord of Hosts, the Lord most high!'

3 With his seraph-train before him,
With his holy Church below,
Thus unite we to adore him,
Bid we thus our anthem flow:

Richard Mant, 1776–1848

INVOCATION. 10 10, 10 10, 10 10. CARL W. LANDAHL, 1908-

Moderately

1. E - ter - nal God, be - fore thy throne we bend, Thy grace to
seek, thy ho - ly Name to bless; Hum - bly our hearts in
grate - ful praise as - cend To thee whose ways are
truth and right-eous - ness. With all the hosts of heaven we thee a -
dore, Ho - ly art thou, the same for ev - er - more! A-men.

2 Lord Jesus Christ, our Saviour and our Friend,
Whom angels praise before the throne on high,
How vast thy love to love us to the end,
And on the cruel Cross to bleed and die.
O blest Redeemer, hear thy children pray:
O Lamb of God, take all our sins away!

3 Spirit of truth, of peace, of joy divine,
Descend to us in all thy saving power;
Kindle a flame of faith and love to shine
Within our yearning hearts this sacred hour;
Show us the Father's will, the Saviour's love,
And fit our souls to dwell with thee above! Amen.

Ernest Edwin Ryden, 1886–

79

KIRBY BEDON. 6 6 4, 6 6 6 4. EDWARD BUNNETT, 1834–1923

In moderate time

1. Shep-herd of ten-der youth, Guid-ing in love and truth
2. Thou art our ho-ly Lord, The all-sub-du-ing Word,
Through de-vious ways, Christ, our tri-um-phant King, We come thy Name to
Heal-er of strife; Thou didst thy-self a-base, That from sin's deep dis-
sing; Hith-er thy chil-dren bring Trib-utes of praise.
grace Thou might-est save our race, And give us life. A-men.

3 Ever be near our side,
Our Shepherd and our guide,
Our staff and song;
Jesus, thou Christ of God,
By thine enduring word
Lead us where thou hast trod,
Make our faith strong.

4 So now, and till we die,
Sound we thy praises high,
And joyful sing;
Let all the holy throng
Who to thy Church belong,
Unite and swell the song
To Christ, our King. Amen.

Clement of Alexandria, cir. 200
Tr. Henry Martyn Dexter, 1821–90

SUOMI. Irregular.

Finnish Folk Melody
Arr. ULRICH S. LEUPOLD, 1909–

Reverently

1. A - rise, my soul, a - rise! Stretch forth to things e - ter - nal,
Though hid from mor - tal eyes, He dwell in light su - per - nal,
2. List to the harps of heaven! Hark to the song vic - to - rious,
To mor - tals is not given To chant its strains all - glo - rious;

And haste thee to the feet of thy Re - deem - er God.
Yet wor - ship him in hum - ble - ness and own him Lord.
The nev - er - end - ing an - them sound - ing through the sky.
Yet sing, my soul, the praise of him who reigns on high.

His ban - quet of love A - waits thee a - bove; Be -
Who bought with his Blood The ran - somed of God; To

hold, the mar - riage fes - tal of the Lamb is come!
him be ev - er - last - ing power and vic - to - ry.
Re - joice, my soul, re - joice, To heaven lift up thy voice:
And let the great A - men Re - sound through heaven a - gain.
Al - le - lu - ia, al - le - lu - ia, al - le - lu - ia!
Al - le - lu - ia, al - le - lu - ia, al - le - lu - ia! A - men.

Johan Kahl, 1721–46
Tr. Ernest E. Ryden, 1886–

DUNDEE (FRENCH). **C. M.** *Scottish Psalter*, 1615

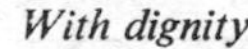
With dignity

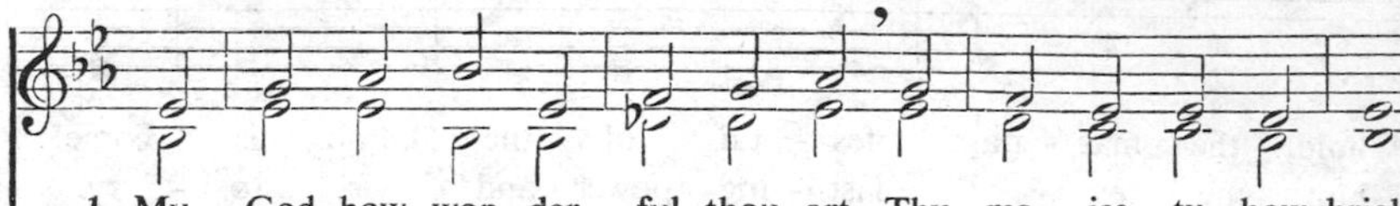

1. My God, how won - der - ful thou art, Thy ma - jes - ty how bright;
2. How dread are thine e - ter - nal years, O ev - er - last - ing Lord,
3. How won - der - ful, how beau - ti - ful The sight of thee must be,

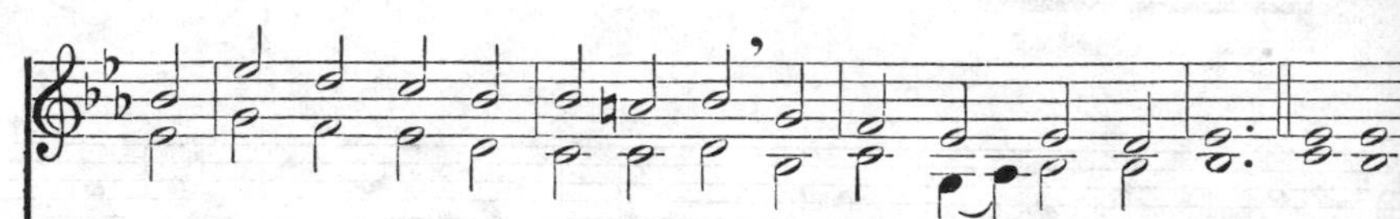

How beau - ti - ful thy mer - cy - seat, In depths of burn - ing light!
By pros-trate spir - its day and night In - ces - sant - ly a -dored!
Thine end-less wis-dom, bound-less power, And awe - ful pur - i - ty! A-men

4 O how I fear thee, living God,
With deepest, tenderest fears,
And worship thee with trembling hope
And penitential tears!

5 Yet I may love thee, too, O Lord,
Almighty as thou art,
For thou hast stooped to ask of me
The love of my poor heart.

6 No earthly father loves like thee;
No mother, e'er so mild,
Bears and forbears as thou hast done
With me, thy sinful child.

7 Father of Jesus, love's reward,
What rapture will it be
Prostrate before thy throne to lie,
And gaze and gaze on thee! Amen.

Frederick William Faber, 1814–

This hymn may also be sung to BEATITUDO (No. 213).

See also:

203 At thy feet, O Christ, we lay
121 Come, Holy Ghost, in love
122 Come, Holy Spirit, God and Lord
136 Come, thou almighty King
429 From all that dwell below the skies
189 Glorious Majesty, before thee
435 Hail, thou once despisèd Jesus
188 Lord Jesus Christ, be present now
397 Love divine, all loves excelling
353 O God of wondrous grace and glory
462 O my soul, on wings ascending
419 O Saviour, precious Saviour
410 The God of Abraham praise
505 Thee will I love, my strength

BERNO. 7 6, 7 6. D.
ARTHUR HENRY MANN, 1850–1929
In moderate time
FIRST TUNE
1. O day of rest and glad - ness, O day of joy and light,
2. On thee, at the cre - a - tion, The light first had its birth;
O balm of care and sad - ness, Most beau - ti - ful, most bright!
On thee, for our sal - va - tion, Christ rose from depths of earth;
On thee the high and low - ly, Be - fore the e - ter - nal throne,
On thee our Lord vic - to - rious The Spir - it sent from heaven,
Sing, 'Ho - ly, ho - ly, ho - ly,' To the great Three in One.
And thus on thee most glo - rious A tri - ple light was given. A-men.

3 Today on weary nations
The heavenly manna falls;
To holy convocations
The silver trumpet calls,
Where Gospel light is glowing
With pure and radiant beams,
And living water flowing
With soul-refreshing streams.

4 New graces ever gaining
From this our day of rest,
We reach the rest remaining
To spirits of the blest.
To Holy Ghost be praises,
To Father, and to Son;
The Church her voice upraises
To thee, blest Three in One. Amen.

Christopher Wordsworth, 1807–85

KOMM, SEELE. 7 6, 7 6. D. JOHANN WOLFGANG FRANCK, 1641–88

In moderate time SECOND TUNE

1. O day of rest and glad - ness, O day of joy and light,
2. On thee, at the cre - a - tion, The light first had its birth;
O balm of care and sad - ness, Most beau - ti - ful, most bright!
On thee, for our sal - va - tion, Christ rose from depths of earth;
On thee the high and low - ly, Be - fore the e-ter - nal throne,
On thee our Lord vic - to - rious The Spir - it sent from heaven;
Sing, 'Ho - ly, ho - ly, ho - ly,' To the great Three in One.
And thus on thee most glo - rious A tri - ple light was given. A-men.

3 Today on weary nations
The heavenly manna falls;
To holy convocations
The silver trumpet calls,
Where Gospel light is glowing
With pure and radiant beams,
And living water flowing
With soul-refreshing streams.

4 New graces ever gaining
From this our day of rest,
We reach the rest remaining
To spirits of the blest.
To Holy Ghost be praises,
To Father, and to Son;
The Church her voice upraises
To thee, blest Three in One. Amen.

Christopher Wordsworth, 1807–8

83 Worship — The Lord's Day

TRURO. L. M.
Psalmodia Evangelica, 1789
With spirit
1. Sweet is the work, my God, my King, To praise thy Name, give thanks and sing, To show thy love by morn - ing light, And talk of all thy truth at night.
2. Sweet is the day of sa - cred rest; No mor - tal cares shall seize my breast; My heart shall tri - umph in my Lord, And bless his works, and bless his word.

3 And I shall share a glorious part
When grace hath well refined my heart;
When doubts and fears no more remain
To break my inward peace again.

4 Then shall I see and hear and know
All I desired or wished below;
And every power find sweet employ
In that eternal world of joy.

Isaac Watts, 1674–1748

MAIDSTONE. 7 7, 7 7. D. WALTER BOND GILBERT, 1829–1910

In flowing style
1. Pleas-ant are thy courts a - bove In the land of light and love;
2. Hap - py birds that sing and fly Round thy al - tars, O most High;
Pleas - ant are thy courts be - low In this land of sin and woe.
Hap - pier souls that find a rest In a heaven-ly Fa-ther's breast.
O, my spir - it longs and faints For the con - verse of thy saints,
Like the wan-dering dove that found No re - pose on earth a - round,
For the bright-ness of thy face, For thy ful - ness, God of Grace!
They can to their ark re - pair And en - joy it ev - er there. A-men.

3 Happy souls, their praises flow
Even in this vale of woe;
Waters in the desert rise,
Manna feeds them from the skies;
On they go from strength to strength,
Till they reach thy throne at length,
At thy feet adoring fall,
Who hast led them safe through all.

4 Lord, be mine this prize to win;
Guide me through a world of sin;
Keep me by thy saving grace;
Give me at thy side a place.
Sun and shield alike thou art;
Guide and guard my erring heart;
Grace and glory flow from thee;
Shower, O shower them, Lord, on me!
Amen

Henry Francis Lyte, 1793–184
Psalm 8

RED WING SEMINARY. 7 7, 7 7, 7 7. JOHN DAHLE, 1853–1931

Quietly
1. Safe - ly through an - oth - er week, God has brought us on our way;
2. While we pray for par-doning grace, Through the dear Re - deem-er's Name,
Let us now a bless - ing seek, Wait - ing in his courts to - day;
Show thy re - con - cil - ed face, Take a - way our sin and shame;
Day of all the week the best, Em - blem of e - ter - nal rest.
From our world-ly cares set free, May we rest this day in thee. A-men.

3 Here we come thy Name to praise,
Let us feel thy presence near;
May thy glory meet our eyes,
While we in thy house appear;
Here afford us, Lord, a taste
Of our everlasting feast.

4 May the Gospel's joyful sound
Conquer sinners, comfort saints;
Make the fruits of grace abound,
Bring relief for all complaints.
Thus may all our Sabbaths prove,
Till we join the Church above. Amen.

John Newton, 1725–1807

This hymn may also be sung to HEATHLANDS (No. 444)

MEINHOLD. 7 8, 7 8, 7 7. Lüneburg *Gesangbuch*, 1686

With feeling
1. Light of light, en - light - en me, Now a - new the day is dawn - ing;
2. Fount of all our joy and peace, To thy liv - ing wa - ters lead me;
Sun of grace, the shad-ows flee, Bright-en thou this ho - ly morn - ing;
Thou from earth my soul re - lease, And with grace and mer - cy feed me;
With thy joy - ous sun-shine blest, Hap-py is my day of rest.
Bless thy word, that it may prove Rich in fruits that thou dost love. A-m

3 Hence all care, all vanity,
For the day to God is holy;
Come, thou glorious Majesty,
Deign to fill this temple lowly;
Naught today my soul shall move,
Simply resting in thy love.

4 Let me with my heart today,
Holy, holy, holy, singing,
Rapt awhile from earth away,
All my soul to thee upspringing,
Have a foretaste inly given
How they worship thee in heaven. Ame

Benjamin Schmolck, 1672–17
Tr. Catherine Winkworth, 1829–78

See also:

169 All people that on earth do dwell
161 Before Jehovah's aweful throne
208 Christ, whose glory fills the skies
136 Come, thou almighty King
467 Dear Lord and Father of mankind
131 Holy, holy, holy, Lord God Almighty
438 Joyful, joyful we adore thee
162 Lo, God is here
496 Still, still with thee
416 When morning gilds the skies

See also: Adoration and Praise (Nos. 403–439)

NEANDER (UNSER HERRSCHER). 8 7, 8 7, 7 7. JOACHIM NEANDER, 1650–80

With dignity

1. O - pen now thy gates of beau - ty, Zi - on, let me en - ter there,
2. Here, O God, I come be - fore thee, Come thou al - so down to me;
Where my soul in joy - ful du - ty Waits on him who an-swers prayer:
Where we find thee and a - dore thee, There a heaven on earth must be:
O how bless-ed is this place, Filled with sol - ace, light, and grace.
To my heart O en - ter thou, Let it be thy tem - ple now. A-men.

3 Here thy praise is gladly chanted,
Here thy seed is duly sown;
Let my soul, where it is planted,
Bring forth precious sheaves alone:
So that all I hear may be
Fruitful unto life in me.

4 Thou my faith increase and quicken,
Let me keep thy gift divine;
Howsoe'er temptations thicken,
May thy word still o'er me shine,
As my guiding star through life,
As my comfort in my strife.

5 Speak, O God, and I will hear thee,
Let thy will be done indeed;
May I undisturbed draw near thee
While thou dost thy people feed;
Here of life the fountain flows,
Here is balm for all our woes. Amen.

Benjamin Schmolck, 1672–1737
Tr. Catherine Winkworth, 1829–78

This hymn may also be sung to DANA (No. 456).

HERR JESU CHRIST, DICH ZU UNS WEND. L. M.

Pensum Sacrum, Görlitz, 1648

FIRST TUNE

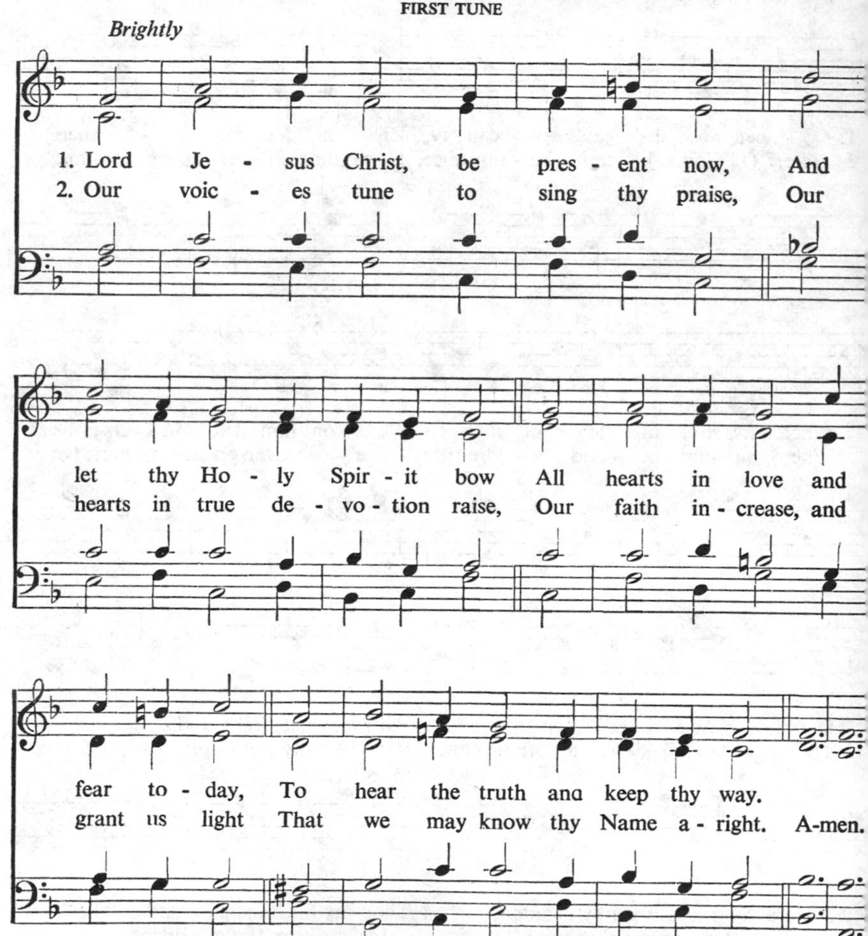
Brightly
1. Lord Je - sus Christ, be pres - ent now, And let thy Ho - ly Spir - it bow All hearts in love and fear to - day, To hear the truth and keep thy way.
2. Our voic - es tune to sing thy praise, Our hearts in true de - vo - tion raise, Our faith in - crease, and grant us light That we may know thy Name a - right. A-men.

3 Then shall we join the hosts that cry,
Thrice-holy is the Lord Most High!
And dwell with God in that blest place
Where we shall see him face to face.

4 Glory to God, the Father, Son,
And Holy Spirit, Three in One;
To thee, O blessèd Trinity,
Be praise throughout eternity! Amen.

Wilhelm II, Duke of Saxe-Weimar, 1598–166
Tr. Catherine Winkworth, 1829–78 a

HERR JESU CHRIST, DICH ZU UNS WEND. L. M.

Pensum Sacrum, Görlitz, 1648
Adapted and harm. by J. S. Bach, 1685–1750

SECOND TUNE

Brightly
1. Lord Je - sus Christ, be pres - ent now, And
2. Our voic - es tune to sing thy praise, Our
let thy Ho - ly Spir - it bow All hearts in love and
hearts in true de - vo - tion raise, Our faith in - crease, and
fear to - day, To hear the truth and keep thy way.
grant us light That we may know thy Name a - right. A-men.

3 Then shall we join the hosts that cry,
Thrice-holy is the Lord Most High!
And dwell with God in that blest place
Where we shall see him face to face.

4 Glory to God, the Father, Son,
And Holy Spirit, Three in One;
To thee, O blessèd Trinity,
Be praise throughout eternity! Amen.

Wilhelm II, Duke of Saxe-Weimar, 1598–1662
Tr. Catherine Winkworth, 1829–78 a.

WACHET AUF. Irregular. PHILIPP NICOLAI, 1556–1608

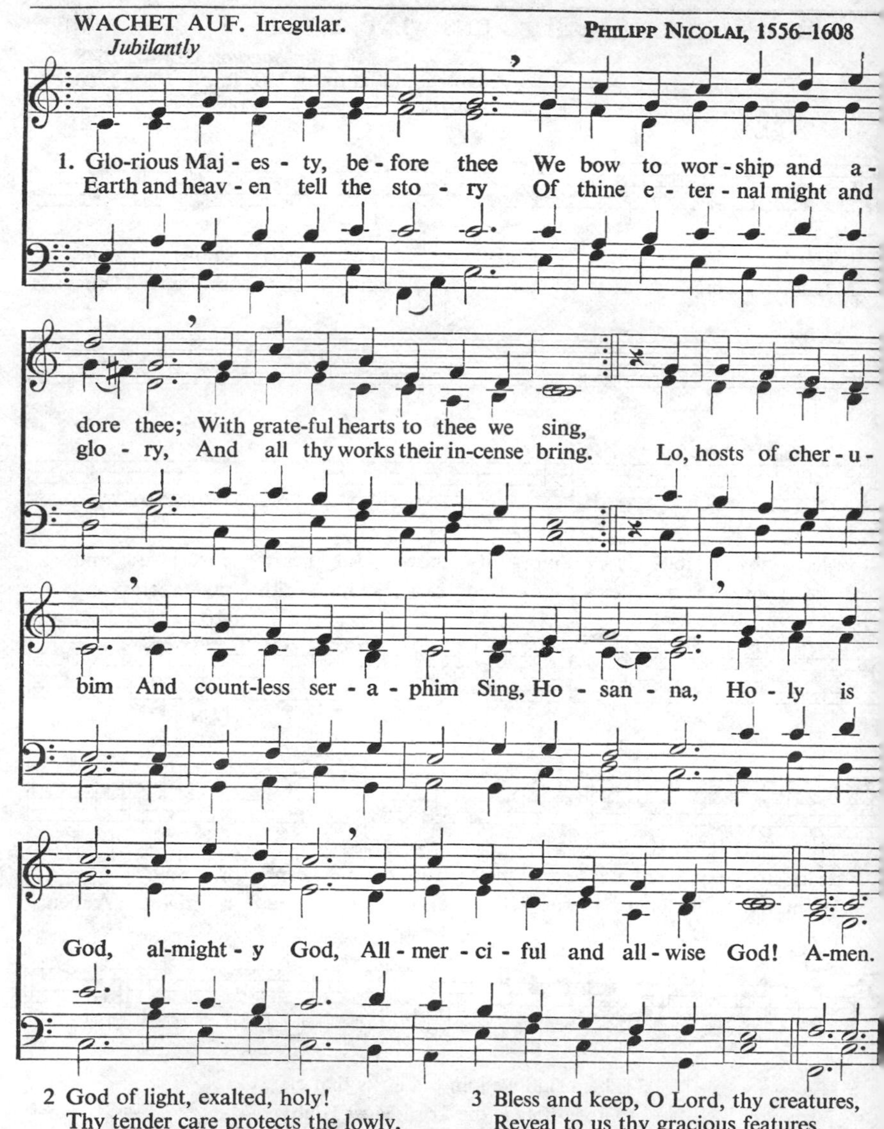
Jubilantly
1. Glo-rious Maj - es - ty, be - fore thee We bow to wor - ship and a -
Earth and heav - en tell the sto - ry Of thine e - ter - nal might and
dore thee; With grate-ful hearts to thee we sing,
glo - ry, And all thy works their in-cense bring.
Lo, hosts of cher - u -
bim And count-less ser - a - phim Sing, Ho - san - na, Ho - ly is
God, al-might - y God, All - mer - ci - ful and all - wise God! A-men.

2 God of light, exalted, holy!
Thy tender care protects the lowly,
Nor leaves thy children to their fate.
Gracious art thou, God our Father,
Thy chosen people thou dost gather
Within thine arms compassionate;
Thou gavest us thy Son,
Through whom thy grace is won,
And thy Spirit
Dwelleth within to cleanse from sin
Whom thine own Son hath died to win.

3 Bless and keep, O Lord, thy creatures,
Reveal to us thy gracious features,
O turn to us thy face with peace.
Here our songs we humbly tender,
Till glorified our tongues shall render
To thee our praise without surcease,
Where hosts of cherubim
And countless seraphim
Sing, Hosanna,
Holy is God, almighty God,
All-merciful and all-wise God! Amen.

Samuel Johan Hedborn, 1783–1849
Tr. August W. Kjellstrand, 1864–1930

LIEBSTER JESU, WIR SIND HIER (DESSAU). 7 8, 7 8, 8 8.

With movement — JOHANN RUDOLPH AHLE, 1625–73

1\. Look up - on us, bless - ed Lord, Take our wan-dering thoughts and guide us;
We have come to hear thy word, With thy teach-ing now pro - vide us,
That, from earth's dis-trac-tions turn-ing, We thy mes-sage may be learn - ing. A-men.

2 For thy Spirit's radiance bright
We, assembled here, are hoping;
If thou shouldst withhold the light,
In the dark our souls were groping:
In each word and thought direct us:
Thou, thou only, canst correct us.

3 Brightness of the Father's face,
Light of Light, from God proceeding,
Make us ready in this place;
Ear and heart await thy leading.
Fill with life and inspiration
Every prayer and meditation. Amen.

Tobias Clausnitzer, 1619–84
Tr. Robert A. S. Macalister, 1870–1950 a.

See also:

173 All creatures of our God
169 All people that on earth
203 At thy feet, O Christ, we lay
161 Before Jehovah's aweful throne
166 Blessing and honor, and glory
123 Come down, O Love divine
127 Come, gracious Spirit, heavenly
121 Come, Holy Ghost, in love
136 Come, thou almighty King
165 Come, we that love the Lord
178 Eternal God, before thy throne
164 God himself is present
135 Holy, holy, holy Lord
131 Holy, holy, holy Lord God Almighty
424 Hosanna to the living Lord
397 Love divine, all loves excelling
201 New every morning is the love
120 O Holy Spirit, enter in
160 Praise, my soul, the King of heaven
408 Praise to the Lord, the Almighty
416 When morning gilds the skies

See also: Adoration and Praise (Nos. 403–439)

SICILIAN MARINERS. 8 7, 8 7, 8 7.
Sicilian Melody, XVIII cent.
In moderate time
FIRST TUNE
1. Lord, dis - miss us with thy bless-ing, Fill our hearts with joy and peace;
Let us each, thy love pos - sess - ing, Tri-umph in re - deem - ing grace.
O re - fresh us, O re - fresh us, Trav'-ling thro' this wil - der - ness. A-men

2 Thanks we give and adoration
For thy Gospel's joyful sound;
May the fruits of thy salvation
In our hearts and lives abound;
Ever faithful
To thy truth may we be found. Amen.

John Fawcett, 1740–18

191

FINNISH SONG. 8 7, 8 7, 8 7. *Suomen Koraalikirja*, 1738

SECOND TUNE

1. Lord, dis - miss us with thy bless - ing, Fill our hearts with joy and peace

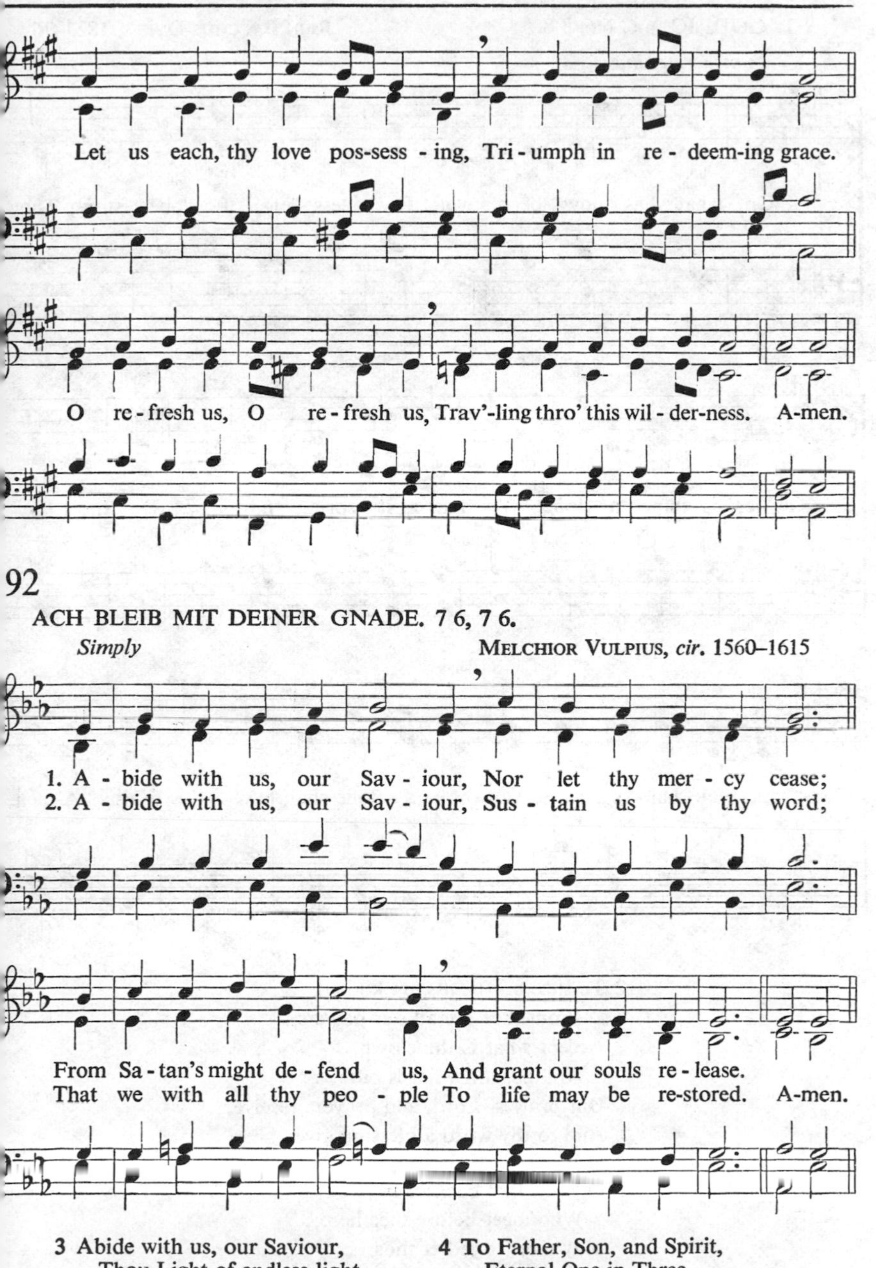
Let us each, thy love pos-sess - ing, Tri - umph in re - deem-ing grace.
O re - fresh us, O re - fresh us, Trav'-ling thro' this wil - der-ness. A-men.
92
ACH BLEIB MIT DEINER GNADE. 7 6, 7 6.
Simply
MELCHIOR VULPIUS, cir. 1560–1615
1. A - bide with us, our Sav - iour, Nor let thy mer - cy cease;
2. A - bide with us, our Sav - iour, Sus - tain us by thy word;
From Sa - tan's might de - fend us, And grant our souls re - lease.
That we with all thy peo - ple To life may be re-stored. A-men.

3 Abide with us, our Saviour,
Thou Light of endless light,
Increase to us thy blessings,
And save us by thy might.

4 To Father, Son, and Spirit,
Eternal One in Three,
As was, and is forever,
All praise and glory be. Amen.

Josua Stegmann, 1588–1632
Tr. Unknown

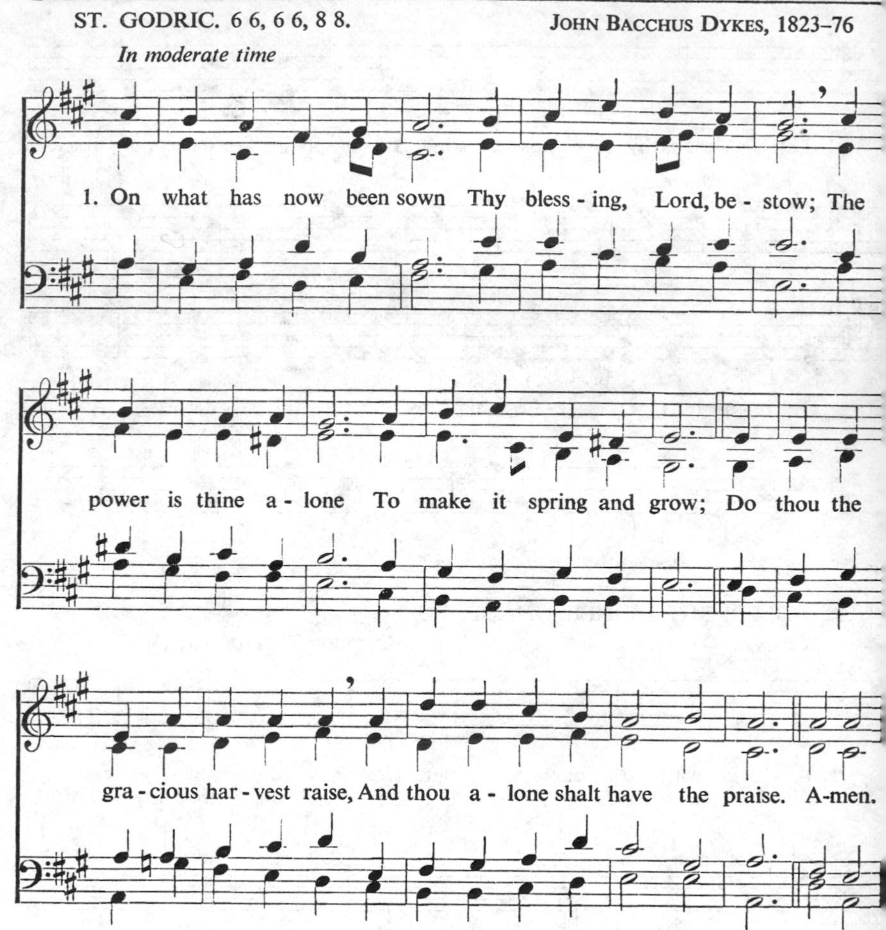
ST. GODRIC. 6 6, 6 6, 8 8.
JOHN BACCHUS DYKES, 1823–76
In moderate time
1. On what has now been sown Thy bless - ing, Lord, be - stow; The
power is thine a - lone To make it spring and grow; Do thou the
gra - cious har - vest raise, And thou a - lone shalt have the praise. A-men.

2 To thee our wants are known,
From thee are all our powers,
Accept what is thine own,
And pardon what is ours;
Our praises, Lord, and prayers receive,
And to thy word a blessing give.

3 O grant that each of us,
Who meet before thee here,
May meet together thus
When thou and thine appear,
And follow thee to heaven our home;
Even so, Amen, Lord Jesus, come! Amen.

John Newton, 1725–180

PSALM 42 (FREU DICH SEHR). 8 7, 8 7, 7 7, 8 8.
Genevan Psalter, 1551
Brightly
Adapted and harm. by J. S. BACH, 1685–1750
1. Praise to thee and ad - o - ra - tion, Bless - ed Je - sus, Son of God,
Who, to serve thine own cre - a - tion, Didst as - sume our flesh and blood.
Grant that I may nev - er stray From thy sa - cred fold a - way,
But with zeal and ho - ly fa - vor Fol - low thee, O bless - ed Sav - iour. A-men.

2 Let me never, Lord, forsake thee,
E'en though bitter pain and strife
On my way should overtake me;
But may I through all my life
Walk in fervent love to thee,
In all woes for comfort flee
To thy birth, thy death and passion,
Till I see thy full salvation. Amen.

Thomas Hansen Kingo, 1634–1703
Tr. Kristen Kvamme, 1866–1938 a.

HERMAS. 6 5, 6 5. D. With Refrain. FRANCES RIDLEY HAVERGAL, 1836–79

Brightly
1. On our way re - joic - ing Glad - ly let us go; Con-quered
2. If with hon - est - heart - ed Love for God and man, Day by
hath our Lead - er, Van-quished is the foe. Christ with - out, our
day thou find us Do - ing what we can, Thou who giv'st the
safe - ty; Christ with - in, our joy; Who, if we be faith - ful,
seed - time Wilt give large in - crease, Crown the head with bless - ings,
Refrain
Can our hope de - stroy? On our way re - joic - ing As we
Fill the heart with peace.

for-ward move, Heark-en to our prais - es, O thou God of love! A-men.

3 Unto God the Father
Joyful songs we sing,
Unto God the Saviour
Thankful hearts we bring,
Unto God the Spirit
Bow we and adore,
On our way rejoicing
Now and evermore. Amen.

John S. B. Monsell, 1811–75

196

ST. FULBERT. C. M. HENRY J. GAUNTLETT, 1805–76

With dignity

1. Al - might - y God, thy word is cast Like seed in - to the ground,
2. Let not the foe of Christ and man This ho - ly seed re - move,

Now let the dew of heaven de - scend And right-eous fruits a - bound.
But give it root in ev - ery heart To bring forth fruits of love. A-men.

3 Let not the world's deceitful cares
The rising plant destroy,
But let it yield a hundredfold
The fruits of peace and joy.

4 Oft as the precious seed is sown
Thy quickening grace bestow,
That all whose souls the truth receive
Its saving power may know. Amen.

John Cawood, 1775–1852 a.

This hymn may also be sung to DUNDEE (FRENCH) (No. 181)

LOBT GOTT, IHR CHRISTEN. C. M. NIKOLAUS HERMANN, *cir.* 1480–1561

Joyfully

1. O hap - py day when we shall stand A - mid the
2. O bless - ed day! From far and near The serv - ants

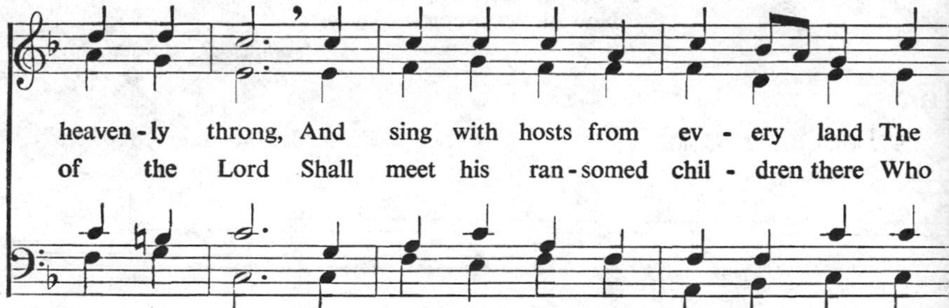
heaven - ly throng, And sing with hosts from ev - ery land The
of the Lord Shall meet his ran - somed chil - dren there Who

new ce - les - tial song, The new ce - les - tial song.
heard God's sav - ing word, Who heard God's sav - ing word. A-men.

3 O what a mighty, rushing flood
Of love without surcease
Shall surge about the throne of God,
In joy and endless peace!

4 Lord, may thy bounteous grace inspire
Our hearts to watch and pray,
That we may join the heavenly choir
Upon that glorious day. Amen.

Wilhelm Andreas Wexels, 1797–186
Tr. George Alfred Taylor Rygh, 1860–194

ELLERS. 10 10, 10 10. EDWARD JOHN HOPKINS, 1818–1901

In moderate time

1. Sav - iour, a - gain to thy dear Name we raise
2. Grant us thy peace up - on our home - ward way;
With one ac - cord our part - ing hymn of praise;
With thee be - gan, with thee shall end the day;
Once more we bless thee ere our wor - ship cease,
Guard thou the lips from sin, the hearts from shame,
Then, low - ly bend - ing, wait thy word of peace.
That in this house have called up - on thy Name. A-men.

3 Grant us thy peace, Lord, through the coming night,
Turn thou for us its darkness into light;
From harm and danger keep thy children free,
For dark and light are both alike to thee.

4 Grant us thy peace throughout our earthly life,
Our balm in sorrow, and our stay in strife;
Then, when thy voice shall bid our conflict cease,
Call us, O Lord, to thine eternal peace. Amen.

John Ellerton, 1826–93

199

ST. MATTHIAS. 8 8, 8 8, 8 8. WILLIAM HENRY MONK, 1823–89

Broadly

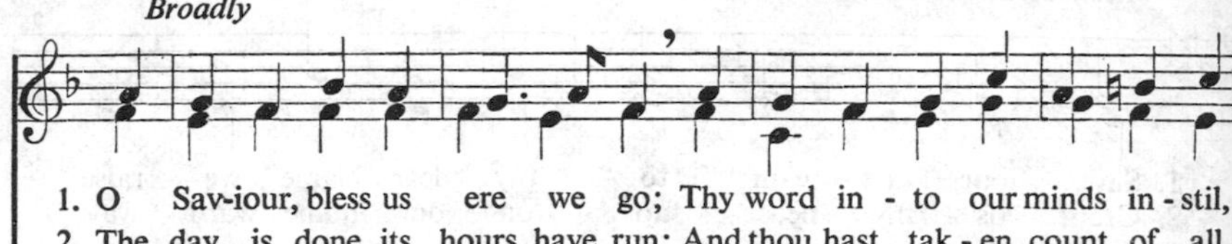

1. O Sav-iour, bless us ere we go; Thy word in - to our minds in - stil,
2. The day is done, its hours have run; And thou hast tak - en count of all,

And make our luke-warm hearts to glow With low - ly love and fer - vent will:
The scan - ty tri-umphs grace hath won, The bro-ken vow, the fre - quent fall:

Refrain

Through life's long day and death's dark night, O gen - tle Je - sus, be our light. A-me

3 Grant us, dear Lord, from evil ways
True absolution and release;
And bless us, more than in past days,
With purity and inward peace:

4 Do more than pardon: give us joy,
Sweet fear, and sober liberty,
And loving hearts without alloy,
That only long to be like thee:

5 Labor is sweet, for thou hast toiled,
And care is light, for thou hast care
Let not our works with self be soiled,
Nor in unsimple ways ensnared:

6 For all we love, the poor, the sad,
The sinful, unto thee we call;
O let thy mercy make us glad;
Thou art our Jesus and our all:

Frederick William Faber, 1814–

PEACE OF GOD. 7 7, 7 7, 7 7. JOHAN P. E. HARTMANN, 1805–1900

In moderate time

1. Peace to soothe our bit - ter woes God in Christ on us be-stows;
Je - sus bought our peace with God With his ho - ly, pre-cious Blood;
Peace in him for sin - ners found Is the Gos - pel's joy - ful sound.

2 Peace to us the Church doth tell,
'Tis her welcome and farewell;
Peace was our baptismal dower,
Peace shall bless our dying hour;
Peace be with you, full and free,
Now and through eternity.

Nikolai F. S. Grundtvig, 1783–1872
Tr. George Alfred Taylor Rygh, 1860–1943

See also:

434 Beautiful Saviour
166 Blessing and honor, and glory
565 Forward! be our watchword
399 Jesus, thy boundless love to me
550 Lead on, O King eternal
560 Onward, Christian soldiers
602 Praise God, from whom all blessings
427 Praise the Lord of heaven
407 Praise the Lord! Ye heavens
436 Rejoice, the Lord is King
555 Rejoice, ye pure in heart
562 The Son of God goes forth to war

See also: Adoration and Praise (Nos. 403–439)

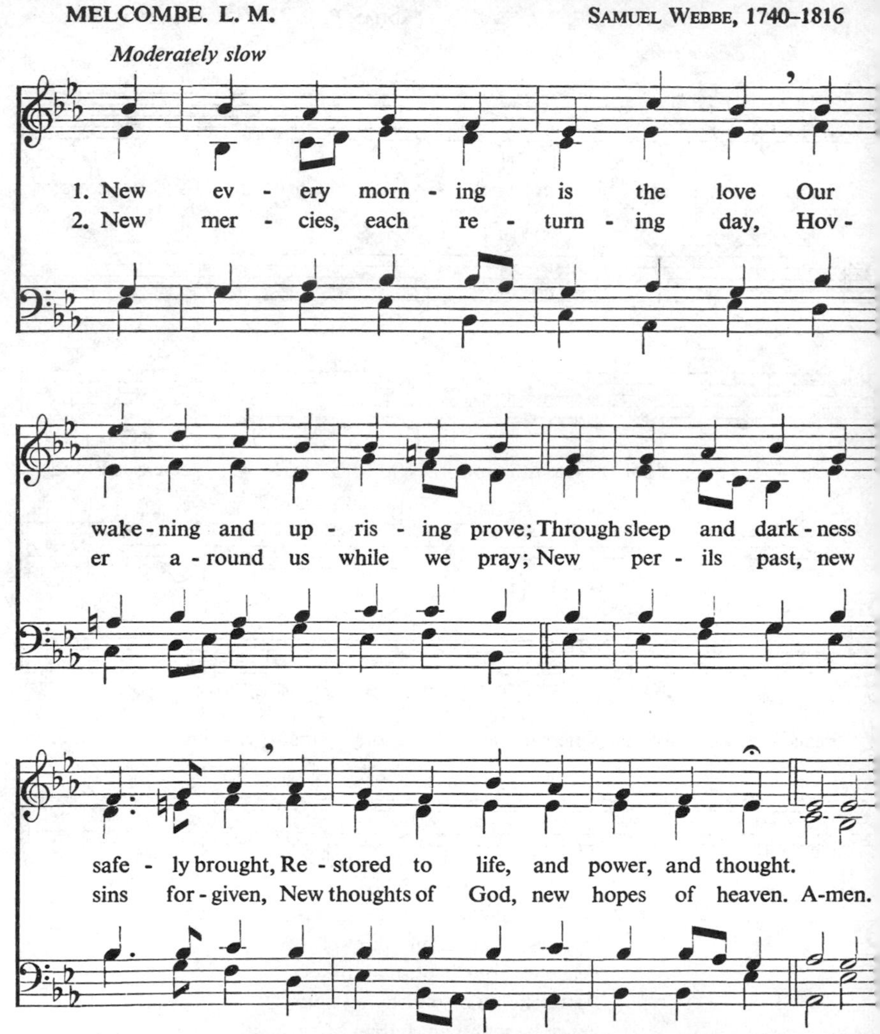
MELCOMBE. L. M.
SAMUEL WEBBE, 1740–1816
Moderately slow
1. New ev - ery morn - ing is the love Our wake - ning and up - ris - ing prove; Through sleep and dark - ness safe - ly brought, Re - stored to life, and power, and thought.
2. New mer - cies, each re - turn - ing day, Hov - er a - round us while we pray; New per - ils past, new sins for - given, New thoughts of God, new hopes of heaven. A-men.

3 If on our daily course our mind
Be set to hallow all we find,
New treasures still, of countless price,
God will provide for sacrifice.

4 Old friends, old scenes, will lovelier be,
As more of heaven in each we see;
Some softening gleam of love and prayer
Shall dawn on every cross and care.

5 The trivial round, the common task,
Will furnish all we ought to ask;
Room to deny ourselves, a road
To bring us daily nearer God.

6 Only, O Lord, in thy dear love,
Fit us for perfect rest above;
And help us, this and every day,
To live more nearly as we pray. Amer

John Keble, 1792–186

MORNING HYMN. L. M.
François H. Barthélémon, 1741–1808
Smoothly, with spirit
1. A - wake, my soul, and with the sun Thy
2. Wake and lift up thy - self, my heart, And
dai - ly stage of du - ty run; Shake off dull sloth, and
with the an - gels bear thy part, Who all night long un -
joy - ful rise To pay thy morn - ing sac - ri - fice.
wea - ried sing High praise to the e - ter - nal King. A-men.

All praise to thee, who safe has kept
And hast refreshed me while I slept:
Grant, Lord, when I from death shall wake
I may of endless light partake.

Lord, I my vows to thee renew;
Disperse my sins as morning dew;
Guard my first springs of thought and will,
And with thyself my spirit fill.

5 Direct, control, suggest, this day,
All I design, or do, or say,
That all my powers, with all their might,
In thy sole glory may unite.

6 Praise God, from whom all blessings flow,
Praise him, all creatures here below;
Praise him above, ye heavenly host;
Praise Father, Son, and Holy Ghost.

Thomas Ken, 1637–1711

This hymn may also be sung to TALLIS' CANON (No. 21)

VOLLER WUNDER. 7 7, 7 7, 7 7. JOHANN GEORG EBELING, 1637–76

FIRST TUNE

In moderate time

1. At thy feet, O Christ, we lay Thine own gift of this new day;
Doubt of what it holds in store Makes us crave thine aid the more;

2. If it flow on calm and bright, Be thy-self our chief de-light;
If it bring un-known dis-tress, Good is all that thou canst bless;

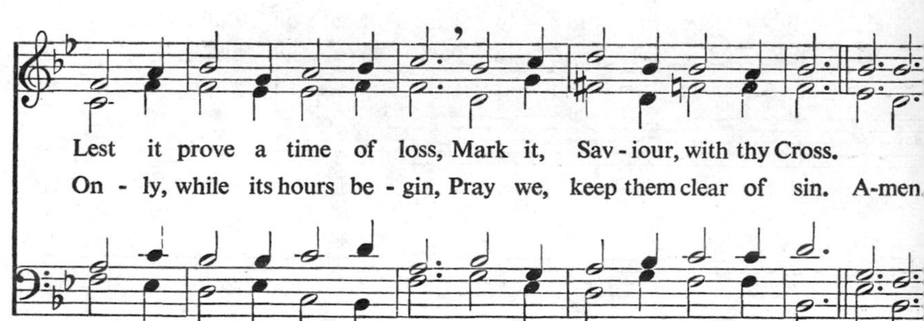
Lest it prove a time of loss, Mark it, Sav-iour, with thy Cross.
On-ly, while its hours be-gin, Pray we, keep them clear of sin. A-men

3 We in part our weakness know,
And in part discern our foe;
Well for us, before thine eyes
All our danger open lies;
Turn not from us, while we plead
Thy compassions and our need.

4 Fain would we thy word embrace,
Live each moment on thy grace,
All our selves to thee consign,
Fold up all our wills in thine,
Think, and speak, and do, and be
Simply that which pleases thee.

5 Hear us, Lord, and that right soon;
Hear, and grant the choicest boon
That thy love can e'er impart,
Loyal singleness of heart;
So shall this and all our days,
Christ our God, show forth thy praise. Amen.

William Bright, 1824–190

BARMOUTH. 7 7, 7 7, 7 7. **Walter Cecil Macfarren, 1826–1905**

SECOND TUNE

In moderate time

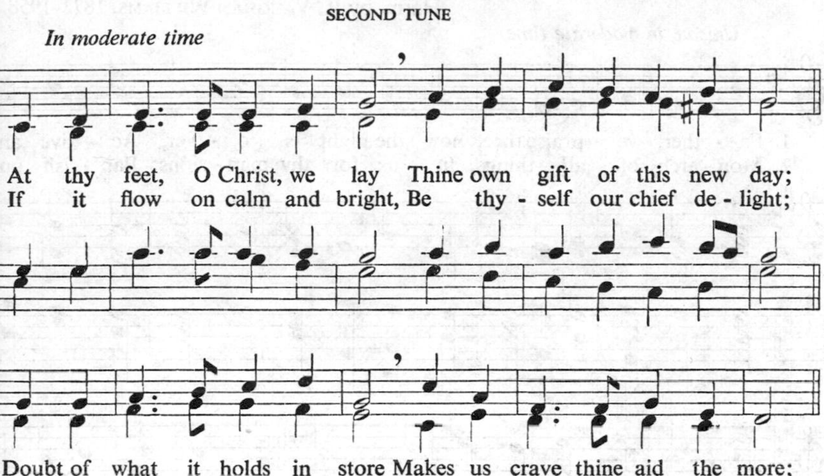
1. At thy feet, O Christ, we lay Thine own gift of this new day;
2. If it flow on calm and bright, Be thy - self our chief de - light;
Doubt of what it holds in store Makes us crave thine aid the more;
If it bring un-known dis - tress, Good is all that thou canst bless;

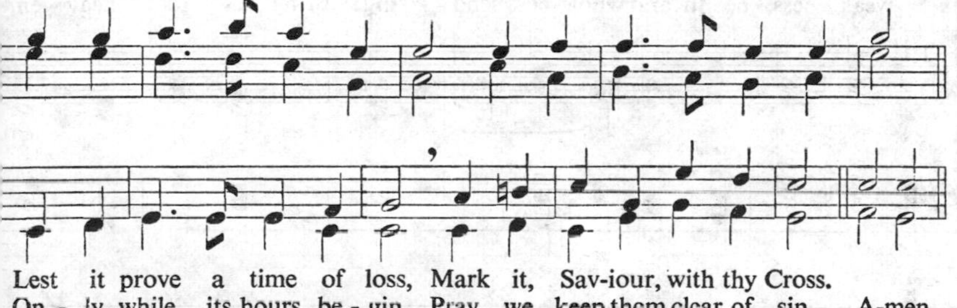
Lest it prove a time of loss, Mark it, Sav-iour, with thy Cross.
On - ly, while its hours be - gin, Pray we, keep them clear of sin. A-men.

3 We in part our weakness know,
And in part discern our foe;
Well for us, before thine eyes
All our danger open lies;
Turn not from us, while we plead
Thy compassions and our need.

4 Fain would we thy word embrace,
Live each moment on thy grace,
All our selves to thee consign,
Fold up all our wills in thine,
Think, and speak, and do, and be
Simply that which pleases thee.

5 Hear us, Lord, and that right boon,
Hear, and grant the choicest boon
That thy love can e'er impart,
Loyal singleness of heart;
So shall this and all our days,
Christ our God, show forth thy praise. Amen.

William Bright, 1824–1901

This hymn may also be sung to HEATHLANDS (No. 444).

CHRISTE SANCTORUM. 11, 11, 11, 5. XVIII cent. French Church Melody
Harm. by R. VAUGHAN WILLIAMS, 1872–1958

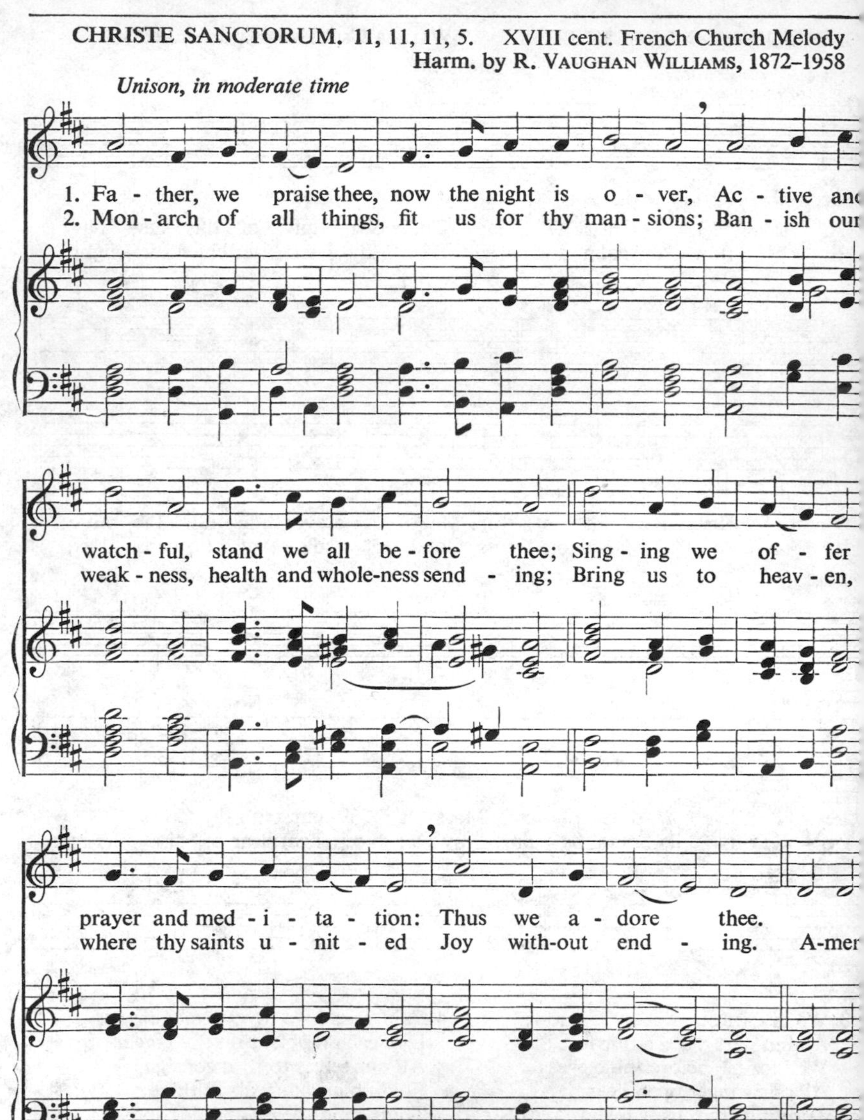
Unison, in moderate time
1. Fa - ther, we praise thee, now the night is o - ver, Ac - tive and
2. Mon - arch of all things, fit us for thy man - sions; Ban - ish our
watch - ful, stand we all be - fore thee; Sing - ing we of - fer
weak - ness, health and whole-ness send - ing; Bring us to heav - en,
prayer and med - i - ta - tion: Thus we a - dore thee.
where thy saints u - nit - ed Joy with-out end - ing. A-men

3 All-holy Father, Son, and equal Spirit,
Trinity blessèd, send us thy salvation;
Thine is the glory, gleaming and resounding
Through all creation. Amen.

Ascribed to St. Gregory, 540–6
Tr. Percy Dearmer, 1867–19

GOTT DES HIMMELS. 8 7, 8 7, 7 7.
HEINRICH ALBERT, 1604–51
With exultation
1. God, who mad - est earth and heav - en, Fa - ther,
Who the day and night hast giv - en, Sun and
2. Praise to thee my soul shall ren - der, Who this
My om - ni - po - tent de - fend - er, Who from
Son, and Ho - ly Ghost,
moon, and star - ry host, Thou whose might - y hand sus -
night hast guard - ed me,
ill doth set me free; Free from dan - ger, an - guish,
tains Earth and all that she con - tains;
woe, Free from the in - fer - nal foe. A - men.

3 Let the night of my transgression
With night's darkness pass away;
Jesus, into thy possession
I resign myself to-day;
In thy wounds I find relief
From my greatest sin and grief.

4 Let my life and conversation
Be directed by thy word;
Lord, thy constant preservation
To thy erring child afford.
Nowhere but alone in thee
From all harm can I be free.

5 Wholly to thy blest protection
I commit my heart and mind;
Mighty God, to thy direction
Wholly may I be resigned.
Lord, my shield, my light divine,
O accept, and own me thine. Amen.

Heinrich Albert, 1604–51
Trs. John Christian Jacobi, 1670–1750
Arthur Tozer Russell, 1806–74
Catherine Winkworth, 1829–78

SPLENDOR PATERNAE. L. M. — Plainsong, Mode I

FIRST TUNE

With movement

1. O Splen - dor of God's glo - ry bright, O thou who bring - est
2. O thou true Sun, on us thy glance Let fall in roy - al
3. The Fa - ther, too, our prayers im - plore, Fa - ther of glo - ry
light from light, O Light of light, light's liv - ing spring,
ra - di - ance; The Spir - it's sanc - ti - fy - ing beam
ev - er - more, The Fa - ther of all grace and might,
O Day, all days il - lu - min - ing!
Up - on our earth - ly sens - es stream.
To ban - ish sin from our de - light. A - men.

4 To guide whate'er we nobly do,
With love all envy to subdue,
To make ill-fortune turn to fair,
And give us grace our wrongs to bear.

5 Rejoicing may this day go hence;
Like virgin dawn our innocence,
Like fiery noon our faith appear,
Nor know the gloom of twilight drear.

6 Morn in her rosy car is borne;
Let him come forth, our perfect morn,
The Word in God the Father one,
The Father perfect in the Son.

7 All laud to God the Father be;
All praise, eternal Son, to thee;
All glory, as is ever meet,
To God the holy Paraclete. Amen.

St. Ambrose, 340–97
Tr. Robert Bridges, 1844–1930

)06

WALTON (GERMANY). L. M. WILLIAM GARDINER'S *Sacred Melodies*, 1815

SECOND TUNE

In moderate time

1. O Splen - dor of God's glo - ry bright, O thou who bring - est
2. O thou true Sun, on us thy glance Let fall in roy - al
3. The Fa - ther, too, our prayers im - plore, Fa - ther of glo - ry

light from light, O Light of light, light's liv - ing spring,
ra - di - ance; The Spir - it's sanc - ti - fy - ing beam
ev - er - more, The Fa - ther of all grace and might,

O Day, all days il - lu - min - ing!
Up - on our earth - ly sens - es stream.
To ban - ish sin from our de - light. A - men.

HAYDN. 8 4 7, 8 4 7. FRANZ JOSEPH HAYDN, 1732–1809

FIRST TUNE

Brightly
1. Come, my soul, thou must be wak-ing; Now is break-ing O'er the earth an-oth-er day. Come to him who made this splen-dor See thou ren-der All thy fee-ble strength can pay.
2. Glad-ly hail the sun re-turn-ing; Read-y burn-ing Be the in-cense of thy powers; For the night is safe-ly end-ed God hath tend-ed With his care thy help-less hours. A-men.

3 Pray that he may prosper ever
Each endeavor,
When thine aim is good and true;
But that he may ever thwart thee
And convert thee,
When thou evil wouldst pursue.

4 Only God's free gift abuse not,
Light refuse not,
But his Spirit's voice obey;
Thou with him shalt dwell, beholding
Light enfolding
All things in unclouded day.

5 Glory, honor, exaltation,
Adoration,
Be to the Eternal One;
To the Father, Son, and Spirit,
Laud and merit,
While unending ages run. Amen.

Friedrich Rudolph Ludwig von Canitz, 1654–9
Tr. Henry James Buckoll, 1803–7

Worship — Morning

MORING. 8 4 7, 8 4 7. KARL JOHAN MORING, 1832–1868

SECOND TUNE

In moderate time

1. Come, my soul, thou must be wak - ing; Now is break - ing
2. Glad - ly hail the sun re - turn - ing; Read - y burn - ing

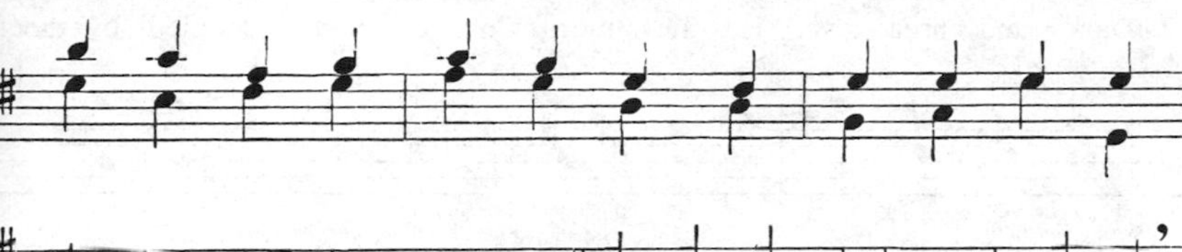

O'er the earth an - oth - er day. Come to him who made this splen-dor;
Be the in - cense of thy powers; For the night is safe - ly end - ed;

See thou ren - der All thy fee - ble strength can pay.
God hath tend - ed With his care thy help - less hours. A-men.

3 Pray that he may prosper ever
Each endeavor,
When thine aim is good and true;
But that he may ever thwart thee
And convert thee,
When thou evil wouldst pursue.

4 Only God's free gift abuse not,
Light refuse not,
But his Spirit's voice obey;
Thou with him shalt dwell, beholding
Light enfolding
All things in unclouded day.

5 Glory, honor, exaltation,
Adoration,
Be to the Eternal One;
To the Father, Son, and Spirit,
Laud and merit,
While unending ages run. Amen.

Friedrich Rudolph Ludwig von Canitz, 1654–99
Tr. Henry James Buckoll, 1803–71

GOUNOD (LUX PRIMA). 7 7, 7 7, 7 7. CHARLES F. GOUNOD, 1818–93

FIRST TUNE

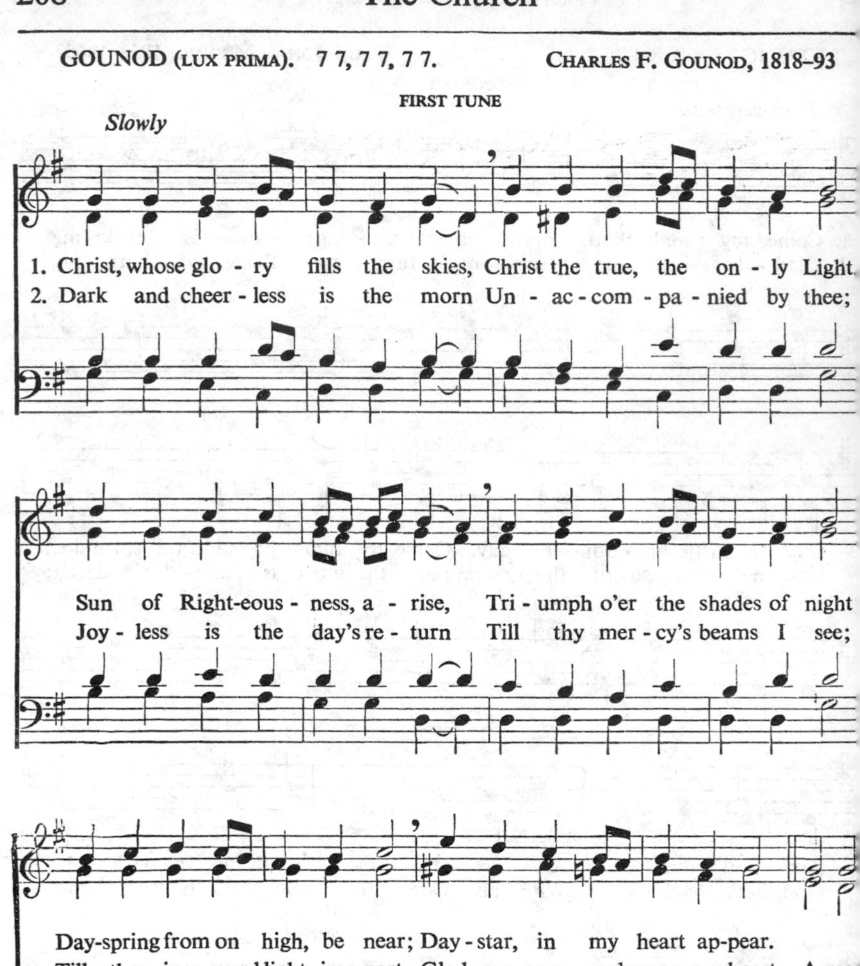
Slowly
1. Christ, whose glo - ry fills the skies, Christ the true, the on - ly Light,
2. Dark and cheer - less is the morn Un - ac - com - pa - nied by thee;
Sun of Right-eous - ness, a - rise, Tri - umph o'er the shades of night
Joy - less is the day's re - turn Till thy mer - cy's beams I see;
Day-spring from on high, be near; Day - star, in my heart ap-pear.
Till they in - ward light im - part, Glad my eyes, and warm my heart. A-men

3 Visit then this soul of mine;
  Pierce the gloom of sin and grief;
Fill me, Radiancy divine,
  Scatter all my unbelief;
More and more thyself display,
Shining to the perfect day. Amen.

Charles Wesley, 1707-

RATISBON. 7 7, 7 7, 7 7. JOHANN GOTTLOB WERNER, *Choralbuch*, 1815

SECOND TUNE

Broadly, in moderate time

1. Christ, whose glo - ry fills the skies, Christ the true, the on - ly Light,
2. Dark and cheer-less is the morn Un - ac - com - pa - nied by thee;

Sun of Right-eous - ness, a - rise, Tri - umph o'er the shades of night;
Joy - less is the day's re - turn Till thy mer-cy's beams I see;

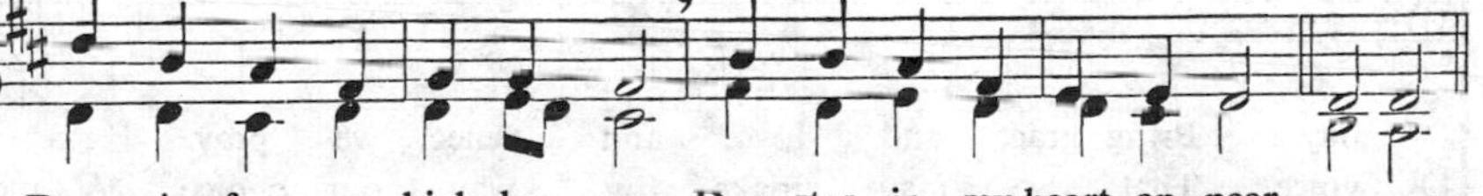

Day-spring from on high, be near; Day - star, in my heart ap - pear.
Till they in - ward light im - part, Glad my eyes, and warm my heart. A-men.

3 Visit then this soul of mine;
Pierce the gloom of sin and grief;
Fill me, Radiancy divine,
Scatter all my unbelief;
More and more thyself display,
Shining to the perfect day. Amen.

Charles Wesley, 1707–88

This hymn may also be sung to DIX (No. 52), or to EASTER GLORY (No. 100).

HURSLEY. L. M. *Katholisches Gesangbuch*, Vienna, 1774

Quietly

1. God of our life, all - glo - rious Lord, Be now and ev - er - more a - dored! In - to the o - pening of this day Bring grace, and love, and peace, we pray.
2. Make clear our path, that we may see Where we must walk to be with thee, And lis - ten al - way for thy voice That we may make thy way our choice. A - men.

3 Give help for doing every task,
Nor let us fail of thee to ask
For grace in speech, for love in deed,
From wrongful actions to be freed.

4 Inspire us now to do some deed
For other's good to help in need;
To rescue and to lead from shame;
To bless with comfort in thy Name.

5 Thus may we walk our way with thee,
Enabled by thy grace to be
A little less unworthy, Lord,
Of thee our Friend, our Holy God.

6 At eventide then will we raise
A grateful heart in songs of praise;
And worship thee, and thy dear Son,
With God the Spirit, ever One. Amen

Paul Zeller Strodach, 1876–19

BARNEKOW. 7 7, 8 8 7. CHRISTIAN BARNEKOW, 1837–1913

Brightly
1. Gold - en light, se - rene and bright, The sky is now a - dorn - ing; As sleep - ing child in moth - er's arm, My God has shield - ed me from harm; I thank him for the morn - ing.
2. Gold - en light, se - rene and bright, Is shed up - on my la - bor; As birds their morn-ing song em - ploy, I praise my God for life and joy To me and to my neigh - bor.

3 Golden light, serene and bright,
To me is life and gladness,
For I am happy every day
I walk upon the narrow way
With God through joy or sadness.

4 Now I pray that God today
Will send to me his blessing;
My daily task I then fulfill
According to his holy will,
His wondrous peace possessing.

Nikolai F. S. Grundtvig, 1783–1872
Tr. Fred C. M. Hansen, 1888–

LANCASTER. C. M. SAMUEL HOWARD, 1710–82

In moderate time

1. Now that the day - star glim - mers bright, We sup - pli - ant - ly pray That he, the un - cre - at - ed Light, May guide us on our way.
2. No sin - ful word, nor deed of wrong, Nor thoughts that id - ly rove, But sim - ple truth be on our tongue, And in our hearts be love.
3. And while the hours in or - der flow, O Christ, se - cure - ly fence Our gates, be - lea - guered by the foe, The gate of ev - ery sense. A - men.

4 And grant that to thine honor, Lord,
Our daily toil may tend;
That we begin it at thy word,
And in thy favor end.

5 To God the Father glory be,
And to his only Son,
And to the Spirit, One and Three,
While endless ages run. Amen.

Latin Hymn, V cen
Tr. John Henry Newman, 1801–9

12

MORGENGLANZ DER EWIGKEIT. 7 8, 7 8, 7 3.

In moderate time FREYLINGHAUSEN'S *Gesangbuch*, 1704

1. Come, thou bright and morn-ing star, Light of light, with-out be - gin - ning,
Shine up - on us from a - far, Like the morn when mists are thin - ning;
2. Let thy grace, like morn - ing dew Fall - ing on the bar - ren plac - es,
Com - fort, quick-en, and re - new All dry souls and dy - ing grac - es;

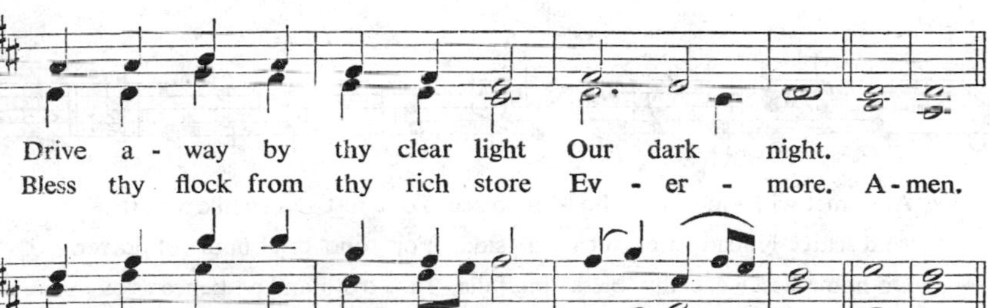
Drive a - way by thy clear light Our dark night.
Bless thy flock from thy rich store Ev - er - more. A - men.

3 May thy fervent love destroy
All cold works, in us awaking
Ardent courage, zeal, and joy,
At the purple morn's first breaking;
Let us truly rise, ere yet
Life has set.

4 Light us to the heavenly spheres,
Sun of grace, in glory shrouded;
Lead us through this vale of tears,
To the land where days unclouded,
Purest joy and perfect peace,
Never cease. Amen.

Christian Knorr von Rosenroth, 1636–89
Tr. Richard Massie, 1800–87

See also:

215 Evening and morning
214 Forth in thy Name, O Lord
131 Holy, holy, holy, Lord God Almighty
438 Joyful, joyful we adore thee
496 Still, still with thee
416 When morning gilds the skies

See also: Adoration and Praise (Nos. 403–439)

213

BEATITUDO. C. M. JOHN BACCHUS DYKES, 1823–76

With movement

1. Be - hold us, Lord, a lit - tle space From dai - ly tasks set free,
2. A - round us rolls the cease - less tide Of bus - iness, toil and care;
3. Yet these are not the on - ly walls Where-in thou mayst be sought;

And met with - in thy ho - ly place To rest a - while with thee.
And scarce-ly can we turn a - side For one brief hour of prayer.
On home-liest work thy bless - ing falls, In truth and pa-tience wrought. A-men.

4 Thine is the loom, the forge, the mart,
The wealth of land and sea,
The worlds of science and of art
Revealed and ruled by thee.

5 Then let us prove our heavenly birth
In all we do and know:
And claim the kingdom of the earth
For thee, and not thy foe.

6 Work shall be prayer, if all be wrought
As thou wouldst have it done;
And prayer, by thee inspired and taught,
Itself with work be one. Amen.

John Ellerton, 1826–9

ANGEL'S SONG (SONG 34). L. M. ORLANDO GIBBONS, 1583–1625

Slowly
Slightly faster
1. Forth in thy Name, O Lord, I go, My dai - ly
2. The task thy wis - dom hath as - signed, O, let me
la - bor to pur - sue, Thee, on - ly thee, re - solved to
cheer - ful - ly ful - fill; In all my works thy pres - ence
know In all I think, or speak, or do.
find, And prove thy good and per - fect will. A - men.

3 Thee may I set at my right hand,
Whose eyes my inmost substance see,
And labor on at thy command,
And offer all my works to thee.

4 Give me to bear thy easy yoke,
And every moment watch and pray,
And still to things eternal look,
And hasten to thy glorious day;

5 For thee delightfully employ
Whate'er thy bounteous grace hath given,
And run my course with even joy,
And closely walk with thee to heaven. Amen.

Charles Wesley, 1707–88

This hymn may also be sung to CANONBURY (No. 538).

DIE GÜLDNE SONNE. 5 5, 5 5, 10, 5 6, 5 6, 10.

JOHANN GEORG EBELING, 1637–76

Cheerfully
1. Eve-ning and morn-ing, Sun-set and dawn-ing, Wealth, peace, and glad-ness, Com-fort in sad-ness, These are thy works; all the glo-ry be thine! Times with-out num-ber, A-wake or in slum-ber, Thine eye ob-serves us, From dan-ger pre-
2. Fa-ther, O hear me, Par-don and spare me; Calm all my ter-rors, Blot out my er-rors, That by thine eyes they may no more be scanned. Or-der my go-ings, Di-rect all my do-ings; As it may please thee Re-tain or re-

serves us, Caus - ing thy mer - cy up - on us to shine.
lease me; All I com - mit to thy fa - ther - ly hand.

3 Griefs of God's sending
Soon have an ending;
Clouds may be pouring,
Wind and wave roaring;
Sunshine will come when the tempest has past.
Joys still increasing
And peace never ceasing,
Fountains that dry not
And roses that die not,
Blooming in Eden, await me at last.

Paul Gerhardt, 1607 76
Tr. Richard Massie, 1800–87

16

ALBANO. C. M. VINCENT NOVELLO, 1781–1861

Slowly

1. From thee all skill and sci - ence flow, All pit - y, care, and love,
2. And part them, Lord, to each and all, As each and all shall need;

All calm and cour - age, faith and hope: O pour them from a - bove!
To rise, like in - cense, each to thee, In no - ble thought and deed. A-men.

3 And hasten, Lord, that perfect day
When pain and death shall cease,
And thy just rule shall fill the earth
With health, and light, and peace;

4 When ever blue the sky shall gleam,
And ever green the sod,
And man's rude work deface no more
The paradise of God. Amen.

Charles Kingsley, 1819–75

This hymn may also be sung to NUN DANKET ALL' UND BRINGET EHR (No. 413).

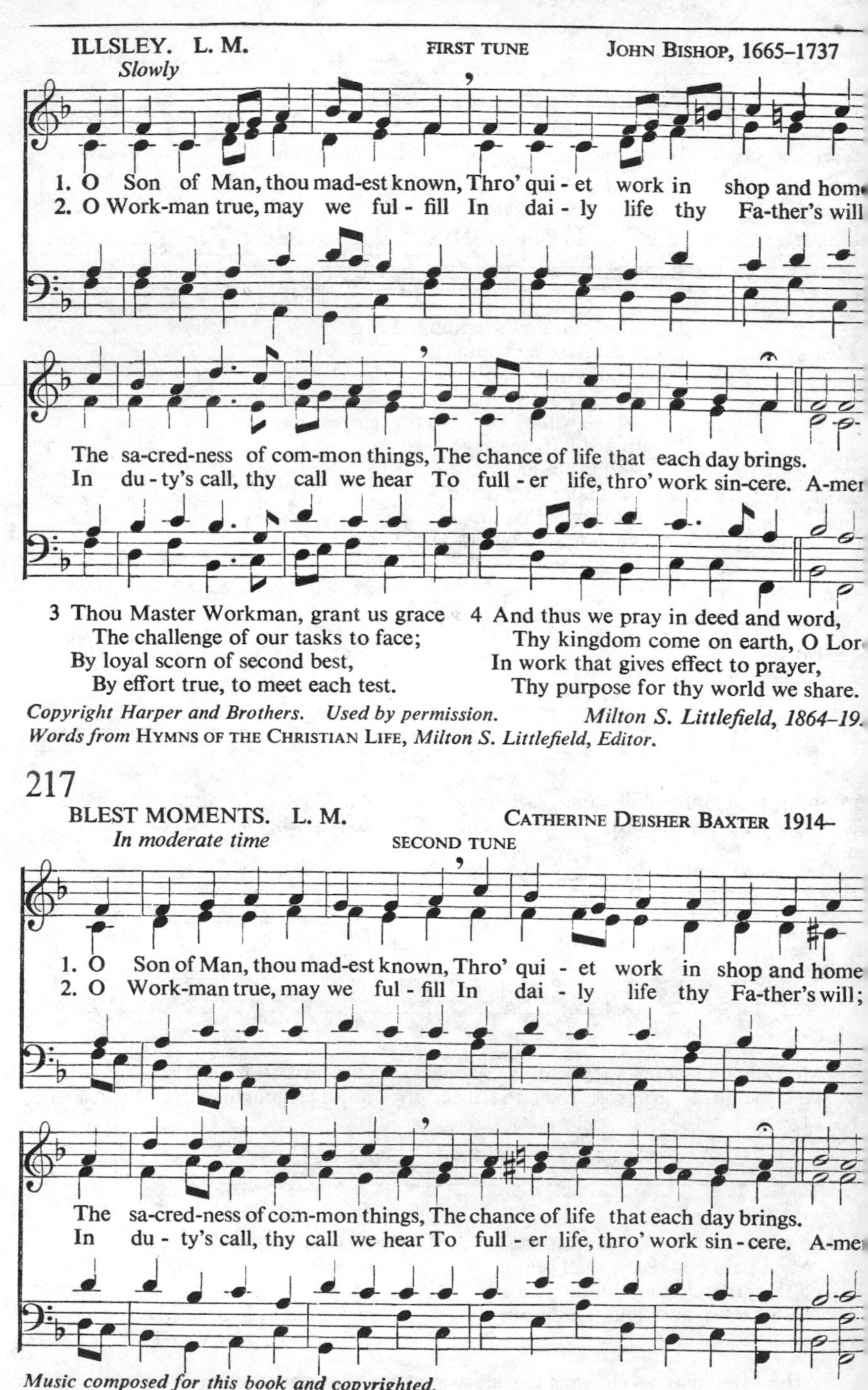
ILLSLEY. L. M.
Slowly
FIRST TUNE
JOHN BISHOP, 1665–1737
1. O Son of Man, thou mad-est known, Thro' qui - et work in shop and hom
2. O Work-man true, may we ful - fill In dai - ly life thy Fa-ther's will
The sa-cred-ness of com-mon things, The chance of life that each day brings.
In du - ty's call, thy call we hear To full - er life, thro' work sin-cere. A-mer
3 Thou Master Workman, grant us grace
The challenge of our tasks to face;
By loyal scorn of second best,
By effort true, to meet each test.
4 And thus we pray in deed and word,
Thy kingdom come on earth, O Lor
In work that gives effect to prayer,
Thy purpose for thy world we share.
Copyright Harper and Brothers. Used by permission.
Milton S. Littlefield, 1864–19.
Words from HYMNS OF THE CHRISTIAN LIFE, Milton S. Littlefield, Editor.
217
BLEST MOMENTS. L. M.
CATHERINE DEISHER BAXTER 1914–
In moderate time
SECOND TUNE
1. O Son of Man, thou mad-est known, Thro' qui - et work in shop and home
2. O Work-man true, may we ful - fill In dai - ly life thy Fa-ther's will;
The sa-cred-ness of com-mon things, The chance of life that each day brings.
In du - ty's call, thy call we hear To full - er life, thro' work sin - cere. A-mer
Music composed for this book and copyrighted.

SKARA. L. M. Karl Ivar Natanael Wideen, 1871–1951

In moderate time
FIRST TUNE
1. Blest are the mo - ments, dou - bly blest, That, drawn from
2. Each field is then a hal - lowed spot, An al - tar
this one hour of rest, Are with a read - y heart be -
is in each man's cot, A church in ev - ery grove that
stowed Up - on the serv - ice of our God!
spreads Its liv - ing roof a - bove our heads. A - men.

3 Look up to heaven! the industrious sun
Already half his race hath run;
He cannot halt or go astray,
But our immortal spirits may.

4 Lord, since his rising in the east,
If we have faltered or transgressed,
Guide, from thy love's abundant source,
What yet remains of this day's course;

5 Help with thy grace through life's short day
Our upward and our downward way,
And glorify for us the west,
When we shall sink to final rest. Amen.

William Wordsworth, 1770–1850

This hymn may also be sung to HAMBURG (No. 503).

WINSCOTT. L. M. SAMUEL SEBASTIAN WESLEY, 1810–76

In moderate time SECOND TUNE

1. Blest are the mo - ments, dou - bly blest, That, drawn from this one hour of rest, Are with a read - y heart be - stowed Up - on the serv - ice of our God!
2. Each field is then a hal - lowed spot, An al - tar is in each man's cot, A church in ev - ery grove that spreads Its liv - ing roof a - bove our heads. A - men.

3 Look up to heaven! the industrious sun
Already half his race hath run;
He cannot halt or go astray,
But our immortal spirits may.

4 Lord, since his rising in the east,
If we have faltered or transgressed,
Guide, from thy love's abundant source,
What yet remains of this day's course;

5 Help with thy grace through life's short day
Our upward and our downward way,
And glorify for us the west,
When we shall sink to final rest. Amen.

William Wordsworth, 1770–1850

This hymn may also be sung to HAMBURG (No. 503).

See also:

240 Angel voices ever singing
202 Awake, my soul, and with the sun
479 I need thee every hour
170 Lord of all being, throned afar
538 Lord, speak to me, that I may speak
451 Teach me, my God and King
545 The wise may bring their learning
544 We give thee but thine own

STRENGTH AND STAY. 11 10, 11 10. JOHN BACCHUS DYKES, 1823–76
Slowly, with breadth
1. O Strength and Stay up - hold - ing all cre - a - tion,
2. Grant to life's day a calm un - cloud - ed end - ing,
Who ev - er dost thy - self un - moved a - bide,
An eve un - touched by shad - ows of de - cay,
Yet day by day the light in due gra - da - tion
The bright-ness of a ho - ly death - bed blend - ing
From hour to hour through all its chang - es guide;
With dawn - ing glo - ries of the e - ter - nal day. A-men.

3 Hear us, O Father, gracious and forgiving,
Through Jesus Christ, thy co-eternal Word,
Who, with the Holy Ghost, by all things living,
Now and to endless ages art adored. Amen.

Ascribed to St. Ambrose, 340–97
Tr. John Ellerton, 1826–93
and Fenton J. A. Hort, 1828–92

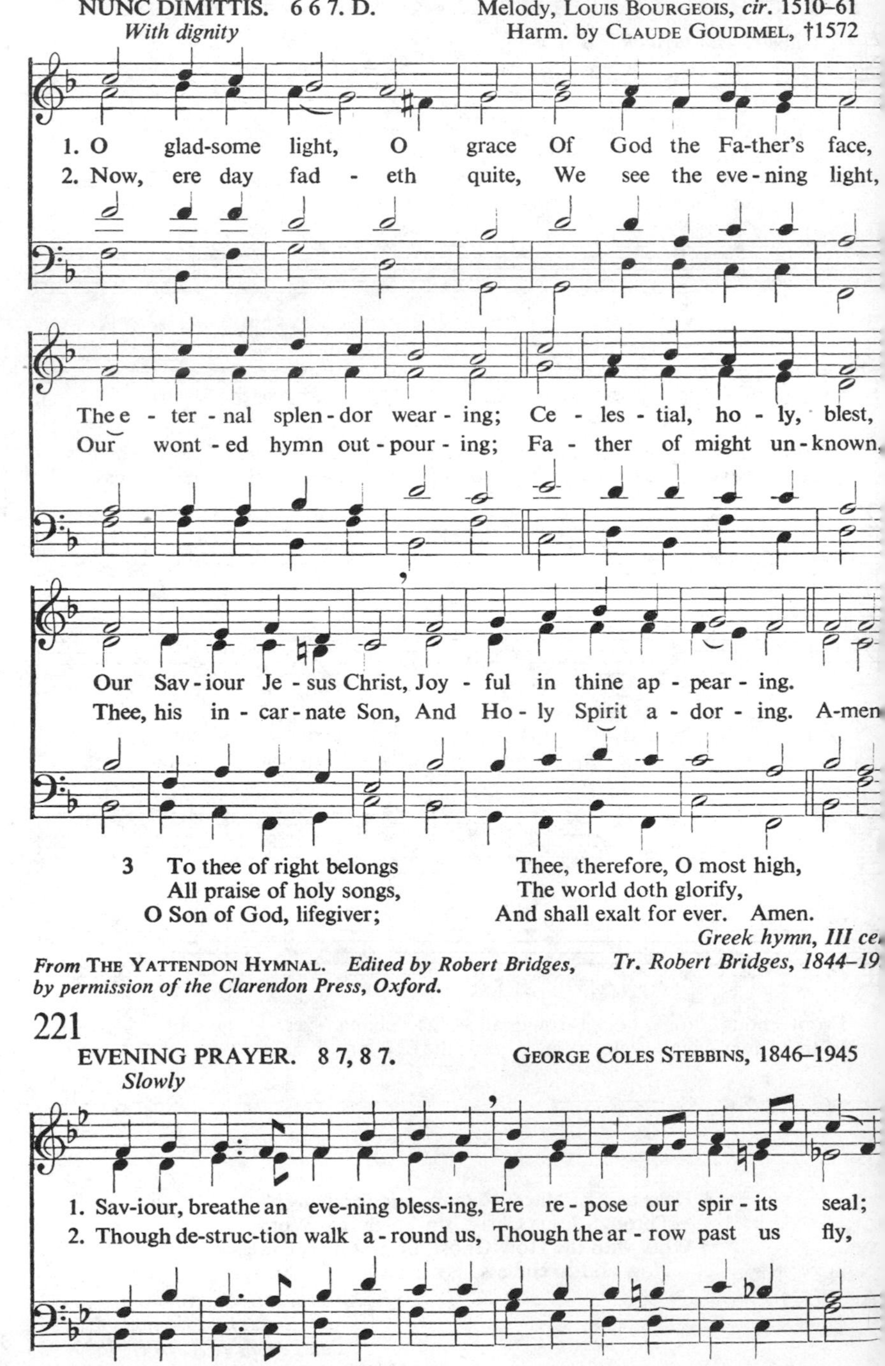
NUNC DIMITTIS. 6 6 7. D.
Melody, LOUIS BOURGEOIS, cir. 1510–61
With dignity
Harm. by CLAUDE GOUDIMEL, †1572
1. O glad-some light, O grace Of God the Fa-ther's face,
2. Now, ere day fad - eth quite, We see the eve-ning light,
The e - ter - nal splen-dor wear - ing; Ce - les - tial, ho - ly, blest,
Our wont - ed hymn out - pour - ing; Fa - ther of might un - known,
Our Sav - iour Je - sus Christ, Joy - ful in thine ap - pear - ing.
Thee, his in - car - nate Son, And Ho - ly Spirit a - dor - ing. A-men
3 To thee of right belongs
All praise of holy songs,
O Son of God, lifegiver;
Thee, therefore, O most high,
The world doth glorify,
And shall exalt for ever. Amen.
Greek hymn, III ce
Tr. Robert Bridges, 1844–19
From THE YATTENDON HYMNAL. Edited by Robert Bridges, by permission of the Clarendon Press, Oxford.
221
EVENING PRAYER. 8 7, 8 7.
GEORGE COLES STEBBINS, 1846–1945
Slowly
1. Sav-iour, breathe an eve-ning bless-ing, Ere re - pose our spir - its seal;
2. Though de-struc-tion walk a - round us, Though the ar - row past us fly,

Sin and want we come con-fess-ing; Thou canst save, and thou canst heal.
An - gel guards from thee surround us; We are safe, if thou art nigh. A-men.

3 Though the night be dark and dreary,
Darkness cannot hide from thee;
Thou art he who, never weary,
Watchest where thy people be.

4 Be thou nigh should death o'ertake us;
Jesus, then our refuge be;
And in Paradise awake us,
There to rest in peace with thee.
Amen.

James Edmeston, 1791–1867
Godfrey Thring, 1823–1903

22

ST. GABRIEL. 8 8, 8 4. FREDERICK A. G. OUSELEY, 1825–99

Quietly

1. The ra-diant morn hath passed a-way, And spent too soon her gold - en store;
2. Our life is but an au-tumn sun, Its glo - rious noon how quick - ly past;
3. O by thy soul - in - spir - ing grace Up - lift our hearts to realms on high;

The shad-ows of de - part - ing day Creep on once more.
Lead us, O Christ, our life-work done, Safe home at last.
Help us to look to that bright place Be - yond the sky, A-men.

4 Where light, and life, and joy, and peace
In undivided empire reign,
And thronging angels never cease
Their deathless strain;

5 Where saints are clothed in spotless white,
And evening shadows never fall,
Where thou, eternal Light of light,
Art Lord of all. Amen.

Godfrey Thring, 1823–1903

TALLIS' CANON. L. M.

THOMAS TALLIS, *cir.* 1505–85

With dignity
1. All praise to thee, my God, this night, For all the blessings of the light; Keep me, O keep me, King of kings, Beneath thine own almighty wings!
2. Forgive me, Lord, for thy dear Son, The ill that I this day have done, That with the world, myself, and thee, I, ere I sleep, at peace may be. A-men.

3 Teach me to live, that I may dread
The grave as little as my bed;
Teach me to die, that so I may
Rise glorious at the aweful day.

4 O when shall I, in endless day,
For ever chase dark sleep away,
And hymns divine with angels sing
In endless praise to thee, my King?

5 Praise God, from whom all blessings flow;
Praise him, all creatures here below;
Praise him above, ye heavenly host;
Praise Father, Son, and Holy Ghost. Amen.

Thomas Ken, 1637–1711

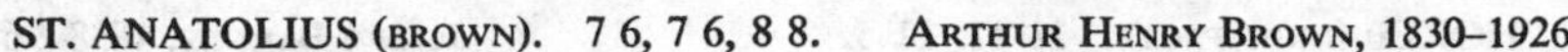

ST. ANATOLIUS (BROWN). 7 6, 7 6, 8 8. ARTHUR HENRY BROWN, 1830–1926

In moderate time

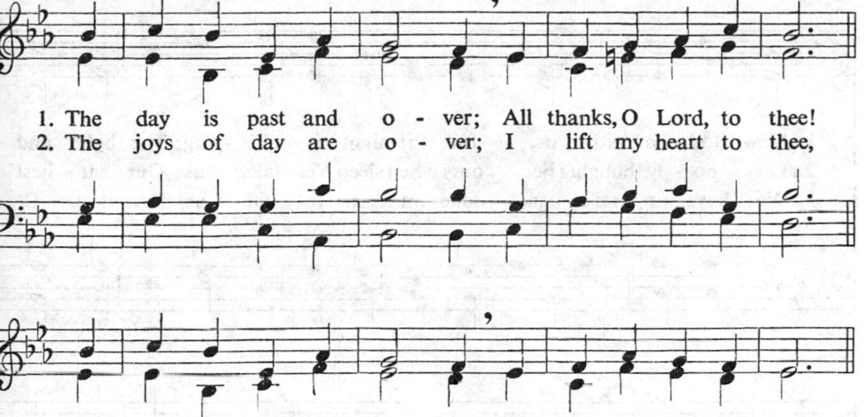
1. The day is past and o - ver; All thanks, O Lord, to thee!
2. The joys of day are o - ver; I lift my heart to thee,
I pray thee that of - fence - less The hours of dark may be.
And call on thee that sin - less The hours of night may be.

O Je - sus, keep me in thy sight, And guard me thro' the com - ing night!
O Je-sus, make their dark-ness light, And guard me thro' the com - ing night. A-men.

3 The toils of day are over;
  I raise the hymn to thee,
And ask that free from peril
  The hours of fear may be.
O Jesus, keep me in thy sight,
And guard me through the coming night.

4 Be thou my soul's preserver,
  O God, for thou dost know
How many are the perils
  Through which I have to go.
Lover of men, O hear my call,
And guard and save me from them all. Amen.

St. Anatolius, †458
Tr. John Mason Neale, 1818–66

HOREB (NIGHTFALL). 11 11, 11 5. JOSEPH BARNBY, 1838–96

Devotionally
FIRST TUNE
1. Now God be with us, for the night is clos - ing; The light and dark - ness are of his dis - pos - ing; And neath his shad - ow here to rest we yield us, For he will shield us.
2. Let ho - ly thoughts be ours when sleep o'er - takes us; Our ear - liest thoughts be thine when morn-ing wakes us; All day serve thee, in all that we are do - ing Thy praise pur - su - ing.
3. We have no ref - uge, none on earth to aid us, Save thee, O Fa - ther, who thine own hast made us; But thy dear Pres - ence will not leave them lone - ly Who seek thee on - ly. A-men.
Rit.

4 Father, thy Name be praised, thy kingdom given;
Thy will be done on earth as 'tis in heaven;
Keep us in life, forgive our sins, deliver
Us now and ever. Amen.

Petrus Herbert, †157
Tr. Catherine Winkworth, 1829–7

LOBET DEN HERREN, ALLE. 11 11, 11 5.
JOHANN CRÜGER, 1598–1662
Devotionally
SECOND TUNE
1. Now God be with us, for the night is clos - ing; The light and
2. Let ho - ly thoughts be ours when sleep o'er - takes us; Our ear - liest
3. We have no ref - uge, none on earth to aid us, Save thee, O
dark - ness are of his dis - pos - ing; And neath his shad - ow
thoughts be thine when morn-ing wakes us; All day serve thee, in
Fa - ther, who thine own hast made us; But thy dear Pres - ence
here to rest we yield us, For he will shield us.
all that we are do - ing Thy praise pur - su - ing.
will not leave them lone - ly Who seek thee on - ly. A-men.

4 Father, thy Name be praised, thy kingdom given;
Thy will be done on earth as 'tis in heaven;
Keep us in life, forgive our sins, deliver
Us now and ever. Amen.

Petrus Herbert, †1571
Tr. Catherine Winkworth, 1829–78

HURSLEY. L. M. *Katholisches Gesangbuch,* Vienna, 1774

Quietly

1. Sun of my soul, thou Sav - iour dear, It is not night if thou be near; O may no earth-born cloud a - rise To hide thee from thy serv - ant's eyes.
2. When the soft dews of kind - ly sleep My wea - ried eye - lids gent - ly steep, Be my last thought, how sweet to rest For - ev - er on my Sav - iour's breast.
3. A - bide with me from morn till eve, For with - out thee I can - not live; A - bide with me when night is nigh, For with - out thee I dare not die.
A - men.

4 If some poor wandering child of thine
Have spurned today the voice divine,
Now, Lord, the gracious work begin;
Let him no more lie down in sin.

5 Watch by the sick; enrich the poor
With blessings from thy boundless stor
Be every mourner's sleep tonight
Like infant's slumbers, pure and light.

6 Come near and bless us when we wake,
Ere through the world our way we take,
Till in the ocean of thy love
We lose ourselves in heaven above. Amen.

John Keble, 1792–18

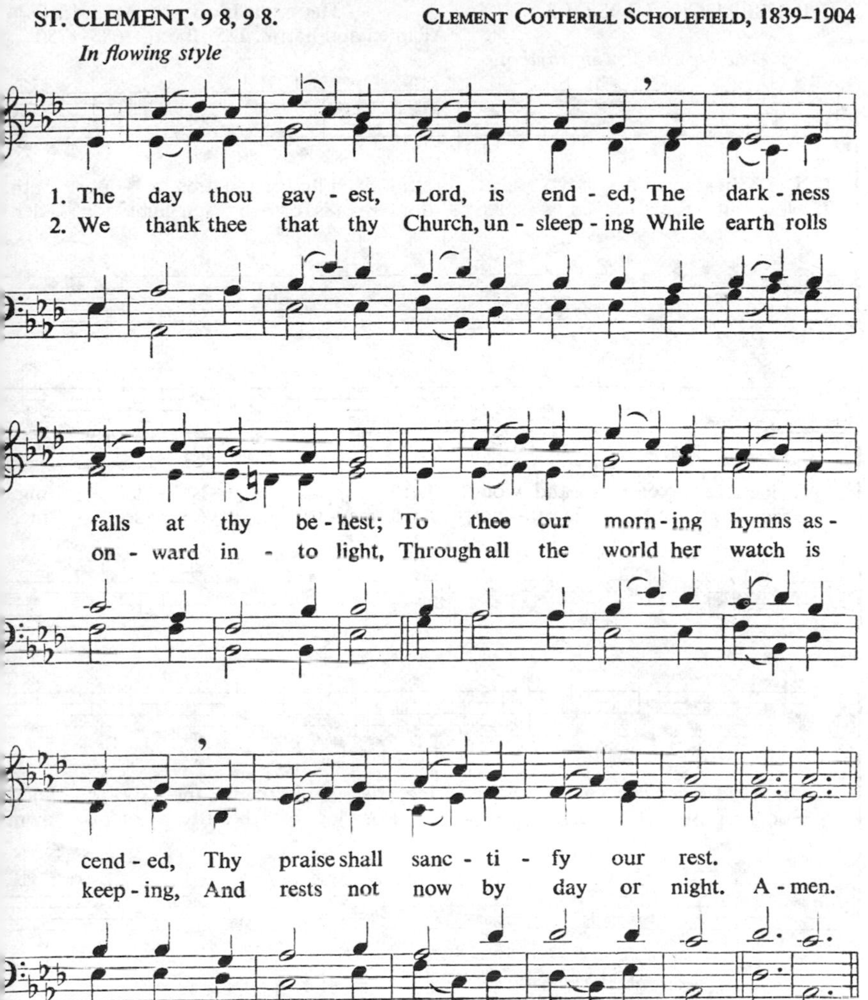
ST. CLEMENT. 9 8, 9 8.
Clement Cotterill Scholefield, 1839–1904
In flowing style
1. The day thou gav - est, Lord, is end - ed, The dark - ness falls at thy be - hest; To thee our morn - ing hymns as - cend - ed, Thy praise shall sanc - ti - fy our rest.
2. We thank thee that thy Church, un - sleep - ing While earth rolls on - ward in - to light, Through all the world her watch is keep - ing, And rests not now by day or night. A - men.

3 As o'er each continent and island
The dawn leads on another day,
The voice of prayer is never silent,
Nor dies the strain of praise away.

4 The sun that bids us rest is waking
Our brethren 'neath the western sky,
And hour by hour fresh lips are making
Thy wondrous doings heard on high.

5 So be it, Lord; thy throne shall never,
Like earth's proud empires, pass away;
Thy kingdom stands, and grows for ever,
Till all thy creatures own thy sway. Amen.

John Ellerton, 1826–93

INNSBRUCK. 7 7 6, 7 7 8. HEINRICH ISAAK, *cir.* 1455–1517
Adapted and harm., J. S. BACH, 1685–1750

Quietly, with flowing rhythm

1. The du-teous day now clos - eth, Each flower and tree re - pos - eth,
2. Now all the heaven-ly splen - dor Breaks forth in star-light ten - der
Shade creeps o'er wild and wood: Let us, as night is fall - ing,
From myr - iad worlds un-known; And man, the mar-vel see - ing,
On God our Mak - er call - ing, Give thanks to him, the Giv - er good.
For - gets his self - ish be - ing, For joy of beau-ty not his own.

3 His care he drowneth yonder,
Lost in the abyss of wonder;
To heaven his soul doth steal:
This life he disesteemeth,
The day it is that dreameth,
That doth from truth his vision seal.

4 Awhile his mortal blindness
May miss God's loving-kindness,
And grope in faithless strife:
But when life's day is over
Shall death's fair night discover
The fields of everlasting life.

Paul Gerhardt, 1607–7
Tr. Robert Bridges, 1844–193

GOUNOD (LUX PRIMA). 8 7, 8 7, 7 7. CHARLES FRANÇOIS GOUNOD, 1818–93

Slowly
1. Sav - iour, now the day is end-ing, And the shades of eve - ning fall,
2. Bless the Gos - pel mes - sage spo-ken In thine own ap - point - ed way;
Let thy ho - ly Dove, de-scend-ing, Bring thy mer - cy to us all;
Give each faint - ing soul a to - ken Of thy ten - der love to - day;
Set thy seal on ev - ery heart, Je - sus, bless us ere we part!
Set thy seal on ev - ery heart, Je - sus, bless us ere we part! A-men.

3 Comfort those in pain or sorrow,
  Watch each sleeping child of thine;
Let us all arise tomorrow
  Strengthened by thy grace divine;
Set thy seal on every heart,
Jesus, bless us ere we part! Amen.

Sarah Doudney, 1843–1926

AR HYD Y NOS. 8 4, 8 4, 8 8, 8 4. Traditional Melody, Welsh

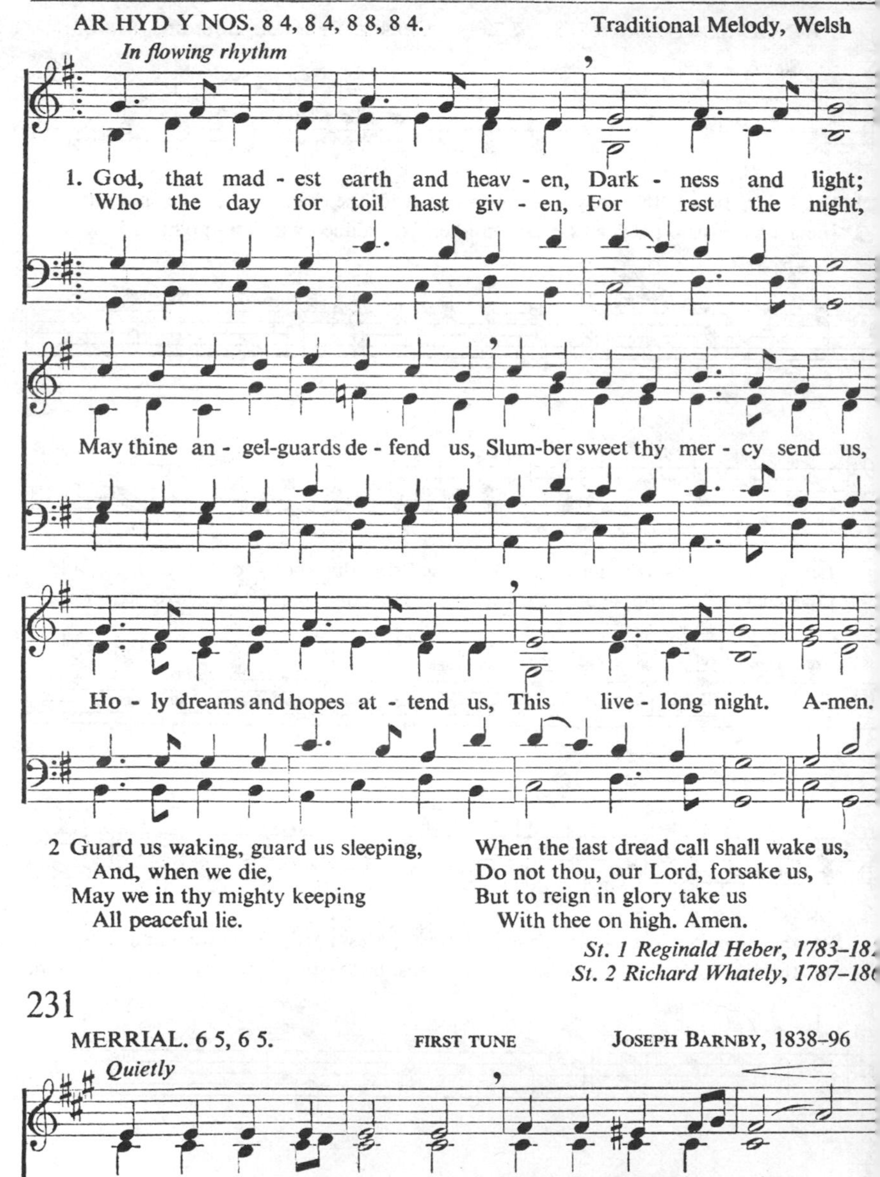
In flowing rhythm
1. God, that mad - est earth and heav - en, Dark - ness and light;
Who the day for toil hast giv - en, For rest the night,
May thine an - gel-guards de - fend us, Slum-ber sweet thy mer - cy send us,
Ho - ly dreams and hopes at - tend us, This live - long night. A-men.

2 Guard us waking, guard us sleeping,
And, when we die,
May we in thy mighty keeping
All peaceful lie.
When the last dread call shall wake us,
Do not thou, our Lord, forsake us,
But to reign in glory take us
With thee on high. Amen.

St. 1 Reginald Heber, 1783–18
St. 2 Richard Whately, 1787–18

231

MERRIAL. 6 5, 6 5. FIRST TUNE JOSEPH BARNBY, 1838–96

Quietly
1. Now the day is o - ver, Night is draw - ing nigh,
2. Now the dark - ness gath - ers, Stars be - gin to peep,
3. Je - sus, give the wea - ry Calm and sweet re - pose;

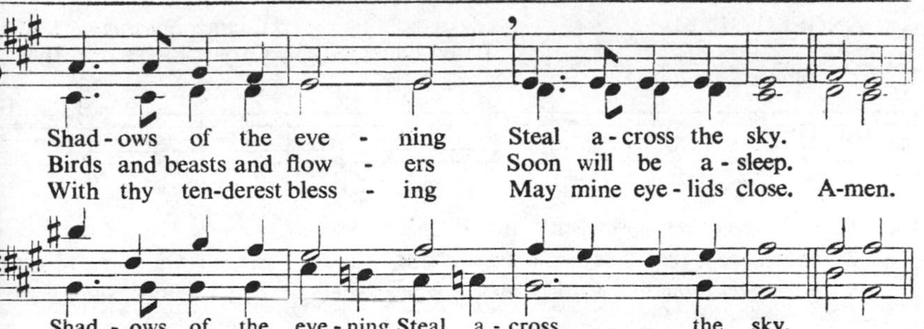
Shad - ows of the eve - ning Steal a - cross the sky.
Birds and beasts and flow - ers Soon will be a - sleep.
With thy ten-derest bless - ing May mine eye - lids close. A-men.
Shad - ows of the eve - ning Steal a - cross the sky.

4 Grant to little children
Visions bright of thee;
Guard the sailors tossing
On the deep blue sea.

5 Comfort every sufferer
Watching late in pain;
Those who plan some evil
From their sin restrain.

6 Through the long night-watches
May thine angels spread
Their white wings above me,
Watching round my bed.

7 When the morning wakens,
Then may I arise
Pure and fresh and sinless
In thy holy eyes.

8 Glory to the Father,
Glory to the Son,
And to thee, blest Spirit,
Whilst all ages run. Amen.

Sabine Baring-Gould, 1834–1924

ords by permission of J. Curwen and Son, Ltd.

31

ST. LUCIAN. 6 5, 6 5. JOHANN C. H. RINCK, 1770–1846

In moderate time

SECOND TUNE

1. Now the day is o - ver, Night is draw - ing nigh,
2. Now the dark - ness gath - ers, Stars be - gin to peep,
3. Je - sus, give the wea - ry Calm and sweet re - pose;

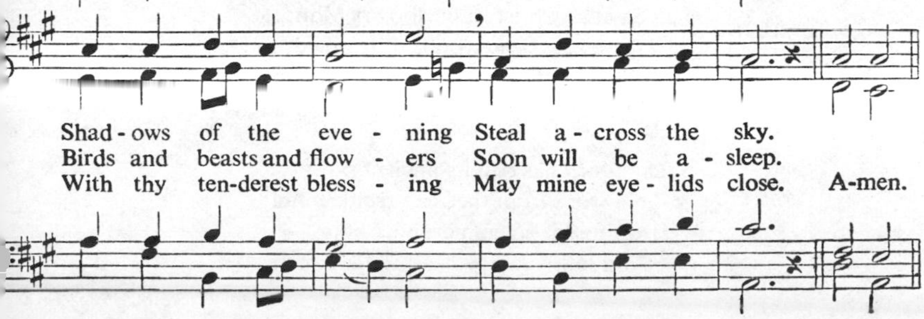

Shad - ows of the eve - ning Steal a - cross the sky.
Birds and beasts and flow - ers Soon will be a - sleep.
With thy ten-derest bless - ing May mine eye - lids close. A-men.

ANGELUS. L. M.

Cantica Spiritualia, 1847
Based on melody by GEORG JOSEPH, *cir.* 1657

In moderate time

1. At e - ven when the sun was set, The sick, O Lord, a - round thee lay; O, in what div - ers pains they met, O, with what joy they went a - way!
2. Once more 'tis e - ven - tide, and we, Op - pressed with var - ious ills, draw near; What if thy form we can - not see? We know and feel that thou art here.
3. O Sav - iour Christ, our woes dis - pel; For some are sick, and some are sad, And some have nev - er loved thee well, And some have lost the love they had. A - men.

4 O Saviour Christ, thou too art Man;
Thou hast been troubled, tempted, tried;
Thy kind but searching glance can scan
The very wounds that shame would hide.

5 Thy touch has still its ancient power;
No word from thee can fruitless fall;
Hear, in this solemn evening hour,
And in thy mercy heal us all. Amen.

Henry Twells, 1823–1900,

CECILE. C. M. D.
PETER JOHNSON, 1870–
Quietly
1. The twi - light shad - ows round me fall, And night comes steal-ing on;
2. My life is but a fleet - ing day, My race how quick - ly run!
But thou, dear Lord, art ev - er near, My day when day is gone,
The dawn and noon - day glo - ry fade With yon - der set - ting sun.
Thy wings in love o'er - shad - ow me, The night with thee is light;
A stran - ger and a pil - grim here, In un-known paths I roam;
I rest in thee, thou change-less One, And wait the morn-ing bright.
Lord, let thy glo - ry light the way That leads me to my home. A-men.

3 By faith I see the better land
Where falls no earthly night,
Where thou dost shine, a radiant sun,
The everlasting Light.
Then grant me, Lord, to walk with thee,
And keep me thine alway,
That with the morn I may awake
Unto the perfect day. Amen.

Ernest Edwin Ryden, 1886–

EVENING PRAISE. 7 7, 7 7 4. With Refrain. WILLIAM F. SHERWIN, 1826–88

Devotionally

1. Day is dy - ing in the west, Heaven is touch - ing
2. Lord of life, be - neath the dome Of the u - ni -

earth with rest; Wait and wor - ship while the night Sets her
verse, thy home, Gath - er us who seek thy face To the

eve - ning lamps a - light Through all the sky.
fold of thy em - brace, For thou art nigh.

Refrain

Ho - ly, ho - ly,

ho - ly Lord God of Hosts! Heaven and earth are full of thee,

Heaven and earth are prais-ing thee, O Lord Most High! A-men.

3 While the deepening shadows fall,
Heart of love, enfold us all;
Through the glory and the grace
Of the stars that veil thy face,
Our hearts ascend.

4 When forever from our sight
Pass the stars, the day, the night,
Lord of angels, on our eyes
Let eternal morning rise,
And shadows end. Amen.

Mary A. Lathbury, 1841–1913

sed by permission of the Chautauqua Institution

35

EVENING PRAYER. 8 7, 8 7. JOHN STAINER, 1840–1901

Unison

1. Je - sus, ten - der Shep-herd, hear me, Bless thy lit - tle lamb to - night;
2. Through this day thy hand has led me, And I thank thee for thy care;

Through the dark-ness be thou near me, Keep me safe till morn-ing light.
Thou hast warmed me, clothed and fed me, Lis - ten to my eve-ning prayer. A-men.

3 Let my sins be all forgiven;
Bless the friends I love so well;
Take me, Lord, at last to heaven,
Happy there with thee to dwell. Amen.

Mary Lundie Duncan, 1814–40

SOLDAU. L.M.

Pre-Reformation melody
Wittenberg Gesangbuch, 1524

In moderate time

1. The fad - ing day a - dorns the west And calls our
2. O Lord, as si - lent shad - ows fall, Thy lov - ing -
wait - ing world to rest; Thou Lord of light and all we know
kind - ness shield us all; And for thy chil - dren near and far
Thy calm and peace on us be - stow.
Set out o'er each a gold - en star. A - men.

3 Of thy protecting hand aware,
May all in sleep invite thy care;
And, strength renewed and darkness gone,
Behold with joy the light of dawn. Amen.

Steingrimur Thorsteinsson, 1830–19
Tr. Jakobina Johnson, 1883–

37 Worship — Evening

ST. HUBERT. 5 5, 8 8, 5 5.
LEICESTER DARWALL, 1813–97
Quietly
1. Round me falls the night; Sav-iour, be my light; Through the hours in dark-ness shroud-ed Let me see thy face un-cloud-ed; Let thy glo-ry shine In this heart of mine.
2. Earth-ly work is done, Earth-ly sounds are none; Rest in sleep and si-lence seek-ing, Let me hear thee soft-ly speak-ing; In my spir-it's ear Whis-per, 'I am near.' A-men.

3 Blessèd, heavenly Light,
Shining through earth's night;
Voice, that oft of love hast told me;
Arms, so strong to clasp and hold me;
Thou thy watch wilt keep,
Saviour, o'er my sleep. Amen.

William R. Romanis, 1824–99

See also:

The Church

THE HOUSE OF GOD

238

CROFT'S 136TH. 6 6, 6 6, 4 4, 4 4. WILLIAM CROFT, 1678–1727

With dignity
FIRST TUNE
1. Lord of the worlds a - bove, How pleas-ant and how fair The
2. O hap - py souls that pray Where God ap - points to hear! O
dwell-ings of thy love, Thine earth - ly tem - ples, are! To thine a -
hap - py men that pay Their con - stant serv - ice there! They praise thee
bode My heart as - pires With warm de - sires To see my God.
still; And hap - py they That love the way To Si - on's hill.

3 They go from strength to strength
Through this dark vale of tears,
Till each arrives at length,
Till each in heaven appears:
O glorious seat,
When God our King
Shall thither bring
Our willing feet!

Isaac Watts, 1674–17
Psalm

DARWALL'S 148TH. 6 6, 6 6, 4 4, 4 4. JOHN DARWALL, 1731–89

SECOND TUNE

With dignity

1. Lord of the worlds a - bove, How pleas - ant and how fair The dwell-ings of thy love, Thine earth-ly tem - ples, are! To thine a - bode My heart as - pires With warm de - sires To see my God.

2. O hap - py souls that pray Where God ap - points to hear! O hap - py men that pay Their con-stant serv - ice there! They praise thee still; And hap - py they That love the way To Si - on's hill.

3 They go from strength to strength
Through this dark vale of tears,
Till each arrives at length,
Till each in heaven appears:
O glorious seat,
When God our King
Shall thither bring
Our willing feet!

Isaac Watts, 1674–1748
Psalm 84

QUAM DILECTA. 6 6, 6 6. HENRY LASCELLES JENNER, 1820–98

In moderate time

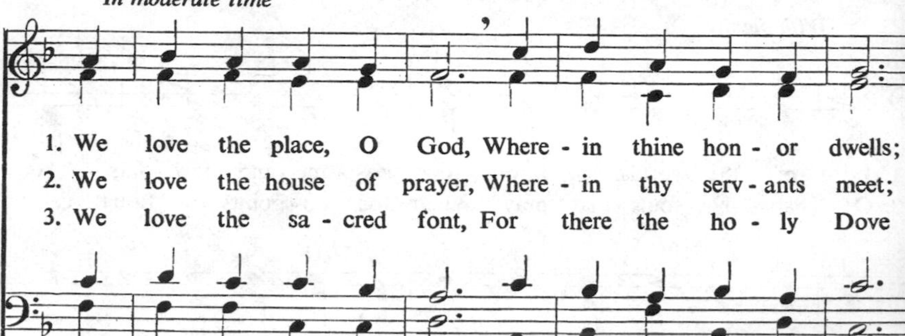
1. We love the place, O God, Where - in thine hon - or dwells;
2. We love the house of prayer, Where - in thy serv - ants meet;
3. We love the sa - cred font, For there the ho - ly Dove

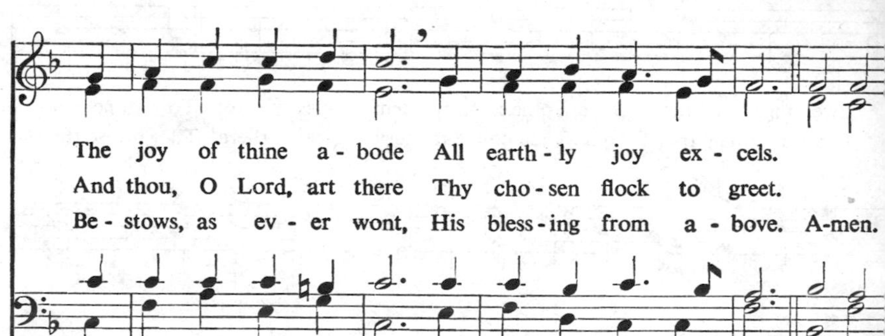
The joy of thine a - bode All earth - ly joy ex - cels.
And thou, O Lord, art there Thy cho - sen flock to greet.
Be - stows, as ev - er wont, His bless - ing from a - bove. A-men.

4 We love thine altar, Lord;
O, what on earth so dear!
For there, in faith adored,
We find thy presence near.

5 We love the word of life,
The word that tells of peace,
Of comfort in the strife,
And joys that never cease.

6 We love to sing below
For mercies freely given;
But O, we long to know
The triumph-song of heaven!

7 Lord Jesus, give us grace
On earth to love thee more,
In heaven to see thy face,
And with thy saints adore. Amen.

William Bullock, 1798–187
Henry Williams Baker, 1821–7

ANGEL VOICES. 8 5, 8 5, 8 4 3. ARTHUR S. SULLIVAN, 1842-1900

Brightly
1. An - gel voi - ces ev - er sing - ing Round thy throne of light,
2. Thou, who art be - yond the far - thest Mor - tal eye can scan,
3. Yea, we know that thou re - joic - est O'er each work of thine;
An gel harps, for ev - er ring - ing, Rest not day nor night;
Can it be that thou re - gard - est Songs of sin - ful man?
Thou didst ears and hands and voi - ces For thy praise com - bine;
Thou-sands on-ly live to bless thee, And con-fess thee Lord of might!
Can we know that thou art near us, And wilt hear us? Yea, we can!
Craftsman's art and music's measure For thy pleas-ure Didst de-sign. A - men.

4 Here, great God, today we offer
Of thine own to thee,
And for thine acceptance proffer,
All unworthily,
Hearts and minds and hands and voices
In our choicest
Melody.

5 Honor, glory, might and merit
Thine shall ever be,
Father, Son, and Holy Spirit,
Blessèd Trinity!
Of the best that thou hast given
Earth and heaven
Render thee. Amen.

Francis Pott, 1832-1909

CROMER, L.M. JOHN AMBROSE LLOYD, 1815–74

With breadth, slowly

1. How bless - ed is this place, O Lord, Where thou art wor - shipped and a - dored; In faith we here an al - tar raise To thy great glo - ry, God of praise!
2. Here let thy sa - cred fire of old De - scend to kin - dle spir - its cold; And may our prayers, when here we bend, Like in - cense sweet to thee as - cend.
3. Here gath - er us a - round thy board To keep the feast with thee, dear Lord, And when in faith our souls draw near, May we dis - cern thy pres - ence here.
A - men.

4 Here let the weary one find rest,
The troubled heart thy comfort blest,
The guilty soul a sure retreat,
The sinner pardon at thy feet.

5 Here thine angelic spirits send
Their solemn praise with ours to blend,
And grant the vision, inly given,
Of this thy house, the gate of heaven. Amen.

Ernest Edwin Ryden, 1886-

This hymn may also be sung to MELCOMBE (No. 201)

REGENT SQUARE. 8 7, 8 7, 8 7. HENRY SMART, 1813–79

Moderately slow, with dignity

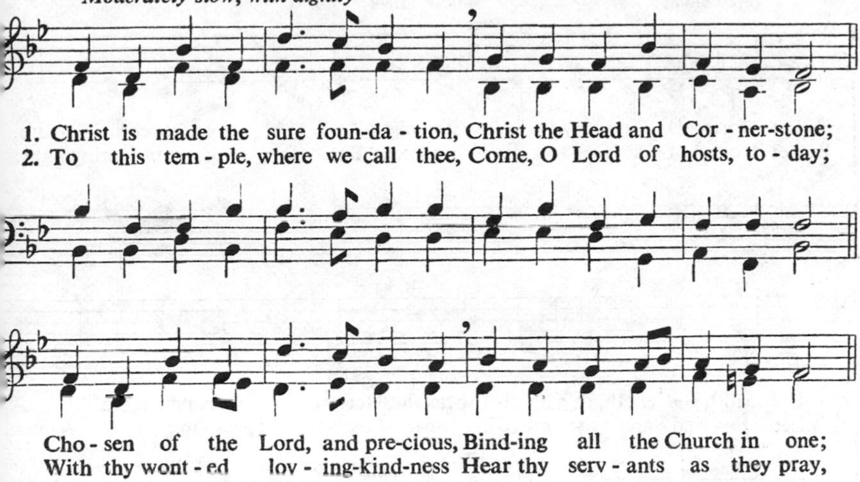

1. Christ is made the sure foun-da - tion, Christ the Head and Cor - ner-stone;
2. To this tem - ple, where we call thee, Come, O Lord of hosts, to - day;

Cho - sen of the Lord, and pre-cious, Bind-ing all the Church in one;
With thy wont - ed lov - ing-kind-ness Hear thy serv - ants as they pray,

Ho - ly Si - on's help for ev - er, And her con - fi - dence a - lone.
And thy full - est ben - e - dic - tion Shed with - in its walls al - way. A-men.

3 Here vouchsafe to all thy servants
What they ask of thee to gain;
What they gain from thee for ever
With the blessèd to retain,
And hereafter in thy glory
Evermore with thee to reign.

4 Laud and honor to the Father,
Laud and honor to the Son,
Laud and honor to the Spirit,
Ever Three and ever One,
One in might, and One in glory,
While unending ages run. Amen.

Latin Hymn, cir. VII cent.
Tr. John Mason Neale, 1818–66 a.

CHELSEA SQUARE. C.M.

Howard Chandler Robbins, 1876–1952
Harm. by Ray Francis Brown, 1897–

With dignity

FIRST TUNE

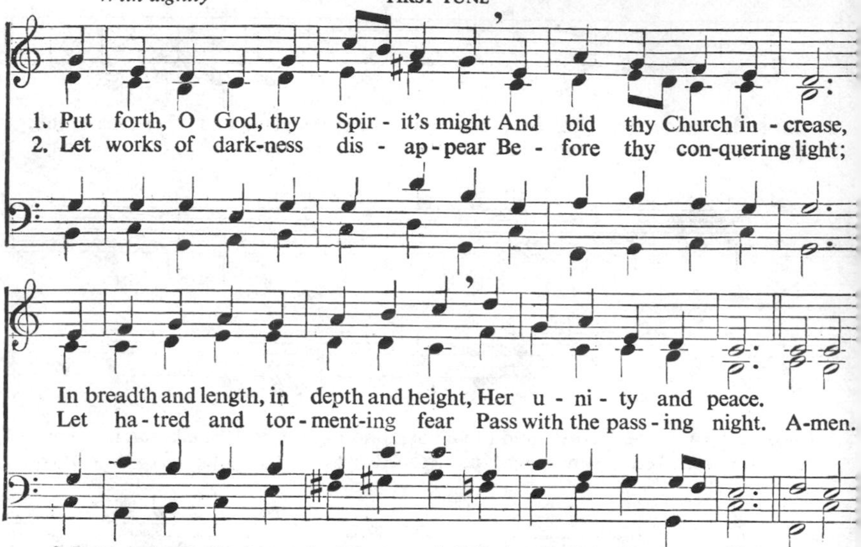

1. Put forth, O God, thy Spir - it's might And bid thy Church in - crease,
In breadth and length, in depth and height, Her u - ni - ty and peace.

2. Let works of dark-ness dis - ap - pear Be - fore thy con-quering light;
Let ha - tred and tor - ment-ing fear Pass with the pass - ing night. A-men.

3 Let what apostles learned of thee
Be ours from age to age;
Their steadfast faith our unity,
Their peace our heritage.

4 O Judge divine of human strife,
O vanquisher of pain!
To know thee is eternal life,
To serve thee is to reign. Amen.

Howard Chandler Robbins, 1876–195

Harmonization by permission of Mrs. Howard Chandler Robbins, Ray Francis Brown and the Church Pension Fund.

243

SPIRITUS DOMINI. C.M.

Roger Cole Wilson, 1912–

With dignity

SECOND TUNE

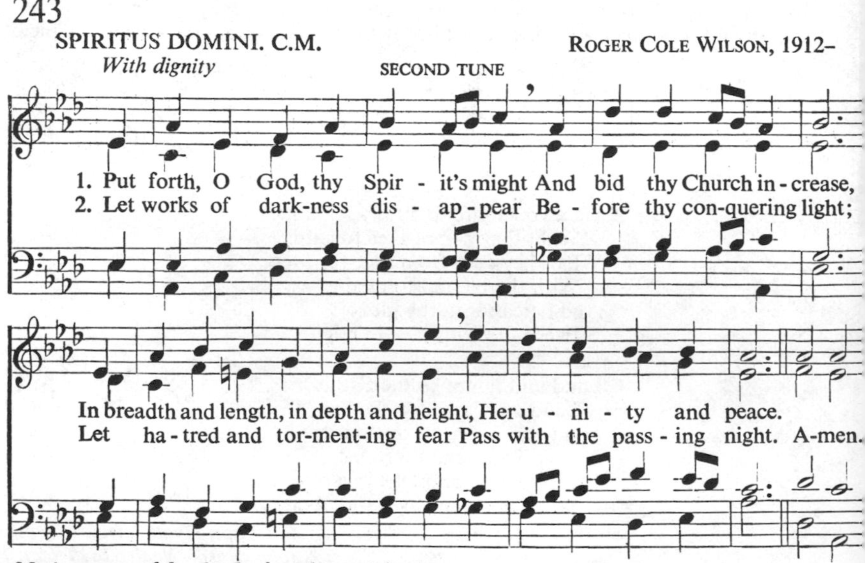
1. Put forth, O God, thy Spir - it's might And bid thy Church in - crease,
2. Let works of dark-ness dis - ap - pear Be - fore thy con-quering light;
In breadth and length, in depth and height, Her u - ni - ty and peace.
Let ha - tred and tor-ment-ing fear Pass with the pass - ing night. A-men.

Music composed for this book and copyrighted

MELCOMBE. L.M. SAMUEL WEBBE, 1740–1816

For Dedication of a Church

Moderately slow
1. All things are thine; no gift have we, Lord of all gifts, to of - fer thee: And hence with grate - ful hearts to - day Thine own be - fore thy feet we lay.
2. Thy will was in the build - ers' thought; Thy hand un - seen a - midst us wrought; Through mor - tal mo - tive, scheme and plan, Thy wise e - ter - nal pur - pose ran. A-men.

3 In weakness and in want we call
On thee for whom the heavens are small;
Thy glory is thy children's good,
Thy joy thy tender fatherhood.

4 O Father, deign these walls to bless;
Fill with thy love their emptiness;
And let their door a gateway be
To lead us from ourselves to thee. Amen.

John Greenleaf Whittier, 1807–92

TANTUM ERGO (DULCE CARMEN). 8 7, 8 7, 8 7.

Essay on the Church Plain Chant, 1782

FIRST TUNE

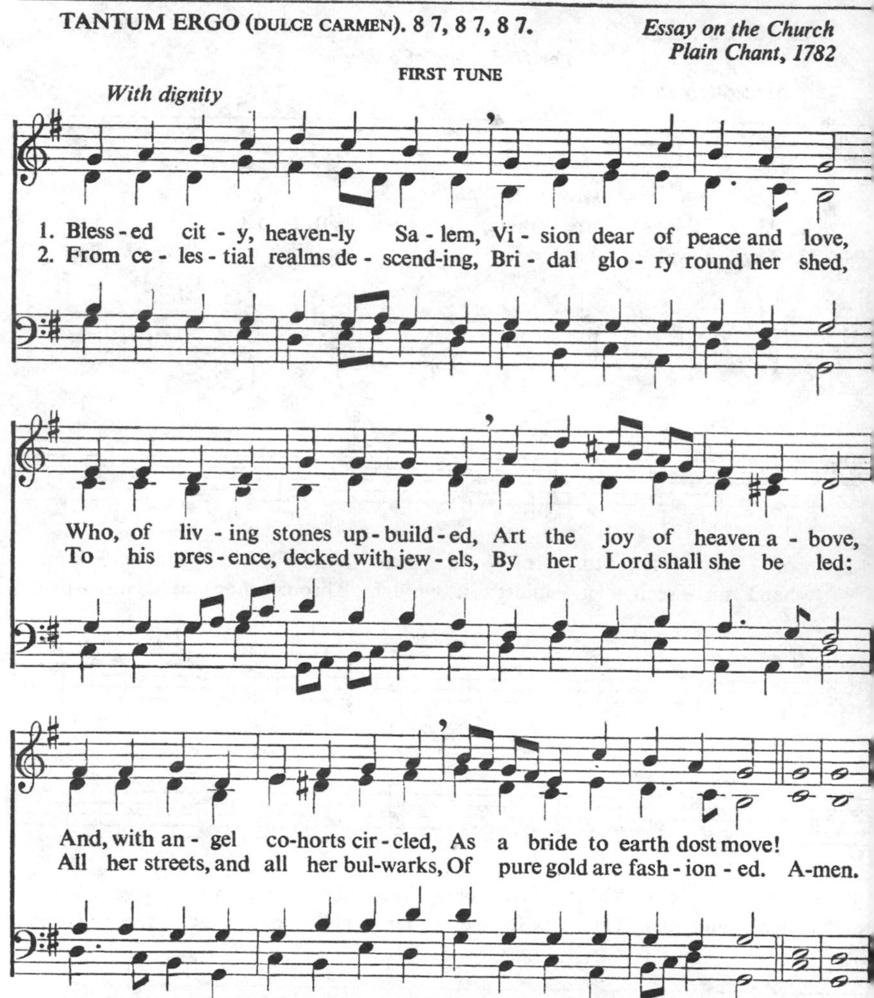
With dignity
1. Bless-ed cit-y, heaven-ly Sa-lem, Vi-sion dear of peace and love,
2. From ce-les-tial realms de-scend-ing, Bri-dal glo-ry round her shed,
Who, of liv-ing stones up-build-ed, Art the joy of heaven a-bove,
To his pres-ence, decked with jew-els, By her Lord shall she be led:
And, with an-gel co-horts cir-cled, As a bride to earth dost move!
All her streets, and all her bul-warks, Of pure gold are fash-ion-ed. A-men.

3 Bright with pearls her portals glitter,
They are open evermore;
And, by virtue of his merits,
Thither faithful souls may soar
Who for Christ's dear Name in this world
Pain and tribulation bore.

4 Many a blow and biting sculpture
Fashioned well those stones elect,
In their places now compacted
By the heavenly architect,
Who therewith hath willed for ever
That his palace should be decked.

5 Laud and honor to the Father;
Laud and honor to the Son;
Laud and honor to the Spirit;
Ever Three and ever One:
Consubstantial, co-eternal,
While unending ages run. Amen.

Latin hymn, cir. VII cent.
Tr. John Mason Neale, 1818-66

245

URBS BEATA. 8 7, 8 7, 8 7. **Plainsong, Mode ii**

SECOND TUNE

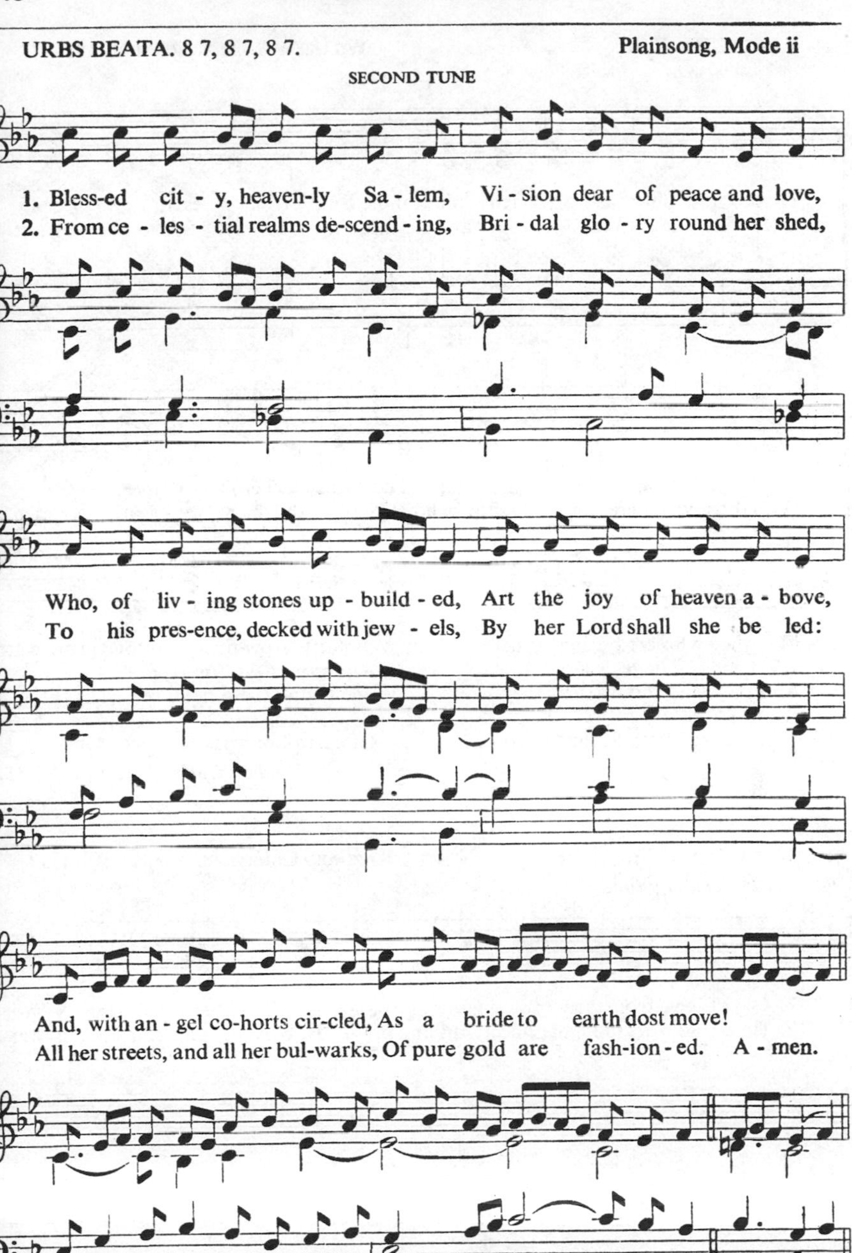
1. Bless-ed cit - y, heaven-ly Sa - lem, Vi - sion dear of peace and love,
2. From ce - les - tial realms de-scend - ing, Bri - dal glo - ry round her shed,
Who, of liv - ing stones up - build - ed, Art the joy of heaven a - bove,
To his pres-ence, decked with jew - els, By her Lord shall she be led:
And, with an - gel co-horts cir-cled, As a bride to earth dost move!
All her streets, and all her bul-warks, Of pure gold are fash-ion - ed. A - men.

Latin hymn, cir. VII cent.
Tr. John Mason Neale, 1818–66

This hymn may also be sung to REGENT SQUARE (No. 242)

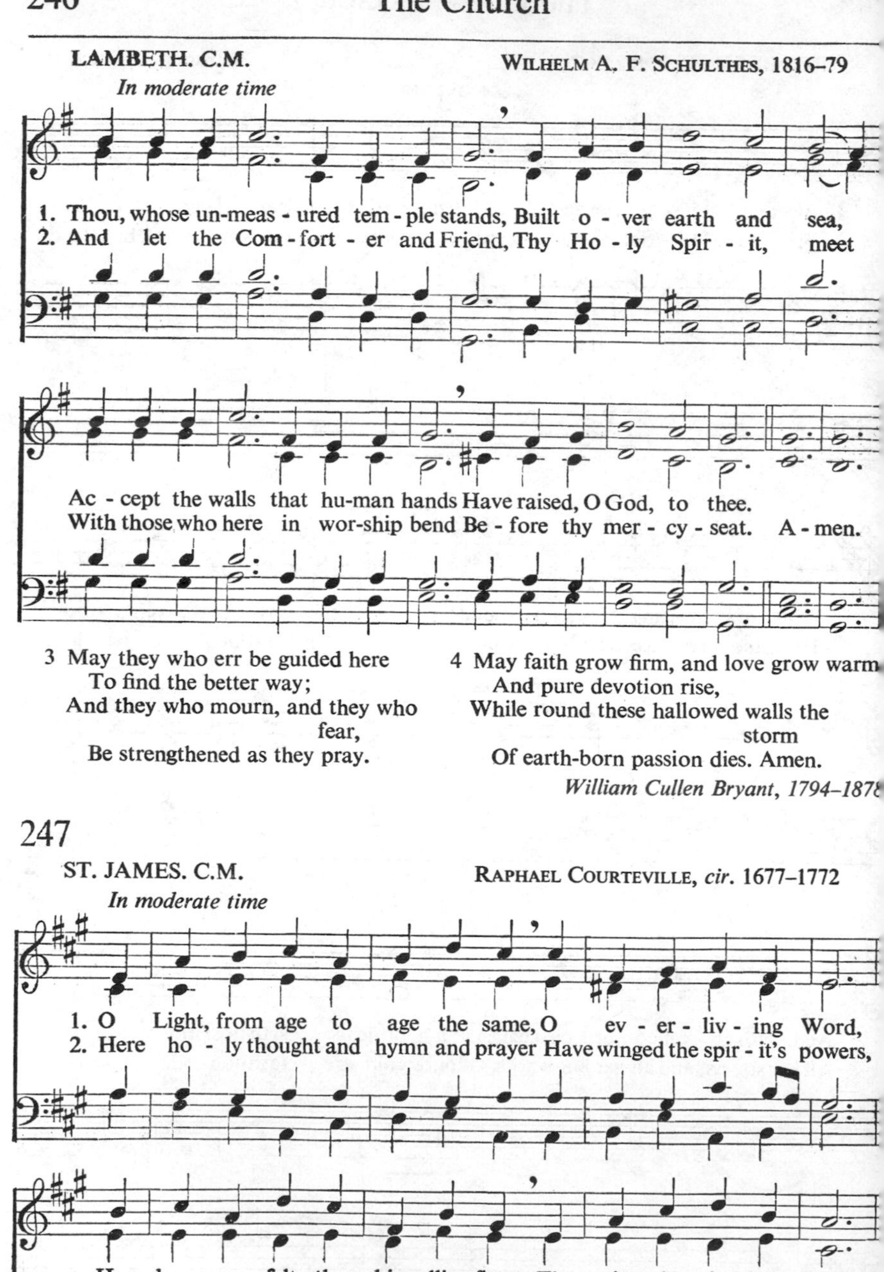
1. Thou, whose un-meas - ured tem - ple stands, Built o - ver earth and sea,
2. And let the Com - fort - er and Friend, Thy Ho - ly Spir - it, meet
Ac - cept the walls that hu-man hands Have raised, O God, to thee.
With those who here in wor-ship bend Be - fore thy mer - cy - seat. A - men.
1. O Light, from age to age the same, O ev - er - liv - ing Word,
2. Here ho - ly thought and hymn and prayer Have winged the spir - it's powers,
Here have we felt thy kin - dling flame, Thy voice with - in have heard.
And made these walls di - vine - ly fair, Thy tem - ple, Lord, and ours.

LAMBETH. C.M. — WILHELM A. F. SCHULTHES, 1816–79

In moderate time

3 May they who err be guided here
To find the better way;
And they who mourn, and they who fear,
Be strengthened as they pray.

4 May faith grow firm, and love grow warm
And pure devotion rise,
While round these hallowed walls the storm
Of earth-born passion dies. Amen.

William Cullen Bryant, 1794–187

247

ST. JAMES. C.M. — RAPHAEL COURTEVILLE, *cir.* 1677–1772

In moderate time

3 What visions rise above the years,
What tender memories throng,
Till each eye fills with happy tears,
Each heart with happy song!

4 Vanish the mists of time and sense;
They come, the loved of yore,
And one encircling providence
Holds all for evermore.

5 O not in vain their toil, who wrought
To build faith's freer shrine;
Not theirs, whose steadfast love and thought
Have watched the fire divine.

6 Burn, holy Fire, and shine more wide!
While systems rise and fall,
Faith, hope, and charity abide,
The heart and soul of all.

Frederick Lucian Hosmer, 1840–1929

248

DANK SEI GOTT IN DER HÖHE. 76, 76. D. BARTHOLOMAEUS GESIUS, *cir.* 1555–1613

With dignity

1. Our Fa - ther, by whose serv - ants Our house was built of old,
Whose hand hath crowned her chil - dren With bless - ings man - i - fold,
2. The change-ful years un - rest - ing Their si - lent course have sped,
New com-rades ev - er bring - ing In com - rades' steps to tread;
For thine un - fail - ing mer - cies Far - strewn a - long our way,
And some are long for - got - ten, Long spent their hopes and fears;
With all who passed be - fore us, We praise thy Name to - day.
Safe rest they in thy keep - ing, Who chang - est not with years.

3 They reap not where they labored,
We reap what they have sown;
Our harvest may be garnered
By ages yet unknown.
The days of old have dowered us
With gifts beyond all praise:
Our Father, make us faithful
To serve the coming days.

4 Before us and beside us,
Still holden in thine hand,
A cloud unseen of witness,
Our elder comrades stand:
One family unbroken,
We join, with one acclaim,
One heart, one voice uplifting,
To glorify thy Name.

George Wallace Briggs, 1875–1959

This hymn may also be sung to HOLY CHURCH (No. 304).

FESTAL DAY. L. M. RALPH P. LEWARS, 1883–

FIRST TUNE

With spirit, in unison

1. Come, all ye peo - ple, come a - way, Come to our glad and fes - tal day; Tell of the deeds that God hath wrought Be - yond de - sert or power of thought.
2. In this fair land our feet are set Where men of ev - ery clime have met; Al - might - y God, with his dear hand Hath kind - ly led the pil - grim band. A - men.

3 Throughout our life his truth and light
Have been our beacon in the night;
Know we in war and peace his care
Of loved ones far away and near.

4 O God, to thee we bring the meed
Of praise, for help in time of need,
For mercies given by thy Son,
For joys which make our cup o'er-run.

5 Grant us, throughout our earthly day,
To love and serve thee all the way;
To labor for thy Kingdom's spread,
For Christ our Lord, for Christ our Head!

6 Father and Son and Spirit blest,
To thee be every prayer addressed,
Who art in threefold Name adored,
From age to age, the only Lord. Amen.

George Rise Seltzer, 1902–

MELCOMBE. L. M. SAMUEL WEBBE, 1740–1816

With spirit SECOND TUNE

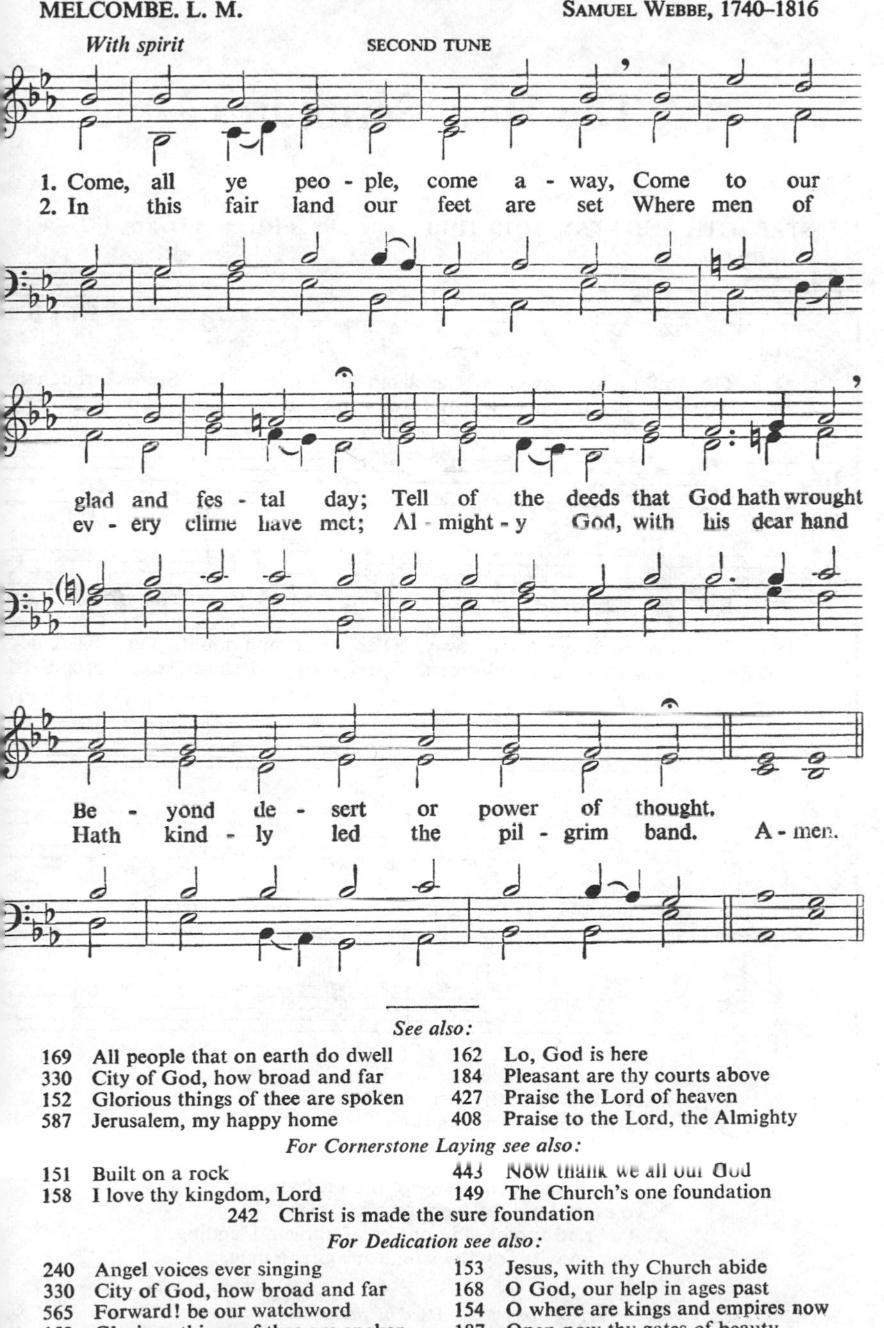
1. Come, all ye peo - ple, come a - way, Come to our glad and fes - tal day; Tell of the deeds that God hath wrought Be - yond de - sert or power of thought.
2. In this fair land our feet are set Where men of ev - ery clime have met; Al - might - y God, with his dear hand Hath kind - ly led the pil - grim band. A - men.

See also:

169 All people that on earth do dwell
330 City of God, how broad and far
152 Glorious things of thee are spoken
587 Jerusalem, my happy home
162 Lo, God is here
184 Pleasant are thy courts above
427 Praise the Lord of heaven
408 Praise to the Lord, the Almighty

For Cornerstone Laying see also:

151 Built on a rock
158 I love thy kingdom, Lord
443 Now thank we all our God
149 The Church's one foundation
242 Christ is made the sure foundation

For Dedication see also:

240 Angel voices ever singing
330 City of God, how broad and far
565 Forward! be our watchword
152 Glorious things of thee are spoken
158 I love thy kingdom, Lord
153 Jesus, with thy Church abide
168 O God, our help in ages past
154 O where are kings and empires now
187 Open now thy gates of beauty
407 Praise the Lord! Ye heavens, adore him

The Holy Scriptures

250

STRENGTH AND STAY. 11 10, 11 10. JOHN BACCHUS DYKES, 1823–76

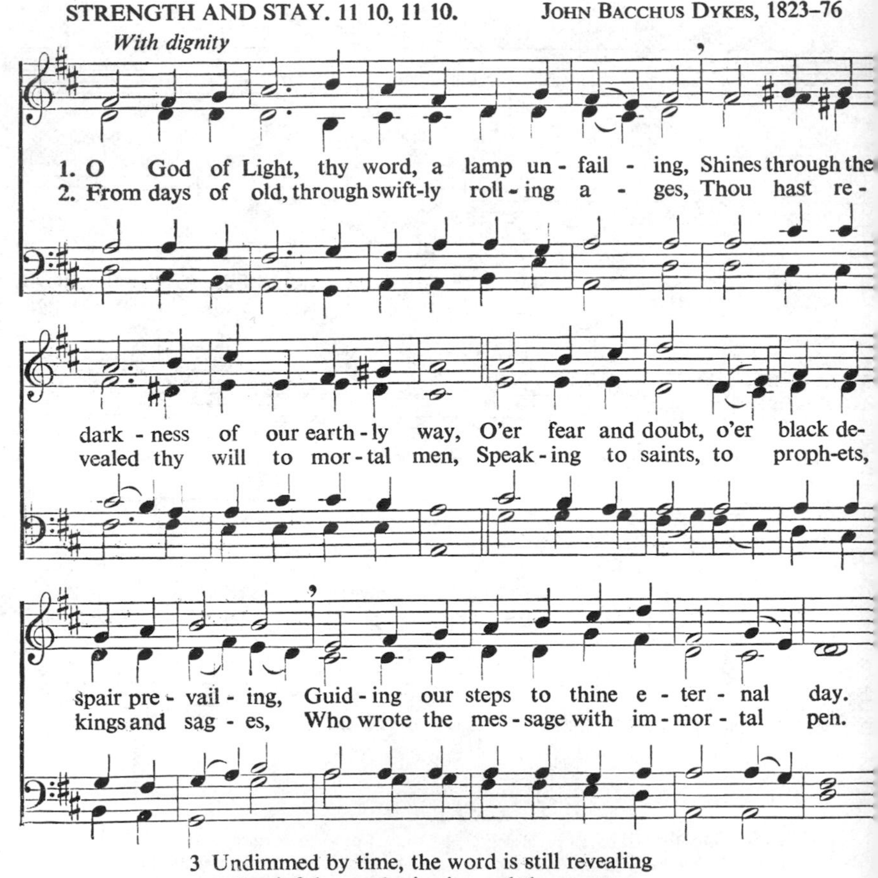

With dignity
1. O God of Light, thy word, a lamp un - fail - ing, Shines through the
2. From days of old, through swift-ly roll - ing a - ges, Thou hast re -
dark - ness of our earth - ly way, O'er fear and doubt, o'er black de-
vealed thy will to mor - tal men, Speak - ing to saints, to proph-ets,
spair pre - vail - ing, Guid - ing our steps to thine e - ter - nal day.
kings and sag - es, Who wrote the mes - sage with im - mor - tal pen.

3 Undimmed by time, the word is still revealing
To sinful men thy justice and thy grace;
And questing hearts that long for peace and healing
See thy compassion in the Saviour's face.

4 To all the world the message thou art sending,
To every land, to every race and clan;
And myriad tongues, in one great anthem blending,
Acclaim with joy thy wondrous gift to man.

Sarah E. Taylor, 1883–1954

This hymn may also be sung to ANCIENT OF DAYS (No. 137).

WOLDER (AUS MEINES HERZENS GRUNDE) 8 6, 8 6, 6 8, 8 6.

DAVID WOLDER'S *Catechismus-Gesangbüchlein, 1598*

In moderate time

1. The Spir - it of the Lord re-vealed His will to saints of old,
Their heart and mind and lips un-sealed His glo - ry to un - fold:
2. The proph-ets passed: at length there came, To so - journ and a - bide,
The Word in - car - nate, to whose Name The proph-ets tes - ti - fied:

In gloom of an - cient night They wit - nessed to the dawn - ing word,
The twi - light o - ver - past, Him - self the ver - y Light of light,

And in the com-ing of the light Pro-claimed the com-ing Lord.
As man with men, re - vealed at last The Fa - ther to our sight. A-men.

3 Eternal Spirit, who dost speak
To mind and conscience still,
That we, in this our day, may seek
To do our Father's will:
Thy word of life impart,
That tells of Christ, the living Way;
Give us the quiet humble heart
To hear and to obey. Amen.

George Wallace Briggs, 1875–1959

MUNICH (MEININGEN). 7 6, 7 6. D. *Meiningen Gesangbuch, 1693*
With spirit Adapted and harmonized by FELIX MENDELSSOHN

1. O Word of God in-car-nate, O Wis-dom from on high,
2. The Church from her dear Mas-ter Re-ceived the gift di-vine,
O Truth un-changed, un-chang-ing, O Light of our dark sky;
And still that light she lift-eth O'er all the earth to shine.
We praise thee for the ra-diance That from the hal-lowed page,
It is the gold-en cas-ket Where gems of truth are stored;
A lan-tern to our foot-steps, Shines on from age to age.
It is the heaven-drawn pic-ture Of Christ, the liv-ing Word. A-men.

3 It floateth like a banner
  Before God's host unfurled;
It shineth like a beacon
  Above the darkling world;
It is the chart and compass
  That o'er life's surging sea,
'Mid mists and rocks and quicksands,
  Still guides, O Christ, to thee.

4 O make thy Church, dear Saviour,
  A lamp of burnished gold,
To bear before the nations
  Thy true light, as of old;
O teach thy wandering pilgrims
  By this their path to trace,
Till, clouds and darkness ended,
  They see thee face to face. Amen.

William Walsham How, 1823–97

253

ISLAND. 8 8 7, 8 8 7 7. HANS TOMISSÖN'S *Psalmebog*, 1569

With dignity

1. How blest are they who hear God's word, Who keep in faith what they have heard, Who dai - ly grow in learn - ing; From light to light shall they in - crease, And tread life's wea - ry path in peace, The balm of joy dis - cern - ing To soothe the spir - it's yearn - ing.
2. Through sor-row's night my sun shall be God's word— a treas - ure dear to me, My shield and buck - ler ev - er. My ti - tle as his child and heir The Fa - ther's hand hath writ - ten there, His prom-ise fail - ing nev - er: 'Thou shalt be mine for - ev - er.'

3 Today his voice with joy I heard,
And, nourished by his holy word,
That bread so freely given,
May stronger faith through grace prevail,
And may its fruits for me avail,
That, after I have striven,
I rest with him in heaven.

Johan Nordahl Brun, 1745–1816
Tr. Hymnal Version, 1955

254

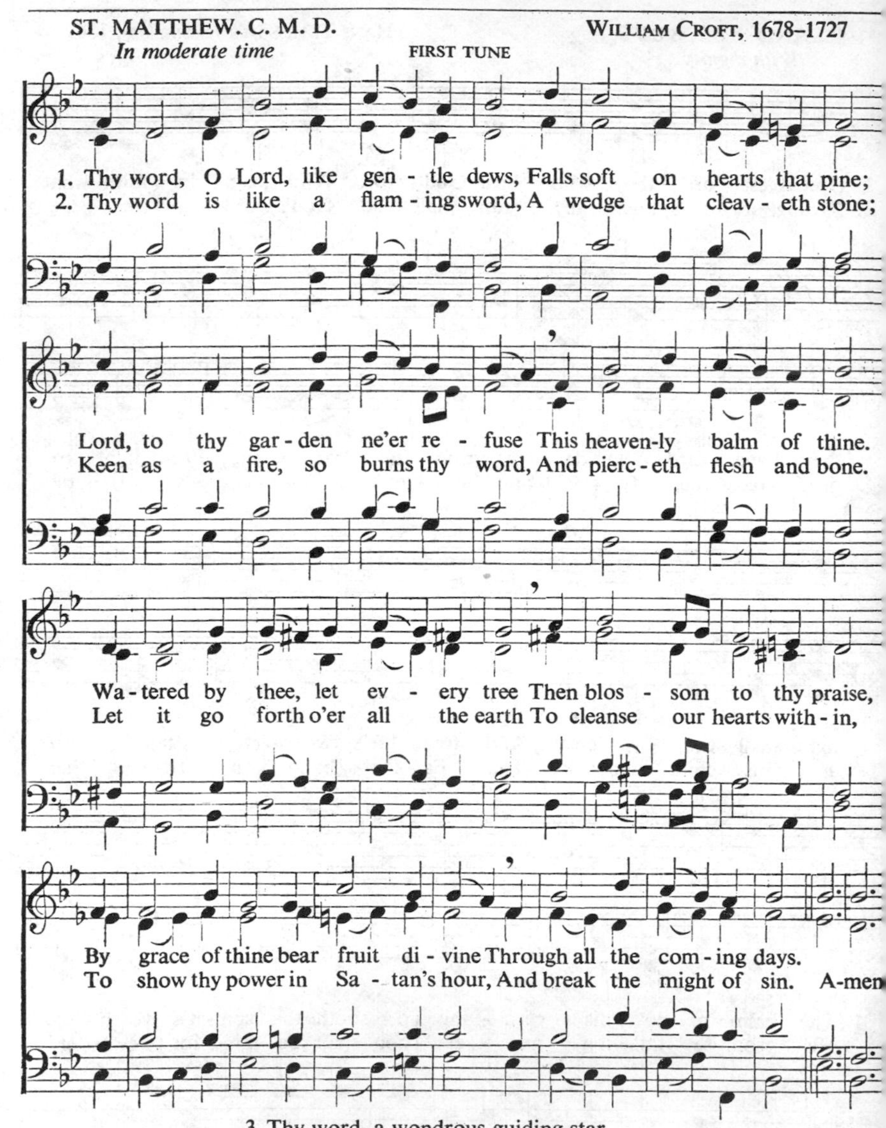
ST. MATTHEW. C. M. D.
WILLIAM CROFT, 1678–1727
In moderate time
FIRST TUNE
1. Thy word, O Lord, like gen - tle dews, Falls soft on hearts that pine;
2. Thy word is like a flam - ing sword, A wedge that cleav - eth stone;
Lord, to thy gar - den ne'er re - fuse This heaven-ly balm of thine.
Keen as a fire, so burns thy word, And pierc - eth flesh and bone.
Wa - tered by thee, let ev - ery tree Then blos - som to thy praise,
Let it go forth o'er all the earth To cleanse our hearts with - in,
By grace of thine bear fruit di - vine Through all the com - ing days.
To show thy power in Sa - tan's hour, And break the might of sin. A-men

3 Thy word, a wondrous guiding star,
  On pilgrim hearts doth rise,
Leads those to God who dwell afar,
  And makes the simple wise.
Let not its light e'er sink in night,
  But in each spirit shine,
That none may miss heaven's final bliss,
  Led by thy light divine. Amen.

Carl Bernhard Garve, 1763–184
Tr. Catherine Winkworth, 1829–7

This hymn may also be sung to ST. LEONARD (No. 54).

RELEASE. C. M. D.
Danish Melody
Broadly
SECOND TUNE
1. Thy word, O Lord, like gen-tle dews, Falls soft on hearts that pine;
2. Thy word is like a flam-ing sword, A wedge that cleav-eth stone;
Lord, to thy gar-den ne'er re-fuse This heaven-ly balm of thine.
Keen as a fire, so burns thy word, And pierc-eth flesh and bone.
Wa-tered by thee, let ev-ery tree Then blos-som to thy praise,
Let it go forth o'er all the earth To cleanse our hearts with-in,
By grace of thine bear fruit di-vine Through all the com-ing days.
To show thy power in Sa-tan's hour, And break the might of sin. A-men.

3 Thy word, a wondrous guiding star,
On pilgrim hearts doth rise,
Leads those to God who dwell afar,
And makes the simple wise.
Let not its light e'er sink in night,
But in each spirit shine,
That none may miss heaven's final bliss,
Led by thy light divine. Amen.

Carl Bernhard Garve, 1763–1841
Tr. Catherine Winkworth, 1829–78

This hymn may also be sung to ST. LEONARD (NO. 54).

CRASSELIUS (DIR, DIR, JEHOVAH). 9 10, 9 10, 10 10.

FREYLINGHAUSEN'S *Gesangbuch*, Halle, 1704

With vigor

1. A - wake, thou Spir - it of the watch - men
Con - tend - ing from the walls of Si - on
2. O Lord, now let thy fire en - kin - dle
And spread the glo - ry of re - demp - tion
(1.) Who nev - er held their peace by day or night,
A - gainst the foe, con - fid - ing in thy might.
(2.) Our hearts, that ev - ery - where its flame may go,
Till all the world thy sav - ing grace shall know.
Through-out the world their cry is ring - ing still,
O har - vest Lord, look down on us and view
And bring - ing peo - ples to thy ho - ly will.
How white the fields; the la - bor - ers, how few! A - men

3 The prayer thy Son himself hath taught us
We offer now to thee at his command;
Behold and hearken, Lord; thy children
Implore thee for the souls of every land:
With yearning hearts they make their ardent plea;
O hear us, Lord, and say, 'Thus shall it be.'

4 Send forth, O Lord, thy strong Evangel
By many messengers, all hearts to win;
Make haste to help us in our weakness;
Break down the realm of Satan, death, and sin:
The circle of the earth shall then proclaim
Thy kingdom, and the glory of thy Name. Amen.

Karl Heinrich von Bogatzky, 1690–1774
Tr. Winfred Douglas, 1867–1944, and Arthur W. Farlander, 1898–1952

256

ST. AGNES. C. M. JOHN BACCHUS DYKES, 1823–76

Slowly, devotionally

1. Fa - ther of mer - cies, in thy word What end - less glo - ry shines!
2. Here the Re - deem - er's wel - come voice Spreads heaven-ly peace a - round,
For ev - er be thy Name a - dored For these ce - les - tial lines.
And life and ev - er - last - ing joys At - tend the bliss - ful sound. A-men.

3 O may these heavenly pages be
My ever dear delight,
And still new beauties may I see
And still increasing light.

4 Divine Instructor, gracious Lord,
Be thou for ever near;
Teach me to love thy sacred word
And view my Saviour there. Amen.

Anne Steele, 1716–78

257

EIN' FESTE BURG. 8 7, 8 7, 6 6, 6 6 7.
MARTIN LUTHER, 1483–1546
With vigor
God's word is our great her - it - age, And shall be ours for ev - er;
To spread its light from age to age Be this our chief en - deav - or; Through life it guides our way, In death it is our stay; Lord, grant while time shall last, Thy Church may hold it fast Through-out all gen - er - a - tions. A-men.

Nikolai F. S. Grundtvig, 1783–1872
Tr. Ole G. Belsheim, 1861–1925 a.

See also:

196 Almighty God, thy word is cast
491 Break thou the bread of life
558 How firm a foundation
323 Spread, O spread, thou mighty word

Holy Baptism

258

PHILIPPINE. L. M. ROBERT EDWIN ROBERTS, 1879–

In moderate time

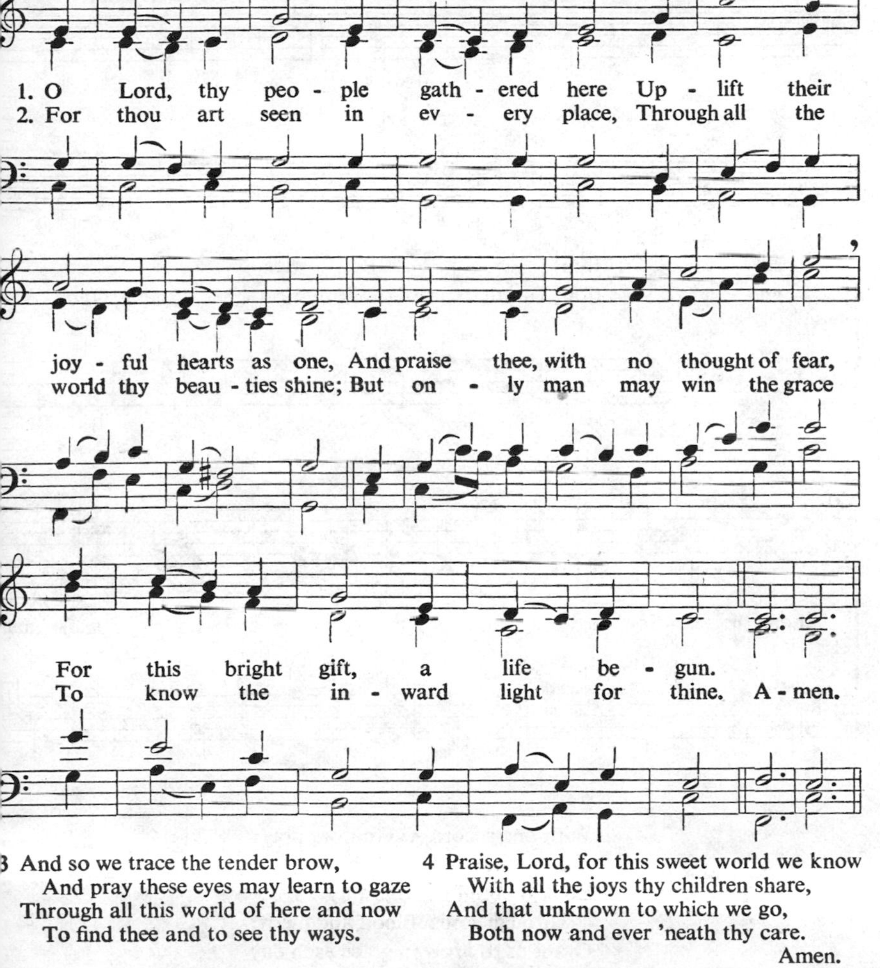
1. O Lord, thy peo - ple gath - ered here Up - lift their
2. For thou art seen in ev - ery place, Through all the
joy - ful hearts as one, And praise thee, with no thought of fear,
world thy beau - ties shine; But on - ly man may win the grace
For this bright gift, a life be - gun.
To know the in - ward light for thine. A - men.

3 And so we trace the tender brow,
And pray these eyes may learn to gaze
Through all this world of here and now
To find thee and to see thy ways.

4 Praise, Lord, for this sweet world we know
With all the joys thy children share,
And that unknown to which we go,
Both now and ever 'neath thy care.
Amen.

Katherine Emily Roberts, 1877–

This hymn may also be sung to GRACE CHURCH (No. 265)

ST. PAUL (ES IST DAS HEIL). 8 7, 8 7, 8 8 7. Wittenberg *Gesangbuch*, 1524

With vigor

1. He that be - lieves and is bap - tized Shall see the Lord's sal - va - tion;
Bap - tized in - to the death of Christ, He is a new cre - a - tion; Through Christ's re-demp-tion he shall stand A - mong the glo-rious heaven-ly band Of ev - ery tribe and na - tion. A-men

2 With one accord, O God, we pray;
Grant us thy Holy Spirit;
Look thou on our infirmity
Through Jesus' Blood and merit;
Grant us to grow in grace each day
By holy baptism, that we may
Eternal life inherit. Amen.

Thomas Hansen Kingo, 1634–170
Tr. George Alfred Taylor Rygh, 1860–194

REGENT SQUARE. 8 7, 8 7, 8 7. **HENRY THOMAS SMART, 1813–79**

Moderately slow, with dignity

1. Je - sus took the babes and blessed them, Brought to him in days of old;
2. Je - sus calls them still with kind-ness Pass-ing ev - ery mor - tal thought;

Fond - ly in his arms ca-ressed them, Bade them wel - come in his fold;
Bids them come, though hu - man blind-ness Still would chide when they are brought;

Warm-ly wel-comed, warm-ly wel-comed When dis-ci - ples' hearts were cold.
Takes and bless-es, takes and bless-es, Whom he hath so dear - ly bought. A-men.

3 Jesus, we would not forbid them,
We would have them brought to thee;
Thou of all their guilt dost rid them,
From the curse dost set them free;
Thine dost make them, thine dost make them,
Thine let them forever be! Amen.

Matthias Loy, 1828–1915

This hymn may also be sung to MANNHEIM (142).

BROCKLESBURY. 8 7, 8 7. CHARLOTTE ALINGTON BARNARD, 1830–69

In moderate time

1. Sav - iour, who thy flock art feed-ing With the Shep-herd's kind - est care,
2. Now, these lit - tle ones re - ceiv-ing, Fold them in thy gra-cious arm

All the fee - ble gen - tly lead-ing, While the lambs thy bos - om share;
There, we know, thy word be - liev-ing, On - ly there se - cure from harm. A-m

3 Never, from thy pasture roving,
Let them be the lion's prey;
Let thy tenderness, so loving,
Keep them through life's dangerous way.

4 Then within thy fold eternal
Let them find a resting-place,
Feed in pastures ever vernal,
Drink the rivers of thy grace. Amen.

William Augustus Muhlenberg, 1796–1

See also:

528 Saviour, teach me, day by day
179 Shepherd of tender youth
335 Sing to the Lord the children's hymn
530 The King of love my shepherd is
522 The Lord's my shepherd, I'll not want

Holy Communion

262

SCHMÜCKE DICH. L. M. D. JOHANN CRÜGER, 1598–1662

Quietly

1. Deck thy - self with joy and glad-ness, Dwell no more, my soul, in sad - ness;
Let the day-light shine up - on thee, Put thy wed - ding gar-ment on thee,
2. Has - ten, then, my soul, to meet him, Ea - ger - ly and glad - ly greet him.
As with - out he stand-eth knock-ing, Quick - ly, thy soul's gate un-lock - ing,

For the Lord of life un - end - ing Un - to thee his call is send - ing:
O - pen wide the fast-closed por - tal, Say - ing to the Lord im - mor - tal,

Come, for now the King most ho - ly Stoops to thee in like-ness low - ly.
'Come, and leave thy serv-ant nev - er, Dwell with - in my heart for-ev - er.' A-men.

3 Jesus, source of life and pleasure,
Truest friend and dearest treasure,
Joy, the sweetest man e'er knoweth;
Fount, whence all my being floweth:

Humbly now I bow before thee,
And in penitence adore thee;
Worthily let me receive thee,
Perfect peace and pardon give me. Amen.

Johann Franck, 1618–77
Tr. John Caspar Mattes, 1876–1948, a.

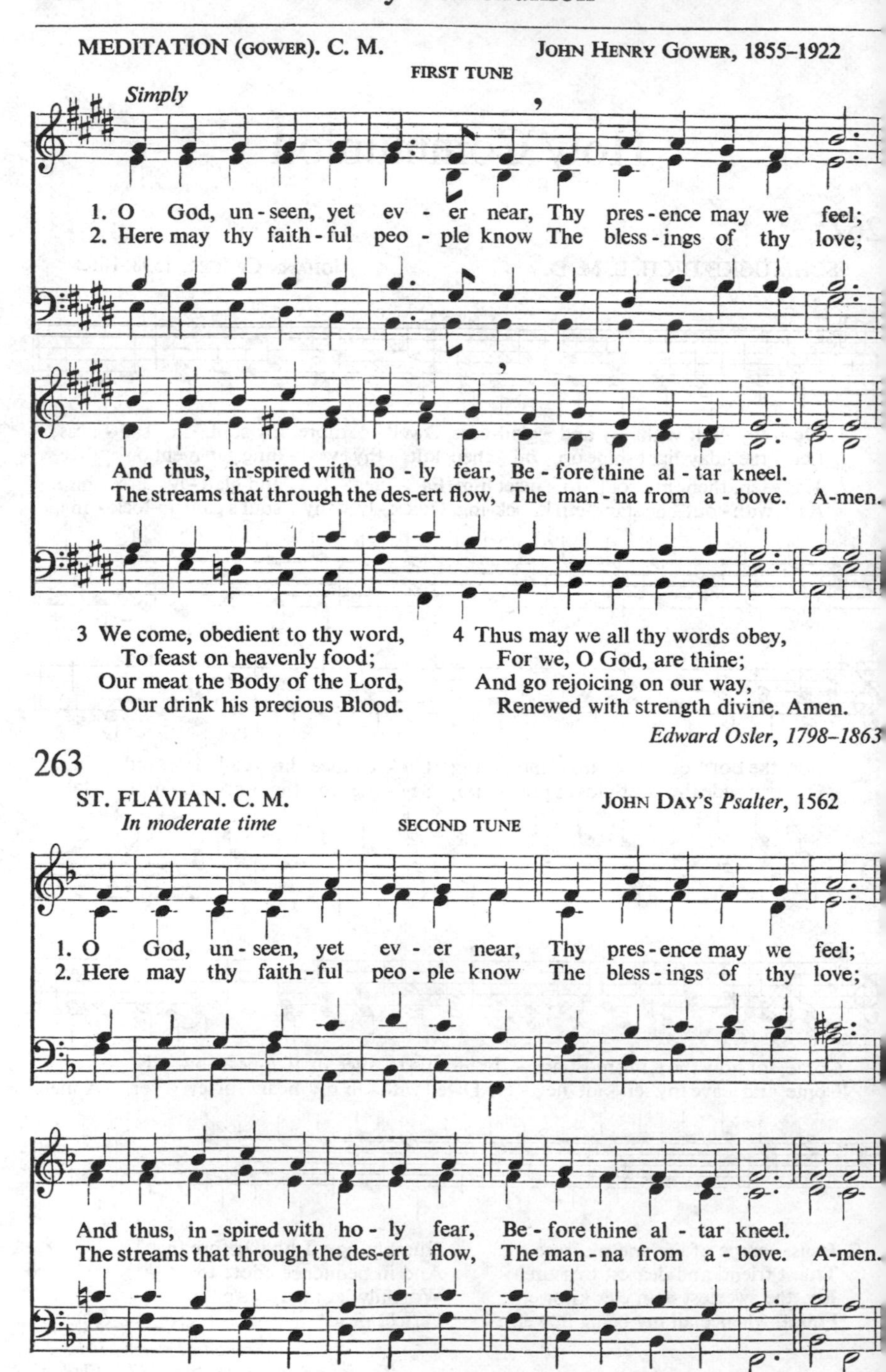
MEDITATION (GOWER). C. M.
JOHN HENRY GOWER, 1855–1922
FIRST TUNE
Simply
1. O God, un-seen, yet ev - er near, Thy pres-ence may we feel;
2. Here may thy faith-ful peo - ple know The bless-ings of thy love;
And thus, in-spired with ho - ly fear, Be-fore thine al - tar kneel.
The streams that through the des-ert flow, The man-na from a - bove. A-men.
3 We come, obedient to thy word,
To feast on heavenly food;
Our meat the Body of the Lord,
Our drink his precious Blood.
4 Thus may we all thy words obey,
For we, O God, are thine;
And go rejoicing on our way,
Renewed with strength divine. Amen.
Edward Osler, 1798–1863
263
ST. FLAVIAN. C. M.
JOHN DAY'S Psalter, 1562
In moderate time
SECOND TUNE
1. O God, un-seen, yet ev - er near, Thy pres-ence may we feel;
2. Here may thy faith-ful peo-ple know The bless-ings of thy love;
And thus, in-spired with ho - ly fear, Be-fore thine al - tar kneel.
The streams that through the des-ert flow, The man-na from a - bove. A-men.

FRANZEN. 7 6, 7 6, 8 7 6.
Danish
Devotionally
HANS TOMISSÖN Psalmebog, 1569
1. Thine own, O lov - ing Sav - iour, Are bid - den here by thee;
2. We hear thine in - vi - ta - tion; We heed, O Lord, thy call;
Thy pas-sion's fruits, thy fa - vor, Thy - self thou giv - est free
Thy word of con - so - la - tion Is spo - ken here for all
To all who by thy grace and love Are mem - bers
Who, drawn un - to thy lov - ing heart, Would seek from
of thy king - dom, Now here, and then a - bove.
thee a bless - ing Ere from thy side they part. A - men.

3 For still in loving favor,
O Christ, thou drawest near
To lead us as our Saviour
Unto a Father dear;
A Father ready to forgive
The lost whom thou didst ransom,
Who by thy death shall live.

4 We would be thine forever
To do thy gracious will,
Let naught from thee us sever,
But keep us faithful still.
Here linger with us, Lord, in love,
Till we shall see thy glory
And feast with thee above. Amen.

Frans Mikael Franzén, 1772–1847
Tr. St. 1–3, Olof Olsson, 1841–1900
St. 4, Ernest Edwin Ryden, 1886–

GRACE CHURCH, L. M. IGNAZ JOSEPH PLEYEL, 1757–1831

FIRST TUNE

Devotionally
1. Lord Je - sus Christ, we hum - bly pray, Re - fresh thy
2. Our trem - bling hearts cleave to thy word, All thou hast
peo - ple here to - day; Be - neath these forms of bread and wine,
said thou dost af - ford; All that thou art we here re - ceive,
En - rich us with thy grace di - vine.
And all we are to thee we give. A - men

3 One bread, one cup, one body, we,
United by our life in thee,
Thy love proclaim till thou shalt come,
To bring thy scattered loved ones home.

4 Lord Jesus Christ, we humbly pray
To keep us steadfast to that day,
That each may be thy welcomed guest
When thou shalt spread thy heavenly feast. Amen.

Henry Eyster Jacobs, 1844–1932

Holy Communion

FILIA. L. M. — Winifred Jacobs Shearer, 1883–

SECOND TUNE

In moderate time

1. Lord Je - sus Christ, we hum - bly pray, Re - fresh thy
2. Our trem - bling hearts cleave to thy word, All thou hast

peo - ple here to - day; Be-neath these forms of bread and wine,
said thou dost af - ford; All that thou art we here re - ceive,

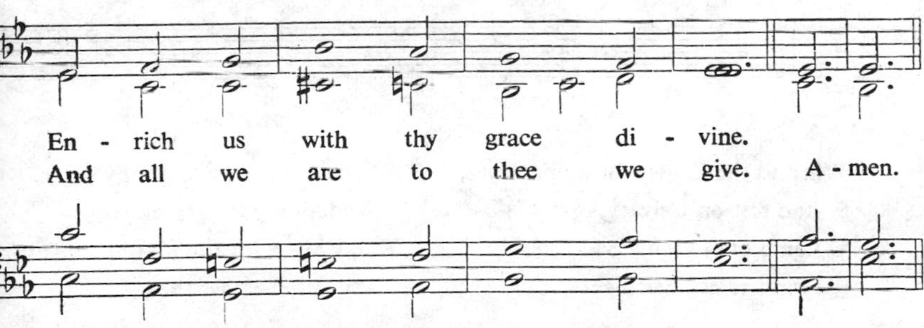

En - rich us with thy grace di - vine.
And all we are to thee we give. A - men.

3 One bread, one cup, one body, we,
United by our life in thee,
Thy love proclaim till thou shalt come,
To bring thy scattered loved ones home.

4 Lord Jesus Christ, we humbly pray
To keep us steadfast to that day,
That each may be thy welcomed guest
When thou shalt spread thy heavenly feast. Amen.

Henry Eyster Jacobs, 1844–1932, a.

DUNDEE (FRENCH). C. M. *Scottish Psalter*, 1615

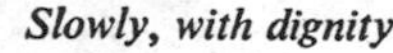
Slowly, with dignity

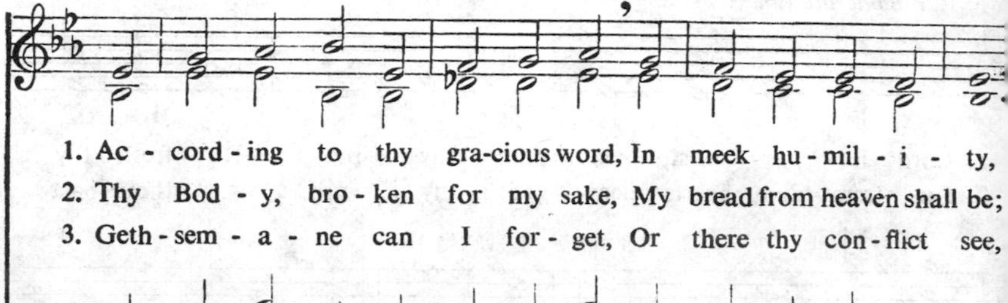
1. Ac - cord - ing to thy gra-cious word, In meek hu - mil - i - ty,
2. Thy Bod - y, bro - ken for my sake, My bread from heaven shall be;
3. Geth - sem - a - ne can I for - get, Or there thy con - flict see,

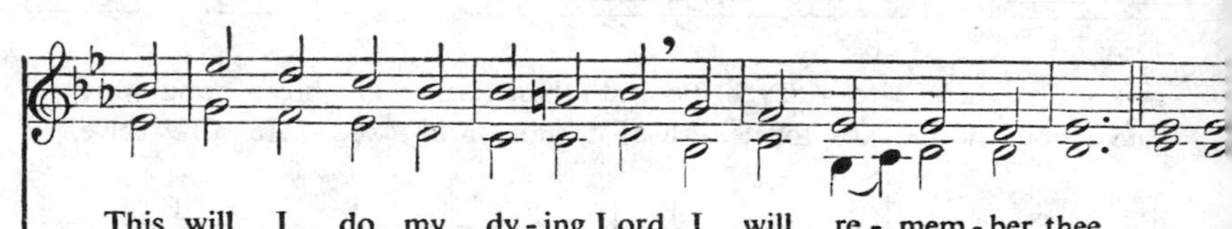
This will I do, my dy - ing Lord, I will re - mem - ber thee.
Thy tes - ta - men - tal cup I take, And thus re - mem - ber thee.
Thine ag - o - ny and blood-y sweat, And not re - mem - ber thee? A-me

4 When to the Cross I turn mine eyes,
And rest on Calvary,
O Lamb of God, my Sacrifice,
I must remember thee!

5 Remember thee, and all thy pains,
And all thy love to me;
Yea, while a breath, a pulse remains,
Will I remember thee.

6 And when these failing lips grow dumb,
And mind and memory flee,
When thou shalt in thy kingdom come,
Jesus, remember me. Amen.

James Montgomery, 1771–18

ANGELUS. L.M. *Cantica Spiritualia*, 1847
Based on melody by GEORG JOSEPH, *cir.* 1657

In moderate time
1. Be still, my soul, for God is near, The great High Priest is with thee now! The Lord of Life him-self is here, Be-fore whose face the an-gels bow.
2. To make thy heart his low-ly throne, Thy Sav-iour God in love draws nigh; He gives him-self un-to his own, For whom he once came down to die. A-men.

3 He pleads before the mercy-seat,
He pleads with God, he pleads for thee;
He gives thee bread from heaven to eat:
His Flesh and Blood in mystery.

4 I come, O Lord, for thou dost call,
To blend my pleading prayer with thine;
To thee I give myself, my all,
And feed on thee, and make thee mine. Amen.

William Dalrymple Maclagan, 1826–1910

ST. GODRIC. 6 6, 6 6, 8 8. JOHN BACCHUS DYKES, 1823–76

In moderate time FIRST TUNE

1. Au - thor of life di - vine, Who hast a ta - ble spread, Fur-

nished with mys - tic wine And ev - er - last - ing bread, Pre - serve the

life thy - self hast given, And feed and train us up for heaven. A-men.

2 Our needy souls sustain
With fresh supplies of love,
Till all thy life we gain,
And all thy fulness prove,
And, strengthened by thy perfect grace,
Behold without a veil thy face. Amen.

Charles Wesley, 1707–8

268

DOLGELLY. 6 6, 6 6, 8 8. 19th cent. Welsh Hymn Melody

Slowly SECOND TUNE

1. Au - thor of life di - vine, Who hast a ta - ble spread, Fur -

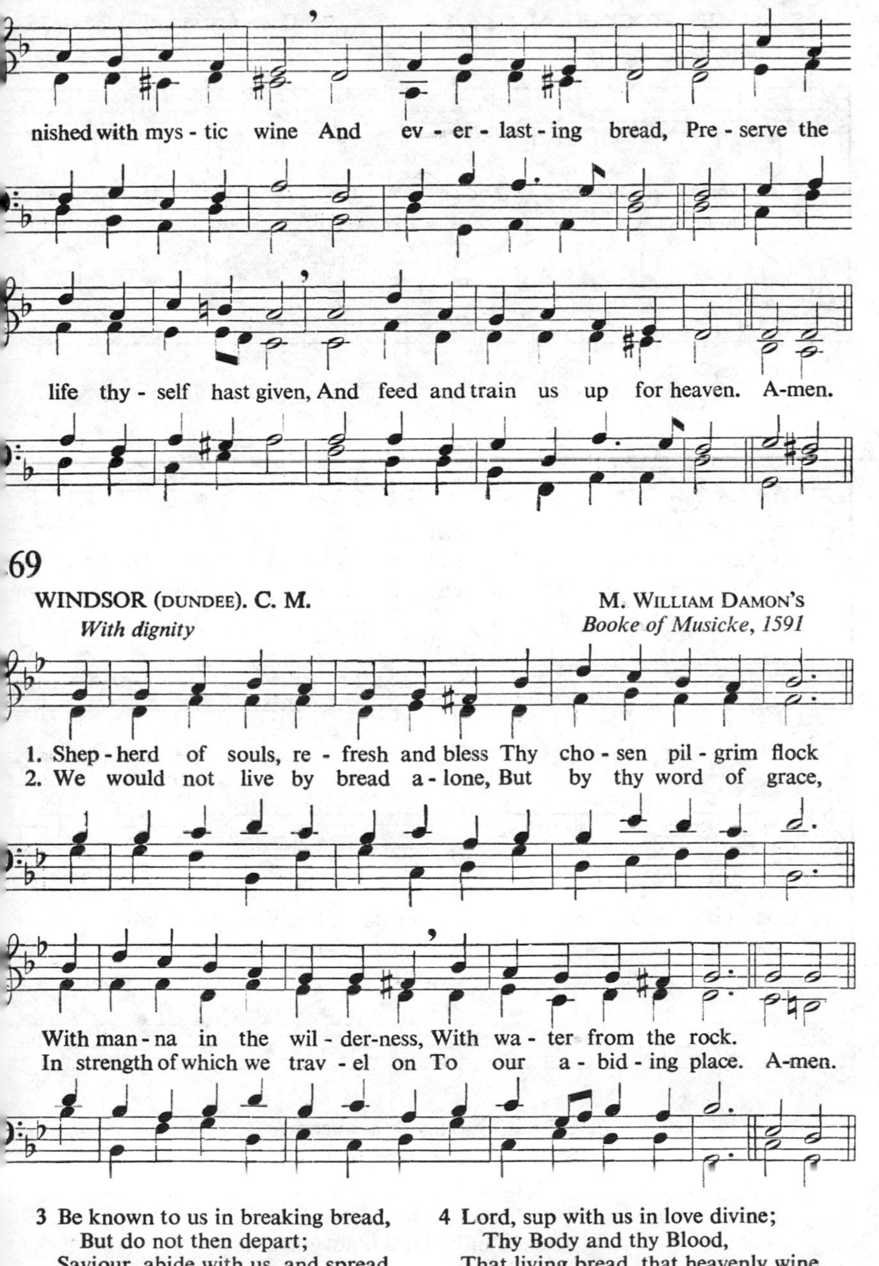

nished with mys - tic wine And ev - er - last - ing bread, Pre - serve the
life thy - self hast given, And feed and train us up for heaven. A-men.
69
WINDSOR (DUNDEE). C. M.
M. WILLIAM DAMON'S
With dignity
Booke of Musicke, 1591
1. Shep - herd of souls, re - fresh and bless Thy cho - sen pil - grim flock
2. We would not live by bread a - lone, But by thy word of grace,
With man - na in the wil - der-ness, With wa - ter from the rock.
In strength of which we trav - el on To our a - bid - ing place. A-men.

3 Be known to us in breaking bread,
But do not then depart;
Saviour, abide with us, and spread
Thy table in our heart.

4 Lord, sup with us in love divine;
Thy Body and thy Blood,
That living bread, that heavenly wine,
Be our immortal food. Amen.

James Montgomery, 1771–1854

This hymn may also be sung to ST. AGNES (No. 481).

ST. JAMES' STOCKHOLM. 8 8 6, 8 8. OLOF AHLSTRÖM, 1756–1835

With joyful dignity

1. A voice, a heaven - ly voice I hear! A - rise, O soul, come and draw near To hal - low and re - vere The day the Lord thy God doth make, And of the bread of life par - take.
2. I come, dear Je - sus, at thy word, A guest un - wor - thy to thy board, My Sav - iour and my Lord. O clothe me with thy right - eous - ness, My soul with thy sal - va - tion bless! A - men

3 O Lord, who my Redeemer art,
Come thou and purify my heart.
From thee I'll ne'er depart,
But wheresoe'er thou leadest me
In constant faith I'll follow thee. Amen.

Johan Olof Wallin, 1779–18
Tr. St. 1, Samuel Magnus Hill, 1851–19
Tr. St. 2, Composi
Tr. St. 3, Ernst William Olson, 1870–19.

INNSBRUCK. 7 7 6, 7 7 8. HEINRICH ISAAK, *cir.* 1450–1527

Quietly, with movement
1. O Bread of life from heav - en, To wea - ry pil - grims giv - en,
2. O fount of grace re - deem - ing, O riv - er ev - er stream-ing
O Man - na from a - bove! The souls that hun - ger feed thou, The
From Je - sus' ho - ly side! Come thou, thy - self be - stow - ing On
rit.
hearts that seek thee lead thou, With thy most sweet and ten - der love.
thirst - ing souls, and flow - ing Till all their wants are sat - is - fied. A-men.

3 O Jesus, by thee bidden,
We here adore thee, hidden
'Neath forms of bread and wine;
Grant, when the veil is riven,
We may behold in heaven
Thy glorious countenance divine. Amen.

Latin hymn, cir. 1661
Tr. St. 1, 2, Philip Schaff, 1819–93
Tr. St. 3, Athelstan Riley, 1858–1945

ADORO TE DEVOTE. 10 10, 10 10. **Plainsong Melody, Mode V (Solesmes)**

In free rhythm. Unison

1. Thee we a - dore, O hid - den Sav - iour, thee,
Who in thy sac - ra - ment art pleased to be;
2. O blest me - mo - rial of our dy - ing Lord,
Who liv - ing bread to men doth here af - ford!
Both flesh and spir - it in thy pres - ence fail,
O may our souls for ev - er feed on thee,
Yet here thy pres - ence we de - vout - ly hail.
And thou, O Christ, for ev - er pre - cious be. A - men.

3 Fountain of goodness, Jesus, Lord and God,
Cleanse us, unclean, with thy most cleansing Blood;
Increase our faith and love, that we may know
The hope and peace which from thy presence flow.

4 O Christ, whom now beneath a veil we see,
May what we thirst for soon our portion be,
To gaze on thee unveiled, and see thy face,
The vision of thy glory and thy grace. Amen.

St. Thomas Aquinas, 1227–74
Tr. James Russell Woodford, 1820–85

273

COENA DOMINI. 10, 10. ARTHUR S. SULLIVAN, 1842–1900

Slowly

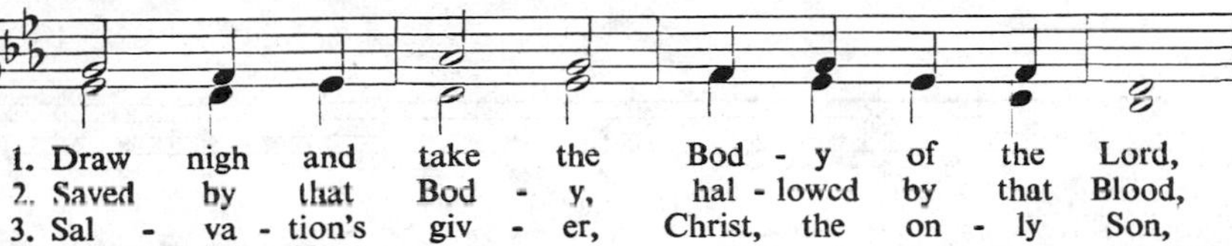
1. Draw nigh and take the Bod - y of the Lord,
2. Saved by that Bod - y, hal - lowed by that Blood,
3. Sal - va - tion's giv - er, Christ, the on - ly Son,

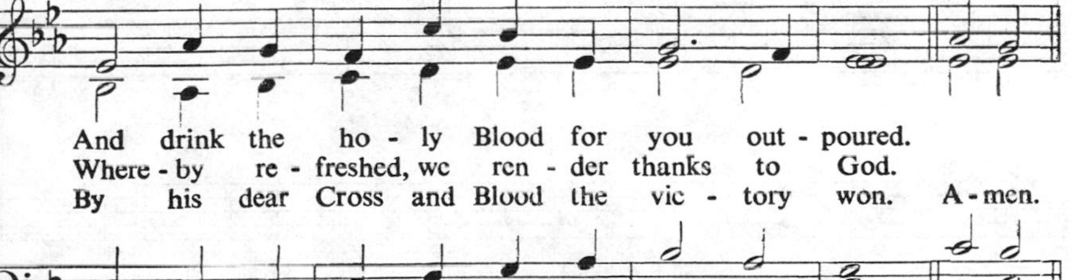
And drink the ho - ly Blood for you out - poured.
Where - by re - freshed, we ren - der thanks to God.
By his dear Cross and Blood the vic - tory won. A - men.

4 Offered was he for greatest and for least,
Himself the Victim, and himself the Priest.

5 Approach ye then with faithful hearts sincere,
And take the pledges of salvation here.

6 He that his saints in this world rules and shields
To all believers life eternal yields;

7 With heavenly bread makes them that hunger whole,
Gives living waters to the thirsty soul.

8 The Judge Eternal, unto whom shall bow
All nations at the last, is with us now. Amen.

Latin Hymn, VII cent.
Tr. John Mason Neale, 1818–66, a.

DAS NEUGEBORNE KINDELEIN. 8 8, 8 8, 8 8.
MELCHIOR VULPIUS, cir. 1560–1615
Devotionally
FIRST TUNE
1. Vic - tim Di - vine, thy grace we claim While thus thy precious death we show;
Once of - fered up, a spot - less Lamb, In thy great tem - ple here be - low, Thou didst for all man - kind a - tone, And stand - est now be - fore the throne.
2. Thou stand - est in the ho - liest place, As now for guilt - y sin - ners slain;
Thy Blood of sprink - ling speaks and prays All - prev - a - lent for help - less man; Thy Blood is still our ran - som found, And spreads sal - va - tion all a - round.
A - men.

3 We need not now go up to heaven
To bring the long-sought Saviour down;
Thou art to all already given,
Thou dost e'en now thy banquet crown:
To every faithful soul appear,
And show thy real presence here. Amen.

Charles Wesley, 1707–88

ST. CHRYSOSTOM. 8 8, 8 8, 8 8.
JOSEPH BARNBY, 1838–96
Devotionally
SECOND TUNE
1. Vic - tim Di - vine, thy grace we claim While thus thy pre - cious
2. Thou stand - est in the ho - liest place, As now for guilt - y
death we show; Once of - fered up, a spot - less Lamb,
sin - ners slain; Thy Blood of sprink - ling speaks and prays
In thy great tem - ple here be - low, Thou didst for all man -
All - prev - a - lent for help - less man; Thy Blood is still our
kind a - tone, And stand - est now be - fore the throne.
ran - som found, And spreads sal - va - tion all a - round. A - men.

3 We need not now go up to heaven
To bring the long-sought Saviour down;
Thou art to all already given,
Thou dost e'en now thy banquet crown:
To every faithful soul appear,
And show thy real presence here. Amen.

Charles Wesley, 1707–88

275

PENITENTIA. 10 10, 10 10. EDWARD DEARLE, 1806–91

Devotionally

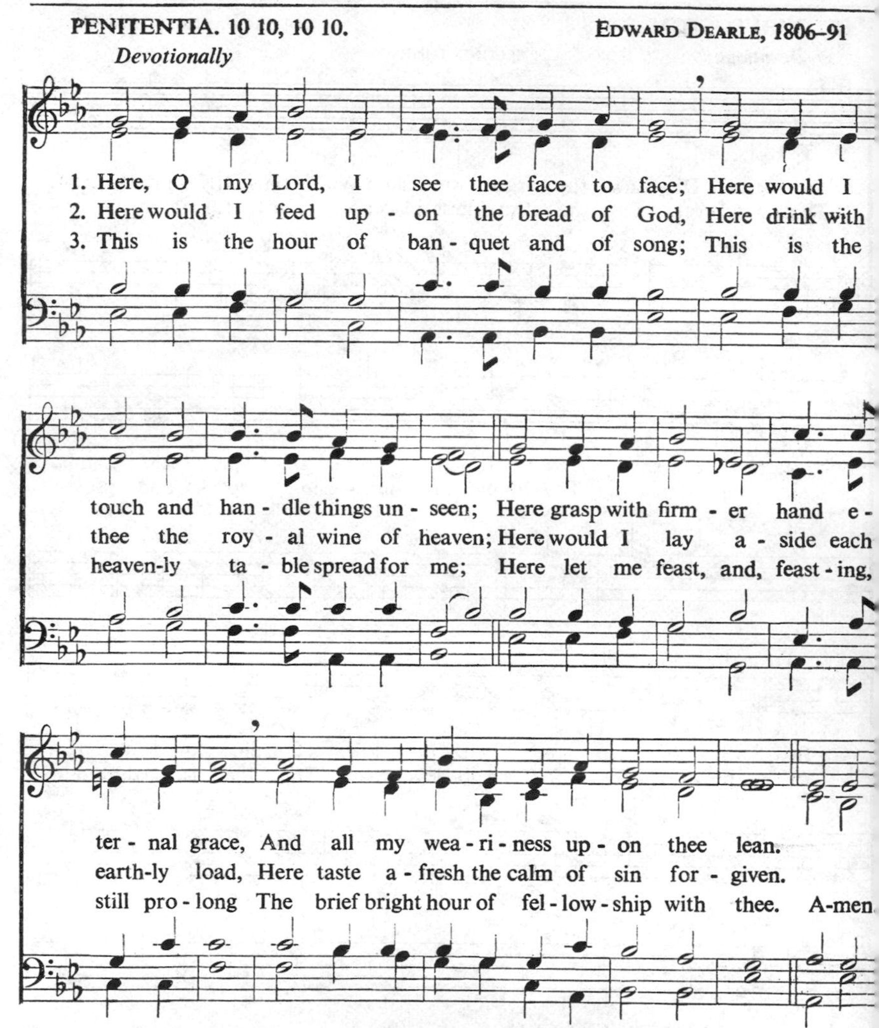
1. Here, O my Lord, I see thee face to face; Here would I touch and handle things unseen; Here grasp with firmer hand eternal grace, And all my weariness upon thee lean.
2. Here would I feed upon the bread of God, Here drink with thee the royal wine of heaven; Here would I lay aside each earthly load, Here taste afresh the calm of sin forgiven.
3. This is the hour of banquet and of song; This is the heavenly table spread for me; Here let me feast, and, feasting, still prolong The brief bright hour of fellowship with thee. Amen

4 I have no help but thine; nor do I need
Another arm save thine to lean upon;
It is enough, my Lord, enough indeed;
My strength is in thy might, thy might alone.

5 Mine is the sin, but thine the righteousness;
Mine is the guilt, but thine the cleansing Blood;
Here is my robe, my refuge, and my peace;
Thy Blood, thy righteousness, O Lord, my God. Amen.

Horatius Bonar, 1808–89

This hymn may also be sung to LANGRAN (No. 366).

ST. FRANCIS. 10 10, 10 10. GIUSEPPE MOSCHETTI, 1908–

Devotionally

1. Not wor - thy, Lord, to gath - er up the crumbs
2. I am not wor - thy to be thought thy child,
3. I hear thy voice: thou bidd'st me come and rest;
With trem - bling hand, that from thy ta - ble fall,
Nor sit the last and low - est at thy board;
I come, I kneel, I clasp thy pierc - ed feet;
A wea - ry, heav - y - la - den sin - ner comes
Too long a wan - derer, and too oft be - guiled,
Thou bidd'st me take my place, a wel - come guest
To plead thy prom - ise and o - bey thy call.
I on - ly ask one rec - on - cil - ing word.
A - mong thy saints, and of thy ban - quet eat. A-men.

4 My praise can only breathe itself in prayer,
My prayer can only lose itself in thee;
Dwell thou forever in my heart, and there,
Lord, let me sup with thee; sup thou with me. Amen.

Edward Henry Bickersteth, 1825–1906

This hymn may also be sung to PENITENTIA (No. 275) or LANGRAN (No. 366).

VERBUM SUPERNUM. L. M. Plainsong Melody, Mode VIII

FIRST TUNE

Unison, in free rhythm
1. O sav - ing Vic - tim, o - pening wide The gate of
heaven to man be - low, Our foes press on from every side, Thine aid sup - ply, thy strength be - stow. A - men.

2 All praise and thanks to thee ascend
For evermore, blest One in Three;
O grant us life that shall not end
In our true native land with thee. Amen.

St. Thomas Aquinas, 1227–74
Tr. Edward Caswall, 1814–78

ST. VINCENT. L. M. SIGISMUND NEUKOMM, 1778–1858

SECOND TUNE

Devotionally
1. O sav - ing Vic - tim, o - pening wide The gate of
heaven to man be - low, Our foes press on from ev - ery
side, Thine aid sup - ply, thy strength be - stow. A - men.

2 All praise and thanks to thee ascend
For evermore, blest One in Three;
O grant us life that shall not end
In our true native land with thee. Amen.

St. Thomas Aquinas, 1227–74
Tr. Edward Caswall, 1814–78

UNDE ET MEMORES. 10 10, 10 10, 10 10. WILLIAM HENRY MONK, 1823–89

Devotionally

1. And now, O Fa - ther, mind - ful of the love That bought us, once for all, on Cal - vary's Tree, And hav - ing with us him that pleads a - bove, We here pre - sent, we here spread forth to thee That on - ly of - fering per - fect in thine eyes, The one true, pure, im - mor - tal sac - ri - fice.
2. Look, Fa - ther, look on his a - noint - ed face, And on - ly look on us as found in him; Look not on our mis - us - ings of thy grace, Our prayer so lan - guid, and our faith so dim: For lo, be - tween our sins and their re - ward We set the pas - sion of thy Son our Lord. A-men.

3 And then for those, our dearest and our best,
By this prevailing presence we appeal;
O fold them closer to thy mercy's breast,
O do thine utmost for their souls' true weal:
From tainting mischief keep them white and clear,
And crown thy gifts with strength to persevere.

4 And so we come; O draw us to thy feet,
Most patient Saviour, who canst love us still;
And by this food, so aweful and so sweet,
Deliver us from every touch of ill:
In thine own service make us glad and free,
And grant us never more to part with thee. Amen.

William Bright, 1824–1901

79

EUCHARISTIC HYMN. 9 8, 9 8. JOHN S. B. HODGES, 1830–1915

Devotionally

1. Bread of the world in mer - cy bro - ken, Wine of the
soul in mer - cy shed, By whom the words of life were
spo - ken And in whose death our sins are dead; A - men.

2 Look on the heart by sorrow broken,
Look on the tears by sinners shed;
And be thy feast to us the token
That by thy grace our souls are fed. Amen.

Reginald Heber, 1783–1826

ECCE PANIS. Irregular. JOHN BACCHUS DYKES, 1823–76

Devotionally, in unison
1. Ver - y Bread, good Shep - herd, tend us, Je - sus, of
thy love be - friend us, Thou re - fresh us,
thou de - fend us, Thine e - ter - nal good - ness
send us In the land of life to see:

2. Thou who all things canst and know - est, Who on earth
such food be - stow - est, Grant us with thy saints, though
low - est, Where the heaven - ly feast thou show - est,
Fel - low - heirs and guests to be. A - men.

St. Thomas Aquinas, 1227–74
Tr. Hymns Ancient and Modern, 1868

PICARDY. 8 7, 8 7, 8 7. XVII cent. French Melody

Unison. In flowing style

1. Let all mor-tal flesh keep si-lence, And with fear and trem-bling stand;
2. King of kings, yet born of Ma-ry, As of old on earth he stood,
Pon-der noth-ing earth-ly-mind-ed, For with bless-ing in his hand
Lord of lords in hu-man ves-ture, In the Bod-y and the Blood
Christ our God to earth de-scend-eth, Our full hom-age to de-mand.
He will give to all the faith-ful His own self for heaven-ly food. A-men.

3 Rank on rank the host of heaven
Spreads its vanguard on the way,
As the Light of light descendeth
From the realms of endless day,
That the powers of hell may vanish
As the darkness clears away.

4 At his feet the six-winged seraph;
Cherubim with sleepless eye,
Veil their faces to the presence,
As with ceaseless voice they cry,
'Alleluia, alleluia,
Alleluia, Lord most high!' Amen.

Liturgy of St. James
Tr. Gerard Moultrie, 1829–85

This hymn may also be sung to ST. THOMAS (HOLYWOOD) (No. 293).

See also:

388 As pants the hart
95 At the Lamb's high feast
491 Break thou the bread of life
569 Come, ye disconsolate
76 Glory be to Jesus
584 Jerusalem the golden
481 Jesus, the very thought
483 Jesus, thou Joy of loving hearts
376 Jesus, thy Blood and righteousness
412 Join all the glorious names
370 Just as I am, without one plea
403 Lord, with glowing heart
397 Love divine, all loves excelling
70 O Lamb of God most holy
480 O thou in all thy might so far
526 The Lord my Shepherd is
522 The Lord's my Shepherd
391 Thou hidden Love of God

OMNI DIE. 8 7, 8 7. CORNER'S *Gesangbuch*, 1631

Slowly, with dignity Arr. by W. S. ROCKSTRO, 1823–95

1. For the bread which thou hast bro - ken; For the
2. By this pledge that thou dost love us, By thy
wine which thou hast poured; For the words which thou hast
gift of peace re - stored, By thy call to heaven a-
spo - ken; Now we give thee thanks, O Lord.
bove us, Hal - low all our lives, O Lord. A - men.

3 With our sainted ones in glory
Seated at our Father's board,
May the Church that waiteth for thee
Keep love's tie unbroken, Lord.

4 In thy service, Lord, defend us,
In our hearts keep watch and ward,
In the world where thou dost send us
Let thy Kingdom come, O Lord. Amen.

Louis FitzGerald Benson, 1855–1930

This hymn may also be sung to BATTY (RINGE RECHT) (No. 63).

JESU, JOY OF MAN'S DESIRING. 8 7, 8 7, 7 6, 8 6. Melody by JOHANN SCHOP, 1600–65, arr. and harm. by J. S. BACH, 1685–1750

Simply; may be sung in unison

Come with us, O bless - ed Je - sus, With us ev - er-
more to be; And in leav - ing now thine al - tar, Let us
nev - er - more leave thee! O let thine an - gel cho - rus
Cease not the heaven-ly strain, But in us, thy lov - ing

chil - dren, Bring . . peace, good will . . . to men. A - men.
John Henry Hopkins, Jr., 1820–91
284
KINGO. L. M.
In moderate time
1. O Je - sus, bless - ed Lord, to thee My heart - felt
2. Break forth, my soul, for joy and say, 'What wealth is
thanks for - ev - er be, Who hast so lov - ing - ly be -
come to me this day, My Sav - iour dwells with - in me
stowed On me thy Bod - y and thy Blood.
now, How blest am I, how good art thou!' A - men.

Thomas Hansen Kingo, 1634–1703
Tr. Arthur James Mason, 1851–1928

This hymn may also be sung to MENDON (No. 415).

285 Post-Communion

AURELIA. 7 6, 7 6. D. SAMUEL SEBASTIAN WESLEY, 1810–76

With breadth and dignity

1. O liv - ing Bread from heav - en, How hast thou fed thy guest!
2. My Lord, thou here hast led me With - in thy ho - liest place,
The gifts thou now hast giv - en Have filled my heart with rest.
And there thy - self hast fed me With treas - ures of thy grace;
O won-drous food of bless - ing, O cup that heals our woes,
And thou hast free - ly giv - en What earth could nev - er buy,
My heart, this gift pos - sess - ing, In thank-ful song o'er-flows!
The Bread of Life from heav - en, That now I shall not die. A-men.

3 Thou givest all I wanted,
The food can death destroy;
And thou hast freely granted
The cup of endless joy.
Ah, Lord, I do not merit
The favor thou hast shown,
And all my soul and spirit
Bow down before thy throne.

4 Lord, grant me that, thus strengthened
With heavenly food, while here
My course on earth is lengthened,
I serve with holy fear;
And when thou call'st my spirit
To leave this world below,
I enter, through thy merit,
Where joys unmingled flow. Amen.

Johann Rist, *1607–6*
Tr. Catherine Winkworth, *1829–7*

ACH GOTT UND HERR. 8 7, 8 7.
As Hymnodus Sacer, 1625
Adapted and harm. by J. S. BACH, 1685–1750
With dignity
1. Strength-en for serv - ice, Lord, the hands That ho - ly
2. Lord, may the tongues which 'Ho - ly' sang Keep free from
things have tak - en; Let ears that now have heard thy songs
all de - ceiv - ing; The eyes which saw thy love be bright,
To clam - or nev - er wak - en.
Thy bless - ed hope per - ceiv - ing. A - men.

3 The feet that tread thy hallowed courts
  From light do thou not banish;
The bodies by thy spirit fed
  With thy new life replenish. Amen.

Syriac, Liturgy of Malabar
Tr. English Hymnal, 1906

See also:

Confirmation

287

LUTHER SEMINARY. C. M. JOHN DAHLE, 1853–1931

Meditatively

1. Lord of the ev - er - last - ing light, Let shine on these to - day A
2. A - noint them free - ly with thy grace, That glad - ly they may share Earth
3. O, may they ev - er turn to thee As Fa - ther and as Friend; Se -

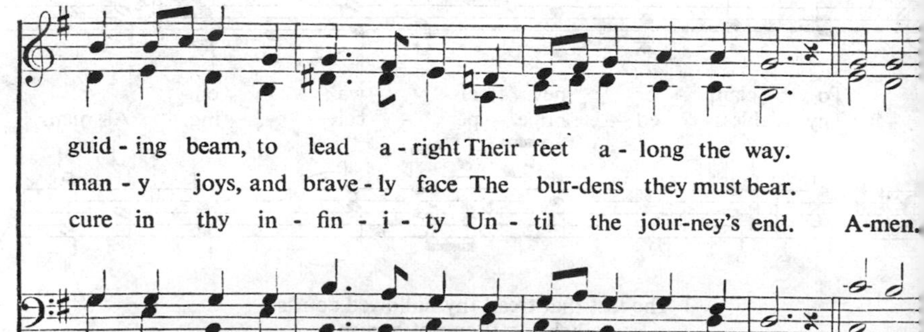
guid - ing beam, to lead a - right Their feet a - long the way.
man - y joys, and brave - ly face The bur-dens they must bear.
cure in thy in - fin - i - ty Un - til the jour-ney's end. A-men.

4 And when, beyond the dusk of time,
They greet the dawn above,
O give them, in that blessèd clime,
Thy endlessness of love. Amen.

Leigh Mitchell Hodges, 1876–195

This hymn may also be sung to BELGRAVE (No. 440).

Confirmation

FRANZEN. 7 6, 7 6, 8 7 6.
Prayerfully

Danish
HANS THOMISSÖN, *Psalmebog*, 1569

1. My Lord, I hear thee plead - ing For love and faith - ful - ness,
2. That hand shall crown with bless - ing Each low - ly, bend - ing head;
Thy love is far ex - ceed - ing The love that I con - fess;
Each heart, thy love con - fess - ing, Shall by that hand be led;
Thy cov - e - nant will ev - er stand On thy e -
I there - fore sing my praise to thee In strains of
ter - nal prom - ise; I take thy prof - fered hand.
al - le - lu - ia, In joy - ful mel - o - dy. A - men.

3 I praise thee, alleluia,
For what thy hand has brought!
I priase thee, alleluia,
For what thy Spirit wrought!
I praise thee with the saints above
For every mercy given,
For faith and hope and love. Amen.

Nikolai F. S. Grundtvig, 1783–1872
Tr. Fred C. M. Hansen, 1888–

BALLERMA. C. M. Adapted by ROBERT SIMPSON, 1790–1832

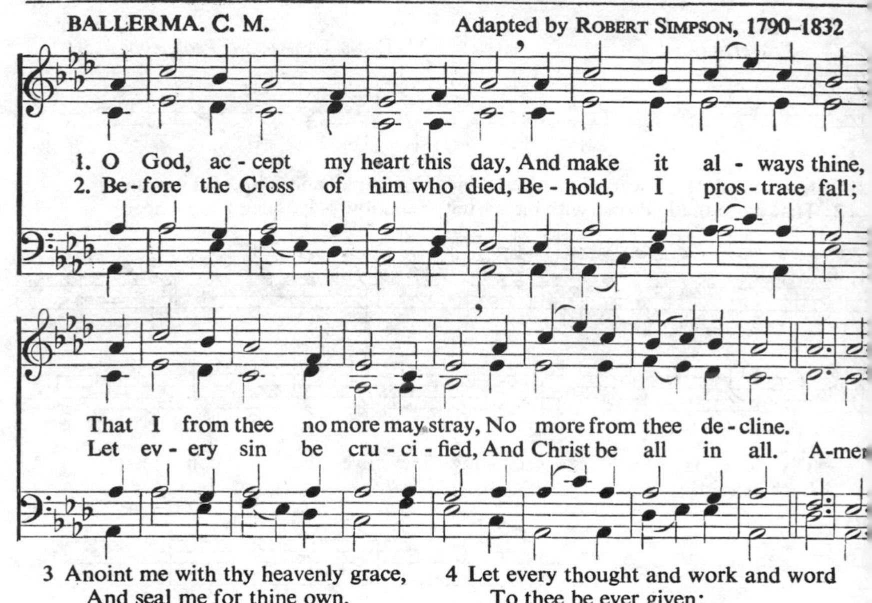
1. O God, ac - cept my heart this day, And make it al - ways thine,
2. Be - fore the Cross of him who died, Be - hold, I pros - trate fall;
That I from thee no more may stray, No more from thee de - cline.
Let ev - ery sin be cru - ci - fied, And Christ be all in all. A-men

3 Anoint me with thy heavenly grace,
And seal me for thine own,
That I may see thy glorious face,
And worship at thy throne.

4 Let every thought and work and word
To thee be ever given;
Then life shall be thy service, Lord,
And death the gate of heaven. Amen.

Matthew Bridges, 1800–

This hymn may also be sung to ST. PETER (No. 291).

290

O DU LIEBE MEINER LIEBE. 8 7, 8 7. D. JOHANN THOMMEN'S *Christen-schatz*, Basel, 1745

In flowing style

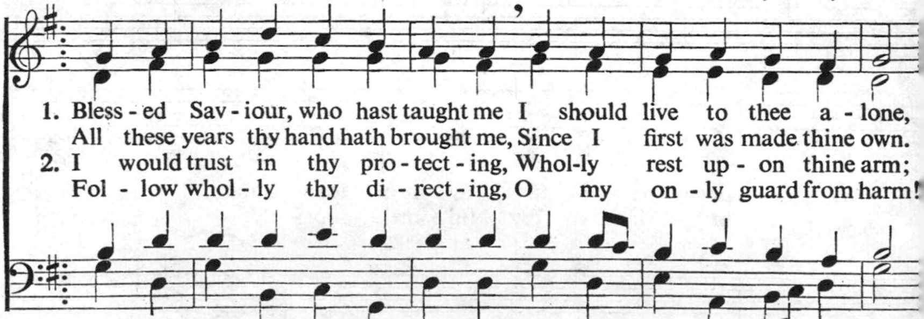

1. Bless - ed Sav - iour, who hast taught me I should live to thee a - lone,
All these years thy hand hath brought me, Since I first was made thine own.
2. I would trust in thy pro - tect - ing, Whol-ly rest up - on thine arm;
Fol - low whol - ly thy di - rect - ing, O my on - ly guard from harm!

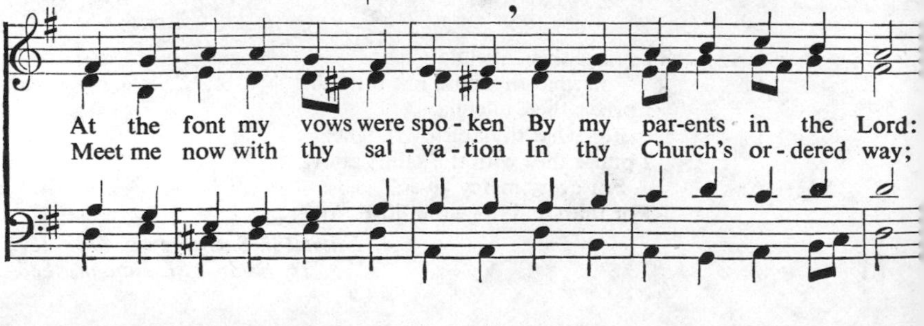

At the font my vows were spo - ken By my par-ents in the Lord:
Meet me now with thy sal - va - tion In thy Church's or - dered way;

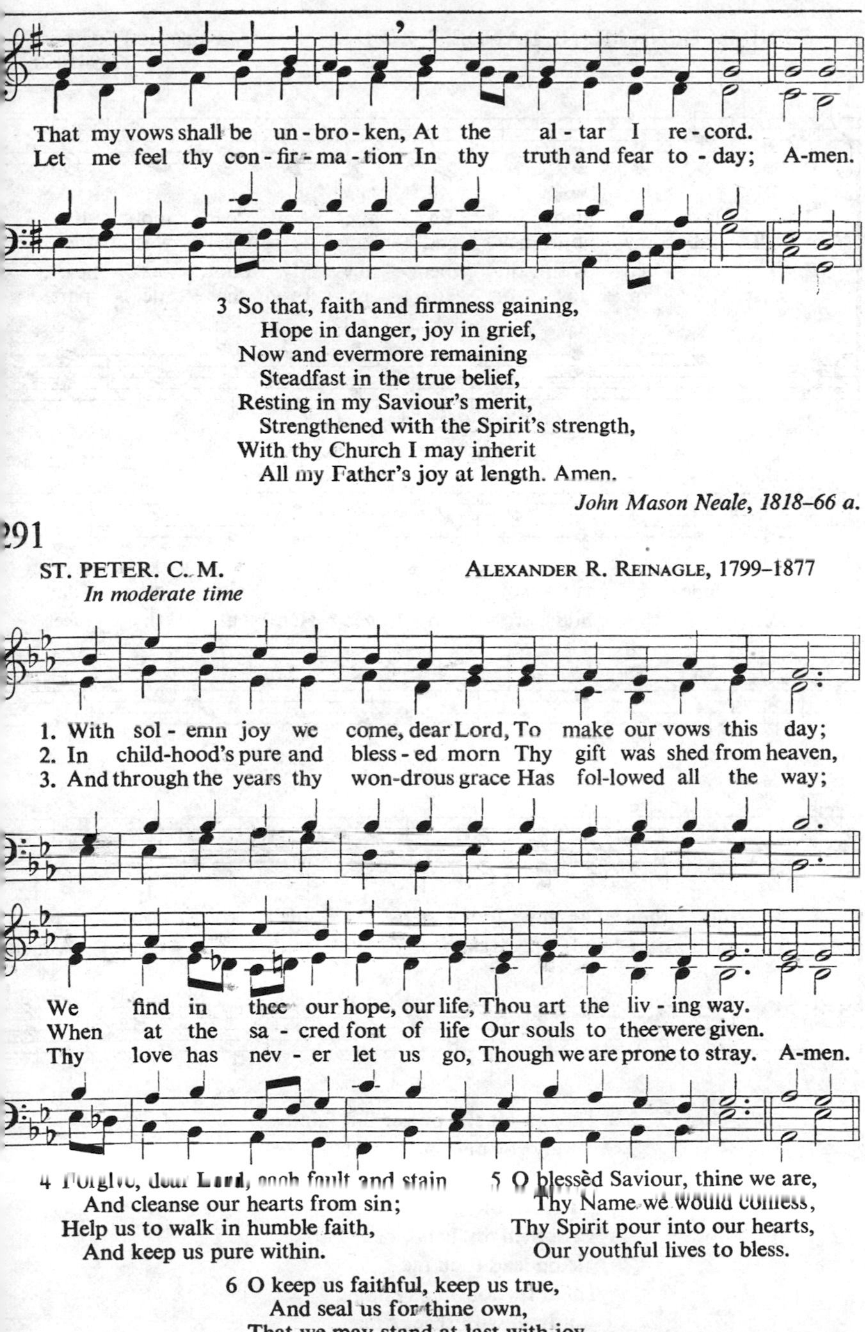
That my vows shall be un-bro-ken, At the al-tar I re-cord.
Let me feel thy con-fir-ma-tion In thy truth and fear to-day; A-men.
1. With sol-emn joy we come, dear Lord, To make our vows this day;
2. In child-hood's pure and bless-ed morn Thy gift was shed from heaven,
3. And through the years thy won-drous grace Has fol-lowed all the way;
We find in thee our hope, our life, Thou art the liv-ing way.
When at the sa-cred font of life Our souls to thee were given.
Thy love has nev-er let us go, Though we are prone to stray. A-men.

3 So that, faith and firmness gaining,
Hope in danger, joy in grief,
Now and evermore remaining
Steadfast in the true belief,
Resting in my Saviour's merit,
Strengthened with the Spirit's strength,
With thy Church I may inherit
All my Father's joy at length. Amen.

John Mason Neale, 1818–66 a.

291

ST. PETER. C. M. ALEXANDER R. REINAGLE, 1799–1877

In moderate time

4 Forgive, dear Lord, each fault and stain
And cleanse our hearts from sin;
Help us to walk in humble faith,
And keep us pure within.

5 O blessèd Saviour, thine we are,
Thy Name we would confess,
Thy Spirit pour into our hearts,
Our youthful lives to bless.

6 O keep us faithful, keep us true,
And seal us for thine own,
That we may stand at last with joy
Before thy great white throne. Amen.

Ernest Edwin Ryden, 1886–

SO NIMM DENN MEINE HÄNDE. 7 4, 7 4. D.
FRIEDRICH SILCHER, 1789–1860
Slowly
1. O take my hand, dear Fa - ther, And lead thou me,
Till at my jour - ney's end - ing I dwell with thee.
2. O cov - er with thy mer - cy My poor, weak heart,
Lest I in joy or sor - row From thee de - part.
A - lone I can - not wan - der One sin - gle day,
Per - mit thy child to lin - ger Here at thy feet,
So do thou guide my foot - steps On life's rough way.
Thy good - ness blind - ly trust - ing With faith com - plete. A-men.

3 Though oft thy power but faintly
May stir my soul,
With thee, my light in darkness,
I reach the goal.
Take then my hand, dear Father,
And lead thou me,
Till at my journey's ending
I dwell with thee. Amen.

Julia Hausmann, 1825–190
Tr. H. Brueckner, 1866–194

ST. THOMAS (HOLYWOOD). 8 7, 8 7, 8 7. Traditional melody, XVIII cent.

Slowly and majestically

1. Lord, to thee I now sur-ren-der All I have, and all I am;
2. Gra-cious God, all thou hast spo-ken In this cov-enant shall take place;

Make my heart more true and ten-der, Glo-ri-fy in me thy Name.
But if I, a-las, have bro-ken These my vows, hide not thy face;

Let o-be-dience, let o-be-dience To thy will be all my aim.
And from fall-ing, and from fall-ing, O re-store me by thy grace! A-men.

3 Help me in this high endeavor,
Father, Son, and Holy Ghost;
Bind my heart to thee for ever
Till I join the heavenly host.
Living, dying,
Let me make in thee my boast. Amen.

Johann Jacob Rambach, 1693–1735
Tr. Charles William Schaeffer, 1813–96

See also:

117 Come, Holy Ghost, our souls inspire
557 Fight the good fight
563 He who would valiant be
550 Lead on, O King eternal
506 Let me be thine forever
392 More love to thee, O Christ
559 My soul, be on thy guard
466 O for a closer walk with God
537 O Master, let me walk with thee
179 Shepherd of tender youth
451 Teach me, my God and King
505 Thee will I love, my strength, my tower

Burial of the Dead

294

JESUS, MEINE ZUVERSICHT (RATISBON). *Praxis Pietatis Melica*, 1653
7 8, 7 8, 7 7.

FIRST TUNE

Jubilantly
1. Je - sus Christ, my sure De - fence And my Sav-iour, ev - er liv - eth;
2. Je - sus, my Re-deem - er, lives! I, too, un - to life must wak - en;
Know-ing this, my con - fi - dence Rests up - on the hope it giv - eth,
He will have me where he is. Shall my cour-age then be shak - en?
Though the night of death be fraught Still with many an anx-ious thought.
Shall I fear? Or could the Head Rise and leave his mem-bers dead? A-men.

3 Nay, too closely am I bound
Unto him by hope for ever;
Faith's strong hand the rock hath found,
Grasped it, and will leave it never;
Not the ban of death can part
From its Lord the trusting heart.

4 Saviour, draw away our heart
Now from pleasures base and hollow,
Let us there with thee have part,
Here on earth thy footsteps follow.
Fix our hearts beyond the skies,
Whither we ourselves would rise. Amen

Luise Henriette von Brandenburg (?), 1627–6
Tr. Catherine Winkworth, 1829–78

94

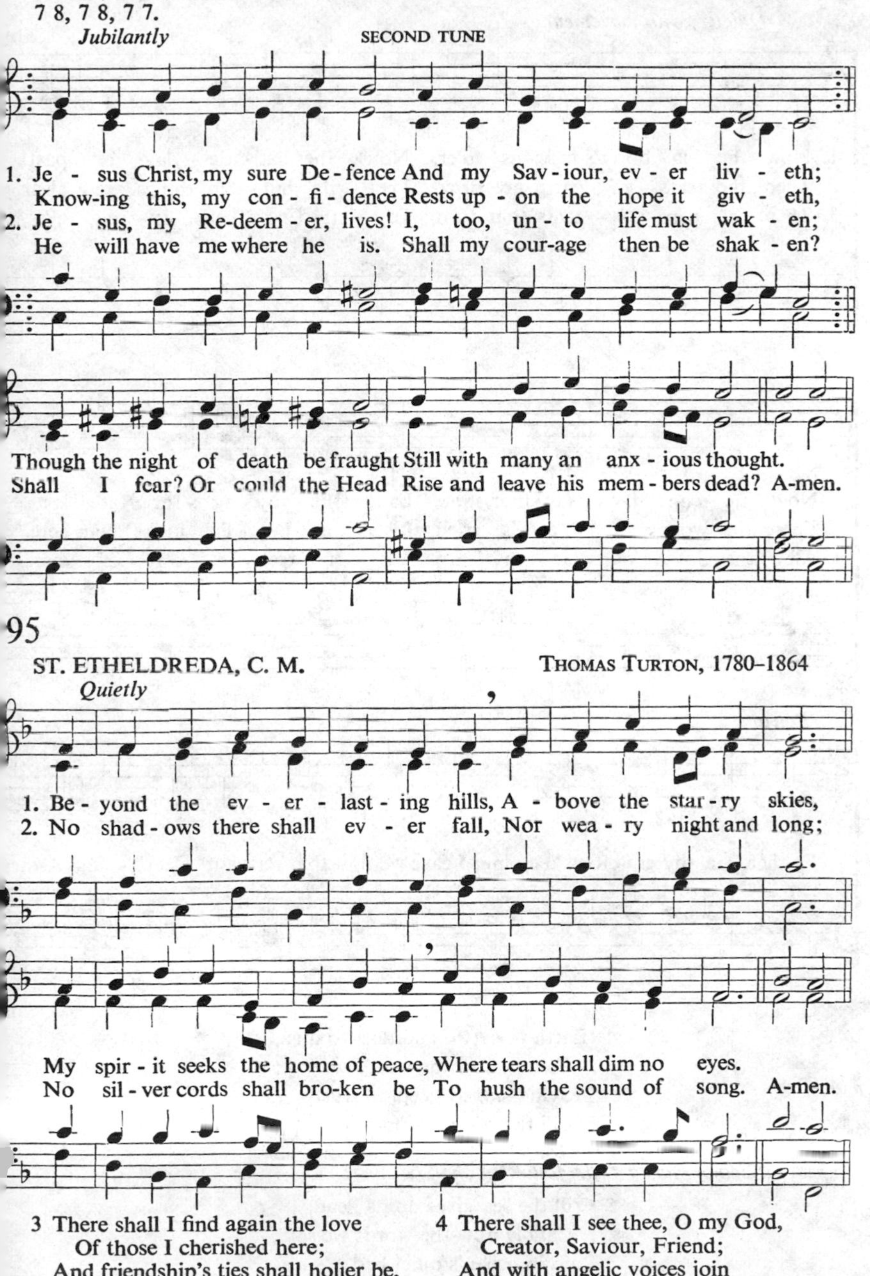
JESUS, MEINE ZUVERSICHT (RATISBON). 7 8, 7 8, 7 7.
Praxis Pietatis Melica, 1653
Jubilantly
SECOND TUNE
1. Je - sus Christ, my sure De - fence And my Sav - iour, ev - er liv - eth;
Know-ing this, my con - fi - dence Rests up - on the hope it giv - eth,
2. Je - sus, my Re-deem - er, lives! I, too, un - to life must wak - en;
He will have me where he is. Shall my cour-age then be shak - en?
Though the night of death be fraught Still with many an anx - ious thought.
Shall I fear? Or could the Head Rise and leave his mem - bers dead? A-men.
95
ST. ETHELDREDA, C. M.
Thomas Turton, 1780–1864
Quietly
1. Be - yond the ev - er - last - ing hills, A - bove the star - ry skies,
2. No shad - ows there shall ev - er fall, Nor wea - ry night and long;
My spir - it seeks the home of peace, Where tears shall dim no eyes.
No sil - ver cords shall bro-ken be To hush the sound of song. A-men.

3 There shall I find again the love
Of those I cherished here;
And friendship's ties shall holier be,
And bonds of love more dear.

4 There shall I see thee, O my God,
Creator, Saviour, Friend;
And with angelic voices join
In worship without end. Amen.

Ernest Edwin Ryden, 1886–

REQUIESCAT. 7 7, 7 7, 8 8. JOHN BACCHUS DYKES, 1823–76

Quietly, with movement

1. Now the la - borer's task is o'er, Now the bat - tle - day is past;
2. There the tears of earth are dried, There its hid - den things are clear,
3. There the pen - i - tents, that turn To the Cross their dy - ing eyes,
Now up - on the far - ther shore Lands the voy - ag - er at last.
There the work of life is tried By a just - er judge than here.
All the love of Je - sus learn At his feet in Par - a - dise.
Refrain
Fa-ther, in thy gra-cious keep-ing, Leave we now thy ser-vant sleep - ing. A-men

4 'Earth to earth, and dust to dust,'
Calmly now the words we say;
Leaving *him* to sleep, in trust,
Till the resurrection-day:

At sea, instead of stanza 4, the following shall be sung:

5 'Till the sea gives up its dead,'
Calmly now the words we say,
Laid in ocean's quiet bed
Till the resurrection-day:

John Ellerton, 1826–9

IAM MOESTA. 9 9, 9 9.
Christliche Geseng Lateinisch und Deutsch, zum Begrebnis,
MARTIN LUTHER, Wittenberg, 1542
With confidence
1. De - spair not, O heart, in thy sor - row, From God's own as -
2. As seed in the spring-time is plant - ed, And rests in the
3. So we, a - mid sor - row and weep - ing, Com - mit - ted, O
sur - an - ces bor - row The prom - ise that Je - sus has
earth un - til grant - ed God's bless - ing of warmth and of
earth, to thy keep - ing, Shall, giv - en new life and per -
giv - en: That life has in death its be - gin - ning.
show - ers, And blos - soms in leaf - lets and flow - ers;
fec - tion, Come forth in the great res - ur - rec - tion. A - men.

4 O Lord, at thy coming in glory,
When all shall bow down and adore thee,
Then forth from the tomb's open portal,
O lead us to mansions immortal. Amen.

Aurelius Clemens Prudentius, 348–413
Tr. Edward Traill Horn III, 1909–

LLEF. L.M. GRIFFITH HUGH JONES, 1849–1919

FIRST TUNE

Moderately slow

1. That day of wrath, that dread - ful day, When heaven and
earth shall pass a - way, What power shall be the
sin - ner's stay? How shall he meet that dread-ful day? A-men.

2 When, shrivelling like a parchèd scroll,
The flaming heavens together roll;
When, louder yet, and yet more dread,
Swells the high trump that wakes the dead;

3 Lord, on that day, that wrathful day,
When man to judgment wakes from clay,
Be thou the trembling sinner's stay,
Though heaven and earth shall pass away! Amen.

Walter Scott, 1771–18
Founded on Dies Ir

WINDHAM. L.M.
DANIEL READ, 1757–1836
SECOND TUNE
Moderately slow
1. That day of wrath, that dread - ful day, When heaven and
earth shall pass a - way, What power shall be the sin - ner's
stay? How shall he meet that dread - ful day? A - men.

2 When, shrivelling like a parchèd scroll,
The flaming heavens together roll;
When, louder yet, and yet more dread,
Swells the high trump that wakes the dead;

3 Lord, on that day, that wrathful day,
When man to judgment wakes from clay,
Be thou the trembling sinner's stay,
Though heaven and earth shall pass away! Amen.

Walter Scott, 1771–1832
Founded on Dies Irae

WEYSE. 9 8, 9 8, 9 8. CHRISTOPH E. F. WEYSE, 1774–1842

With dignity
1. I know of a sleep in Je - sus' Name, A rest from all toil and sor - row; Earth folds in her arms my wea - ry frame, And shel - ters it till the mor - row; The soul is in heaven at home with God, And sor - row is gone for - ev - er.
2. I know of a bless - ed e - ven - tide; And when I am faint and wea - ry, At times with the jour - ney sore - ly tried Through hours that are long and drear - y, Then of - ten I yearn to lay me down And sink in - to peace - ful slum - ber. A-men.

3 I know of a morning bright and fair
When tidings of joy shall wake us,
When songs from on high shall fill the air
And God to his glory take us,
When Jesus shall bid us rise from sleep;
How joyous that hour of waking!

4 O Jesus, draw near my dying bed
And take me into thy keeping,
And say, when my spirit hence is fled
'This child is not dead but sleeping;'
And leave me not, Saviour, till I rise
To praise thee in life eternal. Amen.

Magnus Brostrup Landstad, 1802–8
Tr. Hymnal Version, 195

Marriage

300

O PERFECT LOVE. 11 10, 11 10. **JOSEPH BARNBY, 1838–96**

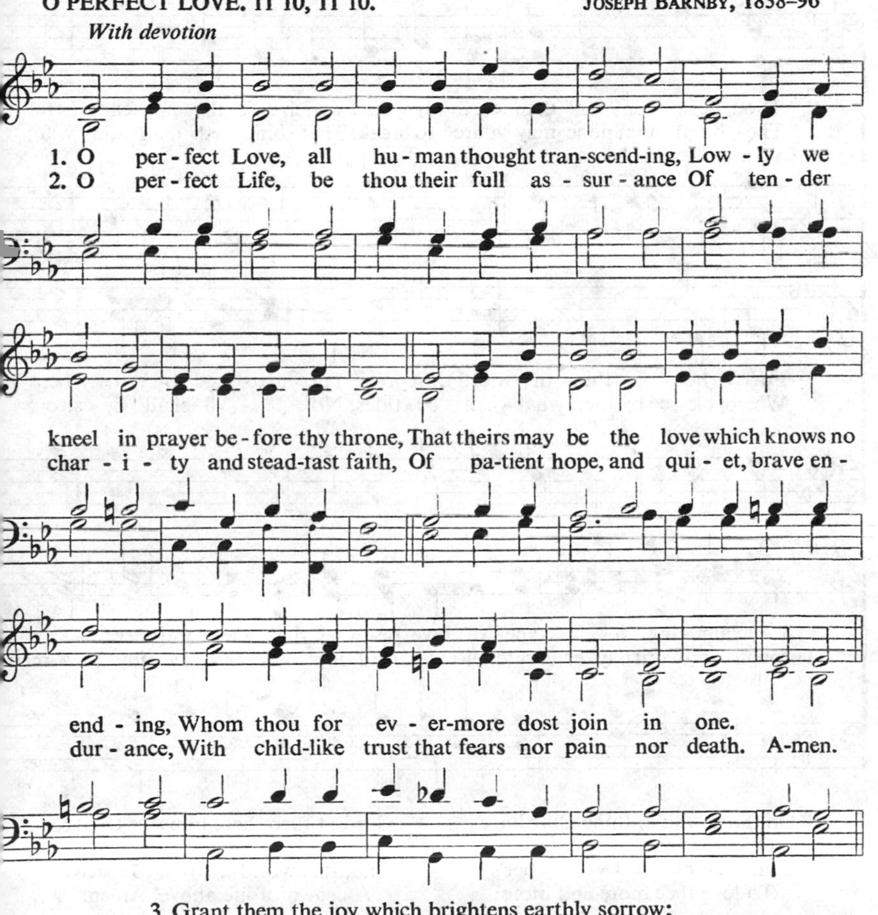

With devotion
1. O per - fect Love, all hu - man thought tran-scend-ing, Low - ly we
2. O per - fect Life, be thou their full as - sur - ance Of ten - der
kneel in prayer be - fore thy throne, That theirs may be the love which knows no
char - i - ty and stead-fast faith, Of pa-tient hope, and qui - et, brave en -
end - ing, Whom thou for ev - er-more dost join in one.
dur - ance, With child-like trust that fears nor pain nor death. A-men.

3 Grant them the joy which brightens earthly sorrow;
  Grant them the peace which calms all earthly strife,
And to life's day the glorious unknown morrow
  That dawns upon eternal love and life. Amen.

Dorothy Frances Gurney, 1858–1932

ISHPEMING. C. M. D.
GERHARD THEODORE ALEXIS, 1889–1927
Joyfully
1. Lord, who at Ca - na's wed-ding feast Didst as a guest ap - pear,
2. The ho - liest vow that man can make, The gold - en thread in life,
Thou, dear - er far than earth - ly guest, Vouch-safe thy pres-ence here;
The bond that none may dare to break, That bind - eth man and wife;
For ho - ly thou in - deed dost prove The mar-riage vow to be,
Which, blessed by thee, what - e'er be - tides, No e - vil shall de - stroy,
Pro - claim - ing it a type of love Be-tween the Church and thee;
Through care-worn days each care di-vides, And dou - bles ev - ery joy. A-men.

3 On those who at thine altar kneel,
O Lord, thy blessing pour,
That each may wake the other's zeal
To love thee more and more;

O grant them here in peace to live,
In purity and love,
And, this world leaving, to receive
A crown of life above. Amen.

St. 1, 3, Adelaide Thrupp, 185.
St. 2, Godfrey Thring, 1823–190.

See also:

397 Love divine, all loves excelling
443 Now thank we all our God
408 Praise to the Lord, the Almighty
530 The King of love my shepherd is

Ordination

302

ST. LAWRENCE, LUND (UPPFAREN ÄR VÅR HERRE). **L. M.** — Swedish Melody, XVII cent.

In flowing style — *For Ministers' Meetings*

1. O pour thy Spir - it from on high; Lord, thine as -
2. With - in thy tem - ple, when they stand To teach the
3. Wis - dom and zeal and faith im - part, Firm - ness with

sem - bled serv - ants bless; Grac - es and gifts to each sup -
truth as taught by thee, Sav - iour, like stars in thy right
meek - ness from a - bove, To bear thy peo - ple on their

ply, And clothe thy priests with right - eous - ness.
hand, The an - gels of the church - es be.
heart, And love the souls whom thou dost love; A - men.

4 To watch and pray and never faint;
By day and night strict guard to keep;
To warn the sinner, cheer the saint,
Nourish thy lambs, and feed thy sheep.

5 Then, when their work is finished here,
In humble hope their charge resign;
When the Chief Shepherd shall appear,
O God, may they and we be thine. Amen.

James Montgomery, 1771–1854

This hymn may also be sung to HAMBURG (No. 503).

303

ERFURT. (ALLGÜTIGER, MEIN PREISGESANG). 8 8 6, 8 8 6.

GEORG PETER WEIMAR, 1734–1800

In moderate time

1. Lord of the Church, we hum-bly pray For those who guide us in thy way,

And speak thy ho - ly word; With love di - vine their hearts in - spire,

And touch their lips with hal-lowed fire, And need - ful grace af - ford. A-men.

2 Help them to preach the truth of God,
Redemption through the Saviour's Blood;
Nor let the Spirit cease
On all the Church his gifts to shower:
To them, a messenger of power,
To us, of life and peace.

3 So may they live to thee alone,
Then hear the welcome word, 'Well done!
And take their crown above;
Enter into their Master's joy,
And all eternity employ
In praise, and bliss, and love. Amen.

St. 1, 2, Edward Osler, 1793–186
St. 3, Charles Wesley, 1707–8

See also:

255 Awake, thou Spirit of the watchmen
121 Come, Holy Ghost, in love
158 I love thy kingdom, Lord
153 Jesus, with thy Church abide
538 Lord, speak to me
314 O Zion, haste
560 Onward, Christian soldiers
541 Rise up, O men of God
564 Soldiers of Christ, arise
510 Take my life, and let it be

HOLY CHURCH. 7 6, 7 6. D. ARTHUR HENRY BROWN, 1830–1926

With spirit

1. Lord of the liv - ing har - vest That whit - ens o'er the plain,
Where an - gels soon shall gath - er Their sheaves of gold - en grain,
Ac - cept these hands to la - bor, These hearts to trust and love,
And deign with them to has - ten Thy king - dom from a - bove. A-men.

2 As laborers in thy vineyard,
Lord, send them out to be
Content to bear the burden
Of weary days for thee;
To ask no other wages,
When thou shalt call them home,
But to have shared the travail
Which makes thy kingdom come.

3 Be with them, God the Father;
Be with them, God the Son;
And God the Holy Spirit;
Most blessèd Three in One!
Make them a royal priesthood
Thee rightly to adore,
And fill them with thy fulness
Both now and evermore. Amen.

John S. B. Monsell, 1811–75

TRURO. L. M. WILLIAMS' *Psalmodia Evangelica*, 1789

With spirit

1. Thou Lord of Hosts, whose guid - ing hand Has brought us
here be - fore thy face, Our spir - its wait for
thy com - mand, Our si - lent hearts im - plore thy peace. A-men.

2 Those spirits lay their noblest powers
As offerings on thy holy shrine:
Thine was the strength that nourished ours;
The soldiers of the cross are thine.

3 While watching on our arms at night
We saw thine angels round us move;
We heard thy call, we felt thy light,
And followed, trusting to thy love.

4 Send us where'er thou wilt, O Lord!
Through rugged toil and wearying fight;
Thy conquering love shall be our sword,
And faith in thee our truest might.

5 Send down thy constant aid, we pray;
Be thy pure angels with us still;
Thy truth, be that our firmest stay;
Our only rest, to do thy will. Amen.

Octavius Brooke Frothingham, 1822–95

This hymn may also be sung to DEUS TUORUM MILITUM (No. 494)

See also:

255 Awake, thou Spirit of the watchmen
557 Fight the good fight
158 I love thy kingdom, Lord
550 Lead on, O King eternal
303 Lord of the Church
519 O God of Bethel
306 O Spirit of the living God
454 O thou whose feet have climbed
541 Rise up, O men of God
564 Soldiers of Christ, arise
510 Take my life, and let it be
446 Ye servants of God, your Master

The Propagation of the Gospel

306

MELCOMBE. L. M. SAMUEL WEBBE, 1740–1816

In moderate time

1. O Spir - it of the liv - ing God, In
2. Give tongues of fire and hearts of love To
3. Be dark - ness, at thy com - ing, light; Con -

all thy plen - i - tude of grace, Wher - e'er the foot of
preach the rec - on - cil - ing word; Give power and unc - tion
fu - sion, or - der in thy path; Souls with - out strength in -

man hath trod, De - scend on our a - pos - tate race.
from a - bove, Wher - e'er the joy - ful sound is heard.
spire with might; Bid mer - cy tri - umph o - ver wrath. A-men.

4 O Spirit of the Lord, prepare
All the round earth her God to meet;
Breathe thou abroad like morning air,
Till hearts of stone begin to beat.

5 Baptize the nations; far and nigh
The triumphs of the Cross record;
The Name of Jesus glorify
Till every kindred call him Lord. Amen.

James Montgomery, 1771–1854

DUKE STREET. L. M.
JOHN HATTON, +1793
With breadth
1. Je - sus shall reign wher - e'er the sun Doth his suc
2. To him shall end - less prayer be made, And prais - es
ces - sive jour - neys run; His king - dom stretch from
throng to crown his head; His Name like sweet per -
shore to shore, Till moons shall wax and wane no more.
fume shall rise With ev - ery morn - ing sac - ri - fice.

3 People and realms of every tongue
Dwell on his love with sweetest song;
And infant voices shall proclaim
Their early blessings on his Name.

4 Blessings abound where'er he reigns;
The prisoner leaps to lose his chains,
The weary find eternal rest,
And all the sons of want are blest.

5 Let every creature rise and bring
Peculiar honors to our King;
Angels descend with songs again,
And earth repeat the loud Amen.

Isaac Watts, 1674–17

ELLACOMBE. C. M. D. WÜRTTEMBERG *Gesangbuch*, 1784

Brightly

1. Lift up your heads, ye gates of brass, Ye bars of i - ron, yield,
And let the King of Glo - ry pass, The Cross is in the field;
That ban - ner, bright - er than the star That leads the train of night,
Shines on their march, and guides from far His serv - ants to the fight.

A holy war those servants wage;
In that mysterious strife,
The powers of heaven and hell engage
For more than death or life.
Ye armies of the living God,
Ye warriors of Christ's host,
Where hallowed footsteps never trod
Take your appointed post.

3 Though few and small and weak your hands,
Strong in your Captain's strength,
Go, to the conquest of all lands;
All must be his at length.
Uplifted are the gates of brass,
The bars of iron yield;
Behold the King of Glory pass:
The Cross hath won the field.

James Montgomery, 1771–1854 a.

MOSCOW (ITALIAN HYMN). 6 6 4, 6 6 6 4. FELICE DE GIARDINI, 1716–96

Joyfully
1. Thou, whose al - might - y word Cha - os and dark - ness heard,
2. Thou, who didst come to bring On thy re - deem - ing wing
And took their flight; Hear us, we hum - bly pray, And where the
Heal - ing and sight, Health to the sick in mind, Sight to the
gos - pel - day Sheds not its glo - rious ray, Let there be light!
in - ly blind, O now to all man - kind Let there be light! A - men

3 Spirit of truth and love,
Life-giving, holy Dove,
Speed forth thy flight!
Move on the waters' face
Bearing the lamp of grace,
And in earth's darkest place
Let there be light!

4 Holy and blessèd Three,
Glorious Trinity,
Wisdom, Love, Might;
Boundless as ocean's tide,
Rolling in fullest pride,
Through the world, far and wide,
Let there be light! Amen.

John Marriott, 1780–1
Revised, Thomas Raffles, 1788–1

MISSIONARY HYMN. 7 6, 7 6. D. LOWELL MASON, 1792–1872

Smoothly, with movement

1. From Green-land's i - cy moun - tains, From In - dia's cor - al strand,
Where Af - ric's sun - ny foun - tains Roll down their gold - en sand,
From many an an - cient riv - er, From many a palm-y plain,
They call us to de - liv - er Their land from er - ror's chain.

2 Can we whose souls are lighted
With wisdom from on high,
Can we to men benighted
The lamp of life deny?
Salvation, O salvation!
The joyful sound proclaim,
Till each remotest nation
Has learned Messiah's Name.

3 Waft, waft, ye winds, his story,
And you, ye waters, roll,
Till, like a sea of glory,
It spreads from pole to pole;
Till o'er our ransomed nature
The Lamb for sinners slain,
Redeemer, King, Creator,
In bliss returns to reign.

Reginald Heber, 1783–1826

CUTTING. 6 6 4, 6 6 6 4.
WILLIAM F. SHERWIN, 1826–88
FIRST TUNE
In moderate time
1. Christ for the world we sing; The world to Christ we bring With lov - ing zeal; The poor and them that mourn, The faint and o - ver-borne, Sin - sick and sor - row-worn, Whom Christ doth heal.
2. Christ for the world we sing; The world to Christ we bring With fer - vent prayer; The way - ward and the lost, By rest - less pas - sions tossed, Re - deemed at count - less cost From dark de - spair.
rit.

3 Christ for the world we sing;
The world to Christ we bring
With one accord;
With us the work to share,
With us reproach to dare,
With us the cross to bear,
For Christ our Lord.

4 Christ for the world we sing;
The world to Christ we bring
With joyful song;
The new-born souls, whose days,
Reclaimed from error's ways,
Inspired with hope and praise,
To Christ belong.

Samuel Wolcott, 1813–8

KIRBY BEDON. 6 6 4, 6 6 6 4.
EDWARD BUNNETT, 1834–1923
SECOND TUNE
In moderate time
1. Christ for the world we sing; The world to Christ we bring
2. Christ for the world we sing; The world to Christ we bring
With lov-ing zeal; The poor and them that mourn, The faint and
With fer-vent prayer; The way-ward and the lost, By rest-less
o - ver-borne, Sin-sick and sor-row-worn, Whom Christ doth heal.
pas-sions tossed, Re-deemed at count-less cost From dark de-spair.

3 Christ for the world we sing;
The world to Christ we bring
With one accord;
With us the work to share,
With us reproach to dare,
With us the cross to bear,
For Christ our Lord.

4 Christ for the world we sing;
The world to Christ we bring
With joyful song;
The new-born souls, whose days,
Reclaimed from error's ways,
Inspired with hope and praise,
To Christ belong.

Samuel Wolcott, 1813–86

This hymn may also be sung to MOSCOW (ITALIAN HYMN) (No. 309)

BEECHER. 8 7, 8 7. D. John Zundel, 1815–82

In moderate time

1. Sav - iour, sprin-kle man - y na-tions; Fruit - ful let thy sor - rows be;
By thy pains and con - so - la - tions Draw the Gen - tiles un - to thee.
Of thy Cross the won - drous sto - ry Be it to the na - tions told;
Let them see thee in thy glo - ry And thy mer - cy man - i - fold. A-men

2 Far and wide, though all unknowing,
Pants for thee each mortal breast;
Human tears for thee are flowing,
Human hearts in thee would rest;
Thirsting as for dews of even,
As the new-mown grass for rain,
Thee they seek, as God of heaven,
Thee as Man for sinners slain.

3 Saviour, lo! the isles are waiting,
Stretched the hand, and strained the sight
For thy Spirit new-creating,
Love's pure flame, and wisdom's light;
Give the word, and of the preacher
Speed the foot and touch the tongue,
Till on earth by every creature
Glory to the Lamb be sung. Amen.

Arthur Cleveland Coxe, 1818–9

This hymn may also be sung to FALFIELD (No. 512)

The Propagation of the Gospel

WEBB. 7 6, 7 6. D. GEORGE JAMES WEBB, 1803–87

Broadly, with movement

1. The morn - ing light is break - ing, The dark - ness dis - ap - pears;
The sons of earth are wak - ing To pen - i - ten - tial tears;
Each breeze that sweeps the o - cean Brings ti - dings from a - far
Of na - tions in com - mo - tion, Pre - pared for Zi - on's war.

2 See heathen nations bending
Before the God we love,
And thousand hearts ascending
In gratitude above;
While sinners, now confessing,
The gospel call obey,
And seek the Saviour's blessing,
A nation in a day.

3 Blest river of salvation,
Pursue thine onward way;
Flow thou to every nation,
Nor in thy richness stay;
Stay not till all the lowly
Triumphant reach their home;
Stay not till all the holy
Proclaim, 'The Lord is come!'

Samuel Francis Smith, 1808–95

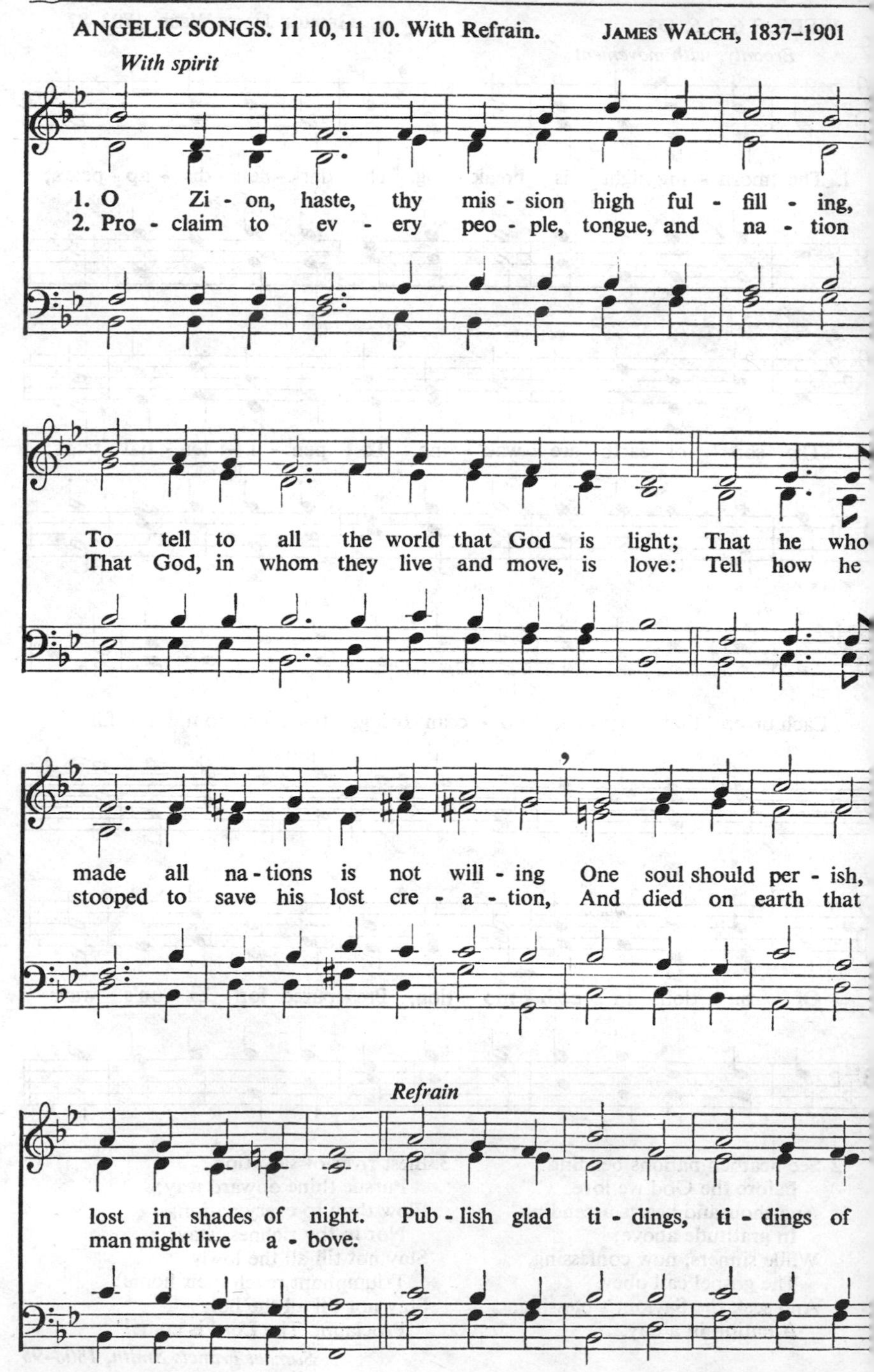
ANGELIC SONGS. 11 10, 11 10. With Refrain.
JAMES WALCH, 1837–1901
With spirit
1. O Zi - on, haste, thy mis - sion high ful - fill - ing,
2. Pro - claim to ev - ery peo - ple, tongue, and na - tion
To tell to all the world that God is light; That he who
That God, in whom they live and move, is love: Tell how he
made all na - tions is not will - ing One soul should per - ish,
stooped to save his lost cre - a - tion, And died on earth that
Refrain
lost in shades of night. Pub - lish glad ti - dings, ti - dings of
man might live a - bove.

peace; Ti - dings of Je - sus, re - demp-tion and re - lease.

3 Give of thy sons to bear the message glorious,
  Give of thy wealth to speed them on their way,
Pour out thy soul for them in prayer victorious,
  And haste the coming of the glorious day.

4 He comes again; O Zion, ere thou meet him,
  Make known to every heart his saving grace;
Let none whom he hath ransomed fail to greet him,
  Through thy neglect, unfit to see his face.

Mary Ann Thomson, 1834–1923

15

WALTHAM. L. M. JOHN BAPTISTE CALKIN, 1827–1905

With spirit

1. Fling out the ban-ner! let it float Sky-ward and sea-ward, high and wide;

The sun that lights its shin - ing folds, The Cross on which the Sav - iour died.

2 Fling out the banner! angels bend
  In anxious silence o'er the sign,
And vainly seek to comprehend
  The wonder of the love divine.

3 Fling out the banner! heathen lands
  Shall see from far the glorious sight,
And nations, crowding to be born,
  Baptize their spirits in its light.

4 Fling out the banner! let it float
  Skyward and seaward, high and wide,
Our glory, only in the Cross,
  Our only hope, the Crucified.

5 Fling out the banner! wide and high,
  Seaward and skyward let it shine:
Nor skill, nor might, nor merit ours;
  We conquer only in that sign.

George Washington Doane, 1799–1859

JUST AS I AM (BARNBY) 8 8, 8 6. JOSEPH BARNBY, 1838–96

FIRST TUNE

In moderate time

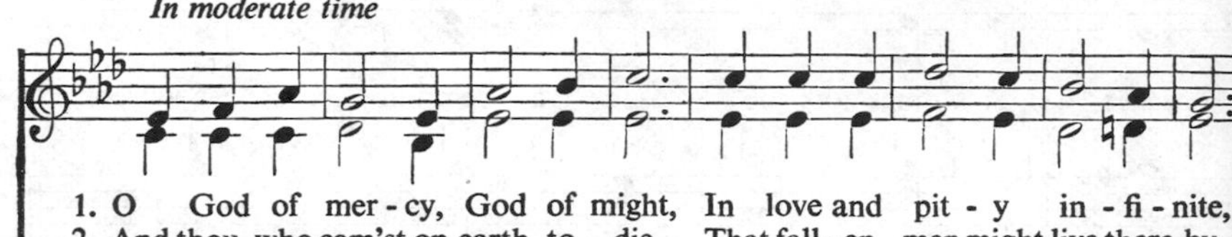

1. O God of mer - cy, God of might, In love and pit - y in - fi - nite,
2. And thou, who cam'st on earth to die That fall - en men might live there-by,

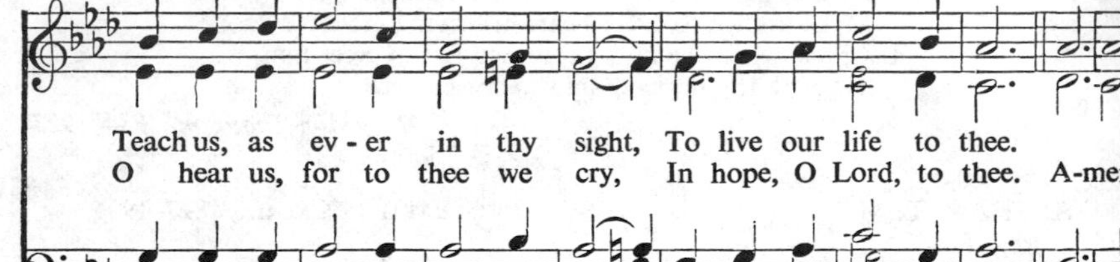

Teach us, as ev - er in thy sight, To live our life to thee.
O hear us, for to thee we cry, In hope, O Lord, to thee. A-men

3 Teach us the lesson thou hast taught,
To feel for those thy Blood hath bought,
That every word and deed and thought
May work a work for thee.

4 For all are brethren, far and wide,
Since thou, O Lord, for all hast died;
Then teach us, whatsoe'er betide,
To love them all in thee.

5 In sickness, sorrow, want, or care,
Whate'er it be, 'tis ours to share;
May we, where help is needed, there
Give help as unto thee.

6 And may thy Holy Spirit move
All those who live, to live in love,
Till thou shalt greet in heaven above
All those who live to thee. Amen.

Godfrey Thring, 1823–190

316

TRANSFIGURATION. 8 8, 8 6. D. OTTO EMANUEL OLSSON, 1879–

SECOND TUNE

With spirit

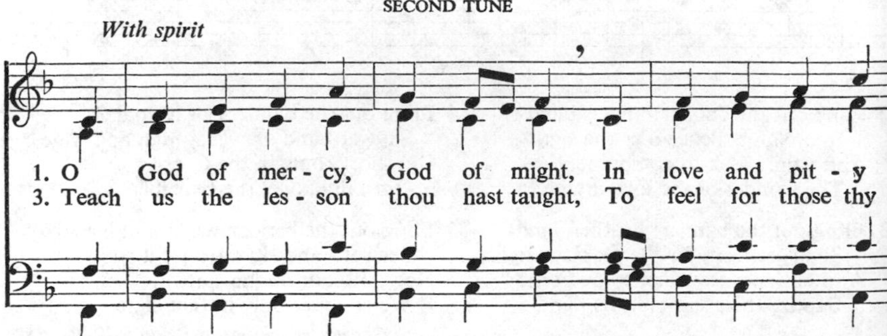

1. O God of mer - cy, God of might, In love and pit - y
3. Teach us the les - son thou hast taught, To feel for those thy

The Propagation of the Gospel

in - fi - nite, Teach us, as ev - er in thy sight, To
Blood hath bought, That ev - ery word and deed and thought May
live our life to thee. 2. And thou, who cam'st on earth to
work a work for thee. 4. For all are breth - ren, far and
die That fall - en men might live there - by, O hear us,
wide, Since thou, O Lord, for all hast died; Then teach us,
for to thee we cry, In hope, O Lord, to thee.
what - so - e'er be - tide, To love them all in thee. A-men.

5 In sickness, sorrow, want, or care,
Whate'er it be, 'tis ours to share;
May we, where help is needed, there
Give help as unto thee.

6 And may thy Holy Spirit move
All those who live, to live in love,
Till thou shalt greet in heaven above
All those who live to thee. Amen.

Godfrey Thring, 1823–1903

FAR OFF LANDS. 76, 76. D.
Moravian Melody
Unison, brightly
1. Re - mem - ber all the peo - ple Who live in far - off lands
In strange and love - ly cit - ies, Or roam the des - ert sands
Or farm the moun-tain pas - tures, Or till the end - less plains
Where chil - dren wade through rice-fields And watch the cam - el - trains. A-men

2 Some work in sultry forests
Where apes swing to and fro,
Some fish in mighty rivers,
Some hunt across the snow.
Remember all God's children,
Who yet have never heard
The truth that comes from Jesus,
The glory of his word.

3 God bless the men and women
Who serve him overseas;
God raise up more to help them
To set the nations free,
Till all the distant people
In every foreign place
Shall understand his kingdom
And come into his grace. Amen.

Percy Dearmer, 1867–19

ELLINGHAM. 10 10, 10 10. SAMUEL SEBASTIAN WESLEY, 1810–76

In moderate time
1. Thy king - dom come! O Fa - ther, hear our prayer;
2. Stum - bling and blind, we strive to do thy will,
Shine through the clouds that dark - en ev - ery - where;
Trust - ing the word thou sure - ly wilt ful - fill,
Thou on - ly light, thou on - ly life and joy,
That men are thine, how - ev - er far they roam,
Show us the hope that noth - ing can de - stroy.
That love shall tri - umph, and thy king - dom come. A-men.

3 Come, through the faith whereby the Church must live;
Come, through the word of truth she has to give;
Come, through her teaching, and her healing, too;
Come, through the work united hearts can do.

4 Thy kingdom come, and come thy glorious Son;
O may our task for him be nobly done!
Faithful and true let all thy servants be,
Till they shall bring all nations home to thee. Amen.

Margaret Rebecca Seebach, 1875–1948

This hymn may also be sung to NATIONAL HYMN (No. 521) or to LONGWOOD (No. 320)

WESLEY. 11 10, 11 10. LOWELL MASON, 1792–1872

FIRST TUNE

With spirit
1. Hail to the bright - ness of Zi - on's glad morn - ing,
2. Hail to the bright - ness of Zi - on's glad morn - ing,
Joy to the lands that in dark - ness have lain!
Long by the proph - ets of Is - rael fore - told;
Hushed be the ac - cents of sor - row and mourn - ing,
Hail to the mil - lions from bond - age re - turn - ing,
Zi - on in tri - umph be - gins her mild reign.
Gen - tiles and Jews the blest vi - sion be - hold.

3 Lo, in the desert rich flowers are springing,
Streams ever copious are flowing along;
Loud from the mountaintops echoes are ringing,
Wastes rise in verdure and mingle in song.

4 See, from all lands, from the isles of the ocean,
Praise to the Saviour ascending on high;
Fallen the weapons of war and commotion,
Shouts of salvation are rending the sky.

Thomas Hastings, 1784–1872

EINER IST KÖNIG. 11 10, 11 10.
JOHANN GEORG HILLE, *cir.* 1730
SECOND TUNE
With spirit
1. Hail to the bright - ness of Zi - on's glad morn - ing,
2. Hail to the bright - ness of Zi - on's glad morn - ing,
Joy to the lands that in dark - ness have lain!
Long by the proph - ets of Is - rael fore - told;
Hushed be the ac - cents of sor - row and mourn - ing,
Hail to the mil - lions from bond - age re - turn - ing,
Zi - on in tri - umph be - gins her mild reign.
Gen - tiles and Jews the blest vi - sion be - hold.

3 Lo, in the desert rich flowers are springing,
Streams ever copious are flowing along,
Loud from the mountaintops echoes are ringing,
Wastes rise in verdure and mingle in song.

4 See, from all lands, from the isles of the ocean,
Praise to the Saviour ascending on high;
Fallen the weapons of war and commotion,
Shouts of salvation are rending the sky.

Thomas Hastings, 1784–1872 a.

LONGWOOD. 10 10, 10 10. JOSEPH BARNBY, 1838–96

Quietly, with dignity

1. Her - alds of Christ, who bear the King's com - mands,
2. Through des - ert ways, dark fen, and deep mo - rass,
Im - mor - tal ti - dings in your mor - tal hands,
Through jun - gles, slug - gish seas, and moun - tain pass,
Pass on and car - ry swift the news ye bring:
Build ye the road, and fal - ter not, nor stay;
Make straight, make straight the high - way of the King.
Pre - pare a - cross the earth the King's high - way. A - men.

3 Where once the crooked trail in darkness wound
Let marching feet and joyous song resound;
Where burn the funeral pyres, and censers swing,
Make straight, make straight the highway of the King.

4 Lord, give us faith and strength the road to build,
To see the promise of the day fulfilled,
When war shall be no more and strife shall cease
Upon the highway of the Prince of Peace. Amen.

Laura Scherer Copenhaver, 1868–1940

This hymn may also be sung to NATIONAL HYMN (No. 521)

LITTLE CORNARD. 6 6, 6 6, 8 8. MARTIN SHAW, 1875–

With spirit
Org.
1. Hills of the North, re - joice; Riv - er and moun - tain - spring,
2. Isles of the south - ern seas, Deep in your cor - al caves
Hark to the ad - vent voice! Val - ley and low - land, sing! Though
Pent be each war - ring breeze, Lulled be your rest - less waves; He
ab - sent long, your Lord is nigh; He judg-ment brings, and vic - to - ry.
comes to reign with bound-less sway, And make your wastes his great high-way.

3 Lands of the East, awake!
Soon shall your sons be free;
The sleep of ages break,
And rise to liberty.
On your far hills, long cold and grey,
Has dawned the everlasting day.

4 Shores of the utmost West,
Ye that have waited long,
Unvisited, unblest,
Break forth to swelling song;
High raise the note, that Jesus died,
Yet lives and reigns, the Crucified.

5 Shout, while ye journey home!
Songs be in every mouth!
Lo, from the North we come,
From East, and West, and South:
City of God, the bond are free,
We come to live and reign in thee!

Charles Edward Oakley, 1832–65

ST. MARIA. C. M. D. WILLIAM GAWLER, *cir.* 1750–1809

Slowly, with dignity

1. E - ter - nal God, whose power up-holds Both flower and flam-ing star,
2. O God of love, whose Spir - it wakes In ev - ery hu - man breast,
To whom there is no here nor there, No time, no near nor far,
Whom love, and love a - lone, can know, In whom all hearts find rest,
No a - lien race, no for - eign shore, No child un-sought, un - known,
Help us to spread thy gra - cious reign Till greed and hate shall cease,
Oh, send us forth, thy proph-ets true, To make all lands thine own!
And kind - ness dwell in hu-man hearts, And all the earth find peace. A-men.

3 O God of truth, whom science seeks
And reverent souls adore,
Who lightest every earnest mind
Of every clime and shore,
Dispel the gloom of error's night,
Of ignorance and fear,
Until true wisdom from above
Shall make life's pathway clear.

4 O God of beauty, oft revealed
In dreams of human art,
In speech that flows to melody,
In holiness of heart;
Teach us to ban all ugliness
That blinds our eyes to thee,
Till all shall know the loveliness
Of lives made fair and free.

5 O God of righteousness and grace,
Seen in the Christ, thy Son,
Whose life and death reveal thy face,
By whom thy will was done,
Inspire thy heralds of good news
To live thy life divine,
Till Christ is formed in all mankind
And every land is thine! Amen.

Henry Hallam Tweedy, 1868–

323

GOTT SEI DANK. 7 7, 7 7. J. A. FREYLINGHAUSEN'S *Gesangbuch*, 1704

With spirit

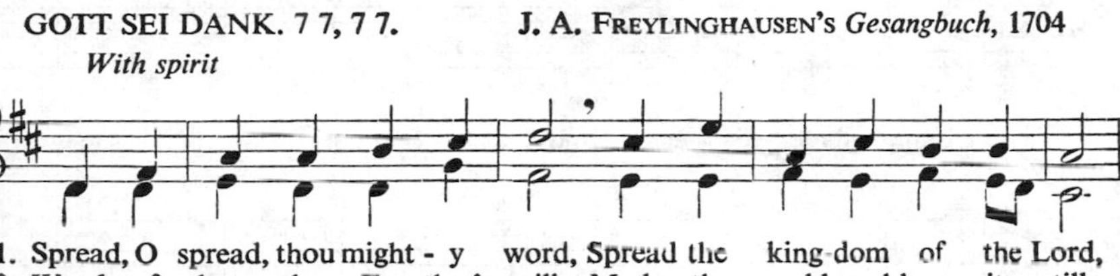
1. Spread, O spread, thou might - y word, Spread the king-dom of the Lord,
2. Word of how the Fa - ther's will Made the world, and keeps it, still;

That to earth's re - mot - est bound Men may heed the joy - ful sound;
How his on - ly Son he gave, Man from sin and death to save;

3 Word of how the Saviour's love
Earth's sore burden doth remove;
How for ever, in its need,
Through his death the world is freed;

4 Mighty word God's Spirit gave,
Man for heavenly life to save;
Word through whose all-holy might
Man can will and do the right;

5 Word of life, most pure and strong,
Word for which the nations long,
Spread abroad, until from night
All the world awakes to light.

Jonathan Friedrich Bahnmaier, 1774–1841
Tr. Catherine Winkworth, 1829–78
Revised, The Hymnal 1940

ST. MATTHEW. C. M. D.
WILLIAM CROFT, 1678–1727
In moderate time
1. Thine arm, O Lord, in days of old Was strong to heal and save;
It tri-umphed o'er dis - ease and death, O'er dark-ness and the grave;
To thee they went, the blind, the dumb, The pal - sied and the lame,
The lep - er with his taint - ed life, The sick with fev - ered frame. A-men.

2 And lo, thy touch brought life and health,
Gave speech and strength and sight;
And youth renewed and frenzy calmed
Owned thee the Lord of light;
And now, O Lord, be near to bless,
Almighty as of yore,
In crowded street, by restless couch,
As by Gennesaret's shore.

3 Be thou our great deliverer still,
Thou Lord of life and death;
Restore and quicken, soothe and bless,
With thine almighty breath.
To hands that work and eyes that see
Give wisdom's heavenly lore,
That whole and sick, and weak and strong,
May praise thee evermore. Amen.

Edward Hayes Plumptre, 1821–91

ST. CRISPIN. L. M. GEORGE J. ELVEY, 1816–93

Devotionally, in moderate time

1. Look from thy sphere of end - less day, O God of mer - cy and of might; In pit - y look on those who stray, Be - night - ed in this land of light.
2. In peo - pled vale, in lone - ly glen, In crowd - ed mart, by stream or sea, How man - y of the sons of men Hear not the mes - sage sent from thee. A - men.

3 Send forth thy heralds, Lord, to call
The thoughtless young, the hardened old,
A wandering flock, and bring them all
To the good Shepherd's peaceful fold.

4 Send them thy mighty word, to speak
Till faith shall dawn and doubt depart,
To awe the bold, to stay the weak,
And bind and heal the broken heart.

5 Then all these wastes, a dreary scene
On which, with sorrowing eyes, we gaze,
Shall grow with living waters green,
And lift to heaven the voice of praise. Amen.

William Cullen Bryant, 1794–1878 a.

HANKEY. 7 6, 7 6 D. With Refrain. WILLIAM GUSTAVUS FISCHER, 1835–1912

In moderate time

1. I love to tell the sto - ry Of un - seen things a - bove,
2. I love to tell the sto - ry, 'Tis pleas - ant to re - peat

Of Je - sus and his glo - ry, Of Je - sus and his love.
What seems, each time I tell it, More won - der - ful - ly sweet.

I love to tell the sto - ry, Be - cause I know it's true;
I love to tell the sto - ry, For some have nev - er heard

It sat - is - fies my long - ings As noth - ing else would do.
The mes - sage of sal - va - tion From God's own ho - ly word.

The Propagation of the Gospel

Refrain
I love to tell the sto - ry; 'Twill be my theme in glo - ry
To tell the old, old sto - ry Of Je - sus and his love.

3 I love to tell the story,
  For those who know it best
Seem hungering and thirsting
  To hear it like the rest.
And when, in scenes of glory,
  I sing the new, new song,
'Twill be the old, old story,
  That I have loved so long.

Katherine Hankey, 1834–1911

See also:

330 City of God, how broad and far
340 From ocean unto ocean
328 Hail to the Lord's Anointed
343 Judge eternal, throned in splendor
418 Let all the world in every corner
303 Lord of the Church
356 Mine eyes have seen the glory
547 Once to every man and nation
302 O pour thy Spirit
327 The Lord will come
329 Thy kingdom come, O God
331 Thy kingdom come! on bended knee
351 Where cross the crowded ways

The Kingdom of God

327

ST. STEPHEN (NEWINGTON). C. M. — WILLIAM JONES, 1726–1800

In moderate time

1. The Lord will come and not be slow, His foot - steps can - not err;
2. Truth from the earth, like to a flower, Shall bud and blos - som then

Be - fore him right-eous-ness shall go, His roy - al har - bin - ger.
And jus-tice, from her heaven-ly bower, Look down on mor - tal men. A-m

3 Rise, God, judge thou the earth in might,
This wicked earth redress;
For thou art he who shalt by right
The nations all possess.

4 The nations all whom thou hast mac
Shall come, and all shall frame
To bow them low before thee, Lord,
And glorify thy Name.

5 For great thou art, and wonders great
By thy strong hand are done:
Thou in thy everlasting seat
Remainest God alone. Amen.

John Milton, 1608
Psalms 82:4; 85:1–3; 86:

This hymn may also be sung to ST. FLAVIAN (No. 138)

WESTWOOD. 7 6, 7 6. D. ROBERT HYSLOP MCCARTNEY, 1844–1905

In moderate time

1. Hail to the Lord's A - noint - ed, Great Da - vid's great - er Son!
2. He comes with suc - cor speed - y To those who suf - fer wrong,
Hail, in the time ap - point - ed, His reign on earth be - gun!
To help the poor and need - y, And bid the weak be strong;
He comes to break op - pres - sion, To set the cap - tive free,
To give them songs for sigh - ing, Their dark - ness turn to light,
To take a - way trans - gres - sion, And rule in e - qui - ty.
Whose souls, con - demned and dy - ing, Were pre - cious in his sight.

3 He shall come down like showers
Upon the fruitful earth;
And love, joy, hope, like flowers,
Spring in his path to birth:
Before him on the mountains
Shall peace, the herald, go;
And righteousness in fountains
From hill to valley flow.

4 Kings shall fall down before him,
And gold and incense bring;
All nations shall adore him,
His praise all people sing:
To him shall prayer unceasing
And daily vows ascend;
His kingdom still increasing,
A kingdom without end.

James Montgomery, 1771–1854
Psalm 72

This hymn may also be sung to AURELIA (No. 285)

329

ST. CECILIA. 6 6, 6 6. LEIGHTON GEORGE HAYNE, 1836–83

Broadly

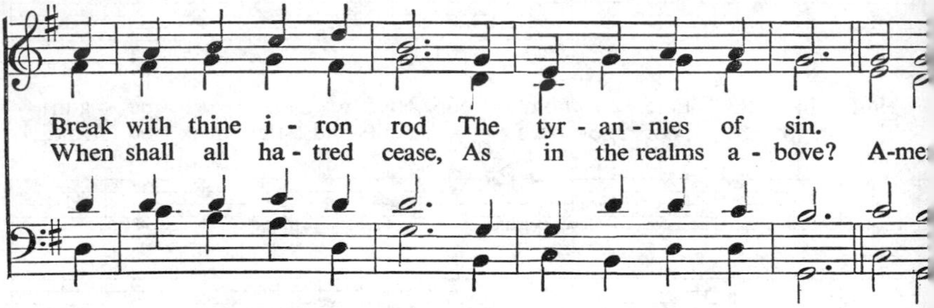

1. Thy king - dom come, O God, Thy rule, O Christ, be - gin;
Break with thine i - ron rod The tyr - an - nies of sin.

2. Where is thy reign of peace And pur - i - ty and love?
When shall all ha - tred cease, As in the realms a - bove? A-men

3 When comes the promised time
That war shall be no more,
And lust, oppression, crime,
Shall flee thy face before?

4 We pray thee, Lord, arise,
And come in thy great might;
Revive our longing eyes,
Which languish for thy sight.

5 Men scorn thy sacred Name,
And wolves devour thy fold;
By many deeds of shame
We learn that love grows cold.

6 O'er heathen lands afar
Thick darkness broodeth yet;
Arise, O Morning Star,
Arise, and never set! Amen.

Lewis Hensley, 1824–1

By permission of the Oxford University Press

330

RICHMOND (CHESTERFIELD). C. M. THOMAS HAWEIS, 1734–1820

FIRST TUNE

Broadly

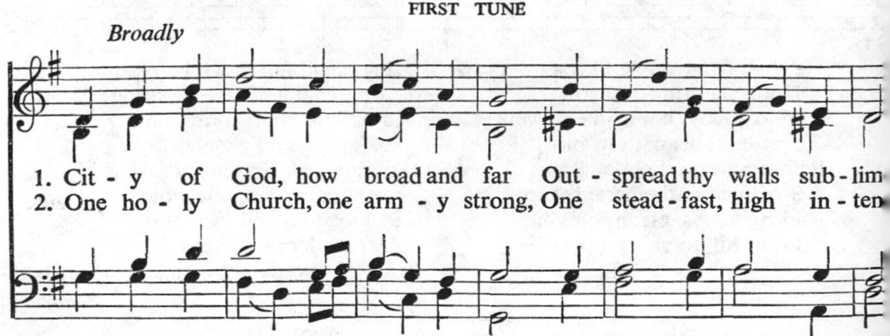
1. Cit - y of God, how broad and far Out - spread thy walls sub - lim
2. One ho - ly Church, one arm - y strong, One stead - fast, high in - ten

The true thy char - tered free - men are Of ev - ery age and clime:
One work-ing band, one har - vest-song, One King om - nip - o - tent.

How purely hath thy speech come down
From man's primeval youth!
How grandly hath thine empire grown
Of freedom, love, and truth!

4 How gleam thy watch-fires through the night
With never-fainting ray!
How rise thy towers, serene and bright,
To meet the dawning day!

5 In vain the surge's angry shock,
In vain the drifting sands:
Unharmed upon the eternal Rock
The eternal city stands.

Samuel Johnson, 1822–82

30

DAYTON. C. M. ROGER COLE WILSON, 1912-

SECOND TUNE

Broadly

1. Cit - y of God, how broad and far Out - spread thy walls sub - lime!
2. One ho - ly Church, one arm - y strong, One stead - fast, high in - tent;

The true thy char-tered free - men are Of ev - ery age and clime:
One work-ing band, one har - vest-song, One King om - nip - o - tent.

usic written for this book and copyrighted

IRISH. C. M.

Irish Folk Song
Hymns and Sacred Poems, Dublin, 1749

Devotionally, in moderate time

1. Thy king - dom come! on bend - ed knee The
2. But the slow watch - es of the night Not
pass - ing a - ges pray; And faith - ful souls have
less to God be - long; And for the ev - er-
yearned to see On earth that king - dom's day.
last - ing right The si - lent stars are strong.

3 And lo, already on the hills
The flags of dawn appear;
Gird up your loins, ye prophet souls,
Proclaim the day is near:

4 The day in whose clear-shining light
All wrong shall stand revealed,
When justice shall be throned in might,
And every hurt be healed;

5 When knowledge, hand in hand with peace,
Shall walk the earth abroad;
The day of perfect righteousness,
The promised day of God.

Frederick Lucian Hosmer, 1840-19

This hymn may also be sung to RICHMOND (No. 330)

FORD COTTAGE. 86, 86, 86. FREDERICK C. MAKER, 1844–1927

With spirit

. O ho - ly cit - y, seen of John, Where Christ, the Lamb, doth reign,
. Hark, how from men whose lives are held More cheap than mer-chan - dise,
With - in whose four-square walls shall come No night, nor need, nor pain,
From wo - men strug-gling sore for bread, From lit - tle chil - dren's cries,
And where the tears are wiped from eyes That shall not weep a - gain!
There swells the sob-bing hu - man plaint That bids thy walls a - rise!

3 Give us, O God, the strength to build
  The city that hath stood
Too long a dream, whose laws are love,
  Whose ways are brotherhood,
And where the sun that shineth is
  God's grace for human good.

4 Already in the mind of God
  That city riseth fair;
Lo, how its splendor challenges
  The souls that greatly dare,
Yea, bids us seize the whole of life
  And build its glory there.

Walter Russell Bowie, 1882–

STOCKHOLM. 11 9, 11 9, 9. Swedish Melody, 1694

With movement

1. Full man - y shall come from the east and the west And sit at the feast of sal - va - tion, With A - bra - ham I - saac, and Ja - cob the blest, O - bey - ing the Lord's in - vi - ta - tion. Have mer - cy up - on us, O Je - sus!
2. May we too give heed when our Sav - iour doth call In ac - cents per - sua - sive and ten - der, And may we be guests at his feast, one and all, Our praise and o - bei - sance to ren - der. Have mer - cy up - on us, O Je - sus! A - men

3 Then ended will be, like a dream that is past,
All trial and trouble and sorrow;
All questions and doubts will be answered at last,
When dawneth eternity's morrow.
Have mercy upon us, O Jesus!

4 Then heaven will ring with an anthem more grand
Than ever on earth was recorded,
When all of the saved shall receive at his hand
The crown to the victors awarded.
Have mercy upon us, O Jesus! Amen

Magnus Brostrup Landstad, 1802-
Tr. Peer Olsen Strömme, 1856-19
Revised, Laurence N. Field, 189

Home and Family

334

ABENDS. L. M. HERBERT STANLEY OAKELEY, 1830–1903

Devotionally, in moderate time

1. O ho - ly Lord, con - tent to fill In low - ly
2. Lead ev - ery child that bears thy Name To walk in
home the low - liest place, Thy child-hood's law a moth - er's
thine own guile - less way, To dread the touch of sin and
Org.
will, O - be - dience meek thy bright - est grace;
shame, And hum - bly, like thy - self, o - bey. A - men.

3 Gather thy lambs within thine arm,
And gently in thy bosom bear;
Keep them, O Lord, from hurt and harm,
And bid them rest forever there.

4 So shall they waiting here below,
Like thee their Lord, a little span,
In wisdom and in stature grow,
And favor with both God and man.
Amen.

William Walsham How, 1823–97

ST. HUGH. C.M. English Traditional Melody

Brightly

1. Sing to the Lord the chil-dren's hymn, His gen - tle love de - clare,
2. He at a moth-er's breast was fed, Though God's own Son was he;

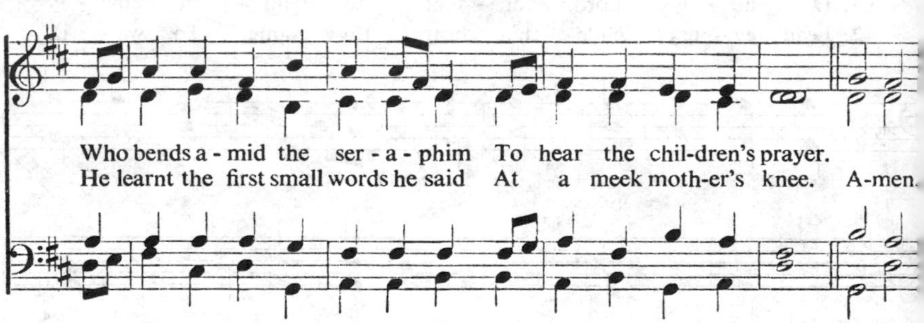

Who bends a - mid the ser - a - phim To hear the chil-dren's prayer.
He learnt the first small words he said At a meek moth-er's knee. A-men.

3 He held us to his mighty breast,
The children of the earth;
He lifted up his hands and blessed
The babes of human birth.

4 Lo! from the stars his face will turn
On us with glances mild;
The angels of his presence yearn
To bless the little child.

5 Keep us, O Jesus Lord, for thee,
That so by thy dear grace
We, children of the font, may see
Our heavenly Father's face. Amen.

Robert Stephen Hawker, 1804–7

336

ALINE. 11 10, 11 10. John Victor Bergquist 1877–1935

Brightly, in moderate tempo

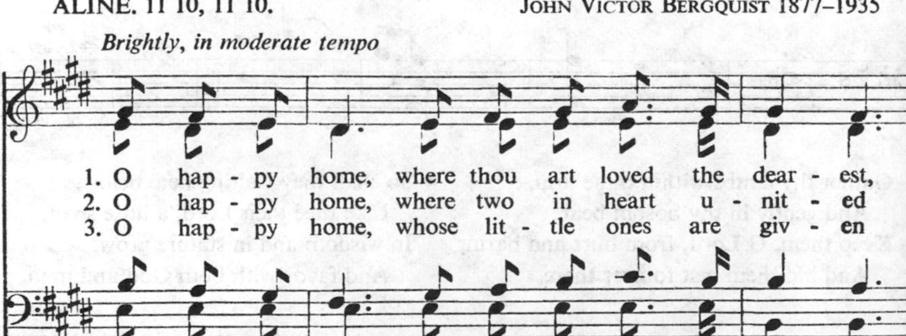
1. O hap - py home, where thou art loved the dear - est,
2. O hap - py home, where two in heart u - nit - ed
3. O hap - py home, whose lit - tle ones are giv - en

Thou lov - ing Friend, and Sav - iour of our race,
In ho - ly faith and bless - ed hope are one,
Ear - ly to thee, in hum - ble faith and prayer,
And where a - mong the guests there nev - er com - eth
Whom death a lit - tle while a - lone di - vid - eth,
To thee, their friend, who from the heights of heav - en
One who can hold such high and hon - ored place.
And can - not end the un - ion here be - gun.
Dost guide and guard with more than moth - er's care.

4 O happy home, where each one serves thee, lowly,
Whatever his appointed work may be,
Till every common task seems great and holy,
When it is done, O Lord, as unto thee.

5 O happy home, where thou art not forgotten
When joy is overflowing, full and free;
O happy home, where every wounded spirit
Is brought, O great Physician, unto thee;

6 Until at last, when earthly toil is ended,
All meet thee in the blessèd home above,
From whence thou camest, where thou hast ascended,
Thy everlasting home of peace and love.

Karl Johann Philipp Spitta, 1801–59
Tr. Sarah Borthwick Findlater, 1823–1907

See also:

Travellers

337

CAIRNBROOK. 8 5, 8 3. EBENEZER PROUT, 1835–1909

Slowly, and softly

1. Ho - ly Fa - ther, in thy mer - cy Hear our anx - ious prayer;
2. Je - sus, Sav - iour, let thy pres - ence Be their light and guide;
Keep our loved ones, now far dis - tant, 'Neath thy care.
Keep, O keep them, in their weak - ness, At thy side. A-men.

3 When in sorrow, when in danger,
When in loneliness,
In thy love look down and comfort
Their distress.

4 May the joy of thy salvation
Be their strength and stay;
May they love and may they praise thee
Day by day.

5 Holy Spirit, let thy teaching
Sanctify their life;
Send thy grace that they may conquer
In the strife.

6 Father, Son and Holy Spirit,
God the One in Three,
Bless them, guide them, save them, keep [them
Near to thee. Amen.

Isabella S. Stephenson, 1843–9

MELITA. 8 8, 8 8, 8 8. JOHN BACCHUS DYKES, 1823–76

With dignity

1. E - ter - nal Fa-ther! strong to save, Whose arm hath bound the rest - less wave,
2. O Sav - iour, whose al - might - y word The winds and waves sub - mis - sive heard,
Who bidd'st the might-y o - cean deep Its own ap - point-ed lim - its keep:
Who walk - edst on the foam - ing deep, And calm a - mid the storm didst sleep:
O hear us when we cry to thee For those in per - il on the sea.
O hear us when we cry to thee For those in per - il on the sea. A-men.

3 O sacred Spirit, who didst brood
Upon the chaos dark and rude,
Who bad'st its angry tumult cease,
And gavest light and life and peace:
O hear us when we cry to thee
For those in peril on the sea.

4 O Trinity of Love and Power,
Our brethren shield in danger's hour;
From rock and tempest, fire and foe,
Protect them wheresoe'er they go;
Thus evermore shall rise to thee
Glad hymns of praise from land and sea.
Amen.

William Whiting, 1825–78

See also:

576 Abide with me, fast falls
471 Come, O thou Traveler unknown
565 Forward! be our watchword
209 God of our life, all-glorious
520 Guide me, O thou great Jehovah
478 He leadeth me
563 He who would valiant be
531 Jesus, Saviour, pilot me
532 Jesus, still lead on
191 Lord, dismiss us
170 Lord of all being, throned
231 Now the day is over

City, Nation, World

339

DARWALL'S 148TH. 6 6, 6 6, 4 4, 4 4. JOHN DARWALL, 1731–89

With dignity

1. Before the Lord we bow, The God who reigns above, And rules the world below, Boundless in power and love. Our thanks we bring In joy and praise, Our hearts we raise To heaven's high King.
2. The nation thou hast blest May well thy love declare, From foes and fears at rest, Protected by thy care. For this fair land, For this bright day, Our thanks we pay—Gifts of thy hand.
3. May every mountain height, Each vale and forest green, Shine in thy word's pure light, And its rich fruits be seen! May every tongue Be tuned to praise, And join to raise A grateful song.

4 Earth, hear thy Maker's voice,
Thy great Redeemer own;
Believe, obey, rejoice,
And worship him alone,
Cast down thy pride,
Thy sin deplore,
And bow before
The Crucified.

5 And when in power he comes,
O may our native land,
From all its rending tombs,
Send forth a glorious band,
A countless throng,
Ever to sing
To heaven's high King
Salvation's song.

Francis Scott Key, 1779–1843

This hymn may also be sung to CROFT'S 136TH (No. 238)

MUNICH (MEININGEN). 76, 76. D. Meiningen *Gesangbuch*, 1693
Adapted and harmonized by FELIX MENDELSSOHN, 1809–47

1. From o - cean un - to o - cean Our land shall own thee Lord,
2. O Christ, for thine own glo - ry, And for our coun - try's weal,
And, filled with true de - vo - tion, O - bey thy sov-ereign word,
We hum - bly plead be - fore thee, Thy - self in us re - veal;
Our prai - ries and our moun-tains, For - est and fer - tile field,
And may we know, Lord Je - sus, The touch of thy dear hand,
Our riv - ers, lakes, and foun-tains, To thee shall trib - ute yield.
And, healed of our dis - eas - es, The temp-ter's power with-stand. A-men.

3 Our Saviour King, defend us,
And guide where we should go;
Forth, with thy message send us,
Thy love and light to show;
Till, fired with true devotion
Enkindled by thy word,
From ocean unto ocean
Our land shall own thee Lord. Amen.

Robert Murray, 1832–1910

This hymn may also be sung to WEBB (No. 551)

ST. GEORGE'S, WINDSOR. 7 7, 7 7. D. GEORGE J. ELVEY, 1816–93

With spirit

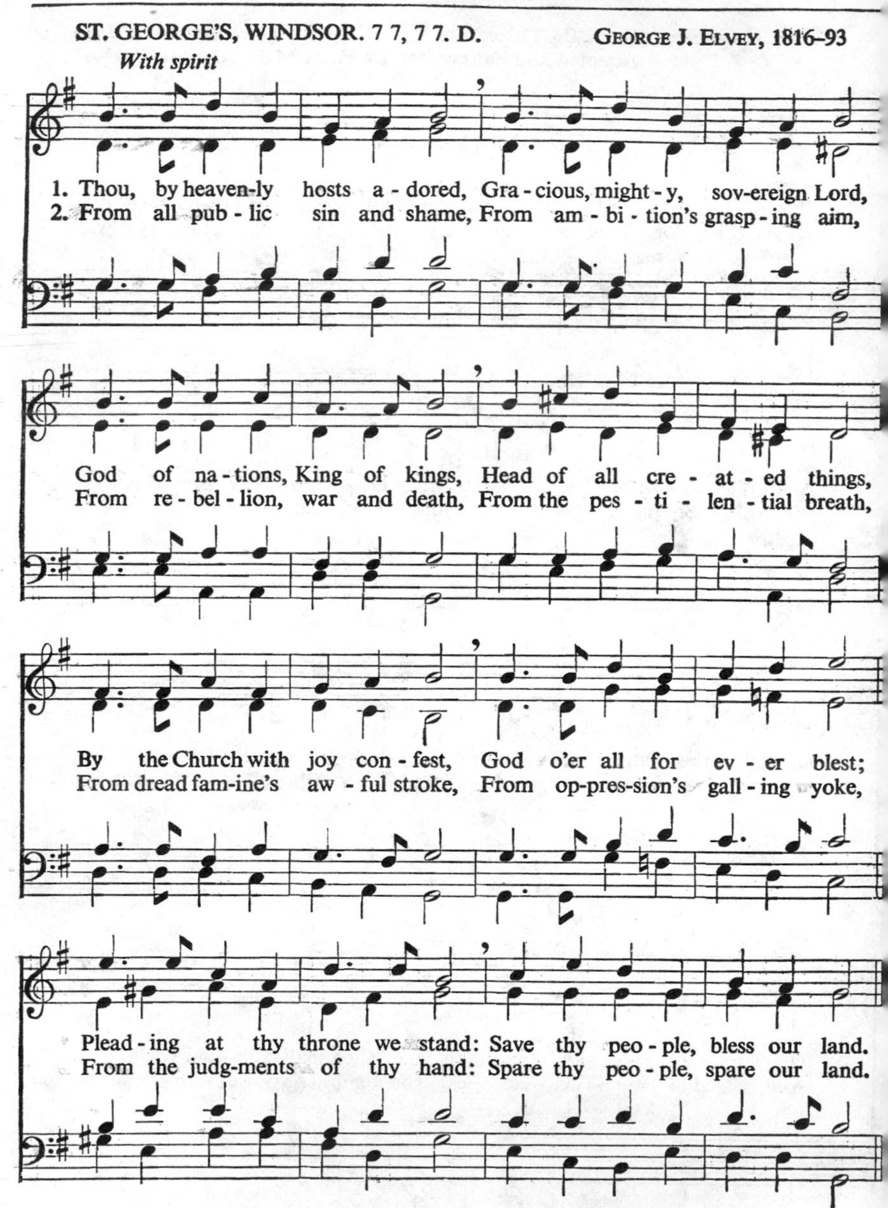
1. Thou, by heaven-ly hosts a - dored, Gra - cious, might - y, sov-ereign Lord,
2. From all pub - lic sin and shame, From am - bi - tion's grasp - ing aim,
God of na - tions, King of kings, Head of all cre - at - ed things,
From re - bel - lion, war and death, From the pes - ti - len - tial breath,
By the Church with joy con - fest, God o'er all for ev - er blest;
From dread fam-ine's aw - ful stroke, From op-pres-sion's gall - ing yoke,
Plead - ing at thy throne we stand: Save thy peo - ple, bless our land.
From the judg-ments of thy hand: Spare thy peo - ple, spare our land.

3 Let our rulers ever be
Men that love and honor thee;
Let the powers by thee ordained
Be in righteousness maintained;
In the people's hearts increase
Love of piety and peace;
Thus united, we shall stand
One wide, free, and happy land.

Henry Harbaugh, 1817–67

This hymn may also be sung to SALZBURG (No. 414) or TICHFIELD (No. 55)

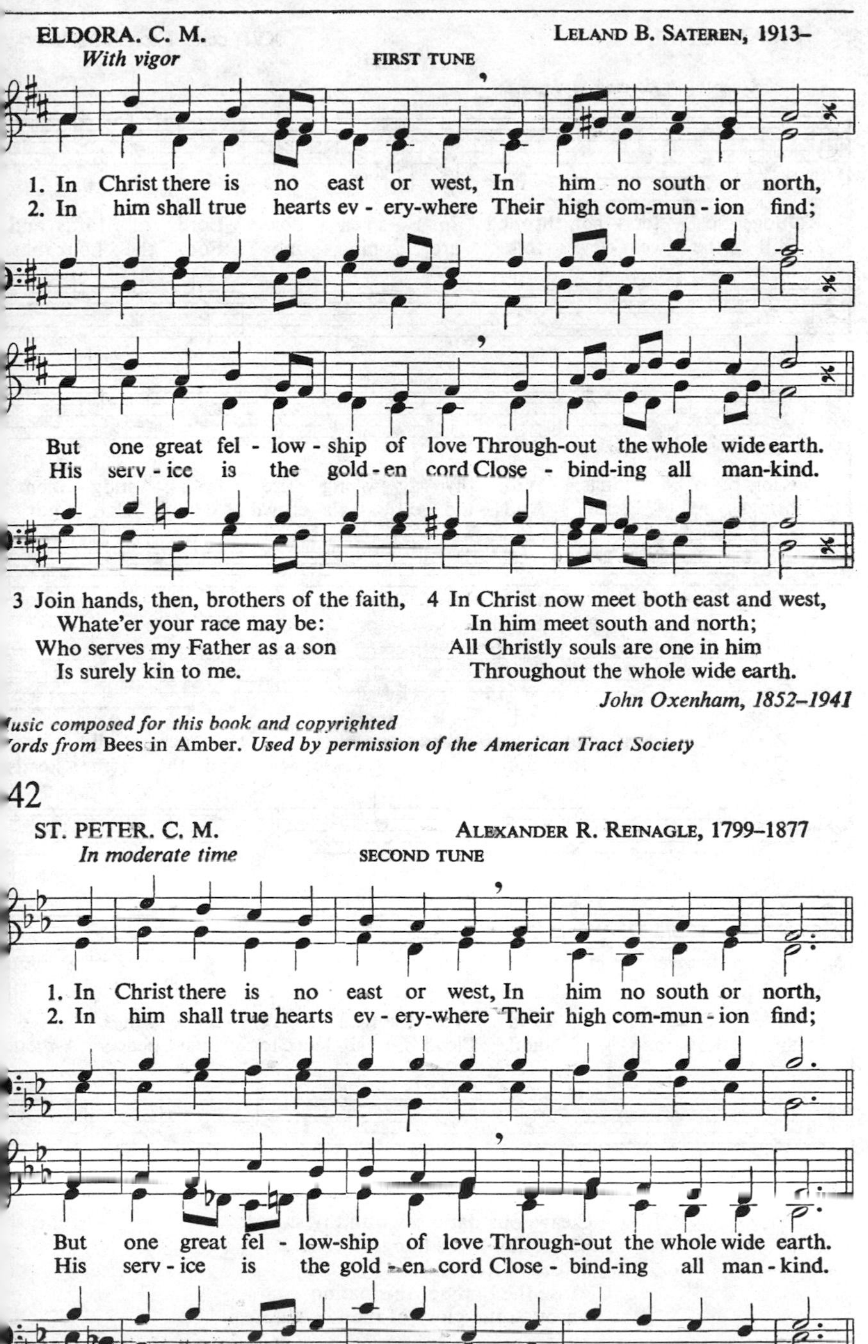
ELDORA. C. M.
LELAND B. SATEREN, 1913–
With vigor
FIRST TUNE
1. In Christ there is no east or west, In him no south or north,
2. In him shall true hearts ev - ery-where Their high com-mun - ion find;
But one great fel - low - ship of love Through-out the whole wide earth.
His serv - ice is the gold - en cord Close - bind-ing all man-kind.
3 Join hands, then, brothers of the faith,
Whate'er your race may be:
Who serves my Father as a son
Is surely kin to me.
4 In Christ now meet both east and west,
In him meet south and north;
All Christly souls are one in him
Throughout the whole wide earth.
John Oxenham, 1852–1941
Music composed for this book and copyrighted
Words from Bees in Amber. Used by permission of the American Tract Society
342
ST. PETER. C. M.
ALEXANDER R. REINAGLE, 1799–1877
In moderate time
SECOND TUNE
1. In Christ there is no east or west, In him no south or north,
2. In him shall true hearts ev - ery-where Their high com-mun - ion find;
But one great fel - low-ship of love Through-out the whole wide earth.
His serv - ice is the gold - en cord Close - bind-ing all man - kind.

PICARDY. 8 7, 8 7, 8 7. **XVII cent. French Melody**

FIRST TUNE

Unison, in flowing style.

1. Judge e - ter - nal, throned in splen - dor, Lord of lords and King of kings, With thy liv - ing fire of judg - ment Purge this land of bit - ter things; Sol - ace all its wide do-min - ion With the heal - ing of thy wings.
2. Still the wea - ry folk are pin - ing For the hour that brings re - lease, And the cit - y's crowd - ed clan - gor Cries a - loud for sin to cease; And the home - steads and the wood - lands Plead in si - lence for their peace. A-men.

3 Crown, O God, thine own endeavor;
Cleave our darkness with thy sword;
Feed the faint and hungry heathen
With the richness of thy word;
Cleanse the body of this nation
Through the glory of the Lord. Amen.

Henry Scott Holland, 1847–19

RHUDDLAN. 8 7, 8 7, 8 7.
Welsh Traditional Melody
SECOND TUNE
Moderately slow
1. Judge e - ter - nal, throned in splen - dor, Lord of lords and
2. Still the wea - ry folk are pin - ing For the hour that
King of kings, With thy liv - ing fire of judg - ment
brings re - lease, And the cit - y's crowd - ed clan - gor
Purge this land of bit - ter things; Sol - ace all its
Cries a - loud for sin to cease; And the home-steads
wide do - min - ion With the heal - ing of thy wings.
and the wood-lands Plead in si - lence for their peace. A-men.

3 Crown, O God, thine own endeavor;
    Cleave our darkness with thy sword;
Feed the faint and hungry heathen
    With the richness of thy word;
Cleanse the body of this nation
    Through the glory of the Lord. Amen.

Henry Scott Holland, 1847-1918

LLANGLOFFAN. 7 6, 7 6. D. Welsh Hymn Melody

In moderate time FIRST TUNE

1. O God of earth and al - tar, Bow down and hear our cry,
2. From all that ter - ror teach - es, From lies of tongue and pen,
Our earth - ly rul - ers fal - ter, Our peo - ple drift and die;
From all the eas - y speech - es That com - fort cru - el men,
The walls of gold en - tomb us, The swords of scorn di - vide,
From sale and prof - a - na - tion Of hon - or, and the sword,
Take not thy thun - der from us, But take a - way our pride.
From sleep and from dam - na - tion, De - liv - er us, good Lord! A-men.

3 Tie in a living tether
The prince and priest and thrall,
Bind all our lives together,
Smite us and save us all;
In ire and exultation,
Aflame with faith, and free,
Lift up a living nation,
A single sword to thee. Amen.

Gilbert Keith Chesterton, 1874–193

KING'S LYNN. 7 6, 7 6. D.

Traditional English Melody
Arr. by R. VAUGHAN WILLIAMS, 1872–1958

In unison, with dignity SECOND TUNE

1. O God of earth and al - tar, Bow down and hear our cry,
2. From all that ter - ror teach - es, From lies of tongue and pen,
Our earth - ly rul - ers fal - ter, Our peo - ple drift and die;
From all the eas - y speech - es That com-fort cru - el men,
The walls of gold en - tomb us, The swords of scorn di - vide,
From sale and prof - a - na - tion Of hon - or, and the sword,
Take not thy thun-der from us, But take a - way our pride.
From sleep and from dam - na - tion, De - liv - er us, good Lord! A-men.

3 Tie in a living tether
The prince and priest and thrall,
Bind all our lives together,
Smite us and save us all;

In ire and exultation,
Aflame with faith, and free,
Lift up a living nation,
A single sword to thee. Amen.

Gilbert Keith Chesterton, 1874–1936

GENEVA. 87, 87. D. GEORGE HENRY DAY, 1883–

Broadly

1. Not a - lone for might - y em - pire Stretch-ing far o'er
2. Not for bat - tle - ship and for - tress, Not for con - quests
land and sea, Not a - lone for boun - teous har - vests, Lift we
of the sword, But for con-quests of the spir - it Give we
up our hearts to thee: Stand - ing in the liv - ing pres - ent,
thanks to thee, O Lord; For the her - i - tage of free-dom,

Mem - o - ry and hope be - tween, Lord, we would with
For the home, the church, the school, For the o - pen
deep thanks-giv - ing Praise thee most for things un - seen.
door to man - hood In a land the peo - ple rule. A-men.

3 For the armies of the faithful,
Souls that passed and left no name;
For the glory that illumines
Patriot lives of deathless fame;
For our prophets and apostles,
Loyal to the living word,
For all heroes of the spirit,
Give we thanks to thee, O Lord.

4 God of justice, save the people
From the clash of race and creed,
From the strife of class and faction,
Make our nation free indeed;
Keep her faith in simple manhood
Strong as when her life began,
Till it find its full fruition
In the brotherhood of man! Amen.

William Pierson Merrill, 1867–1954

This hymn may also be sung to HYFRYDOL (No. 397)

MATERNA. C. M. D.
Samuel A. Ward, 1848–1903
With spirit
1. O beau - ti - ful for spa - cious skies, For am - ber waves of grain,
2. O beau - ti - ful for pil - grim feet, Whose stern, im - pas-sioned stress
For pur - ple moun-tain maj - es - ties A - bove the fruit - ed plain!
A thor - ough-fare for free - dom beat A - cross the wil - der - ness!
A - mer - i - ca! A - mer - i - ca! God shed his grace on thee,
A - mer - i - ca! A - mer - i - ca! God mend thine ev - ery flaw,
And crown thy good with broth - er - hood From sea to shin - ing sea.
Con - firm thy soul in self - con - trol, Thy lib - er - ty in law.

3 O beautiful for heroes proved
In liberating strife,
Who more than self their country loved,
And mercy more than life!
America! America!
May God thy gold refine,
Till all success be nobleness,
And every gain divine.

4 O beautiful for patriot dream
That sees, beyond the years,
Thine alabaster cities gleam,
Undimmed by human tears!
America! America!
God shed his grace on thee,
And crown thy good with brotherhood
From sea to shining sea.

Katherine Lee Bates, 1859–19

ST. MATTHIAS. 8 8, 8 8, 8 8. WILLIAM HENRY MONK, 1823–89

Broadly

1. God of our fa-thers, known of old, Lord of our far-flung bat - tle - line,
2. The tu-mult and the shout-ing dies; The cap-tains and the kings de - part;
Be-neath whose aw - ful hand we hold Do - min-ion o - ver palm and pine;
Still stands thine an- cient sac - ri - fice, An hum-ble and a con - trite heart.
Lord God of hosts, be with us yet, Lest we for-get—lest we for-get!
Lord God of hosts, be with us yet, Lest we for-get—lest we for-get! A-men!

3 Far-called, our navies melt away;
  On dune and headland sinks the fire:
Lo, all our pomp of yesterday
  Is one with Nineveh and Tyre!
Judge of the nations, spare us yet,
Lest we forget—lest we forget!

4 If, drunk with sight of power, we loose
  Wild tongues that have not thee in awe,
Such boastings as the Gentiles use,
  Or lesser breeds without the law—
Lord God of hosts, be with us yet,
Lest we forget—lest we forget!

5 For heathen heart that puts her trust
  In reeking tube and iron shard,
All valiant dust that builds on dust,
  And, guarding, calls not thee to guard,
For frantic boast and foolish word—
Thy mercy on thy people, Lord! Amen.

Rudyard Kipling, 1865–1936

This hymn may also be sung to VATER UNSER (No. 359)

OLD 124th. 10 10, 10 10, 10. Melody in *Genevan Psalter*, 1551

Broadly, with dignity

1. Turn back, O man, for - swear thy fool - ish ways. Old now is earth, and none may count her days, Yet thou, her child, whose head is crowned with flame, Still wilt not hear thine in - ner God pro - claim, 'Turn back, O man, for - swear thy fool - ish ways.'
2. Earth might be fair, and all men glad and wise. Age af - ter age their tra - gic em - pires rise, Built while they dream, and in that dream - ing weep: Would man but wake from out his haunt - ed sleep, Earth might be fair, and all men glad and wise.

3 Earth shall be fair, and all her people one;
Nor till that hour shall God's whole will be done.
Now, even now, once more from earth to sky,
Peals forth in joy man's old, undaunted cry,
'Earth shall be fair, and all her folk be one!'

Clifford Bax, 1886

PAX (KILGORE). 8 7, 8 7, 7 7. CLIVE HAROLD KILGORE, 1889–

1. God of peace, in peace pre - serve us, Hear us, mer - ci - ful Lord God! Let no lust for pow - er swerve us From the way our Mas - ter trod. Guard - ed by thy might - y hand, Safe and free our peo - ple stand.
2. God of love, if foe - men face us Armed with weap - ons forged in hate, Let not pride nor greed de - base us; All our ef - forts con - se - crate That the wrong shall be made right In thy Spir - it, by thy might. A - men.

3 God of mercy, bid the terrors
Of inhuman strife to cease;
Overrule our grievous errors
By thy scepter, Prince of Peace.
Let thine angels speak again,
'Peace on earth, good will toward men.' Amen.

Ernst William Olson, 1870–1958

Music composed for this book and copyrighted

SONG 1. 10 10, 10 10, 10 10. ORLANDO GIBBONS, 1583–1625

In moderate time

1. E - ter - nal Rul - er of the cease-less round Of cir - cling plan-ets
2. We are of thee, the chil-dren of thy love, The broth-ers of thy
sing-ing on their way, Guide of the na - tions from the night pro-foun
well-be - lov - ed Son; De - scend, O Ho - ly Spir - it, like a dove
In - to the glo - ry of the per-fect day: Rule in our hearts, tha
In - to our hearts, that we may be as one; As one with thee, to
we may ev - er be Guid - ed and strength-ened and up-held by thee.
whom we ev - er tend, As one with him, our broth-er and our friend. A-me

3 We would be one in hatred of all wrong,
One in our love of all things sweet and fair,
One with the joy that breaketh into song,
One with the grief that trembleth into prayer,
One in the power that makes the children free
To follow truth, and thus to follow thee.

4 O clothe us with thy heavenly armor, Lord,
Thy trusty shield, thy sword of love divine;
Our inspiration be thy constant word,
We ask no victories that are not thine;
Give or withhold, let pain or pleasure be,
Enough to know that we are serving thee. Amen.

John White Chadwick, 1840–19

51

WALTON (GERMANY). L. M. — WILLIAM GARDINER, 1770–1853

In moderate time

1. Where cross the crowd - ed ways of life, Where sound the
2. In haunts of wretch - ed - ness and need, On shad - owed
cries of race and clan, A - bove the noise of sel - fish
thresh - olds dark with fears, From paths where hide the lures of
strife, We hear thy voice, O Son of Man.
greed, We catch the vi - sion of thy tears. A - men.

From tender childhood's helplessness,
From woman's grief, man's burdened toil,
From famished souls, from sorrow's stress,
Thy heart has never known recoil.

The cup of water given for thee
Still holds the freshness of thy grace;
Yet long these multitudes to see
The sweet compassion of thy face.

5 O Master, from the mountain side,
Make haste to heal these hearts of pain;
Among these restless throngs abide,
O tread the city's streets again;

6 Till sons of men shall learn thy love,
And follow where thy feet have trod;
Till glorious from thy heaven above,
Shall come the city of our God. Amen.

Frank Mason North, 1850–1935

This hymn may also be sung to THANKSGIVING (No. 117)

PAX (ACK, BLIV HOS OSS). L. M. Swedish *Koralbok*, 1697

FIRST TUNE

Devotionally
1. O God of love, O King of peace, Make wars through out the world to cease; The wrath of sin - ful man re - strain; Give peace, O God, give peace a - gain.
2. Re - mem - ber, Lord, thy works of old, The won - ders that our fa - thers told; Re - mem - ber not our sin's dark stain; Give peace, O God, give peace a - gain. A - men.

3 Whom shall we trust but thee, O Lord?
Where rest but on thy faithful word?
None ever called on thee in vain;
Give peace, O God, give peace again.

4 Where saints and angels dwell above,
All hearts are knit in holy love;
O bind us in that heavenly chain;
Give peace, O God, give peace again. Amen.

Henry Williams Baker, 1821–

ST. GREGORY. L. M.

König's *Choralbuch,* 1738
Alt. by William H. Monk, 1823–89

Broadly

SECOND TUNE

1. O God of love, O King of peace, Make wars through - out the world to cease; The wrath of sin - ful man re - strain; Give peace, O God, give peace a - gain.
2. Re - mem - ber, Lord, thy works of old, The won - ders that our fa - thers told; Re - mem - ber not our sin's dark stain; Give peace, O God, give peace a - gain. A-men.

3 Whom shall we trust but thee, O Lord?
Where rest but on thy faithful word?
None ever called on thee in vain;
Give peace, O God, give peace again.

4 Where saints and angels dwell above,
All hearts are knit in holy love;
O bind us in that heavenly chain;
Give peace, O God, give peace again. Amen.

Henry Williams Baker, 1821–77

This hymn may also be sung to QUEBEC (HESPERUS) (No. 370)

MOUNT AIRY. 9 8, 9 8, 8 6.
LUTHER D. REED, 1873–
Harm. by LELAND B. SATEREN, 1913–
Unison, with dignity
1. O God of won - drous grace and glo - ry, Whose law is love, Whose love is life; We wor - ship thee, we bow be - fore thee In days of calm, in hours of strife.
2. Strong Son of God, who liv - est ev - er, Whom death and hell could not con - tain, Who stooped to serve, yet reign - est ev - er; Up - hold the right; let truth re - main.

City, Nation, World

1-3.
In thee we trust; bless thou our land; Our times are
For-give our sins; our lives com-mand; Our times are
4. Give
in thy hand.
4.
peace in our time, O Lord. A-men.

3 O Holy Spirit, pure and mighty,
Whose breath revives the souls of men;
Cleanse thou our hearts, inspire us rightly
To live, and learn, and love again.
We would not build on sinking sand;
Our times are in thy hand.

4 O God, whose grace and power supernal
Endure, though time itself decay,
Our strength renew, with life eternal
Crown all who seek and find the way.
Thy word, O God, the Spirit's sword,
Give peace in our time, O Lord. Amen.

Luther D. Reed, 1873–

Music composed for this book and copyrighted

RUSSIAN HYMN. 11 10, 11 9. ALEXIS FEODOROVICH LWOFF (LVOV), 1799–1870

Majestically

1. God the Om - nip - o - tent! King, who or - dain - est Great winds thy clar - i - ons, light-nings thy sword; Show forth thy pit - y on high where thou reign-est: Give to us peace in our time, O Lord.
2. God the All - mer - ci - ful! earth hath for - sak - en Meek - ness and mer - cy, and slight - ed thy word; Bid not thy wrath in its ter - rors a - wak - en: Give to us peace in our time, O Lord. A-men

3 God the All-righteous One! man hath defied thee,
Yet to eternity standeth thy word;
Falsehood and wrong shall not tarry beside thee:
Give to us peace in our time, O Lord.

4 God the All-wise! by the fire of thy chastening
Earth shall to freedom and truth be restored;
Through the thick darkness thy kingdom is hastening:
Thou wilt give peace in thy time, O Lord.

5 So shall thy children with thankful devotion
Praise him who saved them from peril and sword,
Singing in chorus from ocean to ocean:
'Peace to the nations, and praise to the Lord.' Amen.

Henry F. Chorley, 1808–7.
John Ellerton, 1826–9.

MEIRIONYDD. 7 6, 7 6. D. Welsh Hymn Melody

In moderate time

1. Where rest - less crowds are throng - ing A - long the cit - y ways,
Where pride and greed and tur - moil Con - sume the fe - vered days,
Where vain am - bi - tions ban - ish All thoughts of praise and prayer,
The peo - ple's spir - its wav - er: But thou, O Christ, art there. A-men.

2 In scenes of want and sorrow
And haunts of flagrant wrong,
In homes where kindness falters
And strife and fear are strong,
In busy street of barter,
In lonely thoroughfare,
The people's spirits languish:
But thou, O Christ, art there.

3 O Christ, behold thy people—
They press on every hand!
Bring light to all the cities
Of our belovèd land.
May all our bitter striving
Give way to visions fair
Of righteousness and justice:
For thou, O Christ, art there. Amen.

Thomas Curtis Clark, 1877–1953

BATTLE HYMN, With Refrain. 15 15 15, 6. WILLIAM STEFFE, 1852

Slowly, in unison

1. Mine eyes have seen the glo - ry of the com - ing of
2. He has sound - ed forth the trum - pet that shall nev - er call
the Lord; He is tramp-ling out the vin - tage where the grapes of
re - treat; He is sift - ing out the hearts of men be - fore his
wrath are stored; He hath loosed the fate - ful light - ning of his
judg - ment - seat; O be swift, my soul, to an - swer him; be

[Harmony]
ter - ri - ble swift sword: His truth is march - ing on.
ju - bi - lant, my feet! Our God is march - ing on.
Glo - ry, glo - ry, Hal - le - lu - jah! Glo - ry, glo - ry, Hal - le - lu - jah!
Glo - ry, glo - ry, Hal - le - lu - jah! His truth is march - ing on.

3 In the beauty of the lilies Christ was born across the sea,
With a glory in his bosom that transfigures you and me:
As he died to make men holy, let us die to make men free,
While God is marching on.

Julia Ward Howe, 1819–1910

357

DEUS FORTIS. 10 10, 5 5, 5 5, 3.
With dignity

Norwegian Melody
Arr. by LELAND B. SATEREN, 1913–

1. Might - y God, to thy dear Name be giv - en
2. God is God, though all the earth lay wast - ed;
High - est praise o'er all the earth and heav - en.
God is God, though all men death had tast - ed.
All souls dis - tress - ed, All men op - press - ed,
While na - tions stum - ble, In dark - ness fum - ble,
Their voic - es rais - ing, U - nite in prais - ing Thy glo - ry.
By stars sur - round - ed, Count-less a - bound - eth God's har - vest.

3 Highest hills and deepest vales shall vanish,
Earth and heaven both alike be banished.
As in the dawning
Of every morning
The sun appeareth,
So glorious neareth
God's kingdom.

Petter Dass, 1647–1707
Tr. D. Eivind J. Berggrav, 1884–1959

NATIONAL ANTHEM. 6 6 4, 6 6 6 4. *Thesaurus Musicus*, 1744

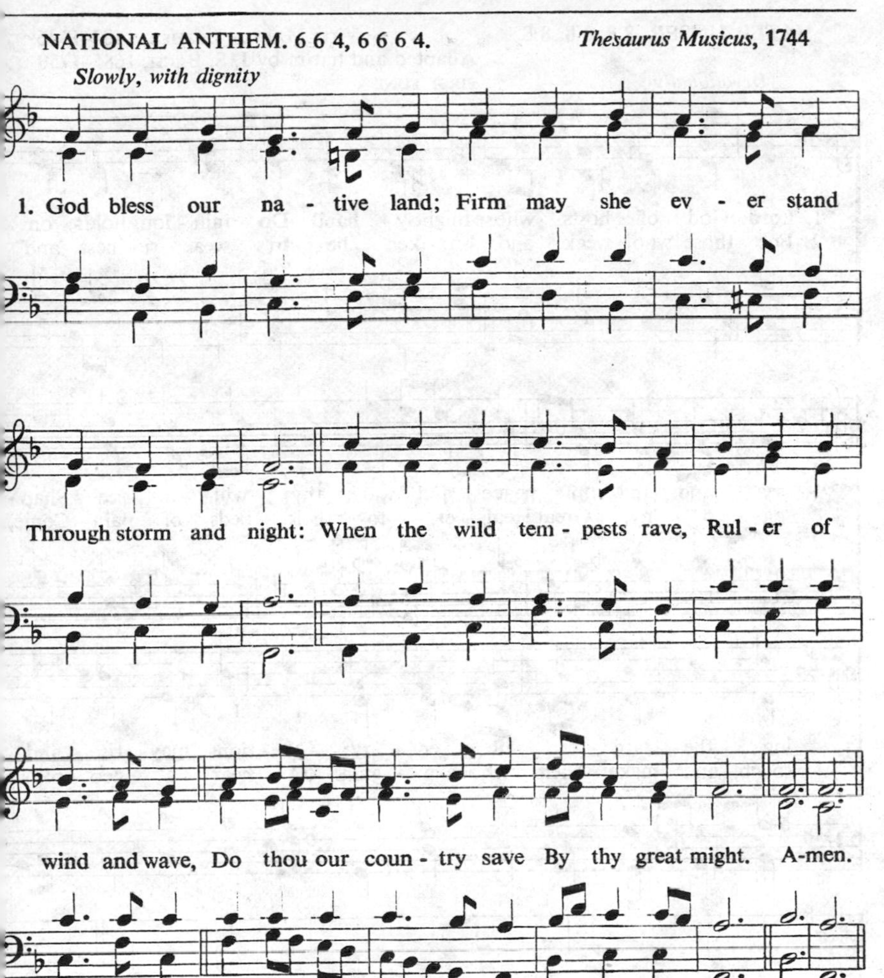
Slowly, with dignity
1. God bless our na - tive land; Firm may she ev - er stand
Through storm and night: When the wild tem - pests rave, Rul - er of
wind and wave, Do thou our coun - try save By thy great might. A-men.

2 For her our prayers shall rise
To God above the skies;
On him we wait.
Thou who art ever nigh,
Guarding with watchful eye,
To thee aloud we cry,
God save the state! Amen.

Based on a German Hymn by Siegfried August Mahlmann, 1771–1826
Charles Timothy Brooks, 1813–83
John S. Dwight, 1813–93

For a higher setting of this tune see No. 360

VATER UNSER. 8 8, 8 8, 8 8.

Arr. MARTIN LUTHER, 1483–1546
Adapted and harm. by J. S. BACH, 1685–1750

FIRST TUNE

Devotionally
1. Lord God of hosts, whose might-y hand Do - min - ion holds on
2. For those who weak and bro - ken lie In wea - ri - ness and
sea and land, In peace and war thy will we see Shap -
ag - o - ny, Great Heal - er, to their beds of pain Come,
ing the larg - er lib - er - ty; Na - tions may rise and
touch, and make them whole a - gain. O hear a peo - ple's
na - tions fall, Thy change - less pur - pose rules them all.
prayers, and bless Thy serv - ants in their hour of stress. A - men.

3 For those to whom the call shall come,
We pray thy tender welcome home;
The toil, the bitterness, all past,
We trust them to thy love at last.
O hear a people's prayers for all
Who, nobly striving, nobly fall.

4 For those who minister and heal,
And spend themselves, their skill, their zeal
Renew their hearts with Christ-like faith,
And guard them from disease and death;
And in thine own good time, Lord, send
Thy peace on earth till time shall end.
Amen

John Oxenham, 1852–1941

SURREY (CAREY). 8 8, 8 8, 8 8. HENRY CAREY, 1692–1743

SECOND TUNE

1. Lord God of hosts, whose might - y hand Do - min - ion
In peace and war thy will we see Shap - ing the
holds on sea and land, Na-tions may rise and na - tions
larg er lib - er - ty;
fall, Thy change-less pur - pose rules them all. A - men.

2 For those who weak and broken lie
In weariness and agony,
Great Healer, to their beds of pain
Come, touch and make them whole again.
O hear a people's prayers, and bless
Thy servants in their hour of stress.

3 For those to whom the call shall come,
We pray thy tender welcome home;
The toil, the bitterness, all past,
We trust them to thy love at last.
O hear a people's prayers for all
Who, nobly striving, nobly fall.

4 For those who minister and heal,
And spend themselves, their skill, their zeal;
Renew their hearts with Christ-like faith,
And guard them from disease and death;
And in thine own good time, Lord, send
Thy peace on earth till time shall end. Amen.

John Oxenham, 1852–1941

AMERICA. 6 6 4, 6 6 6 4.
Thesaurus Musicus, 1744
With dignity
1. My coun-try, 'tis of thee, Sweet land of lib-er-ty,
2. My na-tive coun-try, thee, Land of the no-ble free,
Of thee I sing: Land where my fa-thers died, Land of the
Thy name I love; I love thy rocks and rills, Thy woods and
pil-grims' pride, From ev-ery moun-tain side Let free-dom ring.
tem-pled hills; My heart with rap-ture thrills Like that a-bove. A-men.

3 Let music swell the breeze,
And ring from all the trees
Sweet freedom's song;
Let mortal tongues awake;
Let all that breathe partake;
Let rocks their silence break,
The sound prolong.

4 Our fathers' God, to thee,
Author of liberty,
To thee we sing:
Long may our land be bright
With freedom's holy light;
Protect us by thy might,
Great God, our King. Amen.

Samuel Francis Smith, 1809–9

For a lower setting of this tune see No. 361

NATIONAL ANTHEM. 6 6 4, 6 6 6 4. *Thesaurus Musicus*, 1744

Slowly, with dignity

1. God save our gra - cious Queen, Long live our no - ble Queen,
God save the Queen: Send her vic - to - ri - ous, Hap - py and
glo - ri - ous, Long to reign o - ver us; God save the Queen. A-men.

2 Thy choicest gifts in store
On her be pleased to pour;
Long may she reign:
May she defend our laws,
And ever give us cause
To sing with heart and voice,
God save the Queen. Amen.

Author unknown, XVIII cent.

For the Churches within the British Commonwealth

See also:

426	All hail the power of Jesus' Name	418	Let all the world in every corner
137	Ancient of Days, who sittest	539	O brother man, fold to thy heart
161	Before Jehovah's aweful throne	168	O God, our help in ages past
330	City of God, how broad and far	332	O holy city, seen of John
322	Eternal God, whose power	547	Once to every man and nation
429	From all that dwell	327	The Lord will come and not be slow
521	God of our fathers, whose	329	Thy kingdom come, O God
307	Jesus shall reign where'er the sun	331	Thy kingdom come! on bended knee

Rogation and Harvest

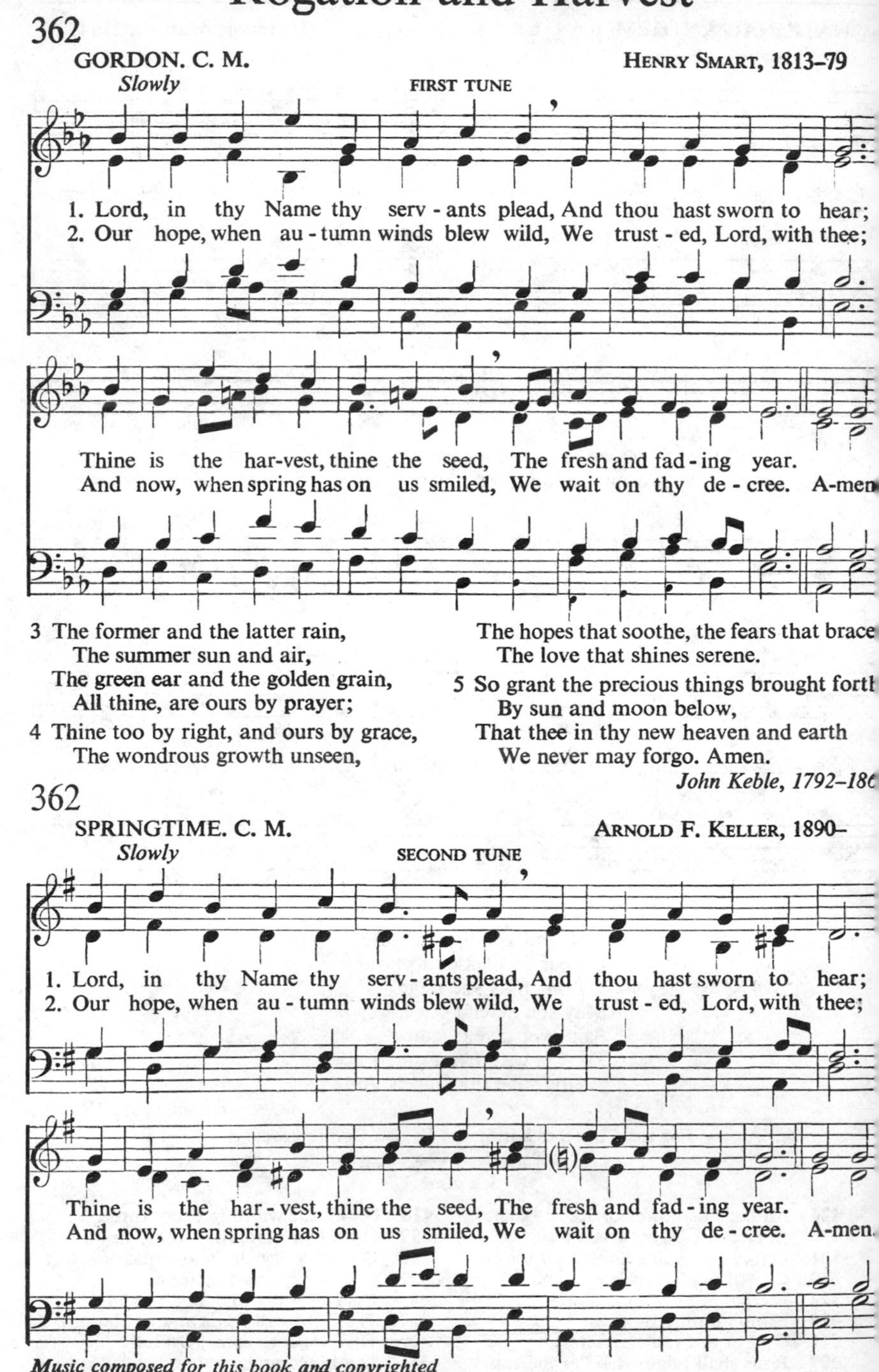
362
GORDON. C. M.
HENRY SMART, 1813–79
Slowly
FIRST TUNE
1. Lord, in thy Name thy serv - ants plead, And thou hast sworn to hear;
2. Our hope, when au - tumn winds blew wild, We trust - ed, Lord, with thee;
Thine is the har-vest, thine the seed, The fresh and fad - ing year.
And now, when spring has on us smiled, We wait on thy de - cree. A-men
3 The former and the latter rain,
The summer sun and air,
The green ear and the golden grain,
All thine, are ours by prayer;
4 Thine too by right, and ours by grace,
The wondrous growth unseen,
The hopes that soothe, the fears that brace
The love that shines serene.
5 So grant the precious things brought fort
By sun and moon below,
That thee in thy new heaven and earth
We never may forgo. Amen.
John Keble, 1792–18
362
SPRINGTIME. C. M.
ARNOLD F. KELLER, 1890–
Slowly
SECOND TUNE
1. Lord, in thy Name thy serv - ants plead, And thou hast sworn to hear;
2. Our hope, when au - tumn winds blew wild, We trust - ed, Lord, with thee;
Thine is the har - vest, thine the seed, The fresh and fad - ing year.
And now, when spring has on us smiled, We wait on thy de - cree. A-men.

ST. GEORGE'S, WINDSOR. 7 7, 7 7. D.
GEORGE J. ELVEY, 1816–93
With spirit
1. Come, ye thank - ful peo - ple, come, Raise the song of har - vest-home;
2. All the world is God's own field, Fruit un - to his praise to yield;
All is safe - ly gath - ered in Ere the win - ter storms be - gin;
Wheat and tares to - geth - er sown, Un - to joy or sor - row grown;
God our Mak - er doth pro - vide For our wants to be sup - plied:
First the blade and then the ear, Then the full corn shall ap - pear:
Come, to God's own tem - ple come, Raise the song of har - vest-home.
Lord of har - vest, grant that we Whole-some grain and pure may be. A-men.

3 For the Lord our God shall come,
And shall take his harvest home;
From his field shall in that day
All offences purge away;
Give his angels charge at last
In the fire the tares to cast;
But the fruitful ears to store
In his garner evermore.

4 Even so, Lord, quickly come
To thy final harvest-home;
Gather thou thy people in,
Free from sorrow, free from sin,
There for ever purified,
In thy presence to abide:
Come, with all thine angels, come,
Raise the glorious harvest-home. Amen.

Henry Alford, 1810–71

WIR PFLÜGEN. 7 6, 7 6. D. With Refrain. JOHANN A. P. SCHULZ, 1747–1800

Briskly

1. We plough the fields, and scat - ter The good seed on the land,
2. He on - ly is the Mak - er Of all things near and far;

But it is fed and wa - tered By God's al - might - y hand;
He paints the way - side flow - er, He lights the eve - ning star;

He sends the snow in win - ter, The warmth to swell the grain,
The winds and waves o - bey him, By him the birds are fed;

The breez - es and the sun - shine, And soft re - fresh - ing rain.
Much more to us, his chil - dren, He gives our dai - ly bread.

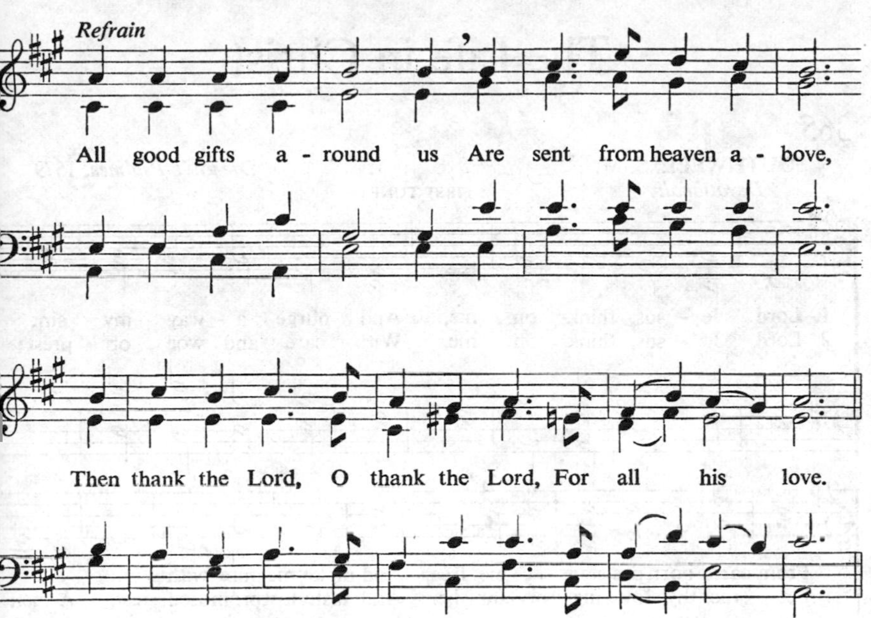
Refrain
All good gifts a - round us Are sent from heaven a - bove,
Then thank the Lord, O thank the Lord, For all his love.

3 We thank thee then, O Father,
   For all things bright and good,
The seed-time and the harvest,
   Our life, our health, our food;
No gifts have we to offer
   For all thy love imparts,
But that which thou desirest,
   Our humble, thankful hearts.

Matthias Claudius, 1740–1815
Tr. Jane Montgomery Campbell, 1817–78

For Rogationtide, see also:

For Harvest, see also:

The Life in Christ

365

SOUTHWELL. S. M. DAMON'S *Psalmes*, 1579

Devotionally FIRST TUNE

1. Lord Je - sus, think on me, And purge a - way my sin;
2. Lord Je - sus, think on me, With care and woe op - prest;
From earth-born pas-sions set me free, And make me pure with - in.
Let me thy lov - ing serv-ant be, And taste thy prom-ised rest. A-men.

3 Lord Jesus, think on me,
  Amid the battle's strife;
In all my pain and misery
  Be thou my health and life.

4 Lord Jesus, think on me,
  Nor let me go astray;
Through darkness and perplexity
  Point thou the heavenly way.

5 Lord Jesus, think on me,
  That, when the flood is past,
I may the eternal brightness see,
  And share thy joy at last.

6 Lord Jesus, think on me,
  That I may sing above
To Father, Spirit, and to thee,
  The strains of praise and love. Amen

Synesius of Cyrene, cir. 375–43
Tr. Allen William Chatfield, 1808–9

365

ST. BRIDE. S. M. SAMUEL HOWARD, 1710–82

Slowly SECOND TUNE

1. Lord Je - sus, think on me, And purge a - way my sin;
2. Lord Je - sus, think on me, With care and woe op - prest;

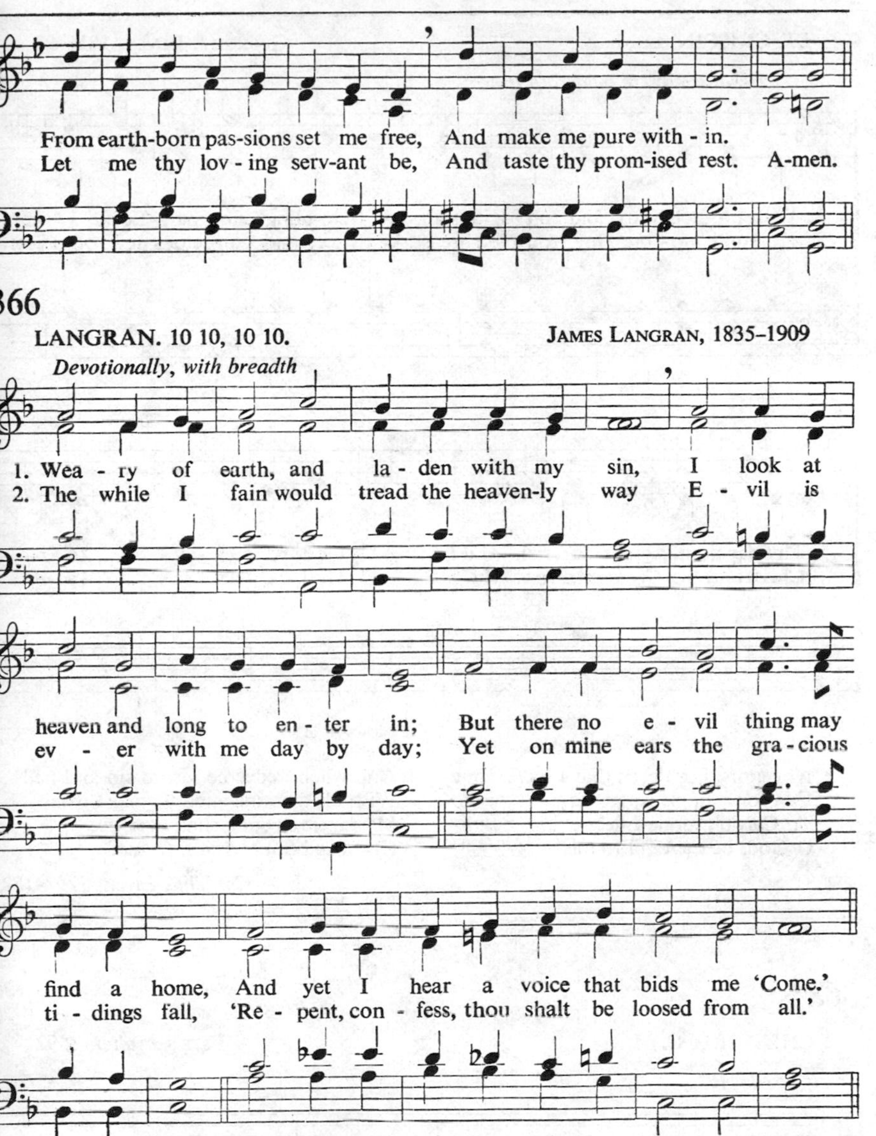
From earth-born pas-sions set me free, And make me pure with - in.
Let me thy lov - ing serv-ant be, And taste thy prom-ised rest. A-men.
366
LANGRAN. 10 10, 10 10.
JAMES LANGRAN, 1835–1909
Devotionally, with breadth
1. Wea - ry of earth, and la - den with my sin, I look at
2. The while I fain would tread the heaven-ly way E - vil is
heaven and long to en - ter in; But there no e - vil thing may
ev - er with me day by day; Yet on mine ears the gra - cious
find a home, And yet I hear a voice that bids me 'Come.'
ti - dings fall, 'Re - pent, con - fess, thou shalt be loosed from all.'

3 O great Absolver, grant my soul may wear
The lowliest garb of penitence and prayer,
That in the Father's courts my glorious dress
May be the garment of thy righteousness.

4 Yea, thou wilt answer for me, righteous Lord;
Thine all the merits, mine the great reward;
Thine the sharp thorns, and mine the golden crown;
Mine the life won, through thine the life laid down.

Samuel John Stone, 1839–1900

367

ST. CRISPIN. L. M. GEORGE J. ELVEY, 1816–93

Devotionally, in moderate time

1. With bro-ken heart and con - trite sigh, A trem-bling sin - ner, Lord, I cry;
Thy par-doning grace is rich and free: O God, be mer - ci - ful to me.

2. I smite up - on my trou-bled breast, With deep and con-scious guilt op-pressed;
Christ and his Cross my on - ly plea: O God, be mer - ci - ful to me.

3 Nor alms, nor deeds that I have done,
Can for a single sin atone;
To Calvary alone I flee:
O God, be merciful to me.

4 And when, redeemed from sin and hell,
With all the ransomed throng I dwell,
My raptured song shall ever be:
God has been merciful to me.

Cornelius Elven, 1797–1873

368

CHESHIRE. C. M. ESTE'S *Psalter*, 1592

Slowly

1. Lord, it be-longs not to my care Wheth-er I die or live;
2. If life be long, I will be glad That I may long o - bey;

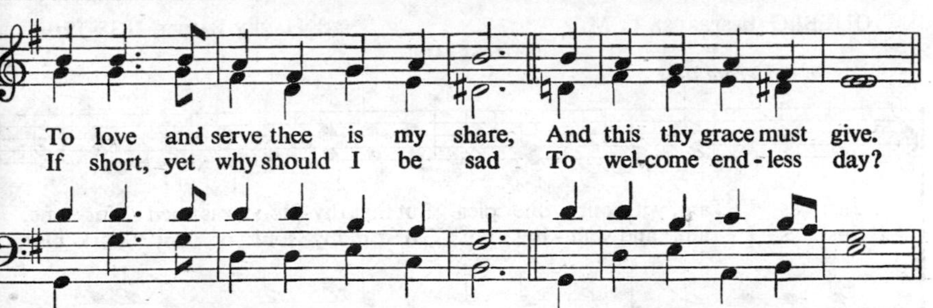
To love and serve thee is my share, And this thy grace must give.
If short, yet why should I be sad To wel-come end-less day?

3 Christ leads me through no darker rooms
Than he went through before;
He that into God's kingdom comes
Must enter by this door.

4 Come, Lord, when grace has made me meet
Thy blessèd face to see;
For if thy work on earth be sweet,
What will thy glory be?

5 My knowledge of that life is small,
The eye of faith is dim;
But 'tis enough that Christ knows all,
And I shall be with him.

Richard Baxter, 1615–91

This hymn may also be sung to TALLIS' ORDINAL (No. 154)

369

LONDON NEW. C. M. *Scottish Psalter*, 1635

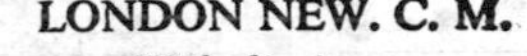
With dignity

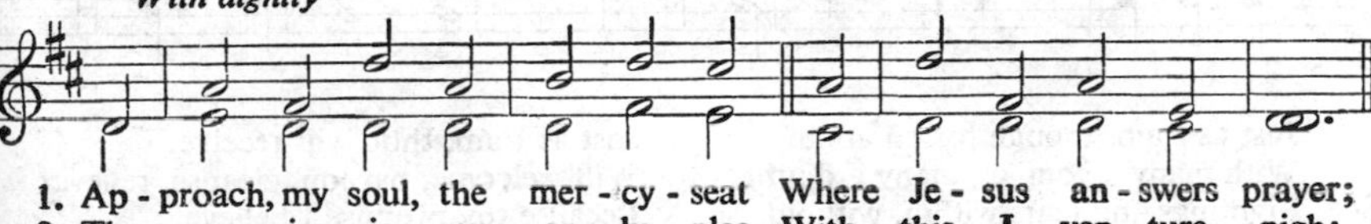
1. Ap-proach, my soul, the mer-cy-seat Where Je-sus an-swers prayer;
2. Thy prom-ise is my on-ly plea, With this I ven-ture nigh;

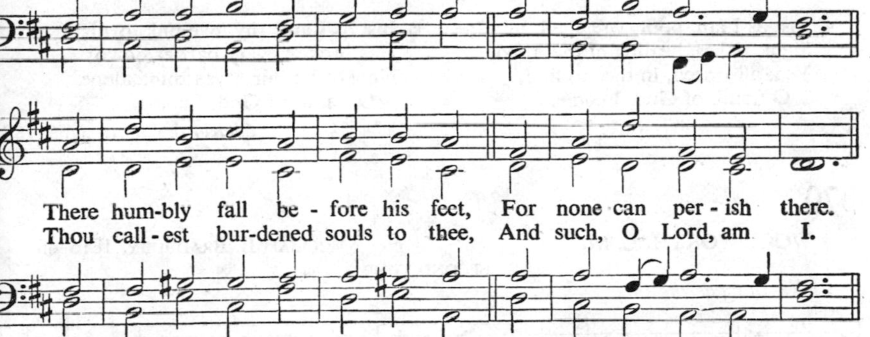
There hum-bly fall be-fore his feet, For none can per-ish there.
Thou call-est bur-dened souls to thee, And such, O Lord, am I.

3 Bowed down beneath a load of sin,
By Satan sorely pressed,
By wars without and fears within,
I come to thee for rest.

4 Be thou my shield and hiding-place,
That, sheltered near thy side,
I may my fierce accuser face,
And tell him, thou hast died.

5 O wondrous Love, to bleed and die,
To bear the cross and shame,
That guilty sinners such as I
Might plead thy gracious Name!

John Newton, 1725–1807

This hymn may also be sung to BELGRAVE (No. 440)

QUEBEC (HESPERUS). L. M. HENRY BAKER, 1835–1910

FIRST TUNE

In moderate time

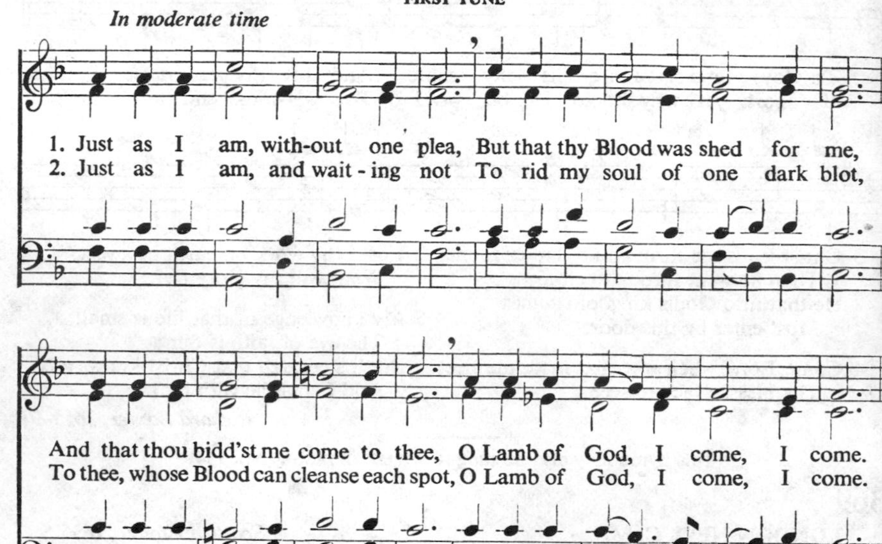
1. Just as I am, with-out one plea, But that thy Blood was shed for me,
2. Just as I am, and wait - ing not To rid my soul of one dark blot,
And that thou bidd'st me come to thee, O Lamb of God, I come, I come.
To thee, whose Blood can cleanse each spot, O Lamb of God, I come, I come.

3 Just as I am, though tossed about
With many a conflict, many a doubt,
Fightings and fears within, without,
O Lamb of God, I come.

4 Just as I am, poor, wretched, blind;
Sight, riches, healing of the mind,
Yea, all I need, in thee to find,
O Lamb of God, I come.

5 Just as I am, thou wilt receive,
Wilt welcome, pardon, cleanse, relieve;
Because thy promise I believe,
O Lamb of God, I come.

6 Just as I am; thy love unknown
Has broken every barrier down;
Now to be thine, yea thine alone,
O Lamb of God, I come.

Charlotte Elliott, 1789–1871

370

WOODWORTH. L. M. WILLIAM B. BRADBURY, 1816–68

SECOND TUNE

In moderate time

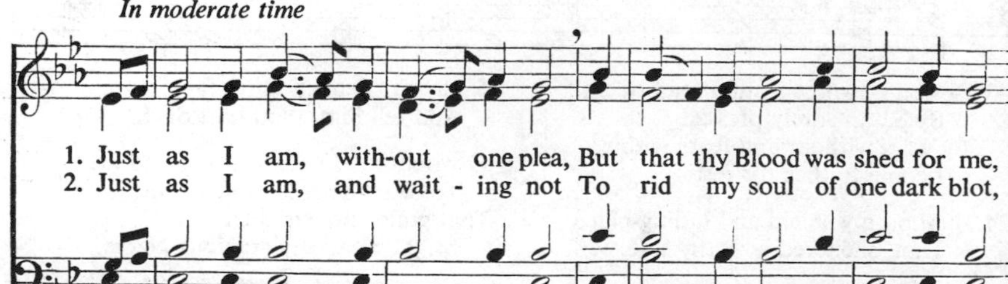
1. Just as I am, with-out one plea, But that thy Blood was shed for me,
2. Just as I am, and wait - ing not To rid my soul of one dark blot,

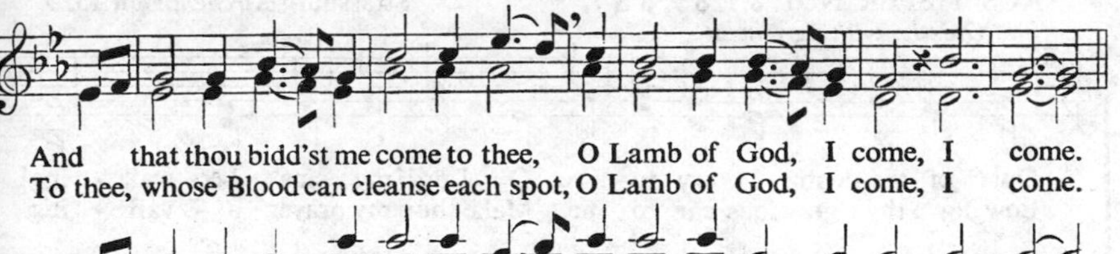
And that thou bidd'st me come to thee, O Lamb of God, I come, I come.
To thee, whose Blood can cleanse each spot, O Lamb of God, I come, I come.

3 Just as I am, though tossed about
With many a conflict, many a doubt,
Fightings and fears within, without,
O Lamb of God, I come.

4 Just as I am, poor, wretched, blind;
Sight, riches, healing of the mind,
Yea, all I need, in thee to find,
O Lamb of God, I come.

5 Just as I am, thou wilt receive,
Wilt welcome, pardon, cleanse, relieve;
Because thy promise I believe,
O Lamb of God, I come.

6 Just as I am; thy love unknown
Has broken every barrier down;
Now to be thine, yea thine alone,
O Lamb of God, I come.

Charlotte Elliott, 1789–1871

371

ST. BERNARD. C. M.

Devotionally

Tochter Sion, Cologne, 1741
Arr. by JOHN RICHARDSON, 1816–79

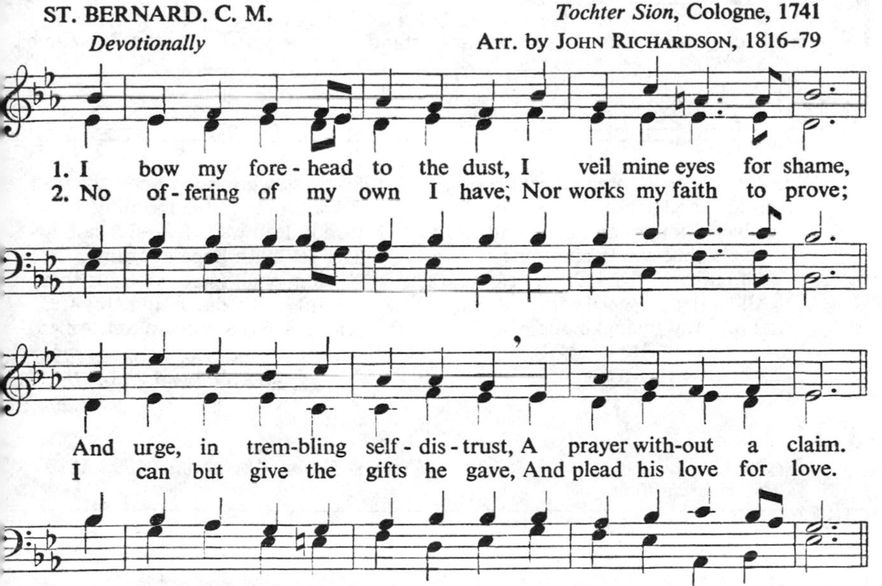
1. I bow my fore-head to the dust, I veil mine eyes for shame,
2. No of-fering of my own I have; Nor works my faith to prove;
And urge, in trem-bling self-dis-trust, A prayer with-out a claim.
I can but give the gifts he gave, And plead his love for love.

3 I dimly guess, from blessings known,
Of greater out of sight;
And, with the chastened Psalmist, own
His judgments too are right.

4 And if my heart and flesh are weak
To bear an untried pain,
The bruisèd reed he will not break,
But strengthen and sustain.

John Greenleaf Whittier, 1807–92

372

AUS TIEFER NOT. 8 7, 8 7, 8 8 7. Strassburg *Kirchenampt*, 1525

Quietly, with movement

1. Out of the depths I cry to thee, O Lord, my sins be-wail-ing!
Bow down thy gra-cious ear to me, Make thou my prayer a-vail-ing.
Mark not my mis-deeds in thy book, But on my sins in mer-cy look,
Or who can stand be-fore thee? A-men.

2 With thee there is forgiveness, Lord,
And love and grace abounding;
The noblest thought and deed and word
Were else but empty sounding.
All guilty in thy sight appear;
All to thy presence come in fear,
And find thy lovingkindness.

3 Like those who watch upon the wall
To welcome in the morning,
My soul doth wait thy quiet call,
Her self with hope adorning.
So may all Israel look for thee,
And in thy day find mercy free,
And plenteous redemption. Amen.

Martin Luther, 1483–154[illegible]
Tr. Edward Traill Horn III, 1909–
Psalm 13[illegible]

373

EVAN. C. M. William Henry Havergal, 1793–1870

In moderate time

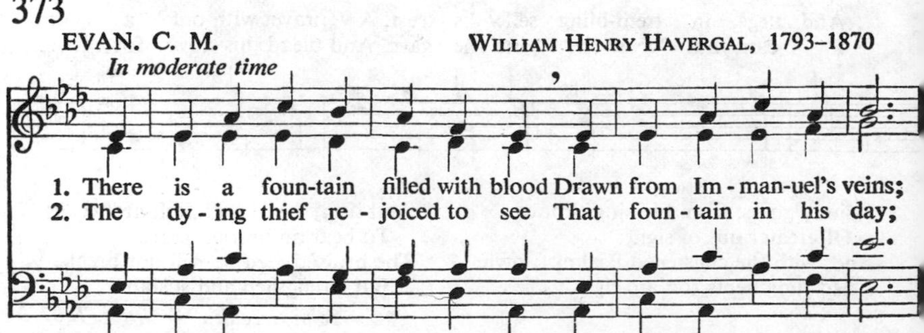

1. There is a foun-tain filled with blood Drawn from Im-man-uel's veins;
2. The dy-ing thief re-joiced to see That foun-tain in his day;

And sin- ners, plunged be - neath that flood, Lose all their guilt - y stains.
And there have I, as vile as he, Washed all my sins a - way.

3 Dear dying Lamb, thy precious Blood
Shall never lose its power
Till all the ransomed Church of God
Be saved, to sin no more.

4 E'er since, by faith, I saw the stream
Thy flowing wounds supply,
Redeeming love has been my theme,
And shall be till I die.

5 Then in a nobler, sweeter song,
I'll sing thy power to save,
When this poor lisping, stammering tongue
Lies silent in the grave.

William Cowper, 1731–1800

74

BRESLAU. L. M.

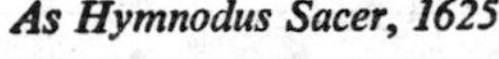
As Hymnodus Sacer, 1625

With dignity

1. God call - ing yet; shall I not hear? Earth's pleasures shall I still hold dear?
2. God call - ing yet; shall I not rise? Can I his lov - ing voice de - spise,

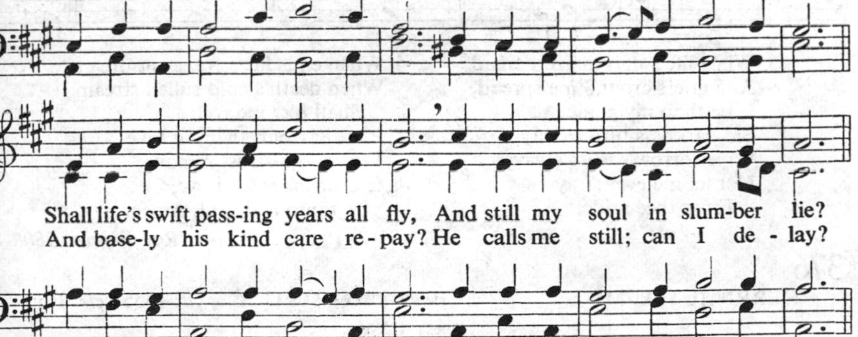
Shall life's swift pass-ing years all fly, And still my soul in slum-ber lie?
And base-ly his kind care re - pay? He calls me still; can I de - lay?

3 God calling yet; and shall he knock,
And I my heart the closer lock?
He still is waiting to receive,
And shall I dare his Spirit grieve?

4 Ah, yield him all; in him confide;
Where but with him doth peace abide?
Break loose, let earthly bonds be riven,
And let the spirit rise to heaven.

5 God calling yet; I cannot stay;
My heart I yield without delay;
Vain world, farewell! from thee I part;
The voice of God hath reached my heart.

Gerhard Tersteegen, 1697–1769
Tr. Sarah Borthwick Findlater, 1823–1907 a.

This hymn may also be sung to HAMBURG (No. 503)

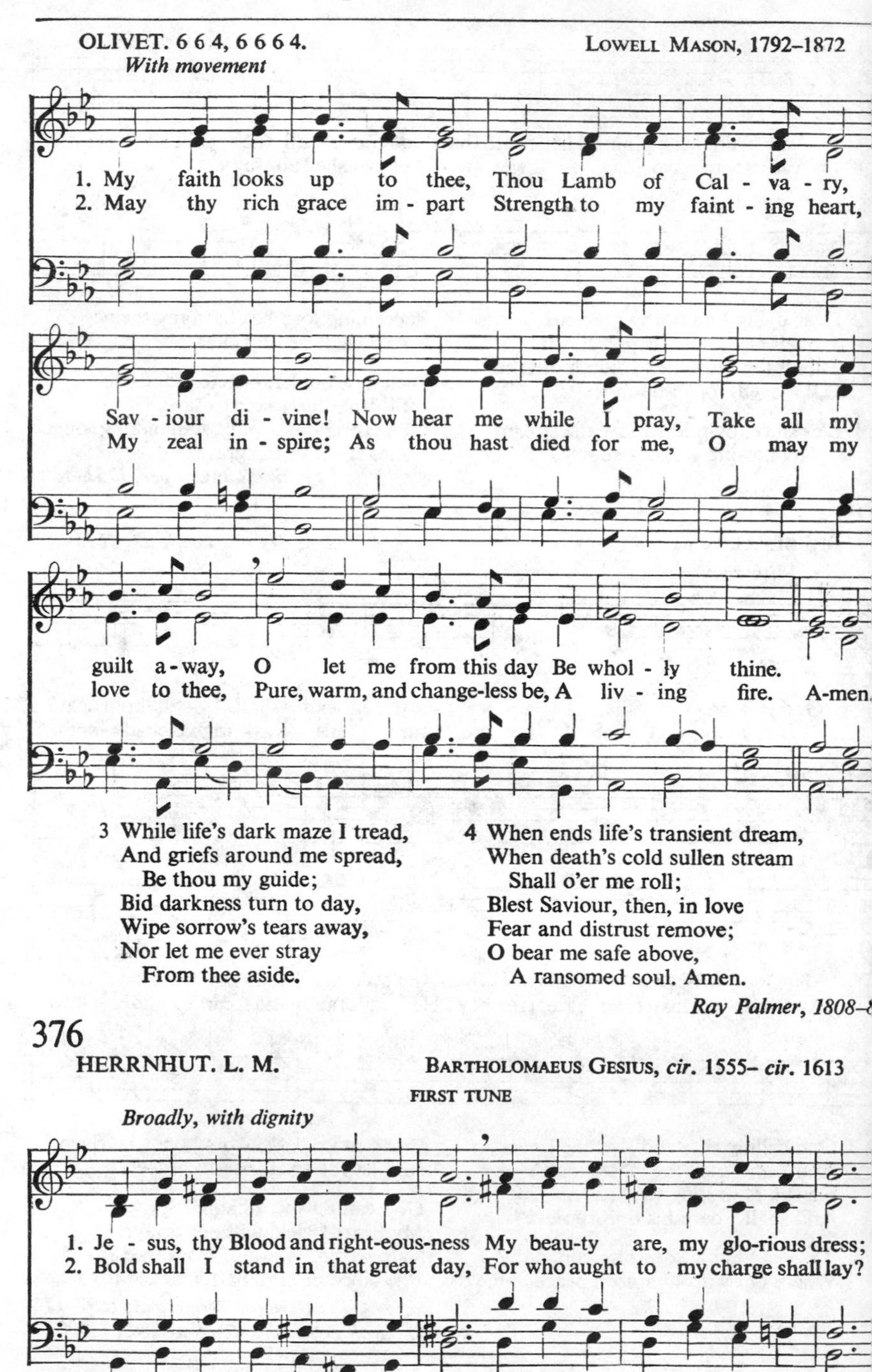
OLIVET. 6 6 4, 6 6 6 4.
LOWELL MASON, 1792–1872
With movement
1. My faith looks up to thee, Thou Lamb of Cal - va - ry, Sav - iour di - vine! Now hear me while I pray, Take all my guilt a - way, O let me from this day Be whol - ly thine.
2. May thy rich grace im - part Strength to my faint - ing heart, My zeal in - spire; As thou hast died for me, O may my love to thee, Pure, warm, and change-less be, A liv - ing fire. A-men.
3 While life's dark maze I tread,
And griefs around me spread,
Be thou my guide;
Bid darkness turn to day,
Wipe sorrow's tears away,
Nor let me ever stray
From thee aside.
4 When ends life's transient dream,
When death's cold sullen stream
Shall o'er me roll;
Blest Saviour, then, in love
Fear and distrust remove;
O bear me safe above,
A ransomed soul. Amen.
Ray Palmer, 1808–
376
HERRNHUT. L. M.
BARTHOLOMAEUS GESIUS, cir. 1555– cir. 1613
FIRST TUNE
Broadly, with dignity
1. Je - sus, thy Blood and right-eous-ness My beau-ty are, my glo-rious dress;
2. Bold shall I stand in that great day, For who aught to my charge shall lay?

Midst flam-ing worlds, in these ar - rayed, With joy shall I lift up my head.
Ful - ly through thee ab-solved I am From sin and fear, from guilt and shame.

3 Lord, I believe thy precious Blood,
Which at the mercy-seat of God
Forever doth for sinners plead,
For me, e'en for my soul, was shed.

4 When from the dust of death I rise
To claim my mansion in the skies,
E'en then shall this be all my plea,
'Jesus hath lived, hath died for me.'

St. 1, Paul Eber, 1511–69
Sts. 2–4, Nicolaus Ludwig von Zinzendorf, 1700–60
Tr. John Wesley, 1703–91 a.

76

O JESU CHRIST, MEINS LEBENS LICHT. L. M. Nürnberg *Gesangbuch*, 1676

SECOND TUNE

Broadly, with dignity

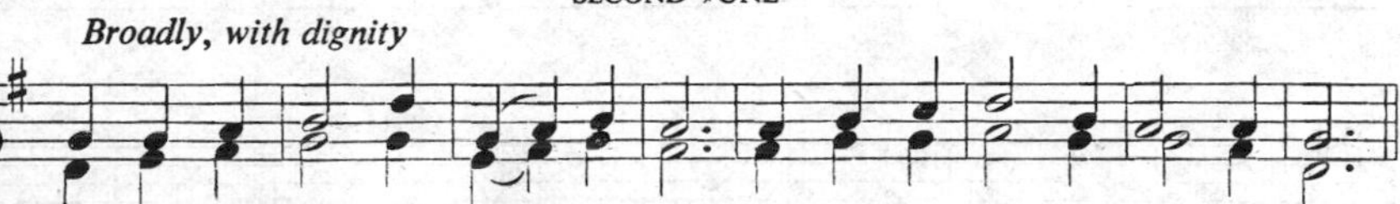

1. Je - sus, thy Blood and right-eous-ness My beau-ty are, my glo-rious dress;
2. Bold shall I stand in that great day, For who aught to my charge shall lay?

Midst flam-ing worlds, in these ar - rayed, With joy shall I lift up my head.
Ful - ly through thee ab-solved I am From sin and fear, from guilt and shame.

3 Lord, I believe thy precious Blood,
Which at the mercy-seat of God
Forever doth for sinners plead,
For me, e'en for my soul, was shed.

4 When from the dust of death I rise
To claim my mansion in the skies,
E'en then shall this be all my plea,
'Jesus hath lived, hath died for me.'

St. 1, Paul Eber, 1511–69
Sts. 2–4, Nicolaus Ludwig von Zinzendorf, 1700–60
Tr. John Wesley, 1703–91 a.

BREAD OF HEAVEN. 7 7, 7 7, 7 7. WILLIAM DALRYMPLE MACLAGAN, 1826–1910

In flowing style

1. Sin - ners Je - sus will re - ceive: Tell this word of grace to all
Who the heaven-ly path - way leave, All who lin - ger, all who fall;
This can bring them back a - gain, 'Christ re - ceiv - eth sin - ful men.'

2 Shepherds seek their wandering sheep
O'er the mountains bleak and cold;
Jesus such a watch doth keep
O'er the lost ones of his fold,
Seeking them o'er moor and fen,
Christ receiveth sinful men.

3 Sick and sorrowful and blind,
I with all my sins draw nigh;
O my Saviour, thou canst find
Help for sinners such as I;
Speak that word of love again,
'Christ receiveth sinful men.'

4 Christ receiveth sinful men,
Even me with all my sin;
Openeth to me heaven again;
With him I may enter in.
Death hath no more sting nor pain,
Christ receiveth sinful men.

Erdmann Neumeister, 1671–17
Tr. Emma Frances Bevan, 1827–19

This hymn may also be sung to PETRA (No. 379)

WENNERBERG. 7 6, 7 6. D.
GUNNAR WENNERBERG, 1817–1901
With vigor
Search me, God, and know my heart, Lord of truth and mer - cy;
Try me, thou who from a - far Know-est all my se - crets;
And if an - y wick - ed way Should be found with - in me,
Bless - ed Sav - iour, lead thou me In the way e - ter - nal. A-men.

Claus August Wendell, 1866–1950
Psalm 139:23, 24

PETRA (REDHEAD NO. 76) 7 7, 7 7, 7 7. RICHARD REDHEAD, 1820–19

FIRST TUNE

Moderately slow

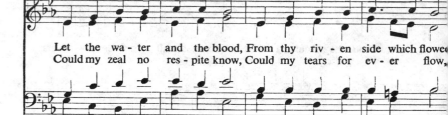

1. Rock of A - ges, cleft for me, Let me hide my - self in thee
2. Not the la - bors of my hands Can ful - fill thy law's de - manc

Let the wa - ter and the blood, From thy riv - en side which flowe
Could my zeal no res - pite know, Could my tears for ev - er flow,

Be of sin the dou - ble cure, Cleanse me from its guilt and power.
All for sin could not a-tone; Thou must save, and thou a - lone. A-me

3 Nothing in my hand I bring,
Simply to thy Cross I cling;
Naked, come to thee for dress;
Helpless, look to thee for grace;
Foul, I to the fountain fly;
Wash me, Saviour, or I die.

4 While I draw this fleeting breath,
When mine eyelids close in death,
When I soar to worlds unknown,
See thee on thy judgment throne,
Rock of Ages, cleft for me,
Let me hide myself in thee. Amen.

Augustus Montague Toplady, 1740

TOPLADY. 7 7, 7 7, 7 7.
THOMAS HASTINGS, 1784–1872
SECOND TUNE
Devotionally
1. Rock of A - ges, cleft for me, Let me hide my - self in thee;
2. Not the la - bors of my hands Can ful - fill thy law's de - mands;
Let the wa - ter and the blood, From thy riv - en side which flowed,
Could my zeal no res - pite know, Could my tears for ev - er flow,
Be of sin the dou - ble cure, Cleanse me from its guilt and power.
All for sin could not a - tone; Thou must save, and thou a - lone. A-men.

3 Nothing in my hand I bring,
Simply to thy Cross I cling;
Naked, come to thee for dress;
Helpless, look to thee for grace;
Foul, I to the fountain fly;
Wash me, Saviour, or I die.

4 While I draw this fleeting breath,
When mine eyelids close in death,
When I soar to worlds unknown,
See thee on thy judgment throne,
Rock of Ages, cleft for me,
Let me hide myself in thee. Amen.

Augustus Montague Toplady, 1740–78

VATER UNSER. 8 8, 8 8, 8 8. Arr. by MARTIN LUTHER, 1483–1546

Devotionally

1. To thee, O Lord, the God of all, With con - trite
heart I hum - bly call, And view my sins a - gainst thee, Lord,
The sins of thought and deed and word; In my dis
tress I cry to thee, O God, be mer - ci - ful to me. A - men

2 My Lord and God, to thee I pray,
O cast me not in wrath away;
Let thy good Spirit ne'er depart,
But draw me closer to thy heart;
This is my penitential plea,
O God, be merciful to me.

3 Let thy belovèd precious Blood
Be to my soul a cleansing flood,
To wash my sins and guilt away;
That, pardoned by thy grace, I may
Go to my house with peace from thee;
O God, be merciful to me. Amen.

Magnus Brostrup Landstad, 1802-
Tr. Carl Doving, 1867–1937

This hymn may also be sung to the Bach arrangement (No. 359)

SCHMÜCKE DICH. L. M. D. JOHANN CRUGER, 1598–1662

Quietly

1. By thy Cross, O Christ, and pas - sion, Thou hast brought us full sal - va - tion;
Thou hast stooped in great com-pas-sion To re - deem a lost cre - a - tion.

Like a shep-herd thou hast sought us In thy heaven-ly fold to gath - er;

With thy pre-cious Blood hast bought us To re - store us to the Fa - ther.

2 Ah, how blest is he who knoweth
That his faith on thee is founded
Whom the Father's love bestoweth
Through eternal grace unbounded.
Thou, O Christ, to every nation
Art a Saviour freely given,
In whose Name is our salvation,
And none else in earth or heaven.

Johan Olof Wallin, 1779–1839
Tr. St. 1, Ernest Edwin Ryden, 1886–
Tr. St. 2, Ernst William Olson, 1870–1958

WELWYN. 11 10, 11 10. ALFRED SCOTT-GATTY, 1847–1918

With movement

1. Now once a - gain for help that nev - er fail - eth,
2. That we may rise and go forth from thine al - tar,
We bring our griev - ous bur - den un - to thee;
To bear the load we could not bear be - fore,
Pour down thy strength, for noth - ing else a - vail - eth,
With mind se - rene, with step that does not fal - ter,
Bless thou the bow - ing head, the bend - ing knee,
Know - ing thy hand will o - pen ev - ery door; A-men.

3 Knowing there will not be so dark a valley
But those who watch may find thy guiding ray,
Knowing there will not be so blind an alley
But it will open on thy broad highway.

4 O Light that led the saints through all the ages,
O Hope that lifted up the martyr's head,
O Comforter of children and of sages,
Lead on, lead on, as thou hast always led! Amen.

Mildred Whitney Stillman, 189

Text and music by permission of the Abbot of Downside Abbey

JESUS, HEAR, 8 7, 8 7. D. ARMAS MAASALO, 1885–1960

With dignity

1. Je - sus, hear my hum-ble plead-ing, Low - ly at thy feet I lie;
Thou for such art in - ter - ced - ing At the Fa-ther's throne on high.
Friend of sin-ners, bless - ed Sav - iour, Let me lin - ger 'neath thy Cross;
Seek-ing there thy gra-cious fa - vor, All things else I count but loss. A-men.

2 Near the mercy-seat abiding
  Let my soul thy glory see;
In thy grace alone confiding,
  Perfect peace I find in thee.
Tune my heart to sing thy praises
  Till I join the heavenly throng
Which through endless ages raises
  Sweetest praise with harp and song. Amen.

Jenny Pohjola, 1899–
Tr. Samuel V. Autere, 1893–
Paraphrase, Ernest Edwin Ryden, 1886–

WIGTOWN. C. M. *Scottish Psalter*, 1635

FIRST TUNE

Devotionally

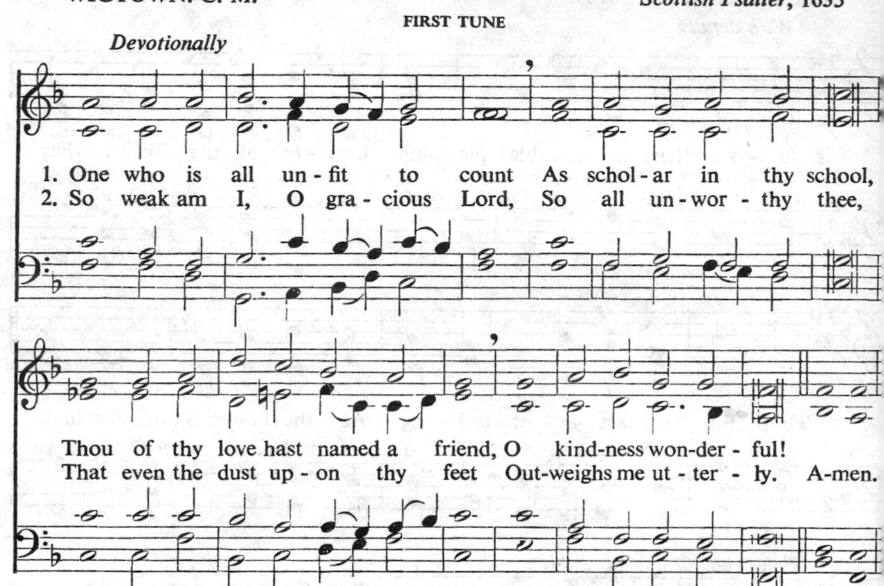
1. One who is all un-fit to count As schol-ar in thy school,
2. So weak am I, O gra-cious Lord, So all un-wor-thy thee,
Thou of thy love hast named a friend, O kind-ness won-der-ful!
That even the dust up-on thy feet Out-weighs me ut-ter-ly. A-men.

3 Thou dwellest in unshadowed light,
All sin and shame above,
That thou shouldst bear our sin and shame,
How can I tell such love?

4 Ah, did not he the heavenly throne
A little thing esteem,
And not unworthy for my sake
A mortal body deem?

5 When in his flesh they drove the nails,
Did he not all endure?
What name is there to fit a life
So patient and so pure?

6 So, Love itself in human form
For love of me he came;
I cannot look upon his face
For shame, for bitter shame.

7 If there is aught of worth in me,
It comes from thee alone;
Then keep me safe, for so, O Lord,
Thou keepest but thine own. Amen.

Narayan Vaman Tilak, 1862–1919
Tr. Nicol Macnicol, 1870–1952

384

CAITHNESS. C. M. Scottish Psalter, 1635

SECOND TUNE

Moderately slow

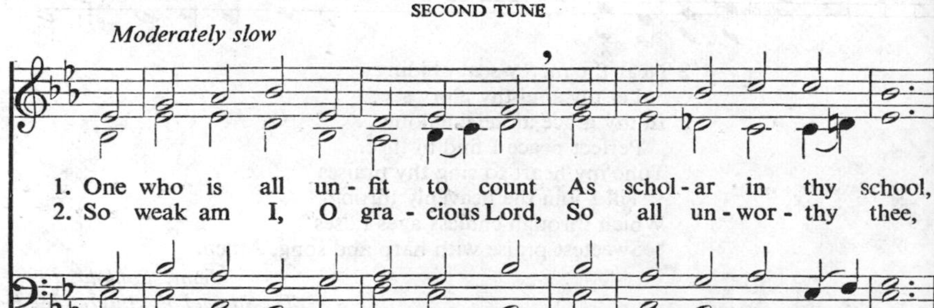
1. One who is all un-fit to count As schol-ar in thy school,
2. So weak am I, O gra-cious Lord, So all un-wor-thy thee,

Thou of thy love hast named a friend, O kind-ness won-der - ful!
That even the dust up - on thy feet Out-weighs me ut - ter - ly. A-men.
385
MELITA. 8 8, 8 8, 8 8.
JOHN BACCHUS DYKES, 1823–76
With dignity
1. My hope is built on noth - ing less Than Je - sus' Blood and right-eous-ness;
2. When dark-ness veils his love - ly face I rest on his un-chang-ing grace;
No mer - it of my own I claim, But whol - ly lean on Je - sus' Name.
In ev - ery high and storm - y gale My an - chor holds with - in the veil.
Refrain
On Christ, the sol - id rock, I stand; All oth - er ground is sink - ing sand.

3 His oath, his covenant, his Blood,
Support me in the whelming flood;
When all around my soul gives way,
He then is all my hope and stay.

4 When he shall come with trumpet sound,
O may I then in him be found,
Dressed in his righteousness alone,
Faultless to stand before the throne!

Edward Mote, 1787–1874

ST. EDITH (ST. HILDA). 7 6, 7 6. D.
In moderate time

JUSTIN H. KNECHT, 1752–1817
EDWARD HUSBAND, 1843–1908

1. O Je - sus, thou art stand - ing Out - side the fast-closed door,
2. O Je - sus, thou art knock-ing; And lo, that hand is scarred,
In low - ly pa - tience wait - ing To pass the thresh - old o'er.
And thorns thy brow en - cir - cle, And tears thy face have marred.
Shame on us, Chris - tian breth - ren, His Name and sign who bear,
O love that pass - eth knowl-edge, So pa - tient - ly to wait;
O shame, thrice shame up - on us, To keep him stand - ing there!
O sin that hath no e - qual, So fast to bar the gate! A-men.

3 O Jesus, thou art pleading
   In accents meek and low,
'I died for you, my children,
   And will ye treat me so?'
O Lord, with shame and sorrow
   We open now the door;
Dear Saviour, enter, enter
   And leave us nevermore. Amen.

William Walsham How, 1823–97

DUKE STREET. L. M.
JOHN HATTON, +1793
With breadth
1. I know that my Re - deem - er lives: What joy the blest as - sur - ance gives! He lives, he lives, who once was dead; He lives, my ev - er - last - ing head!
2. He lives, to bless me with his love; He lives, to plead for me a - bove; He lives, my hun - gry soul to feed; He lives, to help in time of need.

3 He lives, and grants me daily breath;
He lives, and I shall conquer death;
He lives, my mansion to prepare;
He lives, to bring me safely there.

4 He lives, all glory to his Name;
He lives, my Saviour, still the same;
What joy the blest assurance gives:
I know that my Redeemer lives!

Samuel Medley, 1738–99

See also:

486 Alas! and did my Saviour bleed
569 Come, ye disconsolate
467 Dear Lord and Father of mankind
516 Faith of our fathers, living still
594 Give me the wings of faith
558 How firm a foundation
499 I heard the voice of Jesus say
492 I lay my sins on Jesus
401 Jesus, thy love unbounded
395 O for a faith that will not shrink
461 Pass me not, O gentle Saviour
578 Softly and tenderly
495 Sometimes a light surprises
493 There's a wideness in God's mercy
391 Thou hidden Love of God
348 Turn back, O man

388

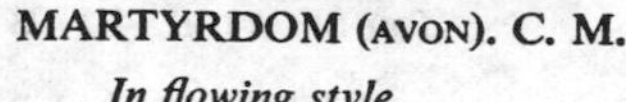

MARTYRDOM (AVON). C. M. HUGH WILSON, 1764–1824

In flowing style

1. As pants the hart for cool - ing streams When heat - ed in the chase,
2. For thee, my God, the liv - ing God, My thirst - y soul doth pine;
So longs my soul, O God, for thee, And thy re - fresh - ing grace.
O when shall I be-hold thy face, Thou Maj - es - ty Di - vine! A-men.

3 Why restless, why cast down, my soul?
Hope still; and thou shalt sing
The praise of him who is thy God,
Thy health's eternal Spring.

4 To Father, Son and Holy Ghost,
The God whom we adore,
Be glory, as it was, is now,
And shall be evermore. Amen.

Nahum Tate, 1652–1715
Nicholas Brady, 1659–1726 a.
Psalm 42

389

WINCHESTER. C. M. THOMAS ESTE'S *Psalter*, 1592

In moderate time

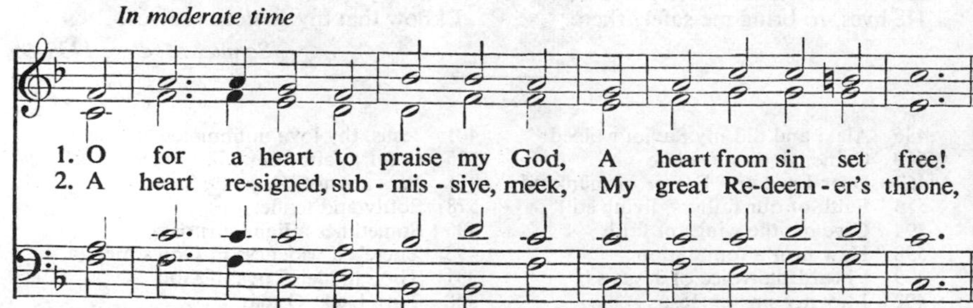
1. O for a heart to praise my God, A heart from sin set free!
2. A heart re-signed, sub - mis - sive, meek, My great Re-deem - er's throne,

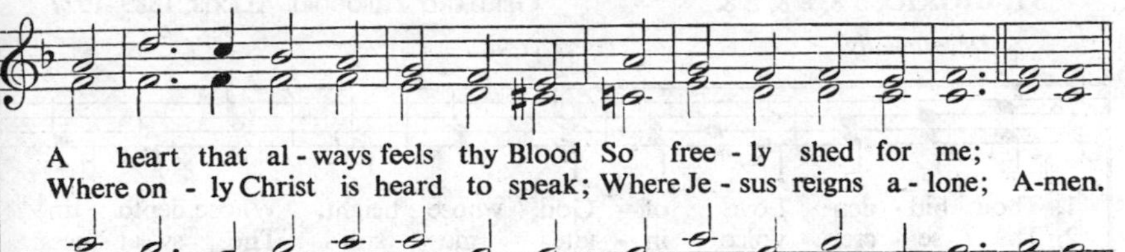
A heart that al - ways feels thy Blood So free - ly shed for me;
Where on - ly Christ is heard to speak; Where Je - sus reigns a - lone; A-men.

3 A humble, lowly, contrite heart,
Believing, true, and clean,
Which neither life nor death can part
From him that dwells within;

4 A heart in every thought renewed
And full of love divine;
Perfect, and right, and pure, and good,
A copy, Lord, of thine.

5 Thy nature, gracious Lord, impart;
Come quickly from above;
Write thy new name upon my heart,
Thy new, best name of love. Amen.

Charles Wesley, 1707–88

390

BEATITUDO. C. M. JOHN BACCHUS DYKES, 1823–76

With movement

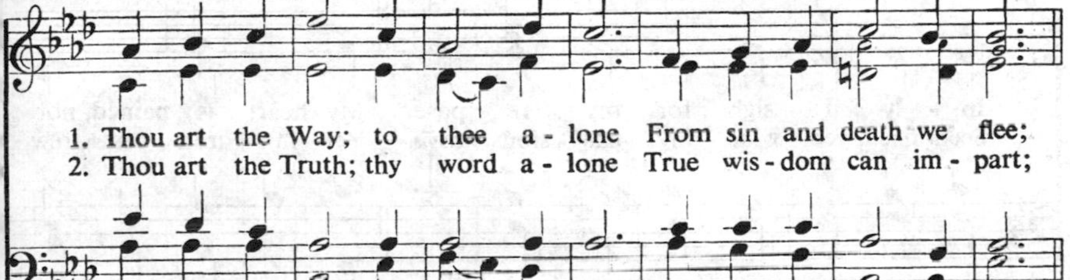
1. Thou art the Way; to thee a - lone From sin and death we flee;
2. Thou art the Truth; thy word a - lone True wis - dom can im - part;

And he who would the Fa - ther seek Must seek him, Lord, by thee.
Thou on - ly canst in - form the mind And pu - ri - fy the heart. A-men.

3 Thou art the Life; the rending tomb
Proclaims thy conquering arm;
And those who put their trust in thee
Nor death nor hell shall harm.

4 Thou art the Way, the Truth, the Life;
Grant us that way to know,
That truth to keep, that life to win,
Whose joys eternal flow. Amen.

George Washington Doane, 1799–1859

This hymn may also be sung to ST. JAMES (No. 247)

ST. INGRID. 8 8, 8 8, 8 8.
GERHARD THEODORE ALEXIS, 1889–1927
Devotionally
FIRST TUNE
1. Thou hid - den Love of God, whose height, Whose depth un - fath - omed no man knows; I see from far thy beau-teous light, In - ly I sigh for thy re - pose. My heart is pained, nor can it be At rest, till it finds rest in thee.
2. Thy se - cret voice in - vites me still The sweet - ness of thy yoke to prove; And fain I would; but, though my will Seem fixed, yet wide my pas - sions rove. Yet hin - dran - ces strew all the way; I aim at thee, yet from thee stray. A-men.

3 Is there a thing beneath the sun
That strives with thee my heart to share?
Ah, tear it thence, and reign alone,
The Lord of every motion there;
Then shall my heart from earth be free,
When it hath found repose in thee.

4 Each moment draw from earth away
My heart, that lowly waits thy call;
Speak to my inmost soul, and say,
'I am thy Love, thy God, thy All!'
To feel thy power, to hear thy voice,
To taste thy love, be all my choice. Amen.

Gerhard Tersteegen, 1697–1769
Tr. John Wesley, 1703–91

This hymn may also be sung to DAVID'S HARP (No. 471)

Aspiration

ST. CHRYSOSTOM. 8 8, 8 8, 8 8. **JOSEPH BARNBY, 1838–96**

SECOND TUNE

Devotionally

1. Thou hid - den Love of God, whose height, Whose depth un - fath - omed
2. Thy se - cret voice in - vites me still The sweet - ness of thy

no man knows; I see from far thy beau - teous light,
yoke to prove; And fain I would; but, though my will

In - ly I sigh for thy re - pose. My heart is pained, nor
Seem fixed, yet wide my pas - sions rove. Yet hin - dran - ces strew

can it be At rest, till it finds rest in thee.
all the way; I aim at thee, yet from thee stray. A - men.

Is there a thing beneath the sun
That strives with thee my heart to share?
Ah, tear it thence, and reign alone,
The Lord of every motion there;
Then shall my heart from earth be free,
When it hath found repose in thee.

4 Each moment draw from earth away
My heart, that lowly waits thy call,
Speak to my inmost soul, and say,
'I am thy Love, thy God, thy All!'
To feel thy power, to hear thy voice,
To taste thy love, be all my choice. Amen.

Gerhard Tersteegen, 1697–1769
Tr. John Wesley, 1703–91

This hymn may also be sung to DAVID'S HARP (No. 471)

MORE LOVE TO THEE. 6 4, 6 4, 6 6, 4 4.
WILLIAM HOWARD DOANE, 1832–1915
Quietly
1. More love to thee, O Christ, More love to thee!
2. Once earth - ly joy I craved, Sought peace and rest;
Hear thou the prayer I make On bend - ed knee;
Now thee a - lone I seek, Give what is best:
This is my ear - nest plea, More love, O Christ, to thee,
This all my prayer shall be, More love, O Christ, to thee,
More love to thee, More love to thee.
More love to thee, More love to thee. A - men.

3 Then shall my latest breath
Whisper thy praise;
This be the parting cry
My heart shall raise;
This still its prayer shall be,
More love, O Christ, to thee,
More love to thee. Amen.

Elizabeth Prentiss, 1818–7

Aspiration

ABERYSTWYTH. 7 7, 7 7. D. JOSEPH PARRY, 1841–1903

FIRST TUNE

With dignity

1. Je - sus, Lov - er of my soul, Let me to thy bos - om fly,
2. Oth - er ref - uge have I none; Hangs my help - less soul on thee;
While the near - er wa - ters roll, While the tem - pest still is high;
Leave, ah, leave me not a - lone, Still sup - port and com - fort me.
Hide me, O my Sav - iour, hide, Till the storm of life is past;
All my trust on thee is stayed, All my help from thee I bring;
Safe in - to the ha - ven guide, O re - ceive my soul at last.
Cov - er my de-fense-less head With the sha-dow of thy wing. A-men.

3 Thou, O Christ, art all I want;
More than all in thee I find;
Raise the fallen, cheer the faint,
Heal the sick, and lead the blind.
Just and holy is thy Name,
I am all unrighteousness;
False and full of sin I am,
Thou art full of truth and grace.

4 Plenteous grace with thee is found,
Grace to cover all my sin;
Let the healing streams abound,
Make and keep me pure within.
Thou of life the fountain art,
Freely let me take of thee;
Spring thou up within my heart,
Rise to all eternity. Amen.

Charles Wesley, 1707–88

393

HOLLINGSIDE. 7 7, 7 7. D.
JOHN BACCHUS DYKES, 1823–76
In flowing style
SECOND TUNE
1. Je - sus, Lov - er of my soul, Let me to thy bos - om fly,
2. Oth - er ref - uge have I none; Hangs my help - less soul on thee;
While the near - er wa - ters roll, While the tem - pest still is high
Leave, ah, leave me not a - lone, Still sup - port and com - fort me.
Hide me, O my Sav - iour, hide, Till the storm of life is past;
All my trust on thee is stayed, All my help from thee I bring
Safe in - to the ha - ven guide, O re - ceive my soul at last.
Cov-er my de - fense - less head With the shad-ow of thy wing. A-me

3 Thou, O Christ, art all I want;
More than all in thee I find.
Raise the fallen, cheer the faint,
Heal the sick, and lead the blind.
Just and holy is thy Name,
I am all unrighteousness;
False and full of sin I am,
Thou art full of truth and grace.

4 Plenteous grace with thee is found,
Grace to cover all my sin;
Let the healing streams abound,
Make and keep me pure within.
Thou of life the fountain art,
Freely let me take of thee;
Spring thou up within my heart,
Rise to all eternity. Amen.

Charles Wesley, 1707–

MARTYN. 7 7, 7 7. D. SIMEON B. MARSH, 1798–1875

THIRD TUNE

In strict time
1. Je - sus, Lov - er of my soul, Let me to thy bos - om fly,
2. Oth - er ref - uge have I none; Hangs my help - less soul on thee;
While the near - er wa - ters roll, While the tem - pest still is high;
Leave, ah, leave me not a - lone, Still sup-port and com - fort me.
Hide me, O my Sav - iour, hide, Till the storm of life is past;
All my trust on thee is stayed, All my help from thee I bring;
Safe in - to the ha - ven guide, O re-ceive my soul at last.
Cov - er my de-fense-less head With the shad-ow of thy wing. A-men.

3 Thou, O Christ, art all I want;
  More than all in thee I find.
Raise the fallen, cheer the faint,
  Heal the sick, and lead the blind.
Just and holy is thy Name,
  I am all unrighteousness;
False and full of sin I am,
  Thou art full of truth and grace.

4 Plenteous grace with thee is found,
  Grace to cover all my sin;
Let the healing streams abound,
  Make and keep me pure within.
Thou of life the fountain art,
  Freely let me take of thee;
Spring thou up within my heart,
  Rise to all eternity. Amen.

Charles Wesley, 1707–88

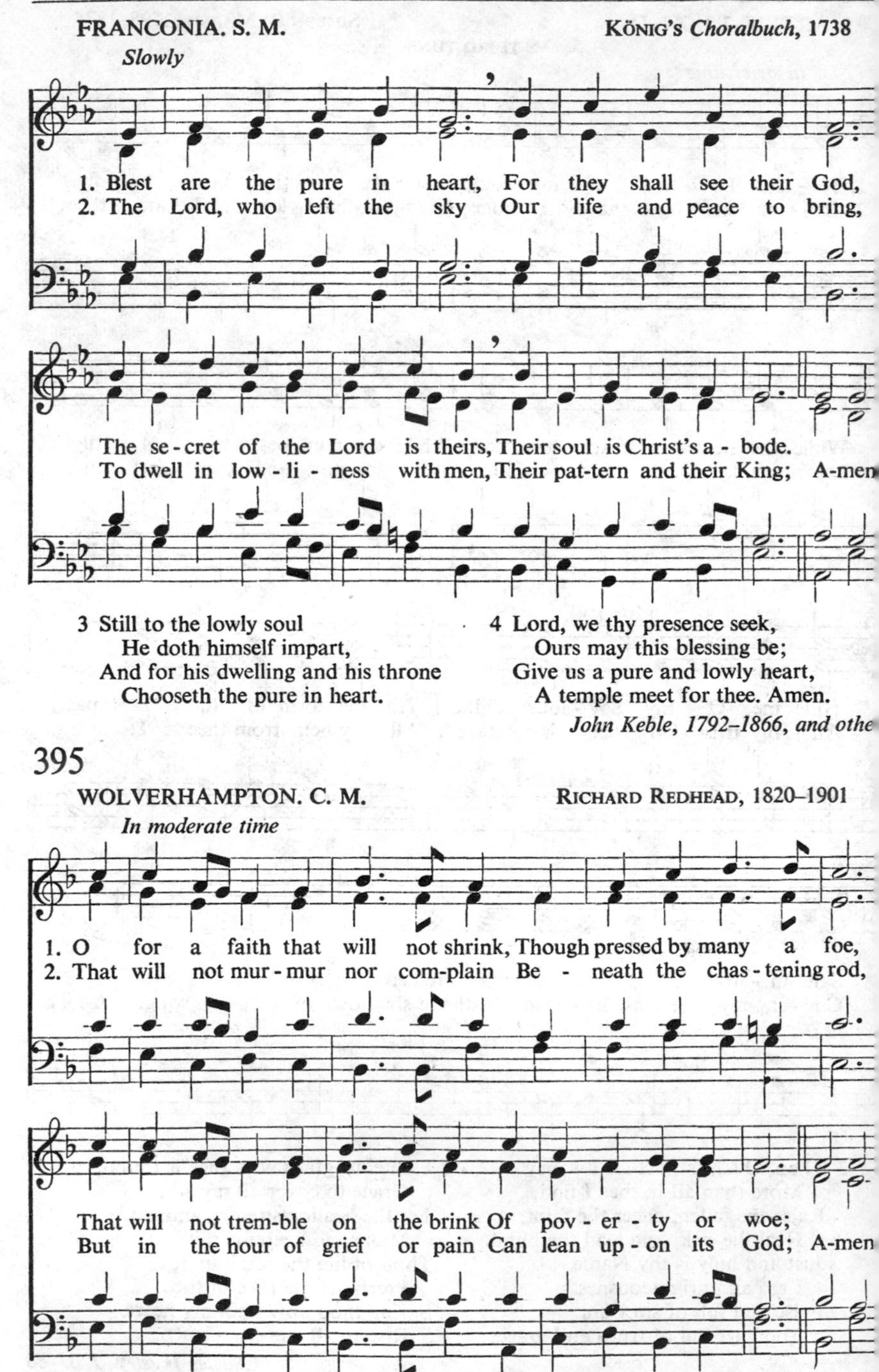
FRANCONIA. S. M.
KÖNIG'S *Choralbuch*, 1738
Slowly
1. Blest are the pure in heart, For they shall see their God,
2. The Lord, who left the sky Our life and peace to bring,
The se-cret of the Lord is theirs, Their soul is Christ's a-bode.
To dwell in low-li-ness with men, Their pat-tern and their King; A-men
395
WOLVERHAMPTON. C. M.
RICHARD REDHEAD, 1820–1901
In moderate time
1. O for a faith that will not shrink, Though pressed by many a foe,
2. That will not mur-mur nor com-plain Be-neath the chas-tening rod,
That will not trem-ble on the brink Of pov-er-ty or woe;
But in the hour of grief or pain Can lean up-on its God; A-men

3 Still to the lowly soul
He doth himself impart,
And for his dwelling and his throne
Chooseth the pure in heart.

4 Lord, we thy presence seek,
Ours may this blessing be;
Give us a pure and lowly heart,
A temple meet for thee. Amen.

John Keble, 1792–1866, and othe

3 A faith that shines more bright and clear
When tempests rage without,
That when in danger knows no fear,
In darkness feels no doubt;

4 A faith that keeps the narrow way
Till life's last hour is fled,
And with a pure and heavenly ray
Lights up a dying bed.

5 Lord, give me such a faith as this,
And then, whate'er may come,
I taste e'en now the hallowed bliss
Of an eternal home. Amen.

William H. Bathurst, 1796–1877

This hymn may also be sung to DUNDEE (FRENCH) (No. 266)

596

I LIFT MY EYES. 9 8, 9 8. RUDOLF LAGI, 1823–68

With movement

1. I lift my eyes unto heaven above, And fold my hands to draw near thee; For thou, dear Lord, dost thy children love, And thou hast promised to hear me.
2. How sweet to bless thee and praise thy Name, For thou, O Christ, art my Saviour; Kind Shepherd, guard me from sin and shame, And let me love thee forever.

3 A little flower in thy garden fair,
My life to thee has been given;
O Saviour, keep me in thy dear care,
And bring me safely to heaven.

4 Dear Lord, I thank thee for all thy love
And gifts divine beyond measure;
A sweeter song I will raise above
To thee, my heart's dearest treasure.

Johan Ludvig Runeberg, 1804–77
Paraphrase, Ernest Edwin Ryden, based on a translation by Ida M. Kaskinen, 1903–

397 Aspiration

HYFRYDOL. 8 7, 8 7. D. ROWLAND HUGH PRICHARD, 1811–87

Slowly, with feeling FIRST TUNE

1. Love di - vine, all loves ex - cel - ling, Joy of heaven, to
Fix in us thy hum - ble dwell - ing, All thy faith - ful
2. Breathe, O breathe thy lov - ing spir - it In - to ev - ery
Let us all in thee in - her - it, Let us find thy
earth come down!
mer - cies crown. Je - sus, thou art all com - pas - sion,
trou - bled breast;
prom - ised rest. Take a - way the love of sin - ning;
Pure un - bound - ed love thou art; Vis - it us with
Al - pha and O - me - ga be; End of faith, as
thy sal - va - tion, En - ter ev - ery trem-bling heart.
its be - gin - ning, Set our hearts at lib - er - ty. A - men.

3 Come, almighty to deliver,
Let us all thy life receive;
Suddenly return, and never,
Never more thy temples leave.
Thee we would be always blessing,
Serve thee as thy hosts above,
Pray, and praise thee without ceasing,
Glory in thy precious love.

4 Finish then thy new creation,
Pure and spotless let us be;
Let us see thy great salvation
Perfectly restored in thee!
Changed from glory into glory,
Till in heaven we take our place,
Till we cast our crowns before thee,
Lost in wonder, love, and praise. Amen.

Charles Wesley, 1707–88

This hymn may also be sung to BEECHER (No. 312)

97 Aspiration

LOVE DIVINE (LE JEUNE). 8 7, 8 7. D. GEORGE F. LE JEUNE, 1841–1904

Broadly SECOND TUNE

1. Love di - vine, all loves ex - cel - ling, Joy of heaven, to earth come down!
2. Breathe, O breathe thy lov - ing spir - it In - to ev - ery trou-bled breast;
Fix in us thy hum-ble dwell-ing, All thy faith - ful mer - cies crown.
Let us all in thee in - her - it, Let us find thy prom-ised rest.
Je - sus, thou art all com - pas - sion, Pure un-bound-ed love thou art;
Take a - way the love of sin - ning; Al - pha and O - me - ga be;
Vis - it us with thy sal - va-tion, En - ter ev - ery trem-bling heart.
End of faith, as its be - gin-ning, Set our hearts at lib - er - ty. A-men.

3 Come, almighty to deliver,
Let us all thy life receive;
Suddenly return, and never,
Never more thy temples leave.
Thee we would be always blessing,
Serve thee as thy hosts above,
Pray, and praise thee without ceasing,
Glory in thy precious love.

4 Finish then thy new creation,
Pure and spotless let us be;
Let us see thy great salvation
Perfectly restored in thee!
Changed from glory into glory,
Till in heaven we take our place,
Till we cast our crowns before thee,
Lost in wonder, love, and praise. Amen.

Charles Wesley, 1707–88

This hymn may also be sung to BEECHER (No. 312)

OLD 130TH. 7 6, 7 6. D. French *Psalter*, Strassburg, 1539

With dignity

1. Mine eyes un - to the moun - tains I lift, whence help goes forth;
2. The shade of the Al - might - y Shields thee up - on the right;
My help comes from Je - ho - vah, Mak - er of heaven and earth.
The sun - light shall not smite thee, Nor yet the moon by night.
Thy foot shall nev - er fal - ter; Thy ev - ery step he keeps;
Thy com - ing in he bless - eth, And from the tem - ple door
The Lord who keep - eth Is - rael, He slum-bers not, nor sleeps.
Thy go - ing out he guid - eth Now and for ev - er - more.

Ernst William Olson, 1870–19
Psalm 1

This hymn may also be sung to FAR OFF LANDS (No. 317)

ST. PETERSBURG (CHERUBIC HYMN). 8 8, 8 8, 8 8.

In moderate time DMITRI STEPANOVITCH BORTNIANSKI, 1752–1825

1. Je - sus, thy bound - less love to me No thought can
2. O grant that noth - ing in my soul May dwell, but
reach, no tongue de - clare; U - nite my thank - ful heart to thee,
thy pure love a - lone; O may thy love pos - sess me whole,
And reign with - out a ri - val there. Thine whol - ly, thine a -
My joy, my treas - ure, and my crown; Strange fires far from my
lone I am; Be thou a - lone my con - stant flame.
soul re - move; May ev - ery act, word, thought, be love.

3 O Love, how cheering is thy ray!
All pain before thy presence flies;
Care, anguish, sorrow, melt away,
Where'er thy healing beams arise.
O Jesus, nothing may I see,
Nothing desire or seek, but thee.

4 Unwearied, may I this pursue,
Dauntless, to this high prize aspire;
Hourly within my soul renew
This holy flame, this heavenly fire;
And day and night be all my care
To guard this sacred treasure there.

Paul Gerhardt, 1607–76
Tr. John Wesley, 1703–91

This hymn may also be sung to DAVID'S HARP (No. 471) or ST. CATHERINE (No. 516)

LOBT GOTT, IHR CHRISTEN. C. M. NIKOLAUS HERMANN, *cir.* 1480–1561

Joyfully
1. O Christ, our hope, our hearts' de - sire, Re - demp - tion's on - ly spring; Cre - a - tor of the world art thou, Its Sav - iour and its King, Its Sav - iour and its King.
2. How vast the mer - cy and the love Which laid our sins on thee, And led thee to a cru - el death To set thy peo - ple free, To set thy peo - ple free.
A-men

3 But now the bonds of death are burst,
The ransom has been paid;
And thou art on thy Father's throne
In glorious robes arrayed.

4 O may thy mighty love prevail
Our sinful souls to spare,
O may we come before thy throne
And find acceptance there!

5 O Christ, be thou our present joy,
Our future great reward;
Our only glory may it be
To glory in the Lord!

6 All praise to thee, ascended Lord;
All glory ever be
To Father, Son, and Holy Ghost
Through all eternity! Amen.

Latin hymn, cir. VIII ce
Tr. John Chandler, 1806–76

This hymn may also be sung to METZLER (No. 453)

Aspiration

EVARTS. 7 6, 7 6. D.

LOWELL MASON, 1792–1872
Based on German Folk Tunes

In moderate time
1. Je - sus, thy love un - bound - ed, So full, so sweet, so free,
Leaves all our thoughts con-found - ed When - e'er we think of thee.
For us thou cam'st from heav - en, For us didst bleed and die,
That, ran-somed and for - giv - en, We might as - cend on high. A-men.

2 We know that thou hast bought us,
And washed us in thy Blood;
We know thy grace hath brought us
As kings and priests to God,
We know that blessèd morning,
Long looked for, draweth near,
When we, at thy returning,
In glory shall appear.

3 O let thy love constrain us
To give our hearts to thee;
Let nothing please or pain us,
Apart, O Lord, from thee;
Our joy, our one endeavor,
Through suffering, conflict, shame,
To serve thee, gracious Saviour,
And magnify thy Name. Amen.

Bosworth's Hymns, 1865

ST. MARGARET. 8 8, 8 8 6. ALBERT LISTER PEACE, 1844–1912

In moderate time

1. O Love that wilt not let me go, I rest my wea - ry
2. O Light that fol-lowest all my way, I yield my flick-erin
soul in thee; I give thee back the life I owe, Tha
torch to thee; My heart re - stores its bor-rowed ray, Tha
in thine o - cean depths its flow May rich - er, full - er be.
in thy sun-shine's blaze its day May bright - er, fair - er be.

3 O Joy that seekest me through pain,
  I cannot close my heart to thee;
I trace the rainbow through the rain,
And feel the promise is not vain
  That morn shall tearless be.

4 O Cross that liftest up my head,
  I dare not ask to fly from thee;
I lay in dust life's glory dead,
And from the ground there blossoms re
  Life that shall endless be.

George Matheson, 1842–19

See also:

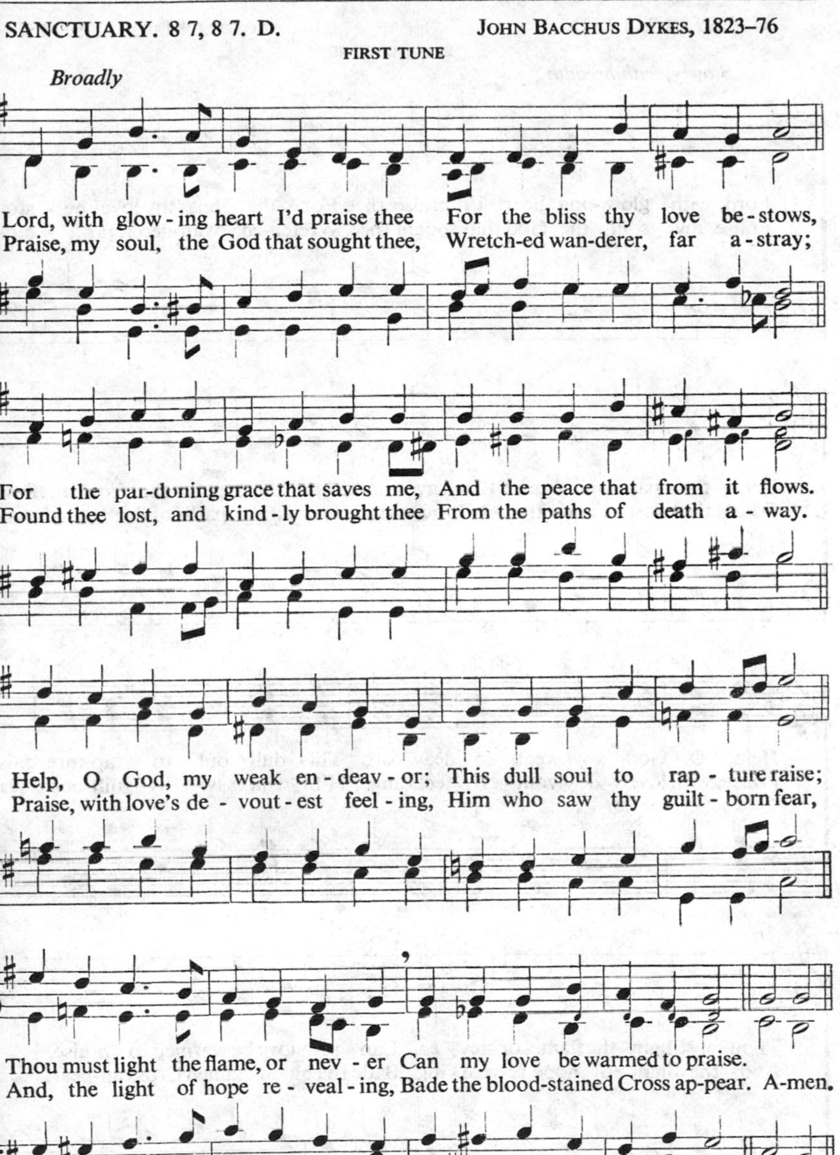
SANCTUARY. 8 7, 8 7. D.
JOHN BACCHUS DYKES, 1823–76
FIRST TUNE
Broadly
Lord, with glow - ing heart I'd praise thee For the bliss thy love be - stows,
Praise, my soul, the God that sought thee, Wretch-ed wan-derer, far a - stray;
For the par-doning grace that saves me, And the peace that from it flows.
Found thee lost, and kind - ly brought thee From the paths of death a - way.
Help, O God, my weak en - deav - or; This dull soul to rap - ture raise;
Praise, with love's de - vout - est feel - ing, Him who saw thy guilt - born fear,
Thou must light the flame, or nev - er Can my love be warmed to praise.
And, the light of hope re - veal - ing, Bade the blood-stained Cross ap-pear. A-men.

3 Lord, this bosom's ardent feeling
Vainly would my lips express;
Low before thy footstool kneeling,
Deign thy suppliant's prayer to bless;

Let thy grace, my soul's chief treasure,
Love's pure flame within me raise;
And, since words can never measure,
Let my life show forth thy praise.
Amen.

Francis Scott Key, 1779–1843

RIPLEY. 8 7, 8 7. D. LOWELL MASON, 1792–1872

SECOND TUNE

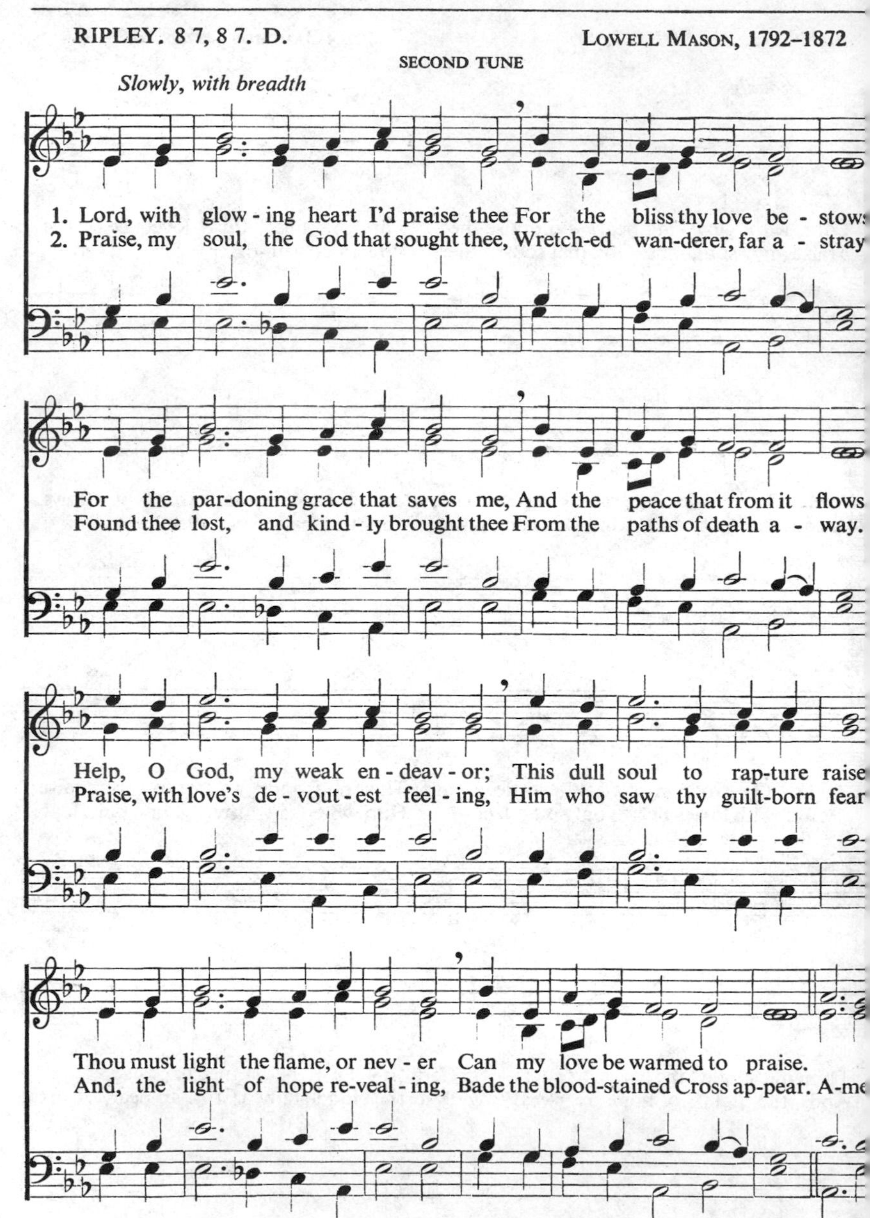
Slowly, with breadth
1. Lord, with glow - ing heart I'd praise thee For the bliss thy love be - stows
2. Praise, my soul, the God that sought thee, Wretch-ed wan-derer, far a - stray
For the par-doning grace that saves me, And the peace that from it flows
Found thee lost, and kind - ly brought thee From the paths of death a - way.
Help, O God, my weak en - deav - or; This dull soul to rap-ture raise
Praise, with love's de - vout - est feel - ing, Him who saw thy guilt-born fear
Thou must light the flame, or nev - er Can my love be warmed to praise.
And, the light of hope re-veal - ing, Bade the blood-stained Cross ap-pear. A-me

3 Lord, this bosom's ardent feeling
Vainly would my lips express;
Low before thy footstool kneeling,
Deign thy suppliant's prayer to bless;

Let thy grace, my soul's chief treasure,
Love's pure flame within me raise;
And, since words can never measure,
Let my life show forth thy praise.

Am

Francis Scott Key, 1779–1

WIE SCHÖN LEUCHTET. Irregular.
PHILIPP NICOLAI, 1556–1608
With movement
1. How bright - ly beams the morn - ing star! What sud - den
Bright - ness of God, that breaks our night And fills the
ra - diance from a - far Doth cheer us with its shin - ing?
dark - ened souls with light, Who long for truth were pin - ing!
New - ly, tru - ly, God's Word feeds us, Right - ly leads us,
Life be - stow - ing. Praise, O praise such love o'er - flow - ing!

2 Through thee alone can we be blest;
Then deep be on our hearts imprest
The love that thou hast borne us;
So make us ready to fulfill
With ardent zeal thy holy will,
Though men may vex or scorn us;
Hold us, fold us, lest we fail thee,
Lo, we hail thee,
Long to know thee!
All we are and have we owe thee.

3 All praise to him who came to save,
Who conquered death and scorned the grave;
Each day new praise resoundeth
To him, the Life who once was slain,
The friend whom none shall trust in vain,
Whose grace for aye aboundeth;
Sing then, ring then, tell the story
Of his glory,
Till his praises
Flood with light earth's darkest mazes!

Philipp Nicolai, 1556–1608
Tr. Hymnal Version, 1955

For another arrangement of music, see No. 33

MONKLAND. 7 7, 7 7. Moravian Melody

Arr. by John Bernard Wilkes, 1785–1869

With dignity

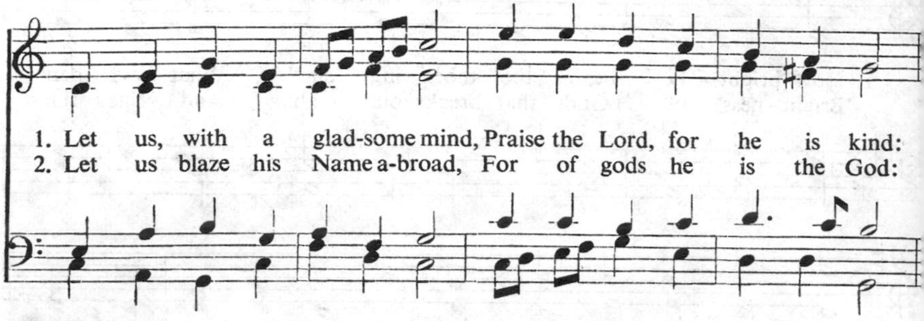

1. Let us, with a glad-some mind, Praise the Lord, for he is kind:
2. Let us blaze his Name a-broad, For of gods he is the God:

Refrain

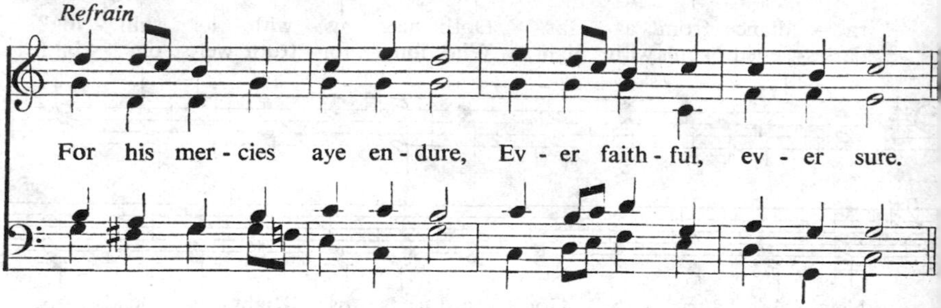

For his mer - cies aye en - dure, Ev - er faith - ful, ev - er sure.

3 He, with all-commanding might,
Filled the new-made world with light:

4 All things living he doth feed;
His full hand supplies their need:

5 He hath, with a piteous eye,
Looked upon our misery:

6 Let us then with gladsome mind
Praise the Lord, for he is kind:

John Milton, 1608–74
Psalm 136

This hymn may also be sung to GOTT SEI DANK (No. 323)

406

ST. PETER. C. M. Alexander Robert Reinagle, 1799–1877

In moderate time

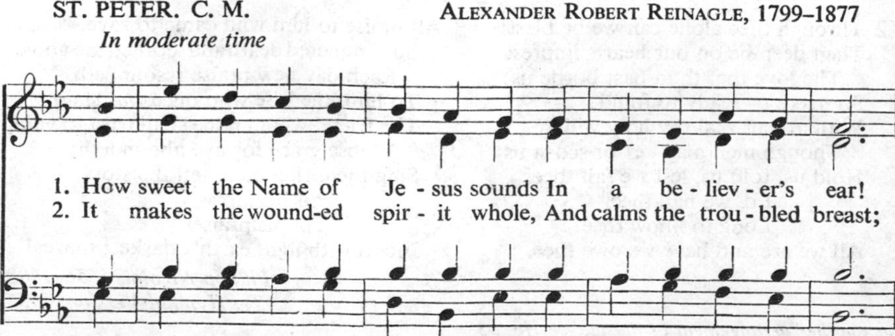
1. How sweet the Name of Je - sus sounds In a be - liev - er's ear!
2. It makes the wound-ed spir - it whole, And calms the trou - bled breast;

It soothes his sor-rows, heals his wounds, And drives a - way his fear.
'Tis man - na to the hun-gry soul, And to the wea - ry rest. A - men.

3 Dear Name! the rock on which I build,
My shield and hiding-place;
My never-failing treasury filled
With boundless stores of grace.

4 Weak is the effort of my heart,
And cold my warmest thought;
But, when I see thee as thou art,
I'll praise thee as I ought.

5 Till then I would thy love proclaim
With every fleeting breath;
And may the music of thy Name
Refresh my soul in death. Amen.

John Newton, 1725–1807

407

ARUNDEL. 8 7, 8 7. JOHN BACCHUS DYKES, 1823–76

With dignity

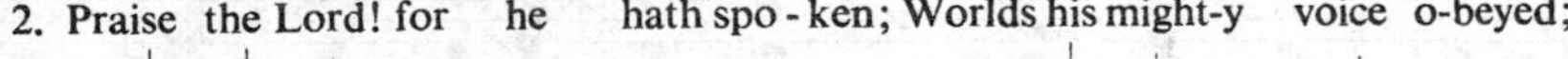
1. Praise the Lord! Ye heavens, a - dore him; Praise him, an - gels, in the height;
2. Praise the Lord! for he hath spo - ken; Worlds his might-y voice o-beyed;

Sun and moon, re - joice be - fore him; Praise him, all ye stars and light.
Laws, which nev-er shall be bro-ken, For their guid-ance hath he made. A-men.

3 Praise the Lord! for he is gracious;
Never shall his promise fail;
God hath made his saints victorious,
Sin and death shall not prevail.

4 Praise the God of our salvation;
Hosts on high, his power proclaim;
Heaven and earth, and all creation,
Laud and magnify his Name! Amen.

London Foundling Hospital Collection, 1796
Psalm 148

LOBE DEN HERREN. 14, 14, 4 7 8.
STRALSUND *Gesangbuch*, 1665
Majestically, with movement
1. Praise to the Lord, the Al - might - y, the King of cre - a - tion;
O my soul, praise him, for he is thy health and sal - va - tion:
2. Praise to the Lord, who o'er all things so won - drous - ly reign - eth,
Shel - ters thee un - der his wings, yea, so gen - tly sus - tain - eth:
All ye who hear, Now to his tem - ple draw near;
Hast thou not seen? All that is need - ful hath been
Join - ing in glad ad - o - ra - tion.
Grant - ed in what he or - dain - eth.
A - men.

3 Praise to the Lord, who doth prosper thy work and defend thee;
Surely his goodness and mercy here daily attend thee.
Ponder anew
What the Almighty can do,
If with his love he befriend thee!

4 Praise to the Lord, O let all that is in me adore him;
All that hath life and breath, come now with praises before him!
Let the Amen
Sound from his people again;
Gladly for aye we adore him. Amen.

Joachim Neander, 1650–8
Tr. Catherine Winkworth, 1829–7
Based on Psalms 103 and 15

CROFT'S 136TH. 6 6, 6 6, 4 4, 4 4. WILLIAM CROFT, 1678–1727

Gravely

1. Ye ho - ly an - gels bright, Who wait at God's right hand, Or
2. Ye bless - ed souls at rest, Who ran this earth - ly race, And
through the realms of light Fly at your Lord's com-mand: As - sist our
now, from sin re - leased, Be - hold the Sav-iour's face, His prais - es
song, Or else the theme Too high doth seem For mor - tal tongue.
sound, As in his sight With sweet de - light Ye do a - bound.

3 Ye saints, who toil below,
Adore your heavenly King,
And onward as ye go
Some joyful anthem sing;
Take what he gives
And praise him still,
Through good or ill,
Who ever lives!

4 My soul, bear thou thy part,
Triumph in God above,
And with a well-tuned heart
Sing thou the songs of love;
Let all thy days
Till life shall end,
Whate'er he send,
Be filled with praise.

Richard Baxter, 1615–91
John Hampden Gurney, 1802–62

LEONI (YIGDAL). 6 6, 8 4. D. Traditional Hebrew Melody XVII Century

May be sung in unison, with spirit

1. The God of A-braham praise, Who reigns en-throned a - bove;
2. Though na - ture's strength de - cay, And earth and hell with - stand,
An - cient of ev - er - last - ing days, And God of love;
To Ca - naan's bound we urge our way At his com - mand.
To him up - lift your voice, At whose su-preme com - mand
The wa - tery deep we pass With Je - sus in our view;
From earth we rise, and seek the joys At his right hand.
And through the howl-ing wil - der - ness Our way pur - sue. A-men.

3 The goodly land we see
With peace and plenty blest;
A land of sacred liberty
And endless rest;
There milk and honey flow,
And oil and wine abound,
And trees of life for ever grow,
With mercy crowned.

4 There dwells the Lord our King,
The Lord our Righteousness,
Triumphant o'er the world and sin,
The Prince of Peace;
On Zion's sacred height
His kingdom he maintains,
And glorious with his saints in light
For ever reigns.

5 Before the great Three-One
They all exulting stand,
And tell the wonders he hath done
Through all their land;
The listening spheres attend
And swell the growing fame,
And sing, in songs which never end,
The wondrous Name.

6 The God who reigns on high
The great archangels sing,
And 'Holy, holy, holy,' cry,
'Almighty King,
Who was, and is, the same,
And evermore shall be:
Eternal Father, great I AM,
We worship thee.'

7 Before the Saviour's face
The ransomed nations bow,
O'erwhelmed at his almighty grace,
Forever new;
He shows his prints of love:
They kindle to a flame,
And sound through all the worlds above,
'Worthy the Lamb.'

8 The whole triumphant host
Give thanks to God on high;
'Hail, Father, Son and Holy Ghost!'
They ever cry;
Hail, Abraham's God, and mine!
I join the heavenly lays.
All might and majesty are thine,
And endless praise. Amen.

Thomas Olivers, 1725–99
Based on the Yigdal

411

GERONTIUS. C. M. JOHN BACCHUS DYKES, 1823–76

Slowly

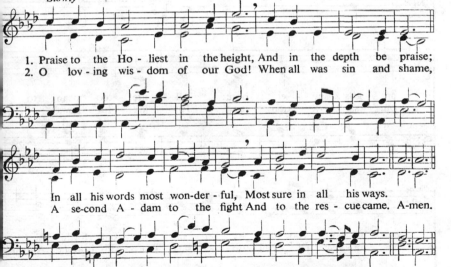

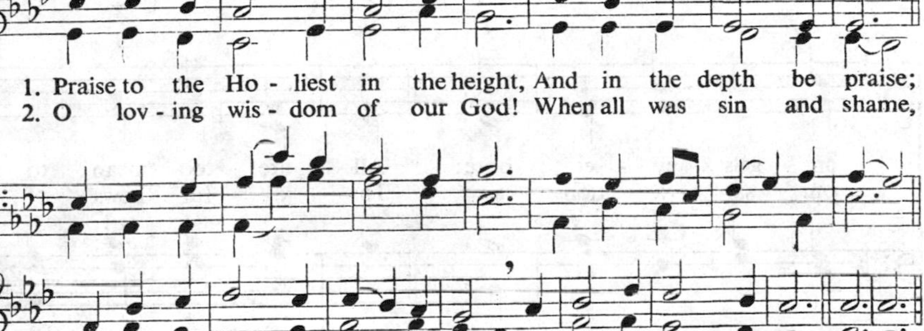
1. Praise to the Ho - liest in the height, And in the depth be praise;
2. O lov - ing wis - dom of our God! When all was sin and shame,

In all his words most won-der - ful, Most sure in all his ways.
A se-cond A - dam to the fight And to the res - cue came. A-men.

3 O wisest love! that flesh and blood,
Which did in Adam fail,
Should strive afresh against the foe,
Should strive, and should prevail;

4 And that a higher gift than grace
Should flesh and blood refine,
God's presence and his very self
And essence all divine.

5 O generous love! that he who smote
In Man for man the foe,
The double agony in Man
For man should undergo;

6 And in the garden secretly,
And on the Cross on high,
Should teach his brethren, and inspire
To suffer and to die.

7 Praise to the Holiest in the height,
And in the depth be praise;
In all his words most wonderful,
Most sure in all his ways. Amen.

John Henry Newman, 1801–90

ST. PETER'S, MANCHESTER. 6 6, 6 6, 8 8. ROGER R. ROSS, 1817–99

Broadly

1. Join all the glo - rious names Of wis - dom, love, and power, That ev - er mor - tals knew, Or an - gels ev - er bore: All are too mean to speak his worth, Too mean to set my Sav - iour forth.
2. Great Proph - et of my God, My tongue would bless thy Name; By thee the joy - ful news Of our sal - va - tion came, The joy - ful news of sins for - given, Of hell sub - dued, and peace with heaven. A-men.

3 Jesus, my great High Priest,
Offered his Blood and died;
My guilty conscience seeks
No sacrifice beside:
His powerful Blood did once atone,
And now it pleads before the throne.

4 O thou Almighty Lord,
My Conqueror and my King,
Thy sceptre and thy sword,
Thy reigning grace, I sing:
Thine is the power; behold I sit
In willing bonds before thy feet. Amen.

Isaac Watts, 1674–1748, a.

NUN DANKET ALL UND BRINGET EHR. C. M.

Joyfully FIRST TUNE JOHANN CRÜGER, 1598–1662

1. Come, let us join our cheer - ful songs With an - gels round the throne;
2. 'Wor - thy the Lamb that died,' they cry, 'To be ex - alt - ed thus';

Ten thou-sand thou - sand are their tongues, But all their joys are one.
'Wor - thy the Lamb,' our lips re - ply, 'For he was slain for us.'

3 Jesus is worthy to receive
Honor and power divine;
And blessings, more than we can give,
Be, Lord, for ever thine.

4 The whole creation join in one
To bless the sacred Name
Of him that sits upon the throne,
And to adore the Lamb.

Isaac Watts, 1674–1748

This hymn may also be sung to DEDHAM (No. 428)

13

CHEERFUL. C. M. MARTIN SHAW, 1875–

Moderately fast SECOND TUNE

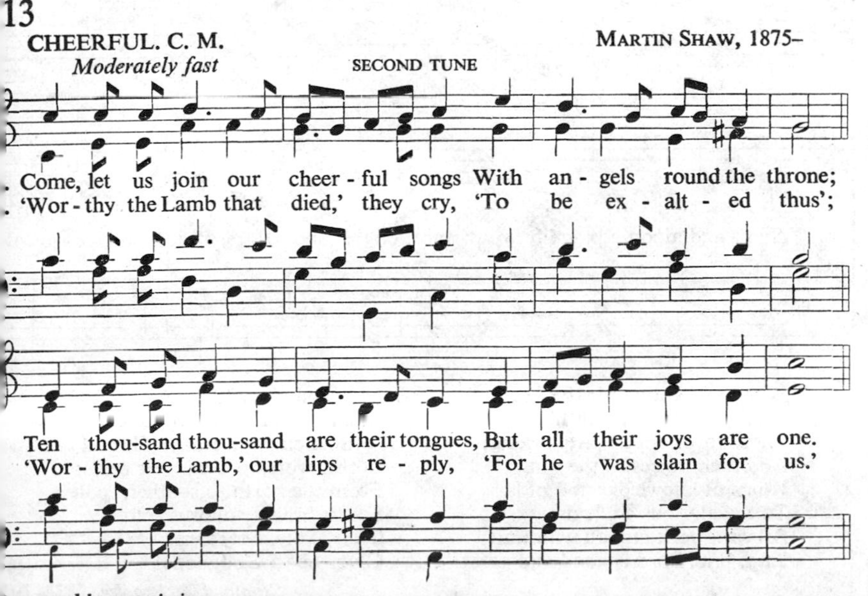
Come, let us join our cheer - ful songs With an - gels round the throne;
'Wor - thy the Lamb that died,' they cry, 'To be ex - alt - ed thus';
Ten thou-sand thou-sand are their tongues, But all their joys are one.
'Wor - thy the Lamb,' our lips re - ply, 'For he was slain for us.'

une used by permission

SALZBURG (ALLE MENSCHEN). 7 7, 7 7. D. JAKOB HINTZE, 1622–1702
With vigor Harm. by J. S. BACH, 1685–1750

1. Let the whole cre - a - tion cry, 'Glo - ry to the Lord on high!'
Heaven and earth, a - wake and sing, 'God is good and there - fore King!'
Praise him, all ye hosts a - bove, Ev - er bright and fair in love;
Sun and moon, up - lift your voice, Night and stars, in God re - joice!

2 Warriors fighting for the Lord,
Prophets burning with his word,
Those to whom the arts belong,
Add their voices to the song.
Kings of knowledge and of law,
To the glorious circle draw;
All who work and all who wait,
Sing, 'The Lord is good and great!'

3 Men and women, young and old,
Raise the anthem manifold,
And let children's happy hearts
In this worship bear their parts;
From the north to southern pole
Let the mighty chorus roll:
'Holy, holy, holy One,
Glory be to God alone!'

Stopford A. Brooke, 1832–19

5 Adoration and Praise

MENDON. L. M.

German Melody
EPHRAIM REED'S *Musical Monitor*, 1824
Adapted by LOWELL MASON, 1792–1872

In moderate time

1. Thee we a - dore, e - ter - nal Lord! We praise thy
2. To thee a - loud all an - gels cry, The heavens and
Name with one ac - cord, Thy saints, who here thy good - ness
all the powers on high; Thee, ho - ly, ho - ly, ho - ly
see, Through all the world do wor - ship thee.
King, Lord God of Hosts, they ev - er sing. A - men.

3 The apostles join the glorious throng,
The prophets swell the immortal song,
The martyrs' noble army raise
Eternal anthems to thy praise.

4 From day to day, O Lord, do we
Highly exalt and honor thee;
Thy Name we worship and adore,
World without end, for evermore!

5 Vouchsafe, O Lord, we humbly pray,
To keep us safe from sin this day;
Have mercy, Lord, we trust in thee;
O let us ne'er confounded be! Amen.

Latin Hymn of IV or V cent.
Thomas Cotterill, 1779–1823, a.

This hymn may also be sung to TRURO (No. 183) or to PARK STREET (No. 110)

LAUDES DOMINI. 666, 666 JOSEPH BARNBY, 1838–96

Brightly

1. When morn - ing gilds the skies, My heart a - wak - ing cries,
2. When mirth for mu - sic longs, This is my song of songs,
May Je - sus Christ be praised. When eve - ning shad - ows fall,
May Je - sus Christ be praised. God's ho - ly house of prayer
This rings my cur - few call, May Je - sus Christ be praised.
Hath none that can com-pare With 'Je - sus Christ be praised.' A-m

3 To him, my highest and best,
Sing I, when love-possest,
May Jesus Christ be praised.
Whate'er my hands begin,
This blessing breaketh in,
May Jesus Christ be praised.

4 No lovelier antiphon
In all high heaven is known
Than 'Jesus Christ be praised.'
There to the eternal Word
The eternal psalm is heard,
'O Jesus Christ be praised.'

5 Ye nations of mankind,
In this your concord find,
May Jesus Christ be praised.
Let all the earth around
Ring joyous with the sound,
May Jesus Christ be praised.

6 Sing, suns and stars of space,
Sing, ye that see his face,
Sing, 'Jesus Christ be praised.'
God's whole creation o'er,
For aye and evermore
Shall Jesus Christ be praised. Ame

German Hymn, XIX ce
Tr. Robert Bridges, 1844–19

ALLELUIA. 87, 87. D.
SAMUEL SEBASTIAN WESLEY, 1810–76
With dignity, in moderate time
1. Al - le - lu - ia! sing to Je - sus, His the scep - tre, his the throne;
2. Al - le - lu - ia! not as or - phans We are left in sor - row now;
Al - le - lu - ia! his the tri - umph, His the vic - to - ry a - lone.
Al - le - lu - ia! he is near us, Faith be-lieves, nor ques-tions how;
Hark! the songs of peace-ful Si - on Thun-der like a might - y flood,
Though the cloud from sight re-ceived him When the for - ty days were o'er,
'Je - sus out of ev - ery na - tion Hath re - deemed us by his Blood.'
Shall our hearts for - get his prom-ise, 'I am with you ev - er-more'? A-men.

3 Allelulia! Bread of Heaven,
Thou on earth our food and stay;
Alleluia! here the sinful
Flee to thee from day to day;
Intercessor, friend of sinners,
Earth's Redeemer, plead for me,
Where the songs of all the sinless
Sweep across the crystal sea.

4 Alleluia! sing to Jesus,
His the sceptre, his the throne;
Alleluia! his the triumph,
His the victory alone;
Hark! the songs of peaceful Sion
Thunder like a mighty flood:
'Jesus out of every nation
Hath redeemed us by his Blood.'
Amen.

William Chatterton Dix, 1837–98

This hymn may also be sung to HYFRYDOL (No. 397)

UNDIQUE GLORIA. 10 4, 6 6, 6 6, 10 4. GEORGE J. ELVEY, 1816–93

With spirit

1. Let all the world in ev - ery cor - ner sing, 'My God and King!
2. Let all the world in every cor - ner sing, 'My God and King!
The heavens are not too high, His praise may thith - er fly;
The Church with psalms must shout; No door can keep them out;
The earth is not too low, His prais - es there may grow.
But, a - bove all, the heart Must bear the long - est part.
Let all the world in ev - ery cor - ner sing, 'My God and King!
Let all the world in ev - ery cor - ner sing, 'My God and King!

George Herbert, 1593–16

ANGEL'S STORY. 7 6, 7 6. D. ARTHUR HENRY MANN, 1850–1929

In moderate time

1. O Sav - iour, pre - cious Sav - iour, Whom yet un - seen we love;
2. O bring - er of sal - va - tion, Who won-drous - ly hast wrought,
O Name of might and fa - vor, All oth - er names a - bove;
Thy - self the rev - e - la - tion Of love be - yond our thought;
We wor - ship thee, we bless thee, To thee a - lone we sing;
We wor - ship thee, we bless thee, To thee a - lone we sing;
We praise thee and con - fess thee, Our ho - ly Lord and King.
We praise thee and con - fess thee, Our gra-cious Lord and King. A-men.

3 In thee all fullness dwelleth,
All grace and power divine,
The glory that excelleth,
O Son of God, is thine.
We worship thee, we bless thee,
To thee alone we sing;
We praise thee and confess thee,
Our glorious Lord and King.

4 O grant the consummation
Of this our song above,
In endless adoration
And everlasting love;
Then shall we praise and bless thee
Where perfect praises ring,
And evermore confess thee,
Our Saviour and our King. Amen.

Frances Ridley Havergal, 1836–79

WILTSHIRE. C. M. GEORGE THOMAS SMART, 1776–1867

Broadly

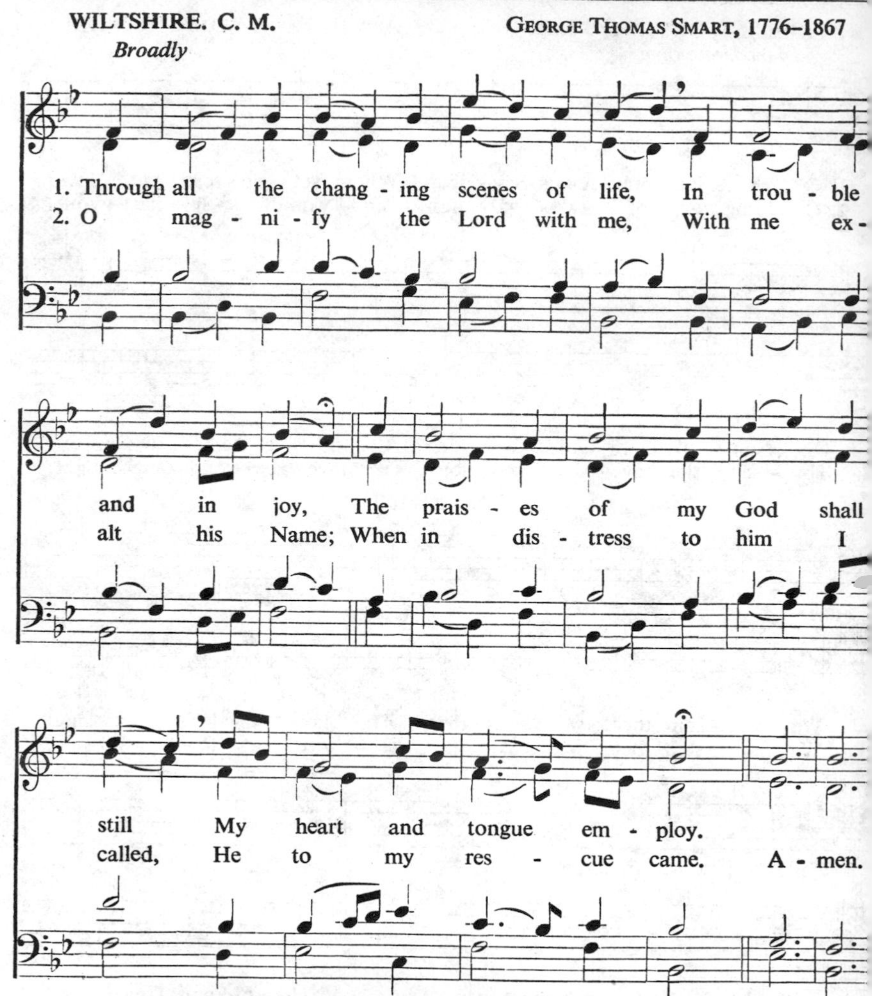
1. Through all the chang - ing scenes of life, In trou - ble and in joy, The prais - es of my God shall still My heart and tongue em - ploy.
2. O mag - ni - fy the Lord with me, With me ex - alt his Name; When in dis - tress to him I called, He to my res - cue came. A - men.

3 The hosts of God encamp around
The dwellings of the just;
Deliverance he affords to all
Who on his succor trust.

4 For God preserves the souls of those
Who on his truth depend;
To them and their posterity
His blessing shall descend.

5 To Father, Son, and Holy Ghost,
The God whom we adore,
Be glory, as it was, is now,
And shall be evermore. Amen.

Nahum Tate, 1652–171
Nicholas Brady, 1659–172
Psalm 3

FLEMMING (INTEGER VITAE). 11 11 11, 5.

FRIEDRICH F. FLEMMING, 1778–1813

In moderate time

1. Praise ye the Fa - ther for his lov - ing - kind-ness; Ten - der - ly
cares he for his err - ing chil - dren; Praise him, ye an - gels,
praise him in the heav - ens, Praise ye Je - ho - vah. A-men.

2 Praise ye the Saviour, great is his compassion;
Graciously cares he for his chosen people;
Young men and maidens, ye old men and children,
Praise ye the Saviour.

3 Praise ye the Spirit, Comforter of Israel,
Sent of the Father and the Son to bless us,
Praise ye the Father, Son, and Holy Spirit,
Praise ye the Triune God. Amen.

Elizabeth Rundle Charles, 1828–96

PRAISE (AF HIMLENS). 8 7, 8 7, 8 8 7.
With vigor
Swedish, 1697
Arr. LELAND B. SATEREN, 1913–
1. Sing praise to God who reigns a - bove, The God of all cre - a - tion, The God of power, the God of love, The God of our sal - va - tion; With heal - ing balm my soul he fills, And ev - ery faith - less mur-mur stills: To God all praise and glo - ry!
2. The an - gel host, O King of kings, Thy praise for ev - er tell - ing, In earth and sky all liv - ing things Be - neath thy shad-ow dwell - ing, A - dore the wis-dom which could span, And power which formed cre - a-tion's plan: To God all praise and glo - ry! A-men.

3 What God's almighty power hath made
His gracious mercy keepeth;
By morning glow or evening shade
His watchful eye ne'er sleepeth:
Within the kingdom of his might
Lo, all is just, and all is right:
To God all praise and glory!

4 Then all my gladsome way along
I sing aloud thy praises,
That men may hear the grateful song
My voice unwearied raises:
Be joyful in the Lord, my heart:
Both soul and body bear your part:
To God all praise and glory! Amen.

Johann Jakob Schütz, 1640–90
Tr. Frances Elizabeth Cox, 1812–97

HOFF. 11 5, 12 9. ERIK CHRISTIAN HOFF, 1830–94

Joyfully

1. O sing, all ye lands, with a ju - bi - lant voice;
2. The Lord, he is God, he hath made us, not we;
Glo - ry be to God! O serve him with glad - ness, be -
Glo - ry be to God! The sheep of his pas - ture we
fore him now re - joice; Sing praise un - to God out of Zi - on!
ev - er - more shall be; Sing praise un - to God out of Zi - on!

3 O enter his gates with thanksgiving and praise;
Glory be to God!
To honor his Name gladsome voices we will raise;
Sing praise unto God out of Zion!

4 For good is the Lord, and his mercy is sure;
Glory be to God!
To all generations his truth shall e'er endure;
Sing praise unto God out of Zion!

Ulrik Vilhelm Koren, 1826–1910
Tr. Harriet Reynolds Krauth Spaeth. 1845–1925, a.
Psalm 100

HOSANNA. 8 8, 8 8, 4 7. JOHN BACCHUS DYKES, 1823–76

With dignity
1. Ho - san - na to the liv - ing Lord! Ho - san - na
2. Ho - san - na, Lord! thine an - gels cry; Ho - san - na,
to the in - car - nate Word! To Christ, Cre - a - tor, Sav - iour, King,
Lord! thy saints re - ply; A - bove, be - neath us, and a - round,
Let earth, let heaven ho - san - na sing! Ho - san - na,
The dead and liv - ing swell the sound; Ho - san - na,
Lord! Ho - san - na in the high - est!
Lord! Ho - san - na in the high - est! A - men.

3 O Saviour, with protecting care
Abide in this thy house of prayer,
Where we thy parting promise claim,
Assembled in thy sacred Name.
Hosanna, Lord!
Hosanna in the highest!

4 But chiefest, in our cleansèd breast,
Eternal, bid thy Spirit rest;
And make our secret soul to be
A temple pure and worthy thee!
Hosanna, Lord!
Hosanna in the highest! Amen.

Reginald Heber, 1783–1826

BOHEMIA. 6 5, 6 5. D.
XIV cent. German Traditional Melody
With dignity
1. Sav - iour, bless - ed Sav - iour, Lis - ten while we sing,
2. Near - er, ev - er near - er, Christ, we draw to thee,
Hearts and voi - ces rais - ing Prais - es to our King.
Deep in ad - o - ra - tion Bend - ing low the knee;
All we have to of - fer, All we hope to be,
Thou for our re - demp - tion Cam'st on earth to die;
Bod - y, soul, and spir - it, All we yield to thee.
Thou, that we might fol - low, Hast gone up on high. A-men.

3 Clearer still and clearer
Dawns the light from heaven,
In our sadness bringing
News of sins forgiven;
Life has lost its shadows,
Pure the light within;
Thou hast shed thy radiance
On a world of sin.

4 Onward, ever onward,
Journeying o'er the road
Worn by saints before us,
Journeying on to God,
Leaving all behind us,
May we hasten on,
Backward never looking
Till the prize is won. Amen.

Godfrey Thring, 1823–1903

426

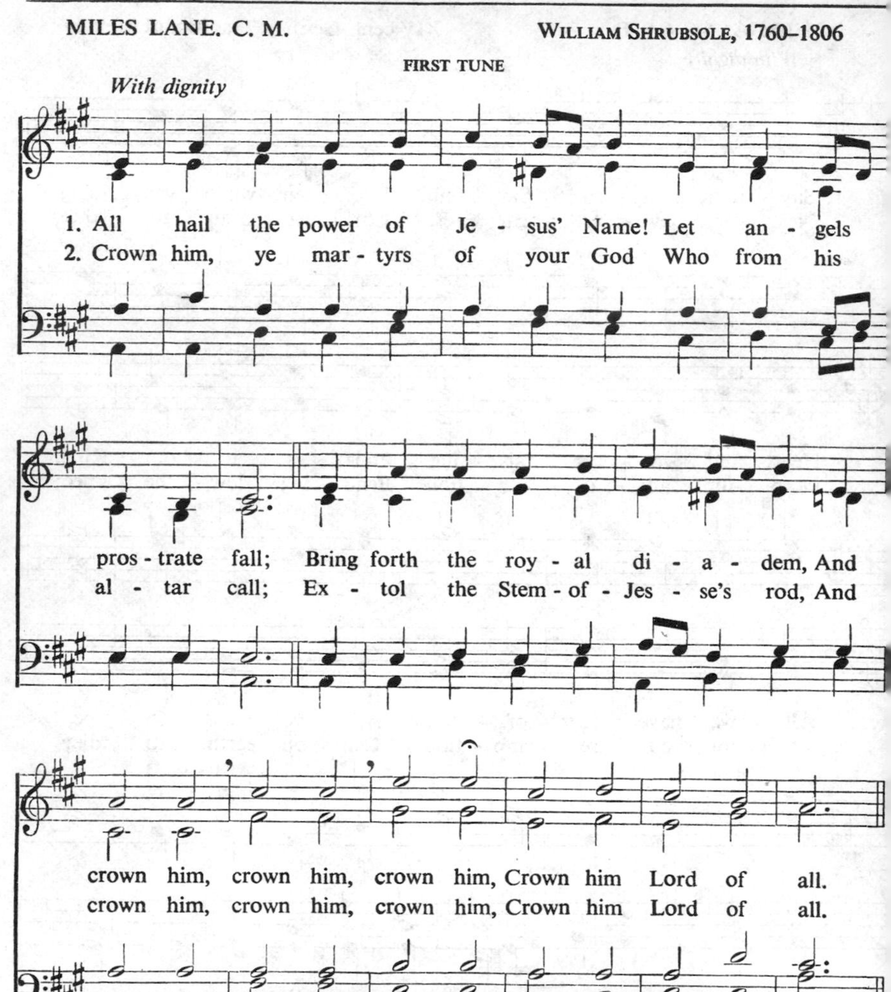
MILES LANE. C. M.
WILLIAM SHRUBSOLE, 1760–1806
FIRST TUNE
With dignity
1. All hail the power of Je - sus' Name! Let an - gels pros - trate fall; Bring forth the roy - al di - a - dem, And crown him, crown him, crown him, Crown him Lord of all.
2. Crown him, ye mar - tyrs of your God Who from his al - tar call; Ex - tol the Stem - of - Jes - se's rod, And crown him, crown him, crown him, Crown him Lord of all.

3 Ye seed of Israel's chosen race,
Ye ransomed of the fall,
Hail him who saves you by his grace,
And crown him Lord of all.

4 Sinners, whose love can ne'er forget
The wormwood and the gall,
Go, spread your trophies at his feet,
And crown him Lord of all.

5 Let every kindred, every tribe,
On this terrestrial ball,
To him all majesty ascribe,
And crown him Lord of all.

6 O that with yonder sacred throng
We at his feet may fall;
We'll join the everlasting song
And crown him Lord of all.

Edward Perronet, 1726–92
John Rippon, 1751–1836

MILES LANE. C. M.
William Shrubsole, 1760–1806
Descant by Edgar C. Robinson
FIRST TUNE
Alternate Version
With dignity
Congregation
1. All hail the power of Je - sus' Name! Let an - gels pros-trate fall;
2. Crown him, ye mar - tyrs of your God Who from his al - tar call;
Choir
Bring forth the roy - al di - a - dem, And crown him,
Ex - tol the Stem - of - Jes - se's rod, And crown him
And crown him,
crown him, crown him, Crown him,
Lord of all.
And crown him
crown him, crown him, Crown him Lord of all.
Edward Perronet, 1726–92
John Rippon, 1751–1836

Descant from Enlarged Songs of Praise by permission of the Oxford University Press

CORONATION. 8 6, 8 6, 8 6. OLIVER HOLDEN, 1765–1844

SECOND TUNE

With dignity, in strict time

1. All hail the power of Je - sus' Name! Let an - gels pros-trate fall;
2. Crown him, ye mar - tyrs of your God Who from his al - tar call;

Bring forth the roy - al di - a - dem, And crown him Lord of all;
Ex - tol the Stem - of - Jes - se's rod, And crown him Lord of all;

Bring forth the roy - al di - a - dem, And crown him Lord of all.
Ex - tol the Stem - of - Jes - se's rod, And crown him Lord of all.

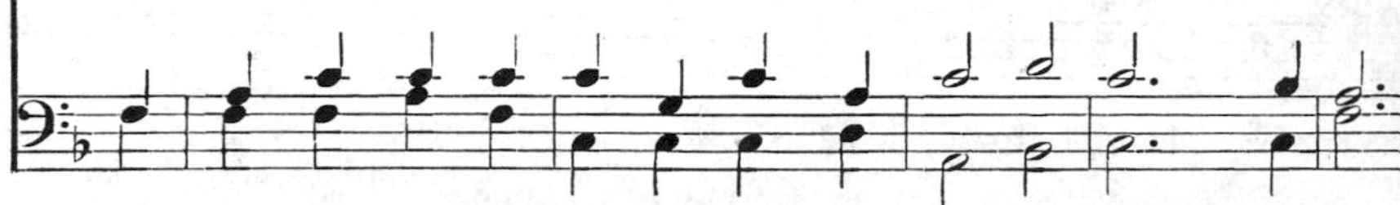

3 Ye seed of Israel's chosen race,
Ye ransomed of the fall,
Hail him who saves you by his grace,
And crown him Lord of all.

4 Sinners, whose love can ne'er forget
The wormwood and the gall,
Go, spread your trophies at his feet,
And crown him Lord of all.

5 Let every kindred, every tribe,
On this terrestrial ball,
To him all majesty ascribe,
And crown him Lord of all.

6 O that with yonder sacred throng
We at his feet may fall;
We'll join the everlasting song
And crown him Lord of all.

Edward Perronet, 1726–92
John Rippon, 1751–1836

DAVID (ST. ALBAN'S). 6 5, 6 5. D. THOMAS MORLEY, 1842–91

In moderate time

1. Praise the Lord of heav - en, Praise him in the height,
Praise him, all ye an - gels, Praise him, stars and light;
Praise him, clouds and wa - ters, Which a - bove the skies,
When his word com-mand - ed, Stab-lished did a - rise. A-men.

2 Praise the Lord, ye fountains
Of the deeps and seas,
Rocks and hills and mountains,
Cedars and all trees;
Praise him, clouds and vapors,
Snow and hail and fire,
Stormy wind, fulfilling
Only his desire.

3 Praise him, fowls and cattle,
Princes and all kings;
Praise him, men and maidens,
All created things;
For the Name of God is
Excellent alone,
Over earth his footstool,
Over heaven his throne. Amen.

Thomas Brierly Browne, 1805–74
Psalm 148

DEDHAM. C. M. William Gardiner, 1770–1853

With dignity FIRST TUNE

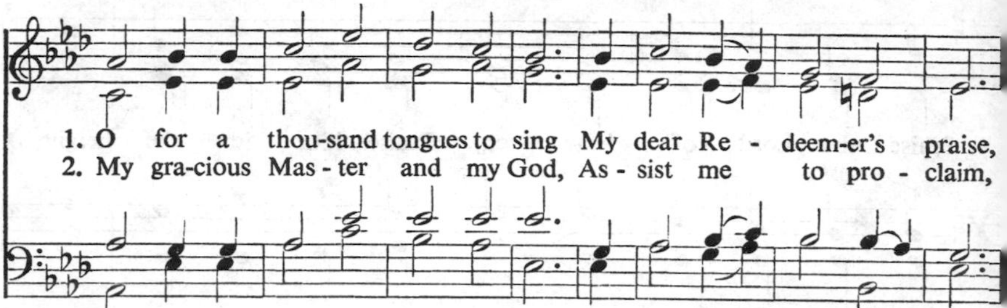

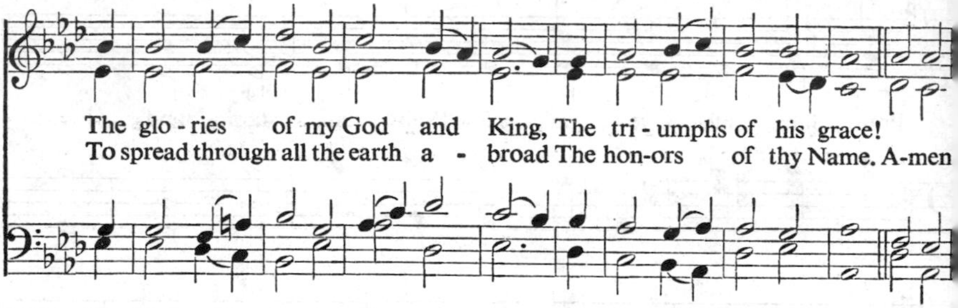

1. O for a thou-sand tongues to sing My dear Re - deem-er's praise,
2. My gra-cious Mas - ter and my God, As - sist me to pro - claim,

The glo - ries of my God and King, The tri - umphs of his grace!
To spread through all the earth a - broad The hon-ors of thy Name. A-men

3 Jesus! the Name that charms our fears,
That bids our sorrows cease,
'Tis music in the sinner's ears,
'Tis life and health and peace.

4 He breaks the power of cancelled sin,
He sets the prisoner free;
His Blood can make the foulest clean,
His Blood availed for me.

5 He speaks, and, listening to his voice,
New life the dead receive,
The mournful broken hearts rejoice,
The humble poor believe.

6 Hear him, ye deaf; his praise, ye dumb,
Your loosened tongues employ;
Ye blind, behold your Saviour come;
And leap, ye lame, for joy.

7 Glory to God, and praise, and love
Be ever, ever given
By saints below and saints above,
The Church in earth and heaven. Amen.

Charles Wesley, 1707–88

This hymn may also be sung to WINCHESTER (No. 389)

428

AZMON. C. M. Carl Gotthilf Gläser, 1784–1829
Arr. by Lowell Mason, 1792–1872

In moderate time SECOND TUNE

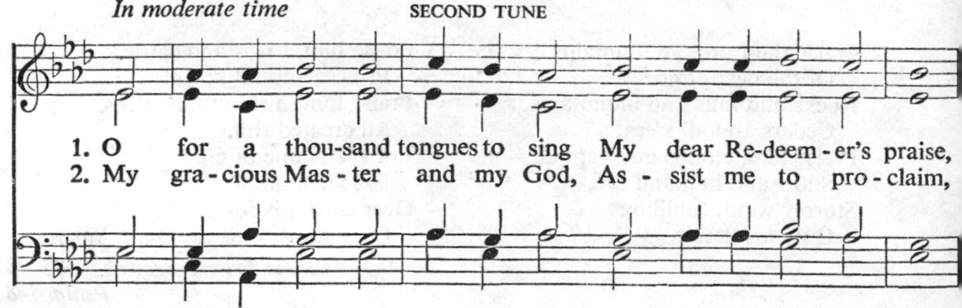
1. O for a thou-sand tongues to sing My dear Re-deem - er's praise,
2. My gra - cious Mas - ter and my God, As - sist me to pro - claim,

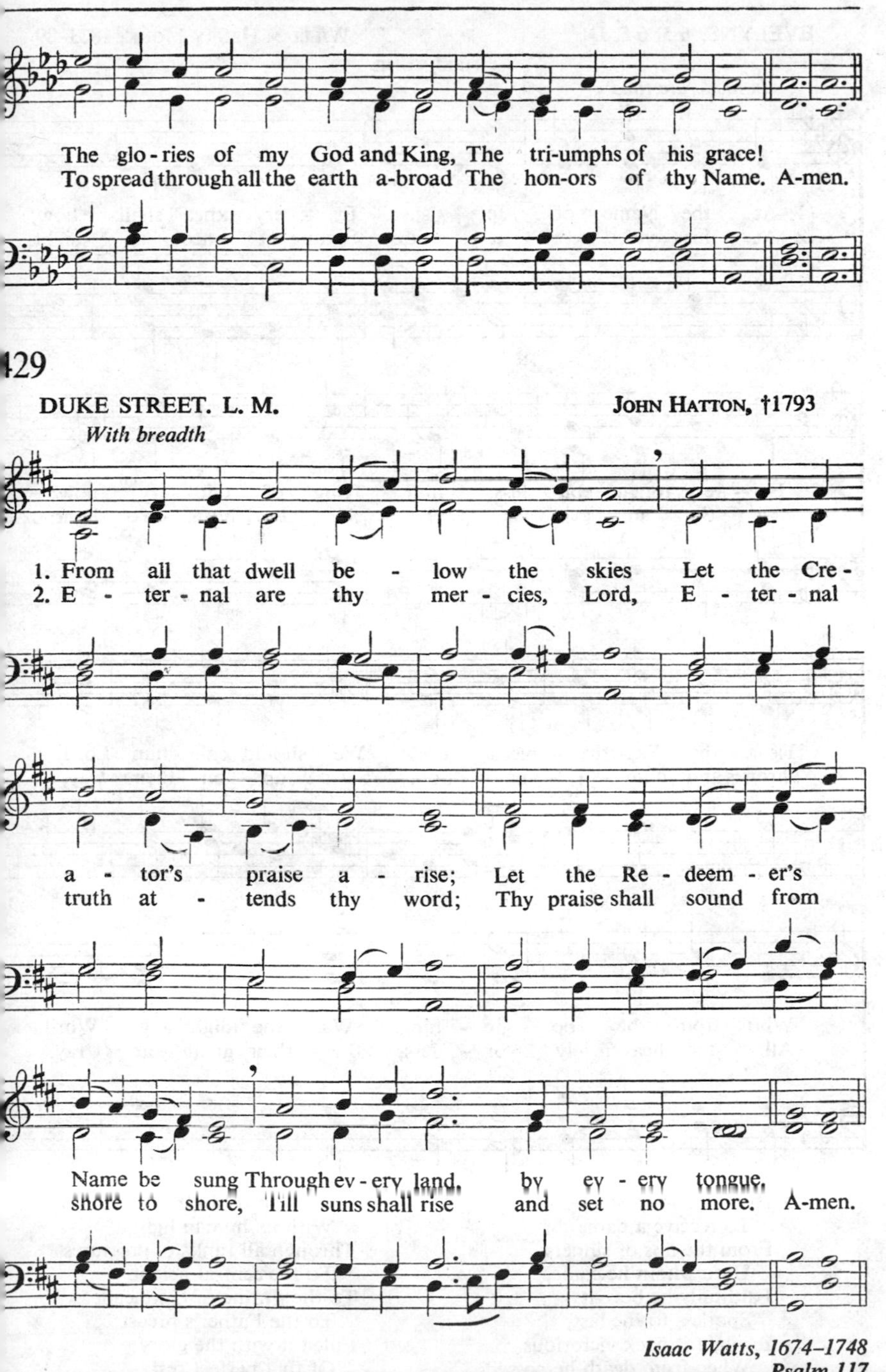
The glo - ries of my God and King, The tri-umphs of his grace!
To spread through all the earth a-broad The hon-ors of thy Name. A-men.
429
DUKE STREET. L. M.
JOHN HATTON, †1793
With breadth
1. From all that dwell be - low the skies Let the Cre -
2. E - ter - nal are thy mer - cies, Lord, E - ter - nal
a - tor's praise a - rise; Let the Re - deem - er's
truth at - tends thy word; Thy praise shall sound from
Name be sung Through ev - ery land, by ev - ery tongue.
shore to shore, Till suns shall rise and set no more. A-men.

Isaac Watts, 1674–1748
Psalm 117

EVELYNS. 6 5, 6 5. D. WILLIAM HENRY MONK, 1823–89

FIRST TUNE

In moderate time
1. At the Name of Je - sus Ev - ery knee shall bow,
2. At his voice cre - a - tion Sprang at once to sight,
Ev - ery tongue con - fess him King of Glo - ry now;
All the an - gel fac - es, All the hosts of light,
'Tis the Fa - ther's pleas - ure We should call him Lord,
Thrones and dom - i - na - tions, Stars up - on their way,
Who from the be - gin - ning Was the might - y Word.
All the heaven - ly or - ders, In their great ar - ray.

3 Humbled for a season,
   To receive a name
From the lips of sinners
   Unto whom he came,
Faithfully he bore it
   Spotless to the last,
Brought it back victorious
   When from death he passed.

4 Bore it up triumphant
   With its human light,
Through all ranks of creatures
   To the central height,
To the throne of Godhead,
   To the Father's breast;
Filled it with the glory
   Of that perfect rest.

5 In your hearts enthrone him;
There let him subdue
All that is not holy,
All that is not true:
Crown him as your captain
In temptation's hour;
Let his will enfold you
In its light and power.

6 Brothers, this Lord Jesus
Shall return again,
With his Father's glory,
With his angel train;
For all wreaths of empire
Meet upon his brow,
And our hearts confess him
King of Glory now.

Caroline Maria Noel, 1817–77

30

ST. ERIK. 6 5, 6 5. D. Swedish Melody, 1697

Brightly SECOND TUNE

1. At the Name of Je - sus Ev - ery knee shall bow,
2. At his voice cre - a - tion Sprang at once to sight,
Ev - ery tongue con - fess him King of Glo - ry now;
All the an - gel fac - es, All the hosts of light,
'Tis the Fa - ther's pleas - ure We should call him Lord,
Thrones and dom - i - na - tions, Stars up - on their way,
Who from the be - gin - ning Was the might - y Word.
All the heaven - ly or - ders, In their great ar - ray.

DIADEMATA. S. M. D. GEORGE J. ELVEY, 1816–93

With dignity

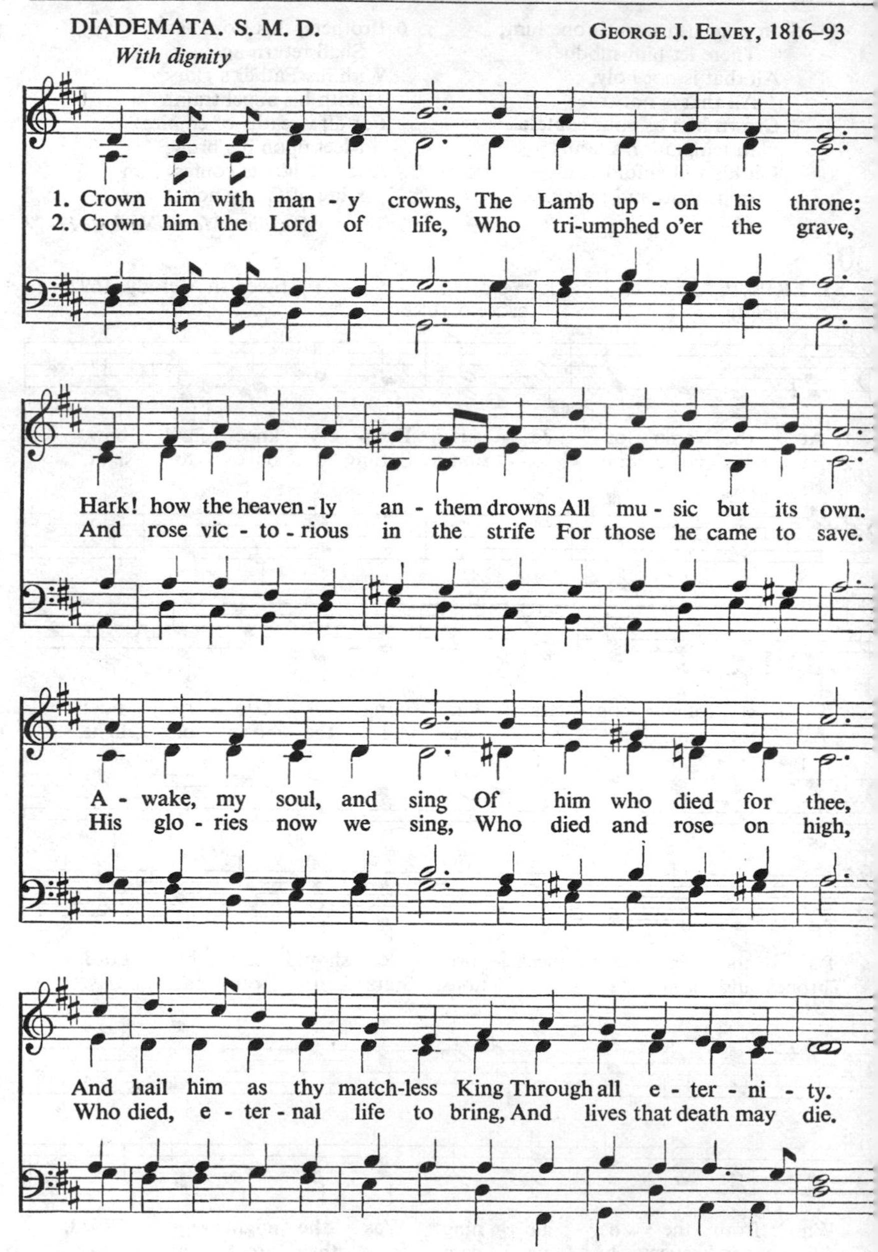
1. Crown him with man - y crowns, The Lamb up - on his throne;
2. Crown him the Lord of life, Who tri-umphed o'er the grave,
Hark! how the heaven - ly an - them drowns All mu - sic but its own.
And rose vic - to - rious in the strife For those he came to save.
A - wake, my soul, and sing Of him who died for thee,
His glo - ries now we sing, Who died and rose on high,
And hail him as thy match-less King Through all e - ter - ni - ty.
Who died, e - ter - nal life to bring, And lives that death may die.

3 Crown him the Lord of love,
Behold his hands and side,
Rich wounds yet visible above
In beauty glorified.

No angel in the sky
Can fully bear that sight,
But downward bends his burning eye
At mysteries so bright.

4 Crown him the Lord of peace,
  Whose power a sceptre sways
From pole to pole, that wars may cease,
  Absorbed in prayer and praise.
His reign shall know no end,
  And round his piercèd feet
Fair flowers of Paradise extend
  Their fragrance ever sweet.

5 Crown him the Lord of years,
  The Potentate of time,
Creator of the rolling spheres,
  Ineffably sublime.
All hail, Redeemer, hail!
  For thou hast died for me;
Thy praise and glory shall not fail
  Throughout eternity.

Matthew Bridges, 1800–94
Godfrey Thring, 1823–1903

32

MONKLAND. 7 7, 7 7.

Moravian Melody
Arr. by JOHN BERNARD WILKES, 1785–1869

With dignity

1. Songs of praise the an - gels sang, Heaven with al - le - lu - ias rang,
2. Songs of praise a - woke the morn When the Prince of Peace was born;

When cre - a - tion was be - gun, When God spake and it was done.
Songs of praise a - rose when he Cap - tive led cap - tiv - i - ty. A-men.

3 Heaven and earth must pass away,
Songs of praise shall crown that day;
God will make new heavens and earth,
Songs of praise shall hail their birth.

4 Saints below with heart and voice
Still in songs of praise rejoice;
Learning here, by faith and love,
Songs of praise to sing above.

5 Hymns of glory, songs of praise,
Father, unto thee we raise,
Jesus, glory unto thee,
With the Spirit, ever be. Amen.

James Montgomery, 1771–1854

MARGARET. Irregular. TIMOTHY RICHARD MATTHEWS, 1826–1910

Smoothly, in moderate time

1. Thou didst leave thy throne And thy king - - ly crown When thou
cam - est to earth for me, But in Beth - le-hem's home Was there
found no room For thy ho - ly na - tiv - i - ty: O
come to my heart, Lord Je - sus; There is room in my heart for thee.

2
Heaven's arches rang
When the angels sang,
Proclaiming thy royal degree;
But in lowly birth
Didst thou come to earth,
And in great humility:
O come to my heart, Lord Jesus;
There is room in my heart for thee.

3
The foxes found rest
And the birds their nest
In the shade of the forest tree;
But thy couch was the sod,
O thou Son of God,
In the desert of Galilee:
O come to my heart, Lord Jesus;
There is room in my heart for thee.

4 Thou camest, O Lord,
With the living word,
That should set thy people free;
But with mocking scorn,
And with crown of thorn,
They bore thee to Calvary:
O come to my heart, Lord Jesus;
There is room in my heart for thee.

5 When the heavens shall ring,
And the angels sing
At thy coming to victory,
Let thy voice call me home,
Saying, 'Yet there is room,
There is room at my side for thee;'
And my heart shall rejoice, Lord Jesus,
When thou comest and callest for me.

Emily E. S. Elliott, 1836–97

34

SCHÖNSTER HERR JESU. 5 5 7, 5 5 8. Silesian Folksong, 1842

Simply
1. Beau - ti - ful Sav - iour, King of Cre - a - tion, Son of
2. Fair are the mead - ows, Fair are the wood-lands, Robed in
God and Son of Man! Tru - ly I'd love thee, Tru - ly I'd
flowers of bloom-ing spring; Je - sus is fair - er, Je - sus is
serve thee, Light of my soul, my joy, my crown.
pur - er, He makes our sor - rowing spir - it sing.

3 Fair is the sunshine,
Fair is the moonlight,
Bright the sparkling stars on high;
Jesus shines brighter,
Jesus shines purer,
Than all the angels in the sky.

4 Beautiful Saviour,
Lord of the nations,
Son of God and Son of Man!
Glory and honor,
Praise, adoration,
Now and for evermore be thine!

Münster Gesangbuch, 1677
Schlesische Volkslieder, 1842
Tr. Joseph Augustus Seiss, 1823–1904

SUPPLICATION. 8 7, 8 7. D. WILLIAM HENRY MONK, 1823-89

FIRST TUNE

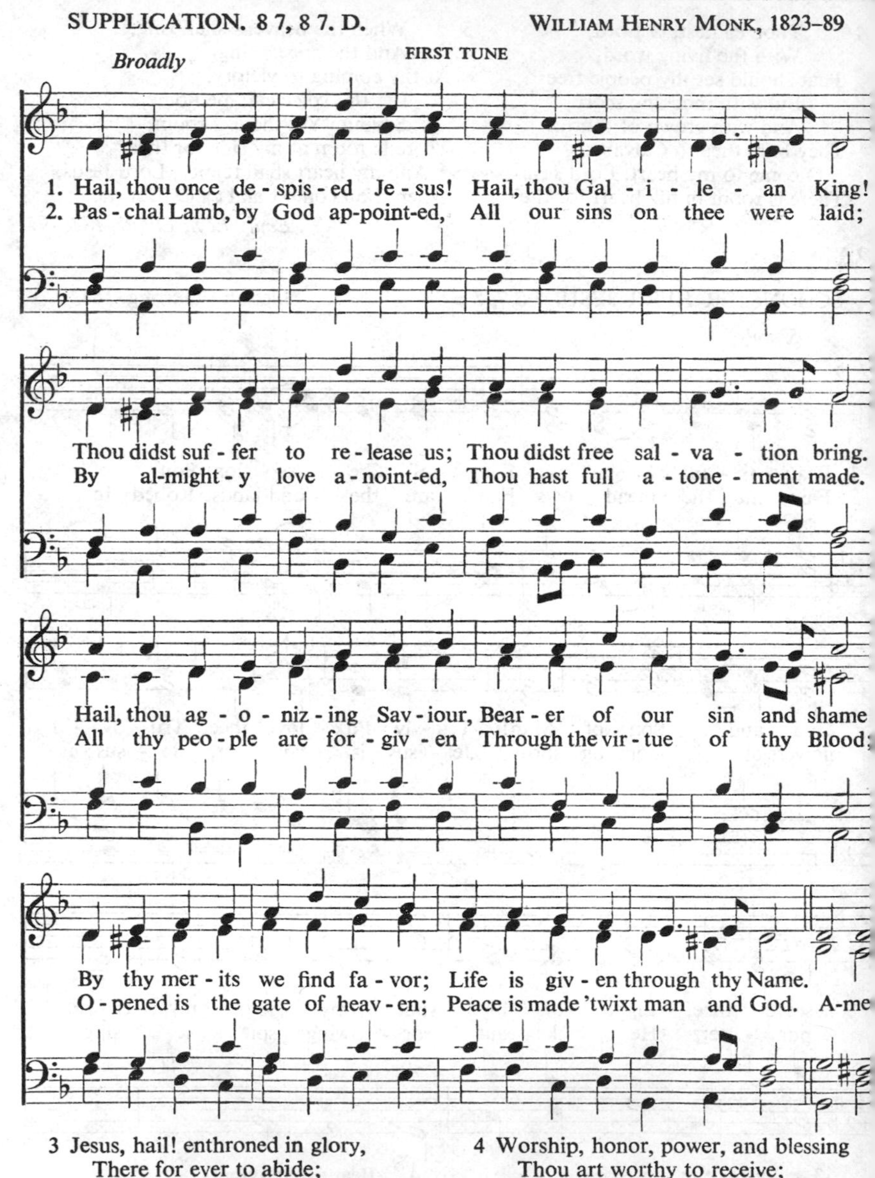
Broadly
1. Hail, thou once de - spis - ed Je - sus! Hail, thou Gal - i - le - an King!
2. Pas - chal Lamb, by God ap-point-ed, All our sins on thee were laid;
Thou didst suf - fer to re - lease us; Thou didst free sal - va - tion bring.
By al-might - y love a - noint-ed, Thou hast full a - tone - ment made.
Hail, thou ag - o - niz - ing Sav - iour, Bear - er of our sin and shame
All thy peo - ple are for - giv - en Through the vir - tue of thy Blood;
By thy mer - its we find fa - vor; Life is giv - en through thy Name.
O - pened is the gate of heav - en; Peace is made 'twixt man and God. A-me

3 Jesus, hail! enthroned in glory,
There for ever to abide;
All the heavenly hosts adore thee
Seated at thy Father's side.
There for sinners thou art pleading,
There thou dost our place prepare,
Ever for us interceding,
Till in glory we appear.

4 Worship, honor, power, and blessing
Thou art worthy to receive;
Loudest praises, without ceasing,
Meet it is for us to give.
Help, ye bright angelic spirits,
Bring your sweetest, noblest lays;
Help to sing our Saviour's merits,
Help to chant Immanuel's praise.
Ame

John Bakewell, 1721–1819, and othe

CONQUEROR (O DURCHBRECHER). 8 7, 8 7. D.

FREYLINGHAUSEN'S *Gesangbuch*, Halle 1704

With movement SECOND TUNE

1. Hail, thou once de - spis - ed Je - sus! Hail, thou
Thou didst suf - fer to re - lease us; Thou didst
2. Pas - chal Lamb, by God ap - point - ed, All our
By al - might - y love a - noint - ed, Thou hast
Gal - i - le - an King!
free sal - va - tion bring. Hail, thou ag - o - niz - ing
sins on thee were laid;
full a - tone - ment made. All thy peo - ple are for -
Sav - iour, Bear - er of our sin and shame! By thy mer - its we find
giv - en Through the vir - tue of thy Blood; O - pened is the gate of
fa - vor; Life is giv - en through thy Name.
heav - en; Peace is made 'twixt man and God. A-men.

3 Jesus, hail! enthroned in glory,
There for ever to abide;
All the heavenly hosts adore thee
Seated at thy Father's side.
There for sinners thou art pleading,
There thou dost our place prepare,
Ever for us interceding,
Till in glory we appear.

4 Worship, honor, power, and blessing
Thou art worthy to receive,
Loudest praises, without ceasing,
Meet it is for us to give.
Help, ye bright angelic spirits,
Bring your sweetest, noblest lays;
Help to sing our Saviour's merits,
Help to chant Immanuel's praise. Amen.

John Bakewell, 1721–1819, and others

JUBILATE. 6 6, 6 6, 8 8, 8 8. HORATIO W. PARKER, 1863–1919

FIRST TUNE

Joyfully
1. Re - joice, the Lord is King! Your Lord and King a - dore;
2. Je - sus, the Sav - iour, reigns, The God of truth and love;
Re - joice, give thanks and sing, And tri - umph ev - er - more:
When he had purged our stains He took his seat a - bove:
Refrain
Lift up your heart, lift up your voice; Re - joice, a - gain I say, re - joice.
Lift up your heart, lift up your voice; Re-joice, a-gain I say re - joice.

3 His kingdom cannot fail,
He rules o'er earth and heaven,
The keys of death and hell
Are to our Jesus given:

4 He sits at God's right hand
Till all his foes submit,
And bow to his command,
And fall beneath his feet:

Charles Wesley, 1707–8

This hymn may also be sung to DARWALL's 148th (No. 339)

LAUS REGIS. 6 6, 6 6, 8 8. **William E. Fischer, 1849-1936**

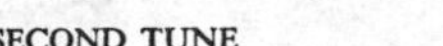
SECOND TUNE

In moderate time

1. Re - joice, the Lord is King! Your Lord and King a - dore;
2. Je - sus, the Sav - iour, reigns, The God of truth and love;

Re - joice, give thanks and sing, And tri - umph ev - er - more:
When he had purged our stains He took his seat a - bove:

Refrain

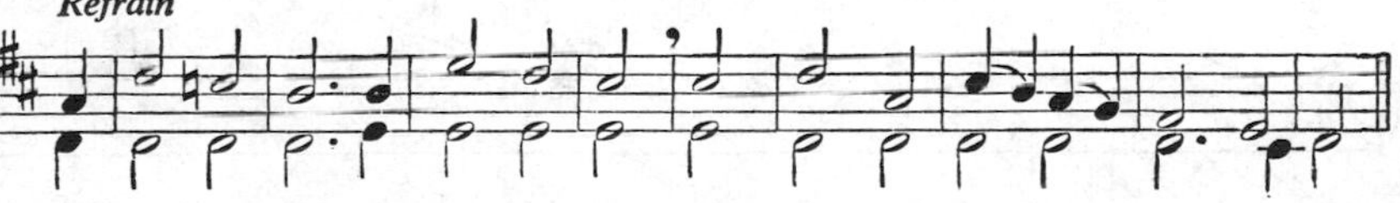

Lift up your heart, lift up your voice; Re - joice, a - gain I say, re-joice.

3 His kingdom cannot fail,
He rules o'er earth and heaven,
The keys of death and hell
Are to our Jesus given:

4 He sits at God's right hand
Till all his foes submit,
And bow to his command,
And fall beneath his feet:

Charles Wesley, 1707–88

This hymn may also be sung to DARWALL's 148th (No. 339)

LASST UNS ERFREUEN. L. M. With Alleluias.

Geistliche Kirchengesänge, Cologne, 1623

In unison, boldly
1. Ye watch-ers and ye ho - ly ones, Bright ser - aphs, cher - u -
2. O high - er than the cher - u - bim, More glo-rious than the
bim, and thrones, Raise the glad strain, Al - le - lu - ia!
ser - a - phim, Lead their prais - es, Al - le - lu - ia!
Cry out, do - min - ions, prince-doms, powers, Vir - tues, arch - an -
Thou bear - er of the e - ter - nal Word, Most gra - cious, mag

Refrain
gels, an - gels' choirs,
ni - fy the Lord,
Al - le - lu - ia, Al - le - lu - ia,
Al - le - lu - ia, Al - le - lu - ia, Al - le - lu - ia!

3 Respond, ye souls in endless rest,
Ye patriarchs and prophets blest,
Alleluia, Alleluia!
Ye holy twelve, ye martyrs strong,
All saints triumphant, raise the song,
Alleluia!

4 O friends, in gladness let us sing,
Supernal anthems echoing,
Alleluia, Alleluia!
To God the Father, God the Son,
And God the Spirit, Three in One,
Alleluia!

John Athelstan Riley, 1858–1945

ALLELUIA. 8 7, 8 7. D. SAMUEL SEBASTIAN WESLEY, 1810–76

With dignity, in moderate time
1. Joy - ful, joy - ful we a - dore thee, God of glo - ry, Lord of love;
2. All thy works with joy sur-round thee, Earth and heaven re - flect thy rays,
Hearts un - fold like flowers be - fore thee, Prais - ing thee, their Sun a - bove.
Stars and an - gels sing a - round thee, Cen - ter of un - bro - ken praise
Melt the clouds of sin and sad - ness, Drive the dark of doubt a - way;
Field and for - est, vale and moun-tain, Flow - ery mead-ow, flash-ing sea,
Giv - er of im - mor - tal glad-ness, Fill us with the light of day.
Chant-ing bird and flow - ing foun-tain, Call us to re - joice in thee. A-me

3 Thou art giving and forgiving,
Ever blessing, ever blest,
Well-spring of the joy of living,
Ocean-depth of happy rest!
Thou our Father, Christ our Brother,
All who live in love are thine;
Teach us how to love each other,
Lift us to the joy divine.

4 Mortals, join the mighty chorus
Which the morning stars began;
Father-love is reigning o'er us,
Brother-love binds man to man.
Ever singing, march we onward,
Victors in the midst of strife;
Joyful music lifts us sunward
In the triumph song of life. Amen.

Henry van Dyke, 1852–19.

NOTTINGHAM (ST. MAGNUS). C. M. JEREMIAH CLARKE, *cir.* 1669–1707

With dignity

1. The head that once was crowned with thorns Is crowned with glo - ry now;
2. The high - est place that heaven af - fords Is his, is his by right,

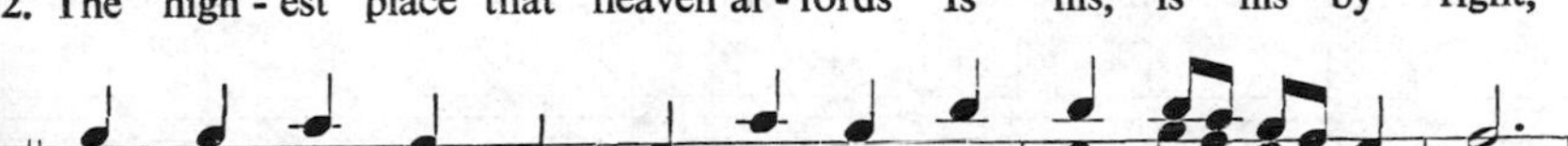

A roy - al di - a - dem a - dorns The might - y Vic - tor's brow.
The King of kings, and Lord of lords, And heaven's e - ter - nal Light;

3 The joy of all who dwell above,
The joy of all below,
To whom he manifests his love
And grants his Name to know.

4 To them the Cross with all its shame,
With all its grace, is given;
Their name an everlasting name,
Their joy, the joy of heaven.

5 They suffer with their Lord below,
They reign with him above;
Their profit and their joy to know
The mystery of his love.

6 The Cross he bore is life and health,
Though shame and death to him;
His people's hope, his people's wealth,
Their everlasting theme.

Thomas Kelly, 1769–1854

See also:

BELGRAVE. C. M. — William Horsley, 1774–1858

FIRST TUNE

In moderate time

1. When all thy mer - cies, O my God, My ris - ing soul sur - veys,
2. Un - num-bered com-forts to my soul Thy ten - der care be-stowed

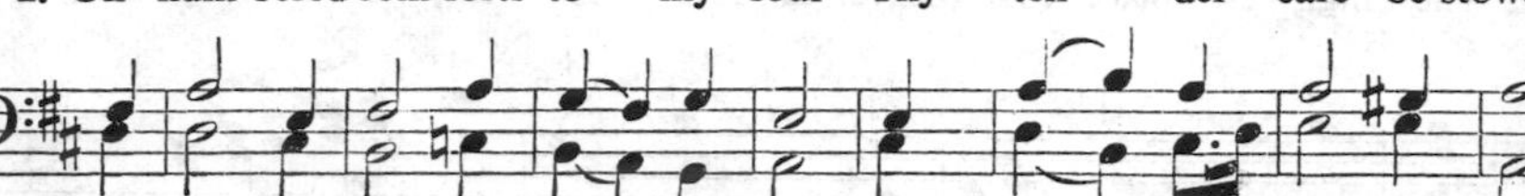

Trans-port - ed with the view, I'm lost In won - der, love, and praise!
Be - fore my in - fant heart con-ceived From whom these com-forts flowed! A-men

3 Ten thousand thousand precious gifts
My daily thanks employ;
Nor is the least a cheerful heart
That tastes those gifts with joy.

4 Through every period of my life
Thy goodness I'll pursue,
And after death, in distant worlds,
The glorious theme renew.

5 When nature fails, and day and night
Divide thy works no more,
My ever grateful heart, O Lord,
Thy mercies shall adore.

6 Through all eternity to thee
A joyful song I'll raise;
But O, eternity's too short,
To utter all thy praise! Amen.

Joseph Addison, 1672–1719

This hymn may also be sung ST. FULBERT (No. 196)

440

EAGLEY. C. M. — James Walch, 1837–1901

SECOND TUNE

In moderate time

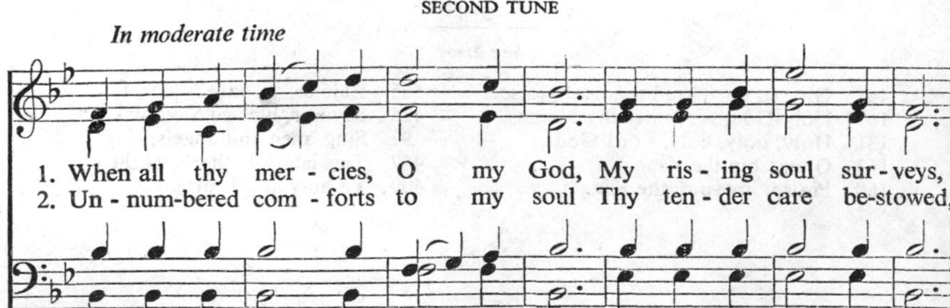
1. When all thy mer - cies, O my God, My ris - ing soul sur - veys,
2. Un - num-bered com - forts to my soul Thy ten - der care be-stowed,

Trans-port-ed with the view, I'm lost In won-der, love, and praise!
Be - fore my in - fant heart con-ceived From whom these com-forts flowed. A-men.

This hymn may also be sung to ST. FULBERT (No. 196)

441

DUKE STREET. L. M. JOHN HATTON, †1793

With breadth

1. Give to our God im - mor - tal praise, Mer - cy and
2. Give to the Lord of lords re - nown, The King of

truth are all his ways. Won - ders of grace to
kings with glo - ry crown, His mer - cies ev - er

God be - long, Re - peat his mer - cies in your song.
shall en - dure, When lords and kings are known no more.

3 He sent his Son with power to save
From guilt and darkness and the grave.
Wonders of grace to God belong,
Repeat his mercies in your song.

4 Through this vain world he guides our feet,
And leads us to his heavenly seat,
His mercies ever shall endure,
When this vain world shall be no more.

Isaac Watts, 1674–1748

CREATION. L. M. D. Adapted from FRANZ JOSEPH HAYDN, 1732–1809

With dignity

1. The spa-cious fir-ma-ment on high. With all the blue e-the-real sky, And span-gled heavens, a shin-ing frame, Their great O-rig-i-nal pro-claim. The un-wea-ried sun from day to day Does his Cre-a-tor's power dis-play, And pub-lish-es to ev-ery land The works of an al-might-y hand.

2 Soon as the evening shades prevail
The moon takes up the wondrous tale,
And nightly to the listening earth
Repeats the story of her birth;
Whilst all the stars that round her burn
And all the planets in their turn,
Confirm the tidings, as they roll,
And spread the truth from pole to pole.

3 What though in solemn silence all
Move round the dark terrestrial ball;
What though no real voice nor sound
Amid their radiant orbs be found;
In reason's ear they all rejoice,
And utter forth a glorious voice;
For ever singing as they shine,
'The hand that made us is divine.'

Joseph Addison, 1672–1719

143

NUN DANKET ALLE GOTT. 6 7, 6 7, 6 6, 6 6.

Majestically JOHANN CRÜGER, 1598–1662

1. Now thank we all our God With heart and hands and voic - es,
Who won-drous things hath done, In whom his world re - joic - es;
Who, from our moth-er's arms, Hath blessed us on our way With
count-less gifts of love, And still is ours to - day. A-men.

2 O may this bounteous God
Through all our life be near us,
With ever joyful hearts
And blessèd peace to cheer us;
And keep us in his grace,
And guide us when perplexed,
And free us from all ills
In this world and the next.

3 All praise and thanks to God
The Father now be given,
The Son, and him who reigns
With them in highest heaven;
The one eternal God,
Whom earth and heaven adore;
For thus it was, is now,
And shall be evermore. Amen.

Martin Rinkart, 1586–1649
Tr. Catherine Winkworth, 1829–78

HEATHLANDS. 7 7, 7 7, 7 7.
HENRY SMART, 1813–79
In moderate time
1. For the beau - ty of the earth, For the beau - ty of the skies,
2. For the beau - ty of each hour Of the day and of the night,
For the love which from our birth O - ver and a - round us lies,
Hill and vale, and tree and flower, Sun and moon and stars of light,
Christ, our God, to thee we raise This our sac - ri - fice of praise.
Christ, our God, to thee we raise This our sac - ri - fice of praise. A-men.

3 For the joy of ear and eye,
For the heart and mind's delight,
For the mystic harmony
Linking sense to sound and sight,
Christ, our God, to thee we raise
This our sacrifice of praise.

4 For the joy of human love,
Brother, sister, parent, child,
Friends on earth and friends above,
For all gentle thoughts and mild,
Christ, our God, to thee we raise
This our sacrifice of praise.

5 For thyself, best gift divine!
To our race so freely given,
For that great, great love of thine,
Peace on earth and joy in heaven,
Christ, our God, to thee we raise
This our sacrifice of praise. Amen.

Folliott Sandford Pierpoint, 1835–1917

This Hymn may also be sung to Dix (No. 52), and Easter Glory (No. 100)

BISHOPGARTH. 8 7, 8 7. D. Iambic.
ARTHUR S. SULLIVAN, 1842–1900
Joyfully
1. To thee, O Lord, our hearts we raise In hymns of ad - o - ra - tion,
2. And now, on this our fes - tal day, Thy boun-teous hand con - fess - ing,
To thee bring sac - ri - fice of praise With shouts of ex - ul - ta - tion.
Up - on thine al - tar, Lord, we lay The first-fruits of thy bless - ing.
Bright robes of gold the fields a - dorn, The hills with joy are ring - ing,
By thee the souls of men are fed With gifts of grace su - per - nal;
The val-leys stand so thick with corn That e - ven they are sing - ing.
Thou, who dost give us dai - ly bread, Give us the bread e - ter - nal.

3 We bear the burden of the day,
And often toil seems dreary;
But labor ends with sunset ray,
And rest comes for the weary.
May we, the angel-reaping o'er,
Stand at the last accepted,
Christ's golden sheaves, for evermore
To garners bright elected.

4 O blessèd is that land of God
Where saints abide for ever,
Where golden fields spread fair and broad,
Where flows the crystal river.
The strains of all its holy throng
With ours today are blending;
Thrice blessèd is that harvest-song
Which never hath an ending.

William Chatterton Dix, 1837–98

LYONS. 10 10, 11 11. JOHANN MICHAEL HAYDN, 1737–1806

With dignity

1. Ye ser - vants of God, your Mas - ter pro - claim,
2. God rul - eth on high, al - might - y to save;
And pub - lish a - broad his won - der - ful Name;
And still he is nigh, his pres - ence we have;
The Name all - vic - to - rious of Je - sus ex - tol;
The great con - gre - ga - tion his tri - umph shall sing,
His king - dom is glo - rious, and rules o - ver all.
As - crib - ing sal - va - tion to Je - sus our King. A - men.

3 Salvation to God, who sits on the throne!
Let all cry aloud, and honor the Son:
The praises of Jesus the angels proclaim,
Fall down on their faces, and worship the Lamb.

4 Then let us adore, and give him his right,
All glory and power, all wisdom and might,
All honor and blessing, with angels above,
And thanks never ceasing, and infinite love. Amen.

Charles Wesley, 1707–88

47 Thanksgiving

WENTWORTH. 8 4, 8 4, 8 4. FREDERICK C. MAKER, 1844–1927

With dignity, but brightly

1. My God, I thank thee, who hast made The earth so bright;
So full of splen - dor and of joy, Beau - ty and light;
So man - y glo - rious things are here, No - ble and right. A-men.

2 I thank thee, Lord, that thou hast made
Joy to abound;
So many gentle thoughts and deeds
Circling us round,
That in the darkest spot of earth
Some love is found.

3 I thank thee, too, that all our joy
Is touched with pain,
That shadows fall on brightest hours,
That thorns remain;
So that earth's bliss may be our guide,
And not our chain.

4 I thank thee, Lord, that here our souls,
Though amply blest,
Can never find, although they seek,
A perfect rest,
Nor ever shall, until they lean
On Jesus' breast. Amen.

Adelaide Anne Procter, 1825–64

ALMSGIVING. 8 8 8, 4. JOHN BACCHUS DYKES, 1823–76

FIRST TUNE

In moderate time
1. O Lord of heaven and earth and sea, To thee all praise and glo - ry be; How shall we show our love to thee, Who giv - est all?
2. The gold - en sun - shine, ver - nal air, Sweet flowers and fruit thy love de - clare, When har - vests rip - en, thou art there, Who giv - est all. A - men.

3 For peaceful homes and healthful days,
For all the blessings earth displays,
We owe thee thankfulness and praise,
Who givest all.

4 Thou didst not spare thine only Son,
But gav'st him for a world undone,
And freely with that blessèd One,
Thou givest all.

5 Thou giv'st the Spirit's blessèd dower,
Spirit of life and love and power,
And dost his sevenfold graces shower
Upon us all.

6 For souls redeemed, for sins forgiven,
For means of grace and hopes of heaven,
Father, all praise to thee be given,
Who givest all. Amen.

Christopher Wordsworth, 1807–8

MEYER (ES IST KEIN TAG). 8 8 8, 4.

JOHANN DAVID MEYER'S
Geistliche Seelen-Freud, Ulm, 1692

SECOND TUNE

In moderate time
1. O Lord of heaven and earth and sea, To thee all praise and glo - ry be; How shall we show our love to thee, Who giv - est all?
2. The gold - en sun - shine, ver - nal air, Sweet flowers and fruit thy love de - clare, When har - vests rip - en, thou art there, Who giv - est all. A - men.

3 For peaceful homes and healthful days,
For all the blessings earth displays,
We owe thee thankfulness and praise,
Who givest all.

4 Thou didst not spare thine only Son,
But gav'st him for a world undone,
And freely with that blessèd One,
Thou givest all.

5 Thou giv'st the Spirit's blessèd dower,
Spirit of life and love and power,
And dost his sevenfold graces shower
Upon us all.

6 For souls redeemed, for sins forgiven,
For means of grace and hopes of heaven,
Father, all praise to thee be given,
Who givest all. Amen.

Christopher Wordsworth, 1807–85

BLOMSTERTID. 7 6, 7 6. D. Swedish *Koralbok*, 1697

With breadth

1. How mar - vel - lous God's great-ness, How glo - ri - ous his might,
2. Each ti - ny flower - et whis - pers The great Life - giv - er's Name;
To this the world bears wit - ness In won - ders day and night.
The might - y moun - tain mass - es His ma - jes - ty pro - claim;
In form of flower and snow - flake, In morn's re - splend-ent birth,
The hol - low vales are hymn - ing God's shel - ter for his own;
In af - ter - glow at e - ven, In sky and sea and earth.
The snow-capped peaks are point - ing To God's al - might - y throne.

3 The ocean's vast abysses
In one grand psalm record
The deep mysterious counsels
And mercies of the Lord;
The icy waves of winter
Are thundering on the strand;
E'en grief's chill stream is guided
By God's all-gracious hand.

4 The starry hosts are singing
Through all the light-strewn sky
Of God's majestic temple
And palace-courts on high;
When in these outer chambers,
Such glory gilds the night,
What the transcendent brightness
Of God's eternal light!

Valdimar Briem, 1848–1930
Tr. Charles Venn Pilcher, 1879–1961, a.

KREMSER. 12 11, 12 11.
17th cent. Netherland Folk Song
Arr. by EDWARD KREMSER, 1838–1914
May be sung in unison, with breadth
1. We praise thee, O God, our Re - deem - er, Cre - a - tor,
2. We wor - ship thee, God of our fa - thers, we bless thee;
3. With voi - ces u - nit - ed our prais - es we of - fer,
In grate - ful de - vo - tion our trib - ute we bring.
Through trou - ble and tem - pest our guide thou hast been;
To thee, great Je - ho - vah, glad an - thems we raise;
We lay it be - fore thee, we kneel and a - dore thee,
When per - ils o'er - take us, es - cape thou wilt make us,
Thy strong arm will guide us, our God is be - side us;
We bless thy ho - ly Name, glad prais - es we bring.
And with thy help, O Lord, our bat - tles we win.
To thee, our great Re - deem - er, for - ev - er be praise. A - men.

Author unknown, 1626
Tr. Julia Bulkley Cady Cory, 1882

See also:

173 All creatures of our God
169 All people that on earth
161 Before Jehovah's aweful throne
166 Blessing and honor, and glory
429 From all that dwell
405 Let us, with a gladsome mind
345 Not alone for mighty empire
160 Praise, my soul
408 Praise to the Lord
436 Rejoice, the Lord is King

ST. ANDREW. S. M. JOSEPH BARNBY, 1838–96

FIRST TUNE

Quietly

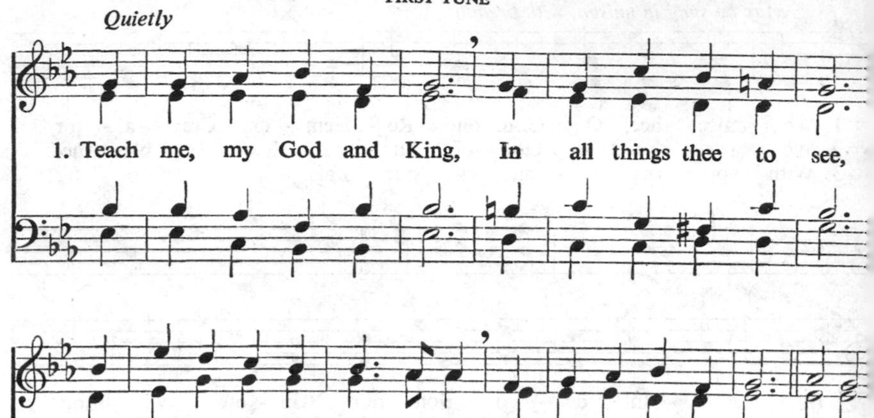
1. Teach me, my God and King, In all things thee to see,
And what I do in an - y-thing, To do it as for thee; A-men

2 To scorn the senses' sway,
While still to thee I tend:
In all I do be thou the way,
In all be thou the end.

3 All may of thee partake;
Nothing so small can be,
But draws, when acted for thy sake,
Greatness and worth from thee.

4 If done to obey thy laws,
E'en servile labors shine;
Hallowed is toil if this the cause,
The meanest work, divine.

5 Thee, then, my God and King,
In all things may I see,
And what I do in anything,
May it be done for thee. Amen.

George Herbert, 1593–163
Alt. John Wesley and other

451

CARLISLE. S. M. CHARLES LOCKHART, 1745–1815

SECOND TUNE

Quietly

1. Teach me, my God and King, In all things thee to see,

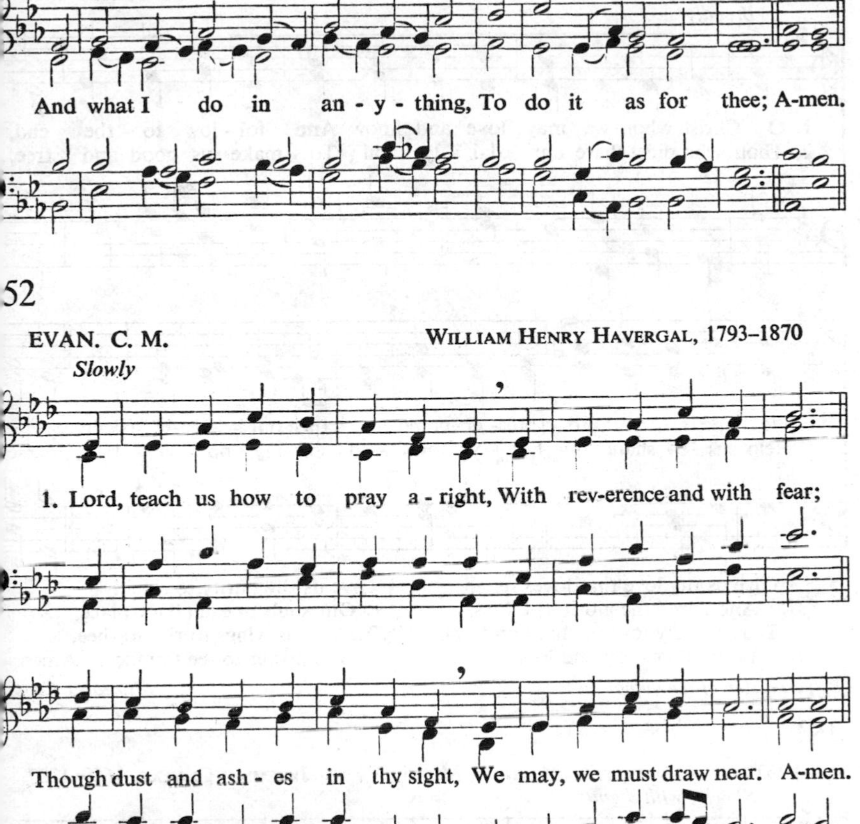
And what I do in an - y - thing, To do it as for thee; A-men.
52
EVAN. C. M.
WILLIAM HENRY HAVERGAL, 1793–1870
Slowly
1. Lord, teach us how to pray a - right, With rev-erence and with fear;
Though dust and ash - es in thy sight, We may, we must draw near. A-men.

2 We perish if we cease from prayer,
O grant us power to pray;
And when to meet thee we prepare,
Lord, meet us by the way.

3 God of all grace, we come to thee
With broken, contrite hearts;
Give what thine eye delights to see,
Truth in the inward parts.

4 Give deep humility; the sense
Of godly sorrow give;
A strong desire, with confidence,
To hear thy voice and live;

5 Faith in the only sacrifice
That can for sin atone;
To cast our hopes, to fix our eyes,
On Christ, on Christ alone;

6 Patience to watch and wait and weep,
Though mercy long delay;
Courage our fainting souls to keep,
And trust thee though thou slay.

7 Give these, and then thy will be done;
Thus strengthened with all might,
We, through thy Spirit and thy Son,
Shall pray, and pray aright. Amen.

James Montgomery, 1771–1854

This hymn may also be sung to WINDSOR (DUNDEE). (No. 269)

453

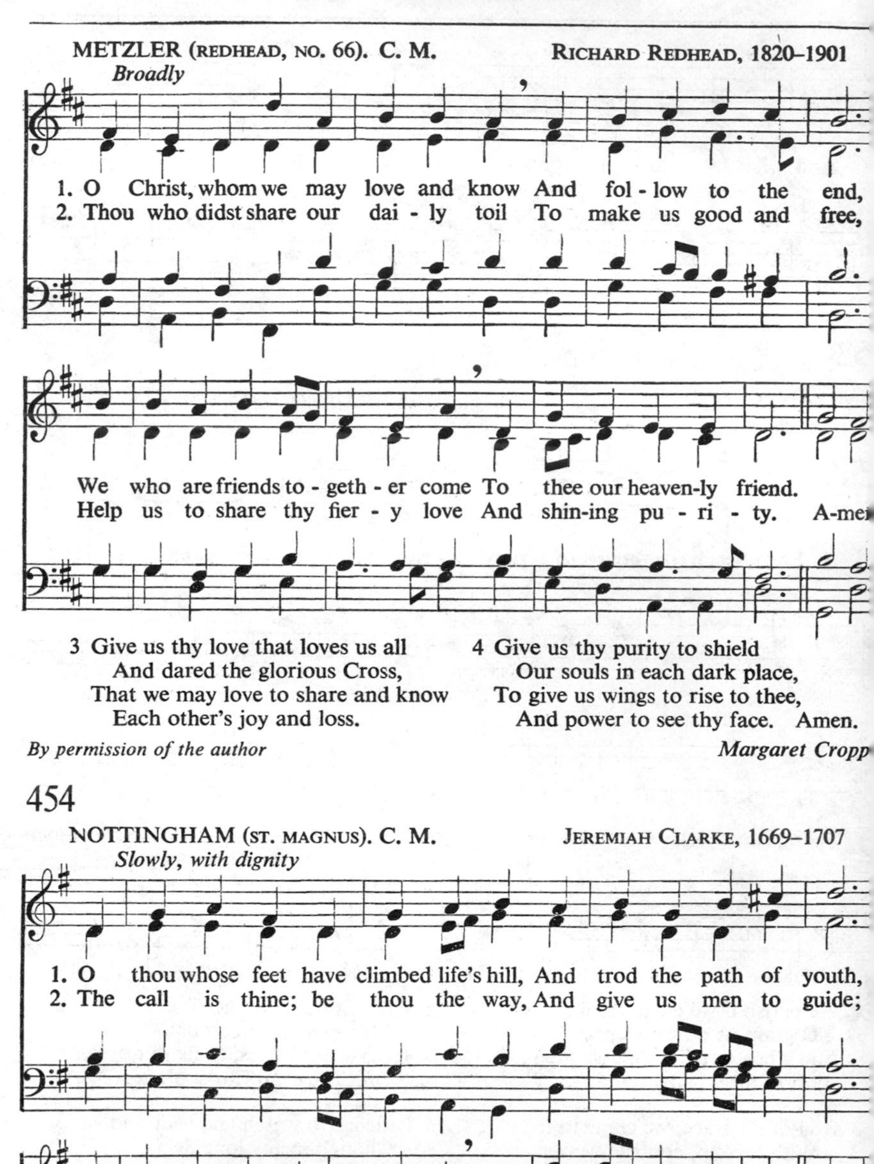
METZLER (REDHEAD, NO. 66). C. M.
RICHARD REDHEAD, 1820–1901
Broadly
1. O Christ, whom we may love and know And fol - low to the end,
2. Thou who didst share our dai - ly toil To make us good and free,
We who are friends to - geth - er come To thee our heaven-ly friend.
Help us to share thy fier - y love And shin-ing pu - ri - ty. A-men.

3 Give us thy love that loves us all
And dared the glorious Cross,
That we may love to share and know
Each other's joy and loss.

4 Give us thy purity to shield
Our souls in each dark place,
To give us wings to rise to thee,
And power to see thy face. Amen.

By permission of the author

Margaret Cropper

454

NOTTINGHAM (ST. MAGNUS). C. M. — JEREMIAH CLARKE, 1669–1707

Slowly, with dignity

1. O thou whose feet have climbed life's hill, And trod the path of youth,
Our Sav - iour and our broth-er still, Now lead us in - to truth.

2. The call is thine; be thou the way, And give us men to guide;
Let wis - dom broad-en with the day, Let hu - man faith a - bide. A-men.

3 Who learn of thee the truth shall find,
Who follow, gain the goal;
With reverence crown the earnest mind,
And speak within the soul.

4 Awake the purpose high which strives,
And, falling, stands again;
Conform the will of eager lives
To quit themselves like men:

5 Thy life the bond of fellowship,
Thy love the law that rules,
Thy Name, proclaimed by every lip,
The Master of our schools. Amen.

Louis FitzGerald Benson, 1855–1930

This hymn may also be sung to TALLIS' ORDINAL (No. 154)

455

WINDSOR (DUNDEE). C. M.

M. William Damon's
Booke of Musicke, 1591

With dignity

1. Lord, as to thy dear Cross we flee, And plead to be for - given,
2. Help us, through good re - port and ill, Our dai - ly cross to bear;

So let thy life our pat - tern be, And form our souls for heaven.
Like thee, to do our Fa - ther's will, Our breth-ren's griefs to share. A-men.

3 Let grace our selfishness expel,
Our earthliness refine,
And in our hearts let kindness dwell,
As free and true as thine.

4 If joy shall at thy bidding fly,
And grief's dark day come on,
We, in our turn, would meekly cry,
'Father, thy will be done.' Amen.

John Hampden Gurney, 1802–62, a.

ALL SAINTS. 8 7, 8 7, 7 7. *Geistreiches Gesangbuch*, Darmstadt, 1698

FIRST TUNE

With dignity

1. One there is a - bove all oth - ers, Well de-serves the name of Friend;
His is love be - yond a broth-er's, Cost - ly, free, and knows no end;
2. Which of all our friends, to save us, Could or would have shed his blood?
But this Sav - iour died to have us Rec - on - ciled in him to God;

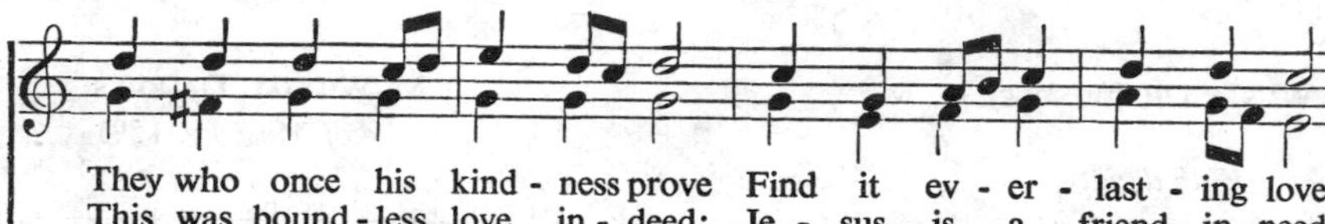

They who once his kind - ness prove Find it ev - er - last - ing love.
This was bound - less love in - deed; Je - sus is a friend in need.

3 When he lived on earth abasèd,
'Friend of sinners' was his Name;
Now, above all glory raisèd,
He rejoices in the same;
Still he calls them brethren, friends,
And to all their wants attends.

4 O for grace our hearts to soften!
Teach us, Lord, at length to love.
We, alas, forget too often
What a friend we have above;
But when home our souls are brought
We will love thee as we ought.

John Newton, 1725–180

456

DANA. 8 7, 8 7, 7 7. ANDREAS PETER BERGGREN, 1801–80

SECOND TUNE

With dignity

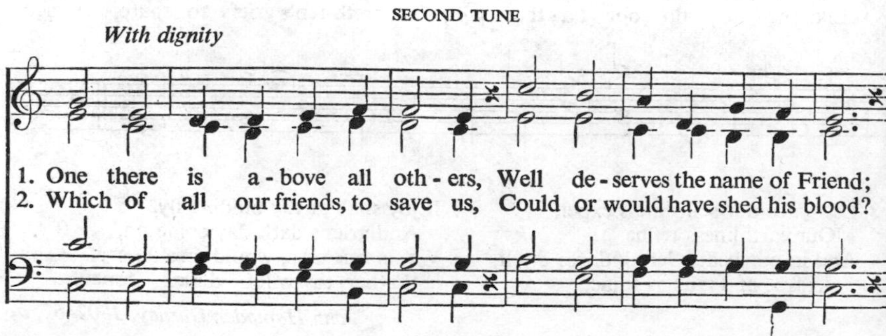
1. One there is a - bove all oth - ers, Well de - serves the name of Friend;
2. Which of all our friends, to save us, Could or would have shed his blood?

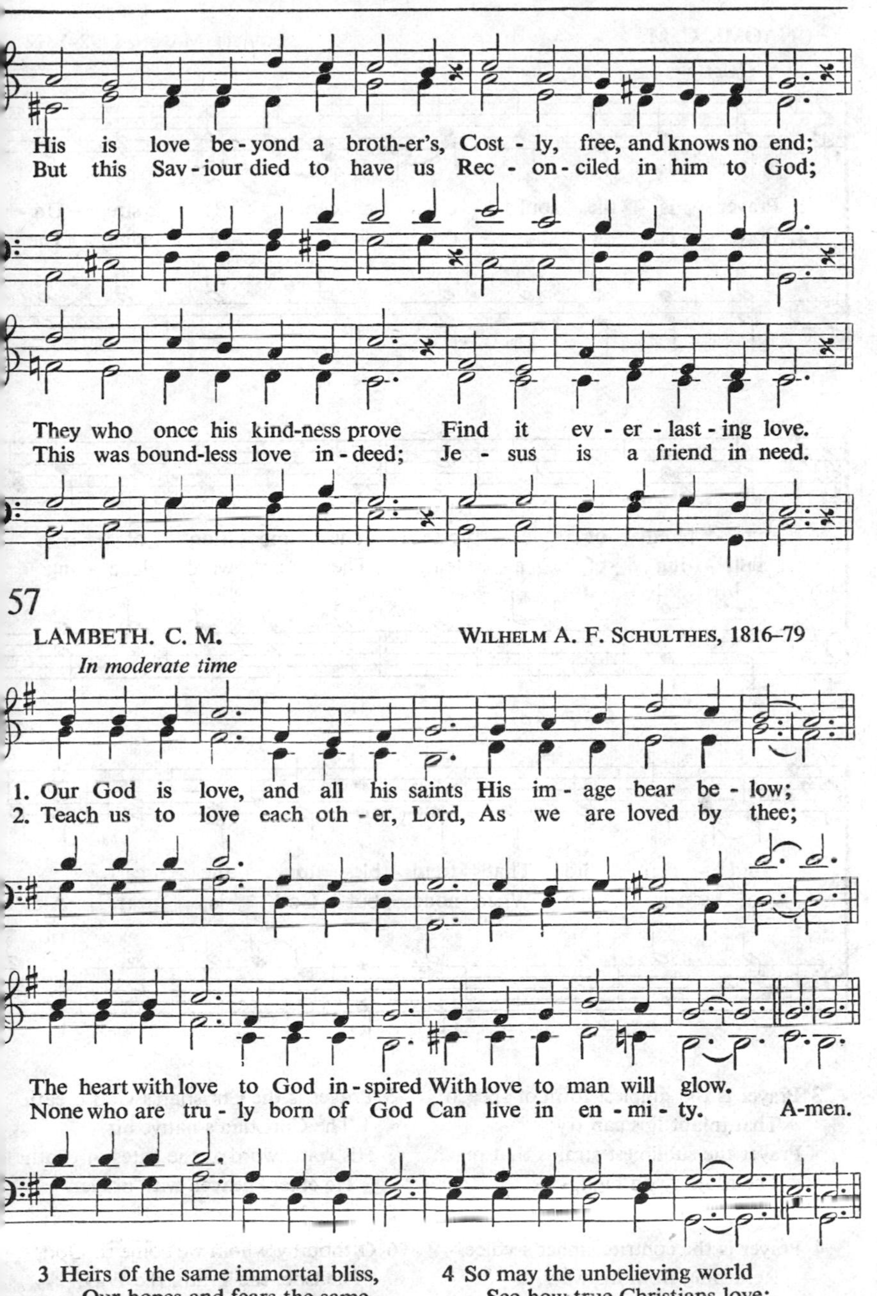
His is love be-yond a broth-er's, Cost - ly, free, and knows no end;
But this Sav-iour died to have us Rec - on-ciled in him to God;
They who oncc his kind-ness prove Find it ev - er - last - ing love.
This was bound-less love in-deed; Je - sus is a friend in need.
57
LAMBETH. C. M.
WILHELM A. F. SCHULTHES, 1816–79
In moderate time
1. Our God is love, and all his saints His im-age bear be - low;
2. Teach us to love each oth - er, Lord, As we are loved by thee;
The heart with love to God in-spired With love to man will glow.
None who are tru - ly born of God Can live in en - mi - ty. A-men.

3 Heirs of the same immortal bliss,
Our hopes and fears the same,
With bonds of love our hearts unite,
With mutual love inflame.

4 So may the unbelieving world
See how true Christians love;
And glorify our Saviour's grace,
And seek that grace to prove. Amen.

Thomas Cotterill, 1779–1823

NAOMI. C. M. LOWELL MASON, 1792–1872

Quietly

1. Prayer is the soul's sin - cere de - sire, Un - ut - tered or ex - pressed; The mo - tion of a hid - den fire That trem - bles in the breast.
2. Prayer is the bur - den of a sigh, The fall - ing of a tear, The up - ward glanc - ing of an eye When none but God is near. A-men

3 Prayer is the simplest form of speech
That infant lips can try;
Prayer the sublimest strains that reach
The Majesty on high.

4 Prayer is the contrite sinner's voice,
Returning from his ways,
While angels in their songs rejoice,
And cry, 'Behold, he prays!'

5 Prayer is the Christian's vital breath,
The Christian's native air,
His watchword at the gates of death:
He enters heaven with prayer.

6 O thou by whom we come to God,
The Life, the Truth, the Way,
The path of prayer thyself hast trod:
Lord, teach us how to pray. Amen.

James Montgomery, 1771–18

ERIE (WHAT A FRIEND). 8 7, 8 7. D.
CHARLES CROZAT CONVERSE, 1832–1918
Quietly
What a friend we have in Je - sus, All our sins and griefs to bear!
What a priv - i - lege to car - ry Ev - ery-thing to God in prayer!
O what peace we of - ten for - feit, O what need-less pain we bear,
All be-cause we do not car - ry Ev - ery-thing to God in prayer!

2 Have we trials and temptations?
  Is there trouble anywhere?
We should never be discouraged,
  Take it to the Lord in prayer.
Can we find a friend so faithful,
  Who will all our sorrows share?
Jesus knows our every weakness;
  Take it to the Lord in prayer.

3 Are we weak and heavy-laden,
  Cumbered with a load of care?
Precious Saviour, still our refuge;
  Take it to the Lord in prayer.
Do thy friends despise, forsake thee?
  Take it to the Lord in prayer;
In his arms he'll take and shield thee,
  Thou wilt find a solace there.

Joseph Scriven, 1820–86

DARMSTADT (O GOTT, DU FROMMER GOTT). 6 7, 6 7, 6 6, 6 6.

AHASUERUS FRITSCH, 1629–1701
Adapted and harm. by J. S. BACH, 1685–1750

Slowly and majestically

1. O God, e - ter - nal source Of love be - yond our know - ing,
Who giv - eth ev - ery gift, Thy bound-less grace be - stow - ing:
Grant sound-ness to our minds And whole-ness to our frame
And par - don to our souls, That we may praise thy Name. A-me

2 O help us to fulfill
On earth our holy calling;
O make us hear thy voice,
And keep our feet from falling.
So may we serve thee here
With all our strength and might,
And may our every deed
Be righteous in thy sight.

3 All praise and thanks to God
The Father now be given,
The Son and him who reigns
With them in highest heaven;
The one, eternal God,
Whom earth and heaven adore,
For thus it was, is now,
And shall be evermore. Amen.

J. Heermann, 1585–1647, and M. Rinkart, 1586–16
Tr. E. T. Horn III, 1909–, and C. Winkworth, 1829–

61 Petition and Intercession

PASS ME NOT. 8 5, 8 5. With Refrain. WILLIAM HOWARD DOANE, 1832–1915
Quietly
1. Pass me not, O gen - tle Sav - iour, Hear my hum - ble cry;
2. Let me at thy throne of mer - cy Find a sweet re - lief;
While on oth - ers thou art call - ing, Do not pass me by.
Kneel - ing there in deep con - tri - tion, Help my un - be - lief.
Refrain
Sav - iour, Sav - iour, hear my hum - ble cry, While on
oth - ers thou art call - ing, Do not pass me by.

3 Trusting only in thy merit,
Would I seek thy face;
Heal my wounded, broken spirit,
Save me by thy grace.

4 Thou the spring of all my comfort,
More than life to me;
Whom have I on earth beside thee,
Whom in heaven but thee?

Fanny Jane Crosby, 1820–1915

WERDE MUNTER. 8 7, 8 7, 7 7, 8 8. JOHANN SCHOP, *cir.* 1600–65

Gently
1. O my soul, on wings as - cend - ing, On the ho - ly mount seek rest,
Where sweet an - gel-harps are blend - ing With the an - thems of the blest.
Let thy fer - vent praise and prayer Come be - fore thy Mak - er there,
Know-ing that, while yet a mor - tal, Thou art near the Fa - ther's por - tal.

2 While upon this earth abiding,
  Let us never cease to pray,
In the blessèd Lord confiding,
  As our fathers in their day.
Be the voice of children raised
To the God our fathers praised;
May his blessing, failing never,
Rest on all his saints forever.

3 Bless us, Father, and protect us
  From all harm in all our ways;
Patiently, O Lord, direct us
  Safely through these fleeting days;
Let thy face upon us shine,
Fill us with thy peace divine;
Praise the Father, Son, and Spirit,
Praise him, all that life inherit.

Johan Olof Wallin, 1779–18
Tr. Compos

SOMETHING FOR JESUS. 6 4, 6 4, 6 6 6, 4. ROBERT LOWRY, 1826–99

Softly and devotionally

1. Sav - iour, thy dy - ing love Thou gav - est me,
2. O'er the blest mer - cy seat, Plead - ing for me,
Nor should I aught with - hold, Dear Lord, from thee;
My fee - ble faith looks up, Je - sus, to thee;
In love my soul would bow, My heart ful - fill its vow,
Help me my cross to bear, Thy won - drous love de - clare,
Some of - fering bring thee now, Some - thing for thee.
Some song to raise, or prayer, Some - thing for thee.

3 Give me a faithful heart,
Likeness to thee,
That each departing day
Henceforth may see
Some work of love begun,
Some deed of kindness done,
Some wanderer sought and won,
Something for thee.

4 All that I am and have,
Thy gifts so free,
In joy, in grief, through life,
Dear Lord, for thee;
And when thy face I see,
My ransomed soul shall be,
Through all eternity,
Something for thee.

Sylvanus Dryden Phelps, 1816–95

HIMMEL. 8 7, 8 7, 7 7. FRIEDRICH HEINRICH HIMMEL, 1765–1814

Broadly, not too fast

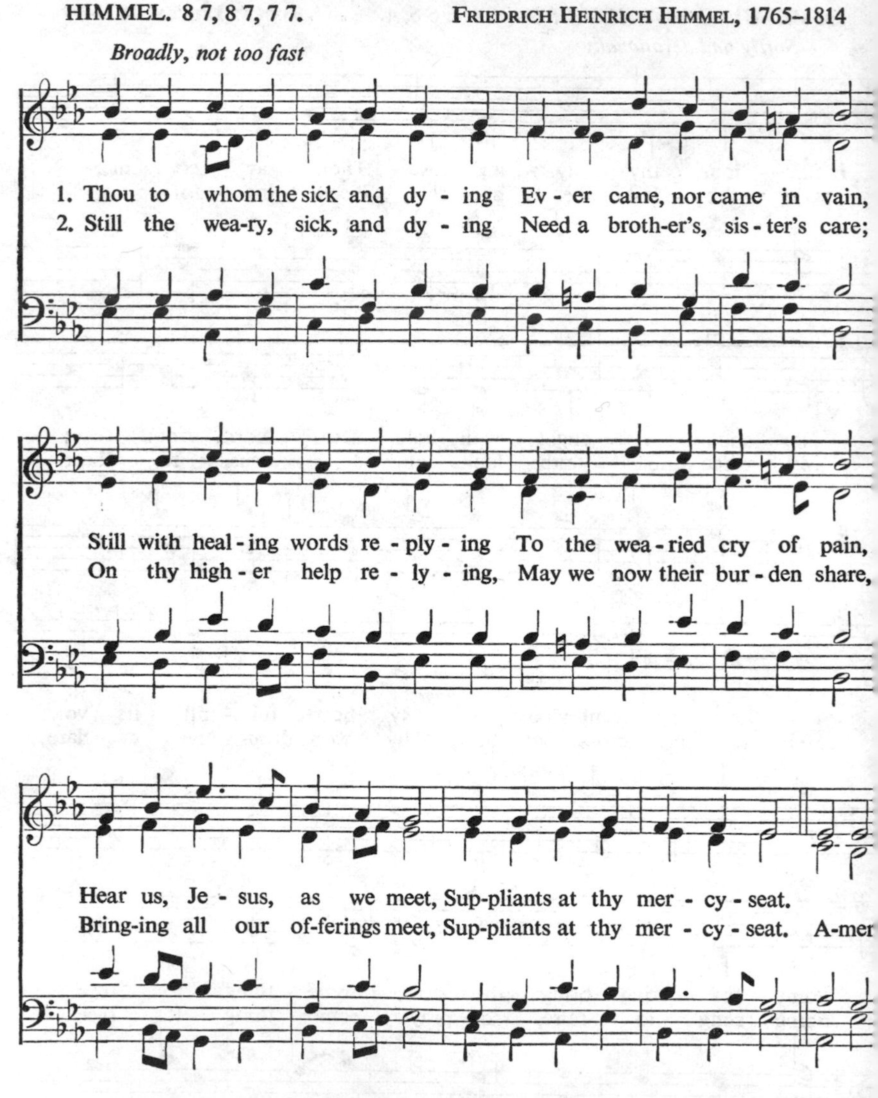
1. Thou to whom the sick and dy - ing Ev - er came, nor came in vain,
2. Still the wea-ry, sick, and dy - ing Need a broth-er's, sis - ter's care;
Still with heal - ing words re - ply - ing To the wea - ried cry of pain,
On thy high - er help re - ly - ing, May we now their bur - den share,
Hear us, Je - sus, as we meet, Sup-pliants at thy mer - cy - seat.
Bring-ing all our of-ferings meet, Sup-pliants at thy mer - cy - seat. A-men

3 May each child of thine be willing,
Willing both in hand and heart,
All the law of love fulfilling,
Ever comfort to impart,
Ever bringing offerings meet,
Suppliant, to thy mercy-seat.

4 So may sickness, sin, and sadness
To thy healing power yield,
Till the sick and sad, in gladness,
Rescued, ransomed, cleansèd, healed,
One in thee, together meet,
Pardoned, at thy judgment-seat.
Amen

Godfrey Thring, 1823–19

ALMSGIVING. 8 8 8, 4. JOHN BACCHUS DYKES, 1823–76

In moderate time

1. My God and Fa - ther, while I stray Far from my
2. If but my faint - ing heart be blest With thy sweet
home, in life's rough way, O teach me from my
Spir - it for its guest, My God, to thee I
heart to say, 'Thy will be done.'
leave the rest, 'Thy will be done.' A - men.

3 Renew my will from day to day,
Blend it with thine, and take away
All that now makes it hard to say,
'Thy will be done.'

4 Then when on earth I breathe no more
The prayer oft mixed with tears before,
I'll sing upon a happier shore,
'Thy will be done.' Amen.

Charlotte Elliott, 1789–1871

See also:

CAITHNESS. C. M. *Scottish Psalter*, 1635

Moderately slow

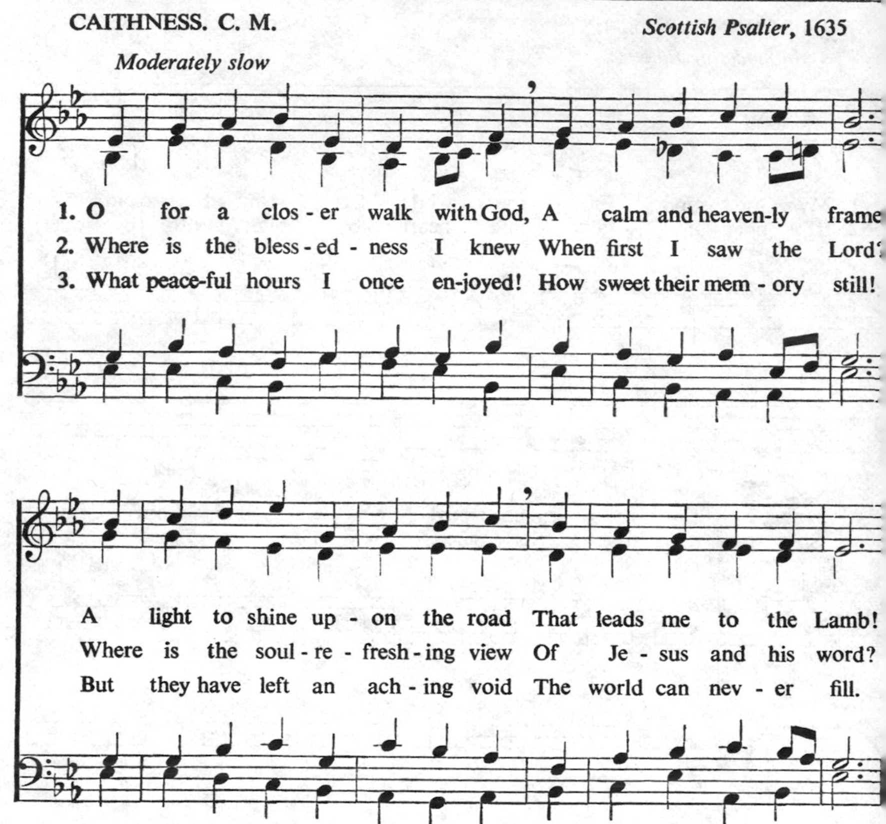
1. O for a clos - er walk with God, A calm and heaven-ly frame
2. Where is the bless - ed - ness I knew When first I saw the Lord?
3. What peace-ful hours I once en-joyed! How sweet their mem - ory still!
A light to shine up - on the road That leads me to the Lamb!
Where is the soul - re - fresh - ing view Of Je - sus and his word?
But they have left an ach - ing void The world can nev - er fill.

4 Return, O holy Dove, return,
Sweet messenger of rest!
I hate the sins that made thee mourn,
And drove thee from my breast.

5 The dearest idol I have known,
Whate'er that idol be,
Help me to tear it from thy throne,
And worship only thee.

6 So shall my walk be close with God,
Calm and serene my frame;
So purer light shall mark the road
That leads me to the Lamb.

William Cowper, 1731–1800

This hymn may also be sung to DEDHAM (No. 428)

REST. 8 6, 8 8 6. FREDERICK C. MAKER, 1844–1927

Quietly

1. Dear Lord and Fa - ther of man-kind, For - give our fool - ish ways;
2. In sim - ple trust like theirs who heard, Be - side the Syr - ian sea,

Re - clothe us in our right - ful mind, In pur - er lives thy
The gra - cious call - ing of the Lord, Let us, like them, with -

ser - vice find, In deep - er rev - erence, praise.
out a word Rise up and fol - low thee. A - men.

3 O Sabbath rest by Galilee,
O calm of hills above;
Where Jesus knelt to share with thee
The silence of eternity,
Interpreted by love!

4 Drop thy still dews of quietness,
Till all our strivings cease;
Take from our souls the strain and stress,
And let our ordered lives confess
The beauty of thy peace.

5 Breathe through the heats of our desire
Thy coolness and thy balm;
Let sense be dumb, let flesh retire;
Speak through the earthquake, wind, and fire,
O still small voice of calm! Amen.

John Greenleaf Whittier, 1807–92

WINCHESTER. C. M. THOMAS ESTE'S *Psalter*, 1592

In moderate time

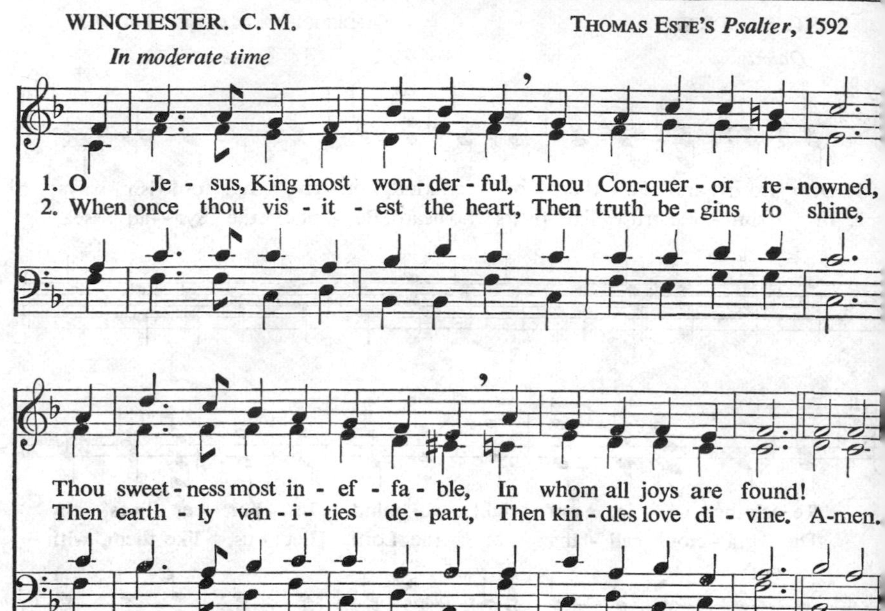
1. O Je - sus, King most won - der - ful, Thou Con-quer - or re - nowned,
2. When once thou vis - it - est the heart, Then truth be - gins to shine,
Thou sweet - ness most in - ef - fa - ble, In whom all joys are found!
Then earth - ly van - i - ties de - part, Then kin - dles love di - vine. A-men.

3 O Jesus, light of all below,
Thou fount of life and fire,
Surpassing all the joys we know,
All that we can desire;

4 May every heart confess thy Name,
And ever thee adore,
And, seeking thee, itself inflame
To seek thee more and more.

5 Thee may our tongues forever bless;
Thee may we love alone,
And ever in our lives express
The image of thine own. Amen.

Ascribed to St. Bernard of Clairvaux, 1091–1153
Tr. Edward Caswall, 1814–78

469

SOUTHWELL (IRONS). C. M. HERBERT S. IRONS, 1834–1905

With dignity

1. Je - sus, these eyes have nev - er seen That ra - diant form of thine;
2. I see thee not, I hear thee not, Yet art thou oft with me;

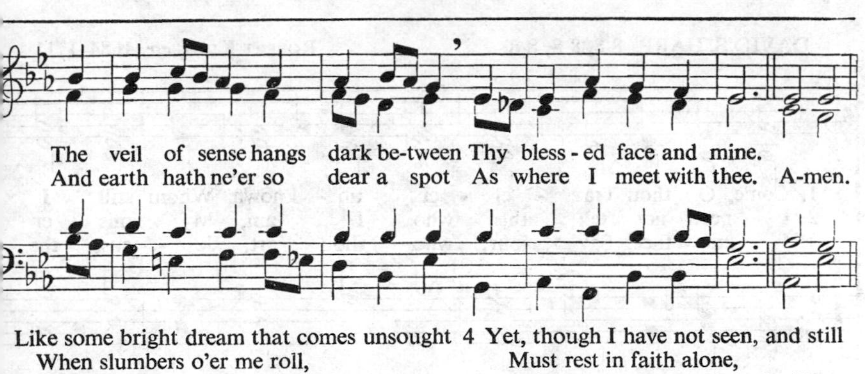
The veil of sense hangs dark be-tween Thy bless - ed face and mine.
And earth hath ne'er so dear a spot As where I meet with thee. A-men.

Like some bright dream that comes unsought
When slumbers o'er me roll,
Thine image ever fills my thought,
And charms my ravished soul.

4 Yet, though I have not seen, and still
Must rest in faith alone,
I love thee, dearest Lord, and will,
Unseen but not unknown.

5 When death these mortal eyes shall seal,
And still this throbbing heart,
The rending veil shall thee reveal
All-glorious as thou art. Amen.

Ray Palmer, 1808–87

This hymn may also be sung to NUN DANKET ALL' UND BRINGET EHR (No. 413)

470

TRENTHAM. S. M. ROBERT JACKSON, 1840–1914

Slowly

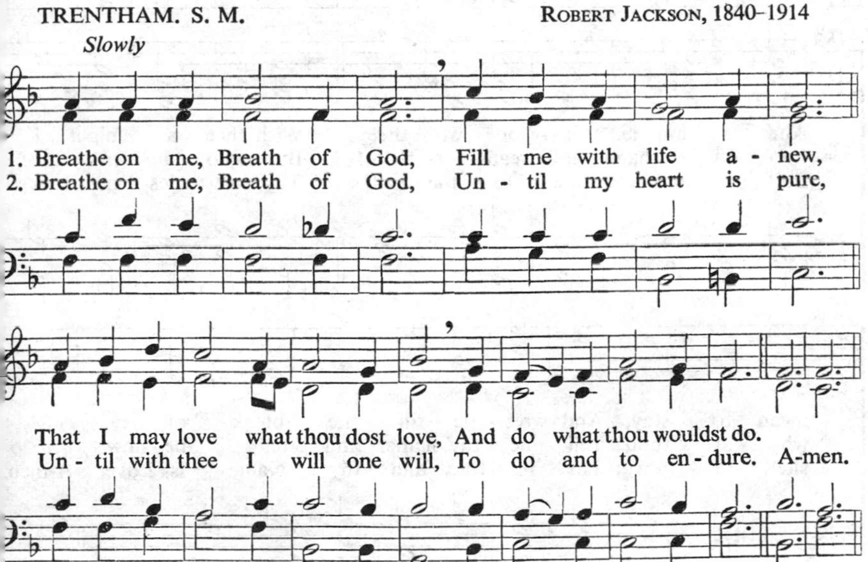
1. Breathe on me, Breath of God, Fill me with life a - new,
2. Breathe on me, Breath of God, Un - til my heart is pure,
That I may love what thou dost love, And do what thou wouldst do.
Un - til with thee I will one will, To do and to en - dure. A-men.

3 Breathe on me, Breath of God,
Unite my soul with thine,
Until this earthly part of me
Glows with thy fire divine.

4 Breathe on me, Breath of God,
So shall I never die,
But live with thee the perfect life
Of thine eternity. Amen.

Edwin Hatch, 1835–89

DAVID'S HARP. 8 8, 8 8, 8 8. ROBERT KING, *cir.* 1684–1711

1. Come, O thou Trav - el - er un - known, Whom still I hold, but can - not see; My com - pa - ny be - fore is gone, And I am left a - lone with thee; With thee all night I mean to stay, And wres - tle till the break of day.
2. I need not tell thee who I am, My mis - er - y or sin de - clare; Thy - self hast called me by my name; Look on thy hands, and read it there! But who, I ask thee, who art thou? Tell me thy name, and tell me now.
3. I know thee, Sav - iour, who thou art, Je - sus, the fee - ble sin - ner's friend; Nor wilt thou with the night de - part, But stay and love me to the end: Thy mer - cies nev - er shall re - move; Thy na - ture and thy Name is Love. A-men.

4 Yield to me now, for I am weak,
But confident in self-despair;
Speak to my heart, in blessings speak,
Be conquered by my instant prayer.
Speak, or thou never hence shalt move,
And tell me if thy name is Love.

5 'Tis Love, 'tis Love, thou died'st for me
I hear thy whisper in my heart!
The morning breaks, the shadows flee;
Pure universal love thou art;
To me, to all, thy mercies move;
Thy nature and thy name is Love. Amer

Charles Wesley, 1707–8

LANGRAN. 10 10, 10 10. JAMES LANGRAN, 1835–1909

Devotionally, with breadth

1. Lead us, O Fa - ther, in the paths of peace; With - out thy
2. Lead us, O Fa - ther, in the paths of truth; Un - helped by

guid - ing hand we go a - stray, And doubts ap - pall, and sor - rows
thee, in er - ror's maze we grope, While pas - sion stains and fol - ly

still in - crease; Lead us through Christ, the true and liv - ing way.
dims our youth, And age comes on, un-cheered by faith or hope. A-men.

3 Lead us, O Father, in the paths of right;
Blindly we stumble when we walk alone,
Involved in shadows of a darkening night;
Only with thee we journey safely on.

4 Lead us, O Father, to thy heavenly rest,
However rough and steep the pathway be,
Through joy or sorrow, as thou deemest best,
Until our lives are perfected in thee. Amen.

William Henry Burleigh, 1812–71

473

PEACE. 10 10, 10 6.
GEORGE WHITEFIELD CHADWICK, 1854–1931
Devotionally
1. I sought the Lord, and af - ter - ward I knew
2. Thou didst reach forth thy hand and mine en - fold;
He moved my soul to seek him, seek - ing me;
I walked and sank not on the storm-vexed sea;
It was not I that found, O Sav - iour true;
'Twas not so much that I on thee took hold
No, I was found of thee.
As thou, dear Lord, on me.
3 I find, I walk, I love, but O the whole
Of love is but my answer, Lord, to thee;
For thou wert long beforehand with my soul,
Always thou lovèdst me.
Anonymous. 188
474
RICHMOND (CHESTERFIELD). C. M.
THOMAS HAWEIS, 1734–1820
Broadly
1. Walk in the light: so shalt thou know That fel - low - ship of love
2. Walk in the light: and thou shalt find Thy heart made tru - ly his

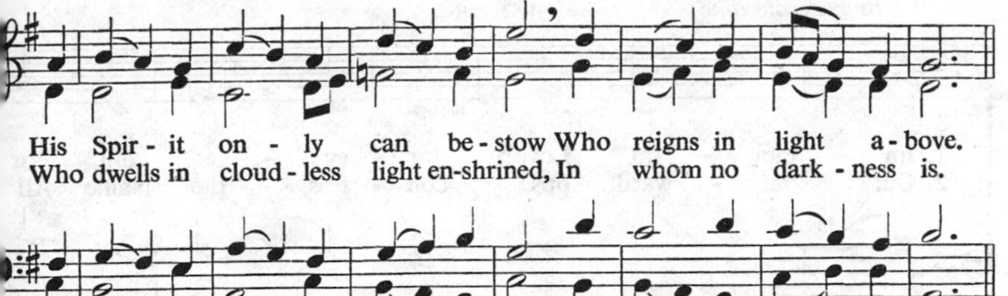
His Spir - it on - ly can be - stow Who reigns in light a - bove.
Who dwells in cloud - less light en-shrined, In whom no dark - ness is.

3 Walk in the light: and thou shalt own
Thy darkness passed away,
Because that light hath on thee shone
In which is perfect day.

4 Walk in the light: and thine shall be
A path, though thorny, bright;
For God, by grace, shall dwell in thee,
And God himself is light.

Bernard Barton, 1784–1849

75

FRANCONIA. S. M. *König's Choralbuch,* 1738

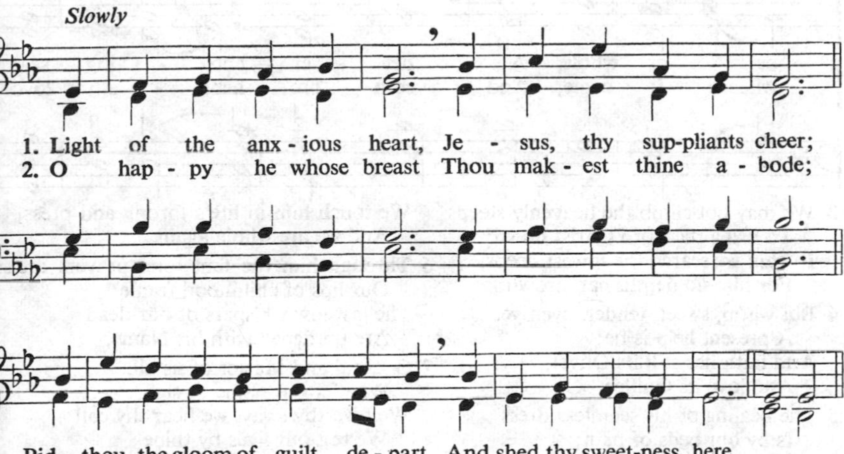
Slowly
1. Light of the anx - ious heart, Je - sus, thy sup-pliants cheer;
2. O hap - py he whose breast Thou mak - est thine a - bode;
Bid thou the gloom of guilt de - part, And shed thy sweet-ness here.
Sweet light that with the pure wilt rest, For they shall see their God. A-men.

3 Brightness of God above,
Unfathomable grace,
Within our hearts implant thy love
And fix thy dwelling-place.

4 To lowly minds revealed,
Our Saviour we adore;
Like tribute to the Father yield,
And Spirit, evermore. Amen.

Ascribed to St. Bernard of Clairvaux, 1091–1153
Tr. Robert Campbell, 1814–68

BISHOPTHORPE (ST. PAUL'S). C. M. JEREMIAH CLARKE, *cir.* 1669–1707

In moderate time FIRST TUNE

1. Im - mor - tal Love, for - ev - er full, For ev - er flow - ing free, For - ev - er shared, for ev - er whole, A nev - er - ebb - ing sea!
2. Our out - ward lips con - fess the Name All oth - er names a - bove; Love on - ly know - eth whence it came, And com - pre - hend - eth love.

3 We may not climb the heavenly steeps
  To bring the Lord Christ down;
In vain we search the lowest deeps,
  For him no depths can drown:

4 But warm, sweet, tender, even yet
  A present help is he;
And faith has still its Olivet,
  And love its Galilee.

5 The healing of his seamless dress
  Is by our beds of pain;
We touch him in life's throng and press,
  And we are whole again.

6 Through him the first fond prayers are sa
  Our lips of childhood frame;
The last low whispers of our dead
  Are burdened with his Name.

7 O Lord, and Master of us all,
  What'er our name or sign,
We own thy sway, we hear thy call,
  We test our lives by thine.

John Greenleaf Whittier, 1807–

476

SERENITY. C. M. WILLIAM VINCENT WALLACE, 1814–65

Devotionally

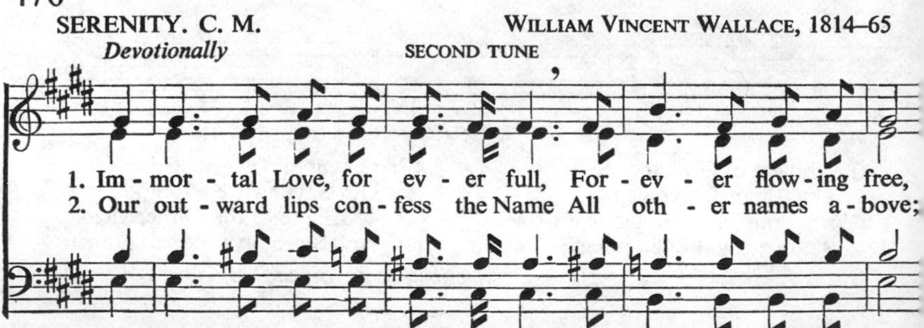
SECOND TUNE
1. Im - mor - tal Love, for ev - er full, For - ev - er flow - ing free,
2. Our out - ward lips con - fess the Name All oth - er names a - bove;

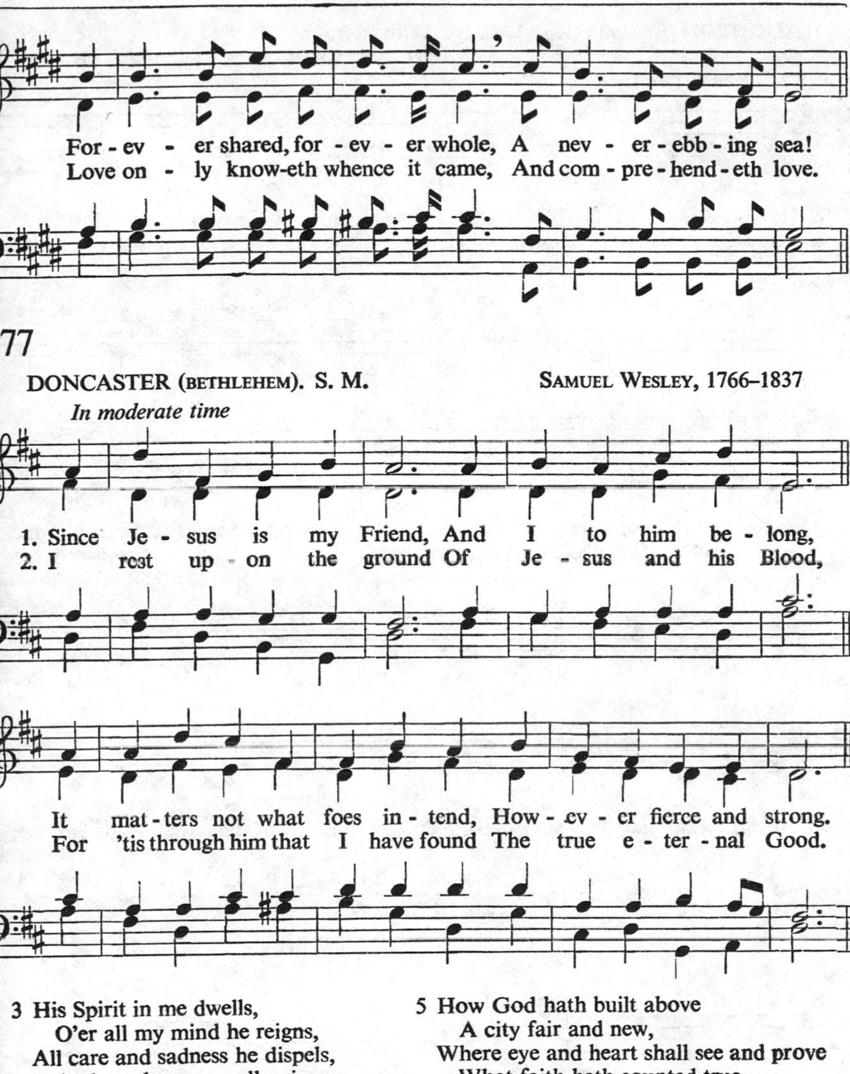
For - ev - er shared, for - ev - er whole, A nev - er - ebb - ing sea!
Love on - ly know-eth whence it came, And com - pre - hend - eth love.
77
DONCASTER (BETHLEHEM). S. M.
SAMUEL WESLEY, 1766–1837
In moderate time
1. Since Je - sus is my Friend, And I to him be - long,
2. I rest up - on the ground Of Je - sus and his Blood,
It mat - ters not what foes in - tend, How - ev - er fierce and strong.
For 'tis through him that I have found The true e - ter - nal Good.

3 His Spirit in me dwells,
O'er all my mind he reigns,
All care and sadness he dispels,
And soothes away all pains.

4 He whispers in my breast
Sweet words of holy cheer,
How he who seeks in God his rest
Shall ever find him near.

5 How God hath built above
A city fair and new,
Where eye and heart shall see and prove
What faith hath counted true.

6 My heart for gladness springs,
It cannot more be sad;
For very joy it laughs and sings,
Sees naught but sunshine glad.

7 The sun that lights mine eyes
Is Christ the Lord I love;
I sing for joy of that which lies
Stored up for me above.

Paul Gerhardt, 1607–76
Tr. Catherine Winkworth, 1829–78

AUGHTON (HE LEADETH ME). L. M. With Refrain.

WILLIAM BATCHELDER BRADBURY, 1816–68

In moderate time

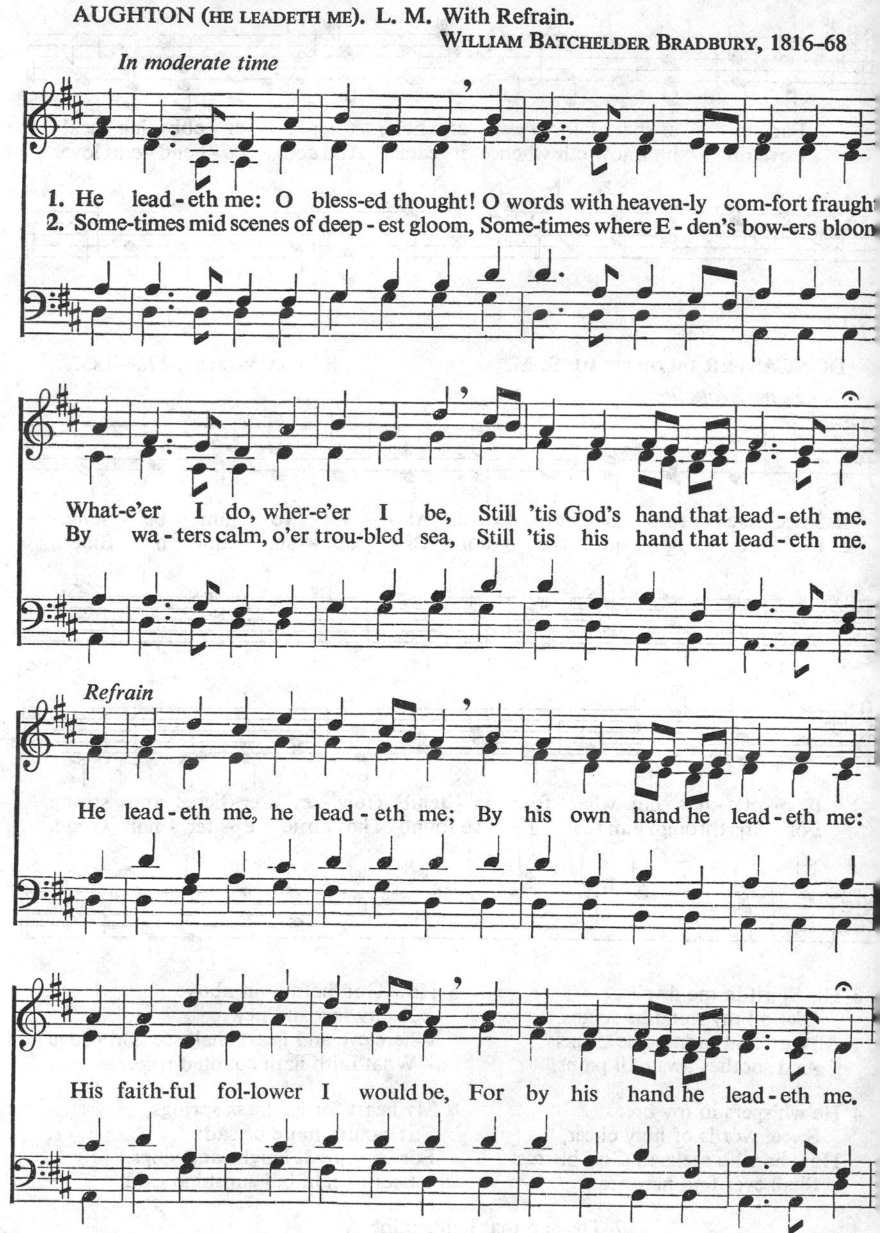
1. He lead-eth me: O bless-ed thought! O words with heaven-ly com-fort fraught
2. Some-times mid scenes of deep-est gloom, Some-times where E-den's bow-ers bloom
What-e'er I do, wher-e'er I be, Still 'tis God's hand that lead-eth me.
By wa-ters calm, o'er trou-bled sea, Still 'tis his hand that lead-eth me.
Refrain
He lead-eth me, he lead-eth me; By his own hand he lead-eth me:
His faith-ful fol-lower I would be, For by his hand he lead-eth me.

3 Lord, I would clasp thy hand in mine,
Nor ever murmur nor repine;
Content, whatever lot I see,
Since 'tis my God that leadeth me.

4 And when my task on earth is done,
When by thy grace the victory's won,
E'en death's cold wave I will not flee,
Since God through Jordan leadeth me.

Joseph Henry Gilmore, 1834–1918, a.

LOWRY. 6 4, 6 4. With Refrain. ROBERT LOWRY, 1826–99

In moderate time
1. I need thee ev - ery hour, Most gra - cious Lord;
No ten - der voice like thine Can peace af - ford.
Refrain
I need thee, O I need thee, Ev - ery hour I need thee;
O bless me now, my Sav - iour, I come to thee. A-men.

2 I need thee every hour,
Stay thou near by;
Temptations lose their power
When thou art nigh.

3 I need thee every hour,
In joy or pain;
Come quickly and abide,
Or life is vain.

4 I need thee every hour,
Teach me thy will;
And thy rich promises
In me fulfill.

5 I need thee every hour,
Most Holy One,
O make me thine indeed,
Thou blessèd Son. Amen.

Annie Sherwood Hawks, 1835–1918
Refrain, Robert Lowry, 1826–99

IRISH. C. M.

Irish Folk Tune
Hymns and Sacred Poems, Dublin, 1749

Devotionally FIRST TUNE

1. O thou in all thy might so far, In

all thy love so near, Be - yond the range of

sun and star, And yet be - side us here:

2 What heart can comprehend thy Name,
Or searching find thee out,
Who art within, a quickening flame,
A presence round about?

3 Yet though I know thee but in part,
I ask not, Lord, for more;
Enough for me to know thou art,
To love thee, and adore.

4 And dearer than all things I know
Is childlike faith to me,
That makes the darkest way I go
An open path to thee.

Frederick Lucian Hosmer, 1840–192

REDEEMER. C. M. ARNOLD F. KELLER, 1890–

Devotionally SECOND TUNE

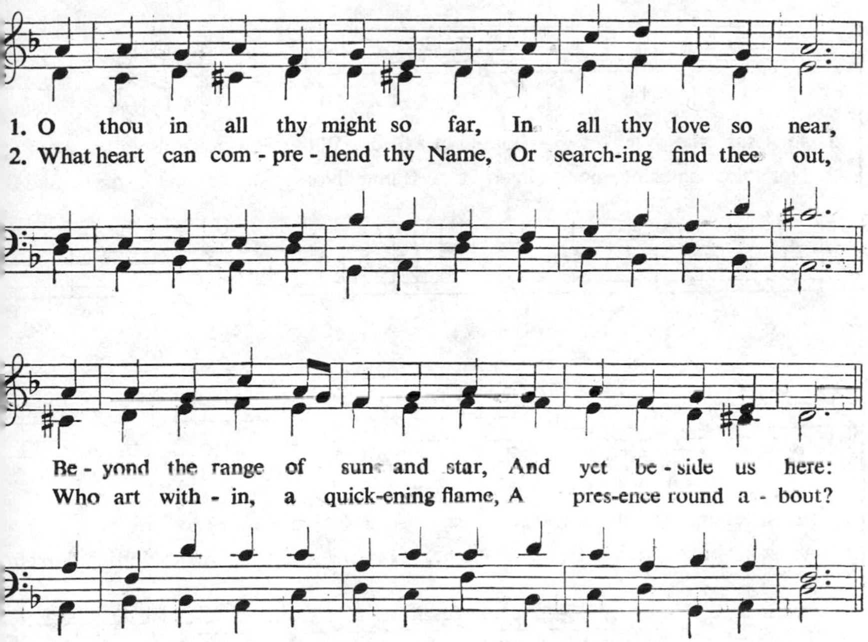

1. O thou in all thy might so far, In all thy love so near,
2. What heart can com - pre - hend thy Name, Or search-ing find thee out,

Be - yond the range of sun and star, And yet be - side us here:
Who art with - in, a quick-ening flame, A pres-ence round a - bout?

3 Yet though I know thee but in part,
I ask not, Lord, for more;
Enough for me to know thou art,
To love thee, and adore.

4 And dearer than all things I know
Is childlike faith to me,
That makes the darkest way I go
An open path to thee.

Frederick Lucian Hosmer, 1840–1929

Music composed for this book and copyrighted

See also:

388 As pants the hart
394 Blest are the pure
123 Come down, O Love divine
121 Come, Holy Ghost, in love
406 How sweet the Name of Jesus
399 Jesus, thy boundless love
571 Peace, perfect peace
378 Search me, God, and know my heart
391 Thou hidden Love of God
508 Make me a captive, Lord
120 O Holy Spirit, enter in
129 Spirit of God, descend upon my heart

481

ST. AGNES. C. M. JOHN BACCHUS DYKES, 1823–76

Devotionally

1. Je - sus, the ver - y thought of thee With sweet-ness fills the breast;
2. Nor voice can sing, nor heart can frame, Nor can the mem - ory find

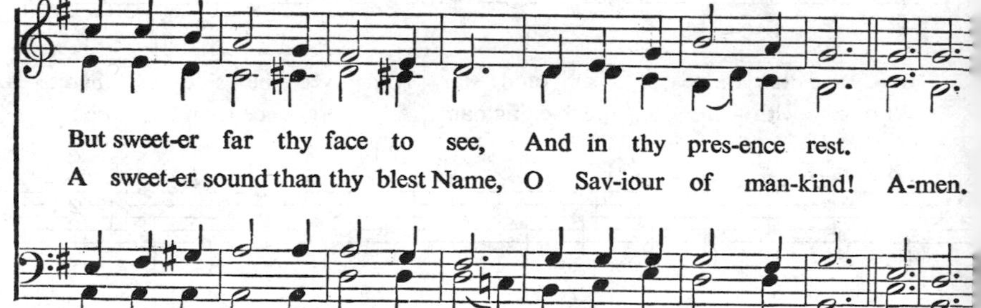

But sweet-er far thy face to see, And in thy pres-ence rest.
A sweet-er sound than thy blest Name, O Sav-iour of man-kind! A-men.

3 O hope of every contrite heart,
O joy of all the meek,
To those who fall, how kind thou art,
How good to those who seek!

4 But what to those who find? Ah, this
Nor tongue nor pen can show;
The love of Jesus, what it is,
None but his loved ones know.

5 Jesus, our only joy be thou,
As thou our prize wilt be;
Jesus, be thou our glory now,
And through eternity. Amen.

Ascribed to St. Bernard of Clairvaux, 1091–1153
Tr. Edward Caswall, 1814–78

ST. CHRISTOPHER. 7 6, 7 6. D. FREDERICK C. MAKER, 1844–1927

Devotionally
1. Be - neath the Cross of Je - sus I fain would take my stand;
2. Up - on that Cross of Je - sus, Mine eye at times can see
The shad - ow of a might-y rock With - in a wea - ry land;
The ver - y dy - ing form of One Who suf - fered there for me;
A home with - in a wil - der-ness, A rest up - on the way,
And from my smit - ten heart, with tears, Two won - ders I con - fess:
From the burn - ing of the noon-tide heat And bur - dens of the day.
The won - der of his glorious love, And my own worth-less - ness.

3 I take, O Cross, thy shadow
For my abiding-place;
I ask no other sunshine than
The sunshine of his face:
Content to let the world go by,
To know no gain nor loss,
My sinful self my only shame,
My glory all, the Cross.

Elizabeth C. Clephane, 1830–69

CHRISTE REDEMPTOR. L. M.

Plainsong Melody, Mode I
Arr. ERNEST WHITE, 1899–

FIRST TUNE

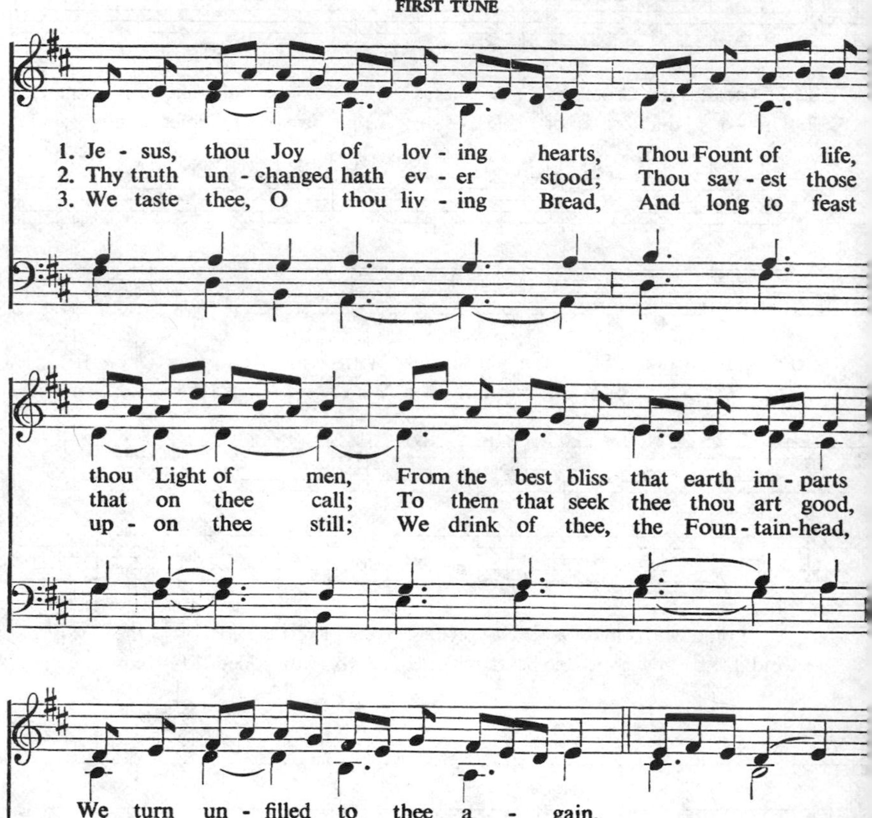
1. Je - sus, thou Joy of lov - ing hearts, Thou Fount of life, thou Light of men, From the best bliss that earth im - parts We turn un - filled to thee a - gain.
2. Thy truth un - changed hath ev - er stood; Thou sav - est those that on thee call; To them that seek thee thou art good, To them that find thee, all in all.
3. We taste thee, O thou liv - ing Bread, And long to feast up - on thee still; We drink of thee, the Foun - tain-head, And thirst our souls from thee to fill.
A - men.

4 Our restless spirits yearn for thee,
Where'er our changeful lot is cast;
Glad, when thy gracious smile we see,
Blest, when our faith can hold thee fast.

5 O Jesus, ever with us stay;
Make all our moments calm and bright;
Chase the dark night of sin away,
Shed o'er the world thy holy light. Amen.

Ascribed to St. Bernard of Clairvaux, 1091–115.
Tr. Ray Palmer, 1808–8

WALTON (GERMANY). L. M. WILLIAM GARDINER'S *Sacred Melodies*, 1815

In moderate time SECOND TUNE

1. Je - sus, thou Joy of lov - ing hearts, Thou Fount of life, thou Light of men, From the best bliss that earth im - parts We turn un - filled to thee a - gain.
2. Thy truth un - changed hath ev - er stood; Thou sav - est those that on thee call; To them that seek thee thou art good, To them that find thee, all in all.
3. We taste thee, O thou liv - ing Bread, And long to feast up - on thee still; We drink of thee, the Foun - tain - head, And thirst our souls from thee to fill. A-men.

4 Our restless spirits yearn for thee,
Where'er our changeful lot is cast;
Glad, when thy gracious smile we see,
Blest, when our faith can hold thee fast.

5 O Jesus, ever with us stay;
Make all our moments calm and bright;
Chase the dark night of sin away,
Shed o'er the world thy holy light. Amen.

Ascribed to St. Bernard of Clairvaux, 1091–1153
Tr. Ray Palmer, 1808–87

484

LONDON NEW. C. M. *Scottish Psalter*, 1635

With dignity

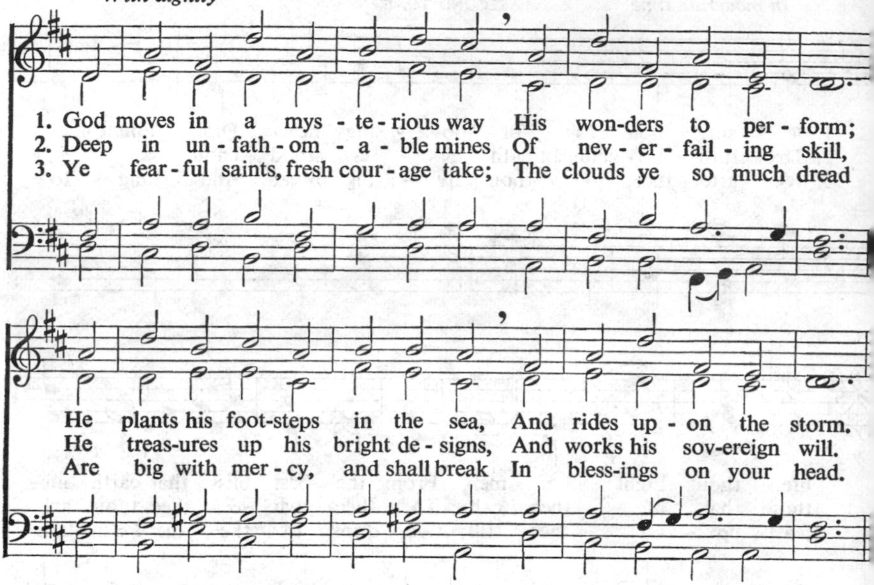

1. God moves in a mys - te - rious way His won-ders to per - form;
He plants his foot-steps in the sea, And rides up - on the storm.

2. Deep in un - fath - om - a - ble mines Of nev - er - fail - ing skill,
He treas-ures up his bright de - signs, And works his sov-ereign will.

3. Ye fear - ful saints, fresh cour - age take; The clouds ye so much dread
Are big with mer - cy, and shall break In bless-ings on your head.

4 Judge not the Lord by feeble sense,
But trust him for his grace;
Behind a frowning Providence
He hides a smiling face.

5 His purposes will ripen fast,
Unfolding every hour;
The bud may have a bitter taste,
But sweet will be the flower.

6 Blind unbelief is sure to err,
And scan his work in vain;
God is his own interpreter,
And he will make it plain.

William Cowper, 1731–1800

This hymn may also be sung to St. Anne (No. 168)

485

KALMAR. 8 7, 8 7, 7 7. Swedish Melody, 1676

With dignity

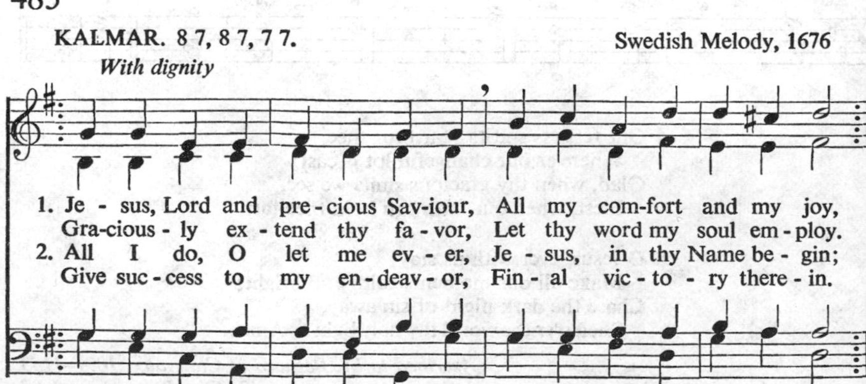
1. Je - sus, Lord and pre - cious Sav-iour, All my com-fort and my joy,
Gra-cious - ly ex - tend thy fa - vor, Let thy word my soul em - ploy.
2. All I do, O let me ev - er, Je - sus, in thy Name be - gin;
Give suc - cess to my en - deav - or, Fin - al vic - to - ry there - in.

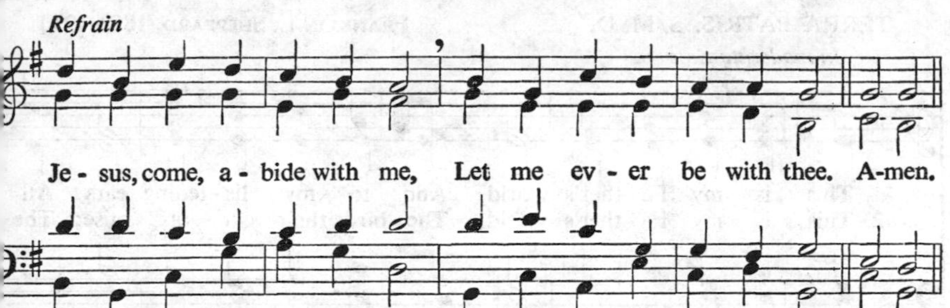
Refrain
Je - sus, come, a - bide with me, Let me ev - er be with thee. A-men.

Let my words and thoughts, O Saviour,
To thy praise and glory tend;
Help me, Lord, that I may gather
Treasures that shall never end.

4 When my days on earth are over,
Let me enter into rest.
Bear me home, O blessèd Saviour,
When to thee it seemeth best.

Jakob Arrhenius, 1642–1725
Tr. Augustus Nelson, 1863–1949

486

MARTYRDOM (AVON). C. M. HUGH WILSON, 1764–1824

In flowing style

1. A - las! and did my Sav - iour bleed, And did my Sov-ereign die?
2. Was it for sin that I had done He groaned up - on the tree?

Would he de - vote that sa - cred Head For sin - ners such as I?
A - maz - ing pit - y, grace un-known, And love be - yond de - gree!

3 Well might the sun in darkness hide,
And shut his glories in,
When Christ, the mighty Maker, died
For man, the creature's sin.

4 Thus might I hide my blushing face,
While his dear Cross appears;
Dissolve my heart in thankfulness,
And melt mine eyes to tears.

5 But drops of grief can ne'er repay
The debt of love I owe.
Here, Lord, I give myself away;
'Tis all that I can do.

Isaac Watts, 1674–1748

TERRA PATRIS. S. M. D. FRANKLIN L. SHEPPARD, 1852–1930

In moderate time

1. This is my Fa-ther's world, And to my lis-tening ears All na - ture sings, and round me rings The mu-sic of the spheres. This is my Fa-ther's world; I rest me in the thought Of rocks and trees, of skies and seas, His hand the won - ders wrought.
2. This is my Fa-ther's world; The birds their car - ols raise; The morn-ing light, the lil - y white, De - clare their Mak - er's praise. This is my Fa-ther's world; He shines in all that's fair; In the rust - ling grass I hear him pass, He speaks to me ev-ery-where.

3 This is my Father's world,
O let me ne'er forget
That though the wrong seems oft so strong,
God is the Ruler yet.
This is my Father's world;
Why should my heart be sad?
The Lord is King, let the heavens ring;
God reigns, let the earth be glad!

Maltbie Davenport Babcock, 1858–190

88 Contemplation

SANDON. 10 4, 10 4, 10 10. CHARLES HENRY PURDAY, 1799–1885

Slowly, with dignity

1. Un - to the hills a - round do I lift up My long -ing eyes;
2. He will not suf - fer that thy foot be moved; Safe shalt thou be.
3. Je - ho - vah is him - self thy keep - er true, Thy change-less shade;
O whence for me shall my sal - va - tion come, From whence a - rise?
No care - less slum - ber shall his eye - lids close, Who keep - eth thee.
Je - ho - vah thy de - fence on thy right hand Him - self hath made.
From God the Lord doth come my cer - tain aid,
Be - hold, he sleep - eth not, he slum - bereth ne'er,
And thee no sun by day shall ev - er smite;
From God the Lord who heaven and earth hath made.
Who keep - eth Is - rael in his ho - ly care.
No moon shall harm thee in the si - lent night. A-men.

4 From every evil shall he keep thy soul,
From every sin;
Jehovah shall preserve thy going out,
Thy coming in.
Above thee watching, he whom we adore
Shall keep thee henceforth, yea, for evermore. Amen.

John Campbell, 1845–1914
Psalm 121

PAX DEI. 10 10, 10 10.
JOHN BACCHUS DYKES, 1823–76
Devotionally, in moderate time
1. O God, I love thee; not that my poor love
2. But, Je - sus, thou art mine, and I am thine;
3. No thought can fath - om and no tongue ex - press
May win me en - trance to thy heaven a - bove,
Clasped to thy bos - om by thy arms di - vine,
Thy griefs, thy toils, thy an - guish meas - ure - less,
Nor yet that stran - gers to thy love must know
Who on the cru - el Cross for me hast borne
Thy death, O Lamb of God the un - de - filed;
The bit - ter - ness of ev - er - last - ing woe.
The nails, the spear, and man's un - pity - ing scorn.
And all for me, thy way - ward sin - ful child. A-men

4 How can I choose but love thee, God's dear Son,
O Jesus, loveliest, and most loving One!
Were there no heaven to gain, no hell to flee,
For what thou art alone I must love thee.

5 Not for the hope of glory or reward,
But even as thyself hast loved me, Lord,
I love thee, and will love thee and adore,
Who art my King, my God, for evermore. Amen.

Latin hymn, XVII cent.
Based on a Spanish hymn of unknown date
Tr. Edward Henry Bickersteth, 1825–1906

90

O JESU. 8 6, 8 6, 8 8. JOHANN BALTHASAR REIMANN, 1702–49

Slowly

1. I look to thee in ev - ery need, And nev - er look in vain;
2. Dis - cour-aged in the work of life, Dis - heart - ened by its load,

I feel thy strong and ten - der love, And all is well a - gain:
Shamed by its fail - ures or its fears, I sink be - side the road;

The thought of thee is might-ier far Than sin and pain and sor - row are.
But let me on - ly think of thee, And then new heart springs up in me.

3 Thy calmness bends serene above,
My restlessness to still;
Around me flows thy quickening life,
To nerve my faltering will:
Thy presence fills my solitude;
Thy providence turns all to good.

4 Embosomed deep in thy dear love,
Held in thy law, I stand;
Thy hand in all things I behold,
And all things in thy hand;
Thou leadest me by unsought ways,
And turn'st my mourning into praise.

Samuel Longfellow, 1819–92

BREAD OF LIFE. 6 4, 6 4. D. WILLIAM F. SHERWIN, 1826–88

Slowly, in flowing style

1. Break thou the bread of life, Dear Lord, to me,
As thou didst break the loaves Be - side the sea;
Be - yond the sa - cred page I seek thee, Lord;
My spir - it pants for thee, O liv - ing Word! A-men.

2 Bless thou the truth, dear Lord,
To me, to me,
As thou didst bless the bread
By Galilee;
Then shall all bondage cease,
All fetters fall;
And I shall find my peace,
My All-in-all! Amen.

Mary A. Lathbury, 1841–19

Used by permission of the Chautauqua Institution

Contemplation

MUNICH (MEININGEN). 7 6, 7 6. D.
Meiningen *Gesangbuch*, 1613
Adapted and harm. by FELIX MENDELSSOHN, 1809–47
Devotionally
1. I lay my sins on Je - sus, The spot - less Lamb of God;
2. I lay my wants on Je - sus; All full - ness dwells in him;
He bears them all, and frees us From the ac - curs - ed load.
He heals all my dis - eas - es, He doth my soul re - deem.
I bring my guilt to Je - sus, To wash my crim - son stains
I lay my griefs on Je - sus, My bur - dens and my cares;
White in his Blood most pre - cious, Till not a spot re - mains.
He from them all re - leas - es, He all my sor - rows shares.

3 I long to be like Jesus,
Meek, loving, lowly, mild;
I long to be, like Jesus,
The Father's holy child.

I long to be with Jesus,
Amid the heavenly throng,
To sing with saints his praises,
To learn the angels' song.

Horatius Bonar, 1808–89

This hymn may also be sung to ST. EDITH (No. 386)

493

OMNI DIE. 8 7, 8 7.
Corner's *Gesangbuch*, 1631
Arr. by W. S. Rockstro, 1823–95
Slowly, with dignity
FIRST TUNE
1. There's a wide - ness in God's mer - cy, Like the wide - ness of the sea; There's a kind - ness in his jus - tice, Which is more than lib - er - ty.
2. There is no place where earth's sor - rows Are more felt than up in heaven; There is no place where earth's fail - ings Have such kind - ly judg - ment given.
3. There is wel - come for the sin - ner, And more grac - es for the good; There is mer - cy with the Sav - iour; There is heal - ing in his Blood.

4 There is grace enough for thousands
Of new worlds as great as this;
There is room for fresh creations
In that upper home of bliss.

5 For the love of God is broader
Than the measures of man's mind,
And the heart of the Eternal
Is most wonderfully kind.

6 There is plentiful redemption
In the Blood that has been shed;
There is joy for all the members
In the sorrows of the Head.

7 'Tis not all we owe to Jesus;
It is something more than all;
Greater good because of evil,
Larger mercy through the fall.

8 If our love were but more simple,
We should take him at his word;
And our lives would be all sunshine
In the sweetness of our Lord.

Frederick William Faber, 1814–

ARMSTRONG. 8 7, 8 7. D. HENRY BRINLEY RICHARDS, 1817–89

Quietly
SECOND TUNE
There's a wide - ness in God's mer - cy, Like the wide - ness of the sea;
There is wel - come for the sin - ner, And more grac - es for the good;
There's a kind - ness in his jus - tice, Which is more than lib - er - ty.
There is mer - cy with the Sav - iour; There is heal - ing in his Blood,
There is no place where earth's sor-rows Are more felt than up in heaven;
There is grace e - nough for thou-sands Of new worlds as great as this;
There is no place where earth's fail - ings Have such kind - ly judg-ment given.
There is room for fresh cre - a - tions In that up - per home of bliss.

3 For the love of God is broader
  Than the measures of man's mind,
And the heart of the Eternal
  Is most wonderfully kind.
There is plentiful redemption
  In the Blood that has been shed;
There is joy for all the members
  In the sorrows of the Head.

4 'Tis not all we owe to Jesus;
  It is something more than all:
Greater good because of evil,
  Larger mercy through the fall.
If our love were but more simple,
  We should take him at his word;
And our lives would be all sunshine
  In the sweetness of our Lord.

Frederick William Faber, 1814–63

DEUS TUORUM MILITUM. L. M. French Church Melody (Grenoble)

FIRST TUNE

In unison, with dignity

1. We sing the praise of him who died, Of him wh[o] died upon the Cross; The sinner's hope let men deride, For this we count the world but loss.
2. Inscribed upon the Cross we see, In shining letters, 'God is Love.' He bears our sins upon the Tree; He brings us mercy from above.

3 The Cross, it takes our guilt away;
It holds the fainting spirit up;
It cheers with hope the gloomy day,
And sweetens every bitter cup.

4 It makes the coward spirit brave,
And nerves the feeble arm for fight;
It takes all terror from the grave,
And gilds the bed of death with light;

5 The balm of life, the cure of woe,
The measure and the pledge of love,
The sinner's refuge here below,
The angels' theme in heaven above.

Thomas Kelly, 1769–1

494

MADAGASCAR. L. M. GORDON C. RUUD, 1920–

SECOND TUNE

With joyful dignity

1. We sing the praise of him who died, Of him who
2. In - scribed up - on the Cross we see, In shin - ing
died up - on the Cross; The sin - ner's hope let
let - ters, 'God is Love.' He hears our sins up -
men de - ride, For this we count the world but loss.
on the Tree; He brings us mer - cy from a - bove.

3 The Cross, it takes our guilt away;
It holds the fainting spirit up;
It cheers with hope the gloomy day,
And sweetens every bitter cup.

4 It makes the coward spirit brave,
And nerves the feeble arm for fight;
It takes all terror from the grave,
And gilds the bed of death with light;

5 The balm of life, the cure of woe,
The measure and the pledge of love,
The sinner's refuge here below,
The angels' theme in heaven above.

Thomas Kelly, 1769–1854

Music composed for this book and copyrighted

This hymn may also be sung to WAREHAM (No. 127)

BENTLEY. 7 6, 7 6. D. — JOHN PYKE HULLAH, 1812–84

Heartily — FIRST TUNE

1. Some-times a light sur - pris - es The Chris - tian while he sings;
2. In ho - ly con - tem - pla - tion We sweet - ly then pur - sue
It is the Lord who ris - es With heal - ing in his wings;
The theme of God's sal - va - tion, And find it ev - er new;
When com - forts are de - clin - ing, He grants the soul a - gain
Set free from pres - ent sor - row, We cheer - ful - ly can say,
A sea - son of clear shin - ing, To cheer it af - ter rain.
Let the un - known to - mor - row Bring with it what it may.

3 It can bring with it nothing
But he will bear us through;
Who gives the lilies clothing
Will clothe his people, too:
Beneath the spreading heavens
No creature but is fed,
And he who feeds the ravens
Will give his children bread.

4 Though vine nor fig tree neither
Their wonted fruit should bear,
Though all the fields should wither,
Nor flocks nor herds be there;
Yet God, the same abiding,
His praise shall tune my voice;
For while in him confiding
I cannot but rejoice.

William Cowper, 1731–180

Contemplation

CRÜGER. 7 6, 7 6. D.

WILLIAM H. MONK, 1823–89
From JOHANN CRÜGER, 1598–1662

In moderate time SECOND TUNE

1. Some-times a light sur - pris - es The Chris - tian while he sings;
2. In ho - ly con - tem - pla - tion We sweet - ly then pur - sue
It is the Lord who ris - es With heal - ing in his wings;
The theme of God's sal - va - tion, And find it ev - er new;
When com-forts are de - clin - ing, He grants the soul a - gain
Set free from pres - ent sor - row, We cheer - ful - ly can say,
A sea - son of clear shin - ing, To cheer it af - ter rain.
Let the un-known to - mor - row Bring with it what it may.

3 It can bring with it nothing
But he will bear us through;
Who gives the lilies clothing
Will clothe his people, too:
Beneath the spreading heavens
No creature but is fed,
And he who feeds the ravens
Will give his children bread.

4 Though vine nor fig tree neither
Their wonted fruit should bear,
Though all the fields should wither,
Nor flocks nor herds be there;
Yet God, the same abiding,
His praise shall tune my voice;
For while in him confiding
I cannot but rejoice.

William Cowper, 1731–1800

WILLINGHAM. 11 10, 11 10.
FRANZ ABT, 1819–85
In moderate time
1. Still, still with thee, when pur - ple morn - ing break - eth,
2. A - lone with thee, a - mid the mys - tic shad - ows,
When the bird wak - eth, and the shad - ows flee;
The sol - emn hush of na - ture new - ly born;
Fair - er than morn - ing, love - li - er than day - light,
A - lone with thee in breath - less ad - o - ra - tion,
Dawns the sweet con - scious - ness, I am with thee.
In the calm dew and fresh - ness of the morn.

3 Still, still with thee, as to each newborn morning
A fresh and solemn splendor still is given,
So does this blessèd consciousness, awaking,
Breathe each day nearness unto thee and heaven.

4 So shall it be at last, in that bright morning,
When the soul waketh and life's shadows flee;
O in that hour, fairer than daylight dawning,
Shall rise the glorious thought, I am with thee.

Harriet Beecher Stowe, 1812–96

This hymn may also be sung to O PERFECT LOVE (No. 300)

Contemplation

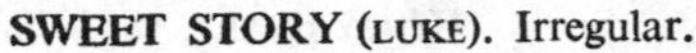

SWEET STORY (LUKE). Irregular.

Greek Melody, arr. WILLIAM B. BRADBURY, 1816–68
Harm. by WINFRED DOUGLAS, 1867–1944

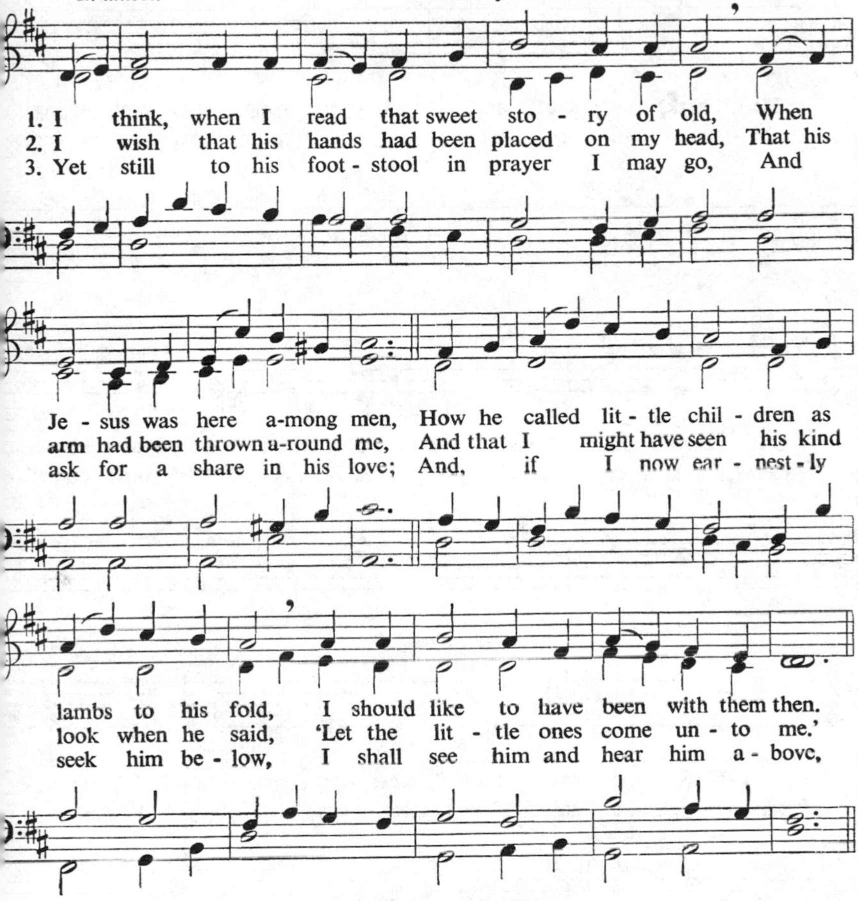

In unison

1. I think, when I read that sweet sto - ry of old, When
2. I wish that his hands had been placed on my head, That his
3. Yet still to his foot - stool in prayer I may go, And

Je - sus was here a-mong men, How he called lit - tle chil - dren as
arm had been thrown a-round me, And that I might have seen his kind
ask for a share in his love; And, if I now ear - nest - ly

lambs to his fold, I should like to have been with them then.
look when he said, 'Let the lit - tle ones come un - to me.'
seek him be - low, I shall see him and hear him a - bove,

4 In that beautiful place he is gone to prepare
For all who are washed and forgiven;
And many dear children are gathering there,
'For of such is the kingdom of heaven.'

5 But thousands and thousands, who wander and fall,
Never heard of that heavenly home;
I should like them to know there is room for them all,
And that Jesus has bid them to come.

6 I long for the joy of that glorious time,
The sweetest and brightest and best,
When the dear little children of every clime
Shall crowd to his arms and be blest.

Jemima Luke, 1813–1906

PILGRIMS. 11 10, 11 10. With Refrain. HENRY SMART, 1813–79

In moderate time

1. Hark! hark, my soul! an - gel - ic songs are swell - ing
2. On - ward we go, for still we hear them sing - ing,
O'er earth's green fields and o - cean's wave - beat shore;
'Come, wea - ry souls, for Je - sus bids you come;'
How sweet the truth those bless - ed strains are tell - ing
And through the dark, its ech - oes sweet - ly ring - ing,
Of that new life when sin shall be no more!
The mu - sic of the Gos - pel leads us home.

Contemplation

Refrain
An - gels of Je - sus, an - gels of light,
Sing - ing to wel - come the pil - grims of the night!

3 Far, far away, like bells at evening pealing,
The voice of Jesus sounds o'er land and sea,
And laden souls, by thousands meekly stealing,
Kind Shepherd, turn their weary steps to thee.

4 Rest comes at length; though life be long and dreary,
The day must dawn, and darksome night be past;
Faith's journeys end in welcome to the weary,
And heaven, the heart's true home, will come at last.

5 Angels, sing on, your faithful watches keeping,
Sing us sweet fragments of the songs above,
Till morning's joy shall end the night of weeping,
And life's long shadows break in cloudless love.

Frederick William Faber, 1814–63

THIRD MODE MELODY. C. M. D.

THOMAS TALLIS, *cir.* 1505–85

FIRST TUNE

Devotionally
1. I heard the voice of Je - sus say, 'Come un - to me and rest;
Lay down, thou wea - ry one, lay down Thy head up - on my breast.'
I came to Je - sus as I was, Wea - ry, and worn, and sad;
I found in him a rest - ing - place, And he hath made me glad.

2 I heard the voice of Jesus say,
'Behold, I freely give
The living water, thirsty one,
Stoop down, and drink, and live.'
I came to Jesus and I drank
Of that life-giving stream;
My thirst was quenched, my soul revived,
And now I live in him.

3 I heard the voice of Jesus say,
'I am this dark world's light;
Look unto me, thy morn shall rise,
And all thy day be bright.'
I looked to Jesus, and I found
In him my star, my sun;
And in that light of life I'll walk
Till traveling days are done.

Horatius Bonar, 1808–8

VOX DILECTI. C. M. D. JOHN BACCHUS DYKES, 1823–76

SECOND TUNE
Unison
1. I heard the voice of Je - sus say, 'Come un - to me and rest;
Lay down, thou wea - ry one, lay down Thy head up - on my breast.'
Harmony
I came to Je - sus as I was, Wea - ry, and worn, and sad;
I found in him a rest - ing-place, And he hath made me glad.

2 I heard the voice of Jesus say,
'Behold, I freely give
The living water, thirsty one,
Stoop down, and drink, and live.'
I came to Jesus and I drank
Of that life-giving stream;
My thirst was quenched, my soul revived,
And now I live in him.

3 I heard the voice of Jesus say,
'I am this dark world's light;
Look unto me, thy morn shall rise,
And all thy day be bright.'
I looked to Jesus, and I found
In him my star, my sun;
And in that light of life I'll walk
Till traveling days are done.

Horatius Bonar, 1808–89

WERE YOU THERE. Irregular.

Negro Spiritual
Harm. by WINFRED DOUGLAS, 1867–1944

With reverence
1. Were you there when they cru - ci - fied my Lord? Were you
2. Were you there when they nailed him to the tree? Were you
there when they cru - ci - fied my Lord? O . . . . ,
there when they nailed him to the tree? O . . . . ,
some-times it caus - es me to trem-ble, trem - ble, trem - ble.
some-times it caus - es me to trem-ble, trem - ble, trem - ble.
Were you there when they cru - ci - fied my Lord?
Were you there when they nailed him to the tree?

3 Were you there when they laid him in the tomb?
Were you there when they laid him in the tomb?
O, sometimes it causes me to tremble, tremble, tremble.
Were you there when they laid him in the tomb?

4 Were you there when he rose up from the tomb?
Were you there when he rose up from the tomb?
O, sometimes it causes me to tremble, tremble, tremble.
Were you there when he rose up from the tomb?

Negro Spiritual

O JESULEIN SÜSS. Irregular.
Cologne, 1623
Bass by J. S. BACH, 1685–1750
Quietly
1. O Je - su so meek, O Je - su so kind, Thou hast ful - filled thy Fa - ther's mind; Hast come from heav - en down to earth In hu - man flesh through hu - man birth. O Je - su so meek, O Je - su so kind!
2. O Je - su so good, O Je - su so meek, To do thy will is all we seek; For all we are or have is thine; Do thou our hearts to thee in - cline. O Je - su so good, O Je - su so meek!

Valentin Thilo, 1607–62
Tr. Geoffrey William Daisley, 1877–1939

FORTITUDO. L. M. L. David Miller, 1919–

Schools and Colleges

With spirit. Unison FIRST TUNE

1. The Lord our God a - lone is strong; His hands built
2. His moun - tains lift their sol - emn forms, To watch in
not for one brief day, His won - drous works, through a - ges
si - lence o'er the land; The roll - ing o - cean, rocked with
long, His wis - dom and his power dis - play.
storms, Sleeps in the hol - low of his hand. A - men.

3 Thou sovereign God, receive the praise
Thy willing servants offer thee;
Accept the prayers that thousands raise,
And let these halls thy temple be.

4 And let those learn, who here shall mee
True wisdom is with reverence crowne
And science walks with humble feet
To seek the God that faith hath foun
Ame

Caleb Thomas Winchester, 1847–19

Music composed for this book and copyrighted

TRURO. L. M. Williams' *Psalmodia Evangelica*, 1789

SECOND TUNE
With spirit
1. The Lord our God a - lone is strong; His hands built
2. His moun - tains lift their sol - emn forms, To watch in
not for one brief day, His won - drous works, through
si - lence o'er the land; The roll - ing o - cean,
a - ges long, His wis - dom and his power dis - play.
rocked with storms, Sleeps in the hol - low of his hand. A-men.

3 Thou sovereign God, receive the praise
Thy willing servants offer thee;
Accept the prayers that thousands raise,
And let these halls thy temple be.

4 And let those learn, who here shall meet,
True wisdom is with reverence crowned,
And science walks with humble feet
To seek the God that faith hath found.
Amen.

Caleb Thomas Winchester, 1847–1920

See also:

295 Beyond the everlasting hills
527 Brief life is here our portion
593 I know not what the future hath
473 I sought the Lord, and afterward
476 Immortal Love, forever full
584 Jerusalem the golden
469 Jesus, these eyes have never seen
401 Jesus, thy love unbounded
570 Majestic sweetness
398 Mine eyes unto the mountains
181 My God, how wonderful thou art
535 Not always on the mount may we
573 O blessèd Sun whose splendor
197 O happy day when we shall stand
583 There is a land of pure delight
503 When I survey the wondrous Cross

HAMBURG. L. M.

Arr. by LOWELL MASON, 1792–1872

FIRST TUNE

In moderate time

1. When I sur - vey the won - drous Cross On which the
2. For - bid it, Lord, that I should boast Save in the

Prince of Glo - ry died, My rich - est gain I
death of Christ, my God; All the vain things that

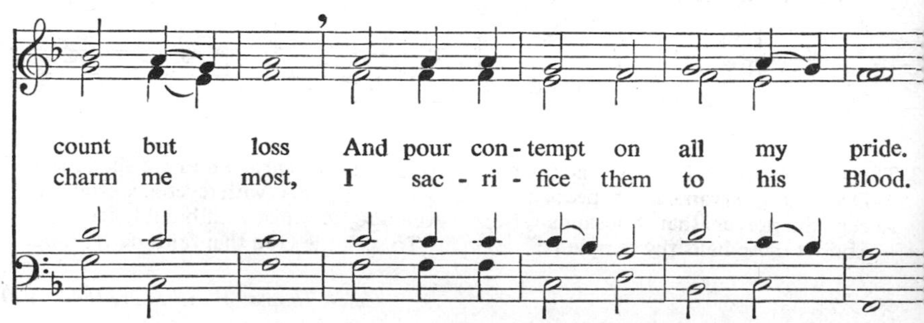
count but loss And pour con - tempt on all my pride.
charm me most, I sac - ri - fice them to his Blood.

3 See, from his head, his hands, his feet,
Sorrow and love flow mingled down;
Did e'er such love and sorrow meet,
Or thorns compose so rich a crown?

4 Were the whole realm of nature mine,
That were an offering far too small;
Love so amazing, so divine,
Demands my soul, my life, my all.

Isaac Watts, 1674–174

HAMBURG (BOSTON). L. M. LOWELL MASON, 1792–1872

ALTERNATE HARMONIZATION

In moderate time
1. When I sur - vey the won - drous Cross On which the
2. For - bid it, Lord, that I should boast Save in the
Prince of Glo - ry died, My rich - est gain I
death of Christ, my God; All the vain things that
count but loss And pour con-tempt on all my pride.
charm me most, I sac - ri - fice them to his Blood. A-men.

3 See, from his head, his hands, his feet,
Sorrow and love flow mingled down;
Did e'er such love and sorrow meet,
Or thorns compose so rich a crown?

4 Were the whole realm of nature mine,
That were an offering far too small;
Love so amazing, so divine,
Demands my soul, my life, my all.

Isaac Watts, 1674–1748

503 Consecration

ROCKINGHAM (COMMUNION). L. M. Arr. by EDWARD MILLER, 1731–1807

SECOND TUNE

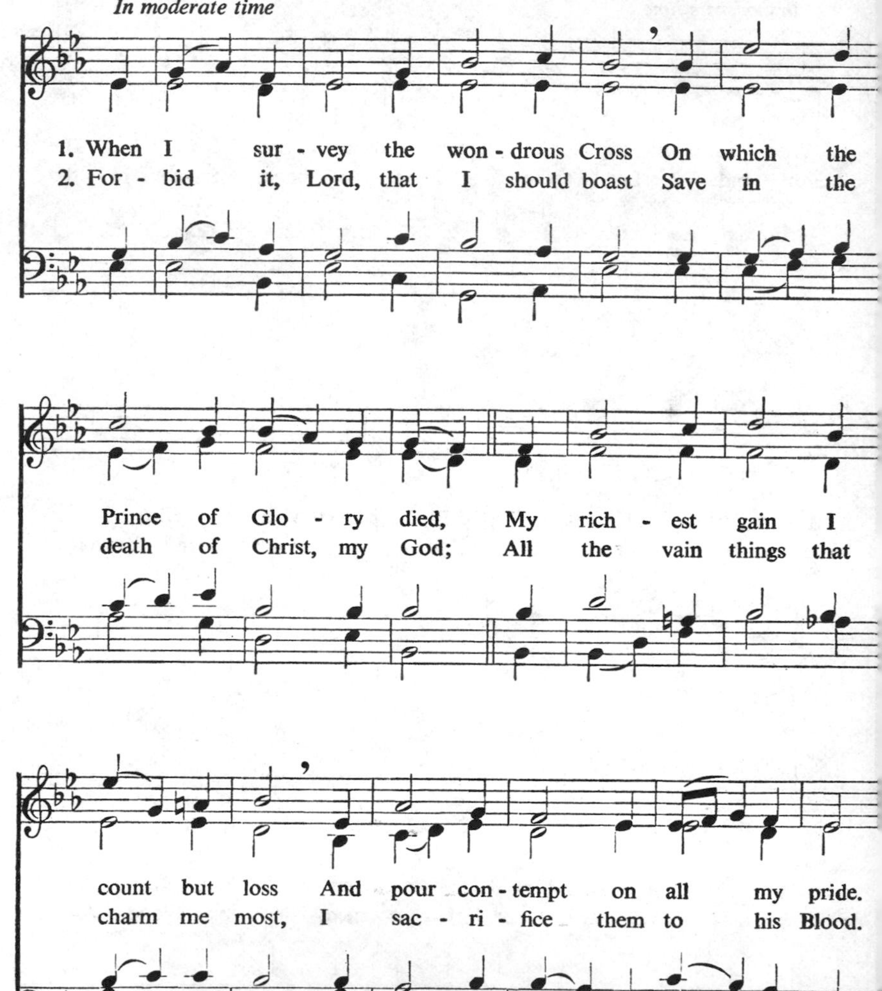
In moderate time
1. When I survey the wondrous Cross On which the Prince of Glory died, My richest gain I count but loss And pour contempt on all my pride.
2. Forbid it, Lord, that I should boast Save in the death of Christ, my God; All the vain things that charm me most, I sacrifice them to his Blood.

3 See, from his head, his hands, his feet,
Sorrow and love flow mingled down;
Did e'er such love and sorrow meet,
Or thorns compose so rich a crown?

4 Were the whole realm of nature mine,
That were an offering far too small;
Love so amazing, so divine,
Demands my soul, my life, my all.

Isaac Watts, 1674–174

ST. CHRYSOSTOM. 8 8, 8 8, 8 8. JOSEPH BARNBY, 1838–96

Devotionally
1. Je - sus, my Lord, my God, my all, Hear me, blest Sav - iour, when I call; Hear me, and from thy dwell - ing place Pour down the rich - es of thy grace.
2. Je - sus, too late I thee have sought; How can I love thee as I ought? And how ex - tol thy match - less fame, The glo - rious beau - ty of thy Name?
Je - sus, my Lord, I thee a - dore, O make me love thee more and more. A - men.

3 Jesus, what didst thou find in me
That thou hast dealt so lovingly?
How great the joy that thou hast brought,
So far exceeding hope or thought!

4 Jesus, of thee shall be my song,
To thee my heart and soul belong;
All that I have or am is thine,
And thou, blest Saviour, thou art mine.

Henry Collins, 1827–1919

ICH WILL DICH LIEBEN. 8 8, 8 8, 8 8. J. B. KÖNIG'S *Choralbuch*, 1738

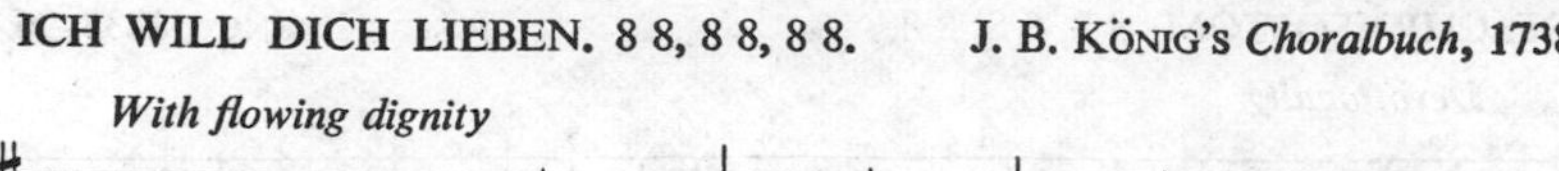

With flowing dignity

1. Thee will I love, my strength, my tower;
Thee will I love, my joy, my crown;
Thee will I love with all my power,
In all thy works, and thee alone;
Thee will I love, till the pure fire
Fill my whole soul with chaste desire.

2 I thank thee, uncreated Sun,
That thy bright beams on me have shined;
I thank thee, who hast overthrown
My foes, and healed my wounded mind;
I thank thee, whose enlivening voice
Bids my freed heart in thee rejoice.

3 Uphold me in the doubtful race
Nor suffer me again to stray,
Strengthen my feet with steady pace
Still to press forward in thy way,
That all my powers, with all their might,
In thy sole glory may unite.

4 Thee will I love, my joy, my crown:
Thee will I love, my Lord, my God;
Thee will I love, beneath thy frown
Or smile, thy sceptre or thy rod.
What though my flesh and heart decay?
Thee shall I love in endless day.

Johann Scheffler, 1624–77
Tr. John Wesley, 1703–91

COPENHAGEN (JEG VIL MIG HERREN LOVE). 76, 76. D.

HARTNACK O. K. ZINCK, 1746–1833

Joyfully
1. Let me be thine for ev - er, My gra-cious God and Lord;
May I for-sake thee nev - er, Nor wan-der from thy word.
Pre-serve me from the maz - es Of er-ror and dis-trust,
And I shall sing thy prais - es For ev - er with the just. A-men.

2 Lord Jesus, bounteous giver
Of light and life divine,
Thou didst my soul deliver;
To thee I all resign.
Thou hast in mercy bought me
With blood and bitter pain,
Let me, since thou hast sought me,
Eternal life obtain.

3 O Holy Ghost, who pourest
Sweet peace into my heart,
And all my soul restorest,
Let not thy grace depart.
And, while his Name confessing,
Whom I by faith have known,
Grant me thy constant blessing;
Make me for aye thine own. Amen.

St. 1, Nikolaus Selnecker, 1532–92
St. 2, 3, Rudolstadt Gesangbuch, 1688
Tr. Matthias Loy, 1828–1915, a.

This hymn may also be sung to the tune NYLAND (No. 574)

ST. CHRYSOSTOM. 7 7, 7 7, 7 7.
JEREMIAH F. OHL, 1850–1941
Devotionally
1. Je - sus, Mas - ter, whose I am, Pur - chased thine a - lone to be, By thy Blood, O spot - less Lamb, Shed so will - ing - ly for me, Let my heart be all thine own, Let me live for thee a - lone.
2. Oth - er lords have long held sway; Now thy Name a - lone to bear, Thy dear voice a - lone o - bey, Is my dai - ly, hour - ly prayer; Whom have I in heaven but thee? Noth - ing else my joy can be. A-men.

3 Jesus, Master, whom I serve,
Though so feebly and so ill,
Strengthen hand and heart and nerve
All thy bidding to fulfill;
Open thou mine eyes to see
All the work thou hast for me.

4 Jesus, Master, I am thine;
Keep me faithful, keep me near;
Let thy presence in me shine
All my homeward way to cheer.
Jesus, at thy feet I fall,
O be thou my all in all. Amen.

Frances Ridley Havergal, 1836–79

LEOMINSTER. S. M. D.
George William Martin, 1828–81
Arr. Arthur S. Sullivan, 1842–1900
In moderate time
1. Make me a cap - tive, Lord, And then I shall be free;
2. My heart is weak and poor Un - til it mas - ter find;
Force me to ren - der up my sword, And I shall con-queror be.
It has no spring of ac - tion sure, It var - ies with the wind.
I sink in life's a - larms When by my - self I stand;
It can - not free - ly move Till thou hast wrought its chain;
Im - pris - on me with - in thine arms, And strong shall be my hand.
En - slave it with thy match-less love, And death - less it shall reign. A-men.

3 My power is faint and low
Till I have learned to serve;
It wants the needed fire to glow,
It wants the breeze to nerve;
It cannot drive the world
Until itself be driven;
Its flag can only be unfurled
When thou shalt breathe from heaven.

4 My will is not my own
Till thou hast made it thine;
If it would reach a monarch's throne
It must its crown resign;
It only stands unbent
Amid the clashing strife,
When on thy bosom it has leant
And found in thee its life. Amen.

George Matheson, 1842–1906

ORIENTIS PARTIBUS. 7 7, 7 7. Office de la Circoncision, Sens, *cir.* 1210

In moderate time

1. Con-quering kings their ti - tles take From the foes they cap - tive make;
2. Yea, none oth - er Name is given Un - to mor - tals un - der heaven,
3. Rath - er glad - ly for that Name Bear the Cross, en - dure the shame;

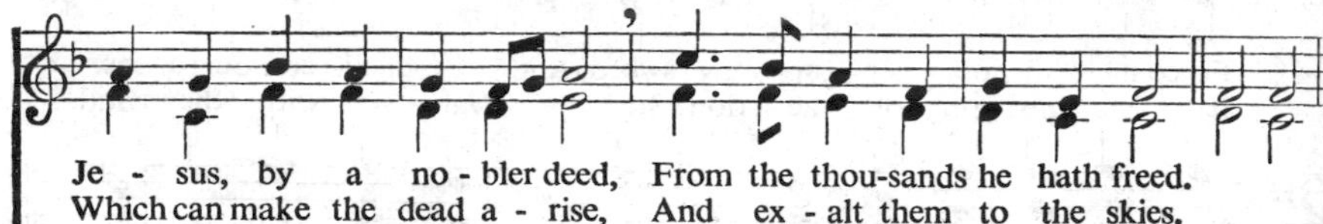

Je - sus, by a no - bler deed, From the thou-sands he hath freed.
Which can make the dead a - rise, And ex - alt them to the skies.
Joy - ful - ly for him to die Is not death but vic - to - ry. A-men.

4 Jesus, who dost condescend
To be called the sinner's friend,
Hear us, as to thee we pray,
Glorying in thy Name to-day.

5 Glory to the Father be,
Glory, Holy Son, to thee,
Glory to the Holy Ghost,
From the saints and angel-host. Amen.

Latin Hymn, XVIII cent.
Tr. John Chandler, 1806–76

This hymn may also be sung to INNOCENTS (No. 511)

510

PATMOS. 7 7, 7 7. WILLIAM HENRY HAVERGAL, 1793–1870

In moderate time

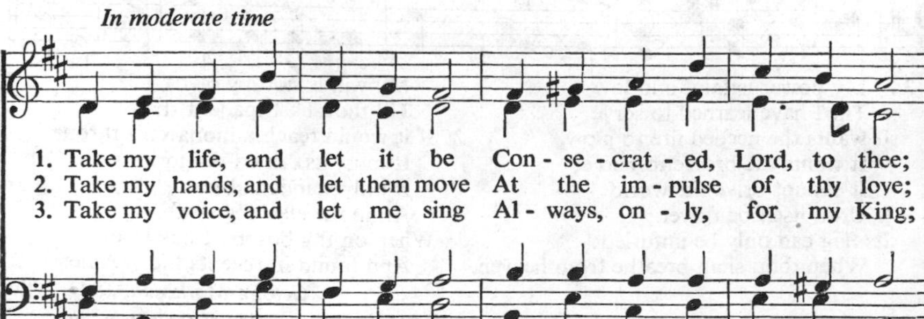
1. Take my life, and let it be Con - se - crat - ed, Lord, to thee;
2. Take my hands, and let them move At the im - pulse of thy love;
3. Take my voice, and let me sing Al - ways, on - ly, for my King;

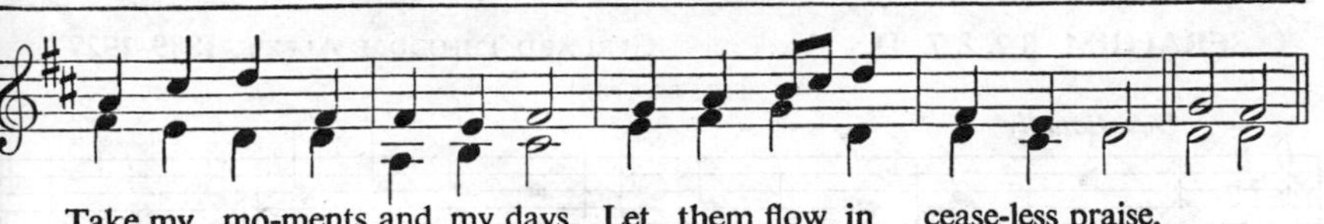

Take my mo-ments and my days, Let them flow in cease-less praise.
Take my feet, and let them be Swift and beau-ti - ful for thee.
Take my lips, and let them be Filled with mes-sag - es from thee. A-men.

4 Take my silver and my gold,
Not a mite would I withhold;
Take my intellect, and use
Every power as thou shalt choose.

5 Take my will and make it thine,
It shall be no longer mine;
Take my heart, it is thine own,
It shall be thy royal throne.

6 Take my love; my Lord, I pour
At thy feet its treasure-store;
Take myself, and I will be
Ever, only, all for thee. Amen.

Frances Ridley Havergal, 1836–79

511

INNOCENTS. 7 7, 7 7. The Parish Choir, London, 1850

In moderate time

1. Thine for ev - er! God of love, Hear us from thy throne a - bove;
2. Thine for ev - er! O how blest They who find in thee their rest!

Thine for ev - er may we be Here and in e - ter - ni - ty.
Sav - iour, Guard-ian, heaven-ly Friend, O de - fend us to the end. A-men.

3 Thine for ever! Lord of life,
Shield us through our earthly strife;
Thou, the Life, the Truth, the Way,
Guide us to the realms of day.

4 Thine for ever! Thou our Guide,
All our wants by thee supplied,
All our sins by thee forgiven,
Lead us, Lord, from earth to heaven.
Amen.

Mary Fawler Maude, 1819–1913

SERAPHIM. 8 7, 8 7. D. GERHARD THEODORE ALEXIS, 1889–1927

FIRST TUNE

Devotionally
1. Je - sus, I my cross have ta - ken, All to leave and fol - low thee;
2. Man may trou - ble and dis-tress me, 'Twill but drive me to thy breast;
Des - ti - tute, de - spised, for - sak - en, Thou from hence my all shalt be.
Life with tri - als hard may press me, Heaven will bring me sweet - er rest.
Per - ish ev - ery fond am - bi - tion, All I've sought, or hoped, or known;
O, 'tis not in grief to harm me, While thy love is left to me;
Yet how rich is my con - di - tion, God and heaven are still my own.
O, 'twere not in joy to charm me, Were that joy un-mixed with thee.

3 Take, my soul, thy full salvation;
Rise o'er sin and fear and care;
Joy to find, in every station,
Something still to do or bear.
Think what Spirit dwells within thee,
What a Father's smile is thine,
What a Saviour died to win thee;
Child of heaven, shouldst thou repine?

4 Haste then on from grace to glory,
Armed by faith, and winged by prayer;
Heaven's eternal day's before thee,
God's own hand shall guide thee there.
Soon shall close thine earthly mission,
Swift shall pass thy pilgrim days;
Hope soon change to glad fruition,
Faith to sight, and prayer to praise.

Henry Francis Lyte, 1793–1847

FALFIELD. 8 7, 8 7. D. ARTHUR S. SULLIVAN, 1842–1900

Broadly, with movement SECOND TUNE

1. Je - sus, I my cross have tak - en, All to leave and fol - low thee;
2. Man may trou - ble and dis - tress me, 'Twill but drive me to thy breast;
Des - ti - tute, de-spised, for - sak - en, Thou from hence my all shalt be.
Life with tri - als hard may press me, Heaven will bring me sweet - er rest.
Per - ish ev - ery fond am - bi - tion, All I've sought, or hoped, or known;
O, 'tis not in grief to harm me, While thy love is left to me;
Yet how rich is my con - di - tion, God and heaven are still my own.
O, 'twere not in joy to charm me, Were that joy un - mixed with thee.

3 Take, my soul, thy full salvation;
Rise o'er sin and fear and care;
Joy to find, in every station,
Something still to do or bear.
Think what Spirit dwells within thee,
What a Father's smile is thine,
What a Saviour died to win thee;
Child of heaven, shouldst thou repine?

4 Haste then on from grace to glory,
Armed by faith, and winged by prayer;
Heaven's eternal day's before thee,
God's own hand shall guide thee there.
Soon shall close thine earthly mission,
Swift shall pass thy pilgrim days;
Hope soon change to glad fruition,
Faith to sight, and prayer to praise.

Henry Francis Lyte, 1793–1847

ST. OLAVE. 6 6, 6 6, 6 6. JOSEPH BARNBY, 1838–96

Quietly
1. Thy life was given for me, Thy Blood, O Lord, was shed
2. Long years were spent for me In wea - ri - ness and woe,
3. And thou hast brought to me Down from thy home a - bove
That I might ran - somed be, And quick - ened from the dead.
That through e - ter - ni - ty Thy glo - ry I might know.
Sal - va - tion full and free, Thy par - don and thy love.
Thy life was given for me, What have I given for thee?
Long years were spent for me, Have I spent one for thee?
Great gifts thou brought-est me, What have I brought to thee?

4 O let my life be given,
My years for thee be spent;
World-fetters all be riven,
And joy with suffering blent.
Thou gav'st thyself for me,
I give myself to thee.

Frances Ridley Havergal, 1836–79

FEDERAL STREET. L. M. HENRY K. OLIVER, 1800–85

In moderate time
1. Je - sus, and shall it ev - er be, A mor - tal
2. A - shamed of Je - sus! soon - er far Let eve - ning
man a - shamed of thee? A - shamed of thee, whom
blush to own a star; He sheds the beams of
an - gels praise, Whose glo - ries shine through end - less days?
light di - vine O'er this be - night - ed soul of mine.

3 Ashamed of Jesus! that dear Friend
On whom my hopes of heaven depend!
No; when I blush, be this my shame,
That I no more revere his Name.

4 Ashamed of Jesus! yes, I may
When I've no guilt to wash away;
No tear to wipe, no good to crave,
No fears to quell, no soul to save.

5 Till then, nor is my boasting vain,
Till then I boast a Saviour slain;
And O may this my glory be,
That Christ is not ashamed of me.

Joseph Grigg, cir. 1720–68
Revised by Benjamin Francis, cir. 1734–99

ANGEL'S STORY. 7 6, 7 6. D. ARTHUR HENRY MANN, 1850–1929

In moderate time FIRST TUNE

1. O Je - sus, I have prom - ised To serve thee to the end;
2. O let me feel thee near me, The world is ev - er near;
Be thou for ev - er near me, My mas - ter and my friend;
I see the sights that daz - zle, The tempt - ing sounds I hear;
I shall not fear the bat - tle If thou art by my side,
My foes are ev - er near me, A - round me and with - in;
Nor wan - der from the path - way If thou wilt be my guide.
But, Je - sus, draw thou near - er, And shield my soul from sin. A-men

3 O let me hear thee speaking
In accents clear and still,
Above the storms of passion,
The murmurs of self-will;
O speak to reassure me,
To hasten or control;
O speak, and make me listen,
Thou guardian of my soul.

4 O Jesus, thou hast promised
To all who follow thee,
That where thou art in glory
There shall thy servant be;
And, Jesus, I have promised
To serve thee to the end;
O give me grace to follow,
My master and my friend. Amen.

John Ernest Bode, 1816–7

Consecration

SEDGWICK. 7 6, 7 6. D.
LEE H. BRISTOL, JR., 1923–
With spirit
SECOND TUNE
1. O Je - sus, I have prom - ised To serve thee to the end;
2. O let me feel thee near me, The world is ev - er near;
Be thou for ev - er near me, My mas - ter and my friend;
I see the sights that daz - zle, The tempt-ing sounds I hear;
I shall not fear the bat - tle If thou art by my side,
My foes are ev - er near me, A - round me and with - in;
Nor wan - der from the path - way If thou wilt be my guide.
But, Je - sus, draw thou near - er, And shield my soul from sin. A-men.

3 O let me hear thee speaking
In accents clear and still,
Above the storms of passion,
The murmurs of self-will;
O speak to reassure me,
To hasten or control;
O speak, and make me listen,
Thou guardian of my soul.

4 O Jesus, thou hast promised
To all who follow thee,
That where thou art in glory
There shall thy servant be;
And, Jesus, I have promised
To serve thee to the end;
O give me grace to follow,
My master and my friend. Amen.

John Ernest Bode, 1816–74

ST. CATHERINE. 8 8, 8 8, 8 8.
HENRI FREDERICK HEMY, 1818–88
Broadly
Adapted by JAMES GEORGE WALTON, 1821–1905
1. Faith of our fa - thers! liv - ing still In spite of dun - geon, fire, and sword; O how our hearts beat high with joy When - e'er we hear that glo - rious word:
2. Our fa - thers, chained in pris - ons dark, Were still in heart and con - science free, And blest would be their chil-dren's fate, If they, like them, should die for thee:
Refrain
Faith of our fa - thers, ho - ly faith, We will be true to thee till death.

3 Faith of our fathers! we will love
Both friend and foe in all our strife;
And preach thee, too, as love knows how,
By kindly words and virtuous life:

Frederick William Faber, 1814–6

Consecration

STEPHANOS. 8 5, 8 3. HENRY WILLIAMS BAKER, 1821–77

Broadly

1. Art thou wea - ry, art thou lan - guid, Art thou sore dis - tressed?
2. Hath he marks to lead me to him, If he be my guide?
3. Hath he di - a - dem, as mon - arch, That his brow a - dorns?

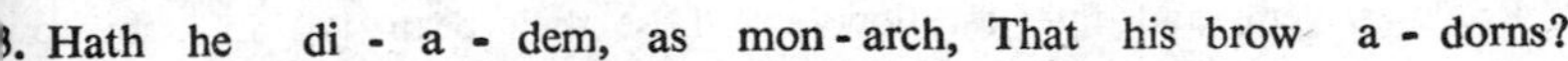

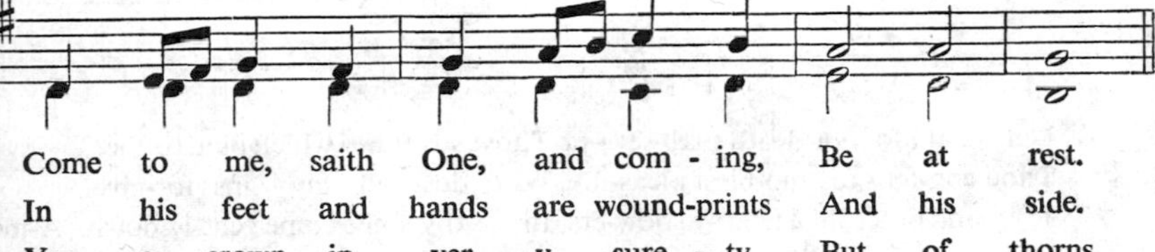

Come to me, saith One, and com - ing, Be at rest.
In his feet and hands are wound-prints And his side.
Yea, a crown in ver - y sure - ty, But of thorns.

4 If I find him, if I follow,
What his guerdon here?
Many a sorrow, many a labor,
Many a tear.

5 If I still hold closely to him,
What hath he at last?
Sorrow vanquished, labor ended,
Jordan passed.

6 If I ask him to receive me,
Will he say me nay?
Not till earth and not till heaven
Pass away.

7 Finding, following, keeping, struggling,
Is he sure to bless?
Saints, apostles, prophets, martyrs,
Answer, Yes!

John Mason Neale, 1818–66, a.
Based on the Greek

MERTON. 8 7, 8 7. WILLIAM HENRY MONK, 1823–89

In moderate time

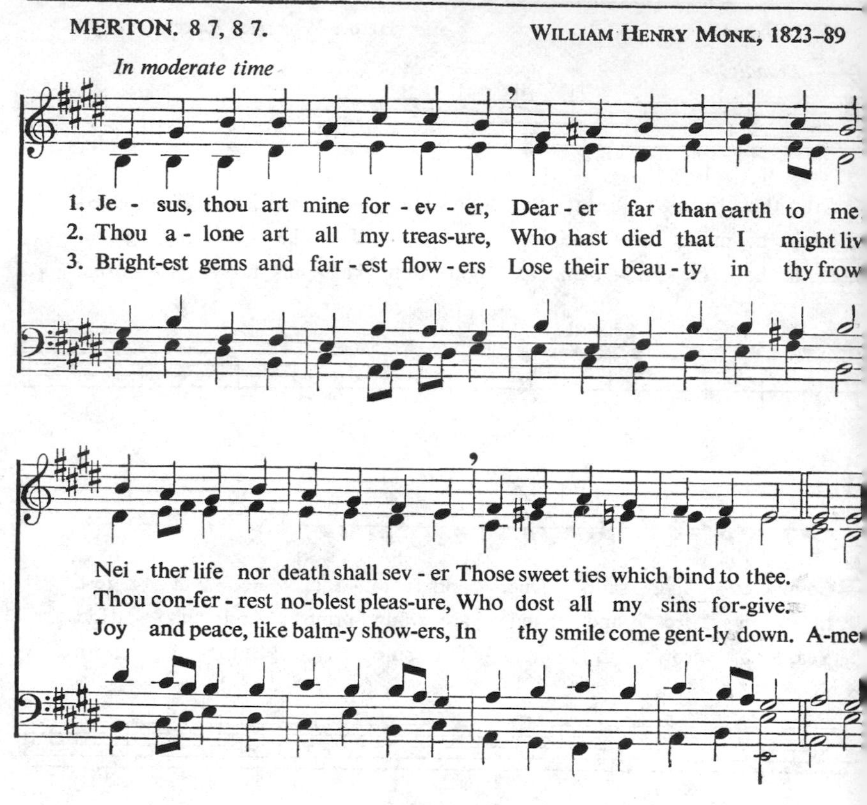
1. Je - sus, thou art mine for - ev - er, Dear - er far than earth to me.
2. Thou a - lone art all my treas-ure, Who hast died that I might liv
3. Bright-est gems and fair - est flow - ers Lose their beau - ty in thy frow
Nei - ther life nor death shall sev - er Those sweet ties which bind to thee.
Thou con-fer - rest no-blest pleas-ure, Who dost all my sins for-give.
Joy and peace, like balm-y show-ers, In thy smile come gent-ly down. A-me

4 Lamb of God! I do implore thee,
Guard, support me, lest I fall;
Let me evermore adore thee,
Be my everlasting All. Amen.

Matthias Loy, 1826–19

See also:

540 Believing fathers oft have told
214 Forth in thy Name, O Lord
563 He who would valiant be
479 I need thee every hour
553 Jesus calls us
399 Jesus, thy boundless love
550 Lead on, O King eternal
538 Lord, speak to me, that I may speak
293 Lord, to thee I now surrender
570 Majestic sweetness sits enthroned
392 More love to thee, O Christ
289 O God, accept my heart this day
402 O Love that wilt not let me go
292 O take my hand, dear Father
379 Rock of Ages, cleft for me
549 Saviour, thee my heart I tender

19 Pilgrimage

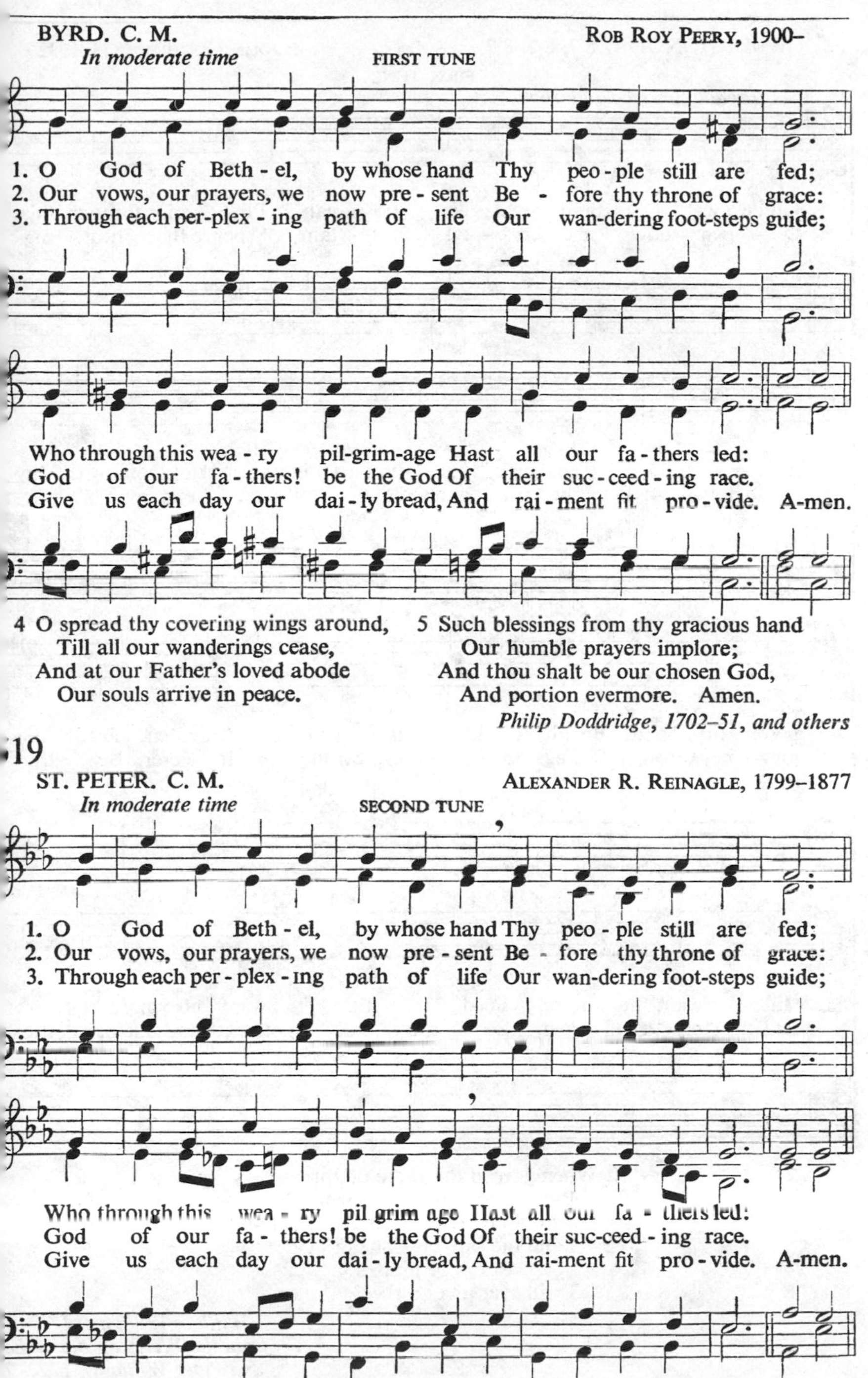
BYRD. C. M.
ROB ROY PEERY, 1900–
In moderate time
FIRST TUNE
1. O God of Beth-el, by whose hand Thy peo-ple still are fed;
2. Our vows, our prayers, we now pre-sent Be-fore thy throne of grace:
3. Through each per-plex-ing path of life Our wan-dering foot-steps guide;
Who through this wea-ry pil-grim-age Hast all our fa-thers led:
God of our fa-thers! be the God Of their suc-ceed-ing race.
Give us each day our dai-ly bread, And rai-ment fit pro-vide. A-men.
4 O spread thy covering wings around,
Till all our wanderings cease,
And at our Father's loved abode
Our souls arrive in peace.
5 Such blessings from thy gracious hand
Our humble prayers implore;
And thou shalt be our chosen God,
And portion evermore. Amen.
Philip Doddridge, 1702–51, and others
19
ST. PETER. C. M.
ALEXANDER R. REINAGLE, 1799–1877
In moderate time
SECOND TUNE
1. O God of Beth-el, by whose hand Thy peo-ple still are fed;
2. Our vows, our prayers, we now pre-sent Be-fore thy throne of grace:
3. Through each per-plex-ing path of life Our wan-dering foot-steps guide;
Who through this wea-ry pil-grim-age Hast all our fa-thers led:
God of our fa-thers! be the God Of their suc-ceed-ing race.
Give us each day our dai-ly bread, And rai-ment fit pro-vide. A-men.

520

CWM RHONDDA. 8 7, 8 7, 8 7. JOHN HUGHES, 1873–1932

FIRST TUNE

Broadly, in moderate time
1. Guide me, O thou great Je - ho - vah, Pil - grim through this
2. O - pen now the crys - tal foun - tain Whence the heal - ing
bar - ren land; I am weak, but thou art might - y, Hold me with thy
stream doth flow; Let the fire and cloud-y pil - lar Lead me all my
power - ful hand; Bread of heav - en, Bread of heav - en, Feed me
jour - ney through; Strong de - liv - erer, Strong de - liv - erer, Be thou
till I want no more, Feed me till I want no more.
still my strength and shield, Be thou still my strength and shield. A-men.

3 When I tread the verge of Jordan,
Bid my anxious fears subside;
Death of death and hell's destruction,
Land me safe on Canaan's side;
Songs of praises
I will ever give to thee. Amen.

William Williams, 1717–91
Tr. from the Welsh by the author
and Peter Williams, 1722–96

20 Pilgrimage

PILGRIM. 8 7, 8 7, 4 7.
JEREMIAH F. OHL, 1850–1941
In moderate time
SECOND TUNE
1. Guide me, O thou great Je - ho - vah, Pil - grim through this bar - ren land; I am weak, but thou art might - y, Hold me with thy power - ful hand; Bread of heav - en, Feed me till I want no more.
2. O - pen now the crys - tal foun - tain Whence the heal - ing stream doth flow; Let the fire and cloud - y pil - lar Lead me all my jour - ney through; Strong de - liv - erer, Be thou still my strength and shield. A - men.
(♯)

3 When I tread the verge of Jordan,
Bid my anxious fears subside;
Death of death and hell's destruction,
Land me safe on Canaan's side;
Songs of praises
I will ever give to thee. Amen.

William Williams, 1717–91
Tr. from the Welsh by the author
and Peter Williams, 1722–96

NATIONAL HYMN. 10 10, 10 10. GEORGE WILLIAM WARREN, 1828–1902

With dignity
1. God of our fa - thers, whose al - might - y hand
2. Thy love di - vine hath led us in the past,
Leads forth in beau - ty all the star - ry band
In this free land by thee our lot is cast;
Of shin - ing worlds in splen - dor through the skies,
Be thou our rul - er, guard - ian, guide, and stay;
Our grate - ful songs be - fore thy throne a - rise.
Thy word our law, thy paths our cho - sen way. A-men

3 From war's alarms, from deadly pestilence,
Be thy strong arm our ever sure defence;
Thy true religion in our hearts increase,
Thy bounteous goodness nourish us in peace.

4 Refresh thy people on their toilsome way,
Lead us from night to never-ending day;
Fill all our lives with love and grace divine,
And glory, laud, and praise be ever thine. Amen.

Daniel C. Roberts, 1841–19

22

CRIMOND. C. M. Melody by JESSIE SEYMOUR IRVINE, 1836–87
Arr. DAVID GRANT, 1833–93

In moderate time

1. The Lord's my Shep - herd, I'll not want. He makes me down to lie In pas - tures green; he lead - eth me The qui - et wa - ters by.
2. My soul he doth re - store a - gain, And me to walk doth make With - in the paths of right - eous - ness, E'en for his own Name's sake.

3 Yea, though I walk in death's dark vale,
Yet will I fear none ill;
For thou art with me; and thy rod
And staff me comfort still.

4 My table thou hast furnishèd
In presence of my foes;
My head thou dost with oil anoint,
And my cup overflows.

5 Goodness and mercy all my life
Shall surely follow me,
And in God's house for evermore
My dwelling-place shall be.

Scottish Psalter, 1650
Psalm 23

This hymn may also be sung to EVAN (No. 452)

LUX BENIGNA. 10 4, 10 4, 10 10. JOHN BACCHUS DYKES, 1823–76

In strict time
FIRST TUNE
1. Lead, kind-ly Light, a - mid the en-cir-cling gloom, Lead thou me on;
2. I was not ev - er thus, nor prayed that thou Shouldst lead me on;
The night is dark, and I am far from home; Lead thou me on.
I loved to choose and see my path, but now Lead thou me on;
Keep thou my feet; I do not ask to see
I loved the gar - ish day, and, spite of fears,
The dis - tant scene; one step e - nough for me.
Pride ruled my will: re - mem - ber not past years.

3 So long thy power hath blest me, sure it still
Will lead me on,
O'er moor and fen, o'er crag and torrent, till
The night is gone;
And with the morn those angel faces smile
Which I have loved long since, and lost awhile.

John Henry Newman, 1801–90

23 Pilgrimage

SANDON. 10 4, 10 4, 10 10.
CHARLES PURDAY, 1799–1885
Slowly, with dignity
SECOND TUNE
1. Lead, kind-ly Light, a - mid the en-cir-cling gloom, Lead thou me on;
2. I was not ev - er thus, nor prayed that thou Shouldst lead me on;
The night is dark, and I am far from home; Lead thou me on.
I loved to choose and see my path, but now Lead thou me on;
Keep thou my feet; I do not ask to see
I loved the gar - ish day, and, spite of fears,
The dis - tant scene; one step e - nough for me.
Pride ruled my will: re - mem - ber not past years.

3 So long thy power hath blest me, sure it still
Will lead me on,
O'er moor and fen, o'er crag and torrent, till
The night is gone;
And with the morn those angel faces smile
Which I have loved long since, and lost awhile.

John Henry Newman, 1801–90

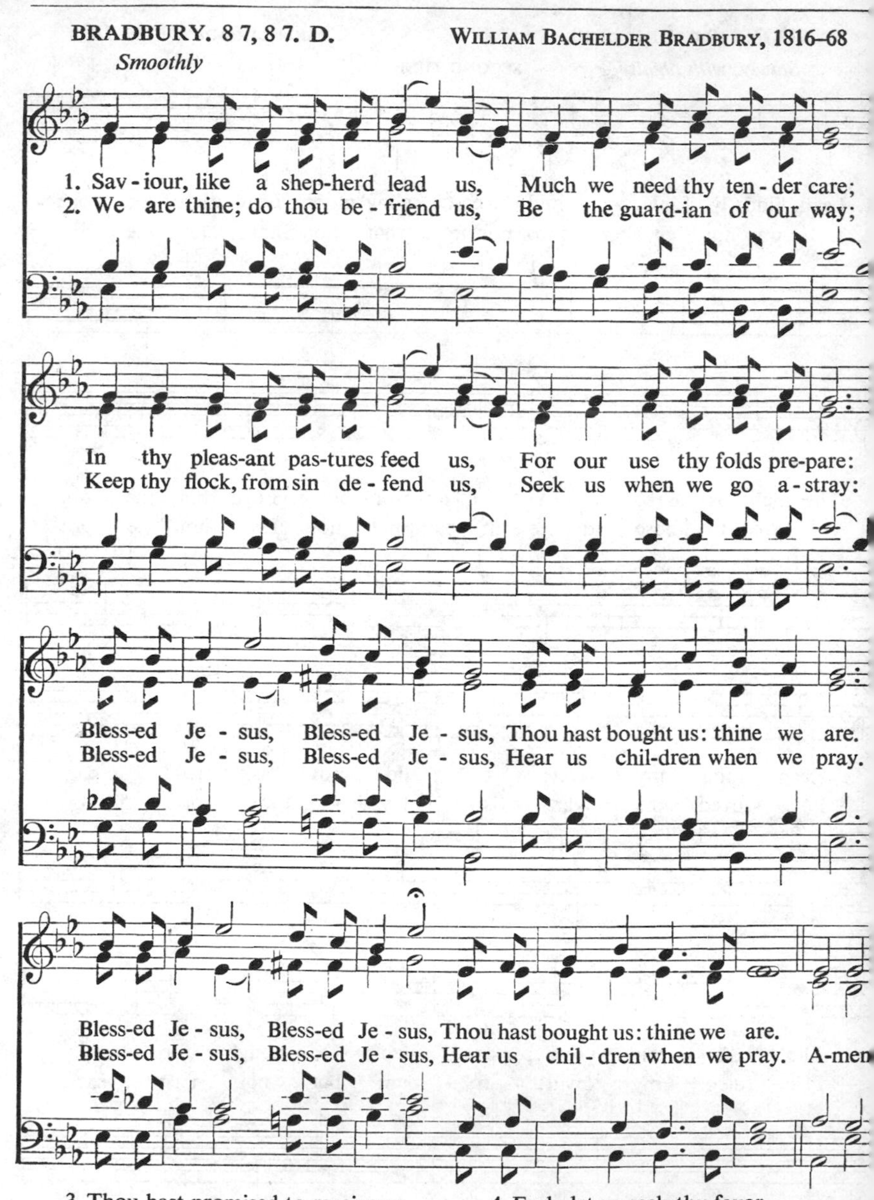
BRADBURY. 8 7, 8 7. D.
WILLIAM BACHELDER BRADBURY, 1816–68
Smoothly
1. Sav - iour, like a shep-herd lead us, Much we need thy ten - der care;
2. We are thine; do thou be - friend us, Be the guard-ian of our way;
In thy pleas-ant pas-tures feed us, For our use thy folds pre-pare:
Keep thy flock, from sin de - fend us, Seek us when we go a - stray:
Bless-ed Je - sus, Bless-ed Je - sus, Thou hast bought us: thine we are.
Bless-ed Je - sus, Bless-ed Je - sus, Hear us chil-dren when we pray.
Bless-ed Je - sus, Bless-ed Je - sus, Thou hast bought us: thine we are.
Bless-ed Je - sus, Bless-ed Je - sus, Hear us chil - dren when we pray. A-men

3 Thou hast promised to receive us,
Poor and sinful though we be;
Thou hast mercy to relieve us,
Grace to cleanse, and power to free:
Blessèd Jesus,
Early let us turn to thee.

4 Early let us seek thy favor,
Early let us do thy will;
Blessèd Lord and only Saviour,
With thy love our bosoms fill:
Blessèd Jesus,
Thou hast loved us, love us still.
Amen

Dorothy Ann Thrupp, 1779–184

WATCHMAN. 7 7, 7 7. D. LOWELL MASON, 1792–1872

With movement
1. Watch-man, tell us of the night, What its signs of prom - ise are.
2. Watch-man, tell us of the night; High - er yet that star as - cends.
Trav - eler, o'er yon moun-tain's height, See that glo - ry - beam - ing star.
Trav - eler, bless - ed - ness and light, Peace and truth its course por-tends.
Watch-man, does its beau-teous ray Aught of joy or hope fore - tell?
Watch-man, will its beams a - lone Gild the spot that gave them birth?
Trav - eler, yes; it brings the day, Prom-ised day of Is - ra - el.
Trav - eler, a - ges are its own; See, it bursts o'er all the earth.

3 Watchman, tell us of the night,
For the morning seems to dawn.
Traveler, darkness takes its flight,
Doubt and terror are withdrawn.
Watchman, let thy wanderings cease;
Hie thee to thy quiet home.
Traveler, lo! the Prince of Peace,
Lo! the Son of God is come!

John Bowring, 1792–1872

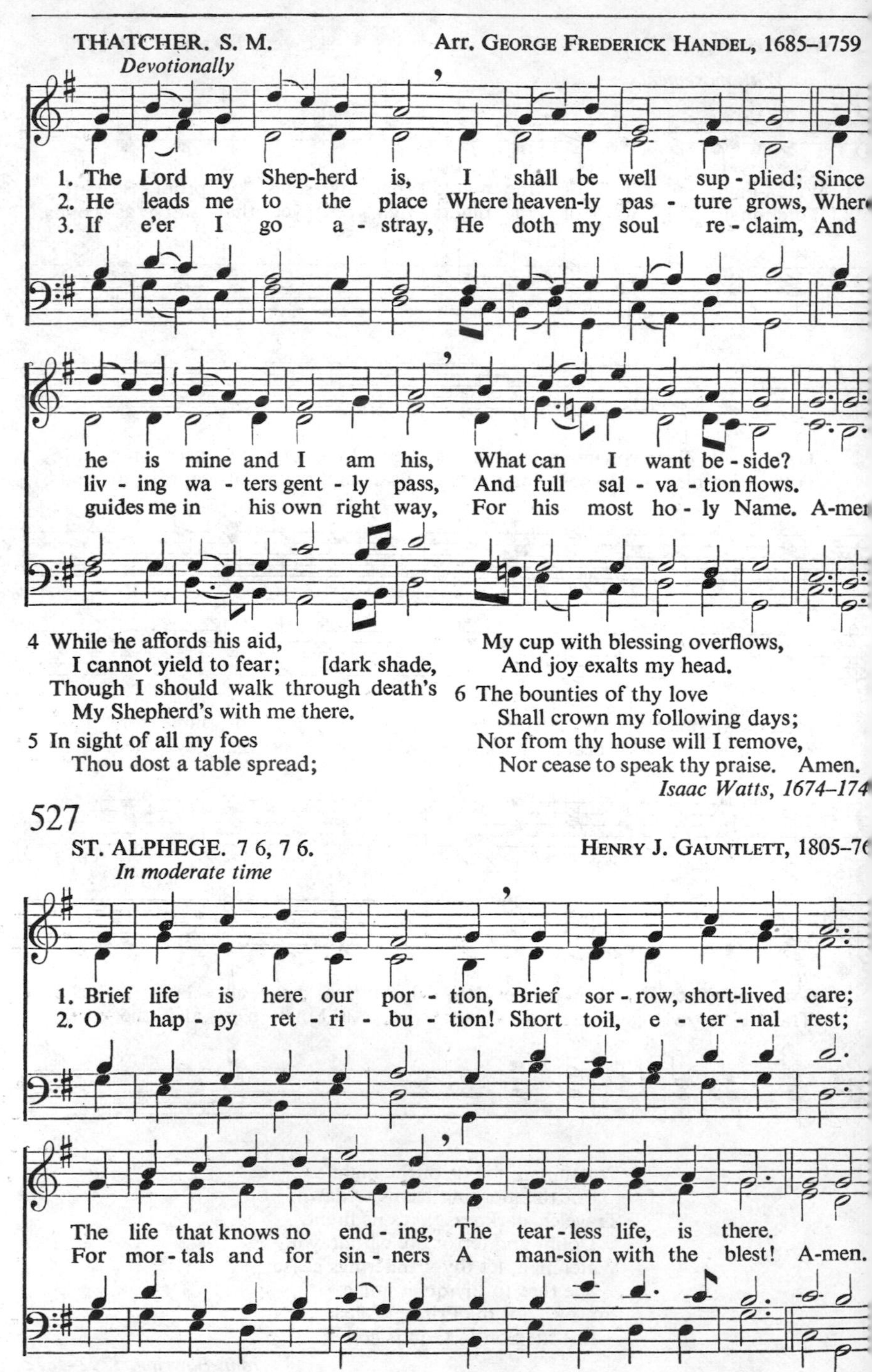
THATCHER. S. M.
Arr. George Frederick Handel, 1685–1759
Devotionally
1. The Lord my Shep-herd is, I shall be well sup-plied; Since he is mine and I am his, What can I want be-side?
2. He leads me to the place Where heaven-ly pas-ture grows, Wher[e] liv-ing wa-ters gent-ly pass, And full sal-va-tion flows.
3. If e'er I go a-stray, He doth my soul re-claim, And guides me in his own right way, For his most ho-ly Name. A-me[n]
4 While he affords his aid,
I cannot yield to fear; [dark shade,
Though I should walk through death's
My Shepherd's with me there.
5 In sight of all my foes
Thou dost a table spread;
My cup with blessing overflows,
And joy exalts my head.
6 The bounties of thy love
Shall crown my following days;
Nor from thy house will I remove,
Nor cease to speak thy praise. Amen.
Isaac Watts, 1674–174[8]
527
ST. ALPHEGE. 7 6, 7 6.
Henry J. Gauntlett, 1805–7[6]
In moderate time
1. Brief life is here our por-tion, Brief sor-row, short-lived care; The life that knows no end-ing, The tear-less life, is there.
2. O hap-py ret-ri-bu-tion! Short toil, e-ter-nal rest; For mor-tals and for sin-ners A man-sion with the blest! A-men.

3 There grief is turned to pleasure,
Such pleasure as below
No human voice can utter,
No human heart can know.

4 And now we fight the battle,
But then shall wear the crown
Of full and everlasting
And passionless renown.

5 And now we watch and struggle,
And now we live in hope,
And Sion, in her anguish,
With Babylon must cope;

6 But he whom now we trust in
Shall then be seen and known,
And they that know and see him
Shall have him for their own.

7 The morning shall awaken,
The shadows shall decay,
And each true-hearted servant
Shall shine as doth the day.

8 There, God our King and portion,
In fullness of his grace,
We then shall see for ever,
And worship face to face.

9 O sweet and blessèd country,
The home of God's elect;
O sweet and blessèd country,
That eager hearts expect!

10 Jesus, in mercy bring us
To that dear land of rest,
Who art, with God the Father
And Spirit, ever blest. Amen.

Bernard of Cluny, XII cent.
Tr. John Mason Neale, 1818–66

This hymn may also be sung to OSLO (No. 586)

528

FERRIER. 7 7, 7 7. JOHN BACCHUS DYKES, 1823–76

In moderate time

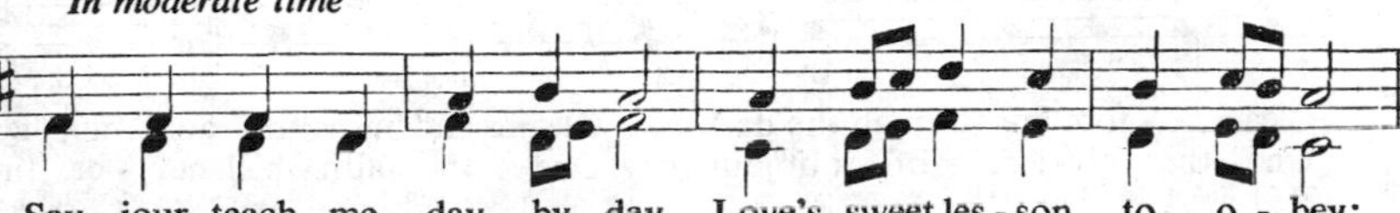

1. Sav - iour, teach me, day by day, Love's sweet les - son to o - bey;
2. With a child's glad heart of love At thy bid - ding may I move,
3. Teach me thus thy steps to trace, Strong to fol - low in thy grace,

Sweet - er les - son can - not be, Lov-ing him who first loved me.
Prompt to serve and fol - low thee, Lov-ing him who first loved me.
Learn-ing how to love from thee, Lov-ing him who first loved me. A-men.

4 Love in loving finds employ,
In obedience all her joy;
Ever new that joy will be,
Loving him who first loved me.

5 Thus may I rejoice to show
That I feel the love I owe;
Singing, till thy face I see,
Of his love who first loved me. Amen.

Jane Eliza Leeson, 1807–82

ST. ASAPH. 8 7, 8 7. D.
WILLIAM SAMUEL BAMBRIDGE, 1842–1923
With movement, broadly
FIRST TUNE
1. Through the night of doubt and sor - row On - ward goes the pil - grim band,
2. One the light of God's own pres - ence O'er his ran-somed peo - ple shed,
Sing - ing songs of ex - pec - ta - tion, March-ing to the prom-ised land.
Chas- ing far the gloom and ter - ror, Bright-ening all the path we tread:
Clear be - fore us through the dark-ness Gleams and burns the guid - ing light;
One the ob - ject of our jour - ney, One the faith which nev - er tires,
Broth-er clasps the hand of broth - er, Step-ping fear-less through the night.
One the ear - nest look-ing for-ward, One the hope our God in - spires;

3 One the strain that lips of thousands
  Lift as from the heart of one;
One the conflict, one the peril,
  One the march in God begun:
One the gladness of rejoicing
  On the far eternal shore,
Where the one almighty Father
  Reigns in love for evermore.

4 Onward, therefore, pilgrim brothers,
  Onward with the Cross our aid!
Bear its shame and fight its battle,
  Till we rest beneath its shade;
Soon shall come the great awakening,
  Soon the rending of the tomb;
Then the scattering of all shadows,
  And the end of toil and gloom.

Bernhardt Severin Ingemann, 1789–186
Tr. Sabine Baring-Gould, 1834–192

MARCHING. 8 7, 8 7. MARTIN SHAW, 1875–

SECOND TUNE

Brightly

1. Through the night of doubt and sor - row On - ward goes the pil - grim band,
2. Clear be - fore us through the dark-ness Gleams and burns the guid - ing light;
3. One the light of God's own pres-ence O'er his ran-somed peo - ple shed,

Sing - ing songs of ex - pec - ta - tion, March-ing to the prom-ised land.
Broth - er clasps the hand of broth - er, Step - ping fear-less through the night.
Chas - ing far the gloom and ter - ror, Bright-ening all the path we tread:

4 One the object of our journey,
One the faith which never tires,
One the earnest looking forward,
One the hope our God inspires;

5 One the strain that lips of thousands
Lift as from the heart of one;
One the conflict, one the peril,
One the march in God begun:

6 One the gladness of rejoicing
On the far eternal shore,
Where the one almighty Father
Reigns in love for evermore.

7 Onward, therefore, pilgrim brothers,
Onward with the Cross our aid!
Bear its shame and fight its battle,
Till we rest beneath its shade;

8 Soon shall come the great awakening,
Soon the rending of the tomb;
Then the scattering of all shadows,
And the end of toil and gloom.

Bernhardt Severin Ingemann, 1789–1862
Tr. Sabine Baring-Gould, 1834–1924

DOMINUS REGIT ME. 8 7, 8 7. Iambic. JOHN BACCHUS DYKES, 1823–76

FIRST TUNE

In moderate time

1. The King of love my shep - herd is, Whose good - ness
2. Where streams of liv - ing wa - ter flow My ran - somed
3. Per - verse and fool - ish oft I strayed, But yet in

fail - eth nev - er; I noth - ing lack if
soul he lead - eth, And where the ver - dant
love he sought me, And on his shoul - der

I am his, And he is mine for ev - er.
pas - tures grow With food ce - les - tial feed - eth.
gent - ly laid, And home, re - joic - ing, brought me. A - men.

4 In death's dark vale I fear no ill
With thee, dear Lord, beside me,
Thy rod and staff my comfort still,
Thy Cross before to guide me.

5 Thou spread'st a table in my sight;
Thy unction grace bestoweth;
And O what transport and delight
From thy pure chalice floweth!

6 And so through all the length of days
Thy goodness faileth never;
Good Shepherd, may I sing thy praise
Within thy house for ever. Amen.

Henry Williams Baker, 1821–77
Psalm 23

ST. COLUMBA. 8 7, 8 7. Traditional Irish Hymn Melody

SECOND TUNE

Tenderly, in moderate time

1. The King of love my shep - herd is, Whose good - ness
2. Where streams of liv - ing wa - ter flow My ran - somed
3. Per - verse and fool - ish oft I strayed, But yet in
fail - eth nev - er; I noth - ing lack if
soul he lead - eth, And where the ver - dant
love he sought me, And on his shoul - der
I am his, And he is mine for ev - er.
pas - tures grow With food ce - les - tial feed - eth.
gent - ly laid, And home, re - joic - ing, brought me. A-men.

4 In death's dark vale I fear no ill
With thee, dear Lord, beside me,
Thy rod and staff my comfort still,
Thy Cross before to guide me.

5 Thou spread'st a table in my sight;
Thy unction grace bestoweth;
And O what transport and delight
From thy pure chalice floweth!

6 And so through all the length of days
Thy goodness faileth never;
Good Shepherd, may I sing thy praise
Within thy house for ever. Amen.

Henry Williams Baker, 1821–77
Psalm 23

531 Pilgrimage

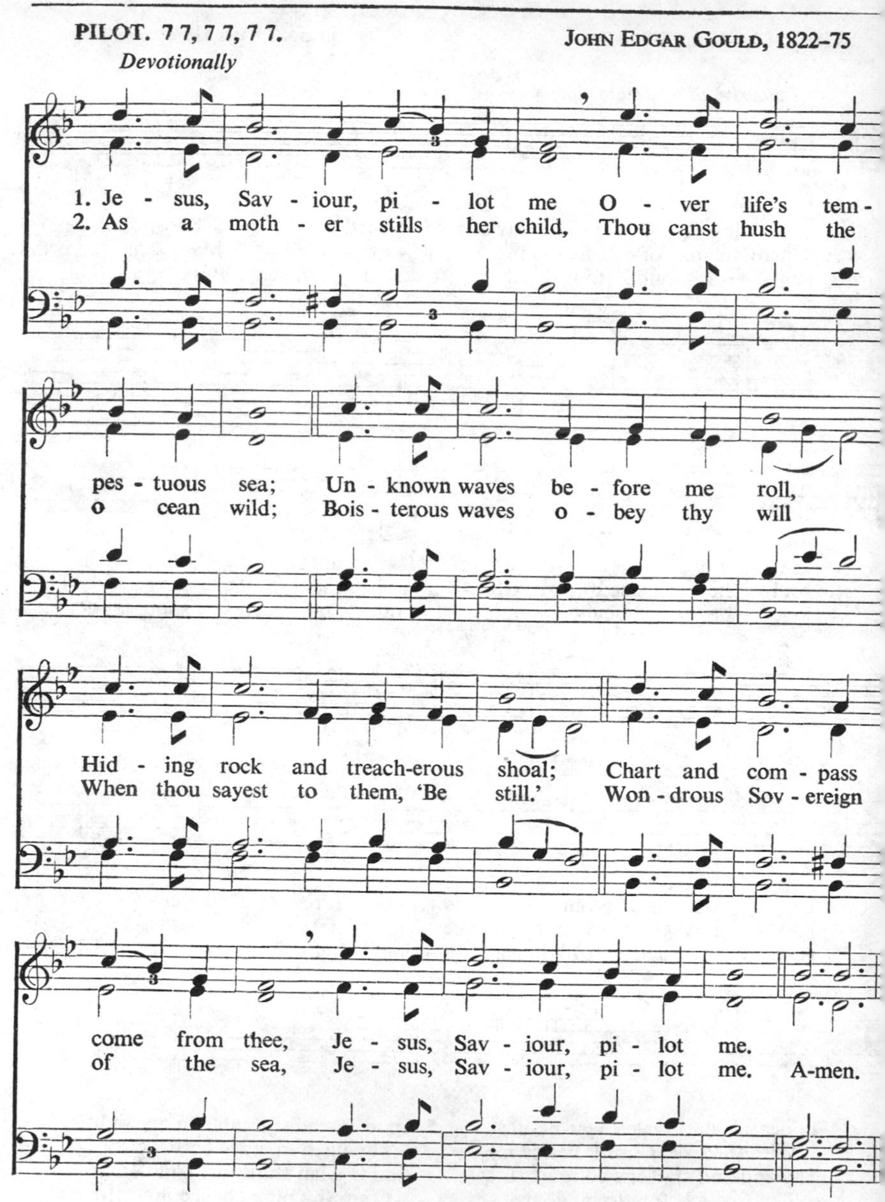
PILOT. 7 7, 7 7, 7 7.
JOHN EDGAR GOULD, 1822–75
Devotionally
1. Je - sus, Sav - iour, pi - lot me O - ver life's tem - pes - tuous sea; Un - known waves be - fore me roll, Hid - ing rock and treach-erous shoal; Chart and com - pass come from thee, Je - sus, Sav - iour, pi - lot me.
2. As a moth - er stills her child, Thou canst hush the o cean wild; Bois - terous waves o - bey thy will When thou sayest to them, 'Be still.' Won - drous Sov - ereign of the sea, Je - sus, Sav - iour, pi - lot me. A-men.
3
3
3
3

3 When at last I near the shore,
And the fearful breakers roar
'Twixt me and the peaceful rest,
Then, while leaning on thy breast,
May I hear thee say to me,
'Fear not, I will pilot thee.' Amen.

Edward Hopper, 1818–88

SEELENBRÄUTIGAM. 5 5, 8 8, 5 5. ADAM DRESE, 1620–1701

Quietly
1. Je - sus, still lead on, Till our rest be won; And, al - though the way be cheer - less, We will fol - low, calm and fear - less; Guide us by thy hand To our fa - ther - land.
2. If the way be drear, If the foe be near, Let not faith - less fears o'er - take us, Let not faith and hope for - sake us; For through man - y a foe To our home we go. A-men.

3 When we seek relief
From a long-felt grief,
When temptations come alluring
Make us patient and enduring;
Show us that bright shore
Where we weep no more.

4 Jesus, still lead on,
Till our rest be won;
Heavenly Leader, still direct us,
Still support, console, protect us,
Till we safely stand
In our fatherland! Amen.

Nicolaus Ludwig von Zinzendorf, 1700–60
Tr. Jane L. Borthwick, 1813–97, a.

HEBRON (MASON). L. M. — LOWELL MASON, 1792–1872

In moderate time

NEW YEAR

1. Great God, we sing that might - y hand By which sup - port - ed still we stand; The o - pening year thy mer - cy shows, Let mer - cy crown it till it close.

2. By day, by night, at home, a - broad, Still are we guard - ed by our God, By his in - ces - sant boun - ty fed, By his un - err - ing coun - sel led. A-men.

3 With grateful hearts the past we own;
The future, all to us unknown,
We to thy guardian care commit,
And, peaceful, leave before thy feet.

4 In scenes exalted or depressed
Thou art our joy, and thou our rest;
Thy goodness all our hopes shall raise,
Adored through all our changing days.
Amen.

Philip Doddridge, 1702–51

534

HOMELAND. 7 6, 7 6. D. — ARTHUR S. SULLIVAN, 1842–1900

In moderate time

FIRST TUNE

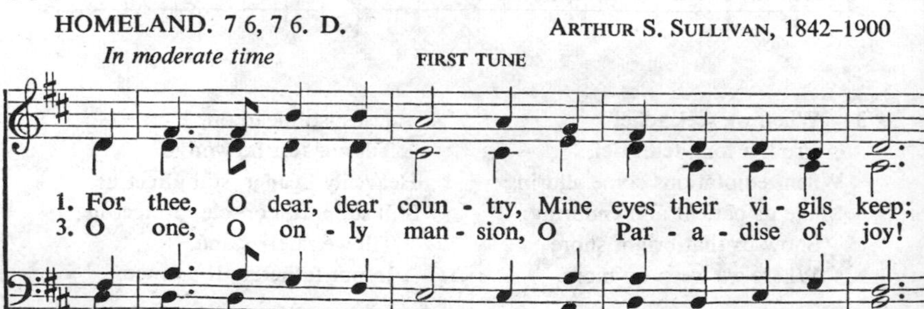
1. For thee, O dear, dear coun - try, Mine eyes their vi - gils keep;
3. O one, O on - ly man - sion, O Par - a - dise of joy!

Pilgrimage

For very-y love, be-hold-ing Thy hap-py name, they weep;
Where tears are ev-er ban-ished, And smiles have no al-loy;
2. The men-tion of thy glo-ry Is unc-tion to the breast,
4. The Cross is all thy splen-dor, The Cru-ci-fied thy praise;
And med-i-cine in sick-ness, And love, and life, and rest.
His laud and ben-e-dic-tion Thy ran-somed peo-ple raise. A-men.

5 Thou hast no shore, fair ocean;
Thou hast no time, bright day;
Dear fountain of refreshment
To pilgrims far away!

6 Upon the Rock of Ages
They raise thy holy tower;
Thine is the victor's laurel,
And thine the golden dower.

7 O sweet and blessèd country,
The home of God's elect;
O sweet and blessèd country,
That eager hearts expect!

8 Jesus, in mercy bring us
To that dear land of rest,
Who art, with God the Father
And Spirit, ever blest. Amen.

Bernard of Cluny, XII cent.
Tr. John Mason Neale, 1818–66

This hymn may also be sung to St. Alphege (No. 527), and to Komm, Seele (No. 595)

ELY CATHEDRAL. 7 6, 7 6. D. T. TERTIUS NOBLE, 1867–1953

SECOND TUNE

With movement

1. For thee, O dear, dear coun - try, Mine eyes their vig - ils keep;
3. O one, O on - ly man - sion, O Par - a - dise of joy!
5. Thou hast no shore, fair o - cean; Thou hast no time, bright day;
7. O sweet and bless - ed coun - try, The home of God's e - lect;

For ver - y love, be - hold - ing Thy hap - py name, they weep;
Where tears are ev - er ban - ished, And smiles have no al - loy;
Dear foun-tain of re - fresh - ment To pil - grims far a - way!
O sweet and bless - ed coun - try, That ea - ger hearts ex - pect!

Pilgrimage

2. The men - tion of thy glo - ry Is unc - tion to the breast,
4. The Cross is all thy splen - dor, The Cru - ci - fied thy praise;
6. Up - on the Rock of A - ges They raise thy ho - ly tower;
8. Je - sus, in mer - cy bring us To that dear land of rest,
And med - i - cine in sick - ness, And love, and life, and rest.
His laud and ben - e - dic - tion Thy ran - somed peo-ple raise.
Thine is the vic - tor's laur - el, And thine the gold - en dower.
Who art, with God the Fa - ther And Spir - it, ev - er blest. A-men.

Bernard of Cluny, XII cent.
Tr. John Mason Neale, 1818–66

LOB SEI DEM ALLMÄCHTIGEN GOTT. L. M.

JOHANN CRÜGER, 1598–1662

With dignity FIRST TUNE

1. Not al - ways on the mount may we Rapt in the heaven ly vi - sion be; The shores of thought and feel - ing know The Spir - it's ti - dal ebb and flow.
2. 'Lord, it is good a - bid - ing here,' We cry, the heaven ly pres - ence near; The vi - sion van - ish - es, our eyes Are lift - ed in - to va - cant skies.

3 Yet hath one such exalted hour
Upon the soul redeeming power,
And in its strength through after days
We travel our appointed ways;

4 Till all the lowly vale grows bright,
Transfigured in remembered light,
And in untiring souls we bear
The freshness of the upper air.

5 The mount for vision: but below
The paths of daily duty go,
And nobler life therein shall own
The pattern on the mountain shown.

Frederick L. Hosmer, 1840–192

This hymn may also be sung to ST. CRISPIN (No. 325)

Pilgrimage

ONEONTA. L. M.
WALTER HENRY HALL, 1862–1935
In moderate time
SECOND TUNE
1. Not al - ways on the mount may we Rapt in the heaven - ly vi - sion be; The shores of thought and feel - ing know The Spir - it's ti - dal ebb and flow.
2. 'Lord, it is good a - bid - ing here,' We cry, the heaven - ly pres - ence near; The vi - sion van - ish - es, our eyes Are lift - ed in - to va - cant skies.

3 Yet hath one such exalted hour
Upon the soul redeeming power,
And in its strength through after days
We travel our appointed ways;

4 Till all the lowly vale grows bright,
Transfigured in remembered light,
And in untiring souls we bear
The freshness of the upper air.

5 The mount for vision: but below
The paths of daily duty go,
And nobler life therein shall own
The pattern on the mountain shown.

Frederick L. Hosmer, 1840–1929

PILGRIM SONG. 9 9, 5 5, 4. ERNEST AUGUST HAGFORS, 1827–1913

In moderate time

1. Lord, as a pil - grim on earth I roam, By foes sur - round - ed, far from my home; What - e'er be - tide me, Walk thou be - side me, Shep - herd di - vine!
2. Though friends for - sake me, thou art the same, Faith - ful for - ev - er is thy blest Name, Thou wilt not leave me, Oft though I grieve thee, Thou Friend di - vine! A - men.

3 Thou art my refuge; grant me, I pray,
Strength for each burden, light on my way,
Balm in my sorrow,
Grace for tomorrow,
Saviour divine!

4 Lord, let thy presence lead all the way,
Until the dawning of that great day
When I shall see thee
Throned in thy glory,
God blest for aye! Amen.

Wilhelmi Malmivaara, 1854–1922
Paraphrase, Ernest Edwin Ryden, 1886–
Based on tr. by Aino Lilja Kantonen-Halkola, 1901–

See also:

590 For ever with the Lord
565 Forward! be our watchword
498 Hark! hark, my soul
478 He leadeth me
472 Lead us, O Father,
191 Lord, dismiss us
168 O God, our help in ages past
515 O Jesus, I have promised
462 O my soul, on wings ascending
555 Rejoice, ye pure in heart
425 Saviour, blessèd Saviour
269 Shepherd of souls

37

MARYTON. L. M.
HENRY PERCY SMITH, 1825–98
In moderate time
1. O Mas - ter, let me walk with thee In low - ly paths of serv - ice free; Tell me thy se - cret; help me bear The strain of toil, the fret of care.
2. Help me the slow of heart to move By some clear, win - ning word of love; Teach me the way - ward feet to stay, And guide them in the home-ward way. A-men.

3 Teach me thy patience; still with thee
In closer, dearer company,
In work that keeps faith sweet and strong,
In trust that triumphs over wrong;

4 In hope that sends a shining ray
Far down the future's broadening way,
In peace that only thou canst give;
With thee, O Master, let me live. Amen.

Washington Gladden, 1836–1918

CANONBURY. L. M.

ROBERT SCHUMANN, 1810–56

In moderate time
1. Lord, speak to me, that I may speak In living echoes of thy tone; As thou hast sought, so let me seek Thy erring children lost and lone.
2. O lead me, Lord, that I may lead The wandering and the wavering feet; O feed me, Lord, that I may feed Thy hungering ones with manna sweet. A-men.

3 O strengthen me, that while I stand
Firm on the Rock, and strong in thee,
I may stretch out a loving hand
To wrestlers with the troubled sea.

4 O teach me, Lord, that I may teach
The precious things thou dost impart;
And wing my words, that they may reach
The hidden depths of many a heart.

5 O fill me with thy fulness, Lord,
Until my very heart o'erflow
In kindling thought and glowing word
Thy love to tell, thy praise to show. Amen.

Frances Ridley Havergal, 1836–7

WELWYN. 11 10, 11 10.
ALFRED SCOTT-GATTY, 1847–1918
With movement
1. O broth - er man, fold to thy heart thy broth - er!
2. Fol - low with rev - erent steps the great ex - am - ple
Where pit - y dwells, the peace of God is there;
Of him whose ho - ly work was do - ing good;
To wor - ship right - ly is to love each oth - er,
So shall the wide earth seem our Fa - ther's tem - ple,
Each smile a hymn, each kind - ly deed a prayer.
Each lov - ing life a psalm of grat - i - tude.

3 Then shall all shackles fall; the stormy clangor
Of wild war-music o'er the earth shall cease;
Love shall tread out the baleful fire of anger,
And in its ashes plant the tree of peace.

John Greenleaf Whittier, 1807–92

Music by permission of the Abbot of Downside Abbey

MEIRINGEN. 8 6, 8 6, 8 8. CHRISTIAN GOTTLOB NEEFE, 1748–98

With spirit
1. Be - liev - ing fa - thers oft have told What things by God were done, When faith - ful men in days of old Their life - long bat - tle won: True broth - ers all, of one ac - cord, We hold one faith, we serve one Lord.
2. A - mid the world's con - fus - ed noise, Where we but dark - ly see, The Christ ap - peals, with sweet, clear voice: 'My broth - ers, fol - low me, Like broth - ers true, of one ac - cord, To hold one faith, to serve one Lord.'
3. His Church our shel - ter, he our guide, Our strength his heal - ing Cross, We range our - selves up - on his side, Where none can suf - fer loss. Like broth - ers true, of one ac - cord, We hold one faith and serve one Lord. A-men

So by thy Spirit mold us, Lord;
Inspire our hearts to pray;
Our hungry souls feed with thy word,
Teach all of us to say:
'True brothers all, of one accord,
We hold one faith, we serve one Lord.'

5 We fain would serve thy Church e'en now,
With hearts from self set free,
Striving to make thy Kingdom grow.
O God, so may it be,
That, brothers true, with one accord
We hold the faith and serve the Lord!
Amen.

Archibald Hamilton Charteris, 1835–1908, a.

FESTAL SONG. S. M.

WILLIAM HENRY WALTER, 1825–93

With spirit

1. Rise up, O men of God! Have done with less - er things;
2. Rise up, O men of God! His king - dom tar - ries long;

Give heart and soul and mind and strength To serve the King of kings.
Bring in the day of broth - er - hood, And end the night of wrong.

3 Rise up, O men of God!
The Church for you doth wait,
Her strength unequal to her task;
Rise up and make her great!

4 Lift high the Cross of Christ!
Tread where his feet have trod;
As brothers of the Son of Man,
Rise up, O men of God!

William Pierson Merrill, 1867–1954

Words by permission of The Presbyterian Tribune

IN BABILONE. 87, 87. D.
XVIII cent. Dutch Melody
Harm. T. TERTIUS NOBLE, 1867–1953
In unison, with breadth
1. Son of God, e - ter - nal Sav - iour, Source of life and truth and grace, Son of Man, whose birth in - car - nate Hal - lows all our hu - man race,
2. As thou, Lord, hast lived for oth - ers, So may we for oth - ers live; Free - ly have thy gifts been grant - ed, Free - ly may thy serv - ants give.
3. Come, O Christ, and reign a - bove us, King of Love, and Prince of Peace; Hush the storm of strife and pas - sion, Bid its cru - el dis - cords cease;
4. Dark the path that lies be - hind us, Strewn with wrecks and stained with blood; But be - fore us gleams the vi - sion Of the com - ing broth - er - hood.

Service

Thou our Head, who, throned in glo - ry, For thine
Thine the gold and thine the sil - ver, Thine the
By thy pa - tient years of toil - ing, By thy
Thou who pray - edst, thou who will - est That thy
own dost ev - er plead, Fill us with thy
wealth of land and sea, We but stew - ards
si - lent hours of pain, Quench our fe - vered
peo - ple should be one, Grant, O grant our
love and pit - y, Heal our wrongs, and help our need.
of thy boun - ty, Held in sol - emn trust for thee.
thirst of pleas - ure, Shame our sel - fish greed of gain.
hope's fru - i - tion: Here on earth thy will be done. A-men.

Somerset Corry Lowry, 1855–1932

armonization by permission of Philip R. Noble

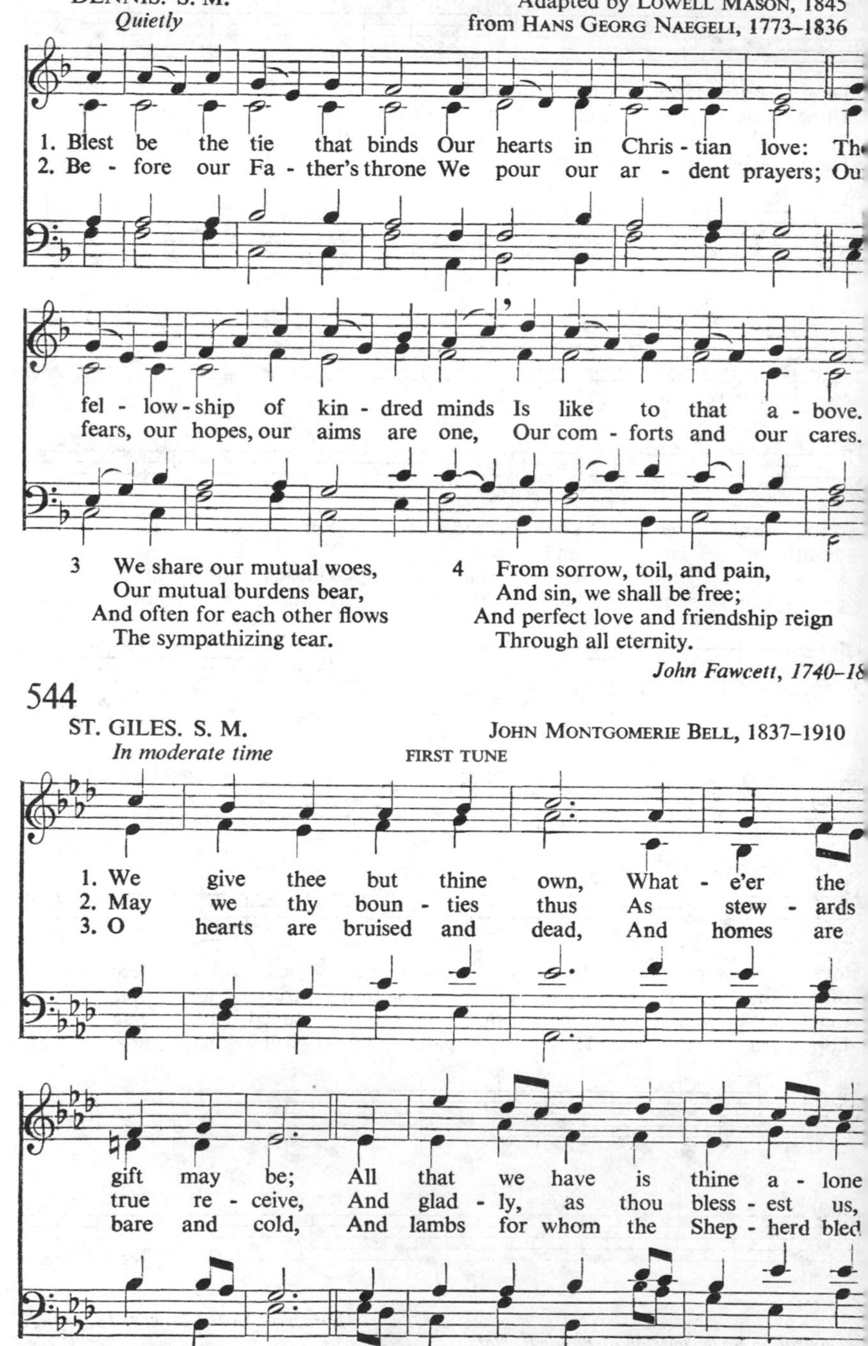
DENNIS. S. M.
Quietly
Adapted by LOWELL MASON, 1845
from HANS GEORG NAEGELI, 1773–1836
1. Blest be the tie that binds Our hearts in Chris - tian love: Th
2. Be - fore our Fa - ther's throne We pour our ar - dent prayers; Ou
fel - low - ship of kin - dred minds Is like to that a - bove.
fears, our hopes, our aims are one, Our com - forts and our cares.

3 We share our mutual woes,
Our mutual burdens bear,
And often for each other flows
The sympathizing tear.

4 From sorrow, toil, and pain,
And sin, we shall be free;
And perfect love and friendship reign
Through all eternity.

John Fawcett, 1740–18

544
ST. GILES. S. M.
In moderate time
FIRST TUNE
JOHN MONTGOMERIE BELL, 1837–1910
1. We give thee but thine own, What - e'er the
2. May we thy boun - ties thus As stew - ards
3. O hearts are bruised and dead, And homes are
gift may be; All that we have is thine a - lone
true re - ceive, And glad - ly, as thou bless - est us,
bare and cold, And lambs for whom the Shep - herd bled

A trust, O Lord, from thee.
To thee our first - fruits give.
Are stray - ing from the fold; A - men.

4 To comfort and to bless,
To find a balm for woe,
To tend the lone and fatherless,
Is angels' work below.

5 The captive to release,
To God the lost to bring,
To teach the way of life and peace,
It is a Christlike thing.

6 And we believe thy word,
Though dim our faith may be;
Whate'er for thine we do, O Lord,
We do it unto thee. Amen.

William Walsham How, 1823–97

This hymn may also be sung to TRENTHAM (No. 470) or HEATH (No. 559)

44

ST. GEORGE (ST. OLAVE). S. M. — HENRY JOHN GAUNTLETT, 1805–76

SECOND TUNE

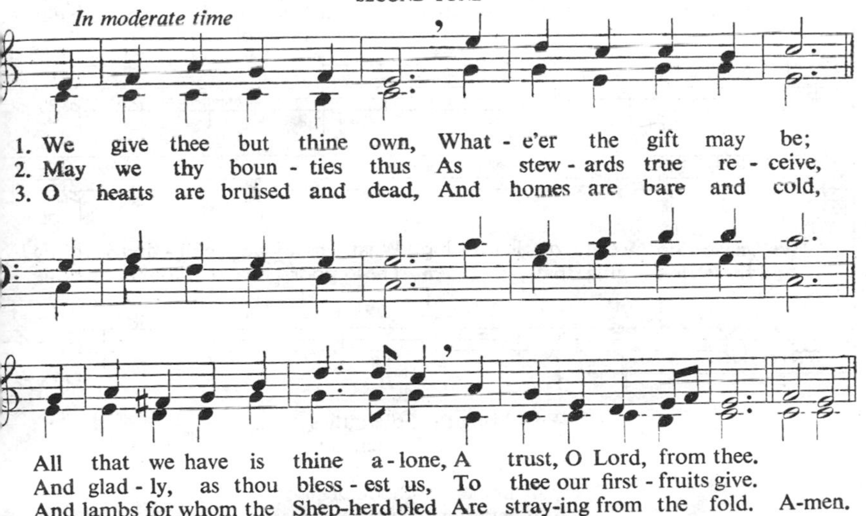
In moderate time
1. We give thee but thine own, What - e'er the gift may be;
2. May we thy boun - ties thus As stew - ards true re - ceive,
3. O hearts are bruised and dead, And homes are bare and cold,
All that we have is thine a - lone, A trust, O Lord, from thee.
And glad - ly, as thou bless - est us, To thee our first - fruits give.
And lambs for whom the Shep-herd bled Are stray-ing from the fold. A-men.

CHRISTMAS MORN. 76, 76. D.
EDWARD JOHN HOPKINS, 1818–1901
In moderate time
1. The wise may bring their learn - ing, The rich may bring their wealth,
2. We'll bring him hearts that love him; We'll bring him thank-ful praise,
And some may bring their great - ness, And some their strength and health;
And young souls meek - ly striv - ing To walk in ho - ly ways;
We, too, would bring our treas - ures To of - fer to the King;
And these shall be the treas - ures We of - fer to the King,
We have no wealth or learn - ing: What shall we chil - dren bring?
And these are gifts that e - ven The poor - est child may bring.

3 We'll bring the little duties
We have to do each day;
We'll try our best to please him,
At home, at school, at play;
And better are these treasures
To offer to our King,
Than richest gifts without them;
Yet these a child may bring.

Book of Praise for Children, 188

WEIMAR. 7 6, 7 6. D. MELCHIOR VULPIUS, 1560–1615

With dignity
1. Let us now our voi - ces raise, Wake the day with glad - ness;
2. Nev - er flinched they from the flame, From the tor - ment nev - er;
God him - self to joy and praise Turns our hu - man sad - ness;
Vain the ty - rant's sharp - est aim, Vain each fierce en - deav - or:
Joy that mar - tyrs won their crown, O - pened heaven's bright por - tal,
For by faith they saw the land Decked in all its glo - ry,
When they laid the mor - tal down For the life im - mor - tal.
Where tri - um - phant now they stand With the vic - tor's sto - ry.

3 Up and follow, Christian men!
Press through toil and sorrow;
Spurn the night of fear, and then,
O the glorious morrow!

Who will venture on the strife,
Who will first begin it?
Who will grasp the Land of Life?
Warriors, up and win it!

St. Joseph the Hymnographer, † 883
Tr. John Mason Neale, 1818–66

This hymn may also be sung to ST. KEVIN (No. 106)

EBENEZER (TON-Y-BOTEL). 8 7, 8 7. D. THOMAS JOHN WILLIAMS, 1869–1944

Unison, with dignity

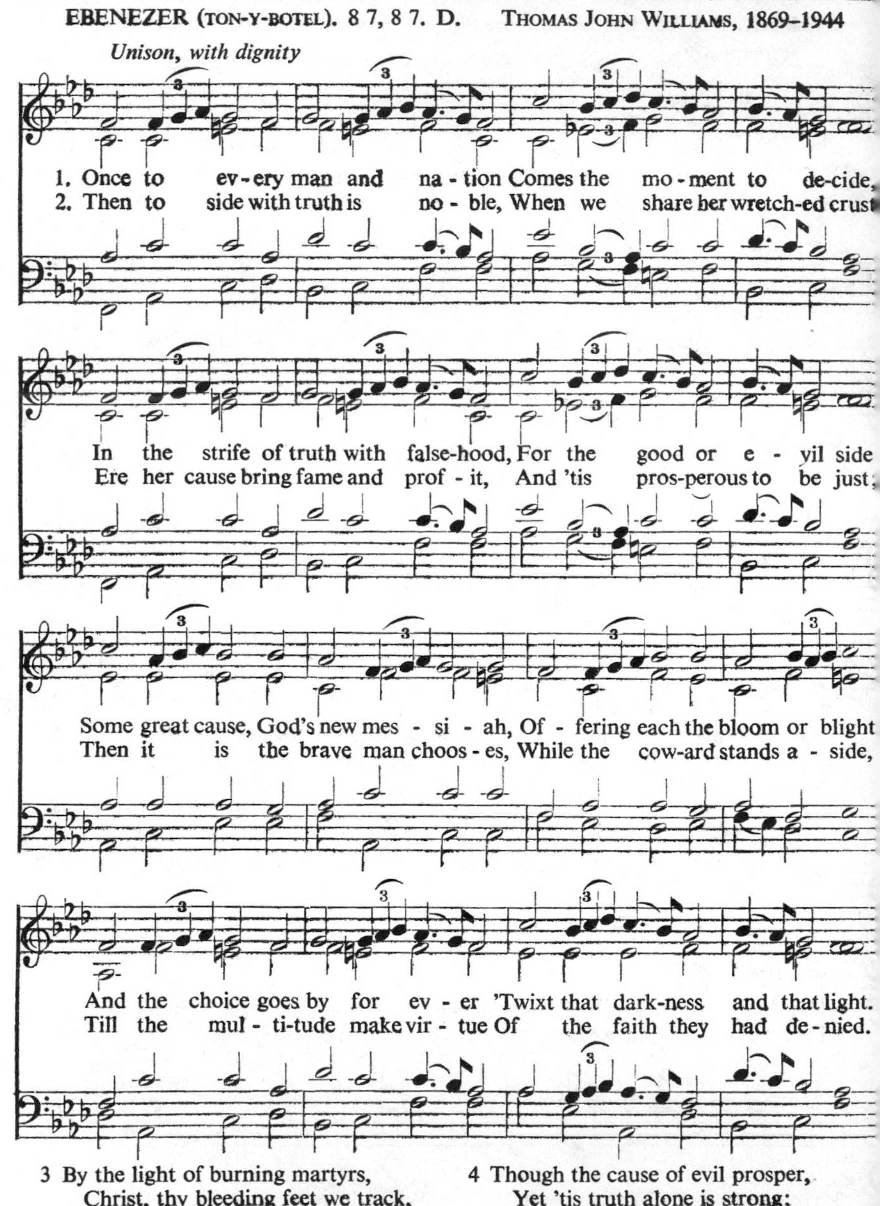
1. Once to ev-ery man and na-tion Comes the mo-ment to de-cide,
2. Then to side with truth is no-ble, When we share her wretch-ed crust
In the strife of truth with false-hood, For the good or e-vil side
Ere her cause bring fame and prof-it, And 'tis pros-perous to be just;
Some great cause, God's new mes-si-ah, Of-fering each the bloom or blight
Then it is the brave man choos-es, While the cow-ard stands a-side,
And the choice goes by for ev-er 'Twixt that dark-ness and that light.
Till the mul-ti-tude make vir-tue Of the faith they had de-nied.

3 By the light of burning martyrs,
Christ, thy bleeding feet we track,
Toiling up new Calvaries ever
With the Cross that turns not back.
New occasions teach new duties;
Time makes ancient good uncouth;
They must upward still and onward
Who would keep abreast of truth.

4 Though the cause of evil prosper,
Yet 'tis truth alone is strong;
Though her portion be the scaffold
And upon the throne be wrong,
Yet that scaffold sways the future,
And, behind the dim unknown,
Standeth God within the shadow,
Keeping watch above his own.

James Russell Lowell, 1819–9[illegible]

LYNNE. 13 10, 11 10. BATES GILBERT BURT, 1878–1948

Unison, with vigor
1. O God of youth, whose Spir - it in our hearts is stir - ring
2. Fill thou our hearts with zeal in ev - ery brave en - deav - or
3. Teach us to know the way of Je - sus Christ, our Mas - ter,
Hope and de - sire for no - ble lives and true,
To right the wrongs that shame this mor - tal life;
Give us his clear - eyed faith, his fear - less heart,
Keep us, we pray thee, stead - fast and un - err - ing;
Give us the val - iant spir - it that shall nev - er
And through life's dark - ness, dan - ger, and dis - as - ter,
With light and love di - vine our souls en - due.
Fal - ter or fail, how - ev - er long the strife.
O may we nev - er from his side de - part.

4 May we be true to him, our Captain of salvation,
Bearing his Cross in service glad and free,
Winning the world to that last consummation
When all its kingdoms shall his kingdom be.

Bates Gilbert Burt, 1878–1948

LOVE DIVINE (LE JEUNE). 87, 87. D.
GEORGE F. C. LE JEUNE, 1841–1904
Broadly
Deaconesses
1. Sav - iour, thee my heart I ten - der, And would yield my - self to thee;
2. Let me do thy will or bear it; I would know no will but thine;
All my powers to thee sur - ren - der, Thine and on - ly thine to be.
Shouldst thou take my life or spare it, I that life to thee re - sign.
Send me, Lord, where thou wilt send me, On - ly do thou guide my way;
Thine I am, O Lord, for ev - er, To thy serv - ice set a - part;
May thy grace through life at - tend me, Glad-ly then shall I o - bey.
Suf - fer me to leave thee nev - er; Seal thine im - age on my heart. A-men

John Burton, 1803–77

See also:

LANCASHIRE. 7 6, 7 6. D.
HENRY SMART, 1813–79
Brightly
1. Lead on, O King e - ter - nal, The day of march has come;
2. Lead on, O King e - ter - nal, Till sin's fierce war shall cease,
Hence-forth in fields of con - quest Thy tents shall be our home:
And ho - li - ness shall whis - per The sweet A - men of peace;
Through days of prep - a - ra - tion Thy grace has made us strong,
For not with swords loud clash - ing, Nor roll of stir - ring drums,
And now, O King e - ter - nal, We lift our bat - tle - song.
But deeds of love and mer - cy, The heaven-ly king-dom comes. A-men.

3 Lead on, O King eternal:
  We follow, not with fears,
For gladness breaks like morning
  Where'er thy face appears:
Thy Cross is lifted o'er us;
  We journey in its light;
The crown awaits the conquest;
  Lead on, O God of might. Amen.

Ernest Warburton Shurtleff, 1862–1917

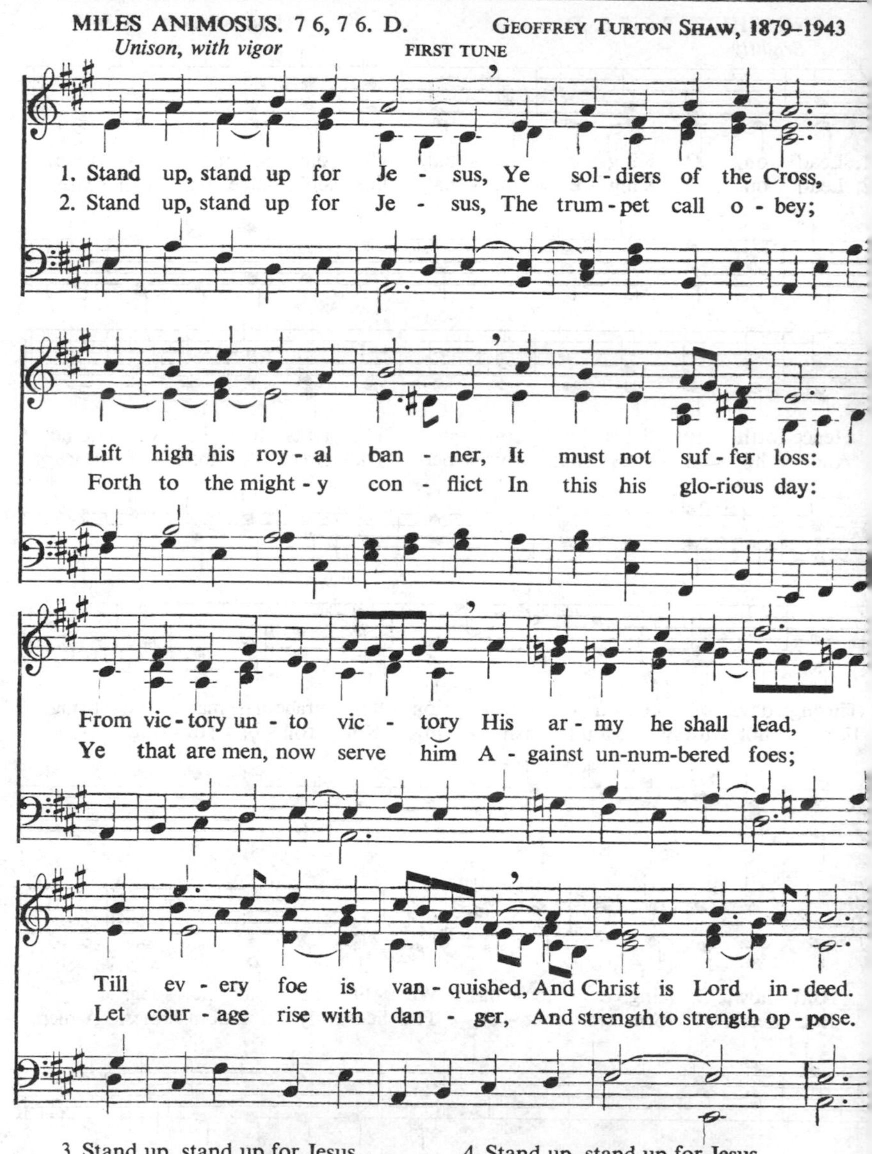
MILES ANIMOSUS. 7 6, 7 6. D.
GEOFFREY TURTON SHAW, 1879–1943
Unison, with vigor
FIRST TUNE
1. Stand up, stand up for Je - sus, Ye sol-diers of the Cross,
2. Stand up, stand up for Je - sus, The trum-pet call o - bey;
Lift high his roy - al ban - ner, It must not suf - fer loss:
Forth to the might - y con - flict In this his glo-rious day:
From vic-tory un - to vic - tory His ar - my he shall lead,
Ye that are men, now serve him A - gainst un-num-bered foes;
Till ev - ery foe is van - quished, And Christ is Lord in - deed.
Let cour - age rise with dan - ger, And strength to strength op - pose.

3 Stand up, stand up for Jesus,
Stand in his strength alone;
The arm of flesh will fail you,
Ye dare not trust your own:
Put on the gospel armor,
Each piece put on with prayer;
Where duty calls or danger,
Be never wanting there.

4 Stand up, stand up for Jesus,
The strife will not be long;
This day the noise of battle,
The next the victor's song:
To him that overcometh
A crown of life shall be;
He with the King of Glory
Shall reign eternally.

George Duffield, 1818–88

WEBB. 7 6, 7 6. D.
GEORGE JAMES WEBB, 1803–87
Broadly, with movement
SECOND TUNE
1. Stand up, stand up for Je - sus, Ye sol - diers of the Cross;
2. Stand up, stand up for Je - sus, The trum - pet call o - bey;
Lift high his roy - al ban - ner, It must not suf - fer loss:
Forth to the might - y con - flict In this his glo - rious day:
From vic - tory un - to vic - tory His ar - my he shall lead,
Ye that are men, now serve him A - gainst un - num-bered foes;
Till ev - ery foe is van-quished, And Christ is Lord in - deed.
Let cour - age rise with dan - ger, And strength to strength op - pose.

3 Stand up, stand up for Jesus,
Stand in his strength alone;
The arm of flesh will fail you,
Ye dare not trust your own:
Put on the gospel armor,
Each piece put on with prayer;
Where duty calls or danger,
Be never wanting there.

4 Stand up, stand up for Jesus,
The strife will not be long;
This day the noise of battle,
The next the victor's song:
To him that overcometh
A crown of life shall be;
He with the King of Glory
Shall reign eternally.

George Duffield, 1818–88

CHRISTMAS. 8 6, 8 6 6.
GEORGE FREDERICK HANDEL, 1685–1759
With spirit
1. A - wake, my soul, stretch ev - ery nerve, And press with vig - or on; A heaven-ly race de - mands thy zeal, And an im - mor - tal crown, And an im - mor - tal crown.
2. A cloud of wit - ness - es a - round Hold thee in full sur - vey; For - get the steps al - read - y trod, And on - ward urge thy way, And on - ward urge thy way.
3 'Tis God's all-animating voice
That calls thee from on high;
'Tis his own hand presents the prize
To thine aspiring eye.
4 Then wake, my soul, stretch every nerve,
And press with vigor on;
A heavenly race demands thy zeal,
And an immortal crown.
Philip Doddridge, 1702–51
This hymn may also be sung to NOTTINGHAM (ST. MAGNUS) (No. 454)
553
GALILEE. 8 7, 8 7.
WILLIAM HERBERT JUDE, 1851–1922
Slowly
1. Je - sus calls us; o'er the tu - mult Of our life's wild, rest - less sea,
2. As of old Saint An-drew heard it By the Gal - i - le - an lake,
3. Je - sus calls us from the wor - ship Of the vain world's gold-en store;

Day by day his clear voice sound-eth, Say - ing, 'Chris-tian fol-low me!'
Turned from home and toil and kin-dred, Leav-ing all for his dear sake.
From each i - dol that would keep us, Say-ing, 'Chris-tian, love me more.' A-men.

4 In our joys and in our sorrows,
Days of toil and hours of ease,
Still he calls, in cares and pleasures,
'Christian, love me more than these.'

5 Jesus calls us! By thy mercies,
Saviour, make us hear thy call,
Give our hearts to thine obedience,
Serve and love thee best of all. Amen.

Cecil Frances Alexander, 1823–95

54

ARLINGTON. C. M. THOMAS AUGUSTINE ARNE, 1710–78

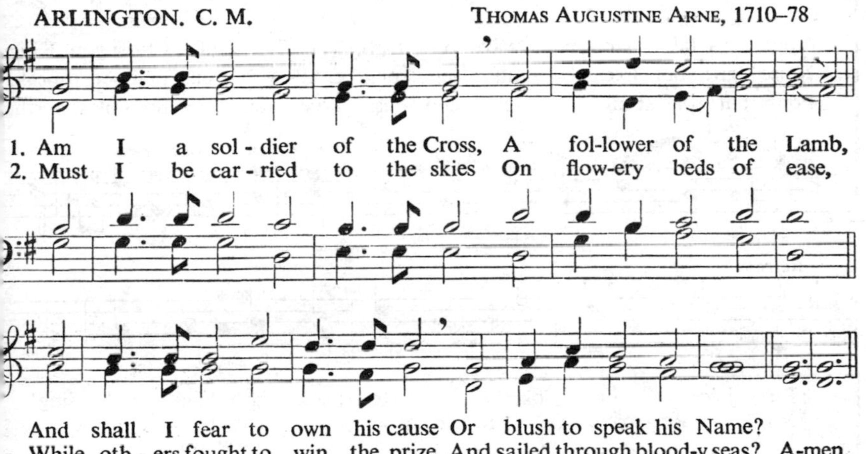
1. Am I a sol - dier of the Cross, A fol-lower of the Lamb,
2. Must I be car - ried to the skies On flow-ery beds of ease,
And shall I fear to own his cause Or blush to speak his Name?
While oth - ers fought to win the prize, And sailed through blood-y seas? A-men.

3 Are there no foes for me to face?
Must I not stem the flood?
Is this vain world a friend to grace
To help me on to God?

4 Sure I must fight, if I would reign—
Increase my courage, Lord—
I'll bear the toil, endure the pain,
Supported by thy word.

5 Thy saints, in all this glorious war,
Shall conquer, though they die;
They see the triumph from afar,
By faith they bring it nigh.

6 When that illustrious day shall rise,
And all thy armies shine
In robes of victory through the skies,
The glory shall be thine. Amen.

Isaac Watts, 1674–1748 a.

This hymn may also be sung to WINCHESTER (No. 389)

MARION. S. M. With Refrain. ARTHUR HENRY MESSITER, 1834–1916

With spirit
1. Re - joice, ye pure in heart, Re - joice, give thanks, and sing;
2. Bright youth and snow-crowned age, Strong men and maid - ens meek,
3. With all the an - gel choirs, With all the saints on earth,
Your fes - tal ban - ner wave on high, The Cross of Christ your King.
Raise high your free ex - ult - ing song; God's won-drous prais - es speak.
Pour out the strains of joy and bliss, True rap - ture, no - blest mirth.
Refrain
Re - joice, re - joice! Re - joice, give thanks, and sing!
Re - joice, re - joice!

4 With voice as full and strong
As ocean's surging praise,
Send forth the hymns our fathers loved,
The psalms of ancient days.

5 Still lift your standard high,
Still march in firm array,
As warriors through the darkness toil
Till dawns the golden day.

6 At last the march shall end,
The wearied ones shall rest,
The pilgrims find their Father's house,
Jerusalem the blest.

7 Then on, ye pure in heart,
Rejoice, give thanks, and sing;
Your festal banner wave on high,
The Cross of Christ your King.

Edward Hayes Plumptre, 1821–9

NEANDER (UNSER HERRSCHER). 8 7, 8 7, 7 7. JOACHIM NEANDER, 1650–1680

With dignity

1. Rise, ye chil - dren of sal - va - tion, All who cleave to Christ the Head;
2. Saints and mar - tyrs long be - fore us Firm - ly on this ground have stood;
3. Fight - ing, we shall be vic - to - rious By the Blood of Christ our Lord;

Wake, a - wake, O might - y na - tion, Ere the foe on Zi - on tread;
See their ban - ner wav - ing o'er us, Con-querors through the Sav-iour's Blood.
On our fore-heads, bright and glo-rious, Shines the wit - ness of his word;

He draws nigh, and would de - fy All the hosts of God most high.
Ground we hold, where - on of old Fought the faith - ful and the bold.
Spear and shield on bat - tle - field, His great Name; we can - not yield.

4 When his servants stand before him
Each receiving his reward,
When his saints in light adore him,
Giving glory to the Lord;
'Victory!' our song shall be
Like the thunder of the sea.

Justus Falckner, 1672–1723
Tr. Emma Frances Bevan, 1827–1909

PENTECOST. L. M. WILLIAM BOYD, 1847–1928

Broadly, with spirit

1. Fight the good fight with all thy might, Christ is thy
2. Run the straight race through God's good grace, Lift up thine

strength, and Christ thy right; Lay hold on life, and
eyes, and seek his face; Life with its way be-

it shall be Thy joy and crown e - ter - nal - ly.
fore us lies, Christ is the path, and Christ the prize.

3 Cast care aside, lean on thy Guide;
His boundless mercy will provide;
Trust, and thy trusting soul shall prove
Christ is its life, and Christ its love.

4 Faint not nor fear, his arms are near;
He changeth not, and thou art dear;
Only believe, and thou shalt see
That Christ is all in all to thee.

John S. B. Monsell, 1811–75

558

ADESTE FIDELES. Irregular. JOHN FRANCIS WADE'S *Cantus diversi*, 1751

In moderate time

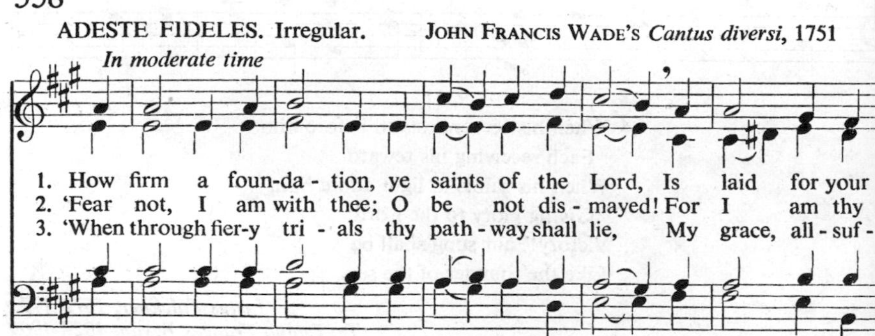
1. How firm a foun-da - tion, ye saints of the Lord, Is laid for your
2. 'Fear not, I am with thee; O be not dis - mayed! For I am thy
3. 'When through fier-y tri - als thy path - way shall lie, My grace, all - suf -

faith in his ex - cel - lent word! What more can he say than to
God, and will still give thee aid; I'll strength-en thee, help thee, and
fi - cient, shall be thy sup - ply: The flames shall not hurt thee; I
you he hath said, Who un - to the Sav - iour for ref -
cause thee to stand, Up - held by my right - eous, om - nip -
on - ly de - sign Thy dross to con - sume, and thy gold
uge have fled, Who un - to the Sav - iour for ref - uge have fled?
o - tent hand, Up - held by my right-eous, om-nip - o - tent hand.
to re - fine, Thy dross to con - sume, and thy gold to re - fine.

4 'E'en down to old age all my people shall prove
My sovereign, eternal, unchangeable love,
And then, when gray hairs shall their temples adorn,
Like lambs they shall still in my bosom be borne.

5 'The soul that on Jesus hath leaned for repose
I will not, I cannot desert to his foes;
That soul, though all hell should endeavor to shake,
I'll never, no never, no never forsake!'

"K" in Rippon's Selection, 1787 a

HEATH. S. M.

MASON and WEBB'S *Cantica Laudis*, 1850

In moderate time

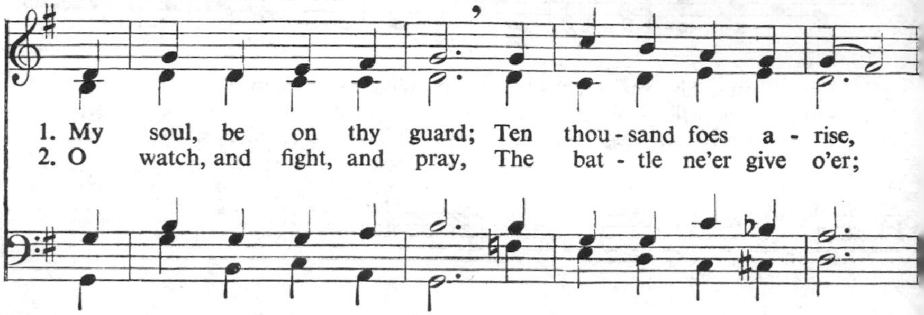

1. My soul, be on thy guard; Ten thou - sand foes a - rise,
2. O watch, and fight, and pray, The bat - tle ne'er give o'er;

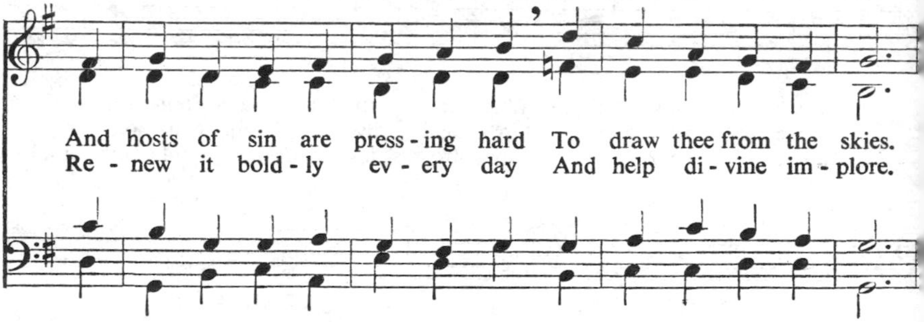

And hosts of sin are press - ing hard To draw thee from the skies.
Re - new it bold - ly ev - ery day And help di - vine im - plore.

3 Ne'er think the victory won
Nor lay thine armor down;
Thine arduous work will not be done
Till thou obtain thy crown.

4 Fight on, my soul, till death
Shall bring thee to thy God;
He'll take thee at thy parting breath
Up to his blest abode.

George Heath, 1750–1822

560

ST. GERTRUDE. 6 5, 6 5. D. With Refrain. ARTHUR S. SULLIVAN, 1842–1900

Broadly

1. On-ward, Chris-tian sol - diers, March-ing as to war, With the Cross of
2. At the sign of tri - umph Sa - tan's le-gions flee; On then, Chris-tian
3. Like a might - y ar - my Moves the Church of God; Broth - ers, we are

Je - sus Go - ing on be - fore. Christ the roy - al Mas - ter Leads a -
sol - diers, On to vic - to - ry! Hell's foun-da - tions quiv - er At the
tread - ing Where the saints have trod. We are not di - vid - ed, All one
gainst the foe; For - ward in - to bat - tle, See, his ban - ners go!
shout of praise; Broth-ers, lift your voic - es, Loud your an-thems raise.
bod - y we, One in hope and doc - trine, One in char - i - ty.
Refrain
On - ward, Chris - tian sol - diers, March - ing as to war,
With the Cross of Je - sus Go - ing on be - fore.

4 Crowns and thrones may perish,
Kingdoms rise and wane,
But the Church of Jesus
Constant will remain;
Gates of hell can never
'Gainst that Church prevail;
We have Christ's own promise,
And that cannot fail.

5 Onward, then, ye faithful,
Join our happy throng;
Blend with ours your voices,
In the triumph-song;
Glory, laud, and honor,
Unto Christ the King;
This through countless ages
Men and angels sing.

Sabine Baring-Gould, 1834–1924

PENITENCE. 6 5, 6 5. D. SPENCER LANE, 1843–1903

Quietly
1. In the hour of tri - al, Je - sus, plead for me,
2. With for - bid - den pleas - ures Should this vain world charm,
Lest by base de - ni - al I de - part from thee;
Or its sor - did treas - ures Spread to work me harm,
When thou seest me wa - ver, With a look re - call,
Bring to my re - mem - brance Sad Geth - sem - a - ne,
Nor from fear or fa - vor Suf - fer me to fall.
Or, in dark - er sem - blance, Cross-crowned Cal - va - ry. A-men.

3 Should thy mercy send me
Sorrow, toil and woe,
Or should pain attend me
On my path below,
Grant that I may never
Fail thy hand to see;
Grant that I may ever
Cast my care on thee. Amen.

James Montgomery, 1771–1854

ALL SAINTS NEW. C. M. D.
HENRY STEPHEN CUTLER, 1824–1902
With spirit
1. The Son of God goes forth to war, A king - ly crown to gain;
2. The mar - tyr first, whose ea - gle eye Could pierce be - yond the grave,
His blood - red ban - ner streams a - far; Who fol - lows in his train?
Who saw his Mas - ter in the sky And called on him to save;
Who best can drink his cup of woe, Tri - um-phant o - ver pain;
Like him, with par - don on his tongue, In midst of mor - tal pain,
Who pa - tient bears his cross be - low, He fol - lows in his train.
He prayed for them that did the wrong: Who fol - lows in his train? A-men.

3 A glorious band, the chosen few,
On whom the Spirit came,
Twelve valiant saints, their hope they knew,
And mocked the cross and flame.
They met the tyrant's brandished steel,
The lion's gory mane;
They bowed their necks the death to feel:
Who follows in their train?

4 A noble army, men and boys,
The matron and the maid,
Around the Saviour's throne rejoice
In robes of light arrayed.
They climbed the steep ascent of heaven
Through peril, toil, and pain:
O God, to us may grace be given
To follow in their train! Amen.

Reginald Heber, 1783–1826

MONKS GATE. 6 5, 6 5, 6 6 6 5. English Traditional Melody

FIRST TUNE

Brightly
1. He who would val - iant be 'Gainst all dis - as - ter,
2. Who so be - set him round With dis - mal sto - ries,
Let him in con - stan - cy Fol - low the Mas - ter.
Do but them - selves con-found, His strength the more is.
There's no dis - cour - age - ment Shall make him once re - lent
No foes shall stay his might, Though he with gi - ants fight;
His first a - vowed in - tent To be a pil - grim.
He will make good his right To be a pil - grim.

3 Since, Lord, thou dost defend
Us with thy Spirit,
We know we at the end
Shall life inherit.
Then fancies flee away!
I'll fear not what men say,
I'll labor night and day
To be a pilgrim.

John Bunyan, 1628–88 a.

ST. DUNSTAN'S. 6 5, 6 5, 6 6 6 5. WINFRED DOUGLAS, 1867–1944

SECOND TUNE

Brightly
1. He who would val - iant be 'Gainst all dis - as - ter,
2. Who so be - set him round With dis - mal sto - ries,
Let him in con - stan - cy Fol - low the Mas - ter.
Do but them - selves con - found, His strength the more is.
There's no dis - cour - age - ment Shall make him once re - lent
No foes shall stay his might, Though he with gi - ants fight;
His first a - vowed in - tent To be a pil - grim.
He will make good his right To be a pil - grim.

3 Since, Lord, thou dost defend
Us with thy Spirit,
We know we at the end
Shall life inherit.
Then fancies flee away!
I'll fear not what men say,
I'll labor night and day
To be a pilgrim.

John Bunyan, 1628–88 a.

FROM STRENGTH TO STRENGTH. S. M. D.

EDWARD WOODALL NAYLOR, 1867–

FIRST TUNE

Unison. Broadly, with marked rhythm
1. Sol - diers of Christ, a - rise And put your ar - mor on,
3. Stand then, in his great might, With all his strength en - dued;
Ped.
Strong in the strength which God sup - plies Through his e - ter - nal Son;
And take, to arm you for the fight, The pan - o - ply of God.
2. Strong in the Lord of Hosts, And in his might - y power;
4. To keep your ar - mor bright At - tend with con - stant care,
Who in the strength of Je - sus trusts Is more than con - quer - or.
Still walk-ing in your Cap-tain's sight, And watch-ing un - to prayer.

5 From strength to strength go on,
  Wrestle and fight and pray;
Tread all the powers of darkness down,
  And win the well-fought day;

6 That, having all things done,
  And all your conflicts past,
Ye may o'ercome through Christ alone,
  And stand entire at last.

Charles Wesley, 1707–88

564

DURHAM (DOVER). S. M. — Williams' *Psalmody*, cir. 1770

SECOND TUNE

Moderately slow

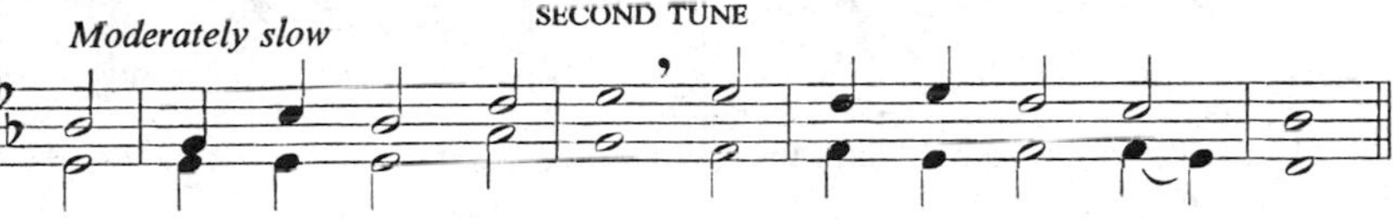

1. Sol - diers of Christ, a - rise And put your ar - mor on,
2. Strong in the Lord of Hosts, And in his might - y power;
3. Stand then, in his great might, With all his strength en - dued;

Strong in the strength which God sup-plies Through his e - ter - nal Son;
Who in the strength of Je - sus trusts Is more than con - quer - or.
And take, to arm you for the fight, The pan - o - ply of God.

4 To keep your armor bright
  Attend with constant care,
Still walking in your Captain's sight,
  And watching unto prayer.

5 From strength to strength go on,
  Wrestle and fight and pray;
Tread all the powers of darkness down,
  And win the well-fought day;

6 That, having all things done,
  And all your conflicts past,
Ye may o'ercome through Christ alone,
  And stand entire at last.

Charles Wesley, 1707–88

565

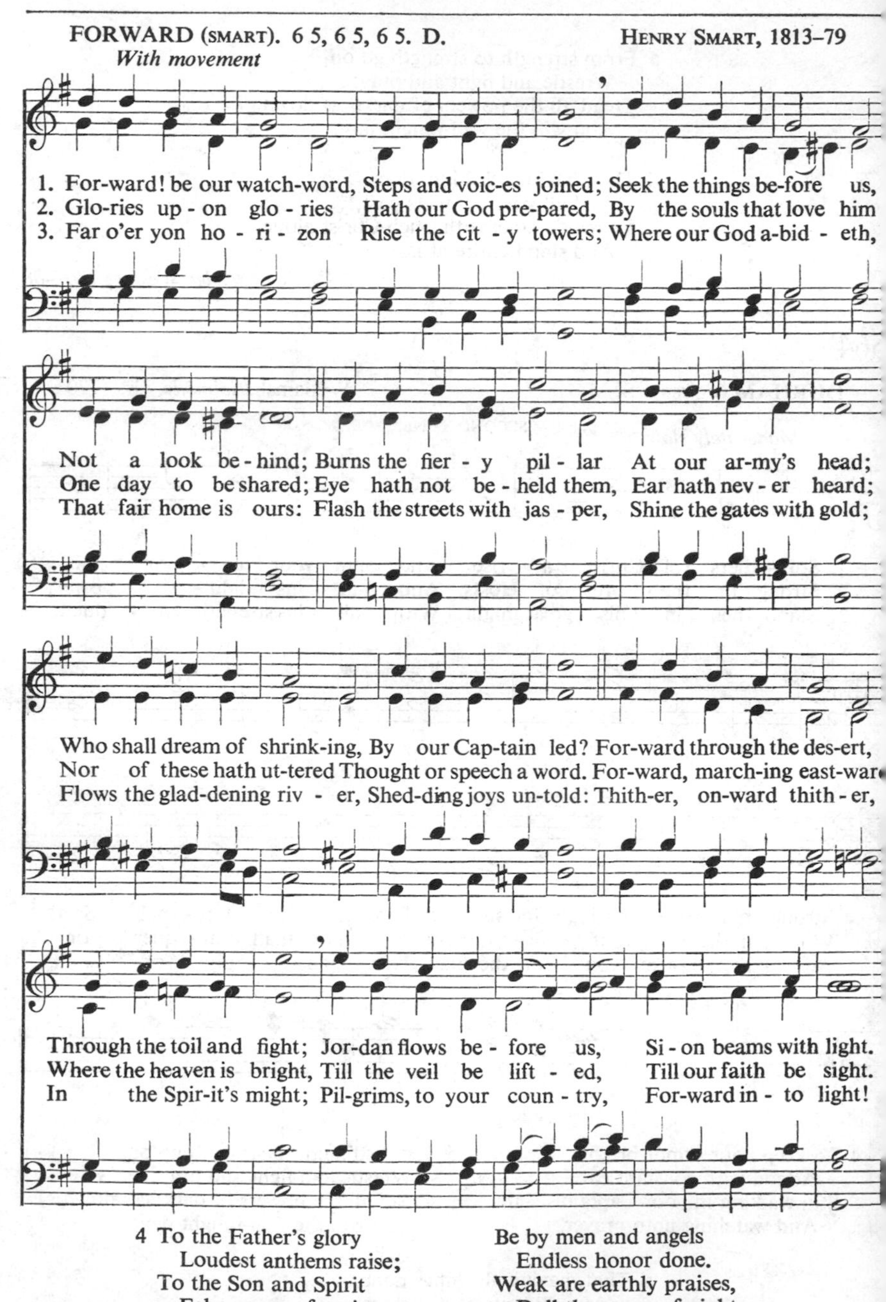
FORWARD (SMART). 6 5, 6 5, 6 5. D.
HENRY SMART, 1813–79
With movement
1. For-ward! be our watch-word, Steps and voic-es joined; Seek the things be-fore us, Not a look be-hind; Burns the fier - y pil - lar At our ar-my's head; Who shall dream of shrink-ing, By our Cap-tain led? For-ward through the des-ert, Through the toil and fight; Jor-dan flows be - fore us, Si - on beams with light.
2. Glo-ries up - on glo - ries Hath our God pre-pared, By the souls that love him One day to be shared; Eye hath not be - held them, Ear hath nev - er heard; Nor of these hath ut-tered Thought or speech a word. For-ward, march-ing east-war Where the heaven is bright, Till the veil be lift - ed, Till our faith be sight.
3. Far o'er yon ho - ri - zon Rise the cit - y towers; Where our God a-bid - eth, That fair home is ours: Flash the streets with jas - per, Shine the gates with gold; Flows the glad-dening riv - er, Shed-ding joys un-told: Thith-er, on-ward thith - er, In the Spir-it's might; Pil-grims, to your coun - try, For-ward in - to light!

4 To the Father's glory
Loudest anthems raise;
To the Son and Spirit
Echo songs of praise;
To the Lord almighty,
Blessèd Three in One,
Be by men and angels
Endless honor done.
Weak are earthly praises,
Dull the songs of night;
Forward into triumph,
Forward into light!

Henry Alford, 1810–71

JUDAS MACCABAEUS. 5 5, 6 5, 6 5, 6 5. With Refrain.
GEORGE FREDERICK HANDEL, 1685–1759
Majestically
1. Thine is the glo - ry, Ris - en, con-quering Son; End - less is the vic - tory Thou o'er death hast won. An - gels in bright rai - ment Rolled the stone a - way, Kept the fold - ed grave clothes Where thy bod - y lay.
2. Lo, Je - sus meets thee, Ris - en from the tomb! Lov - ing - ly he greets thee, Scat-ters fear and gloom; Let his Church with glad - ness Hymns of tri - umph sing, For her Lord now liv - eth; Death hath lost its sting.
3. No more we doubt thee, Glo - rious Prince of Life; Life is nought with- out thee; Aid us in our strife; Make us more than con-querors, Through thy death - less love; Bring us safe through Jor - dan To thy home a - bove.
Refrain
Thine is the glo - ry, Ris - en, con-quering Son; End - less is the vic - tory Thou o'er death hast won. A-men.

Edmond Budry, 1854–1932 Tr. Richard Birch Hoyle, 1875–1939

Words from CANTATE DOMINO. *By permission of the World's Student Christian Federation*

LUTHER LEAGUE HYMN. Irregular. GEORGE C. F. HAAS, 1854–1927

With dignity

1. O Chris - tians, leagued to - geth - er To bat - tle for the right,
2. Then 'on - ward' be the war - cry; And on - ward still, so long

A - rise and don your ar - mor, Put the foe to flight!
As we have self to con - quer, Souls to cheer with song.

We've giv - en our al - le - giance To serve with - out sur - cease
Let sound the mar - tial mu - sic, Ring out the bu - gle call

The might - y Lord of ar - mies And gen - tle Prince of Peace
To ral - ly for the con - flict Our peo - ple one and all.

Refrain
All hail, our glo - rious Sav - iour! We march where thou hast trod,
rit.
To seek thy house of tri - umph, The cit - y of our God.

3 We proudly bear as banner
A cross within the heart,
To show that we have chosen
Christ, the better part.
Then joy and peace and comfort
Shall blossom as a rose,
Until our earthly blessings
The worth of heaven disclose.

Lillian Weaver Cassaday, 1861–1914
Refrain, Margaret Rebecca Seebach, 1875–1948

See also:

150 A mighty fortress is our God
68 Christian, dost thou [illegible]
310 Faith of our fathers
156 Fear not, thou faithful Christian
144 For all the saints
78 Go to dark Gethsemane
568 If thou but suffer God
531 Jesus, Saviour, pilot me
157 Lord of [illegible]
356 Mine eyes have seen
577 Nearer, my God, to thee
395 O for a faith that will not shrink
515 O Jesus, I have promised
547 Once to every man and nation
541 Rise up, O men of God
529 Through the night of doubt

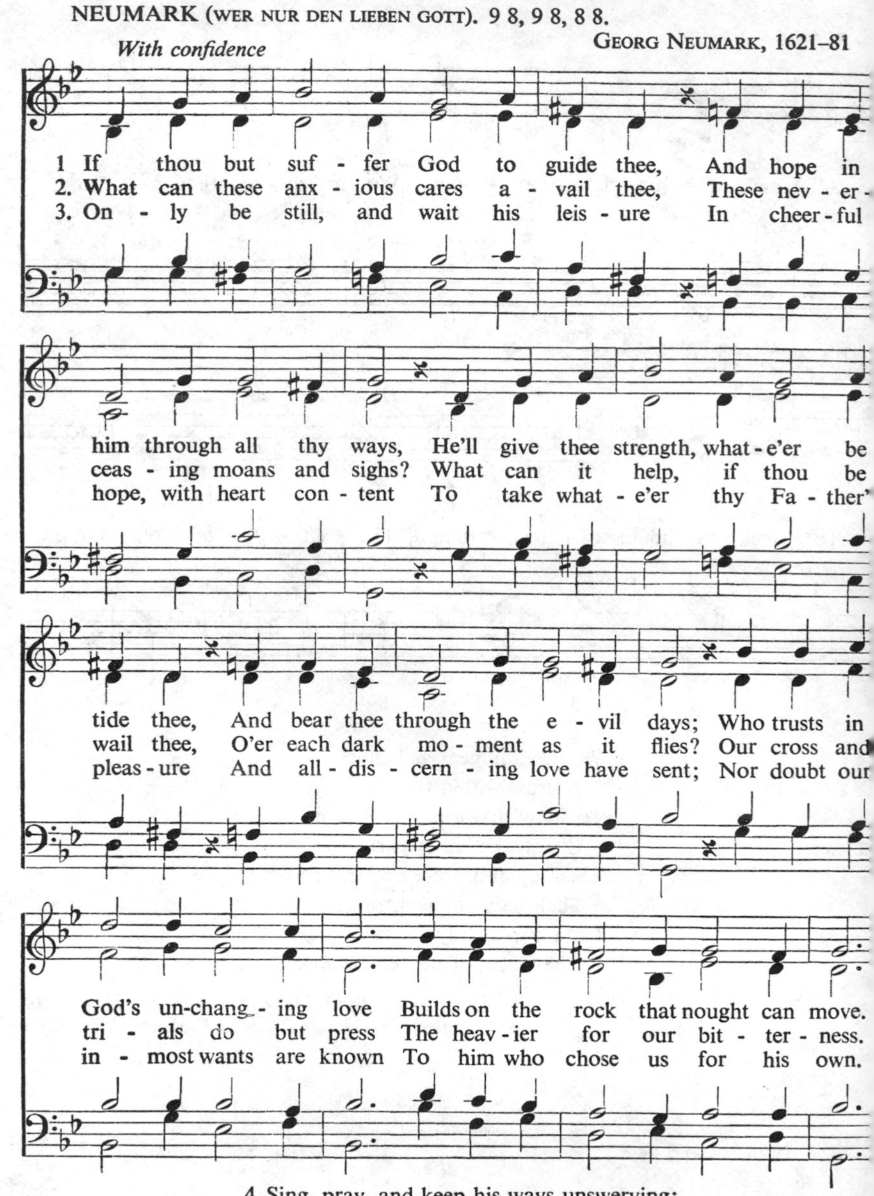
NEUMARK (WER NUR DEN LIEBEN GOTT). 9 8, 9 8, 8 8.
GEORG NEUMARK, 1621–81
With confidence
1 If thou but suf - fer God to guide thee, And hope in
2. What can these anx - ious cares a - vail thee, These nev - er-
3. On - ly be still, and wait his leis - ure In cheer-ful
him through all thy ways, He'll give thee strength, what - e'er be
ceas - ing moans and sighs? What can it help, if thou be
hope, with heart con - tent To take what - e'er thy Fa - ther'
tide thee, And bear thee through the e - vil days; Who trusts in
wail thee, O'er each dark mo - ment as it flies? Our cross and
pleas - ure And all - dis - cern - ing love have sent; Nor doubt our
God's un-chang - ing love Builds on the rock that nought can move.
tri - als do but press The heav - ier for our bit - ter - ness.
in - most wants are known To him who chose us for his own.

4 Sing, pray, and keep his ways unswerving;
In all thy labor faithful be,
And trust his word; though undeserving,
Thou yet shalt find it true for thee:
God never will forsake in need
The soul that trusts in him indeed.

Georg Neumark, 1621-
Tr. Catherine Winkworth, 1829-

CONSOLATION (ALMA REDEMPTORIS MATER). 11 10, 11 10.

SAMUEL WEBBE, 1740–1816

Devotionally

1. Come, ye dis - con - so - late, wher - e'er ye lan - guish;
2. Joy of the des - o - late, light of the stray - ing,
Come to the mer - cy - seat, fer - vent - ly kneel;
Hope of the pen - i - tent, fade - less and pure!
Here bring your wound - ed hearts, here tell your an - guish;
Here speaks the Com - fort - er, ten - der - ly say - ing,
Earth has no sor - row that heaven can - not heal.
'Earth has no sor - row that heaven can - not cure.'

3 Here see the Bread of Life; see waters flowing
Forth from the throne of God, pure from above;
Come to the feast of love; come, ever knowing
Earth has no sorrow but heaven can remove.

St. 1, 2, Thomas Moore, 1779–1852
St. 3, Thomas Hastings, 1784–1872

ORTONVILLE. C. M. THOMAS HASTINGS, 1784–1872

Slowly, with dignity

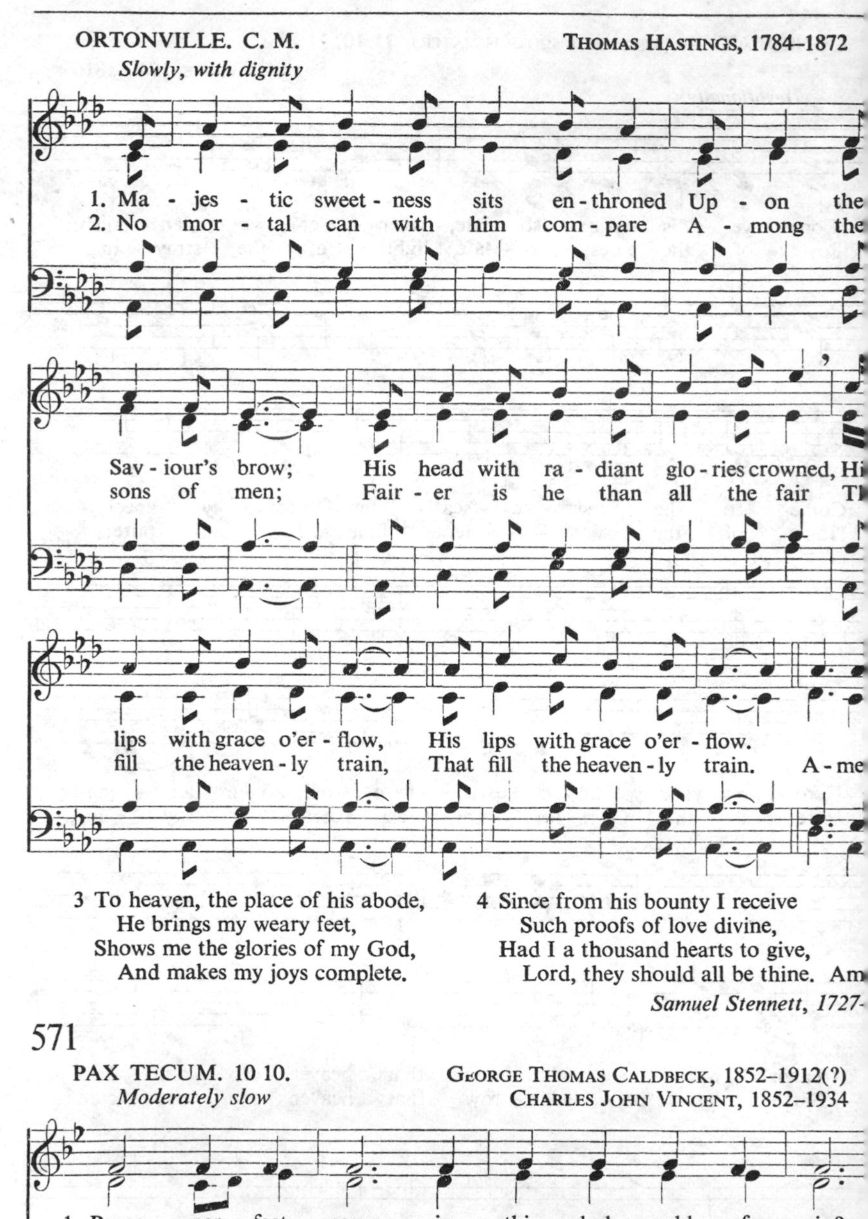
1. Ma - jes - tic sweet - ness sits en - throned Up - on the Sav - iour's brow; His head with ra - diant glo - ries crowned, Hi[s] lips with grace o'er - flow, His lips with grace o'er - flow.
2. No mor - tal can with him com - pare A - mong the sons of men; Fair - er is he than all the fair Th[at] fill the heaven - ly train, That fill the heaven - ly train. A - me[n]

3 To heaven, the place of his abode,
He brings my weary feet,
Shows me the glories of my God,
And makes my joys complete.

4 Since from his bounty I receive
Such proofs of love divine,
Had I a thousand hearts to give,
Lord, they should all be thine. Am[en]

Samuel Stennett, 1727-

571

PAX TECUM. 10 10. GEORGE THOMAS CALDBECK, 1852–1912(?)
CHARLES JOHN VINCENT, 1852–1934

Moderately slow

1. Peace, per - fect peace, in this dark world of sin?
2. Peace, per - fect peace, by throng - ing du - ties pressed?
3. Peace, per - fect peace, with sor - rows surg - ing round?

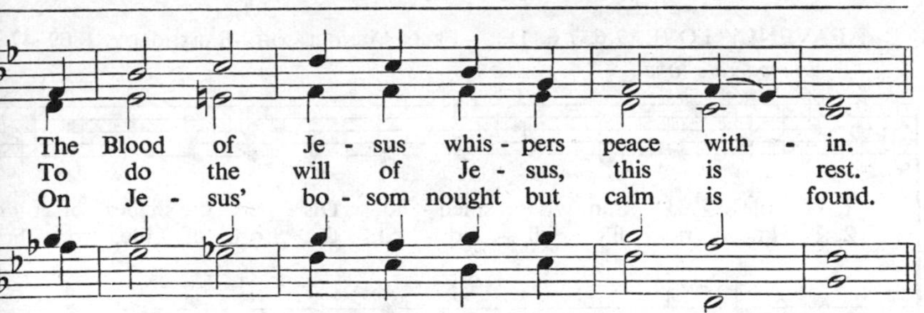
The Blood of Je - sus whis - pers peace with - in.
To do the will of Je - sus, this is rest.
On Je - sus' bo - som nought but calm is found.

4 Peace, perfect peace, with loved ones far away?
In Jesus' keeping we are safe, and they.

5 Peace, perfect peace, our future all unknown?
Jesus we know, and he is on the throne.

6 Peace, perfect peace, death shadowing us and ours?
Jesus has vanquished death and all its powers.

7 It is enough; earth's struggles soon shall cease,
And Jesus call us to heaven's perfect peace.

Edward Henry Bickersteth, 1825–1906

72

SANDELL (TRYGGARE KAN INGEN VARA). L. M. Swedish Melody

Simply

1. Chil-dren of the heaven-ly Fa - ther Safe - ly in his bos-om gath - er;
2. God his own doth tend and nour - ish, In his ho - ly courts they flour - ish.

Nest-ling bird nor star in heav - en Such a ref - uge e'er was giv - en.
From all e - vil things he spares them, In his might - y arms he bears them.

3 Neither life nor death shall ever
From the Lord his children sever;
Unto them his grace he showeth,
And their sorrows all he knoweth.

4 Though he giveth or he taketh,
God his children ne'er forsaketh,
His the loving purpose solely
To preserve them pure and holy.

Caroline V. Sandell Berg, 1832–1903
Tr. Ernst William Olson, 1870–1958

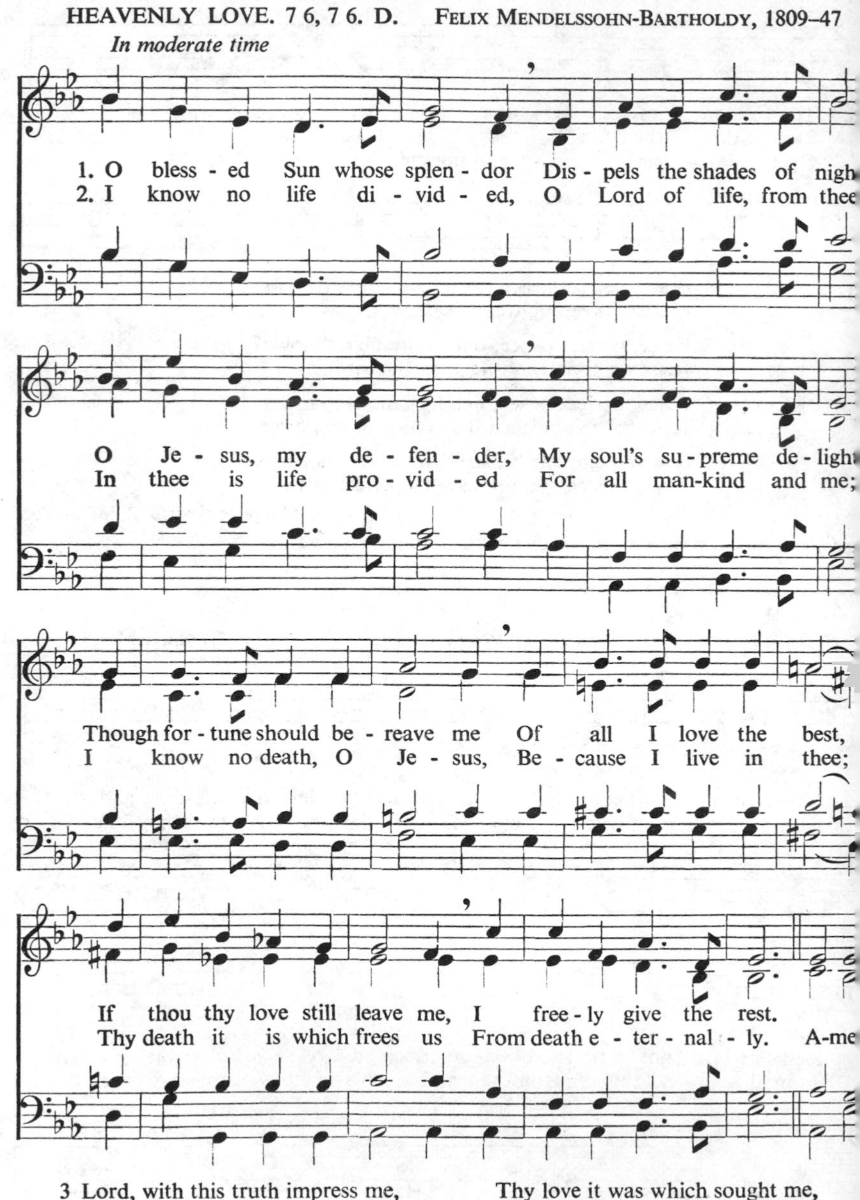
HEAVENLY LOVE. 7 6, 7 6. D.
FELIX MENDELSSOHN-BARTHOLDY, 1809–47
In moderate time
1. O bless - ed Sun whose splen - dor Dis - pels the shades of nigh
2. I know no life di - vid - ed, O Lord of life, from thee
O Je - sus, my de - fen - der, My soul's su - preme de - ligh
In thee is life pro - vid - ed For all man-kind and me;
Though for - tune should be - reave me Of all I love the best,
I know no death, O Je - sus, Be - cause I live in thee;
If thou thy love still leave me, I free - ly give the rest.
Thy death it is which frees us From death e - ter - nal - ly. A-me

3 Lord, with this truth impress me,
And write it on my heart,
To comfort, cheer and bless me,
That thou my Saviour art.

Thy love it was which sought me,
Thyself unsought by me,
And for thy ransom bought me
To live for aye in thee. Amen.

Karl Johann Philipp Spitta, 1801-
Tr. Richard Massie, 1800-

This hymn may also be sung to ST. CHRISTOPHER (No. 482)

NYLAND. 7 6, 7 6. D.
Finnish Melody
Harm. by DAVID EVANS, 1874–1948
With movement
1. In heaven-ly love a-bid-ing, No change my heart shall fear;
2. Wher-ev-er he may guide me, No want shall turn me back;
And safe is such con-fid-ing, For noth-ing chang-es here:
My Shep-herd is be-side me, And noth-ing can I lack.
The storm may roar with-out me, My heart may low be laid,
His wis-dom ev-er wak-eth, His sight is nev-er dim,
But God is round a-bout me, And can I be dis-mayed?
He knows the way he tak-eth, And I will walk with him.

3 Green pastures are before me,
  Which yet I have not seen;
Bright skies will soon be o'er me,
  Where darkest clouds have been.
My hope I cannot measure,
  The path to life is free;
My Saviour has my treasure,
  And he will walk with me.

Anna Laetitia Waring, 1820–1910

JESU, MEINE FREUDE. 6 6 5, 6 6 5, 7 8 6. JOHANN CRÜGER, 1598–1662

Devotionally FIRST TUNE

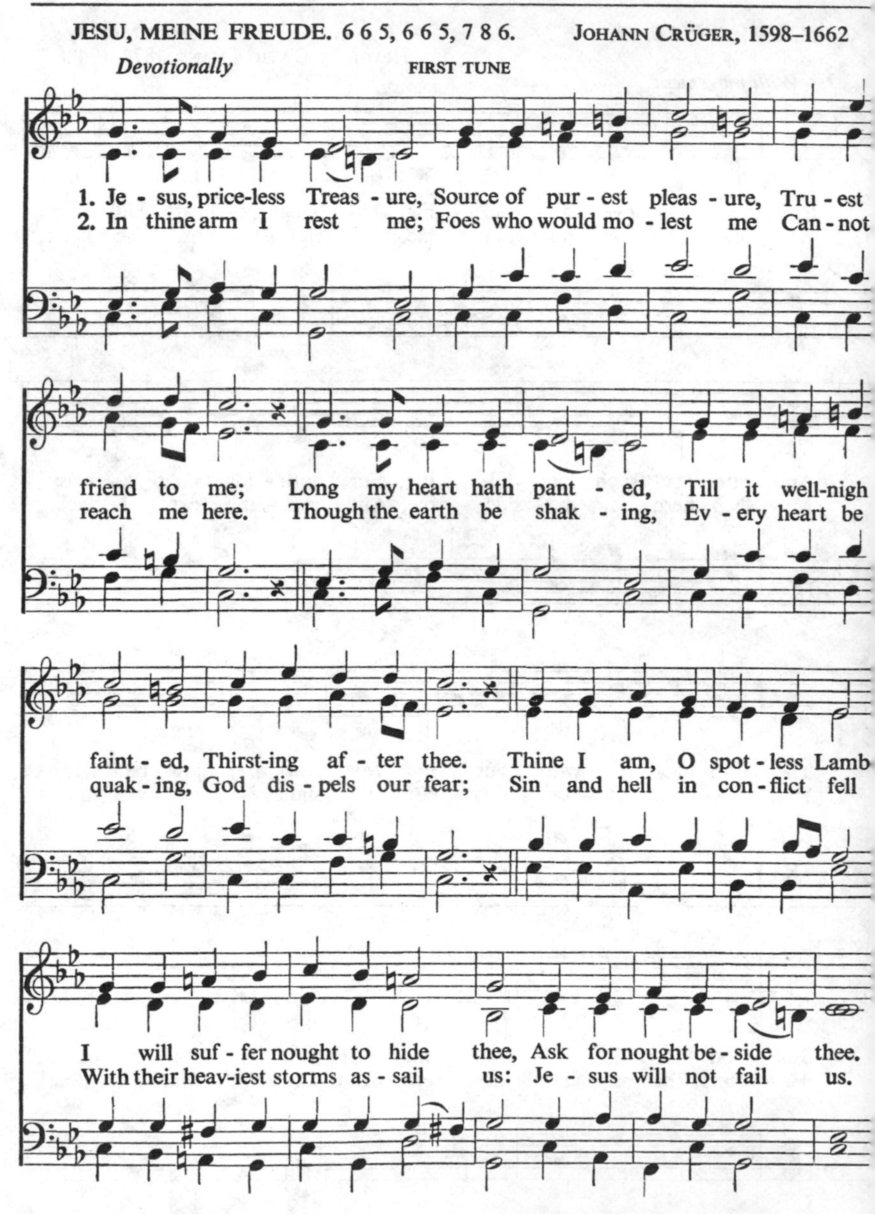
1. Je - sus, price-less Treas - ure, Source of pur - est pleas - ure, Tru - est friend to me; Long my heart hath pant - ed, Till it well-nigh faint - ed, Thirst-ing af - ter thee. Thine I am, O spot - less Lamb I will suf - fer nought to hide thee, Ask for nought be - side thee.
2. In thine arm I rest me; Foes who would mo - lest me Can - not reach me here. Though the earth be shak - ing, Ev - ery heart be quak - ing, God dis - pels our fear; Sin and hell in con - flict fell With their heav-iest storms as - sail us: Je - sus will not fail us.

3 Hence, all thoughts of sadness!
For the Lord of gladness,
Jesus, enters in;
Those who love the Father,
Though the storms may gather,
Still have peace within;
Yea, whate'er we here must bear,
Still in thee lies purest pleasure,
Jesus, priceless Treasure!

Johann Franck, 1618–7
Tr. Catherine Winkworth, 1829–7

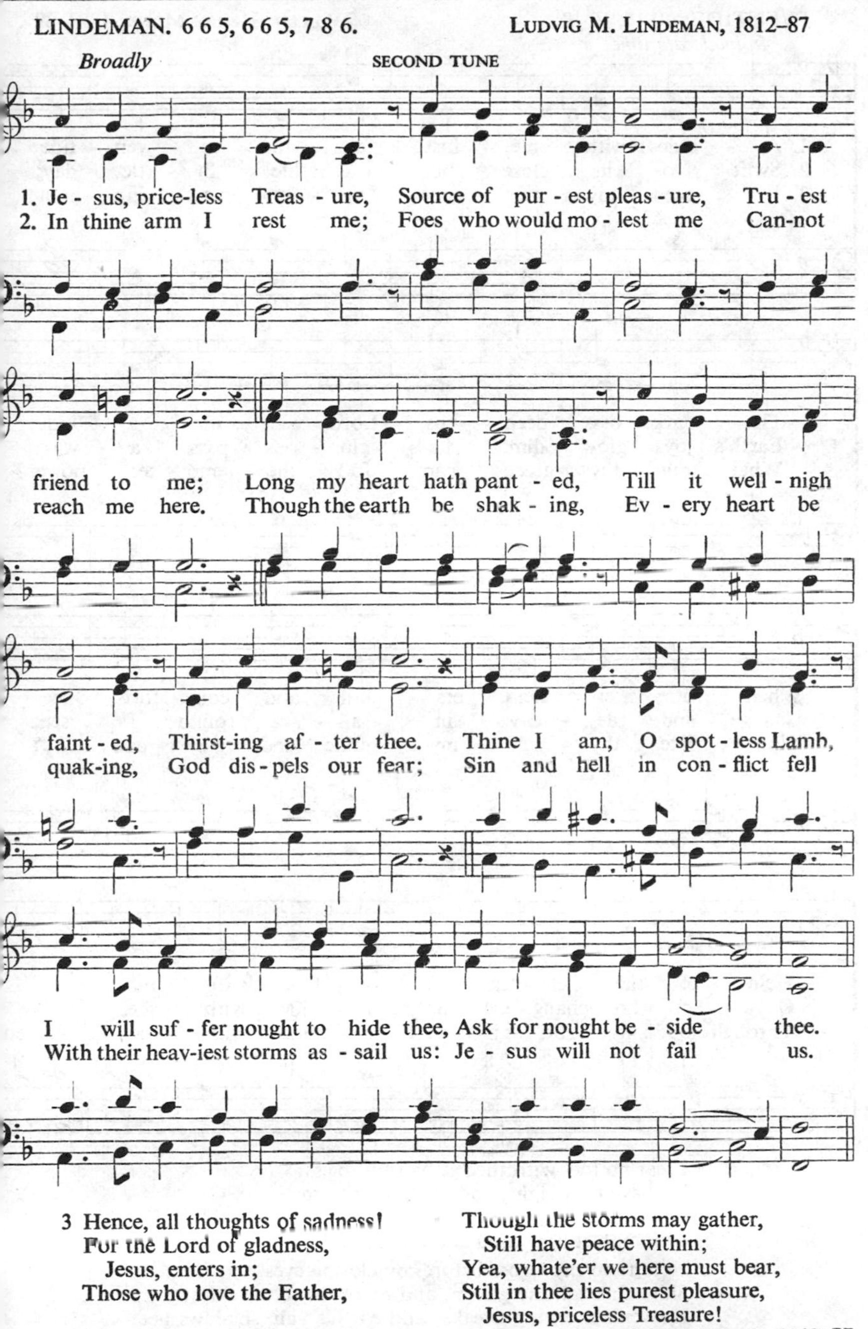
LINDEMAN. 6 6 5, 6 6 5, 7 8 6.
LUDVIG M. LINDEMAN, 1812–87
Broadly
SECOND TUNE
1. Je - sus, price-less Treas - ure, Source of pur - est pleas - ure, Tru - est
2. In thine arm I rest me; Foes who would mo - lest me Can-not
friend to me; Long my heart hath pant - ed, Till it well - nigh
reach me here. Though the earth be shak - ing, Ev - ery heart be
faint - ed, Thirst-ing af - ter thee. Thine I am, O spot - less Lamb,
quak-ing, God dis - pels our fear; Sin and hell in con - flict fell
I will suf - fer nought to hide thee, Ask for nought be - side thee.
With their heav-iest storms as - sail us: Je - sus will not fail us.

3 Hence, all thoughts of sadness!
For the Lord of gladness,
Jesus, enters in;
Those who love the Father,
Though the storms may gather,
Still have peace within;
Yea, whate'er we here must bear,
Still in thee lies purest pleasure,
Jesus, priceless Treasure!

Johann Franck, 1618–77
Tr. Catherine Winkworth, 1829–78

EVENTIDE. 10 10, 10 10.
WILLIAM HENRY MONK, 1823–89
In moderate time
1. A - bide with me, fast falls the e - ven - tide;
2. Swift to its close ebbs out life's lit - tle day;
3. I need thy pres - ence ev - ery pass - ing hour;
The dark - ness deep - ens, Lord, with me a - bide;
Earth's joys grow dim, its glo - ries pass a - way;
What but thy grace can foil the temp - ter's power?
When oth - er help - ers fail and com - forts flee,
Change and de - cay in all a - round I see;
Who like thy - self my guide and stay can be?
Help of the help - less, O a - bide with me.
O thou who chang - est not, a - bide with me.
Through cloud and sun - shine, O a - bide with me.
A-men

4 I fear no foe, with thee at hand to bless;
Ills have no weight, and tears no bitterness.
Where is death's sting? Where, grave, thy victory?
I triumph still, if thou abide with me!

5 Hold thou thy Cross before my closing eyes,
Shine through the gloom, and point me to the skies;
Heaven's morning breaks, and earth's vain shadows flee;
In life, in death, O Lord, abide with me. Amen.

Henry Francis Lyte, 1793–184

BETHANY. 6 4, 6 4, 6 6 6 4. LOWELL MASON, 1792–1872

Brightly
1. Near - er, my God, to thee, Near - er to thee,
2. Though like a wan - der - er, The sun gone down,
3. Then let my way ap - pear Steps un - to heaven;
E'en though it be a cross That rais - eth me,
Dark - ness be o - ver me, My rest a stone,
All that thou send - est me In mer - cy given;
Still all my song shall be, Near - er, my God, to thee,
Yet in my dreams I'd be Near - er, my God, to thee,
An - gels to beck - on me Near - er, my God, to thee,
Near - er, my God, to thee, Near - er to thee.
Near - er, my God, to thee, Near - er to thee.
Near - er, my God, to thee, Near - er to thee.

4 Then with my waking thoughts,
Bright with thy praise,
Out of my stony griefs
Bethel I'll raise;
So by my woes to be
Nearer, my God, to thee,
Nearer to thee.

5 Or, if on joyful wing
Cleaving the sky,
Sun, moon, and stars forgot,
Upward I fly;
Still all my song shall be,
Nearer, my God, to thee,
Nearer to thee.

Sarah Flower Adams, 1805–48

FOR YOU AND FOR ME. 11 7, 11 7. With Refrain.

Quietly WILL LAMARTINE THOMPSON, 1847–1909

1. Soft - ly and ten - der - ly Je - sus is call - ing,
2. Why should we tar - ry when Je - sus is plead - ing,
Call - ing for you and for me; Pa - tient - ly Je - sus is
Plead-ing for you and for me? Why should we lin - ger and
wait - ing and watch - ing, Watch - ing for you and for me.
heed not his mer - cies, Mer - cies for you and for me?
Refrain
Come home, come home, Ye who are wea - ry, come
Come home, Come home,
home; Ear - nest - ly, ten - der - ly, Je - sus

is call - ing, Call - ing, O sin - ner, come home!

3 O, for the wonderful love he has promised,
Promised for you and for me;
Though we have sinned, he has mercy and pardon,
Pardon for you and for me.

Will Lamartine Thompson, 1847–1909

79

NARENZA. S. M. J. LEISENTRIT, *Catholicum Hymnologium*, 1587

With dignity

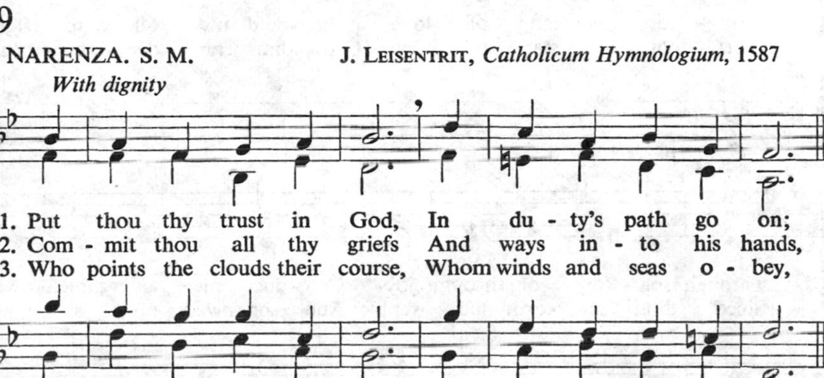
1. Put thou thy trust in God, In du - ty's path go on;
2. Com - mit thou all thy griefs And ways in - to his hands,
3. Who points the clouds their course, Whom winds and seas o - bey,

Walk in his strength with faith and hope, So shall thy work be done.
To his sure truth and ten - dcr care Who earth and heaven com-mands.
He shall di - rect thy wan-dering feet, He shall pre-pare thy way. A-men.

4 Leave to his sovereign sway
To choose and to command;
So shalt thou, wondering, own his way,
How wise, how strong his hand.

5 Thy everlasting truth,
Father, thy ceaseless love
Sees all thy children's wants, and knows
What best for each will prove.

6 Let us, in life, in death,
Thy steadfast truth declare,
And publish with our latest breath
Thy love and guardian care. Amen.

Paul Gerhardt, 1607–76
Tr. John Wesley, 1703–91

DENBY. 6 6, 6 6. D.
CHARLES J. DALE, 1904
Quietly
1. My Je - sus, as thou wilt, O may thy will be mine;
2. My Je - sus, as thou wilt, Though seen through man - y a tear,
In - to thy hand of love I would my all re - sign.
Let not my star of hope Grow dim or dis - ap - pear;
Through sor - row or through joy Con - duct me as thine own,
Since thou on earth hast wept And sor-rowed oft a - lone,
And help me still to say, 'My Lord, thy will be done!'
If I must weep with thee, My Lord, thy will be done! A-men

3 My Jesus, as thou wilt,
All shall be well for me;
Each changing future scene
I gladly trust with thee.
Straight to my home above
I travel calmly on,
And sing, in life or death,
'My Lord, thy will be done!' Amen.

Benjamin Schmolck, 1672–17
Tr. Jane Borthwick, 1813–

ANCIENT OF DAYS (ALBANY) 11 10, 11 10.

With dignity

JOHN ALBERT JEFFERY, 1855–1929

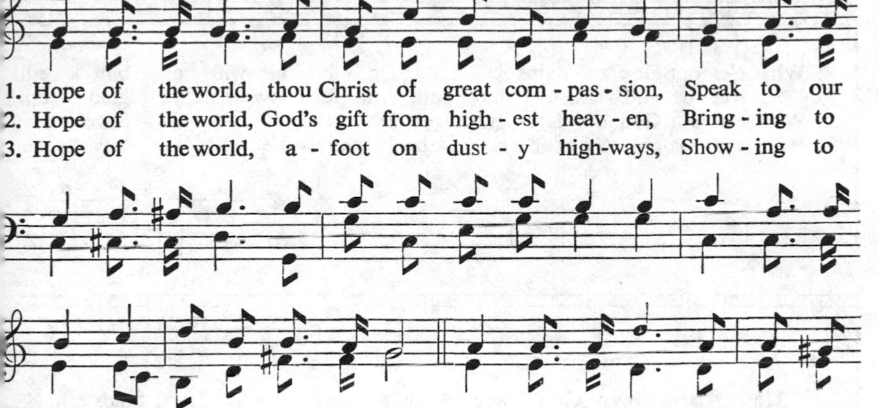
1. Hope of the world, thou Christ of great com - pas - sion, Speak to our
2. Hope of the world, God's gift from high - est heav - en, Bring - ing to
3. Hope of the world, a - foot on dust - y high-ways, Show - ing to

fear - ful hearts by con - flict rent. Save us, thy peo - ple, from con -
hun - gry souls the bread of life, Still let thy Spir - it un - to
wan - dering souls the path of light; Walk thou be - side us lest the

sum - ing pas - sion, Who by our own false hopes and aims are spent.
us be giv - en To heal earth's wounds and end her bit-ter strife.
tempt-ing by - ways Lure us a - way from thee to end - less night. A-men.

4 Hope of the world, who by thy Cross didst save us
From death and dark despair, from sin and guilt;
We render back the love thy mercy gave us;
Take thou our lives and use them as thou wilt.

5 Hope of the world, O Christ, o'er death victorious,
Who by this sign didst conquer grief and pain,
We would be faithful to thy Gospel glorious:
Thou art our Lord! Thou dost for ever reign! Amen.

Georgia Harkness, 1891–

WAS GOTT TUT. 8 7, 8 7, 4 4, 8 8. *Weimar Gesangbuch*, 1681

Confidently
1. What-e'er our God or - dains is right; Ho - ly his will a - bid - eth;
I will be still what - e'er he doth, And fol - low where he guid - eth.
2. What-e'er our God or - dains is right; He nev - er will de - ceive me;
He leads me by the prop - er path; I know he will not leave me,
He is my God; Though dark my road, He holds me
I take, con - tent, What he hath sent; His hand can
that I shall not fall; Where - fore to him I leave it all.
turn my griefs a - way, And pa - tient - ly I wait his day.

3 Whate'er our God ordains is right;
Though now this cup, in drinking,
May bitter seem to my faint heart,
I take it, all unshrinking;
Tears pass away
With dawn of day;
Sweet comfort yet shall fill my heart,
And pain and sorrow shall depart.

4 Whate'er our God ordains is right;
Here shall my stand be taken;
Though sorrow, need, or death be mine,
Yet am I not forsaken;
My Father's care
Is round me there;
He holds me that I shall not fall,
And so to him I leave it all.

Samuel Rodigast, 1649–170
Tr. Catherine Winkworth, 1829–7

See also:

192 Abide with us, our Saviour
482 Beneath the Cross of Jesus
121 Come, Holy Ghost, in love
478 He leadeth me: O blessèd thought
490 I look to thee in every need
146 In heaven above, in heaven above
64 In the Cross of Christ I glory
532 Jesus, still lead on
368 Lord, it belongs not to my care
402 O Love that wilt not let me go
456 One there is above all others
226 Sun of my soul, thou Saviour dear
526 The Lord my Shepherd is
522 The Lord's my Shepherd

583 Life Everlasting

SAWLEY. C. M.
JAMES WALCH, 1837-1901
Devotionally
1. There is a land of pure de - light,
2. There ev - er - last - ing spring a - bides,
3. Sweet fields be - yond the swell - ing flood
Where saints im - mor - tal reign; In - fi - nite day ex -
And nev - er - with - ering flowers; Death, like a nar - row
Stand dressed in liv - ing green; So to the Jews old
cludes the night, And pleas - ures ban - ish pain.
sea, di - vides This heaven - ly land from ours.
Ca - naan stood While Jor - dan rolled be - tween.

4 But timorous mortals start and shrink
To cross this narrow sea,
And linger, shivering on the brink,
And fear to launch away.

5 O could we make our doubts remove,
Those gloomy doubts that rise,
And see the Canaan that we love
With unbeclouded eyes;

6 Could we but climb where Moses stood,
And view the landscape o'er,
Not Jordan's stream, nor death's cold flood
Should fright us from the shore!

Isaac Watts, 1674–1748

EWING. 7 6, 7 6. D. ALEXANDER EWING, 1830–95

With dignity
1. Je - ru - sa - lem the gold - en, With milk and hon - ey blest,
2. They stand, those halls of Si - on, All ju - bi - lant with song,
Be - neath thy con - tem - pla - tion Sink heart and voice op - pressed;
And bright with man - y an an - gel, And all the mar - tyr throng;
I know not, O I know not What joys a - wait us there,
The Prince is ev - er in them, The day - light is se - rene;
What ra - dian - cy of glo - ry, What bliss be - yond com-pare.
The pas - tures of the bless - ed Are decked in glo-rious sheen. A-men.

3 There is the throne of David,
  And there, from care released,
The shout of them that triumph,
  The song of them that feast;
And they, who with their Leader
  Have conquered in the fight,
For ever and for ever
  Are clad in robes of white.

4 O sweet and blessèd country,
  The home of God's elect!
O sweet and blessèd country,
  That eager hearts expect!
Jesus, in mercy bring us
  To that dear land of rest,
Who art, with God the Father
  And Spirit, ever blest. Amen.

Bernard of Cluny, XII cent
Tr. John Mason Neale, 1818–66

ST. ANSELM. 7 6, 7 6. D.
JOSEPH BARNBY, 1838–96
Devotionally
1. Thy word, O God, de - clar - eth No man hath seen or heard
2. With thee, their war - fare end - ed, Thy saints, from earth re-leased,
The joys our God pre - par - eth For them that love their Lord.
Shall keep, with glo - ries splen - did, E - ter - nal ho - ly feast.
Their eyes shall see thy glo - ry, Thy face, thy throne, thy might;
There shall thy sons and daugh - ters The tree of life par - take,
With shouts shall they a - dore thee, The true, e - ter - nal Light.
Shall drink the liv - ing wa - ters, And bread with thee shall break. A-men.

3 Thy constant praises sounding
Before thy great white throne,
They all in joy abounding
Shall sing the song unknown:
Laud, honor, praise, thanksgiving
And glory ever be
To thee, the everlasting
And blessèd Trinity. Amen.

Johann Walther, 1496–1570
Tr. Alfred Ramsey, 1860–1926

OSLO. 7 6, 7 6. D. **Scandinavian Folksong**

In moderate time. May be sung in unison

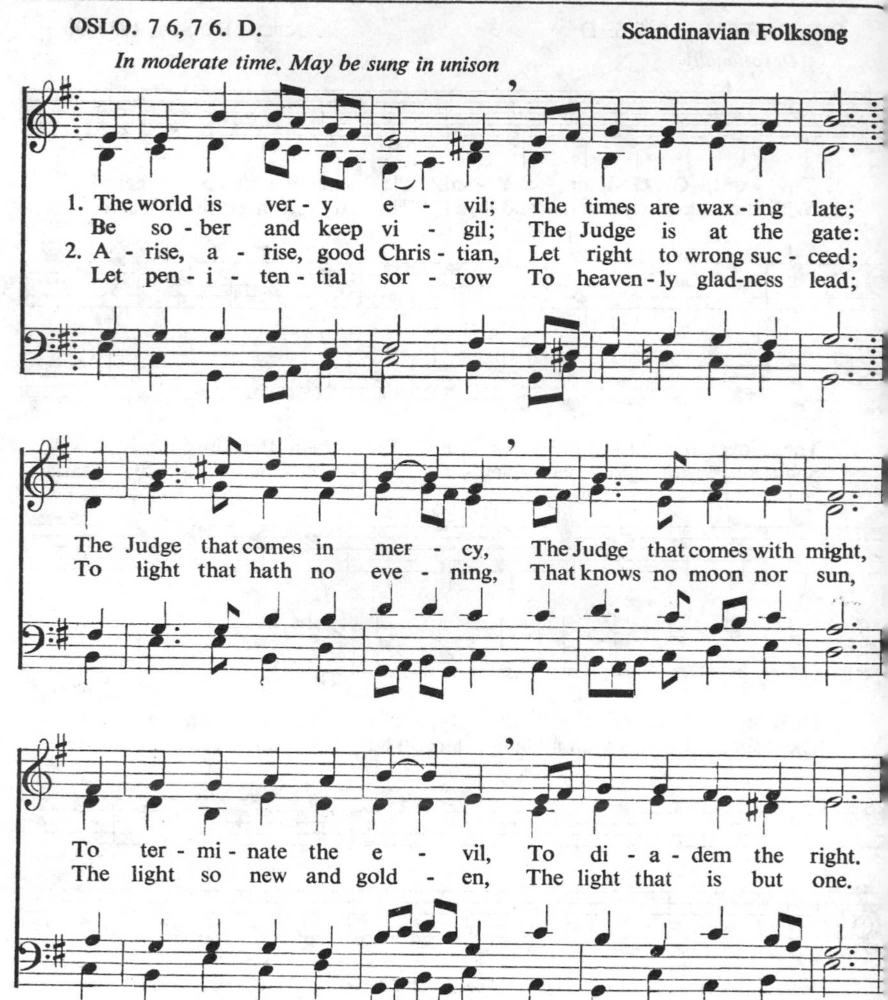
1. The world is very evil; The times are waxing late;
Be sober and keep vigil; The Judge is at the gate:
2. Arise, arise, good Christian, Let right to wrong succeed;
Let penitential sorrow To heavenly gladness lead;
The Judge that comes in mercy, The Judge that comes with might,
To light that hath no evening, That knows no moon nor sun,
To terminate the evil, To diadem the right.
The light so new and golden, The light that is but one.

3 The home of fadeless splendor,
Of flowers that fear no thorn,
Where they shall dwell as children
Who here as exiles mourn;
The peace of all the faithful,
The calm of all the blest,
Inviolate, unvaried,
Divinest, sweetest, best.

4 O happy, holy portion,
Refection for the blest,
True vision of true beauty,
Sweet cure of all distrest!
Strive, man, to win that glory;
Toil, man, to gain that light;
Send hope before to grasp it,
Till hope be lost in sight.

Bernard of Cluny, XII cent.
Tr. John Mason Neale, 1818–66

Harmony from ENLARGED SONGS OF PRAISE *by permission of the Oxford University Press*

This hymn may also be sung to ST. ALPHEGE (No. 527)

587

LAND OF REST. C. M. — Traditional American Melody
Harm. by ANNABEL MORRIS BUCHANAN, 1888–

Quietly, with movement — FIRST TUNE

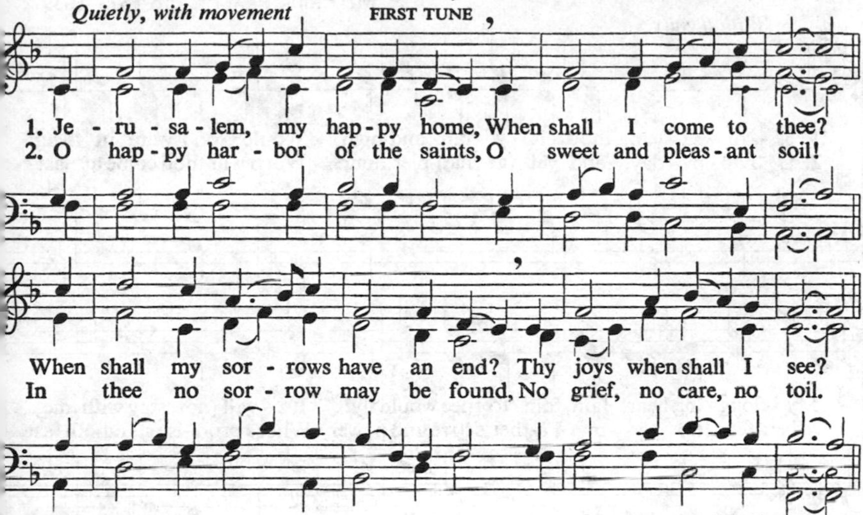

1. Je - ru - sa - lem, my hap - py home, When shall I come to thee?
When shall my sor - rows have an end? Thy joys when shall I see?

2. O hap - py har - bor of the saints, O sweet and pleas - ant soil!
In thee no sor - row may be found, No grief, no care, no toil.

3 Thy gardens and thy gallant walks
Continually are green;
There grow such sweet and pleasant flowers
As nowhere else are seen.

4 Quite through the streets with silver sound
The flood of life doth flow,
Upon whose banks on every side
The wood of life doth grow.

5 There trees for evermore bear fruit,
And evermore do spring;
There evermore the angels sit,
And evermore do sing.

6 Jerusalem, my happy home,
Would God I were in thee!
Would God my woes were at an end,
Thy joys that I might see!

Based on St. Augustine. F. B. P., cir. XVI cent.

587

SOUTHWELL (IRONS). C. M. — HERBERT STEPHEN IRONS, 1834–1905

SECOND TUNE

Slowly, with dignity
1. Je - ru - sa - lem, my hap - py home, When shall I come to thee?
2. O hap - py har - bor of the saints, O sweet and pleas-ant soil!
When shall my sor-rows have an end? Thy joys when shall I see?
In thee no sor - row may be found, No grief, no care, no toil.

JERUSALEM, DU HOCHGEBAUTE STADT. 10 6, 10 6, 7 6, 7 6.
MELCHIOR FRANCK, cir. 1573–1639
With dignity
1. Je - ru - sa - lem, thou cit - y fair and high, Would God I were in thee!
2. O hap - py day, and yet far hap-pier hour, When wilt thou come at last?
My long - ing heart fain, fain to thee would fly! It will not stay with me;
When fear-less to my Fa-ther's love and power, Whose prom-ise stand-eth fast,
Far o - ver vale and moun - tain, Far o - ver field and plain,
My soul I glad - ly ren - der; For sure - ly will his hand
It hastes to seek its foun - tain And quit this world of pain.
Lead her, with guid - ance ten - der, To heaven her fa - ther - land.

3 Saints robed in white before the shining throne
Their joyful anthems raise,
Till heaven's glad halls are echoing with the tone
Of that great hymn of praise,
And all its host rejoices,
And all its blessèd throng
Unite their myriad voices
In one eternal song.

Johann Matthäus Meyfart, 1590–164
Tr. Catherine Winkworth, 1829–7

PARADISE. 8 6, 8 6, 6 6, 6 6.
JOSEPH BARNBY, 1838–96
In moderate time
1. O Par - a - dise, O Par - a - dise, Who doth not crave for rest?
2. O Par - a - dise, O Par - a - dise, The world is grow - ing old;
3. O Par - a - dise, O Par - a - dise, We long to sin no more;
Who would not seek the hap - py land Where they that loved are blest:
Who would not be at rest and free Where love is nev - er cold?
We long to be as pure on earth As on thy spot - less shore:
Refrain in unison
Where loy - al hearts and true - - - Stand ev - er in the light,
All rap-ture, through and through, In God's most ho - ly sight. A-men.

4 O Paradise, O Paradise,
We shall not wait for long;
E'en now the loving ear may catch
Faint fragments of thy song:

5 Lord Jesus, King of Paradise,
O keep us in thy love,
And guide us to that happy land
Of perfect rest above:

Frederick William Faber, 1814–63

CARLISLE. S. M. CHARLES LOCKHART, 1745–1815

Quietly
1. For ev - er with the Lord! A - men, so let it be; Life from the dead is in that word, 'Tis im - mor - tal - i - ty.
2. Here in the bod - y pent, Ab - sent from him I roam, Yet night - ly pitch my mov - ing tent A day's march near - er home.
3. My Fa - ther's house on high, Home of my soul, how near At times to faith's fore - see - ing eye Thy gold - en gates ap - pear!

4 Ah, then my spirit faints
To reach the land I love,
The bright inheritance of saints,
Jerusalem above!

5 For ever with the Lord!
Father, if 'tis thy will,
The promise of that faithful word
E'en here to me fulfill.

6 Be thou at my right hand,
Then can I never fail;
Uphold thou me, and I shall stand;
Fight, and I must prevail.

7 So when my latest breath
Shall rend the veil in twain,
By death I shall escape from death,
And life eternal gain.

8 Knowing as I am known,
How shall I love that word,
And oft repeat before the throne,
'For ever with the Lord!'

James Montgomery, 1771–1854

This hymn may also be sung to KANE (No. 165)

TANTUM ERGO (DULCE CARMEN). 8 7, 8 7, 8 7.

Essay on the Church Plain Chant, 1782

With dignity
1. Light's a - bode, ce - les - tial Sa - lem, Vi - sion whence true
2. There for ev - er and for ev - er Al - le - lu - ia
3. There no cloud nor pass - ing va - por Dims the bright - ness
peace doth spring, Bright - er than the heart can fan - cy,
is out - poured; For un - end - ing, for un - bro - ken,
of the air; End - less noon - day, glo - rious noon - day,
Man - sion of the high - est King; O how glo - rious
Is the feast - day of the Lord; All is pure and
From the Sun of suns is there; There no night brings
are the prais - es Which of thee the proph - ets sing!
all is ho - ly That with - in thy walls is stored.
rest from la - bor, For un - known are toil and care. A-men.

4 Now with gladness, now with courage,
  Bear the burden on thee laid,
That hereafter these thy labors
  May with endless gifts be paid,
And in everlasting glory
  Thou with brightness be arrayed.

5 Laud and honor to the Father,
  Laud and honor to the Son,
Laud and honor to the Spirit,
  Ever Three and ever One,
Consubstantial, co-eternal,
  While unending ages run. Amen.

Ascribed to Thomas à Kempis, 1379–1471
Tr. John Mason Neale, 1818–66

This hymn may also be sung to REGENT SQUARE (No. 242)

EDENGROVE. 8 6, 7 6, 7 6, 7 6. SAMUEL SMITH, 1821–1917

Cheerfully
1. There's a Friend for lit - tle chil-dren A - bove the bright blue sky,
2. There's a rest for lit - tle chil-dren A - bove the bright blue sky,
A Friend who nev - er chang - es, Whose love will nev - er die;
Who love the bless - ed Sav - iour, And to the Fa - ther cry;
Our earth - ly friends may fail us And change with chang-ing years,
A rest from ev - ery trou - ble, From sin and dan - ger free,
This Friend is al - ways wor - thy Of that dear Name he bears.
Where ev - ery lit - tle pil - grim Shall rest e - ter - nal - ly.

3 There's a home for little children
Above the bright blue sky,
Where Jesus reigns in glory,
A home of peace and joy;
No home on earth is like it,
Nor can with it compare;
For every one is happy,
Nor could be happier there.

4 There's a crown for little children
Above the bright blue sky,
And all who look to Jesus
Shall wear it by and by;
A crown of brightest glory,
Which he will then bestow
On those who found his favor,
And loved his Name below.

Albert Midlane, 1825–190

OUR CHRIST. C. M. OSCAR RUDOLPH OVERBY, 1892–

FIRST TUNE

In moderate time

1. I know not what the fu - ture hath
2. I know not where his is - lands lift
3. And so be - side the si - lent sea
Of mar - vel or sur - prise, As - sured a -
Their frond - ed palms in air; I on - ly
I wait the muf - fled oar; No harm from
lone that life and death His mer - cy un - der - lies.
know I can - not drift Be - yond his love and care.
him can come to me On o - cean or on shore.

4 And thou, O Lord, by whom are seen
Thy creatures as they be,
Forgive me if too close I lean
My human heart on thee.

5 And if my heart and flesh are weak
To bear an untried pain,
The bruisèd reed thou wilt not break,
But strengthen and sustain.

John Greenleaf Whittier, 1807–92 a.

DALEHURST. C. M. ARTHUR COTTMAN, 1842–79

SECOND TUNE

In moderate time

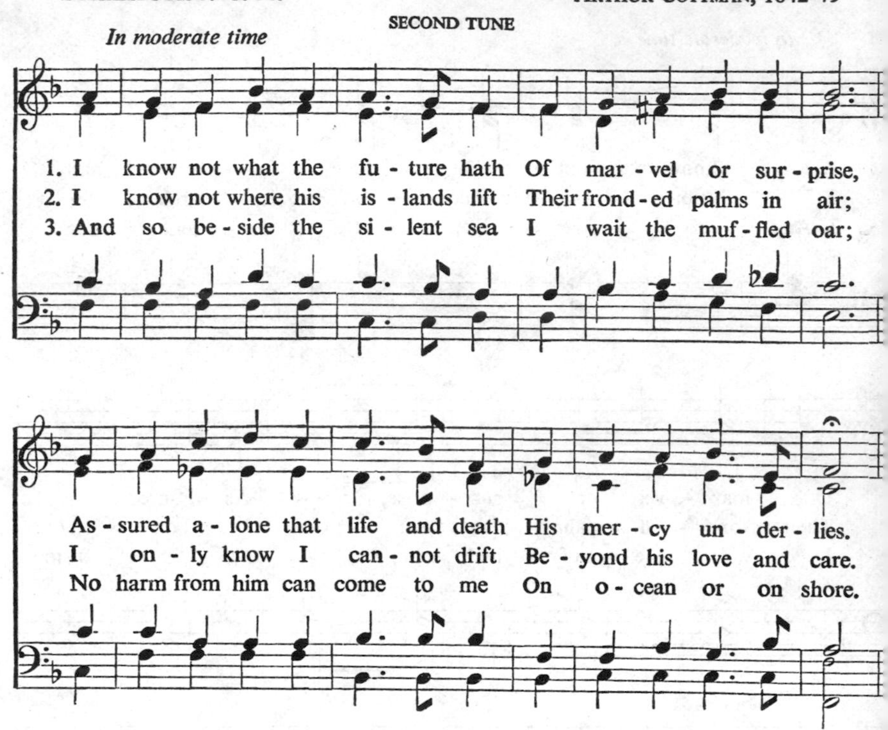
1. I know not what the fu - ture hath Of mar - vel or sur - prise,
2. I know not where his is - lands lift Their frond - ed palms in air;
3. And so be - side the si - lent sea I wait the muf - fled oar;
As - sured a - lone that life and death His mer - cy un - der - lies.
I on - ly know I can - not drift Be - yond his love and care.
No harm from him can come to me On o - cean or on shore.

4 And thou, O Lord, by whom are seen
Thy creatures as they be,
Forgive me if too close I lean
My human heart on thee.

5 And if my heart and flesh are weak
To bear an untried pain,
The bruisèd reed thou wilt not break,
But strengthen and sustain.

John Greenleaf Whittier, 1807–92 a.

See also:

599 Behold a host like mountains
295 Beyond the everlasting hills
245 Blessèd city, heavenly Salem
527 Brief life is here our portion
572 Children of the heavenly Father
297 Despair not, O heart, in thy sorrow
534 For thee, O dear, dear country
598 For those we love within the veil
594 Give me the wings of faith
143 Hark! the sound of holy voices
597 I heard a sound of voices
146 In heaven above, in heaven above
532 Jesus, still lead on
368 Lord, it belongs not to my care
176 O God, the Rock of Ages
197 O happy day when we shall stand
600 O Lord of life, where'er they be
116 To realms of glory in the skies

594

BALLERMA. C. M.
Adapted by ROBERT SIMPSON, 1790–1832
In moderate time
1. Give me the wings of faith to rise With - in the veil, and see The saints a - bove, how great their joys, How bright their glo - ries be.
2. Once they were mourn - ing here be - low, And wet their couch with tears; They wres - tled hard, as we do now, With sins and doubts and fears.

3 I ask them whence their victory came;
They, with united breath,
Ascribe their conquest to the Lamb,
Their triumph to his death.

4 They marked the footsteps that he trod,
His zeal inspired their breast,
And, following their incarnate God,
Possess the promised rest.

5 Our glorious Leader claims our praise
For his own pattern given,
While the long cloud of witnesses
Show the same path to heaven.

Isaac Watts, 1674–1748

This hymn may also be sung to BEATITUDO (No. 390)

KOMM, SEELE. 7 6, 8 6. D. JOHANN WOLFGANG FRANCK, 1641–88

In moderate time FIRST TUNE

1. Ten thou-sand times ten thou - sand In spark - ling rai - ment bright,
2. What rush of al - le - lu - ias Fills all the earth and sky;
The ar - mies of the ran-somed saints Throng up the steeps of light;
What ring - ing of a thou-sand harps Be - speaks the tri - umph high;
'Tis fin - ished, all is fin - ished, Their fight with death and sin;
O day, for which cre - a - tion And all its tribes were made;
Fling o - pen wide the gold-en gates, And let the vic - tors in!
O joy, for all its form-er woes A thou-sand-fold re - paid! A-men.

3 O then what raptured greetings
  On Canaan's happy shore,
What knitting severed friendships up,
  Where partings are no more!
Then eyes with joy shall sparkle
  That brimmed with tears of late;
Orphans no longer fatherless,
  Nor widows desolate.

4 Bring near thy great salvation,
  Thou Lamb for sinners slain;
Fill up the roll of thine elect,
  Then take thy power and reign;
Appear, Desire of Nations,
  Thine exiles long for home;
Show in the heavens thy promised sign,
  Thou Prince and Saviour, come! Amen.

Henry Alford, 1810–71

ALFORD. 7 6, 8 6. D. JOHN BACCHUS DYKES, 1823–76

With spirit, in moderate time
SECOND TUNE
1. Ten thou - sand times ten thou-sand In spark-ling rai - ment bright,
2. What rush of al - le - lu - ias Fills all the earth and sky;
The ar - mies of the ran-somed saints Throng up the steeps of light;
What ring - ing of a thou-sand harps Be - speaks the tri - umph high;
'Tis fin - ished, all is fin - ished, Their fight with death and sin;
O day, for which cre - a - tion And all its tribes were made;
Fling o - pen wide the gold - en gates, And let the vic - tors in!
O joy, for all its form - er woes A thou-sand-fold re - paid! A-men.

3 O then what raptured greetings
  On Canaan's happy shore,
What knitting severed friendships up,
  Where partings are no more!
Then eyes with joy shall sparkle
  That brimmed with tears of late;
Orphans no longer fatherless,
  Nor widows desolate.

4 Bring near thy great salvation,
  Thou Lamb for sinners slain;
Fill up the roll of thine elect,
  Then take thy power and reign;
Appear, Desire of Nations,
  Thine exiles long for home;
Show in the heavens thy promised sign,
  Thou Prince and Saviour, come! Amen.

Henry Alford, 1810–71

QUEDLINBURG. 10 10, 10 10. From a Chorale by J. C. Kittel, 1732–1809

In moderate time FIRST TUNE

1. O what their joy and their glo - ry must be,
2. Tru - ly Je - ru - sa - lem name we that shore,
3. We, where no trou - ble dis - trac - tion can bring,
Those end - less Sab - baths the bless - ed ones see!
Vi - sion of peace, that brings joy ev - er - more;
Safe - ly the an - thems of Si - on shall sing;
Crown for the val - iant, to wea - ry ones rest;
Wish and ful - fil - ment can sev - ered be ne'er,
While for thy grace, Lord, their voic - es of praise
God shall be all, and in all ev - er blest.
Nor the thing prayed for come short of the prayer.
Thy bless - ed peo - ple shall ev - er - more raise. A - men.

4 Low before him with our praises we fall,
Of whom, and in whom, and through whom are all;
Of whom, the Father; and in whom, the Son;
Through whom, the Spirit, with them ever One. Amen.

Peter Abelard, 1079–11
Tr. John Mason Neale, 1818–

O QUANTA QUALIA (REGNATOR ORBIS). 10 10, 10 10. Dactylic.
La Feillée's Méthode du Plain-Chant, 1808
Broadly, with dignity
SECOND TUNE
1. O what their joy and their glo - ry must be,
2. Tru - ly Je - ru - sa - lem name we that shore,
3. We, where no trou - ble dis - trac - tion can bring,
Those end - less Sab - baths the bless - ed ones see!
Vi - sion of peace, that brings joy ev - er - more;
Safe - ly the an - thems of Si - on shall sing;
Crown for the val - iant, to wea - ry ones rest;
Wish and ful - fil - ment can sev - ered be ne'er,
While for thy grace, Lord, their voic - es of praise
God shall be all, and in all ev - er blest.
Nor the thing prayed for come short of the prayer.
Thy bless - ed peo - ple shall ev - er - more raise.
A-men.

4 Low before him with our praises we fall,
Of whom, and in whom, and through whom are all;
Of whom, the Father; and in whom, the Son;
Through whom, the Spirit, with them ever One. Amen.

Peter Abelard, 1079–1142. Tr. John Mason Neale, 1818–66

PATMOS. 7 6, 8 6. D. HENRY JOHNSON STORER, 1860–1935

Broadly, with dignity

1. I heard a sound of voic - es A - round the great white throne,
2. From ev - ery clime and kin - dred, And na - tions from a - far,
With harp - ers harp - ing on their harps To him that sat there - on:
As ser - ried ranks re - turn - ing home In tri - umph from a war,
'Sal - va - tion, glo - ry, hon - or!' I heard the song a - rise,
I heard the saints up - rais - ing, The myr - iad hosts a - mong,
As through the courts of heaven it rolled In won - drous har - mo - nies.
In praise of him who died and lives, Their one glad tri - umph song. A-men

3 I saw the holy city,
The New Jerusalem,
Come down from heaven, a bride adorned
With jeweled diadem;
The flood of crystal waters
Flowed down the golden street;
And nations brought their honors there,
And laid them at her feet.

4 And there no sun was needed,
Nor moon to shine by night,
God's glory did enlighten all,
The Lamb himself the light;
And there his servants serve him,
And, life's long battle o'er,
Enthroned with him, their Saviour King,
They reign for evermore.

5 O great and glorious vision,
The Lamb upon his throne!
O wondrous sight for man to see!
The Saviour with his own:
To drink the living waters
And stand upon the shore,
Where neither sorrow, sin, nor death
Shall ever enter more.

6 O Lamb of God who reignest,
Thou bright and morning Star!
Whose glory lightens that new earth
Which now we see from far;
O worthy Judge eternal,
When thou dost bid us come,
Then open wide the gates of pearl
And call thy servants home. Amen.

Godfrey Thring, 1823–1903

98

MEYER (ES IST KEIN TAG). 8 8 8, 4. JOHANN DAVID MEYER'S *Seelenfreund*, 1692

Moderately slow

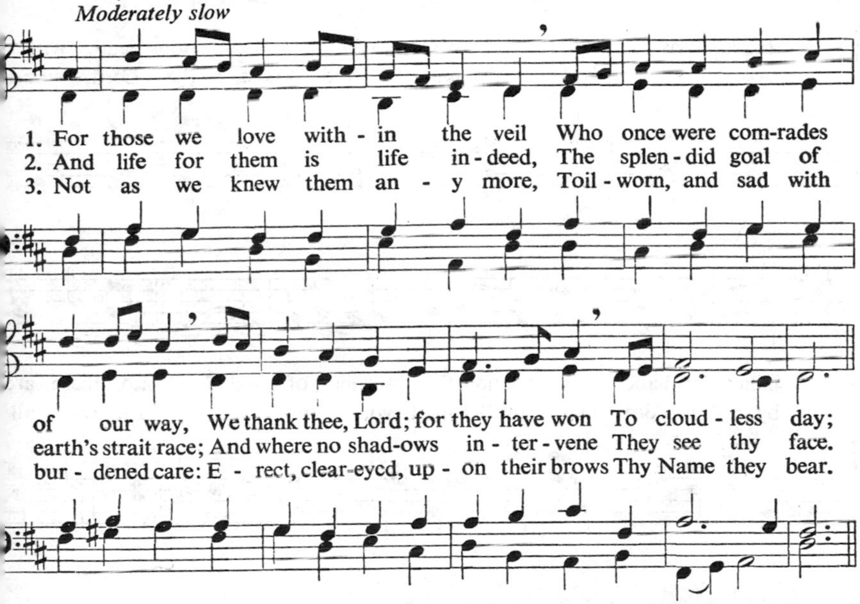

1. For those we love with - in the veil Who once were com-rades
2. And life for them is life in-deed, The splen-did goal of
3. Not as we knew them an - y more, Toil-worn, and sad with

of our way, We thank thee, Lord; for they have won To cloud - less day;
earth's strait race; And where no shad-ows in - ter - vene They see thy face.
bur - dened care: E - rect, clear-eyed, up - on their brows Thy Name they bear.

4 Free from the fret of mortal years,
And knowing now thy perfect will,
With quickened sense and heightened joy,
They serve thee still.

5 O fuller, sweeter is that life,
And larger, ampler is the air;
Eye cannot see nor heart conceive
The glory there;

6 Nor know to what high purpose thou
Dost yet employ their ripened powers,
Nor how at thy behest they touch
This life of ours.

7 There are no tears within their eyes;
With love they keep perpetual tryst;
And praise and work and rest are one,
With thee, O Christ.

William Charter Piggott, 1872–1943

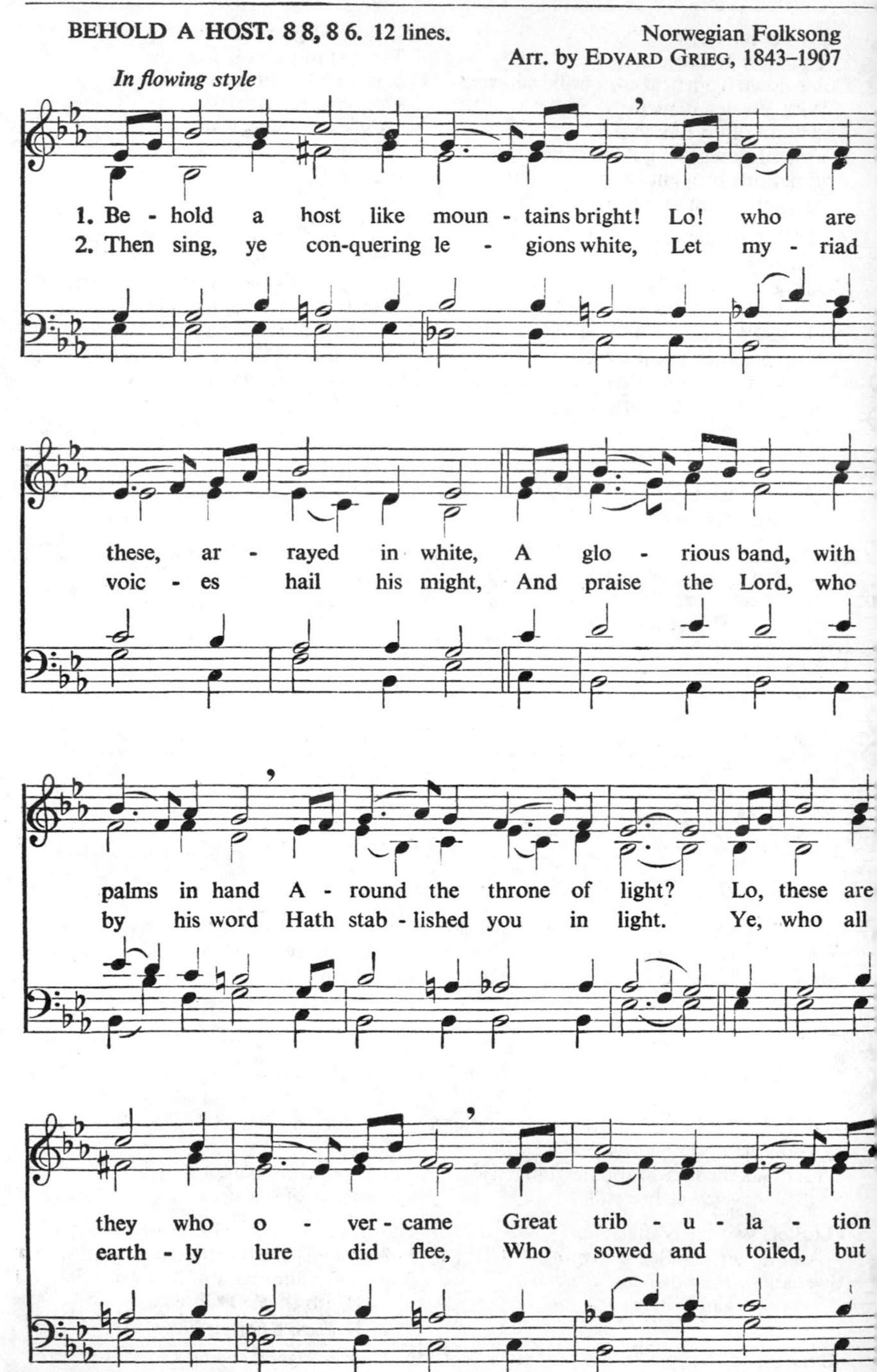
BEHOLD A HOST. 8 8, 8 6. 12 lines.
Norwegian Folksong
Arr. by EDVARD GRIEG, 1843–1907
In flowing style
1. Be - hold a host like moun - tains bright! Lo! who are these, ar - rayed in white, A glo - rious band, with palms in hand A - round the throne of light? Lo, these are they who o - ver - came Great trib - u - la - tion
2. Then sing, ye con-quering le - gions white, Let my - riad voic - es hail his might, And praise the Lord, who by his word Hath stab - lished you in light. Ye, who all earth - ly lure did flee, Who sowed and toiled, but

Commemoration

in his Name, And with his Blood the Lamb of God
tears to see, With rap - ture bring your sheaves and sing
Hath washed a - way their shame. Be - fore God's face they
A heaven - ly mel - o - dy. Lift up your palms, your
sing and pray, Their voic - es blend with an - gels' lay, And
voic - es raise Through heav - en's vault and end - less days. To
all con-spire, a joy - ous choir, To laud him night and day.
God and to the Lamb is due E - ter - ni - ty of praise.

Hans Adolf Brorson, 1694–1764
Hymnal Version, 1955

600

VULPIUS (GELOBT SEI GOTT). 8 8 8. With Alleluias.
MELCHIOR VULPIUS, cir. 1560–1615
Harm. ERNEST MACMILLAN
With exultation
1. O Lord of life, wher - e'er they be, Safe in thine own e - ter - ni - ty, Our dead are liv - ing un - to thee.
2. All souls are thine, and, here or there, The faith - ful rest with - in thy care; One prov - i - dence a - like they share.
3. Thy word is true, thy ways are just; A - bove the re - quiem, 'Dust to dust,' Shall rise our psalm of grate - ful trust.
Al - le - lu - ia! Al - le - lu - ia! Al - le - lu - ia!

4 O happy they in God who rest,
No more by fear and doubt oppressed;
Living or dying, they are blest.
Alleluia!

Frederick Lucian Hosmer, 1840–1929

This hymn may also be sung to VICTORY (No. 90)

See also:

144 For all the saints
141 For all thy saints, O Lord
143 Hark! the sound of holy voices
135 Holy, holy, holy, Lord
584 Jerusalem the golden
145 The saints of God
562 The Son of God goes forth
585 Thy word, O God, declareth
409 Ye holy angels bright
437 Ye watchers and ye holy ones

OLD 124TH. 10 10, 10 10, 10.
Melody in Genevan Psalter, 1551
Broadly, with dignity
1. Praise ye the Lord, ye servants of the Lord: Praise ye his Name; his lordly honor sing: Thee we adore; to thee glad homage bring; Thee we acknowledge; God to be adored For thy great glory, Sovereign, Lord, and King.
2. Father of Christ— of him whose work was done, When by his death he took our sins away: To thee belongeth worship, day by day, Yea, Holy Father, everlasting Son, And Holy Ghost, all praise be thine for aye! Amen.

Apostolic Constitutions, IV cent.
Tr. George Ratcliffe Woodward, 1849–1934, and others

OLD HUNDREDTH. L. M.

Louis Bourgeois, *cir.* 1510–61
Genevan Psalter, 1551

With great dignity
Praise God, from whom all bless - ings flow; Praise
him, all crea - tures here be - low; Praise him a - bove, ye
heaven - ly host; Praise Fa - ther, Son, and Ho - ly Ghost. A-men.

Thomas Ken, 1637–171

BLESSING, AND GLORY, AND WISDOM, AND THANKSGIVING,
AND HONOR, AND POWER, AND MIGHT, BE UNTO
OUR GOD FOR EVER AND EVER.
AMEN.

Indexes

Note: Indexes of Originals of Translated Hymns and of Metres appear in the text edition the Service Book and Hymnal.

AUTHORS, TRANSLATORS, AND SOURCES OF HYMNS

The numbers in parenthesis refer to translations

Index of Authors

Index of Authors

Index of Authors

Index of Composers

COMPOSERS AND SOURCES OF TUNES

The numbers in parenthesis refer to arrangements

Index of Composers

Index of Composers

Index of Composers

Index of Tunes

TUNES

Index of Tunes

Index of Tunes

Index of Tunes

Index of Tunes

LITURGICAL INDEX

Note: Hymns related to the Propers for the Day have been arranged in the following s quence: P. Procession; I. Introit; Ps. Psalm paraphrase following the Old Testament Lesso E. Epistle; Gr. Gradual; G. Gospel.

NITY XXIII	TRINITY XXIV		TRINITY XXV		TRINITY XXVI		TRINITY XXVII	
353	P.	160	P.	127	P.	584	P.	7
520		174		157		589		168
560	I.	165	I.	382	I.	406		434
200		412		561	Ps.	595	I.	8
571	Ps.	488	Ps.	527	E.	327		408
474	E.	317	E.	141		331	Ps.	409
480		459		590		356		596
330		532		594	Gr.	394	E.	586
514	Gr.	490	Gr.	176		583		587
. 488	G.	295	G.	327	G.	197	Gr.	219
332		297		587		588		499
339		578		589		597	G.	590

INDEX OF FIRST LINES

Index of First Lines

Index of First Lines

Index of First Lines

Index of First Lines

Index of First Lines